13th Edition **2021-22**

INDIAN ECONOMY

FOR CIVIL SERVICES, UNIVERSITIES AND OTHER EXAMINATIONS

ABOUT THE AUTHOR

Ramesh Singh is an alumnus of *Delhi School of Economics* and an education consultant with over two and a half decades of experience in guiding the aspirants of Civil Services as well as students preparing for other competitive exams. He is a prolific writer and has authored several books both in English and Hindi for McGraw Hill, including *Indian Economy* (in Marathi also), *Bhartiya Arthavyavastha, Contemporary Essays, Objective Indian Economy and Social Development,* and *1000 Plus Questions on General Science*. He is also a popular columnist of the Publication Division journals *Yojana* and *Kurukshetra.*

A teacher par excellence, he is endowed with an exceptional quality of simplifying the most difficult concepts of economics in an easy-to-understand style, making economics easy for even those who have no background in it. He is the founding-director of the institution *EcoMadeEasy*, which offers courses in economics for a diverse range of exams. He lives in Delhi and keeps himself busy in diverse academic activities.

13th Edition **2021-22**

INDIAN ECONOMY

FOR CIVIL SERVICES, UNIVERSITIES AND OTHER EXAMINATIONS

Ramesh Singh
Director, *EcoMadeEasy*
New Delhi

McGraw Hill Education (India) Private Limited

Published by McGraw Hill Education (India) Private Limited
Registered Office: Anjana Complex No: 5/90A, Butt Road, St. Thomas Mount, Chennai-600016

Indian Economy, 13e

1 2 3 4 5 6 7 8 9 D102542 25 24 23 22 21

Printed and bound in India

Print Edition:

ISBN (13) : 978-93-90727-42-1
ISBN (10) : 93-90727-42-1

e-Book Edition:

ISBN (13) : 978-93-90727-43-8
ISBN (10) : 93-90727-43-X

Typeset at Kaushik Laser Point & Printers, Tis Hazari Court, Delhi - 110 053 and printed at Magic International Pvt. Ltd., Plot No. 26E, Sector-31, (Industrial), Site-IV, Greater Noida 201306
Cover Printer: Magic International Pvt. Ltd., Plot No. 26E, Sector-31, (Industrial), Site-IV, Greater Noida 201306
Cover Image Source: DAL

Cover Designer: Creative Designer

DQQZRRZJDXDRZ

Visit us at: www.mheducation.co.in

Write to us at: info.india@mheducation.com

CIN: U80302TN2010PTC111532

Toll Free Number: 1800 103 5875

In the loving memories of my parents

P.N. Singh

&

R.N. Devi Singh

PREFACE TO THE THIRTEENTH EDITION

It feels great to present the *13th edition 2021-22* of the book—more so after the rigour of revision during the hard times of the pandemic. Being recognised among the **best-sellers** has no doubt been extremely satisfying, however, the challenge to make it the *first pick* for the readers has gone on increasing over the years.

Aimed primarily at the civil services exams conducted by the Union Public Service Commission, the contents of the book are developed with the highest sense of their relevance, the reason it has remained a popular companion for state civil services and other exams too, year after year.

Coming to the economy, while the governments are busy taking stock of the disruption caused by the once-in-a-century event, the *COVID-19* pandemic, the uncertainties related to present and future continue like never before. Indian economy, which was already faced with lower demand and subdued investments, looks to recover faster on the back of increased investments announced for 2021–22 by the Government, which has taken a kind of holiday from the compulsions of sticking to the legislative fiscal targets. We see the Government kickstarting some *long-pending* reforms in the areas such as agriculture market, labour market, MSMEs sector, trade, foreign investment, etc.—all being transformative in nature. These reforms, which are aimed at using the pandemic disruption as an opportunity, are set to have a very deep and long-term impact on the economy.

Salient Features of the Book

- It aims to cover all those concepts and theories which are required to help the reader develop a 'fundamental' and 'application-based' understanding of economics along with its subtle linkages to real policy issues and the areas of governance, polity, diplomacy, ethics, technology, etc. in an *inter-disciplinary* manner— so that economics becomes easy for even those who have 'no background' in it.
- The first chapter aims to present a simplified and application-based insight into *Economics* to 'lessen the fear' of readers, especially those who have no background in the discipline.
- Inter-disciplinary in approach, the book intertwines current developments to give *basic-to-advance* knowledge to the reader in an 'easy-to-understand' style.
- Sectoral areas such as *Agriculture, Industry* and *Services* have been fully updated with latest developments.

- The segments on *inflation* and *price management, banking, insurance, external sector* and *human development* have all been fully revamped and updated as per the changed times.
- *Taxation* and *Budgeting*—the very core of policy making—have been presented in an exam-oriented, updated and simplified style.
- *Burning Socio-Economic Issues* have been 'fully' changed to suit the changed landscapes of the global economy in general and domestic economy in particular.
- Thoroughly revised and updated with all the latest and major official sources such as *Economic Survey 2020–21, Union Budget 2021–22, India 2021*, major reports of the *NITI Aayog* and central ministries.
- *Economic Survey 2020–21* (volume-wise) and *Union Budget 2021–22* have been presented as special coverage.
- Current and relevant *Model Questions* with their *Answers* and *Explanations* for both Preliminary and Main Exams have been covered in exam-oriented way.
- *Glossary*, being among the most useful segments of the book, has been made exam-oriented by simplifying the core 'concepts' and 'terms' in an objective and comprehensive style.

With all the sense of responsibility, I present this book to the readers with the wish that it serves their needs of the exams taking place in 2021 and 2022 in a better way.

Constructive suggestions from the readers are most welcome.

Wishing all the very best to the readers in their endeavour!

Ramesh Singh
www.rameshsingh.org
dr.rmsh@gmail.com

PREFACE TO THE FIRST EDITION

I felt my first serious inclination towards writing when my first article was published in the journal *Mainstream* way back in 1988 while pursuing my post graduation studies at the Delhi School of Economics. My interaction with the students inside and outside the classroom in 1990–91, when India faced a serious financial crisis, made me realise that there was an immediate need of a book on Indian economy, which could educate the students about the various aspects and challenges of the Indian economy in a simple and lucid manner. It took nearly two decades to fulfil this dream of mine.

The book has been designed to cater to the requirements of the General Studies paper for various Civil Services Examinations (Union as well as the States), and the optional Economics. It would also be useful for graduate and postgraduate courses in Economics of various universities. Adequate and required notes and references have been given after consulting and referring to an array of sources. I have taken care of both the objective and the subjective aspects based on my classroom experience of interacting with the students.

I am grateful to Prof. Majid Husain for the inspiration and motivation I got from him to complete this work. I have especially learnt the art and importance of work, punctuality and honesty in a very practical way from him.

Thanks are also due to Mr. Rajesh Kumar Baghel, Mr. Rakesh Kumar, Md. Ishtiaq, and Mr Vikash. I am indebted to my wife, Mrs Ila Singh, for her full support and my two little daughters, Medha and Smiti, for providing the sparkle in an otherwise monotonous work.

Finally, my special thanks to the team from McGraw-Hill, who took great pains to finalise the project and complete it in a record time with all the possible expertise. I welcome from the readers constructive advice and comments, which could guide me in further revision of this book.

Ramesh Singh
www.rameshsingh.org
dr.rmsh@gmail.com

ABOUT THE CIVIL SERVICES EXAMINATION

The Civil Services Examination comprises two successive stages:

(i) Civil Services (Preliminary) Examination (Objective Type) for the selection of candidates for Main Examination; and

(ii) Civil Services (Main) Examination (Written and Interview) for the selection of candidates for the various services and posts.

Scheme and subjects for the Preliminary and Main Examination.

A. PRELIMINARY EXAMINATION

The Examination shall comprise two compulsory Papers of 200 marks each.

Note:

(i) Both the question papers will be of the objective type (multiple choice questions).

(ii) The question papers will be set both in Hindi and English. However, questions relating to English Language Comprehension skills of Class X level will be tested through passages from English language only without providing Hindi translation thereof in the question paper.

B. MAIN EXAMINATION

The written examination will consist of the following papers:

Qualifying Papers:

Paper A: (One of the Indian Language to be selected by the candidate from the Languages included in the Eighth Schedule to the Constitution). **300 Marks**

Paper B: English **300 Marks**

The papers on Indian Languages and English (Paper A and Paper B) will be of Matriculation or equivalent standard and will be of qualifying nature. The marks obtained in these papers will not be counted for ranking.

Papers to be counted for merit

Paper I: Essay **250 Marks**

Paper II: General Studies–I **250 Marks**
(Indian Heritage and Culture, History and Geography of the World and Society)

Paper III:	General Studies –II (Governance, Constitution, Polity, Social Justice and International relations)	**250 Marks**
Paper IV:	General Studies –III (Technology, Economic Development, Bio-diversity, Environment, Security and Disaster Management)	**250 Marks**
Paper V:	General Studies –IV (Ethics, Integrity and Aptitude)	**250 Marks**
Paper VI:	Optional Subject – Paper 1	**250 Marks**
Paper VII:	Optional Subject – Paper 2	**250 Marks**
Sub Total (Written test)		**1750 Marks**
Personality Test		**275 Marks**
Grand Total		**2025 Marks**

Candidates may choose any one of the optional subjects from amongst the list of subjects given below:

List of Optional Subjects for Main Examination:

(i) Agriculture
(ii) Animal Husbandry and Veterinary Science
(iii) Anthropology
(iv) Botany
(v) Chemistry
(vi) Civil Engineering
(vii) Commerce and Accountancy
(viii) Economics
(ix) Electrical Engineering
(x) Geography
(xi) Geology
(xii) History
(xiii) Law
(xiv) Management
(xv) Mathematics
(xvi) Mechanical Engineering
(xvii) Medical Science
(xviii) Philosophy
(xix) Physics
(xx) Political Science and International Relations
(xxi) Psychology
(xxii) Public Administration
(xxiii) Sociology
(xxiv) Statistics
(xxv) Zoology
(xxvi) Literature of any one of the following:

Assamese, Bengali , Bodo, Dogri, Gujarati, Hindi, Kannada, Kashmiri, Konkani, Maithili, Malayalam, Manipuri, Marathi, Nepali, Oriya, Punjabi, Sanskrit, Santhali, Sindhi, Tamil, Telugu, Urdu and English.

TABLE OF CONTENTS

CHAPTER 1

INTRODUCTION

*Economics is the study of how goods and services are produced, distributed and consumed. As resources are always in short supply, the British economist Lionel Robbins in 1935 described the discipline as 'the science of scarcity'.**

In this Chapter...

- More Than A Dismal Science
- Defining Economics
- Micro and Macro
- What is an Economy?
- Economic Systems
- Washington Consensus
- Beijing Consensus
- Santiago Consensus
- National Income
- Comparing GVA & GDP
- Fixed-Base to Chain-Base Method
- Standing Committee on Economic Statistics
- Income Estimates for 2020–21

MORE THAN A DISMAL SCIENCE

Economics has been called a dismal science, precisely a depressing and poor science[1]. Other than this the discipline has also been criticised for being a kind of riddle for common people to comprehend. Last but not the least, it has been called a 'failed science' also (more so after its failure to predict the US *sub-prime crisis* of 2008). Still, nobody can deny the invaluable role played by economics to make this world a better place for humanity.

Understanding economics and its nuances have always been a challenge, especially, for those who come from no background in it. It doesn't mean that those with a background (university-educated) in it are very comfortable—many of such people face an altogether different sort of problem—they *understand* less economics than they *know*! Missing the applicatory dimension of economics is a general problem among such people. Today, emphasis being on the *applications*

1. **Thomas Carlyle,** the Scottish historian, coined this term (in his work *Occasional Discourse on the Negro Question,* 1849) while making a point against the emancipation of the Negro slaves (as per his belief it will leave slaves worse off due to the economic principle of demand and supply). Later on, his belief was also addressed to the 'depressing' (dismal) proposition of T.R. Malthus (in his work *An Essay on the Principle of Population,* 1798) that in future, food supply would not match the rise in population.

* *David Orrel and Borin Van Loon,* **Introducing Economics: A Graphic Guide,** *Faber & Faber, London, 2011, p. 3*

of economics (especially in the competitive exams) 'knowing' economics is not enough rather one is required to have the ability to apply economics in everyday life—and this is only possible if one 'understands' economics!

Making economics easier for both categories of the readers has been one of the prime aims of this book. However this has not been an easy task for two reasons—firstly, keeping the soul of concepts intact while simplifying them and secondly, educating the reader about the contemporary economic issues. Developing a book on Indian Economy would have been an easier task had simplifying economics not been among the aims. This is why along with the analyses of economic issues there flows an undercurrent of economic theory throughout the book. For this, it will be *wiser* on the part of the reader to keep in touch with the footnotes and glossary to feel and comprehend the subject matter in a desired way.

DEFINING ECONOMICS

Simply put, 'economics studies economic activities of the human being' (a *working definition*). Humanities are intricately connected as all aim to study the differentiated human activities—that is why inter-disciplinary approach to study humanities is considered wiser.

What are Economic Activities? In a very simple way, all activities where money is involved can be called economic activities. And wherever money comes in question, there comes the economic motive/gain—several examples can be taken of it—getting job, giving a job, buying and selling something, doing a business, so on and so forth. Things are still a bit complicated! Visiting religious places for prayer is clearly not an economic activity but what about giving alms to beggars there or putting some money on the places of worship or for that matter religious donations. Can we call them our economic activities? It looks difficult to say! Here, other than the activity of prayer all are economic activities!

However, defining economics has not been as easy as it has been presented here—defining every discipline has been a complex and contentious task for that matter. Widely used and quoted definitions of the discipline revolve around the uses of resources and their distribution. Let us feel the technicality involved in a typical definition with the help of two such acclaimed definitions taken as reference—

Economics is the study of how societies use scarce resources to produce valuable commodities and distribute them among different people.[2]

Economics studies how individuals, firms, governments and other organisations within our society make choices and how these choices determine a society's use of its resources.[3]

Economics is the study of 'how society uses its scarce resources' is probably the most used definition which is catchy as well as concise also[4].

MICRO AND MACRO

After the Great Depression (during the 1930s) the domain of economics got divided into two broad branches—the micro- and macro-economics. John Maynard Keynes is considered the *father* of macroeconomics (the branch came into being after the publication of his seminal work, *The General Theory of Employment, Interest and Money,* in 1936).

Simply put, if macroeconomics (macro) is about the forest, microeconomics (micro) is about the trees. While the former deals with the big picture (the forest) the latter deals with the details (the trees) that make up the forest. Micro and macro are the *Greek* words which mean 'small' and 'big', respectively.

---

2. Samuelson, P.A. and Nordhaus, W. D., **Economics,** Tata McGraw Hill Company Ltd., N. Delhi, 2005, p. 4.

3. Stiglitz, J.E. and Walsh, C.E., **Economics,** W. W. Norton & Company, N. York, 2006, p. 6.

4. Mathew Bishop, **Economics-An A-Z Guide,** Economist-Profile Books, UK, London, 2009.

While micro takes a bottoms-up approach to analyse economy, macro takes a top-down approach. Taking an example, while micro tries to understand the choices which consumers make and the income they earn, macro tries to understand the dynamics of inflation and growth. Though, they appear to be different, they are actually interdependent and complementary since there are many overlapping issues between them. For example, a rise in inflation (macro effect) will cause rise in the cost of raw materials leading to rise in prices which consumers will pay (micro effect).

Micro theory evolved from the theories of how prices are determined, macro, on the other hand, is rooted in empirical observations that existing theory could not explain. While there are no competing schools of thought in micro, macro has schools like New Keynesian or New Classical. Since the late 1980s rather these divisions have been narrowing[5].

Econometrics is the third core area of economics other than the micro and macro. This field seeks to apply statistical and mathematical methods to economic analysis. The sophisticated analyses of micro and macro sub-fields would not have been possible without the major advances made in econometrics over the past century or so.

WHAT IS AN ECONOMY?

Economy is economics in action. It is a still-frame picture of the economic activities. A country, a company and a family all have their economies. It is popularly used in case of countries—Indian economy, the US economy, the Japanese economy, etc. While the principles and theories of economics remain the same, economies (of countries) show diversities given the socio-economic diversities countries have.

Sectors & Types of Economies

Economic activities in a country/economy are broadly divided into three main sectors[6] and by their dominance economies get their names also:

Primary Sector The economic activities which take place while exploiting the natural resources fall under it, such as mining, agricultural activities, oil exploration, etc. When agriculture sector (one of the sub-sectors of the primary sector) contributes minimum half of the national income and livelihood in a country it is called an *agrarian economy.*

Secondary Sector It contains all of the economic activities under which the raw materials extracted out of the primary sector are processed (also called industrial sector). One of its sub-sectors, manufacturing, has proved to be the largest employer across the western developed economies. When secondary sector brings in minimum half of the national income and employment in a country it is called an *industrial economy*.

Tertiary Sector All of the economic activities where services are produced falls in this sector, such as education, healthcare, banking, communication, etc. When this sector contributes minimum half of the national income and livelihood in a country it is called a *service economy.* Later on, experts created two more sectors of economy—quaternary and quinary. Though, they are sub-sectors of the tertiary sector.

Quaternary Sector Known also as 'knowledge' sector, the activities related to education, research and development, etc. come under it. The sector plays the most important role in defining the quality of the human resources an economy has.

Quinary Sector All activities where top decisions are made fall under it. The highest level of decision makers in governments (inclusive of their

5. **Rethinking Macroeconomic Policy,** Olivier Blanchard, Giovanni Dell'Ariccia and Paolo Mauro, *International Monetary Fund*, SPN/10/03, February 12, 2010.

6. Todaro, Michael P. and Smith, Stephen C., **Economic Development,** Pearson Education, 8th edition, N. Delhi, p. 440.

bureaucracy) and the private corporate sector fall under it. The number of people involved in this sector is very low rather they are considered the 'brain' behind socio-economic performance of an economy.

Stages of Growth

Looking at the way developed countries did grow, a theory about it was proposed by W.W. Rostow[7] in 1960 as per which economies grow following *five linear stages* through the three main sectors i.e., agriculture, industry and services. However, several countries did show exceptions to this standard pattern—India and many other South East Asian countries such as Indonesia, Philippines, Thailand and Vietnam fall under this category. These countries moved from the stage of agrarian to service economy without much healthier expansion of their industrial sector.

India saw a transition from the dominance of the agriculture to services sector by late 1990s when the contribution of services in her national income crossed 50 per cent mark.

ECONOMIC SYSTEMS

Human life depends on uses (consumption) of certain things (goods and services) some of which, upto a level, are also essential (such as food, water, shelter, cloth, etc.) for survival. How to let people have these things was the *first challenge* for the humanity[8]. This challenge has two dimensions to it—firstly, these things need to be created (produced) and secondly, they should reach (distributed/supplied to) the needy people. For production one needs to set up productive assets for which money needs to be spent (known as investment). But 'who' will invest and 'why'? In the process of taking on this challenge there evolved different types of economic systems (i.e., different ways of *organising an economy*). We can prepare a long list of economic systems, however, three of them are considered the major ones—a brief overview of which follows below.

Market Economy

This is considered the first formal economic system emerging out of the traditional economic system. Its origin is traced back to the work *(An Inquiry into the Nature and Causes of the Wealth of Nations, 1776)* of the Scottish philosopher-economist Adam Smith (1723-90). His main ideas can be summed up, in a simplified way, in the following way:

- It is the self-interest which motivates individuals/firms to do economic activities out of which society gets goods and services supplied with. It means the products society gets is unintended social benefits of someone's self-interested actions. Adam Smith called this motivating factor the *invisible hand* (often called as the 'animal spirit'). This way the questions like 'who' will invest in productive assets and 'why' seem to get answered.
- To attain higher prosperity there should be increasing *division of labour* (specialisation of labour force by breaking down large jobs into small components). Specialisation brings in speed, precision and quality in the labour force.
- For invisible hand to operate properly a suitable environment (i.e., market) determined by the forces of demand and supply (called the market forces) is

7. Walt W. Rostow, *The Stages of Economic Growth: A Non-Communist Manifesto*, Cambridge University Press, London, 1960, pp. 1-5.

8. Enhancing the well-being (life satisfaction) of the mankind has been the *second major challenge* for economics—the efforts in this direction led to the evolution of the ideas of *growth, development, human development* and finally *happiness* (which will be discussed in just the next chapter i.e., Chapter 2).

required. What to produce, how much to produce and at what price to sell (i.e., supply) all such decisions depend on these forces.

- Such an economic system needs to be regulated by *competition* prevailing in the market.
- For efficient operation of the economic activities, government should follow a policy of *laissez faire* (French word which means 'leave it alone' which is generally translated by economists as 'non-interference'). Lesser the government, better the economic performance. Here, non-interference by government means great many different things such as—government playing no or least economic role (producing none of the goods and services), no economic regulation, no taxes imposed, etc.

Adam Smith himself called such an economic system as 'the system of natural liberty'. Rather these ideas were the drivers of two major economic systems—'capitalism' and 'free market economy'. Though, they are based on the same economic environments (demand and supply), there are subtle differences between them:

While capitalism is focused on creation of 'wealth' and ownership of productive assets, free market economy is focused on 'exchange' of wealth (through production and supply of goods and services).

In a capitalist system there might be some government regulation but private owner can have monopoly on the market and thus prevents competition. However, a free market economy is solely based on market forces (demand and supply), and there is little or no government regulation. That is why in free market economy free competition is possible without any intervention from outside forces.

Such an economic system got *first* tried in the USA in 1777 from where capitalism spread across the whole Euro-America (Northern America and Western Europe). These economies enjoyed high prosperity and operated well till got hit with the Great Depression[9] in 1929. By that time great capital was amassed by few (the multi- and trans-national companies) while majority remaining poor—widening inequality in the process over the time. Taxes were imposed but they were very few in number and at very lower rates with state playing negligible welfare role.

Cons of this System Supported by the democratic rights and freedoms, this system had great environment for individual success, innovation and business activities. Though, it looks smoothly operating for over one and half centuries (with subtle changes) it had its own set of limitations which can be summarised precisely in the following way:

- There was almost no tool to look after those who have lower purchasing power (i.e., the poor).
- Negligible to total absence of welfare actions from the state.
- Widening economic inequality even after launching distributive measures such as progressive taxation (in which richer are taxed with higher rates).

The existing set of policy approaches could not help these economies to recover out of the Depression. It was in wake of this crisis that we see the rise of a new branch of economics—the macroeconomics—proposed by the British economist John Maynard Keynes (1883-1949) in his seminal work *The General Theory of*

9. Depression is a stage in economic system which shows certain very sticky traits such as—excessively lower aggregate demand, abnormally lower rate of inflation with higher rates of unemployment and/or lower rates of employment—leading to locking down of production centres. A detailed and objective analysis is presented about depression, recession, etc. in Chapter 7.

Employment, Interest and Money, 1936. Together with analysing the causes which might have caused this crisis, Keynes suggested a new set of policy approach also to help economic recovery. In very simple term, Keynes suggested these economies to include certain traits from the other economic system (Non-Market Economy) to correct the crisis faced by them. After including the Keynesian advices these economies recovered out of the Depression and in this process (practically) the *mixed economic system* evolved.

Non-Market Economy

Rooted (immediately) in the ideas of Karl Marx (1818-83), it had two variants—*socialist* and *communist*. While in the socialist model (ex-USSR, 1917-89) state was having ownership control on only natural resources, in the communist model (China, 1949-85) the state used to have ownership control over labour also. It got also known by its other names such as *State Economy, Command Economy, Centrally Planned Economy*. Basically, this system evolved in 'reaction' to the market economy and was based on the following main beliefs:

- Resources of a country should be used for the wellbeing of all.
- Resources are best used once they are under the ownership of society/community (Socialism/Communism). Thus, all economic roles will be played by the state only.
- No property rights given to individuals guided by the belief that it promotes exploitation of the labourers (i.e., proletariat) and helps a small minority (i.e., bourgeoisie) to get richer over time—resulting into increasing economic inequality.
- Absence of market (i.e., inter-play of demand and supply was totally absent).
- No idea of competition (i.e., total state monopoly in economic sphere).
- People to play economic role (employed in the state-owned enterprises) *according to their ability* and in return to get all facilities from the state *as per their needs*.
- The decisions such as what to produce, how much to produce and how to supply them to people were taken by the state itself.

This system first got tried by the Bolsheviks in the ex-USSR (in 1919) from where it spread across the whole eastern Europe (the so-called socialist bloc countries) of the time, finally getting its purest form in the communist China (in 1949)—emergence of the socialist and communist models of the non-market economy.

Cons of this System Even after being fully committed to the 'wellbeing of masses' and absence of poverty (theoretically, speaking) this system had its own limitations which can be summarised briefly in the following way:

- Though, the aim was to serve all there was no idea of creating capital or wealth—which created a scarcity of investible capital in the coming times.
- State used to prioritise the uses of resources—thus the best or optimum uses of resources (driven by market forces) were denied leading to their misallocation and wastage.
- In the absence of property rights there was no motivation to work hard and tap the animal spirit of the people (as no money was paid to them)—leading to virtual absence of innovation (i.e., research and development)—a process of internal decay.
- Being non-democratic political systems the things like *liberty* and *freedom* were totally absent. Aimed at avoiding exploitation of the labourers at the hand of the capitalist state itself emerged as the sole agent of

exploitation—critics called this 'State Capitalism'.

A process of internal decay was being faced by these economies since early 1970s caused by the in-built shortcomings they had. It was way back in mid-1950s that the Polish philosopher Oskar Lange[10] had advised these economies to embrace 'market socialism' which was outrightly rejected by both Soviet Bloc and China. At last by mid-1980s state economies moved to modify their economic systems by including certain traits of the market economy:

- Ex-USSR, by late 1980s, announced the twin policies of *Perestroika* (restructuring) and *Glasnost* (openness) switching over to mixed economy with fundamental traits of market economy. Similar changes were adopted by the existing East European socialist economies and the CIS (Confederation of Independent States).
- China, by mid-1980s, announced its *Open-Door Policy* embracing mixed economy with fundamental traits of the market economy. Rather China had started preparations for this change by mid-1970 itself but they were not explicit in nature.

In a way the two major and contrasting economic systems of the time had completed the full circle and moved closer borrowing traits from each other—the evolution of the mixed economy (where we find the mixture of traits of both of the economic systems). This event has been also termed as the *end of ideology*—as the ideological divide between these economic systems looked bridged now—eventually ending the long-drawn *Cold War* which originated from this ideological difference.[11]

Mixed Economy

In practice, mixed economic system was already there (by late 1930s) once the market economies adopted certain policy changes (borrowing from the non-market economy) to recover out of the Depression. But first country to announce adopting this system was France (in 1944-45, with the announcement to adopt national planning). The system got further strengthened once the non-market economies started modifying themselves by mid-1980s. It was with few reports of the World Bank that helped world agree on the best model of the economic system:

- World Bank accepted the need of 'state intervention' in the economy (i.e., the market economy) which used to be an ardent advocate of the free market economy. But the time and nature of the intervention cannot be universal.[12]
- World Bank further concluded that neither of the economic systems (market and non-market) are free from flaws and even a novice of economics can agree that the best economic system can be the mixture of the both. But the state and market mix in any country has to be decided by its socio-economic needs of the time as there cannot be a fixed model of mixed economy.[13]

The *chief characteristics* of the mixed economy may be summarised in the following way—

10. Oskar Lange (1904-65) praised the state economy for many of its good traits but advised for inclusion of the good traits of the market economy—naming the new model as 'market socialism' [Galbraith, J.K., ***A History of Economics***, Penguin Books, London, 1991, pp. 188-89].

11. Francis Fukuyama, ***The End of History and the Last Man***, Free Press, New York, USA, 1992.

12. ***The East Asian Miracle: Economic Growth and Public Policy***, World Bank policy research report, World Bank & Oxford University Press, New York, 1993.

13. ***World Development Report 1999/2000: Entering the 21st Century***, World Bank & Oxford University Press, New York, 1999.

- Both state and private sector to have economic roles.
- Private sector to play those roles where invisible hand (the motive of profit) can work properly. Production and supply of the 'private goods' (the goods and services which people use by purchasing them from their own income) is the best example in this case. But state is not prohibited from playing this role.
- Those roles which private sector will not be motivated to play (due to absence of any profit element) should be better taken care of by the state. Supply of the 'public goods' (the goods and services which are consumed by all without making any direct payments from their individual income) is the best example in this case. But private sector is free to play this role also.
- The economic roles played by either state or private sector may not remain fixed for all times to come and may get modified as per the needs of the time.
- Regulation (things like rules, competition, taxation, etc.) of the economic system to be taken care of by the state.

It means, mixed economic system is not a kind of *finality* which the market or non-market economic systems used to be rather continuous change looks its main feature—capable to modify as per the socio-economic needs of the hour. This way, the long-drawn debate about the possible *role of state*[14] in economy also got decided.

Distribution Systems

Along with the three economic systems there evolved three distribution systems also. While capitalist economy distributed the goods and services through market (people buying their needs from the market at a price decided on market principles), state economy distributed them without taking the help of market (directly state used to supply them to the people without any payments). In the case of mixed economy, the distribution system was a hybrid of the former two models of distribution—state and market both being used (certain goods and services people used to buy from market while certain others being supplied by the state either free or at subsidised prices).

Though, we see a kind of consensus emerging in favour of the mixed economic system, the future had much in store. Over the time, it came under influence of several ideologies some of which also left enduring impact on the world economies—major ones have been briefed below.

WASHINGTON CONSENSUS

It is a set of reform policy package which was suggested by the International Monetary Fund, World Bank and the US Department of the Treasury (i.e., the US finance ministry) to the developing countries faced with economic crisis. Since all of these institutions were based in Washington, the policy prescription was called Washington Consensus by the US economist John Williamson[15]. The 10-point reform policy prescriptions are as given below:

1. Fiscal discipline
2. A redirection of public expenditure priorities toward fields offering both high economic returns and the potential to improve income distribution, such as primary health care, primary education, and infrastructure.

14. Joseph E. Stiglitz, ***The Role of State in Economic Development***, the keynote address at the Annual World Bank Conference on Development Economics, New York, 1996.

15. John Williamson, **'What Washington Means by Policy Reform'**, Chapter 2 in John Williamson (ed.), *Latin American Adjustment: How Much Has Happened?*, 1990; Institute for International Economics and John Williamson, **'What Should the Bank Think About the Washington Consensus'**, Background Paper to the World Bank's *World Development Report 2000*, Washington DC, July 1999.

3. Tax reform (to lower marginal rates and broaden the tax base)
4. Interest rate liberalisation
5. A competitive exchange rate
6. Trade liberalisation
7. Liberalisation of FDI inflows
8. Privatisation
9. Deregulation (in the sense of abolishing barriers to entry and exit)
10. Secure property rights

However, in coming times, the term became synonymous to *neo-liberalism* (in Latin America), *market fundamentalism* (as George Soros told in 1998) and even *globalisation* across the world. It has often been used to describe an extreme and dogmatic commitment to the belief that **markets can handle everything.**

But the reality has been different—the *set of polices* was already being recommended by the IMF (International Monetary Fund) and the WB (World Bank) together with the US Treasury, especially during the period of the eighties and early nineties.[16] The prescription was originally intended to address the real problems occurring in Latin America at the time, and their use later to handle a wide array of other situations has been criticised even by original proponents of the policies. The name of the Washington Consensus has often been mentioned as being somewhat unfortunate, especially by its creator. John Williamson[17] says that audiences the world over seem to believe that this signifies a set of neo-liberal policies that have been imposed on hapless countries by the Washington-based international financial institutions and have led them to crisis and misery—there are people who cannot utter the term without foaming at the mouth. He further adds that many people feel that it gives the impression that the points outlined represent a set of rules imposed on developing nations by the United States. Instead, Williamson always felt that the prescription represented a consensus precisely because they were so universal. Many proponents of the plan do not feel that it represents the hard-line *neo-liberal* agenda that anti-free-trade activists say it does. They instead present it as a relatively conservative assessment of what policies can help bring a country to economic stability.

But the policy prescription led to processes which are known as Liberalisation, Privatisation, Globalisation, thus cutting down the role of the State in the economy—more so in the nations which got developmental funding from the WB or went to the IMF in times of the Balance of Payment crises (as in the case of India which commenced its reform process in 1991 under the 'conditions' of the IMF). It was as if the Adam Smith's prescription of 'free market' (liberalism) has taken its rebirth (in *neo-liberalism*).

Experts believe that the US sub-prime crisis of 2008 followed by the great recession across the western developed economies were rooted in the ideas promoted by the Washington Consensus. Post-recession period has seen a clear erosion of faith in market and a rising sentiments in favour of 'state intervention' in the economy (i.e., rising faith in the idea of *development state*).

BEIJING CONSENSUS

Economic rise of China since mid-1980s needs no introduction. Whether this rise was led by any conscious development model has been an issue of scholarly debate. Finally, the idea of Beijing

16. Stiglitz, J.E., **Initiative for Policy Dialogue**, a paper presented at the conference *From the Washington Consensus towards a new Global Governance*, Barcelona, September 2004. The conference was sponsored by the Ford Foundation, the MacArthur Foundation, and the Mott Foundation.

17. Williamson, J., ***Did the Washington Consensus Fail?***, Institute for International Economics, Washington DC, 2002.

Consensus[18] was forwarded by Joshua Cooper Remo in 2004.

Also known as Chinese Model of economic development, this refers to the policies which were followed by Deng Xiaoping since 1976 (the year Mao Zedong died). Later on, this model was seen as an *alternative* to the Washington Consensus (i.e., an anti-Washington Consensus view) for the developing countries. Over the time experts interpreted this model in different ways rather it is believed to be based[19] on three main pillars:

1. Constant experimentation and innovation;
2. Peaceful distributive growth with gradual reforms; and
3. Self-determination and inclusion of selective foreign ideas.

The model received higher attention in wake of the great recession hitting the western economies (when China remained still dynamic)—experts portraying it as China's alternative to the liberal-market approach of the Washington Consensus.[20] Whether the developing countries should embrace the Chinese model has been a contentious issue. Experts believe that the things which worked for China may not work for others looking at the heterogeneity of Chinese performance.[21] Again, in wake of the rise of China, experts almost declared the 'death of market' and 'rise of state-led growth' rather such hurried conclusions might be misplaced because China's best economic performance came when market was the dominant force.[22]

Till 2010 we find rising interest in this model across the developing world but once the Chinese growth took a downturn in recent times, experts have advised double caution in blindly following this model. Some experts believe that the rising protectionism across the world (especially the USA, the UK and other places) has been caused by an inclination towards this model only.

SANTTAGO CONSENSUS

This is yet another alternative to the Wáshington Consensus. It was put forward by the then World Bank group President James D. Wolfensohn[23] (in Santiago) for the developing countries. Core idea of this model is *inclusion* which should not be only economic but social too. This way, this is a socio-economic development model and is bound to have its local characteristics. This way, it looks similar to the Beijing Consensus which also includes the social overtones.

In addition to financial resources the World Bank proposed to harness the incredible power of the information technologies and new spirit of openness and partnership (under the spell of rising globalisation) to make knowledge of global best-practice in development accessible to all. World Bank started building an internal architecture of a 'knowledge bank' for the purpose.

This proposal from the World Bank inspired the world governments to focus more on aspect of inclusive socio-economic growth. We see this happening in India also—with the Government launching the *third generation of economic reforms* in 2002 (which was aimed at making the fruits of reforms inclusive in nature).

18. Joshua Cooper Ramo, The Beijing Consensus, Foreign Policy Centre, London, May 2004.
19. Zhang Weiwei, ***The Allure of Chinese Model***, International Herald Tribune, November 2, 2006.
20. ***Beware the Beijing Model***, The Economist, London, May 26, 2009.
21. John Williamson, ***Is the Beijing Consensus Now Dominant,*** Asia Policy, DC Washington, January 26, 2012.
22. Yasheng Huang, ***Rethinking the Beijing Consensus***, Asia Policy, DC Washington, January 7, 2011.
23. James D. Wolfensohn, ***The Santiago Consensus: From Vision to Reality***, Speech of the President of the World Bank group, Santiago, Chile, April 19, 1998.

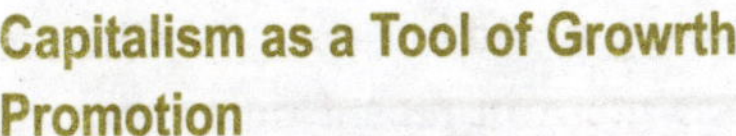

Capitalism as a Tool of Growrth Promotion

Capitalism as an economic system failed in the wake of the Great Depression (1929) and got purposefully modified into the mixed economy. But we find countries coming under the spells of capitalism in coming times too. Two such clear spells can be cited—the *first* under the influence of the Washington Consensus (post-1985) and the *second* after the official acceptance to Globalisation (via the WTO, post-1995). Experts believe that the ensuing Great Recession (after the US sub-prime crisis of 2007) among the developed countries was largely caused by the extreme capitalistic inclinations (neo-liberal policies) found among them. This way, the world has witnessed the devastating effects of capitalism twice by now.

Over the time, a kind of agreement has emerged across the world that though capitalism is not an ideal (or sustainable) type of an economic system rather such policies can be quite helpful in promoting the cause of growth. This is why today, we find countries across the world having capitalistic policy orientation (i.e., *pro-business* policies) under the overall design of a mixed economy—one set of policies (capitalistic) aiming higher growth while the other aiming at effective welfare. Such a clear policy shift has been seen in India too—it was in wake of the criticism to the *Union Budget 2015–16* (of being *pro-rich* or *pro-corporate*) that the erstwhile Finance Minister categorically clarified that the Budget was trying to be pro-corporate as well as pro-poor. Basically, over the time, experts started treating capitalism less as an economic system and more as tool of promoting growth and income.

NATIONAL INCOME

Measuring progress has been a major riddle for experts. Income as an indicator of progress was tried by many before the idea of the gross domestic product (GDP) was put forward by the US-economist Simon Kuznets[24] in 1934. The method tries to calculate (account) a country's income at domestic and national levels—in gross and net forms—having four clear concepts (GDP, NDP, GNP and NNP)—a brief and objective overview is presented below.

GDP

Gross Domestic Product (GDP) is the value of the all *final* goods and services produced within the boundary of a nation during one year period. For India, this calendar year is from 1st April to 31st March.

It is also calculated by adding national private consumption, gross investment, government spending and trade balance (exports-minus-imports). The use of the exports minus imports factor removes expenditures on imports not produced in the nation, and adds expenditures of goods and service produced which are exported, but not sold within the country.

It will be better to understand the terms used in the concept, *'gross'*, which means same thing in Economics and Commerce as 'total' means in Mathematics; *'domestic'* means all economic activities done within the boundary of a nation/ country and by its own capital; *'product'* is used

24. **Simon Kuznets,** an economist at the US National Bureau of Economic Research (NBER), presented the *National Income, 1929-32* report to the U.S. Congress in which he used the concept of GDP to capture the value of total income generated in the country. The concept got used by the US government basically as a tool to understand and measure the recovery process of the economy out of the Great Depression of 1929. The US Presidents Herbert Clark Hoover (tenure 1929-33) and F. Roosevelt (tenure 1933-45) used the concept vigorously. The idea was adopted as *a standard tool to account national income* by the World Bank and International Monetary Fund right since they started their operation in 1944-45. Importance of this contribution can be guessed by the fact that Kuznets was awarded Nobel Economics Prize (in 1971) for this single contribution. Attempts to calculate national income were made earlier too but this was the first *empirical* attempt towards it.

to define 'goods and services' together; and *'final'* means the stage of a product after which there is no known chance of value addition in it.

The different uses of the concept of GDP are as given below:

1. Per annum percentage change in it is the 'growth rate' of an economy. For example, if a country has a GDP of 107 which is 7 rupees higher than the last year, it has a growth rate of 7 per cent. When we use the term 'a growing' economy, it means that the economy is adding up its income, i.e., in quantitative terms.
2. It is a 'quantitative' concept and its volume/size indicates the 'internal' strength of the economy. But it does not say anything about the 'qualitative' aspects of the goods and services produced.
3. This is the most commonly used data in comparative economics. The GDPs of the member nations are ranked by the IMF at *purchasing power parity* (PPP). In 2020, India was the *3rd largest* economy (i.e., the size of its GDP) in the world in PPP terms[25] while at the prevailing rate of rupee's exchange rate (in US dollars) it was slated to lose one rank (being pushed down by the UK) and become the *6th largest* economy in the world in the year— again replacing the UK in 2025 to become *5th largest* and the *3rd largest* by 2030.[26]

25. ***World Economic Outlook***, IMF, Washington, DC, USA, October 2019 and January 2021 and *Economic Survey 2020-21*, vol. 1 & 2, Ministry of Finance, GoI, N. Delhi.
26. ***Centre for Economics and Business Research***, London, UK, December 2020

NDP

Net Domestic Product (NDP) is the GDP calculated after adjusting the weight of the value of 'depreciation'. This is, basically, *net form* of the GDP, i.e., GDP minus the total value of the 'wear and tear' (depreciation) that happened in the assets while the goods and services were being produced. Every asset (except human beings) go for depreciation in the process of their uses, which means they 'wear and tear'. The governments of the economies decide and announce the rates by which assets depreciate (done in India by the Ministry of Commerce and Industry) and a list is published, which is used by different sections of the economy to determine the real levels of depreciations in different assets. For example, a residential house in India has a rate of 1 per cent per annum depreciation, an electric fan has 10 per cent per annum, etc., which is calculated in terms of the asset's price. This is one way how depreciation is used in economics. The other way it is used in the external sector while the domestic currency floats freely as against the foreign currencies. If the value of the domestic currency falls following market mechanism in comparison to a foreign currency, it is a situation of 'depreciation' in the domestic currency, calculated in terms of loss in value of the domestic currency.

Thus, *NDP = GDP – Depreciation.*

This way, NDP of an economy has to be always lower than its GDP for the same year, since there is no way to cut the depreciation to zero. But mankind has developed several techniques and tools such as 'ball-bearing', 'lubricants', etc., to cut the loss due to depreciation.

The **different uses** of the concept of NDP are as given below:

1. For domestic use only: to understand the historical situation of the loss due to depreciation to the economy. Also used

to understand and analyse the sectoral situation of depreciation in industry and trade in comparative periods.

2. To show the achievements of the economy in the area of research and development, which have tried cutting the levels of depreciation in a historical time period.

However, NDP is not used in comparative economics, i.e., to compare the economies of the world. Why this is so? This is due to different rates of depreciation which is set by the different economies of the world. Rates of depreciation may be based on logic (as it is in the case of houses in India—the cement, bricks, sand and iron rods which are used to build houses in India can sustain it for the coming 100 years, thus the rate of depreciation is fixed at 1 per cent per annum). But it may not be based on logic all the time, for example, upto February 2000 the rate of depreciation for heavy vehicles (vehicles with 6-wheels and above) was 20 per cent while it was raised to 40 per cent afterwards—to boost the sales of heavy vehicles in the country. There was no logic in doubling the rate. Basically, depreciation and its rates are also used by modern governments as a tool of economic policymaking, which is the third way how depreciation is used in economics.

GNP

Gross National Product (GNP) is the GDP of a country added with its 'income from abroad'. Here, the trans-boundary economic activities of an economy is also taken into account. The items which are counted in the segment 'Income from Abroad' are:

1. **Private Remiffances:** This is the net outcome of the money which inflows and outflows on account of the 'private transfers' by Indian nationals working outside of India (to India) and the foreign nationals working in India (to their home countries). On this front India has always been a gainer- till the early 1990s from the Gulf region (which fell down afterwards in the wake of the heavy country-bound movements of Indians working there due to the Gulf War) and afterwards from the USA and other European nations. As per the World Bank, in 2019 too, India remained world's top recipient of remittances (US $80 billion) followed by China (US $67 billion), Mexico (US $34 billion) and Philippines (US $26 billion).

2. **Interest on External Loans:** The net outcome on the front of the interest payments, i.e., balance of inflow (on the money lend out by the economy) and outflow (on the money borrowed by the economy) of external interests. In India's case it has always been negative as the economy has been a 'net borrower' from the world economies.

3. **External Grants :** The net outcome of the external grants i.e., the balance of such grants which flow to and from India. Today, India offers more such grants than it receives. India receives grants (grants or loan-grant mix) from few countries as well as UN bodies (like the UNDP) and offers several developmental and humanitarian grants to foreign nations. In the wake of globalisation, grant outflows from India has increased as its economic diplomacy aims at the playing bigger role at international level.

Ultimately, the balance of all the three components of the 'Income from Abroad' segment may turn out to be positive or negative. In India's case it has always been negative (due to heavy outflows on account of trade deficits and interest payments on foreign loans). It means, the 'Income from Abroad' is subtracted from India's GDP to calculate its GNP.

The normal formula is *GNP = GDP + Income from Abroad.* But it becomes GNP = GDP + (– Income from Abroad), i.e., GDP – Income from Abroad, in the case of India. This means that India's GNP is always lower than its GDP.

The **different uses** of the concept GNP are as given below:

1. It is a more exhaustive concept of national income than the GDP as it indicates towards the *'quantitative'* as well as the *'qualitative'* aspects of the economy, i.e., the *'internal'* as well as the *'external'* strength of the economy.
2. It enables us to learn several facts about the production behaviour and pattern of an economy, such as, how much the outside world is dependent on its product and how much it depends on the world for the same (numerically shown by the size and net flow of its 'balance of trade'); what is the standard of its human resource in international parlance (shown by the size and the net flow of its 'private remittances'); what position it holds regarding financial support from and to the world economies (shown by the net flow of 'interests' on external lending/borrowing).

NNP

Net National Product (NNP) of an economy is the GNP after deducting the loss due to 'depreciation'. The formula to derive it may be written like:

NNP = GNP – Depreciation

or,

NNP = GDP + Income from Abroad – Depreciation.

The **different uses** of the concept of NNP are as given below:

1. This is the **'National Income' (NI)** of an economy. Though, the GDP, NDP and GNP, all are 'national income' they are not written with capitalised 'N' and 'I'.
2. This is the *purest form* of the income of a nation.
3. When we divide NNP by the total population of a nation we get the 'per capita income' (PCI) of that nation, i.e., 'income per head per year'. A very basic point should be noted here that this is the point where the rates of depreciation followed by different nations make a difference. Higher the rates of depreciation lower the PCI of the nation (whatever be the reason for it logical or artificial as in the case of depreciation being used as a tool of policymaking). Though, economies are free to fix any rate of depreciation for different assets, the rates fixed by them make difference when the NI of the nations are compared by the international financial institutions like the IMF, WB, ADB, etc.

The 'Base Year' together with the 'Methodology' for calculating the National Accounts were revised by the Central Statistics Office (CSO) in January 2015, which is given in the forthcoming pages.

Cost and Price of National Income

While calculating national income the issues related to 'cost' and 'price' also need to be decided. Basically, there are two sets of costs and prices; and an economy needs to choose at which of the two costs and two prices it will calculate its national income. Let us understand[27] its relevance:

[27] The information on issues like 'cost', 'price', 'taxes' and 'subsidies' are based on the different **Discussion Papers** released by the **Central Statistical Organisation** (GoI) from time to time.

1. **Cost:** Income of an economy, i.e., value of its total produced goods and services may be calculated at either the 'factor cost' or the 'market cost'. What is the difference between them? Basically, 'factor cost' is the 'input cost' the producer has to incur in the process of producing something (such as cost of capital, i.e., interest on loans, raw materials, labour, rent, power, etc.). This is also termed as *'factory price'* or 'production cost/price'. This is nothing but 'price' of the commodity from the producer's side. While the 'market cost' is derived after adding the indirect taxes to the factor cost of the product, it means the cost at which the goods reach the market, i.e., showrooms.

   India officially used to calculate its national income at *factor cost* (though the data at *market cost* was also released which were used for other purposes by the governments, commerce and industry). Since January 2015, the CSO has switched over to calculating it at *market price* (i.e., *market cost*). The market price is calculated by adding the *product taxes* (generally taken as the *indirect taxes* of the Centre and the States) to the factor cost. This way India switched over to the popular international practice. Once the GST has been implemented it will be easier for India to calculate its national income at market price.

2. **Price:** Income can be derived at two prices, constant and current. The difference in the constant and current prices is only that of the *impact of inflation*. Inflation is considered stand still at a year of the past (this year of the past is also known as the 'base year') in the case of the constant price, while in the current price, present day inflation is added. Current price is, basically, the maximum retail price (MRP) which we see printed on the goods selling in the market.

Revised Method

The Central Statistics Office (CSO), in January 2015, released the **new** and **revised** data of National Accounts, effecting two changes:

1. The *Base Year* was revised from 2004–05 to 2011–12. This was done in accordance with the recommendation of the National Statistical Commission (NSC), which had advised to revise the base year of all economic indices every five years.
2. This time, the *methodology* of calculating the National Accounts has also been revised in line with the requirements of the System of National Accounts (SNA)-2008, an internationally accepted standard.

The **major changes** incorporated in this revision are as given below:

1. **Headline growth rate** will now be measured by *GDP at constant market prices*, which will henceforth be referred to as 'GDP' (as is the practice internationally). Earlier, growth was measured in terms of growth rate in *GDP at factor cost and at constant prices.*
2. Sector-wise estimates of Gross Value Added (GVA)[28] will now be given at basic prices[29] instead of factor cost. The relationship

28. GVA, which measures the difference in value between the final good and the cost of ingredients used in its production, widens the scope of capturing more economic activity than the earlier 'factor cost' approach—a sum of the total cost of all factors used to produce a good or service, net of taxes and subsidies.

29. The **basic price** is the amount receivable by the producer from the purchaser for a unit of a good or service produced as output minus any tax payable (such as sales tax or VAT the buyer pays), and plus any subsidy receivable, on that unit as a consequence of its production or sale; it excludes any transport charges invoiced separately by the producer. In other words, the basic price is what the seller collects for the sale, as opposed to what the buyer pays.

between GVA at factor cost, GVA at basic prices, and GDP (at market prices) is given below:

GVA at basic prices = CE + OS/MI + CFC + production taxes less production subsidies.

GVA at factor cost = GVA at basic prices – production taxes + production subsidies.

GDP = GVA at basic prices + product taxes – product subsidies.

[Where, **CE** : compensation of employees; **OS** : operating surplus; **MI** : mixed income; and **CFC** : consumption of fixed capital (i.e., depriction). **Production taxes** or **production subsidies** are paid or received with relation to production and are independent of the volume of actual production. Some examples of **production taxes** are *land revenues, stamps and registration fees* and *tax on profession*. Some **production subsidies** are subsidies to railways, input subsidies to farmers, subsidies to village and small industries, administrative subsidies to corporations or cooperatives, etc. **Product taxes** or **subsidies** are paid or received on per unit of the product. Some examples of product taxes are excise tax, sales tax, service tax and import and export duties. **Product subsidies** include food, petroleum and fertilizer subsidies, interest subsidies given to farmers, households, etc., through banks, and subsidies for providing insurance to households at lower rates].

3. Comprehensive coverage of the *corporate sector* both in manufacturing and services by incorporation of annual accounts of companies as filed with the Ministry of Corporate Affairs (MCA) under their e-governance initiative, MCA21. Use of MCA21 database for manufacturing companies has helped in accounting for activities other than manufacturing undertaken by these companies.
4. Comprehensive coverage of the *financial sector* by inclusion of information from the accounts of stock brokers, stock exchanges, asset management companies, mutual funds and pension funds, and the regulatory bodies including the Securities and Exchange Board of India (SEBI), Pension Fund Regulatory and Development Authority (PFRDA) and Insurance Regulatory and Development Authority (IRDA).
5. Improved coverage of activities of *local bodies* and *autonomous institutions*, covering around 60 per cent of the grants/transfers provided to these institutions.

COMPARING GVA & GDP

Economic growth is estimated using two main methods—demand side and supply side. Under *supply side*, the value-added by the various sectors in the economy (i.e., agriculture, industry and services) are added up to derive the gross value added (GVA). This way, it captures the income generated by all economic actors across the country.

Under the *demand side*, GDP is arrived by adding up all expenditures done in the economy. Broadly speaking there are four sources of expenditures in an economy—namely, private consumption (individuals and households), government, business enterprises, and net exports (exports minus imports). It includes all the taxes received and all subsidies disbursed by the government. Thus, GDP is equal to GVA added with the net taxes (taxes minus subsidies).

While GDP is a good measure in comparative studies (comparing economies), GVA is a better measure to compare different sectors *within* the economy. GVA is more important when looking at *quarterly* growth data, because quarterly GDP is arrived at by apportioning the observed GVA data into different spender categories.

FIXED-BASE TO CHAIN.BASE METHOD

Government is at present exploring the idea of shifting to the *chain-base* method for calculating the GDP from the *fixed-base* (year) method. In the new method GDP estimates are compared with those of the previous year instead of a fixed base year which is revised every five years.

In a fixed-base method, the weights assigned (in the index) to various economic activities (i.e., the goods and services produced) stay unchanged even if the economy changes structurally. Besides, this method does not factor in relative changes in prices and impact on demand. While in a chain-base method weights assigned to economic activities change annually and thus capture structural changes more quickly. The current gig economy India is argued to reflect in the current GDP statistics of India, for instance. The new method will have several *advantages* over the exiting one:

- It will capture structural changes in the economy faster by allowing new activity and items to be added every year. Current GDP estimates are based on data for 2011-12 (the base year) and are due for revision. New items and firms involved in production process will be captured more quickly rather than a gap of 5 years (which practically takes 7-8 years to reflect).
- Comparing India's growth datasets with other countries will get easier and better as this is the best international practice[30] today. In globalising world economy, investment and trade decisions depend heavily in such comparative datasets.
- It is believed to prevent the ongoing controversies related to datasets also.

[30] The US shifted to the chain base or chain-weighted index in 1996 and other developed countries followed—in most of the cases it produced better outcome.

STANDING COMMITTEE ON ECONOMIC STATISTICS

Aimed at looking into collection of economic datasets, the Government by late December 2019, set up the Standing Committee on Economic Statistics (SCES). Headed by the ex-Chief Statistician Pronab Sen, the 28-member broad-based committee has members[31] coming from the UNO, RBI, Ministry of Finance, Niti Aayog, Tata Trust, economists and statisticians from several universities.

The committee has been given *wide-ranging mandate* which includes looking into datasets such as the Periodic Labour Force Survey, Annual Survey of Industries, Annual Survey of Services Sector Enterprises, Annual Survey of Unorganised Sector Enterprises, Time Use Survey, Index of Service Production, Index of Industrial Production, Economic Census and other surveys or statistics brought before it. The new panel subsumed all existing Standing Committees on labour, industry, services, etc.

Experts believe that the Government's step to set up the SCES came in the backdrop of India's failure to comply with the requirements of the **SDDS** (Special Data Dissemination Standard) of the IMF (International Monetary Fund).

[31] *C.P. Chandrasekhar* (Prof. JNU, who later resigned from the panel in opposition to the attack on the students of the university), *Hema Swaminathan* (Prof. IIM Bangalore), and *Jeemol Unni* (Prof. Ahmedabad University) are also its members who were signatories (among a total of 108 economists and social scientists) to the March 2019 *joint statement* to the Government against the alleged 'suppression of statistics'. Incidentally, the chairman of the committee, *Pronab Sen,* has also been critical of the way the data and reports have been handled in recent past.

Several experts in the country had shown their reservations[32] about the economic datasets and their way of publication since early 2015 itself.

SDDS of the IMF Aimed at guiding members to enhance data transparency and help financial market participants to assess the economic statistics of individual countries, the IMF launched the SDDS in 1996. It has over 20 data categories including national income accounts, production indices, employment, and central government operations. As per the report[33] of the IMF, India did show the following three types of deviations from the SDDS:

1. Delays in data dissemination from the periodicity prescribed.
2. Not listing data category in the Advance Release Calendar (ARC) as mandated.
3. Data not disseminated at all for a particular period.

The IMF acknowledged India's deviations but termed them 'non-serious'. However, independent observers see these deficiencies as a result of indifference to data dissemination procedures.

INCOME ESTIMATES FOR 2020-21

India was no exception to the economic challenge posed by the once in a century event of novel pandemic COVID-19. Though, by early 2021, the economy was showing a V-shaped recovery its growth had been badly hit during 2020-21 for which the ***latest*** national income estimates are as given below[34]:

- **GDP** (Gross Domestic Product) is estimated to be ₹ 134.4 lakh crore at constant prices (showing a *negative* growth rate of 7.7 per cent in comparison to 4.2 per cent of the preceding year) and ₹ 194.8 lakh crore at current prices (showing a *negative* nominal growth rate of 4.3 per cent over the preceding year).
- **GVA** (Gross Value Added) is estimated to be ₹ 123.4 lakh crore at constant prices (showing a *negative* growth rate of 7.2 per cent in comparison to 3.9 per cent of the preceding year) and ₹ 175.8 lakh crore at current prices (showing a *negative* growth rate of 4.2 per cent).
- **PCNI** (Per Capita Net National Income) is estimated to be ₹ 1,26,968 at current prices against ₹ 1,34,226 of the preceding year (showing a *negative* growth rate of 5.4 per cent).

The IMF[35] estimated a negative growth rate of 8.0 per cent for India in 2020— though for 2021 and 2022 its growth projections are 11.5 per cent and 6.8 per cent respectively.

32. Two top Government officials (while they were in office)—the former Chief Economic Advisor, *Arvind Subramanian* and the former RBI Governor, *Raghuram Rajan*—had shown their reservations about the national income accounts. In coming days, the list of such critics went on increasing.

33. ***Annual Observance Report of the SDDS for 2018***, IMF, Washington DC, USA, August 2018.

34. ***Economic Survey 2020-21***, vol. 2, p. 50, Ministry of Finance, GoI, N. Delhi.

35. ***World Economic Outlook***, IMF, Washington, DC, USA, January 2021.

CHAPTER 2

GROWTH, DEVELOPMENT AND HAPPINESS

*Happiness is a result of creating strong social foundations, for which it is time to build 'social trust' and 'healthy lives', not guns and walls.**

In this Chapter...

- Introduction
- Progress
- Economic Growth
- Economic Development
- Happiness
- Insights into Human Behaviour
- Nudge & Public Policy
- COVID-19 and Development

INTRODUCTION

Similar to seers and philosophers, economists, were also party to human's quest for a better tomorrow. We have been a witness to a number of notions coming in from the literature of Economics in this area—starting with a very humble and layman's word like 'progress' to technical terms like 'growth', 'development' and 'human development'. With greater dependence on the idea of the 'economic man', the world created immense wealth in the post-War decades. It was in the 1980s that social scientists started finer studies in the area of mankind's actions, finally challenging the very idea of the 'economic man' ('rational man'). Thus starts mankind's urge to introspect the lives of humanity on the planet earth. Meanwhile, humanity was faced with unique riddle of climate change. By now, courtesy the UNO, the world has the World Happiness Report.

PROGRESS

Progress is a general term frequently used by experts to denote betterment or improvement in anything. In economics, the term was used for a long time to show the positive movement in the lives of people and in an economy. It had both quantitative and qualitative aspects to it. After a point of time, some economists started using all the three terms—progress, growth and development—interchangeably to mean almost the same thing. But it was only during the 1960s, 1970s and

* World Happiness Report 2017, SDSN, UNO, Nev'York, 2017

1980s that a clear meaning of these terms really evolved.[1] The term 'progress' became a general term with no specific meaning in economics or denoting both growth and development. But growth and development were allotted their clear-cut meanings.

ECONOMIC GROWTH

A term coming from the life sciences, 'growth' in economics means economic growth. An increase in economic variables over a period of time is economic growth. The term can be used in an individual case or in the case of an economy or for the whole world. The most important aspect of growth is its *quantifiability,* i.e., one can measure it in absolute terms.[2] All the units of measurement may be applied, depending upon the economic variable, where growth is being studied. We have a few examples:

1. An economy might have been able to see growth in food production during a decade which could be measured in tonnes.
2. The growth of road network in an economy might be measured for a decade or any period in miles or kilometres.
3. Similarly, the value of the total production of an economy might be measured in currency terms which means the economy is growing.
4. Per capita income for an economy might be measured in monetary terms over a period.
5. We may say that ***economic growth is a quantitative progress.***

To calculate the ***growth rate*** of an economic variable the difference between the concerned period is converted into percentage form. For example, if a dairy farm owner produced 100 litres of milk last month and 105 litres in the following month, his dairy has a growth rate of 5 per cent over a period of two months. Similarly, we may calculate the growth rate of an economy for any given successive periods. Growth rate is an ***annual concept*** which may be used otherwise with the clear reference to the period for which it is used.

Though growth is a value neutral term, i.e., it might be positive or negative for an economy for a specific period, we generally use it in the positive sense. If economists say an economy is growing it means the economy is having a positive growth otherwise they use the term 'negative growth'.

Economic growth is a widely used term in economics which is useful in not only national level economic analyses and policymaking, but also highly useful in the study of comparative economics. International level financial and commercial institutions go for policymaking and future financial planning on the basis of the growth rate data available for the economies of the world.

ECONOMIC DEVELOPMENT

For a comparatively longer period of time after the birth of economics, economists remained focused on aspects of expanding the quantity of production and income of a country's economy. The main issue economists discussed was—how to increase the quantity of production and income of a country or a nation-state. It was believed that once an economy is able to increase its production, its income will also increase and there will be an automatic betterment (quality increase) in the lives of the people of the economy. There was no conscious discussion over the issue of quality expansion in the lives of the people. Economic growth was considered as a cause and effect for the betterment of the lives of the people. This was the reason why economists, till the 1950s, failed

1. Based on the analyses in Michael P. Todaro and Stephen C. Smith, ***Economic Development***, Pearson Education, 8th Ed., New Delhi, 2004, pp. 9–11.
2. As the IMF and the WB considered this yardstick of development as quoted in Gerald M. Meier and James E. Rauch, ***Leading Issues in Economic Development***, Oxford University Press, New Delhi, 2006, pp. 12–14.

to distinguish between growth and development, though they knew the difference between these terms.

It was during the 1960s and in the later decades that economists came across many countries where the growth was comparatively higher, but the quality of life was comparatively low. The time had come to define economic development differently from what the world meant by economic growth. For economists, development indicates the quality of life in the economy, which might be seen in accordance with the availability of many variables such as:

- The level of nutrition
- The expansion and reach of healthcare facilities—hospitals, medicines, safe drinking water, vaccination, sanitation, etc.
- The level of education
- Other variables on which the quality of life depends

Here, one basic thing must be kept in mind that if the masses are to be guaranteed with a basic minimum level of quality-enhancing inputs (above-given variables such as food, health, education, etc.) in their life, a minimum level of income has to be guaranteed for them. Income is generated from productive activities. It means that before assuring development we need to assure growth. Higher economic development requires higher economic growth. But it does not mean that a higher economic growth automatically brings in higher economic development—a confusion the early economists failed to clarify. We may cite an example here to understand the confusion: two families having same levels of income, but spending differing amounts of money on developmental aspects. One might be giving little attention to health, education and going for saving, and the other might not be saving but taking possible care of the issues of health and education. Here the latter necessarily will have higher development in comparison to the former. Thus, we may have some diverse cases of growth and development:

- Higher growth and higher development
- Higher growth but lower development
- Lower growth but higher development

The above-given combinations, though comparative in nature, make one thing clear, that, just as for higher income and growth we need conscious efforts, same is true about economic development and higher economic development.

Without a conscious public policy, development has not been possible anywhere in the world. Similarly, we can say, that without growth there cannot be development either.

The first such instance of growth without development, which the economists saw, was in the Gulf countries. These economies, though they had far higher levels of income and growth, the levels of development were not of comparable levels. Here started the branch of economics which came to be known as *'development economics'*. After the arrival of the WB and IMF, conscious economic policies were framed and prescribed for the growth and development of less developed economies.

We can say that economic development is quantitative as well as qualitative progress in an economy.[3] It means, when we use the term growth we mean quantitative progress and when we use the term development we mean quantitative as well as qualitative progress. If economic growth is suitably used for development, it comes back to accelerate the growth and ultimately greater and greater population is brought under the arena of development. Similarly, high growth with low development and ill-cared development finally results in fall in growth. Thus, there

3. *World Bank*, ***World Development Report 1991***, Oxford University Press, New York, 1991, p. 4.

is a circular relationship between growth and development. This circular relationship broke down when the Great Depression occurred. Once the concept of the *'welfare state'* got established, development became a matter of high concern for the governments of the world, policymakers and economists alike. A whole new branch of economics—welfare economics has its origin in the concept of welfare state and the immediacy of development.

Measuring Development

Although economists were able to articulate the differences between growth and development (Mahbub ul Haq, a leading Pakistani economist had done it by the early 1970s), it took some more time when the right method of measuring development could be developed. It was an established fact that the goal of progress goes beyond the mere 'increase in income'. International bodies such as the UNO, IMF and WB were concerned about the development of the comparatively underdeveloped regions of the world. But any attempt in this direction was only possible once there was a tool to know and measure the level of development in an economy and the determinants which could be considered as the traits of development. The idea of developing a formula/method to measure the development was basically facing two kinds of difficulties:

1. At one level it was difficult to define as to what constitutes development. Factors which could show development might be many, such as levels of income/consumption, quality of consumption, healthcare, nutrition, safe drinking water, literacy and education, social security, peaceful community life, availability of social prestige, entertainment, pollution-free environment, etc. It has been a really difficult task to achieve consensus among the experts on these determinants of development.
2. At the second level it looked highly difficult to quantify a concept as development constitutes quantitative as well as qualitative aspects. It is easy to compare qualitative aspects such as beauty, taste, etc., but to measure them we don't have any measuring scale.

Human Development Index

The dilemma of measuring the developmental level of economies was solved once the United Nations Development Programme (UNDP) published its first Human Development Report (HDR) in 1990. The report had a human development index (HDI) which was the first attempt to define and measure the level of development of economies. The 'index' was a product of select team of leading scholars, development practitioners and members of the Human Development Report office of the UNDP. The first such team which developed the HDI was led by **Mahbub ul Haq** and **Inge Kaul.** The term 'human development' is a corollary of 'development' in the index.

The HDR measures development by combining three indicators—*Health, Education* and *Standard of Living*—converted into a composite human development index, the HDI. The creation of a single statistic in HDI was a real breakthrough which was to serve as a frame of reference for both 'social' and 'economic' development. The HDI sets a minimum and a maximum for each dimension, called *goalposts*, and then shows where each country stands in relation to these goalposts, expressed as a value between 0 and 1 (i.e., the index is prepared on the *scale of one*). The *three* indicators[4] used to develop the composite index are as given below:

4. UNDP, ***Human Development Report, 2013*** and ***Human Development Report, 2010***, United Nations Development Programme, New York, USA, 2013 and 2010.

The **Education** component of the HDI is now (since HDR-2010) measured by two other indicators:

1. **Mean of years of schooling (for adults aged 25 years):** This is estimated based on educational attainment data from censuses and surveys available in the UNESCO Institute for Statistics database and *Barro and Lee* (2010) methodology.
2. **Expected years of schooling (for children of school entering age):**These estimates are based on enrolment by age at all levels of education and population of official school age for each level of education. Expected years of schooling is capped at 18 years.

These indicators are normalised using a minimum value of zero and maximum values are set to the actual observed maximum value of mean years of schooling from the countries in the time series, 1980–2012, that is 13.3 years estimated for the United States in 2010. The *education index* is the geometric mean of two indices.

The **Health** component is measured by the *life expectancy* at birth component of the HDI and is calculated using a minimum value of 20 years and maximum value of 83.57 years. This is the observed maximum value of the indicators from the countries in the time series, 1980–2012. Thus, the longevity component for a country where life expectancy at birth is 55 years would be 0.551.

The **Standard of Living** component is measured by *GNI* (Gross National Income/ Product) per capita at 'Purchasing Power Parity in US Dollars' (PPP $) instead of GDP per capita (PPP $) of past. The *goalpost* taken for minimum income is $100 (PPP) and the maximum is US $87,478 (PPP), estimated for Qatar in 2012. The HDI uses the logarithm of income, to reflect the diminishing importance of income with increasing GNI.

The scores for the three HDI dimension indices are then aggregated into a composite index using geometric mean. The HDI facilitates instructive comparisons of the experiences within and between different countries.

The UNDP ranked[5] the economies in accordance of their achievements on the above-given three parameters on the scale of one (i.e., 0.000–1.000). As per their achievements the countries were broadly classified into three categories with a range of points on the index:

1. High Human Development Countries: 0.800–1.000 points on the index.
2. Medium Human Development Countries: 0.500–0.799 points on the index.
3. Low Human Development Countries: 0.000–0.499 points on the index.

The *Human Development Report 2020* is discussed in ***Chapter 20.***

The Debate Continues

Though the UNDP commissioned team had evolved a consensus as to what constitutes development, academicians and experts around the world have been debating this issue. By 1995, economies around the world had officially accepted the concept of human development propounded by the UNDP. Basically, the UNDP designed HDR was used by the World Bank since the 1990s to quantify the developmental efforts of the member countries and cheap developmental funds were allocated in accordance. Naturally, the member countries started emphasising on the parameters of income, education and life expectancy in their policy making and in this way the idea of HDI got obligatory or voluntary acceptance around the world.

5. Todaro and Smith, ***Economic Development***, p. 58.

For many years, experts and scholars came up with their own versions of defining development. They gave unequal weightage to the determinants defining development, as well as selected some completely different parameters which could also denote development in a more suitable way. Since quality is a matter of value judgement and a normative concept, there was scope for this representation. Most of such attempts were not prescriptions for an alternative development index, but they were basically trying to show the incompleteness of the HDI, via intellectual satires. One such attempt was made by economists and scholars of the London School of Economics in 1999 which concluded that, Bangladesh was the most developed country in the world with the USA, Norway, Sweden getting the lowest ranks in the index.

Basically, it is very much possible to come out with such an index. As for example, we may say that peace of mind is a necessary element of development and betterment in human life which depends heavily on the fact as to how much sleep we get everyday. House theft and burglary are major determinants of a good night's sleep which in turn depends on the fact as how assured we go to sleep in our homes at night from burglars and thieves. It means we may try to know a good sleep by the data of thefts and burglaries in homes. Since minor house thefts and burglaries are under-reported in police stations, the surveyor, suppose tried to know such cases with data as how many 'locks' were sold in a country in a particular year. In this way a country where people hardly have anything to be stolen or no risk of being burgled might be considered having the best sleep in night, thus the best peace of mind and that is why this will be the most developed country.

Basically, the HDI could be considered as one possible way of measuring development which was evolved by the concerned group of experts with the maximum degree of consensus. But the index which calculates the development of economies on certain parameters might be overlooking many other important factors, which affect the development of an economy and standard of living. As per experts, such other determinants affecting our living conditions might be:

- cultural aspects of the economy,
- outlook towards aesthetics and purity of the environment,
- aspects related to the rule and administration in the economy,
- people's idea of happiness and prestige,
- ethical dimension of human life, etc.

Introspecting Development

Confusion about the real meaning of development started only after the World Bank and the international Monetary Fund came into being. As experts were studying the development process of the developing world, they were also surveying the performance reports of the developed world. As the western world came to be regarded as developed, having top twenty ranks on the HDI, social scientists started evaluating the conditions of life in these economies. Most of such studies concluded that life in the developed world is anything but happy. Crime, corruption, burglaries, extortion, drug trafficking, flesh trade, rape, homicide, moral degradation, sexual perversion, etc.—all kinds of the so-called vices—were thriving in the developed world. It means development had failed to deliver them happiness, peace of mind, a general well-being and a feeling of being in good state. Scholars started questioning the very efforts being made for development around the world. Most of them have suggested a need of redefining development which could deliver happiness to mankind.

Why has development not delivered happiness to the developed world? The answer to this question does not lie in any one objective fact, but touches so many areas of human life. First, whenever economists from the outset talked about progress they meant overall happiness of human life. Social scientists, somehow have been using terms such as progress, growth, development, well-being, welfare as synonyms of 'happiness'. Happiness is a normative concept as well as a state of mind. Therefore, its idea might vary from one economy to the other.[6]

Second, the period in which development was defined, it was considered that with the supply of some selected material resources human life can be improved. These resources were pin-pointed as, a better level of income, proper level of nutrition, healthcare facilities, proper levels of literacy and education, etc.

Happiness is a broader thing than development. The so-called 'development' for which the world has been striving hard for the last many decades is capable of delivering material happiness to mankind. Happiness has its non-material side also. It means, while the world has been trying to maximise its prospects of development, i.e., material happiness, it could not attend the non-material part of happiness. The non-material part of our life is rooted in ethics, religion, spiritualism and cultural values. As development or human development was defined in material terms, it could only deliver us material happiness which is visibly available in the developed world. Due to partial definition of development, the developed world has been able to achieve development, i.e., happiness, but only of material kind. For the non-material part of happiness, we need to redefine our 'ideas' of development.

---

6. There were diverse opinions about the real meaning of 'development'—by mid-1940s upto almost the whole 1950s it meant 5–7 per cent growth rate in an economy—even by the IMF and WB. By the late 1960s new views of development started emerging. **Arthur Lewis** had seen development in the sense of *human freedom* in 1963 itself when he concluded that 'the advantage of economic growth is not that wealth increases happiness, but that it increases the range of human choice.' For him development means a freedom from 'servitude'—mankind could be free to have choices to lead a life full of material goods or in spiritual contemplation (W. Arthur Lewis, The Theory of Economic Growth, Allen & Unwin, London, 1963, p. 420).

For **Dudley Seers** development meant more employment and equality besides a falling poverty ('The Meaning of Development', a paper presented at the 11th World Conference of the Society for International Development, New Delhi, 1969, p. 3). Dudley Seers was later supported by many other economists such as **Denis Goulet** (The Cruel Choice: A New Concept in the Theory of Development, Atheneum, New York, 1971, p. 23), Richard Brinkman (1995), P. Jegadish Gandhi (1996) and many others.

The **International Labour Organization** (ILO) had also articulated by the mid-1970s that economic development must be able to deliver the economic ability that people can meet their basic needs (the concept of 'sustenance') besides the elimination of absolute poverty, creating more employment and lessening income inequalities (Employment, Growth and Basic Needs, ILO, Geneva, 1976). **Amartya Sen** articulated a similar view via his ideas of 'capabilities' and 'entitlements' ('Development: Which Way Now?', Economic Journal 93, December 1983, pp. 754–57).

By 1994, the United Nations looked to including the element of 'capabilities' in its idea of development when it concludes that 'human beings are born with certain potential capabilities and the purpose of development is to create an environment in which all people can expand their capabilities in present times and in future. Wealth is important for human life. But to concentrate exclusively on it is wrong for two reasons. First, accumulating wealth is not necessary for the fulfillment of some important human choices.... Second, human choices extend far beyond economic well-being' (UNDP, Human Development Report 1994, Oxford University Press, New York, 1994, pp. 13–15).

The **World Bank** by 1991 had also changed its views about development and had concluded that for improving the *quality of life* we should include education, health, nutrition, less poverty, cleaner environment, equality, greater freedom and richer cultural life as the goals of development.

Amartya Sen, a leading thinker on the meaning of development attracted attention for articulating human goals of development. He opined that enhancing the lives and the freedoms we enjoy, should be the concerns of development known as the 'capabilities' approach to development (see his Commodities and Capabilities, North Holland, Amsterdam, 1985 and Development as Freedom, Alfred Knopf, New York, 1999).

Somehow a very small kingdom had been able to define development in its own way, which included material as well as non-material aspects of life and named it the Gross National Happiness (GNH). This country is Bhutan.

Gross National Happiness Bhutan, a small Himalayan kingdom and an economic non-entity, developed a new concept of assessing development in the early 1970s—the Gross National Happiness (GNH). Without rejecting the idea of human development propounded by UNDP, the kingdom has been officially following the targets set by the GNH. Bhutan has been following the GNH since 1972 which has the following parameters to attain happiness/development:

- Higher real per capita income
- Good governance
- Environmental protection
- Cultural promotion (i.e., inculcation of *ethical* and *spiritual* values in life without which, it says, progress may become a curse rather than a blessing)

At the level of real per capita income, the GNH and the HDI are the same. Though the HDI is silent on the issue of 'good governance', today it should be considered as being promoted around the world once the World Bank came with its report on it in 1995 and enforced it upon the member states. On the issue of protecting environment, though the HDI did not say anything directly, the World Bank and the UNO had already accepted the immediacy of sustainable development by then and by early 1990s there was a separate UN Convention on the matter (follow up on this convention has been really very low till date which is a different issue).

It means the basic difference between the GNH and the HDI looks at the level of assimilating the ethical and spiritual aspects into our (UNDP's) idea of development.

An impartial analysis sufficiently suggests that material achievements are unable to deliver us happiness devoid of some ethics at its base. And ethics are rooted in the religious and spiritual texts. But the new world is guided by its own scientific and secular interpretation of life and the world has always been suspicious about recognising the spiritual factor in human life. Rather the western idea of secularism was defined after rejecting the very existence of anything like God and also rejecting the whole traditional hypothesis of spiritualism as instances of ignorance and orthodoxy. And there should not be any doubt in accepting it that the western ideology in the name of development has ultimately, dominated the modern world and its way of life. The idea of development which was followed by a large part of the world has been cent per cent 'this-worldly'. And anybody can assess today what kind of happiness the world has been able to achieve in the end.

A recent study by a senior economist from the UNDP on the Bhutanese development experience under the GNH has vindicated the idea of 'gross happiness' which development must result into. As per the study, the period 1984–98 has been spectacular in terms of development with life expectancy increasing by a hopping 19 years, gross school enrolment reaching 72 per cent and literacy touching 47.5 per cent (from just 17 per cent).[7]

After the terror attack on the World Trade Centre in the USA the whole world has gone for a psychic metamorphosis and at least the euphoria of development from this world to that world has been shaken from its very base. The world which is in the process of globalisation at one hand has started introspecting whether multicultural co-existence

7. **Stefan Priesner** a senior economist with the UNDP conducted the study for the John Hopkins University, USA, in 2005.

is possible. The Human Development Report of 2004 was titled as *Cultural Liberty in Today's Diverse World.* We may conclude that mankind is passing through a phase of serious introspection and transition where the dominant view in the world may metamorphose into redefining the very idea of development by including ethical values and spiritualism as important parts. But till now the proponents of development look a bit shy in believing and accepting whole-heartedly that there exists a non-material part of life, which needs to be realised to make our development result into happiness.

HAPPINESS

The *World Happiness Report 2021* was released[8] on 19th March 2021 (one day before the International Day of Happiness). The 149-nation report, 9th in the series (no report was published in 2014), ranks nations based on 'reported happiness' by their citizens. Aimed at 'guiding public policy' of the nations, the report measures and ranks the nations based on the following *six variables*:

1. GDP per capita (at PPP)
2. Social support (someone to count on)
3. Healthy life expectancy at birth
4. Freedom to make life choices
5. Generosity
6. Perception of corruption

Besides considering the data on the above-given six indicators, the report based on the Gallup World Poll, also considered the respondents' vote on three 'subjective' indicators, namely:

1. ***Life evaluations:*** Where the respondents will situate their life on a ladder from 0 at the bottom to 10 at top representing the worst and the best possible life respectively.
2. ***Positive emotions:*** Whether the respondents experienced 'happiness, laugh and enjoyment' on the day they polled and the day before.
3. ***Negative emotions:*** Whether the respondents experienced 'worry, sadness, and anger' on the day they polled and the day before.

Major highlights The major highlights from the report are as given below:

- The top **10 happiest** countries (last year's ranks given in brackets) are—***1st*** Finland (1st), ***2nd*** Denmark (2nd), ***3rd*** Switzerland (3rd), ***4th*** Iceland (4th), ***5th*** The Netherlands (6th), ***6th*** Norway (5th) ***7th*** Sweden (7th), ***8th*** Luxembourg (9th), ***9th*** New Zealand (8th) and ***10th*** Austria (10th).
- Afghanistan is the **least happy** country.
- Ranks of few ***advanced economies***—Australia (11th), Germany (13th), Canada (14th), UK (17th), USA (19th), France (21st), Japan (56th).
- **India** is ranked ***139th*** (up 5 ranks from the report of 2020 in which it has lost 4 ranks in comparison to the report of 2019). The ***9 other countries*** that rank below India are Burundi, Yemen, Tanzania, Haiti, Malawi, Lesotho, Botswana, Rwanda, and Zimbabwe.
- Among ***India's neighbours*** Pakistan is ranked 105th, China 84th, Sri Lanka 129th and Bangladesh 101st.

Trust and benevolence The evidence on the links between trust and well-being suggests that

8. **World Happiness Report 2021** edited by John F. Helliwell, Richard Layard, Jeffrey D. Sachs, Jan-Emmanuel De Neve, Lara B. Aknin, and Shun Wang, Sustainable Development Solutions Network (SDSN), UNO, New York.

trust and benevolence are strong supports for well-being, and also for successful strategies to control COVID-19.

Social capital and political system Quality of social capital and the extent to which people trust their governments and benevolence of others supported not only countries' ability to maintain their happiness 'before' and 'during' the pandemic but reduced the COVID-19 death toll also— by facilitating more effective strategies for limiting the spread of the pandemic while maintaining and building a sense of common purpose.

Compliant citizens and freedom Policies can be very effective when citizens are 'compliant' (as in East Asia) to government directives and more 'freedom-oriented' (as in Australia and New Zealand)— the evidence shows that people's morale improves when the government acts.

Lessons from the Asia-Pacific The region has achieved notable success compared to the North Atlantic region in controlling the pandemic, with far lower mortality rates and greater successful implementation of Non-Pharmaceutical Interventions (NPIs) to stop the spread of the disease (such as border controls, face-mask use, physical distancing, widespread testing, contact tracing, and quarantining/home isolation of infected individuals). These measures in Asia-Pacific were both *top-down* (governments putting strong control policies), and *bottom-up* (public complying with governments' health directives).

The NPIs found lower public compliance in the ***North Atlantic*** countries may be due to their characteristics such as— being more 'individualistic', relative 'looseness' of social norms, higher assertions of 'personal liberty' and demands for 'privacy'.

Mental health Mental health has been one of the casualties both of the pandemic and the resulting lockdowns. On the positive side, the pandemic has shone a light on mental health as never before— this increased public awareness bodes well for future research and better services that are so urgently needed.

Future of work and social capital The impacts of the pandemic on the world of work are likely to endure. Evidence from past recessions and early research from the COVID-19 suggests that 'young people' who come of age in worse macroeconomic conditions are more likely to be driven by financial security in adulthood.

The shift to *remote working* is likely to last long after the crisis has subsided, which will provide future workers with more flexibility and control over their working lives, but at the risk of undermining social capital at work.

WELLBY approach

A new concept, the Well-Being-Adjusted Life Years (WELLBYs), has been introduced in the report to evaluate social progress and make effective policy, which takes into account both— (i) the quality of life, and (ii) the length of life.

As the concept of Quality-Adjusted Life Years (QALYs), is used by health economists to count (only) the individual patient's health-related quality of life, the WELLBY approach, counts the *total* well-being of individual. This approach puts a lower value upon money (unlike customary) relative to life. According to many studies in rich countries, an extra US$ 1 raises WELLBYs by around 1/100,000 points. But an extra year of life increases WELLBYs by around 7.5 WELLBYs. So, the community should value a year of life equally to US$ 750,000 of GDP.

The approach also provides a more complete way of measuring human progress and comparing the performance of different countries. It does this by multiplying average well-being by life expectancy. On this basis, the number of WELLBYs per person rose by 1.3 per cent between 2006-08 and 2017-19, due to higher life expectancy, especially in the less healthy countries— this was a significant reduction in fundamental inequality across the world, and inequality remains lower in 2020 despite COVID-19. The report advises all policy-makers to maximise the WELLBYs of all.

The Meaning of Happiness

The word 'happiness' is quite complex and is not used lightly. Happiness is an aspiration of every human being, and can also be a measure of social progress. Yet, are the citizens of different countries, happy? If they are not, what, if anything, can be done about it? The key to proper measurement must begin with the meaning of the word 'happiness'. As per the WHR 2013, the problem, of course, is that happiness is used in at least **two** ways:

1. As an emotion ['Were you happy yesterday?'], and
2. As an evaluation ['Are you happy with your life as a whole?'].

If individuals were to routinely mix up their responses to these very different questions, then measures of happiness might tell us very little. Changes in reported happiness used to track social progress would perhaps reflect little more than transient changes in emotion. Or impoverished persons who express happiness in terms of emotion might inadvertently diminish society's will to fight poverty. Fortunately, respondents to the happiness surveys do not tend to make such confusing mistakes. Both the WHRs did show that the respondents of the surveys clearly recognise the difference between *happiness as an emotion* and *happiness in the sense of life satisfaction*. The responses of individuals to these different questions are highly distinct. A very poor person might report himself to be happy emotionally at a specific time, while also reporting a much lower sense of happiness with life as a whole; and indeed, people living in extreme poverty do express low levels of happiness with life as a whole. Such answers should spur our societies to work harder to end extreme poverty.

The ***WHR*** is based on the primary measures of subjective well-being;[9] life evaluations;[10] life satisfaction;[11] and happiness with life as a whole.[12] Thus, happiness appears twice, once as an emotional report, and once as part of a life evaluation, giving considerable evidence about the nature and causes of happiness in both its major senses.

The Background

In July 2011 the UN General Assembly passed a historic resolution.[13] It invited member countries to measure the happiness of their people and to use this to help guide their public policies. This was followed in April 2012 by the **first** UN high-level meeting on happiness and well-being, chaired by the Prime Minister of Bhutan. At the same time

9. Guidelines on ***Measuring Subjective Well-being***, OECD, Paris, 2013.
10. Used in the ***World Values Survey, the European Social Survey*** and many other national and international surveys. It is the core 'life evaluation' question recommended by the OECD (2013), and used since the first ***World Happiness Report***.
11. The *Gallup World Poll (GWP)* – the GWP includes the 'life satisfaction' question on a 0 to 10 scale on an experimental basis, giving a sample sufficiently large to show that when used with consistent samples the two questions provide mutually supportive information on the size and relative importance of the correlates.
12. The ***European Social Survey*** contains questions about 'happiness with life as a whole', and about life satisfaction, both on the same 0 to 10 numerical scale. The responses provide the scientific base to support the WHR findings that answers to the two questions give consistent (and mutually supportive) information about the correlates of a good life.
13. UN General Assembly, ***Happiness: Towards a Holistic Approach to Development***, United Nations 19 July 2011.

the **first** *World Happiness Report* was published,[14] followed some months later by the OECD Guidelines setting an international standard for the measurement of well-being.[15]

Re-imagining the Idea of Happiness

Search for a 'happier' life for humanity has been the ultimate aim of not only saints, seers and philosophers, but of economists too. The whole gamut of economics literature on progress, growth and development is ultimately aimed at bringing more 'happiness' into the lives of human beings. Over the time, diverse ideological currents impressed upon the humanity to take variety of 'meanings' out of the highly subjective term 'happiness'—and finally, the humanity is where it is today.

A time also came when many scholars and world leaders raised the ultimate question—are we happier today? And in the wake of this increased 'scrutiny' around the world, there came the UN resolution of 2011 which invited member countries to measure the happiness of their people and to use this to help guide their public policies. The *WHR 2012* itself provides a very interesting and eye-opening inquiry into the state of human happiness in the world. To understand the 'shift' which is expected to take place among policymakers around the world in coming years, it will be better to ***lift some ideas*** from the **first** **WHR:**[16]

1. This is an age of stark contradictions. While at the one hand the world enjoys technologies of unimaginable sophistication, at the other hand, at least one billion people are living without enough to eat. The world economy is propelled to soaring new heights of productivity through ongoing technological and organisational advances; yet it is relentlessly destroying the natural environment in the process. Countries achieve great progress in economic development as conventionally measured; yet along the way countries succumb to new crises of obesity, smoking, diabetes, depression, and other ills of modern life. These contradictions would not come as a shock to the greatest sages of humanity, including **Aristotle** and the **Buddha,** who taught humanity, time and again, that material gain alone will not fulfil our deepest needs. Material life must be harnessed to meet these human needs, most importantly to promote the end of suffering, social justice and the attainment of happiness.

2. The *WHR 2012* took key examples from the USA—the world's economic superpower—which has achieved striking economic and technological progress over the past half century without gains in the self-reported happiness of the citizenry with the following serious 'concerns' of today:
   (i) uncertainties and anxieties are high,
   (ii) social and economic inequalities have widened considerably,
   (iii) social trust is in decline, and
   (iv) confidence in government is at an all-time low.

   Perhaps for these reasons, life satisfaction in the USA has remained nearly constant during the decades of rising Gross National Product (GNP) per capita.

3. The realities of poverty, anxiety, environmental degradation, and unhappiness in the midst of great plenty should not be regarded as mere curiosities. They require our urgent attention, and especially so at

---

14. J. F. Helliwell, R. Layard & J. Sachs (eds.), ***World Happiness Report 2012***, Earth Institute, New York, USA, 2012.

15. OECD; **Guidelines on Measuring Subjective Well-being**, Organisation for Economic Co-operation and Development, Paris, 2013.

16. J. F. Helliwell, R. Layard and J. Sachs (eds.), ***World Happiness Report 2012***, Earth Institute, New York, USA, 2012.

this juncture in human history. For we have entered a new phase of the world, termed the *Anthropocene*[17] by the world's Earth System scientists. The Anthropocene will necessarily reshape our societies. If we continue mindlessly along the current economic trajectory, we risk undermining the Earth's life support systems—food supplies, clean water and stable climate—necessary for human health and even survival in some places. In years or decades, conditions of life may become dire in several fragile regions of the world. We are already experiencing deterioration of life support systems in the dry lands of the Horn of Africa and parts of Central Asia.

On the other hand, if we act wisely, we can protect the Earth while raising quality of life broadly around the world. We can do this by adopting *lifestyles* and *technologies* that improve **happiness** (or life satisfaction) and reduce human damage to the environment. Sustainable Development is the term given to the combination of human well-being, social inclusion and environmental sustainability. There is no doubt in concluding that the 'quest for happiness' is intimately linked to the 'quest for sustainable development'.

4. In an impoverished society, the urge for material gain typically makes a lot of sense. Higher household income (or higher per capita GNP) generally signifies an improvement in the life conditions of the poor. The poor suffer from dire deprivations of various kinds: lack of adequate food supplies, remunerative jobs, access to health care, safe homes, safe water and sanitation, and educational opportunities. As incomes rise from very low levels, human well-being improves. Not surprisingly, the poor report a rising satisfaction with their lives as their meager incomes increase.

On the opposite end of the income spectrum, for most individuals in the high-income world, the basic deprivations have been vanquished. There is enough food, shelter, basic amenities (such as clean water and sanitation), and clothing to meet their daily needs. In fact, there is a huge surfeit of amenities above basic needs. Poor people would swap with rich people in a heartbeat. Yet all is not well. ***The conditions of affluence have created their own set of traps.***

Most importantly, the lifestyles of the rich imperil the survival of the poor. Human-induced climate change is already hitting the poorest regions and claiming lives and livelihoods. It is telling that in much of the rich world, affluent populations are so separated from the poor that there is little recognition, practical or moral, of the adverse spillovers (or 'externalities') from their own behaviour.

5. **Affluence** has also created its own set of afflictions and addictions (problems)—obesity, adult-onset diabetes, tobacco-related illnesses, eating disorders such as anorexia and bulimia, psychosocial disorders, and addictions to shopping, TV and gambling, are all examples of disorders of development. So too is the loss of community, the decline of social trust and the rising anxiety levels associated with the vagaries of the modern globalised economy, including the threats of unemployment or episodes of illness not covered by health insurance in the United States (and many other countries).

17. The Anthropocene is a newly invented term that combines two Greek words: 'anthropo' for human; and 'cene' for new, as in a new geological epoch. The Anthropocene is the new epoch in which humanity, through its technological prowess and population of 7 billion, has become the major driver of changes of Earth's physical systems, including the climate, carbon cycle, water cycle, nitrogen cycle and biodiversity.

6. Higher average incomes do not necessarily improve average well-being, the US being a clear case in point, as noted famously by Professor Richard Easterlin[18]—where GNP per capita has risen by a factor of three since 1960, while measures of average happiness have remained essentially unchanged over the half-century. The increased US output has caused massive environmental damages, notably through greenhouse gas concentrations and human-induced climate change, without doing much at all to raise the well-being even of Americans. Thus, we don't have a trade off between short-run gains to well-being versus long-run costs to the environment; we have a pure loss to the environment without offsetting short-term gains.

The ***parodox*** that Easterlin noted in the US was that at any particular time richer individuals are happier than poorer ones, but over time the society did not become happier as it became richer. This is due to four reasons:

(i) Individuals compare themselves to others. They are happier when they are higher on the social (or income) ladder. Yet when everybody rises together, relative status remains unchanged.

(ii) The gains have not been evenly shared, but have gone disproportionately to those at the top of the income and education distribution.

(iii) The other societal factors—insecurity, loss of social trust, declining confidence in government—have counteracted any benefits felt from higher incomes.

(iv) Individuals may experience an initial jump in happiness when their income rises, but then at least partly return to earlier levels as they *adapt* to their new higher income.

7. These phenomena put a clear limit on the extent to which rich countries can become happier through the simple device of *economic growth*. In fact, there are still other general reasons to doubt the formula of ever rising GNP per person as the route to happiness. While higher income may raise happiness to some extent, the *quest* for higher income may actually reduce one's happiness. In other words, it may be nice to have more money, but not so nice to crave for it. **Psychologists** have found repeatedly that individuals who put a high premium on higher incomes generally are less happy and more vulnerable to other psychological ills than individuals who do not crave higher incomes. Aristotle and the Buddha advised humanity to follow a middle path between asceticism on the one side and craving material goods on the other.

8. Another problem is the creation of new material **'wants'** through the incessant advertising of products using powerful imagery and other means of persuasion. Since the imagery is ubiquitous on all of our digital devices, the stream of advertising is more relentless than ever before. Advertising is now a business of around US $500 billion per year. Its goal is to overcome satiety by creating wants and longings where none previously existed. Advertisers and marketers do this in part by preying on psychological weaknesses and unconscious urges. Cigarettes, caffeine, sugar, and trans-fats, all cause cravings if not outright

18. Among the foremost contributors to the *Happiness Economics*, Easterlin is particularly known for his 1974 article **'Does Economic Growth Improl'e the Human Lot? Some Empirical Evidence'** (his ideas are today known as the ***Easterlin Paradox***, was proposed by him in this article). Here he concluded that contrary to expectation, happiness at a national level does not increase with wealth once basic needs are fulfilled.

addictions. Fashions are sold through increasingly explicit sexual imagery. Product lines are generally sold by associating the products with high social status rather than with real needs.

9. The thinking of becoming happier by becoming richer is challenged by the law of *diminishing marginal utility of income*[19]—after a certain point, the gains are very small. This means that poor people benefit far more than rich people from an added dollar of income. This is a good reason why tax-and-transfer systems among high-income OECD countries on balance take in net revenues from high-income households and make net transfers to low-income households. Put another way, the inequality of household income is systematically lower with net of taxes and transfers than before taxes and transfers.[20]

10. The western economist's logic of ever higher GNP is built on a vision of humanity completely at variance with the wisdom of the sages, the research of psychologists, and the practices of advertisers. Economists assume that individuals are **'rational decision-makers'** who know what they want and how to get it, or to get as close to it as possible, given their budget. Individuals care largely about themselves and derive pleasure mainly through their consumption. The individual's preferences as consumers are a given or change in ways actually anticipated in advance by the individuals themselves. Some economists even say that drug addicts have acted 'rationally', consciously trading off the early benefits of drug use with the later high toll of addiction.

11. We understand that we need a very different model of humanity, one in which we experienced complicated interplay of emotions and rational thought, unconscious and conscious decision-making, **fast** and **slow** thinking. Many of our decisions are led by emotions and instincts, and only later rationalised by conscious thought. Our decisions are easily 'primed' by associations, imagery, social context and advertising. We are inconsistent or 'irrational' in sequential choices, failing to meet basic standards of rational consistency. And we are largely unaware of our own mental apparatus, so we easily fall into *traps* and *mistakes*. Addicts do not anticipate their future pain; we spend now and suffer the consequences of bankruptcy later; we break our diets now because we aren't thinking clearly about the consequences. We also understand (again!) that we are **social animals** through and through. We learn through imitation, and gain our happiness through meeting *social norms* and having a sense of *belonging to the community*.

12. Human beings feel the pain of others, and react viscerally when others are sad or injured. We even have a set of 'mirror neurons' that enable us to feel things from the point of view of others. All of this gives us a remarkable capacity to cooperate even with strangers, and even when there is little chance of reward or reciprocity, and to punish 'non-cooperators', even when imposing punishment on others is costly or puts us at risk.

---

19. Suppose that a poor household at ₹1,000 income requires an extra ₹100 to raise its life satisfaction level (or happiness) by one notch. A rich household at ₹1,000,000 income (one thousand times as much as the poor household) would need one thousand times more money, or ₹100,000, to raise its well-being by the same one notch. Gains in income have to be of equal proportions to household income to have the same benefit in units of life satisfaction.

20. On an average across the OECD countries, cash transfers and income taxes reduce inequality by one third. Poverty is around 60 per cent lower than it would be without taxes and benefits. Even among the working-age population, government redistribution reduces poverty by about 50 per cent *(OECD, 2008)*.

Of course there are limits to such cooperation and fellow feeling. We also cheat, bluff, deceive, break our word, and kill members of an out-group. We engage in identity politics, acting as cruel to outsiders as we are loving to our own group. All these lessons of human nature matter more than ever, more even than when the Buddha taught humanity about the illusions of transient pleasures, and the Greeks warned us against the tempting Siren songs that could pull us off our life's course. For today we have more choices than ever before. In the ancient world, the choice facing most of humanity most of the time was little choice indeed—to work hard to secure enough to eat, and even then to face the risk of famine and death from bad weather or bad luck.

13. Today, we face a set of real choices. Should the world pursue GNP to the point of environmental ruin, even when incremental gains in GNP are not increasing much (or at all) the happiness of affluent societies? Should we crave for higher personal income at the cost of the community and social trust? Should our governments spend even a tiny fraction of the $500 billion spent on advertising each year to help individuals and families to understand better their own motivations, wants and needs as consumers? Should we consider some parts of our society to be 'off bounds' to the profit motive, so that we can foster the **spirit of cooperation, trust** and **community?** A recent analyst[21] of Finland's school system, for example, writes that Finland's excellence (ranking near the top of international comparisons in student performance) has been achieved by fostering a spirit of community and equality in the schools. This is in **sharp contrast** to the education reform strategy at work in the US, where the emphasis is to put on *testing, measurement,* and *teacher pay* according to student test performance.

21. Pasi Sahlberg, **Education Policies for Raising Student Learning: The Finnish Approach;** *Journal of Education Policy, 22*(2), March 2007, World Bank, Washington DC, pp. 147–171.

INSIGHTS INTO HUMAN BEHAVIOUR

The World Bank in its report (*World Development Report 2015: Mind, Society, and Behaviour)* said that development policies become more effective when combined with insights into human behaviour. It further adds that policy decisions informed by **behavioural economics** can deliver impressive improvements in promoting development and well-being in society. It some examples from **India** in the areas of healthcare and education:

- Open defecation dropped 11 per cent from very high levels after a Community-Led Total Sanitation (CLTS) programme was combined in some chosen villages with the standard approach of subsidies for toilet construction and information on the transmission of diseases.
- The likelihood of default on loans became three times less with a simple change in the periodicity of meetings between microfinance clients and their repayment groups to weekly rather than monthly.
- Research showed that boys from backward classes were just as good at solving puzzles as boys from the upper castes when caste identity was not revealed. However, in mixed-caste groups, revealing the boys' castes before puzzle-solving sessions created a significant 'caste gap' in achievement with the boys from backward classes under performing by 23 per cent (making caste salient to the test takers invoked identities, which in turn affected performance, as per the report).

The *Report* has recommended that the presence of a stereotype can contribute to measured ability differences, which in turn reinforce the stereotype and serve as a basis for exclusion, in a vicious cycle—finding ways to break this cycle could increase the well-being of marginalised individuals enormously.

Social Norms, Culture and Development

Economic development is not only dependent on fiscal policy, monetary policy and taxation, but is also rooted in human psychology, sociology, culture and norms. In economics, there has been a bit of resistance in emphasising other aspects of development, because it is thought of giving ground to the neighbouring disciplines.[22] The *World Development Report (WDR)* of 2015 focuses on the behavioural and social foundations of development, and has been very well received.

Government documents (generally, hard-nosed), usually, make no mention of the role of social norms and culture in promoting development and economic efficiency. However, there is now a growing body of literature that demonstrates how certain social norms and cultural practices are vital ingredients for economic efficiency and growth. Groups and societies that are known to be honest and trustworthy tend to do better than societies that do not have this reputation. There have been broad cross-country studies and also laboratory experiments that illustrate this. More generally, what is being argued is that a nation's success depends of course on its resources, human capital and economic policies, for instance fiscal and monetary policies, but also on the cultural and social norms that permeate the society. Societies that are endowed with personal integrity and trustworthiness have the natural advantage, in that no third party is required to enforce contracts. For outsiders the mere knowledge that a particular society is trustworthy is reason to do more business and trade with it. One reason why these 'social' causes of development do not get enough recognition in the literature on economic policy is that the science of *how* these economics-friendly social qualities are acquired is not yet fully understood. Fortunately, the new discipline of **behavioural economics** is beginning to give us some insights into the formation of customs and behaviour:[23]

- It is, for instance, known that buildings and office spaces which are cleaner and aesthetically better maintained result in individuals being more honest and desisting corrupt activity. It is almost as if we have a mental inclination not to defile a good ambience through acts of corruption.
- New York city's notorious high crime was controlled, among other things, by cleaning up the city and removing graffiti from the walls. New York's police department took a decision to deter vandalism and graffiti that scar public spaces. This act of making the city scape more aesthetic somehow made potential criminals less prone to crime.
- One sees casual evidence of this in the behaviour of Delhites using the metro. It has been widely noted that people behave better when they travel on Delhi's well-maintained metro (postponing their bad behaviour to when they come up to the surface again, some would add).

All this is in keeping with the influential *broken windows* theory in sociology, which maintains that, if we control low level, anti-social behaviour and take small steps to improve the environment,

22. Kaushik Basu, Chief Economist, World Bank, *Livemint*, N Delhi, 3 February, 2015.

23. Ministry of Finance, ***Economic Survey 2009–10***, GoI, N Delhi, pp. 34–35.

this will have a natural deterrent effect on larger criminal behaviour and acts of corruption. Also, the sheer recognition and awareness that some collective qualities of citizens, such as honesty and trustworthiness, enable the entire society to do well, prompts individuals to adopt those qualities and overcome the ubiquitous free-rider problem.

There is a growing literature[24] in economics arguing that **pro-social behaviour**, which includes *altruism* and *trustworthiness*, is innate to human beings and, moreover, forms an essential ingredient for the efficient functioning of economies. In other words, human beings have a natural ability to forego personal gains for the sake of other people or because that is what is required because of a promise the person had made. This trait may well have evolutionary roots, but its existence is now well demonstrated in laboratory tests by recent studies.

Values and Economics

There is research[25] in psychology and evolutionary biology which shows that **morality, altruism,** and other-regarding **values** are an innate part of the human mind, even though the social setting in which a person lives can nurture or stunt these traits. However, the recognition that these human and moral qualities can have a large impact on economic development came relatively late to economics. Hence, the literature on this is relatively recent and brief. In fact, recent research shows that having a few 'good' human beings in society can give rise to dynamics through which we end up with an overall better society. There is also evidence that social norms and habits that at first sight seem ingrained in a society can change over short periods of time. By this argument it is possible for a country to nurture and develop the kinds of social norms that enable a more vibrant economy.

In talking about a nation's economic progress, all attention, including both praise and criticism, is usually focused on the government. It is, however, important to recognise that much also depends on civil society, the firms, the farmers and ordinary citizens. The social norms and collective beliefs that shape the behaviour of these agents play an important role in how a nation performs.

Honesty, punctuality, the propensity to keep promises, the attitude towards corruption are matters shaped in great part by norms and social beliefs and the behaviour patterns can become habitual. Moreover, in a democracy like India, what can be done by government depends in great measure on how ordinary people think and what people believe in. That is what electoral politics is all about. An important reason why this got so little attention in the past is because so much of traditional economics was written as if these non-economic facets of life did not matter. But we now know that a market economy cannot function if people are totally self serving. While self-interest is a major driver of economic growth, it is important to recognise that honesty, integrity and trustworthiness constitute the cement that binds society. At times economists treated these social norms, preferences and customs as unalterable. If that were so, there would not be much point

24. Over half a dozen contemporary works have been cited as references by the Ministry of Finance, ***Economic Survey 2010–11***, GoI, N Delhi, p. 40.

25. Several recent literature have been quoted by the ***Economic Survey 2011–12***, Ministry of Finance, GoI, N Delhi, p. 44:
    (i) F. Fukuyama, ***Trust: The Social Virtues and the Creation of Prosperity***, Free Press, New York, 1996.
    (ii) A. S. Guha, and B. Guha, 'The Persistence of Goodness', ***Journal of Institutional and Theoretical Economics***, 2012.
    (iii) M. D. Hauser, ***Moral Minds***, Harper Collins, New York, 2012.
    (iv) T. Hashimoto, 'Japanese Clocks and the History of Punctuality in Modern Japan', ***East Asian Science, Technology, and Society*** 2, 2008.

in analysing their effect. But we do know that these qualities in people can change. Honesty and integrity can be nurtured and aversion to corruption can be shored up.

NUDGE & PUBLIC POLICY

Behavioural economics provides insights to **nudge**[26] people towards desirable behaviour. By now, nudge has been successfully used in India as an instrument of public policy (in the Swachh Bharat Mission (SBM) and Beti Bachao Beti Padhao (BBBP) campaigns) and it can be further used to aim even higher goals[27] such as:

1. from BBBP to BADLAV (Beti Aapki Dhan Lakshmi Aur Vijay Lakshmi);
2. from Swachh Bharat to Sundar Bharat;
3. from 'Give it up'(for the LPG subsidy) to 'Think about the Subsidy'; and
4. from tax evasion to tax compliance.

Nudges can be used in policy making with effective outcomes by taking the following three policy actions:

1. People's behaviour is influenced by social and religious norms. Thus, beneficial norms can be used as positive influencers (friends and neighbours as role models) to modify people's behaviour.
2. As people have an inclination to go for 'default' option in their actions changing the default can be a very effective policy.
3. Policy of reminders and repeated reinforcements help sustained change in behaviour as people find it difficult to sustain good habits.

Common people fail to connect to policy actions of the Governments. For an effective use of nudges in public policy it is essential to relate economics to common person[28] using something that he or she encounters every day, for example, *a plate of food.*

COVID-19 AND DEVELOPMENT

By now, the world has seen several alternative economic/development models among which the Washington Consensus, Santiago Consensus, and Beijing Consensus had wider sways. World has also witnessed as how the meaning of progress metamorphosed into happiness from just being a monetary idea. But these changes have not proved to be enough. The ongoing global pandemic COVID-19 has posed a *serious question* to the development model the world is following! Other than showing world's unpreparedness in fighting such a pandemic it has also started a vigorous debate about the need of a new economic approach to development. The sustainability issue which has been debated by the experts since early 1960s has got a new dimension this time – the *local dimension* of development. Experts have given empirical insights of local approach (by being ethical) in saving environment and creating

26. Nudge literally means to prod (someone) gently with one's elbow in order to attract attention. It is a concept of behavioural science which proposes *positive reinforcement* and *indirect suggestions* as ways to influence the behaviour of individuals or groups. Nudging contrasts with other ways to achieve compliance, such as education, legislation or enforcement—it is different from giving incentives or penalising. The concept of nudge was popularised by **Richard Thaler** and **C. R. Sunstein** in the book ***Nudge: Improving Decisions about Health, Wealth, and Happiness***, Yale University Press, New Haven, CT, 2008. Thaler was awarded Nobel Memorial Prize for Economic Science in 2017 in recognition to his contributions to Behavioural Economics.

27. **Economic Survey 2018-19**, Vol. 1, pp. 30-56, Ministry of Finance, GoI, N Delhi.

28. *Thalinomics: The Economics of a Plate of Food in India*, **Economic Survey 2019-20**, Vol. 1, pp. 260-285, Ministry of Finance, GoI, N Delhi.

happiness but this time round the proposition is to build the local economic model.

Hit with increasing scarcity of resources, degrading environment and visible risks of climate change, the COVID-19 pandemic has made the common people (this time) to ask very fundamental and imaginative questions on mass scale (circulating globally on the *social media* platforms), such as – what are needs of life? how much is enough? what for conspicuous consumption? can this earth sustain our demands? etc. Already, the ideologies like 'minimalism' have been wreaking havoc by slowing demand in economies (as in case of Japan since 2002), now people across the world are inclined to *consume less and less*. In contrast, the contemporary economic model the world follows is based on the foundation of never-ending enhancement in demand (by accelerating consumption!).

The ongoing pandemic has forced the mankind to re-assess the model of development on which it has such a high pride. Alternative economic models are being forwarded again by scholars. Though, it seems quite pessimistic but many are predicting that the world has changed for all time to come! India also has its own share of challenges and needs serious introspection. Where does India stand amidst this crisis? Some feel the ***Atmanirbhar Bharat Abhiyan*** is India's way to explore for an alternative economic model? But does this campaign have co-ordinates to redefine our relationship with nature and meaning of development? [For more on this refer the topic 'The Circularity of Economy in' ***Chapter 21***].

CHAPTER 3

EVOLUTION OF THE INDIAN ECONOMY

*After 1757, when the East India Company took over the governance of Bengal, the British relationship with India became exploitative, as exports to Britain and opium exports to China were financed out of the tax revenue from Bengal. There is not much evidence of significant transfer of European technology to Asia. To understand why, it is useful to scrutinise the experience of China and India, as they accounted for three-quarters of the Asian population and GDP in 1500 AD.**

In this Chapter...

- The Background
- Prime Moving Force: Agriculture vs. Industry
- Planned and Mixed Economy
- Emphasis on the Public Sector

THE BACKGROUND

The economic profile of India was in complete distress at the time of Independence. Being a typical case of colonial economy, India was serving a purpose of development not for herself but for a foreign land—the United Kingdom. Both agriculture and industry were having structural distortions while the state was playing not even a marginal role. During the half century before India became independent, the world was having accelerated development and expansion in its agriculture and industry on the shoulders of the active role being played by the states, with the same happening in the UK itself.[1]

There was not only the unilateral transfer of investible capital to Britain by the colonial state (the 'drain of wealth'), but the unequal exchange was day by day crippling India's commerce, trade and the thriving handloom industry, too. The colonial state practiced policies which were great impediments in the process of development in the country. Throughout the colonial rule, the

1. Bipan Chandra, Mridula Mukherjee and Aditya Mukherjee, ***India After Independence***, Penguin Books, New Delhi, p. 341.

* *Angus Maddison,* **Growth and Interaction in the World Economy: The Roots of Modernity,** *The AEI Press, Washington DC, 2005, p. 60.*

economic vision that the state had was to increase India's capacity to export primary products, and increase the purchase/import of the British manufactured goods and raise revenues to meet the drain of capital as well as meet the revenue requirements of the imperial defence.[2]

The social sector was a neglected area for the British rulers which had a negative impact on the production and productivity of the economy. India remained a continent of illiterate peasants under British rule. At the time of Independence, its literacy was only 17 per cent with 32.5 years of life expectancy at birth.[3]

Industrialisation of India was also neglected by the colonisers—the infrastructure was not built to industrialise India but to exploit its raw materials. Indian capitalists who did emerge were highly dependent on British commercial capital and many sectors of the industry were dominated by British firms, e.g., shipping, banking, insurance, coal, plantation crops and jute.[4]

The pre-independence period was altogether a period of near stagnation showing almost no change in the structure of production or in the levels of productivity—the aggregate real output during the first half of the 20th century estimated at less than 2 per cent a year or less.[5]

The overall economic performance of India under the British rule was very low. According to economic statistician Angus Maddison, there was no per capita growth in India from 1600 to 1870—per capita growth was a meagre 0.2 per cent from 1870 to 1947, compared with 1 per cent in the UK.[6] The per capita incomes of ₹18 for 1899 and ₹39.5 for 1895 in current prices say the true story of the abject poverty Indian masses were faced with.[7] The repeated famines and disease epidemics during the second half of the nineteenth century and the first half of the twentieth century show the greatest socio-economic irresponsibility and neglect of the British government in India at one hand and the wretchedness of the masses at the other.[8]

The political leaders and the industrialists both were very much aware and conscious about the economic inheritance once India became independent. Somehow, these dominant lot of people who were going to lay down the foundation stones of the independent Indian economy were almost having consensual[9] view, even before the Independence, on many major strategic issues:

1. State/governments should be given a direct responsibility for development.
2. An ambitious and vital role to be assigned to the public sector.
3. Necessity for the development of heavy industries.
4. Discouragement to foreign investment.
5. The need for economic planning.

Once India became independent, it was a real challenge for the government of the time to go for a systematic organisation of the economy.

2. Bipan Chandra, 'The colonial legacy' in Bimal Jalan (ed.) ***The Indian Economy: Problems and Prospects***, Penguin Books, New Delhi, Revised Edition, 2004, p. 5.
3. B. R. Tomlinson, ***The Economy of Modern India 1860–1970***, Cambridge University Press, Cambridge, 1993, p. 7.
4. Angus Maddison, ***The World Economy: A Millennial Perspective***, OECD, Paris, 2001, p. 116.
5. A. Vaidyanathan, 'The Indian Economy Since Independence (1947–90)', in Dharma Kumar (ed.), ***The Cambridge Economic History of India***, Vol. II, Cambridge University Press, Cambridge, England, Expanded Edition, 2005, p. 947.
6. Angus Maddison, The World Economy, p. 116.
7. The respective data of Digby and Atkinson have been quoted by Sumit Sarkar, ***Modern India 1885–1947***, Macmillan, New Delhi, 1983, p. 42.
8. Recounted vividly by Mike Davis in his ***Late Victorian Holocaust: El-Nino Famines and the Making of the Third World*** (Verso, London & New York, 2001, p. 162), where he links the monsoon failures in India to El Nino—Southern Oscillation (ENSO) climate fluctuations in the western Pacific. The monsoon failure leading to drought and hunger one year and then to a severe malaria epidemic the next when the rains reappeared and a burst of mosquito abundance afflicted a weakened population.
9. Bipan Chandra et. al., ***India's Struggle for Independence***, p. 15.

This was a task full of every kind of challenges and hurdles as the economy had hardly anything optimistic. The need of delivering growth and development was in huge demand in front of the political leadership as the country was riding on the promises and vibes of the nationalist fervour. It was not a simple task.

Now the decisions which were to be taken by the political leadership of the time were going to shape the very future of India. Many important and strategic decisions were taken only by 1956 which shaped Indian economic journey till date—undoubtedly they heavily dominated the pre-reform period, but the post-reform period is also not completely free of their impact. To understand the nature and scope of the Indian economy in current times it is not only useful but essential to go through the facts, reasons and the delicacies which made the economy evolve and unfold the way it evolved and unfolded. A brief overview follows.

PRIME MOVING FORCE: AGRICULTURE VS. INDUSTRY

A topical issue of the debate regarding India has been the choice for the sector which will lead the process of development. The government of the time opted for industry to be India's prime moving force of the economy. Whether India should have gone for agriculture as its prime moving force for better prospects of development, is a highly debatable issue even today among experts.

Every economy has to go for its development through exploitation of its natural and human resources. There are priorities of objectives set by the economy which is attempted to be realised in a proper time frame. The availability and non-availability of resources (natural as well as human) are not the only issues which make an economy decide whether to opt for agriculture or industry as its prime moving force. There are many more socio-political compulsions and objectives which play their roles in such decision making.

The political leadership selected industry as the leading force of the economy after Independence—this was already decided by the dominant group of the nationalist leaders way back in the mid-1930s when they felt the need for economic planning in India before setting up the National Planning Committee in 1938. Given the available resource base it seems an illogical decision as India lacked all those pre-requisites which could suggest the declaration of industry as its prime moving force:

1. Almost no presence of infrastructure sector, i.e., power, transportation and communication.
2. Negligible presence of the infrastructure industries, i.e., iron and steel, cement, coal, crude oil, oil refining and electricity.
3. Lack of investible capital—either by the government or the private sector.
4. Absence of required technology to support the process of industrialisation and no research and development.
5. Lack of skilled manpower.
6. Absence of entrepreneurship among the people.
7. Absence of a market for industrial goods.
8. Many other socio-psychological factors which acted as negative forces for the proper industrialisation of the economy.

The obvious choice for India would have been the agriculture sector as the prime moving force of the economy because:

1. The country was having the natural resource of fertile land which was fit for cultivation.
2. Human capital did not require any kind of higher training.

By only organising our land ownership, irrigation and other inputs to agriculture, India could have gone for better prospects of development. Once there was no crises of food, shelter, basic healthcare, etc., to the masses, one goal of development could have been realised—a general welfare of the people. Once the masses were able to achieve a level of purchasing capacity, India could have gone for the expansion of industries. India was capable of generating as much surplus income for its masses as was required by the emerging industries for a market success. The People's Republic of China did the same in 1949—taking a realistic evaluation of its resources, it declared agriculture as its prime moving force for the economy. The surplus generated out of agriculture was suitably invested to develop the pre-requisites for industrialisation and the country went for it in the 1970s.

The emergence of industrial China was so vibrant that its impact was felt in the so-called highly developed and industrialised economies of the world—the industrial homework of China catapulted it into a giant.

Was the political leadership of independent India not able to analyse the realities as we did above and conclude that agriculture should have been the moving force of the economy in place of industry? Is it possible that Pandit Nehru in command could have missed the rational analysis of the Indian realities, a giant among the Asian visionaries of the time (Mao was still to emerge on the international scene)? How India could have not opted for agriculture as its prime moving force whose leadership had fought the nationalist movement on the Gandhian fervour of villages, agriculture and rural development. Even if Gandhi was not in the government there were many devout Gandhians in it and no one should doubt that the main internal force which vibrated throughout the governmental decisions were nothing but 'Gandhian Socialism'. There were many decisions which were taken under the influence of the main political force of the times, still some very vital ones were influenced by the visionary hunches of the political leadership mainly being J. L. Nehru. This is why the economic thinking of independent India is considered and said to be nurtured by Nehruvian Economics even today. If we go through the major literatures on the Indian economic history, views of the critiques of the time and the contemporary experts, we may be able to feel the answer as to why India went for industry as its prime moving force in place of an obvious and logical choice of agriculture (we should not be happy to know that even today this is a highly debatable issue among experts):

1. Looking at the resources available, agriculture would have been the obvious choice as the prime moving force (PMF) of the economy (i.e., cultivable land and the human power). But as Indian agriculture was using traditional tools and technology its modernisation as well as future mechanisation (later to some extent) would have been blocked due to the lack of indigenous industrial support. If India would have gone for import this would have required enough foreign reserves and a natural dependence on foreign countries. By choosing industry as the prime moving force, India opted to industrialise the economy as well as modernise the traditional mode of farming.

2. The dominant ideology around the world as well as in the WB and the IMF was in favour of industrialisation as a means to faster growth, which could be translated into faster development. These international bodies were supporting the member countries from every point of view to industrialise. Same was the case with the developed economies. It was possible not only to industrialise faster on these supports of the organisations

but there was a hope for emerging as an industrial exporter in the future. The same kind of support was not offered to an economy that opted for agriculture as the prime moving force. Basically, going for the agriculture sector was considered a symbol of 'backwardness' at that time. The political leadership wanted to carry India ahead, and not in the backward direction. It was only in the 1990s that the world and the WB/IMF changed its opinion regarding the agriculture sector. After the 1990s emphasis on this sector by an economy was no more considered a sign of backwardness.

3. The second World War has proved the supremacy of defence power. For defence a country needs not only the support of science and technology, but also an industrial base. India also required a powerful defence base for herself as a deterrent force. By opting for industries as the prime moving force of the economy India tried to solve many challenges simultaneously—first, industry will give faster growth, second, agriculture will be modernised in time and third the economy will be able to develop its own defence against external threats. Since the economy had also opted for scientific and technological preparedness, its achievements were to sustain the pace of modernisation.

4. Even before Independence, there was a socio-economic consensus among social scientists along with the nationalist leaders, that India needed a boost towards social change as the country lagged behind in the areas of modernisation. A break from the traditional and outmoded way of life and cultivation of a scientific outlook was a must for the country. Such feelings also made the political leadership of the time go in favour of wholehearted industrialisation.

5. By the time India got her independence the might of industrialisation was already proven and there were no doubts regarding its efficacy.

Given above are some of the important reasons that worked to make Indian political leadership go in favour of industry as the economy's prime moving force. Probably, the resource related and temperamental realities of India got marginalised in the hope and wish of a future industrialised and developed India. It is yet impossible to conclude whether the economy has completely failed to do so. Experts have divided opinions on this issue.

The last decade of the 20th century (i.e., the decade of the 1990s) saw major changes taking place in the world economic idea about the agriculture sector. It was no more a symbol of backwardness for an economy that emphasises on the agriculture sector as the engine of growth and development. China had proved to the world how agriculture could be made the prime moving force of an economy and generate internal as well as external strength to emerge as an industrial economy. In the wake of the ongoing reform process, India was introspecting almost all economic policies it followed since Independence. It was time for the agriculture sector to have the prime attention. A major shift[10] took place in the Indian economic thinking when the government announced in 2002 that from now onwards, in place of industry, **agriculture will be the prime moving force** of the economy. This was a policy shift of historic importance which was announced by the highest economic think tank of the country—the Planning Commission—as the economy commenced the Tenth Plan (2002–07).

10. The Government of India had shown such an intention in two regular Union Budgets (i.e., the fiscals 2000–01 and 2001–02) but had not announced the shift officially.

As per the Planning Commission[11] such a policy shift will solve the three major challenges faced by the economy:

1. Economy will be able to achieve food security with the increase in agricultural production. Besides, the agricultural surplus will generate exports in the globalising world economy benefiting out of the WTO regime.
2. The challenge of poverty alleviation will be solved to a great extent as the emphasis will make agriculture a higher income-generating occupation and induce growth in the rural economy by generating more gainful employment.
3. The situation of India as an example of 'market failure' will cease.[12]

Though the world's perception regarding agriculture had changed by the mid-1990s, India recognises the sector as the prime moving force of the economy a bit late, i.e., by 2002. Now, there is a consensus among experts and policymakers regarding the role of agriculture in the Indian economy. Agriculture and allied activities remained the major source of livelihood for nearly half of the Indian population—its share in employment being 48.7 per cent, with 16.5 per cent contribution in the GDP.[13]

Once India started the process of economic reforms, it commenced in the industrial sector—as the economy had got its structure through the successive industrial policies, it looks a normal thing. To the extent the agriculture sector is concerned reforms were initiated a bit late—better say by early 2000s. Three *major reasons* may be cited for this delay:

1. Agriculture being always open for the private sector, it was now difficult to go for further privatisation for encouraging investments. The need was for 'corporate' and 'contract' farming under the leadership of the *corporate world.*
2. Lack of awareness about the contours of the economic reforms among the farm community.
3. The heavy dependency of population on agriculture for livelihood could not permit the government to go for the right kind of agricultural reforms at the right time—first, the industrial sector (via manufacturing) needed expansion to lessen the population dependency on the agriculture sector.

Any one sector in which the governments at the Centre and states have been facing the biggest hurdles has been the farm sector. The major reform needs and the hurdles being faced may be summed up in the following points:

1. A *national agri-market* is the need of the hour, but there lacks a political will among the majority of states to put in place a right kind of Agricultural Produce Market Committees.
2. The need of promoting *corporate investment* in the farm sector is hurdled

11. Planning Commission, ***Tenth Five Year Plan (2002–07)***, Government of India, New Delhi, 2002.

12. It has been argued by economists time and again that India is a typical example of 'market failure'. Market failure is a situation when there are goods and services in an economy and its requirement too, but due to lack of purchasing power the requirements of the people are not translated into demand. Whatever industrial goods and services India had been able to produce they had stagnated or stunted sales in the market as the largest section of the consumers earned their livelihood from the agriculture sector, which is unable to create a purchasing power to the levels required by the market. As agricultural activities will become more gainful and profitable, the masses depending on it will have the level of purchasing capacity to purchase the industrial goods and services from the market. Thus, the Indian market won't fail. The view has been articulated by Amartya Sen and Jean Dreze in their monograph titled ***India: Economic Development and Social Opportunity***, United Nations University, 1996.

13. Ministry of Finance, **Economic Survey 2019-20**, Government of India, Vol. 2, p. 193.

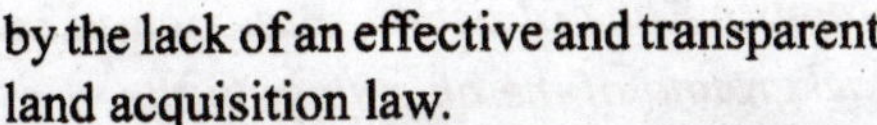

by the lack of an effective and transparent land acquisition law.

3. *Labour reforms* needs fine-tuning to promote industrial farming, which is hurdled by a long tradition of complex kind of labour laws of the country.
4. *Farm mechanisation* is hindered by the lack of investment in industries.
5. *Research and development* needs huge investment from the private sector, but there lacks a conducive atmosphere for it.
6. Right kind of *'downstream and upstream requirements'* together with a proper kind of *'supply chain management'* is absent in the area of agri-goods.
7. Expansion of the right kind of *commodity trading* in agri-commodities.
8. Strengthening the farm sector to face the competition posed by the agricultural sector of the developed world, with regard subsidies and prices, in wake of the globalising world economy.
9. Making farming *remunerative* to check farm crisis of contemporary times.

Experts believe that for taking the right policy steps in the sector there needs a high degree of federal maturity in the country. Increased awareness among farmers together with the right government support to prevent farm distress will serve the purpose in a great way.

PLANNED AND MIXED ECONOMY

Independent India was declared to be a planned and a mixed economy. India needed national planning, which was decided by the political leadership almost a decade before Independence.[14] India was not only facing regional disparities at the level of resources, but inter-regional disparities were also

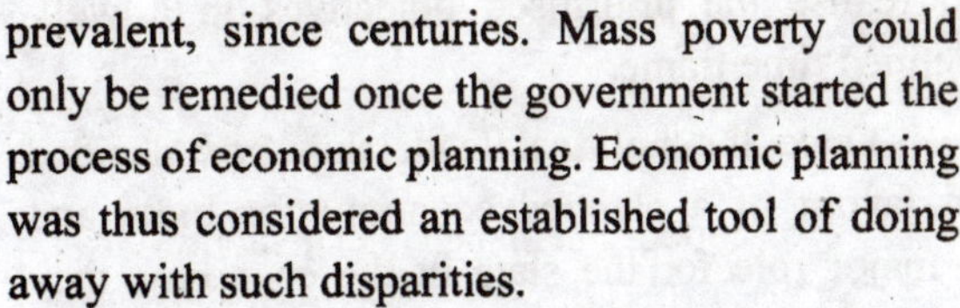

prevalent, since centuries. Mass poverty could only be remedied once the government started the process of economic planning. Economic planning was thus considered an established tool of doing away with such disparities.

Basically, it was the abject poverty of the masses which made the government go for planning so that it could play an active role in the allocation of resources and mobilise them for equitable growth and development. Though India was constitutionally declared a federation of states, in the process of planning, the authority of regulation, directing and undertaking economic activities got more and more centralised in the Union government.[15]

India's decision for a planned economy was also moulded by some contemporary experiences in the world.[16] *Firstly,* the Great Depression of 1929 and the reconstruction challenges after the second World War had made experts to conclude in favour of a state intervention in the economy (opposite to the contemporary idea of 'non-interference' as proposed by Adam Smith). *Secondly,* it was the same time that the command economies (i.e., state economies) of the Soviet Union and the East European countries started making news about their faster economic growth. In the 1950s and 1960s, the dominant view among policymakers around the world was in favour of an active role of the state in the economy. *Thirdly,* a dominant role for the state in the economy to neutralise market failure situations (as happened during the period of the Great Depression when demand fell down to the lowest levels) was gaining ground around the world. For many newly independent developing nations, economic planning was therefore an obvious choice. Economic planning was considered to help states to mobilise resources

14. **National Planning Committee**, GoI, N. Delhi, 1949.

15. Bimal Jalan, ***India's Economic Policy,*** Penguin Books, New Delhi, 1993, p. 2.

16. C. Rangarajan, ***Perspectives on Indian Economy,*** UBSPD, New Delhi, 2004, p. 96.

to realise the prioritised objectives in a well-defined time frame.

Once the political leadership had decided in favour of a planned economy for India and a major role for the state in the economy, they needed to clarify about the organisational nature of the economy—whether it was to be a state economy or a mixed economy—because planning was not possible in a free market economy (i.e., capitalistic economy). The idea of planning in India was inspired from the soviet planning which was a command economy and did not suit the requirements of democratic India, which was till now a privately owned economy.[17] The dominant force behind planning in India, at least after Independence, was Nehru himself who had strong socialist leanings. He thought it was important to define the role of the state in the economy, which was going to be at times similar to the state in the soviet Union and at times completely dissimilar to it. Though there was an example of a capitalistic-democratic system going for planning, France by that time (1947), it had little experience to offer the Indian policymakers (France had gone for a mixed economy by 1944–45). With the basic urge to accelerate the process of economic growth, the planners went to define the respective roles of the state and the market, in the very first plan itself. The following lines look refreshingly ahead of the times and crystal-clear about the scope of the government's role in the economy vis-á-vis the private sector.

'This brings us to the problem of the techniques of planning. A possible approach to the problem is, as mentioned earlier, through a more or less complete nationalisation of the means of production and extensive system of government controls on the allocation of resources and on the distribution of the national product. Judged purely as a technique of planning, this may appear a promising line of action. But, viewed against the background of the objectives outlined above, and in the light of practical considerations, such an expansion of the public sector is, at the present stage, neither necessary nor desirable. Planning in a democratic set-up implies the minimum use of compulsion or coercion for bringing about a realignment of productive forces. The resources available to the public sector have, at this stage, to be utilised for investment along new lines rather than in acquisition of existing productive capacity. Public ownership of the means of production may be necessary in certain cases; public regulation and control in certain others. The private sector has, however, to continue to play an important part in production as well as in distribution. Planning under recent conditions thus means, in practice, an economy guided and directed by the state and operated partly through direct state action and partly through private initiative and effort.'[18] The above-quoted lines are imaginatively ahead of the times. It will be suitable to note here that as 1950s and 1960s made the world experts favour state intervention in the economy, the *East Asian Miracle*[19] of the coming three decades was going to define the very limits of such an intervention. The East Asian economies were able to sustain a high growth rate over three decades and had revived again the discussions regarding the respective roles of the state and the market as well as the nature of the state's role in the economy. The kind of conclusions drawn were very similar to the view presented in India's First Plan itself which was presented by the World Bank in 1993.

The real nature of the Indian brand of mixed economy, though beautifully outlined in 1951 itself, went through a process of detailed evolution

17. Rakesh Mohan, 'Industrial Policy and Control' in Bimal Jalan (ed.), ***The Indian Economy: Problems and Prospects***, p. 101.

18. Planning Commission, ***The First Five Year Plan: A Draft Outline***, GoI, New Delhi, 1951.

19. The ***East Asian Miracle***, World Bank, Washington D.C, 1993.

in the decade of the 1950s.[20] By the end of the 1950s, the concept of the mixed economy was almost buried and rose from hibernation only by mid-1980s and finally early in 1990s, in the wake of the process of economic reforms.

We see the government modifying the process of planning and functions of the Planning Commission in wake of the reform process—an attempt to redefine the roles of government and private sector in the economy. In a sense, India was increasingly getting more dependent on the latter for the promotion of growth and development.

By early 2015, we saw some major changes taking place in the area of planning in India. The Government replaced the existing body, *Planning Commission,* with the *NITI Aayog* (a new economic 'Think Tank'), with the aim of 'overhauling' the very process and method of planning in the country. This move is believed to originate out of India's experiences of development planning spanning over six decades. Co-operative federalism, bottom-up approach, holistic and inclusive development with the need of an Indian model of development are some of the hallmarks of the new design. The move is also seen in light of the changed needs of the economy.

Atmanirbharta Push However, self-reliance had been one of the six major objectives of planning, a renewed push for it has come from the Government in the wake of the *COVID-19* pandemic. In 2020-21, the Government launched the *Atmanirbhar Bharat Abhiyan (Self-Reliant India Campaign)* to support this cause. The Government aims to attaining self-reliance with the help of the *five pillars* of the Abhiyan, namely – Economy, Infrastructure, System, Vibrant Demography and Demand. This is for the ***first time*** that clear pillars have been defined by the Government in this regard.

Some critics have shown their reservations regarding the Abhiyan and have called it similar to the Make in India, a scheme of past. However, some experts, have seen it in the backdrop of the limits of global supply chain (caused by the recent pandemic and similar possibilities in future) – India's urge to redesign her economic space, relationship with environment and economic diplomacy.

EMPHASIS ON THE PUBLIC SECTOR

The state was to be given an active and dominant role in the economy, it was very much decided by the time India became independent. There were no doubts about it in the minds of the people who formed the dominant political force at the time. Naturally, there was going to be a giant structure of the government-controlled enterprises to be known as the public sector undertakings (PSUs). Criticism aside, there was at that time, a strong logic behind the glorification of PSUs. Some of the reasons for heavy investments in the PSUs were purely natural while others were consequential in nature. There were certain highly commendable objectives set for them, some other goals would go on to serve the very soul of the mixed economy. We must go for an impartial and rational analysis of the matter, in the midst of all the criticism of PSUs and the contemporary moves of privatising them, to understand their roles in the Indian economy. We may understand the reasons behind the ambitious expansion of the PSUs in the face of the following major requirements.

1. **Infrastructural Needs :** Every economy whether it is agrarian, industrial or post-industrial, needs suitable levels of infrastructure such as power, transportation and communication. Without their healthy presence and expansion, no economy can grow and develop.

   At the eve of Independence, India was having almost no presence of these

20. We see the process of evolution specially in the industrial policies, India pursued since 1948 to 1956.

three basic requirements. There was just a beginning in the area of railways, and post and telegraph. Power was restricted to selective homes of government and the princely states. [It means, even if India had opted for agriculture as its prime moving force, it had to develop the infrastructure sector.]

These sectors require too much capital investment as well as heavy engineering and technological support for their development. Expansion of the infrastructure sector was considered not possible by the private sector of the time as they could possibly not manage the following components:

(i) heavy investment (in domestic as well as foreign currencies),

(ii) technology,

(iii) skilled manpower, and

(iv) entrepreneurship.

Even if these inputs were available to the private sector, it was not feasible for them as there was no market for such infrastructure. These infrastructures were essential for the economy, but they needed either subsidised or almost free supply as the masses lacked the market-determined purchasing capacity. Under these typical conditions, it was only the government which could have shouldered the responsibility. The government could have managed not only the inputs required for the development of the sector, but could also supply and distribute them to the needy areas and the consumers for the proper growth of the economy. There were no alternatives and that is why the infrastructure sector in India has such a dominant state presence that many areas have obvious government monopolies—as in power, railways, aviation, telecommunication, etc.

2. **Industrial Needs:** India had opted for the industrial sector as its prime moving force, as we saw in the earlier pages. Now there were some areas of industries which the government had to invest in, due to several compulsive reasons. For industrialisation to take place, the presence of certain industries is essential (these industries have been called in the country by different names—*basic industries, infrastructure industries, core industries, core sector*). To the initial group of six industries, in 2013 two new industries (Natural Gas and Fertilisers) were added. The combined weight of these eight industries in the new series of Index of Industrial Production (IIP) is 40.27 per cent. These industries are (their percentage weights in IIP given in brackets)[21]:

(i) Refinery products (11.29)

(ii) Electricity (7.99)

(iii) Steel (7.22)

(iv) Coal (4.16)

(v) Crude Oil (3.62)

(vi) Natural Gas (2.77)

(vii) Cement (2.16)

(viii) Fertilisers (1.06)

Similar to the infrastructure sector, these basic industries also require high level of capital, technology, skilled manpower and articulation in entrepreneurship which was again considered not feasible for the private sector of the time to manage. Even if the private sector supplied goods from the

21. The revised *Index of Industrial Production (IIP)* was released by the **Central Statistics Office** (CSO) on 12th May 2017: Aimed at capturing the structural changes in the economy and improving the quality of representation, the revision includes many things such as—shifting the base year to 2011–12 from 2004–05, changes in the basket of commodities and their weights.

'basic industries', they might not be able to sell their products in the market due to the lower purchasing power of the consumers. Perhaps, that is why again the responsibility of developing the basic industries was taken up by the government.

Out of the six basic industries, the cement industry had some strength in the private sector, while in the iron and steel industry a lone private company was present. The coal industry was controlled by the private sector and crude oil and refining was just a beginning by then. The level of demands of an industrialising India was never to be met by the existing strength of the basic industries. Neither the required level of expansion in them was possible by the existing number of private players. With no choice left, the government decided to play the main role in industrialising the country. In many of them we as a result, see a natural monopoly for the PSUs, again.

3. **Employment Generation:** The PSUs were also seen as an important part of the employment generation strategy. A government in a democratic set up cannot think only economics, but it has to realise the socio-political dimensions of the nation too. The country was faced with the serious problem of poverty and the workforce was increasing at a fast rate. Giving employment to the poor people is a time-tested tool of poverty alleviation. The PSUs were thought to create enough jobs for the employable workforce of the economy.

There was also felt an immediacy for a social change in the country. The poverty of a greater section of the country was somehow connected to the age-old caste system which propitiated the stronghold of the upper castes on the ownership of land, which was the only means of income and livelihood for almost above 80 per cent of the population. Along with the ambitious policy of land reforms, the government decided to provide reservations to the weaker sections of the society in government jobs. The upcoming PSUs were supposed to put such jobs at the disposal of the government which could have been distributed along the decided reservation policy—such reservations were considered an economic tool for social change.

In the highly capital-intensive sectors in which the government companies were going to enter, managing investible funds to set them up was not going to be an easy task. The government did manage the funds with sources like taxation, internal and external borrowing and even taking last refuge in the printing of fresh currencies. The government went to justify the high taxation and heavy public indebtedess in supplying employment to the Indian employable population.

The PSUs were considered by the government as the focus of the 'trickle-down effect'. The government did everything to set up and run the PSUs as the benefits were supposed to percolate to the masses, finally reinforcing growth and development in the country. Employment in the PSUs was seen as the effort of the trickle down theory, simply said. At a point of time, Nehru even mentioned the PSUs as the 'temples of modern India'. The government went to commit even a job in every household via the PSUs—without calculating the dimensions of the future labour force in the country and the required resources to create jobs at such a high scale. But the government went on creating new PSUs without analysing the fiscal repercussions—moreover believing them to be the real engine of equitable growth.

The employment generation responsibility of the PSUs was extended to such an extent by the government that most of them had over-supply of the labour force which started draining its profits on account of salaries, wages, pensions and provident funds (the latter two had late financial impact).

4. **Profit and Development of the Social Sector:** The investment to be made by the government in PSUs was in the nature of asset creation and these entities were to be involved in production activities. It was natural for the government to gain control over the profits and dividends accruing from them. The goods and services the PSUs produced and sold provided disposable income to the government. The government had a conscious policy of spending the income generated by the PSUs. They were to be used in the supply of the 'social goods' or what is called the 'public goods'. And thus, India was to have a developed social sector. By social goods the government meant the universal supply of certain goods and services to the citizen. These included education, healthcare, nutrition, drinking water, social security, etc., in India. It means that the PSUs were also visioned as the revenue generators for the development of the social sector. Due to many reasons the PSUs would not be able to generate as much profit as was required for the healthy development of the social sector. This eventually hampered the availability of public goods in the country. In place of giving profits back to the government, a large number of the PSUs started incurring huge losses and required budgetary support regularly.

5. **Rise of the Private Sector:** As the PSUs took the responsibility of supplying the infrastructure and the basic industries to the economy, a base for the rise of private sector industries was slowly established. With the rise of private sector industries in the country, the process of industrialisation was thought to be completed. Out of the many roles the PSUs were supposed to play, this was the most far-sighted. What happened to the different roles the PSUs were assigned is a totally different matter, to which we will return while discussing the industrial scenario of the country. Here we have analysed why the government of India after Independence went for such an ambitious plan of expansion of the public sector.

Besides, the PSUs were aimed at many other connected areas of developmental concerns, such as, self-sufficiency in production, balanced regional development, spread of small and ancillary industries, low and stable prices, and long-term equilibrium in balance of payment. Over time the PSUs have played a critical role in promoting the growth and development of the country.[22]

By the mid-1980s, there emerged a kind of consensus across the world (including the IMF & World Bank) regarding the inefficiency and under-performance of the PSUs (in the wake of the idea of the Washington Consensus which is said to promote 'neo-liberal' economic policies across the world). In the wake of it, there commenced a process of privatisation and disinvestment of the PSUs among majority of the economies in the world—India being no exception to it. By late 1990s, new studies proved that under-performance and inefficiency could be there in the private

22. Sumit Bose and Sharat Kumar, 'Public-sector Enterprises', in Kaushik Basu and Annemie Maertens (eds.), ***The New Oxford Companion to Economics in India,*** Vol. II, Oxford University Press, New Delhi, 2012, p. 578–83.

sector companies, too. By mid-2000s (in the wake of the US *sub-prime crisis*) a new consensus emerged among the international organisations that state/government need not exit the economy and a kind of slow down towards privatisation moves of the PSUs across the world (the world in a sense is pushing the 'pause' button on neo-liberalism) is under process.

India pursued a less ambitious disinvestment policy from 2003–04 to 2015–16 (the government has decided to own controlling shares among the divested PSUs). Since 2016–17 financial year, the government has decided to restart the process of 'strategic disinvestment' (in which the ownership of the PSUs may also be transferred to the private sector). Such a policy of disinvestment was launched by the government in 2000 which was paused by the UPA-I in 2003–04). The government has also decided in favour of selling increased shares of the PSUs to the foreign institutions, at par with the domestic financial institutions. Such policy moves[23] of the recent times should be seen in the light of certain important contemporary realities—need of promoting investment in the economy; need of the government to quit undesirable areas of economic activities and expanding in the areas of need and where private sector will not enter (welfare actions); revenue generation by stake sale, monetisation of their assets and enhanced profit from the PSUs (by selling majority stakes in the PSUs at one hand the government will de-burden itself from the owner's responsibility, while on the other hand its share of revenue from the divested PSUs will increase as the new owner will run the enterprise on market principles); etc.

---

23 We find such policy advices coming from the *Economic Survey* in past including **Economic Survey 2019-20** and **2018-19**. Further, the Governments have been increasingly acting upon such policy advices (examples may be taken from the **Union Budget 2020-21** and **201 9-20** also).

CHAPTER 4

ECONOMIC PLANNING

*The idea of planning and a planned society is accepted now in varying degrees by almost everyone. But planning by itself has little meaning and need not necessarily lead to good results. Everything depends on the objectives of the plan and on the controlling authority, as well as, of course, the government behind it,**

In this Chapter...

- Introduction
- Definition
- Origin and Expansion of Planning
- Types of Planning

INTRODUCTION

Today, most of the world economies are planned and world has seen major experiments in the area of economic planning by now. India has been a planned economy right since her independence and continues to be so under the policy think tank the Niti Aayog. This thin chapter intends to introduce the reader to the major ***Whats, Hows*** and ***Whys*** of the 'concept of economic planning'— picking real examples from major planned economies of the world including India. Besides being a theoretical foundation it aims to provide a theoretical anchor to ***planning in India*** (the very next chapter).

DEFINITION

A number of definitions have been forwarded by different economists from time to time since the term 'planning' entered the domain of economics. To make us develop a clear understanding of planning, we need to see only a few of them which will enable us to draw out a working definition that fits contemporary time.

A large number of economists and experts have agreed that perhaps the best definition is given by H. D. Dickinson, according to whom, economic planning is, "the making of major economic decisions—what and how much is to

* *New Jawaharlal Nehru,* **The Discovery of India,** *Oxford University Press, 6th Impression (1st Edition 1946, Oxford, London), N. Delhi, 1994, p. 501.*

be produced and to whom it is to be allocated by the conscious decision of a determinate authority, on the basis of a comprehensive survey of the economic system as a whole."

It was the National Planning Committee, set up in 1938 by the Indian National Congress which, for the first time, tried to define planning (in 1940, though, its final report was published in 1949) in India. It could be considered the broadest possible definition of planning: "Planning, under a democratic system, may be defined as the technical coordination, by disinterested experts of consumption, production, investment, trade, and income distribution, in accordance with social objectives set by bodies representative of the nation. Such planning is not only to be considered from the point of view of economics, and raising of the standard of living, but must include cultural and spiritual values, and the human side of life."[1]

By the late 1930s, there was an almost political consensus that independent India will be a planned economy. As India commenced economic planning by the early 1950s, the planning commission of India also went on to define planning. According to the Planning Commission, "Planning involves the acceptance of a clearly defined system of objectives in terms of which to frame overall policies. It also involves the formation of a strategy for promoting the realisation of ends defined. Planning is essentially an attempt at working out a rational solution of problems, an attempt to coordinate means and ends; it is thus different from the traditional hit-and-miss methods by which reforms and reconstruction are often undertaken".[2]

In the post-War period, a large number of the newly independent countries were attracted towards planning. Many new forces of change kept refining the very idea of planning due to the compulsive necessities of industrialisation or the issue of sustainability of the development process. But to carry forward our discussion, we need a working as well as a contemporary definition of planning. We may define it as *a process of realising well-defined goals by optimum utilisation of the available resources.*[3] While doing economic planning the government sets developmental objectives and attempts to deliberately coordinate the economic decision making over a longer period to influence, direct and in some cases even to control the level and growth of a nation's main economic variables (i.e., income, consumption, employment, saving, investment, exports, imports, etc.).[4]

An economic plan is simply a set of specific economic targets to be achieved in a given period of time with a stated strategy. Economic plans may be either comprehensive or partial. A ***comprehensive plan*** sets targets to cover all major aspects of the economy, while a ***partial plan*** may go for setting such targets for a part of the economy (i.e., agriculture, industry, public sector, etc.). Taken broadly, the planning process itself can be described as an exercise in which a government first chooses social objectives, then sets various targets (i.e., economic targets), and finally organises a framework for implementing, coordinating and monitoring the development plan.[5]

One very important thing which should be clear to all is that the idea of planning first emerged in its applied form and after studying and surveying the experiences of different countries which followed it, experts started theorising

1. S. R. Maheshwari, ***A Dictionary of Public Administration***, Orient Longman, New Delhi, 2002, p. 371.
2. Planning Commission, ***First Five Year Plan (1951–56)***, Government of India, New Delhi, 1991, p. 7.
3. After the emergence of the concept of **Sustainable Development** (1987) experts across the world started using the term 'optimum' in place of the hitherto used term 'maximum'.
4. Michael P. Todaro, ***Development Planning: Models and Methods.*** Oxford University Press, Nairobi, 1971.
5. United Nations Department of Economic Affairs, ***Measures for Economic Development of Underdeveloped Countries***, UNO, DEA, New York, 1951, p. 63.

about planning. Thus, in the case of planning, the direction has been from practice to theory. This is why the form and the nature of planning kept changing from country to country and from time to time. As we will see in the following pages, the types of planning itself evolved through time as different countries experimented with it.

As per our working definition, we may say the following things about planning:

1. **Planning is a process:** It means planning is a process of doing something. Till we have some goals and objectives left regarding our lives, the process might continue. With the changing nature of our needs, the nature and scope of the planning process might undergo several changes. Planning is not an end in itself. As processes accelerate and decelerate, change direction and course, so also does planning.

2. **Planning must have well-defined goals:** After the Second World War, several countries went for development planning. As these nations had enormous socio-economic hurdles, they first set some goals and objectives and then started their process of realising them via planning. In due course of time, there emerged a consensus that planning must have some goals and those goals should be well-defined (not vaguely defined)—so that the government's discretionary intervention in the economic organisation could be democratically transparent and justified. Even in the non-democratic nations (i.e., erstwhile USSR, Poland, China, etc.) the goals of planning were clearly defined.[6]

3. **Optimum utilisation of the available resources :** Here we see two catch concepts. *First,* is the way of utilising the resources. Till the idea of sustainability emerged (1987) experts tried to 'maximise' the resource exploitation. But once experts around the world introspected the untenability of such a method of resource utilisation, the sustainable approach was included into planning and here in entered the idea of utilising resources at its 'possible best', so that environmental degradation could be at its minimum and the future generations could also be able to continue with their progress. *Second* is the idea of the natural resources which are available. Resources (i.e., natural as well as human) could be of indigenous origin or exogenous. Most of the countries doing planning tried to utilise their indigenous resources, yet some tried to tap the exogenous resources too, taking leverage of their diplomatic acumen. For example, the first country going for national planning, i.e., Soviet Union, leveraged resources available in the East European countries. India also used exogenous resources for her development planning wherever it was necessary and possible to tap.[7]

By the 1950s, planning had emerged as a method or tool of utilising resources to achieve any kind of goals for policymakers, around the world:

1. Trying to achieve a particular size of family for different countries came to be known as ***family planning***.
2. The process of providing suitable physical and social infrastructure for the erstwhile or the upcoming urban

6. The Gosplan, *First Five Year Plan (1928–33)*, USSR, 1928.

7. Many of the PSUs in the 1950s and the early 1960s were not only set up with natural resources (capital as well as machines) from USSR, Germany, etc., but even the human resource was also tapped from there for few years.

areas came to be known as *town/urban planning*.

3. A country trying to optimise the use of its revenues for different categories of expenditures came to be known as *financial planning*. Financial planning is more popularly known as *budgeting*. Every budget, be it of the government or of the private sector is nothing but an exercises in financial planning.
4. Similarly, at the macro and micro levels, there might be any number of planning processes—agricultural planning, industrial planning, irrigation planning, road planning, house planning, etc.

Simply said, the art of achieving any kind of goal by the use of the resources we have is the process of planning. We may cite a very general example—students of a class are able to join the class at the right time coming from different places of their stay. How they are able to do so? All of them must be planning their time in such a way that they are able to join the class at the same time though their places of residence are not at an equal distance from the class. All might be having their own ways of time planning—some might be having bed-tea, some might not, some might be having breakfast at their place, yet others might think to take their breakfast in the college canteen, etc.

It means that even if we are not consciously planning or have not announced it as yet, we are always planning our days. Same is correct in the case of countries. Many countries announced that they will be planned economies, yet some others didn't go for any such policy announcements. The soviet Union, Poland, China, France, India are examples of the former category while the USA, Canada, Mexico fall in the latter category.[8] But here we are concerned with the conscious process of planning. There will be some methods, some tools and types of planning emerging through time as different countries will start their processes of planning.

ORIGIN AND EXPANSION OF PLANNING

Planning is a method of achieving faster economic progress. It has been tried by different countries at different times and at different levels. We may see them as under:

1. **Regional Planning :** It was at the regional level that planning was used as a part of development policy by any country for the *first time*. It was the USA which started the first regional planning after the Tennessee Valley Authority (TVA) was set up in 1916—for a large-scale rehabilitation in south-eastern USA covering parts of seven states. With the primary aim of flood control, soil conservation and providing electricity, the TVA/the regional plan was also involved in many related activities such as industrial development, forestry, wildlife conservation, town planning, construction of road and rail, encouraging sound agricultural practices and malaria control in the defined region.[9] The US experience of regional planning became such a success in realising its well-defined goals that it emerged as a role model and an object of inspiration for many countries around the world in the coming decades—the Damodar Valley Corporation (DVC) in India (1948), the Volta River Project in Ghana (1966), etc.
2. **National Planning :** The official experiment in the area of national planning is rooted in the Bolshevik Revolution of Russia

8. Though the USA was the first to go for planning, but at the regional level (Tennessee Valley Authority, 1916)—it never announced its intention for national planning.

9. Leong, G.C. and Morgan, G.C., ***Human and Economic Geography***, Oxford University Press, Oxford, 1982, p. 145.

(1917)—the Soviet Union. Dissatisfied with the pace of industrialisation, it was in 1928 that Joseph Stalin announced its policy of central planning for the Soviet Union. The collectivisation of agriculture and forced-draft industrialisation were other radical new policy initiatives announced by Stalin besides economic planning in 1928.[10] The Soviet Union went for its first five year plan for the period 1928–33 and the world was to have its *first* experience of *national planning.* The famous Soviet slogan "great leap forward" was initiated for rapid industrialisation through the introduction of economic planning at the national level. The nature and scope of Soviet planning (called ***the Gosplon***) will have its direct or indirect bearings on all those countries which went for economic planning, be state or capitalist or mixed economies. India was to have direct influence of Soviet planning on its planning process. In the first Soviet Plan, heavy industries was favoured over light industry, and consumer goods were the residual sector after all the other priorities had been met. We see the same emphasis in the Indian planning process.[11] The Soviet model of economic planning spread to the East European countries, especially after World War II and found its purest form of such planning in the People's Republic of China (1949). During the early 1940s, the concept of national planning was borrowed by France and the world saw national planning being initiated by a hitherto capitalist economy as well as by a non-centralised political system (i.e., democratic system). France started economic planning at the national level after announcing itself as a mixed economy.

TYPES OF PLANNING

After the first national planning was started by the Soviet Union, many more countries followed it, but with variations in their methods and practices. Though there are many variants of planning the most important one is on the basis of the type of economic organisation (i.e., state economy, mixed economy). During the course of evolution, planning has been classified into two types, based upon the type of economic system prevalent in the country.

1. **Imperative Planning:** The planning process followed by the state economies (i.e., the socialist or communist) is known as the imperative planning. Such planning is also called as ***directive or target planning***. Such planning had two main variants. In the socialist system, all economic decisions were centralised in the hands of the state with collective ownership of resources (except labour). In the communist system (i.e., China of the past) all resources were to be owned and utilised by the state (including labour). Thus, communist China was the purest example of such planning. In the case of the Soviet Union a little bit of 'market' did exist—even after the collectivisation of agriculture was enacted by Stalin in 1928 only 94 per cent of Soviet peasants could be included in the process.[12] Basic features of such planning are as under:

    (i) *Numerical (i.e., quantitative) targets* of growth and development are set by the

---

10. Alec Nove, ***An Economic History of the USSR***, 3rd ed., Penguin Books, Baltimore, USA, 1990, p. 139.

11. Rakesh Mohan 'Industrial Policy and Controls' in the Bimal Jalan (eds), ***The Indian Economy: Problems and Prospects***, Penguin Books, New Delhi, 2004., p. 101. Also see Bipan Chandra et. al., ***India After Independence***, Penguin Books, New Delhi, 2000, pp. 341–42, as well as A. Vaidyanathan, 'The Indian Economy Since Independence (1947–70)' in Dharma Kumar (ed.), ***The Cambridge Economic History of India***, Vol. II, Cambridge University Press, Cambridge, 1983, pp. 949–50.

12. Samuelson, P. A. and Nordhaus, W. D, ***Economics***, McGraw-Hill Companies Inc., N. York, 2005., p. 591.

plan. As for example, five lakh tonnes of steel, two lakh tonnes of cement, 10,000 kms of national highways, 5,000 primary schools, etc., will be produced/ built in the coming 5 or 6 years.

(ii) As the *state* controls the ownership rights over the resources, it is very much possible to realise the above-cited planned targets.

(iii) almost *no role for the market,* no price mechanism with all economic decisions to be taken in the centralised way by the state/government.

(iv) no private participation in the economy, only the state plays the economic role.

The ***Command Economies*** followed this kind of planning. That is why such economies are also known as the ***Centrally Planned Economies***—the USSR, Poland, Hungary, Austria, Romania, etc., and finally China. Basically, it was the migration of some of the great economists from the Soviet Bloc countries to Britain and the USA that a proper study and discussion started on the very nature and purpose of planning in the command economies. Many of these economists went back to their countries of origin after the Second World War to serve and in some measure, suffer the revolution there.[13] It was their articulate and contemporary economic thinking which formed the basis for the idea of mixed economy in the post-War world. One among them was Oskar Lange, the famous Polish economist, who after returning home to serve as the Chairman of the Polish State Economic Council (as India had the Planning Commission) suggested and coined the concept of *'market socialism'* in the 1950s. His ideas of market socialism were cancelled by not only Poland but also by other state economies of the time.[14]

The peak of this type of planning was reached in China after the Cultural Revolution (1966–69), which led to an economic slowdown in the country, which had adopted a soviet-style central planning system after 1949. Under Deng Xiaoping (1977–97), China decentralised a great deal of economic power with its announcement of the open door policy in 1985 to save the economy. The Chinese ***open door policy*** was an initiative in the direction of 'market socialism' under the communist political design (a popular student demand for political reform in favour of democracy was ruthlessly repressed in Tiananmen Square in 1989). Similarly, the Soviet Union under the leadership of Mikhail Gorbachev began a process of political and economic reforms, called ***prestroika*** (i.e., restructuring) and ***glasnost*** (i.e., openness) in 1985 to save the failed economic experiments in the state economy. Other East European economies followed similar economic reforms from 1989 onwards. Thus, the whole world of the state economies had moved towards market economy by the late 1980s. Since then none of the countries have followed imperative planning.

2. **Indicative Planning:** In the following two decades after the soviet planning

---

13 From Poland two great economists Oskar Lange (1904–65) and Michal Kalecki (1899–1970); from Hungary, William J. Fellner (1905–83), Nicholas Kaldor (1908–86), Thomas Balogh (1905–85) and Eric Roll (1907–95); from post-war Austria Ludwig von Mises (1880–1973), Friedrich A. von Hayek (1899–1992), Fritz Machlup (1902–83), Gottfried Haberler (1900–96) and Joseph A. Schumpeter (1883–1950) [J.K. Galbraith, ***A History of Economics***, Penguin Books, London, 1987, pp. 187–90].

14 It was blasphemous to preach in favour of market in the socialist world at that time—he was not put behind the bars was a great mercy on him. Oskar Lange towards the end of his life told Paul M. Sweezy, the most noted American Marxist scholar, that during this period he did not retire for the night without speculating as to whether he might be arrested before the dawn (J.K. Galbraith, ***A History of Economics***, p. 189).

commenced, the idea of planning got attention from the democratic world. A time came when some such economies started national planning. As they were neither state economies nor communist/socialist political systems, the nature of their planning was different from the command economies. Such planning has been termed as indicative planning by economists and experts. The identifying features of indicative planning may be summed up as under:

(i) every economy following the indicative planning were mixed economies.

(ii) unlike a centrally planned economy (countries following imperative planning) indicative planning works through the market (price system) rather than replaces it.[15]

(iii) side by side setting numerical/ quantitative targets (similar to the practice in the imperative planning) a set of economic policies of indicative nature is also announced by the economies to realise the plan targets.

(iv) the indicative nature of economic policies, which are announced in such planning, basically encourage or discourage the private sector in its process of economic decision making.

After converting to mixed economy by the mid-1940s, France commenced its first six year plan in 1947, which got popularity as the **Monnet Plan** (he was the first chairman of the General Planning Commission and the then Cabinet Minister for planning in France).[16] Later, Monnet Plan became synonymous with indicative planning. This plan is also sometimes described as the *basic sector Planning* as the government had selected eight basic industries as the core of development in which the nature of planning was almost *imperative*, i.e., under state monopoly (these sectors were owned by the private sector till 1944 when France went for their nationalisation).[17] Other economic activities were open for private participation for which indicative kind of policy-planning was essential. France as well as Japan have followed indicative planning with great success. It was in 1965 that the UK commenced such a planning with the National Plan and abandoned in 1966 after being overtaken by events (a balance of payment crisis resulting in a deflationary package of measures). Since then the UK never went for planning.[18]

Though the **first use of** economic planning as an instrument of economic progress was done by the USA (with the Tennessee Valley Authority in 1916 at the regional level), it never went for a *formal* national planning. In the 1940s, some economists had suggested in favour of the use of national planning. We may have a reflex of indicative planning in the USA if we look at the *Presidential Reports* which come after regular intervals. These reports are just 'benchmarks' in the area of resource utilisation and governmental announcements of its objectives—basically trying to motivate the private sector towards the area of public objectives. The indicative planning as it is practised by the mixed economy, any growth target could only be achieved once the public and the private enterprises worked in tandem. This is why besides the plan targets, the governments need to announce some set of indicative policies to encourage and motivate the private sector to

15. ***Collins Internet-linked Dictionary of Economics***, Glasgow, 2006.

16. George Albert Steiner, ***Government's Role in Economic Life***, McGraw-Hill, New York, 1953, p. 152.

17. India had a French influence on its development planning when it followed almost state monopoly in the six infrastructure industries also known as the ***core*** or the ***basic*** industries, i.e., cement, iron and steel, coal, crude oil, oil refinery and electricity.

18. Though the planning agencies the National Economic Development Council (NEDC) and the Economic Development Committees (EDCs) continued functioning, it was in 1992 that the NEDC was abolished (***Collins Dictionary of Economics***, 2006).

accelerate their economic activities in the direction of the plan targets.

After the Second World War, almost all the newly independent countries adopted the route of planned development. Though they followed an overall model of the indicative planning, many of them had serious inclination towards imperative planning. As in the case of India, the heavy bias towards imperative planning could only be reformed once the process of economic reforms was started in 1991.

Today, as there are mostly only mixed economies around the world, any country's development planning has to be only of the indicative type. After the revival of the role and the need of market in promoting growth and development via the Washington Consensus (1985), the World Trade Organisation (1995) and the Santiago/New Consensus (1998) only indicative planning has remained possible with the state playing only a marginal role in the economy, especially in the areas of social importance (i.e., nutrition, healthcare, drinking water, education, social security, etc.).

Some Other Types

There are still many **other types** of planning depending upon the point of view we are looking at. For example, from the territorial point of view, planning could be ***regional*** or ***national***. From the political point of view planning could be ***central***, ***state*** or ***local***. Similarly, from the participatory point of view, planning has been categorised into ***centrslised*** and ***decentrulised***. Again, from the temporal point of view planning could be ***long-term*** or ***short-term*** (in relative sense). Similarly, planning can be ***sectorol*** and ***spatial*** too. While sectoral planning emphasises the specific sector in the economy (i.e., agriculture, industry or the services), in the spatial planning development is seen in spatial framework (which aims at influencing the distribution of people and activities in spaces).

One **major classification** of planning, which has been in news for the past few years, is done on the basis of 'value system' of the society—***systems*** and ***normative*** planning. The systems approach to planning is largely *value-neutral* and remains fully focussed on the economic aspects of development. Socio-cultural variables are not given much importance in it and it goes quite mechanically targeting the planned goals. This emerged as the most favoured type of planning across the world as it was very much in harmony with the idea of secularism, equality and other democratic ideals of modern time. The most important part of this approach was its neutrality to the social diversities. Such an approach to planning suited India quite perfectly as it had very high socio-cultural diversities. The normative approach of planning is *value-based*. This process of planning remains in conformity to the value system of the target population—having quite diversified approach to development. This approach of planning was largely avoided by the world and never tried at macro level till the first decade of the twenty first century. With the rising acceptance to the *behavioural economics* we find normative approach gaining ground across the world. It got faster recognition among the experts and policymakers after two major international events—firstly, it was the publication of the first *World Happiness Report (2012)* and secondly, the *World Development Report 2015 (World Bank)* with latter highlighting the importance and impact of including behavioural dimensions of people in formulating public policies.

The Case of India

The *Economic Survey 2010–11* is the first document of the Government of India which advocates the need for a ***normative approach*** to planning in India. It is believed that until a programme/scheme run by the governments are not able to connect with the customs, traditions and ethos of the population, their acceptability will not be of the desired level among the target population. Establishing an empathic relationship between the programmes/schemes and target population is now considered an important aspect of planning and policymaking. Such a change in the thinking is based on the experiences of India and other countries of the world.

In January 2015, the Government of India replaced the erstwhile body, Planning Commission, by the *NITl Aayog* (a policy *think tank*). If we look into the functions and guiding principles of the new body we come to know that India has officially moved towards ***normative planning***—the new body has to follow a *development model* which is 'all round, all pervasive, all inclusive and holistic'. In this process the NITI Aayog has been further asked to enable the country to draw on the vitality and energy of the bedrock of our *ethos culture* and *sustenance.*

In recent times we see Government employing nudges[19] to modify people's behaviour to take desired socio-economic outcome aimed at development—i.e., using behavioural insights to frame economic policies. All such policy actions are the examples of normative planning.

The ***Atmanirbharta*** (self-reliance) push of the Government is a *value-laden idea* with local overtones (such as 'vocal for local' blurring the lines between nationalism and protectionism) and thus, is guided by ***normative insighrs***— be it aimed at emerging as a 'pharmacy of the world' or exploring the possibilities of an alternative to the global supply chain.[20]

---

19. **Economic Survey 2018-19**, Vol. 1, pp. 30-56 and **Economic Survey 2019-20**, Vol. 1, pp. 260-285, Ministry of Finance, GoI, N. Delhi.

20. **Economic Survey 2020-21**, vol. 2, pp. 97-99, Ministry of Finance, GoI, N. Delhi.

CHAPTER 5

PLANNING IN INDIA

*For the first eight Plans the emphasis was on a growing public sector with massive investments in basic and heavy industries, but since the launch of the Ninth Plan in 1997, the emphasis on the public sector has become less pronounced and the current thinking on planning in the country, in general, is that it should increasingly be of an indicative nature.**

In this Chapter...

INTRODUCTION

It was the Soviet Union which explored and adopted *national planning* for the first time in the world. After a prolonged period of debate and discussion, the First Soviet Plan commenced in 1928 for a period of five years. But the world outside was not fully aware of the modus operandi of development planning till the 1930s. It was the exodus[1] of the east European economists to Britain and the United States in the 1920s and 1930s that made the world aware as to what economic/

1. J.K. Galbraith, ***A History of Economics***, (London: Penguin Books 199), p. 187.

* *Planning Commission, 'An Overview of Planning in India', GoI, N. Delhi, 2013.*

national planning was all about. The whole lot of colonial world and the democracies of the time were fascinated by the idea of planning as an instrument of economic progress. The nationalist leaders with socialistic inclination of the erstwhile British colonies were more influenced by the idea of economic planning. The whole decade of the 1930s is the period in the Indian history when we see nationalists, capitalists, socialists, democrats and academicians advocating for the need of economic planning in India at one point or the other.[2]

Independent India was thus destined to be a planned economy. The economic history of India is nothing but the history of planning.[3] Even if the so-called economic reforms started in 1991–92, all the humble suggestions regarding the contours of reforms were very much outlined by the Planning Commission by then.[4] Once the reforms commenced, the think tank started outlining the major future direction for further plans.[5] Going through the history of planning in India is a highly educational trip in itself—for though the Planning Commission has been a political body, it never hesitated in pointing out good economics time and again. Let us therefore look into the unfolding of the planning process in India.

BACKGROUND

By the decade of the 1930s, the idea of planning had already entered the domain of intellectual and political discussion in India. Many fresh proposals suggesting immediacy of planning in India were put forward, though the erstwhile British government remained almost immune to them. But these humble proposals of planning served their purpose once India became independent and decided to adopt a planned economy.

The Visvesvaraya Plan

The credit of proposing the first blueprint of Indian planning is given to the popular civil engineer and the ex-Dewan of the Mysore state, M. Visvesvaraya. In his book *The Planned Economy of India,* published in 1934, he outlined the broad contours of his plan proposal.[6] His ideas of state planning were an exercise in democratic capitalism (similar to the USA) with emphasis on industrialisation—a shift of labour from agricultural to industries, targeting to double the national income in one decade. Though there was no follow up by the British government on this plan, it aroused an urge for national planning among the educated citizens of the country.

The FICCI Proposal

In 1934, a serious need of national planning was recommended by the Federation of Indian Chambers of Commerce and Industry (FICCI), the leading organisation of Indian capitalists. Its President N.R. Sarkar proclaimed that the days of undiluted laissez-faire were gone forever and for a backward country like India, a comprehensive plan for economic development covering the whole gamut of economic activities was a necessity. Voicing the views of the capitalist class, he further called for a high powered 'National Planning Commission' to coordinate the whole process of planning so that the country could make a structural break with the past and achieve its full growth potential.[7]

2. Bipan Chandra, 'The Colonial Legacy', in Bimal Jalan (ed.), ***The Indian Economy: Problems and Prospects,*** (New Delhi: Penguin books, 2004).
3. ArjunSengupta,'TheplanningRegimesince1951'inN.N.Vohra and Sabyasachi Bhattacharya (eds), ***Looking Back: India in the Twentieth Century*** (New Delhi: National Book Trust, 2001), p. 121.
4. Planning Commission, ***Seventh Five Year Plan (1985–90),*** (New Delhi: Government of India), 1985.
5. Planning Commission, ***The 8th, 9th, 10th and 11th Plans,*** New Delhi: Government of India.
6. Sumit Sarkar, ***Modern India: 1855–1947,*** (New Delhi: Macmillan, 1983), pp. 360–361.
7. Bipan Chandra et al., ***India After Independence, 1947–2000,*** (New Delhi: Penguin Books, 2000), p. 341.

By the late nineteenth century, the economic thinking of the nationalists (such as M.G. Ranade and Dadabhai Naroji) was in favour of a dominant role of the state in the economy and doubted the prudence of the 'market mechanism'. This thinking was further reinforced by the Keynesian ideas in the wake of the Great Depression, the *New Deal* in the USA and the Soviet experiment in national planning. Thus, the Indian capitalist class were also influenced by these events which were voiced in the FICCI articulation for planning.

The Congress

Though the Gandhians and some of the business and propertied representatives were opposed to commit the party to centralised state planning (including Mahatma Gandhi),[8] it was on the initiative[9] of the INC president Subhash C. Bose that the National Planning Committee (NPC) was set up in October 1938 under the chairmanship of J. L. Nehru to work out concrete programmes for development encompassing all major areas of the economy. Basically, the NPC was set up in a conference of the Ministers of Industries of the Congress-ruled States (though other states were also invited to participate) where M. Visvesvaraya, J.R.D. Tata, G.D. Birla and Lala Sri Ram and many others including academicians, technocrats, provincial civil servants, trade unionists, socialists and communists, etc., were also invited. The 15-member NPC with 29 sub-committees and a total of 350 members produced 29 volumes of recommendations.[10] The work of the committee was interrupted when the Second World War broke out and in the wake of the Quit India Movement many of its members including the chairman were arrested, and between 1940 and 1945 the Committee had only a nominal existence. Though the final report of the NPC could only be published in 1949, many developments related to planning took place during the Interim Government upto 1946.

'A series of valuable reports were published which brought together the constructive thinking done by the committee and the sub-committees and the materials collected in the course of their work. The importance of the NPC lies not so much in these reports as in the wide interest it created throughout the country for co-ordinated planning as the only means of bringing about a rapid increase in the standards of living and its emphasis on the need for bringing fundamental changes in the social and economic structure.'[11]

Some of the important developments after the NPC was set up which prepared a foundation for coordinated planning in Independent India are given below:

1. **Post War Reconstruction Committee:** Early in June 1941, the Government of India formed (on popular demand) a Post-War Reconstruction Committee which was to consider various plans for the reconstruction of the economy.[12]
2. **Consultative Committee of Economists:** A consultative committee of economists under the chairmanship of Ramaswamy Mudaliar was set up in 1941 as a 'think tank' to advise the four post-War Reconstruction Committees for executing national plan for the country.

   Though the committee suggested many plans for different areas of the economy, they had negligible practical

8. A. Vaidyanathan. 'The Indian Economy Since Independence (1947–70)', in Dharma Kumar (ed), ***The Cambridge Economic History of India***, Vol.II, (Cambridge: Cambridge University Press, 1983), p. 949.
9. Sumit Sarkar, ***Modern India***, p. 360.
10. Publications Division, ***The Gazetteer of India***, Vol. 3, (New Delhi: Government of India, 1975), p. 2.
11. ***Ibid.***, pp. 2–3.
12. There was a popular view in favour of rapid industrialisation among the important nationalists, economists and the business class of that time.

significance as these suggestions were imbued with academic biases.

3. **Planning and Development Department:** After all possible delays, it was in 1944 that the government created a Planning and Development Department under a separate member of the Viceroy's Executive Council for organising and co-ordinating economic planning in the country. Ardeshir Dalal (the controller of the Bombay Plan) was appointed as one of its acting members. More than 20 panels of experts were set up. The central departments and the governments of the Provinces and Indian states were invited to prepare detailed plans for industrialisation.[12] This Department was abolished in 1946.

4. **Advisory Planning Board:** In October 1946, the Government of India appointed a committee called the 'Advisory Planning Board'[13] to review the planning that had already been done by the British government, the work of the National Planning Committee, and other plans and proposals for planning and to make recommendations regarding the future machinery of planning and also in regard to objectives and priorities. The Board strongly recommended the creation of 'a single, compact authoritative organisation ... responsible directly to the Cabinet ... which should devote its attention continuously to the whole field of development.'[14] This was an emphatic advice for the creation of a National Planning Commission, similar to FICCI's view of 1934, which will have autonomy and authoritative say on the process of development planning, working in tandem with the Union Cabinet and also influencing the developmental decisions of the states. This happened in 1950 with the setting up of the Planning Commission.

The Board, in its Report of January. 1947, emphatically expressed the opinion that the 'proper development of large-scale industries can only take place if political units, whether in the provinces or states, agree to work in accordance with a common plan.'[15] This suggestion worked as a great influence on the planning process of Independent India as it always tried to give unifying nature to development planning. But, this process also induced a serious tendency of centralisation in the Indian planning to which a number of states were to pose objections and straining the centre-state relations, time and again.[16] However, the political leadership, right from the 1920s, was very conscious of the need for decentralised planning in the country.[17]

The Bombay Plan

The Bombay Plan was the popular title of 'A Plan of Economic Development for India', which was prepared by a cross-section of India's leading capitalists. The eight capitalists involved in this plan were Purshotamdas Thakurdas, J.R.D. Tata, G.D. Birla, Lala Sri Ram, Kasturbhai Lalbhai, A.D. Shroff, Ardeshir Dalal and John Mathai.[18] The Plan was published in 1944–45. Out of these eight industrialists, Purshotamdas Thakurdas was one among the 15 members of the National

13. The Board was set up by the Interim Government formed in 1946.
14. Dharma Kumar (ed.), ***The Cambridge Economic History of India***, Vol.II, p. 950.
15. Kalikinkar Datta, ***An Advanced History of India***, 4th Edition (New Delhi: Macmillan, 2006), pp. 955–56.
16. S.N. Jha and P.C. Mathur (eds), ***Decentralisation and local Politics***, (New Delhi: Sage Publications, 2002), pp. 28–30.
17. A.H. Hanson, ***The Process of Planning: A study of India's Five-Year Plans, 1950–1964*** (London: Oxford University Press, 1966), pp. 152–55.
18. Bipan Chandra, 'The Colonial Legacy', p. 23.

Planning Committee (1938);[19] J.R.D. Tata, G.D. Birla and Lala Sri Ram, were members of the sub-committees (29 in total) of the National Planning Committee.[20]

The popular sentiments regarding the need of planning and criss-cross of memberships between the NPC and the Bombay Plan club made possible some clear-cut agreements between these two major plans, which ultimately went to mould the very shape of the Indian economy after Independence. We may have a look at some of the very important agreements:[21]

1. A basic agreement on the issue of the ***agrarian restructuring***—abolition of all intermediaries (i.e., zamindari abolition), minimum wages, guarantee of minimum or fair prices for agricultural products, cooperatives, credit and marketing supports.
2. Agreement on ***rapid industrialisation*** for which both the plans agreed upon an emphasis on heavy capital goods and basic industries (the Bombay Plan had allocated 35 per cent of its total plan outlay on basic industries).
3. Taking clues from the Soviet Planning, the NPC and the Bombay Plan both were in favour of a simultaneous ***development of the essential consumer goods*** industries, but as a low-key affair.
4. Both the plans agreed upon the importance of promoting the ***medium-scale, small-scale and cottage industries*** as they could provide greater employment and required lesser capital and lower order of plants and machineries.
5. Both the plans wanted the ***state to play an active role*** in the economy through planning, controlling and overseeing the different areas of the economy, i.e., trade, industry and banking, through state ownership (public sector) or through direct and extensive control over them.
6. Large-scale measures for ***social welfare*** were favoured by both the plans, which suggested to be based on issues like, right to work and full employment, the guarantee of a minimum wage, greater state expenditure on housing, water and sanitation, free education, social insurance to cover unemployment and sickness and provision of utility services such as electricity and transportation at a low cost through state subsidies.
7. Both the plans agreed upon a planning which could do away with gross ***inequalities***. Through measures like progressive taxation and prevention of concentration of wealth. Inequality was considered undesirable as it tended to restrict the domestic market.

The Gandhian Plan

Espousing the spirit of the Gandhian economic thinking, Sriman Narayan Agarwal formulated The Gandhian Plan in 1944. The plan laid more emphasis on agriculture. Even if he referred to industrialisation, it was to the level of promoting cottage and village-level industries, unlike the NPC and the Bombay Plan which supported a leading role for the heavy and large industries. The plan articulated a 'decentralised economic structure' for India with 'self-contained villages'.

It needs to be noted here that the Gandhians did not agree with the views of the NPC or the Bombay Plan, particularly on issues like centralised planning, dominant role of the state in

[19] Partha Chatterjee, 'Development Planning and the Indian Planning', in Partha Chatterjee (ed.), ***State and Politics in India*** (New Delhi: Oxford University Press, 1997), p. 273.

[20] Rakesh Mohan, 'Industrial Policy and Controls', in Bimal Jalan (ed.), ***Indian Economy: Problems and Prospects*** (New Delhi: Penguin Books, 1994).

[21] Bipan Chandra, 'The Colonial Legacy', pp. 23–31.

the economy and the emphasis on industrialisation being the major ones.[22] For Gandhi, the machinery, commercialisation and centralised state power were the curses of modern civilisation thrust upon the Indian people by European colonialism. It was industrialism itself, Gandhi argued, rather than the inability to industrialise, which was the root cause of Indian poverty. This was until the 1940s that the Congress supported the above-given view of Gandhi to mobilise a mass movement against the colonial rule. But it was in the NPC that the Congress tried to articulate a different view on these issues, almost taking a break from Gandhi's ideas. The very first session of the NPC was brought to an impasse by J.C. Kumarappa (the lone Gandhian on the 15-member NPC) by questioning the authority of the NPC to discuss plans for industrialisation. He said on the occasion that the national priority as adopted by the Congress was to restrict and eliminate modern industrialism. The impasse was normalised after Nehru intervened and declared that most members of the NPC felt that large-scale industry ought to be promoted as long as it did not 'come into conflict with the cottage industries'.[23] This was a long-drawn ideological impasse which made it necessary to articulate the Gandhian view of planning via this plan.

The people's Plan

In 1945, yet another plan was formulated by the radical humanist leader M.N. Roy, Chairman of the Post-War Reconstruction Committee of Indian Trade Union. The plan was based on Marxist socialism and advocated the need of providing the people with the 'basic necessities of life'.[24] Agricultural and industrial sectors, both were equally highlighted by the plan. Many economists have attributed the socialist leanings in Indian planning to this plan. The common minimum programmes of the United Front Government of the mid-nineties (20th century) and that of the United Progressive Alliance of 2004 may also be thought to have been inspired from the same plan. 'Economic reforms with the human face', the slogan with which the economic reforms started in the early 1990s also has the resonance of the People's Plan.

The Sarvodaya Plan

After the reports of the NPC were published and the government was set to go for the five-year plans, a lone blueprint for the planned development of India was formulated by the famous socialist leader Jayaprakash Narayan—the Sarvodaya Plan published in January 1950. The plan drew its major inspirations from the Gandhian techniques of constructive works by the community and trusteeship as well as the Sarvodaya concept of Acharya Vinoba Bhave, the eminent Gandhian constructive worker. Major ideas of the plan were highly similar to the Gandhian Plan like emphasis on agriculture, agri-based small and cottage industries, self-reliance and almost no dependence on foreign capital and technology, land reforms, self-dependent villages and decentralised participatory form of planning and economic progress, to name the major ones.[25] Some of the acceptable ideas of the plan got their due importance when the Government of India promoted five year plans.

By the early 1960s, Jayaprakash Narayan had become highly critical of the Indian planning process, especially of its increasing centralising nature and dilution of people's participation in it. Basically, the very idea of democratic decentralisation was disliked by the established power structure, namely, the MLAs/MPs, the

22. Dharma Kumar, *The Cambridge Economic History of India*, p. 949.

23. Partha Chatterjee, 'Development Planning and the Indian Planning', p. 275.

24. S.K. Ray, *Indian Economy* (New Delhi: Prentice Hall, 1987), p. 369.

25. A.H. Hanson, *The Process of Planning*, p. 175.

bureaucracy and the state-level politicians.[26] This led the Jayaprakash Narayan Committee (1961) to decide against the centralising nature of Indian planning. The committee pointed out that after having accepted Panchayati Raj as the agency responsible for planning and execution of plans, there is 'no longer any valid reason for continuing the individual allocations subjectwise even to serve as a guide.'[27]

Disregarding the humble advice of the committee, central schemes like small farmers development agency (SFDA), drought-prone area programme (DPAP), intensive tribal development programme (ITDP), intensive agricultural district programme (IADP), etc., were introduced by the government and were put totally outside the purview of the Panchayats.

It was only after the 73rd and 74th Amendments effected to the Constitution (1992) that the role of local bodies and their importance in the process of planned development was accepted and the views of Jayaprakash got vindicated.

Some Area-wise Reports

The idea for the need of a planned development of India became more and more popular by the decade of the 1940s. It was under this popular pressure that the Government of India started taking some planned actions in this direction. In the 1940s, we see several area-specific reports being published:[28]

1. Gadgil Report on Rural Credit
2. Kheragat Report on Agricultural Development
3. Krishnamachari Report on Agricultural Prices
4. Saraiya Report on Cooperatives
5. A series of reports on Irrigation (ground water, canal, etc.)

All these reports, though prepared with great care and due scholarship, the government had hardly any zeal to implement the plans on their findings. But independent India was greatly benefited when the planning started covering all these areas of concern.

There is no doubt in drawing the conclusion that prior to Independence, there was thus a significant measure of agreement in India between the Government of India under the Secretary of State, the Indian National Congress, prominent industrialists and the others on the following principles:[29]

1. There should be central planning, in which the state should play an active part, for social and economic development to bring about a rapid rise in the standard of living;
2. There should be controls and licencing in order, among other things, to direct investments into the desired channels and ensure equitable distribution;
3. While there should be balanced development in all sectors of the economy, the establishment of basic industries was specially important. In this, state-owned and state-managed enterprises have an important role to play. There were, however, differences of approach with regard to the specific fields to be allocated to the public and private sectors.

It is highly interesting and important to note that all the above agreements and opinions were reached through an evolutionary manner in the last two-decades before Independence in the deliberations and exercises regarding the need for economic planning in the country.

26. George Mathew, ***Power to the People,*** in M.K. Santhanam (ed.), ***50 Years of Indian Republic*** (New Delhi: Publications Division, Government of India, 200), p. 32.

27. L.C. Jain, et al., ***Grass without Roots*** (New Delhi: Sage Publications, 1985).

28. A.H. Hanson, ***The Process of Planning***, p. 180.

29. Publications Division, ***The Gazatteir of India***, p. 5.

'The plans prepared by the Government of India, the Bombay Plan and other above-discussed plans (except the NPC and the Sarvodaya Plan) suffered from serious limitations. When they were prepared, it was known that transfer of power was to take place quite soon; but the exact form of the future government was not known, the plans consisted largely of proposals of experts, which were not effectively co-ordinated. They had no social philosophy behind them. With the advent of Independence, they became inadequate, though the thinking that had taken place on planning generally and its techniques proved useful for the future.'[30]

MAJOR OBJECTIVES OF PLANNING

Planning for India was an instrument to realise the aspirations and dreams of the future. We know that the foundations of future India were not laid in one day. The cherished dream about future India had evolved through a long-drawn process of the entire period of the freedom struggle. These aspirations and goals got their proper places and due importance in the reports of the National Planning Committee (NPC), in the deliberations of the Constituent Assembly and finally in the Constitution of India. From the margins of the ripening nationalist movement, as well as taking clues from the Soviet and the French styles of planning, the NPC articulated the objectives of planning in India. The process of planning in India tried to include all the aspirations of the nationalist movement as well as of the future generations. But this will be a highly general comment upon the objectives of planning in India. We need to delve into the specific and objective goals of planning in India to further our discussions. Some of the historic deliberations regarding planning will serve our purpose:

1. Reviewing the entire situation, in the light of the social philosophy evolved over decades, the Constituent Assembly came to the conclusion that to guide this 'revolution of rising expectations' into constructive channels, India should make determined efforts through carefully planned large-scale social and economic development and the application of modern scientific and technological improvements, to bring about a rapid and appreciable rise in the standard of living of the people, with the maximum measure of social justice attainable. On the whole it was a call for India becoming a welfare state.[31] This important deliberation does not only call for the necessity of planning for the country, but it also outlines the broader objectives of planning.
2. There are three important features included in the constitutional provisions, which pertain to the objectives of planning in the country:[32]
   (i) 'Economic and social planning' is a concurrent subject. Also, while framing the 'Union', 'State' and 'Concurrent' lists, allocating subjects and other provisions, the Constitution vests power in the Union to ensure co-ordinated development in essential fields of activity, while preserving the initiative and authority of the states in the spheres allotted to them.
   (ii) The Constitution includes provisions for promoting cooperation on a voluntary basis between the Union and the states and among states and groups of states in investigation of matters of common interest, in legislative procedures and in administration, thus avoiding the rigidities inherent in federal constitutions

30. Ibid., p. 5.
31. Ibid.
32. Ibid., pp. 7–10

(Articles 249, 252, 257, 258, 258-A, and 312). In other words, the objective is cooperative federalism.

(iii) The Constitution also sets out in broad outline the pattern of the welfare state envisaged and the fundamental principles on which it should rest.

These are the major cornerstones of planning and its objectives enshrined in the Constitution that will breed enough Union–State tussle in coming decades and make it compulsive for the government to resort to 'reforms with a human face' rhetoric. We can see the methodology of planning taking a U-turn in the era of the economic reforms since the early 1990s.

3. The government resolution announcing the setting up of the Planning Commission (March 1950) started with a reference to the constitutional provisions bearing on the socio-economic objectives of the Constitution. The Fundamental Rights and the Directive Principles of the Constitution assure every citizen, among other things, adequate means of livelihood, opportunities for employment and a socio-economic order based on justice and equality. Thus, the basic objectives[33] of planning were already given in the provisions of the Constitution of India. These were emphatically stated in the First Five Year Plan (1951–56) itself, in the following words:

'The urge to economic and social change under present conditions comes from the facts of poverty and of inequalities in income, wealth and opportunity. The elimination of poverty cannot obviously, be achieved merely by redistributing existing wealth. Nor can a programme aiming only at raising production remove existing inequalities. These two have to be considered together....'

4. The above objectives of planning were time and again emphasised in one form or the other in the coming times. As the Second Five Year Plan (1956–61) said:

'The Plan has to carry forward the process initiated in the First Plan period. It must provide for a larger increase in production, in investment and in employment. Simultaneously, it must accelerate the institutional changes needed to make the economy more dynamic and more progressive in terms no less of social than of economic ends.'

5. The same objectives were repeated by the Sixth Five Year Plan (1980–85) in the following words:

'The basic task of economic planning in India is to bring about a structural transformation of the economy so as to achieve a high and sustained rate of growth, a progressive improvement in the standard of living of the masses leading to eradication of poverty and unemployment and providing a material base for a self-reliant economy.'

6. It will be highly needful to enquire about the objectives of planning in the era of the economic reforms initiated in the fiscal 1991–92 as this new economic policy (NEP) made the experts and economists to conclude many questionable things about the objectives of planning in the country:

(i) The need to shift dependence from wage to self-employment.

(ii) The state is rolling back and the economy is becoming pro-private and sector-wise the social purpose of the planning will be lacking.

(iii) The objectives of planning nearly outlined hitherto have been blurred.

(iv) The promotion of foreign investment will induce the economy into the perils of neo-imperialism, etc.

33 Ibid.

But all the above-given doubts were cleared by the forthcoming plans in straightforward words. We may quote from the following plans:

- 'For the future economic development, the economy will be more dependent upon private participation and the nature of planning will become more indicative with the major objectives of planning remaining the same'. This was announced by the government while launching the economic reforms (July 23, 1991) and commencing the Eighth Five Year Plan (1992–97). 'There was no change in the basic objectives of planning even though there was change in instruments of policy'—this was announced by the government while announcing the new economic policy (1991).
- While the Ninth Plan (1997–2002) was being launched, it was announced that 'The goals of planning in India, which were set by Panditji have not changed. The Ninth Plan does not attempt to reinvent the wheel. At the same time, the goals and targets this Plan attempts to achieve are based on the lessons of experience including the Eighth Plan. They address today's problems and challenges and try to prepare the nation for tomorrow as well.'[34]

Finally, a broad consensus looks evolving through the process of planning and crystallising on the six major objectives of planning[35] in India which are as follows:

34. Deputy Chairman, Planning Commission, May 1999. It is interesting to note here that the composition of the polity in the Centre was dominated by the BJP, while the Deputy Chairman, Planning Commission was K.C. Pant (an old congress man)—continuity in the basic ideas and objectives of planning being maintained.

35. Publications Division, ***India*** (New Delhi: Government of India, various years).

1. **Economic Growth:** Sustained increase in the levels of production in the economy is among the foremost objectives of planning in India, which continues till date and will be so in future, without any iota of doubt in it.
2. **Poverty Alleviation:** Poverty alleviation was the most important issue which polarised the members of the NPC as well as the Constituent Assembly that a highly emphatic decision in favour of a planned economy evolved even before Independence. Several programmes have been launched in India directing the cause of poverty alleviation by all the governments till date and the process continues even today with more seriousness (we see the National Rural Employment Guarantee Programme—NREGP—being launched by the UPA Government in 2006 by passing an Act in the Parliament—the matter has started attracting such high political concern).
3. **Employment Generation:** Providing employment to the poor has been the best tool of economics to alleviate poverty. Thus, this objective of planning in India comes naturally once it commits itself to alleviate poverty. Employment generation in India has been, therefore, part and parcel of the objective of poverty alleviation in India. General programmes and schemes have been launched by the governments from time to time in this direction, some based on the wage employments still, others based on self-employment.
4. **Controlling Economic Inequality:** There were visible economic inequalities in India at the inter-personal as well as at the intra-personal levels. Economic planning as a tool of checking all kinds

of economic disparities and inequalities was an accepted idea by the time India started planning.[36] To fulfil this objective of planning the governments have enacted highly innovative economic policies at times even inviting a tussle with regard to the Fundamental Rights enshrined in the Constitution.

Though Indian Planning has socio-economic objectives to fulfil, only economic planning was made a part of the planning process (technically speaking) and social planning (better called social engineering) was left to the political process. That is why reservation in government jobs and admissions in premier academic institutions, land reforms, promoting inter-caste marriages, etc., do not fall under the purview of the Planning Commission.

5. **Self-reliance:** During the 1930s and 1940s, there was an ardent desire among the nationalists, capitalists and the NPC for making the economy self-reliant in all economic spheres. Self-reliance was defined not as autarchy, but as an effort to strike against a subordinate position in the world economy. As Jawaharlal Nehru asserted: self-reliance, 'does not exclude international trade, which should be encouraged but with a view to avoid economic imperialism.'[37] India still strives for self-reliance in every field of the economy, as well as serving the realities of higher interdependence in the globalising world post-World Trade Organisation (WTO).

In the wake of unprecedented disruptions brought by the **COVID-19** pandemic, the Government has given a renewed push towards self-reliance by announcing the ***Atmanirbhar Bharat Abhiyan*** (Self-Reliant India Campaign) in May 2020. The Abhiyan which is based on five pillars, namely – Economy, Infrastructure, System, Demography and Demand – has been visualised by the experts as India's alternative to rising global protectionism. This is for the *first time* that India has given clear specifications for attaining self-reliance. How India co-ordinates its new brand of self-reliance with globalisation (which India supports vigorously) only coming times can say!

6. **Modernisation:** Modernising the traditional economy was set as a foremost objective of planning. Specially, the agriculture sector of the economy needed an immediate inclusion of modern methods and techniques of farming, dairying, etc. Similarly, in education too, India needs to go for inclusion of modern education system.

India did not miss the chance of accepting the importance of modern science and technology. As the economy had selected industry as its prime moving force (PMF), it was essential to adopt the changing dimensions of science and technology.

The major objectives of planning in India are not only broad but open-ended. That is why it hardly needed any change and modification with changing times. It means, after the completion of one plan the objectives for the new plan are automatically set. Coming to the composition of the objectives, we may confidently conclude that all the aspirations of the Preamble,[38] the Directive

36. Duly discussed by the NPC as well as the Constituent Assembly.

37. ***National Planning Committee Report;*** Also Nehru in ***The Discovery of India.***

38. The Preamble was declared by the Supreme Court as an ***integral part of the Constitution*** and any amendments amounting to a change in its meaning and spirit amounted to the violation of the 'basic feature' of the Constitution (Keshvanand Barti, 1973 and S.R. Bommai, 1994 cases). This further magnified the objectives and role of Planning in India.

Principles of the State Policy,[39] the Fundamental Duties and the Fundamental Rights have got their due place and weightage. All the aspirations of the nationalists and the freedom fighters look resonating in the very soul of the Indian planning system.

The above-given objectives of planning got abolished with the Planning Commission. Under the new body—NITI Aayog—a *holistic and federal* objectives of planning have been set by the GoI (they have been discussed under the sub-title, NITI Aayog at the end of this chapter).

PLANNING COMMISSION

Once the National Planning Committee published its Report (1949), there was a firm inclusion of the need for 'Economic and Social Planning'[40] in the Constitution, the stage was set for the formal launching of planning in the country. Though the economy was run on the principles of planning very much after the Independence itself[41] it was in a piecemeal manner only. For formal planning to begin, for the whole economy at the national level, there was a need for a permanent expert body which could take over the responsibility of the whole gamut of planning, i.e., plan formation, resource aspects, implementation and review—as planning is a technical[42] matter. Thus, in March 1950[43] the Planning Commission (PC) was set up by the government by a Cabinet Resolution (without resorting to legislation). Important details regarding the composition, legal status, etc., of the PC were as under:

1. An ***extra-constitutional*** (i.e., non-constitutional) and ***non-statutory*** body (though planning originates from the Constitution there is no reference to the PC in it).
2. An ***advisory body*** to the Government of India on an array of issues of economic development.
3. A 'think tank' on economic development with the Prime Minister as its ex-officio Chairman and with the provision or a Deputy Chairman.[44] The main function of the Deputy Chairman was to ***co-ordinate*** the work of the Commission.[45]
4. Had an open provision for the number of its membership (as many area experts are required by the particular proposed period of planning) other than six Union Cabinet Ministers as its ***ex-officio members***[46] and a Member Secretary. The Minister of Planning is already an ex-officio member of the PC.[47]

39 As the different Articles of the Directive Principles got interpreted as being complementary parts of the Fundamental Rights, their enforcement became obligatory for the Government in coming times, still broadening the objectives of planning in the country.

40 Distribution of legislative power, List-III, Entry 20.

41 Though formal planning commenced in the fiscal 1951–52, planning has already commenced with the Industrial Policy Resolution, 1948. More so, the Prime Minister of India who headed the NPC had already taken firm decision that India would be a planned economy by August 1937 (Congress Working Committee, Wardha). Thus, the economy takes its first wink in the planned era!

42 Alan W. Evans, 'Economic and Planning', in Jean Forbes (ed.), ***Studies in Social Science and Planning*** (Edinburgh: Scottish Academy Press, 972), p. 121.

43 I. Publications Division, ***The Gazette of India***, p. 10.
II. S.R. Maheshwari (Indian Administration New Delhi: Orient Longman, 2002, p. 121).
III. 'The Indian Economy Since Independence', p. 949.

44 The post of Deputy Chairman was later given a cabinet rank in the Union Council of Minister.

45 Publications Division, ***Gazetteer of India***, p. 11.

46 Publications Division, ***India 2008*** (New Delhi: Ministry of Information and Broadcasting, Government of India, 2009), p. 676.

47 There was a provision of only *three* Cabinet Ministers as its ***ex-officio*** members namely the Finance, Human Resource Development and Defence upto July 2004 when the United Progressive Alliance Government increased it to include the other *three* Cabinet Ministers, viz., the Railways, Agriculture and Information Technology. It has been only once in the history of the PC that it had *six* Cabinet Ministers as its ex-officio members, i.e., in the final years of the Rajiv Gandhi regime (***The Economic Times***, 16 July 2004, N. Delhi Edition).

5. An ***autonomous body*** entitled to form its own views on important issues and place them before the governments. It worked closely with the Union and State cabinets and had full knowledge of their policies.
6. Was invariably ***consulted*** on changes proposed in social and economic policies. To ensure free and full exchange of ideas, the PC had established a ***convention*** that it will not give publicity to differences of views between the Commission and the Union and State governments.
7. ***Linked*** with the Union Cabinet at the secretariat level. The PC was part of the Cabinet organisation and the 'demand for grants' for it was included in the budget demand for the Cabinet Secretariat.
8. Seated at the 'Yojana Bhavan', the Commission had a staff of secretaries and advisers and also a research organisation.[48]
9. The PC was a ***technical body*** with experts and professionals coming from an array of specific areas as per the need of planning of the concerned period (see footnote 42).
10. The Commission had ***executive powers.***[49]

Functions of the Planning Commission

Though the PC was set up with a definite purpose of planning, nobody knew that it would extend its functions over the entire spectrum of administration in the country. It was described as the 'economic Cabinet of the country as a whole' even encroaching upon the constitutional body like the Finance Commission[50] and not being accountable to the Parliament.[51] Through time it built up a heavy bureaucratic organisation[52] which led even Nehru himself to observe—'The Commission which was a small body of serious thinkers has turned into a government department complete with a crowd of secretaries, directors and of course a big building.'[53]

Though the functions of the PC were extended to include timely changes in the planning needs (in the reforms era), its functions were announced by the same government order which did set up the Planning Commission. The order[54] says:

'The Planning Commission will—

1. Make an assessment of the material, capital and human resources of the country, including technical personnel, and investigate the possibilities of augmenting such of those resources as are found to be deficient in relation to the nation's requirements;
2. Formulate a plan for the most effective and balanced utilisation of the country's resources;
3. On a determination of priorities, define the stages in which the plan should be carried out and propose the allocation of

48 Publications Division, *Gazetteer of India*, p. 11.

49 Prima facie a body should have been either constitutional or statutory to wield the executive powers, but as a number of Cabinet Ministers as well as the PM himself were directly involved with the PC, it used to wield executive powers for all practical purposes.

50 Rajamannar was the Chairman of the Fourth Finance Commission. See Ministry of Finance Report of the Fourth Finance Commission (New Delhi: Government of India, 1965) pp. 88–90.

51 By the 1950s it was a general criticism of the PC which looked highly logical. But through the entire period of planning the Government never did think to convert the PC into a constitutional body. Practically enough, the Union Cabinet and the whole Government is accountable to the Parliament for the functions of the PC as it has complete mandate and support of the governments of the time.

52 Appleby, ***Public Administration in India: Report of A Survey***, Ford Foundation, 1953, p. 22.

53 As quoted in D.D. Basu, ***An Introduction to the Constitution of India*** (New Delhi: Wadhwa & Company, 1999), p. 330.

54 Publication Division, ***The Gazetteer of India, Vol. 3***, op. cit., pp. 10–11.

resources for the due completion of each stage;

4. Indicate the factors which are tending to retard economic development, and determine the conditions which, in view of the current social and political situation, should be established for the successful execution of the plan;
5. Determine the nature of the machinery which will be necessary for securing the successful implementation of each stage of the plan in all its aspects;
6. Appraise from time to time the progress achieved in the execution of each stage of the Plan and recommend the adjustments of policy and measures that such appraisal may show to be necessary; and
7. Make such interim or ancillary recommendations as appear to be appropriate either for facilitating the discharge of the duties assigned to it; or on a consideration of the prevailing economic conditions, current policies, measures and development programmes; or on an examination of such specific problems as may be referred to it for advice by Central or State governments.'

With the commencement of the Tenth Plan (2002–07), the government handed over ***two new functions*** to the Planning Commission in 2002, namely:

1. To monitor the plan implementation with special reference to the process of 'economic reforms' with the help of the steering committees.

   It should be noted here that once the process of economic reforms was initiated in the country (early 1990s) there was a diminishing role proposed for the state in the economy in some areas and increased role for the state in some other areas. The re-definition of the state's role in the economy (though it was the contemporary thinking world wide) made most of the experts and the business community to conclude as if there will be no role for planning in the economy. The New Economic Policy (NEP) of 1991–92 was a prima-facie proposal for the expansion of the market economy in the country. But it was not the case altogether. Planning has not become irrelevant though it needed to search for a new orientation. And it was highly essential that the process of planning keeps its relevance to the bigger and the broader process of economic reforms. This particular new function of the PC must be seen in this light.

2. To monitor the progress of various Central Ministries. It should be noted here that for the first time, the PC went to set the 'monitorable targets' for 10 areas indicating development. The Central Ministries have been linked to these monitorable targets. The timely performances of the Ministries are now monitored by the PC as per its new function.

With the inclusion of the above-mentioned two functions in the existing functions (which were already very broad), the PC had emerged as a real 'supercabinet'. Since it was basically the Deputy-Chairman who officiated the general meetings of the Commission, he had a high-level say[55] in articulating the direction and the nature of the economic policies. Through the first new function it articulated the future dimensions of the economic reforms and through the second new function, it influenced the works of the various ministries—ultimately it seems as if the PC had been able to emerge as the real think-tank of development in the country.[56]

The PC had also been able to influence the economic policies of the states since 2002 in a great way. Though the PC did not make the state plans[57] it was able to influence the overall economic policies of the states. It had been possible due to the setting of 'monitorable targets' for states for the same development indicators/areas as was been set for the Centre.[58] The states were liable for being monitored by the PC concerning their performances regarding these monitorable targets. This way the Central Government had started having its say over the state governments via the new functions of the PC.

We may conclude that the PC had been able to unify not only the various economic policies of the Centre, but also those of the states with the help of these two new functions. Earlier, there had always been a lack of congruence among the policies of the various central ministries and the ideas articulated by the PC.

An Epitaph to the Planning Commission

On January 1, 2015, the government formally abolished the PC by replacing it with the newly created body—the NITI Aayog. With this there ended an era in the economic history of independent India. Whether it was better to revive the PC or abolish it has been a matter of much debate among the discipline experts, politicians and the media. The debate, at times, had emotional tones, too. But the government has its own wisdom behind the action (a detailed discussion on it has been included as the last *sub-topic* of this chapter titled **'NITI Aayog')**.

As an 'epitaph' to the PC (may be an 'ode'), it will be quite relevant to have an eye on the report of the Independent Evaluation Office (IEO) on the former which was submitted to the Prime Minister Office by late June 2014. As per it, the PC was created in response to the unique challenges faced by a nascent democracy and a fledgling economy—it conceived a 'top-down approach' to planning that envisaged a dynamic Central government building up the economic and social order of weak states. The report called the PC in its current form and function a hindrance and not a help to India's development. It further added that it

55. It is not without that the Government decides to call in Montek Singh Ahluwalia, an economist of international repute to officiate as the Deputy Chairman of the PC. Every idea and opinion of Mr. Ahluwalia was understood by the coalition partners of the UPA Government as a thing the Government is necessarily going to implement in future. One can imagine the increased role of the office of the PC. There is always a hue and cry every time the Deputy Chairman articulates an idea or opinion. Though the PC is chaired by the PM, it seems that the Deputy Chairman has started availing enough autonomy to speak his mind.

56. Ibid.

57. As per the original mandate, the PC was supposed to formulate the state plans also. By 1960s, with the decision to follow the multi-level planning (MLP) in the country the states started having their own state planning boards (SPBs).

58. In setting these targets the concerned states were consulted approach of planning was followed.

is not easy to reform such a large *ossified body* and it would be better to replace it with a new body that is needed to assist states in ideas, to provide long-term thinking and to help cross-cutting reforms. Some of the **major** recommendations of IEO on the PC are as follows:

1. The PC be scrapped and replaced with the *Reform and Solutions Commission* (RSC), which should be staffed with experts with domain knowledge and kept free from any ministerial administrative structure. The new body should have full-time representation of major trade and industry organisations, civil society representatives, academics, etc., so as to capture their concerns and benefit from their expertise in formulating long–term strategy.
2. The RSC will perform ***three*** main functions:
   - (i) Serve as a solutions exchange and repository of ideas that have been successful in different aspects of development in various states and districts, and in other parts of the world;
   - **(ii)** Provide ideas for integrated systems reform; and
   - **(iii)** Identify new and emerging challenges and provide solutions to preempt them.
3. The current functions of the PC be taken over by other bodies, 'which are better designed to perform those functions'.
4. Since the state governments have better information about local requirements and resources than the central government and central institutions, they should be allowed to identify priorities and implement reforms at the state level, independent of mandatory diktats from the central institutions.
5. The task of long-term economic thinking and coordination can be performed by a new body established to act solely as a 'think tank' within the government.
6. The Finance Commission be made a *permanent body* responsible for the allocation of centrally collected revenue to the states and the finance ministry be tasked with the division of funds among the various central ministries.

The recommendations of the IEO (a brainchild of the PC itself) on the PC were quite surprising, even shocking to few. Whether the new body replacing the PC will be a betterment over the latter and will be able to carve out its desired aims is a matter to be evaluated and analysed in future. Meanwhile, we can visibly find some of the recommendations of the IEO resonating in the newly created body, the NITI Aayog, the replacement for the PC.

Note: While a detailed literature has been included on the NITIAayog' in this chapter, the literature on the PC has been left unchanged for ease of understanding and comparative purpose.

NATIONAL DEVELOPMENT COUNCIL

The National Development Council (NDC) was set up on August 6, 1952 by a Resolution[59] issued from the Cabinet Secretariat. The first Plan recommended its formation with a very concise and suitable observation:

'In a country of the size of India where the states have under the constitution full autonomy within their own sphere of duties, it is necessary to have a forum such as a National Development Council at which, from time to time, the Prime Minister of India and the Chief Ministers of the

59. Cabinet Secretariat, ***Resolution No. 62/CF/50*** (06.08.1952) Government of India, New Delhi.

states can review the working of the plan and of its various aspects.'[60]

There were some strong reasons why the NDC was set up, which may be seen as follows:

1. The Central Plans were to be launched in the states and the UTs with the participation of the state-level personnel. The Planning Commission was not provided with its own implementation staff (though the PC was given the responsibility of plan implementation) for this purpose. Therefore, the consent and co-operation of these federal units was a must.

2. Economic planning as a concept had its origin in the centralised system (i.e., Soviet Union). For India, to democratise/decentralise the very process of planning was not a lesser task/challenge than promoting development itself. Indian planning is rightly said to be a process of trial and error in striking a balance between liberty and progress, central control and private initiative and national planning with local authority.[61]

   The setting up of the NDC can be considered as a step towards decentralised planning.

3. In the constitutional design of the federal rigidities it was necessary to provide the whole planning process a unified outlook. The NDC serves the purpose of diluting the autonomous and rigid federal units of the Union of India.[62]

The NDC initially comprised the Prime Minister of India (de facto Chairman), the Chief Ministers of all States and the Members of the Planning Commission (replaced by the NITI Aayog since January 2015). In the first meeting of the NDC held on November 8–9, 1952, Jawaharlal Nehru stated that NDC is 'essentially a forum for intimate cooperation between the State Governments and the Central Government for all the tasks of national development'. In the *words* of Nehru, setting up of the NDC may be regarded as one of the most significant steps taken for promoting understanding and consultation between the Union and the State Governments on planning and common economic policies.

Considering the recommendations of the 'Administrative Reforms Commission', the NDC was reconstituted and its functions redefined by a Cabinet Resolution on October 7, 1967. The reconstituted NDC comprised the Prime Minister, all Union Cabinet Ministers, Chief Ministers of all States and Union Territories and the Members of the Planning Commission. Delhi Administration was represented in the Council by the Lt. Governor and the Chief Executive Councillor, and the remaining Union Territories by their respective Administrators. Other Union Ministers and State Ministers may also be invited to participate in the deliberations of the council. In the reconstituted Council, the Secretary of the Planning Commission acts as Secretary to the NDC and the Planning Commission was expected to furnish such administrative or other assistance for the work of the Council as may be needed. The basic nature, origin and legal status of the Council are similar to the Planning Commission. The **revised functions**[63] of the NDC are:

1. To consider the proposals formulated for Plans at all important stages and accept them;

60. Planning Commission, First Five year Plan: A Draft Outline (New Delhi: Government of India, 1957), p. 253.
61. Publications Divisions, ***The Gazetteer of India***, p. 10.
62. The Advisory Planning Board (1946) set up by the Interim Government had suggested for such a consultative body with the representatives from the provinces, the princely states and some other interests to advise the Planning Commission for the success of planning in India.
63. Other than the ***Cabinet Resolution,*** it is also quoted is The ***Gazetteer of India*** (Publications Division, The Gazetteer of India, p. 15).

2. To review the working of the Plans from time to time;
3. To consider the important questions of social and economic policy affecting national development; and
4. To recommend measures for the achievement of the aims and targets set out in the national plan, including measures to secure the ***active participation*** and cooperation of the people, improve the efficiency of the administrative services, ensure the fullest development of the less advanced regions and backward sections of the community and through sacrifices borne equally by all citizens, build up resources for national development.[64]

Though the first Plan of India was launched before the arrival of the NDC, the body had many meetings before the terminal year of the plan and useful deliberations (almost all) after due consideration were included by the government into the planning process. But after the death of Jawaharlal Nehru—the greatest champion of democratic decentralisation in the country[65] the NDC had become a small gathering of only those who had the same vested interests with only the Congress CMs participating in its meetings. The CMs belonging to other political parties usually did not come to its meetings; the government hardly gave any importance to their advice. A phase of tussle between the Centre and the states started worsening from here onward with a degradation in principles of the **co-operative federalism,** with every five-year plans which followed. It was only by the mid-1990s that we see the revival of the lost glory of NDC as well as that of the spirit of decentralised planning. This has been possible due to three major reasons:

1. In the era of economic reforms, with greater dependence on the private capital made it necessary to allow states greater autonomy in economic matters. Once the WTO regime started it became an economic compulsion.
2. The enactment of the Constitutional Amendments 73rd and the 74th had made local level planning a constitutional compulsion.
3. And lastly it was the compulsion of coalition politics in the formation of the Union Government which made the Centre to favour the states.

As per the major experts on the issue of decentralised planning, the last of the above given three reasons has played the most important role. By 2002, in the area of development planning we find an enhanced level of federal maturity and we see the last three five years plans (10th, 11th and 12th) adopted by a consensual support of the NDC members.

NDC had its last meeting (57th) in December 2012 and since the new policy think tank NITI Aayog was set up it has not been assigned any work. It is believed that in coming times it will be either abolished or merged with the NITI.

NDC vs GC At the level of composition the NDC and Governing Council (GC) of the NITI Aayog look different in only one way—members of the NITI are not its members while the members of the PC used to be the members of the NDC. Fostering *federal cooperation* is the core objective for both

64. The ***italicised*** words are here highlighting the level of the Government's consciousness about the concerned issues of decentralised planning, regional and individual inequalities to which the planning was to be specially attentive.

65. George Mathew, undoubtedly among the legendary commentator on the Panchayat Raj/democratic decentralisation calls Nehru as 'its most eminent champion at the national level'. Similarly, the reputed historians Bipan Chandra and others call Nehru as 'the greatest champion of planned economic development'. For Nehru the process of planning in the country was to be democratic about which seems very clear, as his writings support.

but the way it was/is done was/is better in case of the GC (as it reaches its decision in absence of the members of the NITI). The opinion of the GC is necessary for the desired functioning of the NITI as the former is an integral part of the latter. This way the GC looks a better body in comparison to the NDC. This rationale gets doubly vetted by the Government's belief that the NITI is 'State's best friend at the Centre' (the 3rd function of the NITI).

CENTRAL PLANNING

The Plans which are formulated by the Central Government and financed by it for the implementation at the national level are known as Central Plans. Over the years, the Centre has launched three such plans and the governments have maintained continuity in their implementation. The three central plans are:

1. Five-Year Plans,
2. Twenty-Point Programme, and
3. Member of Parliament Local Area Development Scheme.

An introductory description of these plans is given as follows:

1. The Five-Year Plans

This is the most important among the central plans and is being continuously implemented one after the other since planning commenced in India. As planning has been a purely political exercise in India, the five-year plans of the country have seen many unstable and critical moments till date. Several new developments related to planning also took place during the years. Given below is a concise summary of the plans as we see their different periods of implementation:

First Plan The period for this plan was 1951–56. As the economy was facing the problem of large-scale foodgrains import (1951) and the pressure of price rise, the plan accorded the highest priority to agriculture including irrigation and power projects. About 44.6 per cent of the plan outlay went in favour of the public sector undertakings (PSUs).

The Plan was launched with all the lofty ideas of socio-economic development, which had frustrating outcomes in the following years.

Second Plan The plan period was 1956–61. The strategy of growth laid emphasis on rapid industrialisation with a focus on heavy industries and capital goods.[66] The plan was developed by Professor Mahalanobis. Due to the assumption of a closed economy, shortages of food and capital were felt during this Plan.

Third Plan The Plan period was 1961–65. The Plan specifically incorporated the development of agriculture[67] as one of the objectives of planning in India besides, for the first times, considering the aim of balanced, regional development.

Enough misfortunes awaited this plan—two wars, one with China in 1961–62 and the other with Pakistan in 1965–66 along the Gujarat border and a severe drought-led famine in 1965–66 had to be faced. Due to heavy drain and diversion of funds, this plan utterly failed to meet its targets.

Three Annual Plans The period of the three consecutive Annual Plans was 1966–69. Though the Fourth Plan was ready for implementation in 1966, the weak financial situation as well as the low morale after the defeat by China, the government decided to go for an Annual Plan for 1966–67. Due to the same reasons the government went for another two such plans in the forthcoming years. The broader objectives of these Annual Plans were

66. Sukhomoy Chakravarti, ***Development Planning: The Indian Experience*** (New York: Oxford University Press, 1989), pp. 9–11.

67. C. Rangarajan, ***Indian Economy: Essays on Money and Finance*** (New Delhi: UPSBD, 1998), p. 272.

inside the design of the Fourth Plan which would have been implemented for the period 1966–71 had the financial conditions not worsened by then.

Some economists as well as the opposition in the Parliament called this period as a discontinuity in the planning process, as the Plans were supposed to be for a period of five years. They named it a period of 'Plan Holiday', i.e., the planning was on a holiday.[68]

Fourth Plan The Plan period was 1969–74. The Plan was based on the Gadgil strategy with special focus to the ideas of growth with stability and progress towards self-reliance. Droughts and the Indo-Pak War of 1971–72 led the economy to capital diversions creating financial crunch for the Plan.

The politicisation of planning started from this plan, which took serious 'populist' design in the coming plans. Frequent double-digit inflations, unreigned increase in the fiscal deficits, subsidy-induced higher non-plan expenditures and the first move in the direction of 'nationalisation' and greater control and regulation of the economy were some of the salient features of this plan, which continued unchanged till the early 1990s. The search for political stability at the Centre converted planning into a tool of real politics with greater and greater 'centralisation' ensuing plan after plan.

Fifth Plan The Plan (1974–79) has its focus on poverty alleviation and self-reliance.[69] The popular rhetoric of poverty alleviation was sensationalised by the government to the extent of launching a fresh plan, i.e., the Twenty-point Programme (1975) with a marginal importance being given to the objective of 'growth with stability' (one of the major objectives of the Fourth Plan).

The planning process got more politicised. The havocs of hyper-inflation led the government to hand over a new function to the Reserve Bank of India to stabilise the inflation (the function which the RBI carries forward even today). A judicious price wage policy was started to check the menace of inflation on the wage-earners. This Plan saw an increase in the socio-economic and regional disparities despite the many institutional, financial and other measures which were initiated by the government to attend to them. The nationalisation policy continued. There was an overall decay in the quality of 'governance'. A nexus of the 'criminal-politician-bureaucrat' seems to emerge for the first time to hijack the political system.[70]

The plan period was badly disturbed by the draconian emergency and a change of the government at the Centre. The Janata Party came to power with a thumping victory in 1977. As the government of the time had then complete say in the central planning in India, how could the new government continue with the Fifth Plan of the last government which had still more than one year to reach its completion. The dramatic events related to Indian planning may be seen objectively as given below:

1. The Janata Government did cut-short the Fifth Plan by a year ahead of its terminal year, i.e., by the fiscal 1977–78, in place of the decided 1978–79.

68. It should be noted here that as per the official version of the Government of India, the planning has been a *continuous process* in the country and there is no term like 'Plan Holiday' in its official documents. The term was given by the critics and popularised by the contemporary media.

69. Experts believe this Plan to be somewhat based on the ideas of D.P. Dhar, the Minister for Planning at that time.

70. **N.N. Vohra Committee Report,** Government of India, N. Delhi, 1993.

2. A fresh Plan, the Sixth Plan for the period 1978–83 was launched by the new government which called it the **'Rolling Plan'**.[71]
3. In 1980, there was again a change of government at the Centre with the return of the Congress which abandoned the Sixth Plan of the Janata Government in the year 1980 itself.
4. The new government launched a fresh new **Sixth Plan** for the period 1980–85. But by that time, two financial years of the Janata Government's Sixth Plan had already been completed. These two years of the Plan were adjusted by the Congress Government in a highly interesting way:
   (i) The first year, i.e., 1978–79 was added to the fifth plan which was cut-short by the Janata Government to four years. And thus the Fifth Plan officially became of 5 years again (1974–79).
   (ii) Now what to do with the second year, i.e., 1979–80. The Congress Government announced this year to be a year of one Annual Plan. This Annual Plan (1979–80) may be considered the lone independent remnant of the 'Rolling Plan' of the Janata Government.

The Sixth Plan (1978–83) which could not become an official plan of India had emphasis on some of the highly new economic ideas and ideals with almost a complete no to foreign investment; new thrust on price control; rejuvenation of the Public Distribution System (PDS); emphasis on small-scale and cottage industries; new lease of life to Panchayati Raj Institutions (PRIs) (i.e., the 2nd Phase of the revival of the PRIs); agriculture and the subject of rural development getting the due; etc., being the major ones.

Sixth Plan This Plan (1980–85) was launched with the slogan of '*Garibi Hatao*' (alleviate poverty).[72] Already, a programme (the TPP) was tested and tried by the same government in the Fifth Plan which tried to improve the standard of living of the poor masses with the 'direct approach' (the idea of poverty alleviation, but such a slogan of '*Garibi Hatao*' was not given to the programme).

The plan gave emphasis on socio-economic infrastructure in the rural areas; eliminating rural poverty and regional disparities (through the IRDP); commencing 'target group' approach[73] together with launching a number of national level programmes and schemes aimed at specific concerns and areas of development ('target group' approach).[74]

71 It should be noted here that there is nothing like the 'Rolling Plan' in the official documents of planning in India. Basically, the origin of the concept of the 'Rolling Plan' goes back to the period when India went for the Annual Plans (1966–69) for the first time and the critics noted it as a ***discontinuity*** in the planning process, calling it a period of the 'plan holiday'. The basic trait of the 'Rolling Plan' was its ***continuity,*** while the Congress commenced its sixth Plan (1980–85) the idea of the 'Rolling Plan' was cancelled, as for the new Government the element of 'rolling' (continuity) was already in the Indian Planning— India was following the approach of the 'perspective planning'. A separate Division of Perspective Planning was already functioning in the Yojana Bhavan since the mid-1970s. The two elements which make a plan a 'perspective plan' are, firstly, the 'continuity' and secondly, 'evaluation-based' planning. For the Congress Government, logically, the planning in India was not only 'rolling' but more than that it was evaluation-based, too.

72 Some experts see this Plan as a symbol of the planning being converted to a complete politics—with utter populism entering into the planning process of India. The circle of the politicisation of planning gets completed with this Plan.

73 'Target group' approach of planning is selecting the group of people where a particular problem is and attacking the problem directly. The TPP was the first such programme in India.

74 Publications Division, ***India 1980–1983*** (New Delhi: Government of India).

Seventh Plan The Plan (1985–90) emphasised on rapid foodgrain production, increased employment creation and productivity in general. The basic tenets of planning, i.e., ***growth, modernisation, self-reliance*** and ***social justice*** remained as the guiding principles.[75] The *Jawahar Rojgar Yojana* (JRY) was launched in 1989 with the motive to create wage-employment for the rural poors. Some of the already existing programmes, such as the IRDP, CADP, DPAP and the DDP were re-oriented.

Till date, the government has been evaluating the achievements of all the developmental programmes, courtesy the youngest PM of India. Somehow, democracy and development got connected with a major change in the thinking of the political elite, which decided to go in for democratic decentralisation to promote development. It laid strong foundations for itself as the constitutional amendments—the 73rd and 74th were possible by the early 1990s.

Though the economy had better growth rates throughout the 1980s, specially in the latter half, yet it was at the cost of bitter fiscal imbalances. By the end of the Plan, India had a highly unfavourable balance of payments situation. Heavy foreign loans on which the governmental expenditures depended heavily during the period, the economy failed to service.[76] The Plan was not laid with a strong financial strategy, which put the economy into a crisis of unsustainable balance of payments and fiscal deficits.[77] India basically tried to attend its growth prospects by commercial and other external borrowings on hard terms, which the economy failed to sustain. In the process of liberalisation, an expansion of internal demand for the home market was permitted without generating equitable levels of exports and ultimately Indian imports were financed by the costly external borrowings. Such an 'inward looking' fiscal policy proved to be a mistake when the external aid environment for the economy was deteriorating.[78]

Two Annual Plans The Eighth Plan (whose term would have been 1990–95) could not take off due to the 'fast-changing political situation at the Centre'.[79] The pathbreaking and restructuring-oriented suggestions of the Eighth Plan, the sweeping economic reforms ensuing around the world, as well as the fiscal imbalances of the late 1980s were the other important reasons for the delay in the launch of the Eighth Plan. The new government, which assumed power at the centre in June 1991, decided to commence the Eighth Plan for the period 1992–97 and that the fiscals 1990–91 and 1991–92 should be treated as two separate Annual Plans. The two consecutive Annual Plans (1990–92) were formulated within the framework of the approach to the Eighth Plan (1990–95) with the basic thrust on maximisation of employment and social transformation.

Eighth Plan The Eighth Plan (1992–97) was launched in a typically new economic environment. The economic reforms were already started (in July 1991) with the initiation of the structural adjustment and macro-stabilisation policies necessitated by the worsening balance of payments, higher fiscal deficit and unsustainable rate of inflation.

This was the first plan which went on for an introspection of the macro-economic policies which the country had been pursuing for many decades. The major concerns and pathbreaking

75. Planning Commission, ***Seventh Five Year Plan (1980–85)*** (New Delhi: Government of India, 1980).
76. Similar financial strategy to promote growth and development had led the soviet Union to economic collapse via the balance of payment crisis during Gorbachev's regime by 1991, as is pointed out by Jeffrey Sachs in ***The End of Poverty*** ((London: Penguin Books, 2005), pp. 131–34).
77. C. Rangarajan, ***Indian Economy***, p. 274.
78. ***Bimal Jalan*** in Bimal Jalan (ed.), 1992, pp. 190 191, op.cit.
79. This is the official version for the delay (Publications Division, ***India 2007*** (New Delhi: Government of India, 2007), p. 680.

suggestions[80] which this Plan articulated may be summarised as follows:

1. An immediate re-definition of the state's role in the economy was suggested;
2. 'Market-based' development advised in areas which could afford it, i.e., a greater role for the private sector in the economy;[81]
3. More investment in the infrastructure sector, especially in the laggard states as the ongoing emphasis on greater private sector investment could not be attracted towards these states;
4. Rising non-plan expenditure and fiscal deficits need to be checked;
5. Subsidies need restructuring and refocussing;
6. Planning immediately needs to be 'decentralised';
7. Special emphasis on 'co-operative federalism' suggested;
8. Greater focus on 'agriculture' and other 'rural activities' was suggested for which the Plan cited empirical evidences as they encourage the economy to achieve enhanced standard of living for its people and to promote the cause of balanced growth—a shift in the mindset of planning.

As the economy moved towards liberalisation, criticism came from every quarter against the move. The process of planning was also criticised on the following counts:

1. As economy moves towards the market economy, the planning becomes 'irrelevant';
2. When the state is 'rolling back', planning makes no sense;
3. The planning process should be 're-structured' in the era of liberalisation; and
4. There should be increased thrust on the 'social sector' (i.e., education, healthcare, etc.)

Ninth Plan The Ninth Plan (1997–2002) was launched when there was an all round 'slowdown' in the economy led by the South East Asian Financial Crisis (1996–97). Though the liberalisation process was still criticised, the economy was very much out of the fiscal imbroglio of the early 1990s. With a general nature of 'indicative planning', the Plan not only did target an ambitious high growth rate (7 per cent), but also tried to direct itself towards time-bound 'social' objectives. There was an emphasis on the seven identified Basic Minimum Services (BMS) with additional Central Assistance for these services with a view to obtaining complete coverage of the population in a time-bound manner. The BMS[82] included:

1. Safe drinking water;
2. Primary health service;
3. Universalisation of primary education;
4. Public housing assistance to the shelter-less poor families;
5. Nutritional support to children;
6. Connectivity of all villages and habitations; and

80. It should be noted here that the kind of economic reforms India started in 1991–92 were ***almost ditto suggested*** by the Eighth Plan. The suggestions were based on India's own experience and the experiences of the world economies after the Second World War. The Sixth and the Seventh Plans had suggested almost on the similar lines which made the Governments of the time go for the so-called 'liberalisation' moves in the mid-1980s.

81. C. Rangarajan, ***Indian Economy***, p. 275–276.

82. Publications Division, ***India 2007***, pp. 682–83.

7. Streamlining of the public distribution system.

The issue of fiscal consolidation became a top priority of the governments for the first time, which had its focus on the following[83] related issues:

1. Sharp reduction in the revenue deficit of the government, including centre, states and the PSUs through a combination of improved revenue collections and control of in-essential expenditures;
2. Cutting down subsidies, collection of user charges on economic services (i.e., electricity, transportation, etc.), cutting down interest, wages, pension, PF, etc;
3. Decentralisation of planning and implementation through greater reliance on states and the PRIs.

Tenth Plan The Plan (2002–07) commenced with the objectives of greater participation of the NDC in their formulation. Some highly important steps were taken during the plan, which undoubtedly points out a change in the planning policy mindset of the government, major ones being:[84]

1. Doubling per capita income in 10 years;
2. Accepting that the higher growth rates are not the only objective—it should be translated into improving the quality of life of the people;
3. For the first time the Plan went to set the 'monitorable targets' for eleven select indicators of development for the Centre as well as for the states;
4. 'Governance' was considered a factor of development;
5. States' role in planning to be increased with the greater involvement of the PRIs;
6. Policy and institutional reforms in each sector, i.e., reforms in the PSUs, legal reforms, administrative reforms, labour reforms, etc;
7. Agriculture sector declared as the prime moving force (PMF) of the economy;
8. Increased emphasis on the social sector (i.e., education, health, etc.);
9. Relevance between the processes of economic reforms and planning emphasised; etc.

Eleventh Plan The Plan targets a growth rate of 10 per cent and emphasises the idea of 'inclusive growth'. In the approach paper, the Planning Commission shows its concerns regarding realising the growth targets on account of the compulsions towards the Fiscal Responsibility and Budget Management Act. In recent times some aberrations in the economy have started to increase the government's concerns in meeting the Plan target of 10 per cent growth. The major concerns are:

1. A higher inflation (above 6 per cent) led to the tightening of the credit policy forcing lower investment in the economy (which will lower production);
2. A stronger rupee is making export earnings shrink fast;
3. Costlier foodgrains and other primary articles playing havoc for the poor masses;
4. Costlier oil prices becoming a burden for the national exchequer; etc.

Not only the government but the Confederation of Indian Industry (CII) as well as the World Bank expressed doubts in the Eleventh Plan realising the ambitious 10 per cent growth.[85]

83. Ministry of Finance, ***Economic Survey*** (1998–200) (New Delhi: Government of India, Various Years); Publications Division, ***India 2007***, p. 683.

84. Planning Commission, ***Tenth Five year Plan (2002–07)***, (New Delhi: Government of India).

85. **World Development Report-2003**, World Bank, N. York, USA, p. 31.

Twelfth Plan The 'Draft Approach Paper' of the Twelfth Plan (2012–17) was prepared by the Planning Commission after widest consultation till date—recognising the fact that citizens are now better informed and also keen to engage. Over 950 civil society organisations across the country provided inputs; business associations, including those representing small enterprises have been consulted; modern electronic and 'social media' (Google Hangout) were used to enable citizens to give suggestions. All state governments, as well as local representative institutions and unions, have been consulted through five regional consultations. Though the Approach Paper for the Plan was approved by the NDC by mid-2011, the Plan Document was finalised much later after the launch of the plan (like the Tenth and Eleventh Plans).

The Draft Approach Paper lays down the major targets of the Plan, the key challenges in meeting them, and the broad approach that must be followed to achieve the stated objectives which are summed-up as follows:

1. Growth rate of 9 per cent is targeted for the Plan. However, in view of the uncertainties in the global economy and the challenges in the domestic economy, the Approach Paper indicates that it could be achieved only if some **difficult decisions** are taken.
2. It emphasises the need to intensify efforts to have 4 per cent average growth in the **agriculture** sector during the Plan period; with foodgrains growing at about 2 per cent per year and non-food grains (notably, horticulture, livestock, dairying, poultry and fisheries) growing at 5 to 6 per cent.
3. The higher growth in agriculture would not only provide broad based income benefits to the rural population but also help restrain **inflationary pressure,** which could arise if high levels of growth are attempted without corresponding growth in domestic food production capabilities.
4. It proposes that the major **flagship programmes** which were instrumental for promoting inclusiveness in the Eleventh Plan should continue in the Twelfth Plan—there is a need to focus on issues of implementation and governance to improve their effectiveness.
5. The Plan indicates that the **energy** needs of rapid growth will pose a major challenge since these requirements have to be met in an environment where domestic energy prices are constrained and world energy prices are high and likely to rise further.
6. For the GDP to grow at 9 per cent, commercial energy supplies will have to grow at a rate between 6.5 and 7 per cent per year. Since India's domestic energy supplies are limited, dependence upon imports will increase. Import dependence in the case of petroleum has always been high and is projected to be **80** per cent in the Twelfth Plan.
7. Even in the case of **coal,** import dependence is projected to increase as the growth of thermal generation will require coal supplies, which cannot be fully met from domestic mines.
8. It suggests the need to take steps to reduce energy intensity of production processes, increase domestic energy supply as quickly as possible and ensure rational energy pricing that will help achieve both objectives, viz., reduced energy intensity of production process and enhance domestic energy supply, even though it may seem difficult to attempt.

9. It draws attention to evolving a holistic **water** management policy aiming at more efficient conservation of water and also in water use efficiency, particularly in the field of agriculture.
10. It argues that a new legislation for **land acquisition** is necessary, which strikes an appropriate balance between the need for fair compensation to those whose land is acquired and whose livelihood is disrupted, and the need to ensure that land acquisition does not become an impossible impediment to meeting our needs for infrastructure development, industrial expansion and urbanisation.
11. It maintains that **health, education** and **skill development** will continue to be the focus areas in the Twelfth Plan, and that there is a need to ensure adequate resources to these sectors—***'universal healthcare'*** proposed by it, emphatically. Simultaneously, it also points to the need to ensure maximum efficiency in terms of outcomes for the resources allocated to these sectors. The need to harness ***private investment*** in these sectors has also been emphasised by the approach.
12. It takes cognizance of the fact that achieving 9 per cent growth will require large **investments** in infrastructure sector development—notes greater momentum to public investment and Public Private Partnerships (PPPs) in infrastructure sector needs to be imparted so that present infrastructure shortages can be addressed early.
13. It has emphasised the importance of the process of **fiscal correction.** However, the paper cautions that fiscal consolidation would imply that total resources available for the Plan in the short run will be limited. Resource limitations imply the need to prioritise carefully and that some ***priority areas,*** e.g., health, education and infrastructure will have to be funded more than others.
14. It also emphasises the need for focusing more on **efficient use** of available resources in view of the resource constraints.

The **appraisal document** for the 12th Plan, prepared by the NITI Aayog estimated a growth rate of maximum 7.75 per cent. Taking clues from the Plans the document made a strong case for clear tax policies and focus on manufacturing sector.

2. Twenty-Point Programme

The Twenty Point Programme (TPP) is the second Central Plan which was launched in July 1975. The programme was conceived for coordinated and intensive monitoring of a number of schemes implemented by the Central and the state governments. The basic ***objective*** was of improving the quality of life of the people, especially of those living below the poverty line. Under this, a thrust was given to schemes relating to poverty alleviation, employment generation in rural areas, housing, education, family welfare and health, protection of environment and many other schemes having a bearing on the quality of life in rural areas.

The programme was restructured in 1982 and 1986. The programme, known as the ***'TPP-86'*** has 119 items grouped into 20 points which are related to the improvement in the quality of life in rural areas. Among the total items, 54 are monitored on the basis of evoluatory criteria, 65 against pre-set physical targets and rest of the 20 important items on monthly basis. The targets are fixed by the Ministries at the Centre in consultation with the states and the UTs. The allocation for the programme is done under the various Five Year Plans.

The 'TPP-86' was restructured and named 'TPP-2006' keeping in view the challenges of the 21st century with particular reference to the process of economic reforms. This was in harmony with the National Common Minimum Programme (NCMP) of the UPA Government.

This was the first programme which had 'direct attack' approach on rural poverty. The forthcoming five year plan (i.e., the 6th Plan, 1980–85), launched with the slogan 'Garibi Hatao', was based on the experiences of the TPP—a right mix of economics and real politic. Over the years, the programme has been implemented uninterrupted by all political parties which came to power at the Centre.

By **mid-2015**, the Ministry of Statistics and Programme Implementation (MOSPI), which monitors the programme, in a report to the Prime Minister's Office, had advised to wrap it up as it has outlived its utility. While the PMO decided to 'restructure' it on the recommendations of the Inter-Ministerial Group, which is presently working on it. It should be noted that the Government has restructured the existing 50 Centrally Sponsored Schemes (CSSs) into 30 under the active participation of the Governing Council of the NITI Aayog.

3. MPLADS

The Member of Parliament Local Area Development Scheme (MPLADS) is the last of the Central Plans and latest to have been launched, too. The scheme was launched on December 23, 1993 with only ₹5 lakh given to each MPs which was increased to ₹1 crore in the year 1994–95. when the MPs did put a demand to increase the sum to ₹5 crore in 1997–98, finally the government enhanced it to ₹2 crore since 1998–99. In April 2011 the corpus was enhanced to ₹5 crore while announcing the new guidelines for the scheme.

Basically, in the early 1990s there came a demand from the MPs cutting across party lines for such a scheme so that the fruits of development could directly reach the masses via their representatives. The government of the time decided to go in for such a scheme and the MPLADS came.

Under this scheme the Members of Parliament[86] recommend some works (i.e., creation of fixed community assets, based on locally felt developmental needs) to the concerned District Magistrate. The scheme is governed by a set of guidelines, which have been comprehensively revised and issued in November 2005. Its performance has improved due to pro-active policy initiatives, focus monitoring and review.[87]

In recent years, many criticisms of the scheme came to the public notice, which concerned either misappropriation of the funds or non-use of the funds, especially from the backward states. The people's representative at the PRI level have been demanding scrapping of the scheme as it infringes the idea of decentralised planning. In it's place, they want the funds to be given to the local bodies directly for the same kind of works specified by the MPLADS.[88]

In May 2014, MOSPI issued the **revised guidelines** for the scheme which is simple, clear

86. For development works the MP, Lower House (the Lok Sabha) may select one or more districts of his/her constituency; the MP, Upper House (the Rajya Sabha) may select any one or more districts from his/her constituency (i.e., a state or an UT); and the nominated MPs may select any one or more districts from their constituency (i.e., the whole country).

87. As the Government reports in Publications Division, ***India 2007***, pp. 711–12.

88. We may especially quote the '21 Point Memorandum' handed over by the ***All India Panchayat Adhyakshas Meet***, mid-2002, N. Delhi to the President and the Central Government of the time.

and understandable to all concerned. The fine points of the guidelines are as given below:

1. It provides not only the list of prohibited items under the scheme, but also that of permissible items.
2. In order to encourage *trusts* and *societies* to work for the betterment of tribal people, the ceiling of ₹50 lakh, stipulated for building assets by trusts and societies in areas occupied by tribals, has been enhanced to ₹75 lakh.
3. Further, to promote cooperative movement and rural development, the Cooperative Societies have also been made eligible under the MPLAD Scheme.
4. The abandoned or suspended MPLAD work to be completed by the states.
5. Natural and man-made calamities can also be allocated funds under it.
6. Now the funds can be allocated by a MP outside of Constituency/State/UTs, too.
7. It can converge with the other approved Central (like MGNAREGA) and State Government schemes.
8. Funds from local bodies can be pooled with MPLADS works.
9. Public and community contribution is made permissible in the scheme.
10. 'One MP–One Idea', an annual competition for best innovation in solving local problems.
11. A proper mechanism for its implementation and auditing have also been put in place.

To provide MPs a greater choice under the scheme, the list of indicative and illustrative shelf of projects has been expanded touching the fields of infrastructure development, drinking water, education, roads, health, sanitation, natural calamity, etc. The scheme has been given more dynamism and flexibility.

MULTT-LEVEL PLANNING

It was by the late 1950s and early 1960s that the states demanded the right to plan at the state level. By the mid-1960s, the states were given the power to plan by the Centre, advising them that they should promote planning at the lower levels of the administrative strata, too, i.e., at the district level planning—via the municipalities and corporations in the urban areas and via block level through panchayats and the tribal boards. By the early 1980s, India was a country of multi-level planning (MLP) with the structure and strata of planning as follows:

First Strata: Centre-Level Planning

At this level three types of Central Plans had evolved over the years—the Five Year Plans, the Twenty-Point Programme and the MPLADS.

Second Strata: State-Level Planning

By the 1960s, the states were planning at the state level with their respective planning bodies, the state Planning Boards with the respective CMs being their de-facto Chairman. The plans of the states were for a term of five years and parallel to the concerned Five Year Plans of the Centre.

Third Strata: District-Level planning

By the late 1960s all the districts of the states were having their own plans with their respective District Planning Boards[89] with the respective District Magistrate being the de-facto chairman. The district-level plans are implemented now via

89 After the implementation of the 74th Constitutional Amendments they have become the District Planning Committees (DPCs).

municipalities or corporations in the urban areas and the panchayats via the blocks in the rural areas.

Fourth Strata: Block-Level Planning

As a part of the district-level planning the block level planning came up which had the District Planning Boards as their nodal body. Below the blocks, India developed the planning at the local level, too.

Fifth Strata: Local Level Planning

By the early 1980s, plans were being implemented at the local level via the blocks and had the District Planning Boards (DPBs) as the nodal agency. Due to socio-economic differentiations among the population, local-level planning in India developed with its three variants,[90] namely:

1. Village-Level Planning
2. Hill Area Planning
3. Tribal Area Planning

Basically, the MLP was started to promote the process of decentralised planning in the country. It was the Indian version of democratic planning which ultimately sought to guarantee the people's participation in the process of planning. But it failed to do so due to many reasons. The reasons have been discussed below:

1. It could not promote people's participation in the formation of the various plans. The basic idea of the MLP model was that once the local-level plans will be handed over to the blocks, the blocks will make their plans and once the blocks hand over their plans to the districts, the district-level plans will be formulated. Similarly, the state plans and finally the Five Year Plan if the Centre will formulate one. By doing so, every idea of planning will have the representation of everybody in the country at the time of plan formation—a special kind of plan empathy would have developed out of this process. But this was not the reality. Every strata made their own plans—lacking the empathy factor.
2. Only central Plans were implemented as the states lacked the required level of finance to support the plans. They ultimately had to be satisfied by implementing the Central Plans which failed to include the states' empathy.
3. As the local bodies in India were not having any constitutional mandate, they just played the complementary roles to the state planning process. As they had no financial independence, their plans, even if they were formulated, remained only on paper.
4. The MLP, thus, failed to include the people's participation in planning, badly betraying the local aspirations.[91]

But at least the failure of MLP made the government to think in the direction of decentralised planning afresh leading to the enactment of the two important Constitutional Amendments—the 73rd and 74th.

WAY TO DECENTRALISED PLANNING

Economic planning was basically an element of the centralised kind of political system (i.e., the

90. While people in some areas have socio-cultural similarities (as in the hill areas with no tribal population and the people living in the plains, i.e., villages) they lack economic similarities. Similarly, while people living in the tribal areas and the hill areas have economic similarities they lack socio-cultural similarities. That is why all these three habitations had three sets of planning patterns.

91. G.V.K. Rao Committee (CAARD), 1985; L.M. Singhvi Committee (CCPPRI), 1986 and Sarkaria Commission, 1988 all discussed this inter-connection (Suresh Mishra, ***Legislative Status of Panchayat Raj in India*** (New Delhi: Indian Institute of Public Administration, 1997).

socialist and the communist). When India decided in favour of a planned economy it was to face double challenges:

1. The first challenge was to realise the objectives of planning in a time-bound frame, and
2. Making economic planning a suitable instrument of development in the democratic set up—to democratise and decentralise the process of planning itself.

The government tried to decentralise the planning process by setting up the NDC and promoting the MLP, but without being able to achieve the desired results. By the late 1980s, a direct link was established[92] between development and democracy. And it was established that the above-given challenges were basically complementary—without solving the second challenge (i.e., decentralisation) the first challenge (i.e., development) cannot be solved. Finally, once the PRIs were given the constitutional status, first time planning became a constitutional exercise at any level, i.e., at the panchayat level.

Though the planning at the central and the state levels are still extra-constitutional activities, it has become constitutional at the level of local bodies. Kerala has shown some pathbreaking good works via local body planning.[93] But still there are many hurdles to be solved before the local bodies are really able to plan for their proper development. These hurdles as per the experts are as under:

1. The financial status of the PRIs is still not stabilised.
2. Which taxes the PRIs can impose are still not clear.
3. The state assemblies have been procrastinating in delegating timely and needful powers to the PRIs.
4. Low level of awareness among the local people regarding their Right to Information and the right functioning of the PRIs.
5. Use of money and muscle power in the PRI elections in some states.

By mid-2002, there took place an all India Panchayat Adhyaksha Sammelan in New Delhi. At the end of the conference, the Panchayat Adhyakshas handed over a '21 Point Memorandum' to the government which specially dealt with the financial status of the PRIs. In July 2002, while the then PM was addressing the annual meet of the District Rural Development Agency (DRDA), he announced that the PRIs will be given 'financial autonomy' very soon. He further added that once there is a political consensus, the government might go in for further constitutional amendment. Unfortunately, the same coalition (i.e., the NDA) did not come to power in the forthcoming general elections. But the UPA Government did not look less serious on the issue of participatory development. By mid-2006, the Planning Commission wrote letters to every Chief Minister of each state that before the Eleventh Plan commences it wants that all the PRIs are duly delegated their functional powers of planning from the concerned states. Otherwise, the funds kept for local development would not flow to the states. This shows the seriousness of the Central Government.

Meanwhile, the Central government is aimed at **redrawing** the contours of decentralised planning in the country. The new development 'think tank'—*NITI Aayog*—has a completely new orientation towards decentralised planning:

92. Governments' failure in including the local aspirations in the process of planned development has been considered by major experts as the foremost reason behind the success of the regional political parties, which has led to the governments of the 'compromises', i.e., coalition governments, at the Centre and in the states via the 'hung parliaments' and the 'hung assemblies', respectively.

93. Jose. George, 'Panchayats and Participatory Planning in Kerala', ***The Indian Journal of Public Administration,*** Vol. XLIII, No. 1, January–March 1997.

1. The body has to design the development policies keeping in mind the needs of *nation, states* and the *PRIs*. This will be one of its kind—a fully 'integrated' planning process.
2. It has to use the '*bottom-up*' approach unlike the one-size-fits-all ('Top-down') approach of the past.
3. To the extent the finalisation of plans and required funds are concerned, all stakeholders will be having their says (through the Governing Council which is composed of the CMs of states and the Chiefs of UTs).
4. Promoting the idea of '*Team India*' which will be working on a common 'National Agenda'.
5. It has to promote the idea of *co-operative federalism,* which is in itself a highly decentralised style of promoting development planning.

By early 2015, we saw a change in the Central Government's outlook towards the fund requirements by the states, viz.,

1. States now get *42 per cent* share in the pool of taxes of the Centre (recommendation of the Fourteenth Finance Commission accepted).
2. States are getting *liberal funding* (loan plus grants) from the Centre to implement the State Plans.
3. One of the aims behind implementing the proposed GST is to the enhance the internal financial capacity of the states as the new tax will increase the gross tax collections of the states.
4. States are now free to go for higher *market borrowings* without any permission from the Centre (but such a move has to come from the Centre). The UDAY (Ujwal Discom Assurance Yojana), launched in 2015–16 is one of such approvals of the Central Government under which states are allowed to issue 'UDAY Bonds' up to 75 per cent of the dues of the electricity distribution companies (Discom) of the states (by mid-2016, the total discom debt in the country amounted to ₹4.3 lakh crore).

THE PLANNING COMMISSION & THE FINANCE COMMISSION

Federal political systems provide independent financial control to the central as well as the state governments so that they are able to perform their exclusive functions.[94] For the same objective, the Constitution of India has made elaborate provisions,[95] i.e., setting up of a Finance Commission to recommend to the President certain measures relating to the distribution of financial resources between the Union and the states. But the powers given to the Finance Commission by the Parliament limited its functions to the extent of finding out revenue gap of the states, besides recommending for the 'grant-in-aids to the states from the Centre. The finance commission cannot determine the capital-related issues of the states (though the Constitution does not classify between the capital or revenue related roles of the commission while determining the Centre's assistance to the states).

In the meantime, to promote the process of planning, an extra-constitutional body, i.e., the Planning Commission was set up even before the First Finance Commission was set up. The Planning Commission played a very vital role in the process of determining Central assistance to the states as all development plans, programmes and projects

94. As *K.C. Wheare* writes about the classical federal constitutions in ***Federal Government*** (New Delhi: Oxford University Press, 1956), p. 97.

95. Articles 270, 273, 275 and 280 of the ***Constitution of India.***

are within its purview. All grants or loans given by the Centre to the states for developmental works are practically dependent on the recommendations of the Planning Commission. And that is why the role of the Planning Commission was said to 'confine'[96] the role of the Finance Commission, i.e., a non-constitutional body eclipsing a constitutional body. P.J. Rajamannar who headed the Finance Commission (1966–69) suggested to clearly define the relative scope and functions of the two commissions by amending the Constitution, and the Planning Commission was advised to be made a statutory body independent of the government. But no such follow ups came from the successive governments at the Centre. But one thing was important, most of the finance commissions devaluated some extra shares in the central taxes (i.e., the income tax and the central excise) and grants-in-aid.

Since the decade of the 1990s, certain events made the Central Government change its mindset regarding the role of the states in the process of development. Major events may be counted as under:

1. The process of economic reforms started in 1991–92 required active economic participation from the states.
2. The constitutional requirement of 'participatory planning' mandated by the 73rd and 74th Constitutional Amendments was enacted in 1993.
3. The arrival of coalition era at the Centre when over a dozen political parties, having regional affiliations came together to form the government.
4. The recommendations of the Tenth Finance Commission followed by a Constitutional Amendment making Alternative Method of Devolution a law in 1995.
5. Various new needs of the time, such as, tax reforms, agricultural development, industrial expansion, etc.

The year 2002 could be considered a watershed in the area of promoting the states' need for financial resources in promoting their developmental requirements. In July 2002, while the government was setting up the Twelfth Finance Commission (2005–10) the then Minister of Finance announced that in future the Planning Commission will be *playing more or less a role of collaborator to the Finance Commission*. In the same announcement, the government made one member of the Planning Commission, a member of the Finance Commission too (a symbol of physical and ideological connection between the two bodies).[97] It was as if the government had accepted the suggestions of the Fourth Finance Commission to a great extent. Though the critics took it as an infringement of a constitutional body by a non-constitutional one, the government clarified by calling it a symbol for promoting the contemporary needs of the economy and fiscal federalism.

Another milestone was created in the enactment of the Fiscal Responsibility and Budget Management (FRBM) Act in 2003, which empowers the state governments to go for market borrowings to fulfil their plan expenditure without prior permission from the Central Government (provided they have enacted their respective Fiscal Responsibility Acts).[98] This

96. Ministry of Finance, ***Report of the Fourth Finance Commission***, p. 88.

97. In the 10th Plan, **Som Pal** was that common member in both the Commissions (who resigned from the PC once the UPA-I came to power). But this arrangement has been followed by the government in all new Commissions since then—with **B.K. Chaturvedi** and **Prof. Abhijit Sen** (Members, PC) being the *Additional Members* of the *13th* and *14th Finance Commissions*.

98. This should be considered a great fiscal freedom to the states (which even the constitution could not foresee) and also making them behave with more responsibility in fiscal matters. More than 20 states have passed their fiscal Responsibility Acts (FRAs) by now and are borrowing from the market for their planned needs.

has boosted the participatory planning in the country by guaranteeing greater autonomous plan participation from the states.

If we look at the tax reforms process, we see a general tendency of enabling the states to collect more and more taxes, the Value Added Tax (VAT) being a glaring example by which almost all states have been able to increase their gross tax revenue receipts. The cause will be served more once the economy goes for the proposed enactment of the Goods and Services Tax (GST).

In January 2015, the NITI Aayog replaced the Planning Commission, thus the comparison between the latter and the Finance Commission no more exits, but it will always have its *academic importance* in the area of development planning in the country. Such experiences of the past will function as directives for the policy makers in the future.

Meanwhile, the new body, the NITI Aayog, is totally different in its approach towards fund allocations (unlike the Planning Commission it does not allocate funds to states) to the states to promote the cause of development planning. Basically, the states now sit in the NITI itself, in a very strong position. The NITI Aayog has been termed by the Central Government as the *'best friend of states in the Centre'*.

A CRITICAL EVALUATION

Planning has been subject to a number of criticisms right since its inception in the country. With the passage of time, not only the number of criticism increased, but more importantly the shortcomings of planning were pointed out. Although after considerable delay, the governments took note of the shortcomings besides taking some major steps. The criticisms stand even today, but with one difference that the government is not only conscious of them but also trying to do away with them. We may briefly discuss the major criticisms of planning in India as well as the follow ups from the government to do away with them as under:

1. Lack of 'Perspective' in Planning

According to experts, if a nation is going for economic planning it must have 'perspective' element in it. To have perspective in planning, two basic elements need to be fulfilled, namely:

1. Planning should be evaluation-based, and
2. 'Long-term' goals should be followed up besides the 'short-term' goals.

In the Indian content, the succeeding plans have been always commenced without the full evaluation of the preceding Plan. This was mainly due to the following reasons:

1. Lack of a nodal body responsible for data collection at the national level;
2. Federal nature of polity made data collection full of delays and also due to higher dependence on the states; and
3. Speedier data delivery was not possible.

After the recommendations of the National Statistical Commission (Chaired by C. Rangarajan), 2000, the government discussed to set up a nodal body for data collection at the pan-India level, cutting across federal hurdles. Computerisation is already being done for speedier data delivery. For the time being the Plans are launched on the basis of projected data (provisional, latest, etc.), which is almost near the real data. But once the above discussed arrangements are in place, Indian planning will be based on evaluation, undoubtedly. In the meantime, the 'Quarterly Review' and the 'Performance Budgeting' of the Union Budgets have brought in the evaluation element to a greater degree.

The First Plan had set long-term goals (for the coming 20 years) besides the short-term goals (for five years). But over the time, falling confidence in mobilising required resources and political uncertainties at the Centre made it a convention to set only short-term targets of planning. This shortcoming seems to be done away with after the commencement of the Tenth Plan. The Plan did not go for setting long-term goals only, but even did set monitorable targets for the Eleventh Plan, too.

Point should be noted here that the government had been conscious about the need for perspective planning as a separate division with the same name, which has been functioning in the Yojana Bhavan since the mid-1970s.

2. Failure in Promoting a Balanced Growth and Development

Indian planning is blamed for failing the objective of a regionally balanced growth and development. Though the Second Plan itself had noticed this fact, the measures taken were not sufficient or were short-sighted. Economic planning at the national level has proved to be a highly effective tool of promoting balanced growth. But in the Indian case it turned out to be the opposite.

To take care of the issue of balanced growth, the planning process has been using the right tools, i.e., allocating plan funds on a sectoral (primary, secondary and federal reasons) basis. But due to political reasons, enough discrepancies cropped up in the method of allocating funds to the states. At the theoretical level, the governments knew the remedies, but at the practical levels politics dominated the planning process. Democratic immaturity and politicisation of the planning process is to be blamed for this.

Now things have changed for the better. The government is following a two-pronged strategy to achieve the objective of a balanced growth and development in the country:

1. Backward regions today are prioritised in directing the Central Government investment (very much the same since the 1950s), but a new beginning in the 'differential development strategy' has been made by the Centre with the Tenth Plan. Under this strategy, the developmental constraints of different states are to be tackled with a differentiation in the strategy. The more needy states get more funds and assistance from the Centre for their planned development, cutting across the political party lines (it is seen today as a symbol of political maturity on the issue of economic development, at least).
2. There is also a complementary strategy of the planning to address the matter of regional imbalance in the country. After the country started the process of economic reforms, the nature of planning was to incline more and more towards indicative planning. The economy was to be more and more dependent on private sector investment for its future development. And the private sector will be, naturally, more interested in investing in the regions, which have better infrastructure support. Since the developed regions have better infrastructure they will attract the highest level of private investment, which will again accelerate the process of imbalanced growth. To tackle this problem, the Centre is promoting the states with lower infrastructure so that they can overcome the disadvantage. The process is slower, but at least the government is addressing the issue, which is not less satisfying and there is no criticism to this strategy. Still balanced growth and development is going to be a great challenge for planning in India.

3. Highly Centralised Nature of Planning

Decentralising the process of planning has been a major goal of the governments since the 1950s. But after Nehru, with every Plan we see greater tendency of centralisation in the planning process. Setting up of the NDC and promoting multi-level planning (MLP) did not serve much purpose in this direction. It has been among the criticised areas of planning in India as the National Planning Committee as well as the First Plan itself had called for 'democratic planning' in the country.

By the mid-1980s, the mindset of the Centre went for a change and the need for decentralised planning got proper attention. Finally, by early 1990s two constitutional amendments (i.e., the 73rd and the 74th) promoted the cause of decentralised planning by delegating constitutional powers to the local bodies. With this, a new era of planning began, but still the planning of local bodies is in a nascent stage due to lack of proper financial provisions for them. Once the financial provisions for local bodies are evolved to the adequate level or the local bodies are given financial autonomy, the process of decentralised planning will surely get a new direction and meaning, as the experts believe.

In the meantime, the Tenth Plan emphasised greater role for the states in the planning process. The Plan started a concerted effort to include the states' participation in the national planning process. The Centre is today more concerned about the developmental constraints of the states and is trying to adequately support the state Plans to the extent possible. In return, the Centre wants greater and transparent fiscal compliance from the states. This approach continued during the Eleventh Plan and so has been committed for the Twelfth Plan, too. After some time we may hope that this criticism of Indian planning will lose it's ground.

It is high time now that the planning process of the nation tries including the mass participation. The ***Economic Survey 2011-12*** rightly devotes a section to dwell into contracts and how the **civil society** and citizens play a key role in fostering economic growth. *'Honesty, punctuality, the propensity to keep promises, the attitude towards corruption are matters shaped in great part by norms and social beliefs and the behaviour patterns can become habitual. Moreover, in a democracy like India, what can be done by government depends in great measure on how ordinary people think and what people believe in,'* it says. The Survey further adds that the **civil society** has been campaigning to put in place new institutions, such as the Lokpal Act, to ensure the quality of service and bring about transparency through steps such as auction of natural resources while the government has either been slow or resisted several changes.[99]

4. Lop-sided Employment Strategy

Planning in India has been tilted heavily in favour of 'capital intensive' industries, especially from the Second Plan onwards. Such industries in the public sector could not generate enough employment. In place of it India should have gone in for 'labour-intensive' industries. In the era of economic reforms, the attitude changed and the planning process is promoting the agriculture sector with an emphasis on agri-industries and agro-exports to create more gainful and quality employment opportunities. The earlier emphasis on 'wage-employment' has shifted towards 'self-employment' to do away with the lop-sided employment strategy of the past.

99. Ministry of Finance, ***Economic Survey 2011–12*** (New Delhi: Government of India, 2012), p. 30.

5. Excessive Emphasis on PSUs

Indian planning emphasised on public sector undertakings (PSUs) for the right reasons, but in the wrong way and for a considerably longer period of time. The state's monopolies in certain areas continued over such a long period that too in losses that there came a demand-supply gap in the major goods and services produced by the PSUs. Though very conducive policy changes were effected after the country started the reform processes, the hangover of the past is still looming large. Several reforms in the PSUs as well as a more liberal approach towards the private sector with market reforms are needed to phase out the discrepancies created by the over emphasis on PSUs.

6. Agriculture Overshadowed by the Industry

Promoting the cause of faster industrialisation over time became so dear to the planning process that the agriculture sector got badly overshadowed. Though the Plans were highlighting or prioritising agriculture, the industrial sector and the PSUs were glorified in such a way that time and resources both were scarce for the agriculture sector. Such a policy always created a situation of food insecurity (even today) for the country and the masses who depended upon agriculture for their livelihood and income (still it is 58.2 per cent)[100] could never increase their purchasing power to a level that the economy could reverse the situation of 'market failure'. In India, even today, industrial growth is badly dependent on agricultural growth.

The Tenth Plan recognises agriculture as the 'core element' of development. This is a welcome ideological change in the strategy of planning. Now the industries can sustain themselves, but the laggard agriculture sector needs some special care and promotion from the government, so that the masses who earn their livelihood from agriculture can benefit out of the WTO-promoted globalisation. The agriculture sector is in urgent need of attention, otherwise, the process of globalisation is going to be ineffective in benefitting the masses.

7. Faulty Industrial Location Policy

There are time-tested theories of 'industrial location' considering the nearness of raw materials, market, cheaper labour, better transportation and communication, etc. But the Plans always prioritised setting up of new industrial units (i.e., the PSUs) in the backward regions of the country, which falsify the theories of industrial location. The government needs to develop all industrial infrastructures besides setting up certain PSUs. As the PSUs require skilled labour force, the regions failed to gain any employment from the PSUs too. The government still continues with the same policy of setting up industries, but now the new PSUs are hardly set up in traditional areas.

8. Wrong Financial Strategy

Mobilising resources to support the highly capital-intensive Plans (courtesy the PSUs) has always been a challenge for the government. To support the Plans, no stones were left unturned namely, going for a highly complex and liberal tax structure, nationalising the banks, etc. Ultimately, tax evasion, the menace of parallel economy and lesser and lesser capital for the private sector were the bane of India. Expansion of subsidies, salaries and the interest burden every year gave an upward push to the non-plan expenditure leading to scarcity of funds to support the plan expenditure (i.e., the developmental expenses).

In the era of reforms, the government has started giving attention to the financial strategy of supporting the Plans in the right way. Besides tax reforms, the financial reforms, as well as fiscal

---

100. Ministry of Finance, Economic Survey 2012–13 (New Delhi: Government of India, 2013), p. 173.

consolidation have been given proper care in recent years.

9. Politicisation of the Planning Process

In a democratic political system, almost every issue of socio-political importance is influenced by politics. It is more correct in the case of lesser matured democracies. The same stands true for the process of planning in our country. Greater and greater politicisation of the planning process culminated in such a design that at times economic planning served the opposite purpose. For example, we know that planning is a tool for promoting regionally balanced growth, but in India in the process of serving vested political interests of the Centre, it resulted into promoting an imbalanced growth.

In recent years, the government has tried to address the major criticism of planning in India. More such constructive steps with better results are expected in future. More aware and better informed citizens will lead to better and better planning in future.

There has been a general anger among the sections of society regarding coalition politics, scams, etc., in recent years. The *Economic Survey 2014-15* rightly *blames coalition politics* and the *federal structure* for tardy decision making in several areas—from oil subsidy to tax reforms, FDI in retail and free movement of foodgrains. Almost everyone outside the government blamed it for *policy paralysis*. The Survey notes it as an area of concern. The Survey notes that *politicians* and *policy makers* can set the ball rolling by acting as *role models*, but it also cited the poor record on enforcement of contract to argue that people's attitude needs to change. '*In these everyday situations (such as hiring a cab or a painter) it is cumbersome to bring in the state and the law courts. Here the main guarantor has to be people's personal integrity and trustworthiness*', it says. The statement comes from a government that has been battling a spate of *corruption scandals*—ranging from those in the telecom sector to Commonwealth Games and criticism over poor governance standards and inability to push through critical decisions.[101]

The *Economic Survey 2012-13* suggested a new objective for the Planning Commission—the global economic and financial crisis which has persisted for the last five years has not only exposed the vulnerability of almost all the countries over the globe to external shocks, but also has lessons for the *planning process*, viz., countries need to have inbuilt social safety nets for facing such eventualities, which affect the weak and vulnerable the most, and wipe out the fruits of growth for years. India with its focus on inclusive development and timely interventions has, however, been able to weather the crisis better than many other countries.[102]

INCLUSIVE GROWTH

Inclusive growth is a growth process which yields broad-based benefits and ensures equality of opportunity for all (*UNDP* and the *11th Plan*). Fundamentally, the ideas of growth and development already include the element of 'inclusiveness' in them, but at times, due to certain reasons, the processes might occur in non-inclusive manner.

It was in 2000–01 that the Government of India came to think clearly about 'inclusiveness' in the economy, while reviewing the performance of the economic reforms. It was found that the reform process enabled economy towards faster and higher 'wealth creation', but all could not be part of it. Only the people with resources (physical or human) were able to get benefits

101. ***Economic Survey 2011–12***, MoF, GoI, N. Delhi, p. 30.
102. Ministry of Finance, ***Economic Survey 2012–13***, p. 269.

out of the reforming economy. It was assessed that the fruits of reforms could not percolate to the ***disadvantaged*** and ***marginalised*** sections of the society. It means, the growth process during reforms was not able to include a big segment of the Indian population. In this backdrop, we see the government adopting a conscious policy towards 'inclusive growth'. Even before reforms commenced in the country, this element was lacking. But during reforms it became more glaring due to the higher pace of growth which the economy attained during this period. Though the government started attending to this issue since 2000–01 itself, it was given real attention in the *11th Plan* (2007–12), where we see a clear policy evolving towards the idea of inclusive growth in the country—'including the disadvantaged and marginalised sections of the society, specially, SCs, STs, OBCs, Minorities and Women' in the processes of growth and development. By the *12th Plan* (2012–17), the focus increased when we see the issue of inclusiveness entering into the very slogan of the Plan—'Faster, Sustainable and More Inclusive Growth'. During the course of time, we see the government evolving a clear *short-term* and *long-term* policy towards the cause of inclusive growth.

Short-term policy

This policy is aimed at supplying those goods and services to the disadvantaged and marginalised sections of society which are bare minimum and are essential in nature. Several Central Sector Schemes and Centrally Sponsored Schemes are run by the governments for this purpose. This policy touches the areas like:

1. Food and nutrition (Annapurna, Antodaya, Mid-Day Meal, and the last being National Food Security Act, etc.);
2. Healthcare and sanitation (National Health Mission, Total Sanitation Campaign, ASHA, Mission Indradhanush, and the last being Swachh Bharat Abhiyan, etc.);
3. Housing (Indira Aawas Yojana, Rajiv Aawas Yojana, etc.);
4. Drinking water (National Rural Drinking Water Programme, etc.);
5. Education (Sarva Shiksha Abhiyan, Rashtriya Madhyamik Shiksha Abhiyan, Model School Scheme, etc.).

The short-term policy has two drawbacks- *Firstly*, the schemes in it are subsidy-based, which incurr heavy drain on the national exchequer (it means it will not be fiscally sustainable in the long run). *Secondly*, the schemes fail to make the target population self-dependent. This is why the government has also evolved a long-term policy in this regard.

Long-term policy

This policy is aimed at bringing in self-dependence in the target population. This policy contains in itself the sustainability element, too. The attempts by the governments may be classified as given below:

1. All the schemes which aim at poverty alleviation and employment generation;
2. All the programmes which promote education at any level;
3. Vocationalisation of education (one such old idea has been the Industrial Training Institutes); and
4. Skill Development (a recent idea).

In recent time, we see increased emphasis on imparting right 'skill' among the population. Towards this, the government decided in 2008–09 to launch a skill development programme in the country through the National Skill Development Corporation (a joint venture not-for-profit company under the Ministry of Finance). There is an overall target of skilling/upskilling 500 million people in India by 2022, mainly by fostering private sector initiatives in skill development programmes and providing funding. The new government at Centre has also given the same call in the *'Skill India'*.

This way, we can see a initiative fool proof policy towards inclusive growth getting evolved by the GoI which is sustainable, too. The Planning Commission *(11th Plan)* says that inclusive growth can only be ensured if there is a degree of empowerment that creates a true feeling of participation so necessary in a democratic polity. Empowerment of disadvantaged and hitherto marginalised groups is therefore an essential part of any vision of inclusive growth. India's democratic polity, with the establishment of the third layer of democracy at the PRIs level, provides opportunities for empowerment and participation of all groups with reservations for SCs, STs and women. These institutions should be made more effective through greater delegation of power and responsibility.

The strategy for inclusive growth in the *11th* and *12th Plans* is not just a conventional strategy for growth to which some elements aimed at inclusion have been added. On the contrary, it is a strategy which aims at achieving a particular type of growth process, which will meet the objectives of *inclusiveness* and *sustainability.* A key feature of the inclusive growth strategy is that growth of 'GDP should not be treated as an end in itself, but only as a means to an end'. This is best done by adopting *monitorable targets*, which would reflect the multi-dimensional **economic** and **social** objectives of inclusive growth. Furthermore, to ensure efficient and timely implementation of the accompanying projects and programmes, these targets need to be disaggregated at the level of the states which implement many of the programmes.

RESOURCE MOBILISATION

Resource mobilisation is a broad term which includes raising and directing the resources (physical and human) of the economy to realise the desired socio-economic objectives. It involves all the economic policies activated by the governments—we can perceive it to be the very essence and the end result of the 'fiscal policies' of both the Centre and the states.

For Indian economy to move on the path of desired growth and development, the Government of India (GoI) needs to take care of the issue of resource mobilisation for various agents in the economy, namely –

1. GoI,
2. State governments,
3. Private sector, and
4. General public

In India, the responsibility of mobilising resources for the *planned* development of the country was given to the Planning Commission (PC). The commission used to take care of the fund requirements of the centre and the state governments. Practically, it was the PC which has to put in place the means by which the required funds for the *planned targets* of the economy were mobilised. These plan targets are set by the GoI through the PC itself. The plan targets set by the states are also duly taken care of the PC in due course of this process. Though the effective responsibilities to mobilise resources ultimately rests with the Ministry of Finance in which the various departments and divisions of the ministry play their diverse and highly focussed roles.

1. **GoI:** To the extent GoI is concerned it needs funds to realise two categories of the **planned targets,** namely:

(i) *Infrastructural targets* (which chiefly include power, transportation and communication; in coming years so many other sectors got attached with it, for example, technology parks, urban infrastructure, etc.); and

(ii) *Social sector targets* (which include education, health, social security, etc.—known as the Human Development related targets since 2010–11). These funds get mobilised through the *Plan Finance-II Division* of the Ministry of Finance.

2. **State Governments:** Other than the fund requirements of the GoI, the states also need funds for their developmental requirements (similar to the GoI)—they get the funds mobilised through three sources: *firstly,* through their own sources of income and market borrowings (after the recommendations of the 13th Finance Commission states are allowed to finance 25 per cent of their Plan Expenditure through market borrowing for which they do not need any permission from the GoI, provided they have effected their Fiscal Responsibility Acts); *secondly,* through the loans they get from the GoI on the advice of the PC (Ministry of Finance, GoI, shows these expenditures in the *Plan Finance-I Division*); and *thirdly,* through the GoI Central Sector Schemes, Centrally Sponsored Schemes and Additional Central Allocations (this includes the fund transfer to the states under 'Special Category States').

3. **Private Sector:** Other than the government, a large amount of fund is required by the private sector to meet their short-term (working capital) and long-term (capital market) requirements. The GoI needs to take care of this issue also—the financial system is managed in such a way that other than the government the private sector is also able to mobilise resources for its various requirements. This becomes even more important in a mixed economy, which is reforming and favours increased participation in the economy from the private sector.

This needs focussed reform in the financial system as it was structured to channelise more funds and resources towards government needs before the reforms commenced. The main idea here is to prevent the governments from 'crowding out' the funds and let it flow smoothly towards the private sector—the process of reforms in the financial sector, tax structure, fiscal policies of the Centre and states, etc., come under it.

4. **General Public:** Other than the government and the private sector, common people of an economy also need funds for their *general spending* and *investment*. The government needs to put in place such a fiscal policy which enables them (too) to have their access to funds. The savings common people do is used as investment provided they are able to save. Other than saving, people must get incentive and enough funds which they might directly invest in the primary or secondary security markets or in financial instruments (shares, bonds, mutual funds, pension funds, insurance, etc.). Common people are the main drivers of 'demand' in an economy. In the periods of reforms, the government sets *twin targets*—at the one hand promoting private sector so that 'supply' can be optimised in the economy (through *'structural reforms'*) and at the other it tries to create adequate 'demand' in the economy (by the process of *'macro-economic stabilisation'*).

The government used different 'means' to mobilise resources since Independence, in order to realise the desired and required kind of developmental goals. A part of resources are mobilised for investment purposes (i.e., the creation of productive assets) for which different *'investment models'* have been tried by now.

INVESTMENT MODELS

Investment is a process of putting money in productive activities to earn income. It can be done *directly* (in different activities in the primary, secondary or tertiary sectors) or *indirectly* (as in financial securities, such as shares, debentures, bonds, mutual funds, etc.). In the case of India, 'Investment Models' are the *means and tools* by which the GoI has tried to mobilise required funds (resources) to promote the different goals of planned development. Since India started the planning process (1951), we see differing ***models*** being tried by the governments to mobilise resources—it has been a kind of 'evolutionary' process. We may understand them in the following 'phases'.

Phase-I (1951–69)

This was the phase of 'state-led' development in which we see the GoI utilising every internal and external means to mobilise required resources. The main areas of resource allocations were for infrastructure and social sector. The famous Mahalanobis Plan gets implemented during this period. In this period, we see the whole financial system, tax system and fiscal policy of the country getting regulated to drive in maximum funds for the government to meet its planning related financial responsibilities.

This phase was marred by visible mismatches between the need and availability of investible fund—there always prevailed a lag between the requirement of funds and their mobilisation. Thus, investment targets of the government got derailed many times (war with China and a limited war with Pakistan also eroded and diverted the resource allocation mechanism). But overall, the government was able to start the process of industrialisation almost from nothing by mobilising heavy funds in favour of the infrastructure sector and infrastructure industries (the core sector)—education, health care also got funds but in a subdued manner as the GoI remained greatly preoccupied with 'glorification of the public sector'. This was the age when GoI used to consider the PSUs as the 'temples of modern India'.

Phase-II (1970–73)

With the enactment of the Industrial Policy of 1970 we see GoI deciding in favour of including 'private capital' in the process of planned development—but not in a big and open way. The idea of 'Joint Sector' comes under which a combination of partners—Centre, state and private sector—could enter the industrial sector. This was done basically, to make private sector come up in areas which were open for them, but due to certain technical and financial reasons they were not able to take part. In due course of time the government did quit such ventures and such industrial settlements came under complete private control.

This is for the first time we see the government inclining on private funding for planned development, but we do not see any private entry in the GoI's monopoly areas of industrial activities (which takes place only after the reform process begins in 1991).

Phase-III (1974–90)

With the enactment of the FERA in 1974 we see the government, for the first time, proposing to take the help of 'foreign capital' in the process of planned development—but not via cash foreign investment—only through the 'technology transfer' route that too up to only 26 per cent of the total project value proposed by the private sector. Basically, under FERA government tightened the flow of foreign currency inflow into the Indian private sector, which started hampering the technological upgradation process and initiation of the state-of-the-art technologies from the world—the technology transfer route was put in place to fill this gap. It means that even if GoI tried to include foreign investment in the developmental process its entry remained restricted in two ways:

1. It was not either 'direct' (as we see FDI during the reform process) or 'indirect' (as the PIS), but via technology transfer.
2. Foreign entities could enter only those industrial areas which were open for the Indian private sector (under Schedule B of the Industrial Policy Resolution, 1956). The 'monopoly' industries under GoI (some of the most attractive industries for the private sector) remained closed for entry.

It also means, that India failed to articulate an *investment model* which could tap the better elements of the foreign capital—state-of-the-art technologies, better work culture and most importantly, scarce investible capital. Experts believe it as a missed opportunity for India. By 1965–66, the South East Asian economies like Malaysia, Indonesia, Thailand and South Korea had opened up their economies for both forms of foreign investments—direct as well as indirect—and the governments there 'decontrolled' the industrial sectors, which were earlier fully under government controls (it should be noted here that these economies had started exactly the same way as India had started after Independence). This gave those economies a chance to tap not only scarce investible fund into their economies, but the state-of-the-art technologies from the world and world class work culture and entrepreneurship, too. Soon these economies came to be known as the Asian Tigers.

The period after 1985 saw dynamism in the area of resource mobilisation—two consecutive Planning Commissions suggested for opening up of the economy and inclusion of the Indian and foreign private capital in industrial areas which were hitherto reserved for the government. It suggested that GoI to withdraw from areas where the private sector was capable and fit to function (for example, infrastructure sector) and concentrate on areas where private sector would not be interested to operate (for example, the social sector). In a sense, during this time, we see an ideological shift in the government towards giving an 'active' or 'central' role to the private sector in the process of economic development. This was an advice for a completely different kind of *investment model*. But due to lack of political will, the governments of the time could not go in for the same. Though, we find the government going for a kind of limited degree of economic reforms through the Industrial Policies of 1985 and 1986 (this should not be taken as Economic Reforms in India which officially starts in 1991 only).

As a **summary** of the investment models up to 1990, we can highlight the following points:

1. Government remains the main investor in the economy and experts believe that India did undue delay in putting in place an *investment model* by which the potential of the private sector could be channelised into the process of developmental investment.
2. Emphasis on the public sector continued together with nationalisation drives also by late 1960s and early 1980s (the PSUs, to a large extent, were privatised by the South East Asian economies by now, making these socially-oriented and loss-making units to catapult into hubs

of profit and real drivers of growth and development).

3. Tax system was structured to raise maximum tax revenue (which led to tax evasion and excessive tax burdens on the citizens).
4. GoI continued cutting its non-plan expenditures so that resources could be allocated for the purpose of planned development (which led to expenditure cuts even in essential areas like education, health care, etc.).
5. Excessive government dependence on the financial system continued 'crowding out' funds, and as a result, the private sector could not mobilise suitable levels of funds for their requirements.
6. Technological upgradation and initiation of new technologies into the economy got hampered due to non-availability of foreign currency to the private sector (GoI, by late 1970, started facing the difficulty of paying its external liabilities, which were mainly created due to the expansion of the PSUs).
7. Main sources of fund in this model were, government's tax revenue, internal borrowings, external borrowings and the freshly printed currencies.

There always prevailed a lag between the requirement of funds and their mobilisation resulting into government investment targets getting derailed most of the times. In the meanwhile, the biggest crisis was building-up in the areas of infrastructure shortcomings. By early 1960s itself the Indian private sector was eager to enter this sector so that adequate levels of infrastructure could be developed. But due to several reasons we see the GoI continuing as the monopoliser in these sectors.

Phase-IV (1991 onward)

Due to prolonged follow-up of weak fundamentals of economics and immediately after Gulf War-I, India headed for a severe Balance of Payment crisis by late 1980s, which made India go to the IMF for financial help. It comes up but at some 'conditions'—the design of the 'conditions' made India to go for a 'restructuring' of the economy under the process of economic reforms commencing in 1991.

Reform era shifted India towards including the 'private sector' (domestic as well as foreign) for the future development of the economy—and here comes a different *investment model*. Main elements of this investment model are as given below:

1. The hitherto monopoly sectors of the industry were opened up for private investment—barring Nuclear Research, Nuclear power and Railways (latter two areas are partially opened)—in all of them direct foreign investments have also been allowed (between 26 to 100 per cent). We see the 'investment model' for *'infrastructure sector'* shifting from 'government-led' to 'private-led'.
2. In coming times, GoI articulated the idea of the Public Private Partnership (PPP) model of investment for this sector, to provide confidence and space to the private sector to enter the sectors (as the private sector was not much interested to participate due to some inter-related problems in the sector, for example lack of 'market reforms'). By the 10th Plan we see private sector putting in around 21 per cent of funds required for the infrastructure projects in the PPP mode which increased up to 32 per cent by the 11th Plan. On the basis of past two

plans the PC projected that private sector will put in around 50 per cent (48 per cent, to be precise) of the funds required for infrastructure development during the 12th Plan (which could not be achieved due to several internal and external reasons till 2015). Here, one point should not be missed that in future the infrastructure sector is to be fully handled by the private sector—as per the idea of the reform process.

3. In 2002, the government, articulated the idea of PPP (Public-Private-People-Partnership) through the 10th Plan (2002–07). The idea has its use at the local level where the resources are to be mobilised for the creation of physical and social infrastructure. It was launched in watershed management successfully. Gujarat had shown highly successful model of this investment in its 'Pani Panchayat'.

4. To support the private sector to mobilise their share of fund in the infrastructure PPP, the government has set up the Infrastructure Development Fund, which also has provision for the Viability Gap Funding (VGF).

5. Inside the general idea of PPP, the government has also put in place some other options of investment models, such as BOT (Build-Operate-Transfer); BOO (Build-Own-Operate); BOOT (Build-Own-Operate-Transfer); BLT (Build-Lease-Transfer); BOLT (Build Operate-Lease-Transfer); DBFO (Design-Build-Finance-Operate); DBOT (Design-Build-Operate-Transfer); DCMF (Design-Construct-Manage-Finance); etc.

6. In the area of mobilising resources for the expansion of the **Social Sector,** we see an increased focus coming from the government. But the government still thinks inadequacy of funds for the proper and timely development of the sector. Thus, by 2012, the GoI proposed plans to include the participation of private sector in the sector, mainly, education and health care through the PPP mode, which is still to be formally launched. Meanwhile, the provision regarding corporate social responsibility (CSR) via the Companies Act, 2013, some additional funds have started flowing to the fund-starved social sector. By early 2015, the government has asked the PSUs to flow their part of the CSR expenditures to the GoI for the newly launched sanitation drive, the Swachch Bharat Abhiyan.

7. So that the *corporate sector* is able to mobilise enough resources for its investment needs in the economy, the governments started to restructure the whole gamut of the tax structure, financial structure and its fiscal policy. Now, as the economy will depend more on private participation for its developmental requirements, the government avoids crowding out the fund from the economy—a process of fiscal consolidation starts in. An increased emphasis comes on the fronts of 'targeting' the subsidies, their better delivery, pension reforms, etc., so that the government could de-burden the financial system from its fund requirements and enough finance flows in the system for the private sector.

8. To take care of the spending and investment requirements of the *general public*, the government is committed to put in place a cheap interest rate regime, right kind of financial environment, a stable inflation and exchange rate besides other instruments. Bringing in 'inclusiveness' in the growth process is now the declared policy stance of the government.
9. Once the new government came to power by mid-2014, we find a renewed synergy in creating conducive environment for the private sector so that the economy could be able to attract enough investible fund to further the process of development. The government looks committed to the cause of improving the *'ease of doing business'* in the country. Aimed to this we find the government busy in putting in place the 'right' kind of land acquisition law, labour law, companies law, tax laws, digitalisation of government processes, etc.

Overall, the current investment model of the economy is **private-led** and for this the GoI proposes to put in place the right kind of financial system, legal framework, labour laws, etc. The main idea of this model is to 'unshackle' the hidden potential of the private sector. To the extent the role of the government is concerned, it will be limited to being a regulator with an increased tone of a 'facilitator' and a caretaker of the well being of the disadvantaged and marginalised sections of the society, so that the face of the economic reform remains 'humane'. In wake of the financial crisis in the western economies, the challenge of mobilising resources has become tougher and it will be really good that the government is able to devise out a working investment model.

CENTRAL SECTOR SCHEMES AND CENTRALLY SPONSORED SCHEMES

The exercise of planned development in India has evolved two type of schemes over the time, viz.,—**Central Sector Scheme and Centrally Sponsored Scheme.** The names are derived from the pattern of funding and the modality for implementation.

The ***Central Sector Schemes*** are 100 per cent funded by the Union Government with states functioning as implementing agencies. These schemes are mainly formulated on subjects from the *Union List*. In addition, the Central ministries also implement some schemes directly in the states/UTs, which are called Central Sector Schemes, but resources under these schemes are not generally transferred to states.

As per the **Union Budget 2016-17,** the existing 1,500 such schemes were restructured into 300 by the GoI to prevent overlapping of expenditure and help in better monitoring and evaluation.

Under the ***Centrully Sponsored Schemes (CSSs)*** a certain percentage of the funding is borne by the Centre and the states in fixed ratios and the implementation is done by the state governments. CSSs are formulated in subjects from the *State List* to encourage states to prioritise in areas that require more attention. Funds are routed either through the Consolidated Fund of the states and or are transferred directly to state/district level autonomous bodies/implementing agencies. As per the *Baijal Committee Report* (1987), CSSs have been defined as the schemes which are funded directly by Central ministries/departments and implemented by the states or their agencies, irrespective of their pattern of financing, unless they fall under the Centre's sphere of responsibility, i.e., the Union List.

Conceptually, both CSS and Additional Central Assistance (ACA) schemes have been passed by the Central Government to the state governments. The difference between the two has arisen because of the *historical evolution* and the way these are being budgeted and controlled and release of funds takes place. In case of CSSs, the budgets are allocated under concerned ministries themselves which look after the entire process of the release of funds, too.

Central Plan Assistance

Financial assistance provided by the GoI to support State's Five Year Plans is called Central Plan Assistance (CPA) or Central Assistance (CA), which primarily comprises the following:

1. **Normal Central Assistance (NCA):** The distribution of the NCA is formula based (Gadgil-Mukherjee Formula) and is untied. Gadgil Formula of determining the Central Assistance to the State is being adopted from the Fourth Plan and revised subsequently—allocation was made by the Planning Commission.
2. **Additional Central Assistance (ACA):** This is provided for implementation of externally aided projects (EAPs), and for which presently there is no ceiling. Unlike NCA, this is scheme based. The details of such schemes are given in the Statement 16 of the Expenditure Budget Vol. I. There can be one time ACA and advance ACA.

   One time ACA are assistance given by the Planning Commission to particular states for undertaking important state specific programmes and schemes. These are one time assistance and thus not recurring. These assistances are discretionary in nature.

   Advance ACA are advances given to *Special Category States* in times of financial stress and recoverable in 10 years.
3. **Special Central Assistance (SCA):** This is provided for special projects and programmes, e.g., Western Ghats Development Programme, Border Areas Development Programme, etc. (in exceptional situations, ACA, may also be provided). This special plan assistance is given only to *Special Category States* to bridge the gap between their planning needs and resources. In other words, SPAs are ACA for the special category states.

CPA is provided, as per scheme of financing applicable for specific purposes, approved by the Planning Commission. It is released in the form of *grants* and/or *loans* in varying combinations, as per terms and conditions defined by the Ministry of Finance, Department of Expenditure. Central assistance in the form of ACA is provided also for various Centrally Sponsored Schemes, viz., Accelerated Irrigation Benefits Programme, Rashtriya Krishi Vikas Yojana, etc., and SCA is extended to states and UTs as additive to Special Component Plan (renamed Scheduled Castes Sub Plan) and Tribal Sub Plan. Funds provided to the states under Member of Parliament Local Area Development Scheme (MPLADS), i.e., ₹5 crore per annum per MP also count as CA central assistance.

CSSs Restructured

For the 12th Plan period (2012–17) the existing 137 CSSs were restructured into 66 schemes, including the 17 *flagship programmes*. The government had set up an expert Committee (Chaired by B.K. Chaturvedi, member of the erstwhile Planning Commission) for the purpose which submitted its report by late-2011.

The *14th FC* recommended that sector-specific transfers from the Union to the states/UTs should be confined to sectors like education, health, drinking water and sanitation. However, in view of the preponderance of CSSs being interventions in key sectors of national importance, the GoI kept **50** of the **66** ongoing CSSs in the *Union Budget 2015–16*. The balance were in the process of being either taken into the Central Sector, or reformulated as new Umbrella Schemes or were transferred to the states. The CSSs funds are released as central assistance to state plans which are routed through the states' budgets (new method as per the *Union Budget 2014–15*). This provides greater autonomy, authority and responsibility to the states in implementation of the schemes.

In **March 2015,** to rationalise the CSSs, a Sub-Group of Chief Ministers was set up in pursuance of the decision taken by the *Governing Council* of the NITI Aayog. The *guiding principles* of the sub-group was defined as—the Union and the states/UTs to work as Team India in the spirit of 'Cooperative Federalism' towards realisation of the goals of VISION 2022 when India will celebrate the 75th year of Independence. The broad objectives of the VISION are:

1. Providing basic amenities to all citizens in an equitable and just manner for ensuring a life with self-respect and dignity, and
2. Providing appropriate opportunities to every citizen to realise her potential.

Accordingly, the existing 50 CSSs were rationalised and restructured into 28 *umbrella* schemes[103] (in normal times number not to exceed 30) by the Union Budget 2016-17. This will avoid overlapping of expenditure, provide visibility and impact. The **major features** of the restructuring are as given below:

1. The CSSs have been divided into — *Core* and *Optional* schemes.
2. The new expenditure sharing pattern for the *Core Schemes* is—for 8 North Eastern (NE) states and 3 Himalayan states 90:10; for other States 60:40 (Centre:States) and for UTs 100 per cent to be borne by the Centre.
3. For *Optional Schemes* the expenditure sharing pattern is—for 8 NE and 3 Himalayan states 80:20; for other states 50:50 (Centre:States) and for the UTs 100 per cent to be borne by the Centre.
4. Amongst the Core Schemes, those for social protection and social inclusion should form the *Core of the Core* and be the first charge on available funds for the National Development Agenda.

103. The process of restructuring basically limited to rationalisation (better called 'rearrangement') of the existing schemes into **umbrella** schemes. But these umbrellas are large enough and include close to 200 schemes. For example, one Core Scheme ***Green Revolution*** (implemented by the Department Agriculture, Cooperation and Farmers' Welfare) contains *17 schemes* under its umbrella which are—Rashtriya Krishi Vikas Yojana; National Food Security Mission; Agriculture Marketing Information; Integrated Scheme on Agricultural Cooperation; Integrated Scheme on Agriculture Census and Statistics; National Agri-Tech Infrastructure; National Mission on Horticulture; National Mission on Oil Seed and Oil Palm; National Project on Agro-Forestry; National Project on Organic Farming; National Project on Soil Health and Fertility; Organic Value Chain Development for North East Region; Paramparagat Krishi Vikas Yojana; Rain-fed Area Development and Climate Change and Sub-Missions on Agriculture Extension; Agriculture Mechanisation; Plant Protection; and Plant Quarantine & Seed and Planting Material). [Source: **Bibek Debroy,** Chairman, **Economic Advisory Council to the PM,** *Indian Express*, Delhi, September 12, 2019].

5. Funds for *Optional Schemes* would be allocated to the states by the Ministry of Finance as a **lump sum,** and states would be *free* to choose which Optional Schemes they wish to implement. In such schemes, states have been given the *flexibility* of *portability* of funds to any other CSSs.
6. Henceforth, the CSSs will come up only in key identified sectors which comprise the *National Development Agenda* (to be decided by the NITI Aayog, in co-ordination with its Governing Council).
7. NITI Aayog to have concurrent jurisdiction in *monitoring* of the schemes in the states and Central ministries.
8. Third-party *evaluation* by NITI Aayog.

In 2019-20, the CSSs were broadly classified under two categories, *Core of the Core Schemes* and *Core Schemes* (funding pattern remaining unchanged). The list of the 30 schemes[104] is given below:

Core of the Core Schemes

1. National Social Assistance Programme
2. Mahatma Gandhi National Rural Employment Guarantee Programme
3. Umbrella Scheme for Development of Schedule Castes
4. Umbrella Programme for Development of Scheduled Tribes
5. Umbrella Programme for Development of Minorities
6. Umbrella Programme for Development of Other Vulnerable Groups

Core Schemes

1. Green Revolution
2. White Revolution
3. Blue Revolution
4. Pradhan Mantri Krishi Sinchai Yojana
5. Pradhan Mantri Gram Sadak Yojana
6. Pradhan Mantri Awas Yojana (PMAY)
7. Jal Jeevan Mission (JJM)
8. Swachh Bharat Mission (Urban)
9. Swachh Bharat Mission (Gramin)
10. National Health Mission
11. National Education Mission
12. National Programme of Mid-Day Meal in Schools
13. Umbrella ICDS
14. Mission for Protection and Empowerment for Women
15. National Livelihood Mission - Ajeevika
16. Jobs and Skill Development
17. Environment, Forestry and Wildlife
18. Urban Rejuvenation Mission: AMRUT and Smart Cities Mission
19. Modernisation of Police Forces
20. Infrastructure Facilities for Judiciary
21. Rashtriya Gram Swaraj Abhiyan (RGSA)
22. PMJAY-Ayushman Bharat
23. Border Area Development Programme (BADP)
24. Shyama Prasad Mukherjee Rurban Mission (SPMRM)

104. ***Union Budget 2020-21***, Ministry of Finance, GoI, N. Delhi. [Before the last revision in the classification, last two (i.e., the BADP and SPMRM) were implemented as the *Optional Schemes*].

At present the schemes are under the process of evaluation before they can be streamlined as per the recommendations of the 15th Finance Commission (FFC). Experts believe that the Commission may suggest a *measurable and performance-based incentives* related to the schemes for states (the Terms of Reference given to the Commission includes 'achievements in implementation of flagship schemes of Government of India, disaster resilient infrastructure, sustainable development goals, and quality of expenditure'). Thus, the schemes are headed for further restructuring.

INDEPENDENT EVALUATION OFFICE

An Independent Evaluation Office (IEO) was created by the GoI in February 2014, at an arm's distance from the government with the objective of strengthening public accountability of some of the important social sector programmes, which account huge resource mobilisation such as the flagship programmes. Conceived on the lines of Independent Evaluation Office (IEO) of the IMF,[105] the body was created on the basis of international experiences, in cooperation with the *World Bank* and the British *DFID* (Department for International Development)—it was modelled on the lines of Mexico's National Council for the Evaluation of Social Development Policy.

The IEO was an independent office attached to the Planning Commission under a Governing Board chaired by the Deputy Chairman of the Planning Commission. The IEO was funded by the Planning Commission and had, as its head, a full-time Director General in the rank and status of Member of the Planning Commission/Union Minister of State. The DG had a tenure of 3 years extendable to 5 years. Its staff was selected by the DG without any interference and to have its independent budget.

It was felt that the government programmes can benefit enormously from concurrent independent evaluation. Presently, concurrent evaluation was done by the concerned ministries as an on-going parallel process. Expert evaluation of programmes that have been in operation was done by the Programme Evaluation Organisation (PEO) of the Planning Commission—the IEO was expected to strengthen this evaluation process. **Main aims** of the office was:

1. To help improve the effectiveness of government policies and programmes by assessing their impact and outcomes.
2. To set guidelines and methodology for all evaluations done by various departments, and agencies and encourage a culture of openness and learning in government systems.
3. To connect India to the best international evaluated evidence in development practice and knowledge to learn from others success and mistakes.

Main features about the functioning of the office may be summed-up as given below:

1. It will conduct independent evaluations of plan programmes—especially flagship programmes—and assess their effectiveness, relevance and impact. Besides, it has the freedom to conduct independent evaluations on any programme which has access to public

105. An Independent Evaluation Office (IEO) functions in the International Monetary Fund (IMF) since 2001, which conducts independent and objective *evaluations* of Fund's policies and activities. Under its Terms of Reference, it is fully independent from the Management of the IMF and operates at arm's length from the Board of Executive Directors with the following *three* missions—(i) Enhancing the learning culture within the Fund, (ii) Strengthening the Fund's external credibility, and (iii) Supporting institutional governance and oversight *(Source: Independent Evaluation Office, IMF, Washington DC, 2014).*

funding or implicit or explicit guarantees from the government.

2. The work programme of the IEO will be prepared through an open process of consultations, including feedback from **civil society** and will be made public.
3. The IEO will prepare the *Terms of Reference* for all independent evaluations, which will be conducted by selected institutes and researchers, selected on competitive basis.
4. IEO will provide guidance to any agency or department of the government to improve the quality of its self evaluation and monitoring system. Such support is intended to bring all evaluations under a common internationally accepted methodology, help achieve better development outcomes and encourage a *culture of learning* in the government.
5. Besides making available on it's website and other public avenues, its reports will be submitted to the Parliament and the Prime Minister's Office.
6. It will also make internationally available findings from independently and professionally evaluated Indian programmes in the spirit of South-South learning and cooperation.
7. IEO will **represent** India as it's independent evaluation authority at international forums on development and effectiveness and will endeavour to improve India's evaluation systems in line with international best practices.

The IEO handed over its first report to the Government in September 2014 and in the following week, the DG of the IEO was relieved from his services. Later on, the IEO was *merged* into the newly constituted (September 2015) monitoring and evaluation body, the Development Monitoring and Evaluation Office (DMEO). The functions and the special features of the IEO still reflect in the new body.

PROGRAMME EVALUATION ORGANISATION

The Programme Evaluation Organisation (PEO) was established in October 1952, as an independent organisation, under the general guidance and direction of the PC with a specific task of evaluating the community development programmes and other Intensive Area Development Schemes. The evaluation set up was further strengthened by the development of methods and techniques of evaluation in the 1st Plan and setting up of evaluation machineries in the States during the 3rd (1961–66) and 4th (1969–74) Plans. Gradually, with the extension of the programmes/schemes in a variety of sectors, viz., agricultural cooperation, rural industries, fisheries, health, family welfare, rural development, rural electrification, public distribution, tribal development, social forestry, etc., the evaluation work undertaken by the PEO was extended to other important CSSs.

The broad **functions** of the PEO include undertaking evaluation of selected programmes/ schemes under implementation, as per the requirement of the various Divisions of the PC, Central Ministries and Departments of the Government of India. The evaluation studies are designed to ***assess:***

1. the performance,
2. the process of implementation,
3. the effectiveness of the delivery systems, and
4. the impact of programmes.

The **objectives** of the PEO:

1. Objective assessment of process and impact of the development programmes,
2. Identifying the areas of success and failures at different stages of administration and execution, and analysis of reasons for success or failure,
3. Examining extension methods and people's reactions thereto and deriving lessons for future improvement in the formulation and implementation of the new programmes/schemes.

The PEO was *merged* into the newly constituted (September 2015) monitoring and evaluation body, the Development Monitoring and Evaluation Office (DMEO). The functions and the special features of the PEO very well reflect in the new body.

DEVELOPMENT MONITORING AND EVALUATION OFFICE

The Development Monitoring and Evaluation Office (DMEO) was constituted by *merging* the erstwhile Program Evaluation Office (PEO) and the Independent Evaluation Office (IEO) in September 2015. As an attached office under the NITI Aayog, it aims at fulfilling monitoring and evaluation (M&E) mandate (i.e., function) of the Aayog. It is entrusted with building M&E ecosystem in the country with the following functions:

1. Monitoring progress and efficacy of policies/ programmes, taking initiatives to help improvements including necessary mid-course corrections.
2. Evaluating implementation of programmes and identification of needed resources to strengthen success and scope of delivery.

As a part of NITI Aayog, DMEO has advisory powers across the Ministries and Departments of the Union Government, and is *one of few* institutions within the government to provide a cross- and inter-ministerial perspective. It has mandate of technical advisory to States also. For M&E the 'output-outcome framework' (as prescribed by the Union Budget 2019-20) has been evolved[106]. This framework has *measurable indicators* for the objectives (i.e., 'outcome') for all of the centrally sponsored schemes and central sector schemes. Sectoral reviews are done by the office on the basis of the outcomes achieved by the schemes.

All of the functions and special features of the erstwhile bodies, the IEO and PEO, are still with the DMEO added with several new and dynamic features to serve the changed developmental needs of the country on the path of transformation.

NITI AAYOG

By mid-2014, India did show a quite strong mandate and a very stable government came at the Centre. We find the new government showing a renewed vigour and zeal in several areas. One such area has been its attempts at 'redefining' the federal polity of the country for the purpose of promoting growth and development. We see a pronounced policy shift in the direction of 'empowering and keeping state in front' by giving them more[107] financial space and responsibilities. Keeping its promises in the direction, the government abolished the

106. To know more about the **Output-Outcome Framework** see GLOSSARY.

107. Such a stance in the process of planning we find in the document of the 10th Plan (2002–07) for the first time when the government of the time (the NDA-led) made the call : **'if states are developed, the nation is developed'**. We find a pronounced shift towards 'decentralised planning' (the Plan was nicknamed as the 'People's Plan'). The new idea of 'monitorable targets' also commenced in this plan giving states more say and accountability in the process of planned development (these targets were continued within the forthcoming Plans). Several other steps were also taken in this Plan aimed at bringing the states in the mainstream of the developmental process, viz., by giving them increased role and accountability.

Planning Commission (PC) and replaced it bv a new body—the NITI Aayog. The acronym **NITI** stands for **National Institution for Transforming India.** We see the government aspiring for the emergence of the 'Team India' in the new body. It will be premature to be conclusive on this shift from 'Planning to NITI' (as the government calls). Even an academic comparison between the old and the new bodies will also not serve enough purpose as it needs some time when the outcome of the change will be available. Judgements on this shift will be only good once it is done after some period of time. In the meantime, India remains a planned economy. The discussion given here is mainly based on the documents and releases which came out from the GoI before and after the NITI Aayog was set up (January 1, 2015). In these documents, the government has not only provided the reasons as why does India need to go in for a new body, but charts out a very encouraging and out of tradition role/function for the new body. An attempt has been made to closely follow the 'government line' of thinking so that the 'spirit' of it is not lost.

Transforming India Transforming India

The government aims at 'transforming the development agenda of India' with the help of the NITI Aayog and has given a slogan, 'from planning to NITI'. India has undergone a paradigm shift over the past six decades—politically, economically, socially, technologically as well as demographically. The role of the government in national development has seen a parallel evolution. Keeping with these changing times, the government decided to set up the **NITI Aayog** as a means to better serve the needs and aspirations of the people of India. The government thinks the new institution to function as a catalyst to the developmental process—nurturing an overall enabling environment, through a *holistic approach* to development going beyond the limited sphere of the public sector and the GoI, which will be built on the foundations of:

1. An empowered role of states as equal partners in national development; operationalising the principle of *Cooperative Federalism.*
2. A knowledge hub of internal as well as external resources, serving as a repository of good governance best practices, and a *Think Tank* offering domain knowledge as well as strategic expertise to all levels of the government.
3. A collaborative platform facilitating *Implementation*; by monitoring progress, plugging gaps and bringing together the various ministries at the Centre and in states, in the *joint pursuit* of developmental goals.

Changing Contours of India

The government agrees that the Planning Commission has served India well. However, India has changed dramatically over the past 65 years at *multiple levels* and across *varied scales.* These transformatory forces have changed the very contours of India—highlighted by the government document in the six areas:

1. **Demographic Shift:** India's population has increased over three-fold to reach 121 crores. This includes an addition of over 30 crore people to Urban India. As well as an increase of 55 crore youth (below the age of 35), which is more than one and a half times the total population of the country then. With increasing levels of development, literacy and communication, the aspirations of the people have soared, moving from *scarcity and survival* to *safety and surplus*. Today, we are looking at a completely different India, and country's governance systems need to be transformed to keep up with the changing India.
2. **Economic Shift:** India's economy has undergone a paradigm shift. It has expanded by over a hundred times, going from a GDP of ₹10,000 crore to ₹100 lakh crore at current

prices, to emerge as one of the world's largest economics. Agriculture's share in the GDP has seen a dramatic drop, from more than 50 per cent to less than 15 per cent. The plan size of ₹43 lakh crore of the 12th Plan dwarfs the plan size of ₹2,400 crore of the 1st Plan. Priorities, strategies and structures dating back to the time of the birth of the Planning Commission, must thus be *revisited.* To align with this shift and sheer scale, India needs to *overhaul* the very *nature* of the planning processes, the government says.

3. **Shift in the Private Sector:** The nature of the Indian economy, and the role of the government in it, has undergone a paradigm shift. Driven by an increasingly open and liberalised structure, India's private sector has matured into a vibrant and dynamic force. The sector is not operating just at the international cutting edge, but also with a global scale and reach. This changed economic landscape requires a new *administrative paradigm* in which the role of the government must evolve from simply allocating resources in a command and control ecosystem, to a far more nuanced one of directing, calibrating, supporting and regulating a *market eco system.* National development must be seen beyond the limited sphere of the 'Public Sector'. Government must, thus, transition from being a 'provider of first and last resort' and 'major player' in the economy, to being a 'catalyst' nurturing an 'enabling environment', where the entrepreneurial spirits of all, from small self-employed entrepreneurs to large corporations, can flourish. This importantly, frees up the government to focus its precious resources on public *welfare* domains such as essential entitlements of food, nutrition, health, education and livelihood of vulnerable and marginalised groups of the society.

4. **Forces of Globalisation:** In recent decades, the world at large has also evolved. We live today in a 'global village', connected by modern transport, communications and media, and networked international markets and institutions. In this milieu, India's economic actions 'contribute' to the global dynamics, while our economy also gets influenced by the happenings far away from us. The framework of *policy making* together with the *functioning of governments* need to incorporate the realities of our continuing integration with the global economic system.

5. **Role of the States:** Indian states have evolved from being mere appendages of the Centre, to being the actual drivers of national development. The development of states must thus become the national goal, as the nation's progress lies in the progress of states. As a consequence, the *one-size-fits-all approach*, often inherent in centralised planning, is no longer practical or efficient. States need to be heard and given the flexibility required for effective implementation. The government quotes Dr. B. R. Ambedkar to bring the point home: 'it is unreasonable to centralise powers where central control and uniformity is not clearly essential or is impracticable'. Thus, while emanating from global experiences and national synergy, India's strategies need to be calibrated and customised to *local needs* and opportunities.

6. **Technology Paradigm:** Technology advancements and information access have unleashed the creative energy of India. They have integrated our varied regions and ecosystems in an interlinked national economy and society, opening up newer avenues of coordination and cooperation. Technology is also playing a substantial role in enhancing transparency as well as efficiency, holding the government more accountable. Thus, India needs to make it central to systems of policy and governance.

Change Must Come

The above-given changes have been recognised by the experts for years now. With changing contours of the economy, the institutions guiding the economy should also change. The government quotes several such *instances* when appropriate changes were advised in the Planning Commission by the experts, committees, even the PC, among others:

1. The ***8th Plan*** (1992–97) document (the very first after the reform process commenced in 1991) categorically stated that, as the role of the government was reviewed and restructured, the role and functions of the PC too needed to be rethought. The PC also needed to be reformed to keep up with changing trends, relieving itself of the old practices and beliefs, which had lost relevance, and adopting new ones based on past experiences of India as well as other nations. Specifically, the PC needed to be in tune with the process of economic reforms.
2. The ***Standing Committee on Finance*** of the 15th Lok Sabha observed in its 35th Report on Demand for Grants (2011–12) that the 'PC has to come to grips with the emerging social realities to re-invent itself to make itself more relevant and effective for aligning the planning process with economic reforms and its consequences, particularly for the poor'. This was the need of making the planning process relevant to the process of economic reforms.
3. The former Prime Minister, Dr. Manmohan Singh, in his farewell address to the PC (April 2014), also urged reflection on 'what the role of the PC needs to be in this new world. Are we still using tools and approaches which were designed for a different era? What additional roles should the Planning Commission play and what capacities does it need to build to ensure that it continues to be relevant to the growth process?' This observation has quite high relevance, as Dr. Singh is himself a not 'noted' economist.

Taking the clues for a change, the government quotes Mahatma Gandhi before going for the change: 'Constant development is the law of life, and a man who always tries to maintain his dogmas in order to appear consistent drives himself into a false position'. The government adds further, keeping true to this principle our institutions of governance and policy must evolve with the changing dynamics of the new India, while remaining true to the founding principles of the Constitution of India, and rooted in our *Bharatiyata* or wisdom of our *civilisational history* and *ethos*. It was, in every sense, a kind of pledge to devise India's own means, methods, tools and approaches to promote development.

For the government, the NITI Aayog is to be the *institution* to give life to these aspirations (discussed above). The Aayog is being formed based on extensive consultation across a spectrum of stakeholders, including inter alia state governments, relevant institutions, domain experts and the people at large.

Functions of NITI Aayog

With the process of maturity and deepening in Indian nationhood, the country has embraced a greater measure of pluralism and decentralisation. This necessitates a *paradigm shift* in Central government's approaches to the governments in the state, as well as at the local levels. The *state governments* and the *local bodies* must be made equal partners in the development process through the following changes:

1. understanding and supporting their developmental needs and aspirations,
2. incorporating varied local realities into national policies and programmes with the required flexibility.

This way the new body, NITI Aayog, is designed to live up to the principle of 'Team

India' with its following **officially demarcated functions:**

1. **Cooperative and Competitive Federalism:** It will be the 'primary platform' for operationalising cooperative federalism, enabling states to have active participation in the formulation of national policy, as well as achieving time-bound implementation of quantitative and qualitative targets through the combined authority of the Prime Minister and the Chief Ministers. This will be by means of systematic and structured interactions between the Union and state governments, to better understand developmental issues, as well as forge a consensus on strategies and implementation mechanisms. The above would mark the replacement of the *one-way* flow of policy from centre-to-state, with a genuine and continuing *Centre-State partnership*. The Aayog is supposed to further this cooperation with the enhanced vibrancy of *Competitive Federalism;* the Centre competing with the states and vice versa, and the states competing with each other, in the joint pursuit of national development.

2. **Shared National Agenda:** It will 'evolve' a shared vision of national development priorities and strategies, with the active involvement of the states. This will provide the framework 'national agenda' for the Prime Minister and Chief Ministers to implement.

3. **State's Best Friend at the Centre:** It will support states in addressing their own challenges, as well as building on strengths and comparative advantages. This will be through various means, such as *coordinating* with ministries, championing their ideas at the Centre, providing 'consultancy' support and 'building capacity'.

4. **Decentralised Planning:** The new body is to 'restructure' the planning process into a 'bottom-up model', empowering states, and guiding them to further empower local governments in developing mechanisms to formulate credible plans at the village level, which are progressively aggregated up the higher levels of the government. The maturing of India's governmental institutions has enabled increasing the specialisation of their functions. There is, thus, a need to separate as well as energise the distinct 'strategy' element of governance from the usual 'process' and 'implementation' element. As a dedicated 'Think Tank' of the government, NITI Aayog will carry out this 'directional' role, strategically charting the future of the nation. It will provide specialised inputs—strategic, functional and technical—to the Prime Minister and the government (Centre as well as the state), on matters critical to the fulfillment of the national development agenda. It means, the new body is to function like a 'think tank'.

5. **Vision & Scenario Planning:** To 'design' medium and long-term strategic frameworks of the big picture vision of India's future—across schemes, sectors, regions and time; factoring in all possible alternative assumptions and counterfactuals. These would be the 'drivers of the national reforms agenda', especially focussed on identifying critical gaps and harnessing untapped potentialities. The same would need to be intrinsically dynamic with their progress and efficacy constantly monitored for necessary mid-course recalibration;

and the overall environment (domestic and global) continuously scanned for incorporating evolving trends and addressing emerging challenges. This would mean a fundamental transition from merely planning for where the nation's money goes, to planning where we want the nation to go. And given its unique position as the aggregator and integrator of all developmental initiatives of the Government of India and the states, the new body would be ideally suited for the same.

6. **Domain Strategies:** To 'build' a repository of specialised domain expertise, both sectoral and cross-sectoral; to assist ministries of the Central and state governments in their respective development planning, as well as problem solving needs. This will especially enable the imbibing of good governance best practices, both national as well as international, especially with regards to structural reforms in the country.
7. **Sounding Board:** To be an 'in-house sounding board' whetting and refining government positions, through objective criticisms and comprehensive counter-views in the economy.
8. **Network of Expertise:** To 'mainstream' external ideas and expertise into government policies and programmes through a collaborative community of national and international experts, practitioners and other partners. This would entail being government's link to the outside world, roping in academia (universities, think tanks and research institutions), private sector expertise, and the people at large, for close involvement in the policymaking process. To bring the point home, the document quotes the Rigveda – 'let us welcome noble thoughts flowing in from all directions'.
9. **Knowledge and Innovation Hub:** The body to be an 'accumulator' as well as 'disseminator' of research and best practices on good governance, through a state-of-the-art Resource Centre which identifies, analyses, shares and facilitates replication of the same. The document further adds, an increasingly mature Indian population has steadily increased the focus on, and demand for, actual delivery and results. To keep up with such enhanced aspirations, the new body will have the mandate to go beyond mere planning and strategising, to facilitating *implementation* of the development agenda as well. This would involve making implementation central to the planning process, through an emphasis on tangible outcomes, realistic targets, strict time lines and robust monitoring and evaluation—a transition from the isolated conceptualisation of merely 'planning', to 'planning for implementation'. It will also act as a 'catalyst' to the government machinery at large—filling gaps, enhancing capabilities and de-clogging bottlenecks, as and where required.
10. **Harmonisation:** To 'facilitate harmonisation' of actions across different layers of the government, especially when involving cross-cutting and overlapping issues across multiple sectors through: communication, coordination, collaboration and convergence among all stakeholders. The emphasis will be on bringing all together on an integrated and holistic approach to development.
11. **Conflict Resolution:** To provide a 'platform' for mutual resolution of inter-sectoral, inter-departmental, inter-state

as well as centre-state issues; facilitating consensus acceptable and beneficial to all, to bring about clarity and speed in execution.

12. **Coordinating Interface with the World:** It will be the 'nodal point' for strategically harnessing global expertise and resources in India's developmental process—coming in from across nations, multi-lateral institutions and other international organisations.

13. **Internal Consultancy:** It will offer an internal 'consultancy' function to Central and state governments on policy and programme design—providing frameworks adhering to basic design principles such as decentralisation, flexibility and a focus on results. This would include specialised skills such as structuring and executing PPPs.

14. **Capacity Building:** To enable 'capacity building' and 'technology upgradation' across governments, benchmarking with latest global trends and providing managerial and technical knowhow.

15. **Monitoring and Evaluation:** It will 'monitor' the implementation of policies and programmes, and 'evaluate' their impact; through rigorous tracking of performance metrics and comprehensive programme evaluations. This will not only help identify weaknesses and bottlenecks for necessary course-correction, but also enable data-driven policymaking; encouraging greater efficiency as well as effectiveness.

The Guiding Principle

The government document has categorically pointed out the very 'purpose' of the new body —in the process of carrying out its functions, the Aayog will be guided by an overall vision of development which is inclusive, equitable and sustainable. The institution is to follow a strategy of empowerment built on human dignity and national self-respect—the document quote Swami Vivekanada to emphasise this: 'to encourage everyone in his struggle to live up to his own highest idea'. The new body is supposed to follow a development model which is ***all round, all pervasive, all inclusive and holistic.***

Antyodaya To prioritise service and upliftment of the poor, marginalised and downtrodden, (the document quotes the idea of 'Antodaya' as articulated by Pandit Deendayal Upadhyay). Development is incomplete and meaningless, if it does not reach the farthest individual. 'Nothing is more dreadfully painful than poverty' (the centuries old sage-poet Tiruvallur has been quoted).

Inclusion To empower vulnerable and marginalised sections, redressing identity-based inequalities of all kinds—gender, region, religion, caste or class—the document quoted from Sankar Dev—'to see every being as equivalent to one's own soul is the supreme means (of attaining deliverance)'. Weaker sections must be enabled to be masters of their own fate, having equal influence over the choices the nation makes.

Village To integrate our villages into the development process, to draw on the vitality and energy of the bedrock of our *ethos, culture* and *sustenance.*

Demographic Dividend To harness our greatest asset, the people of India, by focussing on their development, through *education* and *skilling,* and their *empowerment,* through productive livelihood opportunities.

People's Participation To transform the developmental process into a *people-driven* one, making an awakened and participative citizenry—the driver of good governance. This includes our extended Indian family of the non-resident Indian community spread across the world, whose significant geo-economic and geo-political strength must be harnessed.

Governance To nurture an open, transparent, accountable, pro-active and purposeful style of governance, transitioning focus from *Outlay to Output to Outcome.*

Sustainability Maintain sustainability at the core of our planning and developmental process, building on our ancient tradition of respect for the environment.

Structure of the NITI

The Aayog will be a lean organisation, modelled as a network of expertise, focusing on functionality, flexibility and domain knowledge, with the following 'structure' and 'mechanism':

1. **Chairman:** the Prime Minister of India (de-facto).
2. **Governing Council:** will comprise the Chief Ministers of all states and Lt. Governors of union territories.
3. **Regional Councils:** will be formed to address specific issues and contingencies impacting more than one state or region. Strategy and planning in the Aayog will be anchored from state-level; with regional councils convened by the Prime Minister for identified priority domains, put under the joint leadership of related sub-groups of states (grouped around commonalities which could be geographic, economic, social or otherwise) and central ministries. The regional councils will have the following features:
   - (i) Will have specified tenures, with the mandate to evolve strategy and oversee implementation.
   - (ii) Will be jointly headed by one of the group Chief Ministers (on a rotational basis or otherwise) and a corresponding Central Minister.
   - (iii) Will include the sectoral central ministers and secretaries concerned, as well as state ministers and secretaries.
   - (iv) Will be linked with corresponding domain experts and academic institutions.
   - (v) Will have a dedicated support cell in the Aayog's secretariat.
4. **Special Invitees:** It will have experts, specialists and practitioners with relevant domain knowledge as special invitees nominated by the Prime Minister.
5. **Full-time Organisational Framework:** In addition to PM as its Chairman it will comprise:
   - (i) Vice-Chairperson—to be appointed by the PM.
   - (ii) Members: all as full-time.
   - (iii) Part-time Members: maximum of 2, from leading universities, research organisations and other relevant institutions in an *ex-officio* capacity. Part time members will be on a rotational basis.
   - (iv) Ex-Officio Members: maximum of 4 members of the Union Council of Ministers to be nominated by the PM.
   - (v) Chief Executive Officer: to be appointed by the PM for a fixed tenure, in the rank of Secretary to the Government of India.
   - (vi) Secretariat: as deemed necessary.

Specialised Wings in the NITI Aayog

The Aayog will house a number of specialised 'Wings', as per the government document:

1. **Research Wing:** It will develop in-house sectoral expertise as a dedicated think tank of top notch domain experts, specialists and scholars.

2. **Consultancy Wing:** It will provide a market-place of whetted panels of expertise and funding, for Central and state governments to tap into; matching their requirements with solution providers, public and private, national and international. By playing match-maker instead of providing the entire service itself, NITI Aayog will be able to focus its resources on priority matters, providing guidance and an overall quality check to the rest.

3. **Team India Wing:** It will comprise representatives from every state and ministry and will serve as a permanent platform for national collaboration. Each representative in this Wing will:
   (i) Ensure every state/ministry has a continuous voice and stake in the Aayog.
   (ii) Establish a direct communication channel between the state/ministry and the Aayog for all development related matters, as the dedicated liaison interface.

A national 'Hub-Spoke' institutional model will be developed, with each state and ministry encouraged to build dedicated *mirror institutions*, serving as the interface of interaction. These institutions, in turn, will nurture their own networks of expertise at the state and ministry level. NITI Aayog will function in close cooperation, consultation and coordination with the ministries of the Central government, and state governments. While it will make recommendations to the Central and state governments, the responsibility for taking and implementing decisions will rest with them.

Vehicle of Good Governance

The Aayog will seek to facilitate and empower the critical requirement of good governance, which is people-centric, participative, collaborative, transparent and policy-driven. It will provide critical directional and strategic input to the development process, focussing on deliverables and outcomes. This, along with being as incubator and disseminator of fresh thought and ideas for development, will be the core mission of NITI Aayog. The document, at the end, quotes from Chanakya to emphasise the importance and need of good governance –'good governance is at the root of a nation's wealth, comfort and happiness'.

If we look into the state of governance in the country, we find that it has improved a lot at the level of the Central government but at the state level the situation is still not good.[108] As the lives of citizens depend more on the supplies from the state governments the poor state of governance hits their lives in a big way. The Central government's push in favour of good governance has been practically crippled by the inability or unwillingness of the state governments in this regard. It means that the state of governance can not be improved much till there is an effective co-operation among the governments of the country. Once a very willing beginning has been started under the NITI Aayog ('co-operative federalism' being one of the three foundations on which it is imagined to be built) in this direction it is believed that the quality of governance should improve in the coming years.

We find an intentional attempt by the Government to intertwine the aspect of good governance in the very idea of the NITI Aayog. Not only the word governance but the *established traits of governance*[109] find clear mentions at several places—

108. This was explained in detail by the **Tenth Five Year Plan (2002-07)** citing the example of the *Mid-Day Meal Scheme* run by the Government of India.

109. As per the **UNO/IMF (Report onGood Governance, 1996)** *good governance is the process of decision- making and their implementation which is—consensus oriented, participatory, based on Rule of Law, transparent, accountable, responsive, equitable and inclusive.*

1. In the *Foundations* the NITI Aayog is built on (a collaborative platform facilitating implementation);
2. In the *Guiding Principles* (Participation, Inclusion, Governance and Antodaya);
3. In its *structural composition* (Governing Council as a tool to promote participatory federation); and finally,
4. In its *Functions* (co-operative and competitive federalism, best friend of states at the Centre, decentralised planning, harmonisation, conflict resolution, internal consultancy, capacity building, monitoring and evaluation are effective in improving governance).

It means the very idea of NITI Aayog is very sensitive to the need of good governance in the country and as the institution succeeds in playing its desired role as governance will improve. These are the reasons due to which we see the Government visualising it as the 'vehicle of good governance'.

Concluding Remarks

The idea of NITI Aayog does not look only innovative in its approach but quite contemporary too—imaginatively forging into the emerging idea and the need of including 'happiness' (as the World Happiness Report has suggested) in the policymaking framework.

It gives a call for inclusion of *ethos* and *cultural elements* of India in the development model, delicately linking the issue of growth and development to the 'behavioural' dimensions of the people of India (rightly in sync with the recent proposition of the World Bank in its *World Development Report 2015*). We find several such shining 'stars' in the newly set up body, which will be surely analysed and discussed again and again by analysts, experts, scholars. At the end, we can wisely conclude that the erstwhile PC was aimed at serving some purposes which was suitable for the old time, while the current times require us to carry on the legacy to a new level where we can build India, which can combine and integrate the energy and potential of all who belong to the nation being all open to the world (agreeing categorically to the idea of globalisation).

MAJOR DOCUMENTS OF THE NITI

Aimed at following the idea of *vision and scenario planning,* the NITI Aayog has been working on three documents namely, the Fifteen Year Vision, Seven Year Strategy and Three-Year Action Agenda—while the last two have been already published, work on the first one is still in progress. A brief introduction of these two documents have been given below:

Three-Year Action Agenda

Increasingly liberalised economy and the changed global economic dynamism needed new 'tools' and 'approaches' to promote development process (the five-year plans were not vibrant enough to these changed realities). An outcome of extensive consultations between the governments and various stakeholders (including economists, scientists, journalists, NGOs, industry associations and experts from education, health, culture and other areas), the Draft Three-Year Action Agenda (2017–18 to 2019–20) contains 7 parts and 24 chapters.[110] The action agenda is *actionable* as well as *aspirational* which touches several areas of importance such as:

1. It proposes reduction of the fiscal deficit to 3 per cent of the GDP and the revenue deficit to 0.9 per cent of the GDP by 2019–20.

110. **Draft Three-Year Action Agenda (2017-18 to 2019-20),** NITI Aayog, PMO, N. Delhi, 23rd April, 2017.

2. Doubling farmers' incomes by 2022 together with an emphasis on job creation in industry and services.
3. Generous floor space index (FPI), flexible conversion rules, etc. advised for urban areas.
4. Encouraging development outcomes in the North Eastern Region; Coastal Areas & Islands; North Himalayan states; and Desert and Drought prone states to take care of regional issues.
5. Emphasis on Transport and Digital Connectivity.
6. Under energy section it aims at consumer-friendly measures, reducing the cross-subsidy in the power sector and reforming coal sector by setting up a regulator.
7. Under science and technology emphasis is on developing PPP and creation of a National Science, Technology & Innovation Foundation (to identify national issues) and streamlining of the patent regime.
8. To promote *governance,* shrinking role of the government in undesirable areas.
9. Tackling tax evasion, expanding the tax base and simplifying the tax system and strengthening public procurement.
10. Undertaking judicial system reforms (use of ICT and cutting workload) and police reforms at state level to promote the cause of rule of law.
11. Shift from input-based to outcome-based (with arrangement of 'ranking') in education and skill development.
12. Focus on public health through significantly increasing government expenditure on it.
13. Building an inclusive society.
14. Adopting sustainable practices, tackling city air pollution, policy towards protecting trees sustainable use of water resources.

Seven-Year Strategy Framework

Titled as the *Strategy for New India @75,* it defines clear developmental objectives seeking to make development a 'Jan Andolan' (mass movement) aimed at making India a $3.0 trillion economy by 2022–23.[111] It is a detailed exposition across 41 crucial areas (covered in same number of chapters), that recognizes the progress already made, identifies binding constraints, and suggests the way forward for achieving the objectives. The 41 areas have been discussed into four sections—*Drivers, Infrastructure, Inclusion* and *Governance:*

Drivers focuses on the engines of economic performance with chapters on growth and employment, doubling of farmers' incomes; upgrading the science, technology and innovation ecosystem; and promoting sunrise sectors like fintech and tourism.

Infrastructure deals with the physical foundations of growth which are crucial to enhancing the competitiveness of Indian business as also ensuring the citizens' ease of living.

Inclusion deals with the urgent task of investing in the capabilities of all of India's citizens. The three themes in this section revolve around the dimensions of health, education and mainstreaming of traditionally marginalised sections of the population.

Governance delves deep into how the governance structures can be streamlined

111. **Strategy for New India @75,** NITI Aayog, PMO, N. Delhi, 19th December, 2018.

and processes optimised to achieve better developmental outcomes.

The recommendations of the NITI Aayog in the document are practical and detailed to facilitate time-bound implementation—by 2022, New India will provide a solid foundation for clean, inclusive, sustained and sustainable growth for the next three decades.[112]

NITI PERFORMS

Some experts and most of the political parties (in the opposition benches) were quite sceptical about the very idea of the NITI Aayog. Naturally enough, this scepticism was more due to abrupt disconnect being affected by the Government under which the economic think tank Planning Commission was abolished which was as old as the very existence of Independent India itself. The prevailing breach of trust and lack of cooperation between the Central and State governments were among the major reasons for the indifference shown to the NITI by the experts, the political analysts and the political parties. Though it will be too early to pass a judgement on its performance still *some major examples* can be cited in this regard:

1. Probably, the first major work by the think tank was its smooth deliberations with the states in restructuring the existing 66 Centrally Sponsored Schemes (CSSs) into 30 giving them more impact, visibility and flexibility.
2. The spirit of 'cooperative federalism' has been greatly strengthened through the NITI Aayog. It has been able to lessen the situation of breach of financial trust between the Centre and states. Implementation of the indirect tax reform GST has been greatly enabled by the NITI Aayog.[113]
3. To promote cleanliness and several other variables of human development and ease of doing business the think tank has launched several indices and started ranking the states—ultimately enhancing the spirit of competition among the governments.
4. It has been able to educate and make states aware about the importance of promoting economic reforms in the country.
5. It is through this platform that the states have been encouraged to go for the UDAY Scheme aimed at financial turnaround of the state electricity boards or the DISCOMs. This is an 'optional' scheme but due to increased awareness among the states regarding the importance and the need of the factor market reforms most of the states have opted for it.[114]
6. State governments positively taking part in the NITI Initiative to Yield Aspirational Targets and Actionable Means (Niyatam) under which their administrative, developmental and legal structure are aimed to be streamlined.
7. NITI Aayog's advice of 'land pooling' has been well-received by the states which has smoothened the issue of land acquisition for different purposes in the country.

112. Rajiv Kumar, Vice Chairman, NITI Aayog concludes in the last paragraph of the Preface to the document *Strategy for New India@75*.

113. The policy think tank functioned as 'a forum for fostering cooperative and competitive federalism', as per Arvind Subramanian, the Former Chief Economic Advisor to the Government of India (*Of Counsel— The Challenges of the Modi-Jaitley Economy*, Penguin Random House India, Gurgaon, India, 2018, p. 193).

114. The policy think tank functioned as 'a forum for fostering cooperative and competitive federalism', as per Arvind Subramanian, the Former Chief Economic Advisor to the Government of India (*Of Counsel— The Challenges of the Modi-Jaitley Economy*, Penguin Random House India, Gurgaon, India, 2018, p. 192).

8. By now the NITI Aayog has come up with several reports on a variety of sectors to enhance the process of development in the country taking states as an integral partner which range from sports to irrigation to education, health, etc.
9. Budgetary and extra-budgetary financial allocations to states from the Centre have also become quite smooth unlike past when states used to always have complain against the Planning Commission in this regard.
10. As NITI Aayog monitors and collects developmental data on real-time basis (unlike Planning Commission with almost 2 years of data lag) the element of accountability has improved which has enhanced the quality of governance.

This way, we find NITI emerging into a better think tank than the erstwhile Planning Commission in fostering the spirit of federal cooperation. Besides, in the process of transforming the development agenda of India, it has introduced new tools in this regard based on highly objective methods of monitoring and evaluation.

BEYOND THE PANDEMIC

The COVID-19 pandemic has been rightly called 'once in a century global crisis' by the ***Economic Survey 2020-21*** much in agreement with the international economic organisations— economic damages of which are still being counted across the world. Meanwhile, India looks going beyond the pandemic in a quite imaginative way. To convert the pandemic into an opportunity the Government of India gave call for a 'Self-reliance Campaign' (i.e., the ***Atmonirbhar Bharat Abhiyan***) by early 2020-21. The campaign which is still in the process of evolution includes a diverse range of policy steps put forward in the form of incentives (Production-Linked Incentives for industries), structural reforms (from labour laws to agricultural marketing to PSUs and banking sectors) aimed at making India a US$ 5 trillion economy and a global economic powerhouse by 2024-25.

India's push for self-reliance has been seen by experts and government documents in the following[115] ways:

- Checking India's 'increasing' dependency on the global value chain (in the backdrop of possible future disruptions similar to the COVID-19 pandemic).
- India's urge to check its rising 'trade deficit' with China besides increasing data and privacy vulnerabilities.
- 'Reimagining' the Make in India scheme aimed at 'Assemble in India' and boosting labour-intensive manufacturing sector.
- Developing a 'Pan-India supply chain' which can be integrated to the global value chain to boost exports.
- A changed stance in 'economic diplomacy' aimed at redefining India's place in the emerging global economic order.
- India's version of 'protectionism' with a blend of its strong support for globalisation and multilateralism.
- Emphasis on import-substitution and promoting decentralised industrial expansion (districts to be the unit of focus, in line with the advice of the *Economic Survey 2019-20*).
- Promoting 'circular economy' (a proposal of the NITI Aayog) with an eye on India's commitments towards

115. Based on the comments from an array of national and international *experts* besides the implicit and explicit undertones of the *NITI Aayog* and *Economic Survey 2020-21*, vol. 1, Ministry of Finance, GoI, N. Delhi.

checking climate change. [for details on Circular Economy see *Chapter 21*].

With the help of multiple policy actions, evolving in sync with the global economy, the Government has pledged to transform the economy from ***command and control*** to ***plug and play***— aimed at enabling the businesses and industries to develop and expand in the country.

We can see visible overtones of *pro-corporate* policy stance of the Government today but at the same time deeply rooted in *pro-poor* results in a **quite effective, methodical and transparent way—much better than any time seen in the past.** [116]

116. Based on the *Economic Survey 2020-21,* vol. 1, Ministry of Finance, GoI, N. Delhi (which resonates in the volumes of other *Economic Surveys* and the *Union Budgets* right after 2014-15).

CHAPTER 6

ECONOMIC REFORMS

*An important feature of India's reform programme, when compared with reforms underway in many other countries, is that it has emphasised gradualism and evolutionary transition rather than rapid restructuring or 'shock therapy'. This gradualism has often been the subiect of unfavourable comment by the more impatient advocates of reform, both inside and outside the country.**

In this Chapter...

INTRODUCTION

The economic reforms initiated in 1991 is now into the 30th year. In this period there was hardly a day that some news, news analysis, write-up or article did not appear in the newspapers regarding the reform process. Several highly acclaimed books have been authored on India's economic reforms by some of the best experts of economics from India and abroad. Still students, especially coming from non-economics background, are generally at a loss on the 'pros' and 'cons' of the reform process.

ECONOMIC REFORMS

Popularly, economic reforms denote the process in which a government prescribes declining role for the state and expanding role for the private sector in an economy. So let's unravel the reform process based on the author's classroom interactions with students. It is safer to see economic reform as a policy shift in an economy from one to another or ***'alternative development strategies'***. Economists attribute the differences in the performance of economies to the differences in the 'strategies' they follow. The different strategies of development

* ***Montek S. Ahluwatia Addressing at the inaugural session of the Seminar on 'India's Economic Reforms', Merton College, Oxford University, London, June, 1993.***

evolved through a long period of trial and error by different countries under the influence of different sets of ideologies. But the process has been like an educational trip. To understand the term 'economic reform' and more so to clarify the confusion concerning it in the Indian context, we must see the different 'alternative development strategies' which evolved through time. A brief description is given below:

1. **Planning Model:** Till the rise of the Soviet Union, the prevalent development strategy in the Euro-American countries was the capitalist system of economy, which promoted the principles of laissez-faire and dominant role for private capital in the economy. Once the Soviet Union went for the planning model (later the East European countries and finally China in 1949) most of the developing countries after their independence were influenced by socialism and the governments there took a central role in planned development. As these economies were dominated by foreign colonisers, they worried that opening the economy to foreign investment would lead to a new form of domination, the domination by large multinationals. That is why most of these countries went for 'protectionist' economic policy with ***import substitution*** as one method, side by side. But by the 1970s, the world was having convincing proofs that the socialist as well as the planned economies[1] were inclined to follow their kind of development strategies—either because they had very slow and lower growth rates or were stagnating. The experiences of these economies gave rise to a new ideology which became popular as the *'Washington Consensus'*.

2. **Washington Consensus:** By the early 1980s, a new development strategy emerged. Though it was not new, it was like the old idea getting vindicated after failure of a comparatively newer idea. After the world recognised the limits of a state-dominated economy, arguments in favour of the market, i.e., the private sector, was promoted emphatically. Many countries shifted their economic policy just to the other extreme arguing for a minimal role of the government in the economy. Governments of the socialist or the planned economies were urged/suggested to privatise and liberalise, to sell off state-owned companies and eliminate government interventions in the economy. These governments were also suggested to take measures which could boost the aggregate demand in the economy (*i.e., macroeconomic stability meosures*). The broad outlines of such a development strategy were regarded as being inspired by the *Washington Consensus.*[2]

This consensus is broadly termed as the popular meaning of the 'economic reform' followed by almost all the socialist, communist and planned developing economies during the 1980s in one form or the other[3]—the term economic reform got currency around the world during this period. The term was usually seen as a corollary for promoting 'naked capitalism', openness in the economy and an open attitude towards foreign investments, etc. The governments

1. There were many developing non-socialist countries which also accepted the economic planning as their development strategy (France should not be counted among them as it was a developed economy by then). These countries were following the 'mixed economy' model, but their form was closer to the command economies, i.e., the state economy or the socialist economy.

2. As the strategy was advocated by the IMF, the WB and the US Treasury (i.e., US Ministry of Finance) all located in Washington, it properly came to be known as Washington Consensus.

3. Without changing the broad contours of economic policy, the Government in India had also come under the influence of this consensus, followed a great many ***liberal*** policies (during Rajiv Gandhi's regime) in the 1980s.

of the developing economies were criticised by the political parties in the opposition and the critiques for being soft to the dictates of the IMF and the WB, and becoming a party to promote 'neo-imperialism'.

But these policies, in many cases proved little better than the previous policies in promoting economic growth over an extended period of time. But somehow a mood in favour of the market economy had gained ground. The United Kingdom under Mrs. Thatcher had gone for politically most vocal privatisation moves without any political debates (the only such example of privatisation moves among the democracies, till date).[4] It should be noted here that after the Great Depression of 1929 a 'strong state intervention' was suggested (by J. M. Keynes) and such a policy did really help the Euro-American countries to mitigate the crisis. The favour for the state intervention in the economy was being reversed by the Washington Consensus. But soon this consensus was also to be replaced by another development strategy. More detailed discussion on the Washington Consensus is given in *Chapter 1*.

3. **Mixed Economy:** By the mid-1990s, it had become increasingly clear that neither of the extremes—the Washington Consensus or the state-led planned economy—were the ultimate strategies of development.[5] The success achieved by the East Asian economies even if we take into account their setback due to the financial crisis of 1997–98, stands out in marked contrast to the experiences of other economies of the time who were following the Washington Consensus.[6] The East Asian economies have not only been able to propel higher growth rates, but they have been greatly successful in reducing poverty, promoting education and healthcare, etc.

The East Asian economies had promoted a development strategy, which had its most distinctive feature as the balance they were able to strike between the role of the state/government and the market/the private sector in their economies. This was really a new kind of mixed economy, which was never permanently inclined towards either state intervention or the free market, but always a balanced mix of the state and the market according to the requirement of the socio-economic situation of the economy. The East Asian countries had pursued market-oriented policies that encouraged development of the private sector—augmenting and governing the market, not replacing it.[7]

Technically speaking, shifting of economic policy of a country from one to the other above-given three 'alternative development strategies' is economic reform. But in the history of world economy, it was inclination of the economies towards the market economy, which have been referred as economic reforms. In the Indian case, economic reform has always been used in this sense. Here, one should note that when India started the programme of economic reforms in the early 1990s, the world view was in favour of privatisation, liberalisation, de-nationalisation, etc., as the main plank of economic reforms. But by the mid-1990s, not only the world view has polarised in favour of a mixed economy', but one another change was about to sweep the world economies, i.e., the favour for

4. ***Collins Dictionary of Economics***, Glasgow, 2006, pp. 417–18.
5. World Bank, ***The East Asian Miracle: Economic Growth and Public Policy.*** (Washington DC: Oxford University Press, 1993).

6. ***Ibid.***
7. As is concluded by Stiglitz and Walsh, p. 800, op. cit.

globalisation sponsored by the World Trade Organisation (WTO). Now, the developing economies (mixed economies with planning as their development strategy) as well as the transition economies (Russia and the whole Eastern Europe, and China)—who were already promoting the market-oriented reform process were faced with a dilemma. To prosper and compete in the globalising environment while they needed immediate liberation from their state-dominated mode of economies at one hand, they also needed to strike a balance between the state and the market on the other. Each one of them tried to strike the balance in their own way with mixed results. In India, the governments have not been able to convince the masses that the economy needs reforms and the attempted reforms will benefit all. In every election since the reforms of 1991, the voters have not supported a pro-reform government. Though the process of economic reforms started in India with the slogan ***'reforms with human face'***—the slogan has utterly failed to garner the empathy of the masses. We may hope that in coming times the masses will start connecting with the reforms and will be able to get the message clear, i.e., reforms are to benefit all.

ECONOMIC REFORMS IN INDIA

On July 23, 1991, India launched a process of economic reforms in response to a fiscal and balance-of-payment (BoP) crisis. The reforms were historic and were going to change the very face and the nature of the economy in the coming times. The reforms and the related programmes are still going on with changing emphasis and dimensions, but they are criticised as being slow ever since the UPA Government came to power in May 2004. Back in the mid-1980s, the government had taken its first steps to economic reforms. While the reforms of the 1980s witnessed rather limited deregulation and 'partial liberalisation of only a few aspects of the existing control regime, the reforms started in early 1990s in the fields of industries, trade, investment and later to include agriculture, were much 'wider and deeper'.[8] Though liberal policies were announced by the governments during the reforms of the 1980s itself, with the slogan of 'economic reforms', it was only launched with full conviction in the early 1990s. But the reforms of the 1980s, which were under the influence of the famous ***'Washington Consensus'*** ideology had a crippling impact on the economy. The whole Seventh Plan (1985–90) promoted further relaxation of market regulations with heavy external borrowings to increase exports (as the thrust of the policy reform). Though the thrust increased the growth rate led by higher industrial growth (riding on costly imports supported by foreign borrowings, which the industries would not be able to pay back and service), it also led to a substantial increase in foreign indebtedness that played a major role in the BoP crisis of 1991.[9] The crisis was immediated by the First Gulf War (1991) which had two-pronged negative impact on the Indian foreign exchange (forex) reserves. First, the war led the oil prices to go upward forcing India to use its forex reserves in comparatively shorter period and second, the private remittances from Indians working in the Gulf region fell down fast (due to their emergency evacuation)—both the crises were induced by a single cause, i.e., the Gulf War. But the balance of payments crisis also reflected deeper problems of rising foreign debt, a

8. Jeffrey D. Sachs, Ashutosh Varshney and Nirupan Bajpai, ***India in the Era of Economic Reforms,*** (New Delhi: Oxford University Press, 199), p. 1.

9. J. Barkley Rosser, Jr. and Marina V. Rosser, ***Comparative Economics in a Transforming World Economy,*** 2nd Edition (New Delhi: Prentice Hall of India, 2005), p. 469.

fiscal deficit of over 8 per cent of the GDP and a hyper-inflation (over 13 per cent) situation.[10]

The minority government of the time had taken a highly bold and controversial step in the form of economic reforms criticised throughout the 1990s by one and all—right from the opposition in the Parliament, to the communist parties, to the industrial houses, the business houses, media, experts and by the masses also. By now as the benefits of the reforms have accrued to many, the criticism has somewhat calmed down, but still the reform process is considered as 'anti-poor' and 'pro-rich' by at least the masses—the people who decide the political mandate for the country to rule. At least one belief is followed by everybody, i.e., the benefits of reforms are not tickling to the masses (the ***'aam aadami'***) with the desirable pace.[11] The need of the hour is to go for 'distributive growth', though the reform has led the economy to a higher growth path.

Obligatory Reform

Similar reform process started by some other economies since the 1980s were voluntary decisions of the concerned countries. But in the case of India it was an involuntary decision taken by the government of the time in the wake of the BoP crisis. Under the Extended Fund Facility (EFF) programme of the IMF, countries get external currency support from the fund to mitigate their BoP crisis, but such supports have some obligatory conditionalities put on the economy to be fulfilled. There are no set rules of such conditions already available with the IMF, though they are devised and prescribed to the BoP-crisis-ridden economy at the time of need. A point needs to be referred here is that the conditionalities put upon India were of the nature which required all the economic measures to be formulated by them. It means that the reforms India carried or is carrying out at present were neither formulated by India nor mandated by the public. Yes, there was a large section of experts inside and outside the government who believed in similar economic measures to bring the economy on the right path. Some of them were arguing the same since the 1970s, while many other experts believed in them since the mid-1980s.[12] But why after all was the Rao-Manmohan Government credited to start the reform process in India? It is because they thought it suitable to follow and make it politically possible in India. Imagine, a government proposing to sell the state-owned companies to the private sector or closing them down in a country which has been convinced that these companies will be the 'temples of modern India'. The masses were convinced that the government has bowed down to the diktats of the IMF, the imperialist forces, the multinationals, etc. Even today such feelings are there in several quarters of the economy. The politics of economic reforms damaged India more than the reform has benefitted the country. It would not be an exaggeration if we conclude that economic reforms had no political consensus. Political parties in India are divided on the issue of reforms—the parties together with the masses lack the level of political maturity required for the success of the reform programme. It is right, democratic maturity comes to a multi-party political system, but it takes time. It takes even more time where masses are unaware and ignorant. The emotional issues of religion, caste, etc., play their own roles in such situations.

10. Vijay Joshi and I. M. D. Little, ***India's Economic Reforms, 1991–2001***, (Oxford: Clarendon Press, 1996), p. 17.

11. The feeling is even shared by the government of the present time. One may refer to the similar open acceptance by India's Minister of Commerce at the Davos Summit of the World Economic Forum (2007). In an interview to the ***CNN-IBN*** programme, the Cabinet Minister for Panchayat Raj, and the North East (Mani Shankar Aiyar) on 20 May 2007 opined that benefits of higher growth are going to the selected 'classes' and not to the 'masses'.

12. The Seventh and the Eight Plans have many such suggestions to give to the governments of the time, especially the latter Plan called for the same nature of the reform process, very clearly.

The IMF conditions put forth for India were as under:

1. Devaluation of the rupee by 22 per cent (which was effected in two phases and the Indian rupee fell down from ₹21 to ₹27 per US Dollar).
2. Drastic reduction in the peak import tariff from the prevailing level of 130 per cent to 30 per cent (India completed it by 2000–01 itself and now it is voluntarily cut to the level of 15 per cent).
3. Excise duties (i.e., CENVAT now) to be hiked by 20 per cent to neutralise the revenue short falls due to the custom cut (a major tax reform programme was launched to streamline, simplify and modernise the Indian tax structure which is still going on).
4. All government expenditure to be cut down by 10 per cent, annually (i.e., cutting the cost of running the government and denotes interests, pays, pension PF and subsidies. A pressure on the government to consolidate the fiscal deficit and go for fiscal prudence).

Though India was able to pay back its IMF dues in time, the structural reform of the economy was launched to fulfil the above-given conditions of the IMF. The ultimate goal of the IMF was to help India bring about equilibrium in its BoP situation in the short-term and go for macroeconomic and structural adjustments so that in future the economy faces no such crisis.

There was enough scope for the critics to criticise India's economic reforms as prescribed and dictated by the IMF. The process of economic reforms in India had to face severe criticism from almost every quarter of the economy concerned, although the reforms were aimed to boost growth and deliver competitiveness to the economy.[13]

Reform Measures

The economic reform programme, that India launched, consisted of ***two*** categories of measures:

1. **Macroeconomic Stabilisation Measures:** It includes all those economic policies which intend to boost the aggregate ***demand*** in the economy—be it domestic or external. For the enhanced domestic demand, the focus has to be on increasing the purchasing power of the masses, which entails an emphasis on the creation of gainful and quality employment opportunities.
2. **Structural Reform Measures:** It includes all the policy reforms which have been initiated by the government to boost the aggregate supply of goods and services in the economy. It naturally entails unshackling the economy so that it may search for its own potential of enhanced productivity. For the purchasing capacity of the people to be increased, the economy needs increased income, which comes from increased levels of activities. Income so increased is later distributed among the people whose purchasing power has to be increased—this will take place by properly initiating a suitable set of macroeconomic policies. For the income to get distributed among the target population, it takes time, but the efforts a government initiates to increase the supply, i.e., increasing production becomes visible soon. As production is done by the producers (i.e., the capitalists), *prima facie* the structural

13. Ministry of Finance, ***Economic Survey 1991–92: Part II Sectoral Developments & New Industrial Policy, 1991***, GoI, New Delhi.

reform measures look 'pro-rich' and 'pro-industrialist' or 'pro-capitalist', known with different names. Ignorant people easily get swayed by the logic that everything which is 'pro-rich' has to be necessarily 'anti-poor'. But it was not the case with the process of economic reforms. Unless the economy is able to achieve higher growth (i.e., income) wherefrom the purchasing power of the masses will be enhanced? And increased income takes time to reach everybody. If the economy lacks political stability, this process takes even more time due to short-term goals set by the unstable and frequently changing governments—the exact case is with India.

The LPG

The process of reforms in India has to be completed via three other processes namely, liberalisation, privatisation and globalisation, known popularly by their short-form, the LPG. These three processes specify the characteristics of the reform process India initiated. Precisely seen, liberalisation shows the ***direction*** of reform, privatisation shows the ***path*** of reform and globalisation shows the ultimate ***goal*** of the reform. However, it would be useful to see the real meanings of these terms and the exact sense in which they are being used worldwide and particularly in India.

Liberalisation

The term liberalisation has its origin in the political ideology 'liberalism', which took its form by early nineteenth century (it developed basically in the previous three centuries). The term is sometimes portrayed as a ***meta-ideology*** capable of embracing a broad range of rival values and beliefs. The ideology was the product of the breakdown of feudalism and the growth of a ***market*** or ***capitalist*** society[14] in its place, which became popular in economics via the writings of Adam Smith (its founding father in the USA) and got identified as a principle of ***laissez-faire.***[15]

The term liberalisation has the same connotation in economics as its root word liberalism. Pro-market or pro-capitalistic inclination in the economic policies of an economy is the process of liberalisation. We see it taking place in the whole Euro-America in the 1970s and particularly in the 1980s.[16] The most suitable example of this process could be China of the mid-1980s when it announced its ***'open door policy'.*** Though China lacks (even today) some trademark traits of liberalism, as for example, individualism, liberty, democratic system, etc., still China was called a liberalising economy.

We may take an example from the history of the world economy—putting the USA of the early 20th century and the communist China on the two poles of the scale—thus representing the best historical example of the liberal economy and China being the best example of the 'illiberal' economy. With the USA on the south pole and China on the north any policy movement towards 'the south' is 'liberalisation'. The movement from the south to the north will be known as 'illiberalisation'.

It means that the process of decreasing traits of a state economy and increasing traits of a market economy is liberalisation. Similarly, the opposite will be the process of illiberalisation. Technically speaking, both the processes will be known as the processes of economic reforms, since 'reform' as a term does not say anything about the 'direction'.

---

14. Andrew Heywood, ***Politics***, (New York: Palgrave, 2002), p. 43.
15. Robert Nisbet, ***Prejudices: A Philosophical Dictionary***, (Massachusetts: Harvard University Press, 1982), p. 211.
16. **'Economics: Making Sense of the Modern Economy'** ***The Economist***, London, 1999, pp. 225–26.

All the economic reforms in the world have been from the 'north to the south'. Similar is the case with the process of liberalisation.

It means, in the Indian case the term liberalisation is used to show the direction of the economic reforms—with decreasing influence of the state or the planned or the command economy and increasing influence of free market or the capitalistic economy. It is a move towards capitalism. India is attempting to strike its own balance of the 'state-market mix'. It means, even if the economic reforms have the direction towards market economy it can never be branded a blind-run to capitalism. Since the economy was more like the state economy in the former years, it has to go for a greater degree of mix of the market. But in the long run, liberalism curtails the powers of the Parliament.[17]

Privatisation

The decades of the 1980s and 1990s witnessed a 'rolling back' of the state by the governments, especially in the USA and UK under the inspiration of the New Right priorities and beliefs.[18] The policies through which the 'roll back' of the state was done included deregulation, privatisation and introduction of market reforms in public services. Privatisation at that time was used as a process under which the state assets were transferred to the private sector.[19] The root of the term privatisation goes to this period which got more and more currency around the world once the East European nations and later the developing democratic nations went for it. But during the period several connotations and meanings of the term 'privatisation' have developed. We may see them as follows:

1. Privatisation in its purest sense and lexically means de-nationalisation,[20] i.e., transfer of the state ownership of the assets to the private sector to the tune of 100 per cent. Such bold moves took place only once anywhere in the world without any political fallouts—in the early 1980s of the UK under the Thatcher regime. This route of privatisation has been avoided by almost all democratic systems. In the mid-1990s some West European nations—Italy, Spain and France—besides the USA went for such moves.[21] India never ventured into any such privatisation move.
2. The sense in which privatisation has been used is the process of disinvestment all over the world. This process includes selling of the shares of the state-owned enterprises to the private sector. Disinvestment is de-nationalisation of less than 100 per cent ownership transfer from the state to the private sector. If an asset has been sold out by the government to the tune of only 49 per cent the ownership remains with the state though it is considered privatisation. If the sale of shares of the state-owned assets has been to the tune of 51 per cent, the ownership is really transferred to the private sector even then it is termed as privatisation.
3. The third and the last sense in which the term privatisation has been used around the world, is very wide. Basically, all the economic policies which directly or indirectly seem to promote the expansion of the private sector or the market (economy) have been termed by experts and the governments as the process of privatisation. We may cite few examples from India—de-licencing and de-reservation of the industries, even cuts in the

17. J.K. Galbraith, ***A History of Economics***, (London: Penguin Books,), p. 123, 1780.
18. Andrew Heywood, ***Politics***, p. 100.
19. Stiglitz and Walsh, ***Economics***, pp. 802–3.
20. Collins, Oxford, Penguin, ***Dictionary of Economics***, relevant pages.
21. Samuelson and Nordhaus, ***Economics***, p. 199.

subsidies, permission to foreign investment, etc.[22]

Here we may connect liberalisation to privatisation in India. Liberalisation shows the direction of economic reforms in India, i.e., inclination towards the dominance of market. But how will it be achieved? Basically, privatisation will be ***the path*** to reform. It means, everything which includes promotion of the 'market' will be the path of the reform process in India.

Globalisation

The process of globalisation has always been used in economic terms though it has always taken the political and cultural dimensions. Once economic changes occur it has several socio-political manifestations.[23] Globalisation is generally termed as 'an increase in economic integration among nations'.[24] Even before several nation-states were not even born, the countries around the world had gone for globalisation, i.e., 'a closer integration of their economies'.[25] This globalisation lasted from 1800 to almost 1930, interrupted by the Great Depression and the two Wars which led to retrenchment and several trade barriers were erected since early 1930s.[26]

The concept was popularised by the Organisation of Economic Cooperation and Development (OECD) in the mid-1980s again after the Wars. In its earlier deliberalisation, the organisation had defined globalisation in a very narrow and business-like sense—***'any cross-border investment by an OECD company outside its country of origin for its benefit is globalisation'.*** After this summit of the OECD, proposals for replacing the GATT by the WTO were pushed by the developed economies of the world, better known as the starting of the Uruguay Round of GATT deliberations which ends in Marrakesh (1994) with the birth of WTO. In the meantime, the OECD had defined globalisation officially, (1995) too— 'a shift from a world of distinct national economies to a global economy in which production is internationalised and financial capital flows freely and instantly between countries.'[27]

The official meaning of globalisation for the WTO is movement of the economies of the world towards ***'unrestricted cross border movements of goods and services, capital and the labour force'.*** It simply means that the economies who are signatories to the process of globalisation (i.e., signatories to the WTO) for them there will be nothing like foreign or indigenous goods and services, capital and labour. The world becoming a flat and level-playing field emerging in the due process of time.[28]

For many political scientists (which is today a very dominant force in the world), globalisation is the emergence of a situation when our lives are increasingly shaped by the events that occur at a great distance from us about which the decisions are not taken by our conscious self. One section of experts believe that globalisation subordinates the state, while the other section argues that the local, national and global events constantly interact under it without any subordination of one by the other. Rather, globalisation highlights the deepening as well as broadening of the political process in this sense.[29]

India became one of the founding members of the WTO and was obliged to promote the process of globalisation, though its economic reforms

22. New Industrial Policy, 1991 & several documents of GoI since then.
23. Talcott Parsons, ***The Structure of Social Action***, (New York: McGraw Hill, 1937).
24. Samuelson and Nordhaus, ***Economics***, p. 32.
25. Stiglitz and Walsh, ***Economics***, p. 804.
26. Thomas L. Friedman, ***The World is Flat***, (London: Penguin Books, 2006), 9. Stiglitz & Walsh, ***Economics***, p. 804.
27. As quoted in Andrew Heywood, ***Politics***, p. 139.
28. As Friedman shows in his best-seller, ***The World is Flat***, p. 9.
29. As put by the ***Oxford's Dictionary of Politics***, N. Delhi, 24 pp. 222–25; Andrew Heywood, ***Politics***, p.138.

started with no such obligations. It is a different thing that India started the process of globalisation right after the reforms in 1991.[30]

Now we may connect the three simultaneous processes—the LPG with which India launched its reform programme. The process of liberalisation shows movement of the economy towards the market economy, privatisation is the path/route through which it will travel to realise the ultimate 'goal', i.e., globalisation.

It should be noted here that the Indian idea of globalisation is deeply and frequently inclined towards the concept of welfare state, which keeps coming in the day to day public policy as an emphatic reference. The world, including the IMF, the WB and the developed nations have now increasingly shown their recognition to the fact that the official goal of globalisation of the world economies would not take place without giving the poor of the world a better standard of living. Even if globalisation is complete without including almost one-fifth of the world population, i.e. the poor, will it be called development of the world?

Blend of Protectionism Amidst rising protectionism in the world India also seems fine-tuning its stand on globalisation which has become more visible in the wake of the ***COVID-19*** pandemic. In May 2020, the Government gave a very emphatic call for self-reliance by launching the ***Atmanirbhar Baharat Abhiyan*** (Self-Reliant India Campaign) which aims to boost the MSMEs, agriculture, pan-India supply chain, import-substitution, discouraging imports, boosting exports through expansion of labour-intensive manufacturing industries besides unshackling the economic potential through effective and speedier reforms – while officially remaining committed to multilateralism (i.e., globalisation).

GENERATIONS OF ECONOMIC REFORMS

Though there were no such announcements or proposals while India launched its reforms in 1991, in the coming times, many 'generations' of reforms were announced by the governments.[31] A total of ***three*** generations of reforms have been announced till date, while experts have gone to suggest the ***fourth*** generation, too. We may substantiate the components of the various generations of reforms to properly understand the very characteristics and nature of the reform process in India.

First Generation Reforms (1991-2000)[32]

It was in the year 2000–01 that the government, for the first time, announced the need for the Second Generation of economic reforms and it was launched in the same year. The ones which had been initiated by then (i.e., from 1991 to 2000) were called by the government as the reforms of the First Generation. The broad coordinates of the First Generation of reforms may be seen as under:

1. **Promotion to Private Sector:** This included various important and liberalising policy decisions, i.e., 'de-reservation' and 'de-licencing' of the industries, abolition of the MRTP limit, abolition of the compulsion of the phased-production and conversion of

30. It should be noted here that the whole Euro-America has already started promoting globalisation by the mid-1980s as the WTO deliberations at Uruguay started. The formation of the WTO only gave globalisation an official mandate in 1995, once it started its functions. It means, for India, globalisation was a reality by 1991 itself—one has to move as the dominant forces move.

31. It should be noted here that many economists regard the economic reforms of the mid-1980s as the First Generation reforms. However, the governments of the time have not said anything like that. It was only in the year 2000–01 that India officially talks about the generations of reform for the first time.

32. Based on the ***New Industrial Policy, 1991*** & several ***Economic Surveys*** as well as many announcements by the governments.

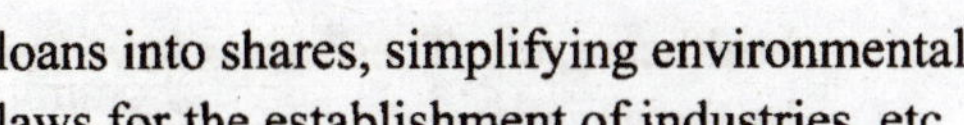

loans into shares, simplifying environmental laws for the establishment of industries, etc.

2. **Public Sector Reforms:** The steps taken to make the public sector undertakings profitable and efficient, their disinvestment (*token*), their corporatisation, etc., were the major parts of it.

3. **External Sector Reforms:** They consisted of policies like, abolishing quantitative restrictions on import, switching to the floating exchange rate, full current account convertibility, reforms in the capital account, permission to foreign investment (direct as well as indirect), promulgation of a liberal Foreign Exchange Management Act (the FEMA replacing the FERA), etc.

4. **Financial Sector Reforms:** Several reform initiatives were taken up in areas such as banking, capital market, insurance, mutual funds, etc.

5. **Tax Reforms:** This consisted of all the policy initiatives directed towards simplifying, broadbasing, modernising, checking evasion, etc.

A major re-direction was ensued by this generation of reforms in the economy—the 'command' type of the economy moved strongly towards a market-driven economy, private sector (domestic as well as foreign) to have greater participation in the future.

Second Generation Reforms (2000- 01 onwards)[33]

The government launched the second generation of reforms in 2000–01. Basically, the reforms India launched in the early 1990s were not taking place as desired and a need for another set of reforms was felt by the government, which were initiated with the title of the Second Generation of economic reforms. These reforms were not only deeper and delicate, but required a higher political will power from the governments. The major components of the reform are as given below:

1. **Factor Market Reforms:** Considered as the 'backbone' for the success of the reform process in India, it consists of dismantling of the Administered Price Mechanism (APM). There were many products in the economy whose prices were fixed/regulated by the government, viz., petroleum, sugar, fertilizers, drugs, etc. Though a major section of the products under the APM were produced by the private sector, they were not sold on market principles which hindered the profitability of the manufacturers as well as the sellers and ultimately the expansion of the concerned industries leading to a demand-supply gap. Under market reforms these products were to be brought into the market fold.

   In the petroleum segment now only kerosene oil and LPG remained under the APM, while petrol, diesel (by March 2014), lubricants have been phased out. Similarly, the income tax paying families don't get sugar from the TPS on subsidies; only urea, among the fertilizers, remain under APM, while many drugs have also been phased out of the mechanism. Opening the petroleum sector for private investment, cutting down the burden of levy on sugar (levy obligation was abolished by mid-2013), etc., are now giving dividends to the economy. But we cannot say that the Factor Market Reforms (FMRs) are complete in India. It is still going on. Cutting down subsidies on essential

[33] Based on the Ministry of Finance, ***Economic Survey 2000–01 (New Delhi: Government of India, 2001);*** and ***Union Budget, 2001–02*** especially besides other official announcements by the GoI in the coming years.

goods is a socio-political question in India. Till market-based purchasing power is not delivered to all the consumers, it would not be possible to complete the FMRs.

2. **Public Sector Reforms:** The second generation of reforms in the public sector especially emphasises on areas like greater functional autonomy, freer leverage to the capital market, international tie-ups and greenfield ventures, disinvestment[34] (*strategic*), etc.
3. **Reforms in Government and Public Institutions:** This involves all those moves which really go to convert the role of the government from the 'controller' to the 'facilitator' or the administrative reform, as it may be called.
4. **Legal Sector Reforms:** Though reforms in the legal sector were started in the first generation itself, now it was to be deepened and newer areas were to be included, such as, abolishing outdated and contradictory laws, reforms in the Indian Penal Code (IPC) and Code of Criminal Procedure (CrPC), Labour Laws, Company Laws and enacting suitable legal provisions for new areas like Cyber Law, etc.
5. **Reforms in Critical Areas:** The second generation reforms also commit to suitable reforms in the infrastructure sector (i.e., power, roads, especially as the telecom sector has been encouraging), agriculture, agricultural extension, education and healthcare, etc. These areas have been called by the government as ***'critical areas'.***[35]

These reforms have two segments. The first segment is similar to the FMRs, while the second segment provides a broader dimension to the reforms, viz., corporate farming, research and development in the agriculture sector (which was till now basically taken care of by the government and needs active participation of the private sector), irrigation, inclusive education and healthcare.

Other than the above-given focus of this generation of reforms, some other important areas were also emphasised:

1. **State's Role in the Reform:** For the first time, an important role to the state was designed, in the process of economic reforms. All new steps of the reforms were now to be started by the state with the centre playing a supportive role.
2. **Fiscal Consolidation:** The area of fiscal consolidation, though it was a major co-ordinate of reform in India since 1991 itself, gets a constitutional commitment and responsibility. The Fiscal Responsibility and Budget Management (FRBM) Act is passed by the Centre and the Fiscal Responsibility Act (FRA) is followed by the states as an era of new commitments to the fiscal prudence starts in the country.
3. **Greater Tax Devolution to the States:** Though there was such a political tendency[36] by the mid-1990s itself, after the second generation reforms

34. Basically 'disinvestment' started in India in its 'token' form, which is selling of government's minority shares in PSUs. While in the Second Generation, the government went for 'strategic' kind of disinvestment, which basically involved the transfer of ownership of the PSUs from the state to the private sector—MFI2, BALCO, etc., being the firsts of such disinvestments. Once the UPA Government came to power in May 2004, the latter form of disinvestment was put on hold. We will discuss it in detail in the chapter on ***Indian Industry.***

35. Ministry of Finance, ***Economic Survey 2000–01.***

36. We see it, especially, when the Coalition Government (i.e., the UF Government) goes to amend the constitution so that the Alternative Method of Devolution (AMD) of the tax suggested by the Tenth Finance Commission becomes a law before the recommendations of the Eleventh Finance Commission. It should be noted that the AMD has increased the gross tax devolution to the states by a hefty 5 per cent.

started, we see a visible change in the central policies favouring greater fiscal leverage to the states. Even the process of tax reforms takes the same dimension. Similarly, the Finance Commissions as well as the Planning Commission start taking greater fiscal care of the states. And for the first time the states had a net revenue surplus collections in the fiscal 2007–08.[37]

4. **Focusing on the Social Sector:** The social sector (especially healthcare and education) gets increased attention by the government with manifold increases, in the budgetary allocation, as well as show of a greater compliance to the performance of the development programmes.

We see mixed results of the second generation reforms though the reforms still continue.

Third Generation Reforms

Announcement of the third generation of reforms were made on the margins of the launching of the Tenth Plan (2002–07). This generation of reforms commits to the cause of a fully functional Panchayati Raj Institution (PRIs), so that the benefits of economic reforms, in general, can reach to the grassroots.

Though the constitutional arrangements for a decentralised developmental process was already effected in the early 1990s, it was in the early 2000s that the government gets convinced of the need of 'inclusive growth and development'. Till the masses are not involved in the process of development, the development will lack the 'inclusion' factor, it was concluded by the government of the time. The Eleventh Plan goes on to ratify the same sentiments (though the political combination at the centre has changed) and views regarding the need for the third generation of reforms in India.

Fourth Generation Reforms

This is not an official 'generation' of reform in India. Basically, in early 2002, some experts coined this generation of reforms which entail a fully 'information technology-enabled' India. They hypothesised a 'two-way' connection between the economic reforms and the information technology (IT), with each one reinforcing the other.

THE REFORM APPROACH

The process of economic reforms commenced in the world by mid-1980s (in Western Europe and Northern America). Once the idea of the Washington Consensus gained ground, we find similar reforms being followed by different countries cutting across continents. Over the time, experts together with the IMF/WB, started classifying such countries into two categories, viz., one which went for the 'Gradualist Approach' and the other which went for the 'Stop-and-Go Approach'.

India's reform process which commenced in 1991 has been termed by experts as gradualist (also called incremental)[38] in nature with traits of occasional reversals, and without any big ideological U-turns—coalitions of various political parties at the Centre and different political parties ruling the states lacked a general sense of consensus on reforms. It reflects the compulsions

37 The Comptroller and Auditor General, *Provisional Report*, May 2007.

38 **Isher J. Ahluwalia**, *Industry* in Kaushik Basu & Annemie Maertens edited ***The New Oxford Companion to Economics in India***, Oxford University Press, N. Delhi, India, 2012, Vol. 2, pp. 371–375.

of India's highly pluralist and participative democratic policy-making process.[39] Though such an approach helped the country to avoid socio-political upheavals/instability, it did not allow the desired economic outcome which could have accrued from the reforms. The first generation of economic reforms could not bring the expected results due to lack of some other set of reforms for which India goes after almost over a decade—the second generation of economic reforms. Similarly, the economic benefits (whatever accrued) remained non-inclusive, in absence of an active public policy aimed at inclusion (commencing via the third generation of economic reforms). This created a kind of disillusionment about the prospects of reforms and failed the governments to muster enough public support in favour of reforms.

Unlike India, several other countries (such as Brazil, Argentina, South Africa, etc.) went for the stop-and-go kind of reforms. In such reforms, the governments first decide the sectors where reforms are needed—then they pin-point the prerequisites (which will create a conducive atmosphere for reforms to take place), and finally both set of the reforms are activated simultaneously. In their cases, economic results from reforms were on the expected lines. Though these nations took high risks on the socio-political front, in their case, in medium-term itself, the governments were able to mobilise enough public support in favour of reforms (which encouraged the governments to go for further reforms). Such reforms do not look possible in the case of India—this is why last few volumes of the Economic Survey (2015–16, 2016–17 and 2017–18) advised in favour of an incremental approach to reforms.

Presently, we see the Government of India pushing for *'transformational reforms'* (as the ***Union Budget 2017-18*** described it). Some of such reforms have been:

1. Inflation targeting and setting up the Monetary Policy Committee by amending the RBI Act, 1934;
2. Restarting of the 'strategic disinvestment' of the PSUs;
3. Demonetisation of the high denomination currency notes (aimed at checking corruption, black money, tax evasion, fake currency and terrorism);
4. Enactment of the new Benami Law (aimed at checking black money);
5. Bankruptcy Law (aimed at promoting the 'ease of doing business'); and
6. Enactment of the Aadhar Act (aimed at rationalising and weeding out corruption in the present subsidy regime); etc.

The transformational reforms are special in this sense that they are aimed at inducing *behavioural changes*[40] in the actions of the targeted group—by far claimed to be quite successful[41] in doing so. For example, almost 83 per cent cases of the debt default during 2016-2020 under the insolvency and bankruptcy code (IBC, 2016) got resolved before commencement of the insolvency process itself—on account of 'behavioural change' among the defaulting debtors.[42]

Though, overall scheme of reforms in India still remains incremental (i.e., gradual) rather the 'transformational reforms' are the examples of non-gradual (stop-and-go) brand of reforms.

39 **Montek S. Ahluwalia,** *Planning* in Kaushik Basu & Annemie Maertens edited ***The New Oxford Companion to Economics in India***, Oxford University Press, N. Delhi, India, 2012, Vol. 2, pp. 530–536.

40 ***Interim Budget 2019–20,*** Ministry of Finance, GoI, N. Delhi.

41 ***World Development Report-2015,*** World Bank, N. York, USA.

42 **Economic Survey 2020-21,** vol. 2, pp. 155-56, Ministry of Finance, GoI, N. Delhi.

Meanwhile, the Government had been advised to go for ***large-scale incremental reforms*** in the country.[43]

The Government was advised[44] to ***must*** use its strong mandate to go for *expeditious reforms* in the economy— we find a series of major structural reforms announced[45] during 2019-21 which were all 'non-gradual' in nature. Moving forward by late 2020-21 certain other long-pending reforms[46] were launched by the Government related to agriculture sector/market, labour law, MSMEs, start-ups, public sector banks (PSBs), etc. Recently, the Government announced to ***speed*** up the process of reforms[47] further by announcing to privatise two PSBs, bringing initial public offer of the LIC, privatising all non-core public sector enterprises, monetisation of public assets, etc.— under the self-reliance campaign (***Atmanirbhar Bharat Abhiyan***).

43. ***Economic Survey 2017–18, Vol. 1,*** Ministry of Finance, GoI, N. Delhi, p. 140.
44. **Economic Survey 2019-20,** Vol. 2, pp. 1-4, Ministry of Finance, GoI, N. Delhi.
45. **Economic Survey 2019-20,** Vol. 2, pp. 29-30, Ministry of Finance, GoI, N. Delhi. Expeditious reforms mean reforms done with *speed* and *efficiency*.
46. **Economic Survey 2020-21,** vol. 2, pp. 38-41, Ministry of Finance, GoI, N. Delhi.
47. **Union Budget 2021-22,** Ministry of Finance, GoI, N. Delhi.

CHAPTER 7

INFLATION AND BUSINESS CYCLE

*Fluctuations in the level of economic activity, alternating between periods of depression and boom, led by one prominent factor, i.e., the expectations of the future demand-intertwined with the inflation-has always been a fascinating topic for economists.**

In this Chapter...

SECTION-A

- Introduction
- Definition
- Why Does Inflation Occur?
- Types of Inflation
- Other Variants of Inflation
- Other Important Terms
- Inflation Targeting
- Monetary Policy Anchor: Headline or Core Inflation?
- GDP Deflator
- Base Effect
- Effects of Inflation
- Inflation in India
- Wholesale Price Index
- Consumer Price Index
- Trends in Inflation
- Producer Price Index
- Housing Price Index
- Service Price Index

SECTION-B

- Introduction
- Depression
- Recovery
- Boom
- Recession
- Growth Recession
- Double-Dip Recession
- Conclusion

* *See Joseph E. Stiglitz and Carl E. Walsh, Economics, 4th Edition (New York: W.W. Norton, 2005), 494-496; Collins internet-linked Dictionary of Economics, Glasgow, Scotland: Harper Collins, 2006), pp. 48-49.*

SECTION-A

INTRODUCTION

For a layman, inflation is just price rise. It becomes a matter of everyday discussion if the prices of daily or weekly items start rising. Whatever impact it might be having on other areas of economy, inflation might take an ugly turn and lead to a political crisis—at least in the developing economies. India has seen governments thrown out of power in elections due to price rise in daily-use items. This is not the case in the developed economies, but inflation takes its political toll there, too. In the developed economies, more aware and informed voters get carried away by the greater impact of higher or lower inflations in the elections. In this chapter, we will try to examine the concept of inflation from all possible dimensions to have an overall understanding.

DEFINITION

A rise in the general level of prices;[1] a sustained rise in the general level of prices;[2] persistent increases in the general level of prices;[3] an increase in the general level of prices in an economy that is sustained over time;[4] rising prices across the board[5]—is inflation. These are some of the most common academic definitions of inflation. If the price of one good has gone up, it is not inflation; it is inflation only if the prices of *most* goods have gone up.[6]

1. Samuelson, Paul A. and Nardhaus, William D., ***Economics***, Tata McGraw-Hill, N. Delhi, 2006, p. 439.
2. McCormick, B.J. et. al, ***Introducing Economics***, Penguin Education, Great Britain, 1974, p. 609.
3. ***Penguin Dictionary of Economics***, Penguin Books, London, 7th Ed., 2003.
4. ***Collins internet-linked Dictionary of Economics***, Harper-Collins Publishers., Glasgow, 2006.
5. Mathew Bishop, ***Pocket Economist***, *The Economist*, London, 2007, p. 121.
6. Stiglitz, Joseph E. and Walsh, Carl E., ***Economics***, W.W. Norton & Company, New York, 2005, p. 509.

Two terms are used to show a fall in general level of prices—*disinflation* and *deflation*. But these terms have very specific meanings in terms of price fall—while disinflation is considered good for the economy (as it brings comfort to the consumers), deflation is not considered good (as it invites the risks of slowdown and even recession in the economy). In practice, the *same term inflation* is used by the experts to show price rise (i.e., inflation has gone up) as well as price fall (i.e., inflation has come down).

The rate of inflation is measured on the basis of price indices which are of two kinds—Wholesale Price Index (WPI) and Consumer Price Index (CPI). A price index is a measure of the average level of prices, which means that it does not show the exact price rise or fall of a single good. The rate of inflation is the rate of change of general price level which is measured as follows:

Rate of inflation (year x) = Price level (year x) –Price level (year x-1)/Price level (year x-1) × 100

This rate shows up in percentage form (%), though inflation is also shown in ***numbers***, i.e., ***digits***. A price index is a weighted average of the prices of a number of goods and services. In the index the total weight is taken as 100 at a particular year of the past (the ***base year***), this when compared to the current year shows a rise or fall in the prices of current year, there is a rise or fall in the '100' in comparison to the base year—and this inflation is measured in digits.

Inflation is measured ***'point-to-point'***. It means that the reference dates for the annual inflation is January 1 to January 1 of two consecutive years (not for January 1 to December 31 of the concerned year). Similarly, the weekly rate of inflation is the change in one week reference being the two consecutive last days of the week (i.e., 5 p.m. of two Fridays in India).

WHY DOES INFLATION OCCUR?

Economists have been giving different explanations throughout the 19th and 20th centuries for the occurrence of inflation—the debate still goes on. But the debate has certainly given us a clearer picture of inflation. We shall see the reasons responsible for inflation in two parts:

1. **Pre-1970s:** Till the rise of the monetarist school, economists used to agree upon two reasons behind inflation:

   (i) ***Demand-Pull Inflation:*** A mismatch between demand and supply pulls up prices. Either the demand increases over the same level of supply, or the supply decreases with the same level of demand and thus the situation of demand-pull inflation arises. This was a Keynesian idea. The Keynesian School suggests cuts in spending as the way of tackling excess demand mainly by increasing taxes and reducing government expenditure.

   In practice, the governments keep tracking the demand-supply matrix to check such inflation. Depending upon the situation, the goods in short supply are imported, interest on loans increased and wages revised.

   (ii) ***Cost-Push Inflation:*** An increase in factor input costs (i.e., wages and raw materials) pushes up prices. The price rise which is the result of increase in the production cost is cost-push inflation. The Keynesian school suggested controls on prices and incomes as direct ways of checking such an inflation and, 'moral suasions' and measures to reduce the monopoly power of trade unions as indirect measures (basically, cost-push inflations chiefly used to happen due to higher wage demanded by the trade unions during the era).

   Today, the governments of the world use many tools to check such inflations—reducing excise and custom duties on raw materials, wage revisions, etc.

2. **Post-1970s:** After the rise of Monetaristic School of Economics in the early 1970s (monetarism developed in opposition to post-1945 Keynesian idea of demand management), the school provided monetarist explanation for inflation, the so-called 'demand-pull' or the 'cost-push' which is excessive creation of money in the economy.

   (i) ***Demand-Pull Inflation:*** For the monetarists, a demand-pull inflation is creation of extra purchasing power to the consumer over the same level of production (which happens due to wage revisions at the micro level and deficit financing at the macro level). This is the typical case of creating extra money (either by printing or public borrowing) without equivalent creation in production/supply, i.e., 'too much money chasing too little output'—the ultimate source of demand-pull inflation.

   (ii) ***Cost-Push Infiation:*** Similarly, for the monetarists, 'cost-push' is not a truly independent theory of inflation—it has to be financed by some extra money (which is created by the government via wage revision, public borrowing, printing of currency, etc.). A price rise does not get automatically reciprocated by consumers' purchasing. Basically, people must have got some extra purchasing power created that's why they start purchasing at higher prices also. If this has not been the reason, people would have cut-down their consumption (i.e., overall demand) to the level of their purchasing capacity and the aggregate demand of goods would have gone down. But this does not happen. It means every cost-push inflation is a result of excessive creation of money—increasing money flow or money supply.

For the monetarists, a particular level of money supply for a particular level of production is healthy for an economy. Extra creation of money over the same level of production causes inflation. They suggested proper monetary policy (money supply, interest rates, printing of currencies, public borrowing etc.), to check situations of inflationary pressure on the economy. Monetarists rejected the Keynesian theory of inflation.

Measures to Check Inflation

Inflation being a socio-economically sensitive issue, governments across the world try several short and long-term policy steps to check it from getting uncomfortable—a brief idea about the steps are given below:

(i) ***Demand side measure:*** In this category mainly, two types of steps are taken. Firstly, the consumers are appealed to cut back the consumption of the items which show higher inflation (called *austerity*). This step has generally failed across the world because it does not work in case of essential items (such as wheat, rice, milk, tea, etc.) and as people who have money, they don't wish to cut down consumption. Secondly, the government may tighten flow of money in the system (known as *monetary measure*)—central bank making money costlier (by increasing repo rate, increasing CRR, etc., in case of India).[7] This step also has its own limitations—it is not effective if the items showing inflation are essential ones (such as wheat, rice, onion, potato, etc., because consumers don't borrow money from banks to buy them). But it can be quite effective if the items are building materials (interest on home loan can be increased to cut back the demand of these items).[8]

(ii) ***Supply side meosure:*** Aimed at increasing the supply of the items showing inflation, the government may go in for upscaling the production or import of the items. This measure also has its own limitations—production may not be upscaled in short-run and import may not reach the country in time.[9] Rather in medium and long-run, production of these items can be upscaled.

(iii) ***Cost side measure:*** Two variety of steps may be taken under it—in short-run cutting taxes can bring in comfort but in the long-run cutting cost of production is the only way out (by scaling up technology).[10]

---

7. While inflation started moving upward, during 2009–13, the RBI went for upward revisions in the repo rate 17 times in a row with no effective outcome as the items showing inflationary pressure were essential ones—wheat, rice, pulses, milk, eggs, fish, meat, etc. *[Several monetary policy reviews of the RBI between 2009–13].*

8. During 2004–05 *(Economic Survey 2004–05)*, when building materials did show higher inflation, the RBI went for upward revision of the interest rate on home loan (actually, by 2002–03 home loan was made extremely cheaper by the Government in order to encourage the housing sector which boosted the demand for building materials in the country).

9. This was visible once in 1998 (by the time imported onions reached India the prices have started touching ₹150 per kg. rising from ₹10 a kilo) and second during 2004–05 (when import of building materials were lobbied down by the Indian producers and their production could not be scaled up). *[Economic Survey 1997–98 and 2004–05].*

10. The Governments have been cutting down custom duty, cenvat, VAT under it mainly—several such instances can be cited between 2004–13.

TYPES OF INFLATION

Depending upon the range of increase and its severity, inflation may be classified into three broad categories.

1. Low Inflation

Such inflation is slow and on predictable[11] lines, which might be called small or gradual.[12] This is a comparative term which puts it opposite to the faster, bigger and unpredictable inflations. Low inflation takes place in a longer period and the range of increase is usually in 'single digit'. Such inflation has also been called as '*creeping inflation*'.[13] We may take an example of the monthly inflation rate of a country for six months being 2.3 per cent, 2.6 per cent, 2.7 per cent, 2.9 per cent, 3.1 per cent and 3.4 per cent. Here the range of change is of 1.1 per cent and over a period of six months.

2. Galloping Inflation

This is a '*very high inflation*' running in the range of double-digit or triple digit (i.e., 20 per cent, 100 per cent or 200 per cent in a year).[14] In the decades of 1970s and 1980s, many Latin American countries such as Argentina, Chile and Brazil had such rates of inflation—in the range of 50 to 700 per cent. The Russian economy did show such inflation after the disintegration of the ex-USSR in the late 1980s.

Contemporary journalism has given some other names to this inflation—*hopping inflation*, *jumping inflation* and *running or runaway inflation*.[15]

11 Samuelson and Nordhaus, ***Economics***, p. 671.

12 ***Collins Dictionary of Economics***, p. 251.

13 Ibid.

14 Samuelson and Nordhaus, ***Economics***, p. 671

15 As popularised by ***The Economist, The Wall Street Journal, The Economic Times*** (India), etc.

3. Hyperinflation

This form of inflation is '*large and accelerating*'[16] which might have the annual rates in million or even trillion.[17] In such inflation not only the range of increase is very large, but the increase takes place in a very short span of time, prices shoot up overnight.

The best example of hyperinflation that economists cite is of Germany after the First World War—in early 1920s. At the end of 1923, prices were 36 billion times higher than two years earlier.[18] This inflation was so severe that paper German currencies (the Deutsche Mark) were more valuable as stove fuel than as actual money.[19] Some recent examples[20] of hyperinflation had been the Bolivian inflation of mid-1985 (24,000 per cent per annum) and the Yugoslavian inflation of 1993 (20 per cent per day). The latest example has been Venezuela which saw an annual inflation of over 53 million per cent by 2019, as per its central bank. The currency of Zimbabwe was declared *worthless* (by the magazine *The Economist*) in wake of rise in annual inflation to 90 billion trillion per cent by 2008.

Such an inflation quickly leads to a complete loss of confidence in the domestic currency and people start opting for other forms of money, as for example physical assets, gold and foreign currency (also known as 'inflation proof' assets) and people might switch to barter exchange.[21]

16 ***Collins Dictionary of Economics***, p. 251.

17 Samuelson and Nordhaus, ***Economics***, p. 671.

18 Thomas Sargent, 'The Ends of Four Big Inflations', in R. Hall, ***Inflations, Causes and Effects*** (as quoted by Stiglitz and Walsh, ***Economics***, p. 513).

19 Stiglitz & Walsh, ***Economics***, p. 512.

20 Sachs, Jeffery, ***The End of Poverty***, Penguin Books, London, 2005, pp. 92–108.

21 Hyperinflation erodes the value of money very fast and that too at a very high scale. We may put it with an example, suppose the annual rate of inflation is 100 per cent, money loses half its value every year. It means that a note of ₹100 will have a value of just ₹3 after five years.

OTHER VARIANTS OF INFLATION

Other than the three broad categories we analysed above, some other variants of inflation are also considered by governments in their policymaking:

1. Bottleneck Inflation

This inflation takes place when the supply falls drastically and the demand remains at the same level. Such situations arise due to supply-side hurdles, hazards or mismanagement which is also known as 'structural inflation'. This could be put in the 'demand-pull inflation' category.

2. Core Inflation

This nomenclature is based on the inclusion or exclusion of the goods and services while calculating inflation. Popular in western economies, core inflation shows price rise in all goods and services excluding ***energy*** and ***food articles***. First used[22] in India in 2000–01 it does not suit our inflation analysis in the right sense because prices here depend more on food articles and energy. Since 2015–16, a new *core-core inflation* is also measured by India which excludes food, fuel & light, transport and communication.

OTHER IMPORTANT TERMS

Inflationary Gap

The excess of total government spending above the national income (i.e., fiscal deficit) is known as inflationary gap. This is intended to increase the production level, which ultimately pushes the prices up due to extra creation of money during the process.

[22] Ministry of Finance, ***Economic Survey, 2000–01***, (New Delhi: Government of India, 2001).

Deflationary Gap

The shortfall in total spending of the government (i.e., fiscal surplus) over the national income creates deflationary gaps in the economy. This is a situation of producing more than the demand and the economy usually heads for a general slowdown in the level of demand. This is also known as the ***output gap***

Inflation Tax

Inflation erodes the value of money and the people who hold currency suffer in this process. As the governments have authority of printing currency and circulating it into the economy (as they do in the case of deficit financing), this act functions as an income to the governments. This is a situation of sustaining government expenditure at the cost of people's income. This looks as if inflation is working as a tax.[23] That is how the term inflation tax is also known as ***seigniorage***. It means, inflation is always at the level to which the government may go for deficit financing—level of deficit financing is directly reflected by the rate of inflation.

It could also be used by the governments in the form of prices and incomes policy under which the companies pay inflation tax on the salary increases above the set level prescribed by the government.[24]

Inflation Spiral

An inflationary situation in an economy which results out of a process of wage and price interaction ***'when wages press prices up and prices pull wages up'***[25] is known as the inflationary spiral. It is also known as the ***wage-price spiral***. This wage-price interaction was seen as a plausible cause of

[23] Stiglitz and Walsh, ***Economics***, p. 511.

[24] ***Penguin Dictionary of Economics***.

[25] Ibid.

inflation in the year 1935 in the US economy, for the first time.[26]

Inflation Accounting

A term popular in the area of corporate profit accounting. Basically, due to inflation the profit of firms/companies gets overstated. When a firm calculates its profits after adjusting the effects of current level of inflation, this process is known as inflation accounting. Such profits are the real profit of the firm which could be compared to a historic rate of inflation (inflation of the base year), too.

Inflation Premium

The bonus brought by inflation to the borrowers is known as the inflation premium. The interest banks charge on their lending is known as the *nominal* interest rate, which might not be the real cost of borrowing paid by the borrower to the banks. To calculate the real cost a borrower is paying on its loan, the nominal rate of interest is adjusted with the effect of inflation and thus the interest rate we get is known as the real interest rate. Real interest is always lower than the nominal interest rate, if the inflation is taking place—the difference is the inflation premium.

Rising inflation premium shows depleting profits of the lending institutions. At times, to neutralise the effects of inflation premium, the lender takes the recourse to increase the nominal rate of interest.[27] In recent times, it was done by the Indian banks in July 2003 to ward off their depleting profits when inflation had crossed the 7 per cent level—the level of inflation was threatening to deplete even the capital base of the banks. Since then the RBI has been following a tighter credit policy as inflation was going beyond the upper limit of its healthy range (i.e., 4–5 per cent in the Indian case).

Phillips Curve

It is a graphic curve which advocates a relationship between inflation and unemployment in an economy. As per the curve there is a 'trade off' between inflation and unemployment, i.e., an inverse relationship between them. The curve suggests that lower the inflation, higher the unemployment and higher the inflation, lower the unemployment.[28] During the 1960s, this idea was among the most important theories of the modern economists. This concept is known after the economists who developed it—Alban William Housego Phillips (1914–75). Bill Phillips (popular name) was an electrical engineer from New Zealand and was an economist at the London School of Economics when he propounded the idea. In 'The Relation between Unemployment and the Rate of Change of Money Wage Rates in the United Kingdom, 1861–1957' (published in *Economica* in 1958), he provided empirical evidence to support his ideas.[29]

By the early 1960s, an economic wisdom emerged around the world that by following a certain kind of monetary policy, unemployment could be checked forever and at the cost of a slightly higher inflation, unemployment could be reduced permanently. The central banks of the developed world started framing the required kind of monetary policies mixing the trade-off between inflation and unemployment. The idea became popular among the developing economies too by the late 1960s, though they were a bit confused, as most of them were fighting the menace of higher inflations (double digit) along with high level of unemployment.[30]

By the early 1970s, two American economists, Milton Friedman (Nobel Laureate, 1976) and Edmund Phelps challenged the idea of

26 J.K. Galbraith, ***A History of Economics***, (London: Penguin Books, 1991), p. 205, pp. 267–70.

27 Patrick Lane, ***Economics*** (London: The Economist, 199), p. 270.

28 Stiglitz and Walsh, ***Economics***, pp. 821–22.

29 ***Penguin Dictionary of Economics***, pp. 297–98.

30 Gerald M. Meier and James E. Ranch, **Leading Issues in Economic Development** (New Delhi: Oxford University Press, 2006), pp. 37–39.

the Phillips Curve. According to them the trade-off between inflation and unemployment was only short-term, because once people came to expect higher inflation they started demanding higher wages and thus unemployment will rise back to its '*natural rate*' (the unemployment rate that occurs at full employment when the economy is producing at potential output, it is usually called the natural rate of unemployment).[31] They advocated that there was no long-term trade-off between inflation and unemployment. In the long run, monetary policy can influence inflation. They suggested that if monetary policy tried to hold unemployment below its natural rate, inflation will be rising to higher level, which is also known as the **non-accelerating inflation rate of unemployment (NAIRU)**.[32] The NAIRU is that rate of unemployment which is consistent with a constant rate of inflation. It means at NAIRU, the upward and downward forces on price (inflation) and wage (unemployment) neutralise each other and there is no tendency of change in the rate of inflation. We may say that the NAIRU is the lowest unemployment rate that an economy can sustain without any upward pressure on inflation rate.

Reflation

Reflation is a situation often deliberately brought by the government to reduce unemployment and increase demand by going for higher levels of economic growth.[33] Governments go for higher public expenditures, tax cuts, interest rate cuts, etc. Fiscal deficit rises, extra money is generally printed at higher level of growth, wages increase and there is almost no improvement in unemployment.

Reflation can also be understood from a different angle—when the economy is crossing through the cycle of recession (low inflation, high unemployment, low demand, etc.) and government takes some economic policy decisions to revive the economy from recession, certain goods see sudden and temporary increase in their prices, such price rise is also known as reflation.

Stagflation

Stagflation is a situation in an economy when inflation and unemployment both are at higher levels, contrary to conventional belief. Such a situation first arose in the 1970s in the US economy (average unemployment rate above 6 per cent and the average rate of inflation above 7 per cent)[34] and in many Euro-American economies. This took place as a result of oil price increases of 1973 and 1979 and anticipation of higher inflation. The stagflationary situation continued till the early 1980s. Conventional thinking that a trade-off existed between inflation and unemployment (i.e., Phillips Curve) was falsified and several economies switched over to alternative ways of economic policies, such as monetaristic and supply-side economics.

When the economy is passing through the cycle of stagnation (i.e., long period of low aggregate demand in relation to its productive capacity) and the government shuffles with the economic policy, a sudden and temporary price rise is seen in some of the goods—such inflation is also known as stagflation. Stagflation is basically a combination of high inflation and low growth.[35]

INFLATION TARGETING

The announcement of an official target range for inflation is known as inflation targeting. It is done by the Central Bank in an economy as a part of

31. Stiglitz and Walsh, *Economics*, p. 822.
32. Samuelson and Nordhaus, *Economics*, pp. 680–87.
33. *Collins Dictionary of Economics*, p. 446.
34. Stiglitz and Walsh, *Economics*, p. 478.
35. C. Rangarajan, *Indian Economy: Essays on Money and Finance*, (New Delhi; UBSPD, 1998), p. 58.

their monetary policy to realise the objective of a ***stable*** rate of inflation[36] (the Government of India asked the RBI to perform this function in the early 1970s).

India commenced inflation targeting 'formally' in *February 2015* when an agreement between the GoI and the RBI was signed related to it—the **Agreement on Monetary Policy Framework**. The agreement provides the aim of inflation targeting in this way—it is essential to have a modern monetary framework to meet the challenge of an increasingly complex economy. Whereas the objective of monetary policy is to primarily maintain *price stability*, while keeping in mind the objective of *growth*.' The highlights of the agreement are as given below:

- The RBI will aim to bring CPI-C Inflation below 6 per cent by January 2016. The target for financial year 2016–17 and all subsequent years shall be 4 per cent with a band of +/– 2 per cent (it means the 'healthy range of inflation' to be 2–6 per cent).
- RBI to publish the Operating Target(s) and establish an Operating Procedure of monetary policy to achieve the target.
  - Any change in the operating target(s) and operating procedure in response to evolving macro-financial conditions shall also be published.
- Every six months, the RBI to publish a document explaining:
  - Source of inflation;
  - Forecasts of inflation for the period between six to eighteen months from the date of the publication of the document; and
- The RBI shall be seen to have failed to meet the target if inflation is:
  - More than 6 per cent for three consecutive quarters for the financial year 2015–16 and all subsequent years.
  - Less than 2 per cent for three consecutive quarters in 2016–17 and all subsequent years.
- If the RBI fails to meet the target it shall set out in a report to the GoI:
  - the reasons for its failure to achieve the target underset in this agreement;
  - remedial actions proposed to be taken by the RBI; and
  - an estimate of the time-period within which the target would be achieved pursuant to timely implementation of proposed remedial actions.
- Any dispute regarding the interpretation or implementation of the agreement to be resolved between the Governor, RBI and the GoI.

It should be noted that the *Urjit Patel Committee* setup by the RBI on monetary policy gave similar advices by early 2014—the move is seen as a follow up to this. This way India joined the club of inflation targeting countries such as USA, UK, European Union, Japan, South Korea, China, Indonesia and Brazil. It was New Zealand which went for inflation targeting in 1989 for the first time in the world.[37]

Many experts view the core inflation (inflation in the price index excluding food, fuel and other volatile components) as the better measure of

36. Samuelson and Nordhaus, ***Economics***, p. 723.

37. New Zealand passed a law to do this with a target of 0 to 2 per cent inflation with a provision that the Governor of the Reserve Bank of New Zealand could be fired if inflation crosses the 2 per cent upper limit—now this target range has been revised to 1 to 3 per cent (Stiglitz and Walsh, ***Economics***, p. 849).

inflation for monetary policy purposes. This is because food and fuel price shocks are transitory as well as mainly supply driven and therefore not a monetary phenomenon. [A detailed discussion on this issue is presented in the *Chapter 12* titled *Banking in India*].

As the first 5-year regime (August 2016-March 2021) of inflation targeting comes to an end, the Government will announce its new regime. As per reports in media, the government was considering a proposal to raise the inflation target under the monetary policy framework to 5 per with a tolerance level of plus and minus 2 per cent from April 2021— aimed at giving the RBI greater leeway to cut policy rates to boost growth in the economy ravaged by the Covid-19 pandemic. The Government decision is awaited on it.

RBI Working Paper Amid growing speculation that the Government may ask the RBI to loosen the inflation target to help push economic growth, an RBI working paper (titled *Measuring Trend Inflation in India* by Harendra Kumar Behera and Michael Debabrata Patra, December 2020) recommended that maintaining the inflation target at 4 per cent is appropriate for the country. The paper finds that there is a steady decline in *trend inflation* to 4.1-4.3 per cent since 2014 and any change in it may have the following impact on the economy—

1. Setting an inflation target *below the trend* may impart a 'deflationary bias' to monetary policy because it will go into overkill relative to what the economy can intrinsically bear in order to achieve the target.
2. Opposite to it, a target fixed *above the trend* renders monetary policy too expansionary and prone to inflationary shocks and unanchored expectations.

Thus, the paper recommends 4 per cent (based on CPI-C) as the appropriate inflation target for India. However, the paper believes that for setting monetary policy, it is necessary to consider significant changes in the overall macroeconomic ecosystem in which policy is conducted. The working paper, which seeks to examine whether the choice of the target for inflation is consistent with its trend, finds that the concept of *trend inflation* is vital for the design and conduct of monetary policy to which actual inflation outcomes are expected to converge after short-run fluctuations from a variety of sources die out.

MONETARY POLICY ANCHOR: HEADLINE OR CORE INFLATION?

In recent times, many experts have suggested *core inflation* (inflation in the price index excluding food, fuel and other volatile components) as the better measure of inflation for monetary policy purposes (i.e., as monetary policy anchor). This belief is based on the fact that food and fuel price shocks are transitory besides being supply-driven and therefore are not monetary phenomenon.

Some recent studies suggest that targeting core inflation maximises welfare. However, these studies consider that 'markets are complete' which allow households to insure against risks of price rise. But as per the *Economic Survey 2020-21*, in the case of developing economies there are two deviations as markets here are not complete:

1. Inability of agents to smooth their lifetime consumption, and
2. Other structural differences such as a high share of food in household consumption expenditure.

Some studies suggest that while under complete markets, the choice of targeting strict core inflation is the best policy, with incomplete markets, headline inflation targeting is welfare improving relative to core inflation targeting. A recent RBI working paper (titled *Are Food Prices Really Flexible? Evidence from India* by G. V. Nadhanael, September 2020), analyses weekly price data on 45 food items in India, for the period 2005-18 (using the data collected by the Directorate of Economics and Statistics, Ministry of Agriculture and Farmers Welfare). The paper finds heterogeneity in the extent of price stickiness among food products. Given wide variations in the price stickiness of food items, the paper suggests that it is important to pay attention to the 'sticky component' of food inflation in addition to core inflation.

Skewflation

Economists usually distinguish between inflation and a relative price increase. 'Inflation' refers to a sustained, across-the-board price increase, whereas 'a relative price increase' is a reference to an episodic price rise pertaining to one or a small group of commodities. This leaves a ***third phenomenon***, namely one in which there is a price rise of one or a small group of commodities over a sustained period of time, without a traditional designation. '**Skewflation**' is a relatively new term to describe this third category of price rise.

In India, food prices rose steadily during the last months of 2009 and the early months of 2010, even though the prices of non-food items continued to be relatively stable. As this somewhat unusual phenomenon stubbornly persisted, policymakers conferred on how to bring it to an end. The term 'skewflation' made an appearance in internal documents of the Government of India, and then appeared in print in the ***Economic Survey 2009-10*** GoI, MoF.

The **skewedness** of inflation in India in the early months of 2010 was obvious from the fact that food price inflation crossed the 20 per cent mark in multiple months, whereas wholesale price index (WPI) inflation never once crossed 11 per cent. It may be pointed out that the skewflation has gradually given way to a lower-grade generalised inflation (with the economy in the middle of 2011 inflating at around 9 per cent with food and non-food price increases roughly at the same level).

Given that other nations have faced similar problems, the use of this term picked up quickly, with the ***Economist*** magazine *(January 24, 2011)*, in an article entitled *'Price Rises in China: Inflated Fears'*, wondering if China was beginning to suffer from an Indian-style skewflation.

GDP DEFLATOR

This is the ratio of the GDP at current prices to that of the constant prices. It is derived by using the following formula—

GDP Deflator = GDP at Current Prices ÷ GDP at Constant Prices × 100

This shows the increase in the value of GDP due to increase in inflation in between the period—base year (i.e., the year of constant prices) and the current year. This is why it is used as a measure of inflation (also known as 'implicit price deflator'). Though, countries use inflation indices to measure inflation, these indices are not able to capture all goods and services produced by them. In case of India, while services are not included in the wholesale price index (WPI), the consumer price index (CPI) contains only those goods and services which households purchase for consumption (such as food, cloth, health, education, etc.) and misses several other goods and services (such as intermediate goods, services required by firms, etc.). Since the deflator covers the entire range of goods and services produced in the economy, it is seen as a more comprehensive measure of inflation.

BASE EFFECT

It refers to the impact of the rise in price level (i.e., last year's inflation) in the previous year over the corresponding rise in price levels in the current year (i.e., current inflation). If the price index had risen at a high rate in the corresponding period of the previous year, leading to a high inflation rate, some of the potential rise is already factored in, therefore, a similar absolute increase in the price index in the current year will lead to a relatively lower inflation rates. On the other hand, if the inflation rate was too low in the corresponding period of the previous year, even a relatively smaller rise in the price index will arithmetically give a high rate of current inflation. For example:

	Price Index				Inflation		
	2017	2018	2019	2020	2018	2019	2020
Jan	100	120	140	160	20	16.67	14.29

The index has increased by 20 points in all the three years, viz., 2018, 2019 and 2020. However, the inflation rate (calculated on 'year-on-year' basis) tends to decline over the three years from 20 per cent in 2018 to 14.29 per cent in 2020. This is because the absolute increase of 20 points in the price index in each year increases the *base year price index* by an equivalent amount, while the absolute increase in price index remains the same. The 'year-on-year' inflation is calculated by the formula :

Current Inflation Rate = [(Current Price Index – Last year's Price Index)] ÷ Last year's Price Index] × 100

EFFECTS OF INFLATION

There are multi-dimensional effects of inflation on an economy both at the micro and macro levels. It redistributes income, distorts relative prices, destabilises employment, tax, saving and investment policies, and finally it may bring in recession and depression in an economy. A brief and objective overview of the effects of inflation is given below:

1. **On Creditors and Debtors:** Inflation redistributes wealth from creditors to debtors, i.e., lenders suffer and borrowers benefit out of inflation. The opposite effect takes place when inflation falls (i.e., deflation).

2. **On Lending:** With the rise in inflation, lending institutions feel the pressure of higher lending. Institutions don't revise the nominal rate of interest as the 'real cost of borrowing' (i.e., nominal rate of interest minus inflation) falls by the same percentage with which inflation rises.

3. **On Aggregate Demand:** Rising inflation indicates rising aggregate demand and indicates comparatively lower supply and higher purchasing capacity among the consumers. Usually, higher inflation suggests the producers to increase their production level as it is generally considered as an indication of higher demand in the economy.

4. **On Investment:** Investment in the economy is boosted by the inflation (in the short-run) because of two reasons:

   (i) Higher inflation indicates higher demand and suggests entrepreneurs to expand their production level, and

   (ii) Higher the inflation, lower the cost of loan (as shown above in no. 2)

5. **On Income:** Inflation affects the income of individual and firms alike. An increase in inflation, increases the 'nominal' value of income, while the 'real' value of income remains the same. Increased price levels erode the purchasing power of the money in the short-run, but in the long-run the income levels also increase (making the nominal value of income going upward). It means, in

a given period of time income may go up due to two reasons, viz., inflationary situation and increased earning. The concept 'GDP Deflator' (GDP at current prices divided by GDP at constant prices) gives the idea of 'inflation effect' on income over a given period.

6. **On Saving:** Holding money does not remain an intelligent economic decision (because money loses value with every increase in inflation) that is why people visit banks more frequently and try to hold least money with themselves and put maximum with the banks in their saving accounts (to minimise the loss in value of money with interest earned on it, provided bank is paying positive interest on saving account). This is also known as the ***shoe leather cost***[38] of inflation (as it consumes the precious time of the people visiting the bank frequently tagging their shoe). It means that saving rate increases. But this happens as a short-term effect of inflation. In the long-run, higher inflation depletes the saving rate in an economy. Just the opposite situation arises when inflation falls or shows falling traits with decreasing saving, in the short-run and increasing saving in the long-run, respectively.

7. **On Expenditure:** Consumption as well as investment both of the expenditures rise as inflation rises. Increased prices make our consumption levels fall as goods and services we buy get costlier. We see a tendency among the people to cut their consumption levels aimed at neutralising the impact of price rise— making consumption expenditure fall. Exact opposite happens once prices head downward.

On the other hand inflations make 'investment' expenditure increase as a result of decreased cost of money/finance (inflation brings benefit to borrower—known as 'inflation premium'). In times of price fall just opposite happens.

8. **On Tax:** On tax structure of the economy, inflation creates two distortions:

(i) Tax-payers suffer while paying their direct and indirect taxes. As indirect taxes are imposed ad valorem (***on value***), increased prices of goods make tax-payers to pay increased indirect taxes (like cenvat, VAT, etc., in India).

Similarly, due to inflation, direct tax (income tax, interest tax, etc.) burden of the tax-payers also increases as tax-payer's gross income moves to the upward ***slabs*** of official tax brackets (but the real value of money does not increase due to inflation; in fact, it falls). This problem is also known as ***bracket creep***—i.e., ***inflation-induced tax increases***.[39] Some economies (as in the US and many European countries) have ***indexed*** their tax provisions to neutralise this distortion on the direct tax payers.

(ii) The extent to which tax collections of the government are concerned, inflation increases the nominal value of the gross tax revenue, while real value of the tax collection does not compare with the current pace of inflation as there is a lag (***delay***) in the tax collection in all economies.

But governments get an advantage on their interest burden, on their borrowings as inflation benefits borrowers. This benefit, however, depends upon the contemporary levels of fiscal deficit and the total national debt.

38. Samuelson and Nordhaus, **Economics**, p. 674.

39. Ibid.

In the case of a government incurring high fiscal deficit (increased borrowing, printing currency), inflation functions as a tax, i.e., ***inflation tax*** via which the government fulfils its expenditure by cutting down the expenditure and consumption of the people.

9. **On Exchange Rate:** With every inflation the currency of the economy ***depreciates*** (loses its exchange value in front of a foreign currency) provided it follows the flexible currency regime. Though it is a comparative matter, there might be inflationary pressure on the foreign currency against which the exchange rate is compared.

10. **On Export:** With inflation, exportable items of an economy gain competitive prices in the world market. Due to this, the volume of export increases (keep in mind that the value of export decreases here) and thus export income increases in the economy. It means export segment of the economy benefits due to inflation. Importing partners of the economy exert pressure for a stable exchange rate as their imports start increasing and exports start decreasing (see the next point).

11. **On Import:** Inflation gives an economy the advantage of lower imports and import-substitution as foreign goods become costlier. But in the case of compulsory imports (i.e., oil, technology, drugs, etc.) the economy does not get this benefit and loses more foreign currency instead of saving it.

12. **On Trade Balance:** In the case of a developed economy, inflation makes trade balance favourable, while for the developing economies inflation is unfavourable for their balance of trade. This is because of composition of their foreign trade. The benefit to export which inflation brings in to a developing economy is usually lower than the loss it incur due to its compulsory imports which become costlier due to inflation.

13. **On Employment:** Inflation increases employment in the short-run, but becomes neutral or even negative in the long run (see the Phillips Curve and the NAIRU in the earlier sections).

14. **On Wages:** Inflation increases the nominal (face) value of wages, while their real value falls. That is why there is a negative impact of inflation on the purchasing power and living standard of wage employees. To neutralise this negative impact the Indian government provides ***dearness allowance*** to its employees twice a year.

15. **On the Self-employed:** Inflation has a neutralising impact on the self-employed people in the long-run. But in the short-run they also get affected as the economy as a whole gets affected.

16. **On the Economy:** All the segments discussed above belong to an economy, but we must know the overall short-term and long-term impacts of inflation on an economy.

Experiences of the world economies in the late 1980s show that a particular level of inflation is healthy for an economy. This specific level of inflation was called as the 'range' of inflation and every economy needs to calculate its own range. Inflation beyond both the limits of the range is never healthy for any economy. In the case of India, it is considered 2 to 6 per cent at CPI(C), which is also known as the 'comfort zone' of inflation in India since 2015. Similarly for Australia, New Zealand, the USA, Canada and the European Union, the healthy range today is 1 to 3 per cent. This is why every economy today utilises ***inflation targeting*** as part of its monetary policy.

Inflation beyond the limits of the decided/prescribed range brings in recession to depression.

(We will see them in Section B of this Chapter, under 'Business Cycle'.)

INFLATION IN INDIA

Every economy calculates its inflation for efficient financial administration as the multi-dimensional effects of inflation make it necessary. India calculates its inflation on two price indices, i.e., the wholesale price index (WPI) and the consumer price index (CPI). While the WPI-inflation is used at the macro-level policymaking, the CPI-inflation is used for micro-level analyses. The inflation at the WPI is the inflation of the economy. Both the indices follow the 'point-to-point' method and may be shown in ***points*** (i.e., digit) as well as in ***percentage*** relative to a particular ***base year***

WHOLESALE PRICE INDEX

The first index number of wholesale prices commenced in India for the week January 10, 1942. It was having the base week ending August 19, 1939 = 100, which was published by the office of the Economic Adviser to the Government of India (Ministry of Industry).[40] Independent India followed the same series with more number of commodities included in the index. Several changes regarding inclusion of commodities, assigning them the logical weights took place in the coming times including revisions in the ***base years*** for the WPI. The WPI base year has been revised five times till date. The base years are as given below:

1. 1952–53 Base Year (112 Commodities) issued from June 1952.
2. 1961–62 Base Year (139 Commodities) issued from July 1969.
3. 1970–71 Base Year (360 Commodities) issued from January 1977.
4. 1981–82 Base Year (447 Commodities) issued from January 1989.
5. 1993–94 Base Year (435 Commodities) issued from July, 1999.
6. 2004–05 Base Year (676 Commodities) released in September 2011.
7. 2011–12 Base Year (697 Commodities) released in May 2017.

Revised WPI

The new series of the WPI was released[41] by the Government with the *revised* base year as 2011–12. The existing base year was 2004–05. The new base year aligns with the base year of other indicators like the Gross Domestic Product (GDP) and Index of Industrial Production (IIP). A Working Group was set up (March 2012) by the Government to advise on the new series of the WPI (headed by Saumitra Chaudhuri, Member, erstwhile Planning Commission). *Key highlights* of the revised series are as given below:

- WPI continues to constitute three major groups—Primary Articles, Fuel and Power, and Manufactured Products. The number of items has been increased from 676 to 697—in all 199 new items have been added and 146 old items have been dropped.
- It is more representative with increase in number of quotations from 5482 to 8331—an increase by 2849 quotations (52 per cent).
- The prices used for compilation do not include indirect taxes in order to remove impact of fiscal policy. This is in consonance

40 Ministry of Finance, **Economic Survey 2006-07** (New Delhi: Government of India, 2007), p. 85.

41 ***Office of Economic Advisor***, Department for Promotion of Industry and Internal Trade (DPIIT), Ministry of Commerce and Industry, GoI, N. Delhi, May 12th, 2017.

Table 7.1

Major Group/Group	Weight		No. of items		No. of Quotations	
	2004-05	2011-12	2004-05	2011-12	2004-05	2011-12
All commodities	100.00	100.00	676	697	5482	8331
Primary articles	20.12	22.62	102	117	579	983
Fuel and power	14.91	13.15	19	16	72	442
Manufactured products	64.97	64.23	555	564	4831	6906

with international practices and will make the new WPI conceptually closer to Producer Price Index (PPI).

- Item level aggregates for new WPI have been compiled using Geometric Mean (GM) following international best practice and as is currently used for compilation of the CPI-C.

The major changes in weights, number of items and quotations between WPI 2004–05 and WPI 2011–12 are given in the ***Table 7.1***

- A new Wholesale Food Price Index (WPFI) has been introduced—combining the Food Articles (belonging to the group Primary Articles) and Food Products (belonging to the group Manufactured Products). Together with the Consumer Food Price Index (CPFI) released by Central Statistics Office, this would help monitor the price situation of food items better.
- To keep pace with the changing structure of the economy it is necessary to follow a dynamic review process of the WPI and related aspects of it. That is why the Government has set up (for the first time) a high level Technical Review Committee (TRC) for this purpose. The committee is headed by the Secretary, Department of Industrial Policy and Promotion (DIPP).

Meanwhile, a ***Working Group*** (headed by Ramesh Chand, member Niti Aayog) was set up by the government in *mid-2019* to look into various issues related to the WPI, such as—revising the current series of 2011-12 to a new base year; reviewing its commodity basket; reviewing the existing system of price collection in particular for manufacturing sector and suggest changes for improvement; and suggesting a roadmap to switch over to PPI from the existing WPI.

CONSUMER PRICE INDEX

India has been measuring inflation at the consumer prices also besides at the wholesale prices. But in place of a single[42] consumer price index (CPI), India was managing with four differing ses of the CPIs due to the socio-economic differentiations found among the consumers (i.e., people's choices of consumption and their purchasing power). Though, in 2011-12, the government announced a new set of consumer indices (i.e., CPI-R, CPI-U and CPI-C), datasets for the older CPIs (to be phased out in coming times) are still announced by the Central Statistical Office (CSO). A brief review of the older CPIs are given below:

1. **CPI-IW:** The Consumer Price Index for Industrial Worker (CPI-IW) is compiled by the Labour Bureau on a monthly basis which measures changes in the retail prices of a fixed *basket* of goods and services (a total of 463 items) being consumed by an average working-class family. To capture the

42. The economies of the Euro-American region have a single CPI as the majority of consumers show the same consumer behaviour (see J.B. Rosser and M.V. Rosser, ***Comparative Economics in a Transforming World Economy*** (Cambridge USA: Prentice Hall, MIT Press, 2004)).

latest consumption pattern the base year[43] of the index was revised to 2016 (from 2001) in October 2020. Besides being a guide for policy making, the index is used for fixing/revising wages, regulating the dearness allowances (DA) of manual workers and employees of central and state governments (i.e., industrial workers from the existing *seven sectors* such as Factories, Mines, Plantation, Railways, Public Motor Transport Undertakings, Electricity Generating & Distributing Establishments and Ports & Docks).

2. **CPI-UNME:** The Consumer Price Index for the Urban Non-Manual Employees (CPI-UNME) has 1984–85 (first base year was 1958–59) as the base year and 146–365 commodities in the basket for which data is collected at 59 centres in the country—data collection frequency is monthly with two weeks time lag.[44]

   This price index has limited use and it is basically used for determining dearness allowances (DAs) of employees of some foreign companies operating in India (i.e., airlines, communications, banking, insurance, embassies and other financial services). It is also used under the Income Tax Act to determine ***capital gains*** and by the CSO (Central Statistical Organisation) for deflating selected services sector's contribution to the GDP at factor cost and current prices to calculate the corresponding figure at constant prices. Since the publication of the CPI (U) started the index was discontinued with from January 2011.

3. **CPI-AL:** The Consumer Price Index for Agricultural Labourers (CPI-AL) has 1986–87 as its base year with 260 commodities in its basket. The data is collected in 600 villages with a monthly frequency and has three weeks time lag.

   This index is used for revising minimum wages for agricultural labourers in different states. As the consumption pattern of agricultural labourers has changed since 1986–87 (its base year), the Labour Bureau proposes to revise the existing base year of this index. For the revision, the consumer expenditure data collected by the NSSO during its 61st NSS Round (2004–05) is proposed to be used.

   The governments at the Centre and states remain vigilant regarding the changes in this index as it shows the price impact on the most vulnerable segment of the society, this segment spends almost 75 per cent of its total income on the purchase of food articles. Governments' failure to stabilise the index in the long range can make them politically volatile and be translated into political debacles. That is why the FCI is always kept ready to supply cheaper foodgrains in the situations of any price rise.

4. **CPI-RL:** There is yet another Consumer Price Index for the Rural Labourers (CPI-RL) with 1983 as the base year, data is collected at 600 villages on monthly frequency with three weeks time lag, its basket contains 260 commodities.

   The agricultural and rural labourers in India create an overlap, i.e., the same labourers work as the rural labourers once the farm sector has either low or no employment scope. Probably, due to this reason this index was dropped by the government in 2001–02.[45] But after the government change at the Centre the index was revived again.[46]

43. **Economic Survey 2020-21**, vol. 2, pp. 166-68, Ministry of Finance, GoI, N. Delhi.
44. Ministry of Finance, ***Economic Survey 2001–02***, p. 90.
45. Ministry of Finance, ***Economic Survey 2001–02***, p. 91.
46. Ministry of Finance, ***Economic Survey 2006–07***, p. 90.

TABLE 7.2: COMPARISION OF WEIGHING DIAGRAM OF THE EXISTING AND REVISED SERIES OF CPI

Group Description	Old Series of CPI (Weights computed on the basis CES 2004-05)			Revised Series of CPI (Weights computed on the basis CES 2011-12)		
	Rutal	Urban	Combd.	Rutal	Urban	Combd.
Food and beverages	56.39	35.81	47.58	34.18	36.29	45.86
Pan, tobacco and intoxicants	2.72	1.34	2.13	3.26	1.36	2.35
Clothing and footwear	5.36	3.91	4.73	7.36	5.57	6.53
Housing	-	22.54	9.77	-	21.67	10.07
Fuel and light	10.42	8.40	9.49	7.94	5.50	6.84
Miscellaneous	24.91	28.00	26.31	27.26	29.53	28.32
Total	100.00	100.00	100.00	100.00	100.00	100.00

Source: *CSO, February 2015. Here, 'Combd.' stands for Combined while '-' stands for 'not available'.*

Revision in the CPI

In 2011-12, Government announced a new set of the consumer price indices—*CPI-R* for the rural market, *CPI-U* for the urban market, and by combining them a 'national' CPI. The national consumer price index is called *CPI-C* (where 'C' stands for Combined). In order to make them more robust, the CPIs were further revised in **2015** by incorporating the following changes:

1. The base year has been changed from 2010 = 100 to 2012 = 100.
2. The basket of items and their weighing diagrams have been prepared using the Modified Mixed Reference Period (MMRP) data of Consumer Expenditure Survey (CES), 2011–12, of the *68th Round* of National Sample Survey (NSS). This has been done to make it consistent with the *international practice* of shorter reference period for most of the food items and longer reference period for the items of infrequent consumption. The weighing diagrams of old series of CPI were based on the Uniform Reference Period (URP) data of CES, 2004–05, of the 61st Round of NSS.

   With this change in the weighing diagrams, the gap between Weight Reference Year and Price Reference Year (Base Year), which was *six years* in the old series, has now been reduced to *six months* only. Due to change in the *consumption pattern* from 2004–05 to 2011–12, the weighing diagrams (share of expenditure to total expenditure) have changed. A comparison of weighing diagrams of the old and revised series is given in *Table 7.2*
3. The number of *Groups,* which was five in the old series, has now been increased to **six** 'Pan, tobacco and intoxicants', which was a Sub-group under the group 'Food, beverages and tobacco', has now been made as a separate group. Accordingly, the group 'Food, beverages and tobacco' has been changed to 'Food and beverages'.
4. Egg, which was part of the sub-group 'Egg, fish and meat' in the old series, has now been made as a separate sub-group. Accordingly, the earlier sub-group has been modified as 'Meat and fish'.
5. The elementary/item indices are now being computed using Geometric Mean (GM) of

TABLE 7.3: All India Weights of different Sub-groups within Consumer Food Price Index

Sub-Group Code	Sub-group Description	Rural	Urban	Combined
(1)	(2)	(3)	(4)	(5)
1.1.01	Cereals and products		22.24	24.77
1.1.02	Meat and fish	9.26	9.23	9.25
1 1.03	Egg	1.05	1.21	1.10
1.1.04	Milk and products	16.34	17.98	16.92
1.1.05	Oils and fats	8.90	9.49	9.11
1.1.06	Fruits	6.10	9.80	7.40
1.1.07	Vegetables	15.78	14.88	15.46
1.1,08	Pulses and products	6.25	5.84	6.11
1.1.09	Sugar and confectionery	3.61	3.28	3.49
1.1 .10	Spices	6.57	6.05	6.39
All Sub-groups of CFPI		**100.00**	**100.00**	**100.00**

***Source:** CSO, February 2015. Here, CPFI stands for Consumer Food Price Index.*

the Price Relatives of Current Prices with respect to Base Prices of different markets in consonance with the international practice. In the old series, Arithmetic Mean (AM) was used for that purpose. The advantage of using GM is that it moderates the volatility of the indices as GM is less affected by extreme values.

6. Prices of PDS items under Antyodaya Anna Yojana (AAY) have also been included for compilation of indices of PDS items, in addition to Above Poverty Line (APL) and Below Poverty Line (BPL) prices being taken in the old series.

7. Sample size for collection of house rent data for compilation of *House Rent Index,* which was 6,684 rented dwellings in the old series, has now been doubled to 13,368 rented dwellings in the revised series.

8. Apart from All-India CPIs (Rural, Urban, Combined) for sub-group, group and general index (all-groups), which were released for the old series, all India Item CPIs (Combined) will also be available.

9. The Consumer Food Price Indices (Rural, Urban, Combined) will be compiled as weighted average of the indices of following sub-groups, as practiced earlier in the old series (only the weights have been revised):

TRENDS IN INFLATION

Inflation has been a highly sensitive issue in India right since Independence and it has been so during the ongoing reforms process period, too. It has an incessant tendency of resulting into 'double digits', taking politically explosive proportions like governments falling at the Centre and state levels due to price rise of the commodities such as edible oil, onion, potato, etc. In such situations the government in general has been taking recourse to tighter money supply to contain the state level disturbances due to price rise of the commodities such as edible oil, onion, potato, etc., although it has contained inflation, but at the cost of higher growth. Price rise got rooted in India's political psyche in such a way that the government did check frequent famines quickly at the cost of long-term endemic hunger and sustained malnutrition.[47]

Decadal inflation in India looks comparatively normal with reference to many developing economies.[48] But it has sporadic incidences of double-digit tendencies mainly due to supply-side shortfalls caused by droughts (monsoon failures), price rise of crude oil in the international market or fund diversions due to wars (the Chinese war of 1962 and the Pakistan wars of 1965–66 and 1971). The decadal inflation in India has been as given below:[49]

1. **During 1950s:** remained at 1.7 per cent.
2. **During 1960s:** remained at 6.4 per cent.
3. **During 1970s:** remained at 9.0 per cent.
4. **During 1980s:** remained at 8.0 per cent.
5. **During 1990s:** remained at 9.5 per cent (though it reached 0.5 per cent by the fourth quarter of the fiscal 1998–99)
6. **During 2000s:** Inflation was at lower levels between 2000–08 (from 3 to 5 per cent). But from 2009 onwards it started moving upward with 'stubborn' tendencies.[50] Between 2009–13, the headline inflation remained stuck at uncomfortable levels, primarily due to 'food articles' *(food inflation)* led by protein-rich items *(protein inflation)* in the consequence of shift in dietary habit, income effect (via MGNREGA kind of schemes), increased wages, increase in prices of commodities in the global market (especially, food articles), costlier fodder, costlier energy and fuel, etc. By late 2010, India had the phenomenon of *'skewflation'* with inflation being in the range of 9–10 per cent.
7. **During 2010s:** From 2010–11 to 2013–14 inflation remained higher—the average inflation at WPI and CPI was 8 per cent and 9.7 per cent, respectively. Food inflation, led by protein items, breached into double digit.[51] Since mid-2014 inflation started moderating—WPI inflation remained in negative (-5.1 per cent by August 2015) and CPI inflation positive of 4.9 per cent end-December 2016)—showing a *wedge* (i.e., difference) of 10 per cent which narrowed down to 0.2 per cent by the end of 2018-19.

During 2019-20, while the WPI did show falling trends and fell down to 1.7 per cent (chiefly caused by supply-glut at wholesale level), the CPI-C ended with 4.8 per cent (caused by increased demand at the retail level and supply bottlenecks). The year did show a much higher price rise in urban areas in comparison to the rural counterpart (in relation to almost all items with food being the prime cause).

TRENDS IN 2020-21 As per the *Economic Survey 2020-21*, the currents trends (April-December) of inflation in the country are as given below:

- The ***CPI-C*** increased to 6.6 per cent in 2020-21 before easing to a 15-month low of 4.6

47 Pranab Bardhan agrees to Amartya Sen (How is India Doing?', **New York Review of Books,** December 1982) in: 'A Political Economy Perspective on Development' in Bimal Jalan ed. **Indian Economy Problems and Prospects,** (New Delhi: Penguin Books, 1992), p. 369.

48 Rosser and Rosser, **Comparative Economics in a Transforming World Economy.**

49 Based on Rangarajan, **Indian Economy.** p. 63; Jalan,

50 Ministry of Finance, **Economic Survey 2013-14** (New Delhi: Government of India, 2014), pp. 75–77.

51 Ministry of Finance, **Economic Survey 2014-15** (New Delhi: Government of India, 2015), Vol. 2, pp. 69–75.

per cent (mainly driven by food inflation, which increased from 0.1 per cent in 2018-19 to 6.7 per cent in 2019-20 and further to 9.1 per cent in 2020-21, owing to build up in vegetable prices).

- Rise in *core inflation* was on account of miscellaneous group which primarily consists of services (inflation in transport & communication, which have maximum weightage in the miscellaneous group, increased to 9.4 per cent compared to 2.4 per cent in 2019-20) further pushed up by the rise in gold and silver prices.
- *WPI* inflation remained negative 0.1 per cent throughout the period rising to 1.2 per cent by December 2020— mainly on account of falling prices of the *fuel & power* (dropping sharply from 11.6 per cent in 2018-19 to negative 1.8 per cent in 2019-20 and further to negative 12.2 per cent in 2020-21).
- *Rural-urban* difference in CPI which was high in 2019-20 saw a decline in 2020-21 and remained close—food inflation almost converging; however, fuel & light inflation did show a divergence (a negative 0.1 per cent for rural areas and 6.7 per cent for urban areas)—rural-urban differential (i.e., the *wedge*) remaining in the range of 1.6 to 2.3 per cent (except housing, which is not compiled for rural areas).

Pandemic Disruption During 2020, due to the disruption caused by the COVID-19 pandemic, two forces were at play. On the one hand, there was a *dampening of demand* owing to lower economic activity. On the other hand, *supply chain disruptions* caused food inflation that continued till the unlocking of the economy— softening by the early 2021. A benign global inflation on account of lower economic activity and sharp fall in crude oil prices worked as a cushion to inflationary pressure in the case of India.

Inflationary Causes

Close analysis of inflationary trends does not pinpoint any one reason for inflationary pressures in India. However, experts have cited all good and bad reasons behind it which can be seen as given below:

1. **Structural Inflation**: With few exceptional years, India has been facing the typical problem of bottleneck inflation (*i.e.. structurul inflotion*) which arises out of shortfalls in the supply of goods, a general crisis of a developing economy, rising demand but lack of investible capital to produce the required level of goods.[52] Whenever the government managed to go for higher growths by managing higher investible capital it had inflationary pressures on the economy (seen during 1970s and 1980s, especially) and growth was sacrificed at the altar of lower inflation (which was politically more justified).[53] Thus, the supply-side mismatch remained a long-drawn problem in India for higher inflation. After some time even if the government managed higher expenditure, most of it went to the non-developmental areas, which did show low growth with higher inflation—signs of a stagnating economy.
2. **Cost-Push Inflation:** Due to 'inflation tax' the price of goods and services in India have been rising as the government took alternative recourse to increase its revenue receipts.[54]

52. Desai, Meghnad, 'Development Perspectives' in I.J. Ahluwalia and I.M.D. Little, (eds), ***India's Economic Reforms and Development***, (New Delhi: Oxford University Press, 1998), p. 41.
53. Jalan Bimal, ***India's Economic Policy***, (New Delhi: Penguin Books, 1992), pp. 52–58.
54. C. Rangarajan, 'Development, Inflation and Monetary Policy', in I.J. Ahluwalia and I.M.D. Little (eds), ***India's***
55. ***Economic Reforms and Development***, (New Delhi: Oxford University Press, 1998), pp. 56–57.

We see it taking place due to higher ***import duties*** on raw materials also.[55] The ***non-value-added*** tax (non-VAT) structure of India in the past was also having cascading effect on the prices of commodities in the country.[56] The government needed higher revenues to finance its planned development, thus the above given factors looked inescapable.

3. **Fiscal Policy:** To finance the developmental requirements of the economy, the governments became trapped in the cyclical process of over-money supply. At first it was done by external borrowings, but by the late 1960s onwards (once ***deficit financing*** got acceptance around the world) the government started taking recourse to heavy internal borrowings as well as printing of fresh currency too. A major part of the government's internal borrowing till 2005-06 was contributed by the Reserve Bank of India (RBI) which led to price rise.[57] For any government deficit if the Central Bank (RBI) is purchasing primary issues of the Government securities or creating fresh advances to the government, the combined effect has to be higher inflation, lower savings rates and lower economic growth[58]—the vices of unsound fiscal policy. The higher fiscal deficit tends to bring about higher interest rates as demand for funds rise, excess demand raises expected inflation and expected depreciation of the currency.[59]

Once the foreign exchange (Forex) reserves started increasing with a faster pace by the early 2000–01 fiscal, its cost of maintenance has been translated into higher prices, as the RBI purchases the foreign currencies it supplies into equivalent rupees into the economy, which creates extra demand and the prices go up.[60]

The higher revenue deficits (driven by high interest payments, subsidies, salaries and pensions, basically) and fiscal deficits make the government supply more money which push the inflation in the upward direction. Once the Fiscal and Budget Management Act came into force in 2003, the scenario improved in the coming times. Though the period from 1999 to 2003 did show high growth with low inflation and the lowest interest rates in India.

Healthy Range of Inflation

Higher inflation and higher growth as a trade-off was questioned in the late-1980s by the developed economies as the economic and social costs of higher inflation also needed policy attention—a costly 'trade-off'.[61] In coming times, most of the world economies went in favour of a stable inflation (i.e., ***inflation targeting***) though the idea has been ***protested***[62] India also started inflation stabilisation (informed targeting at WPI) by the early 1970s. It was in 1973 that inflation crossed the 20 per cent mark on account of the international oil price rise and the government (the Indira Gandhi Government) devised a severe

55. Jalan, **India's Economic Policy**, pp. 191–203.
56. ***Chelliah Committee Report***, 1993.
57. V.M. Dandekar, 'Forty Years After Independence', (New Delhi: Penguin Books, 1992), pp. 81–88. in the Bimal Jalan (ed.), ***Indian Economy: Problems and Prospects.***
58. Y.V. Reddy, ***Lectures on Economic and Financial Sector Reforms in India*** (New Delhi: Oxford University Press, 2002), pp. 176–77.
59. Ashima Goyal, 'Puzzles in India Performance: Deficits without Disaster' in Kirit S. Parikh and R. Radhakrishna (eds), **India Development Report, 2004-05** (New Delhi: IGIDR and Oxford University Press, 2005), pp. 191–208.
60. Kaushik Basu, **India Emerging Economy: performance and Prospects in the 1990,s and Beyond** (New Delhi: Oxford University Press, 2004), pp. 89–103.
61. S. Fisher, 'Modern Central Banking', in F. Capie et. al., **The Future of Central Banking, The Tercentenary Symposium of the Bank of England** (Cambridge: Cambridge University Press, 1994) pp. 262–308.
62. Paul Krugman, 'Stable Prices and Fast Growth: Just Say No', **Economist** 31 (1996): pp. 15–18.

anti-inflation package which included directly restricting the disposable incomes of the people (this measure was used for the *first* time in India[63]). The package had an impact and by March 1975 the inflation calmed down to 5.7 per cent. This was the time when the RBI was given a new function 'inflation stabilisation' and India entered the era of monetary controls for inflation. With inflation targeting, there started a debate concerning the healthy range of inflation for the Indian economy, i.e., by mid-1970s. We may have some official and non-official versions of the suitable range of inflation pointed out from time to time:

1. The *Chakravarty Committee (1985)* treated 4 per cent inflation as acceptable for the economy in its report on the monetary system. He also added that this level of price rise will facilitate the purpose of attracting investment for the desired level of growth.
2. The *Government of India* accepted a range of 4 to 6 per cent inflation as acceptable for the economy citing the world average of 0 to 3 per cent at the time (1997–98).[64]
3. The RBI Governor *C. Rangarajan* advocated that inflation rate must come down initially to 6 to 7 per cent and eventually to 5 to 6 per cent on an average over the years.[65]
4. The *Tarapore Committee* on Capital Account Convertibility recommended an acceptable range of 3 to 5 per cent inflation for the three year period (1997–98 to 1999–2000).[66]

In the recent times (June 2003 onwards) the government/the RBI has maintained a general policy of keeping inflation below 5 per cent mark—at any cost—as if fixing 4 to 5 per cent as the healthy range of inflation for the economy.[67]

The medium-term objective (i.e., target) of the government is to keep inflation in the 4–4.5 per cent range.[68] One thing should be kept in mind that inflation has always been a political matter in the country. Every time the RBI tried to check the rising inflation via monetary measures a majority of experts objected to it by calling it a move to sacrifice growth for lower price levels. A tighter monetary policy decelerates investment and growth, hampers the growth prospects of the middle class in general and the entrepreneurs in particular while the wage-earners as well as the poor segment of society feel relieved (at least in short term).

In **February 2015**, India formally commenced the process of 'inflation targeting'. Now, the new monthly CPI (C), is taken as the measure of **headline inflation** and is tracked by the RBI to **anchor** its monetary policy and the healthy annual range for it is between 2 to 6 per cent.

PRODUCER PRICE INDEX

Producer price index (PPI) is a better measure of inflation in comparison to both WPI and CPI. The ongoing process of economic reforms has increasingly connected India to the world which makes it necessary to evolve right comparative indicators. Inflation being among the most vital economic indicators in comparative economics due to which the government proposed to switch over from the WPI to PPI in 2003-04.

63. Ahluwalia and Little, ***India Economic Reforms and Development***, p. 2.
64. Ministry of Finance, Economic Survey 1997-98 (New Delhi: Government of India, 1998), p. 92.
65. Rangarajan, 'Development, Inflation and Monetary Policy, pp. 61–63.
66. We may refer to almost all the credit and monetary policies announced by the RBI during this period.
67. As the RBI put it in its Credit and Monetary Policy Review of July 31, 2007.
68. It should be noted here that the level of inflation was below 5 per cent till the new Government came to power and the outgoing Government was blamed to freeze the inflation data to a more politically digestible level (i.e., below 5 per cent).
69. The new Government in the process of preparing a producer price index (PPI) has also committed to make the inflation data automated like the share indices.

Special Features The PPI measures price changes from the perspective of the producer, while CPI from the perspective of consumer and WPI from the perspective of wholesale 'mandis'. In practice, the wholesellers charge higher prices to retailers, in turn retailers charge higher prices to consumers and the price increase is translated into the higher consumer prices—thus the PPI is useful in having an idea of the consumer prices in the future.[69] In PPI, only basic prices are used while taxes, trade margins and transport costs are excluded. This index is considered a better measure of inflation as price changes at primary and intermediate stages can be tracked before it gets built into the finished goods stage.[70] Due to its better use many economies have switched over to the PPI—the oldest such series is maintained by the Bureau of Labor Statistics (BLS) for the US economy—the index is capable of measuring prices at the wholesaler or the producer stage—widely used by private business houses in their price targeting.[71]

By *mid-2019*, Government did set up a ***Working Group*** headed by Ramesh Chand, member Niti Aayog, with a wide *term of reference* which includes the following issues related to the existing WPI—

1. Suggesting a new base year of WPI [The last revision in its base year to 2011-12 was done in May 2017];
2. Reviewing the commodity basket of the WPI and decide on the computational methodology to be adopted for monthly WPI/PPI [Since 2011-12 significant structural changes have taken place in the economy and it has become necessary to examine the coverage of commodities, weighting diagram and related issues pertaining to the existing WPI];
3. Reviewing the existing system of *price collection* in particular for manufacturing sector and suggest changes for improvement [Data collection method for manufacturing sector has been weak and unable to capture the sector in the real sense]; and
4. Devising a new PPI and recommend a roadmap to *switch over from WPI to PPI* [It has been a long-drawn plan of the Governments to switch over from WPI to PPI—the first Working Group on it was set up in 2004-05 under the chairmanship of Prof. Abhijit Sen, member of the erstwhile Planning Commission, which got inputs from the IMF also. In 2014, another Working Group was set up under Prof. B. N. Goldar to devise a PPI after the Reserve Bank of India began considering CPI-C inflation as a better gauge over the WPI inflation].

HOUSING PRICE INDEX

India's official Housing Price Index (HPI) was launched in July 2007 in Mumbai. Basically developed by the Indian home loans regulator, the National Housing Bank (NHB) the index is named ***NHB Residex***

Currently, it is published for 50 cities (being expanded to cover 100 cities) on quarterly basis with 2012–13 as base year. Among 50 cities covered are 18 State/UT capitals and 37 Smart cities. NHB is not computing the composite all India housing price index as of now.

Meanwhile, the RBI began compiling a house price index (HPI) in 2007 with a quarterly HPI for Mumbai city (Base 2002–03=100). Since then, it has extended its coverage to nine more cities, revised its base to 2010–11 and started publishing a composite All India HPI. RBI's quarterly HPI is

69 Stiglitz and Walsh, **Economics** p. 517.
70 Ministry of Finance, ***Economic Survey 2006–07***, p. 92.
71 Samuelson and Nordhaus, **Economics** p. 441.

based on transactions data received from housing registration authorities in 10 major cities.

With an overall objective of bringing transparency in the Indian real estate market, the index is expected to serve some highly important and timely purposes:

1. Whether a broker is quoting too high a price for houses in the cities.
2. Banks/housing finance bodies will be able to estimate only if the loan applications are realistic for the properties.
3. This will also show the level of non-performing assets in the housing sector.
4. And most importantly it will serve as a realistic price index for the buyers. (At present a buyer had no means, to judge whether a rise in property price was in the offing with the general level of inflation (i.e., at CPI-C) in the country, or has been scaled up disproportionately. Other than quotes from brokers, there are no means at present to evaluate the changes in price in this sector. At present the only index that gave some idea of housing price changes was the CPI (IW) which being a national index did not show ***regional variations***.)

As per the *Economic Survey 2020-21*, the Covid-19 crisis took a heavy toll on the residential real estate market— total number of transactions falling by 71 per cent on quarterly basis (March-June 2020) and by 67 per cent on yearly basis (June 2019-June 2020). However, during the quarter July 2020 to September 2020, transactions increased by around 150 per cent— reflecting economic recovery in the real estate sector.

SERVICE PRICE INDEX

The contribution of the tertiary sector in India's GDP has been strengthening for the past 10 years and today it stands above 60 per cent. The need for a service price index (SPI) in India is warranted by the growing dominance of the sector in the economy.[72] There is no index, so far, to measure the price changes in the services sector. The present inflation (at the WPI) only shows the price movements of the commodity-producing sector, i.e., it includes only the primary and the secondary sectors—the tertiary sector is not represented by it.

The need[73] for such an index was recommended by the working group (under the Chairmanship of Prof. Abhijit Sen, Member, Planning Commission) set up to revise the WPI (1993–94) series which was reiterated by the National Statistical Commission (headed by C. Rangarajan). The Office of the Economic Adviser, Ministry of Commerce and Industry has been making an effort to develop sector-specific service price index for the country with the technical assistance being received under the World Bank Assisted Economic Reforms Projects (WBAERPs).

Starting in 2005-06, the Office has put in place *Experimental Service Price Index* for a total of seven services—railways, postal, air, telecom, port, banking and insurance services. Evolving a single and national service price index is still in the process.

72. Ministry of Finance, ***Economic Survey 2006–07***, p. 94.

73. 'The number of National Statistical Agencies collecting service producer prices data, though growing, is still small', points out the ***OECD-Eurosat, 2005 Inquiry on National Collection of Services Producer Prices Preliminary Report,*** giving information on 45 such countries. The report further adds that while some such agencies have focused exclusively on the price of services provided to enterprises, others have approached the subject more broadly through the development of services producer price indices with varying approaches and coverage. As per the report, at present, 30 countries collect services producer prices while preliminary works have started in other countries, particularly the European countries under the auspices of the Eurosat. Other than the developed Euro-American economies some other countries which worked as inspiration for India which have such an index are China, Hong Kong, Czech Republic, Slovak Republic, Poland, Lithuania, Israel and Vietnam.

SECTION-B: BUSINESS CYCLE

INTRODUCTION

The discussion on growth and development has shown their internal interdependence. If the quality of life in an economy is to be enhanced, there is a need of conscious public policy which can spend and invest in areas like food, nutrition, health, education, shelter, social security, etc. But for such expenditures and investments, the economy needs equitable level of income, too. The income enhancement in any economy takes place via increasing the level of production in the economy, i.e., real gross national product (GNP). It means, development requires higher growth, i.e., higher levels of economic activities. With the help of suitable kind of economic policies, the government of an economy keeps trying to maintain a higher level of economic activity. But, at times, economy keeps failing in this objective. And, thus economies fluctuate between the best and the worst levels of economic activities which is known in economics as ***boom*** and ***depression***, respectively. They can be called different phases of the economic activities of the economies. In between boom and depression, there might be many other situations of the economic activities, such as—***stagnation, slowdown, recession*** and ***recovery***. The fluctuations in the level of economic activity between the depressions and booms has been called by the economists as ***business cycle*** or ***trade cycle*** with recession and recovery as the main intermediate stages.[74] Stagnation[75] and slowdown may be considered as other intermediate stages of the business cycle. We intend here to understand the actual meanings of each of the stages. Economists have pointed out that the business cycle is characterised by ***four*** phases or ***stages*** in which economies alternate:

1. Depression
2. Recovery
3. Boom
4. Recession

DEPRESSION

Though depression has visited the world economy only once in 1929, economists have pin-pointed enough number of traits to recognise it. The ***major*** traits of depression could be as given below:

1. an extremely low aggregate demand in the economy causes activities to decelerate;
2. the inflation being comparatively lower;
3. the employment avenues start shrinking forcing unemployment rate to grow fast;
4. to keep the business going, production houses go for ***forced labour-cuts*** or ***retrenchment*** (***to cut down production cost and be competitive in the market***) etc.

The economic situations become so chaotic in the phase of depression that governments have almost no control over the economy. The Great Depression of 1929[76] gave rise to the ideas of ***strong government intervention***[77] in the economy, such as deficit financing, monetary management, etc.

What the governments may do if depression visits the economy? The simple answer the world has been able to find is to repeat the policy measures

74. *Collins internet-linked Dictionary of Economics*, Glasgow, 2006 & *Oxford Business Dictionary*, N. Delhi, 2004.

75. Simon Cox (ed.), **Economics** (London: The Economists, 2007), p. 60.

76. A very lively description of the Great Depression has been presented by ***Lee Iacocca*** in his autobiography. This is known as the Great Depression due to its length and depth—the economies could recover fully out of it only by the mid-1940s (*Stiglitz and Walsh, p. 495*).

77. Suggested by John Meynard Keynes in his seminal work ***The General Theory of Employment, Interest and Money*** (New York: Harcourt, 1935).

of 1929. The best way to avoid depression is not to let it visit. This is why every modern economy keeps extra vigil on the major symptoms of its economy so that the prevention measures can be taken in time and depression is avoided.

RECOVERY

An economy tries to come out of the low production phase to survive. The low production phase might be depression, recession or slowdown with the former being the worst and rare, governments take many new fiscal and monetary measures to boost demand and production and ultimately a recovery in an economy is managed. The business cycle of recovery may show the following ***major*** economy traits:

1. an upturn in aggregate (total) demand which has to be accompanied by increase in the level of production;
2. production process expands and new investments become attractive;
3. as demand goes upward, inflation also moves upward making borrowing cheaper for investors;
4. with an upturn in production, new employment avenues are created and unemployment rate starts declining; etc.

With the above symptoms, people's income go for a certain increase which creates new demand and a cycle of demand and production (supply) starts playing hand-in-hand to recover the economy. To recover an economy, governments usually go for tax breaks, interest cuts, an increase in salaries of its employees, etc. Assimilation of innovations by the entrepreneurs and search for new frontiers of enterprise do play a very vital role in the process of recovery provided these activities are at first incentives by the governments.

The Euro-American economies recovered out of the Great Depression with the help of the measures cited above. Such recoveries have been seen many times around the world when economies recovered from slowdown or the recessionary phases. The best example of recent times could be cited from India of 1997 to 2002 when the economy suffered severe bouts of slowdown and recession.[78]

BOOM

A strong upward fluctuation in the economic activities is called boom.[79] As economies try to recover out of the phases of slowdown, recession and depression at times the measures taken by the governments as well as the private sector might put economic activities as such which the economic systems fail to digest. This is the phase of the ***boom***. The ***major*** economic traits of boom may be listed as given below:

1. an accelerated and prolonged increase in the demand;
2. demand peaks up to such a high level that it exceeds sustainable output/production levels;
3. the economy heats up and a demand-supply lag is visible;
4. the market forces mismatch (***i.e., demand and supply, disequilibirium***) and tend to create a situation where inflation starts going upward;
5. the economy might face structural problems like shortage of investible capital, lower savings, falling standard of living, creation of a sellers' market.

The phase of recovery is considered good for the economy and it reaches the stage of boom which is considered better. But the boom has its negative side also. Boom is usually followed by price rise.[80] As a boom is a strong upward fluctuation in an

78. ***Economic Surveys, 1996–97 to 2002–03,*** MoF, GoI, N. Delhi.
79. Stiglitz & Walsh, op. cit., p. 945.
80. Samuelson and Nordhaus, op. cit. pp. 680–84.

economy, the supply-side pattern of the economy starts lagging behind the pace of the accelerated aggregate demand.[81] But the dilemma of recovery puts every economy on the path to boom—this has been the experience in the developed world during the 1990s, especially in the US economy. The same scenario developed in India after the economy recovered from the recessionary period of 1996–97 by the year 2002–03 when the rate of inflation peaked to almost 8 per cent for a few months. Majority of the experts felt that Indian economy at that time was passing through a phase of boom and we have seen how the government has been facing difficulty in containing inflation around the 5 per cent mark. Even the government accepted that the economy was over-heating by mid-2007. *The symptoms of overheating are as follows:*

1. there is a downturn in the aggregate demand on overall fall in the demand;
2. as demand falls, the level of production (output) in the economy also falls;
3. as producers cut down their production levels, new employment opportunities are not created—thus employment growth rate falls;
4. as demand keeps on falling, usually producers start cutting down their labour force to adjust their overhead expenditure and the cost of production (labour-cut is not 'forced' here but, 'voluntary')—resulting in increase in the unemployment rate;
5. if the government fails to rescue the economy from the phase of recession, the dangerous stage of ***depression*** remains the logical follow up;
6. the rate of inflation always remains at lower levels—discouraging new investments and lending.

81. Stiglitz and Walsh, op. cit. pp. 495–796.

RECESSION

This is somewhat similar to the phase of 'depression' — we may call it a *mild form* of depression — fatal for economies as this may lead to depression if not handled with care and in time. The financial crises which followed the US 'sub-prime crisis' in almost the whole Euro-American economies has basically brought in 'severe recessionary' trends there. Major traits of recession, to a great extent, are similar to that of 'depression' [except the point (iv) of the Depression, discussed earlier]—may be summed up as follows:

1. there is a general fall in demand as economic activities takes a downturn;
2. inflation remains lower or/and shows further signs of falling down;
3. employment rate falls/unemployment rate grows;
4. industries resort to 'price cuts' to sustain their business.

In the financial year 1996–97, the Indian economy was taken up by the cycle of recession—basically due to a general downturn in domestic as well as foreign demands, initiated by the South East Asian Currency Crisis of mid-1990s.[82] The whole plan of economic reforms in India was derailed and it was only by the end of 2001–02 that the economy was able to recover. What may a government do to rescue the economy from the phase of recession? The usual remedies are given below:

1. Direct and indirect taxes should be cut down, so that the consumers have higher disposable incomes (income after paying direct tax, i.e., income tax) on the one hand and the goods should become cheaper on the other hand, thus there is hope that the demand might pick up.
2. The burden of direct taxes, especially the income tax, dividend tax, interest tax

82. ***Economic Survey, 1996–97***, MoF, GoI, N. Delhi.

are slashed to enhance the disposable income (***i.e., income after direct tax payment***).

3. Salaries and wages should be revised by the government to encourage general spending by the consumers (as the Government of India implemented the recommendations of the fifth pay commission without much deliberation in 1996–97).
4. Indirect taxes such as custom duty, excise duty (cenvat), sales tax, etc., should be cut down so that produced goods reach the market at cheaper prices.
5. The government usually goes on to follow a cheap money supply policy by slashing down interest rates across the board and the lending procedure is also liberalised.
6. Tax breaks are announced for new investments in the productive areas, etc.

All the above-given measures were taken up by the United Front Government in 1996–97 to pull the economy out of the menace of the recession.[83] The forthcoming government took several other such measures by the end of 1998–99 onwards (the NDA Government). Ultimately, the measures taken up by the governments accompanied by a general recovery in the world economy, the Indian economy started recovering from the bout of recession. Many experts had already predicted a possibility of depression with a zero per cent rate of inflation.[84] Although this did not happen.[85]

83. ***Economic Survey, 1996–97,*** MoF, GoI, N. Delhi.

84. It should be noted here that as an impact of recession the rate of inflation (at WPI) had been falling down throughout the mid 1998–99 fiscal finally to the level of 0.5 per cent for a fortnight (***Economic Survey, 1998–99,*** GoI, N. Delhi).

85. The literature of Economics and the empirical world experiences suggest that the phase of recession has all the symptoms of depression except one. Every thing being the same till producers are cutting the labour by force 'involuntarily (***i.e. forced labour cut***) it is the starting of depression—to be competitive in the market every producer starts 'forced labour cuts'—ultimately putting the economy into the grip of a full grown depression.

The World Bank and IMF define recession technically also. Any economy seeing fall in its GDP for two consecutive quarters is said to be hit with *technical recession*. Though, to declare global recession the agencies go into data related to employment, demand of oil, etc., it is defined with the help of global economic growth rate also—global growth rate falling below 2.5 per cent is considered technical recession (2.5 per cent is the *threshold* growth rate for technical global recession).

GROWTH RECESSION

An expression coined by economists to describe an economy that is growing at such a slow pace that more jobs are being lost than are being added. The lack of job creation makes it 'feel' as if the economy is in a recession, even though the economy is still advancing. Many economists believe that between 2002 and 2003, the United States' economy was in a phase of growth recession. In fact, at several points over the past 25 years the U.S. economy is said to have experienced a growth recession. That is, in spite of gains in real GDP, job growth was either non-existent or was being destroyed at a faster rate than new jobs were being added.

Experts have revived this term in the wake of the ongoing financial crises in the Euro-American economies since 2008. The situation is better described by the term ***'double-dip recession'.***

DOUBLE-DIP RECESSION

The concept of 'recession' in the USA and Euro Zone is quite precise and technical—'*two consecutive quarters of falling* GDP'—is how it is defined in these economies. And the idea of the 'double-dip recession' is an extension of it.

A double-dip recession refers to a recession followed by a short-lived recovery, followed by another recession—the GDP growth sliding back to negative after a quarter or two of positive growth. The causes for such a recession vary but often include a slowdown in the demand for goods and services because of layoffs (forced job cuts) and spending cutbacks done in the previous downturn. A double-dip (which may be even 'triple-dip') is a worst-case scenario—fear/speculation of it moves the economy into a deeper and longer recession and recovery becomes too difficult. As the world saw in the case of the Euro Zone crisis—there was a fear of such a recession by first quarter of 2013. (For discussion on '**Retrocession**' see *Glossary*).

CONCLUSION

Business cycles are basically fluctuations in the production levels of economies above and below the trend of the equilibrium levels.[86] But why do economies fluctuate? There are many factors which are said to be responsible for it, as per the experts:

1. Economic instability and uncertainty (due to logical or illogical expectations) may discourage investments thereby reducing growth in the long term.
2. A lack of the creative destruction (i.e. innovation) may put the economy in a slump or slowdown in its overall production.
3. Anti-inflationary government policies (especially when general elections are nearing) may direct the attraction of investors in the economy.
4. Unforeseen disasters may cause economies to fluctuate.

86. Cox, Simon, op. cit., p. 58.

CHAPTER 8

AGRICULTURE AND FOOD MANAGEMENT

*India is now faced with a problem of plenty-with supply outpacing demand-India has surpluses in most food categories which bring down food inflation resulting in stalling a large channel of income transfer from food consumers (mostly rich) to food producers (mostly poor).**

In this Chapter...

- Introduction
- Kharif & Rabi
- Food Philosophy of India
- Land Reforms
- Green Revolution
- Cropping Patterns
- Animal Rearing
- Food Management
- Buffer Stock
- Storage
- Farm Subsidies
- Food Security
- PDS & Food Subsidy
- Agriculture Marketing
- Model Contract Farming Act
- COVID-19 and Agri-Reforms
- Supply Chain Management
- Irrigation
- Farm Mechanisation
- Seed Development
- Fertilisers
- Pesticides
- Agri-Credit
- Agriculture Extension Services
- PMFBY
- WTO and the Indian Agriculture: Prospects and Challenges
- WTO and Agricultural Subsidies AMS
- National Food Security Act
- Food Processing
- Major Policy Initiatives
- Doubling Farm Income
- Cash Support to Farmers
- Women Farmers
- Climate Smart Agriculture
- Way Forward

* *See Agricultural Reforms, Neelkanth Mishra in Abhijit Banerjee, Gita Gopinath, Raghuram Rajan and Mihir Sharma edited* **What the Economy Needs Now,** *pp. 96-103, Juggernaut Books, N. Delhi, 2019.*

INTRODUCTION

Agriculture remains the most important sector of the Indian economy, whether it be the pre-independence or the post-independence periods. This fact is emphatically proved by the large number of people who depend on it for their livelihood. Before starting any discussion on Indian agriculture, we must look into its *special features:*

1. From the monetary point of view the share of the agriculture sector in the economy remains at *17.8 per cent of the GVA (Gross Value Added).*[1] In the fiscal 1950-51 agriculture accounted for 55.4 per cent of the GDP.
2. The share of agriculture has been falling in the country's gross income, while industrial and services sectors' shares have been on a rise constantly. But from the livelihood point of view still *54.5 per cent* of the people of India depend on the agriculture[2] sector. This makes it a more important sector than the industry and the services (for Nepal and Tanzania the dependency for livelihood on agriculture is still higher at 93 per cent and 81 per cent, respectively). It means that around 55 per cent of the population lives with only 18 per cent of the total income of the Indian economy—this fact clearly substantiates the reason why the people who depend on agriculture are poor. In the developed economies such as the USA, France, Norway, the UK and Japan, agriculture contributes only 2 per cent of their GDP with only 2 per cent of the people dependent on this sector for their livelihood.
3. Agriculture is not only the biggest sector of the economy, but also the biggest private sector too. It is the only profession which still carries no burden of individual income tax.
4. This is the biggest *unorganised sector* of the economy accounting for more than 90 per cent share in the total unorganised labour-force (93.4 per cent of the total labour force of the economy, i.e., 40.0 crores is employed in the unorganised sector).[3]
5. India occupies[4] a leading position in global agricultural trade having a share of 2.5 per cent in the world agricultural trade—the USA, Saudi Arabia, Iran, Nepal and Bangladesh as major export destinations. What is *noteworthy* is that since the economic reforms began, India has remained consistently a 'net exporter' of agri-products (in 2019-20, value of exports being ₹2.52 lakh crore against import of ₹1.47 lakh crore).
6. According to the export figures, agriculture is deeply related to industrial growth and the national income in India—1 per cent increase in the agricultural growth leads to 0.5 per cent increase in industrial output (growth) and 0.7 per cent increase in the national income of India.[5]
7. The industrial sector was selected as the *'prime moving force'* of the economy in the late 1940s. But due to market failure the sector failed to lead the economy after independence. Without increasing the income of the people who depend on agriculture for their livelihood, the market was not going to support the industries. As a result, the Government of India announced agriculture as the prime moving force of the economy in 2002.[6]

1 **Economic Survey 2020-21,** vol. 2, pp. 230-32, Ministry of Finance, GoI, N. Delhi.

2 **Economic Survey 2020-21,** vol. 2, p. 230, Ministry of Finance, GoI, N. Delhi.

3 **Labour Bureau,** Ministry of Labour and Employment, GoI, N. Delhi, March 2021.

4 ***Economic Survey 2020-21,*** Vol. 2, p. 237, Ministry of Finance, GoI, N. Delhi.

5 This correlation has been pointed out by many great economists in India since 1960s, for example, by ***Raj Krishna (1976), S. Chakravarty (1974–79)*** and ***C. Rangarajan (1982)*** to quote some of the most important names.

6 Planning Commission, ***Approach Paper to the Tenth Five Year Plan*** (New Delhi: Government of India, 2002).

8. With 1 per cent increase in the share of agriculture in India's total exports, the money which flows into agriculture is calculated to be ₹8,500 crores.[7]

9. A total of 66.1 per cent of the cropped area in the country still depends on the uncertainties of monsoon for their irrigational requirements—meanwhile attention is being given on enhancing *water productivity* and *irrigation efficiency*[8].

10. **Foodgrain** production[9] is estimated to reach a *record* level of 296.65 million tonnes (MT) in 2020-21 (it was 291.95 MT in 2019-20). The country is headed for a *record* production of several crops such as—rice (118.5 MT), wheat (108.3 MT), nutri cereals (46.23 MT)[10] in the year.

AGRICULTURE IN 2020-21

The resilience of India's agriculture sector can be seen from the fact that despite the disruptions of COVID-19 it had a robust growth of 3.4 per cent during 2020-21 We see the industry and services having negative growth rates (-9.6 per cent and -16 per cent, respectively) during the same period.

The renewed thrust given by the Govemment on several fronts such as---credit, market reforms, food processing, dairying, animal husbandry fisheries, farm insurance and farm income support-had their positive impact on the sector.

Source: *Economic Suruey 2020-21, vol. 2, pp. 230-60, Ministru of Finance, Gol, N. Delhi.*

KHARIF & RABI

There are certain special terms used to understand the cropping seasons of India. The agricultural crop year in India is from *July to June*. The Indian cropping season is classified into two main seasons: (i) kharif and (ii) rabi based on the monsoon. The kharif cropping season is from *July to October* during the South-West/Summer Monsoon and the rabi cropping season is from *October to March* (North-East/Returning/Winter Monsoon). The crops grown between March and June are summer crops, known as *jayads*.

Pakistan and Bangladesh are two other countries that are using the term 'kharif' and 'rabi' to describe their cropping patterns. The terms 'kharif' and 'rabi' originate from Arabic language where kharif means *autumn* and rabi means *spring*.

The kharif crops include rice, maize, sorghum, pearl millet/bajra, finger millet/ragi (cereals), arhar (pulses), soyabean, groundnut (oilseeds), cotton, etc. The rabi crops include wheat, barley, oats (cereals), chickpea/gram (pulses), linseed, mustard (oilseeds) etc.

FOOD PHILOSOPHY OF INDIA

Indian food philosophy[11] is generally seen divided into three phases with their own objectives and challenges:

The First Phase

This phase continued for the first three decades after Independence. The main aim and the struggle of this phase was producing as much foodgrains as required by the Indian population, i.e., achieving *physical access* to food.

7 This was the general opinion of the experts throughout the 1990s, but the official document which accepted this contention was the ***Foreign Trade Policy 2002–07***, of the Ministry of Commerce. This View continued with the government in all its forthcoming trade policies till about four decades.

8 **Economic Survey 2015-16, Vol. 2,** Ministry of Finance, GoI, p. 103.

9 *Fourth Advance Estimates,* **Economic Survey 2020-21,** vol. 2, p. 234, Ministry of Finance, GoI, N. Delhi..

10 For *detailed discussion* on 'nutri cereals' see the entry NUTRI CEREALS in **Glossary**.

11 ***Indian Council of Agricultural Research (ICAR),*** N. Delhi, 1998.

The idea of the Green Revolution at the end of this phase at least gave India the confidence of realising the objective. At the end of the 1980s, India was a self-sufficient country with regard to food.

The Second Phase

Meanwhile India was celebrating its success of the first phase, a new challenge confronted the country—achieving *economic access* to food. The situation went on worsening and by early 2000 there was a paradoxical situation in the country when it was having more than three times buffer stocks of foodgrains in the central pool, but in several states people were dying due to lack of food—a complete mockery of the logic behind maintaining buffer stock, success of green revolution and the concept of India being a welfare state.[12] The Supreme Court intervened after a PIL was filed by the People's Union for Civil Liberties (PUCL) and a national level Food for Work Programme came up (to be merged with the National Rural Employment Guarantee Scheme). The courts took the governments on task if foodgrains rot either in godowns or destroyed in oceans to manage market price for the foodgrains, or if the Centre had to go for exporting wheat at very low price. In this process India emerged as the *seventh largest* exporter of wheat (2002). Basically, we were exporting the share of wheat which was not consumed by many Indians due to lack of economic reach to food.

As the inputs of the Green Revolution were costlier, its output naturally were to be costlier. To fight the situation there should have been a time-bound and target-oriented macro-economic policy support, which could deliver comparative increase in the purchasing capacity of the masses to make food affordable for them. India badly failed in it. The crisis was managed by throwing higher and higher subsidies ultimately affecting government expenditure on the infrastructural shortcomings in the agriculture sector. Even after providing higher food subsidies, some people failed to purchase food and they were left with no option but to die of hunger.

India is still in this phase and trying to solve the crisis through twin approach, firstly, by creating maximum number of gainful employment, and secondly, by cutting cost of foodgrains (via the second green revolution based on biotechnology).

It must be kept in mind that the food self-sufficiency happiness was a temporary thing for India. By the mid 1990s, India realised that its foodgrain production was lagging behind its population increase. It means India is still fighting to achieve physical reach to the required level of food.

The Third Phase

By the end of the 1980s, world experts started questioning the very way world was carrying on with different modes of production. Agricultural activity was one among them which had become hugely based on industries (chemical fertilisers, pesticides, tractors, etc.). All developed economies had declared their agriculture to be an industry.[13]

It was time to look back and introspect. By the early 1990s, several countries started going for ecologically friendly methods and techniques of industrial, agricultural and services sectors development. The much-hyped Green Revolution was declared ecologically untenable and the world headed for organic farming, green farming, etc.

It meant that achieving physical and economic reach to food was not the only challenge India was facing, but such aims should not be realised at the cost of the precious ecology and biodiversity—a

12. Publication Division, **India 2000** (New Delhi: Government of India, 2001); Ministry of Finance, ***Economic Survey 2000–01***, (New Delhi: Government of India, 2001).

13. ***Brundtland Report*** on Sustainable Development after the deliberations at the summit ***"Our Common future"***, 1987.

new challenge. India needed a new kind of green revolution which could deliver the physical, economic as well as *ecological access* to food—the Second Green Revolution—an all-in-one approach towards the agriculture sector.

LAND REFORMS

The official stance and emphasis on land reforms in India have been changing over the time in wake of the emerging issues, which may be seen in the following two phases.

Phase-I

This phase commences just after Independence.

All economies were agrarian before they were industrialised, only their periods vary. Once democratic systems developed, the first thing the developed countries of today did was to complete the agrarian reforms in a time-bound way. As land remains the means of livelihood for the larger section of society in an agrarian economy, the successful completion of agrarian reforms benefitted the maximum number of people thereby improving their economic conditions. At the time of Independence, India was a typical agrarian economy and had inherited a very inequitable agrarian system. Land reforms will be a major plank of independent India and as part of the agrarian reforms it was made clear by the pledge of the Indian National Congress in 1935 itself. Land reforms in India had three objectives similar to the other economies which opted for it in the past:

1. Removing *institutional discrepancies* of the agrarian structure inherited from the past which obstructed increasing agricultural production, such as, the size of agricultural holding, land ownership, land inheritance, tenancy reforms, abolition of intermediaries, introduction of modern institutional factors to agriculture, etc.
2. The other objective of the land reforms in India was related to the issue of ***socio-economic inequality*** in the country. The high inequality in land ownership not only had its negative economic impact on the economy; but it was badly intertwined with the caste system in India and the allocation of social prestige and status by the society at large.[14] More than 80 per cent of the population from its livelihood inherited the agrarian system which had inequitable ownership of the asset, i.e., land to earn income. The government wanted to go for a restructuring of land ownership in the economy on logical grounds and with public welfare approach. This objective of land reforms got enough socio-political attention as it tried to dismantle the age-old agrarian structure in the country. It became such a hot issue that land reforms in India got a 'bad-name', synonymous to land-grabbing by the government and allotting them to the landless masses.
3. The third objective of land reforms in India was highly contemporary in nature, which did not get enough socio-political attention—it was the objective of *increasing agricultural production* for solving the inter-related problems of poverty, malnutrition and food insecurity.

To realise the objectives of land reforms, the government took three main steps which had many internal sub-steps:

I. **Abolition of Intermediaries:** Under this step, the age-old exploitative land tenure systems of the Zamindari, Mahalwari and Ryotwari were fully abolished.

14. L.I. Rudolph and S.H. Rudolph, ***In Pursuit of Lakshmi: The Political Economy of the Indian State*** (Bombay: Orient Longman, 1987), pp. 45–50.

2. **Tenancy Reforms:** Under this broader step, three inter-related reforms protecting the land tenants were effected:
   - **(i)** *Regulation of rent* so that a fixed and rational rate of rent could be paid by the share-croppers to the land owners;
   - **(ii)** *Security of tenure* so that a share-cropper could feel secure about his future income and his economic security; and
   - **(iii)** *Ownership rights to tenants* so that the landless masses (i.e., the tenants, the share-croppers) could get the final rights for the land they plough—*'land to the tillers'*.
3. **Reorganisation of Agriculture:** This step again has many inter-related and highly logical provisions in the direction of rational agrarian reforms:
   - **(i)** *Redistribution of land* among the landless poor masses after promulgating timely *ceiling laws*,—the move failed badly with few exceptions, such as West Bengal, Kerala and partially in Andhra Pradesh.
   - **(ii)** *Consolidation of land* could only succeed in the regions of the Green Revolution (i.e., Haryana, Punjab and western Uttar Pradesh) and remained marred with many loopholes and corruption.
   - **(iii)** *Cooperative farming,* which has a high socio-economic moral base, was only used by the big farmers to save their lands from the draconian ceiling laws.

The whole attempt of land reforms in India is considered a big failure by majority of experts. Many consider the issue of land reforms in India as the most complex socio-economic problem of human history.[15] Data regarding the numerical achievements of land reforms have been highly discouraging.[16]

1. Tenancy reforms provided tenants with rights, but only on 4 per cent of the total operated areas in the country (14.4 million hectares of operated area by 11 million tenants by 1992).
2. Redistribution of ownership rights of land took place, but only upto 2 per cent of the total operated area in the country (less than 2 million hectares among the 4.76 million people by 1992).
3. Taken together, the whole process of land reforms could benefit only 6 per cent of the operated area of the country with a negligible socio-economic positive impact.

It was the failure of land reforms which made the government easily attracted towards the new policy of the Green Revolution in the coming times—land reforms had failed to increase agricultural production, thus the government opted for the route of increasing productivity to reach the same goal, i.e., initiation of new techniques of agriculture.

Reasons for Failure of Land Reforms

Out of the many reasons forwarded by the experts responsible for the failure of the land reforms in India, the following three could be considered the most important ones:

1. Land in India is considered a symbol of social prestige, status and identity unlike the other economies which succeeded in their land reform programmes, where it is seen as just an economic asset for income-earning.

15. This was the view of the majority of experts around the world by the late 1960s.

16. P.S. Appu, ***Land Reforms in India: A Survey of Policy, Legislation and Implementation,*** (Mussouri: Land Reforms Unit, Lal Bahadur Shastri National Academy of Administration, 1995), pp. 232–33.

2. Lack of political will which was required to affect land reforms and make it a successful programme.
3. Rampant corruption in public life, political hypocrisy and leadership failure in the Indian democratic system.

Land Reforms & Green Revolution

Once the government launched the Green Revolution, the issue of land reforms almost got marginalised due to the following reasons:

1. There is an inherent diabolic relationship between the Green Revolution and the land reforms as the former suits bigger and economic land holdings, while the latter intended to fragment the land among a large number of the masses.
2. The land reforms were socially opposed by the land-owning caste lobbies, while there was no such opposition to the Green Revolution.
3. The level of legislative attempts taken by the governments regarding the land reforms till date had almost no positive socio-economic impact on the country, while the Green Revolution was having all potential of proving higher yields of foodgrains.
4. The subsidised supplies of foodgrains under PL480 were hampering India from carving out its independent diplomacy, as well as there has always remained a doubt about the regular supplies of wheat.
5. International pressure as well as the suggestions from the World Bank besides the success stories of the Green Revolution from the countries where it had increased the yield of wheat.

Phase-II

The second phase of land reforms can be traced in the process of economic reforms. Economic reforms exposed the economy to the new and emerging realities, such as, land acquisition and leasing, food-related issues and the agricultural provisions of the World Trade Organization (WTO). We see a shift *(Economic Survey 2012–13)* in the thinking of the Government of India towards the issue of land reforms—a clear three step policy looks emerging:

1. Mapping land carefully and assigning conclusive title,
2. Devising a fair but speedy process of land acquisition, and
3. Putting in place a transparent and effective land leasing policy.

Land is probably the single most valuable asset in the country today. Not only could greater liquidity for land allow more resources to be redeployed efficiently in agriculture, it could ease the way for land-utilising businesses to set up. Perhaps, as important, it could allow land to serve as collateral for credit.

The issue of 'inconclusive' land ownership has been a major developmental concern and matter of high litigation in the country. Presently, a scheme[17] the Digital India Land Records Modernisation Programme (DILRMP), is being run as a central sector scheme aimed at moving from *presumptive title* (where registration of a title

17 Aimed at achieving a conclusive land ownership titles,the Department of Land Resources, Ministry of Rural Development launched the *National Land Records Modernisation Programme (NLRMP)* in 2008—by merging the Computerisation of Land Records (CLR) and Strengthening of Revenue Administration and Updating of Land Records (SRA&ULR) schemes of late 1980s. The NLRMP was to be completed by the end of 2016-17 (the terminal year of the 12th Plan) but remained unfinished due to several reasons (states' apathy being one major reason). In 2014, the programme was **revamped** as the *Digital India Land Records Modernisation Programme (DILRMP).* Started as a centrally sponsored scheme (financed by both centre and state), in 2016-17, the programme evolved into a central sector scheme (fully financed by the centre). Aimed at providing a system of updated and automated land records, the programme has three major components, namely—(i) Computerisation of land record, (ii) Survey/re-survey, and (iii) Computerisation of Registration.

does not imply the owner's title is legally valid) to *conclusive title* (where it does). Successful completion of the programme is supposed to speed up the process of development in the country together with saving the precious time in land-related litigation. However, the programme has been slow and uneven across states—to speed up the process lessons may be taken from some state initiatives[18] such as the Bhoomi Project in Karnataka, the Rajasthan Urban Ceiling Act 2016 and the use of blockchain technology to prevent property fraud in Andhra Pradesh.

Meanwhile, a new central sector scheme, the *Swamitva*, was launched (for the period 2020-24) by the Government in 2020-21 to provide the *record of rights* to village household owners in rural areas and issue 'Property Cards' (which has been given different names by different states). It will bring in several benefits such as— streamlined planning, revenue collection, clarity of property rights, easier borrowings and decrease in property disputes.

Moving onwards, the Government of India passed the *Land Acquisition Bill, 2013*. The bill, besides proposing to amend the *Land Acquisition, Rehabilitation and Resettlement Act, 2011* proposed to put in place a transparent, effective and speedy laws regarding the need of land reforms related to leasing and acquisition. By 2015, the new government at the Centre proposed a new land bill *(Right to Fair Compensation and Transparency in Land Acquisition, Rehabilitation and Resettlement Bill, 2015)*, which aimed at removing the inadequacies of the Land Act of 2013. Faced with extreme opposition by the political parties, experts and media the Bill (which was already enforced through Presidential Ordinance) was repealed by the Government. Later on the NITI Aayog was asked to look into advising an effective, fair and transparent land acquisition policy for the country (NITI Aayog suggested a *Model Land Leasing Law in 2016*).

Finer points (as per the relevant official documents) related to this PHASE may be summed up in the following way:

1. Leasing seems a better choice in face of farmer's opposition seen in recent times in different states toward attempts at land acquisition. Again, if the country needs to attract investment from the organised private sector (domestic or foreign) land leasing seems a better option than land acquisition.
2. Corporate farming has not taken place in the country in a big scale, especially in the areas of foodgrains production, which India needs to ensure food security and compete in the global grain market, in particular, and the agri-market in general. This has become even more important in the wake of the Right to Food given to a large segment of the population.
3. Giving primacy to 'leasing' will solve several problems:
   - **(i)** It will keep land ownership in the hands of the existing farmers;
   - **(ii)** It will prevent mass landlessness and unemployment among the farmers;
   - **(iii)** Farmers will get a permanent source of income (in the meantime, they might be imparted skills and provide better employment in industries); and
   - **(iv)** It will make land easily available for use of public and private purposes.

18. *Land Market Reforms*, Maitreesh Ghatak in Abhijit Banerjee, Gita Gopinath, Raghuram Rajan and Mihir Sharma edited **What the Economy Needs Now**, p. 83, Juggernaut Books, N. Delhi, 2019. It is referenced with ***Land Acquisition and Compensation in Singur: What Really Happened?*** by Maitreesh Ghatak, Sandip Mitra, Dilip Mukherjee and Anusha Nath, *Economic & Political Weekly*, Vol. 48 (21), 2013.

Meanwhile, the **Model Land Leasing Law** advised by the Niti Aayog in 2016 has been well-received by the states and some of them have already tried *land pooling* quite successfully, by early 2020. In this context, the example of Andhra Pradesh[19] has been quite successful which does not offer monetary compensation for the land taken today rather offers a developed piece of land in the future city (25 per cent of every fertile acre pooled to be returned as developed area in future city). The pro-active inter-mediation of state governments the process of land acquisition looks coming out of the troubled times. But the new concern is the *rising cost of land acquisition*—beginning with the financial year 2013-14 it has increased by over 300 per cent till December 2020—from ₹0.8 crore per hectare to ₹2.85 crore per hectare (as per the platform *Bhoomi Rashi*, Ministry of Road Transport and Highways).

- In the wake of the process of globalisation, if the country intends to bring in benefits to agriculture sector it needs to enhance its agriculture production to surplus levels—and for this India needs to garner in the investment potential of the private sector. This cannot happen till the country is able to bring out effective land leasing and acquisition policies.
- The recent emphasis on the promotion of the 'manufacturing sector' and 'smart cities' is hugely dependent on smoother and speedier process of land acquisition. Without expanding the industrial sector to its optimum levels, the agriculture sector can emerge a remunerative profession—the country needs to migrate the extra labour force of the agriculture sector to industry, smoothly.

19. *Land Market Reforms*, Maitreesh Ghatak in Abhijit Banerjee, Gita Gopinath, Raghuram Rajan and Mihir Sharma edited **What the Economy Needs Now**, p. 82, Juggernaut Books, N. Delhi, 2019.

- The issue of land acquisition is to establish a logical equation with 'environmental issue', in order to make the process of development sustainable (Niti Aayog gives a right call for it).

It should be noted that while the Government of India has changed its orientation towards the issue of land reforms, the states in India are still trying to accelerate and continue the process of land reforms of *PHASE I* (but due to enough resistance from the land-owning section in the country, the process does not seem happening, politically).

Agriculture Holdings

The 10th *Agriculture Census 2015-16* was released by the Government in October 2018 (the Census is conducted after every 5 years). As per the report, the average size of land holding is decreasing due to rapid fragmentation caused by high population growth. The *major highlights* of the Census are as given below (all comparisons made in reference to the last and the 9th Census 2010–11):

- The total area under farming fell from 159.6 million hectares (Mha) to 157.14 Mha.
- Small and marginal farmers (owning less than two hectares) account for 86.2 per cent of all farmers in India, but own just 47.3 per cent of the crop area. In comparison, semi-medium and medium land holding farmers (owning between 2-10 hectares) account for 13.2 per cent of all farmers, but own 43.6 per cent of crop area.
- The proportion of small and marginal farmers grew from 84.9 per cent to 86.2 per cent, while the total number of operational holdings grew from 138 million to 146 million.
- The number of small and marginal farms rose by about 9 million during the period.

- The small and marginal farmers (around 126 million in number) own about 74.4 Mha of land—or an average holding of just 0.6 hectares each—not enough to produce surpluses which can financially sustain their families, explaining the rising distress in Indian agriculture.
- For all farmers put together, the size of average land holding declined from 1.15 hectares to 1.08 hectares.
- The farmers holding 10 hectares and more account for just 0.57 per cent and had a share of 9.04 per cent in the operated area.
- State-wise data from the survey showed that Uttar Pradesh accounted for the largest number of operational holdings or farmers at 23.8 million followed by Bihar (16.4 million) and Maharashtra (14.7 million).
- Among operated or farmed areas, Rajasthan topped the list with 20.9 Mha, followed by Maharashtra (19.9 Mha) and Uttar Pradesh (17.45 Mha).
- The proportion of farms that are operated by women rose from 12.8 per cent to 13.9 per cent, signifying that more women are managing farm operations (the process of feminisation of farm sector is going on).

GREEN REVOLUTION

It is the introduction of new techniques of agriculture, which became popular by the name of Green Revolution (GR) in early 1960s—at first for *wheat* and by the next decade for *rice*, too. It revolutionised the very traditional idea of food production by giving a boost by more than 250 per cent to the productivity level.[20] The Green Revolution was centred around the use of the High Yielding Variety (HYV) of seeds developed by the US agro-scientist Norman Borlaug doing research on a British Rockfellor Foundation Scholarship in Mexico by the early 1960s. The new wheat seeds which he developed *in vivo* claimed to increase its productivity by more than 200 per cent. By 1965, the seeds were successfully tested and were being used by farmers in food deficient countries such as Mexico, Taiwan.

Components of the Green Revolution

The Green Revolution was based on the timely and adequate supply of many inputs/components. A brief review on the Green Revolution is given below:

1. **The HYV Seeds:** These seeds were popularly called the *'dwarf'* variety of seeds. With the help of repeated mutations, Mr. Borlaug had been able to develop a seed which was raised in its nature of nutrients supplied to the different parts of the wheat plant—against the leaves, stem and in favour of the grain. This made the plant dwarf and the grain heavier—resulting in high yield.[21]

   These seeds were non-photosynthetic, hence non-dependent on sun rays for targeted yields.

2. **The Chemical Fertilizers:** The seeds were to increase productivity provided they got sufficient level of nutrients from the land. The level of nutrients they required could not be supplied with the traditional composts because they have low concentration of nutrients content and required bigger area while sowing—it meant it will be shared by more than one seed. That is why a high concentration fertilisers were required, which could be given to the targeted seed only—the only option was the chemical fertilisers—urea (N), phosphate (P) and potash (K).

20. *Consultative Group on International Agricultural Research* (CGIAR), World Bank, Washington DC, 1971.

21. *International Maize and Wheat Improvement Centre* (CIMMYT), Mexico, 1971.

3. **The Irrigation:** For controlled growth of crops and adequate dilution of fertilizers, a controlled means of water supply was required. It made two important compulsions—firstly, the area of such crops should be at least free of flooding and secondly, artificial water supply should be developed.

4. **Chemical Pesticides and Germicides:** As the new seeds were new and non-acclimatised to local pests, germs and diseases than the established indigenous varieties, use of pesticides and germicides became compulsory for result-oriented and secured yields.

5. **Chemical Herbicides and Weedicides:** To prevent costlier inputs of fertilisers not being consumed by the herbs and the weeds in the farmlands, herbicides and weedicides were used while sowing the HYV seeds.

6. **Credit, Storage, Marketing/Distribution:** For farmers to be capable of using the new and the costlier inputs of the Green Revolution, availability of easy and cheaper credit was a must. As the farmlands suitable for this new kind of farming was region-specific (as it was only Haryana, Punjab and western Uttar Pradesh in India) storage of the harvested crops was to be done in the region itself till they were distributed throughout the country. Again, the countries which went for the Green Revolution were food-deficient and needed the new yield to be distributed throughout the country and a proper chain of marketing, distribution and transport connectivity was necessary. All these peripheral infrastructure were developed by the countries going for the Green Revolution with softer loans coming from the World Bank—India being the biggest beneficiary.[22]

[22] Publication Division, **India 2002** (New Delhi; Government of India, 2013).

Impact of the Green Revolution

The Green Revolution had its positive as well as negative socio-economic and ecological impacts on the countries around the world, we will specially study India here.

1. **Socio-economic Impact:** Food production increased in such a way (wheat in 1960s and rice by 1970s) that many countries became self-sufficient (self sufficiency of food must not be confused with the idea of food security) and some even emerged as food exporting countries.

   But the discrepancy in farmers' income, it brought with itself increased the inter-personal as well as inter-regional disparities/inequalities in India. Rise in the incidence of malaria due to water-logging, a swing in the balanced cropping patterns in favour of wheat and rice putting pulses, oilseeds, maize, barley on the margins, etc., were negative impacts.

2. **Ecological Impact:** The most devastating negative impact of the Green Revolution was ecological. When the issues related with it were raised by the media, scholars, experts and environmentalists, neither the governments nor the masses (what to say of the farmers of the GR region—they were not educated enough to understand the side effects of the inputs of the GR) were convinced. But a time came when the government and other government agencies started doing studies and surveys focused around the ecological and environmental issues. The major ones among them may be glanced in their chronological order:

   (i) ***Critical Ecological Crisis:*** On the basis of on-field studies[23] it was found

[23] Based on various empirical studies in the 1990s conducted separately by ***Vandana Shiva, C.H. Hanumantha Rao, ICAR, Planning Commission, etc.***

that critical ecological crises in the GR region are showing up—

(a) *Soil fertility being degraded:* Due to the repetitive kind of cropping pattern being followed by the farmers as well as the excessive exploitation of the land; lack of a suitable crop combination and the crop intensity, etc.

(b) *Water table falling down:* As the new HYV seeds required comparatively very high amount of water for irrigation—5 tonnes of water needed to produce 1 kg of rice.

(c) *Environmental degradation:* Due to excessive and uncontrolled use of chemical fertilizers, pesticides and herbicides have degraded the environment by increasing pollution levels in land, water and air. In India it is more due to *deforestation* and extension of cultivation in ecologically fragile areas. At the same time, there is an excessive pressure of animals on forests—mainly by goats and sheeps.

(ii) *Toxic Level in Food Chain:* Toxic level in the food chain of India has increased to such a high level that nothing produced in India is fit for human consumption. Basically, unbridled use of chemical pesticides and weedicides and their industrial production combined together had polluted the land, water and air to such an alarmingly high level that the whole food chain had been a prey of high toxicity.

Conclusion

The above studies and the reports were eye-openers in the area of ecologically non-sustainable kind of agriculture as well as a big question mark on it. This made agro-scientists suggest in favour of an *evergreen revolution* which could be really 'green'. As per the *Economic Survey 2018-19,* India needs a tremendous transformation from the philosophy of 'green revolution' led productivity to 'green method' led sustainability such as 'zero budget natural farming' to eliminate chemical pesticides and promote good agronomic practices that are eco-friendly and less water consuming.

CROPPING PATTERNS

The set and combination of crops which farmers opt for in a particular region, in their farm practices, is cropping pattern of the region. Multiplicity of cropping systems has been one of main features of Indian agriculture and it is attributed to rainfed agriculture and prevailing socio-economic situations of the farming community.

The cropping pattern in India has undergone significant changes over time. As the cultivated area remains more or less constant, the increased demand for food, because of increase in population and urbanisation, puts agricultural land under stress, resulting in *crop intensification* and *crop substitution* of food crops with commercial crops.

Cropping systems of a region are decided, by and large, by a number of soil and climatic parameters, which determine the overall agro-ecological setting for nourishment and appropriateness of a crop or set of crops for cultivation. Nevertheless, at farmers' level, potential productivity and monetary benefits act as guiding principles, while opting for a particular crop or a cropping system. These decisions with respect to choice of crops and cropping systems are further narrowed down under influence of several other forces related to infrastructure facilities, socio-economic and technological factors, all operating interactively at the micro-level. These factors are:

1. **Geographical factors:** Soil, landforms, precipitation, moisture, altitude, etc.

2. **Socio-cultural factors:** Food habits, festivals, tradition, etc.
3. **Infrastructure factors:** Irrigation, transport, storage, trade and marketing, post-harvest handling and processing, etc.
4. **Economic factors:** Financial resource base, land ownership, size and type of land holding, household needs of food, fodder, fuel, fibre and finance, labour availability, etc.
5. **Technological factors:** Improved varieties of seeds and plants, mechanisation, plant protection, access to information, etc.

Prevalent Cropping Systems

Multiplicity of cropping systems has been one of the main features of Indian agriculture. This may be attributed to the following two major factors:

1. Rainfed agriculture still accounts for over 92.8 million hectare or 65 per cent of the cropped area. A large diversity of cropping systems exists under rainfed and dryland areas with an over-riding practice of intercropping, due to greater risks involved in cultivating larger area under a particular crop.
2. Due to prevailing socio-economic situations, such as, dependency of large population on agriculture, small land-holding size, very high population pressure on land resource, etc.

Improving household food security has been an issue of supreme importance to many million farmers of India, with the following farm holdings:

1. 56.15 million marginal (<1.0 ha),
2. 17.92 million small (1.0–2.0 ha), and
3. 13.25 million semi-medium (2.0–4.0 ha).

They together are 90 per cent of the 97.15 million operational holdings. An important consequence of this has been that crop production in India remained to be considered, by and large, a *subsistence* rather than *commercial* activity. One of the typical characteristics of subsistence farming is that most of the farmers resort to grow a number of crops on their farm holdings, primarily to fulfil their household needs and follow the practice of rotating a particular crop combination over a period of 3–4 year, interchangeably on different farm fields.

Under the influence of all the above factors, the cropping systems remain dynamic in time and space, making it difficult to precisely determine their spread using conventional methods, over a large territory. However, it has been estimated that more than **250** double cropping systems are followed throughout the country. Based on the rationale of spread of crops in each district in the country, *30 important cropping systems* have been identified—rice-wheat, rice-rice, rice-gram, rice-mustard, rice-groundnut, rice-sorghum, pear lmillet-gram, pearl millet-mustard, pearl millet-sorghum, cotton-wheat, cotton-gram, cotton-sorghum, cotton-safflower, cotton-groundnut, maize-wheat, maize-gram, sugarcane-wheat, soybean-wheat, sorghum-sorghum, groundnut-wheat, sorghum-groundnut, groundnut-rice, sorghum-wheat, sorghum-gram, pigeon pea-sorghum, groundnut, sorghum-rice, groundnut-sorghum and soybean-gram.

Changes in the Cropping Patterns

Due to various reasons, the cropping pattern of Indian farmers have undergone changes over the time—we can see them in following three phases.

Pre-Green Revolution Period In this phase we see Indian farmers going in for a cropping system (generally), which was primarily decided by the socio-cultural and economic factors—more or less they were closer to being *sustainable* as they had developed through the long process of trial and error of their forefathers. A combination of crops we see being grown by farmers across the country with judicious mixture of crops till the Green Revolution. This was a period of subsistence farming with high dependency of population for livelihood on it. The nature of the cropping pattern was too stubborn to change by incentives.

Green Revolution Period Under the spell of the New Agricultural Strategy (NAS), more popularly as the Green Revolution, 1965 onwards, we see a *major shift* in the cropping pattern of Indian farmers. The main forces of change were economic, infrastructural and technological in nature. Initiation of high yielding varieties of seeds, financial supports of chemical and other inputs together with the provisions of minimum support price (MSP) gave major shift to the farmers' choices of crops. In the GR regions we see a highly repetitive kind of cropping pattern with the 'wheat-rice' having predominance. In coming times, the Government of India started announcing MSPs for many other crops, which had its own impact on the farmers' choices of crops in their cropping systems.

This period was primarily guided by the singular objective of attaining self-sufficiency in food, which may lead the nation to attain food security. By the late 1980s, India was able to manage self-sufficiency in foodgrains. We see the emergence of big farmers in the GR regions for whom at least farming did not remain subsistence —*commercial dimension* enters the Indian farm practices, for the first time.

This is the period when the traditional cropping pattern of India got exposed to new inputs of farming and geographical dimensions of crop selection were undermined. Soon (by 1996–97), the government came to know that the GR farm practices were ecologically damaging and unsustainable. The Government of India officially adopts the idea of *sustainable* agriculture by 1997.

Reform Period Another wave of change in the cropping pattern comes with the process of economic reforms commencing in 1991, which brings in new opportunities together with the challenges in the area of farm sector:

1. The issue of food security continued to give pressure on policymakers as foodgrains production was not able to keep pace with the population growth rate. The situation becomes even more serious with Food Rights (NFSA) given to a large population of the country recently.
2. Globalisation brought in new opportunities of farm exports together with the challenge of cheap production (need of farm mechanisation and commercial farming so that Indian farm products can compete in the global market) in wake of the agricultural provisions of the World Trade Organisation. It made India think of mobilising huge investments in the sector. India accepts agriculture as an industry (2000) giving green signal to *corporate* and *contract* farmings.
3. Ecologically sustainable farming becomes the need of the hour due to ensuing danger of climate change and environment related constraints.
4. The Government of India proposes for the Second Green Revolution in 2002 with inclusion of the genetically modified foods (GMFs).

Current Scenario Today, the cropping pattern in India is highly skewed towards *water intensive* crops which is primarily due to incentive structures like MSP, heavily subsidised electricity, water and fertilizers. The concerns[24] arising out of it together with their remedies are as given below:

24 **Economic Survey 2018-19,** Vol. 2, p. 177, Ministry of Finance, GoI, N. Delhi.

- Around 89 per cent of groundwater extracted is used for irrigation (as per the latest *Asian Water Development Outlook 2016* of the Asian Development Bank) and crops such as paddy and sugarcane consume more than 60 per cent of irrigation water.
- A divergence is seen between land productivity and irrigation water productivity[25] in the major sugarcane producing states in the country reflecting the urgent need to focus on irrigation water productivity to raise agricultural productivity. The states like Tamil Nadu, Karnataka, Maharashtra and Andhra Pradesh which have high land productivity tend to have very low irrigation water productivity, reflecting inefficient use of water and the need to re-calibrate the cropping pattern.
- Fertilizer response ratio has been declining over time indicating declining responsiveness of soil fertility to fertilizer application. There is a need to use optimal dose of fertilizers based on soil health status together with promotion of neem coated urea, micro nutrients, organic fertilizers and water-soluble fertilizers.

Organic and natural farming techniques including Zero Budget Natural Farming (ZBNF) can improve both water use efficiency and soil fertility. The main aim of ZBNF is to eliminate chemical pesticides and promote good agronomic practices that are eco-friendly and less water consuming.

ANIMAL REARING

The economics of animal rearing plays a very vital role in the country. The agriculture sector in India is predominantly a mixed crop-livestock (animals, birds and fishes) farming system. Animal rearing has always remained an integral part of it. Animal rearing (which includes rearing of cows, camels, buffaloes, goats, pigs, sheep, etc.), besides directly contributing to the national income and socio-economic development, plays the following **vital functions** in the country:

- Supplements family income and generates gainful employment in the rural sector;
- Particularly helps the landless labourers, small and marginal farmers and women (economic empowerment of women);
- Provides cheap nutritional food;
- Functions as the best insurance against drought, famine and other natural calamities;
- It is more *inclusive* in nature; and
- Promotes the cause of *sustainable* agriculture.

Major Highlights (as per the *Economic Survey 2020-21* and other *official sources*) related to the allied sectors (called livestock sector also) of agriculture, which includes animal rearing, dairying and fisheries, are as given below:

- **Economic Significance:** With a CAGR (compound annual growth rate) of **8.24** per cent in the last 5 years, the livestock sector has contribution of **28.63** per cent in total agricultural GVA (Gross Value Added) at constant prices and **4.2** per cent in the total GVA of India (in 2018-19, as per the National Accounts Statistics, 2020).
- **Livestock Population and Production:** As per the latest FAOSTAT (Food and Agriculture Organisation Statistics) production data, India is the *3rd largest* producer of egg in the world (a total of 114.38 billion in 2019-20) with a growth rate of 10.19 per cent and per capita availability of 86 eggs per annum. Poultry production in India has taken a quantum leap in the last four decades, emerging from use of unscientific farming

 *Irrigation Water Productivity* (IWP) is defined as ratio of the crop output to irrigation water applied (kg/m^3), as irrigation being an economic activity farmer incurs expenditure on it. Thus, IWP is a practical indicator to estimate the crop output obtained with respect to the actual irrigation water applied.

practices to commercial production systems with state-of-the-art technology.

- **Dairy Sector:** India is the *largest* producer of milk in the world—during 2019-20, the total production was 198.4 million tonnes and the growth rate was 5.68 per cent. The per capita availability (pca) of milk was 407 grams per day in 2019-20 (against the global pca of 298 grams)—while consumption of milk is higher in rural areas (57 per cent) the pca is higher in urban areas (592 ml) in comparison to the rural counterpart (404 ml).

  As per a study of the NDDB (National Dairy Development Board), the demand of milk and milk products for India in 2030 is projected to be 266.5 million tonnes.

- **Fisheries:** India is the *2nd largest* fish producing country in the world accounting for 7.58 per cent of the global production—the total production being 14.16 million tons and marine products' export of 1.26 million tons (in 2019-20). The sector contributes 1.24 per cent to the GVA and 7.28 per cent to the agricultural GVA. The sector provides livelihood to over 28 million people in the country, especially to the marginalized and vulnerable communities, and has promoted meaningful socio-economic development. To harness the untapped potential of the sector, the Government has taken several policy initiatives in recent times:

  - *Blue Revolution*, a centrally sponsored scheme was launched in 2015-16 for a 5-year period to catalyse the Integrated, Responsible and Holistic Development and Management of the Fisheries Sector, which ended in March 2020.
  - *Fisheries and Aquaculture Infrastructure Development Fund (FIDF)*, a dedicated fund for the sector was established by late 2018 for setting up fisheries projects by entrepreneurs.
  - *Kisan Credit Cards* are being issued to fishers and fish farmers (by mid-January 2021, a total of 44,673 cards were issued while additional 4.04 lakh applications were at various stages of issuance).
  - *Pradhan Mantri Matsya Sampada Yojana (PMMSY),* a flagship scheme, was launched in May, 2020 as a part of Atma Nirbhar Bharat Package by the Government, realising the potential, scope and importance of the sector—with the following aims:
    - Enhancing fish production to 22 million tons by 2024-25 at an average annual growth rate of about 9 per cent.
    - Increasing aquaculture productivity to 5 tons per hectare (existing national average is 3 tons).
    - Doubling export earnings (to ₹1 lakh crores) and generating about 55 lakh jobs.
    - Providing insurance coverage to fishing vessels (to be introduced for the first time).
    - Enhancing domestic fish consumption and attracting investments in the sector from other sources.

- **Pig Rearing Scheme:** This scheme is aimed to assist farmers/landless labourers/co-operatives and the tribals particularly in the North-Eastern states by rearing pigs under stall fed condition for quality pork production and organised pork marketing in rural areas and semi-urban areas. The main objectives of the scheme are:

- Encourage commercial rearing by adopting scientific methods and infrastructure creation;
- Production and supply of improved germ plasm;
- Organise stakeholders to popularise scientific practices;
- Create supply chain for the meat industry;
- Encourage value addition for better income.

▶ **Animal Health:** With the improvement in the quality of livestock through launching of extensive cross-breeding programmes, the susceptibility to various diseases, including exotic diseases has increased. In order to reduce morbidity and mortality, efforts are being made by the state/UT governments to provide better health care through polyclinics/veterinary hospitals/dispensaries/first-aid centres including mobile veterinary dispensaries. For the prevention of various diseases, 27 veterinary vaccine production units are working with dominance of the public sector (20 are in the public sector and rest in the private sector). The 'Livestock Health & Disease Control' is being run as a centrally sponsored scheme to assist the attempts of the states and UTs in the area.

Suggestions for further development of the sector are:

▶ Developing progeny tested semen for artificial insemination.

▶ Expansion of fodder availability through innovative means.

▶ Facilities of animal health centres need to be upgraded and the disease control systems made more effective on the veterinary side.

▶ In the drylands and mountain ecosystems, livestock contributes anywhere between 50 to 75 per cent of the total household income of the rural population. Support to these massive and highly diverse livestock populations in these regions is lacking.

▶ Raising the capability of the rural poor to conserve and manage their livestock resources, and enable them to derive sustainable incomes from these resources.

▶ Decentralisation and convergence of policy support for these options is crucial for diversification of livelihoods in small-holder farming.

Recent Policy Initiatives

With the aim of promoting the livestock sector the Government has taken the following major policy initiatives in recent times—

AHIDF (Animal Husbandry Infrastructure Development Fund) was set up by late 2020 as a part of the Atma Nirbhar Bharat Abhiyan stimulus package with a corpus of ₹15000 crores. The fund will incentivise investments by individual entrepreneurs, private companies including SMEs, farmers producers' organisations (FPOs) to establish—

1. dairy processing and value addition infrastructure,
2. meat processing and value addition infrastructure, and
3. animal feed plant.

The beneficiaries will be provided 3 per cent interest subvention with a 2-year moratorium for the loan and 6 years repayment period thereafter. A credit guarantee fund (CGF) of ₹750 crores to be managed by NABARD, will also be set up exclusively for the MSMEs. To ease out the application process, SIDBI has put in place an online system for applicants.

NADCP (National Animal Disease Control Programme), a central sector scheme, was launched to control FMD (Foot & Mouth Disease) and Brucellosis. Hundred per cent of the cattle, buffalo, sheep, goat and pig and bovine female calves of 4-8 months of age are to be vaccinated under it in the next 5 years (2019-2024).

RKA (Rashtriya Kamdhenu Aayog) was set in 2019-20 to upscale sustainable genetic upgradation, production and productivity of cows. The commission will also look after effective implementation of laws and welfare schemes for cows.

FOOD MANAGEMENT

Managing enough food in the domestic market has been the prime focus of the government since Independence. Meeting the physical target of food together with the challenge of enabling Indians to procure food for their consumption was also there. Over the year, we see the government devising various ways and means to handle the twin challenges. Once, the country joined the WTO, a new need was felt for producing surplus and competing with the world, so that the benefits of globalisation could also be reaped by the agriculture sector. This section discusses the challenges to management of food in the country.

Minimum Support Price

Minimum Support Price (MSP) is a form of market intervention by the Government of India to insure agricultural producers against any sharp fall in farm prices—a guarantee price to save farmers from distress sale. The MSPs are announced at the beginning of the sowing season for certain crops on the basis of the recommendations of the Commission for Agricultural Costs and Prices (CACP, 1985). The major objectives are to support the farmers from distress sales and to procure food grains for public distribution. In case the market price for the commodity falls below the announced minimum price due to bumper production and glut in the market, government agencies purchase the entire quantity offered by the farmers at the announced minimum price.

Commencing with 'wheat' for the 1966–67, currently the MSPs are announced for **23** commodities including seven cereals (paddy, wheat, barley, jowar, bajra, maize and ragi); five pulses (gram, arhar/tur, moong, urad and lentil); eight oilseeds (groundnut, rapeseed/mustard, toria, soyabean, sunflower seed, sesamum, safflower seed and niger seed); copra, raw cotton and raw jute. The MSPs are fixed at *incentive level*, to fulfil the following purposes:

1. to induce more investment by farmers in the farm sector,
2. to motivate farmers to adopt improved crop production technologies, and
3. to enhance production and thereby farmers income.

In the absence of such a guaranteed price, there is a concern that farmers may shift to other crops causing shortage in these commodities. The agricultural price policy in India emerged in the backdrop of *food scarcity* and *price fluctuations* provoked by *drought, floods* and *international prices* for exports and imports.

Aimed at making farming remunerative the Government announced to fix the *MSP for crops 50 per cent* above their production cost since 2018–19. The new MSP is fixed by the CACP over the *Cost A2+Fl* (where, *Cost A2* includes all paid out costs borne by the farmer on seeds, fertilisers, pesticides, hired labour, leased-in land, fuel, irrigation, etc. and the *Fl* is imputed cost of unpaid family labour). While farm activists demand it to be fixed over the *Cost C2* (which is a more comprehensive cost that factors in rentals and interest forgone on owned land and fixed capital assets on top of *Cost A2+Fl*).

Experts have concluded that the current MSP for common paddy is ₹1750 per quintal (fixed over the Cost A2+Fl) while it would be ₹2340 per quintal had it been fixed over the Cost C2. The *M. S. Swaminathan* headed Commission on Farmers (of 2004) had suggested it to be fixed above the Cost C2.

Market Intervention Scheme

The Market Intervention Scheme (MIS) is similar to MSP, which is implemented on the request of state governments for procurement of perishable and horticultural commodities in the event of fall in market prices. The scheme is implemented when there is at least 10 per cent increase in production or 10 per cent decrease in the ruling rates over the previous normal year. Proposal of MIS is approved on the specific request of the state/UT governments, if the states/UTs are ready to bear 50 per cent loss (25 per cent in case of North-Eastern states) incurred on its implementation.

Procurement Prices

In 1966–67, the Government of India announced a 'procurement price' for wheat, a bit higher than its MSP (the purpose being security of food procurement for requirement of the PDS). The MSP was announced before sowing, while the procurement price was announced before harvesting—the purpose was to encourage farmers to sell a bit more and get encouraged to produce more. But this increased price hardly served the purpose as a suitable incentive to farmers. It would have been better had it been announced before sowing and not after harvesting. That is why since the fiscal 1968-69 the government announced only the MSP, which is also considered the effective procurement price.[26]

Issue Price

The price at which the government allows offtake of foodgrains from the FCI (the price at which the FCI sells its foodgrains). The FCI has been fetching huge losses in the form of food subsidies. The foodgrains procured are transported to the godowns of the FCI located across the country (counted in the buffer stock). From here they head to the sale counters—to the TPDS or Open Market Sale. The transportation, godowning, the cost of maintaining the FCI, carriage losses, etc., make the foodgrains costlier (the additional expenses other than the MSP is known as the 'economic cost of foodgrains'). To make the foodgrains affordable to the consumers, the issue prices for foodgrains are set lower than the total cost of procurement and distribution—the gap converts into the 'food subsidy'.

Economic Cost of Foodgrains

The economic cost of foodgrains consists of three components, namely the MSP including central bonus (the price paid to farmers), procurement incidentals, and the cost of distribution.

The economic cost of foodgrains has witnessed significant increase in the last few years proportionate to increase in the MSPs (as per the *Economic Survey 2019-20*, an increase of 1 per cent in the MSP leads to a 0.48 per cent increase in the economic cost in case of wheat). In **2020-21**, the economic cost[27] of rice and wheat have increased

26. **New Agricultural Strategy, 1965**, the CACP, 1967 and **Ministry of Agriculture** GoI, N. Delhi.

27. **Economic Survey 2020-21**, vol. 2, p. 251, Ministry of Finance, GoI, N. Delhi.

to ₹ 37.24 and ₹ 26.84 per kilogram respectively—from ₹ 26.16 and ₹ 19.08 in 2013-14.

High economic cost necessitated a detailed review of the open-ended procurement policy, especially in states that offer high bonus on top of MSP and those that impose high taxes and statutory levies, as well as stocking and distribution policies. In this regard, the government set up a *High Level Committee (HLC)* in 2015 (Shanta Kumar as its Chairman) to suggest inter alia *restructuring* or *unbundling* of the FCI with a view to improve its operational efficiency and financial management.

Open Market Sale Scheme

The FCI has been undertaking sale of wheat at pre-determined prices (reserve prices) in the open market from time to time, known as the Open Market Sale Scheme (OMSS). This is aimed at serving the following *objectives:*

1. to enhance market supply of foodgrains;
2. to exercise a moderating influence on open market prices; and
3. to offload surplus stocks.

Under the Open Market Sale Scheme (Domestic), the government now adopts a policy of differential prices to encourage sale of older stock first—sticking to the following policy stance:

1. Keeping the reserve price above MSP, but reasonably below the acquisition cost or economic cost of wheat, so that the buyers remain attracted to purchase of wheat from the *mandis* during the harvest season and the market remains competitive.
2. Maintaining that the market price during the lean season does not increase much and inflation remains under check.

Price Stabilisation Fund

The Government of India, by late *March 2015,* launched the Price Stabilisation Fund (PSF) as a Central Sector Scheme to support market interventions for price control of perishable agri-horticultural commodities. The cost to be borne between the centre and the states in equal ratio (in case of the North Eastern-states, the respective share will be 75:25). The scheme will commence with only two crops, viz., onion and potato.

BUFFER STOCK

Buffer stock refers to a 'reserve' of commodity to offset price fluctuations and unforeseen emergencies. Introduced in 1969 (4th Plan, 1969-74), under it, Government of India maintains a buffer stock of selected *foodgrains* (wheat and rice) in the Central Pool for:

1. Meeting the prescribed minimum buffer stock norms for food security,
2. Monthly release of foodgrains for supply through Targeted Public Distribution System (TPDS) and Other Welfare Schemes (OWS),
3. Meeting emergency situations arising out of unexpected crop failure, natural disasters, etc., and
4. Price stabilisation or market intervention to augment supply so as to help moderate the open market prices.

Central Pool consists of stocks held by FCI, stocks of the Decentralised Procurement Scheme of the participating states and the state government agencies (SGAs). The minimum stocking norms (for two cereals wheat and rice), set by the Government, is to be maintained on *quarterly basis* and revised after every five years—the combined stock limit for wheat and rice, after the last revision of *January 2015* is given below in the table:

Table 8.1 Revised Buffer Stock

As on	Existing since April, 2005 (in million tonnes)	Revised
1st April	21.2	21.04
1st July	31.9	41.12
1st Oct	21.2	30.77
1st Jan	25.0	21.41

In the last revision, its nomenclature[28] was changed to *Foodgrain Stocking Norms* (from the existing 'Buffer Norms and Strategic Reserve').

To control prices of **pulses**, Government decided in October 2015 to create a 1.5 million tonnes of buffer stock of pulses (which was later increased to 2 million tonnes)—to be procured by the FCI, NAFED (National Agricultural Cooperative Marketing Federation of India Limited), and SFAC (Small Farmers Agri-business Consortium).

While four months requirement of foodgrains for issue under TPDS and OWS are earmarked as 'operational stocks', the surplus over that is treated as 'buffer stock' (physically both are merged into one and are not distinguishable). According to the present practice, the Government treats the food stock over and above the minimum norms as 'excess stock' and liquidates them from time to time through exports, open market sales or additional allocations to states.

The present foodgrain procurement policy has been criticised on various counts—excessive dependence on wheat and rice (which is a water-guzzling crop), stockpiling of foodgrains in godowns much above the buffer norms, financial pressure on the governments, export controls on FCI, concerns of rising agricultural subsidies related to the agriculture clause of the WTO being the major ones. Look into the existing foodgrains procurement by the FCI, the Government had set up a *High-Level Committee* in 2015 (Reorienting the Role and Restructuring of FCI, headed by Shanta Kumar) which advised major changes, which are under the Government consideration.

Decentralised Procurement Scheme

The decentralised procurement (DCP) scheme was operationalised by the government in 1997 (together with the Centre and some of the states also procure foodgrains from the farmers, locally). Under this scheme, the designated states procure, store and also issue foodgrains under the TPDS. The difference between the economic cost of the states and the Central Issue Price (CIP) is passed on to the states by the Government of India as subsidy. The decentralised system of procurement, helps to cover more farmers under the MSP operations, improves efficiency of the PDS, provides varieties of foodgrains more suited to local taste, and reduces the transportation costs of the FCI.[29]

The Government of India urged ***all states*** to adopt the DCP scheme so that costs of distribution can be saved and outreach of price support mechanism to the farmers in hitherto weaker areas can be improved. To overcome the problem of gaps in the flow of information about procurement operations on day-to-day basis, an *Online Procurement Monitoring System (OPMS)* has been evolved for reporting and monitoring on a daily basis, procurement operations for wheat, paddy and coarse grains in the country.

States offering bonus over and above the MSP announced by the Government had a distortionary effect on the food procurement process of the Government of India. Checking procurement and its cost from rising, Government took two steps—

28. ***Economic Survey 2019-20***, Vol. 2, pp. 211-212, Ministry of Finance, GoI, N. Delhi.

29. Ministry of Finance, ***Economic Survey 2011–12***, (New Delhi: Government of India, 2012).

firstly, a limit was put on its procurement from the states paying bonus over and above the MSP upto the needs of TPDS and OWS, and secondly, FCI stopped taking part in MSP operations in the case of non-DCP states declaring bonus.

STORAGE

By 2020, the total storage capacity[30] available with FCI and state agencies for storage of foodgrains was **819.19 LMT**, comprising covered godowns of 669.10 LMT and Covered and Plinth (CAP) facilities of 150.09 LMT. Out of the total available storage capacity of 819.19 LMT, FCI has a capacity of 407.76 LMT while state agencies have a capacity of 411.43 LMT. The stock of rice and wheat in the Central Pool was 529.59 LMT on ***January l, 2021***. The CWC (Central Warehousing Corporation) is operating 423 warehouses throughout the country with a total operational storage capacity of around 117 LMT with an overall capacity utilisation of 86 per cent by December 2020. Some areas of concerns related to India's storage system, outlined by some official documents of recent times are briefed below:

1. The CAP of 132 lakh MT capacity cannot be treated as scientific storage.
2. Public agencies do not have warehouses for proper storage of even half of the wheat and rice procured by them.
3. In the wake of persistent seasonal inflation in perishables like fruits and vegetables, there was no effective strategy to control inflation on a sustainable basis.
4. Cold storage capacity for all type of food items is just 29 MT *(Planning Commission 2012)*. The production of potato alone is about 35 MT.
5. Cold storage facility is available for only 10 per cent of fruits and vegetables produced in India *(Planning Commission 2012)*.

To bridge the gap between the requirement and availability of scientific storage capacity is the immediate need of the hour. For this, it is advisable to promote the policies by which private sector investment can be attracted to it. To augment storage capacity, few recent steps[31] taken by the Government, are as given below:

1. Construction of godowns under the *PEG* (Private Entrepreneurs Guarantee Scheme) being implemented in PPP (Public Private Partnership) mode in 24 states.
2. Construction of *Steel Silos* in PPP mode to modernise storage infrastructure and improve shelf life of stored foodgrains with a capacity of 100 LMT is being implemented.
3. Online Depot Management System (ODMS), also known as Depot Online System (DOS), being implemented by FCI to optimise costs and improving functional efficiency. It will *automate* the entire process of depot operations including receipt of foodgrains at the depot, storage, maintenance activities and issue of foodgrains.

FARM SUBSIDIES

Farm subsidies form an integral part of the government's budget. In the case of developed countries, the agricultural or farm subsidies compose nearly 40 per cent of the total budgetary outlay, while in India's case it is much lower (around 7.8 per cent of the agricultural GDP) and of different nature.

30. ***Economic Survey 2020-21,*** Vol. 2, p. 252, Ministry of Finance, GoI, N. Delhi.

31. ***Economic Survey 2019-20,*** Vol. 2, pp. 215, Ministry of Finance, GoI, N. Delhi.

Direct Farm Subsidies These are the kinds of subsidies in which direct cash incentives are paid to the farmers in order to make their products more competitive in the global markets. The developed countries (USA and Europe) spend huge amounts of their annual budgets on the agriculture, farm and fisheries subsidies. Direct farm subsidies are helpful as they provide the right levels of purchasing power to the farmer and can significantly help in raising the standards of living of the rural poor. They also help in checking the misuse of public funds as they help in the proper identification of the beneficiaries.

Indirect Farm Subsidies These are the farm subsidies which are provided in the form of cheaper credit facilities, farm loan waivers, reduction in irrigation and electricity bills, fertilizers, seeds and pesticides subsidy as well as the investments in agricultural research, environmental assistance, farmer training, etc. These subsidies are also provided to make farm products more competitive in the global market.

The subsidies provided on the fertilizers as 'input' subsidies are in the form of *indirect* subsidies. But if the government does not incentivise the farmer by an effective cost reduction in prices of the fertilizers, but provides direct cash incentives after the produce, is known as a *direct* subsidy.

The World Trade Organization (WTO) has put some ceilings on the amount of direct and indirect subsidies being provided by the various developing and developed nations due to the fact that these subsidies *distort the free market forces* which have their own implications.

First thoughts are encouraging. A panel headed by Montek Singh Ahluwalia (the then Deputy Chairman, *Planning Commission)* recommended that the power ministry, instead of paying power-distribution companies, hand out electricity subsidies **directly** to farmers through a smart card linked to the unique identity number.

India spends about ₹1,60,000 crore every year or roughly 2 per cent of its GDP on subsidies, ***all indirectly.*** For example, in fertilizers, which accounts for two-thirds of total subsidies, the government fixes a low selling price and compensates the producers by paying the difference between the selling price and the actual production costs (plus a pre-decided profit margin) as subsidy. *Important issues* related to farm subsidies are as given below:

1. The indirect subsidy has been blamed for benefiting big farmers more than the small and medium farmers, for whom the subsidy is intended. This is because the bulk of the subsidised fertilizers is picked up by the rich farmers, because the small and marginal farmers account for just 37 per cent of the farm land.
2. Indirect subsidy has also discouraged improvements in production processes since manufacturers have no incentive to increase efficiency. This will also play a big part in bringing down India's overall subsidy bill. For instance, according to industry estimates, the money spent on poor farmers could potentially come down to ₹37,000 crore from the current ₹100,000 crore.
3. Another advantage of cash subsidies is that it will free up the distribution system and allow the people who receive the subsidy to choose where they buy their goods from. The complexity is not so much in the transfer of funds, as it is in the identification of the beneficiaries.

Other Countries The idea of disbursing subsidies directly to the beneficiaries is becoming popular among the development thinkers and policymakers. It's already a part of policy in many parts of the world—predominantly, in Latin America where 16 countries have this practice, and also in other countries such as Jamaica, Philippines, Turkey and Indonesia.

The biggest and most cited of such programmes is Brazil's *Bolsa Familia*. It started in 2001, with a programme aimed at education. It expanded in 2003 to include a range of services like food and fuel, and now covers 2.6 million families in that country. The government *transfers cash* straight to a family, subject to conditions such as school attendance, nutritional monitoring, pre-natal and post-natal tests. By many measures, the programme is a success. Brazil's poverty levels dropped by 15 percentage points between 2003 and 2009, at least a sixth, thanks to Bolsa Familia (economic growth played a big part, too). Millennium Development Goals initiative, which in 2000 sought to halve poverty by 2015, doesn't even mention cash transfers. But, Brazil achieved the goals 10 years ahead of the deadline. And the cost of these transfers has been 0.4 per cent of GDP.

The big question is not whether a direct cash transfer is the perfect solution, but whether it's an improvement over the existing systems. The evidence—its success in other parts of the world—and the poor performance of indirect subsidies so far would suggest so. Looking at it, the GoI has already started a pan-India scheme to disburse all forms of subsidies directly, through the ***Direct Benefit Transfer (DBT)*** since 2015-16 onwards.

FOOD SECURITY

India attained self-sufficiency in food by late 1980s, though food security still evades the country. Food security means making food available at affordable prices at all times, to all, without interruptions. Though India's GDP growth has been impressive and the agricultural production has also increased over the past few decades, hunger and starvation still persist among the poorer sections of the population.

State of Hunger & Malnutrition As per the latest *State of Food Security and Nutrition in the World-2020* report of the FAO (UNO), the state of hunger and malnutrition in India is very worrisome:

- 14.0 per cent of population is under-nourished (that is 18.34 crore).
- 50.4 per cent of women in reproductive age (15-49 years age group) are anaemic.
- 36.6 per cent of the children aged under five are stunted (too short for their age).
- 19.6 per cent of children under five suffer from wasting (meaning their weight is too low for their height).

India is ranked 94th out of 107 countries in the latest[32] *Global Hunger Index-2020*. As per it, India is suffering from a serious hunger problem. Some *India-specific* findings of the report are as given below:

- Ranked below Pakistan (88), Bangladesh (75), Nepal (73) and Sri Lanka (64).
- 9.5 per cent of children (6-23 months of age) are given a minimum acceptable diet.
- 14 per cent population is undernourished.
- The highest child stunting rate (37.8 per cent) against global average of 20.7 per cent.

32. The *Global Hunger Index* (published since 2006), is jointly published by the international non-profit agencies **Concern Worldwide** (Dublin, Ireland) and **Welthungerhilfe** (Bonn, Germany), to track and measure hunger at the global, regional, and country levels—with the main aim to trigger action towards reducing global hunger.

The ***Index*** is prepared on the basis of four indicators—child mortality, undernourishment, child wasting (weight for age) and child stunting. This time the major focus of the index was on the relation between climate change and hunger together with the impact of extreme weather on food production and food security also. The Index measures countries on a 100 points scale, where a score of 0 (zero) is considered as best performing countries and 100 is the worst.

Two important things need attention regarding India's food security:

1. Around 23 per cent of India's population is BPL and a greater portion (one conservative estimate suggests that 75 per cent of their household income is spent on food).

2. There is a strong correlation between stability in agricultural production and food security. Volatility in agricultural production impacts food supplies and can result in spikes in food prices, which adversely affect the lowest income groups of the population.

Therefore, along with provision of food subsidy, stability in agricultural commodity prices is essential for making the poorer sections food secure. It means, in the direction of assuring food security, India needs to tackle mainly two hurdles:

1. **Enhancing its food production:** If food (i.e., foodgrains) is to be supplied to all today India will face deficit of around 30 million tonnes of foodgrains. This shows the food insecurity dimension of India.

2. **Strengthening supply chain:** Managing the issues like storage, transportation, proper retailing and integrating the segmented agri-markets into a national agrimarket.

Due to high level of undernourishment and volatility in agricultural prices, India has one of the largest number of food schemes in the World to ensure food security:

1. There is entitlement feeding programmes like the Integrated Child Development Scheme (ICDS – covers all children under six, pregnant and lactating mothers).
2. Mid Day Meal Schemes (MDMS).
3. Food subsidy programmes like the Targeted Public Distribution System (through which the National Food Security Act is being implemented).
4. Annapurna (10 kgs of free food grain for destitute poor).
5. Employment Programmes like Mahatma Gandhi National Rural Employment Guarantee Scheme (100 days of employment at minimum wages) to ensure food security.
6. To address the issue of 'anaemia' and 'micro-nutrient' deficiency and to promote nutrition security in the country, a centrally sponsored pilot scheme on *Fortification of Rice & its Distribution under Public Distribution System* was approved for a period of 3 years beginning in 2019-20. The pilot scheme will focus on 15 districts, preferably one district per state during the initial phase of implementation. *[Economic Survey 2020-21].*
7. With the objective of providing nation-wide portability of ration card under National Food Security Act (NFSA) through ***One Nation One Ration Card*** System, a central sector scheme, the IM-PDS (Integrated Management of Public Distribution System) was launched in 2020-21 (to be completed by March 2022). This system will enable the ration card holders to lift their entitled foodgrains from any fair price shop (FPS) of their choice anywhere in the country by using their same/existing ration card.

By *April 2021,* the facility was seamlessly enabled in 32 States/UTs covering nearly 69 crores beneficiaries (86 per cent of the total NFSA population) in the country. Under this system, equivalent food subsidy is provided through DBT (Cash Transfer instead of subsidised foodgrains) to the beneficiaries in Chandigarh and Puducherry. *[Economic Survey 2020-21].*

Till the vulnerable population is not enabled with the market-linked purchasing capacity, these programmes will be relevant in case ensuring food security in the country. There is a need to run these schemes with utmost focus of the beneficiaries.

PDS & FOOD SUBSIDY

The Public Distribution System (PDS was changed to Targeted PDS in 1997) strives to ensure food security through timely and affordable distribution of foodgrains to the BPL population as this section cannot afford to pay market prices for their food. This involves procurement of foodgrain at MSP by the Government, building up and maintenance of food stocks, their storage, and timely distribution, making foodgrains accessible at reasonable prices to the vulnerable sections of the population.

Food subsidy comprises of (i) subsidy provided to FCI for procurement and distribution of foodgrains under NFSA (National Food Security Act), OWS (Other Welfare Schemes) and maintaining their strategic reserve; and (ii) subsidy provided to States for undertaking 'decentralised procurement'. The acquisition and distribution costs of foodgrains for the central pool together constitute the economic cost. The difference between the economic cost and the Central Issue Price (CIP is the price at which beneficiaries get the foodgrains) gives the quantum of food subsidy.

There have been certain anomalies in India's food management under the PDS which need immediate attention:

- The percentage distribution of the economic cost of wheat and rice has been rising fast. The pooled cost of foodgrains *(MSP plus the Bonus which are offered by the individual states)* accounts for *two-thirds* of the economic cost of wheat and rice. This has made the economic cost of foodgrains to the Food Corporation of India (FCI) increase over the years.
- Increasing costs of labour, fertilisers, pesticides and other inputs have made production of crops costlier over the time. This forced the government to keep on increasing the MSPs of the crops, too.
- The increase in the food subsidy bill is determined by the rate at which the MSPs for wheat and rice increase and the *economic cost* of handling grains (their procurement, stocking and distribution to the targeted households). This has been the major factor for ballooning food subsidy bill.
- The procurement incidentals of wheat and rice consist of costs related to mandi charges and taxes, cost of gunny bags, *arhatiya* commission, *mandi* labour, forwarding charges, internal movement, storage charges, interest, administrative charges and others. Out of these costs, *mandi* charges and taxes constitute more than **40** per cent of the total costs.

Rise in Subsidy In the last few years, there has been a tremendous rise in the food subsidy bill—the annual growth reaching 30 per cent by 2020-21 (estimated to be ₹1,65,000 crore) from the 5 per cent of 2013-14 (₹85,000 crore).There have been many reasons[33] for the rising food subsidy in the present time:

- The NFSA has wider coverage than the erstwhile TPDS.
- The Antyodaya beneficiaries also get foodgrains at the NFSA prices.

---

33 **Economic Survey 2020-21,** vol. 2, pp. 251-52 and **Economic Survey 2019-20,** vol. 2, pp. 213-14, Ministry of Finance, GoI, N. Delhi.

- Under NFSA the categorisation of APL and BPL was abolished.
- Coverage under the Act was also delinked from the poverty estimates as it was substantially high to ensure that all the vulnerable and needy sections of the society get its benefit.
- The build-up of the foodgrain stocks much higher than their buffer norms.
- Increase in economic cost and real MSP.
- Decline in sale to the APL households.

While the economic cost has increased, the selling prices (CIP) for NFSA beneficiaries have not been revised from ₹2 and ₹3 per kg for wheat and rice, respectively. These rates were fixed under the Act initially for a period of three years from the date of commencement of the Act (July, 2013) and thereafter were to be fixed by the Government from time to time, while not exceeding the MSP. As no revision has been done since then it has resulted in widening of the gap between the economic cost and the CIP and increasing food subsidy bills.

While the interests of the vulnerable sections of the population need to be safeguarded, the food subsidy also needs to be rationalised as it distorts market for foodgrains, pulls inflation down and challenges the sustainability of food security in the country.

AGRICULTURE MARKETING

India's agrimarket is presently regulated by the Agricultural Produce Market Committee (APMC) Act enacted by the state governments. There are about 2,477 principal regulated agrimarkets and 4,843 sub-market yards regulated by the respective APMCs in India. Thus, India has not one, not 29 (number of states) but thousands of agricultural markets. This Act notifies agricultural commodities produced in the region such as cereals, pulses, edible oilseeds, fruits and vegetables and even chicken, goat, sheep, sugar, fish, etc., and provides that first sale in these commodities can be conducted only under the aegis of the APMC through the commission agents licensed by the APMCs set up under the Act.

The typical *amenities* available in or around the APMCs are: auction halls, weigh bridges, godowns, shops for retailers, canteens, roads, lights, drinking water, police station, post-office, bore-wells, warehouse, farmers amenity center, tanks, water treatment plant, soil-testing laboratory, toilet blocks, etc. Various taxes, fees/ charges and cess levied on the trades conducted in the *mandis* are also notified under the Act.

As per the *Economic Survey 2014-15*, the APMCs of the states levy multiples fees of substantial magnitude which are non-transparent and hence work as a source of political power. The functioning of the APMCs have always been a matter of debate among experts and policymakers alike—**major issues** being the following:

- They charge a market fee from buyers, and they also charge a licensing fee from the commissioning agents who mediate between buyers and farmers.
- They also charge small licensing fees from a whole range of functionaries (warehousing agents, loading agents, etc.).
- In addition, commissioning agents charge commission fees on transactions between buyers and farmers.
- The levies and other market charges vary widely in the states. Statutory levies/mandi tax, VAT, etc., are a major source of market distortions.
- Such high taxes at the first level of trading have significant cascading effects on commodity prices, as the commodities pass through the supply chain. For rice, these charges can be as high as 14.5 per cent in Andhra Pradesh

(excluding the state VAT) and close to 10 per cent in Odisha and Punjab.

- Even the model APMC Act (described below) treats the APMC as an arm of the state, and, the market fee, as the tax levied by the state, rather than fee charged for providing services. This is a crucial provision which acts as a major impediment to creating national common market in agricultural commodities. Removal of this provision will pave the way for creating competition and a national common market for agricultural commodities.
- Moreover, though the market fee is collected just like a tax, the revenue earned by the APMCs does not go to the state exchequer and hence does not require the approval of the state legislature to utilise the funds thus collected. Thus, APMC operations are independent of scrutiny.
- The rate of commission charged by the licensed commission agents is exorbitant, because, unlike direct taxes, which are levied on net income, the commission is charged on the entire value of the produce sold. The license fee charged from various market licensed operators is nominal, but the small number of licences granted creates a premium, which is believed to be paid in cash.
- There is a perception that the positions in the market committee (at the state level) and the market board (which supervises the market committee) are occupied by politically influential persons. They enjoy a cosy relationship with the licensed commission agents who wield power by exercising monopoly power within the notified area, at times by forming cartels. The resistance to reforming APMCs is perceived to be emanating from these factors.

Model APMC Act

Since the State APMC Acts created fragment markets for agricultural commodities and curtailed the freedom of farmers to sell their produce other than through the commission agents and other functionaries licensed by the APMCs, the Ministry of Agriculture (GoI) developed a *Model APMC Act, 2003* and has been pursuing the state governments to modify their respective Acts along its line. The Model APMC Act provides the following new things:

1. Direct sale of farm produce by the farmer to contract farming sponsors;
2. Setting up 'special markets' for 'specified agricultural commodities'—mostly perishables;
3. Permits private persons, farmers and consumers to establish new markets for agricultural produce in any area;
4. A single levy of market fee on the sale of notified agricultural commodities in any market area;
5. Replaces licensing with registrations of market functionaries, which would allow them to operate in one or more different market areas;
6. Establishment of consumers' and farmers' markets to facilitate direct sale of agricultural produce to consumers;
7. Creation of marketing infrastructure from the revenue earned by the APMCs;
8. Provides some freedom to the farmers to sell their produce directly to the contract-sponsors or in the market set up by private individuals, consumers or producers;

9. Increases the competitiveness of the market of agri-produce by allowing common registration of market intermediaries.

Though slow but majority of states did reform their APMCs in reference to the Model Act with differentiated success—Karnataka Model considered the ideal one. The Government working closely with the states has taken several *recent initiatives* in the direction of freeing up the agri-market in the country:

1. A comprehensive advisory issued to the states to go beyond the provisions of the Model Act and declare the entire state a *single market* with one licence valid across the entire state and removing all restrictions on movement of agricultural produce within the state.
2. The **NAM** (National Agriculture Market) through an Agri-Tech Infrastructure Fund (ATIF) was established by Government of India in July 2015, which will provide a common *e-market platform* of regulated wholesale markets in states/UTs (those states/UTs that are desirous to join the platform). The SFAC (Small Farmers Agribusiness Consortium).
3. On the request of the central government, a number of state governments have exempted the marketing of fruits and vegetables from the purview of the APMC Act.
4. For augmenting infrastructure facilities, the *Union Budget 202 1-22* allowed the APMCs to get funds from the Agriculture Infrastructure Funds.

MODEL CONTRACT FARMING ACT

The Model Agriculture Produce & Livestock Contract Farming and Services (Promotion & Facilitation) Act, 2018 was released by the Government in May 2018. Salient *features* of the Act are as given below:

- Contract farming to be outside the ambit of APMC Act.
- Farmers have been considered weaker in case of contract farming.
- Other than contract farming, it covers all 'services contracts' related to pre-production, production and post-production (it means the whole value chain is covered).
- Contracted produce covered under crop and livestock insurance.
- No permanent structure can be developed on farmers' land or premises.
- No right, title of interest of the land shall vest in the sponsor (i.e., the contact farmer).
- If farmers authorise, FPOs (Farmer Producer Organisations), FPCs (Farmer Producer Companies) can be contract farmers.
- The entire pre-agreed quantity of agri produce to be bought by the contact farmer.
- RARC (Registering and Agreement Recording Committee) or an officer to be appointed for online registration of the contract agreement (at district, block and taluka levels).
- CFFG (Contract Farming Facilitation Group) to be set up to promote contract farming (at village and panchayat levels).
- To settle disputes an accessible and simple mechanism to be set at lowest level possible.
- In structure, the Act is facilitative and promotional rather than being regulatory.

The Act is supposed to enhance India's agricultural production together with securing a remunerative income for the farmers—by integrating farmers with bulk buyers, agro-industries. Though an informal contract farming was there in the country for commercial crops (like cotton, sugarcane, tobacco, tea, coffee, rubber and dairy) it was absent in case of other agri-products. Such an initiative from the Government was long due since contract farming was allowed by the Government in 2000.

COVID-19 AND AGRI-REFORMS

The ongoing coronavirus pandemic has brought serious economic consequences for the economy and has invited multiple disruptions. In the wake of it the Government launched a major push towards self-reliance by announcing the *Atmanirbhar Bharat Abhiyan* in May 2020. The campaign includes following three historic policy decisions (June 2020) towards agricultural reforms:

1. **Essential Commodities Act amended:** The Act of 1955 has been amended to help both farmers and consumers while bringing in price stability – by creating competitive market environment and preventing wastage of agri-produce that happens due to lack of storage facilities. While India has become *surplus* in most agri-commodities, farmers have been unable to get better prices due to lack of investment in cold storage, warehouses, processing and export as the entrepreneurial spirit gets dampened due to hanging sword of the Act. Farmers suffer huge losses when there are bumper harvests, especially of perishable commodities. With adequate processing facilities, much of this wastage can be reduced. Following benefits are expected from this reform move:
    - Commodities like cereals, pulses, oilseeds, edible oils, onion and potatoes will be *removed* from list of essential commodities – will remove fears of private investors of excessive regulatory interference in their business operations.
    - The *freedom* to produce, hold, move, distribute and supply will lead to harnessing of economies of scale and attract private sector and foreign direct investment into agriculture sector.
    - It will help drive up investment in cold storages and modernisation of food supply chain.
    - In situations such as war, famine, extraordinary price rise and natural calamity, such agricultural foodstuff can be regulated. However, the installed capacity of a value chain participant and the export demand of an exporter will remain *exempted* from such stock limit imposition so as to ensure that investments in agriculture are not discouraged.
2. **Barrier-free trade:** To promote barrier-free trade of farm produce the *Farming Produce Trade and Commerce (Promotion and Facilitation) Act, 2020* has been passed. Farmers in India today suffer from various restrictions in marketing their produce. There are restrictions for farmers in selling agri-produce outside the notified APMCs (Agricultural Produce Marketing Committees) market yards. The farmers are also restricted to sell the produce only to registered licensees of the state governments. Further, barriers exist in free flow of agriculture produce between various states owing to the prevalence of various APMC legislations enacted by the states. This historic step in unlocking the vastly regulated agriculture markets in the country is expected to bring in the following benefits to the agriculture sector:
    - It will create an ecosystem where the farmers and traders will enjoy freedom

of choice of sale and purchase of agri-produce.

- It will also promote barrier-free *inter-state* and *intra-state* trade and commerce
- outside the physical premises of markets notified under state APMC legislations.
- It will open more choices for the farmer, reduce marketing costs for the farmers and help them in getting better prices.
- It will also help farmers of regions with *surplus produce* to get better prices and consumers of regions with shortages, lower prices.
- For ensuring a seamless trade an 'electronic transaction platform' is to be set up.
- Farmers not to be charged any cess or levy for sale of their produce under it.
- A separate dispute resolution mechanism to be set up for the farmers.

The move is aimed at creating additional trading opportunities outside the APMC market yards to help farmers get remunerative prices by inducing additional competition–paving the way for creating *One India, One Agriculture Market.*

3. **Freedom to engage with buyers:** To empower farmers to engage with all possible buyers, the Government has passed the *Farmers (Empowerment and Protection) Agreement on Price Assurance and Farm Services Act, 2020.* Indian Agriculture is characterised by fragmentation due to small holdings and has certain weaknesses such as weather dependence, production uncertainties and market unpredictability. This makes agriculture risky and inefficient in respect of both input and output management. The ordinance is expected to bring in the following benefits to the farm sector:

- Empower farmers for engaging with processors, wholesalers, aggregators, large retailers, exporters etc., on a level playing field without any fear of exploitation.
- It will transfer the *risk* of market unpredictability from the farmer to the sponsor and also enable the farmer to access modern technology and better inputs.
- It will reduce cost of marketing and improve income of farmers.
- Farmers will engage in *direct marketing* thereby eliminating intermediaries resulting in full realisation of price.
- Farmers have been provided adequate protection – sale, lease or mortgage of farmers' land is totally prohibited and farmers' land is also protected against any recovery.
- Provision for effective dispute resolution mechanism with clear redressal time lines.

This Act will act as a catalyst to attract private sector investment for building supply chains for farm produce to *global markets* and enable farmers to get access to technology and advice for high value agriculture.

Postscript The new farm laws have been criticised by the farm leaders and the political parties in opposition alike and the country has seen a prolonged farm protest (mainly participated by the farmers from Haryana, Punjab and the western Uttar Pradesh) since late November 2020. While farm leaders were demanding total recall of these laws, the Government offered to postpone their enactment (by 18 months) and invited farmers for talks— the stalemate continued through April 2021.

Agri Commodity Trading

Agri commodity trading is aimed at stabilising prices by market-based *price discovely.* Prices of agri-goods in India are set or influenced by the MSPs and the wholesale prices (controlled by the wholesalers). These prices are not error-free as they are not market-based. In this context, agri-commodity market explores market-oriented price determination which brings in multiple *benefits* to the economy in general and farm community in particular:

1. Stable prices benefit sellers (farmers and traders) as well as buyers (traders and food processing industry);
2. Price volatilities due to seasonal variations are minimised;
3. Stock variations due to export and import are also taken care of; and
4. A market-based *price discovery* gives right signal to all stakeholders.

Historical Background During the pre-Independence era, India had a flourishing market for commodities such as cotton, edible oils, etc. In 1952, futures' trading in most commodities was banned due to shortages of essential commodities, which resulted from wars and natural calamities. The ban was lifted in 2002 and several national and regional exchanges were set up (under the regulatory control of the SEBI) for trading commodities:

1. **National Com modity and Derivatives Exchange (NCDEX)**—the largest agri-commodity exchange where agri-commodities account for around 99.9 per cent of its turnover (rest of the 0.1 per cent is the share of bullion).
2. **National Multi-Commodity Exchange (NMCE)**—almost entire turnover is in agri-commodities (around 99 per cent).
3. **Multi Commodity Exchange (MCX)**—agri-commodities account for around 3 per cent of its total trading turnover.
4. **Indian Commodity Exchange (ICEX)**—around 2 per cent of its turnover comes from the agri-commodities.

Presently, agri-commodities account for around 12 per cent of India's commodity trading while rest non-agri goods account for 88 per cent (such as metal, crude etc). By *April 2021* (as per SEBI), **91** agri-commodities were notified for future trading in the country which includes 17 cereals and pulses (such as wheat, rice, maize, bajra, jowar, ragi, tur, urad, moong, masoor, yellow peas etc); 12 oilseeds, oilcakes & edible oils (such as sunflower, safflower, soy complex, sesamum, linseed, coconut, castor complex etc); 13 spices (such as turmeric, cardamom, ginger, cloves, pepper, jeera etc); 4 fibres (art silk yarn, cotton complex, jute and all jute products, mesta, staple fibre yarn); 2 sweeteners (gur and sugar); 4 plantation crops (cocoa, coffee, rubber and tea); 1 dry fruit (almond) and 13 'Other' goods (such as egg, mentha oil, isabgol, beetlenut, camphor, *onion* and *potato* etc). Majority of them are today actively traded on the commodity exchanges rather at times, trading is also prohibited in case of many of them by the SEBI in wake of extra speculation and volatility.

Agri commodity trading is undergoing for a transformation as the *three* biggest bottlenecks—storage, logistics and financing (which used to plague it resulting into huge harvest and post-harvest losses)—finally being eliminated with a synergistic combination of technology, physical infrastructure and stronger regulation. Looking ahead, it appears that the Indian agri-commodities segment is headed for better days. *[see Chapter 14 for more details on Commodity Trading].*

Upstream & Downstream Requirements

'Upstream' and 'downstream' are business terms applicable to the production processes that exist within several industries. Upstream, downstream and midstream make up the stages of the production process for different industries.

Upstream The upstream stage of the production process involves searching for and extracting raw materials—it does not do anything with the material itself, such as processing the materials. In upstream, firms simply find and extract the raw material. Thus, any industry that relies on the extraction of raw materials commonly has an *upstream stage* in its production process. In a more general sense, upstream can also refer to any part of the production process relating to the extraction stages.

Downstream The downstream stage in the production process involves processing the materials collected during the upstream stage into a finished product. It further includes the actual sale. End users will vary depending on the finished product. Regardless of the industry involved, the downstream process has direct contact with customers through the finished product.

Midstream Several points in between the two points (the place where raw is extracted and till it reaches the final consumer as finished product) are taken as the midstream. It depends on the reference point as how many or which stage is considered as the midstream by an industry.

Whether an activity is upstream or downstream depends on the point of analysis in a supply chain. A manufacturer considers suppliers as upstream and customers as downstream. Within a manufacturer, control over activities in the supply chain is subject to a company's management. Even so, a manufacturing activity that occurs prior to another is considered an upstream activity. Control over activities outside the company is subject to inter-company negotiations, cooperation and technology.

Industries, to have a smooth and uninterrupted functioning, depend heavily on the upstream and downstream requirements. In the case of *India*, we find several bottlenecks in both the processes:

1. In the case of the private sector, the downstream process seems better. But it is not so. Upto the level of 'wholesale' it is somewhat organised, but the retail trading is quite fragmented. India's *retail business* remains least organised. Organised retail is yet to evolve in the country, thus, the levels of uncertainties, potential of market access, monitoring and regulation of retail market are too weak.
2. Upstream processes are also not up-to-the-mark. From the stage where the wholesale comes into picture, things look better. But outsourcing the raw from the local producers is an uphill task in the country. Due to this the upstream segment of the economy has remained too weak and fragmented.
3. The industrial and manufactured sectors have been managing their upstream and downstream requirements, but their heavy dependence on the unorganised sector is a challenging issue in front of India.
4. In the case of agricultural products, the situation is even worse. Agrimarkets of regulations by the APMCs did not allow India to establish a common and single market. This has hampered not only the growth and business prospects, but it has also crippled the agricultural sector in a very serious way. It has taken the heaviest toll on the agriculture sector which still remains a non-remunerative profession.
5. As India is to compete in the global market, its immediately needs to

strengthen it upstream and downstream process. For this, India is advised to pick the best practices from around the world and integrate itself with the developed world with the better ways and the state-of-the-art tools and means.

SUPPLY CHAIN MANAGEMENT

A *supply chain* is a network of facilities and distribution options that performs the functions of procurement of materials, transformation of these materials into intermediate and finished products, and the distribution of these finished products to customers. Supply chains exist in both services, and manufacturing organisations, although the complexity of the chain may vary greatly from industry to industry and firm to firm.

Traditionally, marketing, distribution, planning, manufacturing, and the purchasing organisations along the supply chain operated independently. These organisations have their own objectives and these are often conflicting. Marketing's objective of high customer service and maximum sales conflict with manufacturing and distribution goals. Many manufacturing operations are designed to maximise output and lower costs with little consideration for the impact on inventory levels and distribution capabilities. Purchasing contracts are often negotiated with very little information beyond historical buying patterns. The result of these factors is that there is not a single, integrated plan for the organisation—there were as many plans as businesses. Clearly, there is a need for a mechanism through which these different functions could be integrated. Supply chain management is a strategy through which such an integration can be achieved.

Supply chain management is typically viewed to lie between fully vertically integrated firms, where the entire material flow is owned by a *single firm*, and those where each channel member operates independently. Therefore, coordination between the various players in the chain is key in its effective management. Supply chain management can be compared to a well-balanced and well-practiced 'relay team'—such a team is more competitive when each player knows how to be positioned for the hand-off. The relationships are the strongest between players who directly pass the baton, but the entire team needs to make a coordinated effort to win the race.

Supply chain management, then, is the active management of supply chain activities to maximise customer value and achieve a sustainable competitive advantage. It represents a conscious effort by the supply chain firms to develop and run supply chains in the most effective and efficient ways possible. Supply chain activities cover everything, such as:

1. Product development,
2. Sourcing,
3. Production,
4. Logistics, and
5. Information systems (for proper coordination).

The organisations that make up the supply chain are 'linked' together through *physical* flows and *information* flows. Physical flows involve the transformation, movement, and storage of goods and materials. They are the most visible piece of the supply chain. But just as important are information flows—information flows allow the various supply chain partners to coordinate their long-term plans, and to control the day-to-day flow of goods and material up and down the supply chain.

FDI in Upstream, Downstream and Supply Chain Management

This segment of India has seen least organised development, even in the reforms period. Due to lack of proper 'market reforms' in the area of agricultural products (as APMCs of different states have failed to develop) which hampered so many aspects of it—storage, grading, packaging, etc. It is believed that this field needs huge investments from the corporate sector. The corporate sector has not been much attracted to this sector. Main factors for the unwillingness among the private sector to put in their money in it are, scarcity of capital, logistics, experience and non-conducive policy framework in the agriculture market. This is the reason why the Government of India has allowed more freedom to FDI in retail chain development. It is expected that the willing foreign firms will not only bring in the needed fund to the sector, but alongwith them India will get international experience and best practices.

To compete in the globalising world markets and to gain economic benefits out of globalisation, India needs the following features in its supply chain management:

1. An organised retail sector
2. Proper levels of logistics
3. Fully updated data of raw materials, production, cropping pattern, etc.
4. International class packaging, care to. wards phyto-sanitary aspects

It is felt that the above-cited features will be easier to manage for the top global players as they have fund, experience and a willingness to expand their businesses in the growing regions of the world.

It is believed that the new Model Contract Farming Act 2018 will bring in a new synergy in the supply chain management of agri-goods in the country as it aims to free up the agri-product market for agri-exporters, food processing industries and the bulk buyers—given the opportunity, the Government expects higher investments (specially FDI) in the sector from the private players. It will help the growth and expansion of agri-commodity futures also which have been also opened for the foreign portfolio investment.[34]

IRRIGATION

The Planning Commission[35] classified irrigation projects/schemes in India on the following lines:

1. **Major Irrigation Schemes**—those with cultivable command areas (CCA) of more than 10,000 hectares.
2. **Medium Irrigation Schemes**—those with cultivable command areas (CCA) between 2,000 and 10,000 hectares.
3. **Minor Irrigation Schemes**—those with cultivable command area (CCA) upto 2,000 hectares. Expansion of irrigation facilities, along with consolidation of the existing systems, has been the main part of the strategy for increasing production of foodgrains.

There is **need** to expand the acreage under irrigation along with adoption of appropriate technologies for efficient utilisation of water through suitable pricing to raise agricultural productivity in India. This could be done through– (i) Adoption of irrigation technologies which improve efficiency in the use of water is imperative in a scenario where flood irrigation has resulted in wastage of water. (ii) Focus on efficient irrigation technologies is important with increasing water shortages owing to climate change and indiscriminate wastage of water in agriculture and other uses.

Having *'more crop per drop'* through efficient irrigation technologies should be the motto to improve productivity in agriculture which can ensure food and water security in the future.

34. Greater possibilities in the areas of wholesale and retail will create greater incentives for the private sector to put more money not only into agri-supply chain but they will get more and integrated with the ***agri-commodity contract market*** too.

35. ***Planning Commission***, GoI, N. Delhi, 1961.

Irrigation Potential & Use

As per the latest[36] available data, out of 140 million ha (hectares) of net sown area in the country, net *irrigated area* is about 68.38 million ha (48.8 per cent) and remaining 51.2 per cent is under *rainfed*. Out of the net irrigated area, about 40 per cent is irrigated through canal systems and 60 per cent is irrigated through groundwater. The overall irrigation efficiency of the major and medium irrigation projects is estimated to be around **38** per cent. The efficiency of *surface* irrigation system can be improved from about 35-40 per cent to around 50-60 per cent and that of *groundwater* from about 65-70 per cent to 72-75 per cent. An important challenge facing the irrigation sector in India is the growing gap between Irrigation Potential Created (IPC) and Irrigation Potential Utilized (IPU), and uneven distribution of water over the length of the canal system—caused mainly by the following factors:

- lack of proper operation and maintenance,
- incomplete distribution system,
- non-completion of command area development,
- changes in cropping pattern, and
- diversion of irrigated land for other purposes.

There is need to arrest the declining trend in efficient utilisation of irrigation potential and also reverse it. A larger share of funds available under the Mahatma Gandhi National Rural Employment Guarantee Scheme (MGNREGS) and other employment generating schemes need to be deployed for promotion of irrigation—*for creation and maintenance of community assets, de-silting and repair of tanks and other water bodies.*

Irrigation Efficiency

Agricultural productivity can be boosted in a big way by enhancing irrigation efficiency in the use of irrigation systems. Over the time, the conventional systems of irrigation have become non-viable in many parts of India[37] due to:

- increasing shortages of water,
- wastage of water through over irrigation, and
- concerns of salination of soil.

Economically and technically efficient irrigation technologies like – *drip* and *sprinkler* irrigation – can improve water use efficiency, reduce costs of production by reducing labour costs and power consumption. With this technology, additional area can be irrigated with the same amount of water compared to conventional method of irrigation. In addition, water deficient, cultivable waste land and undulating land areas can be brought under cultivation due to ease of irrigation. There is also good scope for using this technology in closely spaced crops like rice, wheat, onion, potato etc. Farm income has seen a substantial gain[38] caused by multiple benefits which accrue out this technology:

- Saving of irrigation water from 20 to 48 per cent;
- Energy saving from 10 to 17 per cent;
- Saving of labour cost from 30 to 40 per cent;
- Saving of fertilisers from 11 to 19 per cent; and
- Increase in crop production from 20 to 38 per cent.

To promote the cause of enhancing water productivity and irrigation efficiency, Government has taken the following steps in the direction:

- Pradhan Mantri Krishi Sinchayee Yojana (PMKSY) was launched in 2015-16 with the motto of *Har Khet Ko Paani* for providing end-to-end solutions in irrigation supply chain (i.e.,

36. **Ministry of Agriculture & Farmers Welfare**, GoI, N. Delhi, December 2020.

37. NITI Aayog, *Task Force on Agriculture*, 2015, as quoted Ministry of Finance, **Economic Survey 2015-16**, Vol. 2, p. 104.

38. **Economic Survey 2019-20**, Vol. 2, pp. 198-199, Ministry of Finance, GoI, N. Delhi.

water sources, distribution network and farm level applications).

- Per Drop More Crop component of PMKSY (PMKSY-PDMC) was launched in 2015-16 aimed at water use efficiency at farm level.

3. Micro Irrigation Fund (MIF) has been created with NABARD (with a corpus of ₹5000 crore) to facilitate the States in mobilising the resources for expanding coverage of micro irrigation.

Water Productivity

Water productivity in India is very low. The overall irrigation efficiency of the major and medium irrigation projects in India is estimated at around 38 per cent. As per the *NITI Aayog*, efficiency of the *surface irrigation* system can be improved from about 35-40 per cent to around 60 per cent and that of *groundwater* from about 65-70 per cent to 75 per cent. Water productivity needs to be enhanced by the following methods:

- tapping, harvesting and recycling water,
- efficient on-farm water management practices,
- micro irrigation,
- use of waste water, and
- resource conservation technologies.

In order to promote judicious use of water ensuring *'more crop per drop'* of water in agriculture for drought proofing, the GoI recently launched the PMKSY aiming at providing water to every field of agriculture.

FARM MECHANISATION

India needs to introduce better equipment for each farming operation in order to reduce drudgery, to improve efficiency by saving on time and labour, improve productivity, minimise wastage and reduce labour costs for each operation. Agricultural mechanisation in case of India is increasingly needed as:

- Due to shortage of labour for agricultural operations owing to rural-urban migration, shift from agriculture to services and rise in demand for labour in non-farm activities, there is need to use labour for agricultural operations judiciously, which makes a strong case for mechanisation of farming.
- Indian agriculture has a high proportion of female workforce in both the cultivation and processing stages of farming. Therefore, ergonomically designed tools and equipment for reducing drudgery, enhancing safety and comfort and also to suit the needs of women workers would help in better adoption of technologies in agriculture.
- An effective use of agricultural machinery helps in timely farm operations for *quick* rotation of crops on the same land (necessary in wake of shrinking land). By raising a second crop or multi-crops from the same land, there is improvement in the cropping intensity and making agricultural land commercially more viable (NABARD, 2018).

Though, farm mechanisation has improved in the recent times, which stands at 45 per cent, it is much lower in comparison to USA (95 per cent), Brazil (75 per cent) and China (57 per cent). There are intra-national disparities also visible with northern India having higher mechanisation compared to other regions. Tractor industry and farm mechanisation (sales of tractor and power tillers) in the country had compounded annual growth rate (CAGR) of 10 per cent and 7.53 per cent during 2016-2018, respectively.

Important reasons for lower agricultural mechanisation in the country, as per a study (NABARD, 2018) are—economies of operation due to small holdings, access to power, credit cost and procedures, uninsured markets and low awareness. In recent times (since 2014-15 onwards), Government has taken several *new steps* to promote[39] farm mechanisation in the country—

- Under the Sub-Mission on Agricultural Mechanisation (launched in 2014–15) assistance is provided to State governments to impart training/ demonstration, provide assistance to farmers for procurement of agricultural machineries and for setting up of Custom Hiring Centre.
- The latest agricultural machineries, like laser leveller, happy seeders, combine harvesters and power weeders are being promoted.
- Under the new Central Sector Scheme on 'Promotion of Agricultural Mechanisation for In-Situ Management of Crop Residue in the States of Punjab, Haryana, Uttar Pradesh and NCT of Delhi' (2018-19 to 2019-20), the agricultural machines and equipment for in-situ crop residue management (aimed at fighting the *stubble burning* in the region) are provided with 50 per cent subsidy to the individual farmers and 80 per cent subsidy for establishment of Custom Hiring Centres.
- Realising the linear relationship between availability of farm power and farm yield, farm power availability is to be enhanced from 2.02 kW per ha to 4.0 kW per ha by 2030 (to cope up with increasing demand for foodgrains).

39. **Economic Survey 2019-20,** Vol. 2, pp. 196-198, Ministry of Finance, GoI, N. Delhi. The Survey has quoted the latest study of 2018 by NABARD in this regard.

SEED DEVE LOPMENT

Seed is the basic input for increasing productivity in agriculture. It is estimated that the quality of seed accounts for 20 to 25 per cent of productivity.[40] Thus, the adoption of quality seeds needs promotion in India. There are multiple challenges to the development and adoption of quality seeds in the form of:

- Inadequate research inputs for development of new seeds especially,
- Early ripening and resistant (to pest, moisture variations, etc.) varieties,
- High cost of seeds for small and marginal farmers,
- Shortage of supply of quality seeds,
- Non-resolution of issues related to adoption of Genetically Modified Seeds, and
- Inadequate number of players restricting competition.

The **issues**[41] that require immediate attention are:

- **Affordability:** Open pollinated varieties of seeds can be developed by farmers from their own harvested crops. However, for high-yielding hybrid varieties, the farmer has to depend on the market for each crop which gets very costly for the small and marginal farmers.
- **Availability:** Quality seeds have shortage in supply. While there is a demand for banning non-certified seeds, certification *per-se* does not ensure quality seeds. Presence of more players (both public and private) and

40. As per the *DAC&FW (Department of Agriculture, Cooperation & Farmers Welfare)* – as quoted by the **Economic Survey 2015-16,** Vol. 2, p. 105.

41. Ministry of Finance, **Economic Survey 2015-16, pp.** 105-107.

competition in the market for seeds would improve this situation.

- **Research and development of seeds and seed technology :** The first Green Revolution was driven by indigenously developed High Yielding Varieties (HYVs) of seeds for paddy and wheat. Inadequate research and genetic engineering has been a constraint in the development of seeds and seed technologies in major crops during the past few decades in India. There is need to encourage development of seed technologies in both private and public sectors to initiate another round of Green Revolution. This development should cover all agricultural segments.

- **GM crops and seeds :** Concerns about its affordability, environmental and ethical issues, risks to the food chain, disease spread and cross pollination have resulted in their non-introduction.

FERTILISERS

In improving agricultural output, fertiliser is a critical and expensive input. Since the Green Revolution (mid-1960s), there has been a sharp increase in the use of fertilisers in India. To facilitate and promote the use of fertilisers, the Government has been providing fertiliser subsidy to farmers. Today, the fertiliser subsidies stand at around **8** per cent of the total agricultural GDP.[42]

However, the use of fertilisers has not resulted in commensurate growth in agricultural productivity. The declining response ratio or marginal productivity of fertilisers since the 1970s is a pointer to their inefficient use in Indian agriculture. The yield of grain per kilogram use of NPK fertiliser has declined from 13.4 kg grain per ha in 1970 to 3.6 kg grain per ha in irrigated areas by 2018-19.

In the post Green Revolution agriculture scenario, there have been **imbalances** in the use of fertilisers such as:

1. Excessive dependence on urea owing to low/distorted prices of fertilisers, especially urea and regional imbalance in the use,
2. Neglect/low use of compost, manure and other forms of natural nutrient providers,
3. Discontinuing practices of inter and rotational cropping,
4. Diversion of the subsidised fertilisers to non-agricultural use,
5. Indiscriminate use of fertilisers has not proportionally improved the yield of crops, but has resulted in the depletion of soil fertility and salination of soil in many areas.

Certain *improvements in fertilisation* needed in the Indian farm sector may be summed up as follows:

- **Crop-responsive & balanced use of fertilisers :** There is need to facilitate the optimal use of fertilisers depending on the soil health and fertility status. Linking the *soil health card* to provide profile of the soil and fertiliser on the basis of the same profile utilising fertiliser, (even if not subsidised) can improve the yield of crops.

- **Micro nutrients & organic fertilisers:** Indian soils show deficiency of micro nutrients (like boron, zinc, copper and iron) in most parts of the country which limit crop yields and productivity. Fertilisers which supplement micro nutrients can provide an additional yield in cereals in the range of 0.3 to 0.6

42 Ministry of Finance, **January 2021**, MoF, GoI, N. Delhi.

ton per hectare.[43] This deficiency can be overcome if there by expansion in the use of organic fertiliser. Besides, being cheaper to use organic composting and manure it can help improve and retain soil fertility too., There is great scope for enhancing the use of organic fertilisers as around 67 per cent of Indian soil is characterised by low organic carbon.

3. **Nutrient management:** To maintain soil health and productivity, judicious use of chemical fertilisers, bio-fertilisers and locally available organic manures like farmyard manure, compost, vermi-compost and green manure based on soil testing is necessary.

   With over 12 crore farm holdings in India, it is a big challenge to provide soil-testing facilities for overcoming the multi-nutrient deficiencies in soils so as to improve agricultural output. Use of information technology and providing soil fertility maps to farmers can go a long way in efficient nutrient management.

4. **Regional disparity in fertiliser consumption :** India has wide regional disparities in the consumption of fertilisers. This may be attributed to the availability of irrigation facilities in the high consuming states (since irrigation is a requirement for proper absorption of fertilisers). It is necessary to reduce the disparities through appropriate soil-testing facilities and other policy measures.

Rising fertiliser subsidy bill (estimated to be ₹80,000 crores in 2019-20 in comparison to about ₹70,000 crores of 2018-19), has been a major concern in the area of fiscal management for the country. Aimed at *rationalising* fertiliser subsidy, the Government has taken some important steps[44] in recent years:

- All fertiliser subsidies are being disbursed through the Direct Benefit Transfer (DBT) system since late 2016-17. Under this system, the subsidies are released to the fertiliser companies on the basis of actual sales made by the retailers to the beneficiaries (identifying them through Aadhaar Card, KCC, Voter Identity card, etc.).
- The New Urea Policy-2015 has been notified with multiple aims—maximising indigenous urea production, promoting energy efficiency, and rationalising subsidy burden.
- In case of P (phosphate) and K (potash) fertilisers, the Government is implementing the Nutrient Based Subsidy (NBS) scheme under which a fixed amount of subsidy is given based on their content.

PESTICIDES

Due to the presence of weeds, pests, diseases and rodents, the crop yield losses range from 15 to 25 per cent in India. Even though pesticides are essential for improving crop yields, per hectare pesticide use is much lower in India in comparison with other countries. Presently, India uses a low amount of 0.5 kg per ha pesticide compared to 7.0 kg per ha in the USA, 2.5 kg per ha in Europe, 12 kg per ha in Japan and 6.6 kg per ha in Korea. Besides, there are certain concerns regarding pesticides use in the country:

- Use of pesticides without following proper guidelines,

---

43. As per the conducted by the *Indian Council of Agricultural Research (ICAR)* – quoted by the **Economic Survey 2015–16**, Vol. 2, p.108.

44. **Economic Survey 2019-20**, Vol. 2, p. 208, Ministry of Finance, GoI, N. Delhi.

- Use of sub standard pesticides, and
- Lack of awareness about pesticide use.

These practices have given rise to *pesticide residues* being found in food products in India, posing major threats to the environment and human beings. Some **policy steps** which may be suggested in this regard are:

- Farmers need to be educated about the classification of insecticides on the basis of their toxicity and their suitability for aerial application.
- The CIBRC (Central Insecticide Board and Registration Committee) has issued guidelines for the application of pesticides, their dosage, minimum intervals to be maintained, and the levels of toxicity. This information needs to be widely disseminated among farmers.
- Greater focus on IPM (Integrated Pest Management) which will encompass a judicious mix of pest control methods by leveraging the cultural, mechanical, biological methods and need-based use of chemical pesticides. It gives preference to the use of bio-pesticides and bio-control agents, too.
- Being environment friendly, nontoxic and cost effective, bio-pesticides need to be promoted among small farmers to improve productivity in agriculture.

AGRI-CREDIT

Agri-credit is an important mediating input for agriculture to improve productivity. Access to institutional credit enables the farmer to enhance productivity by investing in machinery and purchase of variable inputs like fertilisers, quality seeds, and manure and providing funds till the farmer receives payment from sale of produce, which is at times delayed and staggered. Input use by farmers is sensitive to credit flows to the agriculture sector. Some of the concerns regarding agri-credit are as given below:

1. Predominance of *informal sources* of credit: farmers still avail as much as 40 per cent of the funds from informal sources – 26 per cent of the total agricultural credit flow from the local money lenders (highly exploitative lenders).[45] In respect of high interest rates, **DBT** may be considered to replace subvention of interest rates. The intermediation and refinance model to promote agricultural credit needs to be revisited and replaced with DBT that shall subsidise the interest paid by the farmer, instead of subsidising refinance to financial institutions.
2. The ratio of agricultural credit to agricultural GDP has increased from 10 per cent in 1999-2000 to around 45 per cent by 2017–18. However, the share of long-term credit (for more than 5 years) in agriculture or investment credit has declined from 55 per cent in 2006-07 to 33 per cent in 2017-18. The decline in the share of long-term credit in agriculture needs to be arrested and reversed.
3. There is regional disparity in the distribution of agricultural credit. The coverage is very low in the north-eastern and eastern regions of the country.
4. Crop loans being short-term (for less than 15 months) in nature are meant to meet the current expenditure till the crop is harvested fail to promote major investments in agriculture. Farm loans upto ₹3 lakh are disbursed at an interest rate of 7 per cent per annum (effective interest rate becomes 4 per cent after 3 per cent interest subvention).

Agricultural credit has been boosted by the Government in recent years—the *Union Budget 2021-22* has set a target of ₹16.5 lakh crores for 2020-21 (up from ₹15 lakh crore of 2020-21).

45. **NSSO,** 70th Round data quoted by the **Economic Survey 2015-16**, Vol. 2, p. 110.

However, the regional distribution of agricultural credit in country is highly skewed[46] specially in North Eastern, Hilly and Eastern States. The share of North Eastern States is less than 1 per cent in total agricultural credit disbursement while in case of the Southern States it is upto 15 per cent.

COVID-19 Impact In the wake of the ongoing coronavirus pandemic to help farmers fight the economic hardships, the Government has announced a slew of measures. As the part of India's move towards self-reliance, the *Atmanirbhar Bharat Abhiyan* has the following package of farm liquidity support:

- Loan moratorium of 3 months given to farmers (3 crore farmers with agricultural loans of ₹ 4.22 lakh crore availed this benefit).
- Interest Subvention and Prompt Repayment Incentive on crop loans, due from 1st March, extended up to 31st May, 2020.
- New Kisan Credit Cards (₹ 25 lakh) sanctioned with a loan limit of ₹ 25,000 crores.
- 63 lakh loans of ₹ 86, 600 crores agricultural loans approved (between March 1st to April 30th, 2020).
- Refinancing of agri-credit of ₹ 29,500 crore provided by NABARD, to Cooperative Banks Regional Rural Banks in March, 2020.
- Support of ₹ 4,200 crore provided under RIDF (Rural Infrastructure Development Fund) to sates during March, 2020 for rural infrastructure.
- Working capital limit of ₹ 6,700 crore sanctioned for procurement of agriculture produce to state government entities since March, 2020.

46. **Economic Survey 2019-20**, Vol. 2, p. 208, Ministry of Finance, GoI, N. Delhi.

AGRICULTURE EXTENSION SERVICES

Another key input to farm sector is 'agriculture extension services (AES)'. These services can improve productivity by providing timely advisory services to farmers to adopt best practices, technology, meet with contingencies, market information etc. The AES (also called 'rural advisory services') has been defined[47] as 'consisting of all the different activities that provide the information and services needed and demanded by farmers and other factors in rural settings to assist them in developing their own technical, organisational and management skills and practices so as to improve their livelihoods and well-being'.

Though there are multiple agencies in India offering agricultural advisory services the system is not efficient enough due to the following reasons:[48]

- Lack of functional autonomy,
- Rigid hierarchical structures leading to lack of innovative methods of providing extension services, and
- Coordination failures at multiple levels.

For the improvement of the AES in the country the suggested policy steps are:

- Implementing a new scheme or additional outlays in existing schemes.
- Need of 'one-stop-shop' that offers both hardware and software solutions to raise the incomes of farmers, especially small and marginal farmers.
- Need of an approach which is 'neutral to input, crop and region'.

47. *GFRAS (Global Forum for Rural Advisory Services)*, 2010–quoted by the **Economic Survey 2015-16**, Vol. 2, p. 111.
48. NITI Aayog, **Task Force on Agriculture**, 2015.

- Minimising wastage in inputs as well as produce, till it leaves the farm gate.
- Efforts to enhance post harvest processing/value added activities at the farm.
- Need to share with the farmer, information on weather, in order to improve yield, and minimise damage to crops.

7. Promoting inter and rotational cropping and efficient utilisation of the inputs.
8. Need to shift to demand-driven agricultural advisory services.
9. Need of a virtual connect, using IT (mobile and internet) and integration of agricultural extension services.

Over the time, the GoI has taken variety of initiatives[49] to strengthen the AES in the country, major ones being – *Kisan TV* set up; broadcasting of agri-information by AIR; *Agri-Clinic & Agri-Business* (by agriculture graduates); Extension education institutes set up; model training courses for horticulture, animal husbandry, etc started; National Centre for Management of Agricultural Extension (acronym for which is *MANAGE*) set up as an apex institute to train middle and senior level officers of the states/UTs; digital agricultural platform, the *CAPS* (Cyber Agro-Physical Systems) launched to make farming viable, self-sustaining and internationally competitive; and Agriculture Education Portal *EKTA* (Ekikrit Krishi Shiksha Takniki Ayaam) launched for integrated online information management with 9 Mobile Apps dedicated to mango, pomegranate, onion, garlic, black pepper, etc.

49. **Economic Survey 2019-20**, Vol. 2, p. 203, Ministry of Finance, GoI, N. Delhi.

PMFBY

The Government of India launched a new agricultural insurance scheme in January 2016. The new scheme[50]—Pradhan Mantri Fasal Bima Yojana (PMFBY)—has been termed as a *path breaking scheme for farmers' welfare.* The highlights of this scheme are as given below:

- There will be a uniform premium of only 2 per cent to be paid by farmers for all kharif crops and 1.5 per cent for all rabi crops.
- In case of annual commercial and horticultural crops, the premium to be paid by farmers will be only 5 per cent.
- The premium rates to be paid by farmers are very low and balance premium will be paid by the government to provide full insured amount to the farmers against crop loss on account of natural calamities.
- There is no upper limit on Government subsidy. Even if balance premium is 90 per cent, it will be borne by the Government.
- 25 per cent of the likely claim will be settled directly on farmers account and there will be one insurance company for the entire state as well as farm level assessment of loss for localised risks and post harvest loss.
- Earlier, there was a provision of capping the premium rate which resulted in low claims being paid to farmers. This capping was done to limit Government outgo on the premium subsidy. This capping has now been removed and farmers will get claim against full sum insured without any reduction.
- The use of technology will be encouraged to a great extent. Smartphones will be used

50. **Government of India**, N. Delhi, January 13th, 2016.

to capture and upload data of crop cutting to reduce the delays in claim payment to farmers. Remote sensing will be used to reduce the number of crop cutting experiments.

The scheme replaced the existing NAIS (National Agricultural Insurance Scheme) of 1999 and is being implemented by both private and public sector companies. Though, the scheme is voluntary for states, at present, 27 states/UTs are implementing it. The scheme was made more farmer-friendly and flexible after its *revamp* in February 2020—with the following major changes[51]:

- Direct Benefit Transfer (DBT) was introduced in 2017-18 to help farmers receive claims directly in their bank accounts—a deliberate step to weed out ghost/duplicate through Aadhar based verification.
- National Crop Insurance Portal has been launched to provide interface among all stakeholders.
- Provision of 12 per cent interest rate per annum to be paid by the Insurance Company to farmers for delay in settlement of claims beyond 10 days.
- State Governments to pay 12 per cent interest rate for delay in release of state share of subsidy beyond three months to Insurance Companies.
- Increase in time for change of crop name for insurance from 1 to upto 2 working days.
- Time for intimation of loss due to localised calamities and post-harvest losses has been increased from 48 hours to 72 hours;
- Participation for farmers made voluntary as earlier, the loanee farmers (58 per cent of the total farmers) would compulsorily be brought under this scheme.
- States have been provided flexibility to rationalise the sum insured so that adequate benefits can be availed by farmers.

Aadhar seeding has helped in speedy claim settlement directly into the farmer accounts. Today, the scheme covers over 5.5 crore farmers every year—even during COVID-19 lock down period around 70 lakh farmers benefitted out of it.

WTO AND THE INDIAN AGRICULTURE: PROSPECTS AND CHALLENGES

With the operationalisation of the provisions of the World Trade Organization (WTO), the process of globalisation commenced in the major parts of the world—the non-member countries, in the coming few years, also started negotiating for entry into the club. There has always been an air of confusion among the members and the non-members of the WTO in assessing the pros and cons of globalisation on the health of their economies. The sector which has created the highest number of deliberations in the WTO as well as views and counterviews has been agriculture—an area of utmost concern for the developed and the developing worlds alike. India is no exception to it, better say it has been among the few countries in the world spear-heading the campaign against the biased provisions of the WTO concerning agriculture.

India was sceptical about the issue even before joining the organisation, but once it became a part of it, it started assessing the situation objectively and moved towards crisis mitigation. Globalisation as such opened unlimited prospects

51. Economic Survey 2020-21, vol. 2, p. 239, Ministry of Finance, GoI, N. Delhi.

for the economies, but at the same time brought several challenges too. Yes, the challenges were different in nature for the developed and the developing countries. We need to enquire the prospects and the challenges brought by the WTO for Indian agriculture.

Had the agriculture of the leading and politically vocal developing economies not been of subsistence level, the course of the world would have been completely different. It is the biggest hurdle in the process of globalisation and the success of the World Trade Organization. Yes, the process of converting the sector into an industry has already started in most of the leading developing economies amidst tough resistance from the farmers, political parties and the NGOs alike.

The Prospects

The oldest and the first document regarding the impact of the implementation of the provisions of the WTO, Uruguay Round (1995–2005) was prepared jointly by the World Bank, the GATT[52] and the OECD[53]. According to the joint document, the WTO provisions were supposed to have the following positive impacts on the world trade:

1. By 2005 there will be an addition of $745 billion in the world merchandise trade.[54]
2. The *GATT Secretariat* provided a full break-up of the above-projected trade increase in the following way:
   (i) The clothing sector to have a share of 60 per cent.
   (ii) The agricultural, forestry and fisheries products to have a share of 20 per cent.
   (iii) The processed food, beverages and drinks to have a share of 19 per cent.

It means that due to the implementation of the WTO provisions, there will be only *one per cent* increase in the trade of all other goods excluding the above-cited sectors. It was a highly inflated view and became a matter of debate around the world. But the areas which were projected to have very high increase in their trade were not mere projections either. Member countries went home and started going for their own studies, estimations and projections—India being no exception. We must see the assessment of India:

1. The products which were projected to have the maximum increase in their trade, India had a traditional great export potential in them. It means the WTO has a great prospect for agriculture in store as maximum goods fell in the agriculture sector. Assuming that India's share in the world exports improves from 0.5 per cent to 1.0 per cent, and India is able to take advantage of the opportunities that are created, the trade gains may conservatively be placed at $2.7 billion extra exports per year. A more generous estimate will range from $3.5 to $7 billion worth extra exports.[55]
2. The NCAER (National Council for Applied Economic Research) survey of the WTO on the Indian economy is cited as the best document in this area. The survey[56] had all important things to say on this issue:

52. General Agreement on Trade and Tariff (GATT) was a multi-lateral arrangement (not an ***organisation*** like WTO whose deliberations are binding on the member countries) promoting multi-lateral world trade. Now the GATT has been replaced by the WTO (***since January. 1995***).

53. ***Organisation for Economic Cooperation and Development*** (OECD) was set up as a world body of the developed economies from the Euro-American region, which today includes countries from Asia, too (such as Japan and South Korea). The first idea of 'globalisation' was proposed by the OECD in the early 1980s at one of its Annual Meet (***at Brussels***).

54. Merchandise trade does not include services.

55. Ministry of Finance, Economic Survey 1994–95 (New Delhi: Government of India, 1995).

56. ***NCAER Survey*** headed by its chairman Rakesh Mohan, GoI, 1994.

(i) The exports of agricultural products will be boosted by the WTO accepted regime.

(ii) Only the foodgrains trade that too of wheat and rice were projected to be around $270 billion.

(iii) The survey also pointed out that almost 80-90 per cent of the increased supply of foodgrains to the world is going to originate from only two countries China and India as they are having the scope for increasing production.

(iv) But the survey painted a very wretched picture about the preparedness of Indian agriculture sector to exploit the opportunities. It concluded China to be far better than India is this matter.

(v) It suggested almost every form of preparedness for the agriculture sector (at a glance we may have been on the Second Green Revolution in India—basically the revolution is modelled on the findings and suggestions of the survey).

(vi) Lastly, the survey ended at a high note of caution and concern that if India fails in its preparations to make agriculture come out as a winner in the WTO regime the economy will emerge as the biggest importer of agricultural products. At the same time the cheaper agri-imports might devastate Indian agricultural structure and the import-dependence may ruin the prospects of a better life for millions of poor Indians.

(vii) Even if India does not want to tap the opportunities of the globalising world it has to gear up in the agriculture sector since the world market will hardly be able to fulfil the agri-goods demands of India by 2025. It means, it is only India which can meet its own agri-goods demand in the future.

There is no doubt that the WTO has brought probably *the last opportunity* to make our masses have better income and standard of living via better income coming from agriculture. But provided we go for the right kind of preparation at the right time. There are enough prospects, undoubtedly.

The Challenges[57]

If the WTO brings high prospects for Indian agriculture, it also brings in some hard-boiled challenges in front of it. These could be seen as individual challenges of the similar economies as well as joint challenges of such economies. The *first* category of challenges pertains to the area of relevant preparations, investment and restructuring of agriculture. And the *second* category of challenges are nothing less than a revision in the very agricultural provisions of the WTO itself (around which today revolves the success and failure of the organisation itself). We may take a look at the challenges before the Indian agriculture:

1. **Self-sufficiency of Food :** Due to inflow of cheaper foodgrains from the world it would not remain economically viable in India to produce them and farmers might incline in favour of the profitable agri-products. This will make India heavily dependent upon the world market for its food supplies, marring its achievement of food self-sufficiency.

57. The challenges and their possible remedies discussed in this sub-topic are based on some of the finest and timely debates and articles which appeared in many renowned journals and newspapers between the period 1994 and 2007. For better understanding of the readers only the consensual as well as the less-complex parts have been provided here.

This will have serious political and ethical outcomes for India.[58]

2. **Price Stability :** Dependence on the world market for the supply of agricultural products and specially for foodgrains will never be safe for India. As the international market for the products is highly speculative and full of variations (due to natural factors) the price stability will be always in danger—fluctuations hamper the producers and consumers of agri-goods in India. It would be very tough to fight *dumping* of surplus agri-goods from other countries.

3. **Cropping Pattern :** The cropping pattern of agriculture might take a very imbalanced shape, which will be highly detrimental to the ecology at large[59] as the farmers will always be in favour of going for the crops and commodities which have comparative price advantage.

4. **Weaker Sections:** The benefits of globalisation may not be neutral to areas, crops and the people. There will never prevail a certainty as to which area/region or crops or the people are going to benefit from globalisation in which year. At the same time globalisation is a process where profits can be made, but it is a market-based concept. Those who are unable to produce due to lack of capital, investment and entrepreneurship will have no gains from it. They will be net consumers or buyers. Since India has a vast population of the weaker sections (as other third world countries have) this population will neither be able to increase its income nor be able to purchase the agri-foods having no price stability.

   It means that the weaker sections of India might miss this chance of growth and development. We need to make the benefits of globalisation reach these people, too. This could be done by a timely and society-oriented public policy which is a big challenge.[60]

5. **WTO Commitments:** There are certain time-bound obligatory commitments of India towards the provisions of the WTO in the area of agriculture, which are highly detrimental to the people and the economy. We may see this challenge from two angles:

   (i) According to the agricultural provisions, the total subsidies forwarded by the government to the sector must not cross 10 per cent of the total agricultural outputs. At the same time, exemptions to farmers are to be withdrawn—hampering the public distribution system badly. India's subsidies are still far below this limit, but commitments pose a threat to the sovereign decision making.

   (ii) The subsidies (with different names) to agriculture, which are forwarded by the developed countries are highly

 58. Almost 50 per cent of the Indian population spends 75 per cent of its total income on the purchase of foodgrains—this is why their standard of life and nutrition depends on the indigenously grown food in a great way. Once the self-sufficiency is lost their lives will depend upon the ***diplomatic uncertainties*** of its regular supply. It will have serious political outcomes for the political scenario of India. Similarly, irregular supply of the foodgrains will create a high ethical dilemma, too.

59. Farmers might go for highly repetitive kind of cropping pattern creating problems for soil fertility, water crisis, etc. This will have highly adverse effects on the agriculture insurance companies, too.

60. The primary examples of corporate and contract farming have given enough hints that economically weaker sections of society have meagre chances of benefitting from the globalisation of agriculture—with major profits going to the corporate houses. Naturally, the governments (centre and states) will need to come up with highly effective policies which could take care of the economic interests of the masses.

The policies may focus on areas such as ***healthcare, education, insurance, housing, social security,*** etc. Already the governments have started emphasising the delivery and performance of the ***social sector*** but in the future, more focused and accountable programmes in the sector will be required.

detrimental to Indian agriculture and they are very high, too.[61]

None of the above-given challenges are easy to fight. These are not to be fought by India alone, but almost all developing countries are to face it. Once the WTO comes into operation, many experts from India and abroad have provided ways to fight these challenges, which may be summed up in the following way:

1. To fight the challenges related to self-sufficiency in food, the price stability and the cropping pattern a judicious mix of suitable kind of agricultural and trade policies will be the need of the hour. To the extent agricultural policy is concerned, India has a limited level of freedom. But the WTO regime does not allow the member countries to impose higher tariff or tariff itself to ward off cheaper agri-goods from entering the economy—this is the main reason behind the above challenges. It means it is essential to modify, change or revise the provisions of the WTO.

Similarly, the issue of agricultural subsidies (*the Boxes*) need to be equitably defined so that they do not look biased. Here also the provisions of the WTO need revision.

To fight out this typical challenge, experts suggested that the *WTO is not God-given.* Its provisions may go in for change if concerted efforts are made by the member countries in this direction. Like-minded nations who face the same kind of crises should come together and go for a joint effort, from inside the WTO, for the revisions or relaxations in its provisions. Morality related and ethical issues might be used as eye-openers and a handy tool to have the attention of the developed nations and the WTO alike.

Prima facie this suggestion looked as a preach easier said than done. Post-1995 saw a polarisation of like-minded countries inside the WTO that finally culminated into failure of the *Seatle Round* of the WTO deliberations. The most powerful country in the world failed to convene a meeting that too in its most distant region (the Alaska)—a moral triumph of the poor over the rich. This incidence while indicating a possible failure of the WTO itself, boosted the morale of the developing countries to go for stronger groupings and even sub-groupings under the WTO.

After the Doha Round the USA had hinted to forget multilateralism and indicated its intentions towards bilateralism. The European Union had the same intentions, but it did not show it as openly as the USA. The year 2002 came as a watershed period for the WTO when the EU in its new diplomatic move announced to hear the agriculture-related issues of the developing nations. The USA announced the intentions few days after the EU announcement—just few days before the *Cancun Meet* of the WTO. The Hongkong deliberation of the WTO, though it did not give anything concrete to the developing world, provided enough hope, there is no doubt in it. The real picture emerges in the next meet for which the different pressure groups had serious deliberations on alternatives of bargaining power.

The second level suggestion to India was in the area of preparedness for the WTO regime. India was required to set new and internationally best standards in the area of production by boosting areas such as—research and development, biotechnology, information technology, health and phytosanitary matters. This will make Indian

61. Some of the developed economies are still forwarding subsidies to the agricultural areas to the tune of 180–220 per cent! Again, the justification for such high subsidies have been provided by defining agriculture subsidies according to their ease—highly blurring and confusing.

goods and services compete in the international market.[62]

WTO AND AGRICULTU RAL SUBSIDIES[63] AMS

The subsidies provided by the government to the agricultural sector (i.e., domestic support) is termed by the WTO as Aggregate Measure of Support (AMS).[64] It is calculated in terms of *product* and *input* subsidies. The WTO argues that the product subsidies like minimum support prices and input subsidies (non-product) like credit, fertilisers, irrigation and power will cut production cost of farming and will give undue advantage to such countries in their access to the world market—such subsidies are called to cause *'distortions'* to the world trade. Such subsidies are not permitted in one sense as they have a minimum permissible limit *de minimis* under the provisions which is 5 per cent and 10 per cent of their total agricultural output in the case of developed and developing countries, respectively.

The Boxes

The agricultural subsidies, in the WTO terminology have in general been identified by 'boxes' which have been given the colours of the traffic lights—*green* (means permitted), *amber* (means slow down, i.e., to be reduced) and *red* (means forbidden).

In the agriculture sector, as usual, things are more complicated. The WTO provisions on agriculture has nothing like *red box* subsidies, although subsidies exceeding the reduction commitment levels is prohibited in the *'amber box'*. The *'blue box'* subsidies are tied to programmes that limit the level of production. There is also a provision of some exemptions for the developing countries sometimes called the 'S & D box'.[65]

We may see them individually though they are very much connected in their applied form. The objective meaning of each one of them becomes clear, once one has gone through all of them.

Amber Box

All subsidies which are supposed to distort production and trade fall into the amber box, i.e., all agricultural subsidies except those which fall into the blue and green boxes.[66] These include government policies of *minimum support prices* (as MSP in India) for agricultural products or any help directly related to production quantities (as power, fertilisers, pesticides, irrigation, etc).

Under the WTO provisions, these subsidies are subject to reduction commitment to their minimum level—to 5 per cent and 10 per cent for the developed and the developing countries, respectively, of their total value of agricultural outputs, per annum accordingly. It means, the subsidies *directly related* to production promotion above the allowed level (which fall in either the blue or green box) must be reduced by the countries to the prescribed levels.

In the current negotiations, various proposals deal with issues like deciding the amount by which such subsidies should be reduced further, and whether to set product-specific subsidies or to continue with the present practice of the *'aggregate'* method.

Blue Box

This is the *amber box with conditions.* The conditions are designed to reduce distortions. Any subsidy that would normally be in the amber box, is placed in the blue box if it requires farmers to

62. Because even the agriculture related provisions are modified the global market will always run after the agri-products which are the best—pricewise, qualitywise, etc.

63. A simplified and 'easy-to-understand' analysis done on the basis of the documents of the ***Information and Media Relations Division*** of the World Trade Organisation Secretariat, Geneva, Switzerland, October, 2007.

64. Defined in ***Article 1*** and ***Annexures 3 & 4,*** Agreement on Agriculture (AoA), WTO, 1994.

65. WTO, ***Article 6.2, AoA***, 1994.

66. WTO, ***Article 6, AoA***, 1994.

go for a certain production level.[67] These subsidies are nothing but certain direct payments (i.e., direct set-aside payments) made to farmers by the government in the form of assistance programmes to encourage agriculture, rural development, etc.

At present there are no limits on spending on subsidies in the blue box. In the current negotiations, some countries want to keep blue box as is because they see it as a crucial means of moving away from distorting the amber box subsidies without causing too much hardship. Others want to set limits or reduction commitments on it while some advocate moving these subsidies into the amber box.

Green Box

The agricultural subsidies which cause minimal or no distortions to trade are put under the green box.[68] They must not involve price support.

This box basically includes all forms of government expenses, which are not targeted at a particular product, and all direct income support programmes to farmers, which are not related to current levels of production or prices. This is a *very wide box* and includes all government subsidies like—public storage for food security, pest and disease control, research and extension, and some direct payments to farmers that do not stimulate production like restructuring of agriculture, environmental protection, regional development, crop and income insurance, etc.

The green box subsidies are allowed without limits provided they comply with the policy-specific criteria.[69] It means, this box is exempt from the calculation under subsidies under the WTO provisions because the subsidies under it are not meant to promote production thus do not distort trade. That is why this box is called *'production-neutral box'*. But the facts tell a different story.[70]

In the current negotiations, some countries argue that some of the subsidies forwarded under this box (by the developed economies) do seriously distort trade (opposed to the view of minimal distortion as used by Annexure 2)— it is the view of the developing countries. These countries have raised their fingers on the direct payments[71] given by the developed countries to their farmers via programmes like income insurance and income-safety schemes,[72] environmental protection, etc. Some other countries take the opposite view and argue that the current criteria are adequate, and advocate to make it more flexible (so that it could be increased) to take better care of non-trade concerns such as environmental protection and animal welfare.

S&D Box

Other than the above-discussed highly controversial boxes of agricultural subsidies, the WTO provisions have defined yet another box, i.e., the Social and Development Box (S & D Box)[73] allows the developing countries for some subsidies to the agriculture sector under certain conditions. These conditions revolve around *human development issues* such as poverty, minimum social welfare, health support, etc., specially for the segment of population living below the poverty line. Developing countries can

67. WTO, ***Article 6, Para 5*** AoA, 1994.
68. WTO, ***Annexure 2, AoA***, and ***Para 1*** AoA, 1994.
69. WTO, ***Annexure 2, AoA***, AoA, 1994.
70. Basically, a large part of this box is used by the farmers in the USA and the European Union as basic investments in agriculture. India as well as other like-minded countries have this view and want this box to be brought under the AMS i.e. under the reduction commitments. The USA at the Hongkong Ministerial meet (December 2005) announced to abolish such subsidies in the next 12 year commencing 2008. The EU also proposed to reduce its 'trade distorting subsidies' by 70 per cent. None of them used the name green box which shows some internal vagueness.
71. WTO, ***Para 5, Green Box, AoA,*** 1994.
72. WTO, ***Para 7, Green Box, AoA,*** 1994.
73. WTO, ***Para 8,*** **Green Box,** ***AoA,*** 1994.

forward such subsidies to the extent of less than 5 per cent of their total agricultural output.[74]

Export Subsidies

For export subsidy the WTO has provisions in two categories:

1. Reduction in the total budgetary support on export subsidies, and
2. Reduction in the total quantity of exports covered by the subsidy.

Higher reduction commitment for the developed countries and lower for the developing countries are the provisions. But the developed nations forward such an inflated support to their agricultural exports that even after the committed reductions it will be highly priced distorting against the agri-exports of the developing countries. It is therefore opposed by the developing countries.

Sanitary and Phytosanitary Measures

The provisions of the WTO allow member countries to set their own health and safety standards provided they are justified on scientific grounds and do not result in arbitrary or unjustified barrier to trade. The provisions encourage use of international standards and also include certain special and differential treatment in favour of developing countries.[75]

Though this provision has realised the scope of unjustified kind of health and phytosanitory measures on the developing countries, the developed nations have been beautifully able to do so by validating their health and related rules on scientific grounds. Such instances have distorted trade in favour of these countries and the developing countries' agriculture has been the real loser. The developing countries accuse such measures as the non-tarrif barriers used by the developed nations to block goods from the developing nations.

NAMA

The Non-Agricultural Products Market Access (NAMA) is a part of the WTO provisions which deals with the idea of encouraging market reach to the non-agricultural goods of the member countries.[76] But the encouragement was objected/opposed by the developing countries, especially pointing to the non-tariff barriers enforced by the developed countries. At the Doha Ministerial Conference (November 2001), ministers agreed to start negotiations to further liberalise trade of non-agricultural products. By early 2002, a Negotiating Group on NAMA was created. The members at the meet decided to go for tariff reductions on non-agricultural products adopting the **Swiss Formula**.

One major concern that the members took note was of the small and vulnerable economies for whom a flexibility was committed while going for tariff reductions. For India, market access is not an issue of tariffs alone, but it means elimination of tariff peaks and tariff escalation in the markets of the developed countries. It will also end the abuse of anti-dumping laws and remove non-tariff barriers (NTBs) used to block goods from developing countries.

Swiss Formula

A variety of alternative methods are possible in the process of tariff reductions—some are more common than others. Some are based on *formulas*. But one thing should be kept in mind that whatever formula be agreed upon it does not have value unless it is properly implemented. Even after a formula or combination of formulas has been agreed upon, the final outcome of tariff

74. WTO, ***Article 6.2, AoA***, 1994.

75. WTO, ***Article 14, AoA***, 1994.

76. As per the provisions of the WTO ***fishes, fisheries products*** and ***forest products*** don't fall under agriculture and have been classified as the non-agricultural products.

reductions may depend on the bargaining capacity between countries.

The **Swiss Formula**[77] belongs to the classification of formulas known as having harmonising impact. Since such a formula prescribes a higher/steeper cut on higher tariffs and lower cuts on lower tariffs it is seen to harmonise the rates by bringing the final rates becoming closer and bridging the gap.

The formula was proposed by Switzerland in the Tokyo round negotiations of GATT (1973-79). But Switzerland opposes using this method in the current agriculture negotiations—it prefers the **Uruguay Round formula.**

The Uruguay Round (1986-94) negotiations in agriculture produced an agreement for developed countries to cut tariffs on agricultural products by an average of 36 per cent over six years (6 per cent per year) with a minimum tariff cut of 15 per cent on each product for the period. It was a version of *flat rate* method of tariff reductions.

NATIONAL FOOD SECU RITY ACT

The National Food Security Act was enacted by the Ministry of Consumer Affairs, Food and Public Distribution by end-December 2013. India's most ambitious and world's largest social welfare programme provides legal right to about 82 crore people for subsidised foodgrains—a historic initiative towards ensuring food and nutritional security. Major highlights of the programme are as given below:

- It will cover upto 75 per cent rural and 50 per cent urban population (around two thirds of the total population) with uniform entitlement of 5 kg foodgrains per month at highly subsidised prices of ₹3, ₹2 and ₹1 per kg for rice, wheat and coarse grains, respectively. The *poorest of poor* households continue to receive 35 kg foodgrains per household per month under the *Antyodaya Anna Yojna* at the same subsidised prices.
- It provisions for special focus on nutritional support to women and children—*pregnant* women and *lactating* mothers, besides being entitled to nutritious meals as per the prescribed nutritional norms will also receive maternity benefit of at least of ₹6,000. *Children* in the age group of 6 months to 14 years will be entitled to take home ration or hot cooked food as per prescribed nutritional norms.
- Eldest woman of eighteen years of age or above will be head of the household for issue of ration card, and if not available, the eldest male member is to be the head of the household.
- For effective implementation, the Act also contains provisions for **reforms** in PDS through *doorstep delivery* of foodgrains, application of information and communication technology (ICT) including end-to-end computerisation, leveraging *'Aadhaar'* for identification of beneficiaries, diversification of commodities under TPDS, etc.
- The Act provisions state and district level **redressal mechanism** with designated officers. The states will be allowed to use the existing machinery for District Grievance Redressal Officer (DGRO), State Food Commission, if they so desire, to save expenditure on establishment of new redressal set up. It also provides for **penalty** on public servants or authority, if found guilty of failing to comply with the relief recommended by the DGRO.
- Provisions have also been made for disclosure of records relating to PDS, **social audits** and setting up of Vigilance Committees in order to ensure transparency and accountability.

By now, the NFSA is being implemented (under the existing TPDS) in all States/UTs

77. WTO, ***"Formula Approaches to Tariff Negotiations"*** (Revised), Oct. 2007.

covering about 80 crore persons. In Chandigarh, Puducherry and urban areas of Dadra & Nagar Haveli, it is being implemented in *cash transfer mode*, under which food subsidy is being transferred into the bank accounts of the beneficiaries who then have a choice to buy foodgrains from open market.

Identification of beneficiaries under it is under two categories—households covered under Antyodaya Anna Yojana (AAY) and Priority Households (within the coverage determined for the State/UT). While the Priority Households are entitled to receive 5 kg foodgrain per person per month, the AAY households (which constitute the poorest of the poor), continue to receive 35 kg of foodgrains per household per month. To ensure adequate availability of wheat and rice and to keep a check on the open market prices, the Government has taken several steps[78] in recent times:

- State Governments, particularly those undertaking Decentralized Procurement (DCP), are being encouraged to maximise procurement of wheat and rice.
- Strategic reserves of 5 million tonnes of foodgrains over the operational stocks are maintained to be used in extreme situations.
- Sale of wheat and rice is undertaken through Open Market Sale Scheme (OMSS) (Domestic) so as to check inflationary trend in prices of foodgrains.
- Commencing PDS reforms such as *One Nation - One Ration Card*, Aadhaar authenticated distribution through *e-POS* machines.

In the wake of the rising food subsidy burden, there is a case for revision in the prices of wheat and rice charged to the beneficiaries which has not been revised since the Act commenced in July, 2013. Meanwhile, the MSPs for the crops and the economic cost of procurement have gone up regularly.

COVID-19 Impact The ongoing disruptions caused by the coronavirus pandemic forced upon the country a mass return-migration of labourers from urban areas. Arranging food supplies for these labourers became a challenging task for the economy. Aimed at supplying enough food to these labourers, the Government announced a slew of measures:

- **Short-term measure:** Migrants who were neither NFSA nor State Card beneficiaries in the state they are stationed, were provided *free supply* of 5 kg of foodgrains per person and 1 kg chana per family per month for two months. It was expected to benefit about 8 crore migrants. While the cost of this support was fully borne by the Centre (₹3,500 crore) states were carrying the responsibilities of implementation, identification and distribution.
- **Long-term measure:** Under the PM's Technology Driven Systems Reforms all migrants to be enabled to access Public Distribution System (Ration) from any FPS (Fair Price Shop) in India by March 2021 – *One Nation One Ration Card* – intra-state portability introduced in 20 states. All States/UTs are to complete full FPS automation by March 2021.

FOOD PROCESSING

Indian food processing industry (FPI)[79] has not grown with the pace which we see in the developed countries—there has been certain reasons for it:

- India has a lower urban population (around 30 per cent of the population).

78. **Economic Survey 2019-20**, Vol. 2, pp. 209-210, Ministry of Finance, GoI, N. Delhi.

79. The analyses are based on several volumes of ***Economic Survey, India*** and the relevant documents of the Government of India between the period 2005 and 2015.

- Whatever urban population India has it does not have the *typical* urban food habits. As majority of it is second or third generation in the urban areas they still continue with the non-urban/rural food habits detrimental to the consumption of the agro-processed items.

3. In recent times, there has come enough awareness among the population across the country regarding the chemicals which are used in the agro-processing industries—creating a general tendency to avoid such food articles (much damage has been done to the industry by the 'fast foods', adulteration in food items such as sweets, milk, etc.).
4. A wave across the world towards consuming more 'which comes on plants' than 'what is produced in plants'. A similar wave of 'slow food' has gained popularity across Europe and other parts of the world originating from France.

Moreover, India's agro-processing policy today guided by the following **drivers:**

- As urban population rises and urban food habits evolve, there will be increased demand for processed foods as it happened across the urbanising developed world. The economy has already started having an informed and increased demand in such food items as 'dietary habits' are in the process of shift (NSSO, 2014).
- External dimension to it was also accepted by the government by mid-1990s. As per a joint GATT-OECD study, processed food are supposed to account for around 19 per cent of the increased trade after the provisions of the WTO are implemented.
- A very high percentage of food items which have short shelf life get wasted in India. It does not look good for a country which is crippled by the short-supply of food and high rate of hunger.

Importance

While increased productivity is an essential component of a vibrant agricultural sector, improved post-harvest handling and processing is essential to ensure value addition, reduction in wastage and to make good quality products reach the markets. Too often, even when the yields are high, producers lose income due to poor post-harvest practices.

Aim: Food processing aims to make food more *digestible, nutritious* and *extend the shelf life*. Due to the seasonal variations high levels of wastage or shortages can arise if adequate measures are not taken to preserve and store the food. Food processing covers all the processes that food items go through from the *farm to the consumers' plate*. It includes basic cleaning, grading and packaging as in case of fruits and vegetables and also alteration of the raw material to a stage just before the final preparation. Value addition processes to make 'ready-to eat' food like bakery products, instant foods, flavored and health drinks, etc., are also included in this *definition.*

Food processing *offers* an opportunity for the creation of sustainable livelihoods and economic development for the rural communities. Food processing has come a long way in the last few decades. The everchanging lifestyles, food habits and tastes of customers globally have altered the dynamics of the industry. Food processing benefits all the sections of the society:

- *Farmers* get better returns, higher yield, and lower the risks drastically;

- *Consumers* get access to a greater variety, better prices and new products;
- *Economy* gets benefit via creation of new business opportunities, while the workforce gets employment.

With a huge production base, India can easily become one of the leading food suppliers to the world while at the same time serving the vast growing domestic market of over a billion people. India's large market size with growing incomes and changing life styles also creates incredible market opportunities for food producers, food processors, machinery makers, food technologists and service providers in this sector.

Growth in the food processing sector is also expected to open up a lot of opportunities for players having strong linkages in the agri-value chain. Significant investment opportunities are yet to be tapped in the areas of *supply chain management, cold storages, financing, retailing* and *exports*.

Historically, agriculture and FPI have been plagued by factors such as:

- Low public investment,
- Poor infrastructure,
- Inadequate credit availability, and
- High levels of fragmentation.

Rules and Regulations

Rules and regulations regarding the industry is as given below:

- Most food processing enterprises have been exempted from industrial licensing under the Industries (Development and Regulation) Act, 1951 with the exception of beer and alcoholic drinks, and items reserved for the small scale sector.
- For foreign investment, automatic approval is given even up to 100 per cent equity for a majority of processed foods.
- For manufacture of items reserved for MSEs, FDI is permissible under automatic route up to 24 per cent.

Economic Importance

Given the tremendous attention by the Government in recent years, the industry has started showing its expansion. The economic importance[80] of the sector can be gauged by the following statistics:

- During the last 5 years ending 2018-19, the sector had an average annual growth rate of around 9.99 per cent. It constituted 8.98 per cent and 11.3 per cent of GVA in Manufacturing and Agriculture sector respectively in 2018-19 (at 2011-12 prices).
- According to the latest Annual Survey of Industries for 2016-17, the total number of persons engaged in registered food processing sector was 18.54 lakhs.
- Unregistered food processing sector supports employment to 51.11 lakh workers as per the NSSO 73rd Round, 2015-16 and constitutes 14.18 per cent of employment in the unregistered manufacturing sector.
- The value of processed food exports during 2018-19 was of the order of US $35.30 billion accounting for about 10.70 per cent of India's total exports (total exports US $330.08 billion). The value of import of processed food during 2018-19 was US $19.32 billion which is 3.76 per cent of India's total imports.

MAJOR POLICY INITIATIVES

PMKSY The Pradhan Mantri Kisan *SAMPADA* Yojana (PMKSY) was launched as a central sector scheme by the Government in 2016-17 which provides subsidy-based support to create robust modern infrastructure for agriculture and agro-

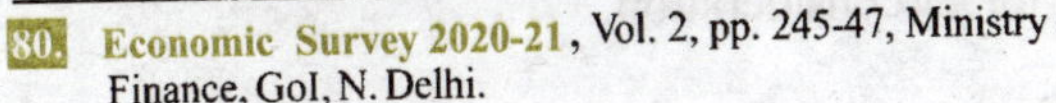

80. **Economic Survey 2020-21**, Vol. 2, pp. 245-47, Ministry of Finance, GoI, N. Delhi.

based industries along the entire value-chain. This umbrella scheme consists the following components:

- Mega Food Parks
- Integrated Cold Chain and Value Addition Infrastructure
- Infrastructure for Agro-processing Clusters
- Creation of Backward and Forward Linkages
- Creation/Expansion of Food Processing & Preservation Capacities
- Operation Greens

Mega Food Parks Scheme (MFPS) The Mega Food Parks Scheme *aims* to accelerate the growth of the food processing industry in the country by facilitating establishment of strong food processing infrastructure backed by an efficient supply chain. Under this scheme, capital grant of 50 per cent of the project cost is provided in general areas and 75 per cent in difficult and ITDP (Integrated Tribal Development Programme) notified areas (with a ceiling of ₹50 crore). Each Mega Food Park takes about 30-36 months to be completed.

Cold Chain, Value Addition and Preservation The Scheme for Cold Chain, Value Addition, and Preservation Infrastructure was approved in 2008 with an *objective* to provide integrated and complete cold chain, value addition and preservation infrastructure facilities without any break, for perishables from the farm gate to the consumer. The assistance under the scheme includes financial assistance (grant-in-aid) of 50 per cent of the total cost of plant and machinery and technical civil works in general areas and 75 per cent for the North Eastern region and difficult areas (subject to a maximum of ₹10 crore).

Modernisation of Abattoirs The Ministry has approved 10 projects in first phase which are at various stages of progress. Two projects have been completed. A proposal for up-scaling the scheme is under consideration.

Technology Upgradation Under the Scheme for Technology Upgradation, Establishment, Modernisation of FPIs, financial assistance is provided in the form of 'grants-in-aid' for the setting up of new food processing units as well as technological upgradation and expansion of existing units in the country. The GoI extends financial assistance in the form of grant-in-aid to entrepreneurs at 25 per cent of the cost of Plant & Machinery and Technical Civil Works subject to a maximum of ₹50 lakhs in general areas or 33.33 per cent subject to a maximum of ₹75 lakhs in difficult terrains. The Scheme has now been transferred to the states with the launching of the National Mission on Food Processing (NMFP) in the 12th Plan.

Quality Assurance, Codex Standards, R & D and Promotional Activities In the global market today, quality and food safety gives a competitive edge which is an important factor for the enterprises producing processed foods and providing services. Apart from domestic standards for food products, processes and management practices, Codex prescribes international standards for safety and quality of food as well as codes of good manufacturing practices, which are accepted worldwide. Further, equal emphasis is required to be accorded to R&D activities for the development of innovative products, cost effective processes and efficient technologies for the food processing sector. The scheme for Food Safety Codex and R&D has been successful in making a dent in this area in the country.

PM-FME The Prime Minister-Formalisation of Micro Food Processing Enterprises (PM-FME) was launched by late 2020-21 (under the Atma Nirbhar Bharat Abhiyan) as a Centrally Sponsored Scheme for the period 2020-25. *One District One Product* (ODOP) approach is to be adopted under it to reap 'benefit of scale' in terms of procurement of inputs, availing common services and marketing of products. States identify 'one food product per district' keeping in view the existing clusters and availability of raw material under it. The scheme also places focus on *waste to wealth* products, minor forest products and *Aspirational Districts* (112 most backward districts of the country have been identified by the Niti Aayog as Aspirational Districts). The existing micro food processing units to get the following supports under it:

- Credit-linked capital subsidy (35 per cent of project cost with a maximum of ₹ 10 lakh) to be given to the units led by individual, FPOs (Farmers Producer Organisations), producer cooperatives and SHGs (Self Help Groups).
- Credit-linked grant (35 per cent of the project cost) for development of common infrastructure including common processing facility, lab, warehouse, cold storage, packaging and incubation centre through FPOs/SHGs/cooperatives or state-owned agencies or private enterprise for use by micro units in the cluster.
- SHGs (Self Help Groups) to get seed capital (₹ 40,000) for working capital and purchase of small tools.
- 50 per cent grant for branding and marketing.

The scheme has picked popularity very fast and by *April 2021* a total of 35 States/UT had identified hundreds of food products under it.

Operation Greens A central sector scheme, the *Operation Greens* was launched in 2018-19 for integrated development of Tomato, Onion and Potato (TOP) value chain with *five* main objectives—enhancing value realisation for TOP farmers and linking them to market; price stabilisation by targeted interventions; reducing post-harvest losses by creation of farm gate infrastructure, agro-logistics and storage; increasing food processing capacities; and setting up market intelligence network to collect real time data of demand and supply.

Under *Atmanirbhar Bharat Abhiyan,* the scheme has been extended from TOP crops to the other notified horticulture crops for a period of six months together with transport subsidy for any fruit and vegetable through Indian Railways.

Production-Linked Incentive (PLI) Scheme A Production-Linked Incentive (PLI) Scheme was introduced by the Government in *November 2020* in 10 key sectors, including food processing sector, for enhancing India's manufacturing capabilities and improving exports. The food segments identified include ready to eat/ready to cook—marine products, processed fruits & vegetables, mozzarella cheese, and innovative/organic products of SMEs. The scheme also supports branding and marketing abroad.

Institutional Support

A range of institutional support has been put in place by the Government to help the industry grow and get global class— a brief description is given below:

- **Indian Institute of Crop Processing Technology (IICPT):** Indian Institute of Crop Processing Technology (IICPT) formerly known as Paddy Processing Research Centre (PPRC), Thanjavur is an autonomous organisation under the administrative control of MoFPI. It has been in existence for the last three decades. As other commodities such as millets, pulses and oil seeds are gaining importance, it was decided in 2001 to expand the mandate of this Institute to include the above commodities also. The institute is being upgraded into a national level institute now.
- **National Meat and Poultry Processing Board (NM P PB):** The GoI established the National Meat and Poultry Processing Board 2009. The Board is an autonomous body and was initially funded by the GoI for 2 years and is to be managed by the industry

self. This industry-driven institution has been launched to work as a *National Hub* for addressing all key issues related to the meat and poultry processing sector for its systematic and proper development. The Board serves as a *single window* service provider for producers, manufacturers and exporters of meat and meat products, for promoting the meat industry as a whole.

- **Indian Grape Processing Board:** The GoI, in 2009, gave its approval for the establishment of the Indian Grape Processing Board (IGPB) at Pune, Maharashtra which is close to the principal grape growing and processing areas in the country. The functions and objectives of the IGPB are:
  - To focus on R&D, extension, quality upgradation, market research, information, domestic and international promotion of *Indian wine*.
  - To foster sustainable development of Indian wine industry.
  - To formulate a vision and action plan for the growth of Indian wine sector including R&D for quality upgradation in new technologies.

  During three years of its existence, the Board has focused on the promotion of *Wines of India* in the domestic as well as international market by participating in important and relevant exhibitions, fairs, consumer awareness and training programmes, undertaking advocacy work with the various state governments/central ministries on various issues related to taxes/levies and promotion aspects. The Board is going to implement a traceability programme 'wine-net' for standards and quality in wine sector.

- **National Institute of Food Technology, Entrepreneurship & Management (NIFTEM):** For developing a vibrant food processing sector, India needs not only world-class food technologists to undertake R&D in frontier areas, develop new products, processes, technologies and machineries, set food standards and protocol testing, but also business leaders and managers well versed with the requisite mix of technologies, management and entrepreneurship who can exploit major opportunities in the expanding global food trade.

  In the emerging global scenario, there is a need for setting up of an institution of global excellence, which could cater to the needs of the booming food processing sector, various stakeholders such as entrepreneurs, industry, exporters, policymakers, government and other research institutions. NIFTEM was conceived by MoFPI to create an international *Center of Excellence* in the field of Food Sciences & Food Technology. NIFTEM will grow into an apex world class institute to promote cooperation and networking among existing institutions both within the country and various international bodies. The institute will offer high quality educational, research and management programme specific to the food industry, provide referral advice on food standards, disseminate knowledge on the food sector and provide business incubation facility. It is situated (2006) at Kundli, Sonipat (Haryana).

DOU BLING FARM INCOME

Remunerative farming is not a precondition for enriching farm community only but it is considered the biggest incentive to enhance the agricultural output, too. This is why enhancing farm income has emerged among the most immediate policy concerns for the government in recent times. Recently, a shift has been seen in the Government's strategy towards the agriculture sector—from increasing farm output to increasing farm income.

Aimed at *doubling the farmers' income by 2022*, the Government of India has announced a 'seven-point strategy'. The details of the strategy are as given below:

- Focus on irrigation with bigger budgets aimed at 'per drop, more crop'.
- Provision of quality seeds and nutrients based on soil health.
- Strengthening warehousing and cold chains to prevent post-harvest crop losses.
- Promoting value addition through food processing.
- Creation of a national farm market, removing distortions and e-platform.
- Mitigating risks at affordable cost through suitable kind of farm insurance.
- Promoting ancillary activities like poultry, beekeeping and fisheries.

Agri-experts together with the foremost Indian agriculture scientist M.S. Swaminathan have appreciated this initiative of the Government. The challenge of doubling farmers' income within the prescribed time frame is very much possible supported by a good strategy, well-designed programmes, adequate resources and good governance.

CASH SUPPORT TO FARMERS

In the wake of rising farm distress, the Government of India, announced a Central Sector Scheme (these schemes are fully financed by the Central Government)—the *Pradhan Mantri Kisan Samman Nidhi (PM-KISAN)*—in 2019-20 (to be implemented from 2018 Kharif season). The scheme provides assured income support of ₹6,000 per year (in 3 equal instalments of ₹2,000 each) to the beneficiaries covering all farmers who own land upto 2 hectares. Initially launched for only the small and marginal farm families across the country holding cultivable land upto 2 hectares, its ambit was later expanded (w.e.f. June, 2019) to cover all farmer families irrespective of the size of their land holdings. The scheme is expected to benefit over 15 crore farmers, as per the Government.

The Scheme excludes affluent farmers such as Income Tax payers in last assessment year, professionals like Doctors, Engineers, Lawyers, Chartered Accountants, etc. and pensioners drawing at least ₹10,000 per month). Special provisions have been made for the North-Eastern States where land ownership rights are community based, Forest Dwellers and Jharkhand, which does not have updated land records and restrictions on transfer of land.

Taking clues form the Central Government, some states have also launched income or investment support schemes[81] in recent times which are of two kinds—inclusive or exclusive of the PM-KISAN—as given below:

- **Rythu Bandhu:** Launched from Kharif 2018, this Government of Telangana scheme provides investment support of ₹4,000 per acre per season (for 2 seasons) to all farmers (55 lakh) towards purchase of inputs like seeds, fertilisers, etc. as initial investment before the crop season. It is estimated to support 55 lakh farmers *(rythus)* in the state. This scheme is independent of the PM-KISAN.
- **KALIA:** The Krushak Assistance for Livelihood and Income Augmentation (KALIA) Scheme was launched in 2018-19 Rabi season onwards by the Odisha government—aimed to accelerate agricultural prosperity and elimination of poverty. The scheme is independent of the PM-KISAN and has following components of it:

81. **Economic Survey 20 19-20**, Vol. 2, pp. 195-196, Ministry of Finance, GoI, N. Delhi.

- Small and marginal farmers get a financial support of ₹25,000 per farm family over five seasons to purchase inputs like seeds, fertilisers, pesticides, labour and other investments.
- Landless agricultural households get a financial assistance of ₹12,500 for agricultural allied activities such as small goat rearing unit, mini-layer unit, duckery units, fishery kits for fisherman, mushroom cultivation and bee-keeping, etc.
- Vulnerable cultivators/landless agricultural labourers get a financial assistance of ₹10,000 per family per year for their sustenance.
- The scheme also has life and accident insurance covers for the farmers at very nominal premiums.

▶ **Krishak Bandhu :** The scheme of the West Bengal state launched from Rabi season of 2018-19 gives ₹10,000 per year as income support for two crops to all 75 lakh farmers (including landless farmers also). This scheme is independent of the GoI scheme PM-KISAN.

▶ **MMKAY:** The Mukhya Mantri Krishi Ashirwad Yojana (MMKAY) of the Jharkhand state gives a grant-in-aid of ₹5,000 per acre per year to the farmers who have arable land upto 5 acres, to reduce their dependence on loans. The cash support is given in two instalments through Direct Benefit Transfer. The scheme is estimated to benefit over 22 lakh farmers in the state. The state implements PM-KISAN also.

▶ **Rythu Bharosa:** Launched by the Andhra Pradesh state government in 2019-20 Kharif season, the scheme provides ₹13,500 income support to all farmers owning upto 5 acres of land—₹6,000 of the PM-KISAN plus ₹7,500 as the state component (as the state implements PM-KISAN also). It is estimated to benefit over 67 lakh farmers in the state.

▶ **Shift from Loan Waiver to Cash Support:** The instance of states opting for farm income/investment support schemes[82] over farm loan waiver programmes has been *appreciated* by the Reserve Bank of India. Since 2014-15, a total of 10 states have announced farm loan waiver programmes of ₹2,31,260 lakh crores. In comparison, the total expenditures of states on income/investment support schemes are estimated to be ₹32,861 crores for 2019-20 (up from ₹16,250 crores of 2018-19). To ensure timely payments to farmers and minimising inclusion and exclusion errors, the RBI has suggested the states to take two important steps in this regard:

- Digitisation of land records, and
- Linking with Aadhar-seeded bank accounts.

WOMEN FARMERS

In agriculture sector, women play a significant and crucial role. Right from the main crop production to livestock, horticulture, post-harvest operations, agro and social forestry, fisheries and marketing, they are involved at every possible level of farm activity (this was rightly recognised by the National Commission on Women, 2001). For sustainable development of the agriculture and rural economy, the contribution of women to agriculture and food production cannot be ignored.

Globally, there is empirical evidence that women have a decisive role in ensuring 'food security' and 'preserving local agro-biodiversity'. Rural women are responsible for the integrated management and use of diverse natural resources

82. **State Finances: A Study of Budgets**, Reserve Bank of India, October 2019, N. Delhi.

to meet the daily household needs *(Food and Agriculture Organisation, 2011)*.

But in this sector also India has high *gender disparity*. As per the Census 2011, out of total female main workers, 55 per cent were agricultural labourers and 24 per cent were cultivators. However, only 12.8 per cent of the operational holdings were owned by women. Moreover, there is concentration of operational holdings (25.7 per cent) by women in the marginal and small holdings categories. With growing rural to urban migration by men, there is **feminisation** of agriculture sector in the country, with increasing number of women in multiple roles—as cultivators, entrepreneurs, and labourers.

This requires that women farmers should have enhanced access to resources like land, water, credit, technology and training which needs critical analysis in the context of India. In addition, the entitlements of women farmers will be the key to improve agriculture productivity. Towards this, Government has been implementing *various schemes* which help improve the entitlements of women farmers, which will prove to be advantageous in bridging the policy gaps which exist in the sector. The following measures[83] have been taken to ensure mainstreaming of women in agriculture sector:

- Earmarking at least 30 per cent of the budget allocation for women beneficiaries in all ongoing schemes and programmes.
- Initiating women centric activities.
- Focus on women self-help group (SHG) by delivering micro-credit and right information together with involving them in the decision-making bodies.
- Recognising the critical role of women in agriculture, the Ministry of Agriculture and Farmers Welfare has declared 15th October of every year as Women Farmer's Day.

Indian farm sector needs a gender specific policy framework to adjust with the existing and emerging realities in the sector. Such a nuanced policy intervention will not only enhance food security but promote gender equality, extension services, sustainability and all-round development in the rural areas.

CLIMATE SMART AGRICULTURE

Climate change can impact the farm sector in different ways—increased variability in temperature, rainfall, extreme weather events like drought and flood. These incidences ultimately hit the farm community in a very negative way. To fight out these uncertainties, development of a climate resilient agro-system is the need of the hour.

It is in this backdrop that the new concept of Climate Smart Agriculture (CSA) has emerged.[84] It is an approach that helps to guide actions needed 'to transform and reorient agricultural systems to effectively support development and ensure food security under changing climate'. It aims to provide stakeholders the means to identify agricultural strategies suitable to their local conditions. The CSA aims to tackle *three* main objectives:

1. Sustainably increasing agricultural productivity and incomes;
2. Adapting and building resilience to climate change; and
3. Reducing and/or removing greenhouse gas emissions wherever possible.

Though, this new concept is at a nascent stage in India, the Government has already started taking policy initiatives in this direction.

82. ***Economic Survey 2017–18***, Vol. 2, pp. 103-104, Ministry of Finance, Government of India, N. Delhi.

84. ***Economic Survey 2017–18***, Vol. 2, pp. 113-114, Ministry of Finance, GoI, N. Delhi.

At present, *climate resilient technologies* are being demonstrated in 446 model villages under KVK (Kisan Vikas Kendra) covering 23 states under National Innovations on Climate Resilient Agriculture (NICRA). In addition, 651 contingency plans have been prepared to manage various weather aberrations such as droughts, floods, cyclones, hailstorms, heat and cold waves.

WAY FORWARD

The *Economic Survey 2020-21*, in agreement with the previous volumes of it, says that the objective of inclusive development in India cannot be realised without the development of rural sector which crucially depends on agriculture—it is an *engine of broad-based growth* (says the *Economic Survey 2017-18*). Progress of the sector has a bearing on the fate of the largest low-income group in India. There is a need for a *paradigm* in how we view agriculture from a rural livelihood sector to a modern business enterprise—in this context, both production and post production needs urgent reforms to enable sustainable and consistent growth. Following suggestions[85] have been given by the document in this regard:

- *Production and productivity* related—expansion of irrigation, adoption of hybrid and improved seeds, increasing variety replacement ratio and augmentation in seed testing facilities.
- *Post-production* related—arrangement of adequate storage and remunerative markets, integration with nutritional outcomes (by means of food fortification), village level procurement centres, linkages between production and processing, development of rural markets, option of selling outside the APMC markets, warehouse upgradations, better freight operations by railways, dedicated freight corridors (most of them are being taken up by the Government).
- *Input optimisation*—by all business enterprises (of knowledge and materials both).
- *From producer to entrepreneur* — imparting farmers basic education and training to transform farmers from a producer to an entrepreneur (rural agricultural schools for hands-on training may be explored in this regard).
- Allied sectors— looking at animal husbandry, dairying and fisheries becoming significant source of farm income and employment, measures need to be taken to increase their productivity enhancing their market access.
- *Extension services*—need strengthening to provide farmers about improved agricultural practices, guidance of their uses and other services.
- *Food subsidy*—While it is difficult to reduce the economic cost of food management in view of rising commitment towards food security, there is a need to consider the revision of CIP (Central Issue Price is the price at which foodgrains are sold by FCI to the beneficiaries) to reduce the 'bulging food subsidy' bill (which is becoming unmanageably large).

85. Economic Survey 2020-21, vol. 2, p. 257-58, Ministry of Finance, GoI, N. Delhi.

CHAPTER 9

INDUSTRY AND INFRASTRUCTURE

Rapid growth of unskilled-labour-intensive sectors is likely to create many more opportunities for the poor than rapid growth of capital- and skilled-labour-intensive sectors. Such a shift would reinforce rather than impede aggregate growth.*

In this Chapter...

- Introduction
- New Industrial Policy, 1991
- Disinvestment
- Performance of CPSEs
- MSME Sector
- Sectoral Concerns
- Textile And Apparels
- FDI Policy Measures
- Ease of Doing Business
- Make in India
- Start-up India
- COVID-19 and Industrial Reforms
- Indian Infrastructure
- Power
- UDAY Scheme
- Railways
- Roads
- Civil Aviation
- Telecom
- Minerals
- Maritime Agenda 2010–20
- Smart Cities
- Private Sector and Urbanisation
- PPP Models
- Petroleum & Natural Gas
- Renewable Energy
- National Hydrogen Mission
- Logistics Sector
- Housing & Urban Infrastructure
- Housing Policy
- COVID-19 and Rental Housing
- National Infrastructure Pipeline
- Recent Challenges
- Way Forward

* *See Arvind Panagariya,* **India: The Emerging Giant,** *pp. 282 and 475, Oxford University Press, N. Delhi, 2013.*

INTRODUCTION

Many of the western economies have already written their success stories of industrialisation leading to accelerated growth and development by the time India became an independent economy. Independent India needed to rejuvenate its economy from a completely dilapidated state. The country had many tasks in front of it—the abject mass poverty, shortage of foodgrains, healthcare, etc., calling for immediate attention. The other areas of attention included industry, infrastructure, science and technology and higher education, to name a few. All these areas of development required heavy capital investment as they had been severely avoided by the colonial ruler for the last 150 years or so. Increasing the growth of the economy and that too with a faster pace was the urgent need of the economy. Looking at the pros and cons of the available options, India decided that the industrial sector should be the 'prime moving force' (PMF) of the economy—the logical choice for faster growth (a fully established idea at that time, the world over). The secondary sector will lead the economy, was well-decided in the 1930s itself by the dominant political forces among the freedom fighters.

As the government of the time had decided upon an active role for the governments in the economy, naturally, the industrial sector was to have a dominant state role—the expansion of the government-owned companies (i.e., the PSUs) to glorious heights. In many ways the development of the Indian economy has been the development of the government sector. Once this idea of state's role in the economy went for a radical change in the early 1990s with the process of economic reforms, the hangover or the drag of it is still visible on the economy. The industrial policies which the governments announced from time to time basically moulded the very nature and structure of the economy. Any discussion on the Indian economy must start with a survey of the industrial policies of the country. Here we have a brief review of the various industrial policies of India till date.

INDUSTRY IN 2020-21

The COVID- 19 pandemic, a 'once in a century' crisis, brought unprecedented economic disruption and made industrial growth rate to fall to the nadir of a negative 57.3 per cent in April 2020—however, recovering back to a negative of 1.9 per cent by November 2020 once the unlocking process began. As per the latest estimates on Gross Value Added (GVA), the sector is expected to record a growth of ***negative* 9.6** per cent with an overall contribution in GVA of 25.8 per cent in 2020-21 (the contribution of the sector has been constantly declining since 2011-12).

By early 2021 , a V-shaped recovery was witnessed stemming from remedial measures, reforms, and the stimulus package announced by the Government under the *Atmanirbhar Bharat* package. Further improvement and fuming up in industrial activities are foreseen with the Government enhancing capital expenditure, the vaccination drive and the resolute push forward on long pending reform measures—the reforms undertaken are probably one of the most comprehensive among the maj or economies of the world.

Source: *Economic Survey 2020-21, vol. 1, pp. 261, Ministry of Finance, GoI, N. Delhi.*

Review of Industrial Policies Upto 1986

For a better understanding of the Indian economy, it is advisable to look into the various industrial polices. The official stances keep changing with every upcoming industrial policy. Understanding these policies becomes even more important to understand the finer aspects of the reform process which the country will commence by the early 1990s. Here, a brief review of India's industrial policies are being discussed to serve the purpose.

Industrial Policy Resolution, 1948

Announced on 8 April, 1948 this was not only the first industrial policy statement of India, but also decided the model of the economic system (i.e., the mixed economy), too. Thus, it was the *first* economic policy of the country. The major highlights of the policy are given below:

1. India will be a mixed economy.[1]
2. Some of the important industries were put under the *Central List* such as coal, power, railways, civil aviation, arms and ammunition, defence, etc.
3. Some other industries (usually of medium category) were put under a *State List* such as paper, medicines, textiles, cycles, rickshaws, two-wheelers, etc.
4. Rest of the industries (not covered by either the central or the state lists) were left open for private sector investment—with many of them having the provision of compulsory licencing.
5. There was a 10-year period for review of the policy.

Industrial Policy Resolution, 1956

The government was encouraged by the impact of the industrial policy of 1948 and it was only after eight years that the new and more crystallised policies were announced for the Indian industries. The new industrial policy of 1956 had the following major provisions:

1. **Reservation of Industries:** A clear-cut classification of industries (also known as the **Reservation of Industries**) were affected with three schedules:
   (i) ***Schedule A:*** This schedule had 17 industrial areas in which the Centre was given complete monopoly. The industries set up under this provision were known as the Central Public Sector Undertakings (CPSUs) later getting popularity as 'PSUs'. Though the number of industries were only 17, the number of PSUs set up by the Government of India went to 254 by 1991. These included those industrial units too which were taken over by the government between 1960 to 1980 under the *nationalisation* drives.[2] These industries belonged to Schedules B and C (other than Schedule A).
   (ii) ***Schedule B:*** There were 12 industrial areas put under this schedule in which the state governments were supposed to take up the initiatives with a more expansive follow up by the private sector. This schedule also carried the provisions of compulsory licencing. It should be noted here that neither the states nor the private sector had monopolies in these industries unlike Schedule A, which provided monopoly to the Centre.[3]
   (iii) ***Schedule C:*** All industrial areas left out of Schedules A and B were put under this in which the private enterprises had the provisions to set up industries. Many of them had the provisions of licencing and have *necessarily* to fit into the framework of the social and economic policy of the state and were subject to control and regulation in terms of the Industries Development and

1. Here this should be noted that India will be a planned economy, was well-decided before this industrial policy which articulated for an ***active role*** of the state in the economy. The main objective of planning pointed out at this time was ***poverty alleviation*** by a judicious exploitation of the resources of the country. Only a 'mixed economy' did fit such a wish (***Conference of State Industry Ministers, 1938***).

2. The nationalisation of industrial units allowed the government to enter the unreserved areas, which consequently increased its industrial presence. Though the nationalisation was provided a highly rational official reason of ***greater public benefit,*** the private sector always doubted it and took it as an insecurity and major unseen future hurdle in the expansion of private industries in the country.

3. The Central government had always the option to set up an industry in any of these 12 industrial areas. This happened in the coming years via two methods—first, through *nationalisation* and second, through the *joint sector*.

Regulation (IDR) Act and other relevant legislations.[4]

The above classification of industries had an in-built bias in favour of government-owned companies (i.e., the CPSUs) which went according to the ideas of the planning process, too. Thus, expansion of the public sector became almost a directive principle of economic policy and the PSUs did expand in the coming times.[5]

It was this industrial policy in which the then PM Pandit Jawaharlal Nehru had termed the PSUs the *'temples of modern India'*, symbolically pointing to their importance.[6] There was a time soon after Independence when the PSUs were regarded as the principal instrument for raising savings and growth in the economy.[7] The rapid expansion of PSUs accounted for more than half of the GDP of the economy by 1988–89.[8]

2. **Provision of Licencing:** One of the most important developments of independent India, the provision of compulsory licencing for industries, was cemented in this policy. All the schedule B industries and a number of schedule C industries came under this provision. This provision established the so-called *'Licence-Quota-Permit'* regime (*raj*) in the economy.[9]
3. **Expansion of the Public Sector:** Expansion of the public sector was pledged for the accelerated industrialisation and growth in the economy—glorification of government companies did start with this policy. The emphasis was on heavy industries.
4. **Regional Disparity:** To tackle the widening **regional disparity**, the policy committed to set up the upcoming PSUs in the comparatively backward and underdeveloped regions/areas in the economy.[10]
5. **Emphasis on Small Industries:** There was emphasis on small industries as well as the khadi and village industries.
6. **Agricultural Sector:** The agricultural sector was pledged as a priority.

Importance

This is considered as the most important industrial policy of India by the experts as it decided not only the industrial expansion but structured the very nature and scope of the economy till 1991 with minor modifications. All the industrial policies were nothing but minor modifications in it except the new industrial policy of 1991 which affected deeper and structural changes in it with which India started a wider process of economic reforms.

Industrial Policy Statement, 1969

This was basically a licencing policy which aimed at solving the shortcomings of the licencing policy started by the Industrial Policy of 1956. The experts and industrialists (newcomers) complained that the industrial licencing policy was serving just the opposite purpose for which it was mooted. Inspired by the socialistic ideals and nationalistic feelings the licencing policy had the following reasons:

4. Industrial Policy Resolution, 1956 (30 October).

5. V. M. Dandekar, ***Forty Years After Independence*** in Bimal Jalan edited ***Indian Economy: Problems and Prospects,*** Penguin Books, New Delhi, 2004, p. 63.

6. This statement we get in the ***Second Five Year Plan (1956–61),*** too.

7. Bimal Jalan, ***India's Economic Policy*** (New Delhi: Penguin Books, 1992), p. 23.

8. V.M., Dandekar, **'Forty years After Independence'**, p. 64.

9. These industries which were set up after procuring ***'licences'*** from the government had fixed upper limits of their production known as ***'quota'*** and they needed to procure timely 'permit' (i.e., permission) for the supply of, raw materials—that is why such a name was given to the whole system.

10. Such a commitment went completely against the *'theory of industrial location'*.

1. Exploitation of resources for the development of all;
2. Priority of resource exploitation for the industries;
3. Price-control of the goods produced by the licenced industries;
4. Checking concentration of economic power;
5. Channelising investment into desired direction (according to the planning process).

In practice, the licencing policy was not serving the above-given purpose properly. A powerful industrial house was always able to procure fresh licences at the cost of a new budding entrepreneur. The price regulation policy via licencing was aimed at helping the public by providing cheaper goods, but it indirectly served the private licenced industries ultimately (as central subsidies were given to the private companies from where it was to benefit the poor in the form of cheaper goods). Similarly, the older and well-established industrial houses were capable of creating hurdles for the newer ones with the help of different kinds of trade practices forcing the latter to agree for sell-outs and takeovers. A number of committees were set up by the government to look into the matter and suggest remedies.[11] The committees on industrial licencing policy review not only pointed out several shortcomings of the policy, but also accepted the useful role of industrial licencing.[12] Finally, it was in 1969 that the new industrial licencing policy was announced which affected the following major changes in the area:

1. The Monopolistic and Restrictive Trade Practices (MRTP) Act was passed. The Act intended to regulate the trading and commercial practices of the firms and checking monopoly and concentration of economic power.
2. The firms with assets of ₹25 crore or more were put under obligation of taking permission from the Government of India before any expansion, greenfield venture and takeover of other firms (as per the MRTP Act)..Such firms came to be known as the *'MRTP Companies'*. The upper limit (known as the *'MRTP limit'*) for such companies was revised upward to ₹50 crore in 1980 and ₹100 crore in 1985.[13]
3. For the redressal of the prohibited and restricted practices of trade, the government did set up an *MRTP Commission.*

Industrial Policy Statement, 1973

The Industrial Policy Statement of 1973 introduced some new thinking into the economy with major ones being as follows:

1. A new classificatory term i.e., *core industries* was created. The industries which were of fundamental importance for the development of industries were put in this category such as iron and steel, cement, coal, crude oil, oil refining and electricity. In the future, these industries came to be known as *basic industries, infrastructure industries* in the country.
2. Out of the six core industries defined by the policy, the private sector may apply for licences for the industries which were not a part of schedule A of the Industrial Policy,

11. There were four specific committees set up on this issue, namely ***Swaminathan Committee (1964), Mahalanobis Committee (1964), R.K. Hazari Committee (1967)*** and ***S. Dutt Committee (1969).*** The Administrative Reform Commission (1969) also pointed out the short comings of the industrial licencing policy perpetuated since 1956.

12. ***Dutt Committee*** (New Delhi: Government of India, 1969).

13. The upward revision was logical as it was hindering the organic growth of such companies—neither the capacity addition was possible nor an investment for technological upgrading.

1956.[14] The private firms eligible to apply for such licences were supposed to have their total assets at ₹20 crore or more.

3. Some industries were put under the *reserved list* in which only the small or medium industries could be set up.[15]
4. The concept of *'joint sector'* was developed which allowed partnership among the Centre, state and the private sector while setting up some industries. The governments had the discretionary power to exit such ventures in future. Here, the government wanted to promote the private sector with state support.
5. The Government of India had been facing the foreign exchange crunch during that time. To regulate foreign exchange the Foreign Exchange Regulation Act (FERA) was passed in 1973.[16] Experts have called it a *'draconian'* Act which hampered the growth and modernisation of Indian industries.
6. A limited permission to foreign investment was given, with the multinational corporations (MNCs) being allowed to set up subsidiaries in the country.[17]

14. Out of the six core industries only the cement and iron & steel industries were open for private investment with the rest fully ***reserved*** for the central public sector investment.

15. This is considered a follow up to such suggestions forwarded by the ***Industrial Licensing Policy Inquiry Committee*** (S. Dutt, Chairman) (New Delhi: Government of India, 1969).

16. The FERA got executed on 1 January, 1974. The private sector in the country always complained against this act and doubted its official intentions.

17. This limited permission was restricted to the areas where there was a need of foreign capital. Such MNCs entered the Indian economy with the help of a partner from India—the partner being the major one with 74 per cent shares in the subsidiaries set up for by the MNCs. The MNCs invested via ***technology transfer route.*** Basically, this was an attempt to make up for the loss being incurred by the FERA. This was the period when most of the MNCs had the chances to enter India. Once economic reforms started by 1991, many of them increased their holdings in the Indian subsidiaries with the Indian partner getting the minority shares or a total exit.

Industrial Policy Statement, 1977

The Industrial Policy Statement of 1977 was chalked out by a different political set up from the past with a different political fervour—the dominant voice in the government was having an anti-Indira stance with an inclination towards the Gandhian-socialistic views towards the economy. We see such elements in this policy statement:

1. Foreign investment in the *unnecessary areas* were prohibited (opposite to the IPS of 1973 which promoted foreign investment via technology transfer in the areas of lack of capital or technology). In practice, there was a complete 'no' to foreign investment.[18]
2. Emphasis on village industries with a redefinition of the small and cottage industries.
3. Decentralised industrialisation was given attention with the objective of linking the masses to the process of industrialisation. The District Industries Centres (DICs) were set to promote the expansion of small and cottage industries at a mass scale.
4. Democratic decentralisation got emphasised and the khadi and village industries were restructured.
5. Serious attention was given on the level of production and the prices of essential commodities of everyday use.

Industrial Policy Resolution, 1980

The year 1980 saw the return of the same political party at the Centre. The new government revised the Industrial Policy of 1977 with few exceptions

18. The permission of working was withdrawn in the case of the already functioning soft drink MNC the ***Coca Cola.*** The ongoing process of entry to the computer giant ***IBM*** and automobile major ***Chrysller*** was soon called off. These instances played a highly negative role when India invited FDI in the post-1991 reform era.

in the Industrial Policy Resolution, 1980. The major initiatives of the policy were as given below:

1. Foreign investment via the technology transfer route was allowed again (similar to the provisions of the IPS, 1973).
2. The 'MRTP Limit' was revised upward to ₹50 crore to promote setting of bigger companies.
3. The DICs were continued with.
4. Industrial licencing was simplified.
5. Overall liberal attitude followed towards the expansion of private industries.

Industrial Policy Resolution, 1985 & 1986

The industrial policy resolutions announced by the governments in 1985 and 1986 were very much similar in nature and the latter tried to promote the initiative of the former. The main highlights of the policies are:

1. Foreign investment was further simplified with more industrial areas being open for their entries. The dominant method of foreign investment remained as in the past, i.e., *technology transfer,* but now the equity holding of the MNCs in the Indian subsidiaries could be upto 49 per cent with the Indian partner holding the rest of the 51 per cent shares.
2. The *'MRTP Limit'* was revised upward to ₹100 crore—promoting the idea of bigger companies.
3. The provision of industrial licencing was simplified. Compulsory licencing now remained for 64 industries only.[19]
4. High level attention on the sunrise industries such as telecommunication, computerisation and electronics.
5. Modernisation and the profitability aspects of public sector undertakings were emphasised.
6. Industries based on imported raw materials got a boost.[20]
7. Under the overall regime of FERA, some relaxations concerning the use of foreign exchange was permitted so that essential technology could be assimilated into Indian industries and international standard could be achieved.
8. The agriculture sector was attended with a new scientific approach with many *technology missions* being launched by the government.

These industrial policies were mooted out by the government when the developed world was pushing for the formation of the WTO and a new world economic order looked like a reality. Once the world had become one market, only bigger industrial firms could have managed to cater to such a big market. Side by side sorting out the historical hurdles to industrial expansion perpetuated by the past industrial policies, these new industrial policy resolutions were basically a preparation for the *globalised* future world.

These industrial provisions were attempted at liberalising the economy without any slogan of 'economic reforms'. The government of the time had the mood and willingness of going for the kind

19. A total number of 95 industries had the compulsions of licencing till then. These industries belonged to Schedules B and C of the Industrial Policy Resolution, 1956.

20. This was similar to the policy being followed by Gorbachev in the USSR with the similar fiscal results—a severe balance of payment (BoP) crisis by end 1980s and the early 1990s (J. Barkley Rosser Jin and Marina V. Rosser, ***Comparative Economics in A Transforming World,*** (New Delhi: PHI & MIT Press, 2004), pp. 469–75).

of economic reforms which India pursued post-1991 but it lacked the required political support.[21]

The industrial policies conjoined with the overall micro-economic policy followed by the government had one major loophole that it was more dependent on foreign capital with a big part being costlier ones. Once the economy could not meet industrial performance, it became tough for India to service the external borrowings—the external events (the Gulf war, 1990–91) vitiated the situation, too. Finally, by the end of 1980s India was in the grip of a severe balance of payment crisis with higher rate of inflation (over 13 per cent) and higher fiscal deficit (over 8 per cent).[22] The deep crisis put the economy in a financial crunch, which made India opt for a new way of economic management in the coming times.

NEW INDUSTRIAL POLICY, 1991

It were the industrial policies of past which had shaped the nature and structure of the Indian economy. The need of the hour was to change the nature and structure of the economy by early 1990s. The Government of India decided to change the very nature of the industrial policy which will automatically lead to change in the nature and scope of the economy. And here came the New Industrial Policy of 1991.

With this policy the government kickstarted the very process of reform in the economy, that is why the policy is taken *more as a process than a policy*.

Background India was faced with severe balance of payment crisis by June 1991. Basically, in early 1990s, there were inter-connected set of events, which were growing unfavourable for the Indian economy:

1. Due to the Gulf War (1990–91), the higher oil prices were fastly[23] depleting India's foreign reserves.
2. Sharp decline in the private remittances from the overseas Indian workers in the wake of the Gulf War[24], specially from the Gulf region.
3. Inflation peaking at nearly 17 per cent.[25]
4. The gross fiscal deficit of the Central Government reaching 8.4 per cent of the GDP.[26]
5. By the month of June 1991, India's foreign exchange had declined to just *two weeks* of import coverage.[27]

India's near miss with a serious balance of payments crisis was the proximate cause that started India's market liberalisation measures in 1991 followed by a gradualist approach.[28] As the reforms were induced by the crisis of the BoP, the initial phase focussed on macroeconomic stabilisation while the reforms of industrial policy, trade and exchange rate policies, foreign investment policy, financial and tax reforms as well as public sector reforms did also follow soon.

---

21. The ***Seventh Five Year Plan (1985–90)*** as well as the ***Sixth Five Year Plan (1980–85)*** had already suggested the government to re-define the role of the state in the economy and permit the private sector into those areas of industries where the presence of the government was non-essential, etc. But such a radical approach might not be digested by the country as it was like 'rolling back' the state. This is why the government of the time looks not going for full-scale economic reforms or vocal moves of liberalisation.
22. Vijay Joshi and I.M.D. Little, ***India's Economic Reforms, 1991–2001,*** (Oxford: Clarendon Press, 1996), p. 17.
23. Ministry of Finance, Economic Survey 1990–91 (New Delhi: Government of India, 1991); Ministry of Finance, Economic Survey 1991–92 (New Delhi: Government of India, 1992).
24. Jeffrey D. Sachs, Ashutosh Varsheny and Nirupam Bajpai, ***India in the Era of Economic Reform*** (New Delhi: Oxford University Press, 1999), p. 1.
25. Department of Economic Affairs, **'Economic Reforms: Two Years After and the Task Ahead'**, Discussion Paper (New Delhi: Government of India, 1993), p. 6.
26. Ibid.
27. Bimal Jalan, ***India's Economic Crisis: The Way Ahead,*** (New Delhi: Oxford University Press, 1991), pp. 2–12.
28. Sach, Varseny and Bajpai, ***India in the Era of Economic Reforms***, p. 2.

The financial support India received from the IMF to fight out the BoP crisis of 1990–91 were having a tag of conditions to be fulfilled by India. These IMF conditionalities required the Indian economy to go for a structural re-adjustment. As the nature and scope of the economy were moulded by the various industrial policies India did follow till date, any desired change in the economic structure had to be induced with the help of another industrial policy. The new industrial policy, announced by the government on 23 July, 1991 had initiated a bigger process of economic reforms in the country, seriously motivated towards the structural readjustment naturally obliged to 'fulfill' IMF conditionalities.[29] The major highlights of the policy are as follows:

1. **De-reservation of the Industries:** The industries which were reserved for the Central Government by the IPR, 1956, were cut down to only eight. In coming years many other industries were also opened for private sector investment. At present there are only two industries which are fully or partially reserved for the Central Government:
   (i) Atomic energy and nuclear research and other related activities, i.e., mining, use management, fuel fabrication, export-import, waste management, etc., of radioactive minerals (none of the nuclear powers in the world have allowed entry of private sector players in these activities, thus no such attempts look logical in India, too).
   (ii) Railways (many of the functions related to the railways have been allowed private entry, but still the private sector cannot enter the sector as a full-fledged railway service provider).
2. **De-licencing of the Industries:** The number of industries put under the compulsory provision of licencing (belonging to Schedules B and C as per the IPR, 1956) were cut down to only 18. Reforms regarding the area were further followed and presently there are only *four industries*[30] which carry the burden of compulsory licencing:
   (i) Aero space and defence related electronics
   (ii) Gun powder, industrial explosives and detonating fuse
   (iii) Dangerous chemicals
   (iv) Tobacco, cigarette and related products
3. **Abolition of the MRTP Limit:** The MRTP limit was ₹100 crore so that the mergers, acquisitions and takeovers of the industries could become possible. In 2002, a competition Act was passed which has replaced the MRTP Act. In place of the MRTP commission, the Competition Commission has started functioning (though there are still some hitches regarding the compositional form of the latter and its real functions and jurisdictions).
4. **Promotion to Foreign Investment:** Functioning as a typical closed economy, the Indian economy had never shown any good faith towards foreign capital. The new industrial policy was a pathbreaking step in this regard. Not only the draconian

29. Rakesh Mohan, 'Industrial Policy and Control's, in Bimal Jalan (ed.), ***The Indian Economy: Problems and Prospects*** (New Delhi: Penguin Books, 1992), pp. 92–123.

30. In 1985–86 there were just 64 industries under the compulsory licencing provision. By the fiscal 2015–19 the number remained five Publications Division, **India 2019** (New Delhi: Government of India, 2019). Though the numbers are still five, all these five industries have many internal areas which today carry no obligation of licencing. As for example, the electronic industry was under this provision and entrepreneurs needed licences to produce radio, TV, tape-recorder, etc., what to ask of mobile phones, computers, DVDs and i-pods. Now only those electronic goods carry licencing provision which are related to either the aero-space or the defence sectors—thus we see a great number of electronic industries freed from the licencing provision the item 'electronics' still remains under it. Similarly while 'drug & pharma' still belong to the licenced industries, dozens of drugs and pharmaceuticals have been made free of it. The six industries have gone for high-level internal de-licencing since the reforms started.

FERA was committed to be diluted, but the government went to encourage foreign investment (FI) in both its forms—direct and indirect. The direct form of FI was called as the foreign direct investment (FDI) under which the MNCs were allowed to set up their firms in India in the different sectors varying from 26 per cent to 100 per cent ownership with them—*Enron* and *Coke* being the flag-bearers. The FDI started in 1991 itself. The indirect form of foreign investment (i.e., in the assets owned by the Indian firms in equity capital) was called the *portfolio investment scheme* (PIS) in the country, which formally commenced in 1994.[31] Under the PIS the *fo reign institutional investors* (FIIs) having good track record are allowed to invest in the Indian security/stock market. The FIIs need to register themselves as a stock broker with SEBI. It means India has not allowed *individual fo reign investment* in the security market still, only *institutional investment* has been allowed till now.[32]

5. **FERA Replaced by FEMA:** The government committed in 1991 itself to replace the draconian FERA with a highly liberal FEMA, which came into effect in the year 2000–01 with a sun-set clause of two years.[33]

6. **Location of Industries:** Related provisions were simplified by the policy which was highly cumbersome and had time-consuming process. Now, the industries were classified into 'polluting' and 'non-polluting' categories and a highly simple provision deciding their location was announced:
   (i) Non-polluting industries might be set up anywhere.
   (ii) Polluting industries to be set up at least 25 kms away from the million cities.

7. **Compulsion of Phased Production Abolished:** With the compulsion of phased production abolished, now the private firms could go for producing as many goods and models simultaneously.[34] Now the capacity and capital of industries could be utilised to their optimum level.

8. **Compulsion to Convert Loans into Shares Abolished:** The policy of nationalisation started by the Government of India in the late 1960s was based on the sound logic of *greater public benefit* and had its origin in the idea of *welfare state*—it was criticised by the victims and the experts alike. In the early 1970s, the Government of India came with a new idea of it. The major banks of the country were now fully nationalised (14 in

31. Ministry of Finance, ***Economic Survey, 1994–95,*** (New Delhi: Government of India, 1995).

32. It becomes very complex and tough to regulate the individual foreign investment in the share market though it is an easier way of attracting foreign exchange. It should be noted that the South East Asian economies which faced financial crisis in 1996–97 all had allowed individual foreign investment in their share market. As the Indian security market was learning the art of regulation in its nascent phase, the government decided not to allow such foreign investment. The logic was vindicated after the South East Asian currency crisis when India had almost no shocks (Ministry of Finance, Economic Survey 1996–97 (New Delhi: Government of India, 1997).

33. The delayed action by the government in the foreign exchange liberalisation was due to the delayed comfort the economy felt regarding the availability of foreign exchange.

34. This was another hurdle which the private sector industries have been complaining about. As the industrial products were completely new to the Indian market and its consumers alike, the government followed this policy with the logic to provide enough time for indigenization of the industrial products i.e.,development of awareness about the product and its servicing, maintenance, etc. As for example, the MNC subsidiary Phillips India was allowed to produce a highly simple radio ***Commandar*** and ***Jawan*** models for comparatively longer periods of time then they were allowed to come up with the smaller fashionable radio sets or two-in-ones and three-in-ones. Such provisions hampered their full capacity utilisation as well as achieving the economy of scale had also been tougher. The new industrial policy of 1991 did away with such impediments. By that time, the Indian consumer as well as the market was fully aware of the modern industrial goods.

number by that time), which had to mobilise resources for the purpose of planned development of India. The private companies who had borrowed capital from these banks (when the banks were privately owned) now wanted their loans to be paid back. The government came with a novel provision for the companies who were unable to repay their loans (most of them were like it)—they could opt to convert their loan amounts into equity shares and hand them over to the banks. The private companies which opted this route (this was a compulsory option) ultimately became a government-owned company as the banks were owned by the Government of India—this was an *indirect* route to nationalise private firms. Such a compulsion which hampered the growth and development of the Indian industries was withdrawn by the government in 1991.[35]

The picture presented by the New Industrial Policy of 1991 was taken by many experts, the opposition in the Parliament and even the public figures as well as the business and industry of the country as a *'rolling back'* of the state. The glorious role given to the state by the Nehruvian economy seemed completely toppled down. Any one idea the new policy challenged was an emphatic good bye to the 'control regime' perpetuated till now by the government. There was a coalition of interests of politicians, bureaucrats, multinationals as well as the domestic industrial and business houses whose interests were sheltered and by the control regime.[36] Thus, a memorandum to the government requesting not to dismantle the control regime by the major industrial houses of India as well as arrival of the '*Swadeshi Jagaran Manch*' were not illogical. But the governments continued with the reform programme with politically permissible pace and a time came when the same industrial houses requested the government (2002) to expedite the process of reform. Now the Indian industry and business class has been able to understand the economics of 'openness' and a different kind of the mixed economy. But the process of reforms have still to go miles before its real benefits start reaching the masses and development together with reform could be made a mass movement.

This is why experts have suggested that only assuming that reforms will benefit the masses will not be enough to make it happen politically, but the governments, the administrative agencies and the economists all need to link it positively to *mass welfare*—it might require to create a popular climate and form the political coalitions in favour of the argument that privatisation and accordingly restructured labour laws are basically aimed at creating jobs, better job prospects, alleviating poverty, enriching education and providing healthcare to the masses.[37] In the coming times, the government went from one to another generations of the reforms, setting new targets and every time trying to make reforms socio-politically possible.

35. Combined with nationalisation, this ***indirect route*** to nationalisation failed to provide the confidence among the entrepreneurs that the industrial units they are intending to set up will be owned by them. This discouraged entrepreneurship in India while taking risk. The abolition of this compulsion was an indirect indication by the government of no more direct or indirect nationalisation in future. This has served the purpose, there is no doubt in it.

36. This nexus of the interests of the vested groups to the control regime of the economy has been beautifully elaborated by Rakesh Mohan in **'Industrial Policy and Controls'** pp. 92–123. He also points out that the control system perpetuating the academic and intellectual ideological leanings negated the very need for re-examination of the system. The 'planners' and the 'bureaucrats' were able to preserve their powers via the control regime did everything to maintain the status quo, Rakesh Mohan further adds.

37. First of the series of such suggestions came from Sach, Varshney and Bajpai, ***India in the Era of Economic Reforms***, p. 24).

DISINVESTMENT

Government-owned firms, namely[38] the public sector undertakings (PSUs) and public sector enterprises (PSEs), played a foundational role in India's development process. Realising the changed situations, the Government decided to 'redefine' (disinvestment and privatisation) the role for these firms once reform process began in 1991. By that time, the Government had invested a total of ₹2.4 lakh crores in 244 firms (the journey with 5 firms and a modest investment of ₹29 crores in March, 1951). Rather the process of setting up new Government firms did not stop and by 2019, Government[39] is invested with ₹16.41 lakh crores in a total number of 348 such firms.

Disinvestment is the process of 'selling ownership' in a company. Technically, the term may be used in case of any company (i.e., privately-owned company), but in practice, it is used only in case of a government-owned company. Disinvestment commenced in the country with three inter-related co-ordinates:

1. As a tool[40] of public sector reforms;
2. As a part of the economic reform process (i.e., as part[41] of the *de-reservation of industries*); and
3. As a tool of resource[42] mobilisation for budgetary needs.

The approach towards public sector reforms in India has been much more cautious than that of the other developing countries. India did not follow the radical solution to it—under which outright privatisation of commercially viable PSUs is done and the unviable ones are completely closed.[43] There was an emphasis on increasing functional autonomy of public sector organisations to improve their efficiency in the 1980s in India as part of the public sector reforms. Once the process of economic reforms started in the early 1990s, disinvestment became a part of the public sector reforms. The C. Rangarajan Commission on Disinvestment of the Public Sector Enterprises (1991) went on to suggest the government on the issue in a highly commendable and systematic way, taking empirical notes from the experiences of disinvestment around the world. The government started the process of disinvestment in 1991 itself. In 1997 the government did set up a Disinvestment Commission to advise upon the various aspects of the disinvestment process. The

38. See **GLOSSARY** for a detailed discussion on the PSEs and PSUs.

39. **Economic Survey 2019-20**, Vol. 2, pp. 221-222, Ministry of Finance, GoI, N. Delhi.

40. Publication Division, **India 1991** (New Delhi: Government of India, 1992).

41. The de-reservation of industries had allowed the private sector to enter the areas hitherto reserved for the Central Government. It means in the coming times in the unreserved areas the PSUs were going to face the international class competitiveness posed by the new private companies. To face up the challenges the existing PSUs needed new kind of technological, managerial and marketing strategies (similar to the private companies). For all such preparations there was a requirement of huge capital. The government thought to partly fund the required capital out of the proceeds of disinvestment of the PSUs. In this way disinvestment should be viewed in India as a way of increasing investment in the divested PSUs (which we see taking place in the cases of BALCO, VSNL, etc.).

42. Right since 1991 when disinvestment began, governments have been using the disinvestment proceeds to manage fiscal deficits in the budget at least up to 2000–01. From 2000–01 to 2002–03 some of the proceeds went for some social sector reforms or for labour security. After 2003 India established National Investment Fund to which the proceeds of disinvestment automatically flow and is not regarded as a ***capital receipt*** of the Union Government. This idea of Indian experiment with disinvestment was articulated by ***Sach, Varshney and Bajpai, India in the Era of Economic Reforms***, pp. 62–63.

43. As was done by **Margaret Thatcher** in the UK in the mid-1980s. Her brand of privatisation was driven by the conviction that government control makes PSUs inherently less efficient and privatisation therefore improves its economic efficiency and is good for the consumers. However, this idea has been rejected around the world on the empirical bases. ***A PSUs could also have comparable economic efficiency even being under full government control.*** This was followed by Mrs. Thatcher (1979–90) forcefully in Great Britain conjoined with the supply-side economics as was done by Ronald Reagan (1981–89) in the United States as discussed by P.A. Samuelson and W.D. Nordhaus, ***Economics*** (New Delhi; Tata McGraw Hill, 2005), p. 703.

financial year 1999–2000 saw a serious attempt by the government to make disinvestment a political process to expedite the process of disinvestment in the country—first a Disinvestment Department and later a full-fledged Ministry of Disinvestment was set up.[44] The new government (UPA) dismantled the Ministry of Disinvestment and today only the Department of Disinvestment is taking care of the matter, working under the Ministry of Finance.

Types of Disinvestment

Since the process of disinvestment was started in India (1991), its consisted of *two official types.* A brief discussion on them is given below:

1. **Token Disinvestment:** Disinvestment started in India with a high political caution—in a symbolic way known as the *token disinvestment* (presently being called as 'minority stake sale'). The general policy was to sell the shares of the PSUs maximum upto the 49 per cent (i.e., maintaining government ownership of the companies). But in practice, shares were sold to the tune of 5–10 per cent only. This phase of disinvestment though brought some extra funds to the government (which were used to fill up the fiscal deficit considering the proceeds as the 'capital receipts') it could not initiate any new element to the PSUs, which could enhance their efficiency. It remained the major criticism of this type of disinvestment, and experts around the world started suggesting the government to go for it in the way that the ownership could be transferred from the government to the private sector. The other hot issue raised by the experts was related to the question of using the *proceeds* of disinvestment.

2. **Strategic Disinvestment:** In order to make disinvestment a process by which efficiency of the PSUs could be enhanced and the government could de-burden itself of the activities in which the private sector has developed better efficiency (so that the government could concentrate on the areas which have no attraction for the private sector such as social sector support for the poor masses), the government initiated the process of strategic disinvestment. The government classifying the PSUs into *'strategic'* and *'non strategic'* announced in March 1999 that it will generally reduce its stake (share holding) in the *'non strategic'* public sector enterprises (PSEs) to 26 per cent or below if necessary and in the *'strategic'* PSEs (i.e., arms and ammunition; atomic energy and related activities; and railways) it will retain its majority holding.[45] There was a major shift in the disinvestment policy from selling small lots of share in the profit-making PSUs (i.e., token disinvestment) to the strategic sale with change in management control both in profit and loss-making enterprises. The essence of the strategic disinvestment was:

   1. The minimum shares to be divested will be 51 per cent, and
   2. The wholesale sale of shares will be done to a *'strategic partner'* having international class experience and expertise in the sector.

   This form of disinvestment commenced with the Modern Food Industries Ltd. (MFIL). The second PSUs was the BALCO which invited every kind of criticism from the opposition political parties, the Government of Chattisgarh and experts, alike. The other PSUs were CMC Ltd, HTL, IBPL, VSNL, ITDC (13 hotels),

44. A former media expert, Arun Shourie remained the Minister for the whole term of the NDA government. Some highly accelerated and successful disinvestments were done during this period but not without controversies.

45. *Concept Classification of the PSEs,* Government of India, 1999.

Hotel Corporation of India Ltd. (3 hotels), Paradeep Phosphate Ltd (PPL), HZL, IPCL, MUL and Lagan Jute Manufacturing Company Ltd. (LJMC)—a total number of 13 public sector enterprises, were part of the *'strategic sale'* or *'strategic disinvestment'* of the PSEs.[46] The new government at the Centre did put this policy of strategic disinvestment on the hold practically and came up with a new policy in place.

Disinvestment Policy

India's disinvestment policy[47] has evolved over time since it commenced in 1991. It has two major features—'ideology' behind the policy and the 'policy' itself. The *ideology* behind the policy is:

1. Public ownership of PSUs to be promoted as they are wealth of nation;
2. Government to hold minimum 51 per cent shares in case of 'minority stake sale'; and
3. Upto 50 per cent or more shares might be sold off under 'strategic disinvestment'.

The current *policy* of disinvestment followed by the government is as given below:

1. *Minority Stake Sale* (the policy of November 2009 continues):
   (i) Listed PSUs to be taken first to comply to minimum 25 per cent norm;
   (ii) New PSUs to be listed which have earned net profit in three preceding consecutive years;
   (iii) 'Follow-on' public offers on case by case basis once capital investment needed; and
   (iv) DIPAM (Department of Investment and Public Asset Management) to identify PSUs and suggest disinvestment in consultation with respective ministries.
2. *Strategic Disinvestment* i.e., selling 50 per cent or more shares of the PSUs (announced in February 2016):
   (i) To be done through consultation among Ministries/Departments and NITI Aayog;
   (ii) NITI Aayog to identify PSUs and advise on its different aspects; and
   (iii) CGD (Core Group of Secretaries on Disinvestment) to consider the recommendations of NITI Aayog to facilitate a decision by the CCEA (Cabinet Committee on Economic Affairs) and to supervise/monitor the implementation process.

Current Policy

In the process of gradual evolution, the disinvestment policy was further tweaked by the Government in **Union Budget 2021-22** with its objectives and features redefined:

Objectives of the Policy

1. Minimising presence of CPSEs including financial institutions and creating new investment space for private sector.
2. Post disinvestment, economic growth of CPSEs and financial institutions to be through infusion of private capital, technology and best management practices.
3. Disinvestment proceeds to finance various social sector and developmental programmes.

Policy Features

1. Policy covers existing CPSEs, Public Sector Banks and Public Sector Insurance Companies.

---

46. Publications Division, ***India 2003*** (New Delhi: Government of India, 2004).

47. Miinistry of Finance, Department of Investment and Public Asset Management, Government of India, N. Delhi, March 2017.

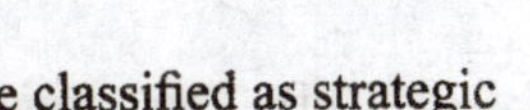

2. Various sectors will be classified as strategic and non-strategic sectors.
3. The *strategic sectors* classified are:
   (i) Atomic energy, Space and Defence
   (ii) Transport and Telecommunications
   (iii) Power, Petroleum, Coal and other minerals
   (iv) Banking, Insurance and financial services
4. In strategic sectors, there will be bare minimum presence of the public sector enterprises. The remaining CPSEs in the strategic sector will be privatised or merged or subsidiarised with other CPSEs or closed.
5. In *non-strategic sectors,* the CPSEs will be privatised, otherwise shall be closed.

Comprehensive Management of Public Assets Since 2016, disinvestment has become a part of the broader policy known as the *comprehensive management of government investments in the public assets.* Before announcing the current disinvestment policy, the Government changed the name of the existing Department of Disinvestment to the Department of Investment and Public Asset Management (DIPAM) along with its *mandate* from taking care of disinvestment to *Comprehensive management of the Government's investment in the CPSEs.* Under it, the following 'four actions' are to be taken in regard to the CPSEs:

1. Achieving optimum return and accelerating growth.
2. Leveraging assets by capital and financial restructuring.
3. Improving investors' confidence through capital market exposure.
4. Rationalising decision-making process for efficient management.

The policy considers the CPSEs as an important financial asset and aims to use them for realising a variety of goals such as—economic return, investment, growth acceleration, etc. The steps like monetisation of assets, for debt management and capital expenditures, buyback of shares by the PSUs having huge surplus, merger and acquisition among the PSUs in the same sector, and launch of exchange traded funds (ETFs), etc. are being taken under it.

As private sector keeps exploring all possibilities to employ their investment in the best possible way (and run their firms on 'business line'), Government also looks aiming at similar policy in case of the public assets. Such a policy shift in case of the CPSEs, however, has come very late (which was proposed by the late 1980s itself and looked essential once economic reforms commenced in the country). The policy will not only unshackle the hidden economic potential of the CPSEs but also help in creating a healthy market for growth and expansion of the private sector in particular and economy in general.

Proceeds of Disinvestment: Debate Concerning the Use

In the very next year of disinvestment, there started a debate in the country concerning the suitable use of the proceeds of disinvestment (i.e., accruing to the government out of the sale of the shares in the PSUs). The debate has by now evolved to a certain stage coming off basically in three phases:

Phase I This phase could be considered from 1991–2000 in which whatever money the governments received out of disinvestment were used for fulfilling the budgetary requirements (better say bridging the gap of fiscal deficit).[48]

Phase II This phase which has a very short span (2000–03) saw two new developments. *First,* the government started a practice of using the proceeds not only for fulfilling the need of fiscal deficit but

48. Ministry of Finance, Various issue of the ***Economic Survey*** (New Delhi: Government of India).

used the money for some other good purposes, such as—re-investment in the PSEs, pre-payment of public debt and on the social sector. *Second,* by the early 2000–01 a broad consensus emerged on the issue of the proposal by the then Finance Minister.[49] The proposal regarding the use of the proceeds of disinvestment was as given below:

Some portions of the disinvestment proceeds should be used:

1. in the divested PSU itself for upgrading purposes
2. in the turn-around of the other PSUs
3. in the public debt repayment/pre-payment
4. in the social infrastructure (education, healthcare, etc.)
5. in the rehabilitation of the labour-force (of the divested PSUs) and
6. in fulfilling the budgetary requirements.

Phase III Two major developments of this phase are as given below:

1. **National Investment Fund:** In January 2005, the Government of India decided to constitute a 'National Investment Fund' (NIF)[50] which has the following *salient features*:

   (i) The proceeds from disinvestment will be channelised into the NIF, which is to be maintained outside the Consolidated Fund of India.

   (ii) The corpus of the National Investment Fund will be of a permanent nature.

   (iii) The Fund will be professionally managed, to provide sustainable returns without depleting the corpus, by selected Public Sector Mutual Funds *(they are, UTI Asset Management Company Ltd.; SBI Funds Management Company Pvt. Ltd.; LIC Mutual Fund Asset Management Company Ltd.).*

   (iv) 75 per cent of the annual income of the Fund will be used to finance selected social sector schemes, which promote education, health and employment. The residual 25 per cent of the annual income of the Fund will be used to meet the capital investment requirements of profitable and revivable PSUs that yield adequate returns, in order to enlarge their capital base to finance expansion/ diversification.

   The income from the NIF investments was utilised on selected social sector schemes, namely the Jawaharlal Nehru National Urban Renewal Mission (JNNURM), Accelerated Irrigation Benefits Programme (AIBP), Rajiv Gandhi Gramin Vidyutikaran Yojana (RGGVY), Accelerated Power Development and Reform Programme, Indira Awas Yojana and National Rural Employment Guarantee Scheme (NREGS).

2. **Restructuring of NIF:** In November 2009, the government approved a change in the policy on utilisation of disinvestment proceeds. In view of the difficult situation caused by the global slowdown of 2008–09 and a severe drought in 2009–10, a *one-time exemption* was accorded to disinvestment proceeds being deposited into NIF—to be operational for the fiscals 2009–12, which was further extended to 2012–13, in view of the persistent difficult condition of the economy. All disinvestment proceeds *(in place of the income accruing out of the*

49. It was proposed by Yashwant Sinha and thus got popularity as the ***'Yashwant Formula'*** of using disinvestment proceeds. Being his personal proposal, the Government of the time was not officially bound to it. However, the idea got support inside and outside of the Parliament and looked having an impact on the government's thinking about the issue.

50. Ministry of Finance, Disinvestment Policy Announcement, Department of Disinvestment (New Delhi: Government of India, 2005).

investment of the NIF corpus) obtained during the three year period were to be used for selected social sector schemes.

Current Policy: In January 2013 (which was further revised in February 2013), the government approved *restructuring* of the NIF and decided that the disinvestment proceeds with effect from the fiscal year 2013–14 will be credited to the existing *'Public Account'* under the head NIF and they would remain there until withdrawn/invested for the approved purposes as decided by the *Union Budget*. It was decided that the NIF would be utilised for the following purposes:

(i) Subscribing to the shares being issued by the CPSE including PSBs and public sector insurance companies, on *rights basis* so as to ensure 51 per cent government ownership in them.

(ii) *Preferential allotment* of shares of the CPSE to promoters, so that government shareholding does not go down below 51 per cent in all cases where the CPSE is going to raise fresh equity to meet its Capex [51] programme.

(iii) *Recapitalisation* of public sector banks and public sector insurance companies.

(iv) Investment by the government in RRBs, IIFCL, NABARD, Exim Bank;

(v) Equity infusion in various metro projects;

(vi) Investment in Bhartiya Nabhikiya Vidyut Nigam Limited and Uranium Corporation of India Ltd.;

(vii) Investment in Indian Railways towards capital expenditure.

This way, the policy regarding the use of disinvestment proceeds became *quite flexible* since 2013-14 and gives the Government freedom to spend them as per the socio-economic needs of the hour—for any kind of expenditures (revenue or capital). As per the ***Union Budget 2021-22,*** the proceeds will be used to finance various social sector and developmental programmes of the government.

Targets of Proceeds Proceeds of disinvestment are classified as 'non-debt Capital Receipts' of the Government and create no labilities—that is why they have emerged as an attractive source of fund for the Government to finance the budgetary allocations. The Government has been setting increasing targets for the proceeds in recent years—a target of ₹2.10 lakh crores was set for 2020-21, however, the realisation had been of only ₹15,220 crores by January 2021 due to the COVID-19 pandemic crisis, as per the *Economic Survey 2020-21*. For the year 2021-22, the *Union Budget 202 1-22* has set a target to mobilise ₹1.75 lakh crores through disinvestment process.

PERFORMANCE OF CPSEs

The public sector enterprise policy[52] enunciated by the Government in November 2020, spells a *complete change in paradigm* as compared to its policy of import substitution and self-sufficiency (which became the basis of the Mahalanobis Plan in 1956). However, the inherent inefficiencies leading to low productivity in the PSEs, high-cost structure and strained public finances led the Government to privatise the PSUs after 1991. Thus, began the journey of privatisation and disinvestment in the country. By now, several measures have been taken to reduce their (i.e., the

51. The Prime Minister's Office has been monitoring the CAPEX (Capital Expenditure) programme and investment plans of selected Central Public Sector Enterprises (CPSEs) since 2012–13. The purpose of this exercise was to enhance investment in the economy, utilising the substantial cash surpluses that are available with some of the CPSEs to drive economic growth.

52. **Economic Survey 2020-21,** vol. 2, p. 273-75, Ministry of Finance, GoI, N. Delhi.

Government) presence in commercial activities—through the stock market route and strategic sale. This 'policy to withdraw' has been a subject of discussion in several *Economic Surveys* (more specifically 2000-01, 2001-02, 2002-03) which reflects Government deliberations on it.

Under the *Atmanirbhar Bharat Mission*, the government has proposed to *rationalise* the participation of the CPSEs in commercial activities with their presence limited only in the 'strategic sectors'—numbers cut down to only ***four***—others to be either merged or privatised or brought under holding companies. The enterprises of 'non-strategic sectors' would be privatised. This initiative is expected to bring healthy competition in sectors and will also assist the Government to focus extensively on 'strategic sectors.' So that the retained enterprises are able to meet the expectations of the Government, certain other reforms have also been suggested by the *Economic Survey 2020-21* which are as given below:

1. Revamping their Boards and structure.
2. Enhancing operational autonomy of their Boards coupled with strong norms of corporate governance.
3. Listing on stock exchange for greater transparency

Besides disinvestment and rationalisation, certain separate steps have also been taken by the Government regarding these enterprises in recent times—revamping of 'performance monitoring system' to make it more objective and forward-looking (based on sectoral indices and benchmarks); timely closure of sick and loss-making enterprises; and disposal of their assets being the major ones.

MSME SECTOR

As per the SMSE Act, 2006 the MSME are classified in two classes—*manufacturing* and *service* enterprises—and they are defined in terms of investment in plant & machinery. The Micro, Small and Medium Enterprises (MSMEs) play a very vital role in the economy—**3.6** crore such units employ **8.05** crore people and contribute **37.5** per cent to the country's GDP. The sector has huge potential for helping address structural problems like, unemployment, regional imbalances, unequal distribution of national income and wealth. Due to comparatively low capital costs and their forward-backward linkages with other sectors, they are headed to play a crucial role in the success of the Make in India initiative.

Realising the importance of the sector, over the time, the government has undertaken a number of schemes for the establishment of new enterprises and development of existing ones like:

1. PMEGP (Prime Minister's Employment Generation Programme),
2. CGTMSE (Credit Guarantee Trust Fund for Micro and Small Enterprises)
3. CLCSS (Credit Linked Capital Subsidy Scheme) for Technology Upgradation,
4. SFURTI (Scheme of Fund for Regeneration of Traditional Industries), and
5. MSECDP (Micro and Small Enterprises-Cluster Development Programme)

Some of the *recent initiatives* undertaken by the government for the promotion and development of the MSMEs, have been as given below:

1. **UAM (Udyog Aadhar Memorandum):** The UAM scheme, notified in September 2015, to promote ease of doing business. Under it, entrepreneurs just need to file an *online* entrepreneurs' memorandum to get a unique Udyog Aadhaar Number (UAN)—a significant improvement over the earlier complex and cumbersome procedure.
2. **Employment Exchange for Industries:** To facilitate *match making* between

prospective job seekers and employers an employment exchange for industries was set up in June 2015 (in line with Digital India).

3. **Framework for Revival and Rehabilitation of MSMEs:** Under this (May 2015), banks need to constitute a Committee for Distressed MSMEs to prepare a Corrective Action Plan (CAP) for them.
4. **ASPIRE (Promoting Innovation and Rural Entrepreneurs):** Launched in March 2015 with the objective of setting up a *network* of technology and incubation centres to accelerate entrepreneurship and promote start-ups for innovation and entrepreneurship in rural and agriculture-based industry.

Enhancing ease of doing business for the sector and their faster growth have been given special attention by the Government in the last few years—with following policy steps[53] taken till *early 2020:*

- Loans up to ₹1 crore to be approved online within 59 minutes;
- Interest subvention of 2 per cent to all GST registered firms;
- PSUs to compulsorily procure 25 per cent (up from 20 per cent) with 3 per cent reserved for women entrepreneurs—through GeM portal;
- 20 Technology Centres (TCs) and 100 Extension Centres (ECs) to be established;
- Government to bear 70 per cent of the cost for establishing Pharma clusters;
- Returns under 8 labour laws and 10 Union regulations to be filed once in a year;
- Establishments to be visited by an Inspector will be decided through a computerised random allotment;
- Single consent under air and water pollution laws;
- Returns to be accepted through self-certification and only 10 per cent units to be inspected; and
- For minor violations under the Companies Act, entrepreneurs no longer have to approach court but can correct them through simple procedures.

COVID-19 Impact In the aftermath of the *COVID-19 pandemic,* the Government was quick to recognise the role of MSMEs in reviving the economy. Under the *Atmanirbhar Bharat Abhiyan* (Self-Reliant India Campaign), several measures were announced by the Government to provide them immediate relief and help grow – the major ones are as given below:

- The distinction between manufacturing and service sector MSMEs has been abolished and an upward revision in their *definition* has been adopted:
  - *Micro* enterprises investment capital increased to ₹1 crore (from existing ₹25 lakh) and ₹5 crores of turnover (from ₹1 crore).
  - *Small* enterprises investment capital to ₹10 crores of investment (from ₹5 crores) and ₹50 crores of turnover (from ₹2 crores).
  - *Medium* enterprises investment increased to ₹50 crores (from ₹10 crores) of investment and ₹250 crores of turnover (from ₹5 crores).
- Collateral-free automatic *loan* of ₹3.0 lakh crore (Government to provide guarantee for the loans) for meeting operational liabilities, buy raw material and restart businesses.
- Approval of ₹20,000 crore as 'subordinate debt' to provide equity support to the stressed

53. Economic Survey 2019-20, Vol. 2, pp. 229-230, Ministry of Finance, GoI, N. Delhi.

MSMEs (estimated to benefit around 2 lakh enterprises).

- *Fund of Funds* (of ₹50,00 crore) to be created for equity infusion for MSMEs which will also help them get listed in stock exchanges.
- Disallowing global tenders in procurements upto ₹200 crore (to create more opportunities for the MSMEs).
- Clearing of the dues of MSMEs by the Government and PSUs within 45 days.
- A robust ICT (information and communication technology) based system *Champions* launched to help and handhold MSMEs.
- The MSMEs are the backbone of Indian economy – around 6 crore such enterprises account for around 29 per cent of India's GDP, contribute over 50 per cent of exports and employ over 11 crore people (as per the latest data from the Government, May 2020). Undoubtedly, they are small economic engines and have a crucial role to play in building a stronger and *self-reliant* India.

SECTORAL CONCERNS

Expansion of industrial activities has been among the primary policy concerns of the Government. Looking at the critical role played by the sectors like steel and coal in the economy and scope of employment and export expansion in textile and apparels, we see the Government taking some focused steps in this regard— a brief summary of the recent developments in the areas are being given below.

Steel

Steel is one of the critical inputs to industries, urban development and infrastructure development. India is the 2nd largest producer as well as consumer of steel (after China) in the world. However, its per capita total finished steel consumption was around 74.7 kg during 2019-20 as against the global average of 229 kg. Further, the capacity utilization in crude steel plants continues to be low.

In light of the role this critical input plays in developmental process, the Government announced the NPS-2017 (National Steel Policy-2017) with vision of expansion in production capacity while being globally competitive. The policy aims at achieving a crude steel capacity of 300 million tonnes (MT) and a finished steel capacity of 230 MT with a per capita consumption of 158 kg by *2030-31.*

By late 2020-21, the Government took the following initiatives[54] under the *Atmanirbhar Abhiyan* to enhance the domestic production of steel:

- 'Speciality Steel' (4 products) was included for incentives under the Production Linked Incentive (PLI) scheme.
- MSMEs (which are members of Engineering Export Promotion Council) to be supplied steel at 'export parity price' under the duty drawback scheme.
- Domestically produced iron and steel to be given preference in Government procurement (where estimate exceeds ₹ 25 crores).
- Domestic industry to be protected (against unfair trade practices adopted by other countries) by imposing anti-dumping duty and countervailing duty.

Coal

In India, coal is the one of the most important and abundant fossil fuel and accounts for 55 per cent of its energy needs. It is not only the primary source of energy in the country but is also used as

54. **Economics Survey 2020-21**, vol.2, pp. 281-82, Ministry of Finance, GoI, N. Delhi.

an intermediary by many industries such as steel, sponge iron, cement, paper, brick-kilns, etc. In 2020-21 (April-October), India's coal production was 337.52 MT (3.3 per cent lower than the previous year). For 2019-20 the production of raw coal was 729.1 MT (a growth of just 0.05 per cent over the previous year). The contraction in production was due to disruption caused by the COVID pandemic. India is an importer of coal also and imported 248.54 MT of it in 2019-20 (5.7 per cent higher than the previous year). Keeping in mind country's heavy dependence on coal, in till early 2021, the Government has taken a number of measures (as per the *Economic Survey 2020-21*) to *strike a balance* between energy needs and environment friendliness:

A. **Steps towards Clean Coal** By early 2021 about 54,500 hectares (ha) land had been brought under green cover by planting 132 million trees which created estimated carbon sink of 2.7 lakh tonnes of CO_2 equivalent per year. By 2030, the plan is to cover 20,000 ha of additional area by planting 50 million trees.

- Two Coal Bed Methane (CBM) Projects with considerable potential for carbon footprint reduction are in the pipeline.
- Surface coal gasification projects (100 MT of coal) with relatively lesser carbon footprint to be set up by 2030.
- First mile connectivity (transportation of coal from pitheads to dispatch points) projects are in the pipeline.

B. **Amendment in Act & Rules and other Measures**

- Mineral Laws (Amendment) Act, 2020 was enacted in March 2020 by bringing several amendments into the Coal Mines (Special Provisions) Act, 2015.
- Over 36 coal blocks allocated through auction for coal mining to the private sector.
- Of the auction of 38 coal mines for commercial mining in June 2020, 19 were successfully auctioned with a success rate of 50 per cent (as compared to 30 per cent in the past).

TEXTILE AND APPARELS

The textile and apparel industry plays an important role in the overall social and economic development of the country. The industry has high contribution in the economy—2 per cent of the GDP, 11 per cent of total manufacturing GVA, and direct and indirect employment to about 10.5 crore people. The sector is the 2nd largest employment generator in the country (next only to agriculture). Most importantly, a major part of this workforce being women, it plays a vital role in *women empowerment* and in the overall social development of the country.

India is the 6th largest exporter of textile and apparel products (after China, Germany, Bangladesh, Vietnam, and Italy) and is well known in the global market for many products including cotton yarn, fashion garments, hand-made carpets, etc. The designing capability of this industry is respected worldwide, which has helped the country to build its image as an industrial powerhouse. The sector is, however, vulnerable to several internal and external economic challenges that affect its overall performance. Besides schemes specific to silk, jute, wool, handloom and handicraft sectors, the Government is implementing the following *major schemes* (as per the *Economic Survey 2020-21*) cutting across sectors to strengthen the industry—

ATUFS The Amended Technology Upgradation Fund Scheme (ATUFS), is a revised version of

TUFS (Technology Upgradation Funds, 1999) and has the objective to modernise and upgrade the technology of the textile industry.

SITP The Scheme for Integrated Textiles Park (SITP) is for providing world class infrastructure facilities—of the 56 sanctioned textile parks, 23 were completed by April 2021.

SAMARTH The Scheme for Capacity Building in Textiles Sector (Samarth), a flagship scheme, is a placement-oriented programme targeting skill development of 10 lakh youth (2017-20) in the entire value chain of textiles (excluding Spinning & Weaving) in the organised sector.

PLI Scheme

With the objective to boost domestic manufacturing and cut import bills the Government introduced (March 2020) a *production-linked incentive (PLI)* scheme— companies will get 'incentives' on their incremental sales over the next 5 years period. Till April 2021, ***13 sectors*** were put under the scheme for which a total amount of around ₹1,97,291 lakh crores had been allocated by the Government. The list of the sectors is as given below:

1. Three sectors announced in *March 2020* (with an approved financial outlay of ₹ 51,311 crores over the 5 years) are—
   (i) Mobile Manufacturing and Specified Electronic Components
   (ii) Critical Key Starting materials/ Drug Intermediaries and Active Pharmaceutical Ingredients
   (iii) Manufacturing of Medical Devices.
2. Ten sectors selected by early *November 2020* (with an approved financial outlay of ₹ 1,45,980 crores over the 5 years) are—
   (i) Advance Chemistry Cell (ACC) Battery
   (ii) Electronic/Technology Products
   (iii) Automobiles & Auto Components
   (iv) Pharmaceuticals drugs
   (v) Telecom & Networking Products
   (vi) Textile Products: MMF segment and technical textiles
   (vii) Food Products
   (viii) High Efficiency Solar PV Modules
   (ix) White Goods (ACs & LED)
   (x) Specialty Steel

These sectors are highly capital-intensive (longer-term Government investments look very difficult into them) which bear benefits over a longer period of time. By offering these sectors incentive, the Government has not only designed a way out to promote investment into them but has tried making the whole PLI structure compliant to India's commitments to WTO by making it 'non-discriminatory' and 'neutral' with respect to domestic sales and exports.

The Incentives Under the scheme, the incentives (in the forms of sops and bonuses) are to be given as percentage of their production turnover (above a minimum floor value) and investment expenditures (on plant, machinery, equipment, research and development and transfer of technology) incurred by the manufacturing companies. However, investments done by companies on land and buildings for the project will not be considered for any incentives.

As per the *Economic Survey 2020-21,* the scheme will make Indian manufacturers globally competitive, attract investment in the areas of core competency and cutting-edge technology, ensure efficiencies, create economies of scale, enhance exports, provide conducive manufacturing ecosystem, and make India an integral part of the global supply chain especially for the sectors identified under the scheme.

As per some *critics,* the scheme will shield domestic firms from market competition—fuelled by the recent policies of import bans, higher import tariffs and decision to stay out of the RCEP (Regional Comprehensive Economic Partnership)— will weaken the market forces and hamper the process of privatisation and economic reforms.

FDI POLICY MEASURES

Foreign direct investment (FDI) is an important driver of economic growth which helps in—sustaining high growth rate, increasing productivity, a major source of non-debt financial resources, and employment generation. A favourable policy regime and sound business environment facilitate FDI flows.

The government has taken various reforms to liberalising and simplifying the FDI policy to provide *ease of doing business* climate in the country that will also lead to larger FDI inflows. A number of sectors have been liberalised, including defence, construction, broadcasting, civil aviation, plantation, trading, private sector banking, satellite establishment and operation and credit information companies. By early 2017, the government had taken the following policy steps to promote FDI in the economy:

- Upto 74 per cent (from the existing 49 per cent) FDI permitted in the *insurance* under the automatic route with certain safeguards *(Union Budget 2021-22)*.
- 100 per cent FDI permitted in manufacturing of *medical devices*; the *white label ATM* and *railway* infrastructure.
- 100 per cent FDI allowed in marketing of food products produced and manufactured in India *(Union Budget 2016–17)*.
- To undertake important banking sector reforms and public listing of general insurance companies undertake significant changes in FDI policy *(Union Budget 2016–17)*.
- Reforms in FDI policy in the areas of Insurance and Pension, Asset Reconstruction Companies, Stock Exchanges *(Union Budget 2016–17)*.
- A new policy for management of the PSUs, including strategic disinvestment—this is supposed to have liberal provisions for the FDI *(Union Budget 2019–20)*.

The FDI equity flows[55] to the country have been on the upswing since 2012-13—

- 2020-21 (April-September) the total FDI equity flows were **US$30.0 billion**.
- For 2019-20, the total FDI equity inflows were US$49.98 billion (as compared to US$44.37 billion during 2018-19).

The bulk of FDI equity flow was in the *non-manufacturing* sector leading to a reduction in the share of manufacturing sector. Within the *manufacturing* sector, industries like automobile, telecommunication, metallurgical, non-conventional energy, chemical (other than fertilisers), food processing, and petroleum & natural gas get the bulk of FDI equity flows— these industries together accounted for about 67 per cent of FDI equity flows into the manufacturing sector in 2019-20.

COVID-19 Impact In April 2020, the Government announced a change in the FDI policy and put into effect the requirement of 'prior clearance' for investments from countries with which India shares its land border. Similar provision has been put in place for any existing or future FDI in an Indian entity, directly or indirectly, where the resulting ownership falls within the same criteria. The FPI (foreign portfolio investment) route of foreign investment was left unchanged. The move

55. **Economics Survey 2020-21**, vol.2, pp. 280-81, Ministry of Finance, GoI, N. Delhi.

is aimed at checking 'opportunistic takeover' due to the *COVID-19 pandemic,* especially from China.

EASE OF DOING BUSINESS

Doing Business report, an annual publication (since 2004) of the World Bank Group ranks the countries of the world on the basis of their 'regulations that enhance business activity and those that constrain it'. Popularly known as 'ease of doing business report' it measures the state of business regulation in countries on the following 12 parameters[56] however, in ranking the last two parameters (in the list below) are not included:

1. Starting a business,
2. Dealing with construction permits,
3. Getting electricity,
4. Registering property,
5. Getting credit,
6. Protecting minority investors,
7. Paying taxes,
8. Trading across borders,
9. Enforcing contracts,
10. Resolving insolvency, and
11. Employing workers, and
12. Contracting with governments.

For ranking countries, the report analyses regulation that encourages efficiency and supports freedom to do business—through field surveys and interviews with corporate lawyers and company executives asking following *three questions* about government—

1. When do governments change regulation with a view to developing their private sector?
2. What are the characteristics of reformist governments?
3. What are the effects of regulatory change on different aspects of economic or investment activity?

In the *Doing Business 2020* report India has been ranked **63rd** among the 190 countries. This shows a jump of 14 ranks over the preceding report. Though, only two cities, Delhi and Mumbai are included in the report it speaks enough about the business regulatory environment in the country. The report has recognised India as one of the ten economies that have improved the most (from 142nd in 2014 to 63rd in 2019).

Though, India has been able to improve[57] its rank in 7 out of 10 parameters, it needs to work on other indicators to improve its ranking further to be ranked within the top 50 economies. India continues to trail in parameters such as Revoking Insolvency, Registering Property, Paying Taxes, and Enforcing Contracts. To get included among the top 30 countries (as the Government has targeted under its Output-Outcome Framework Document), India requires a nuts-and-bolts approach of feedback loops, monitoring and continuous adjustment.

MAKE IN INDIA

Make in India was launched in September 2014 by the GoI to encourage multinational as well as domestic companies to manufacture their products in India. The initiative is set to boost entrepreneurship, not only in manufacturing but in relevant infrastructure and *service sectors* as well. **Major features** of the initiative are as given below:

Vision is to attract both capital and technological investment in India enabling it to become the top

56. **Doing Business 2020**, World Bank, Washington DC, USA, 2020.

57. **Economics Survey 2020-21**, vol.2, pp. 276-78, Ministry of Finance, GoI, N. Delhi.

global FDI, surpassing even China and the United States.

Objective To focus on job creation and skill enhancement in 25 key sectors of the economy, including automobiles, aviation, biotechnology, defence manufacturing, electrical machinery, food processing, oil & gas, and pharmaceuticals, among others.

Logo is inspired from Ashoka Chakra – is a striding lion made of cogs, symbolising manufacturing, strength and national pride.

The initiative also aims at imposing *high quality standards* and the dimensions of *sustainability*. Key policies to be followed are: ease of doing business, getting away with archaic laws, 100 Smart Cities, disinvestment of the PSUs, skills and jobs for the youth, etc. Major *challenges* to the initiatives include – creating a healthy business environment, removal of unfavourable factors, more focus on Indian's MSMEs, lack of world class research and development (R&D), and comparisons with China's 'Made in China' campaign.

The initiative is based on *four pillars* — new processes; new infrastructure; new sectors; and new mindset. The **major steps** taken by the government in this regard are as summed-up below:

1. An interactive portal for dissemination of information and interaction with investors has been created with the objective of generating awareness about the investment opportunities and prospects of the country, to promote India as a preferred investment destination in markets overseas and to increase Indian share of global FDI.
2. *Invest India* set up as the national investment promotion and facilitation *agency*.
3. With the objective of promoting investment in the country, a full-fledged Investment Facilitation Cell has been set up under the Make in India initiative, primarily to support all investment queries as well as to *handhold and liaise* with various agencies on behalf of potential investors.
4. As envisaged by the *National Manufacturing Policy 2011*, Make in India seeks to enable the sector to contribute 25 per cent to the GDP and create 100 million additional jobs by 2022.
5. A number of steps to enhance the skills of workers/the unemployed in India in order to improve their employability.
6. In order to tap the creative potential and boost entrepreneurship in India, the *Start-up India* and *Stand-up India* campaign has been announced.
7. An innovation promotion platform called *AIM* (Atal Innovation Mission) and a techno-financial, incubation and facilitation programme called *SETU* (Self-Employment and Talent Utilization) are being implemented to encourage innovation and start-ups in India.
8. For supporting the financial needs of the *small* and *medium* enterprise sector and promote start-ups and entrepreneurship, various steps taken through Make in India–
   (i) The *India Aspiration Fund* has also been set up under the SIDBI for *venture capital financing* to the MSME sector.
   (ii) SIDBI Make in India Loan for Small Enterprises *(SMILE)* launched to offer quasi-equity and

term-based short-term loans to Indian SMEs on liberal terms.

(iii) A Micro Units Development Refinance Agency *(MUDRA)* Bank set up to provide development and refinance to commercial banks/NBFCs/cooperative banks for loans given to *micro-units*. MUDRA follows a 'credit-plus approach' by also providing several other services such as – financial literacy and addressing skill gaps, information gaps, etc.

During 2019-20, Government took the following major steps to attract more investment in manufacturing sector and boost the Make in India[58] campaign:

- Income Tax rate cut down to 15 per cent (effective rate to be 17.01 per cent inclusive of surcharge & cess) for companies incorporated on or after October 1, 2019 to attract investment in manufacturing and boost Make in India. Minimum Alternate Tax has also been dropped for such companies.
- To provide level playing field, custom duty was increased on certain items such as specified electrical/electronic/ telecom equipment and hardware, Poly Vinyl Chloride, specified articles of nylon, etc.
- The introduction of GST has integrated India into a single common market by breaking barriers to inter-state trade and commerce. By eliminating cascading of taxes and reducing transaction costs, it has enhanced ease of doing business and has provided an impetus to 'Make in India' campaign.

Assemble in India for the World The current environment (in the wake of Sino-US trade tension and rising protectionism across the world) presents[59] India an 'unprecedented' opportunity to chart a China-like, labour-intensive, export trajectory and thereby create unparalleled job opportunities. For this India needs to integrate *Assemble in India for the world* into Make in India. By doing so there is a possibility for India to raise its export market share (in the world exports) to about 3.5 per cent by 2025 and 6 per cent by 2030. Besides, this will create 4 crore well-paid jobs by 2025 and 8 crores by 2030. Other than suggesting to make India's trade policy as an enabler, the Survey has articulated a clear-headed strategy to grab this opportunity. A boost to Make in India may not only enhance exports but replace imports of products in which India has sufficient scope for expansion in domestic manufacturing.

START-UP INDIA

The Start-up India scheme was launched by the GoI in January 2016 with a slogan, *Start-up India* and *Stand-up India*. The mission/scheme aims to build a strong ecosystem for nurturing innovation, driving sustainable economic growth and generating large-scale employment opportunities. Apart from the technology sector the start-up movement will extend to a wide array of other sectors including agriculture, manufacturing, healthcare and education; and from existing tier 1 cities will extend to tier 2 and tier 3 cities including semi-urban and rural areas. The proposed *action plan (Economic Survey 2015–16)* for the firms is as given below:

58. Economic Survey 2019-20, Vol. 2, pp. 28-61, Ministry of Finance, GoI, N. Delhi.

59. Economic Survey 2019-20, Vol. 1, pp. 100-127, Ministry of Finance, GoI, N. Delhi.

- Creating a compliance regime based on self-certification to reduce the regulatory burden and keep compliance cost low.
- Setting up Start-up India hub to create a single point of contact for the entire Start-up ecosystem and enable knowledge exchange and access to funding.
- Rolling out of mobile app and portal to serve as the single platform for start-ups to interact with government and regulatory institutions and various stakeholders.
- Relaxed norms of public procurement.
- Legal support and fast-tracking of patent examination at lower costs to promote awareness of IPR (Intellectual Property Rights).
- Faster and easier exit norms.
- Providing funding support through a fund of funds with a corpus of ₹10,000 crore.
- Credit Guarantee Fund to catalyse entrepreneurship.
- Tax exemption on capital gains.
- Income Tax exemption for three years.
- Launch of AIM (Atal Innovation Mission) with the SETU (Self-Employment and Talent Utilisation) programme to serve as a platform for promotion of world-class innovation hubs, start-up businesses and other self-employment activities, particularly in technology-driven areas.
- Building innovation centres at national institutes to propel successful innovation through augmentation of incubation and R&D efforts.
- Setting up of 7 new research parks (modelled on the research park at IIT Madras).
- Promoting start-ups in the biotechnology sector.
- Launching of innovation-focused programmes for students to foster a culture of innovation in the field of science and technology.

To encourage the Startups, the Government has taken several new initiatives in the area:

- Acknowledging the need to reduce the regulatory burden self-certification allowed (under three labour laws and six environment laws).
- Startup India Hub has been developed as a single point of contact for them enabling them to exchange knowledge and access fund.
- A Fund of Funds for Startups (FFS) with a corpus of ₹10,000 crores has been created which is being managed by SIDBI.
- Several steps have also been taken to promote Industry-Academia Partnership and Incubation. With an aim to foster and facilitate Bio-entrepreneurship, Bio-clusters, Bio-Incubators, Technology Transfer Offices (TTOs) and Bio-Connect, offices are being established in research institutes and universities across India.
- Seed Fund and Equity Funding support is also provided to bio-tech Startups under the initiative.

The policy steps taken by the Government have left a very positive impact on innovation and entrepreneurship in the country. There is a need of encouraging start-ups at the district level to have an inclusive effect of income generation felt at grassroot level. The *present situation* (based on the data base of the World Bank and the Ministry of Corporate Affair) of start-ups[60] in the country is as given below:

- Today, India ranks *3rd* in number of new firms in the world (the number

60. **Economics Survey 2020-21**, vol.2, pp. 279-80, Ministry of Finance, GoI, N. Delhi.

increasing from 70,000 in 2014 to 1,24,000 in 2018).

- By December 2020, there were a total of 41,061 start-ups in the country reporting a total of 39,000 jobs.
- Birth of new firms is very heterogeneous across the districts and sectors—moreover, it is dispersed and not restricted to just a few cities.
- In formal sector while new firms grew with an annual growth rate of 3.8 per cent between 2006-14, for the period 2014-18 the growth rate has been 12.2 per cent.
- Reflecting India's new economic structure (i.e. comparative advantage in the services sector), new firm creation in services is significantly higher than that in manufacturing, infrastructure or agriculture.
- A 10 per cent increase in registration of new firms in a district yields a 1.8 per cent increase in GDDP (gross district domestic product)—being maximal in manufacturing and services sectors.
- Entrepreneurship is fostered by the factors like, literacy, education, quality of physical infrastructure and ease of doing business (like flexible labour laws).

Start-ups drive economic growth (wealth creation), create employment and foster a culture of innovation which will turn the youths *from job seekers to job givers*—and thus can emerge as the tool to tap the demographic dividend.

COVID-19 AND I NDUSTRIAL REFORMS

In the wake of coronavirus pandemic, India announced a major drive towards self-reliance by launching the ambitious *Atmanirbhar Bharat Abhiyan* in May 2020. Under the campaign, the following industrial reform measures were announced by the Government—

Defence Import of some weapons banned; defence production to be indigenised; provision of a separate budget for defence capital procurement; FDI limit in defence manufacturing under automatic route raised to 74 per cent (from 49 per cent); and Ordnance Factory Board (OFB) to be corporatised and listed on stock market (to improve autonomy, efficiency and accountability).

Space Private participation to be encouraged; creation of a level playing field for private players allowing them to use ISRO facilities and participate in future projects on space travel and planetary exploration; and geo-spatial data policy to be eased to make remote-sensing data available more widely to technology entrepreneurs.

Aviation 6 more airports to be auctioned on PPP (private public partnership) mode; 12 more airports to invite private investment; airspace restrictions eased to make flying more efficient; and MRO (maintenance, repair and operations) tax structure to be rationalised to make India an MRO hub.

Minerals Government monopoly on coal removed and commercial mining introduced (on a revenue sharing basis); private sector to be allowed to bid for 50 coal blocks; and private players to be allowed to undertake exploration activities.

Power Power utilities and distribution companies in Union Territories to be privatised (based on a new tariff policy).

Atomic Research Atomic research reactors to be set up in PPP mode for the production of medical isotopes; facilities to be set up in PPP mode for food preservation using irradiation technology; and TDICs (technology development cum incubation centres) to be set up to link robust start-up ecosystem to nuclear sector.

Social Infrastructure To boost private investment in social infrastructure the viability gap funding (VGF) quantum has been increased to 30 per cent (Centre plus state combined) of the project cost (which used to be 20 per cent as in case of other sectors). The scheme is estimated for an expenditure of ₹8,100 crore.

The measures announced aim at involving greater participation from the private sector. For fulfilling the aims of *self-reliance,* the policy decisions are 'bolder' and 'speedier' in approach but they seem to be need of the hour to unshackle the hidden potential of the economy.

INDIAN INFRASTRUCTURE

An Introduction

Infrastructure is the 'lifeline' of an economy as protein is the lifeline of the human body. Whichever sector be the prime moving force of an economy, i.e., primary, secondary or tertiary, suitable level of infrastructure presence is a pre-requisite for growth and development. This is why the Government of India has always given priority to the developmental aspects of the sector. But the level of preparedness and performance had been always less than required by the economy. Which sector is called the infrastructure? *Basically, the goods and services usually requiring higher investment, considered essential for the proper functioning of an economy is called the infrastructure of an economy.*[61] Such sectors might be as many as required by a particular economy such as power, transportation, communication, water supply, sewerage, housing, urban amenities, etc.

There are three sectors which are considered as the infrastructure universally around the world namely power, transportation and communication. Since, infrastructure benefits the whole economy, it has been often argued by the economists that the sector should be funded by the government by means of taxation, partly not wholly.

Indian infrastructure sector is clearly overstrained and has suffered from underinvestment in the post-reforms period.[62] Infrastructure bottlenecks are always constraint in achieving a higher growth for the economy. India needs massive investment, both from the public and private sectors, to overcome infrastructure bottlenecks. Investments by the public and private sectors are not alternatives, but complimentary to each other as the required investment is very high. Public investment in the sector depends upon the ability to raise resources (capital) in the public sector and this in turn depends upon the ability to collect the user charges from the consumers. To make this happen following *three* factors are extremely important:

1. Reform of the power sector,
2. Introduction of road user charges (either directly via tolls or indirectly via a cess on petrol diesel), and
3. Rationalisation of railway fares.

Experts[63] have suggested for expanding public investment in the sector supplemented duly by a vigorous effort of attracting private investment (domestic as well as foreign). Creating the conducive environment to attract private investment in infrastructure should include:

1. Simplification and transparency in the clearance procedures;
2. Unbundling an infrastructure project so that the private sector may go for only those unbundled segment of the project whose they are able to bear; and

61. ***Oxford Dictionary of Business***, (New Delhi: Oxford University Press, 2004).

62. ***India Infrastructure Report 1994.*** (New Delhi: Government of India, 1994).

63. One of such major suggestion was forwarded by Sachs, Varsheny and Bajpai, ***India in the Era of Economic Reforms***, p. 79.

3. Providing credible and independent regulatory framework so that the private players get fair treatment.

Official Ideology

Putting in place the quality and efficient infrastructure services is essential to realise the full potential of the growth impulses surging through the Indian economy. There is now a widespread consensus[64] (clearly accepted by the Planning Commission) that exclusive dependence on the government for the provision of all infrastructure services introduces difficulties concerning adequate scale of investment, technical efficiency, proper enforcement of user charges, and competitive market structure. At the same time, complete reliance on private production, particularly without appropriate regulation, is also not likely to produce optimal outcomes.[65] India, while stepping up public investment in infrastructure, has been actively engaged in finding the appropriate policy framework, which gives the private sector adequate confidence and incentives to invest on a massive scale, but simultaneously preserves adequate checks and balances through transparency, competition and regulation.

The approach towards infrastructure has gone for a *transformational change* since the new policy think tank Niti Aayog came into being. The Seven-Year Strategy Framework (titled as 'Strategy for New India @75') document of the Niti has devoted a full section on it (out of its four sections). The document believes that infrastructure is the physical foundations of growth and development which are crucial to enhancing the competitiveness of Indian businesses as also ensuring the citizens' *ease of living*. The sector needs an unprecedented scale of investment that is why the Government is exploring all possible models of resource mobilisation—the hybrid annuity model (HAM) of the public private partnership (PPP) mode is expected to emerge an effective tool in this regard.

POWER

Electricity is essential for economic activity and is also required in leisure time. In last few decades, the power sector has witnessed substantial transformation from both the demand (universal electrification) and supply-side (the advent of green energy)— with commendable progress made in the generation and transmission of electricity in India. The total installed capacity has increased to 3,73,436 MW by late 2020 (2,31,321 MW of thermal, 45,699 MW of hydro, 6,780 MW of nuclear, and 89,636 MW of renewables and others).

As per the Government, a perceptible decline has been seen in energy deficit— which may be partially attributed to enhanced energy efficiency and improved energy intensity (energy intensity is defined as the quantity of energy required to produce a unit of output). Thus, lower the energy intensity better it is. As per the *Econo mic Survey 2020-21,* the energy intensity of India (at 2011-12 prices) decreased from 65.6 toes (tons of oil equivalent) per crore rupees in 2011-12 to 55.43 toe per crore rupees in 2018-19 while, during the period, the per capita consumption increased from 0.47 toe to 0.58 toe respectively.

In 2014, the Government launched the IPDS (Integrated Power Development Scheme) to facilitate state utilities (i.e., DISCOMs) to ensure quality and reliable 24x7 power supply in the urban areas. By September 2020, distribution strengthening was been completed in 442 of the 546 circles. Further, the country has already accomplished two major landmarks in the arena of rural electrification:

64. Ministry of Finance, ***Economic Survey,*** 2006–07, (New Delhi: Government of India, 2007).

65. ***India Infrastructure Report 2007*** (New Delhi: Government of India, 2011).

1. 100 per cent village electrification under Deen Dayal Upadhyaya Gram Jyoti Yojana, and
2. Universal household electrification under the Saubhagya (the Pradhan Mantri Sahaj Bijli Har Ghar Yojana).

T&D losses have been declining since 2001-02 (32.86 per cent) but are still substantial. As per the latest available data *(Economic Survey 2020-21)* compared to the T&D losses of the peer countries (6 per cent in China, 10 per cent in S. Africa, 13 per cent in Russia, 17.5 per cent in Brazil), India's T&D losses are very high (21.5 per cent) against the global average of around 8.5 per cent and S. Korea being the best at 3.6 per cent only.

Without improving the performance of the electricity distribution companies (DISCOMs) of the state governments efforts towards 100 per cent village electrification, 24 × 7 power supply and clean energy cannot bear fruit. Power outages also adversely affect national priorities like 'Make in India' and 'Digital India'. In addition, default on bank loans by financially stressed DISCOMs has the potential of seriously impacting the banking sector and the economy at large.

UDAY SCHEME

For financial and operational turnaround of DISCOMs and to ensure a sustainable permanent solution to the problem, the *UDAY* (Ujwal DISCOM Assurance Yojana) was launched by the GoI, in November 2015. The scheme also aims to reduce interest burden of the DISCOMs, cost of power and their AT&C (Aggregate Transmission & Technical) losses.

Due to legacy issues, DISCOMs are trapped in a vicious cycle with operational losses being funded by debt. Outstanding debt of DISCOMs were ₹4.3 lakh crore by 2014-15, with interest rates upto 14-15 per cent and AT&C losses as high as 22 per cent. The scheme assures the rise of vibrant and efficient DISCOMs through a permanent resolution of past as well as potential future issues of the sector. It empower DISCOMs with the opportunity to break even in the next 3 years. This is to take place through *four* initiatives:

1. Improving operational efficiencies;
2. Reduction of cost of power;
3. Reduction in interest cost; and
4. Enforcing financial discipline.

Operational efficiency to be improved via steps such as – compulsory smart metering, upgradation of transformers, meters, etc., *energy efficiency* via steps like efficient LED bulbs, agricultural pumps, fans & air-conditioners etc.—to reduce the average AT&C loss from around 22 per cent to 15 per cent and eliminate the gap between ARR (Average Revenue Realised) and ACS (Average Cost of Supply) by 2018-19.

Reduction in cost of power would be achieved through measures such as increased supply of cheaper domestic coal, coal linkage rationalisation, liberal coal swaps from inefficient to efficient plants, coal price rationalisation based on GCV (Gross Calorific Value), supply of washed and crushed coal, and faster completion of transmission lines. NTPC alone is expected to save ₹0.35 unit through higher supply of domestic coal and rationalisation and swapping of coal which will be passed on to DISCOMs.

The *salient features* of the scheme are as given below[66]:

- States shall take over 75 per cent of the DISCOM debt—50 per cent in 2015-16 and 25 per cent in 2016-17. This will reduce the interest cost to 8-9 per cent, from as high as 14-15 per cent.
- GoI will not include the debt taken over by the states in the calculation of fiscal

66. Ministry of Finance, Economic Survey 2015-16, pp. 137–138.

deficit of the States in the financial years 2015-16 and 2016-17.

- States will issue non-SLR including SDL (State Development Loan) bonds in the market or directly to the respective banks and Financial Institutions (FIs).
- DISCOM debt not taken over by the State shall be converted by the Banks and FIs into loans or bonds with interest rate not more than the bank's base rate plus 0.1 per cent. Alternately, this debt may be fully or partly issued by the DISCOM as State guaranteed DISCOM bonds at the prevailing market rates which shall be equal to or less than bank base rate plus 0.1 per cent.
- States to take over the future losses of DISCOMs in a graded manner.
- States accepting UDAY and performing as per operational milestones will be given additional/priority funding through Deendayal Upadhyaya Gram Jyoti Yojana (DDUGJY), Integrated Power Development Scheme (IPDS), Power Sector Development Fund (PSDF) or other such schemes of Ministry of Power and Ministry of New and Renewable Energy. States not meeting operational milestones will be liable to forfeit their claim on IPDS and DDUGJY grants.
- Such States shall also be supported with additional coal at notified prices and, in case of availability through higher capacity utilisation, low cost power from NTPC and other Central PSUs.
- UDAY is optional for all States. However, States are encouraged to take the benefit at the earliest as benefits are dependent on the performance.

Basically, financial liabilities of DISCOMs are the contingent liabilities of the respective States and need to be recognized as such. Debt of DISCOMs is *de facto* borrowing of States which is not counted in *de jure* borrowing. However, credit rating agencies and multilateral agencies are conscious of this de facto debt in their appraisals. The 14th Finance Commission also had similar observations. Similarly, the new scheme, DDUGY (Deendayal Upadhyaya Gram Jyoti Yojana), was launched to promote rural electrification. The budgetary support for continuation of the RGGVY (Rajiv Gandhi Grameen Vidyutikaran) in 12th and 13th Plans, has also been carried forward to the new scheme.

UDAY accelerates the process of reform across the entire power sector and will ensure that power is accessible, affordable and available for all. UDAY truly heralds the *uday* (rise), of a **'Power'**ful India.

AT&C Losses Due to lack of adequate investment on 'transmission and distribution' (T&D) works, the T&D losses have been consistently on the higher side, and reached to the level of 32.86 per cent in the year 2000–01. The reduction of these losses was essential to bring economic viability to the state utilities (SEBs). As the T&D loss was not able to capture all the losses in the network, concept of *Aggregate Technical and Commercial (AT&C)* loss was introduced. AT&C loss captures technical as well as commercial losses in the network and is a true indicator of total losses in the system.

High technical losses in the system are primarily *due to* inadequate investments over the years for system improvement works, which has resulted in unplanned extensions of the distribution lines, overloading of the system elements like transformers and conductors, and lack of adequate reactive power support.

The commercial losses are mainly due to:

1. low metering efficiency,
2. theft, and
3. pilferages

This may be eliminated by improving metering efficiency, proper energy accounting & auditing and improved billing & collection efficiency. Fixing of accountability of the personnel/feeder managers may help considerably in reduction of AT&C loss.

Aimed mainly at bringing down the AT&C of the state Discoms, Uday is the 4th scheme sponsored by the Government—the APRDP (Accelerated Power Development and Reform Programme) in 2001; Restructured-APRDP in 2008; and the IPDS (Integrated Power Development Scheme) in 2014 which subsumed the R-APRDP.

UDAY's Performance As per the Government, the performance of the scheme cannot be called very positive. Of the 28 states that implemented it, 10 have shown either reduced losses or profits in 2019-20. Also, even as most states registered an improvement in reducing the ACS-ARR gap and in bringing down AT&C losses, they are way behind in achieving the targets as per the UDAY schedule (similar to the earlier attempts at it).

During 2020-21, the Government released a loan of ₹ 90,000 crores to the states' DISCOMs to clear their past dues of the power producers. States were asked to reduce AT&C losses and also reduce the ACS-ARR gap which will earn them additional net borrowing space of 0.25 per cent of their GSDP (gross state domestic product) in the year.

Meanwhile, the *Union Budget 2021-22* has announced to introduce a revamped, reforms-based and result-linked **new** *Power Distribution Sector Scheme* (believed to be a replacement for the existing UDAY scheme)— for which a sum of ₹3,05,984 crores has been allocated over a period of 5 years. Besides, the Budget also announced to give consumers alternative to choose the DISCOMs (which is aimed at enhancing competitiveness of the DISCOMs).

RAILWAYS

Indian Railways (IR) with over 67,580 route kms, is the *3rd largest* network in the world under single management. During 2019-20, IR carried 1.2 billion tonnes of freight and 8.1 billion passengers—making it the world's largest passenger carrier and 4th largest freight carrier. IR endeavours to provide safe, efficient, and competitive means of transport by adopting technological changes including through development of specific indigenous systems in signalling to avert train collision and to enable real time management of trains, in keeping with the *Atmanirbhar Bharat Mission* and by maintaining cleanliness standards under Swachh Bharat Abhiyan.

Indian Railways (IR) is faced with a number of challenges. For speedy capacity creation, IR recognises the importance of enhancing project execution capabilities. Considering the enormity of the resources required for plan investment in rail infrastructure, and given the limitation of public resources, efforts are on by IR to generate sufficient *internal surplus*, and tap innovative methods of financing, to meet these needs.

The focus is on prioritising investments in important areas like dedicated freight corridors, high speed rail, high capacity rolling stock, last mile rail linkages and port connectivity, and attracting private and FDI investments to supplement available resources. Major *initiatives* taken by the GoI are as given below:

- Various measures to improve passenger amenities, infrastructure and services, and initiatives under Make in India, freight initiative, resource mobilisation initiative and green initiatives, etc.
- Mobile application for freight operations – Parichaalan – has been introduced.

- IR is installing solar panels on rooftops of coaches for the train lighting system. Solar plants of 50 MW to come up on the rooftops of IR buildings.
- Diamond Quadrilateral network of High Speed Rail connecting major metros (Delhi, Mumbai, Kolkata and Chennai) to come up.
- *Safety* got the highest priority— as a result, the number of train accidents came down to 55 in 2019-20 (from 104 in 2016-17) despite a substantial increase in the traffic volume.
- Private players allowed to operate in the Railways sector through the PPP mode under the ***New India New Railway*** initiative— over 150 pairs of train services identified for the introduction of 151 modern train sets or rakes through private participation.

  The private entity shall be responsible for financing, procuring, operating, and maintenance of the trains and shall have the freedom to decide on the fare to be charged from its passengers. Selection of the private entities is being done through a two-stage competitive bidding process, which is expected to be completed by *May 2021* and the private trains are likely to be introduced in *2023-24.*
- Kisan Rail service was introduced (in Union Budget 2020-21) to provide better market opportunity by transporting perishables and agri-product, including milk, meat, and fish.
- ***National Rail Plan*** (NPR) was developed in 2020-21, to develop capacity (both infrastructure and rolling stock) ahead of demand. It aims at developing adequate rail infrastructure by 2030 to cater to the projected traffic requirements up to 2050— to increase the modal share of rail in freight from the current level of 27 per cent to 45 per cent.

High Speed Train Project The feasibility report of the Japan International Cooperation Agency (JICA) was approved by the GoI in December 2015. A new special purpose vehicle with 50 per cent equity participation from the Ministry of Railways and 50 per cent from the state governments of Maharashtra and Gujarat will be set up to implement the project. *Major features* of the project are as given below:

- Project completion cost is approximately ₹97,636 crore (including price escalation, interest during construction and import duties) – average per km cost of construction works out to be ₹140 crore. To be completed in 7 years.
- Japan's ODA (official development assistance) will be ₹79,165 crore (81 per cent of project cost) for 50 years with 0.1 per cent interest and a 15-year moratorium.
- Total length of the proposed corridor will be 508 km between the Bandra Kurla complex in Mumbai and Sabarmati/Ahmedabad in Gujarat – to cover 12 stations with a maximum design speed of 350 kmph (with a 320 kmph operating speed).

Train 18 India's first engine-less, semi high-speed train (160 kmph), the *Train18* (rechristened *Vande Bharat Express*) was launched in February 2019. The train is equipped with the finest amenities (such as—comfortable 180-degree rotational reclining chairs, mobile charging points, diffused lighting and reading lights, GPS passenger information service, CCTV cameras, talkback facility to connect with the driver in case of emergency, sensor-controlled bathroom fitting for differently-abled people and modular toilets with bio-discharge vacuum systems).

Designed and built by Integral Coach Factory, Chennai (under the Make in India initiative) it is estimated to cost 40 per cent less than a similar train imported from Europe. Its successor called *Train 20* is also being developed which will replace the existing long-distance trains of today in the coming years.

 ROADS

India runs on the road—be it the passenger or goods movement—road transport is the dominant mode of transportation. The transport sector has a share of 4.6 per cent in the country's GVA of which roughly 67 per cent is contributed by road transport. Today India has the *2nd* largest road network (**63.86** lakh kms) in the world after the USA (66.45 lakh km).

Under the proactive policy approach of the Government, road network expanded faster—during the last decade (2009-19), the national highways recorded a CAGR (compound annual growth rate) of 7.25 per cent followed by rural roads (6.25 per cent) and urban roads (4.27 per cent). The pace at which roads have been constructed has grown significantly from 12 kms per day in 2014-15 to *30 kms per day* in 2019-20 it moderated in 2020-21 (mostly on account of the COVID-19 shock).

Financing of the NHDP A part of the fuel cess imposed on petrol and diesel is allocated to the NHAI for funding the implementation of the NHDP. The NHAI leverages the cess flow to borrow additional funds from the debt market. Till date, such borrowings have been limited to funds raised through 54 EC (capital gains tax exemption) bonds and the short-term overdraft facility. Government has also taken loans for financing projects under the NHDP from the World Bank, Asian Development Bank and Japan Bank for International Cooperation which are passed on to the NHAI partly in the form of grants and partly as loan. The NHAI has also availed a direct loan of US$ 180 million from the ADB for the Surat-Manor Expressway Project.

Special Accelerated Road Development Programme for North-East region (SARDP-NE) aims at improving road connectivity to state capitals, district headquarters, and remote places of the north-east region. Development of roads in Left Wing Extremism *(LWE)*-affected areas in the states of Andhra Pradesh, Bihar, Chhattisgarh, Jharkhand, Madhya Pradesh, Maharashtra, Odisha, and Uttar Pradesh is continuing; Prime Minister's Reconstruction Plan *(PMRP)* for Jammu and Kashmir, launched in November 2014.

Pradhan Mantri Gram Sadak Yojna (PMGSY) Launched to provide single all-weather road connectivity to eligible unconnected habitations having population of 500 persons and above in plain areas and 250 persons and above in hill states, tribal (Schedule V) areas, desert (as identified in the Desert Development Programme) areas, and LWE-affected districts as identified by the Ministry of Home Affairs. Rural roads has also been identified as one of the *six components* of Bharat Nirman which has the goal of providing all-weather road connectivity to all villages with a population of 1,000 (500 in the case of hilly or tribal areas).

Bharatmala Pariyojana: Launched in 2015–16, this is a new umbrella program for the highways sector that focuses on optimising efficiency of freight and passenger movement across the country. It *aims* at bridging critical infrastructure gaps through effective interventions like development of Economic Corridors, Inter Corridors and Feeder Routes, National Corridor Efficiency Improvement, Border and International connectivity roads, Coastal and Port connectivity roads and Green-field expressways. The *objective* of the program is to achieve optimal resource allocation for a holistic highway development.

CIVIL AV IATION

India's aviation market is one of the fastest growing in the world. Its domestic traffic has more than doubled from around 61 million in 2013-14 to around 137 million in 2019-20, a growth of over 14 per cent per annum. As per the *Economic Survey 2020-21,* from the *third largest* domestic aviation market, it is expected to become the *third largest* overall (including domestic and international traffic) by the year 2024-25.

Airport infrastructure development continues to be a matter of concern. Upgradation of many airports, including construction of new terminals, upgradation in 37 non-metro airports, for improving air navigation services the Airport Authority of India (AAI) is installing the new ATS automation system. In order to address issues concerning viability of the civil aviation sector, particularly the airline industry, a Working Group of 2019 gave the following recommendations:

- state governments should rationalise the value added tax (VAT) on aviation turbine fuel (ATF),
- foreign airlines be permitted to invest in domestic airlines undertakings,
- direct import of ATF by airlines for their own consumption be allowed,
- airlines should be asked to prepare their turnaround plans,
- fare structure should be reviewed by airlines to cover the cost of their operations,
- an economic regulatory framework suggested with regard to excessive/ predatory pricing.

Air passenger travel and aircraft movements were severely hit by the COVID-19 pandemic, though, as per the *Economic Survey 2020-21,* they were predicted to reach pre-COVID level by early 2021 as a result of swift and decisive interventions and effective measures put in place by the Government.

TELECOM

The telecom is among the three-basic infrastructure of an economy. In case of India, it plays even bigger role for implementation of the JAM (JanDhan Aadhar Mobile) trinity based social sector schemes and other pro-development initiative of the Government. The sector has been recognised all over the world as a powerful tool for development and poverty reduction. As part of the Digital India Campaign, the Government has laid considerable emphasis on broadband for all. Efforts are being made to address the digital divide by extending inclusive internet access to every citizen. The sector has grown with a rapid pace in the last few years and as per the *Economic Survey 2020-21,* it stands at a very strong position:

- The wireless telephony constitutes 98.3 per cent of all subscriptions whereas the share of landline telephones now stands at only 1.7 per cent.
- The overall tele density in India stood at 86.6 per cent by the end of November 2020, whereas tele density in rural and urban areas were 59.1 per cent and 139.0 per cent respectively.
- The number of internet subscribers (both broadband and narrowband put together) stood at 776.45 million at the end of September 2020 as compared to 636.73 million in March 2019.
- The wireless data usage grew at exponential rate during the calendar year 2019 and was at 76.47 Exa bytes which has already reached 75.21 Exa byte during January-September 2020.
- Average wireless data consumption per subscriber per month increased from 9.1 GB in March 2019 to 12.2 GB in June 2020. The reduced cost of data could enable affordable internet access at a rapid pace. As on June-2020, the cost of wireless data stood at ₹ 10.55 per GB.

For achieving the goal of Digital India, the *BharatNet* is among the most ambitious projects of the Government. Under the project, network infrastructure is being established for Broadband Highways, accessible on a non-discriminatory basis to provide affordable broadband services to citizens and institutions in rural areas, in partnership with States and the private sector. By January 2021, about 4.87 lakh kms of optical fiber cable were laid to cover 1.63 lakh Gram Panchayats (GPs) and nearly 1.51 lakh GPs had become service ready.

MINERALS

Minerals play a vital role in the process of development and they are slated to play even greater role in the coming times as economy moves for electric vehicles and the fourth industrial revolution. Though, India has huge reserves of important minerals, the country has not been able to realise its mining potential due to several legislative and procedural reasons. To unshackle the hidden potential of the sector, the Government amended (in 2015) the MMDR (Mines and Mineral Development and Regulation) Act, 1957— heralding major structural reforms in the sector:

- The move towards grant of mineral concessions through *auction* as against the earlier method of 'first-come-first-served' brought in transparency and removed discretion in the grant of mineral concessions.
- Establishment of the NMET (National Mineral Exploration Trust) for providing impetus to exploration.
- Uniform lease period of 50 years.
- Dispensing of the requirement of previous approval of the Central Government for grant of mineral concession other than for atomic minerals, coal and lignite.
- Establishing DMF (District Mineral Foundation) for benefit of people and areas affected by mining.

In 2020-21, the Government took the following new steps[67] in furthering the reform process:

- The MMDR Act was amended in January 2020 to provide transfer of all valid statutory clearances vested with the old lessee to the new successful bidder up to a period of two years for all brownfield mines (so that there is no disruption in production and supply of raw material in the industry).
- At present after auction of mines, the successful bidder applies for clearances and after obtaining clearances production starts. Generally, getting clearances takes longer times, anywhere around 3 to 4 years and consequently production is delayed. For immediate start of production after auction, approach adopted in the amended Act is that States need to obtain the clearances before auction—as a result, production will start without any delay (because clearances are already available).
- To boost growth, employment and to bring state of art technology in the mining sector in general and in exploration in particular, under *Atmanirbhar Bharat Abhiyan,* in 2020-21, the Government announced the following structural reforms:
  - Introduction of a seamless composite exploration-cum-mining-cum-production regime.
  - 500 mining blocks to be offered through an open and transparent auction process.

67. Economic Survey 2020-21, vol. 2, pp. 300-02, Ministry of Finance, GoI, N. Delhi.

- Joint auction of bauxite and coal mineral blocks.
- Removal of distinction between captive and non-captive mines.
- Mineral index for different mineral.
- Rationalisation of stamp duty.
- Schedule of Charges (SoC) approved (first time) for exploration projects which will be funded from the NMET.
- So that appropriate and timely policy intervention could be devised, the AIMS (Aluminium Import Monitoring System) and CIMS (Copper Import Monitoring System) to be set up to monitor the import of aluminium and copper.

MARITIME AGENDA 2010-20

The **objective** of the Maritime Agenda 2010–20 is not only creating more capacity but setting up ports on a par with the best international ports in terms of performance:

- A target of 3,130 MT port capacity has been set for the year 2020. More than 50 per cent of this capacity is to be created in the non-major ports as the traffic handled by these ports is expected to increase to 1,280 MT.
- This enlarged scale of operation is expected to reduce transaction costs considerably and make Indian ports *globally competitive.*
- Proposed investment in major and non-major ports by 2020 is expected to be around ₹2,96,000 crore.
- Most of the investment to come from the private sector including FDI (up to 100 per cent under the automatic route is permitted for construction and maintenance of ports), and private sector to fund most of the projects through PPP or on 'build operate transfer' (BOT) or 'build operate own transfer' (BOOT) basis.
- Private-sector participation will not only increase investment in the ports infrastructure, it is expected to improve operations of the ports through the induction of the latest technology and better management practices.
- Public funds will be mainly deployed for common use infrastructure facilities like deepening of port channels, rail and road connectivity from ports to hinterland, etc.

SMART CITIES

The GoI has launched the Smart Cities Mission (SCM) with the collaboration of states and UTs for urban development. The *purpose* of the mission is—to drive economic growth and improve the quality of life of people by enabling local area development and harnessing technology, especially technology that leads to smart outcomes.

The Mission targets *promoting* cities that provide core infrastructure and give a decent quality of life to its citizens, a clean and sustainable environment and application of 'smart' solutions. The focus is on sustainable and inclusive development and the idea is to look at compact areas and create a replicable model which will act like a lighthouse to other aspiring cities. The smart city includes the following *core* infrastructure development:

- adequate water supply;
- assured electricity supply;
- sanitation, including solid waste management;
- efficient urban mobility and public transport;
- affordable housing, especially for the poor;
- robust IT connectivity and digitalisation;
- good governance, especially e-Governance and citizen participation;

- sustainable environment;
- safety and security of citizens, particularly women, children and the elderly; and
- health and education.

Strategy The strategic components of area-based development in the mission are:

- city improvement (retrofitting);
- city renewal (redevelopment);
- city extension (greenfield development); and
- a pan-city initiative in which smart solutions are applied.

Retrofitting will introduce planning in an existing built-up area to achieve smart city objectives, along with other objectives, to make the existing area more efficient and liveable. In retrofitting, an area consisting of more than 500 acres will be identified by the city in consultation with citizens. Redevelopment will effect a replacement of the existing built-up environment and enable co-creation of a new layout with enhanced infrastructure using mixed land use and increased density. Redevelopment envisages an area of more than 50 acres, identified by urban local bodies (ULBs) in consultation with citizens.

Greenfield development will introduce most of the smart solutions in a previously vacant area (more than 250 acres) using innovative planning, plan financing and plan implementation tools (e.g. land pooling/land reconstitution) with provision for affordable housing, especially for the poor. Greenfield development is required around cities in order to address the needs of the expanding population.

Finance: The Mission will cover 100 cities which have been distributed among the states and UTs on the basis of equitable criteria. The distribution of smart cities will be reviewed after two years of the implementation of the mission.

The Smart City Mission will be operated as a Centrally Sponsored Scheme (CSS) and the central government proposes to give it financial support to the extent of ₹48,000 crore over five years, i.e. on an average ₹100 crore per city per year. An equal amount, on a matching basis, will have to be contributed by the state/ULB; therefore, nearly one lakh crore of government/ULB funds will be available for smart cities development. In the first phase of implementation, *twenty* cities have been shortlisted to roll out the programme.

The migration from the rural areas to the cities is increasing with a higher pace. A *neo middle class* is emerging which has aspirations of better living standards. With all these challenges to the successful implementation of the mission, the centre of attention is the citizen. In other words, a smart city will work towards ensuring the best for all people, regardless of social status, age, income levels and gender, only when *citizens will actively participate* in governance and reforms. Smart Cities Mission requires involvement of *smart people* in the process of making decisions on deploying smart solutions, implementing reforms, doing more with less, maintaining oversight during implementation and designing post-project structures in order to make the smart city developments sustainable.

As per the *Economic Survey 2020-21*, a total of 1987 projects were already completed by December 2020, while 4375 projects were under completion— with total tendered projects worth ₹ 1.66 lakh crores.

Other Urban Infrastructure With increasing urbanisation, opportunities as well as challenges related to urban infrastructure are also increasing. In this context, up to early 2016, the government has taken various *new initiatives* to improve urban infrastructure:

- *SBM (Swachh Bharat Mission)* aims at making India *free from open defecation* and at achieving 100 per cent scientific management of municipal solid waste in 4041 statutory towns/cities in the country. The targets set for the mission which have to be achieved by 2 October 2019.

- *HRIDAY* (National Heritage City Development and Augmentation Yojana) aims at preserving and revitalising the soul and unique character of *heritage cities* in India. In the first phase, it contains 12 cities – Ajmer, Amaravati, Amritsar, Badami, Dwarka, Mathura, Puri, Varanasi, Velankanni, Kanchipuram, Gaya and Warangal.
- *AMRUT* (Atal Mission for Rejuvenation and Urban Transformation) aims at improving basic urban infrastructure in 500 cities/towns which will be known as *mission cities/towns*. This is a Centrally Sponsored Scheme (CSS) funded by GoI, States and the local bodies.

A number of other initiatives in the existing scheme of the policy framework have also been taken – public transport through Bus Rapid Transit Systems (BRTS) approved for 11 cities under the JNNURM (Jawaharlal Nehru National Urban Renewal Mission); Buses and Metro Rail Projects to be equipped with ITS (Intelligent Transport System).

PRIVATE SECTOR AND URBANISATION

Proper urban planning becomes an important issue for India as it is urbanising fast. Given the Government push to the Smart City scheme, it will be needful to tap the potential of every possible candidate in this regard. One of such candidate is the private sector. There are few examples where we find the sector able to develop praiseworthy townships—in certain areas beating the public sector also—though they have their own limitations, too. Two such cases have been cited by the **Economic Survey 2016-17** (quoting case studies)[68] in this regard—of two different time periods:

1. **Gurgaon:** It was in 2001 when Haryana government removed restrictions on the land acquisition process and empowered the HUDA (Haryana Urban Development Authority) and allowed private builders to develop township on the erstwhile agricultural land—and here started the development of today's Gurgaon. Today the city is under the control of HUDA, Municipal Corporation of Gurgaon (created in 2008) and the private builders. In Gurgaon, the private sector has stepped in to address many of the failings of the public sector, with mixed success:
   - (i) Corrected the failure of the public sector by creating private sewage, water, electricity, security and fire prevention.
   - (ii) Rapid Metro in Gurgaon was built by DLF and Infrastructure Leasing & Financial Services Limited (IL&FS), with HUDA providing the requisite land.
   - (iii) Roads are of good quality.
   - (iv) Shortfall in transport facilities is covered by the private modes of transport.

   Precisely speaking, private players have addressed most challenges but they have been unable to provide services beyond their own property line as cooperation lacks amongst them and the authorities. The public authorities have had limited success in providing the city with large scale infrastructure. The failures of the city are also well known:
   - (i) It suffered from lack of cohesive urban plan and its explosive growth has

68. **Economic Survey 2016-17** (Vol. 1, p. 313) cites the studies of S. Rajagopalan & A. Tabarrok, ***Lessons from Gurgaon, India's Private City***, in D. Anderson & S. Moroni (Ed.), Cities and Private Planning, Cheltenham, UK: Edward Elgar, 2014.

outpaced the planning efforts (like in any other Indian cities).

(ii) Multiple layers of local and higher authorities, having greater power to extract rents, have increased the transaction costs for the private builders. Different private builders have to seek different political patronage as otherwise none would manage to function.

(iii) Competition among private suppliers has produced two failures:

(a) Prices of water, electricity, sewage, and so forth are close to marginal cost but average cost is far too high (because of the failure to exploit economies of scale).

(b) Competitive suppliers have produced negative externalities such as excess pollution with diesel fumes, over used common resources by dumping sewage waste and, groundwater dissipation leading to unsustainable level of water table. A vibrant civil society could have been able to put checks on such issues (but city being quite young this is almost absent by now).

2. **Jamshedpur:** This is a private township and one of the best-governed cities in India. Jamshedpur Utilities and Services Company Ltd. (JUSCO), a wholly-owned subsidiary of Tata Steel, is responsible for provisioning of the basic services here. The township is widely regarded as having some of the best urban infrastructure in the country and JUSCO is considered a *model provider*. It has a grown up civil society which checks negative externalities of the urban expansion. The township was rated the second best in the country by *ORG Marg Nielsen* (the worldwide market research firm) on its 'quality-of-life index' in 2008, and in 2010 the city was ranked 7th of 441 cities and towns in India on 'sanitation' and 'cleanliness' by the Ministry of Urban Development.

India needs to take few important lessons from the experience of the above-cited examples—so that the privately developed townships are ideal ones:

(i) Private sector can develop quite a competitive urban centres.

(ii) Private sector will have to bear the burden of higher transaction costs, if the city is managed by multiple authorities. Such costs would also be higher if initial cohesive development plan for the city is not put in place. Post-growth infrastructure development costs are much higher and at times prohibitive.

(iii) The active role of *civil society* can prevent excessive exploitation of resources and reduce the impact of negative externalities associated with rapid urbanisation. We see this being present in the latter but absent in the former.

PPP MODELS

Managing adequate amount of fund for infrastructure development has been always a challenge for India. In reform era, the government evolved the idea of public private partnership (PPP) for the sector aimed at attracting investments from the private sector (domestic as well as foreign). We see an encouraging contribution coming from the private sector in this regard also. But by 2013–14, the PPPs started getting unattractive for the private sector—primarily caused by the in-built flaws in the PPP models together with regulatory reasons—although external reasons have been also there (slowdown in the country's economy due to recession among the western economies).

Various volumes of the *Economic Survey* together with the *Kelkar Committee* on the PPP have discussed about the various flaws in the existing model of the PPP, primarily used for the development of road projects in the country. In this backdrop, a better PPP model was announced by the Government by early 2016—the *Hybrid Annuity Model (HAM)*. A brief review of the major PPP models (few of them are non-PPP models, too) are given below:

1. **BOT-TOLL:** The 'Build-Operate-Transfer-Toll' was one of the earliest models of PPP. Other than sharing the project cost (with the Government) the private bidder was to build, maintain, operate the road and collect toll on the vehicular traffic. The bid was given to the private company offering to share maximum toll revenue to the government. The private party used to cover 'all risks' related to—land acquisition, construction (damage), inflation, cost over-runs caused by delays and commercial. The government was responsible for only regulatory clearances.

   Due to inherent drawbacks, this model proved to be unsustainable for the private bidder—undue delay in land acquisition due to litigation, cost over-runs and uncertainties in traffic movement (commercial risk)—made the road projects economically unviable.

2. **BOT-Annuity:** This was an improvement over the BOT-TOLL model aimed at reversing the declining interest of the private companies towards road projects by mainly reducing the risk for the private players. Other than sharing the project cost the private player was to build, maintain and operate the road projects without any responsibility of collecting toll on the traffic. The private players were offered a fixed amount of money annually (called 'annuity') as compensation—the party bidding for the minimum 'annuity' used to get the project. Toll collection was the responsibility of the Government.

   This was different from the previous model (BOT-TOLL) in one sense—private players were not having any commercial risk (traffic)—but they remained very much exposed to other risks (land acquisition delays, inflation, cost over-runs, construction). Even this model, over the time proved to be unviable for the private sector due to the leftover risks they were exposed to.

3. **EPC Model:** The PPP model which was seen to be a better way out to promote the infra projects were visibly failing by the year 2010 and Government was unable to attract the private players towards the road sector. It was in this backdrop that the Engineering-Procurement-Construction (EPC) Model was announced. In this model, project cost was fully covered by the Government (it means, it was not a PPP model and was like normal contracts given to the bidders) together with majority of the risks—land acquisition, cost over-runs due to delay, inflation and commercial.

   The private developers were supposed to design, construct and hand over the road projects to government—maintenance, operation and toll collection being the government's responsibilities. Contract was given to the private player who offered to construct roads at the lowest cost/price guaranteeing the desired quality levels. It means, the private player in this model was only exposed to the construction-related risks which is a normal risk involved in any contract given by the government to the private party.

EPC Model could have been a temporary way out to develop road projects as it was fully funded by the government—reform era had aimed to attract investment from the private players by evolving a 'business model' for the road sector—need was to develop a new PPP model. In this backdrop we see the government coming up with a new PPP model for the road projects—the Hybrid Annuity Model.

4. **HAM:** Hybrid Annuity Model (HAM) is a mix of EPC and BOT-ANNUITY models. In this model the project cost is shared by the government and the private player in ratio of 40:60, respectively. The private player is responsible to construct and hand over the roads to the government which will collect toll (if wishes)—maintenance remaining the responsibility of the private player till the annuity period. Private player is paid a fixed sum of economic compensation (called 'annuity', similar to the BOT-ANNUITY model of past) by the government for a fixed tenure (normally 15 years, though it is flexible). The private player which demands lowest annuity (in bidding) gets the contract.

   In this model, most of the major risks are covered by the government—land acquisition, clearances, operation, toll collection and commercial while the risks related to inflation and cost over-runs are shared in ratio of the project cost sharing. But the private sector is still exposed to the construction and maintenance risks (delays from the government side in clearances and land acquisition have chances to enhance the degree of risks private players are exposed to). But overall, this is the best PPP model for the time devoid of most of the flaws of past. Private sector has shown good response to this model. By early 2018, this model was notified by the Government for other infra sectors too.

5. **Swiss Challenge Model:** Government of India, for the first time, announced the use of this model for redevelopment of railway stations in the country (by late 2015). This is a very flexible method of giving contracts (i.e., public procurement) which can be used in PPP as well as non-PPP projects.

   In this, one bidder is asked by the government to submit the proposal for the project which is put in public domain. Afterwards, several other bidders submit their proposals aimed at improving and beating the original (first) bidder—finally an improved bid is selected (called counter proposal). If the original bidder is not able to match the counter proposal, the project is awarded to the counter bidder. Government has made it an online method.

   Though, the Government of India used this model for the first time, this has already been used by several states by now—Karnataka, Andhra Pradesh, Rajasthan, Madhya Pradesh, Bihar, Punjab and Gujarat—for roads and housing projects. In 2009, the Supreme Court approved the method for award of contracts.

6. **PPP Model for other sectors:** Though, the idea of PPP model was originally evolved for the infrastructure sector, in recent times, there have been proposals for its uses in other areas, too—such as education, healthcare and even agriculture. The model is getting popular support from the urban local bodies in the country and it is believed that in the *Smart Cities* scheme it could play a very lucrative role. Recently, the **Economic Survey 201 6-17** suggested[69] the government to create a new institution as a PPP to compete with and complement existing institutions to procure stock and dispose pulses.
7. **PPPP Model:** Experts have suggested public private people partnership (PPPP) model, too for certain sector in the country. Though such a model has been in use since 2000–01 itself in agriculture sector to promote participatory irrigation development—in the Command Area Development Programme of 1974 (renamed as Command Area Development and Watershed Management Programme in 2004)—in which individual financial contributions come from the farmers (around 15 per cent of the total cost) to develop field channels and drains.

It is believed that in the area of developing, maintaining and protecting local public assets this model could be highly effective. In future, the local bodies—urban as well as rural—may be using this model to develop social and economic infrastructure.

69. Basically, the **Economic Survey 2016–17** (Vol. 1, pp. 156 & 170) has supported the advice of the ***Committee on Incentivising Pulses Production Through Minimum Support Price (MSP) and Related Policies*** headed by Arvind Subramanian, Chief Economic Adviser (report submitted in September, 2016)—the expert committee was set up by the government on account of the price volatility of pulses seen during 2015–16.

PETROLEUM & NATURAL GAS

India is the 3rd largest energy consumer in the world after USA and China. With a share of 5.8 per cent of the world's primary energy consumption, the Indian energy consumption basket is primarily dominated by Coal and Crude Oil. Today, the Government is aimed at mixing more gas in India's energy basket. In the absence of a global gas market for benchmarking domestic gas prices in India, various formulae have been suggested. Since October 2014 a formula based on producer and consumer markets is being used to arrive at domestic gas prices in India. It was expected that the formula would balance the interest of producers and consumers in the country.

However, market-determined arm's length pricing for domestic gas, with an effective regulator, to provide adequate incentive for investment and also ensure competitiveness and transparency remains the *first-best solution* that merits consideration. It would reflect the appropriate gas price in relation to alternative fuels. In the medium-term, being a large consumer, India may be able to be a *price setter* for gas prices in the region. Possible steps to address the concerns of the sector are as given below:

- Petroleum products and natural gas should be included under the Goods and Services Tax (GST), or at least its exclusion should not be indicated in the Constitution Amendment Bill.
- The cess collections could be used to support construction of a network of gas pipelines, which is of crucial importance for providing clean energy to deprived regions of the country. The progress is somewhat constrained at

present by having been linked to revival of fertiliser units and development of small industries in areas along the gas highway projects. Alternatively, in order to promote the gas pipeline network, Viability Gap Funding (VGF) may be provided for promoting pipeline assets creation and development of efficient markets.

- Impetus is required for construction of not only cross-country pipelines but also city gas distribution. The present system of bidding by the Petroleum and Natural Gas Regulatory Board (PNGRB) is lopsided and long-drawn-out and needs to be reformed since it has constrained development of the gas network.
- Expansion of the PNG/CNG (Compressed Natural Gas) network could help provide gas connections to rural areas.
- Rationalisation of LPG subsidy is essential. It may be useful to cap subsidy to 10 LPG cylinders for each household (that being the maximum used for usual domestic cooking) while aligning taxes and duties on domestic and commercial LPG users.
- Import of Liquefied Natural Gas (LNG) for use in the power industry is exempt from customs duty while LNG for all other uses attracts 5 per cent customs duties. There should be no exemptions for any sector.
- In order to develop a cost-effective and revenue-neutral mechanism for swapping of gas across producing and consuming states for the national gas grid, it is important to make special tax provision for sale of natural gas under the Central Sales Tax Act 1956. Natural gas and LNG may be treated as declared goods to bring about tax parity with crude oil and make prices uniform across states.

Meanwhile, India has entered into exploring the *unconventional* resources of energy such as the *CBM (Coal Bed Methane)* and *Shale Oil & Gas*. The estimated CBM resources are about 92 TCF (trillion cubic feet) of which only 9.9 TCF has so far been confirmed – current production is about 1 million cubic metre per day. In the *Shale Oil & Gas* areas, presently, the assessment process is going on in 50 blocks. Commercial production is yet to begin.

In order to encourage greater participation of private sector in oil and natural gas sector, some recent steps *(till April 2021)* taken by the Government are as given below:

- Bidding of exploration blocks without any production or revenue sharing to Government.
- More functional freedom given to public sector oil companies for collaboration and private sector participation for production enhancement.
- A gas exchange is planned in order to bring market-driven pricing in the energy market.
- 5,000 compressed biogas (CBG) plants to be set up by 2023.
- 100 per cent Foreign Direct Investment (FDI) allowed in natural gas, petroleum products and refineries.
- An Independent Gas Transport System Operator being set up for facilitation and coordination of booking of common carrier capacity in all-natural gas pipelines on a non- discriminatory open access basis *(Union Budget 2021-22)*.

RENEWABLE ENERGY

India's renewable energy potential has been assessed (in the medium-term) at 8, 96,602 MW, which includes the potential from *solar* (7,48,990 MW), *wind* (1,00,000 MW), *small hydro* (20,000 MW) and *biomass* (26,800 MW) power.

Apart from grid power requirement, renewable energy sources are also being used for distributed generation, lighting, pumping and motive power requirement in remote and inaccessible areas. India is graduating from Mega watts to Gig watts in the generation of clean renewable energy. The target from various renewable energy sources has been increased by the GoI to **175 GW** by the year **2022**—solar and wind to contribute 100 GW and 60 GW, respectively. The *major steps* taken by the government to boost the sector in recent times are as given below:

1. **Solar Rooftop:** Grid-connected rooftops systems to come up by 2019–20 under the National Solar Mission (NSM).
2. **Solar Parks:** 25 solar parks and ultra mega solar power projects with an aggregate capacity of 20,000 MW to be set up in the next five years (from 2015–16 to 2019–20).
3. **Solar Projects under the NSM:** In February 2015, the government announced to set up 15,000 MW of grid-connected solar PV power projects under the NSM by 2018–19.
4. **Solar Pumps:** Target of installing of one lakh solar pumps for irrigation and drinking water by 2016.
5. **Solar Cities :** Approval granted for 56 solar city projects under the Development of Solar Cities Programme.

- The Surya Mitra: This scheme was launched in May 2015 for creating 50,000 trained personnel within a period of five years (2015–16 to 2019–20).

In addition to the above, major policy initiatives taken by the government up to April 2021 which include:

1. National Offshore Wind Energy Policy 2015 to exploit the vast 7600 km coastline for development of offshore wind energy in the Indian Exclusive Economic Zone (EEZ),
2. Inclusion of renewable energy in the *priority sector* and bank loans up to ₹15 crore limit to borrowers categories for purposes like solar-based power generators, biomass-based power generators, windmills, micro-hydel plants and for nonconventional energy-based public utilities like street lighting systems, and remote village electrification. For individual households this is up to ₹10 lakh per borrower.
3. Investments in renewable energy are on *automatic route*, i.e. automatic approval for up to **74** per cent *foreign equity participation* in a JV and **100** per cent foreign investment as equity is permissible with the approval of the Foreign Investment Promotion Board (FIPB).
4. Approval to the amendments in the National Tariff Policy 2005, for promotion of renewable power.

NATIONAL HYDROGEN MISSION

The Government announced a major push towards clean energy by launching the National Hydrogen Mission in the Union Budget 2021-22— taking clues form the world mood which is seeing hydrogen (which has high energy density and versatility) to emerge as the top clean fuel for the future. A broad-based research development and demonstration programme on hydrogen energy and fuel is supported by the Government (i.e., the Ministry of New and Renewable Energy).

A *transportation* project supported by the ministry to Banaras Hindu University, IIT Delhi, and Mahindra & Mahindra has resulted in development and demonstration of internal combustion engines for two wheelers, three wheelers, and mini buses that run on hydrogen fuel. Two *hydrogen refuelling* stations have been established (one each at Indian Oil R&D Centre, Faridabad and National Institute of Solar Energy, Gurugram).

LOGISTICS SECTOR

Logistics is the backbone of supply chain (management of flows of goods from the point of origin to the point of consumption). It includes transportation, inventory management, warehousing, materials handling, packaging, and integration of information. Largely 'unorganised', the sector has remained 'unexplored' in India. As per the latest **Economic Survey 2017-18**, *major statistics* which highlight the importance of India's logistics sector are as given below:

- India's logistics industry is around US$ 160 billion worth and has a compound annual growth rate (CAGR) of 7.8 per cent during last five years.
- With the implementation of GST, the Indian logistics market is expected to reach about US$ 215 billion in 2020, growing at a CAGR of 10.5 per cent.
- It provides employment to more than 22 million people.
- With a 10 per cent cut in the cost of logistics exports are estimated to grow by 5-8 per cent.

Though, in terms of overall performance India jumped to 35th rank (from 54th in 2014) in the latest Logistics Performance Index-2016 (World Bank), the sector faces numerous challenges which need immediate attention form the Government:

- High cost impacting domestic and global competitiveness,
- Under-developed material handling infrastructure,
- Fragmented warehousing, multiple regulatory and policy making bodies,
- Lack of seamless movement across modes,
- Lack of integrated IT infrastructure and modern technology.

Government has identified the action points to develop this sector in an integrated way. These action points are—adopting new technology, improved investment, skilling, removing bottlenecks, improving intermodal transportation, automation, single window system for giving clearances, and simplifying processes. To strengthen the sector the Government has created a new Logistics Division (in the Department of Commerce). The sector has been put in the *Harmonized Master List of Infrastructure Sub-sector* (given 'infrastructure status' by late 2017) which will benefit it in many ways:

1. Cheaper fund/credit (at lower rates of interest) on longer tenure fund will be facilitated.
2. Simplified process of approval (for construction of multimodal logistics (parks) facilities which includes both storage and transportation).
3. Increased market accountability through regulatory authority and will attract investments from debt and pension funds.

Apart from increasing trade, better performance in logistics will augment the programme like Make in India, and also enable India to become an important part of the global supply chain.

HOUSING & URBAN INFRASTRUCTURE

India is witnessing rapid urbanisation. According to Census 2011, India's urban population is projected to grow to about 60 crores by 2030 (from 37.7 crores). Urbanisation in India has become an important and irreversible process, and it is an important determinant of economic growth and poverty reduction. Though the cities are engines of growth, a rapid pace of urbanisation poses significant challenges to basic infrastructure services such as water supply, sanitation, solid waste and wastewater management. Some recent steps taken by the Government in this regard are as given below:

- **Deendayal Antyodaya Yojana - National Urban Livelihoods Mission** is being run in all the statutory towns to address the 'social and occupational vulnerabilities' of the urban poor. Under the mission, urban poor are imparted skill training for self and wage employment and assisted in setting up self-employment ventures by providing credit at subsidised rates of interest. The Mission also provides for *shelters* for urban homeless and infrastructure for street vendors.
- **PM Street Vendor's Atmanirbhar Nidhi (PM SVANidhi)** was launched (June 2020) as part of the *Atmanirbhar Bharat Abhiyan* for providing micro-credit facility to the street vendors to restart their businesses post COVID-19 lockdowns. This scheme targets to benefit over 50 lakhs street vendors who had been vending on or before March 24, 2020, in urban areas including those from surrounding peri-urban/rural areas.

Under the Scheme, the vendors can avail a working capital loan of up to ₹ 10,000, which is repayable in monthly instalments in the tenure of one year. On timely/early repayment of the loan, an interest subsidy of 7 per cent per annum will be credited to the bank accounts of beneficiaries through Direct Benefit Transfer on quarterly basis.

HOUSING POLICY

With increasingly fluid population, India needs a housing policy which suitably enables horizontal or spatial mobility (i.e., mobility within and between cities) and vertical mobility (i.e., to climb socio-economic ladder) as opportunities arise. Once the Government is aiming at *Housing for All,* concerns of the twin issues— ***rental*** and ***vacant*** houses— need proper deliberations, which was touched by the *Economic Survey 2017-18* for the first time in the following way—

Housing is a key policy priority of the Government today. With increasingly 'fluid' population the housing policy need to enable horizontal or spatial mobility (i.e., movement within and between cities) and vertical mobility (to climb socio-economic ladder) as opportunities arise. The **Economic Survey 2017-18** highlighted certain factors in this regard when the country is going for an ambitious scheme—*Housing for All.* Two basic issues related to the sector is rental and vacant houses.

Rental Housing Such housing is important for both horizontal and vertical mobility as it allows people to access suitable housing without actually having to buy it. Across the income spectrum, rental housing is an important foothold into a city for new arrivals, until they purchase their own homes. For rural migrants, in particular, whose financial portfolios may already be tied up in land and livestock, it is access to shelter that is more important than investing in their own houses that is subject to local market risk. Nonetheless, the share of rental housing has actually been declining in Indian cities since independence from 54 per cent in 1961 to 28 per cent in 2011. Though the country has witnessed a decline in the share of rentals, it is not uniform—it has been sharper in the northern states (excluding the mountain states). Rental is more prevalent in urban areas (31 per cent) than the rural (5 per cent), as per the Census 2011—with more urbanised states having higher percentages of renting.

Vacant Housing Despite the shortage of housing in urban India (more than 18 million households in 2012), there is also a trend increase in vacant houses (11.1 million in 2011 from 6.5 million of 2001). As per the Census 2011 vacant houses constitute around 12 per cent of the share of the total urban housing stock. The number and share of vacant houses for some major cities are—Mumbai has the highest number of total vacant houses (0.48 million), followed by Delhi (0.3 million) and Bengaluru (around 0.3 million). In terms of share of vacant houses to total residential stock, Gurgaon ranks highest (26 per cent). The phenomenon of high vacancy rates is not fully understood but unclear property rights, weak contract enforcement and low rental yields may be important factors. The spatial distribution of the new real estate may also be an issue as the vacancy rates generally increase with distance away from the denser urban cores.

Home ownership is encouraged as part of socio-economic policy in most part of the world including India. While there is nothing wrong in encouraging home ownership, it needs to be recognised that the rental market is also an important part of the urban eco-system. Housing needs of India are complex and policies have been mostly focused on building more homes and on home ownership. In recent decades several factors have constrained this market in the country, such as—rent control, unclear property rights and difficulties with contract enforcement. India needs a *holistic housing policy* which is capable to resolve the existing constraints to the sector and the issues of rental and vacant housing.

PMAY-U

The Pradhan Mantri Awas Yojana-Urban (PMAY-U) was launched in June, 2015 to provide *pucca house* with basic amenities to all eligible[70] urban poor by 2022, a part of the 'Housing for All' (Pradhan Mantri Awas Yojana). By early 2020, a validated (by states and UTs) demand of 1.12 crore houses were registered. It is one of the *largest* housing schemes of the world covering complete urban India.

Urban habitats and cities are the epicentres of economic growth which contribute over 60 per cent of India's GDP. The construction sector accounts for 8.2 per cent of GDP and employs about 12 per cent of the workforce. Therefore, the investment made under PMAY-(U) not only provides pucca houses to the eligible families to achieve the goal of 'Housing for All' but also triggers *multiplier effect* on the overall economy. The scheme is being implemented through following four verticals:

1. *In Situ Slum Development (ISSR)* works using land as a resource with private participation in which the Government of India gives a grant of ₹1 lakh per house.
2. *Credit Linked Subsidy Scheme (CLSS)* provides subsidy to economically weaker section (EWS) and lower income group (LIG) for new house or incremental housing. The EWS and LIG are defined as a household with upto ₹3 lakh annual income and house sizes upto 30 and 60 square metres, respectively. Both of the beneficiaries get an upfront subsidy at the rate of 6.5 per cent for loans upto ₹6 lakhs.

---

70. **Economic Survey 2019-20**, Vol. 2, pp. 249-251, Ministry of Finance, GoI, N. Delhi **Press Release** of the Ministry of Finance, December 31, 2019.

3. *Affordable Housing in Partnership (AHP)* is being run with public or private sector including parastatal agencies in which a Central assistance of ₹1.5 lakh per EWS house is given (35 per cent constructed houses are reserved for EWS category).
4. *Beneficiary Led House Construction/ Enhancement (BLC)* is a segment which promotes houses for individuals of EWS category under which a Central assistance of ₹1.5 lakh per beneficiary is given.

Out of 1.03 crore houses approved till early 2020, 60 lakhs have been grounded for construction, of which 32 lakh houses have been completed and delivered. As per the Government, the scheme is expected to complete its target much before the deadline year 2022.

COVID-19 AND RENTAL HOUSING

In the wake of coronavirus pandemic, a mass return-migration of labourers was seen from the major urban centres towards villages of the country. This looked quite contradictory to the nationwide lockdown when citizens were advised by the governments to keep inside their homes. As most of these labourers stopped getting work it became almost impossible for them to live in cities and manage even food what to ask of paying rent (in such a situation the landlords simply asked their renters to vacate the houses). This made government seriously notice the problem which migrant labour and urban poor face in getting houses near their place of work at affordable rent.

In the wake of economic disruptions caused by the pandemic, the Government, in May 2020, launched the *Atmanirbhar Bharat Abhiyan* aimed at self-reliance – which has a series of measures touching diverse areas of the economy. One of its measures is related to the arrangement of rental houses for the migrant labour and urban poor – under which the Government announced to launch the *Affordable Rental Housing Complex (ARHC)* scheme. The scheme, under the PMAY (PM Awas Yojana), aims to provide ease of living to the migrant and urban poor at affordable rent by—

1. Converting government funded housing in the cities into Affordable Rental Housing Complexes (under PPP mode);
2. Incentivising manufacturing units, industries, institutions, associations to develop and operate Affordable Rental Housing Complexes (on their private land); and
3. Incentivising central and state government agencies/organisations to develop and operate Affordable Rental Housing Complexes.

NATIONAL INFRASTRUCTURE PIPELINE

Government has set a target to achieve the GDP of US$ 5 trillion by 2024-25. To achieve this goal India needs to invest about US$ 1.4 trillion (₹100 lakh crores) during 2020–25 in infrastructure—and to further sustain the growth by 2030 another US$ 4.5 trillion. To enable[71] economy, achieve the target of investment in the sector, the Government launched (on December 31, 2019) the project National Infrastructure Pipeline (NIP). The NIP captures the infrastructure vision of the country for the period 2020-25. This is the *first-ever* exercise undertaken in the country. Designed on PPP mode this has the following main features:

- The sectoral shares are—on energy (24 per cent), roads (19 per cent), urban infra (16 per cent), and Railways (13 per cent).

71. **Economic Survey 2019-20**, Vol. 2, pp. 232-233, Ministry of Finance, GoI, N. Delhi **Press Release** of the Ministry of Finance, December 31, 2019.

- Funding will be shared equally by Centre and States (39 per cent each) while 22 per cent is supposed to come from private sector (Government expects the private participation to increase to 30 per cent by 2025).

Around 42 per cent of the projects under it were supposed to be launched by *early 2020*, deliberations on rest of the projects were in the process. The *Task Force* which advised for the launch of the NIP, has also recommended for required changes by Centre and States in several key areas such as—

1. Developing a robust bond market for infrastructure companies,
2. Speedy resolution of infrastructure disputes,
3. Optimal risk sharing through better and balanced PPP contracts, and
4. Sanctity and enforceability of contracts.

The investment target under the NIP looks tough given the past experience of investment done in infrastructure, which has been about US$ 1.1 trillion during the whole decade of 2007–2018. However, the period in reference is considered the toughest times for infrastructure projects in the country when they faced hurdles such as—profit hit with global slowdown, delays in project clearance, delays in land acquisition, lack of funding, being the main ones.

Government hopes that a bouquet of well-prepared projects would be able to attract investment from central and state governments, urban local bodies, banks and financial institution, private equity funds, and private investors, both local and foreign.

RECENT CHALLENGES

Infrastructure sector has been faced with some long-standing challenges in the country. In the period of reforms Government aimed to involve the synergy of the private sector into it. The public private partnership model was taking ground year after year. But due to certain internal and external factors the sector almost got derailed by late 2013–14. As per various Government documents these factors are as given below:

1. Project delays which cause high cost over-runs. Though, the situation has improved after the new Government took control but still around 348 such projects are lingering in the pipeline of approvals at various states. By February, 2018, the Government announced to classify such projects into different sub-categories which can give right information (other than calling all of them as 'stalled' projects).
2. Delays in land acquisition. With the Land Act of 2015 being withdrawn and an effective 'land pooling' policy put in place things have started improving in this regard. Some states have surplus land in the pooling arrangement (such as Andhra Pradesh).
3. Scarcity of fund due to longer gestation period. With the help of Infrastructure Investment Trusts, 5/25 Refinancing scheme, debt restructuring things improved but not much. Since late 2017–18, the Government is pursuing insolvency procedure (under the newly enforced Bankruptcy and Insolvency Act) and things look taking pace.
4. Weaknesses of the existing PPP models also took a heavy toll. Though it has been improved by the new model of it—hybrid annuity model (HAM). Though, the model was put in place for only road sector it was notified for other infra sectors also by late 2017.
5. Slowdown in the economy kick-started by the global financial crisis of 2008 together with a state of 'policy paralysis' prevailing in the domestic economy since 2010 onwards.

After the new Government took control the state of policy paralysis is no more there but there are several complex legacy factors which need to be addressed in an effective way.

6. A typical 'twin balance sheet crises' taking grip over the economy (declared so by the *Economic Survey*) by late 2016–17. Due to this while on one hand the public sector banks are unfit to promote lending (which have been the lead lenders to the sector) hit with high non-performing assets (NPAs) on the other hand big private corporates are not eligible to borrow (due to high losses) and invest in the economy.

WAY FORWARD

To maintain growth momentum in the fast-moving world, India needs to develop industry and infrastructure. The scope[72] for *Industry 4.0* (4th Industrial Revolution) and *Next Generation* infrastructure is enormous, the opportunity which India cannot afford to miss. Industry 4.0 encompasses automation whereas next generation infrastructure brings physical infrastructure and technology like internet of things (IoT) and automation together to maximise the efficiency of physical infrastructure. Together with timely investment, there is a need of suitable policy interventions to enable India tap the benefits of these emerging ideas.

The year after the crisis of COVID-19 pandemic will require[73] sustained and calibrated measures to facilitate the process of economic recovery and to enable the economy to get back to its long-term growth trajectory. In this regard, the revival of the industrial and infrastructure sector will be key to overall economic growth and macroeconomic stability. In the words of the Economic Survey 2020-21, the year can be summarised in the lines of Saint Francis of Assisi, *'Start by doing what's necessary, then do what's possible, and suddenly you are doing the impossible'* because as Albert Einstein said, *'In the midst of every crisis, lies great opportunity.'* In a sense, the Survey has given call to start from the scratch and move towards the long-term and sustained economic recovery.

72. **Economic Survey 2019-20,** Vol. 2, p. 251, Ministry of Finance, GoI, N. Delhi **Press Release** of the Ministry of Finance, December 31, 2019.

73. **Economic Survey 2020-21,** vol. 1, p. 303-04, Ministry of Finance, GoI, N. Delhi.

CHAPTER 10

SERVICES SECTOR

*India's dynamic services sector has grown rapidly in the last decade with almost 72.4 per cent of the growth in India's GDP in 2014-15 coming from this sector. Unlike other developing economies, the Indian growth story has been led by services-sector growth which is now in double digits. **

In this Chapter...

- **Introduction**
- **Performance Overview**
- **Services Trade**
- **Sectoral Situation**
- **IT-BPM Services**
- **Ports, Shipping and Waterways**
- **Offshore Fund Management**
- **Manufacturing vs. Services**
- **Global Negotiations**
- **Restrictions and Regulations**
- **The Need for Reforms**
- **COVID-19 and Services Sector**
- **Way Forward**

INTRODUCTION

India's services sector has not only outperformed other sectors of the Indian economy, but has also played an important role in India's integration with world trade and capital markets. India's liberalisation of services has been a challenging process in several sub-sectors, but clearly those services where integration through trade and FDI has gone further are also the ones that have exhibited more rapid growth along with positive spillovers on the rest of the economy.

There is, however, a concern[1] about the *sustainability* of a services-led growth process which largely stems from exports of skill-based services. The prevailing view is that for services growth to be sustained, the sector cannot remain dependent on external demand. It must also be driven by internal demand. More broad-based growth within the services is also required to

1. Rupa Chanda, in Kaushik Basu and Annemie Maertens (eds) 'Services-led Growth' ***The New Oxford Companion to Economics in India***, Vol. II (New Delhi: Oxford University Press, 2012), pp. 624–32.

* *Ministry of Finance,* **Economic Survey 2014-15,** *Vol. 2 (New Delhi: Government of India, 2015), p. 106.*

ensure balanced, equitable and employment-oriented growth, with backward and forward linkages to the rest of the economy. In this regard further infrastructural and regulatory reforms and FDI liberalisation in services can help diversify the sources of growth withing India's services sector and provide the required momentum.

SERVICES IN 2020-21

The lockdown and social distancing measures bad a significant impact on the contact-intensive services sector, which contracted by almost 16 per cent in the first half of the 2020-21. Services sector's significance in the Indian economy has been steady, with the sector now accounting for over 54 per cent of the economy and almost four-fifths of total FDI inflows.

The services sector activity, which had contracted for five consecutive months since March 2020 as the Covid-19 pandemic dented demand, started . to pick up since September 2020. The IHS Markit India Services Business Activity Index also known as Services Purchasing Managers' Index (PMI), which was at an 85-month high of 57.5 in February 2020, fel l to its lowest level of 5.4 in April 2020- however, a V-shaped recovery was witnessed once gradual unlocking began in the country— PMI getting back to 52.3 in December 2020.

Source: *Economic Survey 2020-21, vol. 1, pp. 304-06, Ministry of Finance, GoI, N. Delhi.*

In recent years, there has been a debate in the country regarding the selection of the sector which can lead the growth process in the country. This debate originated from the fact that the services sector contributed over 62 per cent in the GDP during the decade 2001-12. But the debate was somewhat solved by the *Economic Survey 2014-15* in favour of the *manufacturing sector*. The Survey has gone to quote several empirical studies of recent times linking both services and manufacturing sectors to a great many real issues—potential to create employment, need of skilled and unskilled labour force, formality and informality of the sector, etc. For this, the idea of 'Make in India' has acclaimed timely action from the government. Again, the importance of expanding the Railways and enhancing public investment in it have also been pointed out.[2] These findings are also in line with several other studies of the recent times.[3]

PERFORMANCE OVERVIEW

The contact intensive services sector was severely impacted, particularly sub-sectors such as tourism, aviation, and hospitality due to lockdown measures in the wake of the Covid-19 pandemic in 2020. A brief overview[4] is given below for 2020-21 (April-September) in comparison to the corresponding period of the previous year—

- A contraction of 16 per cent led by sub-sectors particularly 'Trade, hotels, transport, communication & services related to broadcasting', which contracted by 31.5 per cent. The Gross Value Added (GVA) of the sector is estimated to have a negative growth rate of 8.8 per cent in 2020-21 (against 5.5 per cent in 2019-20.
- Sub-sectors 'Trade, hotels, transport, communication & broadcasting services', 'Financial, real estate & professional services', and 'Public administration, defence & other services' are estimated to contract by 21.41 per cent, 3.68 per cent and 0.82 per cent respectively.
- Rail freight traffic growth nosedived to (–)35.3 per cent in April 2020 before rising back sharply to 15.5 per cent YoY in September

2. For a detailed description See Ministry of Finance, ***Economic Survey 2014–15***, Vol. 1. Though, the theme of the analysis has been included in this book itself, in the Chapter-9 **'Industry and Infrastructure'.**

3. *India Development Report 2015,* Oxford University Press, N. Delhi, 2015..

4. Economic Survey 2020-21, vol. 1, pp. 305-08, Ministry of Finance, GoI, N. Delhi.

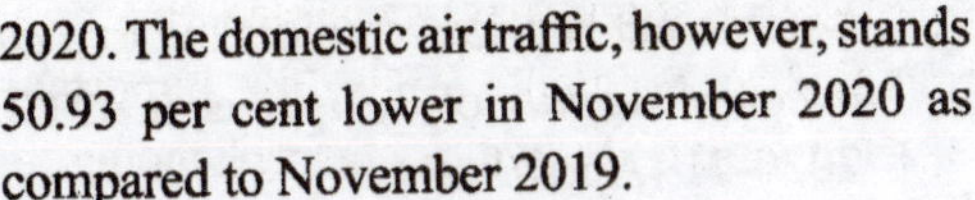

2020. The domestic air traffic, however, stands 50.93 per cent lower in November 2020 as compared to November 2019.

- Bank credit growth YoY to services sector had moderated significantly between September 2018 and December 2019. However, credit growth to the services sector was stronger in 2020, increasing to 8.76 per cent at the end of November 2020 as compared to 4.84 per cent a year ago.
- The IHS Markit India Services Business Activity Index also known as *Services Purchasing Managers' Index (PM!)*, which was at an 85-month high of 57.5 in February 2020, fell to its lowest level of **5.4** in April 2020. As mobility restrictions were lifted and business resumed, Services PMI recovered sharply to 54.1 in October 2020. The index softened to *52.3* in December 2020, although a print above 50 still means expansion.

Services in States The sector accounts for more than 50 per cent of the GSVA (Gross State Value Added) in 15 out of the 33 states and UTs. In eight states, it accounts for more than 60 per cent of GSVA. Chandigarh and Delhi stand out with a particularly high share of services in GSVA of over 85 per cent while Sikkim's share remains the lowest at 27.02 per cent.

It must be noted that even states with relatively lower share of services in GSVA, such as Tripura, Uttarakhand Andhra Pradesh, Gujarat, Madhya Pradesh, Jharkhand, Odisha, and Arunachal Pradesh have witnessed strong services sector growth in the recent years.

FDI Inflows India is a today world's **9th** largest foreign direct investment (FDI) recipient as per the latest *World Investment Report 2020* (of UNCTAD)— 3 rank improvement from the last report. Interestingly, despite the Covid-19 pandemic, services emerged as the largest recipient of gross FDI equity (excluding re-invested earnings) witnessing a strong growth during 2020-21 (April-September)— reaching to US$ 23.91 billion— showing a 34 per cent growth over the previous year (accounted for almost four-fifth of the total gross FDI equity inflows into India during this period).

The jump in FDI equity inflows was driven by strong inflows into the *Computer Software & Hardware* sub-sector, wherein FDI inflows increased to US$ 17.55 billion (over 336 per cent higher over the corresponding period last year). High growth in FDI inflows was also present in subsectors such as Retail Trading, Agriculture Services, and Education.

SERVICES TRADE

World trade and global supply chain were severely impacted by the COVID-19 pandemic in 2020. While WTO (World Trade Organisation) projects the global merchandise trade volume growth to fall by 9.2 per cent in 2020, the IMF expects volume of global trade in goods and services to contract by 10.4 per cent in 2020. WTO services trade activity index indicated a decline in global trade in commercial services of 4.3 per cent in the first three months of 2020. India's trade in services did also get hit hard by the pandemic showing a mixed performance[5] during 2020-21 (April-September):

- India has a significant presence in the services sector exports— remained among the *top ten* trading countries in commercial services in 2019 accounting for 3.5 per cent of world services exports. Notwithstanding the setback witnessed in the wake of the pandemic, India's services sector remained relatively resilient when compared to merchandise trade.
- The sector provided steady flow of current receipts even though exports from a few sub-

5. **Economic Survey 2020-21**, vol. 1, pp. 310-12, Ministry of Finance, GoI, N. Delhi.

sectors were adversely affected. Net services export receipts amounted to US$ 41.67 billion in 2020-21 as compared with US$ 40.47 billion a year ago.

- Services *export* growth moderated to 2.5 per cent in 2019-20 from 6.6 per cent in 2018-19 as receipts primarily on account of transportation, insurance and communication services. With contraction in global demand and implementation of the pandemic induced lockdown measures, services exports declined by 7.87 per cent in 2020-21 as against a growth of 6.39 per cent in the corresponding period of previous year. Among other major sectors, business services exports recorded a growth of 2.48 per cent in H1 of 2020-21.
- With significant drop in foreign tourist arrivals owing to the mobility restrictions imposed worldwide, travel receipts witnessed a decline of 73.49 per cent in 2020-21 as against a growth of 8.21 per cent in corresponding period of the previous year.
- Services *imports* exhibited sharper decline of 13.95 per cent in 2020-21 in comparison with services exports. Among the major sectors, payments for overseas travel fell by 55.09 per cent due to restrictions on outbound travel from India. Payments for transport services (accounting for over 16 per cent share in total services imports) recorded a decline of 25.9 per cent in 2020-21. Payment for imports of business services, which accounted for 43.41 per cent of total services imports, increased by 4.22 per cent in the year.
- Sharper decline in services imports over exports led to an increase in net services receipts by 2.1 per cent in 2020-21 (April-June) over the previous year. Sharp contraction in merchandise trade deficit and a stable net services receipts led to a *current account surplus* of 3.9 per cent of GDP in 2020-21 (April-June).

The data on India's trade in services in 2020-21 (July-September) was showing signs of revival with exports increasing by 8.4 per cent quarter-on-quarter (QoQ) and imports increasing by 13.2 per cent QoQ, resulting in improvement of 2.3 per cent QoQ in net services exports.

As projected by *Gartner* (October 2020), although the global IT spending is expected to decline by 5.4 per cent in 2020, it will rebound with the onset of recovery phase in 2021. Even though projections of world trade volume of goods and services are optimistic for 2021, duration and containment of the pandemic and effectiveness of government policy responses to revive the economy would be key factors in shaping India's services trade.

SECTORAL SITUATION

The lockdown and social distancing measures taken in the wake of the COVID-19 pandemic took a heavy toll on the performance of services sector which had a negative growth rate of 16 per cent in the first half of the 2020-21. A brief account of the sectoral performance is given below:

Tourism

Tourism is a major engine of economic growth that contributes significantly in terms of GDP (5 per cent), foreign exchange earnings and employment (11 per cent). However, the COVID-19 pandemic has had a debilitating impact on world travel and tourism, including India. As per the *World Tourism Barometer* of the United Nation's World Tourism Organization (December 2020 edition), international arrivals fell by 72 per cent globally over the first ten months of 2020— was *the worst year* on record in the history of tourism. A brief account[6] of tourism is a given below:

- In order to evacuate Indians stranded abroad after the breakout of the COVID-19 pandemic and the resultant lockdowns across the world, *Vande Bharat Mission* was launched in early May. Under this Mission, which is currently in its ninth phase, the government established Transport Bubbles with countries to repatriate its citizens (by January 2021, India had Air Bubbles with 24 countries).

  Transport Bubbles (or Air Travel Arrangements) are temporary arrangements between two countries aimed at restarting commercial passenger services when regular international flights are suspended as a result of the pandemic, which are reciprocal in nature, meaning airlines from both countries enjoy similar benefits.

- The tourism sector in India had been performing well with FTAs (Foreign Tourist Arrivals) growing at 14 per cent to 10.04 million and FEEs (Foreign Exchange Earnings) at 19.1 per cent to US$ 27.31 billion in 2017. However, the sector underwent a slowdown in 2018 and 2019 before declining sharply in 2020. The FTAs in 2019 stood at 10.93 million compared to 10.56 million in 2018. In terms of growth, the growth rate of FTAs declined from 14 per cent in 2017 to 5.2 per cent in 2018 and further to 3.5 per cent in 2019. FEEs from tourism stood at US$ 30.06 billion in 2019 as compared to US$ 28.59 billion in 2018. In terms of growth, the FEEs declined from 19.1 per cent in 2017 to 4.7 per cent in 2018, picking up slightly to 5.1 per cent in 2019.

- India ranked 23rd in the world in terms of international tourist arrivals in 2019, falling slightly from the 22nd position in 2018. The country accounts for 1.23 per cent of world's international tourist arrivals and 4.97 per cent of Asia & Pacific's international tourist arrivals (Table 7). India ranks 12th in the world and 7th in Asia & Pacific in terms of tourism foreign exchange earnings, accounting for over 2 per cent of the world's tourism foreign exchange earnings.

- India ranked 34th in Travel and Tourism Competitiveness Index, improving significantly from its rank of 65 in 2013.

- Foreign tourists from the top 10 countries visiting India are from Bangladesh, USA, UK, Australia, Canada, China, Malaysia, Sri Lanka, Germany and Russia. They accounted for 67 per cent of the total foreign tourist arrivals in India in 2019. Among the foreign tourists, 57.1 per cent tourists visited for leisure, holiday and recreation, 14.7 per cent for business purposes, and 12.7 per cent was Indian diaspora.

- The top five states attracting domestic tourists are Tamil Nadu, Uttar Pradesh, Karnataka, Andhra Pradesh and Maharashtra (about 71 per cent of the total in 2019).

- The top five states attracting foreign tourists are Tamil Nadu, Maharashtra, Uttar Pradesh, Andhra Pradesh and Rajasthan (around 69.4 per cent of the total in 2019).

Aimed at facilitating international tourism, the Government has taken several new initiatives in recent years:

1. e-Tourist Visa regime started for 46 countries in September 2014 which is now available for 169 countries. With this, foreign tourist arrivals to India on e-Visas have increased from 4.45 lakh in 2015 to 29.28 lakh in 2019 and stood at 8.37 lakh in January-March 2021.
2. e-Visa scheme has been further liberalised which has five categories now—'e-Tourist Visa', 'e-Business

---

6. **Economic Survey 2020-2 1**, vol. 1, pp. 305-08, Ministry of Finance, GoI, N. Delhi.

Visa', 'e-Medical Visa', 'e-Conference Visa' and 'e-Medical Attendant Visa'.

IT-BPM SERVICES

The IT-BPM industry (Information Technology and Business Process Management) of has been the *flag-bearer* of India's exports over the last 20 years. While 1999-2000 to 2009-10 was a decade of growth, the last decade has been that of consolidation and the industry succeeded in 'decoupling' revenue and employee growth. A brief account[7] about its performance is as follows:

- Over the last decade, the industry grew by *102* per cent reaching US$ 190.5 billion in revenues in 2019-20. It also added 1.8 million employees, up 70 per cent over the last 10 years.
- Over the last six years, IT services has constituted the majority share (over 50 per cent) of the IT-BPM sector, with about US$ 97 billion in revenues in 2019-20. Software & Engineering Services constituting a share of 21 per cent in the sector and US$ 40.2 billion in revenue in 2019-20. BPM services industry has maintained its share at 19.8 per cent, while the Hardware services have been declining in share each year but maintaining growth in revenues.
- A significant part (about 84 per cent) of the IT-BPM industry (excluding hardware and e-commerce) continues to be export driven, with export revenues in excess of US$ 146 billion in 2019-20.
- Out of the total US$ 146.55 billion in exports of the IT-BPM sector in 2019-20, IT services contributed US$ 79.1 billion, accounting for 54 per cent of the exports. BPM and Software Products & Engineering services accounted for the remaining 46 per cent with each accounting for a roughly equal share of about 23 per cent.
- The USA remained the biggest recipient of exports, amounting to US$ 91 billion (62 per cent share) in 2019-20 followed by UK amounting US$ 24.7 billion (17 per cent share). Europe (excluding UK) and Asia-Pacific account for 11.4 per cent and 7.6 per cent of the export earnings of India, respectively.
- The Indian *start-up* ecosystem has been progressing well, despite the Covid-19 pandemic. Faced with a myriad of challenges at the onset of the pandemic, the ecosystem defied the odds and had a record number of 12 start-ups that reached unicorn status. The country is home to 38 unicorns at present, as per the NASSCOM Tech Start up Report 2021. The US and China have 243 and 227 unicorns, respectively.

In 2020-21, a number of significant *structural reforms* were undertaken to drive innovation, technology adoption and efficiency in the IT-BPM sector such as:

- **Relaxation of OSP Terms & Conditions:** Aimed to improve the Ease of Doing Business of the IT Industry particularly Business Process Outsourcing (BPO) and IT Enabled Services, the Government simplified (November 2020) the Other Service Provider (OSP) guidelines of the Department of Telecom—reducing the compliance burden of the BPO industry and enables to *Work from Home (WFH)* and *Work from Anywhere.* Major changes include— no registration requirements for Other Service Providers and Business Process Outsourcing services engaged in data related operations have been taken out of the ambit of OSP; no requirement of bank guarantees, requirement for static IPs, frequent reporting obligations,

7. Economic Survey 2020-21, vol. 1, pp. 316-19, Ministry of Finance, GoI, N. Delhi.

publication of network diagram, penal provisions etc.

- **Consumer Protection Act, 20 19:** The Act (enforced in July 2020) empowers consumers and protects their rights through its various notified rules and provisions such as Consumer Protection Councils, Consumer Disputes Redressal Commissions, Mediation, Product Liability and punishment for manufacture or sale of products containing adulterant/spurious goods. Moreover, every e-commerce entity is required to provide information relating to return, refund, exchange, warranty/ guarantee, delivery, modes of payment, grievance redressal, payments, charge-back options, etc., including country of origin which are necessary for enabling the consumer to make an informed decision at the pre-purchase stage on its platform.

Further, the Act introduces the concept of *product liability* and brings within its scope, the product manufacturer, product service provider and product seller, for any claim for compensation. The Act includes establishment of the *Central Consumer Protection Authority* (CCPA) to promote, protect and enforce the rights of consumers.

PORTS, SHIPPING AN D WATERWAYS

Ports in India handle around 90 per cent of export-import cargo by volume and 70 per cent by value in India. With 13 major ports and about 200 minor ports, a brief account of its performance[8] is given below:

- India had a 1 per cent share in world fleet as on January 2020 (total numbers of ships owned by Indian companies stood at 1,431 in 2019-20, up from 1,210 in 2014-15).
- The cargo capacity of major ports was 1,534.91 MTPA (Million Tonnes Per Annum) by March 2020 (up from 871.52 MTPA of March 2014) which handled traffic of 704.92 MT during 2019-20.
- Ports including Deendayal (Kandla), Paradip, JNPT, Vishakhapatnam, and Chennai had the highest cargo capacities as of March 2020.
- A consistent growth of around 6 per cent was maintained in overall port traffic between 2015-16 and 2018-19 but it decelerated to 1.98 per cent in 2019-20 before falling sharply (by negative of 39 per cent) in 2020 owning to the lockdown in the wake of COVID-19 pandemic— recovering to over 2 per cent growth by November 2020.
- The *turnaround time of ships,* which is a key indicator of efficiency of the ports sector, has declined to *2.62* days in 2020-21 (April-September) from 4 days in 2014-15. The shipping turnaround time has declined across all major ports and is now the lowest at the Cochin port (1.66 days) and the highest at the Mormugao port (3.94 days). As per the latest UNCTAD data, the median ship turnaround time globally is *0.97* days, suggesting that India has room to further improve upon the efficiency at ports.

To harness India's coastline (14,500 km), the Government has embarked on the ambitious *Sagarmala Programme* to promote port-led development in the country with the vision to reduce logistics cost of exports-imports and domestic trade with minimal infrastructure investment. The programme includes the following chief features:

- Reducing the cost of transporting domestic cargo,
- Lowering logistical cost of bulk commodities by locating future industrial capacities near the coast,

8. **Economic Survey 2020-21,** vol. 1, pp. 320-21, Ministry of Finance, GoI, N. Delhi.

- Improving export competitiveness by developing port proximate discrete manufacturing clusters, etc.

Meanwhile, the *Union Budget 2021-22* made the following major announcements for the sector:

- Major ports will be moving from managing their operational services on their own to a model where a private partner will manage it for them—7 of the 13 major ports will be offered on Public Private Partnership mode in 2021-22.
- Flagging of merchant ships by Indian shipping companies to be on subsidy support— with the objectives to enable greater training and employment opportunities for Indian seafarers and enhancing their share in global shipping.
- Recycling of Ships Act, 2019 was enacted and India acceded to the Hong Kong International Convention (HKC)—around 90 ship recycling yards at Alang (in Gujarat) have already achieved HKC-compliant certificates. Recycling capacity of around 4.5 million Light Displacement Tons (LDT) will be doubled by 2024 besides efforts to be made to bring more ships to India from Europe and Japan.

Space Sector

The space programme of India has grown exponentially since its modest beginnings five decades ago, moving from providing simple mapping services in the 1960s to many more uses currently. This includes design and development of a series of launch vehicles and related technologies, satellites and related technologies for earth observation, telecom and broadband, navigation, meteorology and space science, R&D in space sciences, and most recently, planetary exploration. The latest[9] position of the country's space sector is as given below:

- India spent about US$ 1.8 billion on space programmes in 2019-20. However, India's government space expenditure still lags behind that of the major players in the space sector, such as *USA*, which spent about 10 times more than India in the space sector in 2019. *China,* which has become a key player in the space sector in the recent years, also spent about six times more than India in 2019.
- India has launched around 5-7 satellites per year in the recent years with no failures, barring one in 2017. On the other hand, Russia, USA and China dominate the satellite launching services with 19, 25 and 34 satellites respectively in 2019.

There have been *three key areas* of focus for India's space programme, namely:

1. Satellite communication, with INSAT/GSAT system as the backbone to address the needs for telecommunication, broadcasting and satellite-based broadband infrastructure in the country.
2. Earth observation and using space-based information for weather forecasting, disaster management, national resource mapping and governance.
3. Satellite-aided navigation including *GAGAN* and *NavIC*.

In terms of player and applications, the space activity in the world is undergoing tremendous changes. This has been marked by a shift in engagement of space activities—from

9. Economic Survey 2020-21, Vol. 2, pp. 322-23, Ministry of Finance, GoI, N. Delhi.

government agencies pursuing *national needs* and space exploration activities to non-governmental (private sector) agencies aggressively pursuing *commercial needs*. Space systems are also being actively used for *national security* purposes by most countries.

Commercialising Space Sector India's space programme is one of the most well-developed in the world and has achieved numerous successes through its state-owned agency, the ISRO (Indian Space Research Organisation) which is responsible for driving the space activities in India. Aimed at making India a manufacturing hub of space assets, the Government started the process of commercialisation by attracting talent and investment from the private sector in the sector— with the following major steps[10] taken in this direction:

- With the long-term vision of making the country self-reliant and technologically advanced, the Government in June 2020, opened up the space sector enabling the participation of Indian *private sector* in the entire gamut of space activities.
- New Space India Limited (NSIL), a Central Public Sector Enterprise has been mandated to transfer the technologies emanating out of Indian space programme and enable Indian industry to scale up high-technology manufacturing base.
- The Indian National Space Promotion and Authorisation Centre (IN-SPACe) has been set up for promoting industries and attracting investment in space sector.
- ISRO to share its infrastructure, transfer technology know-how for production and spin-off.

As per Satellite Industry Association Report (2020), the global space economy in 2019 was pegged at US$ 366 billion, growing by about 1.7 per cent over 2018. The commercial satellite industry is accounting for nearly 75 per cent of global space business. Technology innovations and demand drives the need for higher bandwidth capacity, throughput speeds, improved optical, radar and thermal imaging. PwC estimates that the Indian space economy is valued at US$ 7 billion, which is around 2 per cent of the global space economy.

The recent reforms announced by Government of India for unlocking the space potential of India stresses the need to enable the private industry to be the co-traveller in India's space journey. Today, as per industry estimates, there are more than *40 start-ups* working in India with funding, teams and structure on space and satellite projects complementing the efforts of government. This number is likely to increase in coming years with technology to play a big role.

OFFSHORE FUND MANAGEMENT

The Government has identified the financial services sector as one of the *Champion* Services Sectors to enable on-shoring of the India-related financial services which are currently being rendered from global financial centres. This would provide an impetus to financial services exports and high-skilled employment. Despite India's strong performance in services exports, India's financial services exports have remained *stagnant*, averaging about US$ 5 billion in the recent years. As a result, the share of financial services exports in overall services exports has almost halved from 4.2 per cent in 2011–12 to 2.3 per cent in 2018–19.

One type of financial services that is currently being rendered from global financial centres and could be potentially brought on-shore is the *asset management* activity of offshore funds. These offshore funds located in tax and regulatory friendly jurisdictions (such as Singapore, Luxembourg, Ireland, Hong Kong

10. **Economic Survey 2020-21**, vol. 1, p. 323, Ministry of Finance, GoI, N. Delhi.

and London), pool investments from offshore investors and invest in India via the Foreign Portfolio Investment (FPI), Private Equity (PE) or Foreign Venture Capital Investment (FVCI) route. Such funds include the India-focused offshore funds which invest only in India, and the Regional/ Global diversified funds with partial investment allocation to India. As foreign investment into India continues to increase in the coming years, on-shoring the fund management activity of offshore funds to India would benefit the economy in the following[11] ways:

1. Contributing to the continued expansion of India's asset management industry which has been witnessing significant growth in the recent years. The Asset Managers Roundtable of India (AMRI) estimates that fund management activity of almost 25 per cent of FPI, PE and FVCI funds' total Assets Under Management (AUM) could be potentially on-shored to India by ***2020,*** and potentially a greater share of AUM in the coming years. Assuming total AUM of FPIs at US$ 542 billion and total AUM of PE & FVCIs at US$ 326 billion by 2020, this implies that nearly US$ 136 billion of FPI funds and US$ 82 billion of PE & FVCI funds, i.e., US$ 217 billion in total assets, could be potentially managed on-shore in India by 2020, according to AMRI estimates.
2. Generating *employment* for high-skilled finance professionals.
3. Gain through the management fee (received by fund managers for managing the offshore funds) would constitute as financial services exports. Based on a conservative assumption of 1 per cent management fee (compared to 2 per cent globally), the AMRI estimates that on-shore management of US$ 217 billion in assets of offshore funds could yield about US$ 2.2 billion in fund management fees and therefore financial services exports in 2020. At present, the fund management activity of these offshore funds is being undertaken by fund managers, often of Indian origin, located in offshore jurisdictions since their presence in India would create tax implications for the offshore fund's profits.

The Challenges In April 2016, the government introduced 'safe harbour' provisions as Section 9A, *Income Tax Act (1961)* under which, on satisfying a set of eligibility conditions, the offshore fund would not be considered a 'resident' for tax purposes solely based on its fund manager being located in India. However, most offshore funds have been unable to utilize the 'safe harbour' provisions since they have to satisfy a total of *17 stringent eligibility conditions* (related to the fund's structure, investor composition, investment activity and fund manager's activity and remuneration). Some of these conditions are not in sync with the structure and investment pattern of offshore funds and nature of FPI inflows into India, and lead to *dual compliance burden* for offshore investors since they are also required to comply with RBI and SEBI regulations related to end-investors in FPIs and *round-tripping*[12].

In comparison, in key fund management jurisdictions such as USA, UK, Singapore and Hong Kong, the eligibility conditions under 'safe harbour' provisions for offshore funds are fewer and less stringent in many cases, with discretion available to tax authorities to evaluate the offshore fund's structure and investment pattern and allow for exceptions on a case-by-case basis.

11. **Economic Survey 2019-20,** Vol. 2, pp. 260-263, Ministry of Finance, GoI, N. Delhi.

12. **See GLOSSARY** for details on 'Round Tripping'.

In view of the above challenges, the Commerce Ministry's *High-Level Advisory Group (HLAG) Report* (September 2019) recommended simplifying the tax framework and removing tax residency risk for offshore funds wanting to on-shore their fund management activity given that the offshore fund and fund manager are registered with SEBI and compliant with SEBI regulations. Operationalising the 'safe harbour' regime of Section 9A, *Income Tax Act (1961)* would enable on-shoring the fund management activity of India-focused offshore funds, and potentially, regional/global offshore funds with partial allocation to India.

MANUFACTURING VS. SERVICES

All the focus being on the manufacturing exports in India has distracted attention from what might be a no less noteworthy development[13]. In past few years, it is India's exports of services that has changed in the most significant, and perhaps alarming, way. One can see the problem looking at market shares. India's share of world exports of services, after surging in the mid-2000s, has flattened out.

What makes this development puzzling is that in recent years the composition of Indian exports of services is more favourable than that of Indian exports of manufactured goods. More of the former goes to the United States, and more of the latter to Asia. Since Asia has slowed down more rapidly, India's exports of manufactures should have been more affected. Furthermore, in 2015, the rupee has depreciated strongly against the dollar which should have helped India's exports of services.

These developments have longer-term implications. Realising India's medium-term growth potential of 8-10 per cent will require rapid growth of exports. How rapid this should be is suggested by comparing India's export performance in services with China's performance in manufacturing at a comparable stage of the growth surge.

China's global market share in manufacturing exports beginning in 1991 and India's global market share beginning in 2003 were roughly similar. The magnitude of the challenge becomes evident when examining China's trajectory over the last fifteen years.

To achieve a similar trajectory, India's competitiveness will have to improve so that its services exports, currently about 3 per cent of world exports, capture nearly 15 per cent of world market share. That is a sizeable challenge, and recent trends suggest that a major effort at improving competitiveness will be necessary to meet it.

GLOBAL NEGOTIATIONS

India aims to position itself as a key player in world services trade. To promote services exports, the government has taken a number of policy initiatives – SEIS (Service Exports from India Scheme) for increasing exports of notified services from India; organising GES (Global Exhibitions on Services); and SCs (Services Conclaves). Besides, some initiatives in sectors like tourism and shipping have also been taken in this regard. Given the potential of India's services exports, services-sector negotiations both at multilateral and bilateral and regional levels are of vital importance to India. Some of the recent negotiations[14] are as given below.

WTO Negotiations

Though, the 11th Ministerial Conference (MC) of the WTO ended without a Ministerial Declaration

13. *Economic Survey 2015–16,* Vol. 2, pp. 167-68, Ministry of Finance, GoI, N. Delhi.

14. *Economic Survey 2017–18,* Vol. 2 & *Economic Survey 2016–17,* Vol. 2, Ministry of Finance, GoI, N. Delhi.

or any substantive outcome, India saw certain favourable outcome from the 10th MC of the multi-lateral trade body *(Economic Survey 2017–18)*:

1. Implementation of preferential treatment in favour of services and service suppliers of least developed countries (LDC) and increasing LDC participation in services trade;
2. To maintain the current practice of not imposing customs duties on electronic transmissions (e-Commerce) until the next Ministerial Conference to be held in 2017.
3. India, together with 20 other members have notified preferential treatment to LDCs in services trade. India has offered this in respect of:
   (i) Market access
   (ii) Technical assistance and capacity building; and
   (iii) Waiver of visa fees for LDC applicants for business and employment.

Before the 11th MC of the WTO India made a presentation a proposal to the WTO for a global pact to boost services trade. The proposal—Trade Facilitation in Services (TFS)—is mainly aimed at 'ensuring'—easier norms for movement of foreign skilled workers/professionals across borders for short-term work; portability of social security contributions; reasonable fees for immigration; cross-border insurance coverage; boosting medical tourism; and publication availability of relevant information for cross-border supply of services. *World Bank* data shows the growing share of services in the world economy, the sources said, adding, however, that global trade flows in services remain subject to numerous border and behind-the-border barriers *(Ministry of Commerce and Industry)*.

Bilateral Agreements

The bilateral agreements signed by India in recent times are:

1. Comprehensive bilateral trade agreements signed, including trade in services, with the governments of Singapore, South Korea, Japan and Malaysia. An FTA in services and investment was signed with the Association of South East Asian Nations (ASEAN) effective since mid-2015.
2. India has joined the **RCEP** (Regional Comprehensive Economic Partnership) pluri- lateral negotiations. The proposed FTA includes the 10 ASEAN countries and its six FTA partners, viz. Australia, China, India, Japan, South Korea and New Zealand. The RCEP is the only mega-regional FTA of which India is a part.
3. India is also engaged in bilateral **FTA** negotiations including trade in services with Canada, Israel, Thailand, the EU, the EFTA (European Free Trade Association), Australia and New Zealand. Dialogue is under way with the US under the India-US Trade Policy Forum (TPF), with Australia under the India-Australia JMC (Joint Ministerial Commission), with China under the India-China Working-Group on Services, and with Brazil under the India-Brazil Trade Monitoring Mechanism (TMM).

RESTRICTIONS AND REGULATIONS

One major issue in services is the domestic barriers and regulations. Domestic regulations, in strict WTO terms, include licensing requirements, licensing procedures, qualification requirements, qualification procedures, and technical standards but here other restrictions and barriers are also considered. While there are many domestic regulations in our major markets, which deny market access to us and therefore need to be negotiated at multilateral and bilateral levels, there are also many domestic regulations in India which hinder the growth of this sector.

Since domestic regulations perform the role of tariffs in regulating services, there is need to list the domestic regulations in India which need to be curbed to help growth of the sector and its exports, while retaining those which are necessary for regulating the sector at this stage. An indicative list of some important domestic regulations in India which need to be examined for suitable policy reforms[15] in the services sector is as follows:

Trade and Transport Services

Some constraints in these sectors include restrictions on inter-state movement of goods which could ease with the adoption of the model *Agriculture Produce and Marketing Committee (APMC) Act* by many states; the *Multimodal Transportation of Goods Act 1993* which needs revision to ease the existing restrictions on transportation and documentation through different modes of transport, particularly restrictions in the *Customs Act*, which do not allow seamless movement of goods; and restrictions on free movement of cargo between *Inland Container Depots (ICDs), Container Freight Stations (CFSs)* and *Ports*.

Construction Development

In this sector, bottlenecks result from continuation of restrictions under the *Urban Land Ceiling and Regulation Act (ULCRA)* in some states namely Andhra Pradesh, Assam, Bihar, and West Bengal, which have not yet repealed it and the confusion in the process required for clearance of buildings even after the repeal of ULCRA by passing of the Urban Land (Ceiling and Regulations) Repeal Act 1999 by the other states.

There is also lack of clarity on the role of states as facilitators in the *land acquisition* policy resulting in increasing number of court litigations adding to risk profile of builders/projects thereby restricting lenders from extending finance to such builders/projects.

There are also restrictions on floor area ratio (FAR) in many states; and other restrictions like the application of bye laws/regulations and its exemptions, e.g., increase in FAR which varies from project to project and is sometimes discriminatory. Obtaining environment clearance is another major hindrance.

Accountancy Services

While the accountancy professionals were hitherto allowed to operate either as a partnership firm or as a sole proprietorship firm or in their own name since the Indian regulations do not permit exceeding 20 professionals under one firm, the emergence of *Limited Liability Partnership (LLP)* structure is likely to address this impediment. However, the number of statutory audits of companies per partner is restricted to 20.

FDI is also not allowed in this sector and foreign service providers are not allowed to undertake statutory audit of companies as per the provisions of the laws in India. There are also domestic regulations like prohibition on the use of individual *logos* for partnership and single proprietorship accounting firms. These regulations need to be relaxed and streamlined to facilitate tie-ups and penetrate foreign markets given the potential for exporting these services by the outsourcing mode.

15. H.A.C. Prasad and R. Sathish, Working Paper No. 1/2010-DEA on 'Policy of India's Services Sector, 2010' with updates from concerned Departments and Institutions, as quoted in, Ministry of Finance, (New Delhi: Government of India, ***Economic Survey 2013–14***, p. 228).

Legal Services

In this sector, FDI is not permitted and international law firms are not authorised to advertise and open offices in India. Foreign service providers can neither be appointed as partners nor sign legal documents and represent clients. The *Bar Council* is opposed to entry of foreign lawyers/law firms in any manner. Indian advocates are not permitted to enter into profit-sharing arrangements with persons other than Indian advocates.

Education Services

These come under the *Concurrent List* with multiple controls and regulations by central and state governments and statutory bodies. Regulations of minimum of 25 acres of land to establish a medical college restricts the setting up of medical colleges in cities like Delhi. *Patient load factor* regulations related to establishment of new medical colleges also need to be in tune with present day equipment-intensive patient care and modern practices and procedures of medical education.

THE NEED FOR REFORMS

Indian services sector have the potential to garner higher economic benefits to the country. But there are many issues both general and sector specific including domestic regulations which hinder the growth prospects of the services sector. If these issues are addressed deftly the sector could lead to exponential gains for the economy. The need of policy reforms[16] in this regards are outlined in the following way:

16 H.A.C. Prasad, R. Sathish, and Salam Shyamsunder Singh (2014), working paper 1/2014-DEA on 'Emerging Global Economic Situation: Opportunities and Policy Issues for Services Sector' and updates from some ministries and institutions, as quoted in, Ministry of Finance, ***Economic Survey 2013–14*** (New Delhi: Government of India, 2017), p. 190.

General Issues

There are some general issues related to the policy framework which hamper the healthy growth and expansion of the services sector in the country. They are broadly related to the following areas:

Nodal Agency and Marketing Despite having strong growth potential in various services sub-sectors, there is no single nodal department or agency for services. An inter-ministerial committee for services has been set up to look into this. But services activities cover issues beyond trade and a more proactive approach and proper institutional mechanism is needed to weed out *unwanted regulations* and tap the opportunities in the services sector in a coordinated way. There is also need for promotional activities for service exports like,

1. Setting up a portal for services,
2. Showcasing India's competence also in non-software services in trade exhibitions,
3. Engaging dedicated brand ambassadors and experts.

Disinvestment There is plenty of scope for disinvestment in services PSUs under both central and state governments. Speeding up disinvestment in some services-sector PSUs could not only provide revenue for the government but also speed up the growth of these services.

Credit Related The issues here include 'collateral free' soft loans to support the sector's cash needs and possibility of considering even export or business orders as collateral for credit-worthy service firms.

Tax and Trade Policy Related These include use of 'net' instead of 'gross' foreign exchange criteria for export benefit schemes, the issue of *retrospective* amendments of tax laws like,

1. Amendment to the definition of royalty to include payment of any rights via any medium for use of computer software,

2. Tax administrative measures to tackle delay in refunds,
3. Introducing VAT (value added tax) refund for foreign tourists, and
4. Addressing the issue of bank guarantees based on past performance to avail export promotion benefits in services.

COVID-19 AND SERVICES SECTOR

With a view to convert the coronavirus disruptions into an opportunity, the Government has given an emphatic call for 'self-reliance' and launched an ambitious ***Atmanirbharta Bharat Abhiyan***. The package (₹ 20 lakh crores) announced under the campaign are in the nature of relief as well as financial stimulus which touches diverse sectors of the economy – one of the most significant part of it is devoted to the MSMEs – which includes today most of the start-ups in the country. The measures related to these enterprises are expected to help them grow faster and play crucial role in economic revival and making the country self-reliant, in the following ways—

1. By revising the *definition* criteria for the MSMEs the Government has given them chance to get bigger and listed on the stock exchange platforms.
2. As the *distinction* between manufacturing and services MSMEs has been abolished, the services sector has got a big boost.
3. The arrangement of collateral-free loans, subordinate debt and creation of *fund of funds* will be a big game-changer in case of the MSMEs and thus to services sector.

[For more details on the package for the MSMEs, refer *Chapter 9*].

WAY FORWARD

India is export hub for software services— its IT outsourcing service market is expected to witness 6-8 per cent growth between 2021-2025 (with only home healthcare industry expected to reach US$ 10 billion by 2025). As per the Government, the services sector has large potential, but the same has not been harnessed fully. The sector should take the COVID-19 crisis as an opportunity, and not as a challenge— the world is going to be different post-COVID, as new norms are setting in, in terms of work, education, entertainment, health etc. In this context the following actions will be highly helpful in further expansion of the sector in India and abroad:

- The sector needs to develop competitive advantage by adopting newer technologies and required skill sets— with focus on quality, exploring new destinations and services.
- The large pool of skilled manpower, especially in the areas of IT & ITeS, is available at relatively low cost needs to be harnessed.
- Rapidly increasing population of youth looking to migrate from agriculture to other sectors will be a boon to the sector.
- There is no reason why the sector depends so much on imports, when we have a large and varied skilled workforce.
- Indian missions abroad should start pitching in effectively to explore Indian exports there.

The most successful segment in the services, is the IT and allied services, and it flourished on its own capabilities, and without seeking much of the Government's support, which many a times comes with the bureaucratic strings and control as well. The Government also has priorities and limitations— it can make focused and policy interventions, help the sector in its nascent stages (i.e., at start-up level), help them grow, check the unfair practices, but can't be seen providing support all the time. [17]

---

17. **India Brand Equity Foundation (IBEF),** April 2021, Ministry of Commerce and Industry, GoI, N. Delhi.

(a) administrative processes to avoid delays [illegible]

Introducing VAT/GST and added tax refund for foreign tourists; and

Addressing the issue of bank guarantees based on past performance to avail export promotion benefits in services.

COVID-19 AND SERVICES SECTOR

[illegible] of the [illegible] disruption [illegible] opportunity, the Government has given an emphatic call for self-reliance and launched an ambitious *Atmanirbhar Bharat Abhiyan*. The package (₹ 20 lakh crore) announced under the [illegible] as well as [illegible] economic [illegible] of the most important parts of it is devoted to the MSMEs, which include today most of the start-ups in the country. The measures related to these enterprises are expected to help them grow faster and play crucial role in economic revival and making the country self-reliant in the following ways—

(i) By revising the definition criteria for the MSMEs, the Government has given them chance to get bigger and listed on the stock exchange in future.

(ii) As the distinction between manufacturing and services MSMEs has been abolished, the services sector has got a big boost.

(iii) The arrangement of collateral-free loans, subordinate debt and creation of *Fund of Funds* will be a big game changer in case of the MSMEs and thus to services sector.

[For more details on the package for the MSMEs refer Chapter 9.]

WAY FORWARD

India's export hub for software services — the IT outsourcing service market is expected to witness 6-8 per cent growth between 2021–2023 (with only [illegible]

home healthcare industry expected to reach US$ 10 billion by 2020 as per the Government, the services sector has large potential but the same has not been harnessed fully. The sector should take the COVID-19 crisis as an opportunity, and act as [illegible] the world is going to be different post-COVID [illegible] in terms of [illegible] entertainment, health etc. In the coming [illegible] following [illegible] highly [illegible] both [illegible] and abroad.

- The sector needs to develop competitive advantage by adopting newer technologies and required skill sets—with focus on quality, exploring new destinations and [illegible].
- The large pool of skilled manpower, especially for the areas of IT & ITeS, is available at relatively low cost needs to be harnessed.
- [illegible] looking to migrate [illegible] to other [illegible] will [illegible] sector.
- There is no reason why the sector depends so much on imports, when we have a large and valued skilled workforce.
- Indian missions abroad should start pitching in effectively to explore Indian export [illegible] there.

The most successful segment in the services is the IT and allied services and it flourished by its own capabilities, and without seeking much of the Government's support, which many a times comes with the bureaucratic strings and corruption as well. The Government also has priorities and [illegible]. It can make focused and policy interventions, help the sector in its nascent stages (i.e., at start-up level), help them grow, check the unfair practices, but must be seen providing support all the time.

[illegible] India Brand Equity Foundation (IBEF), March 2021, Ministry of Commerce and Industry, GoI, N. Delhi.

CHAPTER 11

INDIAN FINANCIAL MARKET

A well-developed financial system should effectively harness domestic savings; facilitate the efficient allocation of domestic and foreign savings to productive investments; allow households and firms to share risk; and support consumption and expenditure smoothening–to meet these goals, the financial system needs a strong banking system as well as a deep equity and bond markets.*

In this Chapter...

- Introduction
- Indian Money Market
- Mutual Funds
- DFHI
- Indian Capital Market
- Financial Regulation

 INTRODUCTION

The market of an economy where funds are transacted between the fund-surplus and fund-scarce individuals and groups is known as the financial market *(definition)*.[1] The basis of transaction is either *interest* or *dividend*. This market might have its organised (institutionalised) as well as non-organised (unregulated/non-institutionalised) segments in an economy.

Financial markets in every economy are having two separate segments today, one catering to the requirements of *short-term funds* and the other to the requirements of *long-term funds*.[2] The short-term financial market is known as the **money market**, while the long-term financial market is known as the **capital market.** The money market fulfils the requirements of funds for the period upto 364 days (*i.e., short term*) while the capital market does the same for the period above 364 days (*i.e., long term*).[3] A brief discussion on the Indian financial market is given below:

1. Based on the discussion in P.A. Samuelson and W.D. Nordhaus, ***Economics*** (New Delhi: Tata McGrawHill, 2005), pp. 543–45.

2. Based on J.E. Stiglitz and C.E. Walsh, ***Economics*** (New York: W.W. Norton & Company, 2006), pp. 612–14.

3. See Reserve Bank of India, ***Report on Currency and Finance*** (New Delhi: Government of India, multiple years).

*See Financial Sector Development and Reforms, Eswar Prasad, pp. 183-192 in Abhijit Banerjee, Gita Gopoinath Raghuram Rajan and Mihir S. Sharma edited **What the Economy Needs Now,** Juggernaut Books, N. Delhi, 2019.

INDIAN MONEY MARKET

Money market is the short-term financial market of an economy. In this market, money is traded between individuals or groups (i.e., financial institutions, banks, government, companies, etc.), who are either *cash-surplus* or *cash-scarce.* Trading is done on a rate known as *discount rate* which is determined by the market and guided by the availability of and demand for the cash in the day-to-day trading.[4] The 'repo rate' of the time (announced by the RBI) works as the guiding rate for the current 'discount rate'. Borrowings in this market may or may not be supported by collaterals. In the money market the *financial assets*, which have quick conversion quality into money and carry minimal transaction cost, are also traded.[5] Money market may be *defined* as a market where short-term lending and borrowing take place between the cash-surplus and cash-scarce sides.

The market operates in both 'organised' and 'unorganised' channels in India. Starting from the 'person-to-person' mode and converting into 'telephonic transaction', it has now gone *online* in the age of internet and information technology. The transactions might take place through the intermediaries (known as brokers) or directly between the trading sides.

Need for Money Market Income generation (i.e., growth) is the most essential requirement of any economic system. In the modern industrial economies, creation of productive assets is not an easy task, as it requires investible capital of long-term nature. Long-term capital can be raised either through bank loans, corporate bonds, debentures or shares (i.e., from the capital market). But once a productive asset has been created and production starts there comes the need of another kind of capital, to meet the day-to-day shortfalls of working capital. It means that only setting-up of firms does not guarantee production as these firms keep facing *fund mismatches* in the day-to-day production process. Such funds are required only for a short period (days, fortnights or few months) and are needed to meet shortfalls in working capital requirements. This requires creation of a different segment of the financial market which can cater to the short-term requirements of such funds for the enterprises—known as the **money market** or the **working capital market.** The short-term period is defined as upto 364 days.

The crucial role money market plays in an economy is proved by the fact that if only a few lakhs or crores of rupees of working capital is not met in time, it can push a firm or business enterprise to go for lock-out, which has been set-up with thousands of crores of capital. If lock-out happens, the firm might default in its payments, losing its age-old credit-worthiness, consequently creating a chain of negatives in the economic system. This is why it is essential for every economy to organise a strong and vibrant money market which has wider geographic presence (the reason why it is today internet-based).

Money Market in India The organised form of money market in India is just close to three decades old. However, its presence has been there, but restricted to the government only.[6] It was the **Chakravarthy Committee** (1985) which, for the first time, underlined the need of an organised money market in the country[7] and the **Vaghul Committee** (1987) laid the blue print for its development.[8] Today, money market in India

4. In the capital market, money is traded on interest rate as well as on dividends. Long-term loans are raised on well-defined interest rates, while long-term capital is raised on dividends through the sale of shares.

5. Such financial assets are known as 'close substitutes for money.'

6. The only instrument of the money market was the Treasury Bills, which were sold by tender at weekly auctions upto 1965. But later these bills were made available throughout the week at discount rates by the Reserve Bank of India.

7. Sukhomoy Chakravarthy, ***Review of the Working of the Monetary System*** (New Delhi: Reserve Bank of India, 1985).

8. M. Vaghul, ***Working Group on Money Market*** (New Delhi: Reserve Bank of India, 1987). The committee was set up in 1986, and came to be known as the Vaghul Committee.

is not an integrated unit and has two segments—*Unorganised Money Market* and *Organised Money Market.*

1. **Unorganised Money Market:** Before the government started the organised development of the money market in India, its unorganised form had its presence since the ancient times—its remnant is still present in the country. Their activities are not regulated like the organised money market, but they are recognised by the government. In recent years, some of them have been included under the regulated organised market (for example, the NBFCs were put under the regulatory control of the RBI in 1997). The unorganised money market in India may be divided into three differing categories:

   (i) ***Unregulated Non-Bank Financial Intermediaries:*** Unregulated Non-Banking Financial Intermediaries are functioning in the form of *chit funds, nidhis* (operate in South India, which lend to only their members) and loan companies. They charge very high interest rates (i.e., 36 to 48 per cent per annum), thus, are exploitative in nature and have selective reach in the economy.

   (ii) ***Indigenous Bankers:*** Indigenous bankers receive deposits and lend money in the capacity of an individual or a private firms. There are, basically, four such bankers in the country functioning as non-homogenous groups:

   (a) *Gujarati Shroffs:* They operate in Mumbai, Kolkata as well as in industrial, trading and port cities in the region.

   (b) *Multani or Shikarpuri Shroffs:* They operate in Mumbai, Kolkata, Assam tea gardens and North Eastern India.

   (c) *Marwari Kayas:* They operate mainly in Gujarat with a little bit of presence in Mumbai and Kolkata.

   (d) *Chettiars:* They are active in Chennai and at the ports of southern India.

   (iii) ***Money Lenders:*** They constitute the most localised form of money market in India and operate in the most exploitative way. They have their two forms:

   (a) The professional money lenders who lend their own money as a profession to earn income through interest.

   (b) The non-professional money lenders who might be businessmen and lend their money to earn interest income as a subsidiary business.

Today, India has **eight** organised instruments of the money market which are used by the prescribed firms in the country, but the unorganised money market also operates side by side—there are certain reasons[9] behind this:

(i) Indian money market is still under-developed.

(ii) Lack of penetration and presence of the instruments of the organised money market.

(iii) There are many needful customers in the money market who are currently outside the purview of the organised money market.

(iv) Entry to the organised money market for its customers is still restrictive in nature—not allowing small businessmen.

9. Based on the suggestions of experts belonging to the Indian financial market.

2. **Organised Money Market:** Since the government started developing the organised money market in India (mid-1980s), we have seen the arrival of a total of **eight** instruments designed to be used by different categories of business and industrial firms. A brief description of these instruments follows:

   (i) ***Treasury Bills (TBs):*** This instrument of the money market though present since Independence got organised only in 1986. They are used by the Central Government to fulfil its short-term liquidity requirement upto the period of 364 days. There developed **five types** of the TBs in due course of time:

   (a) 14-day (Intermediate TBs)

   (b) 14-day (Auctionable TBs)

   (c) 91-day TBs

   (d) 182-day TBs

   (e) 364-day TBs

   Out of the above five variants of the TBs, at present only the **91-day TBs, 182-day TBs** and the **364-day TBs** are issued by the government. The other two variants were discontinued in 2001.[10]

   The TBs other than providing short-term cushion to the government, also function as short-term investment avenues for the banks and financial institutions, besides functioning as requirements of the CRR and SLR of the banking institutions.

   (ii) ***Certificate of Deposit (CD):*** Organised in 1989, the CD is used by **banks** and issued to the depositors for a specified period ranging less than one year—they are negotiable and tradable in the money market. Since 1993 the RBI allowed the **financial institutions** to operate in it—IFCI, IDBI, IRBI (IIBI since 1997) and the Exim Bank—they can issue CDs for the maturity periods above one year and upto three years.

   (iii) ***Commercial Paper (CP):*** Organised in 1990 it is used by the **corporate houses** in India (which should be a listed company with a working capital of not less than ₹5 crore). The CP issuing companies need to obtain a specified credit rating from an agency approved by the RBI (such as CRISIL, ICRA, etc). Aimed to broaden investor participation, in October 2019, the SEBI allowed *listing* of the Commercial Papers.

   (iv) ***Commercial Bill (CB):*** Organised in 1990, a CB is issued by the **All India Financial Institutions** (AIFIs), **Non-Banking Finance Companies** (NBFCs), **Scheduled Commercial Banks, Merchant Banks, Co-operative Banks** and the **Mutual Funds.** It replaced the old Bill Market available since 1952 in the country.

   (v) ***Call Money Market (CMM):*** This is basically an **inter-bank** money market where funds are borrowed and lent, generally, for one day—that is why this is also known as **over-night borrowing market** (also called **money at call**). Fund can be borrowed/raised for a maximum period upto 14 days (called **short notice**). Borrowing in this market may take place against securities or without securities.[11] Rate of interest in this market 'glides' with the 'repo

10. Ministry of Finance, ***Economic Survey 2001–02*** (New Delhi: Government of India, 2002); Ministry of Finance, Economic Survey 2009–10 (New Delhi: Government of India, 2010).

11. The State Bank of India (operates in this market as lender as it is in a comfortable cash position) lends against government securities, while others lend against the 'deposit receipts' of the borrowing banks. The SBI functions as the 'lender of intermediate resort' (while the RBI functions as the 'lender of last resort').

rate' of the time the principle remains, very simple—longer the period higher the interest rate. Depending upon the availability and demand of fund in this market the real call rate revolves nearby the current repo rate.

The scheduled commercial banks, co-operative banks operate in this market as both the borrowers and lenders while LIC, GIC, Mutual Funds, IDBI and NABARD are allowed to operate as only lenders in this market.

(vi) ***Money Market Mutual Fund (MF):*** Popular as Mutual Funds (MFs) this money market instrument was introduced/organised in 1992 to provide short-term investment opportunity to **individuals**. The initial guidelines for the MF have been liberalised many times. Since March 2000, MFs have been brought under the preview of SEBI, besides the RBI. At present, a whole lot of financial institutions and firms are allowed to set up MFs, viz., commercial banks, public and private financial institutions and private sector companies. By December 2020, there were **43** mutual fund companies operating in the country managing a total asset of ₹31.02 lakh crores with a growth of 16.9 per cent over December 2019 *(Economic Survey 2020-21)*.

(vii) ***Repos and Reverse Repos:*** In the era of economic reforms there developed two new instruments of money market—**repo** and **reverse repo.** Considered the most dynamic instruments of the Indian money market they have emerged the most favoured route to raise short-term funds in India. 'Repo' is basically an acronym of the **rate of repurchase.** The RBI in a span of four years, introduced these instruments—**repo** in December 1992 and **reverse repo** in November 1996.

Repo allows the banks and other financial institutions to borrow money from the RBI for short-term (by selling government securities to the RBI). In **reverse repo**, the banks and financial institutions purchase government securities from the RBI (basically here the RBI is borrowing from the banks and the financial institutions). All government securities are dated and the interest for the repo or reverse repo transactions are announced by the RBI from time to time. The provision of repo and the reverse repo have been able to serve the liquidity evenness in the economy as the banks are able to get the required amount of funds out of it, and they can park surplus idle funds through it. These instruments have emerged as important tools in the management of the monetary and credit policy in recent years.[12]

Accepting the recommendations of the **Urjit Patel Committee**, the RBI in April 2014 (while announcing the first *Bi-monthly Credit & Monetary Policy-2014–15*) announced to introduce **term repo** and **term reverse repo** This is believed to bring in higher stability and better signalling of interest rates across different loan markets in the economy.

(viii) ***Cash Management Bill (CMB):*** The Government of India, in consultation with the RBI, decided to issue a new short-term instrument, known as Cash

12 Reserve Bank of India, ***Report on Currency and Finance*** (New Delhi: Government of India, 1999); Reserve Bank of India, Report on Currency and Finance (New Delhi: Government of India, 2000).

Management Bills, since August 2009 to meet the temporary cash flow mismatches of the government. The Cash Management Bills are *non-standard* and *discounted instruments* issued for maturities less than 91 days.

The CMBs have the *generic character of Treasury Bills* (issued at discount to the face value); are tradable and qualify for *ready forward facility;* investment in it is considered as an eligible investment in government securities by banks for SLR.

It should be noted here that the existing Treasury Bills serve the same purpose, but as they were put under the WMAs (Ways & Means Advances) provisions by the Government of India in 1997, they did not remain a discretionary route for the government in meeting its short-term requirements of funds at will (see 'Fiscal Consolidation in India', sub-topic in **Chapter 18** *Public Finance* for details). CBM does not come under the similar WMAs provisions.

MUTUAL FUNDS

Of all investment options, mutual funds are touted to be the best tool for wealth creation over the long term. They are of several types, and the risk varies with the kind of asset classes these funds invest in. As the name suggests, a mutual fund *is a fund that is created when a large number of investors put in their money, and is managed by professionally qualified persons with experience in investing in different asset classes—shares, bonds, money market instruments like call money, and other assets such as gold and property.* Their names usually give a good idea about what type of asset class a fund, also called a scheme, will invest in. For example, a **diversified equity fund** will invest in a large number of stocks, while a **gilt fund** will invest in government securities, while a **pharma fund** will mainly invest in stocks of companies from the pharmaceutical and related industries.

Mutual funds, first of all came in the money market (regulated by the RBI), but they have the freedom to operate in the capital market, too. This is why they have provision of dual regulator—the RBI and SEBI. Mutual funds are compulsorily registered with the Securities and Exchange Board of India (SEBI), which also acts as the **first wall of defence** for all investors in these funds. For those who do not understand how mutual funds operate but are willing to invest, the move by SEBI is seen as a big relief.

Each mutual fund is run by a group of qualified people who form a company, called an *asset management company (AMC)* and the operations of the AMC are under the guidance of another group of people, called *trustees.* Both, the people in the AMC as well as the trustees, have a *fiduciary responsibility,* because these are the people who are entrusted with the task of managing the hard-earned money of people who do not understand much about managing money.

A fund house or a distributor working for the fund house (which could be an individual, a company or even a bank) are qualified to sell mutual funds. The fund house allots the 'units' of the MF to the investor at a price that is fixed through a process approved by SEBI, which is based on the net asset value (NAV). In simple terms, NAV is the total value of investments in a scheme divided by the total number of units issued to investors in the same scheme. In most mutual fund schemes, NAVs are computed and published on a daily basis. However, when a fund house is launching a scheme for the first time, the units are sold at ₹10 each. There are **three types** of schemes offered by MFs:

1. **Open-ended Schemes:** An open-ended fund is one which is usually available from an MF on an ongoing basis, that

is, an investor can buy or sell as and when they intend to at a NAV-based price. As investors buy and sell units of a particular open-ended scheme, the number of units issued also changes every day and so changes the value of the scheme's portfolio. So, the NAV also changes on a daily basis. In India, fund houses can sell any number of units of a particular scheme, but at times fund houses restrict selling additional units of a scheme for some time.

2. **Closed-ended Schemes:** A close-ended fund usually issues units to investors only once, when they launch an offer, called *new fund offer (NFO)* in India. Thereafter, these units are listed on the stock exchanges where they are traded on a daily basis. As these units are listed, any investor can buy and sell these units through the exchange. As the name suggests, close-ended schemes are managed by fund houses for a limited number of years, and at the end of the term either money is returned to the investors or the scheme is made open ended. However, there is a word of caution here that usually, units of close ended funds which are listed on the stock exchanges, trade at a high discount to their NAVs. But as the date for closure of the fund nears, the discount between the NAV and the trading price narrows, and vanishes on the day of closure of the scheme.

3. **Exchange-Traded Funds (ETFs):** ETFs are a mix of open-ended and close-ended schemes. ETFs, like close-ended schemes, are listed and traded on a stock exchange on a daily basis, but the price is usually very close to its NAV, or the underlying assets, like gold ETFs.

If investments have been done in a well-managed MF, the advantages outweigh disadvantages in the long term, which is 10 years or more. There is a very high probability for investors of making more money than by investing in other risk-free investments such as FDs, public provident fund etc. Advantages of investing in MFs include:

(i) diversification of portfolio,

(ii) good investment management services,

(iii) liquidity,

(iv) strong government-backed regulatory help,

(v) professional service, and

(vi) low cost for all the benefits.

An investor, by investing in a mutual fund scheme that has blue chip stocks in its portfolio, indirectly gets an exposure to these stocks. Compared to this, if the same investor wants to have each of these stocks in his portfolio, the cost of buying and managing the portfolio will be much higher.

Mutual funds invest the investors money in both the **loan** and **share** markets. Buyers of MF units are given choice/option as in which of the markets they wish their money to be invested by the fund managers of the MF. This way investors get the following choices:

1. *Loan* (100 per cent of the funds will be invested in the loan market),
2. *Share* (100 per cent of the funds will be invested in the share market), and
3. *Balance* (60 per cent of the funds will be invested in the loan market while the rest 40 per cent in the share market—this provision keeps changing depending upon the health of the share market—clearly announced by the MFs).

By *October 2017*, the SEBI announced to classify the mutual fund schemes into *five broad categories* to cut through the clutter and make it easier for investors to compare plans with similar characteristics—Debt, Equity, Hybrid, Solution-oriented (such as retirement and children funds), and other schemes.

Every class is further finely divided, making for a total of *36 different scheme* categories such as Dividend Yield Equity Fund, which would focus on dividend-yielding stocks, or Banking and PSU Debt Fund, which invests a minimum 80 per cent of its corpus in debt paper issued by state-owned firms and lenders. A fund house will be allowed to have only one scheme per category to ensure that there is no duplication.

DFHI

The Discount and Finance House of India Limited[13] (DFHI) was set up in April 1988 by the RBI jointly with the public sector banks and financial investment institutions (i.e., LIC, GIC and UTI). Its establishment was an outcome of the long-drawn need of the following two types:

1. to bring an equilibrium of liquidity in the Indian banking system, and
2. to impart liquidity to the instruments of the money market prevalent in the economy.

In 2004, the RBI transferred its total holding in the DFHI to the State Bank of India arm SBI Gilts Limited. Its new name is SBI DFHI. It functions as the biggest 'primary dealer' in the economy and functions on commercial basis. It deals in all kinds of instruments in the money market without any upper ceiling. Operating in 'two way' (as a lender and borrower) its objective is to provide needful liquidity and stability in the financial market of the country.

13 It was in 1979 that the Chore Committee for the first time recommended for a discount house to level the liquidity imbalances in the banking system. The government became active after the recommendations of the Working Group on the Money Market (i.e., the Vaghul Committee, 1987) and finally established DFHI in 1988. The Vaghul Committee suggested to set up a discount finance institution which could deal in short-term money market instruments so that liquidity could be provided to these instruments. The committee also recommended the house to operate on 'commercial basis', which was accepted by the government while setting up DFHI.

INDIAN CAPITAL MARKET

The long-term financial market of an economy is known as the 'capital market'. This market makes it possible to raise *long-term money* (capital), i.e., for a period of minimum 365 days and above. Creation of productive assets is not possible without a string capital market—the market gained more importance once most of the economies in the world started industrialising. Across the world, banks emerged as the first and the foremost segment of the capital market. In coming times many other segments got added to it, viz., insurance industry, mutual funds, and finally the most attractive and vibrant, the security/stock market. Organised development of capital market together with putting in place the right regulatory framework for it, has always been a tough task for the economies. It is believed today that for strong growth prospects in an economy presence of a strong and vibrant capital market is essential.

Though the capital market of India is far stronger and better today in comparison to the periods just after Independence, the process of emergence has not been easy and smooth. Once India opted 'industry' as its prime moving force, the first challenge was to raise long-term funds for industrial establishments and their expansion. As banks in India were weak, small and geographically unevenly distributed they were not in a position to play the pivotal role they played in case of the industrialising Western economies. This is why the government decided to set up 'financial institutions' which could play the role of banks (till banks gain strength and presence) and carry on the responsibilities of 'project financing'.

Project Financing

After Independence, India went for intensive industrialisation to achieve rapid growth and development. To this end, the main responsibility was given to the Public Sector Undertakings (PSUs). For industrialisation we require capital, technology and labour, all being typically difficult to manage in the case of India. For capital requirement, the government decided to depend upon internal and external sources and the government decided to set up financial institutions (FIs). Though India was having banks, but due to low saving rate and lower deposits with them, the upcoming industries could not be financed through them. The main borrowers for industrial development were the PSUs. To support the capital requirement of the 'projects' of the public sector industries, the government came up with different types of financial institutions in the coming years. The industrial financing supported by these financial institutions was known as 'project financing' in India. An overview of India's capital in present time is given below:

1. **Financial Institutions:** The requirement of project financing made India to go for a number of FIs from time to time, which are generally classified into four categories:[14]

   (i) ***All India Financial Institutions (AIFIs):*** The all India FIs are IFCI (1948); ICICI (1955); IDBI (1964); SIDBI (1990) & IIBI (1997). All of them were public sector FIs except ICICI, which was a joint sector venture with initial capital coming from the RBI, some foreign banks and FIs. The public sector FIs were funded by the Government of India.

   By 1980s, all Indian banks acquired wider capital base and by early 1990s when the stock market became popular, it became easier for the corporate world to tap cheaper capital from these segments of the capital market.[15] The era of economic reforms had given the same option to the PSUs to tap new capital. As the AIFIs had more or less fixed rate of interest as compared to the banks which could mobilise cheaper deposits to lend cheaper—the AIFIs seemed to become irrelevant. The AIFIs witnessed a sharp decline in recent years.[16] At this juncture the government decided to convert them into **Development Banks**[17] (suggested by the Narasimhan Committee-I) to be known as the All India Development Banks (AIDBs). In 2000, the government allowed ICICI to go for a **reverse merger** (when an elder enterprise is merged with a younger one) with the ICICI Bank—the first AIDB emerged with no obligation of project financing—such entities in coming times will be known as the **universal banks**[18] (allowed to set up as many financial institutions they wish to, such as insurance, merchant banks, mutual funds, etc.). In a similar move, the IDBI was reverse merged with the IDBI Bank in 2002 and the second AIDB emerged. But it has still the obligation of carrying its project financing duties.

14. *Industrial Finance Corporation of India Act, 1948*, Government of India, New Delhi.

15. Ministry of Finance, *Economic Survey 2000-01*, (New Delhi: Government of India, 2010).

16. Ministry of Finance, *Economic Survey 2006-07*, (New Delhi: Government of India, 2007).

17. **Narasimhan Committee on the Financial System (CFS), 1991** suggested for the conversion of the AIFIs into Development Banks.

18. It was the **S.H. Khan Committee on Development Financial Institutions (DFIs), 1998** which forwarded the concept/idea of Universal Banking in India.

In 2002, the government, proposed to merge IFCI and IIBI with the nationalised bank PNB to create a big **Universal Bank.** It is believed that PNB was unwilling to go for this merger as these FIs were running at heavy losses. This move was part correct as per the recommendations of the Narasimhan Committee-II (to the extent merger is concerned, following its 3-Tier Banking Structure of India), but part against it (the committee has advised not to merge weak banks/FIs with either weak or strong banks/FIs).[19] Presently, the government is trying to make IFCI and IIBI to turn around their business and emerge as profitable entities—they are busy recovering their dues and improving their balance sheet.

New DFI: In the *Union Budget 2021-22,* the Government highlighted the need of a 'professionally managed' development financial institution (DFI) which could act as a provider, enabler and catalyst for infrastructure financing in the economy. As infrastructure sector needs long-term debt financing, presence of such an institution was felt since long. Taking steps towards it, the Budget announced to set up a new DFI which will have a lending portfolio of ₹5 lakh crores in the next 3 years (a corpus of ₹20,000 crores was allocated for it).

(ii) ***Specialised Financial Institutions (SFIs)***[20]**:** Two new FIs were set up by the Central Government in the late 1980s to finance **risk** and **innovation** in the area of industrial expansion; this was India's trial in the area of **venture capital funding.**

(a) *IFCI Venture Capital Funds Ltd (IFCI Venture), 2000:* It was promoted as a Risk Capital Foundation (RCF) in 1975 by IFCI Ltd., a society to provide financial assistance to first generation professionals and technocrat entrepreneurs for setting up own ventures through soft loans, under the Risk Capital Scheme.

In 1988, RCF was converted into a company—Risk Capital and Technology Finance Corporation Ltd. (RCTC)—when it also introduced the Technology Finance and Development Scheme (TFDS) for financing development and commercialisation of indigenous technology. Besides, under Risk Capital Scheme, RCTC started providing financial assistance to entrepreneurs by way of direct equity participation. Based on IFCI Venture's credentials and strengths, Unit Trust of India (UTI), entrusted RCTC with the management of a new venture capital fund named **Venture Capital Unit Scheme (VECAUS-III)** in 1991 with its funds coming from the UTI and IFCI. To reflect the shift in the company's activities, the name of RCTC was changed to IFCI Venture Capital Funds Ltd. (IFCI Venture) in February 2000.

In order to focus on Asset Management Activities, IFCI Venture discontinued Risk Capital and Technology Finance Schemes in 2000–01 and continued managing VECAUS-III. In 2007,

---

19. Ministry of Finance, *Economic Survey 2011-12* (New Delhi: Government of India, 2011), pp. 115–16.

20. The write-up is based on information available from SEBI, RBI and different announcements/published reports of the Ministry of Finance, since 1996 onwards.

as UTI had ceased to carry out its activities and its assets vested with **Specified Undertaking of the Unit Trust of India (SUUTI),** the portfolio of VECAUS-III under management of IFCI Venture was transferred to SUUTI.

(b) *Tourism Finance Corporation of India Ltd (TFCI), 1989:* The Government of India had, on the recommendations of the National Committee on Tourism *(Yunus Committee)* set up under the aegis of the Planning Commission, decided in 1988, to promote a separate All India Financial Institution for providing financial assistance to tourism-related activities/projects. In accordance with the above decision, the IFCI Ltd. along with other all-India financial/investment institutions and some nationalised banks promoted a Public Limited Company under the name of 'Tourism Finance Corporation of India Ltd. (TFCI)' to function as a Specialised All-India Development Financial Institution to cater to the financial needs of the tourism industry.

TFCI was incorporated as a Public Limited Company in 1989 and became operational with effect from 1989. TFCI was notified as a Public Financial Institution in January 1990. Its promoter, the IFCI, holds major share (41.6 per cent) in it, while the rest of the shares are with the 'public' (26 per cent), public sector banks, public insurance companies and public mutual fund (i.e., UTI Mutual Fund Ltd.).

(iii) *Investment Institutions (IIs):* Three investment institutions also came up in the public sector, which are yet another kind of FIs, i.e., the LIC (1956), the UTI (1964) and the GIC (1971).

In the present time they are no more known as DIIs (Domestic Investment Institutions) or DFIs (Domestic Financial Institutions). LIC is now the public sector insurance company in the life segment, GIC was been converted into a public sector re-insurance company in 2000, while UTI was converted into a mutual fund company in 2002. Now these investment institutions (IIs) are no more like the past. LIC is now called an 'insurance company', part of the Indian Insurance Industry and is the lone public sector playing in the life insurance segment competing with the private life insurance companies. Similarly, the UTI is now part of the Indian Mutual Fund industry and the lone such firm in the public sector competing with other private sector mutual funds. Similarly, the erstwhile four public sector general insurance companies are part of India's general insurance industry and competing with private companies in the area (they were Holding Companies of the GIC—now these are owned by the GoI directly and GIC only looks after its 're-insurance' business). This is why we do not get the use of the term 'IIs' in recent times in any of the GoI official documents.

(iv) ***State Level Finance Institutions (SLFIs):*** In the wake of states involvement in the industrial development, the central government allowed the states to set up their own financial institutions (after the states demanded so). In this process two kinds of FIs came up:

(a) *State Finance Corporations (SFCs):* First came up in Punjab (1955) with other states following its example. There are 18 SFCs working presently.

(b) *State Industrial Development Corporations (SIDCs):* A fully dedicated state public sector FI to the cause of industrial development in the concerned states. First such FIs were set up (1960) in Andhra Pradesh and Bihar.

Almost all of the SFCs and SIDCs are at present running in huge losses. They may be re-structured on the lines of the AIFIs, but there is lack of will from the states and private financiers who are not interested to go in for their takeovers as such.

2. **Banking Industry:** With the passage of time, the industry saw its nationalisation (1969 and 1980) and again opening up for private sector entry (1993–94) to emerge as the most dependable segment of Indian financial system—in a way its mainstay. By April 2020, there were a total of 163 scheduled commercial banks operating in India—18 public sector banks (PSBs), 53 RRBs (with over 13 under consideration for amalgamation with their parent PSBs), 41 Indian private sector banks (including 10 Small Banks, 7 Payment Banks and 3 Local Area Banks), 46 foreign banks except the scheduled and non-scheduled state co-operative banks—with 74 per cent foreign direct investment (FDI) allowed in the private sector banks (49 per cent under automatic route and above 49 per cent under non-automatic route).[21]

In the wake of the economic reforms the government has promised speedier expansion of the banking sector. But the entry of new private players in the banking sector has been slow, hampering the growth and expansion of the sector. But in a *recent release* the RBI has committed to allow new banks to come up on regular basis—in **April 2014** the RBI allowed two new private sector banks to start their operations. [for a detailed discussion on the banking sector refer the *Chapter 12*].

3. **Insurance Industry:** After Independence, for the purpose of expanding the industry, one after another the life and non-life insurance businesses were nationalised by the government (in 1956 and 1970, respectively), and the public sector insurance companies did serve the better purpose in the areas of providing safety net and nation-building. In the wake of the process of economic reforms a restructuring of the sector was started and the industry was opened for domestic and Foreign Private Players (with the FDI limit increased in 2021-22 to of 74 per cent from 26 per cent of 1999) and an independent regulator – the Insurance Regulatory Development Authority (IRDAD being set up in 1999. Since then many private players have entered the industry. By April 2021, a total of 54 insurance companies were operating in India of which 24 were in life segment while 30 in non-life segment—1 public sector life insurer (LIC), 4 public sector general insurer, 2 specialised insurers (AICIL and ECGC), 1 public sector re-insurer (GIC Re) and 10 foreign re-insurers.[22] The expansion and penetration insurance in the country have increased during the reform period, but not as per the expectations of the governments and, as per the experts and the IRDA, several reasons have been responsible for this.

4. **Security Market:** After the government's attempts to formally organise the security and

21. As per the **Reserve Bank of India,** Mumbai, April 2020.

22. **Annual Report 2018-19** (IRDAI) and **Economic Survey 2020-21,** vol. 2, p. 149, Ministry of Finance, GoI, N. Delhi.

stock market of India, the segment has seen accelerated expansion. Today, it is counted among the most vibrant share markets of the world and has challenged the monopoly of banks in the capital market of the country.[23] The security market of India is regulated by SEBI. India has developed a regulated 'forward market' also where hundreds of commodities and derivatives are traded on spot and non-spot basis—regulated by FMC which merged into SEBI by late 2015.

FINANCIAL REGULATION

India has a multiple regulatory architecture in the financial sector. The design has developed complexities over the time due to: the *number* of regulatory, quasi-regulatory, non-regulatory-but-still-regulating bodies; *overlapping ambiguous* operational design and their influence.[24] A brief overview of the financial regulatory framework is being give here.

Regulatory Agencies

India has product-wise regulators—Reserve Bank of India (RBI) regulates credit products, savings and remittances; the Securities and Exchange Board of India (SEBI) regulates investment products; the Insurance Regulatory and Development Authority (IRDA) regulates insurance products; and the Pension Fund Regulatory and Development Authority (PFRDA) regulates pension products. The Forward Markets Commission (FMC) regulates commodity-based exchange-traded futures (which was merged with the SEBI by late 2015).

Certain entities, primarily engaged in one product (i.e., the insurance companies) also offer other products making it difficult for product-based regulation (this came to light in the PFRDA-IRDA controversy of early 2010s). Thus, most regulation turns out to be entity-based. Another example is of *cooperative banks*, which, except in terms of their ownership structure, are very much like other banks—they take deposits and give loans. Still, their regulation is largely left to the Registrar of Cooperatives.

Quasi-regulatory Agencies

Several other government bodies perform quasi-regulatory functions—National Bank for Agriculture and Rural Development (NABARD), Small Industries Development Bank of India (SIDBI), and National Housing Bank (NHB). NABARD supervises regional rural banks as well as state and district cooperative banks. NHB regulates housing finance companies, and SIDBI regulates the state finance corporations (SFCs).

Central Ministries

Certain ministries of the GoI are also involved in policy making in the financial system. Ministry of Finance (MoF) is most prominently involved, through its representatives on the Boards of SEBI, IRDA and RBI. MoF and Ministry of Small Scale Industries have representatives on SIDBI Board, and Ministry of Urban Development is represented on the NHB Board. MoF representatives are also on Boards of public sector banks (PSBs) and Development Financial Institutions (DFIs). Forward Market Commission (FMC), which used to regulate the commodity exchanges and brokers, under the Ministry of Consumer Affairs, shifted to the Ministry of Finance in 2014 (merged with the SEBI, MoF by September, 2015).

State Governments

Through the Registrar of Cooperatives, who are under the departments of agriculture and

23. Ministry of Finance, ***Economic Survey 2012–13*** (New Delhi: Government of India, 2013), p. 116.

24. **Financial Sector Legislative Reforms Commission** report, March 2013, N. Delhi.

cooperation, the state governments regulate the cooperative banking institutions in their respective states. The state government have also sometimes claimed a regulatory role in certain other cases. Though it never became an open battle, the Andhra Pradesh government's ordinance directing operations of Micro Finance Institutions (MFIs)—many of them NBFCs registered with and regulated by RBI—falls into this space.

Such actions by state government have been matters of contention in the past as well, and some of them have gone to the courts, too (the judgement on the court cases to clarify the *RBI vs. State Government* issue are before the Supreme Court).

Special Statutes for Certain Financial Intermediaries

Some key financial services intermediaries like SBI (and its Associate Banks before their consolidation with SBI in 2017–18), Public Sector Banks, LIC and GIC are governed by their own statutes. These statutes give a special status to these institutions vis-á-vis the other institutions performing the same functions. Earlier, IFCI, UTI and IDBI also operated under special statutes, but now their special statutes have been repealed.

Establishment of FSDC

Few years back, an important addition was made to the regulatory architecture—the Financial Sector Development Council (FSDC) was set up which replaced the High Level Committee on Capital Markets. The council is convened by Ministry of Finance and does not have statutory authority—it is structured as a *council of regulators*—Finance Minister as chairman. It has a permanent secretariat.

The council resolves inter-agency disputes; looks after the regulation of financial conglomerates that fall under various regulators' purview; and performs wealth management functions dealing with multiple products.

The *FSLRC* (Financial Sector Legislative Reforms Commission), set up (headed by Justice B. N. Srikrishna) to ***examine*** the regulatory structure and the laws governing the financial sector, submitted its report by early 2013. In a broad sense, the commission has recommended for changeover from an 'area-based' division of regulators to a 'task-based' division. Major highlights of the recommendations are as follows:

1. Developing a 'horizontal structure' whereby, the basic regulatory/ monitoring functions to be done by a UIA (Unified Financial Agency)—in place of each agency (like SEBI, IRDA, etc.) looking after one financial type and area. It will eliminate *regulatory overlap* (due to which the ULIP controversy happened between the SEBI and IRDA).
2. Setting up a FRA (Financial Redressal Agency) to handle consumer complaints, regardless of area. It means, regulator not to oversee the consumer complaints.
3. FSAT (Financial Sector Appellate Tribunal) to be set up to hear the appeals of entire financial sector.
4. Advice to set up three other agencies which will oversee banking, besides the RBI.

The advices of the commission are under government's consideration with some of them in the process of getting adopted, too.

CHAPTER 12

BANKING IN INDIA

*Banks are perhaps the most important financial intermediary. In the nineteenth century, banks mainly lent money to firms to help finance their inventories - which were held as collateral–in the cases of defaulters banks seized them. Gradually, banks expanded their lending activities–to finance houses and commercial real estates – holding the buildings as collateral. Emergence of information technology has presented special problems to these traditional forms of finance–if the idea does not pan out, the firm may go bankrupt, but there is no collateral– there is little of value that the creditor can seize.**

In this Chapter...

* *See Joseph E. Stiglitz and Carl E. Walsh, Economics, 4th Edition (New York: W.W. Norton, 2006), p. 205.*

INTRODUCTION

The sense in which we today use the term banking has its origin in the western world. It was introduced in India by the British rulers, way back in the 17th century.

Since then a number of changes have taken place in the sector and today Indian banks are among the finest in the emerging market economics well-directed towards becoming global.

NBFCs

Bank is a financial institution engaged primarily in mobilising deposits and forwarding loans. The deposits and loans are highly differentiated in nature. Banks are regulated by the Central bank of the country—in case of India, the RBI (Reserve Bank of India). The another category of financial institution—the ***non-bank***—is almost similar in its functions but *main* difference (though, highly simplified) being that it does not allow its depositors to withdraw money from their accounts.

NBFCs (Non-Banking Financial Companies)[1] are fast emerging as an important segment of Indian financial system. It is an *heterogeneous group* of institutions (other than commercial and co-operative banks) performing financial intermediation in a variety of ways, like accepting deposits, making loans and advances, leasing, hire purchase, etc. They *can not* have certain activities as their principal business—agricultural, industrial and sale-purchase or construction of immovable property.

They raise funds from the public, directly or indirectly, and lend them to ultimate spenders. They advance loans to the various wholesale and retail traders, small-scale industries and self-employed persons. Thus, they have broadened and diversified the range of products and services offered by a financial sector. Gradually, they are being recognised as *complementary* to the banking sector due to their:

1. customer-oriented services;
2. simplified procedures;
3. attractive rates of return on deposits; and
4. flexibility and timeliness in meeting the credit needs of specified sectors.

RBI, the regulator of the NBFCs, has given a very wide definition of such companies (a kind of 'umbrella' definition)—'a financial institution formed as a company involved in receiving deposits or lending in any manner.' Based on their liability structure, they have been classified into two broad categories:

1. deposit-taking NBFCs (NBFC-D), and
2. non-deposit taking NBFCs (NBFC-ND).

It is *mandatory* for a NBFC to get itself registered with the RBI as a *deposit taking* company. For registration they need to be a *company* (incorporated under the Companies Act, 1956) and should have a minimum NOF (net owned fund)[2] of ₹2 crore.

To *obviate dual* regulation, certain category of the NBFCs which are regulated by other financial regulators are exempted from the regulatory control of the RBI:

1. **RBI** update, 11 March, 2016 and the **Business.gov.in**, Government of India, April 2016.

2. The term 'NOF' means, net owned funds (*paid-up capital* and *free reserves* minus *accumulated losses, deferred revenue expenditure* and *other intangible assets*) less, (i) investments in shares of subsidiaries/companies in the same group and all other NBFCs; and (ii) the book value of debentures, bonds, outstanding loans and advances, including hire-purchase and lease finance made to, and deposits with, subsidiaries/companies in the same group, in excess of 10 per cent of the owned funds.

- Venture capital fund, merchant bank, stock broking firms (SEBI registers and regulates them);
- Insurance company (registered and regulated by the IRDA);
- Housing finance company (regulated by the National Housing Bank);
- Nidhi company (regulated by the Ministry of Corporate Affairs under the Companies Act, 1956);
- Chit fund company (by respective state governments under Chit Funds Act, 1982).

Some of the ***important regulations*** relating to acceptance of deposits by the NBFCs are:

- Allowed to accept and/or renew public deposits for a minimum period of 12 months and maximum period of 60 months.
- Cannot accept demand deposits (i.e., the saving and current accounts).
- Cannot offer interest rates higher than the ceiling rate prescribed by the RBI.
- Cannot offer gifts, incentives or any other additional benefit to the depositors.
- Should have minimum investment grade credit rating.
- Their deposits are not insured.
- The repayment of deposits by NBFCs is not guaranteed by RBI.
- Need to maintain Capital Adequacy Ratio (CAR) norm as prescribed by the RBI.

New NBFCs With the objective to promote financial inclusion, ease of financial transactions and infusing greater dynamism in the financial system, in 2017-18, the RBI introduced two new categories of the NBFCs—

1. **NBFC-P2P:** The NBFC Peer to Peer (NBFC-P2P) provide services of loan facilitation to lenders and borrowers on electronic platform (but they are not allowed to raise their own funds by accepting deposits)—matching the right lender with the right borrower as a moderator of interactions between lenders and borrowers. They also provide ancillary services such as loan recovery, credit assessment, profile verification, etc.
2. **NBFC-AA:** The NBFC Account Aggregator (NBFC-AA) gather the scattered financial data (related to banking, insurance, mutual funds, stock market transactions, etc.) of an individual or company and present them in a manner that allows the reader to easily understand and analyse them. Such consolidated financial information is quite helpful in applying for a loan and other financial transactions. Several new age digital lending app-based NBFCs have come up in this segment.

Regulatory Changes For the ease of regulation and providing greater operational flexibility the following changes[3] were made by the RBI in relation of the NBFCs:

- Existing 3 categories of the NBFCs (asset finance companies, investment companies and loan companies) were merged into a new category—NBFC-Investment and Credit Companies (NBFC-ICCs).
- Now onwards they will be regulated by their activity rather than entity.
- Deposit taking NBFC-ICC will invest upto 20 per cent of its net assets in unquoted shares of another company (which is not a subsidiary or a company in the same group of the NBFC).

3. **Reserve Bank of India,** Ministry of Finance, GoI, N. Delhi, February 22, 2019.

- Excluding core investment companies (CICs)[4] the exposures to all of them will be risk weighted as per credit ratings (similar to corporates).

As per the *Economic Survey 2020-21*, the sector in 2020-21 has been crossing through hard times and had a mixed performance:

- Credit growth of NBFCs has been slowing down since 2017-18 (primarily caused by the panic due to *defaulters* of some large NBFCs beginning with the IL&FS) which to a negative of 6.6 per cent in September 2020.
- Total assets of NBFCs increased to ₹ 33.91 lakh crore in March 2020 (16.01 per cent higher that 2019-20). Banks continued to support NBFCs with their lending expanding 9.2 per cent year-on-year basis till October 2020 (well above the overall bank credit growth)—around 6.6 per cent of banks' credit going to them. However, mutual funds lending to NBFCs continued to contract in 2020-21 also.
- As against the regulatory requirement of 15 per cent, their *CRAR* (capital to risk-weighted assets ratio) was 22.05 per cent by June 2020 (up from 20.62 per cent in March 2020).
- Asset quality of the sector deteriorated moderately with GNPAs (gross non-performing assets) ratio at 6.44 per cent by June 2020 (against 6.30 per cent of March 2020).

4. CICs are a kind of NBFC (on the basis of their *activity*) which invest in different kinds of securities (shares and debt)—not less than 90 per cent of their net assets. They can't engage in 'trading' of the instruments they hold. They need to register with the RBI if their asset size is above ₹100 crores and access public funds (through instruments like Commercial Paper, debentures, inter-corporate deposits and borrowings from banks/financial institutions)—are called *Systemically Important Core Investment Companies (CICs-ND-SI)*.

RESERVE BANK OF INDIA

In the wake of the banking crisis of early 20th century, world felt a need of central banking body for the first time. Following the global clue, in India also such a body, the Reserve Bank of India[5], was set up on April 1, 1935 in accordance with the provisions of the RBI Act, 1934, in Calcutta (got shifted to Bombay in 1937). Set up under *private ownership* like a bank it was given two extra functions—regulating banking industry and being the banker of the Government. To better serve the purpose, during mid-1940s, a view emerged across the world in favour of a government-owned central bank—and governments started taking them over. In India also, in 1949 the RBI was nationalised. After nationalisation it stopped being a 'bank' in technical sense (as it stopped accepting deposits from general public). The RBI has been given quite complex and challenging functions which has been summarised in its **Preamble** as given below:

'To regulate the issue of Bank notes and keeping of reserves with a view to securing monetary stability in India and generally to operate the currency and credit system of the country to its advantage; to have a modern monetary policy framework to meet the challenge of an increasingly complex economy, to maintain price stability while keeping in mind the objective of growth.'

As per the changing needs of time, the RBI Nationalisation Act of 1949 has been amended several times by the Government and its functions broadened. Its current functions may be summarised objectively in the following way:

1. **Monetary Authority:** It includes formulation, implementation and monitoring of the monetary policy. The broad objective is—maintaining price

5. Based on the **RBI Nationalisation Act, 1949** and future amendments; and the **RBI website**, April, 2020.

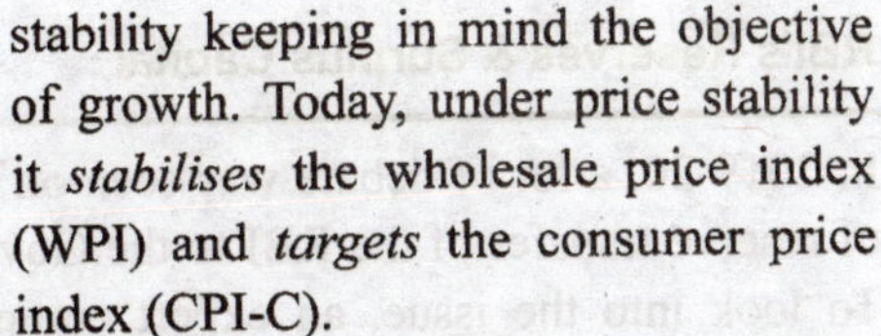

stability keeping in mind the objective of growth. Today, under price stability it *stabilises* the wholesale price index (WPI) and *targets* the consumer price index (CPI-C).

2. **Currency Authority:** It includes issuing of new currency notes and coins (except the currency and coins of rupee one or its denominations, which are issued by Ministry of Finance itself) as well as exchanging or destroying those ones which are not fit for circulation. This function includes the distribution responsibility of the currencies and coins also (of those ones also which are issued by the Ministry of Finance). The broad objective is—keeping adequate supplies of quality currencies and coins.

3. **Regulator and Supervisor of the Financial System:** It includes prescribing broad parameters of banking operations within which the banking and financial system operates. The broad objective of this function is—maintaining public confidence in the system, protecting depositors' interest and providing cost-effective banking services to the public.

4. **Manager of Foreign Exchange:** In includes broad functions like—managing the FEMA (Foreign Exchange Management Act, 1999); keeping the Forex (foreign exchange) reserves of the country; stabilising the exchange rate of rupee; and representing the Government of India in the IMF and World Bank (and other international financial agencies of which India is member). Objective of this function is—facilitating external trade and external payments; and promoting orderly development/maintenance of foreign exchange market in the country.

5. **Regulator and Supervisor of Payment and Settlement Systems:** It includes functions like introducing and upgrading safe and efficient modes of payment systems in the country to meet the requirements of the public at large. The objective is maintaining public confidence in payment and settlement system.

6. **Banker of the Governments and Banks (known also as the Related Functions):** It includes three category of functions—firstly, performing the Merchant Banking[6] functions for the central and state governments; secondly, acting as their Bankers; and thirdly, maintaining banking accounts of the SCBs (scheduled commercial banks)—domestic, foreign, public and private—operating in the country. The broad objectives are enabling governments and the banks mobilise enough liquidity for their functioning under which it lends or manages borrowing plans of the governments and provides short-term and long-term loans to the banks (as *Lender of Last Resort*).

7. **Developmental Function:** Unlike most of the central banks in the world, the RBI was given some developmental functions also. Playing this role, it did set up developmental banks like—IDBI, SIDBI, NABARD, NEDB (North Eastern Development Bank), Exim Bank, NHB. Gradually, the ownership of these banks is being transferred from the RBI to the Government of India (aimed at enhancing regulatory freedom and professionalism of the central bank

6. See **GLOSSARY** for more details on 'Merchant Banks'.

and enabling the Government to take care of the dynamic requirements of development in a better way).

The RBI operates today with its 27 regional offices, most of them situated in state capitals and its affairs are governed by a *central board* of directors. The Government constitutes the board by appointing or nominating the directors for a period of four years in the following way:

1. **Official Directors:** Governor and not more than four Deputy Governors.
2. **Non-Official Directors:** 10 nominated from various fields and 2 government officials. It also includes 4 Directors coming 1 each from the 4 local boards of RBI (also known as sub-offices, they are situated at Chennai, Kolkata, Mumbai and New Delhi).

RBI's Subsidiaries There are 4 fully-owned subsidiaries of the RBI, namely—Deposit Insurance and Credit Guarantee Corporation of India (DICGC), Bharatiya Reserve Bank Note Mudran Private Limited (BRBNMPL), Reserve Bank Information Technology Private Limited (ReBIT), and Indian Financial Technology and Allied Services (IFTAS).

New Financial Year Aimed at aligning its financial year with the government's financial year, in February 2020, the RBI decided[7] to shift to April-March as its new financial year from 2020-21 (from its existing financial year July-June). Thus, the RBI will do away with nearly eight decades of practice—it used to follow January-December financial year before it was changed to July-June in 1940. Such a change was recommended by the *Jalan Committee* (set up by the RBI on the *Economic Capital Framework*, 2019).

RBI's Reserves & Surplus Capital

In 2019-20, a lot of debate was seen on the issue of reserve transfer of the RBI to the Government. To look into the issue, an expert committee on Economic Capital Framework was set up by the RBI (headed by Bimal Jalan) in 2019, which could advise the manner in which it should share *surplus capital* with the Government. On its advice, the RBI transferred an amount of ₹1.76 lakh crore to the Government and affected *several changes* related[8] to the issue:

- Giving a clearer distinction between the two components of 'economic capital'—realized equity and revaluation balances—the committee recommended that realised equity could be used for meeting all risks/losses as they were primarily built-up from retained earnings, while revaluation balances could be reckoned only as risk buffers against market risks as they represented unrealised valuation gains and hence were not distributable.
- The revaluation balance of the central bank should not be distributed.
- The entire net income can be transferable to the government only if realised equity is above its requirement. If it is below the lower bound of requirement, risk provisioning will be made to the extent necessary and only the residual net income (if any) transferred to the Government.
- On the issue of the RBI's economic capital, the committee reviewed the status, need and justification of the various reserves, risk provisions and risk buffers maintained by the RBI and recommended their continuance.
- On the risk provisioning for market risk, the committee has recommended the adoption

7 The decision was taken by the **Central Board** of the RBI on February 15, 2020 and sent to the Government for consideration.

8 **Expert Committee to Review the Extent Economic Capital Framework,** headed by Dr. Bimal Jalan and the follow-up action of the RBI, August 26, 2019.

of Expected Shortfall (ES) methodology under stressed conditions (in place of the extant Stressed-Value at Risk) for measuring the RBI's market risk on which there was growing consensus among central banks as well as commercial banks over the recent years.

- While central banks are seen to be adopting ES at 99 per cent confidence level (CL), the committee has recommended the adoption of a target of ES 99.5 per cent CL keeping in view the macroeconomic stability requirements.
- As per the report, realised equity is also required to cover credit risk and operational risk. This risk provisioning made primarily from 'retained earnings' is cumulatively referred to as the Contingent Risk Buffer (CRB) and has been recommended to be maintained within a range of 6.5 per cent to 5.5 per cent of the RBI's balance sheet, comprising 5.5 to 4.5 per cent for monetary and financial stability risks and 1.0 per cent for credit and operational risks.

The committee based its recommendations on the consideration of the role of central banks' financial resilience, cross-country practices, statutory provisions and the impact of the RBI's public policy mandate and operating environment on its balance sheet and the risks involved.

MONETARY POLICY

Considered as the most dynamic and sensitive function of a central bank (i.e., RBI in case of India) this macroeconomic policy is related to monetary matters—chiefly aimed at regulating the size and cost of fund/money in the economic system. From being announced twice a year (before *slack* and *busy* seasons) today the policy is a *bi-monthly* affair announced 6 times in a financial year after the monetary policy committee (MPC) came into being in 2016. Committee-based approach to monetary policy is supposed to add *value* and *transparency* to monetary policy with *statutory* responsibility given to the RBI for targeting inflation (CPI-C) while keeping in mind the objective of growth. The MPC (has to meet 4 times minimum every year) has a total of 6 members nominated by RBI and the Ministry of Finance in equal numbers including the RBI Governor as its Chairman who avails the right of casting vote in case of a tie in decisions. The actual tone of the monetary policy stance of RBI is set by its first monetary policy of the year announced beginning every financial year—gaining its clues from the annual budget announcements. There are few types of ***monetary policy stances*** which keep coming into media from time to time:

1. *Neutral stance* means interest rates may move either way—upward or downward.
2. *Calibrated tightening* means interest rates can only move upward.
3. *Accommodative stance* (also known as *expansionary stance*) means injection of more funds into the financial system. Falling 'headline inflation' inspires RBI for it and such a stance is aimed at expansion in lending, investment and growth.
4. *Contractionary stance* means syphoning out of fund from the financial system. Such a stance is generally followed once more than optimum fund is believed to be available in the financial system. At times, it is also aimed at taming inflation in long-term.
5. *Hawkish stance* means the contractionary stance aimed at checking inflation from rising (linked to the statutory goals of inflation targeting the 'headline inflation').

To put in place the desired kind of monetary policy, RBI uses a range of instruments and tools—a brief description follows:

Cash Reserve Ratio

Banks operating in the country are under regulatory obligation to maintain 'reserve ratios' of two kinds, one of it being the *cash reserve ratio* (the other being 'statutory liquidity ratio'). Under it, all scheduled commercial banks operating in the country are supposed to maintain a part of their total deposits with the RBI in cash form as the cash reserve ratio (CRR). The RBI could fix[9] it between 3 to 15 per cent of the 'net demand and time liabilities' (NDTL) of the banks. In the wake of the ongoing process of banking reforms, certain changes[10] were affected by the RBI in relation to the ratio since late 1990s:

1. Aimed at enabling banks to lend more and cut interest rates on loans they offer, in 1999–2000, the RBI started paying banks an interest income on their CRR. The payment of interest was discontinued by late 2007 in the wake of rising prices (to check aggregate demand in the economy).
2. The ratio which used to be generally on the higher side, was drastically cut down to 4.5 per cent in 2003 (from the peak of 15 per cent in 1992).
3. A major development came in 2007 when by an amendment (in the RBI Act, 1949), the Government abolished the lower ceiling (called 'floor') on the CRR and gave the RBI greater flexibility in fixing this ratio. It means, it is now possible for the RBI to fix the CRR below 3 per cent also.

9. As per the **RBI Act, 1949**, Section 42, sub-section (1). Rather, this provision has been amended several times since then. See *GLOSSARY* for more detail on NDTL.

10. It was a follow-up to the recommendations of the **Committee on Financial System, 1991** (Narasimham Committee- I), headed by *M. Narasimham*. The Committee had advised the RBI to pay the banks an interest on CRR so that banks could pass this benefit to borrowers and lending can be promoted to enhance private investment in line with the objective of the ongoing economic reform process.

In February 2020, in a *first of its kind* move, the RBI allowed[11] banks to lend to— automobiles; residential housing; and micro, small and medium enterprises (MSMEs), without maintaining the mandatory CRR. This provision will remain open till July 31, 2020. The move is aimed at enhancing lending activity to these sectors which have been hit hard with slowdown in recent times. Simply put, the RBI allowed banks to use the CRR money which otherwise would have been deposited by the banks with the RBI. As a result of this exemption given to banks, the RBI will lose a part of its income since the CRR deposits are used by the RBI in its daily business operations.

In *March 2021*, the CRR was 3 per cent of the NDTL of the banks—one per cent change[12] in it today makes a difference of around ₹1.37 lakh crore on the cash flow in the financial system.

Statutory Liquidity Ratio

Banks operating in the country are under regulatory obligation to maintain 'reserve ratios' of two kinds, one of it being the *statutory liquidity ratio* (the other being the 'cash reserve ratio'). Under it, all scheduled commercial banks operating in the country are supposed to maintain[13] a part of their total deposits (i.e., their NDTL) with themselves in non-cash form (i.e., in 'liquid assets')—the ratio could be fixed by the RBI between 25 to 40 per cent. In practice, banks cannot invest this fund in the liquid assets of their choice rather they are forced to invest in the Government securities (i.e., G-Secs) of various kinds. Banks earn income on this investment as per the configuration of their investments in the G-Secs. In the wake of the ongoing process of banking reforms, certain

11. **Sixth Bi-monthly Monetary Policy**, RBI, February 6, 2020.

12. *6th Bi-monthly Policy Statement*, **Reserve Bank of India**, March 2021.

13. Based on the **RBI Nationalisation Act, 1949** and future amendments; and the **RBI website**, April, 2020.

changes[14] were affected by the RBI in relation to the ratio since late 1990s:

1. The ratio was drastically cut down to 25 per cent (the floor) in 1997 from the existing level of 32 per cent.
2. By an amendment (in the RBI Act, 1949) done in 2007, the lower ceiling (the floor) of 25 per cent was removed by the Government. This way, the SLR may be fixed by the RBI below 25 per cent also. Since then the SLR have shown a falling tendency.

In *March 2021*, the SLR was at **18** per cent of the NDTL of the banks. With one per cent change in this ratio today banks either lose or gain choice of investing around a fund of ₹1.37 lakh crores.

Bank Rate

The interest rate which the RBI charges on its **long-term** lendings is known as the Bank Rate. The clients who borrow through this route are the Government of India, state governments, banks, financial institutions, co-operative banks, NBFCs, etc. The rate has direct impact on long-term lending activities of the concerned lending bodies operating in the Indian financial system. The rate was realigned[15] with the MSF (Marginal Standing Facility) by the RBI in February 2012. By **March 2021**, it was at 4.25 per cent.

14. These changes were made as a follow-up to the recommendations of the **Committee on Financial System, 1991** (Narasimham Committee- I), headed by *M. Narasimham*. The Committee had advised the RBI to stop forcing banks to invest in the G-Secs and allow them to select the liquid assets of their choice for investing this fund. Once banks will earn market-based interest rate on this fund (that will be always higher than the interest they earn from G-Secs) they can lend more loans and cheaper loans which will promote private investment in the economy in line with the broad objective of the economic reform process. The RBI was advised to simply abolish this compulsive investment by banks in the G-Secs for maintaining the SLR.

15. Through an RBI announcement on 15th February, 2012.

Repo Rate

The rate of interest the RBI charges from its clients on their ***short-term*** borrowing is the repo rate in India.[16] Basically, this is an abbreviated form of the 'rate of repurchase' and in western economies it is known as the 'rate of discount'.[17]

In practice it is not called an interest rate but considered a discount on the dated government securities, which are deposited by institution to borrow for the short term. When they get their securities released from the RBI, the value of the securities is lost by the amount of the current repo rate. The Call Money Market of India (inter-bank market) operates at this rate and banks use this route for *overnight* borrowings. This rate has direct relation with the interest rates banks charge on the loans they offer (as it affects the operational cost of the banks). The rate was 4 per cent in **March 2021.**

In October 2013, RBI introduced ***term repos*** (of different tenors, such as, 7/14/28 days), to inject liquidity over a period that is longer than overnight. It has several purposes to serve—stronger money market, stability, and better costing and signalling of the loan products.

Long Term Repo

Aimed at promoting enhanced lending and cutting the cost of short-term funds for the banks, in a first of its kind move, in **February 2020** *(6th Bi-monthly Monetary Policy of 2019-20)*, the RBI announced to offer long term repo operation (LTRO) of ₹1.50 lakh crores at a fixed rate (i.e., at the Repo rate). The tenure of the LTRO will be from *one to three* years. This was aimed at ensuring permanent and deeper liquidity in the financial system together with enhancing lending by cutting cost of funds for the banks (enabling them to lend cheaper loans).

16. **RBI Act, 1934 and Banking Regulation Act, 1949.**

17. Stiglitz and Walsh, ***Economics,*** pp. 629–30.

Reverse Repo Rate

It is the rate of interest the RBI pays to its clients who offer short-term loan to it. At present **(March 2021)** the rate is at 3.35 per cent.

It is reverse of the repo rate and this was started in November 1996 as part of Liquidity Adjustment Facility (LAF) by the RBI. In practice, financial institutions operating in India park their surplus funds with the RBI for short-term period and earn money. It has a direct bearing on the interest rates charged by the banks and the financial institutions on their different forms of loans.

This tool was utilised by the RBI in the wake of over money supply with the Indian banks and lower loan disbursal to serve twin purposes of cutting down banks losses and the prevailing interest rate.[18] It has emerged as a very important tool in direction of following cheap interest regime—the general policy of the RBI since reform process started.

Marginal Standing Facility (MSF)

MSF[19] is a new scheme announced by the RBI in its Monetary Policy, 2011–12 which came into effect from May, 2011. Under this scheme, banks can borrow overnight upto 1 per cent of their net demand and time liabilities (NDTL) from the RBI, at the interest rate 1 per cent (100 basis points) higher than the current repo rate. In an attempt to strengthen rupee and checking its falling exchange rate, the RBI increased the gap between 'repo' and MSF to 3 per cent (late July 2013).

The MSF rate has been floated as a *penal rate* and since mid-2015 RBI has maintained it 1 per cent higher than the prevailing repo rate. By end **March 2021** it is at 4.25 per cent, fully aligned with the Bank rate (i.e., equal to the Bank rate).

Other Tools

Other than the above-given instruments, RBI uses some other important to activate the right kind of the credit and monetary policy:

1. **Call Money Market:** The call money market is an important segment of the money market where borrowing and lending of funds take place on over night basis. Participants in the call money market in India currently include scheduled commercial banks (SCBs)—excluding regional rural banks, cooperative banks (other than land development banks), insurance. Prudential limits, in respect of both outstanding borrowing and lending transactions in the call money market for each of these entities, are specified by the RBI.

   In recent times, several changes have been introduced by the RBI in this market. By ***April 2016,*** banks were allowed to borrow only 1 per cent of their NDTL (net demand and time liabilities, i.e., total deposit of the banks, in layman term) under overnight facility at repo rate. For the rest of 0.75 per cent of their NDTL, they may use the *term repos* of different tenors. In a sense, since late 2013, RBI has been discouraging banks to use repo route and switch over to term repos for their requirements of the short-term funds. Promoting stability and signalling better cost of loans are the main objectives of this changed stance.

2. **Open Market Operations (OMOs):** OMOs are conducted by the RBI via the sale/purchase of government securities (G-Sec) to/from the market with the *primary aim* of modulating rupee liquidity conditions in the market. OMOs are an effective quantitative policy tool in the armoury of the RBI, but

---

18. Ministry of Finance, ***Economic Survey 2001-02,*** (New Delhi: Government of India, 2002).

19. The write-up is based on the RBI's *Credit & Monetary Policy, 2011–12* (in which the scheme was introduced); and the *European Central Bank*, Frankfurt, Germany and *Federal Reserve System* (also known as the *Federal Reserve*, and informally as the *Fed*) Washington DC, USA.

are constrained by the stock of government securities available with it at a point in time. Other than the institutions, now individuals will also be able to participate in this market (the decision was taken in 2017 while it is yet to be implemented).

3. **Liquidity Adjustment Facility (LAF):** The LAF is the key element in the monetary policy operating framework of the RBI (introduced in June 2000). On daily basis, the RBI stands ready to lend to or borrow money from the banking system, as per the need of the time, at fixed interest rates (repo and reverse repo rates). Together with moderating the fund-mismatches of the banks, LAF operations help the RBI to effectively transmit *interest rate signals* to the market. The recent changes regarding a ***cap*** on the repo borrowing and provision of the ***term repo*** have changed the very dynamics of this facility after 2013.

4. **Market Stabilisation Scheme (MSS):** This instrument for monetary management was introduced in 2004. Surplus liquidity of a more enduring nature arising from large capital inflows is absorbed through sale of short-dated government securities and treasury bills. The mobilised cash is held in a separate government account with the Reserve Bank. The instrument thus has features of both, SLR and CRR.

5. **Standing Deposit Facility Scheme (SDFS):** The new scheme has been proposed by the *Union Budget 2018–19*. Such a tool was proposed by the RBI in November 2015 itself. The scheme is aimed at helping RBI to manage liquidity in a better way, especially when the economy is flush with excess fund (as was seen after the demonetisation of the high value currency notes post-November 2016).

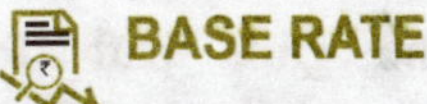

BASE RATE

Base Rate is the interest rate below which Scheduled Commercial Banks (SCBs) will lend no loans to its customers—its means it is like prime lending rate (PLR) and the benchmark prime lending rate (BPLR) of the past and is basically a floor rate of interest. It replaced[20] the existing idea of BPLR on 1 July, 2010.

The BPLR system (while the existing system was of PLR), introduced in 2003, fell short of its original objective of *bringing transparency* to lending rates. This was mainly because under this system, banks could lend below BPLR. This made a bargaining by the borrower with bank-ultimately one borrower getting cheaper loan than the other, and blurred the attempts of bringing in transparency in the lending business. For the same reason, it was also difficult to assess the transmission of *policy rates* (i.e., repo rate, reverse repo rate, bank rate) of the Reserve Bank to lending rates of banks. The Base Rate system is **aimed at** enhancing transparency in lending rates of banks and enabling better assessment of transmission of monetary policy.

After its deregulation by the RBI in 2010, banks fix their own base rates. Thus, in practice base rate shows differentiation—changing from bank to bank according to differentiation in the operational costs of the banks. Banks were not allowed to lend any loan below their base rates. In **March 2021,** the base rate of the banks was in the range of **7.30-8.80** per cent.

By the *fiscal 2015–16*, several new initiatives were taken by the RBI in the area of credit and monetary policy management—*major ones* are being given below:

- Transition to a bi-monthly monetary policy cycle.

20. ***Reserve Bank of India, Announcement,*** 5 April, 2010 (New Delhi: Government of India).

- Recognition of the glide path for disinflation (recommendation of Urjit Patel Committee report implemented). Under it, the CPI (C) is used by the RBI as the 'Headline Inflation' for monetary management.
- A Monetary Policy Framework has been put in place – an agreement in this regard was signed between the Government of India and the RBI late February 2015. Under the framework, the RBI is to 'target inflation' at 4 per cent with a variation of 2 per cent. It means, the 'range of inflation' is to be between 2 to 6 per cent (of the CPI-C).
- Besides the existing repo route, term repos have been introduced for three set of tenors—7, 14 and 28 days.
- RBI is progressively reducing banks' access to overnight liquidity (at the fixed repo rate), and encouraging the banks to increase their dependency on the term repos. By March 2016, banks were allowed to borrow only up to 1 per cent of their NDTL from the Call Money Market—0.25 per cent through repo and the rest of 0.75 per cent through term repo. This aims to improve the transmission of policy impulses across the interest rate spectrum and providing stability to the loan market.
- In 2016–17, individuals were also allowed by the RBI to participate in the government security market (similar to the developed economies like the USA).

MCLR

From the financial year ***2016–17*** (i.e., from 1st April, 2016), banks in the country have shifted to a new methodology to compute their lending rate. The new methodology—***MCLR*** (Marginal Cost of funds based Lending Rate)—which was articulated by the RBI in December 2015. The *main features* of the MCLR are:

- It will be a tenor linked internal benchmark, to be reset on annual basis.
- Actual lending rates will be fixed by adding a spread to the MCLR.
- To be reviewed every month on a pre-announced date.
- Existing borrowers will have the option to move to it.
- Banks will continue to review and publish 'Base Rate' as hitherto.

As per the RBI, 'for monetary transmission to occur, lending rates have to be sensitive to the policy rate'. But this was not occurring by now. During 2015–16, the RBI reduced the policy rate (repo rate) by a total of **1.25** per cent. But in comparison, banks reduced the lending rate by maximum **0.6** per cent. By now, banks have been using either of the following *three methods* to compute their Base Rate:

1. average cost of funds,
2. marginal cost of funds, or
3. blended cost of funds (liabilities).

As per the RBI, the MCLR will bring in the *following* benefits:

- transmission of policy rate into the lending rates of banks to improve;
- computation of the interest rates by banks will get more transparent;
- cost of loan will be fairer to the borrowers as well as the banks.
- it will help the banks to become more competitive and enhance their long-run value.

By late *March 2021,* the MCLRs of banks were in the range of 6.55-7.05 per cent. As the idea of the MCLR did not bring in the desired results (i.e., the healthy monetary transmission), RBI announced (in its 5th bi-monthly monetary policy statement of December 2018) that from *April 2019* all new floating loans extended by banks will be 'benchmarked' (i.e., linked to) to *one of* the following *four* RBI-prescribed **'external'** benchmarks:

1. Repo rate,
2. 91-day Treasury Bill yield,
3. 182-day Treasury Bill yield,
4. Any other benchmark produced by the FBIL (Financial Benchmarks India Private Ltd).[21]

It means that the actual lending rates will not remain linked to the internal data of the banks (as the case has been for MCLR) and banks will be forced to link the interest rates of their new loans with an external and market-determined benchmark. After a short delay banks started switching over to the external benchmarks from *October 2019*. Meanwhile, the process has not resulted into a much better monetary transmission.

COVID-19 AND MONETARY MEASURES

In 2020-21, the liquidity situation remained surplus—as a result of special monetary measures undertaken by the RBI in the wake of COVID-19 induced disruptions— with currency in circulation (CIC), Government cash balances and forex operations by the RBI remaining the main drivers of it. While CIC withdrawals and build-up of Government cash balances resulted in *liquidity drainage* from the banking system, the forex operations of the RBI enhanced liquidity infusion. Several *conventional* and *unconventional* measures (as per the *Economic Survey 2020-21*) were taken by the RBI to manage the liquidity in the economy between February-December 2020, which are as given below:

- Infusion of ₹2.7 lakh crores of fund through OMO (Open Market Operation).
- A total of ₹30,000 crores was infused through OMOs in State Development Loans (SDLs) as a special case.
- TLTROs (Targeted Long Term Repo Operations) of up to three years' tenor for a total amount of ₹1.13 lakh crore for investment in corporate bonds, commercial papers (CPs), and non-convertible debentures, in addition to injection of ₹ 1.25 lakh crore through Long Term Repo Operations (LTROs).
- CRR requirement of banks reduced to 3 per cent (from 4 per cent) augmenting primary liquidity in the banking system by about ₹ 1.37 lakh crore.
- MSF (Marginal Standing Facility) limit for borrowing overnight increase to 3 per cent (from 2 per cent) by dipping into their SLR (Statutory Liquidity Ratio) allowing the banks to raise an additional fund of ₹1.37 crore.
- Special Liquidity Facility for MFs (Mutual Funds) of ₹50,000 crore.
- Refinance facility worth ₹75,000 crore for the AIFIs (All India Financial Institutions) i.e., the NABARD, NHB, SIDBI and EXIM Bank.
- Two 6-month US *Dollar and Rupee swaps* (Sell/Buy) were conducted (March 16 and 23) which infused US$2.7 billion of the foreign currency. This was done to cool down

21. RBI recognises FBIL as an 'independent benchmark administrator'. The company (set up by December 2014) has been jointly promoted by Fixed Income Money Market & Derivative Association of India (FIMMDA), Foreign Exchange Dealers' Association of India (FEDAI) and Indian Banks' Association (IBA).

theheating of forex market as a result of sell off by foreign investors.

MONETARY TRANSMISSION

Monetary policy plays a very vital role in the allocation of funds from the financial system. For this, lending rates decided by the banks must be sensitive to the policy rates (i.e., repo, reverse repo, MSF and bank rate) announced by the central bank—known as 'monetary transmission'. But in recent years, a healthy monetary transmission has been lacking in the system. Since 2015-16 itself, the RBI has been concerned about a general lack of monetary transmission in the financial system. Till ***April 2020,*** steps like enforcing the MCLR and external benchmarks on banks for deciding their lending rates, have been taken by the RBI.

But monetary transmission[22] remained weak throughout almost 2019-20 even after a hefty **2.5** per cent cut in the Repo Rate by the RBI between February 2019 and December 2020. However, the transmission of policy repo rate changes to deposit and lending rates improved since March 2020 as a result of diverse steps taken by the RBI such as—operation twist[23], repo rate cuts, large liquidity surplus, accommodative monetary policy stance, and the introduction of external benchmark-based pricing of loans.

The WALR (weighted average lending rate) on fresh rupee loans declined by 0.94 per cent between March 2020 and November 2020 in response to the reduction of 1.15 per cent in the policy repo rate and comfortable liquidity conditions. In the current easing phase (February 2019 to November 2020), the change in the WALR on outstanding rupee loans has shown significant improvement since March 2020. Of the 0.83 per cent decline in WALR on outstanding loans in February 2019 to November 2020 period, 0.67 per cent decline was noted since March 2020.

Across bank groups, Private Sector Banks exhibited greater transmission in terms on fresh loans, however Public Sector Banks exhibited greater transmission on outstanding loans for the entire easing cycle. Private Sector Banks also reduced deposit rates more than Public Sector Banks.

LIQUIDITY MANAGEMENT FRAMEWORK

A liquidity management framework (LMF) was provisioned by the RBI in 2014 to check volatility in the inter-bank call money market (CMM) and allow banks manage their needs of short-term capital. As per the last revision done by the RBI in *February 2020*, the LMF guidelines were as given below:

- The combined repo borrowings of all banks put together on a day cannot be more than 1 per cent of the combined NDTL of the banks (known as the upper ceiling on repo borrowing).
- Individual banks can borrow not more than 1 per cent of their NDTL under repo operation—0.25 per cent of it as overnight repo and rest of the 0.75 per cent as term repo for 7/14/28 days.
- After exhausting the option of the various repos, banks can borrow upto 1 per cent of their NDTL directly from the RBI for one day (called overnight) under the marginal standing facility (MSF).
- The long-term repo started by the RBI in February 2020 is an extra window over and above the 1 per cent upper cap on the repo operation.

22. **Economic Survey 2020-21,** vol. 2, pp. 133-38, Ministry of Finance, GoI, N. Delhi.
23. See Glossary for details an ***Operation Twist.***

In a push to bring in more 'stability' and better 'interest rate signalling' in the loan market, the RBI has been trying to inspire banks to think in longer term in their operations. Aimed at making banks follow prudential norms, the *Basel III* norms also has put a clear check on *short-termism* followed by banking industry.

NATIONALISATION AND DEVELOPMENT OF BANKING IN INDIA

The development of banking industry in India has been intertwined with the story of its nationalisation. Once the Reserve Bank of India (RBI) was nationalised in 1949 and a central banking was in place, the government considered the nationalising of selected private banks in the country due to the following ***major*** reasons:

1. As the banks were owned and managed by the private sector the services of the banking were having a narrow reach—the masses had no access to the banking service;
2. The government needed to direct the resources in such a way that greater public benefit could take place;
3. The planned development of the economy required a certain degree of government control on the capital generated by the economy. Nationalisation of banks in India took place in the following stages.

Emergence of the SBI

The Government of India, with the enactment of the *SBI Act, 1955* ***partially nationalised*** the three Imperial Banks (mainly operating in the three past Presidencies with their 466 branches) and named them the State Bank of India—the first public sector bank emerged in India. The RBI had purchased 92 per cent of the shares in this partial nationalisation.

Satisfied with the experiment, the government in a related move ***partially nationalised*** eight more private banks (with good regional presence) via the *SBI (Associates) Act, 1959* and named them as the Associates of the SBI—the RBI had acquired 92 per cent stake in them as well. Later on, the State Bank of Bikaner & Jaipur was created (by merging the State Bank of Jaipur and State Bank of Bikaner, as they used to operate in the same region). Following the banking consolidation process, by 2017–18 the SBI and its Associates (7+1) were amalgamated into one bank—the SBI.

Emergence of Nationalised Banks

After successful experimentation in the partial nationalisations the government decided to go for complete nationalisation. With the help of the *Banking Nationalisation Act, 1969,* the government nationalised a total number of 20 private banks:

1. 14 banks with deposits were more than ₹50 crore of nationalised in July 1969, and
2. 6 banks with deposits were more than ₹200 crore of nationalised in April 1980.

After the merger of the loss-making New Bank of India with the Punjab National Bank (PNB) in September 1993, the total number of nationalised banks came down to 19. Aimed at streamlining their operation and size, the Government started a process of merger and amalgamation of the PSBs in 2020—after the completion of this process the number of the PSBs reduced to only 12.

After the nationalisation of banks the government *stopped* opening of banks in the private sector though some foreign private banks were allowed to operate in the country to provide the external currency loans. After India ushered in the era of the economic reforms, the government started a comprehensive banking system reform in the fiscal 1992–93. Three related developments allowed the further expansion of banking industry in the country:

1. In 1993, the SBI was allowed access to the capital market with permission given to sell its share to the tune of 33 per cent through *SBI (Amendment) Act, 1993*.

   At present the Government of India has 59.73 per cent shares in the SBI. (*It was on 9 July, 2007 that the entire equity stake of the RBI was taken over by the Government of India. Thus, the RBI is no more the holding bank of the SBI and its Associates*.)

   On 10 October, 2007 the government announced its proposal of selling the shares of the SBI and cutting down its stake in it to 53 per cent level so that the bank can go for capitalisation.

2. In 1994 the government allowed the nationalised banks to have access to the capital market with a ceiling of 33 per cent sale of shares through the *Banking Companies (Amendment) Act, 1994*.

   Since then many nationalised banks have tapped the capital market for their capital enhancement—Indian Overseas Bank being the first in the row. Though such banks could be better called the public sector banks (as the Government of India holds more than 50 per cent stake in them) they are still known as the nationalised banks.

3. In 1994, itself the government allowed the opening of private banks in the country. The first private bank of the reform era was the UTI Bank. Since then a few dozens Indian and foreign private banks have been opened in the country.

CONSOLIDATION OF BANKS

In the backdrop of the recommendations of financial sector reforms (M. Narasimham, 1991 and 1998), we find a broader process of banking consolidation of the public sector banks (PSBs) commencing in the country by 1993-94 itself. However, certain confusion remained as how[24] much of the Government ownership in them should be disinvested with. The *broader objective* of banking consolidation is helping the PSBs emerge as significant global players for which the most essential aspect will be broadening[25] of their capital base. In this direction, the following actions have been taken by the Government.

Merger It is aimed at creating bigger and stronger banks besides reducing operational cost and broadening capital base of the banks. Mainly starting with the mergers of the Associates of SBI (all 7 such banks merged into 1 by 2017-18), the biggest such exercise was affected in August 2019 when 10 PSBs were merged into four (their number came down to 12). As per the *Union Budget 2021-22,* in 2021-22, other 2-3 banks are to be merged.

Disinvestment Both of the routes of disinvestment are to be followed in case of the banks— 'minority' stake sale and 'strategic' (which may result into privatisation also) aimed at infusing fresh capital and managerial professionalism. The Government has clearly announced in the *Union Budget 2021-22* to privatise all 'non-strategic' public sector enterprises (which include some of the PSBs too) while maintaining ownership control in the 'strategic' ones limited to only *four* in number (which will include few of the PSBs also besides some other financial institutions). For more on the

24 As per the ***Strategic Disinvestment Statement of 1999,*** the government had decided to cut its holding in them to 26 percent. The policy was put on hold once the UPA Government came to power.

25 Y.V. Reddy, ***Lectures on Economic and Financial Sector Reforms in India*** (New Delhi: Oxford University Press, 2002), pp. 137–57.

'strategic PSEs' see the topic on disinvestment in *Chapter 9*.

Strategic Partners The Government had decided (in the disinvestment policy announced in October 1999) to sell the majority stakes of the banks to only a 'strategic partner' in case of their privatisation— in whose hands the banks can grow due to their world-class experience (during 1999-2000 this route was used by the Government to privatise the PSEs such as the BALCO, Modern Foods, VSNL, etc). Though, such specific stance of strategic disinvestment was not announced by the Government till April 2021, however, it may be expected any day.

Summary The Government believes that India needs global sized banks to become a US$ 5 trillion economy by 2024-25. Today, India has only one bank in top 100 global bank list (i.e., SBI at 55th position) while China and the USA have 18 banks and 12 in the list respectively.

As per the *Chief Economic Adviser K.V. Subramanian* (August 2020), India is the 5th largest economy in the world— so, if the Indian banking sector was proportional to the size of its economy, it should have been where South Korea is, which has 6 banks in the global top hundred. He further added that even countries that are a fraction of India's size for example Finland, Denmark, Belgium, Austria, Norway have at least 1 bank in the global top hundred— Sweden and Singapore which are one-sixth and one-eighth the size of Indian economy, respectively, have 3 banks in the list.

REGIONAL RURAL BANKS (RRBs)

The Regional Rural Banks (RRBs) were first set up on 2 October, 1975 (only 5 in number) with the aim to take banking services to the doorsteps of the rural masses specially in the remote areas with no access to banking services with twin duties to fulfill:

1. To provide credit to the weaker sections of the society at concessional rate of interest who previously depended on private money lending, and
2. To mobilise rural savings and channelise them for supporting productive activities in the rural areas.

The GoI, the concerned state government and the sponsoring nationalised bank contribute the share capital of the RRBs in the proportion of 50 per cent, 15 per cent and 35 per cent, respectively. The area of operation of the RRB is limited to notified few districts in a state.

Following the suggestions of the *Kelkar Committee*, the government stopped opening new RRBs in 1987—by that time their total number stood at 196. Due to excessive leanings towards social banking and catering to the highly economically weaker sections, these banks started incurring huge losses by early 1980s. For restructuring and strengthening of the banks, the governments set up two committees—the *Bhandari Committee* (1994–95) and the *Basu Committee* (1995–96). Out of the total, 171 were running in losses in 1998–99 when the government took some serious decisions:

1. The obligation of concessional loans abolished and the RRBs started charging commercial interest rates on its lendings.
2. The target clientele (rural masses, weaker sections) was set free now to lend to any body.

After the above-given policy changes, the RRBs started coming out of the red/losses. The CFS has recommended to get them merged with their managing nationalised or public sector banks and finally make them part of the would-be three-tier banking structure of India. By **April 2021**, as per the RBI, there were 43 RRBs operating in the country.

CO-OPERATIVE BANKS

Banks in India can be broadly classified under two heads—commercial banks and co-operative banks. While commercial banks (nationalised banks, State Bank group, private sector banks, foreign banks and regional rural banks) account for an overwhelming share of the banking business, co-operative banks also play an important role. Initially *set up to* supplant indigenous sources of rural credit, particularly money lenders, today they mostly serve the needs of agriculture and allied activities, rural-based industries and to a lesser extent, trade and industry in urban centres. Co-operative banks have a *three tier structure*—

1. Primary Credit Societies-PCSs (agriculture or urban),
2. District Central Co-Operative Banks-DCCBs, and
3. State Co-Operative Banks-SCBc (at the apex level).

UCBs Primary credit societies (PCSs) in urban areas that meet certain specified criteria can apply to RBI for a banking license to operate as urban co-operative banks (UCBs). They are registered and governed under the co-operative societies acts of the respective states and are covered by the Banking Regulation Act, 1949—thus are under dual regulatory control. The *managerial aspects* of these banks—registration, management, administration, recruitment, amalgamation, liquidation, etc. are controlled by the state governments, while the matters related to *banking* are regulated by RBI.

Traditionally, the area of operation of the UCBs is confined to metropolitan, urban or semi-urban centres and caters to the needs of small borrowers including MSMEs, retail traders, small entrepreneurs, professionals and the salaried class. However, there is no formal restriction as such and today UCBs can conduct business in the entire district in which they are registered, including rural areas. Well managed primary UCBs with deposits of over ₹50 crore are also allowed to operate in more than one state subject to certain norms.

As they are covered by the RBI Act, 1934 (2nd Schedule) they have certain rights and obligations—*rights* of obtaining refinance and loans from the RBI and *obligations* such as maintenance of cash reserves, submission of returns to the RBI etc. Presently, there are 29 UCBs.

DCCBs & SCBs As their names suggest, they operate at the district and state levels. One district can have no more than one DCCB with a number of DCCBs reporting to the SCB. They were under supervision of the RBI—later on this function was delegated to the NABARD.

Problems of these Banks

Co-operative banks play a very vital role in India's financial system. But they have been faced with certain long-drawn problems also—we may have brief look at them:

- Regulation remains the biggest issue as they are under dual regulatory control—the UCBs come under the RBI and the Registrar of Co-operative Societies (RCS) of the respective states while the DCCBs and SCBs come under the NABARD, the RBI and the RCSs. Given the close links between politicians and co-operatives and the fact that the RCS functions under the state government, in practice this dual (or triple) custody of the co-operative banks has, in practice, led to poor supervision and control. Besides, most co-operative banks are lacking in skill and expertise.
- Recruitments are politicised as are appointments at most levels.
- Income recognition and prudential norms that were introduced for commercial banks

in the early 1990s (under the process of banking reforms) are still to be this sector.

Co-operative banks have been in news mostly for fraudulent deals. Due to multiplicity of regulatory control of the federal nature it becomes really difficult to comply these banks to the prudential norms. Meanwhile, the Government of India decided (in the ***Union Budget 2017–18)*** to bring the co-operative banks into the ambit of the 'core banking' structure. Under the core banking solution (CBS), customers are able to avail banks' services across all of the branches rather the branch where the account is—making them customers of the bank rather than of a branch.

Regulatory Changes In 2020-21, the Government took an effective step (by amending the Banking Regulation Act, 1949) in this direction under which the RBI was given greater *regulatory powers* in case of the UCBs—accordingly, the following changes[26] have come in force:

- RBI can issue directions relating to the management of UCBs including approval for appointment of Chairman/MD/CEO, removal and remuneration of MD/CEO.
- Board of these banks should have not less than 51 per cent members having special knowledge/practical experience in specified areas.
- The statutory restriction on grant of director-related loans has been widened and common directorship across banks prohibited.
- RBI has been vested with powers of approval of the appointment/removal of statutory auditors of UCBs.
- RBI to specify the guidelines for raising capital by UCBs (by issuing equity, preference, special shares, debentures, bonds.
- RBI can supersede the Board of Directors of a UCB (in case of a UCB having operations confined to a single State, to be done in consultation with the concerned State Government).
- RBI to sanction voluntary or compulsory amalgamation and to prepare scheme for reconstruction of a UCB with the approval of the Central Government.
- Winding up of a UCB by High Court at the instance of the RBI.
- Priority sector lending (PSL) target for UCBs increased to 75 per cent (from 40 per cent).
- Co-operative banks declared as eligible lending institutions under interest subvention scheme for MSMEs.
- Compulsory reporting of large loans (loans of ₹5 crore and above) given by the UCBs to the CRILC (Central Repository of Information on Large Credits).
- The exposure norms for 'single borrower' and a 'group of borrowers' decreased to 15 per cent and 25 per cent, respectively (from 25 per cent and 40 per cent) for the UCBs.

FINANCIAL SECTOR REFORMS

The process of economic reforms initiated in 1991 had redefined the role of government in the economy—in coming times the economy will be dependent on the greater private participation for its development.[27] Such a changed view to development required an overhauling in the investment structure of the economy. Now the private sector was going to demand high investible capital out of the financial system. Thus, an emergent need was felt to restructure the whole financial system of India.

26. **Economic Survey 2020-21,** vol. 2, pp. 139-40, Ministry of Finance, GoI, N. Delhi.

27. Repeated by the Government of India many times, i.e., the ***New Industrial Policy 1991; the Union Budget 1992–93; Eighth Five Year Plan (1992–97) Draft Approach;*** etc.

The three decades after nationalisation had seen a phenomenal expansion in the geographical coverage and financial spread of the banking system in the country. As certain weaknesses were found to have developed in the system during the late eighties, it was felt that these had to be addressed to enable the financial system to play its role ushering in a more efficient and competitive economy.[28] Accordingly, a *high level* committee on Financial System (CFS) was set up on 14 August, 1991 to examine all aspects relating to *structure, organisation, function* and *procedures* of the financial system—based on its recommendations, a comprehensive reform of the banking system was introduced in the fiscal 1992–93.

The CFS based its recommendations on certain *assumptions*[29] which are basic to the banking industry. And the suggestions of the committee became logical in light of this assumption, there is no second opinion about it. The assumption says that *'the resources of the banks come from the general public and are held by the banks in trust that they are to be deployed for maximum benefit of the depositors.'*. This assumption automatically implied:

1. That even the government had no business to endanger the solvency, health and efficiency of the nationalised banks under the pretext of using banks as resources for *economic planning, social banking, poverty alleviation,* etc.
2. Besides, the government had no right to get hold of the funds of the banks at low interest rates and use them for financing its consumption expenditure (i.e., revenue and fiscal deficits) and thus defraud the depositors.

28. Announced by the government while setting up the M. Narasimham ***Committee on Financial System*** on 14 August, 1991. See also Publication Division, India 2011 (New Delhi: Government of India, 2002).

29. Reserve Bank of India, ***Committee on Financial Systems,*** 1991.

The recommendations of the CFS (**Narasimham Committee I**) were ***aimed*** at:

1. ensuring a degree of operational *flexibility;*
2. *internal autonomy* for public sector banks (PSBs) in their decision making process; and
3. greater degree of *professionalism* in banking operation.

Recommendation of CFS

The CFS recommendation[30] could be summed up under five sub-titles:

1. **On Directed Investment:** The RBI was advised not to use the CRR as a principal instrument of monetary and credit control, in place it should rely on open market operations (OMOs) increasingly. Two proposals advised regarding the CRR:
   (i) CRR should be progressively reduced from the present high level of 15 per cent to 3 to 5 per cent; and
   (ii) RBI should pay interest on the CRR of banks above the basic minimum at a rate of interest equal to the level of banks' one year deposit.

   Concerning the SLR it was advised to cut it to the minimum level (i.e., 25 per cent) from the present high level of 38.5 per cent in the next 5 years (it was cut down to 25 per cent in October 1997). The government was also suggested to progressively move towards market-based borrowing programme so that banks get economic benefits on their SLR investments.

   These suggestions were directed to the goal of making more funds available to the banks, converting idle cash for use, and

30. Ibid.

cutting down the interest rates banks charge on their loans.

2. **On Directed Credit Programme:** Under this sub-title the suggestions revolved around the compulsion of priority sector lending (PSL) by the banks:

   (i) Directed credit programme should be phased out gradually. As per the committee, agriculture and small scale industries (SSIs) had already grown to a mature stage and they did not require any special support; two decades of interest subsidy were enough. Therefore, concessional rates of interest could be dispensed with.

   (ii) Directed credit should not be a regular programme—it should be a case of extraordinary support to certain weak sections—besides, it should be temporary, not a permanent one.

   (iii) Concept of PSL should be redefined to include only the weakest sections of the rural community such as marginal farmers, rural artisans, village and cottage industries, tiny sector, etc.

   (iv) The 'redefined PSL' should have 10 per cent fixed of the aggregate bank credit.

   (v) The composition of the PSL should be reviewed after every 3 years.

3. **On the Structure of Interest Rates:** The major recommendations on the structure of interest rates are:

   (i) Interest rates to be broadly determined by market forces;

   (ii) All controls of interest rates on deposits and lending to be withdrawn;

   (iii) Concessional rates of interest for PSL of small sizes to be phased out and subsidies on the IRDP loans to be withdrawn;

   (iv) Bank rate to be the anchor rate and all other interest rates to be closely linked to it; and

   (v) The RBI to be the sole authority to simplify the structure of interest rates.

4. **On Structural Reorganisation of the Bank:** For the structural reorganisation of banks some major suggestions were given:

   (i) Substantial reduction in the number of the PSBs through mergers and acquisitions—to bring about greater efficiency in banking operations;

   (ii) Dual control of RBI and Banking Division (of the Ministry of Finance) should go immediately and RBI to be made the primary agency for the regulation of the banking system;

   (iii) The PSBs to be made free and autonomous;

   (iv) The RBI to examine all the guidelines and directions issued to the banking system in the context of the independence and autonomy of the banks;

   (v) Every PSB to go for a radical change in work technology and culture, so as to become competitive internally and to be at par with the wide range of innovations taking place abroad; and

   (vi) Finally, the appointment of the Chief Executive of Bank (CMD) was suggested not to be on political considerations but on professionalism and integrity. An independent panel of experts was suggested which should recommend and finalise the suitable candidates for this post.

5. **Asset Reconstruction Companies/Fund:** To tackle the menace of the higher non-performing assets (NPAs) of banks and

financial institutions, the committee suggested setting up of asset reconstruction companies/funds (taking clue from the US experience).

The committee directly blamed the Government of India and the Ministry of Finance for the sad state of affairs of the PSBs. These banks were used and abused by the GoI, the officials, the bank employees and the trade unions, the report adds. The recommendations were revolutionary in many respects and were opposed by the bank unions and the leftist political parties.

There were some other major suggestions of the committee which made it possible to get the following[31] things done by the government:

(i) Opening of new private sector banks permitted in 1993;

(ii) Prudential norms relating to income recognition, asset classification and provisioning by banks on the basis of objective criteria laid down by the RBI;

(iii) Introduction of capital adequacy norms (i.e., CAR provisions) with international standard started;

(iv) Simplification in the banking regulation (i.e., via board for financial supervision in 1994); etc.

The recommendations of the CFS became a kind of milestone for the Governments of future to promote financial and banking sector reforms. We can see the imprint of the committee's advices even today on most of the actions taken in this direction on the broader framework of the reforms initiated by the Government.

31 Based on Y.V. Reddy, ***Lectures on Economic and Financial Sector Reforms in India, 2002.***

BANKING SECTOR REFORMS

The government commenced a comprehensive reform process in the financial system in 1992–93 after the recommendations of the CFS in 1991. In December 1997 the government did set up another committee on the banking sector reform (BSR) under the chairmanship of M. Narasimham.[32] The objective of the committee is objectively clear by the ***terms of reference*** it was given while setting up:

'To review the progress of banking sector reforms to date and chart a programme of financial sector reforms necessary to strengthen India's financial system and make it internationally competitive.'

The **Narasimham Committee-II** (popularly called by the Government of India) handed over its reports in April 1998, which included the following major suggestions:[33]

1. Need for a stronger banking system for which mergers of the PSBs and the financial institutions (AIFIs) were suggested—stronger banks and the DFIs (development financial institutions, i.e., AIFIs) to be merged while weaker and unviable ones to be closed.
2. A 3-tier banking structure was suggested after mergers:

   (i) *Tier- 1* to have 2 to 3 banks of international orientation;

   (ii) *Tier- 2* to have 8 to 10 banks of national orientation; and

   (iii) *Tier- 3* to have large number of local banks.

32 Ministry of Finance, ***Economic Survey 1998–99,*** (New Delhi: Government of India, 1999).

33 Based on the Report of the ***Committee on Banking Sector Reforms,*** April 1998 (Chairman: M. Narasimham).

The first and second tiers were to take care of the banking needs of the corporate sector in the economy.

3. Higher norms of Capital-to-Risk—Weighted Adequacy Ratio (CRAR) suggested—increased to 10 per cent.
4. Budgetary recapitalisation of the PSBs is not viable and should be abandoned.
5. Legal framework of loan recovery should be strengthened (the government passed the *SARFAESI (Act, 2002)*.
6. Net NPAs for all banks suggested to be cut down to below 5 per cent by 2000 and 3 per cent by 2002.
7. Rationalisation of branches and staffs of the PSBs suggested.
8. Licencing to new private banks (domestic as well as foreign) was suggested to continue with.
9. Banks' boards should be depoliticised under RBI supervision.
10. Board for Financial Regulation and Supervisions (BFRS) should be set up for the whole banking, financial and the NBFCs in India.[34]

The recommendations of the BFR committee were more pin-pointed than the CFS (which was also headed by the same Chairman, M. Narasimham) and they did set a broader outline for the future reforms of the banking industry in the country, especially for the public sector banks. We find the Government agreeing with its advices even today on great many fronts of banking reforms.

34 An integrated system of regulation and supervision was suggested by the Committee so that soundness of the financial system could be ensured—the concept of a financial ***super-regulator*** gets vindicated, as opines Y. V. Reddy, in ***Lectures on Economic and Financial Sector Reforms in India***, 38, Ibid.

DRI

The differential rate of interest (DRI) is a lending programme launched by the government in April 1972 which makes it obligatory upon all the public sector banks in India to lend 1 per cent of the total lending of the preceding year to ***'the poorest among the poor'*** at an interest rate of 4 per cent per annum.

Priority Sector Lending

All Indian banks have to follow the compulsory target of priority sector lending (PSL). The priority sector in India are at present the sectors—agriculture, small and medium enterprises (SMEs), road and water transport, retail trade, small business, small housing loans (not more than ₹10 lakhs), software industries, self help groups (SHGs), agro-processing, small and marginal farmers, artisans, distressed urban poor and indebted non-institutional debtors besides the SCs, STs and other weaker sections of society.[35] In 2007, the RBI included five minorities—Buddhists, Christians, Muslims, Parsis and Sikhs under the PSL. In its ***new guidelines*** of March 2015, the RBI added *'medium enterprise, sanitation and renewable energy'* under it.[36] The PSL target must be met by the banks operating in India in the following way:

1. **Indian Banks:** need to lend 40 per cent to the priority sector every year (public sector as well as private sector banks, both) of their total lending. There is a sub-target also—18 per cent of the total lending must go to agriculture and 10 per cent of the total lending or 25 per cent of the priority sector lending (whichever be

35 See Publication Division, ***India 2007*** (New Delhi: Government of India, 2008) and **Economic Survey, 2006–07.**

36 RBI, **New Guidelines on the PSL**, 2 March, 2015.

higher) must be lent out to the weaker sections. Other areas of the priority sector to be covered in the left amount, i.e., 12 per cent of the total lending.

2. **Foreign Banks:** (having less than 20 branches) have to fulfil only 32 per cent PSL target which has sub-targets for the exports (12 per cent) and small and medium enterprises (10 per cent). It means they need to disburse other areas of the PSL from the remaining 10 per cent of their total lending (***lesser burden***).

The Committee on Financial System (CFS, 1991) had suggested to immediately cut it down to 10 per cent for all banks and completely phasing out of this policy for the betterment of the banking industry in particular and the economy in general. The committee also suggested to shuffle the sectors covered under PSL every three years. No follow up has been done from the government except cutting down PSL target for the foreign banks from 40 per cent to 32 per cent (remaining same for those which have less than 20 branches). Meanwhile, some new areas have been added to the PSL.

NPAs AND STRESSED ASSETS

Non-Performing Assets (NPAs) are the *bad loans* of the banks. The criteria to identify such assets have been changing over the time. In order to follow international best practices and to ensure greater transparency, the RBI shifted to the current policy in 2004. Under it, a loan is considered NPA if it has not been serviced for ***one term*** (i.e., 90 days). This is known as *'90 day' overdue norm.* For agriculture loans the period is tied with the period of the concerned crops—ranging from two crop seasons to one year overdue norm.[37]

NPAs were classified into three types:

1. **Sub-standard:** remaining NPAs for less than or equal to 12 months;
2. **Doubtful:** remaining NPAs for more than 12 months; and
3. **Loss assets:** where the loss has been identified by the bank or internal/ external auditors or the RBI inspection, but the amount has not been written off.

Current Situation

The NPAs of the banks, especially those of the public sector banks (PSBs) have been rising fast since 2011-12 itself rather they became a matter of concern for the RBI by late 2017. However, during 2020-21 (April-September), the banks (public as well as private) not only fetched profit but saw a decline[38] in their NPAs and stresses assets:

- GNPAs ratio (i.e., NPAs as a percentage of Gross Loan) of Scheduled Commercial Banks (SCBs) *decreased* to 7.5 per cent by end-September 2020 (from 8.2 per cent at the end-March 2020).
- RSAs (Restructured Standard Assets) ratio of SCBs *decreased* to 7.9 per cent by end-September 2020 (from 8.6 per cent at the end-March 2020).
- GNPA ratio of the PSBs *decreased* to 9.4 per cent by end-September 2020 (from 10.25 per cent at the end-March 2020) and during the same period their Stressed Assets ratio decreased to 9.96 per cent (from 10.75 per cent).
- NNPAs ratios (i.e., NPAs as percentage of their capital) also declined and stood at 2.1 per cent for SCBs and 2.85 per cent for PSBs as at the end-September 2020. Though, various reasons (as reported by

37. Reserve Bank of India, 'Master Circular - Income *Recognition, Asset Classification, Provisioning and Other Related Matters'*, July 2013.

38. **Economic Survey 2020-21**, vol. 2, pp. 131-33, Ministry of Finance, GoI, N. Delhi.

the Government documents since 2013–14) have been cited for the recent upsurge in the NPAs of the PSBs, by now the major ones are being considered as given below:[39]

- Global and domestic macro-economic instabilities due to which a slowdown was seen in the economy diluting the capability of the borrowers to service the loans.
- Delays in project approvals resulting into high cost over-runs. This dented the loan servicing capability of the borrowers in a big way.
- Aggressive lending by the banks to high corporate leverage.
- High incidences of 'wilful defaults'.
- Cases of loan frauds.
- Instances of corruption in the banking institutions.

Looking at the rising NPAs and stressed assets, the Government commenced a multi-pronged policy framework to resolve the NPA crisis faced by the public sector banks.

Resolution of the NPAs

At one hand, while the RBI tried to check the NPAs from rising by announcing new guidelines for the banks, on the other hand, it took several steps to 'resolve' the problem. By *February 2017* (since 2014–15), the RBI has implemented a number of schemes to facilitate resolution of the NPAs problem of the banks—briefly discussed below:

5/25 Refinancing This scheme offered a larger window for revival of stressed assets in the infrastructure sectors and 8 core industries. Under this scheme lenders were allowed to extend the tenure of loans to 25 years with interest rates adjusted every 5 years, so tenure of the loans matches the long gestation period in the sectors. The scheme thus aimed to improve the credit profile and liquidity position of borrowers, while allowing banks to treat these loans as standard in their balance sheets, reducing provisioning costs against NPAs. However, with amortisation spread out over a longer period, this arrangement also meant that the companies faced a higher interest burden, which they found difficult to repay, forcing banks to extend additional loans (called 'evergreening'). This in turn has aggravated the initial problem.

ARCs (Assets Reconstruction Companies) ARCs were introduced to India under the SARFAESI Act (2002), as specialists to resolve the burden of NPAs. But the ARCs (most are privately-owned) finding it difficult to resolve the NPAs they purchased, are today only willing to purchase such loans at low prices. As a result, banks have been unwilling to sell them loans on a large scale. Since (2014) the fee structure of the ARCs was modified (requiring ARCs to pay a greater proportion of the purchase price *up-front* in cash to the banks) purchases of NPAs by them have slowed down further—only about 5 per cent of total NPAs were sold during 2014–15 and 2015–16.

SDR (Strategic Debt Restructuring) In June 2015, RBI came up with the SDR scheme to provide an opportunity to banks to convert debt of companies (whose stressed assets were restructured but which could not finally fulfil the conditions attached to such restructuring) to 51 per cent equity and sell them to the highest bidders—ownership change takes place in it. By end-December 2016, only 2 such sales had materialised, in part because many firms remained financially unviable, since only a small portion of their debt had been converted to equity.

AQR (Assets Quality Review) Resolution of the problem of bad assets requires sound recognition of such assets. Therefore, the RBI emphasised

39. As the then RBI Governor Raghuram Rajan said deposing to the ***Parliamentary Accounts Committee*** in September 2016.

AQR, to verify that banks were assessing loans in line with RBI loan classification rules. Any deviations from such rules were to be rectified by March 2016.

S4A (Scheme for Sustainable Structuring of Stressed Assets) Introduced in June 2016, in it, an independent agency is hired by the banks which decides as how much of the stressed debt of a company is 'sustainable'. The rest ('unsustainable') is converted into equity and preference shares. Unlike the SDR arrangement, this involves no change in the ownership of the company.

The various schemes launched by the RBI to resolve the issues of NPAs and stressed assets of the banks could not bring in the desired results due to several reasons and apprehensions. Finally, these schemes were put on hold and the *regime* of insolvency and bankruptcy law commenced by late 2017-18. In this regard the RBI was vested with the power (via an amendment in the banking regulation act) to direct banks to initiate corporate insolvency resolution process (CIRP) against defaulting borrowers. A *brief discussion* is given below on the historic insolvency and bankruptcy law and its performance till date.

Insolvency and Bankruptcy

By now several measures were put in place by the Government/RBI to resolve the 'twin balance sheet' (TBS) crisis faced by the economy but they could not bring out effective results. Finally, we see the Government moving to make the insolvency procedure effective to address the issue. The lenders (banks) and borrowers (private corporate sector) both have been paying a high financial cost of country's complex and time-taking process of insolvency and bankruptcy process. The new Insolvency and Bankruptcy Code, 2016 (IBC) was amended and enforced by the Government in November 2017. There has been a significant amount of progress in this regard—the entire mechanism for the Corporate Insolvency Resolution Process (CIRP) has been put in place. A number of rules and regulations have been notified to create the institutions and professionals necessary for the process to work. A large number of cases have entered the insolvency process.

A major factor behind the effectiveness of the new Code has been the *adjudication* by the Judiciary—it prescribes *strict time limits* for various procedures under it. In spite of the large inflow of cases to NCLT benches across India, these benches have been able to admit or reject applications for CIRP admissions with few delays. In addition, appellate courts, including the NCLAT, High Courts and the Supreme Court have also disposed appeals quickly and decisively. In this process, a rich case-law has evolved, reducing future legal uncertainty. In the CIRP, the Committee of Creditors (CoC) invites resolution plans from resolution applicants, and may select one of these plans. The Code originally *does not specify* any restrictions on who these resolution applicants might be though it declares some persons are ineligible to submit resolution plans:

1. an undischarged insolvent;
2. a wilful defaulter;
3. a borrower whose account has been identified as a non-performing asset for over a year and who has not repaid the amount before submitting a plan;
4. a person convicted of an offence punishable with two or more years of imprisonment;
5. a person disqualified as a director under the Companies Act, 2013;
6. a person prohibited from trading in securities;

7. a person who is the promoter or in the management of a company which has indulged in undervalued, preferential, or fraudulent transactions;
8. a person who has given guarantee on a liability of the defaulting company undergoing resolution or liquidation, and has not honoured the guarantee;
9. a person who is subject to any of the above disabilities in any jurisdiction outside India; or
10. a person who has a connected person disqualified in any manner above.

Amendments in the Code The Government has been *proactively* addressing the issues that come up in implementation of the IBC, 2016. To ensure proper operationalisation of it, till 2020-21, the Government had affected *three* important amendments in it:

1. The first amendment introduced *Section 29A*, which deals with the provision introduced to bar promoters from bidding for their own companies. It prevented defaulters from regaining control of their companies at a cheaper value.
2. The second amendment introduced *Section 12A* to provide creditors option to withdraw insolvency application within 30 days of filing the petition. The amendment also stated that ***home buyers*** shall be treated as financial creditors. This move was aimed at mainly two issues—firstly, giving home buyers a voice in the insolvency proceedings as they, also provide funding for projects by making advance payments, and secondly, to discourage real estate developers from defaulting on commitments not only to banks but also to their customers.
3. The third amendment has been primarily focused upon the revival of a CD (Corporate Debtor) by ensuring timely admission and completion of the resolution process. The amendment ensures that 14 days period deadline given to the NCLT for admitting or rejecting a resolution application shall be strictly adhered to. The amendment further specifying the mandatory time frame of 330 days to complete the Corporate Insolvency Resolution Process (CIRP) without exception, tries to instil discipline amongst the stakeholders to avoid inordinate delays in the insolvency resolution process.

   The Government also reaffirms its stance as a facilitator in the third amendment by specifically making a resolution plan binding on the Central Government, State Governments or a local authority to whom debt in respect of payment of dues is owed.

Performance of the IBC The experience of the IBC, though it is of just over 3 years, has been quite satisfactory and eye-opening for the country. A brief review[40] about its performance is as given below:

- A total of 4,117 applications were admitted till December 2020 (since its inception in 2016).
- Nearly 23 per cent of the cases admitted were settled or withdrawn after the commencement of Corporate Insolvency Resolution Process (CIRP).
- Out of the 1420 cases for which the CIRP process has been completed, liquidation as an outcome has happened nearly 3.6 times the resolution.

The data given above does not tell the real story about the Code— because 73 per cent (799 cases) of cases under liquidation and 33 per cent of cases (101 cases) under resolution had been

40. **Economic Survey 2020-21,** vol. 2, pp. 151-53, Ministry of Finance, GoI, N. Delhi.

brought in from the regime (i.e., the scrapped Board for Industrial and Financial Reconstruction). Most of these cases have been considered to be *dead corpus* with most of the net worth being eroded by the time they entered CIRP. Having been able to revive 101 of such cases is an achievement in itself. The CIRP for non-BIFR legacy has yielded 195 resolutions and 288 liquidations till date. This also means that the resolution rate for non-BIFR legacy cases is more than 'three times' higher at 40 per cent when compared to BIFR cases.

In view of the COVID-19 pandemic, the IBC was amended (through an Ordinance in June 2020) and insolvency process was suspended till December 2020 (in all 1966 cases)—as a result the number of cases declined.

Behavioural Change The Code has brought significant behavioural changes among the creditors and debtors and is redefining debtor-creditor relationship with the following results:

- The inevitable consequence of a resolution process (i.e., the control/management of the firm move away from existing promoters/managers, most probably, forever) *debtors*to operate below the optimum level of efficiency.
- It encourages the debtors to settle default expeditiously with the creditor at the earliest, preferably outside the Code. In many instances debtors settled their debts on their own or settled immediately after an application was filed with the National Company Law Tribunal (NCLT) before it was admitted.
- Of the total of 18,892 applications (since 2016) that were dealt with, 14,884 cases (involving defaults of ₹5.15 lakh crore) were withdrawn by September 2020, before they were admitted while 897 processes were closed mid-way by December 2020.

Thus, around 83 per cent of the CDs got resolved on the way, before the official commencement of CIRP on account of *behavioural change* among the defaulting debtors. Only 7 per cent of the CDs went for the entire process yielding either resolution or liquidation (remaining 10 per cent were undergoing the process).

Status of Large Accounts Banks started insolvency process in case of 12 large accounts (with huge outstanding) on the direction of the RBI in June 2017—a total of ₹3.45 lakh crore as against liquidation value of ₹73,220 crores. Of these, resolution plans for 8 and liquidation for 2 were approved by December 2020.

NPAs Recovery on Backseat

On account of the outbreak of the COVID-19 pandemic, the focus on resolution and recovery of stressed assets had to take a backseat[41] and several supportive measures were announced by the Government to help stakeholders tide the unprecedented economic disruption, namely—*suspension* of fresh insolvency proceedings under Insolvency & Bankruptcy Code for defaults (arising between March 25, 2020 to March 25, 2021); *loan moratorium* (from March 1, 2020 to August 31, 2020); etc.

For COVID-19 related Stress, a **Resolution Framework** was announced by the RBI to enable the lenders to implement a resolution plan for different segment of borrowers (corporate, MSMEs, personal loans)—once a resolution plan has been invoked lenders are permitted to grant additional moratorium of up to *two* years to the borrowers (in this regard the RBI had appointed the *K.V. Kamath Committee* to suggest parameters for resolution plans).

41. Economic Survey 2020-21, vol. 2, pp. 132-33, Ministry of Finance, GoI, N. Delhi.

The above measures, which provided asset classification reliefs to borrowers, would affect the true recognition of financial stress on the borrower accounts. However, the larger objective of financial stability in the wake of pandemic demanded *prudential forbearance* which was exercised through clear boundaries and disincentives embedded in the reliefs. Moreover, the risk recognition has not been completely suspended as the lenders are required to make provisions of at least 10 per cent in respect of accounts which availed of asset classification benefits under these reliefs.

Wilful Defaulter

There are many people and entities who borrow money from lending institutions but fail to repay. However, not all of them are called wilful defaulters. As is embedded in the name, a wilful defaulter is one who does not repay a loan or liability, but apart from this there are other things that define a wilful defaulter. According to the RBI, a wilful defaulter is one who:

- is financially capable to repay and yet does not do so;
- or one who diverts the funds for purposes other than what the fund was availed for;
- or with whom funds are not available in the form of assets as funds have been siphoned off;
- or who has sold or disposed the property that was used as a security to obtain the loan.

Diversion of fund includes activities such as using short-term working capital for long-term purposes, acquiring assets for which the loan was not meant for and transferring funds to other entities. *Siphoning of funds* means that funds were used for purposes that were not related to the borrower and which could affect the financial health of the entity.

However, a lending institution cannot term an entity or an individual a wilful defaulter for a one-off case of default and needs to take into account the repayment track record. The default should be established to be intentional and the defaulter should be informed about the same. The defaulter should also be given a chance to clarify his stand on the issue. Also, the default amount needs to be at least ₹25 lakh to be included in the category of wilful defaults.

If an entity's or individual's name figures in the list of wilful defaulters, the following restrictions get in action on them:

- Barred from participating in the capital market.
- Barred from availing any further banking facilities and to access financial institutions for five years for the purpose of starting a new venture.
- The lenders can initiate the process of recovery with full vigour and can even initiate criminal proceedings, if required.
- The lending institutions may not allow any person related to the defaulting company to become a board member of any other company as well.

SARFAESI Act, 2002

GoI finally cracked down on the **wilful defaulters** by passing the *Securitisation and Reconstruction of Financial Assets and Enforcement of Security Interest (SARFAESI) Act, 2002*.

The Act gives far reaching powers to the banks/FIs concerning NPAs:

1. Banks/FIs having 75 per cent of the dues owed by the borrower can collectively proceed on the following in the event of the account becoming NPA:

(i) Issue notice of default to borrowers asking to clear dues within 60 days.

(ii) On the borrower's failure to repay:

(a) take possession of security and/or

(b) take over the management of the borrowing concern and/or

(c) appoint a person to manage the concern.

(iii) If the case is already before the BIFR, the proceedings can be stalled if banks/FIs having 75 per cent share in the dues have taken any steps to recover the dues under the provisions of the ordinance.

2. The banks/FIs can also sell the security to a securitisation or Asset Reconstruction Company (ARC), established under the provisions of the Ordinance. [The ARC is sought to be set up on the lines similar to the USA, few years ago.]

Public Sector Asset Rehabilitation Agency (PARA)

To resolve the twin problems of 'balance sheet syndrome' (of the banks as well as the corporate sector), the ***Economic Survey 2016–17*** has suggested the Government to set up a *public sector asset rehabilitation agency* (PARA)—charged with the largest and most complex cases of the 'syndrome'. Such initiatives were successfully able to handle the 'twin balance sheet' (TBS) problems in the countries hit by the South East Currency Crises of mid-1990s. As per the Survey, the Agency charged with working out the largest and most complex cases. Such an approach could eliminate most of the obstacles currently plaguing loan resolution.

- coordination problem as in this case, the debts would be centralised in one agency;
- it could be set up with proper incentives by giving it an explicit mandate to maximise recoveries within a defined time period; and
- it would separate the loan resolution process from concerns about bank capital.

The ***Survey*** outlined seven reasons in support of its suggestion for setting up the PARA—which are as given below:

1. **It's not just about banks, it's a lot about companies.** So far, the NPAs issues revolved around the capital of the bank and how to fund them so that they start giving loans again. But more important issue is to find out a way to resolve the NPAs created by the corporate houses (as why they are stressed).
2. **It is an economic problem, not a morality play.** Diversion of funds (wilful defaults) have undoubtedly been one reason behind non-payment of the debts. But a large number of loan defaults have been caused by unexpected changes in the economic environment—timetables, exchange rates, and growth rate assumptions going wrong.
3. **The stressed debt is heavily concentrated in large companies.** This is an opportunity, because TBS could be overcome by solving a relatively small number of cases. But it presents an even bigger challenge, because large cases are inherently difficult to resolve.
4. **Many of these companies are unviable at current levels of debt requiring debt write-downs in many cases.** Cash flows in the large stressed companies have been deteriorating over the past few years, to the point where debt reductions of more than 50 per cent will often be needed to restore viability. The only alternative would be to convert

debt to equity, take over the companies, and then sell them at a loss.

5. **Banks are finding it difficult to resolve these cases, despite a proliferation of schemes to help them.** Among other issues, they face severe coordination problems, since large debtors have many creditors, with different interests. If PSBs grant large debt reductions, this could attract the attention of the investigative agencies. But taking over large companies will be politically difficult as well.
6. **Delay is costly.** Since banks can't resolve the big cases, they have simply refinanced the debtors—deteriorating the situation. But this is costly for the government, because it means the bad debts keep rising, increasing the ultimate recapitalisation bill for the government and the associated political difficulties. Delay is also costly for the economy, because impaired banks are scaling back their credit, while stressed companies are cutting their investments.
7. **Progress may require a PARA.** The ARCs (Asset Reconstruction Companies) haven't proved any more successful than banks in resolving bad debts. But international experience shows that a professionally run central agency with government backing (not without its own difficulties) can provide the solution in this regard.

Since 2017-18 the Government has been hinting at the idea of the PARA (using its globally popular name—the **Bad Bank**) but final decision to set it up was still awaited. Recently, the *Union Budget 2021-22* proposed setting up of a *bad bank* under the ARC (asset reconstruction company), AMC (asset management company) and AIF (alternative investment funds) model to acquire, manage and turnaround bad loans.

The ARC will acquire bad loans from banks at a negotiated price (at a discount) and pay by way of cash and security receipts. The funds for buying the bad loans will come from the sponsors (government and banks, etc.) as well as alternative investment funds. The AMC will acquire, manage and turnaround bad loans against which it will charge a fee.

CAPITAL ADEQUACY RATIO

At first sight bank is a business or industry a segment of the service sector in any economy. But the failure of a bank may have far greater damaging impact on an economy than any other kind of business or commercial activity. Basically, modern economies are heavily dependent on banks today than in the past—banks are today called the backbone of economies. Healthy functioning of banks is today essential for the proper functioning of an economy. As credit creation (***i.e., loan disbursals***) of banks are highly risky business, the depositors' money depends on the banks' quality of lending. More importantly, the whole payment system, public as well as private, depends on banks. A bank's failure has the potential of creating chaos in an economy. This is why governments of the world pay special attention to the regulatory aspects of the banks. Every regulatory provision for banks tries to achieve a simple equation, i.e., ***'how the banks should maximise their credit creation by minimising the risk and continue functioning permanently'***. In the banking business risks are always there and cannot be made 'zero'—as any loan forwarded to any individual or firm (irrespective of their credit-worthiness) has the risk of turning out to be a bad debt (***i.e., NPA in India***)—the probability of this being 50 per cent. But banks must function so that economies can function. Finally, the central banks of the world started devising tools to minimise the risks of banking at *one hand* and providing cushions (shock-absorbers) to the banks at the *other hand* so that banks do not go bust (i.e., shut down after becoming bankrupt). Providing cushion/shock-absorbers to banks has seen three major developments:[42]

1. The provision of keeping a ***cash ratio*** of total deposits mobilised by the banks (known as the CRR in India);
2. The provision of maintaining some assets of the deposits mobilised by the banks with the banks themselves in ***non-cash form*** (known as the SLR in India); and
3. The provision of the capital adequacy ratio (CAR) norm.

The capital adequacy ratio (CAR) norm has been the last provision to emerge in the area of regulating the banks in such a way that they can sustain the probable risks and uncertainties of lending. It was in 1988 that the central banking bodies of the developed economies agreed upon such a provision, the CAR—also known as the **Basel Accord.**[43] The accord was agreed upon at Basel, Switzerland at a meeting of the Bank for International Settlements (BIS).[44] It was at this time that the **Basel-I** norms of the capital adequacy ratio were agreed upon—a requirement was imposed upon the banks to maintain a certain amount of free capital (***i.e., ratio***) to their ***assets***[45] (i.e., loans and investments by the banks) as a cushion against probable losses in investments and loans. In 1988, this ratio capital was decided to be 8 per cent. It means that if the total investments and loans forwarded by a bank amounts to ₹100, the bank needs to maintain a ***free capital***[46] of ₹8 at that particular time. ***The capital adequacy ratio is the percentage of total capital to the total risk—weighted assets*** (see footnote 46).

CAR, a measure of a bank's capital, is expressed as a percentage of a bank's risk weighted credit exposures:

CAR= Total of the Tier 1 & Tier 2 capitals ÷ Risk Weighted Assets

Also known as 'Capital to Risk Weighted Assets Ratio (CRAR)' this ratio is used to protect depositors and promote the stability and efficiency of financial systems around the world. Two types of capital were measured as per the **Basel-II** norms: *Tier 1* capital, which can absorb losses without a bank being required to cease trading, and *Tier 2* capital, which can absorb losses in the event of a winding-up and so provides a lesser degree of protection to depositors. The new norms (**Basel III**) has devised a third category of capital, i.e., *Tier 3* capital.

The RBI introduced the ***capital-to-risk weighted assets ratio*** (CRAR) system for the banks operating in India in 1992 in accordance with the standards of the BIS—as part of the

42. Through various legislations, since the ***RBI Nationalisation Act, 1949*** and the ***Banking Regulation Act, 1949*** were enacted – and further ***Amendments*** to the Acts, Ministry of Finance, Government of India, New Delhi.

43. Simon Cox (ed.), 'Economics', ***The Economist***, 2007, p. 75.

44. The ***BIS*** is today a central bank for central bankers set up in 1930 in a round tower near Basel railway station in Switzerland as a private company owned by a number of central banks, one commercial bank (Citibank) and some private individuals. Today it functions as a meeting place for the bank regulators of many countries, a multilateral regulatory authority and a ***clearing house*** for many nations' ***reserves*** (i.e. foreign exchange). See Tim Hindle, 'Pocket Finance' ***The Economist***, 2007, pp. 35–36.

45. Investments made and loans forwarded by banks are known as risky assets.

46. The capital of a bank was classified into Tier-I and Tier-II. While Tier-I comprises share capital and disclosed reserves, Tier-II includes revaluation reserves, hybrid capital and subordinated debt of a bank. As per the provision, Tier-II capital should not exceed the Tier I capital. The risk-weighting depends upon the type of assets—for example it is 100 per cent on private sector loans, while only 20 per cent for short-term loans.

financial sector reforms.[47] In the coming years the Basel norms were extended to term-lending institutions, primary dealers and non-banking financial companies (NBFCs), too. Meanwhile, the BIS came up with another set of CAR norms, popularly known as **Basel-II**. The RBI guidelines regarding the CAR norms in India have been as given below:

- Basel-I norm of the CAR was to be achieved by the Indian banks by March 1997.
- The CAR norm was raised to 9 per cent with effect from March 31, 2000 (Narasimham Committee-II had recommended to raise it to 10 per cent in 1998).[48]
- Foreign banks as well as Indian banks with foreign presence to follow Basel-II norms, w.e.f. 31 March, 2008 while other scheduled commercial banks to follow it no later than 31 March, 2009. The Basel-II norm for the CAR is 12 per cent.[49]

Why to Maintain CAR?

The basic question which comes to mind is as to why do the banks need to hold capital in the form of CAR norms? ***Two reasons***[50] have been generally forwarded for the same:

1. Bank capital helps to prevent bank failure, which arises in case the bank cannot satisfy its obligations to pay the depositors and other creditors. The low capital bank has a negative net worth after the loss in its business. In other words, it turns into insolvent capital, therefore, acts as a cushion to lessen the chance of the bank turning insolvent.
2. The amount of capital affects returns for the owners (equity holders) of the bank.

Basel Accords

The Basel Accords (i.e., Basel I, II and now III) are a set of agreements set by the Basel Committee on Bank Supervision (BCBS), which provides recommendations on banking regulations in regards to capital risk, market risk and operational risk. The purpose of the accords is to ensure that financial institutions have enough capital on account to meet obligations and absorb unexpected losses. They are of paramount importance to the banking world and are presently implemented by over 100 countries across the world. The BIS Accords were the outcome of a long-drawn-out initiative to strive for greater international uniformity in prudential capital standards for banks' credit risk. The objectives of the accords could be summed up[51] as:

1. to strengthen the international banking system;
2. to promote convergence of national capital standards; and
3. to iron out competitive inequalities among banks across countries of the world.

The Basel Capital Adequacy Risk-related Ratio Agreement of 1988 (**i.e., Basel I**) was not a legal document. It was designed to apply to internationally active banks of member countries of the Basel Committee on Banking Supervision (BCBS) of the BIS at Basel, Switzerland. But the details of its implementation were left to national

47. The RBI is a member of the Board of the BIS. The financial sector reforms commenced in India in the fiscal 1992–93 after the report submitted by the Narasimham Committee on Financial system (CFS).
48. Ministry of Finance, ***Committee on Banking Sector Reforms*** (M Narasimham Committee-II), (New Delhi: Government of India, April 1998).
49. Ministry of Finance, ***Economic Survey 2006–07***.
50. D. M. Nachane, Partha Ray and Saibal Ghosh, ***India Development Report 2004–05*** (New Delhi: Oxford University Press, 2005), p. 171.
51. Ibid, p. 172.

discretion. This is why Basel I looked G10-centric.[52]

The first Basel Accord, known as **Basel I** focuses on the capital adequacy of financial institutions. The capital adequacy risk (the risk a financial institution faces due to an unexpected loss), categorises the assets of financial institution into five risk categories (0 per cent, 10 per cent, 20 per cent, 50 per cent, 100 per cent). Banks that operate internationally are required to have a risk weight of 8 per cent or less.

The second Basel Accord, known as **Basel II,** is to be fully implemented by 2015. It focuses on three main areas, including minimum capital requirements, supervisory review and market discipline, which are known as the *three pillars*. The focus of this accord is to strengthen international banking requirements as well as to supervise and enforce these requirements.

The third Basel Accord, known as **Basel III,** is a comprehensive set of reform measures aimed to strengthen the regulation, supervision and risk management of the banking sector. These measures aim to[53]:

1. improve the banking sector's ability to absorb shocks arising from financial and economic stress, whatever the source be;
2. improve risk management and governance; and
3. strengthen banks' transparency and disclosures.

The capital of the banks has been classified into ***three tiers*** as given below:

1. **Tier 1 Capital:** A term used to describe the capital adequacy of a bank—it can absorb losses without a bank being required to cease trading. This is the **core measure** of a bank's financial strength from a regulator's point of view (this is the *most reliable* form of capital). It consists of the types of financial capital considered the most reliable and liquid, primarily stockholders' equity and disclosed reserves of the bank—equity capital can't be redeemed at the option of the holder and disclosed reserves are the liquid assets available with the bank itself.
2. **Tier 2 Capital:** A term used to describe the capital adequacy of a bank—it can absorb losses in the event of a winding-up and so provides a lesser degree of protection to depositors. Tier II capital is secondary bank capital (the *second most reliable* forms of capital). This is related to Tier 1 Capital. This capital is a measure of a bank's financial strength from a regulator's point of view. It consists of accumulated after-tax surplus of retained earnings, revaluation reserves of fixed assets and long-term holdings of equity securities, general loan-loss reserves, hybrid (debt/equity) capital instruments, and subordinated debt and undisclosed reserves.
3. **Tier 3 Capital:** A term used to describe the capital adequacy of a bank—considered the *tertiary capital* of the banks which are used to meet/support market risk, commodities risk and foreign currency risk. It includes a variety of debt other than Tier 1 and Tier 2 capitals. Tier 3 capital debts may include a greater number of subordinated issues, undisclosed reserves and general loss reserves compared to Tier 2 capital. To qualify as Tier 3 capital, assets must be limited to 250 per cent of a bank's Tier

52. G-10 comprises Belgium, Canada, France, Germany, Italy, Japan, The Netherlands, Sweden, UK and USA; later the group incorporated Luxembourg, Switzerland and recently Spain into its fold.
53. ***Bank of International Settelements,*** Basel, Switzerland, 15 May, 2012.

1 capital, be unsecured, subordinated[54] and have a minimum maturity of two years.

Disclosed Reserves are the total liquid cash and the SLR assets of the banks that may be used any time. This way they are part of its *core capital* (Tier 1). *Undisclosed Reserves* are the unpublished or hidden reserves of a financial institution that may not appear on publicly available documents such as a balance sheet, but are nonetheless real assets, which are accepted as such by most banking institutions, but cannot be used at will by the bank. That is why they are part of its *secondary capital* (Tier 2).

Basel III Provisions

The Basel III provisions[55] have defined the capital of the banks in different way. They consider common equity and retained earnings as the predominant component of capital (as the past), but they restrict inclusion of items such as deferred tax assets, mortgage-servicing rights and investments in financial institutions to no more than 15 per cent of the common equity component. These rules aim to improve the *quantity* and *quality* of the capital.

While the key capital ratio has been raised to 7 per cent of risky assets, according to the new norms, Tier-I capital that includes common equity and perpetual preferred stock will be raised from 2 to 4.5 per cent starting in phases from January 2013 to be completed by January 2015. In addition, banks will have to set aside another 2.5 per cent as a *contingency* for future stress. Banks that fail to meet the buffer would be unable to pay dividends, though they will not be forced to raise cash.

The new norms are based on renewed focus of central bankers on 'macro-prudential stability'. The global financial crisis following the crisis in the US sub-prime market has prompted this change in approach. The previous set of guidelines, popularly known as *Basel II* focused on 'macro-prudential regulation'. In other words, global regulators are now focusing on financial stability of the system as a whole, rather than micro regulation of any individual bank.

Banks in the West, which are market leaders for the most part, face low growth, an erosion in capital due to sovereign debt exposures and stiffer regulation. They will have to reckon with a permanent decline in their returns on equity thanks to enhanced capital requirements under the new norms. In contrast, Indian banks—and those in other emerging markets such as China and Brazil—are well-placed to maintain their returns on capital consequent to Basel III. Financial experts have opined that Basel III looks changing the economic landscape in which banking power shifts towards the emerging markets.

Basel III Compliance of the PSBs & RRBs

The capital to risk weighted assets ratio (CRAR) of the scheduled commercial banks of India was 13.02 per cent by March 2014 (Basel-III) falling to 12.75 per cent by September 2014. The regulatory requirement for CRAR is 9 per cent for 2015. The decline in capital positions at aggregate level, however, was on account of deterioration in capital positions of PSBs. While the CRAR of the scheduled commercial banks (SCB) at 12.75 per cent as of September 2014 was satisfactory, going forward the banking sector, particularly PSBs will require substantial capital to meet regulatory requirements with respect to additional capital buffers.

54. Subordinated debt ranks below other debts with regard to claims on assets or earnings (also known as a 'junior debt'). In the case of default, such creditors get paid out until after the senior debtholders were paid in full. Thus, such capitals of banks are more risky than unsubordinated debt.

55. *Reserve Bank of India,* MoF, GoI, New Delhi, May 5, 2012.

In order to make the PSBs and RRBs compliant to the *Basel III* norms,[56] the government has been following a recapitalisation programme for them since 2011–12. A *High Level Committee* on the issue was also set up by the government which has suggested the idea of 'non-operating holding company' (HoldCo) under a special Act of Parliament (action is yet to come regarding this).

The Governments have been infusing fresh capital into the PSBs since 2012-13 itself to make them comply to the *Basel III norms* through different means—budgetary supports, scheme (i.e., the Indradhanush Scheme of 2015-16) and Recapitalisation Bonds (initiated in 2019-20). As per the latest *Economic Survey 2020-21,* the CRAR of the SCBs *increased* to 15.8 per cent by end-September 2020 (from 14.7 per cent in March 2020)—on account of improvement seen in the CRARs of both Public and Private sector banks.

Stock of Money

In every economy it is necessary for the central bank to know the stock (amount/level) of money available in the economy only then it can go for suitable kind of credit and monetary policy. Saying simply, credit and monetary policy of an economy is all about changing the level of the money flowing in the economic system. But it can be done only when we know the real flow of money. That's why it is necessary to first assess the level of money flowing in the economy.

Following the recommendations of the *Second Working Group on Money Supply (SWG)* in 1977, RBI has been publishing four *monetary aggregates* (component of money), viz., M_1, M_2, M_3 and M_4 (are basically short terms for Money-1, Money-2, Money-3 and Money-4) besides the Reserve Money. These components used to contain money of differing liquidities:

M_1 = Currency & coins with people + Demand deposits of Banks (Current & Saving Accounts) + 'Other' deposits of the RBI.

M_2 = M_1 + Demand deposits of the post offices (i.e., saving schemes' money).

M_3 = M_1 + Time/Term deposits of the Banks (i.e., the money lying in the Recurring Deposits & the fixed Deposits).

M_4 = M_3 + total deposits of the post offices (both, Demand and Term/Time Deposits).

Now the RBI has started[57] publishing a set of new monetary aggregates following the recommendations of the *Working Group on Money Supply: Analytics and Methodology of Compilation* (Chairman, Dr. Y. V. Reddy) which submitted its report in June 1998. The Working Group recommended compilation of four monetary aggregates on the basis of the balance sheet of the banking sector in conformity with the norms of progressive liquidity: M_0 (monetary base), M_1 (narrow money), M_2 and M_3 (broad money). In addition to the monetary aggregates, the Working Group had recommended compilation of three liquidity aggregates namely, L_1, L_2 and L_3, which include select items of financial liabilities of non-depository financial corporations such as development financial institutions and non-banking financial companies accepting deposits from the public, apart from post office savings

56. **Basel III** norms prescribe a minimum regulatory capital of 10.5 per cent for banks by 1 January, 2019. This includes a minimum of 6 per cent ***Tier I*** capital, plus a minimum of 2 per cent ***Tier II*** capital, and a 2.5 per cent capital conservation buffer. For this buffer, banks are expected to set aside profits made during good times so that it can be drawn upon during periods of stress.

57. The working group was set up in December 1997 under the chairmanship of Y. V. Reddy (the then Deputy Governor, RBI) which submitted its report in June 1998.

banks. **The New Monetary Aggregates** are as given below:

> *Reserve Money* (M_0) = Currency in circulation + Bankers' Deposits with the RBI + 'Others'[58] deposits with the RBI.
>
> *Narrow Money* (M_1) = Currency with the Public + Demand Deposits with the Banking System + 'Others' deposits with the RBI.
>
> $M_2 = M_1$ + Savings Deposits of Post-office Savings Banks.
>
> *Broad Money* $(M_3) = M_1$ + Time Deposits with the Banking System.
>
> $M_4 = M_3$ + All deposits with Post Office Savings Banks (excluding National Savings Certificates).

While the Working Group did not recommend any change in the definition of reserve money and M_1, it proposed a new *intermediate monetary aggregate* to be referred to as NM_2 comprising currency and residents' short-term bank deposits with contractual maturity up to and including one year, which would stand in between narrow money (which includes only the non-interest-bearing monetary liabilities of the banking sector) and broad money (an all-encompassing measure that includes long-term time deposits). The new broad money aggregate (referred to as NM_3 for the purpose of clarity) in the Monetary Survey would comprise, in addition to NM_2, long-term deposits of residents as well as call/term borrowings from non-bank sources, which have emerged as an important source of resource mobilisation for banks. The critical *difference* between M_3 and NM_3 is the treatment of non-resident repatriable fixed foreign currency liabilities of the banking system in the money supply compilation.

There are **two basic changes** in the new monetary aggregates. *First,* since the post office bank is not a part of the banking sector, ***postal deposits*** are no longer treated as part of money supply, as was the case in the extant M_2 and M_4. *Second,* the residency criterion was adopted to a limited extent for compilation of monetary aggregates. The Working Group made a recommendation in favour of compilation of monetary aggregates on residency basis. Residency essentially relates to the country in which the holder has a centre of economic interest. Holdings of currency and deposits by the non-residents in the rest of the world sector, would be determined by their portfolio choice. However, these transactions form part of balance of payments (BoP). Such holdings of currency and deposits are not strictly related to the domestic demand for monetary assets. It is therefore argued that these transactions should be regarded as external liabilities to be netted from foreign currency assets of the banking system. However, in the context of developing countries such as India, which have a large number of expatriate workers who remit their savings in the form of deposits, it could be argued that these non-residents have a centre of economic interest in their country of origin. Although in a macro-economic accounting framework all non-resident deposits need to be separated from domestic deposits and treated as capital flows, the underlying economic reality may point otherwise. In the Indian context, it may not be appropriate to exclude all categories of non-resident deposits from domestic monetary aggregates as non-resident rupee deposits are essentially integrated into the domestic financial system. The new monetary aggregates, therefore, exclude only non-resident repatriable foreign currency fixed deposits from deposit liabilities and treat those as external liabilities. Accordingly,

58 'Others' deposits with RBI comprise mainly: (i) deposits of quasi-government; other financial institutions including primary dealers, (ii) balances in the accounts of foreign Central Banks and Governments, and (iii) accounts of international agencies such as the International Monetary Fund.

from among the various categories of non-resident deposits at present, only Foreign Currency Non-Resident Accounts (Banks) [FCNR(B)] deposits are classified as external liabilities and excluded from the domestic money stock. Since the bulk of the FCNR(B) deposits are held abroad by commercial banks, the monetary impact of changes in such deposits is captured through changes in net foreign exchange assets of the commercial banks. Thus, now the new monetary aggregates NM_2 and NM_3 as well as liquidity aggregates L_1, L_2, and L_3 have been introduced, the components of which are elaborated as follows:

NM_1 = Currency with the Public + Demand Deposits with the Banking System + 'Other' Deposits with the RBI

NM_2 = NM_1 + Short Term Time Deposits of Residents (including the contractual maturity of one year)

NM_3 = NM_2 + Long-term Time Deposits of Residents + Call/Term Funding from Financial Institutions

L_1 = NM_3 + All Deposits with the Post Office Savings Banks (excluding National Savings Certificates)

L_2 = L_1 + Term deposits with Term Lending Institutions and Refinancing Institutions (FIs) + Term Borrowing by FIs + Certificates of Deposit issued by FIs

L_3 = L_2 + Public Deposits of Non-Banking Financial Companies

Data on M_0 are published by the RBI on *weekly* basis, while those for M_1 and M_3 are available on *fortnightly* basis. Among liquidity aggregates, data on L_1 and L_2 are published *monthly*, while those for L_3 are disseminated *quarterly*. The working group advised for the quarterly publication of **Financial Sector Survey** to capture the dynamic linkages between banks and rest of the organised financial sector.

Components of Money Stock

As per the latest *Handbook of Statistics* of the RBI, the components of money at the end of *July 2020* were as give below:

1. Currency in Circulation = ₹26.72 lakh crore
2. Cash with Banks = ₹96,267 crore
3. Currency with Public = Currency in Circulation – Cash with Banks (₹25.76 lakh crore)
4. 'Others' Deposits with the RBI = ₹39,707 crore
5. Bankers' Deposits with the RBI = ₹4.69 lakh crore
6. Demand Deposits = ₹16.48 lakh crore
7. Time Deposits = ₹133.61 lakh crore

Reserve Money (M_0) = ₹31.81 lakh crore [1+4+5]

Narrow Money (M_1) = ₹46.64 lakh crore [3+4+6]

Broad Money (M_3) = ₹176.26 lakh crore [7+M_1]

Money Multiplier

Money multiplier is measured as the ratio of M_3 and M_0 (i.e., M_3 divided by M_0). It was mostly increasing from 1980s onwards up to 2016-17, however, been declining since then. As per the *Economic Survey 2020-21* by March 2020, it was 5.5 (down from 5.6 of the previous year).

However, adjusted for reverse repo (analytically, similar to banks' deposits with the central bank)—it turned out to be even lower at 4.8 by March 2020. Money multiplier has declined from the *recent peak* of 5.8 in October 2018 to 5.5

as on January 1, 2021. In comparison, during the same period, money multiplier adjusted for reverse repo has declined sharply from 5.7 to 4.5. This *shows* that the money supply has responded only partially to reserve money growth, reflecting that the liquidity transmission in the economy remains impaired. The gap between money multiplier and adjusted money reflected the large amount of funds parked by banks under reverse repo window (with the RBI).

Liquidity of Money

As we move from M_1 to M_4 the liquidity (inertia, stability, spendability) of the money goes on decreasing and in the opposite direction, the liquidity increases.

Narrow Money

In banking terminology, M_1 is called narrow money as it is highly liquid and banks cannot run their lending programmes with this money.

Broad Money

The money component M_3 is called broad money in the banking terminology. With this money (which lies with banks for a known period) banks run their lending programmes.

Money Supply

In general discussion we usually use money supply to mean money circulation, money flow in the economy. But in banking and typical monetary management terminology the level and supply of M_3 is known as money supply. The growth rate of broad money (M_3), i.e., *money supply*, was not only lower than the indicative growth set by the Reserve Bank of India, but it also witnessed continuous and sequential deceleration in the last 7 quarters and moderated to 11.2 per cent by December 2012. Aggregate deposits with the banks were the major component of broad money counting for over 85 per cent remaining almost stable. The sources of broad money are net bank credit to the government and to the commercial sector. These two together accounted for nearly 100 per cent of the broad money in 2012–13, compared to 89 per cent in 2009–10.

High Power Money

The central banks of all the countries are empowered to issue the currency. The currency issued by the central bank is called 'high power money' because it is generally backed by supporting 'reserves' and its value is guaranteed by the government and it is the source of all other forms of money. The currency issued by the central bank in fact, is a liability of the central bank and the government. In general, therefore, this liability must be backed by an equal value of assets consisting mainly, gold and foreign exchange reserves. In practice, however, most countries[59] have adopted a 'minimum reserve system'.

Under the *minimum reserve system* the central bank is required to keep a certain minimum reserve of gold and foreign securities and is empowered to ***issue currency to any extent.*** India adopted this system in October 1956. The RBI was required to hold a reserve worth of only ₹515 crore consisting of foreign securities worth ₹400 crore and gold worth ₹115 crore. In 1957, however, the minimum reserves were further reduced to only gold reserve of ₹115 crore and the rest in the form of rupee securities, mainly due to the scarcity of

59. In past, there were two other systems—*first* belongs to Great Britain in which no reserve was maintained upto a certain limit of currency issued, called 'fiduciary system' and *second* known as the 'proportional reserve system' in which, generally, 40 per cent reserve was maintained, adopted by France and the USA in 1928 and by India during 1935–56, replaced in October 1956 by a 'minimum reserve system'.

foreign exchange to meet essential import bill. A gold reserve of ₹115 crore against the currency of ₹17,00,000 crore in circulation today, makes only 0.7 per cent reserve which is of no consequence. This makes the Indian currency system a 'managed paper currency system'. In India, there are two sources of *high power money* supply:

1. RBI and
2. Government of India.

The RBI issues currency notes of rupees 2, 5, 10, 20, 50, 100, 500 and 2000 denominations which RBI calls as the 'Reserve Money'. The RBI issues currency of one rupee notes and coins including coins of smaller denominations on behalf of the Government of India which accounts for around 2 per cent of the total high power money.

Minimum Reserve

The RBI is required to maintain a reserve equivalent of ₹200 crores in gold and foreign currency with itself, of which ₹115 crores should be in gold. Against this reserve, the RBI is empowered to issue currency to any extent. This is being followed since 1957 and is known as the Minimum Reserve System (MRS).

CREDIT RATING

Credit rating is an assessment of the *creditworthiness* of a borrower (individuals, corporations/businesses, and governments) which is shown in quantified form. This helps in knowing the potential risk involved in investment and lending as ratings aim to predict the repayment ability of the borrower.

While credit 'rating' is given to businesses and governments, individual is given credit 'score' (which is calculated on the basis of individual's credit history). Ratings are broadly of two categories—*short-term* credit rating reflects the likelihood of a borrower's default within the year while *long-term* credit rating predicts likelihood of a borrower's default in any given period of time (of more than one year). While credit rating is shown using a *letter-based* or *alphanumeric* system with symbols (such as AAA, AA+, A+, A-, A1+, A1- etc.), credit score is shown in numbers (usually varying between 300-900).[60]

Beginning with the Moody's in 1909, today world has several rating agencies operating. India recognises the following six agencies for its sovereign rating:

1. Fitch Ratings (Fitch)
2. Moody's Investors Services (Moody's)
3. Standard and Poor's (S&P)
4. Dominion Bond Rating Service (DBRS)
5. Japanese Credit Rating Agency (JCRA)
6. Rating and Investment Information Inc. (R&I)

Credit rating industry is very concentrated in the world—only 3 agencies (Moody's, S&P, and Fitch) controlling almost the entire global market. In India, the SEBI (Securities and Exchange Board of India) authorises and regulates all credit rating agencies—there are *7 credit rating agencies* (CRISIL, ICRA, CARE, India Ratings, Acuite Ratings, Brickwork Ratings, and Infomerics) operating in the country (sovereign rating is not done by them).

A favourable sovereign rating helps countries attract enhanced funds from the foreign investors. Rating agencies broadly rate countries as either *investment grade* or *speculative grade*, with the latter projected to have a higher likelihood of default on borrowings. The threshold of **Investment grade** is considered to be **BBB-** for *S&P* and *Fitch* and **Baa3** for *Moody's*. *Table 12.1* presents the rating scale comparison between S&P, Moody's and Fitch.

60. **Economic Survey 2020-21**, vol. 1, pp. 84-120, Ministry of Finance, GoI, N. Delhi.

TABLE 12.1: RATING SCALE COMPARISON BETWEEN SOME MAJOR CREDIT RATING AGENCIES

Interpretation	Fitch and S&P	Moody's
Highest quality	AAA	Aaa
High quality	AA+ AA AA–	Aa1 Aa2 Aa3
Strong payment capacity	A+	A1
	A	A2
	A–	A3
Adequate payment capacity	BBB+ BBB BBB–	Baa1 Baa2 Baa3
Likely to fulfil obligations, on going uncertainty	BB+ BB BB–	Ba1 Ba2 Ba3
High-risk obligations	B+ B B–	B1 B2 B3
Vulnerable to default	CCC+ CCC CCC–	Caa1 Caa2 Caa3
Near or in bankruptcy or default	CC C D	Ca C D

Source: *Economic Survey 2020-21, vol. 1, p. 87, Ministry of Finance, GoI, N. Delhi.*

India's Rating Grievance

India has had a long-standing *sense of grievance* against international credit rating agencies— that it has consistently been rated below expectation as compared to its performance on various parameters during the period 2000-20. An analysis of the ratings shows discrepancies in the approach of the agencies (that seems *biased*) which may be understood in the following way:

- In the history of sovereign credit ratings, the world's 5th largest economy has *never* been rated as the lowest rung of the investment grade (BBB-/Baa3). Reflecting the economic size and thereby the ability to repay debt, the 5th largest economy has been predominantly rated AAA (UK and other countries). *China* and *India* are the only exceptions to this rule (China was rated A-/A2 in 2005 and India was rated BBB-/Baa3 in 2020).
- India's sovereign credit ratings do not reflect its fundamentals. Within its sovereign credit ratings cohort – countries rated between A+/A1 and BBB-/Baa3 (for S&P and Moody's) India is a clear outlier on several parameters and is rated significantly lower than mandated by the effect on the sovereign rating of the parameter which include— GDP growth rate, inflation, general government debt (combined debt of centre and states as per cent of GDP), cyclically adjusted primary balance (as per cent of potential GDP), current account balance (as per cent of GDP), political stability, rule of law, control of corruption, investor protection, ease of doing business, short-term external debt (as per cent of reserves), reserve adequacy ratio and sovereign default history. These anomalies have been there for the last two decades.
- Credit ratings map the probability of default (which reflects the willingness and ability of borrower to meet its obligations). India's willingness to pay is unquestionably demonstrated through its *zero sovereign default* history. Not only this, India has very low sovereign debt in foreign currencies and has a very comfortable forex reserves using which the total of short-term debt of private sector together with the entire sovereign and non-sovereign external debt can be paid off. Today, India's forex reserves can cover an additional 2.8 standard deviation negative event (i.e., an event that can be expected to manifest with a probability of less than 0.1 per cent after meeting all short-term debt).

As per *Survey,* as ratings did not capture India's fundamentals, they also did not have major adverse impact on select economic indicators (such as Sensex return, foreign exchange rate and yield on government securities). Therefore, the document has advised the Government to not remain beholden to a noisy and *biased* ratings and should instead reflect a 'mind without fear' (quoting a line from Rabindranath Tagore).

However, despite ratings not reflecting fundamentals, they can be 'pro-cyclical' (see *GLOSSARY* for more) and can affect the inflows of foreign investments of developing countries. That is why the Survey has given a call to make the methodology of the credit rating agencies more transparent, less subjective and better attuned to reflect the fundamentals of economies.

NON-RESIDENT INDIAN DEPOSITS

Foreign Exchange Management (Deposit) Regulations, 2000 permits Non-Resident Indians (NRIs) to have deposit accounts with authorised dealers and with banks authorised by the Reserve Bank of India (RBI) which include:[61]

- Foreign Currency Non-Resident (Bank) Account [FCNR(B) Account]
- Non-Resident External Account (NRE Account)
- Non-Resident Ordinary Rupee Account (NRO Account)

FCNR(B) accounts can be opened by NRIs and Overseas Corporate Bodies (OCBs) with an authorised dealer. The accounts can be opened in the form of term deposits. Deposits of funds are allowed in Pound Sterling, US Dollar, Japanese Yen and Euro. Rate of interest applicable to these accounts are in accordance with the directives issued by RBI from time to time.

NRE accounts can be opened by NRIs and OCBs with authorised dealers and with banks authorised by RBI. These can be in the form of savings, current, recurring or fixed deposit accounts. Deposits are allowed in any permitted currency. Rate of interest applicable to these accounts are in accordance with the directives issued by RBI from time to time.

NRO accounts can be opened by any person resident outside India with an authorised dealer or an authorised bank for collecting their funds from local bonafide transactions in Indian Rupees. When a resident becomes an NRI, his existing Rupee accounts are designated as NRO. These accounts can be in the form of current, savings, recurring or fixed deposit accounts.

There were two more NRI deposit accounts in operation, viz., *Non-Resident (Non-Repatriable) Rupee Deposit Account* and *Non-Resident (Special) Rupee Account*—an amendment to Foreign Exchange Management (Deposit) Regulations, in 2002, discontinued the acceptance of deposits in these two accounts from April 2002 onwards.

Repatriation of funds in FCNR(B) and NRE accounts is permitted. Hence, deposits in these accounts are included in India's *external debt* outstanding. While the principal of NRO deposits is non-repatriable, current income and interest earning is repatriable. Account-holders of NRO accounts are permitted to annually remit an amount up to US$ 1 million out of the balances held in their accounts. Therefore, deposits in NRO accounts too are included in India's *external debt.*

SMALL & PAYMENT BANKS

By mid-July 2014, the RBI issued the *draft guidelines* for setting up small banks and payment banks. The guidelines said that both are 'niche' or 'differentiated' banks with the common objective

61. As per the latest update by the ***RBI***, April, 2021.

of furthering *financial inclusion*. It is in pursuance of the announcement made in the *Union Budget 2014–15*. The details regarding the provisions to set up such banks and their operational criteria are as given below:

The *guidelines* to set up both the banks are same—

- The minimum capital requirement would be ₹100 crore.
- Promoter contribution would be at least 40 per cent for the first five years. Excess shareholding should be brought down to 40 per cent by the end of fifth year, to 30 per cent by the end of 10th year and to 26 per cent in 12 years from the date of commencement of business.
- Foreign shareholding in these banks will be as per current FDI policy.
- Voting rights to be in line with the existing guideline for private banks.
- Entities other than promoters will not be permitted to have shareholding in excess of 10 per cent.
- The bank should comply with the corporate governance guidelines, including 'fit and proper' criteria for Directors as issued by RBI.
- Operations of the bank should be fully networked and technology driven from the beginning.

Small Banks

The purpose of the small banks is to provide a whole suite of basic banking products such as *deposits* and supply of *credit*, but in a *limited area of operation*. The *objective* of the Small Banks to increase financial inclusion by provision of savings vehicles to under-served and unserved sections of the population, supply of credit to small farmers, micro and small industries, and other unorganised sector entities through high technology low-cost operations. Other features of the small banks are as follows:

- Resident individuals with 10 years of experience in banking and finance, companies and Societies will be eligible as promoters to set up small banks. NFBCs, microfinance institutions (MFIs), and Local Area Banks (LABs) can convert their operations into those of a small bank. Local focus and ability to serve smaller customers will be a key criterion in licensing such banks.
- For the initial three years, prior approval will be required for branch expansion.
- The area of operations would normally be restricted to contiguous districts in a homogenous cluster of states or union territories so that the Small Bank has a 'local feel' and culture. However, if necessary, it would be allowed to expand its area of operations beyond contiguous districts in one or more states with reasonable geographical proximity.
- The bank shall primarily undertake *basic banking activities* of accepting deposits and lending to small farmers, small businesses, micro and small industries, and unorganised sector entities. It cannot set up subsidiaries to undertake non-banking financial services activities. After the initial stabilisation period of five years, and after a review, the RBI may liberalise the scope of activities for small banks.
- The promoters' other financial and non-financial services activities, if any, should be distinctly ring-fenced and not co-mingled with banking business.
- A robust risk management framework is required and the banks would be subject to

all prudential norms and RBI regulations that apply to existing commercial banks, including maintenance of CRR and SLR.

7. In view of concentration of area of operations, the Small Bank would need a diversified portfolio of loans, spread over it area of operations.

8. The maximum loan size and investment limit exposure to single/group borrowers/issuers would be restricted to 15 per cent of capital funds.

9. Loans and advances of up to ₹25 lakhs, primarily to micro enterprises, should constitute at least 50 per cent of the loan portfolio.

10. For the first three years, 25 per cent of branches should be in unbanked rural areas.

By April 2021, a total of 10 Small Banks were operating in the country.

Payments Banks

The **objective** of payments banks is to increase financial inclusion by providing small savings accounts, payment/remittance services to migrant labour, low income households, small businesses, other unorganised sector entities and other users by enabling high volume-low value transactions in deposits and payments/remittance services in a secured technology-driven environment.

- Those who can promote a payments banks can be a non-bank PPIs, NBFCs, corporate's, mobile telephone companies, super market chains, real sector cooperatives companies and public sector entities. Even banks can take equity in Payments Banks.
- Payments Banks can accept demand deposits (only current account and savings accounts). They would initially be restricted to holding a maximum balance of ₹100,000 per customer. Based on performance, the RBI could enhance this limit.
- The banks can offer payments and remittance services, issuance of prepaid payment instruments, internet banking, functioning as business correspondent for other banks.
- Payments Banks cannot set up subsidiaries to undertake NBFC business.
- As in the case of small banks, other financial and non-financial services activities of the promoters should be ring-fenced.
- The Payments Banks would be required to use the word 'Payments' in its name to differentiate it from other banks.
- No credit lending is allowed for Payments Banks.
- The float funds can be parked only in less than one year G-Secs.

By April 2021, a total of 2 Payment Banks were operating in the country.

New Umbrella Entity

In August 2020, the RBI released the framework for a new financial entity, the New Umbrella Entity (NUE), for retail payments. Their scope of activities shall be—to set-up, manage and operate new payment system(s) in the retail space comprising of but not limited to ATMs, White Label PoS; Aadhaar based payments and remittance services; newer payment methods, standards and technologies; monitor related issues in the country and internationally; take care of developmental objectives like enhancement of awareness about the payment systems.

The NUE will be set up as a company with minimum paid-up capital of ₹500 crore with no single promoter owning more than 40 per cent of its shares. By *April 2021*, the RBI was in the process of scrutinising and finalising the applications filed by the eligible entities.

FINANCIAL INCLUSION

Financial inclusion is an important priority of the government. The objective is to ensure the excluded sections, i.e., weaker sections and low income groups, access to various financial services such as a basic savings bank account, need-based credit, remittance facility, insurance and pension. The government has recently launched an effective scheme to promote the cause of financial inclusion—the PMJDY.

Pradhan Mantri Jan-Dhan Yojana

To achieve the objective of financial inclusion by extending financial services to the large hitherto unserved population of the country and to unlock its growth potential, the Pradhan Mantri Jan-Dhan Yojana (PMJDY) was launched on 28 August 2014. The Yojana envisages:

- Universal access to banking facilities with at least one basic banking account for every household.
- Financial literacy, access to credit and insurance.
- The beneficiaries will receive a *RuPay* Debit Card having inbuilt accident insurance cover of ₹1 lakh.
- In addition, there is a life insurance cover of ₹30,000 to those who opened their bank accounts for the first time between 15 August 2014 and 26 January 2015 and meet other eligibility conditions of the Yojana.

The Yojana had entered the *Guinness World Records* for opening most bank accounts during the week starting 23 August, 2014 as part of the financial campaign.

GOLD INVESTMENT SCHEMES

Two new gold investment schemes were launched by the Government of India by November 2015—the Sovereign Gold Bonds and Gold Monetisation Schemes. The schemes are aimed at twin objectives:

1. Reducing the demand for physical gold; and
2. Shifting a part of the gold imported every year for investment purposes into financial savings.

Brief feature of the schemes are as given below:

Sovereign Gold Bonds

These are issued by RBI on behalf of the GoI in rupees and denominated in grams of gold and restricted for sale to the resident Indian entities only, both in demat and paper form. The minimum and maximum investment limits are two grams and 500 grams of gold per person per fiscal year, respectively. The rate of interest for the year 2015–16 was 2.75 per cent per annum, payable on a half yearly basis. The tenor of the Bond is for a period of 8 years with exit option from 5th year onwards. KYC norms are the same as that for gold. Exemption from capital gains tax is also available. Redemption is made in the rupee value equivalent to the price of gold at the time of maturity.

Gold Monetisation Scheme

In this scheme, BIS (Bureau of Indian Standards) certified CPTCs (Collection, Purity Testing Centres) collect the gold from the customer on behalf of the banks. The minimum quantity of gold (bullion or jewellery) which can be deposited is 30 grams and there is no limit for maximum deposit.

Gold Saving Account can be opened with any of the designated bank and denomination in grams of gold for short-term period of 1–3 years, a medium-term period of 5–7 years and a long-term period of 12–15 years. The CPTCs transfer the gold to the refiners. The banks will have a tripartite/bipartite legal agreement with refiners and CPTCs.

For the year 2020–21 interest rate is fixed at 2.25 per cent and 2.5 per cent for the medium- and long-term, respectively. Redemption is made in cash/gold for short term and in cash for medium and long term deposits. The difference between the current borrowing cost for the government and the interest rate paid by the government under the medium/long term deposit will be credited to the Gold Reserve Fund.

In 2019-20 the RBI liberalised the gold-monetisation scheme, allowing charitable institutions, the Centre, states, and government entities to deposit the precious metal. Individuals, corporate entities, mutual funds, and exchange-traded funds were already allowed to deposit gold under the scheme. The aim of the scheme was to mobilise *idle gold* lying with households and temples into the system, and consequently, reduce imports.

This move will help government agencies to deposit gold confiscated by them. Charitable institutions can now take advantage to deposit their unaccounted gold without disclosing their identity. In the past, several complaints were received by the government about money laundering by charitable trusts (they used to accept money eligible for donation tax benefit and give cash back to the donor). To prevent money laundering, a 30 per cent tax has been imposed on charitable trusts for donations received from unidentified persons. It means, now, donors will deposit unaccounted gold and get cash after a deduction of 30 per cent from these trusts. But this also allows the unaccounted gold to find its way into the scheme. Some experts believe that money collected by depositors like this could also be used to fund election campaigns.

Under the scheme, a depositor has to give gold to a collection centre, which are also hallmarking centres. These centres issue certificates of purity after melting the gold, which is sent to refineries for converting into bars. Banks issue deposit receipts after collecting purity certificates from depositors.

MUDRA BANK

As per the Government of India, large industries provide employment to only 1.25 crore people in the country while the *micro units* employ around 12 crore people. There is a need to focus on these 5.75 crore self-employed people (owners of the micro units) who use funds of ₹11 lakh crore, with an average per unit debt of merely ₹17,000. Capital is the key to the small entrepreneurs. These entrepreneurs depend heavily on the local money lenders for their fund requirements.

Looking at the importance of these enterprises, the Government of India launched (April 2015) the *Micro Units Development and Refinance Agency Bank (MUDRA Bank)* with the aim of *funding* these *unfunded* non-corporate enterprises. This was launched as the PMMY (Prime Minister Mudra Yojana). Important features of the MUDRA Bank are as given below:

- Under this banking model, the micro units can avail up to ₹10 lakh loan through refinance route (through the Public and private sector banks, NBFCs, MFIs, RRBs, District Banks, etc).
- The products designed under it are categorised into three buckets of finance named Shishu (loan up to ₹50,000), Kishor (₹50,000 to ₹5 lakh) and Tarun (₹5 lakh to ₹10 lakh).
- Though the scheme covers the traders of fruits and vegetables, in general, it does not refinance the agriculture sector.
- There is no fixed interest rate in this scheme. As per the Government of India, presently, banks are charging the interest rates between Base Rate plus one per cent to 7 per cent per annum. Interest rates on

the loans are supposed to vary according to the risk involved in the enterprises seeking loans. There is no general subsidy offered on interest rates except if the loan is linked to some other government scheme.

In the wake of the disruption caused by the *COVID-19 pandemic* several relief measures were announced by the RBI. As loans were restructured and permission given to not declare a loan as NPAs as forbearance will have negative impact on the loans disbursed under the scheme[62] and the stressed assets under it may rise. Out of the total loan of ₹4.11 lakh crore forwarded by the public sector banks under the scheme till March 2020, about *4.92* per cent had turned into NPAs (which was 2.92 per cent by March 2019).

DIGITAL PAYMENTS INDEX

During 2020-21, digital payments witnessed jump both in volume and value across all categories—overall transactions worth ₹19.35 lakh crore done via UPI and ₹1.02 lakh crore via RuPay cards (till October 2020). To capture the extent of digitisation of payments across the country over different time periods, the RBI has constructed a composite Digital Payments Index (DPI). The index is based on the following *5 parameters* (their weights given in brackets along them):

1. Payment Enablers (25 per cent),
2. Payment Infrastructure – Demand-side factors (10 per cent),
3. Payment Infrastructure– Supply-side factors (15 per cent),
4. Payment Performance (45 per cent), and
5. Consumer Centricity (5 per cent).

The index has March 2018 as its base (i.e., DPI score of March 2018 being 100). The DPI for March 2019 and March 2020, as per the RBI, were 153.47 and 207.84 respectively—indicating a growth of over 100 per cent in 2 years.[63]

62. **Ministry of finance,** GoI, N. Delhi, April 2021 and **Economic survey 2020-21.** vol. 1, pp. 200-234, Minitry of Finance, GoI, N. Delhi.

63. **Economic Survey 2020-21**, vol. 2, p. 143, Ministry of Finance, GoI, N. Delhi.

CHAPTER 13

INSURANCE IN INDIA

*Insurance is a kind of gambling in reverse–a major form of 'risk spreading'–person's risk which would be large, is spread around to make it small for a large number of people–in this process it serves two purposes-provides social security net to people and helps in nation-building by makeing available investible capital.**

In this Chapter...

- Definition
- Insurance Industry
- AICIL
- Insurance Reforms
- Reinsurance
- Deposit Insurance and Credit Guarantee Corporation (DICGC)
- Export Credit Guarantee Corporation (ECGC)
- National Export Insurance Account (NEIA)
- Insurance Penetration & Density
- New Reform Initiatives
- National Digital Health Mission
- Third Party Insurance
- New Policy Steps
- COVID-19 Cover
- Insurance Industry Today
- Way Forward

 DEFINITION

In economic terms, anything used to cut down the risk is known as insurance. But in familiar terms, insurance is provided by an insurance company which covers a person's life (called life segment) or covers loss of assets, property (called non-life or general segment). The insurance policies are purchased at fixed premiums.

 INSURANCE INDUSTRY

Insurance has a deep-rooted history in India. It finds mention in the writings of Manu *(Manusmrithi)*, Yagnavalkya *(Dharmasastra)* and Kautilya *(Arthasastra)*. The writings talk in terms of **pooling of resources** that could be re-distributed in times of calamities such as fire, floods, epidemics and famine. This was probably

* *See Paul A. Samuelson and William D. Nordhaus, Economics, (New Delhi: Tata McGraw Hill, 2005), pp. 2010-12. See* LIBNA, *1956 and GIBNA, 1971 of the GoI.*

a precursor to modern day insurance. Ancient Indian history has preserved the earliest traces of insurance in the form of marine trade loans and carriers' contracts. Insurance in India has evolved over time heavily drawing from other countries (England in particular).

LIC

The life insurance business/industry in the country was nationalised by the Government of India in 1956 and a fully government-owned company, the Life Insurance Corporation of India (LIC) was set up (at that time 245 Indian and foreign companies were playing in the life segment of insurance). Opening of private life insurance companies was prohibited at that time. The LIC was called an investment institution by the government.

The nationalisation was motivated by twin objectives—*first*, to spread the message of life insurance for greater social security and *secondly*, to mobilise people's savings (collected as premiums) for nation building. The LIC had been the biggest investor in the government's process of planned development purchasing government securities (G-Secs.) and equities of the big asset Public Sector Undertakings (PSUs).

GIC

In 1971, the government nationalised the private sector companies (107 Indian and foreign companies) playing in the general insurance segment and a government company, the General Insurance Corporation of India (GIC) was formed in 1972. The GIC started operation on January 1, 1973 with its four holding companies:

1. National Insurance Company Ltd.
2. New India Assurance Company Ltd.
3. Oriental Fire and Insurance Company Ltd.
4. United India Insurance Company Ltd.

In the era of economic reforms, two major changes took place in this area:

1. In November 2000, the GIC was notified as the Indian Reinsurer[1] (to be known as GIC Re).
2. In March 2002 the GIC was withdrawn from holding company status of the four public sector general insurance companies. Now these four companies are directly owned by the Government of India.[2]

AICIL

The public sector insurance company, Agriculture Insurance Company of India Limited (AICIL) was set up by the Government of India in December 2002 (commenced its business in April 2003). This is a *dedicated agri-insurance* company and aims 'to serve the needs of farmers better and to move towards a sustainable actuarial regime'.

This company was responsible to look after the National Agriculture Insurance Scheme (NAIS) which was launched in 1999. Since *January 2016*, the company is looking after the newly launched PMFBY (Prime Minister Fasal Bima Yojana)[3] which subsumed the existing agri-insurance schemes—the NAIS and the Modified NAIS (of 2010). Till the AICIL was not set up, the agri-insurance responsibility of the government was being looked after by the General Insurance Corporation (GIC).

AICIL is jointly promoted by public sector insurance companies and development financial institutions—majority shares owned by the GIC

1. Publication Division, India 2002, (New Delhi: Government of India, 2003).
2. Ministry of Finance, Economic Survey 2002–03, (New Delhi: Government of India, 2003).
3. Ministry of Finance, **Union Budget 2016–17** (New Delhi: Government of India, 2016); and Ministry of Finance, **Economic Survey 2015–16** (New Delhi: Government of India, 2016).

(35 per cent) and NABARD (30 per cent) while the four public sector general insurance companies own 8.75 per cent each in it.

Public Sector Insurance Companies

At present, there are 6 public sector *insurance companies* in India. Out of it one deals in the life segment (LIC); four are involved in the non-life (general) insurance segment; and one is the dedicated agri-insurer. Other than these companies, there is one *re-insurance company*, the GIC Re (wholly owned by the GoI).

INSURANCE REFORMS

Under the process of economic reforms an Insurance Reforms Committee (IRC) was set up in April 1993 under the chairmanship of the ex-RBI Governor R. N. Malhotra. The committee handed over its report (January 1994) with the following major suggestions:[4]

1. Decontrolling insurance sector, i.e., allowing Indian as well as foreign private sector insurance companies to enter the sector (the government did it in 1999 passing the *IRDA Act*).
2. Restructuring the LIC and the GIC and cutting down the government's holding in them to 50 per cent (no follow up still, but the private insurance companies demanding it anxiously. The NDA government had taken steps in this area, but the UPA government has no such plans.) Late 2012, the government started sale of the LIC shares but to public sector undertakings—seen as a welcome move.
3. Delinking GIC and its four subsidiaries (which was done in 2000).
4. Discarding the system of licensing of surveyors by the controller of Insurance.
5. Restructuring the Tariff Advisory Committee.
6. Setting up a regulatory authority for the insurance industry (the IRDA set up in 2000).

IRDA

The Insurance Regulatory and Development Authority (IRDA) was set up in 2000 (the Act was passed in 1999) with one chairman and five members (two as full time and three as part-time members) appointed and nominated by the government. The authority is responsible for the regulation, development and supervision of the Indian insurance industry.

Today, 54 insurance companies are operating in India of which 24 are in life segment while 30 in non-life segment—1 public sector life insurer (LIC), 4 public sector general insurer, 2 specialised insurers (AICIL and ECGC), 1 public sector re-insurer (GIC Re) and 10 foreign re-insurers.

The Government allows a maximum of 74 foreign direct investment (FDI) in insurance sector (increased from 49 per cent by the *Union Budget 2021-22*) and 100 per cent in 'insurance intermediaries' (since 2019-20).[5]

REINSURANCE

Insurance is a very risky business. While the insurance companies offer insurance to its clients, they themselves get exposed to very high financial risks. Re-insurance business emerged out of this reality. When an insurance company buys insurance cover for its insurance business, a new segment comes into being i.e., re-insurance.

Experts believe that in absence of re-insurance, insurance industry in a country will

4 R. N. Malhotra headed Insurance Reforms Committee, Government of India, N. Delhi, January 1994.

5 **Union Budget 2021-22** and **Annual Report 2018-19** (IRDAI), Ministry of Finance, GoI, N. Delhi. For more on *Insurance Intermediaries* see **GLOSSARY**.

not grow to the level of the social requirement—as insurance companies will either not provide insurance cover in several areas or they will charge very high premiums on the policies they offer (to neutralise the risk). Keeping this thing in mind, the Government of India took initiative to convert the existing public sector general insurer, the GIC, into a re-insurance company (in 2000). Known as the GIC Re, it remains the only reinsurance company in the country till now. Over the time, this emerged as a major player in the global reinsurance industry. Reinsurance industry is regulated by the IRDA in the country.

Reinsurance industry had a very low penetration in India. Lack of competition has been cited as a major factor behind it—it had only one player by now. To promote competition and vibrancy the IRDA announced (late 2015) to open up the industry for the entry of foreign companies.

By *April 2021,* a total of 10 foreign reinsurance companies were operating in India which included the top reinsurance companies of the world (the German company *Munich Re* being the largest, the Swiss company *Swiss Re* being the 2nd largest and the German company *Hannover Ruck SE* being the 3rd largest in the world).

DEPOSIT INSURANCE AND CREDIT GUARANTEE CORPORATION (DICGC)

DICGC was set up by merging the Deposit Insurance Corporation (1962) and the Credit Guarantee Corporation (1971) in 1978. While Deposit Insurance had been introduced in India out of concerns to protect depositors, ensure financial stability, instil confidence in the banking system and help mobilise deposits, the establishment of the Credit Guarantee Corporation was essentially in the realm of affirmative action to ensure that the credit needs of the hitherto neglected sectors and weaker sections were met. The essential concern was to persuade banks to make available credit to not so creditworthy clients. After the merger, the focus of the DICGC had shifted onto credit guarantees. This owed in part to the fact that most large banks were nationalised. With the financial sector reforms undertaken in the 1990s, credit guarantees have been gradually phased out and the focus of the Corporation is veering back to its core function of Deposit Insurance with the objective of averting panics, reducing systemic risk and ensuring financial stability.

Insurance cover available on bank deposits was increased from the existing ₹1 lakh to ₹5 lakhs by the Government on **February 1, 2020.** The move announced in the *Union Budget 2020-21* was believed to come in the wake of the recent crisis related to the Mumbai-based urban cooperative bank, the PMC (Punjab and Maharashtra Cooperative). For deposit insurance, depositors do not pay any premium, rather a nominal premium is collected by the DICGC from the banks. The scheme covers all banks operating in India including private sector, co-operative and even branches of foreign banks in India with certain exemptions like—deposits of foreign governments, deposits of central/state governments and inter-bank deposits.

Background In 2017-18, the Government proposed the *Financial Resolution and Deposit Insurance (FRDI) Bill* which aimed to reform the existing provisions related to deposit insurance and credit guarantee. The Bill was criticised for the clause which allowed 'writing down of the liabilities of the failed bank'. This clause was inferred by stakeholders as the 'bail-in' clause (when a financial help comes in from within the bank/financial institution). The Joint Parliamentary Committee also had certain apprehensions related to it. Government withdrew the Bill in July 2018 and announced the need of more time to examine the related issues.

Since 1991, the deposit insurance limit has been upto only ₹1 lakh. Many countries revised their deposit insurance limits after the global financial crisis of 2008. The limit was increased upto US$ 2.5 lakh in USA and US$ 1.15 lakh in UK (set around 3-4 times of the per capita income of these economies). Emerging market economies like Brazil and China have set this limit at 9 times of their per capita income. In case of India it was still less than its per capita income (which was estimated to be ₹1,11,782 at constant market price, as per the *Economic Survey 2017-18*).

EXPORT CREDIT GUARANTEE CORPORATION (ECGC)

The overseas projects undertaken by the Indian companies face many political and commercial risks in the importing countries. To provide adequate credit insurance cover to such firms, the government has set up the Export Credit Guarantee Corporation of India Ltd. (ECGC) under the Ministry of Commerce and Industry, for medium- and long-term exports. But owing to its own limitations, at times it is difficult for ECGC to cover pure commercial risks in issues like long repayment period, the large value of contracts, difficult economic and political conditions of the importing country, together with the fact that reinsurance cover is generally not available for such projects.[6] Many times such projects look necessary considering the economic and political relationship of India with the proposed importing country. It means that in the absence of credit insurance cover, the ability of Indian exporters to go for such export projects is hampered. It should be noted that in many developed economies such projects are covered and underwritten on government account[7].

NATIONAL EXPORT INSURANCE ACCOUNT (NEIA)

For facilitating the service of the ECGC (discussed above), the Government of India did set up the National Export Insurance Account (NEIA) in March 2006 to promote medium- and long-term export by providing credit insurance support in the cases where ECGC was not able to provide credit cover on its own because of purely commercial reasons:[8]

1. The corpus given to the account was ₹66 crore, raised to ₹246 crore by 2007-08 and was enhanced to ₹2,000 crore in the Eleventh Plan (2007-12).
2. Resources of the NEIA will be the corpus, the premium income, interest income and recovery of all the claims paid.
3. As per the provision, an exposure equal to ten times corpus can be taken by the NEIA.

The NEIA can cover projects which fulfil the following criteria:[9]

1. The project by itself should be commercially viable;
2. The project should be strategically important for India, with regard to economic and political relationship of India with the importing country; and

6. Due to its underwriting constraint, the ECGC is unable to cover such projects on its own.

7. As for example the USA, France, the UK and many other Euro-American economies underwrite such medium and long-term projects in the governments' account. The SEIA also covers only medium- and long-term export projects.

8. Announced while setting up the NEIA, Ministry of Commerce and Industry, Government of India, N. Delhi, 9 March, 2006.

9. Ibid.

3. The exporter should be capable of executing the contract, as evident from his previous track record.

The use and benefits of the NEIA need to be publicised among its beneficiaries. Meanwhile, many export projects pertaining to Indonesia, Vietnam, Iran, Sudan, etc., are under way. The NEIA will facilitate potential project exporters to enter the international trade area, as it is expected[10] to be so. In the era of globalisation it has been praised as a welcome development by the experts and the trade people alike.

INSURANCE PENETRATION & DENSITY

The growth in the insurance sector is internationally measured based on the standard of insurance penetration. Insurance penetration is defined as the ratio of premium underwritten in a given year to the Gross Domestic Product (GDP). Likewise, insurance density is another well recognised benchmark and is defined as the ratio of premium underwritten in a given year to total population (measured in US dollars for convenience of comparison). The Indian insurance business has in the past remained under-developed with low levels of insurance penetration.

The latest[11] data (for 2019) of insurance penetration and density in India are as given below:

1. **Insurance Penetration:** India's insurance penetration was **3.76** per cent in 2019 (up from 2,71 per cent in 2001 but much lower from the peak of 5.20 per cent in 2009)—2.82 per cent for life segment and 0.94 per cent for non-life segment (i.e., general insurance). The comparative figures for Malaysia, Thailand and China in 2019 were much better at 4.72, 4.99 and 4.30 per cent respectively. Globally insurance penetration was 7.23 per cent (3.35 per cent for the life segment and 3.88 per cent for the non-life segment respectively) in 2019. Although the penetration is lower in India for both, it is particularly low for non-life insurance as compared to other countries (it being less popular among the people).
2. **Insurance Density:** India's insurance density was **US$ 78** in 2019 (up from US$ 11.5 in 2001)—US$ 58 for life segment and US$ 19 for non-life segment. The comparative figures for Malaysia, Thailand and China in 2019 were much higher at US$ 536, US$ 389 and US$ 430 respectively. Globally insurance density was US$ 818 in 2019 (US$ 379 for the life segment and US$ 439 for the non-life segment respectively). The USA has particularly high insurance density in the non-life category (around US$ 5,600).

Reasons for Underdevelopment of Insurance

As per the various volumes of the Annual Reports published by the IRDA and other Government documents, there have been several reasons responsible for the underdevelopment of the insurance penetration and density in the country:

1. Complex and delayed claim settlement procedures;
2. Vague and incomprehensible rules and regulations of the insurance companies;
3. Lack of education and awareness among the masses;
4. Lower income levels of the population;

10. S. Prabhakaran, Executive Director, ECGC, Mumbai in Survey of Indian Industry 2007, The Hindu, p. 84.
11. **Economic Survey 2020-21,** vol. 1, pp. 147-48, Ministry of Finance, GoI, N. Delhi.

5. Socio-cultural factors;
6. Lack of level playing field in the industry; and
7. Less vibrancy in the regulatory framework.

Recently enacted Insurance Laws (Amendment) Act, 2015 is supposed to have positive impact on regulatory framework as well as insurance penetration.

Policy Initiatives

Committed to expand and strengthen, the insurance industry in the country (following the recommendations of the Malhotra Committee Report, 1993), the Government of India has taken the following policy initiatives[12] in recent years:

1. **Health Insurance:** The Insurance Regulatory Development Authority (IRDA) has been taking a number of proactive steps as part of the initiatives for the spread of health insurance. It had set up a National Health Insurance Working Group in 2003, which provided a platform for the various stakeholders in the health insurance industry to work together and suggest solutions on various relevant issues in the sector. The IRDA is also co-ordinating with and supporting insurance industry initiatives in standardising certain key terminology used in health insurance documents, for better comprehension and in the interest of policyholders. The General Insurance Council, comprising all non-life insurers, evolved a consensus on a uniform definition of 'pre-existing diseases' and its exclusion wording, which has earlier been an expression with many definitions, still more interpretations, and certainly a whole lot of grievances. Such standardisation, effective 1 June, 2008 will help the insured by minimising ambiguity and also by better comparability of health insurance products. Also, with effect from 1 October, 2011, portability in health insurance has been started in which an insured, if not happy with services or the product of the existing insurer, can change to another insurer whilst enjoying the benefits (especially that of pre-existing diseases) of her/his existing policy.
2. **Micro Insurance:** Micro insurance regulations issued by the IRDA have provided a fillip to propagating micro insurance as a conceptual issue. With the positive and facilitative approach adopted under the micro insurance regulations, it is expected that all insurance companies would come out with a progressive business approach and carry forward the spirit of regulations thereby extending insurance penetration to all segments of the society.

NEW REFORM INITIATIVES

With a view to removing archaic and redundant provisions in the insurance laws, empowering the Insurance Regulatory and Development Authority (IRDA) to enable more effective regulation, and enhancing the foreign equity investment cap in an Indian insurance company with the safeguard of Indian ownership and control, the government has implemented the Insurance Laws (Amendment) Act, 2015.

The Act paved the way for **major reform** related amendments in the Insurance Act, 1938, the General Insurance Business (Nationalisation) Act, 1972 and the Insurance Regulatory and Development Authority (IRDA) Act, 1999. It provides greater powers to the IRDAI by which the insurance regulatory framework is supposed to become more flexible, effective and efficient.

12 Ministry of Finance, Economic Survey 2011–12, (New Delhi: Government of India, 2012), pp. 128–29.

Major changes[13] made (with further policy changes) are a s given below:

1. **Promotion of Foreign Investment:** The permissible limit of the FDI (foreign direct investment) in insurance sector was increased to 74 per cent (from the existing 49 per cent) in 2021-22 and allowed foreign ownership and control with safeguards. Under the new structure, the majority of Directors on the Board and key management persons would be resident Indians, with at least 50 per cent of Directors being Independent Directors, and specified percentage of profits being retained as general reserve.

   Greater availability of capital for the capital intensive insurance sector would lead to greater distribution reach to under/un-served areas, more innovative product formulations to meet diverse insurance needs of citizens, efficient service delivery through improved distribution technology and enhanced customer service standards.

2. **Capital Requirement in Government Companies:** The public sector general insurance companies (four), presently required as per the General Insurance Business (Nationalisation) Act, 1972 to be 100 per cent government owned, are now allowed to raise capital. This will enable them to have additional capital for the purposes of business expansion in the rural/social sectors and enhanced competitiveness. The Government of India ownership to be maintained minimum at 51 per cent.

3. **Consumer Welfare:** It will enable the interests of consumers to be better served through provisions like those enabling penalties on intermediaries/ insurance companies for misconduct and disallowing multi-level marketing of insurance products in order to curtail the practice of mis-selling—

   (i) The amended Law has several provisions for levying higher penalties ranging from ₹1 crore to ₹25 crore for various violations including mis-selling and misrepresentation by agents/ insurance companies.

   (ii) With a view to serve the interest of the policy holders better, the period during which a policy can be repudiated on any ground, including mis-statement of facts etc., will be confined to three years from the commencement of the policy and no policy would be called in question on any ground after three years.

   (iii) The amendments provide for an easier process for payment to the nominee of the policyholder, as the insurer would be discharged of its legal liabilities once the payment is made to the nominee.

   (iv) It is now obligatory in the law for insurance companies to underwrite third party motor vehicle insurance as per IRDAI regulations. Rural and social sector obligations for insurers are retained in the amended laws.

4. **Empowerment of IRDAI:** The Act will entrust responsibility of appointing insurance agents to insurers and provides for IRDAI to regulate their eligibility, qualifications and other aspects—

13. **Union Budget 2020-22; Economic Survey 2017-18;** and **IRDAI**, April 2020; Ministry of Finance, GoI, N. Delhi.

(i) It enables agents to work more broadly across companies in various business categories; with the safeguard that conflict of interest would not be allowed by IRDAI through suitable regulations.

(ii) IRDAI is empowered to regulate key aspects of Insurance Company operations in areas like solvency, investments, expenses and commissions and to formulate regulations for payment of commission and control of management expenses.

(iii) It empowers the Authority to regulate the functions, code of conduct, etc., of surveyors and loss assessors. It also expands the scope of insurance intermediaries to include insurance brokers, re-insurance brokers, insurance consultants, corporate agents, third party administrators, surveyors and loss assessors and such other entities, as may be notified by the Authority from time to time.

(iv) Further, properties in India can now be insured with a foreign insurer with prior permission of IRDAI; which was earlier to be done with the approval of the Central Government.

5. **Health Insurance:** The Act defines 'health insurance business' inclusive of travel and personal accident cover and discourages non-serious players by retaining capital requirements for health insurers at the level of ₹100 crore, thereby paving the way for promotion of health insurance as a separate vertical.

6. **Promoting Reinsurance Business in India:** It enables foreign reinsurers to set up *branches* in India and defines 're-insurance' to mean 'the insurance of part of one insurer's risk by another insurer who accepts the risk for a mutually acceptable premium', and thereby excludes the possibility of 100 per cent ceding of risk to a re-insurer, which could lead to companies acting as front companies for other insurers.

7. **Strengthening of Industry Councils:** The Life Insurance Council and General Insurance Council have now been made *self-regulating bodies* by empowering them to frame bye-laws for elections, meetings and levy and collect fees, etc., from its members. Inclusion of representatives of *self-help groups* and *insurance cooperative societies* in insurance councils has also been enabled to broad base the representation on these Councils.

8. **Robust Appellate Process:** Appeals against the orders of IRDAI are to be preferred to SAT as the amended law provides for any insurer or insurance intermediary aggrieved by any order made by IRDAI to prefer an appeal to the Securities Appellate Tribunal (SAT).

9. **Capital Market Reforms:** In March 2019, the IRDA announced the redesigned initial public offering (IPO) guidelines for insurance companies which are looking to divest equity through the IPO route. Now insurance companies are allowed to invest up to 10 per cent in additional *Tier I* bonds issued by banks (which are raising capital to comply to Basel III norms).

Thus, the amendments incorporate enhancements in the insurance laws in keeping with the evolving insurance sector scenario and regulatory practices across the *globe*. The amendments will enable the regulator to create an operational framework for greater innovation, competition and transparency, to meet the insurance needs of citizens in a more complete and subscriber-friendly manner. The amendments are expected to enable the sector to achieve its full growth potential and contribute towards the overall growth of the economy and job creation.

NATIONAL DIGITAL HEALTH MISSION

The National Digital Health Mission[14] was launched by the Government in August 2020 (on the 74th Independence Day) aimed at making medical services accessible to all citizens of the country. The mission is slated to maintain the health records of citizens in 'digital' form – which will have the following features:

1. Unique Health ID to be given to citizens.
2. Health Card to be given to citizens.
3. Citizens can share their health data to third party.

The voluntary healthcare programme aims to integrate doctors, hospitals, pharmacies, insurance companies and make a digital health infrastructure—as its *backbone*. The health accounts of citizens will contain details of every test, every disease, the doctors visited, the medicines taken and the diagnosis. The mission is expected to revolutionise the healthcare and related sectors in an unprecedented way besides fulfilling the aim of the universal healthcare (National Health Policy-2017) with diversity of uses:

1. **Healthcare Sector:** The mission will strengthen the healthcare sector in multiple ways—The citizens who need to procure healthcare services from the private or public sector healthcare agencies need to just share their unique health identity number and their whole medical history will be available to the medical service provider. This will not only speed up the delivery of the health services but cut down the mistakes and repetition of diagnosis and prescriptions. It will strengthen the healthcare sector by—boosting the Government idea of 'tele-consultation' and 'virtual consultation' (announced in *Mission Mode Interventions* in the healthcare sector); synchronisation of the health schemes with the digital health data of the beneficiaries; synchronising the Aadhar numbers of the beneficiaries for cash transfers; and boosting the Ayushman Bharat scheme in a big way.
2. **Insurance Industry:** For insurance industry medical history of the insured person is quite important as they are used for the calculation of actuarial and chargeable premiums. Insurance industry together with the insured individual both suffer due to absence of authentic medical history of the citizens–insurance companies suffer as they need to settle insurance claims of concealed health issues while the insured persons bear the burden of higher premium charges than they would have been if medical history were concealed by others (as the company has to recover its losses!).

Naturally, once the authentic medical history will be available to the insurance sector, the premiums of the insurance policies can be planned in a better and rational way. Due to this the premium for people in good health will fall down while the people who have medical histories need to cough up a bit higher premium. But overall, this will enhance the operational transparency of the insurance sector. Thus, for the insurance industry (especially, the health insurance segment), the mission is expected to be a boon.

---

14. **Ministry of Health and Family Welfare,** August 2020, GoI, N. Delhi.

3. **Lifestyle Improvement:** When health data of citizens are known, a lot of measures can be taken to improve the lifestyle of the insured citizens (which can be customised also) which will reduce the incidence of diseases and manhour losses. The insurance regulator (IRDAI) has already allowed insurers to provide such wellness services to customers of health insurance products.

The incidence of lifestyle diseases is rising very fast in the country. We know that such diseases can be only checked by changing the lifestyle of the people. The Government has been giving much emphasis on this aspect in recent times under which the themes like healthy diet, yoga, exercises, walking, cycling to work, etc. are being promoted.

THIRD PARTY INSURANCE

The 'third-party' insurance is provided by non-life insurance companies on vehicles. This insurance covers the risk on other than the 'two parties' (i.e. the car and the owner, in case of a car) involved in an insurance policy. The policy does not provide any benefit to the insured; however, it covers the insured's legal liability for death/disability of third-party loss or damage to the third-party property. This insurance is also known as 'act only' cover. In India, it is mandatory (under the Motor Vehicle Amendment Act, 2019) for all new two wheelers to have a five-year third-party insurance and cars and commercial vehicles to have a three-year third-party insurance.

The cost of a comprehensive cover is several times that of a stand-alone third-party cover, since damage claims are more frequent than third-party claims. Until now, the premium for motor third-party insurance was calculated on the basis of a schedule of rates provided by the Tariff Advisory Committee, an arm of the IRDAI (the insurance regulator). But IRDA has done away with the motor tariff. The compensation to the victim is largely decided by the earning capacity of the accident victim.

To make insurance policies of vehicles cheaper, insurance companies have been charging a very low premium for such policies. Due to this, insurance companies have not been settling third-party insurance claims quicker (majority of case going for litigation). But in recent years, the IRDAI has taken various steps to strengthen this segment of the non-life insurance. By early 2020-21, the IRDAI announced a market-linked increase in the insurance premium for the third-party insurance together with enforcing a stricter regulatory regime for quicker settlement of the third-party claims.

NEW POLICY STEPS

Enhancing insurance penetration and promoting greater social security of the citizens through inclusive insurance have got special attention from the Government in recent times and several steps have been taken in this direction by the time *(April 2021)*:

PMSBY (Pradhan Mantri Suraksha Bima Yojana) It offers a renewable one-year accidental-death-cum-disability cover to all subscribing bank account holders in the age group of 18 to 70 years for a premium of ₹12 per annum per subscriber.

The risk coverage available will be ₹2 lakh for accidental death and permanent total disability and ₹1 lakh for permanent partial disability, for a one-year period stretching from 1 June to 31 May.

PMJJBY (Pradhan Mantri Jeevan Jyoti Bima Yojana) The scheme offers a renewable one-year term life cover of ₹2 lakh to all subscribing bank account holders in the age group of 18 to 50 years.

NHPS (National Health Protection Scheme): In September 2018, Government launched the NHPS under Ayushman Bharat to provide coverage of up to ₹5 lakh to more than 50 crore vulnerable families (10 crore families). The scheme is expected to increase penetration of health insurance in India from 34 per cent to 50 per cent.

ANANDA In November 2020, LIC of India launched its *first* software application, ANANDA (an acronym for 'Atmanirbhar Agents New Business Digital App') for the on-boarding process with the aid of the agent/broker to get life insurance policy through *paperless module.* Several other insurance companies are in the process of bringing in such App-based insurance platforms—over 120 digital insurance **start-ups** (popularly known as InsurTech) are at present operating in the country.

COVID-19 COVER

The ongoing COVID-19 pandemic did put the insurance firms, especially the health insurers in jitters, given the rising numbers of coronavirus cases and possible consequent claims. By early *June 2020*, the IRDAI advised the General Insurance Council to work on a reasonable and standardised cost structure for COVID-19 treatment – based on the feedback from the Council, the authority unveiled (on 5th June, 2020) a standard COVID-19 product. The major features of the new health insurance product are as given below:

- The policy tenure will be for one year, which can be given on a *family floater basis* with minimum entry age of 18 years and maximum of 65 years with lifelong renewability. The minimum sum insured should be ₹50,000 and the maximum will be ₹5 lakh.
- The base covers to be offered on *indemnity basis*, whereas add-ons should be made available on benefit basis.
- It will cover the costs of *pre-hospitalisation* medical expenses (inclusive of the costs of diagnostics) incurred for a period of 30 days prior to the date of hospitalisation together with the *post-hospitalisation* medical expenses incurred for a period of 60 days from the date of discharge.
- To cover intensive care unit (ICU) expenses up to 5 per cent of sum insured, capped at ₹ 10,000 per day; room charges up to 2.5 per cent, capped at ₹,000; capped expenses incurred on road ambulance up to ₹2,000 per hospitalisation; and day care treatment – with a maximum sum insured of ₹5 lakh.
- For the add-on cover, if the person is quarantined due to diagnosis or suspected infection, then the company will pay 1 per cent of sum insured per day, up to ₹3,000 per day. In the case of daily hospital cash, the company will pay 0.5 per cent of sum insured per day for every 24 hours of hospitalisation on positive diagnosis of COVID-19.
- Expenses incurred on hospitalisation under *AYUSH (Ayushman Bharat)* will be covered without any sub-limits.
- To comply with *portability* provisions and premium payment provisions on monthly, quarterly, half-yearly and yearly basis (premium to be on pan-India basis with no geographic location or zone-based pricing allowed).
- These provisions apply on all *existing health insurance policies* which cover hospitalisation charges.

To facilitate the ease of insurance cover during the pandemic the following regulatory measures[15] were undertaken by the IRDAI:

- KYC process simplified—to be done in paperless mode through Aadhaar.

15. **Economic Survey 2020-21**, vol. 1, p. 149, Ministry of Finance, GoI, N. Delhi.

non-bank

- Short-term health insurance for COVID-19 (upto March 31, 2021) with the following guidelines—
  - All life, general and health insurers allowed to offer COVID-19 specific short-term health insurance policies.
  - Policy term of minimum of 3 months and maximum of 11 months.
  - Life insurers are permitted to issue benefit-based policies only. General and Health insurers can issue both indemnities based and benefit-based policies.
  - Insurers shall comply with pricing norms regulations and guidelines.
  - Waiting period not to exceed 15 days, with no separate add-ons are permitted (lifelong renewability, migration and portability not applicable).

Guidelines were issued for *Corona Rakshak* policy which is a standard benefit-based policy and *Corona Kavach* Policy, a standard health policy which will be offered on indemnity basis and insurers were asked to launch the product from July 10, 2020.

As per the IRDAI (April 2021), the insurance industry has been able to adapt to challenge posed by the pandemic and was resilient in providing services to policyholders without any disruption. As per the NIA (National Insurance Academy), risks are becoming quite complex and insurance industry would have to reinvent itself for the next decade—the use of advanced risk analytics and automation will be needed to deal with the changing landscape.

INSURANCE INDUSTRY TODAY

India's insurance industry is expected to reach the size of US$ 300 billion by the end of 2025. The projected growth rates for life and non-life segments of industries are 15 and 18 per cent annually upto 2025—the entry of digital insurance platforms (presently there are around 120 InsurTech *start-ups* operating in the country) playing a catalytic role. The future of the insurance industry is bright in the country—supported by the demographic factors such as growing middle class, young insurable population and growing awareness of the need for protection and retirement planning. The major features[16] of the industry in India, in the back drop of the global scenario, are as given below:

- India's share in global insurance market is 1.92 per cent—with 9.3 per cent growth rate in insurance premium (against global growth rate of 1.5 per cent).
- India's *life insurance* business is ranked **10th** in the world (among 88 countries) with a 2.61 per cent share. However, growth rate of premium collection in India was 7.7 per cent—much higher than the global rate of 0.2 per cent.
- India's *non-life insurance* sector is ranked **15th** in the world (among 88 countries) with a 1.1 per cent share. However, growth rate of premium collection in India was 14 per cent—much higher the global rate of 3 per cent.
- The share of life insurance business for India is very high at 73.85 per cent (rest 26.15 per cent is the share of non-life insurance business). Globally, the share of life

16. **Economic Survey 2020-21**, vol. 1, pp. 147-49; and **Annual Report 2018-19**, IRDAI, pp. 4-5, Ministry of Finance, GoI, N. Delhi.

insurance is 54.30 per cent (rest 45.70 per cent is the share of non-life insurance).

- The market share of private players in the life rose to 31.3 per cent per cent in 2019-20 (up from 11 per cent in 2003-04).
- The market share of private players in the non-life insurance market rose to 56 per cent in 2020-21 (till April 2020) from 15 per cent in 2003-04.

WAY FORWARD

However, several steps have been taken by the Government in recent times to promote and expand the insurance sector, there are still certain challenges which need attention—some of the major[17] ones are being outlined below:

- Insurance *penetration* and *density* both are low in comparison to the Asian peers and global average. Participation from the rural areas still remains very deficient as insurance companies (specially the private ones) remain focused on the urban population.
- Insurance companies are facing lack of capital and have bad financial health, especially the public sector companies. Though, the Government has infused ₹25 billion till 2020-21, they require an additional fund of around ₹100-120 billion in order to meet the stipulated solvency margin. Private insurers are also faced with capital crunch which became even more serious once the RBI did put a ceiling on banks' holdings in insurance companies at 30 per cent. The Government decision *(Union Budget 2021-22)* to permit upto 74 per cent foreign direct investment (FDI) is expected to bring in relief in this regard. Low capital makes it difficult for the companies to face new risks.
- The *general insurance* industry recorded a decrease in profits, with public-sector general insurers posting losses, and their private-sector counterparts recording a slight fall in profits in 2018-19. Though, premiums have been growing, the industry is experiencing underwriting losses[18] which increased by 45.5 per cent in 2018-19. Taking lessons from the state of banks' NPAs and recent defaulters of the NBFCs, this needs immediate attention:
  - Product pricing is a matter of concern in the non-life segment also. Since 2007, except for motor third-party insurance, companies have had a free market approach to premium pricing—undercutting (reducing) premium prices to maintain market under excessive competition.
  - There is overcrowding in some segments. instead of searching for newer areas (such as home insurance, home appliances insurance, etc.) major private companies have overcrowded certain sectors, such as crop and motor insurance.
  - There are certain issues in the crop insurance segment. While the debate in this segment revolves around whether public or private insurers are better, the need is for their coexistence.
- To maintain profitability, insurance companies are becoming increasingly dependent on their investment portfolio (in stocks and debts). They have also resorted to harmful practices, for example, undercutting premiums.

17. Based on diverse sources including the paper, **India's Insurance Sectror: Challenges and Opportunities** by Saon Ray, Vasundhara Thakur and Kuntala Bandyopadhyay, Indian Council for Research on International Economic Relations (ICRIER) Working Paper 394, July 2020.

18. **Annual Report 2018-19,** IRDAI, Ministry of Finance, GoI, N. Delhi.

- The public sector insurance companies need to be privatised to provide the private players the much-needed level-playing field (however, the stake sale of the LIC was started by the Government few years back. It is for the first time an initial public offer[19] has been proposed in 2021-22).
- Growth of the industry is also restricted by the predominance of traditional distribution channels—there is a need of enhancing/ diversifying them. Online and point-of-sale kind of new channels are emerging but their market share is still insignificant.
- New challenge has emerged once the cover for the COVID-19 pandemic has started. er challenges for insurers. In absence of patient profiles, morbidity rates, and cost of treatment, etc. it will be very difficult for the insurance companies to underwrite risk[20] —as a result insurer may under- or over-price their products. However, the recently launched *National Digital Health Mission* is expected to play an effective role in this regard once the mission has covered a sizable number of citizens.

19. **Union Budget 2021-22**, Ministry of Finance, GoI, N. Delhi.

20. As per the size and business operations, insurance companies compute their need of minimum capital (using the risk-based capital method)—the IRDAI, 2017, Ministry of Finance, GoI, N. Delhi.

CHAPTER 14

SECURITY MARKET IN INDIA

*Had there been no security market–undoubtedly, the most fascinating segment of the financial market–there won't have been the big MNCs and TNCs in the world. Once the world moves towards the process of globalisation, the potential of this market has increased exponentially–its capacity of resource mobilisation is just anybody's guess!**

In this Chapter...

- **Definition**
- **Primary and Secondary Markets**
- **Stock Exchange**
- **SEBI**
- **Spot Exchanges**
- **Important Terms of Stock Market**
- **Foreign Financial Investment**
- **Angel Investor**
- **QFIs SCHEME**
- **RFPIs**
- **Participatory Notes (PNs)**
- **Credit Default Swap (CDS)**
- **Securitisation**
- **Corporate Bond in India**
- **Inflation-Indexed Bonds**
- **Gold Exchange Traded Funds**
- **CPSE ETF**
- **Pension Sector Reforms**
- **Regulatory Measures amidst COVID-19**
- **Financial Stability Development Council (FSDC)**
- **Financial Sector Assessment Programme (FSAP)**
- **Financial Action Task Force (FATF)**
- **Real Estate & Infrastructure Investment Trusts**
- **COVID-19 Interventions**
- **ESG Investment**
- **Social Stock Exchange**
- **Stock Market-Economy Disconnect**

DEFINITION

The segment of a financial market of an economy from long-term capital is raised via instruments such as shares, securities, bonds, debentures, mutual funds, and is known as the security market of that economy.

A security market has components such as a security regulator (SEBI in India), stock exchanges, different share indices, brokers,

* *As many documents of the WTO, World Bank and OECD have accepted many times.*

FIIs, jobbers, etc. There are different kinds of transactions which take place in a security market such as badla, reverse badla, future trading, insider trading (not allowed), private placement, etc.

PRIMARY AND SECONDARY MARKETS

Every security market has two complementary markets—primary and the secondary. The market in which the instruments of security market are traded (procured) directly between the capital-raiser and the instrument purchaser is known as the primary market. As for example, a share being directly purchased by anybody from the issuer which may be the company itself. The person is known as the primary shareholder. The market where the instruments of security market are traded among the primary instrument holders is known as the *secondary market*. Such transactions need an institutionalised floor for their trading which is made available by the stock exchanges.

STOCK EXCHANGE

A physically existing institutionalised set-up where instruments of security stock market (shares, bonds, debentures, securities, etc.) are traded. It serves the following major functions:

1. Makes a floor available to the buyers and sellers of stocks and liquidity comes to the stocks. It is the single most important institution in the secondary market for securities.
2. Makes available the prices of trading as an important piece of information to the investors.
3. By following institutionalised rules and procedures, it ensures that the participants in the stock market live up to their commitments.
4. Passes updated informations to the enlisted companies about their present stockholders (so that they can pass on dividends etc., to them).
5. By publishing its 'Index', it fulfils the purpose of projecting the moods of the stock market.

World's first stock exchange was established in Antwerp, Belgium (then part of the Netherlands) in 1631, the London Stock Exchange opened in 1773 and then Philadelphia Stock Exchange (the first in the New World) opened in 1790.[1] The first stock exchange in India, the Bombay Stock Exchange known as *The Native Share and Stock Brokers' Association* was set up in 1870 (under a tree!).[2]

Top five largest stock exchanges (on the basis of market capitalisation) of the world in their decreasing order are—the New York Stock Exchange, the NASDAQ, the Tokyo Stock Exchange, the London Stock Exchange and the Bombay Stock Exchange.[3]

Trading in the stock exchanges takes place via the mediators known as the *brokers*, the *jobbers*, the *market-maker* (discussed later in this chapter).

As per the latest information,[4] presently, there are a total number of 26 stock exchanges operating in India—7 at the national level and rest 19 at the regional level (one of it, Coimbatore Stock Exchange recently sought for withdrawal of recognition, the matter is sub-judice under SEBI). A brief account of the 'national level stock exchanges' is given below.

NSE

The National Stock Exchange of India Ltd. (NSE) was set up in 1992 and became operationalised in

1. Marc Levinson, ***Guide to Financial Markets*** (London: The Economist, 2006), p. 152.
2. V. Raghunathan, ***Stock Exchanges and Investments*** (New Delhi: Tata McGraw Hill, 1994).
3. Marc Levinson, ***Guide to Financial Markets***, pp. 153–54; Ministry of Finance, ***Economic Survey 2005–06*** (New Delhi: Government of India, 2006).
4. MoF, GoI, dated 22 April, 2013.

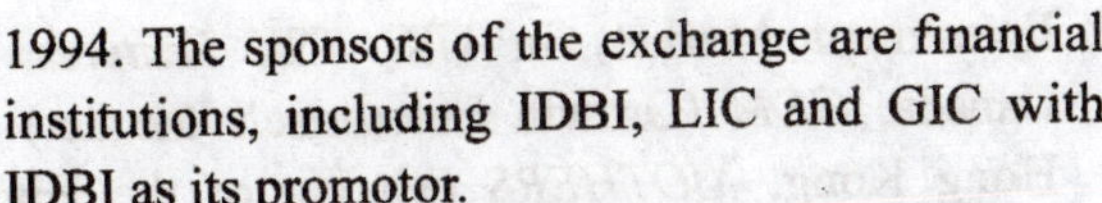

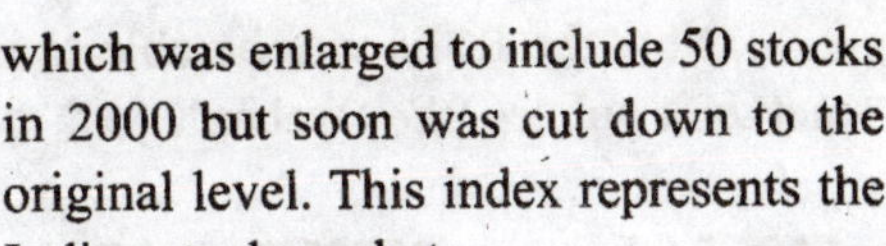

1994. The sponsors of the exchange are financial institutions, including IDBI, LIC and GIC with IDBI as its promotor.

It has a 50 share index and a 500 share index known as S&P CNX-50 (Nifty Fifty) and S&P CNX-500, respectively.

OTCEI

Though the Over the Counter Exchange of India Ltd. (OTCEI) was set up in 1989, it could commence trading only in 1992. India's first fully computerised stock exchange was promoted by the UTI, ICICI, SBI Cap among others, in order to overcome problems such as lack of transparency and delays in settlements prevalent in the older stock exchanges. Another important goal of the exchange was to allow stock market exposure to comparatively smaller companies (companies with paid-up capital from ₹30 lakh to ₹25 crore are enlisted here). Trading in this exchange takes place via market-makers and commission is fixed.

ISE

The Interconnected Stock Exchange of India (ISE) is basically a single floor of India's 15 regional stock exchanges (RSEs), set up in 1998. The RSEs were provided increased reach through this. It is a web-based exchange.

BSE

The Bombay Stock Exchange Ltd. (BSE), earlier a regional stock exchange, converted into a national one in 2002. The *biggest* in India, it accounts for almost 75 per cent of total stocks traded in India and is the *fifth* largest in the world (on the basis of market capitalisation).

There are at present four indices connected with the BSE:

1. **Sensex:** The sensitive index (i.e., Sensex) is a 30 stocks index of the BSE which was enlarged to include 50 stocks in 2000 but soon was cut down to the original level. This index represents the Indian stock market.
2. **BSE–200:** This is a 200 stock share index of the BSE (including the 30 stocks of the Sensex) which has its Dollar version too—*the Dollex*.
3. **BSE–500:** In mid-1999, the BSE came up with a 500-stock index representing major industries and many sub-sectors of the economy with information technology getting a significant weightage.
4. **National Index:** An index of 100 stocks being quoted nationwide (Bombay, Delhi, Kolkata, etc.) was developed to give broader/wider representation of the stock market since the Sensex consists of only 30 stocks. The 30 stocks of the sensex are included in the National Index.

This index is computed by the Statistics Department of the BSE hence it is called the BSE National Index (BSENI).

Indo Next

A new stock exchange to promote liquidity to the stocks of the small enterprises (SMEs) was launched in 2005 jointly and for medium the BSE and the FISE (Federation of Indian Stock Exchanges, representing 18 regional stock exchanges).

It is better known as the *BSE Indo Next.* It was also an effort to rejuvenate the RSEs which were facing falling volumes of trading on their floors. Due to absence of trading at the RSEs, the stocks of the SME, has become illiquid.

The BSE will transfer all its B1 and B2 groups to this exchange. The RSEs also transfer their enlisted companies to the new exchange.

Now the RSEs will be able to use the BSE network online—the 'Webex'.

SME Exchanges: BSESME and Emerge [5]

SME exchange is a stock exchange dedicated for trading the shares of small and medium scale enterprises (SMEs) who, otherwise, find it difficult to get listed in the main exchanges. The concept originated from the difficulties faced by SMEs in gaining visibility or attracting sufficient trading volumes when listed along with other stocks in the main exchanges.

To be listed on the SME exchange, the post-issue paid-up capital of the company should not exceed ₹25 crores. This means that the SME exchange is not limited to the small and medium scale enterprises (which are defined under the 'Micro, Small And Medium Enterprises Development Act, 2006' as enterprises where the investment in plant and machinery does not exceed ₹10 crores). As of now, to get listed in the main boards like, National Stock Exchange, the minimum paid-up capital required is ₹10 cr and that of the BSE is ₹3 cr. Hence, those companies with paid-up capital between ₹10 cr to ₹25 cr have the option of migrating to the Main Board/ or to the SME exchange. The companies listed on the SME exchange are allowed to migrate to the Main Board as and when they meet the listing requirements of the Main Board. There shall be compulsory migration of the SMEs from the SME exchange, in case the post-issue paid-up capital is likely to go beyond the ₹25 crore limit.

World over, trading platforms/exchanges for the shares of SMEs are known by different names such as Alternate Investment Markets or Growth Enterprises Market, SME Board etc. Some of the known markets for SMEs are *AIM* (Alternate Investment Market) in UK, *TSX Ventures* in Canada, *GEM* (Growth Enterprise's Market) in Hong Kong, *MOTHERS* (Market of the High-Growth and Emerging Stocks) in Japan, *Catalist* in Singapore and *Chinext*, the latest initiative in China [see 'World Federation of Exchanges' for latest comparative idea].

Globally, most of these SME exchanges are still at an evolving stage considering the many hurdles they face:

1. Declining prices of listed stocks and their illiquidity.
2. A gradual reduction in new listings and decline in profits of the exchanges etc., (for instance, *AIM* had three predecessors; *CATALIST* succeeded *SESDAQ* with new regulations and listing requirements).
3. In most jurisdictions, idea of a separate exchange for SMEs have become unviable and hence tend to be platforms of existing exchanges, perhaps cross-subsidised by the main board/exchange.

In India, similarly, after the two previous attempts—*OTCEI* (Over the Counter Exchange of India, 1989) and *Indonext*—the market regulator, SEBI, on May 18, 2010 permitted setting up of a dedicated stock exchange or a trading platform for SMEs. The existing bourses/stock exchanges in India, BSE and NSE went live on March 13, 2012 with a separate trading platform for small and medium enterprises (SMEs). BSE has named its SME platform as **BSESME**, while NSE has named it as **Emerge**.

Unlike in India, many of these SME exchanges in various countries operate at a global level, due to smallness of the market, allowing for listing by both domestic as well as foreign companies. Though the names suggest that they are set up for SMEs, these exchanges hardly follow the definition of SMEs in their

5. This section is based on various sources—the SEBI, NSE, BSE, 'World Federation of Exchanges', select issues of *The Economist* and news reportings of *The HT Live Mint, The Business Line and The Economic Times.*

respective jurisdictions. Also, many of them follow a 'Sponsor-supervised' market model, where sponsors or nominated advisors decide if the listing applicant is suitable to be listed or not, i.e., generally no quantitative entry criteria like track record on profitability or minimum paid-up capital or net worth, etc., are specified to be listed in these exchanges. Instead, they are designed as 'buyers beware' markets for informed investors. SEBI has also designed the SME exchanges in a similar format with provisions for ***'market making'*** for the specified securities listed on the SME exchange.

As is the case globally, certain relaxations are also provided to the issuers whose securities are listed on the SME exchange in comparison to the listing requirements in the Main Board (such as in BSE and NSE, in the case of India), which include:

1. Publication of financial results on 'half yearly basis', instead of 'quarterly basis', making it available on their websites rather than publishing it.
2. Option of sending a statement containing the salient features of all the documents instead of sending a full Annual Report.
3. No continuous requirement of minimum number of shareholders, though at the time of IPO there needs to be a minimum of 50 investors, etc.
4. The existing eligibility norms like track record on profits, net worth/net tangible assets conditions, etc., have been fully relaxed for SMEs as is the case globally.
5. However, no compromise has been made to corporate governance norms.

Common Facts about National Stock Exchanges

Before the arrival of national level stock exchanges, India was not having any exchange of national status—better say there was no Indian stock market, but stock markets showing only regional pictures. Besides, the national stock exchanges did solve some major problems of stock market, we may also call their arrivals as part of the stock market reforms in India. The common features of these exchanges are:

1. All are situated in Mumbai;
2. All do screen-based trading (SBT);
3. All have their trading terminals in the major cities of the country;
4. All are web-enabled;
5. All are limited liability companies;
6. The brokers registered here have no say in either the ownership or the management of the exchanges;
7. All are counted among the best and the most technology-equipped stock exchanges in the world.[6]

Players in the Stock Exchanges

Broker is a registered member of a stock exchange who buys or sells shares/securities on his client's behalf and charges a commission on the gross value of the deal—such brokers are also known as *commission brokers*.

Brokers who offer services such as investment advice, clients' portfolio planning, credit when a client is buying on margin other than their traditional commission job are known as *full service brokers*. In India such brokers are just coming up.

Jobber A jobber is a broker's broker or one who specialises in specific securities catering to the need of other brokers—in India also known as '*Taravaniwallah*' (in the BSE).[7] A jobber is

6. P. Chidambaram while presenting the ***Union Budget 2006–07***, (New Delhi; Government of India, 2006).
7. Surendra Sundararajan, ***Book of Financial Terms*** (New Delhi: Tata McGraw Hill, 2004), p. 117.

located at a particular trading post on the floor of the stock exchange and does buying and selling for small price differences, called the *spread.* He has no contact with the investing public.

In the London Stock Exchange he is called a *market-maker* while in the New York Stock Exchange he is called a *specialist.* The Bombay Stock Exchange has made it mandatory for every company with a share capital of over ₹3 crore to appoint jobbers or market-makers if it seeks enlistment. Such an arrangement enables investors to buy and sell shares on the stock exchange and thus liquidity increases.

Market-Maker Functions as an intermediary in the market ready to buy and sell securities. He simultaneously quotes two-way rates—like a jobber basically with the only difference that he quotes two-way rates, for buying and selling at the same time.[8]

On the floor of India's OTCEI, only market-makers are allowed to play. In the money market of India, the Discount and Finance House of India (DFHI) is the chief market-maker.[9]

Since he quotes the selling price while buying a particular share, he makes market for that share, hence such a name.

The NASDAQ of the USA is a market-maker's stock exchange where they are connected by the web-enabled trading terminals.

SEBI

The regulator of Indian stock market, set up under the *Security and Exchange Board of India Act, 1992* (as a non-statutory body set on 12 April, 1988 through a government resolution in an effort to give the Indian stock market an organised structure) with its head office in Mumbai. Its initial paid-up capital was ₹50 crore provided by the promoters—the IDBI, the IFCI and the ICICI.

The Board of SEBI comprises nine members excluding the chairman—one member each from the Ministries of Finance and Law, one member from the RBI and two other members appointed by the central government. It has four full-time members (including the chairman).

Main functions/powers of the Board as per the *SEBI Act, 1992* are:

1. Registering and stock exchanges, merchant banks, mutual funds, underwriters, registrars to the issues, brokers, sub-brokers, transfer agents and others.
2. Levying various fees and other charges (as 1 per cent of the issue amount of every company issuing shares are kept by it as a caution money in the concerned stock exchange where the company is enlisted).
3. Promoting investor education.
4. Inspection and audit of stock exchanges and various intermediaries.
5. Performing other concerned functions as may be prescribed from time to time.

Commodity Trading

Commodity trading happens similar to 'stocks' (shares, securities, debentures, bonds) trading in the stock market. However, commodities are actual physical goods such as corn, silver, gold, crude oil, etc. Futures are contracts for commodities that are traded at a futures exchange like the Chicago Board of Trade (CBOT). Futures contracts have expanded beyond just commodities, now there are futures contracts on financial markets like foreign currencies, interest rates, etc.

Commodity futures serve a great purpose in any economy. As we see in the case of agricultural

8. Tim Hindle, op. cit., p. 129.
9. Surender Sundararajan, ***Book of Financial Terms,*** p. 134.

commodity—their prices play a key role in determining the fortune of the agriculture and food processing industry in India. These prices undergo a *large degree of fluctuation*. Reasons for price fluctuation are crop failure, bad weather, demand-supply imbalance, etc. This fluctuation, in turn, leads to a 'price risk'. This price risk is largely borne by the farmer and the industries where agricultural commodities are used as raw material. Commodity exchanges are associations that determine and enforce rule, and set procedures for trading of commodities. The main objective of the exchange is to protect the participants from adverse movement in prices by facilitating futures trading in commodities.

If the participants *hedge* themselves against this price risk, then they would be able to insulate themselves against the inherent price fluctuations associated with agricultural commodities. One of the methods of doing this would be by using commodity exchanges as a trading platform. Apart from hedging against price risk, a commodity exchange helps in production and procurement planning as one can buy in small lots. Further as the exchange consists of various informed industry participants, *price discovery* is more efficient and discounts the local and global factors.

Let us take a very simple example to understand how trading on commodity exchanges help industry participants. A farmer who is producing wheat can sell 'wheat futures' on a commodity exchange. This will help him lock in a sale price of a specified quantity of wheat at a future date. Hence the farmer would now be able to get an assured price for his produce in future and any decline in the price of wheat would not impact his earnings. On the other hand, a user industry (e.g., a flour mill) could purchase the wheat futures from the exchange. Hence the flour mill would now be able to fix its future purchase cost for a specified quantity of wheat. Therefore, any increase in the price of wheat in future would not impact its cost of production.

By April 2021, a total of **91** commodities were notified by the SEBI for trading on the commodity exchange platforms which were proposed for a 'review' in 2021-22. It is believed that some new products may be introduced based on the learnings from the *COVID-19* pandemic. There are 21 national and regional commodity exchanges in the country—the 6 national exchanges are:

1. National Commodity and Derivatives Exchange (NCDEX)
2. National Multi-Commodity Exchange (NMCE)
3. Multi Commodity Exchange (MCX)
4. Indian Commodity Exchange (ICEX)
5. ACE Derivatives & Commodity Exchange (ACE).
6. Universal Commodity Exchange (UCE).

Improvements in Warehousing The government has been incentivising private investments in warehousing through various subsidies and tax sops. Under the purview of the Warehousing Development and Regulatory Authority (WDRA), a new breed of storage facilities has come up which are scientifically developed—supported by value-added services, such as weighing, testing, certification and even come equipped with 24 × 7 physical security with a number of them sport CCTV-led remote monitoring facilities from a central location.

The most interesting feature of these modern-day warehouses is that they possess an IT backbone, which enables real-time stock updates. As these warehouses undergo regular physical audits, both by internal and external teams, the physical integrity of the stock—both in terms of quality and quantity—can easily be ascertained at any point of time. These state-of-the-art, high-tech warehouses enable the stakeholders to gain finance—using electronic Negotiable Warehouse Receipts (e-NWRs).

Regulation and Reform While the FMC (Forward Markets Commission) regulated the commodity markets since 1952, it was perceived as lacking the power to control wild fluctuations in prices and other irregularities. Accordingly, in 2015, FMC was merged with SEBI (with reputation of being superior in terms of surveillance, risk-monitoring and enforcement mechanisms, and a more robust regulatory body for the sector). Subsequently, SEBI has initiated several reforms measures:

- Allowing stock brokers to deal in commodity derivatives (common broking businesses for equities and commodities),
- Permitting the NSE and BSE to commence commodity trading,
- Allowing the FPIs to participate in commodity derivatives contracts traded in stock exchanges subject to certain stipulations,
- Allowing the Category III Alternative Investment Funds (AIFs) to trade in commodity markets.

As per the experts, India's commodity trading market is at the cusp of transformation as multiple changes are taking place in the related areas such as—infrastructure, logistics, electronic warehousing, transportation, etc.

SPOT EXCHANGES

In India, spot exchanges refer to electronic trading platforms which facilitate purchase and sale of specified commodities, including agricultural commodities, metals and bullion by providing *spot delivery contracts* in these commodities.

This market segment functions like the equity segment in the main stock exchanges. Alternatively, this can be considered as a guaranteed direct marketing by sellers of the commodities. Spot exchanges leverage on the latest technology available in the stock exchange framework for the trading of goods. This is an innovative Indian experiment in the trading of goods and is distinct from what is commonly known as 'commodity exchanges' which trade in *futures contracts* in commodities.

Spot exchange has been **defined** by the Warehousing Development and Regulatory Authority (Electronic Warehouse Receipts) Regulations, 2011 as 'a body corporate incorporated under the Companies Act, 1956 and engaged in assisting, regulating or controlling the business of trading in electronic warehouse receipts.' However, present day spot exchange deals not just with warehouse receipts—this is an electronic market where a farmer or a trader can *discover* the prices of commodities on a national level and can buy or sell goods *immediately* (i.e., on the 'spot') to anyone across the country. All contracts on the exchange are *compulsory delivery contracts*—it means that all outstanding positions at the end of the day are marked for delivery, which implies that seller has to give delivery and buyer has to take the delivery.

The facilities provided by the spot exchange, like a normal stock exchange, include clearing and settlement of trades. Trades are settled on guaranteed basis (i.e., in case of default by any person exchange arranges for the payment of money/good) and the exchange collects various margin payments, to ensure this. The exchange also offers various other services, such as, quality certification, warehousing, warehouse receipt financing, etc.

Spot Exchanges in India

At present, there are **four** spot exchanges operating in the country:

1. The National Spot Exchange Ltd. (NSEL), set up in 2008, is a national level commodity

spot exchange promoted by the Financial Technologies India Ltd. (FTIL) and National Agricultural Cooperative Marketing Federation of India Limited (NAFED). After the FTIL was found involved in irregularities, the FMC (Forward Market Commission), by *end-March 2014* asked it to exit the spot exchange.

2. NCDEX Spot Exchange Ltd. (established in October 2006 by NSE).
3. Reliance Spot Exchange Ltd. (R-Next).
4. Indian Bullion Spot Exchange Ltd. (an online over the counter spot exchange).

Advantages of Spot Exchanges

Spot exchange provides various advantages over the traditional way of trading in commodities:

1. Efficient price determination as price is determined by a wider cross-section of people from across the country, unlike the traditional 'mandis' where price discovery for commodities used to happen only through local participation.
2. Ensures transparency in price discovery—anonymity ensures convergence of different price perceptions, as the buyer or seller merely expresses their desire to trade without even meeting directly.
3. Ensures participation in large numbers by farmers, traders and processors across the country and eliminate the possibility of cartelisation and other such unhealthy practices prevalent in the commodity markets.
4. It brings in some best practices in commodity trading like, system of grading for quality, creating network of warehouses with assaying facilities, facilitating trading in relatively smaller quantities, lower transaction cost, etc.
5. Bank finance available against the goods in the warehouse on easier terms improves holding capacity and can actually incentivise farm production and hence reduce rural poverty.
6. Since the trades are guaranteed (by the exchange), counter party risk is avoided.

Raising Capital in the Primary Market

There are three ways in which a company raises capital in the primary market.

Public Issue A public offer is open for all Indian citizens, the most broad-based method of raising capital and the most prestigious, too (the Reliance Industries Ltd. is the biggest company of India in this category).

Rights Issue Raising capital from the existing shareholders of a company, it means it is a preferential kind of issue restricted to a certain category of the public only.

Private Placement Raising capital by selling shares to a select group of investors, usually financial institutions (FIs) but may be to individuals also. This is done through a proc s of direct negotiations (completely opposite to the public issue). The advantage of this route is the substantial saving a share issuing company makes on marketing expenses (but the risk of shifting loyalties of the investors in this route is also the highest).

Recent times have seen such capital raising by many companies privately placing their shares to the foreign institutional investors (FIIs) as a route to source foreign exchange in India, and that too quickly.

IMPORTANT TERMS OF STOCK MARKET

Short Selling

Sale of a share which is not owned. This is done by someone after borrowing shares from stockbrokers promising to replace them at a future date on the hope (speculation) that the price will fall by then. He fetches profit if price of the share really fell down by the future date of replacement and sustains a loss if the price increased. Recently, short selling has been allowed in India by SEBI.

Bear and Bull

A person who speculates share prices to fall in future and so sells his shares and earns profit is a *bear*. He earns profit out of a falling market. Basically, here he is short selling the shares.

Opposite to bear, bull is a person who speculates share prices to go up in future so either stops selling the select group of shares for that time to be reached (he is basically taking long position on those shares) or starts purchasing that select group of shares.

Thus, a bear increases the number of shares in a stock market activating a general fall in the index—a bearish market. Opposite to it, a bull creates a scarcity of shares in the stock market activating a general rise in the share prices and the index—a bullish market.

Brokers play as a bear for some stocks and as a bull for some other stocks, while a bear broker is a non-entity, a bull is remembered for long time to come—Harshad Mehta was known as the Great Bull.

Book Building

A provision allowed by SEBI to all Initial Public offers (IPOs) in which individual investors are reserved and allotted shares by the company. But the issuer has to disclose the price (at which shares have been allotted the size of the issue and the number of shares offered to the public).

IPO

Initial Public Offer (IPO) is an event of share issuing when a company comes up with its share/ securities issued for the first time.

Price Band

A process of public issue where the company gives a price range (known as price band) and it is left upon the share applicants to quote their prices on it—the highest bidders getting the shares. This is a variant of share issue at premium but considered a safer choice.

Scrip Share

A share given to the existing shareholders without any charge—also known as *bonus share.*

Sweat Share

A share given to the employees of the company without any charge.

Rolling Settlement

An important reform measure started in the Indian stock market in mid-2001 under which all commitments of sale and purchase result into payment/delivery at the end of the 'X' days later (where 'X' stands for 5 days. Some shares have X as one, two or three days, too). Today, all shares are covered under this provision.

Badla

When the buyers want postponement of the transaction—in Western world called *Contango.*

Undha Badla

When the sellers want postponement of the transaction—also known as the *reverse badla* or *backwardation.*

Futures

A trading allowed in shares where a future price is quoted for the shares and the payment and delivery takes place on the pre-determined dates.

Depositories

Started in 1996 under which stocks are converted into *'paperless form'* (dematerialisation of shares shortly known as the 'demat'). At present, two public sector depositaries (Mumbai) are functioning in India set up under the *Depositories Act, 1996*:

1. NSDL (National Securities Depositories Ltd.)
2. CDSL (Central Depositories Services Ltd.)

Spread

The difference between the buying and selling prices of a share is called spread. Higher the liquidity of a share lower its spread and vice versa. Also known as Jobber's *Turn* or *Margin* or *Hair cut.*

Kerb Dealings

The transactions of stocks which take place outside the stock exchanges—unofficially and take place after the normal trading hours.

NSCC

The National Securities Clearing Corporation (NSCC), a public sector company set-up in 1996 takes the *counter party risk* of all transactions done at the NSE just as an intermediary guarantees all trades.

Demutualisation

A process started (2002) by SEBI under which ownership, management and trading membership was to be segregated from each other. No broker was to be on the Board of Directors or an office-bearer in a stock exchange.

This has been done in the case of all stock exchanges except three regional stock exchanges (RSEs) in India.

Authorised Capital

The limits upto which shares can be issued by a company—also known as the *nominal* or *registered* capital. This is fixed in the Memorandum of Association (MoA) and the article of association (AoA) of a company as required by the *Companies Act (Law).*

Paid-up Capital

The part of the authorised capital of a company that has actually been paid by shareholders. A difference may arise because all shares authorised might not be *issued* or issued shares are only partly paid-up.

Subscribed Capital

The amount actually paid by the shareholders or have been committed by them for contribution.

Issued Capital

The amount which is sought by a company to be raised by issuing shares which cannot exceed the authorised capital of the company.

Greenshoe Option

A provision under which a company issuing shares for the first time is allowed to sell some additional shares to the public—usually 15 per cent, is also known as ***over-allotment provision***. It gets its name from the first company (Greenshoe Company, USA) which was allowed such an option.

Penny Stocks

The share which remains low-priced at a stock exchange for a comparatively longer period. Speculators may start hoarding them for hefty margins, this was seen in India in mid-2006. And since such stocks get hoarded, ultimately their market prices increase. The speculators earn profit after offloading (selling) these shares at high prices and others who purchase these shares ultimately might fetch huge losses because price rise of these stocks are unintentional or each intentional manipulation and nothing else.

ESOP

The Employee Stock Ownership Plan (ESOP) enables a foreign company to offer its shares to employees overseas. It was allowed in India (February 2005) provided that the MNC has minimum 51 per cent holding in its Indian company. Earlier a permission from the RBI was required for such an option.

SBT

Screen Based Trading (SBT) is trading of stock based on the electronic medium, i.e., with the help of computer monitor, internet, etc. First such trading was introduced in New York in 1972 by the bond broker ***Cantor Fitzgerald***. India introduced it in 1989 at the OTCEI. Now it is carried out at all exchanges.

OFCDs

Debentures are the debt instruments which may be issued by a listed or non-listed firm to raise funds in a security market. They are of many types, viz., *Redeemable, Non-redeemable, Partially Convertible* and *Fully Convertible*. In case of 'fully convertible debentures' an 'option' (that is why the name OFCDs, i.e., Optionally Fully Convertible Debentures) is given to the debenture-holders who may wish to convert their OFCDs into shares (after expiry of the period fixed by the debenture issuing firm—known as 'lock-in' period). But the 'rate' will be decided by the company (e.g., how many shares against how many debentures). For debenture-holders the 'option' to convert debenture into shares is profitable and/or safer once either of the following situations are correct:

1. The firm is likely to make high profit (so the shareholder can earn higher dividend), or
2. Firm's share-price is likely to rise in the share market (profit can be made by selling shares).

But suppose the firm has weak balance sheet (going bankrupt), then it is better to keep hold on the debenture rather than converting them into shares, because when a company is liquidated (i.e., its assets sold off), the debenture holders get ***primacy*** over shareholders in payment. It means OFCD is a bit tricky thing and is the only suitable route to invest in the security market for the investors who have some knowledge and understanding of share prices, company performance, etc.

Recently, the OFCDs issued by **Sahara** (an NBFC under regulatory control of the RBI) were in news due to some irregularities – it was a simple case of certain loopholes in the regulation of OFCDs and some violations by Sahara:

1. Actually, an OFCD issue process has to be completed within 10 working days (Sahara continued for over two years).
2. If the OFCD is being issued through the 'Private Placement' route only 50 individuals/institutions can subscribe to it (Sahara issued it to over 23 million people and raised over ₹24,000 crores).

Such tricky instruments being issued to novice public was a clear case of financial irregularities.

3. Unlisted companies do not come under the regulatory control of SEBI. In place they are regulated by the Ministry of Corporate Affairs (both the Sahara firms which issued OFCDs are unlisted). But SEBI contended that it can regulate even an unlisted firm if it issues OFCD, as the SEBI Act, 1992 contains the term OFCDs. There was really some regulatory confusion. This is why the government added a 'clause' in the *Companies (Amendment) Act, 2012* which gives SEBI **undisputed jurisdiction** over any investment scheme involving more than 50 investors whether the company is listed or unlisted. Meanwhile, Sahara has been ordered to return the total capital it raised through OFCDs with an interest of 15 per cent per annum.

Derivatives

Derivative is a product whose value is derived from the value of one or more basic variables, called bases (underlying asset, index or reference rate), in a contractual manner.

The underlying asset can be equity, forex, commodity or any other asset. For example, wheat farmers may wish to sell their harvest at a future date to eliminate the risk of a change in prices by that date. Such a transaction is an example of a derivative. The price of this derivative is driven by the spot price of wheat which is the 'underlying'.

In the Indian context the *Securities Contracts (Regulation) Act, 1956* [SC(R)A] **defines derivative** to include:

1. A security derived from a debt instrument, share, loan whether secured or unsecured, risk instrument or contract for differences or any other form of security.
2. A contract, which derives its value from the prices, or index of prices, of underlying securities.

Derivatives are securities under the SC(R)A and hence the trading of derivatives is governed by the regulatory framework under the SC(R)A and are allowed to be traded on the floors of the stock exchanges.

Indian Depository Receipts (IDRs)

As per the **definition** given in the *Companies (Issue of Indian Depository Receipts) Rules, 2004*, IDR is an instrument in the form of a depository receipt created by the Indian depository in India against the underlying equity shares of the issuing company. In an IDR, foreign companies would issue shares, to an Indian depository [say the National Security Depository Limited (NSDL)], which would in turn issue depository receipts to investors in India. The actual shares underlying IDRs would be held by an Overseas Custodian, which shall authorise the Indian depository to issue of IDRs.

Just try to understand in a simple way. An IDR is a mechanism that allows investors in India to invest in listed foreign companies, including multinational companies, in Indian rupees. IDRs give the holder the opportunity to hold an interest in equity shares in an overseas company. IDRs are denominated in Indian Rupees and issued by a Domestic Depository in India. They can be listed on any Indian stock exchange. Anybody who can invest in an IPO (Initial Public Offer) is/are eligible to invest in IDRs. *In other words, what ADRs/GDRs are for investors abroad with respect to Indian companies, IDRs are for Indian investors with respect to foreign companies.*

Shares 'at Par' and 'at Premium'

An ordinary share in India, in general, is said to have a *par value (face value)* of ₹10, though some shares issued earlier still carry a par value of ₹100. Par value implies the value at which a share is originally recorded in the balance sheet as 'equity capital' (this is the same as 'ordinary share capital'). SEBI guidelines for *public issues* by new companies established by individual promoters and entrepreneurs, require all new companies to offer their shares to the public *at par,* i.e., at ₹10. However, a new company set up by existing companies (and of course existing companies themselves) with a track record of *at least five years* of consistent profitability are allowed to issue shares at a **premium.**

When a company issues shares at a premium, it is able to raise the required amount of capital from the public by issuing a fewer number of shares. For example, while a *new company* promoted by first time entrepreneurs intending to raise say, ₹1 crore, has to offer 10 lakh ordinary shares at ₹10 each (at par), an *existing company* may raise the same amount by offering only 2 lakh shares at ₹50 each (close to the market value of its shares). The latter is said to have issued its share at a '*subscription price*' of ₹50 (₹10 in the case of the former company), at a premium of ₹40 (being the excess of subscription price over par value). In such a situation in India, the company's books of accounts will show ₹10 towards *share capital account* and ₹40 towards *share premium account*. It means that the higher the premium, the fewer will be the number of shares a company will have to service. For this very reason, following the policy of free pricing of issues in 1993, many companies came out with issues at prices so high that in many cases they were higher than their market prices, leading to under-subscription of such issues. The companies are, however, learning fast about the pitfalls of high pricing of shares and it is only a matter of time before the issue prices become more realistic.

FOREIGN FINANCIAL INVESTMENT

India opened its capital market for foreign portfolio investment/foreign institutional investment (FPI/FII) in 1994—at present, there are 10,131 such firms registered with the SEBI.[10] Today, they are one of the biggest drivers of India's financial markets and have invested around ₹12.51 trillion (US$ 171.81 billion) in India between FY02-18.[11] Highly developed primary and secondary markets have attracted FIIs/FPIs to the country. Their investments are regulated by SEBI while the ceilings on such investments are maintained by the RBI. Almost all *types* of them are today active in the market—Hedge Funds, Foreign Mutual Funds, Sovereign Wealth Funds, Pension Funds, Trusts, Asset Management Companies, Endowments, University Funds, etc.

Major Regulatory Initiatives SEBI announced several regulatory changes to encourage safe and higher foreign portfolio investment in the country *during 2018-19*—

- Direct overseas listing of Indian companies allowed.
- The KYC (Know-Your-Client) requirement relaxed.
- Foreign entities allowed to participate in the commodity derivatives.
- NRIs allowed to invest through FPI route.
- The timeline for public issue of debt securities reduced to 6 days (from 12 days).

10. Ministry of Finance, GoI, N. Delhi, April 2019.
11. India Brand Equity Foundation (IBEF), Department of Commerce, Ministry of Commerce and Industry, Government of India, N. Delhi, April 2021.

- FPIs allowed to invest up to 25 per cent in Category III Alternative Investment Funds (AIF).
- FPIs allowed to invest in the Real Estate Investment Trusts (REITs) and Infrastructure Investment Trust (InvITs).

Today, India is being viewed as a potential opportunity by investors, with the economy having the capacity to grow tremendously. Buoyed by strong support from the government, FII investments have been strong, even after the disruption caused the COVID-19 pandemic, and are expected to grow in the coming times.

Classification The FPIs have been classified[12] by the SEBI into three broad categories, namely:

- **Category I:** The government entities/ institutions investing in Indian security market on behalf of the Central Bank.
- **Category II:** The financial institutions, mutual funds, etc., which duly regulated in the countries of their origin.
- **Category III:** The financial institutions which do not fall under either of the above-given categories.

Investment by FPIs There were net inflows to the tune of ₹2.1 lakh crore on account of the foreign portfolio investors in the Indian capital market during 2020-21 (up to December), as compared to net inflows of ₹0.81 lakh crore during the same period in previous year. As per the *Economic Survey 2020-21*, the total cumulative investment by FPIs increased by 5.4 per cent to US$ 273.6 billion (on December 31, 2020).

ANGELINVESTOR

A new term in India's financial market, introduced in the *Union Budget 2013-14* which announced that SEBI will soon prescribe the provisions by which the **angel investor** can be recognised as *Category I AIF[13] venture capital funds.*

Angel investor is an investor who provides financial backing to entrepreneurs for 'starting their business'. Angel investors are usually found among an entrepreneur's family and friends but they may be from outside also. The capital they provide can be a one-time injection of seed money or ongoing support to carry the company through difficult times—in exchange they may like owning share in the business or provide capital as loan (in case of a loan they lend at more favourable terms than other lenders, as they are usually investing in the *person* rather than the viability of the business). Other than investible capital, these investors provide technical advices and also help the 'start-up' business with their lucrative contacts.

They are focused on helping the business succeed, rather than reaping a huge profit from their investment. Angel investors are essentially the *exact opposite* of a venture capitalist in their 'intention' (who has high profit prospects as their prime focus). But in one sense both—an *angel investor* and a *venture investor*—serve the same purpose for the entrepreneur (who is in dire need of investible capital).

QFIs SCHEME

In the Budget 2011-12, the government, for the first time, permitted qualified foreign investors (QFIs), who meet the know-your-customer (KYC) norms, to invest directly in Indian mutual funds. In January 2012, the government expanded this scheme to allow QFIs to directly invest in Indian equity markets. Taking the scheme forward,

12. **Security and Exchange Board of India,** Ministry of Finance, GoI, N. Delhi, April 2019.

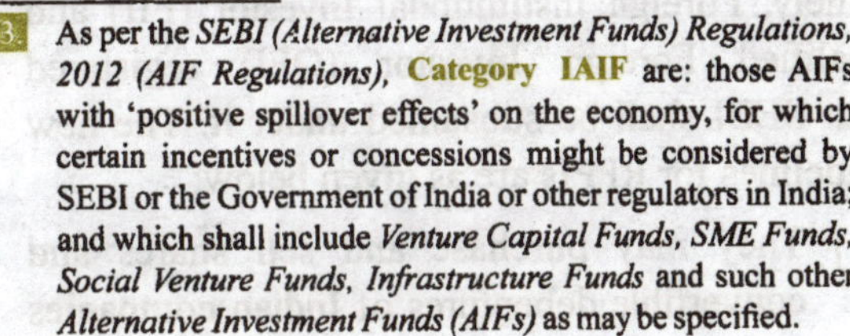
13. As per the *SEBI (Alternative Investment Funds) Regulations, 2012 (AIF Regulations),* **Category IAIF** are: those AIFs with 'positive spillover effects' on the economy, for which certain incentives or concessions might be considered by SEBI or the Government of India or other regulators in India; and which shall include *Venture Capital Funds, SME Funds, Social Venture Funds, Infrastructure Funds* and such other *Alternative Investment Funds (AIFs)* as may be specified.

as announced in *Budget 2012-13*, QFIs have also been permitted to invest in corporate debt securities (CDSs) and MF debt schemes subject to a total overall ceiling of US $ 1 billion.

In *May 2012*, QFIs were allowed to open individual non-interest-bearing rupee bank accounts with authorised dealer banks in India for receiving funds and making payment for transactions in securities they are eligible to invest in. In *June 2012*, the definition of QFI was expanded to include residents of the member countries of the Gulf Cooperation Council (GCC) and European Commission (EC) as the GCC and EC are members of the Financial Action Task Force (FATF).

The speedier moves in the area of promoting higher foreign investment (FIs) in India should be seen in the light of two broad perspectives, viz.,

1. India's rising current account deficit (which crossed an all-time high of 6.7 per cent by *March 2013*) which is creating heavy drain of foreign exchange; and
2. The objective of attracting more FIs while the Western economies are under the spell of recession (cashing in the opportunity).

RFPIs

In *March 2014*, the RBI simplified foreign portfolio investment norms by putting in place an easier registration process and operating framework with an aim to attract inflows. From now onwards, the portfolio investor registered in accordance with the SEBI guidelines shall be called Registered Foreign Portfolio Investor (RFPI)—the existing portfolio investor class, namely, Foreign Institutional Investor (FII) and Qualified Foreign Investor (QFI) registered with SEBI shall be subsumed under it. The new guidelines for RFPIs are as given below:

1. They may purchase and sell shares and convertible debentures of Indian companies through a registered broker on recognised stock exchanges in India as well as purchase shares and convertible debentures, which are offered to public in terms of relevant SEBI guidelines.
2. Such investors can acquire shares or convertible debentures in any bid for, or acquisition of, securities in response to an offer for *disinvestment* of shares made by the central government or any state government.
3. These entities would be eligible to invest in *government securities* and corporate debt, subject to limits specified by the RBI and SEBI from time to time.
4. Such investors would be permitted to trade in all exchange-traded derivative contracts on the stock exchanges, subject to the position limits as specified by SEBI from time to time.
5. RFPI may offer cash or foreign sovereign securities with AAA rating or corporate bonds or domestic government securities, as collateral to the recognised stock exchanges for their transactions in cash as well as derivative segment of the market.

All investments made by that FIIs/QFIs in accordance with the regulations prior to registration as RFPI shall continue to be valid and taken into account for computation of aggregate limit.

PARTICIPATORY NOTES (PNs)

A Participatory Note (PN or P-Note) in the Indian context, in essence, is a *derivative* instrument issued in foreign jurisdictions, by a SEBI registered FII, against Indian securities—the Indian security instrument may be equity, debt, derivatives or may even be an index. PNs are also known as *Overseas Derivative Instruments*, *Equity Linked Notes*, *Capped Return Notes*, and *Participating Return Notes*, etc.

The investor in PN does not own the underlying Indian security, which is held by the FII who issues the PN. Thus, the investors in PNs derive the economic benefits of investing in the security without actually holding it. They benefit from fluctuations in the price of the underlying security since the value of the PN is linked with the value of the underlying Indian security. The PN holder also does not enjoy any voting rights in relation to security/shares referenced by the PN.

Reasons for the popularity of PNs

The reasons why PNs became such a popular route for foreign investors to invest in the Indian security market may be understood through the following points:

1. One of the primary reasons for the emergence of the PN (an 'off-shore derivative instrument', i.e., an ODI) is the restrictions on foreign investments. For example, a foreign investor intending to make portfolio investments in India was required to seek FII registration for which he is required to meet certain eligibility criteria. Lack of full *Capital Account Convertibility* further enhances the entry barriers from the perspective of a foreign investor. However, since *January 2012*, the Indian government has taken a decision to give direct access to such prospective 'foreign individual investors' who were hitherto banned to invest in equity of Indian companies.
2. The off-shore derivative market allows investors to gain exposure to the local shares without incurring the time and costs involved in investing directly. In return, the foreign investor pays the PN issuer a certain basis *point(s)* of the value of PNs traded by him as *costs*. For instance, directly investing in the Indian securities markets as an FII, has significant cost and time implications for the foreign investor. Apart from seeking FII registration, he is required to establish a domestic broker relationship, a custodian bank relationship, deal in foreign exchange and bear exchange rate fluctuation risk, pay domestic taxes and/or filing tax return, obtain or maintain an investment identity, etc. These investors would rather look for derivatives alternatives to gain a cost-effective exposure to the relevant market.
3. Besides reducing transactions costs, PNs also provide customised tools to manage risk, lower financing costs and enhance portfolio yields. For instance, PNs can also be designed for longer maturities than are generally available for exchange-traded derivative.
4. PNs also offer an important *hedging tool* to a foreign investor already registered as an FII. For example, an FII may wish to obtain 'long' exposure to a particular Indian security. The FII can hedge the downside exposure to the listed security, already purchased by purchasing a 'cash settled put option'. Although the Indian exchanges offer options contract, these contracts have a maximum life period of three months, beyond which the FII shall have to rollover its positions, i.e., purchase a fresh option contract. Alternatively, it can avail a PN which can be customised to cater to its hedging requirements.
5. Potential investors who would like to take direct Indian exposure in future, may make initial investments through the PN route so as to get a flavour of future anticipated returns.
6. Further, trading in ODI/PNs gives an opportunity to offshore entities to have a commission based business model. This route provides ease to subscribers as it bypasses the direct route which may be resource heavy for them.

7. And *lastly,* it was a highly 'safe and lucrative route' to invest the 'unaccounted', 'even illegal' money into the Indian security market for huge profits (during the booming period). Experts even imagined that it may be allowing the 'black money' of India (stashed away from India through 'hawala' kind of illegal channels and deposited in the tax havens of the world in 'Swiss Bank' kind of financial institutions) to get invested back in the market. Again, 'terrorist organisations' might have been using this route, too.

PNs are *thus* issued, to provide access to a set of foreign investors who intend to reduce their overall costs and the time involved in making investments in India. In other words, the attraction of investing in PNs is primarily one of efficiency (from an infrastructure and time perspective) for which they are willing to forego certain benefits of directly holding the local securities (for example, title and voting rights), whilst also assuming other risks.

Regulation of PNs

PNs are market instruments that are created and traded overseas. Hence, Indian regulators cannot ban the issue of PNs. However, they can be regulated, as SEBI does—when a PN is traded on an overseas exchange, the regulator in that jurisdiction would be the authority to regulate that trade. PNs have been used by FIIs, since FIIs were permitted to invest in the securities market (1994)—they were not specifically dealt with under the regulations until 2003. According to the *SEBI Regulation, 2004* (and further amended in 2008) with the *objective* of tightening regulations in this regard:

1. **PNs can be issued only to those entities which are regulated by the relevant regulatory authority in countries of their incorporation and are subject to compliance of 'know your client' (KYC) norms.**
2. **Down-stream issuance or transfer of the instruments can also be made only to a regulated entity.**
3. **Further, the FIIs who issue PNs against underlying Indian securities are required to *report* the issued and outstanding PNs to SEBI in a prescribed format.**
4. **In addition, SEBI can call for any information from FIIs concerning off-shore derivative instruments (ODIs) issued by it.**
5. **In order to monitor the investment through these instruments, SEBI on *31 October, 2001*, advised FIIs to submit information regarding issuance of derivative instruments by them, on a monthly basis. These reports require the communication of details such as name and constitution of the subscribers to PNs, their location, nature of Indian underlying securities, etc.**
6. **FIIs cannot issue PNs to non-resident Indians (NRIs) and those issuing PNs are required to give an undertaking to the effect.**
7. **SEBI has also mandated that QFIs (qualified foreign investors), the recently allowed foreign investor class, shall not issue PNs.**

SEBI in consultation with the government had decided in *October 2007*, to place certain restrictions on the issue of PNs by FIIs and their sub-accounts. This decision was taken with a view to moderate the surge in foreign capital inflows into the country and to address the 'know-your-client' concerns for PN holders. However, it was found that such restrictions were ineffective. Therefore, SEBI in October 2008 reviewed its earlier decision and decided to remove these restrictions in the light of the above factors. Rather, more attention is given to effective disclosures. As per a SEBI decision of October 2013, the Category III FIIs are not allowed to issue PNs.

The Concerns Related to PNs

Being derivative instruments and freely tradable, PNs can be easily transferred, creating multiple layers, thereby obfuscating the real beneficial owner. It is in this respect that concerns about the *identity of ultimate beneficial* owner and the source of funds arises.

For the reason that such instruments are issued outside of India, these transactions are outside the purview of SEBI's surveillance and it is the FII which acts as mini-exchange overseas. The actual transactions in the underlying securities are executed by the FIIs only at its discretion, as and when necessary and there is no one-to-one correspondence between transactions in the underlying instruments and issuance of PNs.

The ex-post reporting requirement enjoined upon the FII in respect of PNs on a monthly basis effectively keeps the transactions in PNs out of the real time market surveillance mechanism and beyond the enforceability jurisdiction of SEBI.

There are also concerns that some of the money coming into the market via PNs could be the *'unaccounted wealth'* camouflaged under the guise of FII investment. However, this has not been proved so far. SEBI has indeed been successful in taking action against the FIIs who were non-compliant and those who had misreported offshore derivatives [as happened when SEBI took actions against two FIIs—*Barclays* in December 2009 and *Societe Generale* in January 2010]

At present, PNs are issued by large financial sector conglomerates which not only have strong presence in the global investment banking arena but also have asset management arms which invest across a number of securities markets globally. These entities are originally incorporated in well-regulated and developed jurisdictions like the US, UK, etc. Further, these entities also possess the financial wherewithal to issue PNs, complemented by skilled personnel who are adept at risk management and financial engineering activities.

International Situation

PN like products are not necessarily used to invest in restricted markets, but also reported to be available in the open developed/advanced economies like Japan, Hong Kong, Singapore, Australia, the USA and UK. In response to market manipulation concerns, in December 1999, *Taiwan Securities and Futures Commission* had amended its FII regulations to require periodic disclosure by FIIs of all offshore derivative activities linked to local shares, but this requirement was subsequently removed in June 2000 (as the Ashok Lahiri Committee Report says). *China*'s *Securities Regulatory Commission* requires entities to file reports related to these products with minimal 'reporting requirements that emphasise only on the quota utilised by them'. *Other Asian countries* like Hong Kong, Singapore and Japan have reportedly 'no restrictions' or requirements on PNs. Malaysia, Indonesia and Philippines which are restricted markets though, are having no reporting requirements in this regard.

Hedge Fund

This term has come up from another term ***hedging,*** a process by which businesses insulate themselves from the risk of price changes.[14] Hedge funds are the lot of investible (free floating capital) capital which move very swiftly towards the more profitable sectors of an economy.

At present, such funds easily move from the stock market of one economy to the other—away from the low profit fetching to high profit fetching ones. As stock markets fall and rise such funds change markets accordingly. By nature they are temporary. The period for which they continue

14. P.A. Samuelson and W.D. Norhdaus, ***Economics*** (New Delhi: Tata McGraw Hill, 2007), p. 207.

flowing into an economy there is naturally a boom time. But when they quit for a more attractive economy, the same economy might not be able to manage the accelerated foreign currency outflow and there are chances of imminent foreign currency crisis. This has been in news for the last two years in India where stock market has been in boom, riding on the FIIs inflow via Participatory Notes (PNs).

ECB Policy

A prospective borrower can access external commercial borrowings (ECBs) under two routes, namely the 'automatic route' and the 'approval route'. ECBs not covered under the automatic route are considered on case-by-case basis by the RBI under the approval route. The High Level Committee on ECB took a number of decisions in *September 2011* to expand the scope of ECBs which include:

1. High networth individuals (HNIs) who fulfil the criteria prescribed by SEBI can invest in IDFs.
2. IFCs have been included as eligible issuers for FII investment in the corporate bonds long-term infra category.
3. ECB would be permitted for refinancing of rupee loans of infrastructure projects on the condition that at least 25 per cent of such ECBs shall be used for repayment of the said rupee loan and 75 per cent invested in new projects in the infrastructure sector (but only under the approval route).
4. Refinancing of buyer's/supplier's credit through ECBs for the purchase of capital goods by companies in the infrastructure sector was approved. This would also be permitted only under the approval route.
5. ECBs for interest during construction (IDC) that accumulates on a loan during the project execution phase for companies in the infrastructure sector would be permitted. This would be subject to the condition that the IDC is capitalised and is part of the project cost.
6. Renminbi (RMB)—the Chinese currency —was approved as an ***acceptable currency*** for raising ECBs subject to/limit of US $ 1 billion within the existing ECB ceiling (allowed only through the approval route).
7. The existing ***ECB limits*** under the automatic route were enhanced from US $ 500 million to US$ 750 million for eligible corporates. For borrowers in the *services sector*, the limit has been enhanced from US$ 100 million to US$ 200 million and for *NGOs* engaged in *micro-finance* activities from the existing US$ 5 million to US$ 10 million.

Till **April 2020,** the norms for ECB were further simplified and streamlined by the government—major steps taken in this regard were as given below:

1. Enhancing the limit for refinancing rupee loans through ECB from 25 per cent to 40 per cent for Indian companies in the power sector;
2. Allowing ECB for capital expenditure on the maintenance and operation of toll systems for roads and highways so long as they are a part of the original project subject to certain conditions, and also for low cost housing projects;
3. Reducing the withholding tax from 20 per cent to 5 per cent for a period of three years (July 2012–June 2015) on interest payments on ECBs;
4. Introducing a new ECB scheme of US $10 billion for companies in the manufacturing and infrastructure sectors;
5. Permitting the Small Industries Development Bank (SIDBI) as an

eligible borrower for accessing ECB for on-lending to the micro, small and medium enterprises (MSMEs); and

6. Permitting the National Housing Bank (NHB)/Housing Finance Companies to avail themselves of ECBs for financing prospective owners of low cost/ affordable housing units.

7. In *December 2015*, the RBI announced a *new ECB framework* which was more attuned to the current economic and business environment—from regulatory perspective, now, the ECBs will have three main clear-cut categories—
   (i) Medium-term foreign currency-denominated ECB;
   (ii) Long-term foreign currency-denominated ECB (with minimum average maturity of 10 years); and
   (iii) Indian rupee-denominated ECB.

   The new lenders comprise overseas regulated financial institutions, sovereign wealth funds, pension funds, insurance companies, etc. and has an exhaustive list of permissible end-users with only a small negative list for long-term foreign currency-denominated ECB and INR-denominated ECB.

8. In order to facilitate rupee-denominated borrowing from overseas, the government decided *(December 2015)* to put in place a framework for issuance of rupee-denominated overseas bonds (such bonds have got a popular tag of the *masala bonds*).

These bonds will have minimum maturity of 5 years. These bonds can not be issued for real estate and capital markets sectors. Withholding tax of 5 per cent will be applicable on interest income from these bonds, but the capital gains arising in case of appreciation of the rupee will be exempted from tax.

CREDIT DEFAU LT SWAP (CDS)

CDS is in operation in India since October 2011 – launched in only corporate bonds. The eligible participants are commercial banks, primary dealers, NBFCs, insurance companies and mutual funds.

CDS is a credit derivative transaction in which two parties enter into an agreement, whereby one party (called as the 'protection buyer') pays the other party (called as the 'protection seller') periodic payments for the specified life of the agreement. The protection seller makes no payment unless a credit event relating to a pre-determined reference asset occurs. If such an event occurs, it triggers the Protection Seller's settlement obligation, which can be either cash or physical (India follows physical settlement). It means, ***CDS is a credit derivative that can be used to transfer credit risk from the investor exposed to the risk*** (called protection buyer) ***to an investor willing to take risk*** (called protection seller).

It operates like an insurance policy. In an insurance policy, the insurance firm pays the loss amount to the insured party. Similarly, the buyer of the CDS—the bank or institution that has invested in a corporate bond issue—seeks to mitigate the losses it may suffer on account of a default by the bond issuer. Credit default swaps allow one party to 'buy' protection from another party for losses that might be incurred as a result of default by a specified reference instrument (a bond issue in India). The 'buyer' of protection pays a premium to the seller, and the 'seller' of protection agrees to compensate the buyer for losses incurred upon the occurrence of any one of the several specified 'credit events'. *Thus CDS offers the buyer a chance to transfer the credit risk of financial assets to the seller without actually transferring ownership of the assets themselves.*

Let us try to understand it by an example. Suppose Punjab National Bank (PNB) invests in ₹150 crore bond issued by TISCO. If PNB wishes to *hedge* losses that may arise from a default of TISCO, then PNB may buy a credit default swap from a financial institute, suppose, Templeton. PNB will pay fixed periodic payments to Templeton, in exchange for default protection (just like premium of an insurance policy).

CDS can be *used for different purposes* in a financial system, viz.,

1. Protection buyers can use it to hedge their credit exposure while protection sellers can use it to participate in credit markets, without actually owning assets.
2. The protection buyer can transfer credit risk on an entity without transferring the under lying instrument, reap regular benefit in terms of lower capital charge, seek reduction of specific concentrations in credit portfolio and go short on credit risk.
3. The protection seller will be able to diversify his portfolio, create exposure to a particular credit, have access to an asset which may not otherwise be available, and increase the yield on his portfolio.
4. Banks can use it to transfer risk to other risk takers, create capital for more lending.
5. Distribute risk widely throughout the system and prevent concentrations of risk.

Some analysts have serious **apprehensions** about CDS. *George Akerlof*, Nobel prize-winning economist, in 1993, predicted that the next meltdown will be caused by CDS. In 2003, investment legend *Warren Buffet* called them as 'weapons of mass destruction'. The former US Federal Reserve Chairman *Alan Greenspan*, who betted big on CDS said after the 'sub prime' crisis that 'CDS are dangerous'. A leading US weekly the *Newsweek* described CDS, 'the monster that ate Wall Street'. Many Indian experts had the opinion that 'CDS will not stabilise the economy rather could lead to destabilisation'.

CDS contract are dangerous because they can be manipulated for mischief. It's all about the insurable interest which is never there as it is used for *speculation*. A derivative that amounts to an insurance contract with no insurable interest is bad. But do the speculators have insurable interest? No they don't have any. The US 'sub prime' crisis was a fallout of such CDS contracts—one defaulting and another claiming the 'protection' finally resulting into the defaulter of the insuring company—overnight the biggest US insurance giant, AIG went bankrupt. So happened with many US banks also.

The most damaging aspect of CDS is that the credit risk of one country/region gets exported to another country/region very smoothly and silently. Thus, there is a serious chance of 'contagion effect' suppose there are defaulters there, the thing which happened during the US 'sub prime' crisis.

SECURITISATION

This is the process of issuing 'marketable securities' backed by a pool of existing assets such as auto or home loans. After an asset is converted into a marketable security, it is sold to an investor who then receives interest and principal out of the cash flow generated from servicing of the loan. Financial institutions such as NBFCs and microfinance companies convert their loans into marketable securities and sell them to investors. This helps them get liquid cash out of assets that otherwise would be stuck on their balance sheets.

Global experience shows that if the value of the underlying asset falls then securitised assets lose value as it had happened during the US 'sub-prime crisis'—home loans against which securitised assets were sold to insurance companies and banks lost value, which in turn resulted in a crisis. To prevent such crises, the RBI has taken some precautionary steps in this regard. It has asked companies to hold securities for a certain minimum period:

1. While NBFCs need to keep assets for six months, a minimum retention requirement of 5-10 per cent to ensure that they have a continuing stake in the performance of securitised assets.
2. Micro Finance Institutions (MFIs) need to hold them for three months.

Since it was allowed in India by the RBI, it has been in news – whether the 'securitisations trusts' will need to pay tax on it. Meanwhile, the *Government in 2015* cleared the air on the issue. There should not be any additional income-tax if the income distributed by the trust is received by a person who is exempted from tax. This is expected to bring back mutual funds into the securitisation market.

CORPORATE BOND IN INDIA

Economic vibrancy coupled with sophisticated state–of–the–art financial infrastructure has contributed to rapid growth in the equity market in India. In terms of market features and depth, the Indian equity market ranks among the best in the world. In parallel, the government securities market has also evolved over the years and expanded, given the increasing borrowing requirements of the government. In contrast, the corporate bond market has languished both in terms of market participation and structure. NBCs are the main issuers and very small amounts of finance are raised by companies directly. The ***Economic Survey 2010-11,*** cites many reasons for the less-developed bond market in India:

1. Predominance of banks loans;
2. FII's participation is limited;
3. Pensions and insurance companies and household are limited participants because of lack of investor confidence; and
4. Crowding out by government bonds.

The *Economic Survey 2011-12* concluded[15] that there is now ample empirical research to corroborate Schumpeter's conjecture that financial development facilitates real economic growth. The depth of the financial markets and availability of diverse products should, therefore, not be treated as mere adornment, but as critical ingredients of inclusive growth.

Banks in India accounted for 14.4 per cent of the financing of large firms in 2000-01, which rose further to 17.8 per cent in 2010-11. The *bond market*, on the other hand, has been miniscule in comparison. The thinness of the bond market has been somewhat compensated by foreign borrowing done by Indians, which rose sharply over the last decade. Further, India is characterised by a disproportionate amount of secured borrowing. The small size of unsecured borrowing may, at first sight, not seem to be a matter of concern, but it could be a reflection of the weakness of contract enforcement and lack of adequate information. If contracts were quickly enforced and lenders had information on borrowers, they would be more willing to give unsecured loans. This would give

15. Ministry of Finance, Economic Survey 2011-12 (New Delhi: Government of India, 2012), 34; quotes many contemporary references to bring the point home.

(a) R. Rajan, and L. Zingales, 'Financial Dependence and Growth,' *American Economic Review*, Vol. 88, 1998; (b) S. Banerji, K. Gangopadhyay, I. Patnaik, and A, Shah, 'New Thinking on Corporate Debt in India', mimeo.; (c) C. K. G. Nair, 2012; 'Financial Sector Reforms: Refining the Architecture,' in R. Malhotra (ed.), *A Critical Decade: Policies for India's Development,* (New Delhi: Oxford University Press, 2012) (d) T. A. Bhavani, and N. R. Bhanumurthy, *Financial Access in Post-Reform India*; (e) P. Bolton, and X. Freixas, 'How can Emerging Market Economies Benefit from a Corporate Bond Market?', in E. Borzenstein, K. Cowan, B. Eichengreen, and U. Panizza (eds), *Bond Markets in Latin America*, (Massachusetts: MIT Press, 2008).

a nimbleness to the financial markets which they presently lack.

There are ***many reasons*** why bond markets are important for an emerging economy. Prominent among these is the fact that they lead to more efficient entrepreneurship and greater value creation. When an entrepreneur takes a loan or issues bonds, all additional profit over and above the pre-fixed repayment amount accrues to the entrepreneur. So he or she is better incentivised to take sharper decisions. By having a weak bond market, we may be foregoing this efficiency. And further, this efficiency gap may well mean that there is less lending and hence less investment and entrepreneurship in the economy than is feasible. Further, as India tries to garner 500 billion dollars from the private sector in the Twelfth Plan for investment in the infrastructure sector, having an active bond market would be a valuable avenue for raising money.

There can be many reasons why, despite these advantages, the bond market has not developed adequately. One reason has to do with what economists call 'multiple equilibria'. Consider a situation where the bond market is small. If someone buys bonds and later wishes to sell these off, he anticipates difficulty. Since the bond market is not active, he may not easily be able to sell the bonds and thus he will hold simply because he cannot find a buyer. Hence, this may lead to discourage someone from buying the bonds in the first place. If everybody reasons like this, the bond market remains thin. Hence, the need is for a push that nudges the market to another equilibrium, where people readily buy bonds because they know that they can easily sell these off and this becomes a self-fulfilling prophesy and sustains the large bond market.

There is effort currently on to try to boost India's debt and bond markets, and success in this can give another fillip to growth. With the intervention of the ***Patil Committee (2005)*** recommendations, the corporate bond market is slowly evolving. With bank finance drying up for long term infrastructure projects, in view of asset liability problems faced by the banking system, the need for further development of a deep and vibrant corporate bond market can hardly be overemphasised. Some major initiatives for further development of corporate bond markets, taken by the Government in recent times are as given below:

1. Banks allowed to take limited membership in SEBI-approved stock exchanges for the purpose of undertaking proprietary transactions in the corporate bond markets.
2. To enhance liquidity in the corporate bond markets, the IRDA has permitted insurance companies to participate in the repo market. The IRDA has also permitted insurance companies to become users of *'credit default swap'* (CDS).
3. The minimum **haircut**[16] (i.e., the difference between prices at which a market maker can buy and sell a security) requirement in corporate debt repo have been reduced from the existing 10 per cent; 12 per cent; 15 per cent to 7.5 per cent; 8.5 per cent; 10 per cent for AAA/ AA+/AA-rated corporate bonds.
4. MFs have been permitted to participate in CDS in corporate debt securities, as users.
5. Revised guidelines on CDS for corporate bonds by the RBI provide that

16. ***Haircut*** is the difference between prices at which a *market maker* can buy and sell a security. The term comes from the fact that market makers can trade at such a *thin spread*. It also means that the percentage by which an asset's market value is reduced for the purpose of calculating capital requirement, margin and collateral. When they are used as collateral, securities will generally be devalued since a cushion is required by the lending parties in case the market value falls.

in addition to listed corporate bonds, CDS shall also be permitted on *unlisted* but rated corporate bonds even for issues other than infrastructure companies.

6. Users shall be allowed to **unwind**[17] their CDS-bought position with the original protection seller at a mutually agreeable or FIMMDA (Fixed Income Money Market and Derivatives Association of India) price. If no agreement is reached, then unwinding has to be done with the original protection seller at FIMMDA price.
7. CDS shall be permitted on securities with original maturity up to *one year* like CPs, certificates of deposit, and non-convertible debentures with original maturity less than one year.

During 2020-21, the RBI took a number of measures to strengthen the corporate bond market in India. It accepted many of the recommendations of the *Khan Committee* (August 2016) to boost investor participation and market liquidity in the corporate bond market. The new measures as announced by the RBI include:

1. Commercial banks permitted to issue rupee-denominated bonds overseas *(masala bonds)* for their capital requirements and for financing infrastructure and affordable housing.
2. Brokers registered with the Securities and Exchange Board of India (SEBI) and authorised as market makers in corporate bond market permitted to undertake repo/reverse repo contracts in corporate debt securities. This move will make corporate bonds *fungible* and thus boost turnover in the secondary market.
3. Banks allowed to increase the partial credit enhancement they provide for corporate bonds to 50 per cent from 20 per cent. This move will help lower-rated corporates to access the bond market.
4. Permitting primary dealers to act as *market makers* for government bonds, to give further boost to government securities by making them more accessible to retail investors.
5. To ease access to the foreign exchange market for hedging in 'over the counter' (OTC) and exchange-traded currency derivatives, the entities exposed to exchange rate risk allowed to undertake hedge transactions with simplified procedures, up to a limit of US$30 million at any given time.
6. Pension and provident fund together with insurance companies have been allowed to invest in the corporate bonds.
7. Corporate bonds rated 'BBB' or equivalent declared as investment grade (as initiated by the *Union Budget 2018–19)*—till now only 'AA' rated corporate bonds were entertained as investment grade.
8. Introduction of an electronic platform for repos operation in corporate bonds.
9. Inclusion of them in the RBI liquidity adjustment facility (LAF).
10. FIIs allowed to invest in the corporate bonds through stock exchanges and primary issuance—overall ceiling of US$ 51 billion (with US$ 25 billion ceiling for G-Secs).

17. ***Unwind*** is used to close out a position that has offsetting investments or the correction of an error. Unwinds occur when, for example, a broker mistakenly sells part of a position when an investor wanted to add to it. The broker would have to unwind the transaction by selling the erroneously purchased stock and buying the proper stock. One type of investing that features unwind trading is *arbitrage investing (as happens in the CDS)*. If, for the sake of illustration, an investor takes a long position in stocks, while at the same time selling puts on the same issue, he will need to unwind those trades at some point. Of course, this entails covering the options and selling the underlying stock. A similar process would be followed by a broker attempting to correct a buying or selling error.

Presently, corporate bonds meet around 31 per cent of the long-term funds of the country's corporate sector. The corporate bond market has been expanding with faster pace as banks have been unwilling to lend to the corporates for the last 5-6 years. As per the latest available data (of the SEBI), the outstanding value of domestic corporate bonds in the country was ₹25.6 lakh crore by September 2020 that was around 16 per cent of the GDP (against 160 per cent of GDP in case of the USA).

As India aspires to a US$ 5 trillion economy by 2024-25, it needs to scale up the corporate bond market so that needful amount of long-term funds could be mobilised by the corporate sector— they offer an avenue for long-term funding, where banks generally prefer short-term lending. As per the *Union Budget 2021-22*, the government is to form a permanent institution that will buy and sell corporate bonds in the country. This step is likely to stimulate the shallow secondary market, which usually turns dry in times of crisis.

INFLATION-INDEXED BONDS

To protect the returns of investors from the vagaries of inflation, the Reserve Bank of India plans to introduce inflation-indexed bonds (IIBs)—it was proposed by the *Union Budget 2013-14*. The government hopes this will help increase *financial savings instead of buying gold*. In the recent years, the rate of return on debt investments has often been below inflation, which effectively means that inflation was eroding savings. Inflation indexed bonds provide returns that are always in excess of inflation, ensuring that price rise does not erode the value of savings.

In 2013-14, RBI launched two such bonds —the first one in June 2013 linked with the WPI which had a very weak retail response and second one in *December 2013* linked with CPI. The latter one is called as **Inflation Indexed National Savings Securities-Cumulative (IINSS-C)** with a 10 years tenure. These are internationally known as *inflation-linked securities* or simply *linkers*. Interest rate on these securities would be linked to final combined consumer price index [CPI (Base: 2010=100)]. Interest rate would comprise two parts: fixed rate (1.5 per cent) and inflation rate, based on three-month lag to CPI—thus, if a bond is being valued in December, the reference rate will be CPI of September. The new offering should attract higher attention from savers, especially due to its link to CPI instead of wholesale price index (WPI), which is a less accurate gauge of inflation. CPI is considered a more accurate gauge of the impact of inflation on consumers because it takes into account increases in the cost of education, food, transportation, housing and medical care; in WPI, the emphasis is on measuring the prices of traded goods and services.

It was in 1997 that the IIBs were issued for the first time in India—named as the *Capital Indexed Bonds (CIBs)*. But there remains a difference between these two bonds. While the CIBs provided inflation protection only to principals the new product IIBs provides inflation protection to both the components—principal and interest payments.

GOLD EXCHANGE TRADED FUNDS

Gold Exchange Traded Funds (ETFs) are *open-ended mutual fund schemes* that closely track the price of physical gold. Each unit represents *one gram* of gold having 0.995 purity, and the ETF is listed on stock exchanges. The net asset value of each unit is calculated based on the prices of physical gold prevailing on that day and is designed to provide returns that would closely track the returns from physical gold.

e-Gold

e-Gold is another purchase option, involving investments in units traded on the National Spot

Exchange Limited (NSEL). Here, the investor is required to have a demat account with an affiliate of NSEL. e-Gold's brokerage and transaction charges are lower than *gold ETFs* as there are no fund management charges. One can take delivery of gold or sell it in the exchange.

But there is also a *negative point* here from the tax angle—under e-Gold, one has to hold the yellow metal for 36 months to enjoy *long-term capital gain* benefits, and this is taxed at 20 per cent. For ETFs (Exchange Traded Funds) and gold funds, the holding period to be classified as long-term is only one year. After a year, ETF and gold funds will suffer 10 per cent tax without indexation and 20 per cent after indexation. For a small investor, gold ETF would appear to be the best option, as it meets his needs without difficulties in terms of creating a separate demat account, tax implications and wealth tax.

CPSE ETF

The Central Public Sector Enterprises Exchange Traded Fund (CPSE ETF) comprising the shares of 10 blue chip PSUs was listed on the BSE and NSE platforms on 4 April, 2014. The Government of India expected to raise a corpus of ₹3,000 crore through the fund while it got over-subscribed to the tune of ₹4,300 crores.

This scheme is conceived by the Government of India as a means to *disinvest* a part of its holding in Public Sector Units (PSUs) and would be managed by ***Goldman Sachs Asset Management (India) Pvt. Ltd***., a *mutual fund company* that specialises in managing exchange traded funds.

ETF is a security that tracks an index, a commodity or a basket of assets such as an index fund, but trades like a stock on an exchange – the CPSE ETF tracks the CPSE Index (of 10 PSUs included in the ETF). CPSE Index has been constructed by including companies that meet the following criteria:

1. Owned 55 per cent or more by the GoI and listed on the NSE;
2. Large PSUs (those having more than ₹1,000 crores as average free float market capitalisation for six months period ending June 2013); and
3. With a consistent dividend payment record (at least 4 per cent for 7 years immediately prior to or 7 out of 8/9 years immediately prior to June 2013).

The ten blue-chip PSUs which meet the above criteria and their weightages are: ONGC (26.72 per cent); GAIL (India) (18.48 per cent); Coal India (17.75 per cent); REC (7.16 per cent); Oil India (7.04 per cent); IOC (6.82 per cent); Power Finance Corp. (6.49 per cent); Container Corp. (6.40 per cent); Bharat Electronics (2 per cent) and Engineers India Ltd. (1.13 per cent).

CPSE ETF will invest the corpus in the above-given companies as per the given weightage. Hence, subject to the tracking error and expenses, CPSE ETF's returns will closely correspond to the CPSE Index returns.

Meanwhile, the Government has announced **(Union Budget 2017-18)** to launch a new ETF with diversified CPSE stocks and other Government holdings in the fiscal 2017-18.

PENSION SECTOR REFORMS

Pension has been the integral part of government jobs in India. Pension serves two important socio-economic objectives:

1. It facilitates the flow of long-term savings for development, i.e., *nation-building*; and
2. Also helps establish a credible and sustainable *social security system* in the country.

The New Pension Scheme, now renamed as National Pension System (NPS) was introduced by the Government on December 22, 2003 and it was made mandatory for Central Government employees (except armed forces) who join service w.e.f. January 1, 2004. The Scheme was extended to the State Governments and as of now 28 State Governments have notified NPS for their employees. The Scheme was extended to all citizens of the country on voluntary basis from May 2009. Although, the NPS is perhaps one of the cheapest financial products available in the country, in order to make it affordable for the economically disadvantaged, the government in September 2010 introduced a lower cost version, known as ***Swavalamban Scheme,*** which enables groups of people to join the NPS at a substantially reduced cost. As per existing scheme under NPS, Swavalamban could be availed either in 'unorganised sector' or in *'NPS Lite'.* NPS Lite is a model specifically designed to bring NPS within easy reach of the economically disadvantaged sections of the society—it is extremely affordable and viable due to its optimised functionalities, available at reduced charges. Under the Swavalamban scheme, the government provides subsidy to each NPS account holder and the scheme has been extended until 2016-17.

A customised version of the core NPS model, known as the *NPS Corporate Sector Model* was introduced from December 2011 to enable 'organised-sector' entities to move their existing and prospective employees to the NPS under its Corporate Model. All pubic sector banks have been asked to provide a link on their website to enable individual subscribers to open online NPS accounts.

As per the *Economic Survey 2012-13,* the pension reforms in India have generated widespread interest internationally but before universal inclusion of poorer sections of Indian society into the pension network is a reality, the economy needs to solve the following *major challenges* :

1. Lower levels of financial literacy, particularly among workers in the unorganised sector;
2. Non-availability of even moderate surplus;
3. Lukewarm response so far from most of the state/UT governments to a co-contributory Swavalamban Scheme; and
4. Lack of awareness, on the supply side, about the NPS and of access points for people to open their accounts individually have been major inhibiting factors.

During 2015-16, the government launched a new pension scheme, the ***APY (Atal Pension Yojana).*** The scheme provides a defined pension, depending on the contribution and its period. The subscribers to it will receive a minimum pension of ₹1000, 2000, 3000, 4000 or 5000 per month, from the age of 60 years, depending on their contributions, which are themselves based on the age of joining the scheme.

The scheme is open to all bank account holders. The central government co-contributes 50 per cent of the total contribution subject to a maximum of ₹1,000 per annum, to each eligible subscriber's account, for a period of five years (from 2015-16 to 2019-20), who joined the APY between 1 June 2015 and 31 March 2016 and who is not a member of any statutory social security scheme and is not an income tax payer.

AUM of NPS The asset under management (AUM) under NPS increased to ₹4.94 lakh crore by September 2020, as compared to ₹3.71 lakh crore the previous year— showing a year-on-year growth of *33.3* per cent. Maximum growth was registered by All-Citizen model (52.3 per cent) followed by Atal Pension Yojana (46.1 per cent), Corporate Sector (34.8 per cent) and State Government Sector (30.7 per cent).

Changes in NPS Some major steps[18] taken by the Government in 2019-20 related to the NPS are as given below:

1. **Choice of Fund:** Similar to subscribers of the private sector, government subscribers also allowed to choose any pension funds including private sector funds (can be changed once in a year).

2. **Choice of Investment Pattern:** Government employees may exercise one of the following choices of Investment Pattern twice in a financial year—

   (i) For both existing and new subscribers, the fund will be allocated among the three existing public sector fund managers under the guidelines of the PFRDA.

   (ii) Government employees who prefer a fixed return with minimum amount of risk have been given an option to invest 100 per cent of the funds in Government securities.

   (iii) Government employees who prefer higher returns shall be given the options of the following two Life Cycle based schemes—

   (a) Conservative Life Cycle Fund with maximum 25 per cent exposure to equity.

   (b) Moderate Life Cycle Fund with maximum exposure of 50 per cent to equity.

REGULATORY MEASURES AMIDST COVID-19

In view of the COVID-19 pandemic, the following regulatory measures were taken by the Pension Fund Regulatory & Development Authority of India:

- Extension for submission of various compliance by the Pension Funds and Custodian.
- Extension of time limit for submission of annual accounts and other annual submissions.

  The partial withdrawal from NPS has been allowed for treatment of COVID-19.
- Online on-boarding on NPS allowed through Aadhaar-based offline paperless KYC verification.
- Online registration of Atal Pension Yojana subscribers through Bank's own web-portal, without using net-banking for their savings bank customers allowed.

FINANCIAL STABILITY DEVELOPMENT COUNCIL (FSDC)

An apex level body, the FSDC, was set up by the GoI in December 2010. It was in line with the G-20 initiative which came in wake of the financial crises among the western economies triggered by the 2007-08 'sub-prime' crisis of the USA. The Council has the following *objectives:*

1. To strengthen and institutionalise the mechanism for maintaining financial stability,
2. To enhance inter-regulatory coordination, and
3. To promote financial-sector development.

The council is *chaired* by the Finance Minister and has *heads* of financial-sector regulatory authorities, the Finance Secretary and/or Secretary of the Department of Economic Affairs, Secretary of the Department of Financial Services, and the Chief Economic Adviser as members. Without prejudice to the autonomy of regulators, the Council ***monitors:***

---

18. **Economic Survey 2019-20,** Vol. 2, pp. 130-132, Ministry of Finance, GoI, N. Delhi.

1. macro-prudential supervision of the economy, including functioning of large financial conglomerates,
2. inter-regulatory coordination and financial-sector development issues, and
3. *financial literacy* and *financial inclusion.*

FINANCIAL SECTOR ASSESSMENT PROGRAMME (FSAP)

The *IMF Board* decided in September 2010, to include 25 *systemically* important economies, including India, under the Financial Stability Assessment Programme (FSAP) for members with systemically important financial sectors. The joint IMF-World Bank Financial Stability Assessment Programme (FSAP) was conducted for India in *January 2013* which assessed Indian financial system in relation to the highest international standards. The **assessment** recognises that the Indian financial system remained *largely stable* on account of a sound regulatory and supervisory regime. However, the assessment identifies *some gaps* in[19]—

1. International and domestic supervisory information sharing and co-operation;
2. Consolidated supervision of financial conglomerates; and
3. Some limits on the *de jure* independence of the regulators (RBI and IRDA).

Despite having reservations on few issues, overall the Indian authorities expect the FSAP exercise to play a *significant role* in shaping India's post-crisis initiatives to strengthen the regulatory and supervisory architecture based on the evolving international consensus as well as careful examination of their relevance in the India-specific context. As a member of the FSB[20], BCBS[21] and IMF, India is actively participating in post-crisis reforms of the international regulatory and supervisory framework under the aegis of

19. RBI, 16th January, 2013.

20. The **FSB** was established in April 2009 as the successor to the Financial Stability Forum (FSF). The FSF was founded in 1999 by the G-7 for enhancing cooperation among the various national and international supervisory bodies and international financial institutions so as to promote stability in the international financial system. In November 2008, the leaders of the G-20 countries called for a larger membership of the FSF. As announced in the G-20 Leaders Summit of *April 2009*, the expanded FSF was re-established as the *Financial Stability Board (FSB)* with a broadened mandate to promote financial stability. The FSB is chaired by *Mark Carney*, Governor of the Bank of Canada. Its secretariat is located in Basel, Switzerland, and hosted by the Bank for International Settlements.

Its ***objective*** is to coordinate at the international level the work of national financial authorities and international standard setting bodies and to develop and promote the implementation of effective regulatory, supervisory and other financial sector policies. [*Source*: Financial Stability Board Secretariat, Bank for International Settlements, Basel, Switzerland].

21. The **BCBS** (Basel Committee on Banking Supervision) provides a forum for regular cooperation on banking supervisory matters. The Committee's members, today, come from 27 nations including India. The present Chairman of the Committee is *Stefan Ingves*, Governor of Sveriges Riksbank. It is located at the Bank for International Settlements (BIS) in Basel, Switzerland.

Its ***objective*** is to enhance understanding of key supervisory issues and improve the quality of banking supervision worldwide. It seeks to do so by exchanging information on national supervisory issues, approaches and techniques, with a view to promoting common understanding. At times, the Committee uses this common understanding to develop guidelines and supervisory standards in areas where they are considered desirable. In this regard, the Committee is ***best known*** for its international standards on ***Capital Adequacy*** *(i.e. Basel I, Basel II and Basel III, by now)*; the ***Core Principles for Effective Banking Supervision***; and the ***Concordat*** on cross-border banking supervision.

The *Committee* encourages contacts and cooperation among its members and other banking supervisory authorities. It circulates to supervisors throughout the world both published and unpublished papers providing guidance on banking supervisory matters. Contacts have been further strengthened by an *International Conference of Banking Supervisors (ICBS)* which takes place every two years. [*Source*: BIS, Basel, Switzerland].

the **G-20**. India remains committed to adoption of international standards and best practices, in a phased manner and calibrated to local conditions, wherever necessary, as it is a country characterised by complex and diverse socio-political and economic conditions.

FINANCIAL ACTION TASK FORCE (FATF)

The FATF is an inter-governmental policy making body that has a ministerial mandate to establish international standards for combating *money laundering* and *terrorist financing. India joined the FATF as its 34th member in June 2010. At present, the FATF has 36 members comprising 34 countries and two organisations (European Union and Gulf Cooperation Council).*

REAL ESTATE & INFRASTRUCTURE INVESTMENT TRUSTS

The SEBI firmed up regulations that will govern Real Estate Investment Trusts (REITs), and the Infrastructure Investment Trusts (InvITs).[22] The long-pending proposal of 2008, the trusts have the **objective** of enabling the cash-strapped real estate and infrastructure developers to have easy access to funds. They create a new investment avenue for institutions and high net worth individuals, and eventually ordinary investors.

REITs

Major provisions announced by the SEBI for the REITs are as given below:

1. To be close-ended real estate investment schemes that will invest in property with the aim of providing returns to unit holders.
2. The returns will be derived mainly from rental income or capital gains from real estate.
3. Allowed to invest in commercial real estate assets, either directly or through special purpose vehicles (SPVs). In SPVs, a REIT must have a controlling interest of at least 50 per cent of the share capital and will have to hold at least 80 per cent of their assets directly in properties.
4. To raise funds only through an initial offering and units of REITs have to be mandatorily listed on a stock exchange, similar to initial public offering (IPO) and listing for equity shares.
5. Required to have assets worth at least ₹500 crore at the time of an initial offer and the minimum issue size has to be ₹250 crore. The minimum subscription size for units of a REIT on offer will be ₹2 lakh and at least 25 per cent of the units have to be offered to the public.
6. Will be able to raise money through follow-on offers, rights issues or qualified institutional placements and the trading lot for such units will be ₹1 lakh.

According to the norms, although a REIT may raise funds from any type of investors, resident or foreign, initially only wealthy individuals and institutions will be allowed to subscribe to REIT unit offers. The market regulator said a REIT may have up to three sponsors, with each holding at least 5 per cent and collectively holding at least 25 per cent for a period of at least three years from the date of listing. Subsequently, the sponsors' combined holding has to be at least 15 per cent throughout the life of the REIT.

Similar to the practice in the US, Australia, Singapore and other nations where REITs are common, SEBI has decided to allow these trusts to invest primarily in completed revenue-

22. Economic Survey 2007-08, pp. 229-234, Ministry of Finance, GoI, N. Delhi.

generating properties. To ensure that REITs generate continuous returns, SEBI said at least 80 per cent of the REIT's assets has to be invested in completed and revenue generating properties. And only up to 20 per cent of assets can be invested in properties that are being developed, mortgage-backed securities, debt of companies in the real estate sector, equity shares of listed companies that derive at least 75 per cent of their income from real estate, government securities, or money market instruments. No REIT can invest more than 10 per cent in properties that are under construction.

InvITs

SEBI also announced the launch of **InvITs** which are *somewhat similar* to REITs. However, an initial offer will not be mandatory for InvITs though listing will be mandatory for both publicly and privately placed InvITs. *Major provisions* are as given below:

1. It can invest in infrastructure projects, either directly or through an SPV (Special Purpose Vehicle). In case of Public-Private-Partnership (PPP) projects, such investments will be only through an SPV.
2. While listing, the collective holding of sponsors of an InvIT has to be at least 25 per cent for at least three years.
3. Required to have a holding worth at least ₹500 crore in the underlying assets, and the initial offer size of the InvIT has to be at least ₹250 crore.
4. Any InvIT, which looks to invest at least 80 per cent of its assets in completed and revenue generating infrastructure assets, has to raise funds only through a public issue of units, with a minimum 25 per cent public float and at least 20 investors.
5. The minimum subscription size and trading lot of such a listed InvIT has to be ₹10 lakh and ₹5 lakh, respectively. A publicly offered InvIT may invest the remaining 20 per cent in under-construction infrastructure projects and other permissible investments.

An InvIT that proposes to invest more than 10 per cent of its assets in under-construction infrastructure projects can raise funds only through private placement from qualified institutional buyers with a minimum investment and trading lot of ₹1 crore and from at least five investors, where single holding cannot be more than 25 per cent.

Recent Developments To promote the real estate and infrastructure trusts, a friendlier tax regime was put in place by the GoI through two successive *Union Budgets*, 2014-15 and 2015-16. However, the idea of the trusts could not get much momentum. Basically, due to subdued market conditions in the sectors attracting investors—new (greenfield) project or a trust—has remained difficult by now. Majority of the existing projects in the sectors are running into losses with weak balance sheets of their developers, unable to even service their bank loans.

To push the cause of the trusts, in 2019-20, the security market regulator, SEBI, permitted the Foreign Portfolio Investment (FPI) in the trusts. How much interest the FPIs will show in the trusts it will be known only in future, meanwhile, experts believe that real momentum in the sectors can be only expected once economy comes out of the spell of economic slowdown.

COVID-19 INTERVENTIONS

In the wake of the ongoing COVID-19 pandemic, the security market of India also got disrupted due to lockdown. To ease the economic hardship and face up the challenges the security market regulator (the SEBI), after discussing issues with all stakeholders, announced the following measures pertaining to raising of capital and corporate debt market aimed at fighting the challenge:

- Several relaxations announced – extension of date for filings to stock exchanges (like quarterly and annual financial results), corporate governance reports, shareholding pattern, among others.

- One-time relaxation in primary market fund raising norms to make it easier for companies to raise capital amid the COVID-19 pandemic.
- Rights issues are now considered successful if the minimum subscription received is 75 percent (in place of existing norm of 90 per cent).
- In case of fast track issues, the eligibility criteria of average market capitalisation of public shareholding of the issuer has been relaxed to ₹100 crore from the earlier ₹250 crore.
- The validity of observation letters (OLs) for initial public offerings (IPOs), rights issues and new fund offer (NFO) documents for mutual funds extended by 6 months.
- Relaxations given to market intermediaries such as stock brokers, depository participants and share transfer agents (RTAs).
- Deadlines for implementation of stewardship code for mutual funds, overhaul of regulations governing portfolio management services (PMS), mutual funds and alternative investment fund (AIFs) extended.

Earlier (by late May 2020), the SEBI had directed companies that have publicly traded securities, including shares and bonds, to disclose broad-ranging details about the financial fallout from the *coronavirus pandemic*. The regulator found that listed companies (that too a very small number of them) had only offered sketchy details related to shutdown of operations and updates about sanitation and safety measures at offices. Listed entities to ensure that all investors have access to timely, adequate and updated information – will now have to evaluate and disclose the impact of pandemic on their businesses, both qualitatively and quantitatively.

ESG INVESTMENT

In past few years world has seen the emergence of a new concept in stock markets— a new set of the environmental, social, and governance (ESG) criteria for the listed companies. These criteria precisely have the following meanings[23] embedded in them:

- Environmental criteria look into company's approach towards the nature (which may include aspects like energy use, pollution, waste disposal, natural resource conservation, treatment of animals, etc.).
- Social criteria examine company's relations with employees, suppliers, customers, privacy, data protection and the communities where it operates.
- Governance deals with company's leadership, executive pay, audits, internal controls, and rights of shareholders.

These value-laden criteria are being increasingly (especially, in western countries) screened by the socially conscious investors before making their investment decisions— these criteria help investors find companies with values that match their own. The ESG investing (which is also called *impact investing*) is being taken as sustainable and socially responsible investing which can leave impact not only on our surrounding but also on the pattern of our investments. Such investments in a sense make investors believe that they are able to avoid and discourage the companies whose practices signal risk factors (as seen in the cases—the 2010 oil spill of BP and 2015 emission scandal of Volkswagen)— share prices of both falling by over 10 per cent as investors' backlash.

23. Based on several documents of the SEBI, RBI and Ministry of Finance, GoI, N. Delhi, April 2021.

As business practices are getting more conscious of these criteria, investment firms are increasingly tracking their performance. In 2020, financial services companies such as *JPMorgan Chase, Wells Fargo,* and *Goldman Sachs* published their annual reports in which extensive review was given in this regard.

Case with India As per the stock market regulator, the SEBI, the focus on ESG further increased—in line with global trend, investors in India also did show increased interest in ESG investment during 2020-21. As a consequence of this, the regulator in April 2021, committed to announce relevant ESG guidelines soon.

SOCIAL STOCK EXCHANGE

Social Stock Exchange (SSE) allows the listing of social enterprises (non-profit and for-profit, both) on stock exchanges aimed at providing them additional channel to raise fund. Today, such exchanges are operating in several countries[24] like the UK, Canada, Singapore, S. Africa, Kenya and Brazil. In India, social enterprises[25] operate in several forms, which can be broadly classified into two categories:

1. *Non-Profit Organisations (NPOs)* which are usually structured as non-governmental organisations (Section 8 Companies, Trusts or Societies).
2. For-Profit Enterprises (FPEs) which operate as private limited companies, partnerships or sole proprietorships.

These enterprises depend mainly on philanthropic funds from governments, international donors or companies (chiefly through their corporate social responsibility) and a dearth of funding has always been felt. Given the sustainable development goals of the UNO, India has also been realising the need of inclusive and socially responsible development. In tandem, the corporate sector has begun to adopt a variety of measures to ensure that their activities are not causing harm to society or the environment. Investing has also shifted towards an Environmental Social Governance (ESG) framework.

In this backdrop, it was in the *Union Budget 2019-20* that the Government proposed to set up a social- stock exchange under the ambit of the SEBI for social enterprises so that they can raise capital as equity, debt or as units like a mutual fund. Accordingly, on the recommendations of a Working Group (under the Chairmanship of Ishaat Hussain), the SEBI announced (in June 2020) the guidelines (which was in the stage of public feedback by April 2021) for setting up of the SSE in the country. As per the SEBI, the exchange[26] can be housed within the existing stock exchanges (such as BSE and/or NSE), which will help it leverage the existing infrastructure and client relationships of the exchanges to onboard investors, donors, and social enterprises (for-profit and non-profit). The SSE will have two primary roles:

1. To effectively deploy the fundraising instruments and structures available under the regulatory guidelines towards social enterprises:
   (i) For FPEs: Equity and Social Venture Funds (SVFs).
   (ii) For NPOs: Zero coupon zero principal bonds, SVFs, Mutual Funds (MFs), various pay-for-

24. Though, in the USA we don't find any SSE as such, we find a similar platform called the *MissionMarkets* (MM) launched in 2010 which works on 'impact investing' (i.e., environmental, social, and governance criteria). But MM do not contain start-ups as social enterprises rather the companies which have incorporated social responsibility into their existing for-profit business models.

25. By **April 2021**, over 3.1 million non-profit organisations (NPOs) were operating in India which precisely means—more than double the number of schools and 250 times the number of government hospitals—one NPO for 400 Indians.

26. **Security and Exchange Board of India**, June 2020 and Union Budget 2019-20, Ministry of Finance, GoI, N. Delhi.

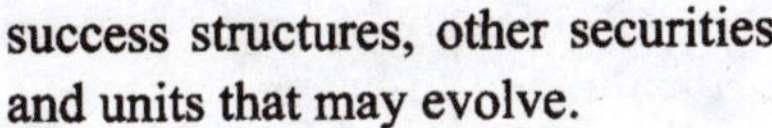

success structures, other securities and units that may evolve.

(iii) For Section 8 Companies: Equity and Debt.

2. To foster overall sector development by creating a capacity building unit which will be responsible for:

(i) Encouraging the setting up of a Self-Regulatory Organization (SRO) that will bring together existing Information Repositories (IRs), in the immediate term for extending requisite support to SSE.

(ii) Implementing the reporting standard for all social enterprises that benefit from the SSE.

(iii) Operating the *capacity building fund* for enhancing reporting capabilities by NPOs (particularly the smaller NPOs). Creating awareness and driving adoption of this fund among NPOs, philanthropists, and donors.

(iv) Actively raising awareness and promoting the fundraising instruments/structures available on the SSE among social enterprises and non-profit organisations.

Both these roles are equally important to ensure that the SSE makes a meaningful impact. In order to benefit from the SSE an NPO must commit to reporting in accordance with the minimum standard. In addition, an NPO may choose to register with an IR (Information Repositories) in order to further signal credibility and legitimacy to investors and funders. As per the working group, this report was the first important phase of a long journey and more will need to be done in subsequent years so that the market for such king of funding matures over the time.

Market and socialist have been strange bedfellows and until few decades back world used to consider them mutually exclusive affairs. But this dichotomy seems changing—a third dimension is on emergence which includes social business, impact investing (i.e., ESG) and now the social stock exchanges.

STOCK MARKET-ECONOMY DISCONNECT

Almost during the whole of 2020-21 a clear disconnect[27] was seen between the stock markets and the economy in the country. As per the SEBI, such a disconnect was never witnessed before. Typically, stock markets have been barometers of the economy and move in the direction the economy moves or at least it is expected to move. However, after the onset of the pandemic, several institutions, including the Financial Stability Board and the RBI, have raised concerns of an increasing disconnect of the financial markets with the real economy and a possible risk it may pose to systemic stability.

India has been seeing such unprecedented market movements like many global markets as measures were being taken to tackle the pandemic and its after effects. The sharp swings in the market from the *lows* of March 2020 to the *historic highs* in January 2021 have also increased volatility in the market. The fall, recovery and the overall market movement since March 2020 and till date have been significant and unprecedented. Not only this, the functioning of corporates as well as their fund-raising practices changed during the pandemic. Meanwhile, the jury is out and is busy in guessing game—the country is yet to get an official version of explanation for the phenomenon—jeopardising the already low reputation (due to failure of predicting the 2007-08 global financial crisis) of the economists again at global as well domestic level!

27. Based on the statements passed by the *SEBI, RBI,* other Government sources and media reporting, chiefly of *The Economist, The Wall Street Journal* and *Bloomberg.*

CHAPTER 15

EXTERNAL SECTOR IN INDIA

*No country in today's globalised world can be fully insulated from what happens in the global economy and India is no exception to the rule. As the country is increasingly integrated into the world, it cannot remain impervious to developments abroad. The unfolding of the Euro zone crisis and uncertainty surrounding the global economy have impacted the Indian economy causing drop in growth, higher current account deficit and declining capital inflows.**

In this Chapter...

- Definition
- Forex Reserves
- Forex Management and Impossible Trinity
- External Debt
- Fixed Currency Regime
- Floating Currency Regime
- Managed Exchange Rates
- Foreign Exchange Market
- Exchange Rate in India
- Major Terms
- Current Account
- Capital Account
- Balance of Payment (BoP)
- Convertibility
- IMF Conditions on India
- Special Economic Zone
- Foreign Investment
- COVID-19 and FDI Policy
- ECB Liberalised
- Trade Facilitation
- Export Promotion Schemes
- Trade Logistics
- India's Trade
- Current Trade Opportunity
- India as Pharmacy of The World
- Exchange Rate Monitoring
- BIPA & BIT
- RTAs by India
- The Quad
- Deglobalisation and India
- COVID-19 and Multilateralism
- Way Forward

* *As many documents of the WTO, World Bank and OECD have accepted many times.*

DEFIN ITION

All economic activities of an economy which take place in foreign currency fall in the external sector such as export, import, foreign investment, external debt, current account, capital account, balance of payment, etc. (*definition*)[1].

FOREX RESERVES

The total foreign currencies (of different countries) an economy possesses at a point of time is its 'foreign currency assets/reserves'.[2] The Forex Reserves (short for 'foreign exchange reserves') of an economy is its 'foreign currency assets' added with its *gold reserves, SDRs* (Special Drawing Rights) and *Reserve Tranche Position (RTP)* in the IMF.[3] In a sense, the Forex reserves is the upper limit upto which an economy can mobilise foreign currency if need be.

Major facts related to India's *forex reserves* and its management, as per the *Economic Survey 2020-21,* were as given below:

- Forex reserves reached an *all-time high* of US$ 586.1 billion (on 8th January 2021).
- Forex was able to cover about 8 months of country's imports.
- India was the 5th largest forex reserves holder in the world (after China, Japan, Switzerland and Russia).
- International financial liabilities of India was 210.7 per cent of forex reserves (down from 229.7 per cent in March 2020).

1. Based on J.E. Stiglitz and C.E. Walsh, ***Economics***, (New York: W.W. Norton and Company, 2006), pp. 757-58.
2. Based on P.A. Samuelson and W.D. Nordhaus, ***Economics***, (New Delhi: Tata McGraw Hill, 2005), p. 604.
3. Ibid., pp. 605–07.

FOREX MANAGEMENT AND IMPOSSIBLE TRINITY

The ***key*** behind the record forex reserves by the early 2021, was the large current account surplus (due to low imports rather than higher exports) supported by robust inflows of FDI as well as FPI— which led to large BoP surplus. The current account balance, in economic terms, is synonymous with the Savings-Investment balance. A current account surplus implies a higher level of national savings relative to investment. A rise in forex reserves also represents investments in bonds and securities of other countries (which implies that investments are being done outside India). A developing country like India needs to spend on domestic investments to spur its growth. However, this surplus gives adequate space for increased investment expenditures.

Faced with a large BoP surplus, the RBI is faced with two options— *firstly,* absorb the surplus (by buying it from the forex market) and accumulate more forex reserves or *secondly,* let the ₹ appreciate. With inflation largely attributed to supply-side disruptions and expected to stabilize, RBI chose to intervene in the forex market, accumulate reserves, which prevented one-sided appreciation of ₹ and supplemented expansionary monetary policy (i.e., reduction in the repo rate). However, RBI had to fine balance the headline inflation in a sustainable manner and yet stimulate growth.

As per the *Economic Survey 2020-21,* accumulation of forex reserves resulted in the concomitant release of ₹ in the system which helped the Government's higher borrowings as inflation remained lower. But once the headline inflation went above the policy band (of 4+/-2 per cent), RBI had to confront the classic conundrum of *impossible trinity*[4] (i.e., the Mundell-Fleming

4. For more on the concept of ***Impossible Trinity,*** see the section ***Trilemmas*** in **Chapter 18.**

trilemma) – maintain an open capital account, stable exchange rate, and still conduct independent monetary policy.

Robust export earning is considered the key to sustainable management of external sector and the Government is committed to boost exports via trade facilitation— by cutting down the transaction costs and time— and enhancing export competitiveness.

EXTERNAL DEBT

As India started managing its balance of payment in a more prudent way after the reform period, its external debt position has also improved in a big way.

As a standard practice, India's external debt statistics are released by the RBI with a lag of one quarter. As per the *Economic Survey 2020-21*, the latest details of India's external debt during 2020-21 (upto September 2020) were as give below:

- Total external debt was **US$ 556.2 billion** (0.4 per cent down from March 2020).
- The *largest* component of it, the ECBs (External Commercial Borrowings), was at US$ 207 billion (down by 5.8 per cent from March 2020).
- The *2nd largest* component of it, the stock of NRI deposits, was at US$ 137.3 billion (up by 5.1 per cent from March 2020).
- The *3rd largest* component of it, the trade credit (import-financing) was at US$ 99.4 billion (down by 2.0 per cent from march 2020).
- *Government debt* was at US$ 103.6 billion (up by around 2.5 per cent from March 2020).
- Ratio of *Government debt* to total debt was at 22.0 per cent (up from 21.2 per cent of March 2020).
- External debt as a *ratio to GDP* was at 21.6 per cent (up from 20.6 per cent in March 2020).
- Ratio of *forex reserves to total debt* was at 97.4 per cent (up from 85.2 per cent in March 2020)— boosted by the increase in forex reserves.
- Ratio of *short-term debt to forex reserves* was at 45.5 per cent (down from 49.4 per cent in March 2020)— due to sizeable increase in forex reserves.
- Ratio of *short-term debt* to total debt at 'original maturity' was at 18.5 (down from 19.1 per cent of March 2020) while at 'residual maturity' was at 44.6 per cent (up from 42.4 per cent of March 2020).
- Ratio of *concessional debt* to total debt was at 9.0 per cent (up from 8.8 per cent of March 2020).
- *Debt service ratio* was at 9.7 per cent (up from 6.5 per cent of March 2020). This means that India was paying 9.7 per cent of its export earnings to pay its external debt (inclusive of principal and interest).

FIXED CURRENCY REGIME

The fixed currency regime[5] is a method of regulating exchange rates of world currencies brought by the IMF. In this system, the exchange rate of a particular currency was fixed by the IMF keeping the currency in front of a basket of important world currencies (they were UK£, US

5. Ibid., pp. 610–11.

$, Japanese ¥, German Mark DM and the French Franc FFr). Different economies were supposed to maintain that particular exchange rate in future. Exchange rates of currencies were modified by the IMF from time to time.

FLOATING CURRENCY REGIME

The floating currency regime[6] is a method of regulating exchange rates of world currencies based on the market mechanism (*i.e.*, demand and supply). In the follow-up to the fixed currency system of exchange rate determination, it was the UK which blamed the system for its payment crisis of the late 1960s. Looking at the major loopholes in this system, the UK government decided to switch over to the floating currency regime in 1973—the same year the IMF allowed an option to its member countries to go for either of the currency systems.

In the floating exchange rate system, a domestic currency is left free to float against a number of foreign currencies in its foreign exchange market and determine its own value. Such exchange rates are also called *market driven* or *based* exchange rates, which are regulated by factors such as the demand and supply of the domestic and the foreign currencies in the economy concerned.

MANAGED EXCHANGE RATES

A managed-exchange-rate system is a hybrid or mixture of the fixed and flexible exchange rate systems in which the government of the economy attempts to affect the exchange rate *directly* by buying or selling foreign currencies or *indirectly*, through monetary policy[7] (i.e., by lowering or raising interest rates on foreign currency bank accounts, affecting foreign investment, etc.).

Today, most of the economies have shifted to this system of exchange rate determination. Almost all countries tend to intervene when the markets become *disorderly* or the *fundamentals* of economics are challenged by the exchange rate of the time. Some of the major examples of the managed exchange-rate system have been given below[8]:

1. Some countries allow to *free float* their currencies and allow the market forces to determine their exchange rate with rare government intervention. This is the idea from which the *floating currency regime* basically emerged. The USA and the EU are the major examples in this category.
2. Some economies have *managed but flexible* exchange rates, under which the governments buy or sell its currency to reduce day-to-day volatility of currency fluctuations and sometimes go for systematic intervention for desired objectives. Canada and Japan fall in this category, besides many developing countries. India, too, falls under this category which follows the *dual currency regime* since 1992–93 financial year.[9]
3. Some economies, particularly small ones, peg their currencies to a major currency or to a *basket* of currency in a fixed exchange rate—known as the *pegging of currencies*. At times, the peg is allowed to glide smoothly upward or downward—a system which is known as *gliding* or *crawling peg*. Some economies have a *hard fix* of a currency

6. Ibid., pp. 611–15.

7. Ibid., p. 615.

8. The discussion is based primarily on Samuelson and Nordhaus, ***Economics***, 613–15 and D. Salvatore, ***International Economics*** (New Jersey: John Wiley and Sons, 2004) pp. 717–22.

9. Ministry of Finance, ***LERMS, Union Budget 1992–93***, (New Delhi: Government of India, 1992).

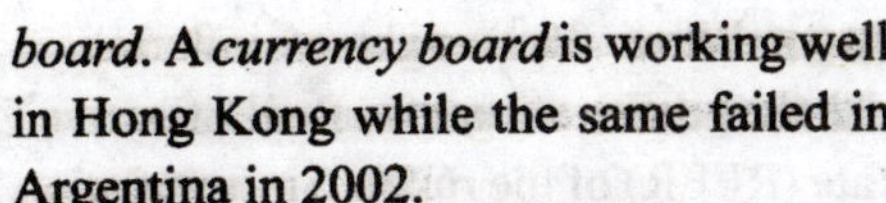

board. A *currency board* is working well in Hong Kong while the same failed in Argentina in 2002.

FOREIGN EXCHANGE MARKET

The market where different currencies can be bought and sold is called the foreign exchange market.[10] Out of the trades in different currencies, the exchange rate of the currency is determined by the economy.[11] This is an institutional framework for the exchange of one national currency for another.[12] This is particularly correct either in the case of a free float exchange (i.e., floating currency) regime or in a managed or hybrid exchange rate system. It is not allowed at all either in a *fixed currency system or a hard fix* (in a hard fix this happens once the currency to which the hard fix has been done itself starts fluctuating).

EXCHANGE RATE IN INDIA

Indian currency, the 'rupee', was historically linked with the British Pound Sterling till 1948 which was fixed as far back as 1928. Once the IMF came up, India shifted to the fixed currency system committed to maintain rupee's external value (i.e., exchange rate) in terms of gold or the US ($ Dollar). In 1948, ₹ 3.30 was fixed equivalent to US $ 1.

In September 1975, India delinked rupee from the British Pound and the RBI started determining rupee's exchange rate with respect to the exchange rate movements of the basket of world currencies (£, $, ¥, DM, Fr.). This was an arrangement between the fixed and the floating currency regimes.

In 1992–93 financial year, India moved to the floating currency regime with its own method which is known as the 'dual exchange rate'.[13] There are two exchange rates for rupee, one is the 'official rate' and the other is the 'market rate'. Here the point should be noted that it is the everyday's changing market-based exchange rate of rupee which affects the official exchange rate and not the other way round. But the RBI may intervene in the forex market via the demand and supply of rupee or the foreign currencies. Another point which should be kept in mind is that none of the economies have till date followed an ideal free-floating exchange rate. They require some mechanism to intervene in the foreign exchange market because this is a highly speculative market.

MAJOR TERMS

Trade Balance The monetary difference of the total export and import of an economy in one financial year is called trade balance. It might be positive or negative, known to be either favourable or unfavourable, respectively, to the economy.

Trade Policy Broadly speaking, the economic policy which regulates the export-import activities of any economy is known as the trade policy. It is also called the foreign trade policy or the Exim Policy. This policy needs regular modifications depending upon the economic policies of the economies of the world or the trading partners.[14]

Depreciation This term is used to mean two different things. In foreign exchange market, it is a situation when domestic currency loses its value in front of a foreign currency if it is market-driven. It means depreciation in a currency can only take place if the economy follows the floating exchange rate system.

In domestic economy, depreciation means an asset losing its value due to either its use, wear and tear or due to other economic reasons. Depreciation here means *wear and tear*. This is also known as *capital consumption*. Every economy has an official annual rates for different assets at which fixed assets are considered depreciating.

10. Stiglitz and Walsh, ***Economics***, p. 757.
11. Samuelson and Nordhaus, ***Economics***, p. 604
12. D. Salvatore, ***International Economics***, p. 7.
13. Ministry of Finance, ***LERMS***.
14. D. Salvatore, ***International Economics***, pp. 235–36.

Devaluation In the foreign exchange market, when exchange rate of a domestic currency is cut down by its government against any foreign currency, it is called devaluation. It means official depreciation is devaluation.

Revaluation A term used in foreign exchange market which means a government increasing the exchange rate of its currency against any foreign currency. It is official appreciation.

Appreciation In foreign exchange market, if a free floating domestic currency increases its value against the value of a foreign currency, it is appreciation. In domestic economy, if a fixed asset has seen increase in its value, it is also known as appreciation. Appreciation rates for different assets are not fixed by any government as they depend upon many factors which are unseen.

LERMS

India announced the Liberalised Exchange Rate Mechanism System (LERMS) in the Union Budget 1992–93 and in March 1993 it was operationalised. India delinked its currency from the fixed currency system and moved into the era of floating exchange-rate system under it.

Indian form of exchange rate is known as the 'dual exchange rate', one exchange rate of rupee is official and the other is market-driven.[15] The market-driven exchange rate shows the actual tendencies of the foreign currency demand and supply in the economy vis-á-vis the domestic currency. It is the market-driven exchange rate which affects the official rate and not the other way round.

NEER The Nominal Effective Exchange Rate (NEER) of the rupee is a weighted average of exchange rates before the currencies of India's major trading partners.

15. Ministry of Finance, **LERMS, Union Budget 1992 93**, GoI, MoF, N. Delhi.

REER When the weight of inflation is adjusted with the NEER, we get the Real Effective Exchange Rate (REER) of the rupee. Since inflation has been on the higher side in recent months, the REER of the rupee has been more against it than the NEER.

EFF The Extended fund Facility (EFF) is a service provided by the IMF to its member countries which authorises them to raise any amount of foreign exchange from it to fulfil their BoP crisis, but on the conditions of structural reforms in the economy put by the body. It is the first agreement of its kind. India had signed this agreement with the IMF in the financial year 1981–82.

Hard Currency It is the international currency in which the highest faith is shown and is needed by every economy. The strongest currency of the world is one which has a high level of liquidity. Basically, the economy with the highest as well as highly diversified exports that are compulsive imports for other countries (as of high-level technology, defence products, life saving medicines and petroleum products) will also create high demand for its currency in the world and become the hard currency. It is always scarce.

Upto the Second World War, the best hard currency was the Pound Sterling (£) of the UK, but soon it was replaced by the US Dollar. Some of the best hard currencies of the world today are the US Dollar, the Euro(€), Japanese Yen (¥) and the UK Sterling Pound (£). Meanwhile, by late 2015, the IMF allowed the SDR to be denominated in the Chinese 'Yuan'–paving the way for a new hard currency which was implemented in 2016.

Soft Currency A term used in the foreign exchange market which denotes the currency that is easily available in any economy in its forex market. For example, rupee is a soft currency in the Indian forex market. It is basically the opposite term for the hard currency.

Hot Currency Hot currency is a term of the forex market and is a temporary name for any hard currency. Due to certain reasons, if a hard currency is exiting an economy at a fast pace for the time, the *hard* currency is known to be *hot*. As in the case of the SE Asian crisis, the US dollar had become hot.

Heated Currency A term used in the forex market to denote the domestic currency which is under enough pressure (heat) of depreciation due to a hard currency's high tendency of exiting the economy (since it has become hot). It is also known as *currency under heat* or *under hammering*.

Cheap currency A term first used by the economist J. M. Keynes (1930s). If a government starts re-purchasing its bonds before their maturities (at full-maturity prices), the money which flows into the economy is known as the cheap currency, also called cheap money.

In the banking industry, it means a period of comparatively lower/softer interest rates regime.

Dear Currency This term was popularised by economists in the early 1930s to show the opposite of the cheap currency. When a government issues bonds, the money which flows from the public to the government or the money in the economy in general is called dear currency, also called *dear money*.

In the banking industry, it means a period of comparatively higher/costlier interest rates regime.

CURRENT ACCOU NT

Current account Curre has two meanings—one is related to the banking sector and the other to the external sector:

1. In the banking industry, a business firm's bank account is known as current account. The account is in the name of a firm run by the authorised person or persons in which no interest is paid by the bank on the deposits. Every withdrawal from the account takes place by cheques with limitations on the number of deposits and withdrawals in a single day. The *overdraft* facility or the *cash-cum-credit* (c/c Account) facility to business firms is offered by the banks on this account only.
2. In the external sector, curre current account refers to the account maintained by every government of the world in which every kind of current transactions is shown—basically this account is maintained by the central banking body of the economy on behalf of the government. Current transactions of an economy in foreign currency all over the world are—export, import, interest payments, private remittances and transfers.

All transactions are shown as either inflow or outflow (credit or debit). At the end of the year, the current account might be positive or negative. The positive one is known as a surplus current account, and the negative one is known as a deficit current account. India had surplus current accounts for three consecutive years (2000–03)—the only such period in Indian economic history.

During the first half of 2020-21, India had a current account surplus of 3.1 per cent (of GDP) i.e., US$ 34.7 billion. This surplus was generated due to steep contraction in merchandise imports and lower travel services outflows leading to a sharper fall in current payments (by 30.8 per cent) than current receipts (15.1 per cent). As per the *Economic survey 2020-21,* it is expected that the annual current account surplus would be of at least 2 per cent— after a period of **17 years** in this period.

During the last decade, India's current account always remained in deficit (averaging at 2.2 per cent) which reversed in the last quarter of 2019-20 with a modest surplus of 0.1 per cent with successive surpluses in the coming quarters of 2020-21.

CAPITAL ACCOU NT

Every government of the world maintains a capital account, which shows the capital kind of transactions of the economy with outside economies. Every transaction in foreign currency (inflow or outflow) considered as capital is shown in this account—external lending and borrowing, foreign currency deposits of banks, external bonds issued by the Government of India, FDI, PIS and security market investment of the QFIs (Rupee is fully convertible in this case).

There can be deficit or surplus in this account like the current account.

BALANCE OF PAYMENT (BOP)

The outcome of the total transactions of an economy with the outside world in one year is known as the balance of payment (BoP) of the economy.[16] Basically, it is the net outcome of the current and capital accounts of an economy. It might be favourable or unfavourable for the economy. However, negativity of the BoP does not mean it is unfavourable. A negative BoP is unfavourable for an economy if only the economy lacks the means to fill the gap of negativity.

The BoP of an economy is calculated on the principles of accountancy (*double-entry book-keeping*)[17] and looks like the balance sheet of a company—every entry shown either as credit (inflow) or debit (outflow). If there is a positive outcome at the end of the year, the money is automatically transferred to the foreign exchange reserves of the economy. And if there is any negative outcome, the same foreign exchange is drawn from the country's forex reserves. If the forex reserves are not capable of fulfilling the negativity created by the BoP, it is known as a BoP crisis and the economy tries different means to solve the crisis in which going for forex help from the IMF is the last resort.

CONVERTIBILITY

An economy might allow its currency full or partial convertibility in the current and the capital accounts. If the domestic currency is allowed to convert into the foreign currency for all current account purposes, it is a case of full current account convertibility. Similarly, in cases of capital outflow, if the domestic currency is allowed to convert into the foreign currency, it is a case of full capital account convertibility. If the situation is of partial convertibility, then the portion allowed by the government can be converted into foreign currency for current and capital purposes. It should always be kept in mind that the issue of currency convertibility is concerned with foreign currency *outflow* only.

Convertibility in India

India's foreign exchange earning capacity was always poor and hence it had all possible provisions to check the foreign exchange outflow, be it for current purposes or capital purposes (remember the draconian FERA). But the process of economic reforms has changed the situation to unidentifiable levels.

Current Account

Current account is today fully convertible (operationalised on 19 August, 1994). It means that the full amount of the foreign exchange required by someone for current purposes will be made available to him at official exchange rate and there could be an unprohibited outflow of foreign exchange (earlier it was partially convertible). India was obliged to do so as per Article VIII of

---

16. Samuelson and Nordhaus, ***Economics***, p. 601.

17. It means that each external transaction is recorded/entered twice—once as a credit and once as a debit of an equal amount. This is because every transaction has two sides—we sell something and we receive payment for it; similarly, we buy something and we have to pay for it (See Salvatore, ***International Economics***, p. 432).

the IMF which prohibits any exchange restrictions on current international transactions (keep in mind that India was under pre-conditions of the IMF since 1991).

Capital Account

After the recommendations of the S.S. Tarapore Committee (1997) on Capital Account Convertibility, India has been moving in the direction of allowing full convertibility in this account, but with required precautions. India is still a country of partial convertibility (40:60) in the capital account, but inside this overall policy, enough reforms have been made and to certain levels of foreign exchange requirements, it is an economy allowing full capital account convertibility.

1. Indian corporates are allowed full convertibility in the automatic route upto $ 500 million overseas ventures (investment by Ltd. companies in foreign countries allowed) per annum.
2. Indian corporates are allowed to prepay their external commercial borrowings (ECBs) via automatic route if the loan is above $ 500 million per annum.
3. Individuals are allowed to invest in foreign assets, shares, etc., upto the level of $ 2,50,000 per annum.
4. Unlimited amount of gold is allowed to be imported (this is equal to allowing full convertibility in capital account via current account route, but not feasible for everybody) which is not allowed now.

The Second Committee on the Capital Account Convertibility (CAC)—again chaired by S.S. Tarapore—handed over its report in September 2006 on which the RBI/the government is having consultations.

IMF CONDITIONS ON INDIA

The BoP crisis of the early 1990s made India borrow from the IMF which came on some conditions. The medium term loan to India was given for the restructuring of the economy on the following conditions:

1. Devaluation of rupee by 22 per cent (done in two consecutive fortnights—rupee fell from ₹21 to ₹27 against every US Dollar).
2. Drastic custom cut to a peak duty of 30 per cent from the erstwhile level of 130 per cent for all goods.
3. Excise duty to be increased by 20 per cent to neutralise the loss of revenue due to custom cut.
4. Government expenditure to be cut by 10 per cent per annum (the burden of salaries, pensions, subsidies, etc.).

The above-given conditions to which India was obliged were vehemently opposed by the Indian corporate sector, opposition in the Parliament and majority of Indians. But by the end of 1999–2000, when India saw the multiple benefits accruing out of the ongoing reforms, there was no ideological opposition to the idea. It should always be kept in mind that the nature of structural reforms India went through was guided and decided by these pre-conditions of the IMF.

This is how the direction of structural reforms of an economy is regulated by the IMF in the process of strengthening the BoP position of the crisis-driven economy. The purpose has been served in the Indian case. India has not only fulfilled these conditions but it has also moved ahead.

SPECIAL ECONOMIC ZONE

The special economic zone (SEZ) policy was announced by the government in 2000 which was concretised through the SEZ Act, 2005. It mainly aims to develop 'export hubs' in the country to promote growth and development. As an idea it was not new—India had set up *Asia's first* 'export processing zone' (EPZ) in Kandla in 1965 itself. Later on, the idea got another encouragement through the 'export oriented units' (EOUs). After the SEZ policy was formalised through an Act, the EOUs and EPZs are open to conversion to SEZ.

The SEZs can be set up by either the GoI, States or even private sector—in all three sectors of the economy—agriculture, industry and services. As per the Ministry of Commerce and Industry, the principal objectives behind creating SEZs in the country include:

1. generation of additional economic activity,
2. promotion of exports of goods and services,
3. promotion of investment from domestic and foreign sources,
4. creation of employment opportunities, and
5. development of infrastructure facilities.

Recent steps taken by the Government to strengthen SEZs in the country are given below[18]:

- Minimum Land Area requirement for setting up of new SEZs has been reduced to 50 per cent for multi-product and sector-specific SEZs.
- Sectoral broad-banding has been introduced to encompass similar and related areas under the same sector.
- A new sector 'agro-based food processing' sector has been introduced to encourage agro-based industries in SEZs (food processing getting government's nod by late 2016 for 100 per cent FDI is expected to give a big push to it).
- Dual use of facilities like Social and Commercial infrastructure by SEZs and non-SEZs entities has been allowed in order to make SEZ operations more viable.
- Online processing of various activities relating to SEZ for improving 'ease of doing business'.
- 'SEZ India' mobile app launched to help the SEZs to track their transactions on SEZ Online System (launched in January 2017).

By ***April 2021,*** the Government had approved 511 proposals for setting up SEZs (in addition to 9 SEZs of the GoI and 13 of States/private sector which were setup prior to the enactment of the SEZs Act, 2005)—out of which 301 SEZs are operational. Today, the SEZs are invested with ₹5.1 lakh crore and have created 18.20 lakh employment. They have 21 per cent share in India's total exports.

In recent times, the SEZs have lost their original synergy due to global economic slowdown which followed the great recession among the developed economies and the COVID-19 pandemic.

FOREIGN INVESTMENT

Though the importance of foreign investment in the economy was realised by the Government by the late 1980s, it was only liberalised after the country commenced the process of the economic reforms in 1991. In 1991 itself, India opened up to inflows of direct and indirect forms of foreign investments—more emphasis being on the former for being more durable and beneficial to the economy. Since then, much water has flown in the area and today India is among the highest recipients of FDI (foreign direct investment) in the world—in 2016–17 being the topmost recipient in

18. **Ministry of Commerce and Industry,** Government of India, N. Delhi, March 2021.

the world (it is one of the aims of the 'Make in India' initiative).

By now, most of the sectors are open for 100 per cent FDI while all categories of the investors are allowed to invest in the security market of the country. Pushing in favour of enhanced inflows of foreign investment, related policy was further *liberalised* with the following changes:

1. The 'single brand retail trading' (SBRT) is now open for 100 per cent FDI under automatic route.
2. The 'construction' and 'real estate brokerage' are open to receive 100 per cent FDI under automatic route.
3. 'Aviation' sector is allowed to receive 49 per cent FDI under automatic route (it includes the public sector aviation company Air India also).
4. Foreign institutional investments/ foreign portfolio investments (FIIs/FPIs) has been allowed in 'power distribution' over and above the FDI limit of 49 per cent under automatic route. Earlier, it used to be allowed but under the overall FDI limit.
5. The marketplace-based model of 'e-Commerce' sector has been allowed to receive 100 per cent FDI under the automatic route. But this ease came with a rider—sales of any vendor through them or its group companies limited to 25 per cent of the total sales of such vendor.
6. In the case of FDI in the 'pharma sector', the reference to Drugs and Cosmetics Act has been dropped—making things easier for the investors.
7. In the wake of the *COVID- 19 pandemic,* the Government gave an emphatic call for self-reliance (under the newly launched campaign, the *Atmanirbhar Bharat Abhiyan*) and raised the FDI limits in defence sector to 74 per cent (from existing 49 per cent) under automatic route. India already allows 100 per cent FDI in the sector on case-by-case basis.
8. Upper limit of FDI was increased to 74 per cent (from 49 per cent) in the insurance sector by the *Union Budget 2021-22,* which was a long-awaited demand from the capital-starved industry.

Capital Flows

As per the *Economic Survey 2020-21,* the net capital flows were modest during the year (April-September) at US$ 16.5 billion, as against US$ 40.0 billion in the comparative period of the previous year— mainly due to net repayments of ECBs (external commercial borrowings) and decline in banking capital. However, there was an increase in net foreign investment to US$ 31.4 billion in the first half of 2020-21 (against US$ 28.7 billion in the corresponding period of the previous year). Other features[19] of the foreign capital flows were as given below:

1. **FDI Inflows:** During 2020-21 (April-October), net FDI flows recorded an inflow of US$ 27.5 billion (14.8 per cent higher than same period of the previous year)— an endorsement of India's status as a preferred investment destination amongst the global investors.

   Computer software and hardware sector attracted the highest FDI equity inflows of US$ 17.6 billion in 2020-21 (April-September) against US$ 4.0 billion in the corresponding period of the previous year. *Singapore* continues to be the top investing

19. **Economic Survey 2020-21,** vol. 1, pp. 105-07, Ministry of Finance, GoI, N. Delhi.

country, in terms of FDI equity inflows, while US has taken second position, as against being at 4th spot during corresponding period a year ago.

2. **FPI Inflows:** A high *sell-offs* by FPI was seen in March 2020 reflecting recessionary fears among global investors at the onset of the pandemic. However, it witnessed a strong rebound (especially in equity market) afterwards and the net FPI flows recorded US$ 28.5 billion during 2020-21 (April-December) as against US$ 12.3 billion in corresponding period of the last year.

   Indian equity market during the period was supported by factors such as— abundant liquidity in global market, better corporate earnings, better management of COVID-19 pandemic, and the addition of Indian stocks to Morgan Stanley Capital International (MSCI) Global Standard indices.

3. **Other Capital Flows:** Among other forms of capital flows, banking capital recorded a net outflow of US$ 8.9 billion in the first half of 2020-21 (higher than US$ 5.7 billion in first half of 2019-20). With repayments exceeding fresh disbursals, net outflows on *ECBs* increased to US$ 5.7 billion in 2020-21 (April-September). Net inflow on account of *non-resident deposits* was US$ 4.9 billion (lower than US$ 5.0 billion in the first half of 2019-20).

COVID-19 AND FDI POLICY

The ongoing coronavirus pandemic has brought unprecedented economic disruptions in the economy which have impacted the limited stock companies very hard. This has made these companies vulnerable to shocking takeovers from the buyers who can manage huge funds. Taking note of the situation, the Government changed the FDI policy in April 2020.

As per the new FDI norms, now 'prior clearance' in India's companies will be required for investments from the countries with which India shares its land border. This norm applies on all existing and future FDIs in an Indian company. However, the indirect foreign investment (i.e., foreign portfolio investment) has been left unchanged. The move is aimed at checking 'opportunistic takeover' due to the *COVID-19 pandemic*, especially from China. This step from the Government is believed to have come in the wake of a 1.75 per cent stake purchase by the People's Bank of China (the central banking body of China) in the HDFC Bank.

ECB LIBERALISED

With the changing dynamics of economy, India's needs for foreign loans have also gone for a change. Though the RBI has been quite careful about higher exposure to the external loans, its overall policy stance regarding it has been liberal. Following this stance, the *external commercial borrowing (ECB)* norms were further liberalised[20] by the RBI, which are as given below:

- All eligible borrowers to raise up to US$ 750 million per financial year under the automatic route (with sector-wise limits being abolished).
- The list of eligible borrowers enlarged—all entities eligible to receive FDI, port trusts, units in SEZs, SIDBI, Exim Bank and registered microfinance entities.
- Public sector oil marketing companies can borrow upto US$ 10 billion for working capital purposes with a minimum average

20. Reserve Bank of India, Ministry of Finance, Government of India, N. Delhi, March 2020.

maturity period of 3 years under the automatic route without mandatory hedging[21]. This move is aimed at curbing volatility in the forex market arising out of dollar demand for crude oil purchases.

Manufacturing companies allowed upto US$ 50 million of ECB per year with the maturity of 1 year.

- In the case of ECB being raised from a foreign equity holder (and utilised for working capital, general corporate purposes or repayment of rupee loans), the maturity period will be 5 years.

In place of putting sectoral cap, the RBI decided to set an overall prudential limit on the ECB at 6.5 per cent of the GDP. It was for the first time that the RBI put such an open idea in the public domain—till now it was managed through its internal benchmark which never used to be available in the public domain.

As per the *Economic Survey 2020-21*, during the first half of 2020-21, the ECBs had the following features:

- Total ECBs stood at US$ 163.8 billion (was lower in March 2020 at US$ 164.7 billion).
- Commercial loans and securitized borrowings were the highest in ratio (91.2 per cent) which were predominantly denominated in US$ (77.2 per cent) and accessed mainly by non-financial corporations (74.5 per cent).
- While the average maturity of the ECBs was 6 years, the cost of ECBs was at 1.9 per cent which was higher than observed in the recent years.

21. To understand the concept 'hedging' related to ECB in a bit more detail, see the entry FOREIGN CLRRENCY HEDGING in the *Glossary* at the end of the book.

- To the extent the *drivers of ECBs* are concerned, we see both country-specific *push factors* (idiosyncratic) and generic and global *pull factors* (the latest Survey quoted some global studies ranging between 2011-17 to outline them):
  - *Country-specific (push) factors*—economic activity (growth rate), exchange rate, interest rate, inflation, status of corporate bond market, degree of openness in capital account, and the regulatory framework.
  - *Generic and Global (pull) factors*—rates of interest, global growth and inflation.

The slowdown in the economic activity in the first half of 2020-21 may have caused ebbing of appetite for ECBs among the Indian corporate houses. The ongoing COVID-19 pandemic is expected to 'adversely impact' the export earnings of external commercial borrowers— which would adversely impact their repayment capacity—thereby a source of *potential vulnerability* in coming times.

India, as a capital scarce country with high scope of investment, has been encouraging capital inflows but of stable and long-term kinds which are least prone to sudden stoppage or exits. Accordingly, the motivation has been to minimize currency risk by 'mandatory hedging' and 'rollover risk' by stipulating average minimum maturity while enabling firms to access foreign borrowing by fixing a dynamic limit as a ratio to GDP coupled with regulation of their uses.

TRADE FACILITATION

With an aim to reduce trade barriers caused by inefficient and overly burdensome regulatory administrative procedures, the Trade Facilitation

Agreement (TFA), negotiated at WTO, came into force in February 2017. A National Committee on Trade Facilitation (NCTF) was, accordingly, constituted in August 2016 (with the Cabinet Secretary as the Chair). A National Trade Facilitation Action Plan (NTFAP) for 2017-2020 containing specific activities to further ease out the bottlenecks to trade was prepared.

For the period 2020 to 2023, a new NTFAP is under preparation, to take additional reforms to bolster trade facilitation efforts and transform the cross-border clearance eco-system through efficient, transparent, risk-based, coordinated, digital, seamless and technology-driven procedures. India has been making proactive strides in TFA implementation under the guidance of NCTF. Many of the commitments, as per the *Economic Survey 2020-21,* which are otherwise due by 2022, have already been notified to WTO as implemented such as—

- Establishment of a Single Window (Article 10.4); Risk Management for clearance of goods (Article 7.4), being the major ones. The transparency notifications covering information on import and export procedures, enquiry points, single windows, etc. were also in April, 2019.
- Further, various regulatory relaxation measures were extended for facilitating trade during COVID-19, which include— 24x7 clearance; dedicated single window; condonation of delay in filing import declarations; waiver of late filing fees; undertakings instead of bond being the major ones.

These initiatives reflect India's commitment towards facilitation of trade with an emphasis on transparency and openness. India has been at the forefront in undertaking initiatives aimed at maximizing predictability and automation in trade, reflecting in the consistent improvement on the *United Nation's Global Survey on Digital and Sustainable Trade.*

EXPORT PROMOTION SCHEMES

India officially acknowledges (as per the *Economic Survey 2020-21*) that in the interconnected global economy of today, efforts to streamline, speed up and coordinate trade procedures will enhance trade and help the country integrate itself with global production and supply chain. To lend continuity, the Foreign Trade Policy, 2015-2020 has already been extended by one year (i.e., up to March 2021). Other than 'trade facilitation', the Government has launched the following major schemes[22] to promote exports from the country:

RoDTEP (Remission of Duties and Taxes on Exported Products): The MEIS (Merchandise Exports from India Scheme) of 2015 was challenged by the USA in WTO in early 2018—with final report of the WTO panel observing it a 'prohibited subsidy'— thus it needed to be withdrawn (though India put an appeal in the WTO regarding it). Meanwhile, in order to continue supporting the industry and to eliminate any uncertainty amongst the exporting community, Government rolled out a new *WTO compliant scheme,* namely RoDTEP, for all export goods with effect from January 2021.

Under this scheme, duties and taxes levied at the Central, State and local levels (such as electricity duties and VAT on fuel used for transportation) which are not getting exempted or refunded under any other existing mechanism will be refunded to exporters in their ledger account with Customs. The credits can be used to pay basic customs duty on imported goods or transferred to other importers— facilitating ease of transactions for exports.

22. **Economic Survey 2020-21** and **2019-20**, vols. 2, Ministry of Finance, GoI, N. Delhi.

PLI (Production-Linked Incentive) The scheme (announced in 2020-21) which applies on 13 eligible sectors (for more, see the chapter on *Industry and Infrastructure*) is expected to make Indian manufacturers globally competitive; attract investment in the areas of core competency and cutting-edge technology; ensure efficiencies; create economies of scale; establish backward linkages with MSMEs; enhance exports; and make India an integral part of the *global supply chain.*

SEIS (Services Exports from India Scheme) Under this scheme, rewards (in the form of 'duty credit scrips') are given to the exporters of services on their net foreign exchange earnings. The scrips (just like MEIS) are transferable and can be used to pay certain central duties and taxes. The service exporters are eligible for SEIS at the rate of 5 per cent and 7 per cent of the net foreign exchange earnings (NFEE).

EPCG (Export Promotion Capital Goods Scheme) This scheme allows exporters to import capital goods (except certain specified items under the scheme) for pre-production, production and post-production at *zero* customs duty. In return, the exporters are required to fulfil the export obligation to the tune of *six times* the import duties, taxes and cess saved amount on capital goods (to be fulfilled in 6 years). These imports are also exempt from the IGST till March 2020.

AAS (Advance Authorization Scheme) Advance Authorization (AA) is issued to allow duty free import of inputs (such as fuel, oil and catalyst), which are physically incorporated in export products.

DFIA (Duty Free Impo rt Authorization) This is issued on post export basis for products for which Standard Input Output Norms (SION) have been notified. One of the objectives of the scheme is to facilitate transfer of the authorization or the inputs imported as per SION, once export is completed. Provisions of DFIA Scheme are similar to Advance Authorization Scheme.

IES (Interest Equal ization Scheme) Launched for a period of 5 years (2015-20), the scheme is being implemented by the DGFT (Directorate General of Foreign Trade) through RBI for pre- and post- Shipment Rupee Export Credit—eligible exporters avail interest equalization at the rate of 3 per cent per annum (increased to 5 per cent in November 2018 for MSME sector).

EOU/EHTP/STP/BTP Scheme The objectives of these four schemes, i.e., Export Oriented Units (EOU), Electronic Hardware Technology Park (EHTP), Software Technology Parks (STP) and Bio-Technology Parks (BTP) are to promote exports, enhance foreign exchange earnings, attract investment for export production and employment generation. The units (other than trading firms) undertaking to export their entire production of goods and services (except permissible sales in DTA) may be set up under the schemes which are permitted to import inputs without payment of customs duty.

DES (Deemed Exports Scheme) Deemed Exports refer to those transactions in which the goods supplied do not leave the country and the payment for such supplies is received either in Indian rupees or in free foreign exchange. Under the scheme, exemption (or refund) of duties on manufactured products is given to ensure a *level playing field* to domestic manufacturers.

TMA (Transport and Marketing Assistance for Specified Agriculture Products Scheme) Launched in February 2019, it aims to mitigate the disadvantage of higher *cost of transportation* of export of specified agriculture products due to trans-shipment and to promote brand recognition for Indian agricultural products in specified overseas markets (for the period between March 2019 and March 2020).

TIES (Trade Infrastructure for Export Scheme) The scheme has the objective to assist Central and State Government Agencies for the creation of appropriate *infrastructure* for the growth of exports from the States. The scheme provides financial assistance in the form of grant-in-aid to Central/ State Government owned agencies for setting up or for upgradation of export infrastructure as per the guidelines of the scheme.

TRADE LOGISTICS

The ongoing COVID-19 pandemic has underscored the need for a *resilient logistics sector* that can respond to emergencies and supply chain disruptions. Despite the sector being plagued by some 'structural issues' such as highly fragmented ownership; few large players; lack of consolidation in operations; sub-optimal modal share with freight movement highly skewed towards road sector; lack of an integrated approach by user sectors (multiple line ministries and agencies); absence of consistent policies and regulations; among others, India has made remarkable progress[23] in logistics sector.

- India's rank has improved significantly in trading across borders parameter of Ease of Doing Business index from 146 in 2018 to 68 in 2020. The parameter assesses the time and cost associated with the 'logistical process' of exporting and importing goods.
- The Logistics Performance Index (LPI), released by the World Bank, assesses relative logistics efficiency of countries. On this index, India was ranked 44 out of 160 countries in 2018 (up from rank of 54 in 2014).
- India is among nine countries having area above ten-lakh square kilometre out of 24 countries analysed by LPI in 2018, with a score above three. India performs above average after controlling for the level of development and better than some of its BRICS peers.

23. Economic Survey 2020-21, vol. 2, pp. 117-19, Ministry of Finance, GoI, N. Delhi.

The *National Logistics Policy* was in an advanced stage (by April 2021) of roll-out with a vision to develop a modern, efficient and resilient logistics services sector that builds on dynamic processes, technology and professional manpower to seamlessly integrate multiple modes of transportation and inventory management to provide more reliable, cost-effective, greener, safer and equitable logistics solutions.

Some major **Process Reforms** done by the Government in recent times, which have contributed towards improving logistics efficiency are—

- Reduction in waiting time for inter-state border crossing due to GST;
- Revision in axle load norms for heavy vehicles leading to better carrying capacity;
- Introduction of paperless EXIM trade process through E-Sanchit; faceless assessment by 'Turant Customs' by Central Board of Indirect Taxes and Customs (CBIC);
- Installation of scanners at major ports; implementation of Port Community System *1X* at all important ports;
- Radio Frequency Identification (RFID) tagging of all EXIM containers for track and trace; and
- Mandatory electronic toll collection system (i.e., FASTag) for reducing time loss at toll plaza.

Some major **Infrastructure initiatives,** at various stages of implementation, are—

1. *Bharatmala Pariyojana* is a new umbrella programme for the highways sector that envisages building more than 80,000 km of roads, highways, greenfield expressways, bridges with an investment of around US$ 107 billion.

2. *Sagarmala* aims at Port Modernization & New Port Development, Port Connectivity Enhancement, Port-linked Industrialization, Coastal Community Development and giving impetus to Coastal Shipping. By now, 508 projects have been identified and 111 waterways have been declared 'National Waterways' for which the work is going on in phases.
3. *Multi-Modal Logistics Parks* shall act as hubs for freight movement enabling freight aggregation, distribution and multi-modal transportation. They would provide modern mechanized warehousing space and value-added services such as customs clearance with bonded storage yards, warehousing management services, etc.
4. *Dedicated Freight Corridors (DFCs)* aims at reduction in unit cost of transportation with higher speed of freight trains and better turnaround of wagons. Around 70 per cent of freight is expected to shift to DFC, freeing up capacity on Indian Railways.
5. *Trade Infrastructure for Export Scheme (TIES)* aims to assist the creation of appropriate infrastructure for the growth of exports from the States.

Some **Digital and Technological initiatives** under development are—

1. *Logistics Planning and Performance Monitoring Tool (LPPT)* will allow real-time monitoring of operational performance and asset utilization of various logistics infrastructure such as ports, airports, various corridors comprising national and state highways, Inland Container Depots (ICDs), etc.
2. *India Logistics Platform (iLOG)* - Several IT-based solutions have been deployed by government over the years such as Indian Customs EDI Gateway (ICEGATE) and Single Window Interface for Trade (SWIFT) developed for trade facilitation; Port Community System (PCS) for cargo handling at seaports; Freight Operations Information System (FOIS) by Indian Railways and VAHAN (National Vehicle Registration System). However, each system owner has adopted a different approach, leaving critical gaps that require manual or offline processing at various stages.
3. *Component Systems* that would be latched with the iLOG with Aadhaar and Blockchain-based security protocols include— truck visibility & positioning platform (integrated with e-way bill and Vahan); National e-registry of warehousing; digital trucking; logistics account number (LAN); digital green corridor; and digital port decongestion and container tracking & management system.

Today, the logistics sector employs over 12 million labour force in the country, involved mainly in land transportation, warehousing (storage and packaging), supply chain, courier and express services. To impart right set of skills to this workforce, a curriculum on *logistics and supply chain* is being developed for classes 9 and 10 at the school level— to be introduced in Industrial Training Institutes (ITIs) and polytechnics under PMKVY (Pradhan Mantri Kaushal Vikas Yojana), DDU-GKY (Deen Dayal Upadhyay Grameen Kaushalya Yojana) and the state skill missions.

INDIA'S TRADE

India's trade fell sharply during 2020-21, like other countries in the world. The decline in imports outweighed that in exports – leading to smaller trade deficit of US$ 9.8 billion as compared to US$ 49.2 billion in the first quarter but registering a trade surplus in the month of June, 2020 after a gap of 18 years. The trade deficit during the April-December, 2020-21 was US$ 57.5 billion as compared to US$ 125.9 billion in the corresponding period last year. Major **features** of India's trade, as per the *Economic Survey 2020-21*, during 2020-21 (April-November) are as given below:

- **Top 10 export items:** Drug formulations (7.1 per cent share) emerged as the 2nd largest exports; Iron & Steel (4.4 per cent share); with sharp fall in exports of motor vehicles/cars (which remains no in the list).
- **Top export destinations:** USA continues to be the largest export market for India, while China has occupied the 2nd position, moving up from 3rd spot in previous year. Exports to China constituted around 7.8 per cent (against 5.4 per cent in 2019). Malaysia is a new entrant among the top 10 export destinations, as compared to last year, while Nepal no longer occupies position among the top 10 destinations.
- **Top 10 import origins:** China continues to be the largest import source for India in 2020-21 (April-November) with share of imports rising to 17.7 per cent from 14.5 per cent in corresponding period a year ago. While Switzerland is no more among the top 10 import sources, Germany is the *new addition* in the list accounting for 3.7 per cent share of total imports.
- Crude Petroleum continues to be the *highest* imported commodity (14.3 per cent share); Gold & Silver (fall in share to 5.6 per cent from 6.3 per cent) slipping to *third* position from second earlier. Computer hardware and peripherals is one of the new additions in the list of top 10 import commodities (with 3.0 per cent share) due to more people working from home.
- India had the most favourable trade balance with USA, followed by Bangladesh and Nepal. The highest trade deficit is with China, followed by Iraq and Saudi Arabia.
- **Invisibles:** Net *services receipts* amounting to US$ 41.7 billion remained stable in the first half of the 2020-21 (US$ 40.5 billion in corresponding period a year ago), notwithstanding a sharp contraction in travel receipts owing to the international mobility restrictions imposed at the onset of the pandemic and falling remittances. Resilience of the services sector was primarily driven by software services, which accounted for 49 per cent of total services exports.
- Net *private transfer* receipts, mainly representing remittances by Indians employed overseas, totalling US$ 35.8 billion in the first half of 2020-21 declined by 6.7 per cent over the corresponding period of previous year. It is pertinent to note that as per the *World Migration Report 2020*, India has the largest number of migrants living abroad (17.5 million) and was the top recipient of remittances of US$ 83.3 billion in 2019.

As per the World Bank, remittance flows to low and middle-income countries (LMICs) are estimated to decline in 2020, by around 7.2 per cent. For India, remittances are projected to fall by about 8.9 per cent to US$ 76 billion in 2020.

Net outgo due to *cross border income* payments associated with the production and ownership of financial and other non-produced assets, which had been moving upward since 2011-12, declined in 2019-20—in the first half of 2020-21, there was a net outflow of primary income of US$ 16.8 billion (as against outflow of US$14.7 billion in corresponding period a year ago).

CURRENT TRADE OPPORTUNITY

The dynamics of global trade has gone for much change in recent times. Two factors have played a very vital role in this change, one being the rise of protectionism in the world and the Sino-US trade tensions. After the outbreak of the COVID-19 pandemic, several MNCs having their production bases in China were searching for alternative bases to continue their production. Thus, the current environment for international trade presents India an unprecedented opportunity to chart a China-like, labour-intensive, export trajectory and thereby create unparalleled job opportunities. To tap this opportunity, India should act[24] in the following direction—

- 'Assemble in India for the world' should be integrated into the 'Make in India'. By doing so, India can raise its export market share to about 3.5 per cent by 2025 and 6 per cent by 2030. Job creation out of this will be 4 crores by 2025 and 8 crores by 2030.
- The increased exports can contribute about 25 per cent for making India a $5 trillion economy by 2025.

The remarkable export performance of China in comparison to India is driven primarily by deliberate specialization at large scale in labour-intensive sectors, especially 'network products' (products which are used in information technology for networking), where production occurs across Global Value Chains (GVCs) operated by the MNCs. China used this strategy to export primarily to rich countries. In a similar way, India should focus on enabling *assembling operations* at the highest possible level in network products.

India's insecurity on trade front related to regional and preferential trade agreements can be overcome by tapping this opportunity—by promoting the cause of manufacturing industries. By evaluating the impact of India's trade agreements (for the period 1993–2018), we find that India's exports have increased by 13.4 per cent for manufactured products and 10.9 per cent for total merchandise while imports increased by 12.7 per cent for manufactured products and 8.6 per cent for total merchandise. This way, we find a clear gain of 0.7 per cent in trade balance surplus per year for manufactured products and 2.3 per cent per year for total merchandise.

INDIA AS PHARMACY OF THE WORLD

The ongoing COVID-19 pandemic presented both an opportunity and a challenge for India to emerge[25] as the pharmacy of the world— showing its vulnerabilities as well as its potential in this regard. The global pharmaceutical market is set to exceed US$ 1.5 trillion by 2023— against this backdrop, the Indian pharma industry is currently valued at US$ 41 billion and is expected to grow to US$ 65 billion by 2024 and about US$ 120-130 billion by 2030. Certain encouraging facts related to pharma industry of the country are as given below:

- *3rd* largest in the world, in terms of volume (after China and Italy) and *14th* largest in terms of value.
- Share in global exports almost doubled to 2.6 per cent in 2019 from 1.6 per cent of 2010—*11th* position (with top positions going to Germany, Switzerland and USA).

24. Economic Survey 2019-20, Vol. 1, pp. 100-127, Ministry of Finance, GoI, N. Delhi.

25. Economic Survey 2020-2 1, vol. 1, pp. 97-99, Ministry of Finance, GoI, N. Delhi has quoted *Report of the High-Level Advisory Group*, 2019 (headed by S. S. Bhalla) of the Department of Commerce among other latest studies of recent times.

- Emerged as a global hub for generic medicines (on the back of being a raw material base and a skilled workforce).
- Has the largest number of US-FDA compliant pharma plants (more than 262 including APIs) outside of USA.
- India's pharma sector has high value of TSC (trade specialization coefficient), closer to 1, consistently from 2014-15 (the value of TSC lies between -1 and 1, wherein a higher TSC value denotes stronger export competitiveness of the country).

During 2020-21 (April-October), India had US$ 11.1 billion of pharma exports showing an impressive growth rate of 18.0 per cent— increasing in total exports to 7.3 per cent (from 5.1 per cent)— making it the 3rd largest exported commodity. The commitment to supply COVID-19 vaccines to other countries has made India the epicentre for its manufacturing. According to data available from US-FDA, Indian pharma companies have garnered nearly **45** per cent of all new Abbreviated New Drug Applications (ANDAs) approvals during the first nine months of 2020-21 (which hints at export potential in the coming years). But before India emerges as the pharmacy of the world, certain *challenges* are also there, namely—

1. Its excessive dependence on China for sourcing Active Pharmaceutical Ingredients (APIs) and Key Starting Materials (KSMs).
2. Disproportionate dependence on USA for pharma exports.
3. Excessive dependence on manufacturing of the generic formulations.

Government has taken a few focused initiatives to get over these challenges during 2020-21, namely— PLI (Production Linked Incentive) Scheme announced for enhancing manufacturing capacities and exports besides for bulk drugs (which applies on Drug Intermediates, APIs and medical devices); and scheme for promotion of Parks for bulk drugs and medical devices. To emerge as the *pharmacy of the world,* the industry needs a broad-based development strategy led by the following components:

1. Broadening of market base together with product categories— for example, tapping the opportunities in newer product classes such as biosimilars, gene therapy and specialty drugs and increasing exports to large and traditionally underpenetrated markets (such as Japan, China, Africa, Indonesia, Russia/CIS countries, Brazil and Latin America).
2. Restructuring of the existing regulatory framework together with upgrading and building capacities at various National Institute of Pharmaceutical Education and Research (NIPERs).
3. Boosting R&D expenditure to move up in value chain from generics to Novel Chemical Entities (i.e., new complex pharmaceuticals).

EXCHANGE RATE MONITORING

Indian currency has seen frequent exchange rate volatility in recent times. External variables have been changing more frequently than any time in past. This forces India to closely monitor the exchange rate dynamics of the world, its major trade partners and the emerging competitors in its export market. India needs (as per the Economic Survey 2016-17) to *rethink its exchange rate policy outlook* and go for a shift in it—this becomes even more clear by considering the following points:

1. International trading opportunities are becoming scarcer in the aftermath of three major events—global financial crisis, the eurozone crisis and the stock market

meltdown of China (2015). The world 'export-GDP ratio' has declined since 2011. Going forward, a sharp rise in the US dollar is expected with a corresponding decline in the currencies of India's competitors, notably China and Vietnam. Already, since July 2015, the yuan has depreciated about 11.6 per cent (form July 2015 to December 2016) against the dollar and, as a consequence, the rupee has appreciated by 6 per cent against the yuan. Given the situation there has been a continuous pressure of capital outflows on India.

2. To sustain high growth rate, India needs support of exports in the coming times. And this is only possible once rupee's exchange rate is able to maintain the competitive edge over its competitors in the export market. The rise of countries such as Vietnam, Bangladesh, and the Philippines is a new matter of concern which compete with India across a range of manufacturing and services.
3. India's present exchange rate management policy gives unusually high weight to UAE (due to high oil imports and a trans-shipment point for India's exports). But this trade has almost nothing to do with India's export competitiveness. The policy currently considers overall trade in place of the sectoral situations and their relations with the exchange rate. Due to this, India gives heavy weight to euro, even though it is really Asian countries which are India's main competitors (not Europe).
4. Ever since the developed countries came under the grip of Great Recession, we have seen 'unconventional monetary policy' being pushed by most of them—with effective interest rates running in negatives, too. While the central banks in the west have been aiming to push up inflation and growth through it, RBI has been balancing them (till *March 2017*). Given the situation, it looks advisable for the RBI (through 'Monetary Policy Committee') to recalibrate its monetary policy outlook.

RBI's policy on the exchange rate of the rupee has been to allow it to be *determined* by market forces. Interventions come from it but only to maintain orderly market conditions by containing excessive volatility. For this, RBI does not use any reference to any pre-determined target level or band.

COVID-19 Impact & RBI's Interventions In the months following the outbreak of the pandemic, India experienced an unprecedented outflow of FPI (of US$ 15.92 billion in March 2020) in comparison to cumulative inflows of US$ 1.42 billion in the previous two months— resulting in high volatility in the rupee. In the wake of it, several conventional and unconventional tools were deployed by RBI in order to ensure financial stability and orderly conditions in financial markets— and was largely successful in controlling the element of exchange volatility.

Large stimulus given by central banks in advanced economies resulted in heightened capital flows into emerging markets including India— which caused asset price inflation as well as appreciation in several local currencies including rupee. As per the *Economic Survey 2020-21*, the judicious interventions in forex markets were, therefore, required to prevent a large one-sided appreciation in the rupee— as was done by RBI.

BIPA & BIT

Attracting adequate amounts of foreign investments was one of the major aims of the process of economic reforms which commenced in 1991. Accordingly, a Model BIT (Bilateral Investment Treaty) was crafted by the Government in 1993. Since then India has signed 83 such treaties called the Bilateral Investment Promotion and Protection

Agreements (BIPAs) with different countries—the first one with the UK in 1994 and the last with the UAE signed in 2018. They aim to increase foreign investments[26] both ways—inflows and outflows.

Objective These agreements aim to increase the comfort level and boost the confidence of investors by assuring—a level playing field, non-discriminatory treatment, and an independent forum for dispute settlement.

New BIT In the wake of the changes which have occurred in India and around the world since the first Model BIT was announced, the Government finalised a new[27] *Model BIT in 2016* which is being used for 're-negotiation' of the existing BIPAs, CECAs (Comprehensive Economic Cooperation Agreements), CEPAs (Comprehensive Economic Partnership Agreements) and the FTAs (Free Trade Agreements). The essential features of the new model BIT are given below:

- An 'enterprise-based' definition of investment
- Non-discriminatory treatment through due process
- National treatment
- Protections against expropriation
- A refined Investor State Dispute Settlement (ISDS) provision under which investors to first exhaust local remedies before going for international arbitration[28]
- The ISDS to award monetary compensation alone
- Excludes matters such as government procurement, taxation, subsidies, compulsory licenses and national security (to preserve regulatory authority of Government)

Meanwhile, re-negotiation process under the new Model BIT has faced resistance from some countries, though out of the 83 BITs, by now, 72 are already enforced while rest of them are under the process of re-negotiation.

RTAs BY INDIA

In general, multilateral trade agreements are the first best solutions for deepening global trade and development as they are founded on the core principles of non-discrimination. Meanwhile, RTAs (Regional Trade Agreements) are efforts by nations aimed at deepening economic relations, usually with neighbouring countries, and tend to be *largely political* in nature. With the multilateral trade negotiations process under the WTO being a painfully slow one requiring broad-based consensus, RTAs have progressively assumed greater importance and a growing share in international trade.

While RTAs are broadly *compliant* with WTO mandates and remain broadly *supportive* of the WTO process, they remain ***second-best*** solutions that are discriminatory in nature against non-members and are inefficient as low cost producing non-members lose out to members. While bilateral RTAs have no equity considerations, mega-regional trading groups may not necessarily be equitable if membership is diverse and small countries may lose out either way—if they are part of it, they may not have much say and if they are not, they may stand to lose.

India has always stood for an open, equitable, predictable, non-discriminatory and rule-based international trading system and views RTAs as

26. These agreements aim at only foreign direct investment (FDI) as since 1993–94 itself rupee is fully convertible in the case of the foreign indirect investment (the Foreign Portfolio Investment-FPI).

27. *India Brand Equity Foundation (IBEF)*, **Ministry of Commerce & Industry**, GoI, N. Delhi, March 2019.

28. Normally, investment disputes arising between the host nation and the investor are resolved by the *ICSID (International Centre for Settlement of Investment Disputes)*, an agency of the World Bank group. But as India is not its member, 'a clause' in the BIPAs/BITs is dedicated to serve this purpose. However, these agreements crafted by India serve more purposes than the purpose served by the ICSID such as promoting investment, exploring possibilities of investments and allowing local resolution of the disputes among others.

building blocks in the overall objective of trade liberalization as well as complementing the multilateral trading system under the WTO.

By **April 2021,** there[29] were 16 RTAs of India in force which included 10 FTAs (free trade agreements) and 6 PTAs (preferential trade agreements) while 22 trade negotiations were in progress:

- **FTAs in force:** The 10 FTAs, spanning trade, investment and technological cooperation, signed by India are—with Sri Lanka; the SAFTA (South Asian Free Trade Area) S. Korea CEPA, Japan CEPA and Malaysia CECA.
- **PTAs in force:** The 6 PTAs signed by India are— APTA (Asia Pacific Trade Agreement); the GSTP (Global System of Trade Preference, which includes 44 countries); SAARC Preferential Trading Agreement (SAPTA); with Afghanistan, MERCOSUR and Chile.
- **Ongoing Trade negotiations:** There were 24 ongoing trade negotiations of India with the countries/block such as—EU BTIA; Sri Lanka; Thailand; Mauritius; New Zealand FTA; Singapore; BIMSTEC; GCC; Canada; Australia; Malaysia; ASEAN; Korea; Iran; Peru; Bangladesh and Chile.

THE QUAD

The Quad[30] is the acronym used for the Quadrilateral Security Dialogue (QSD) which is also called the *Asian NATO*. This is an informal strategic forum of Australia, India, Japan and the USA— which has remained primarily involved in summits, exchange of information and military exercises between them— later on upscaling to ministerial and leadership level meetings.

Origin Its origin is traced back to the Indian Ocean Tsunami of 2004 when a temporary joint rescue operation was run by Australia, India, Japan and USA (in which the world recognised not only India's naval-military preparedness but its significance in the Asia-Pacific region). However, the rescue mission ended after handing over charge to the UNO. Meanwhile, a new framework has taken birth— the Quadrilateral, or Quad— with the Japanese PM (Shinzo Abe) voicing his long-standing idea of an 'arc of prosperity and freedom' that encompassed India, and brought it into a tighter maritime framework with Japan, USA and Australia (which were already close military allies). The plan for a meeting of the Quad was firmed up when Prime Minister Manmohan Singh visited Tokyo in December 2006.

The evolving idea of Quad encountered growing concerns in China and soon we see its dilution. Contrary to general perception, Australia wasn't the first to go slow on Quad, rather it was the USA, which felt that angering China would hamper its larger strategic efforts (move to sanction Iran in the UN Security Council and the 6-nation talks on North Korea). Thus, experts believed the forum getting in a kind of hibernation with the formal withdrawal of Australia from it in 2008 (the phase between 2008-15 is called *Quad 1.0*).

Situating Quad Experts have seen the diplomatic-military initiative of Quad as a response to the increased Chinese economic dominance, which of late started showing up in the form of *military dominance* of the world in general and Asia-Pacific in particular (the border related skirmishes with India, S. Korea, Japan and its incursions in the China Sea being the major examples of the latter).

---

29. **Ministry of Commerce and Industry,** April 2021 and **Economic Survey 2019-20,** vol. 2, pp. 105-08, Ministry of Finance, GoI, N. Delhi.
30. Based on several official press releases by nations concerned and contemporary media reporting and analyses (*The Economist, The Guardian, The Wall Street Journal* being the main ones).

Certain other attempts to reign in the Chinese economic dominance of recent times have been the TPP (Trans-Pacific Partnership) and its companion the TTIP (Trans-Atlantic Trade and Investment Partnership) which fizzled out due to the reluctance of the USA to be their part (under Donald Trump regime), though their revival is being predicted in 2021 once the new regime (under Joe Biden) came to power in the country.

Revival During 2017-19, we see a kind of revival (which is popularly called *Quad 2.0*) of the forum— main thrust coming from the USA (under Donald Trump, in the wake of his protectionist policies leading to a fierce Sino-US trade tension). Some recent instances of its revival can be seen in the following developments:

- The coming together of the *naval chiefs* of the four countries in India in 2018 (the Raisina Dialogue) is considered the *first indications* of the revival of the Quad's security structure.
- By late September 2019, the *1st ministerial* (external affairs) level meeting took place in New York where collective efforts to advance a "free, fair, open, prosperous and inclusive Indo-Pacific" was discussed.
- The *2nd ministerial* meeting was held in Tokyo in October 2020, though no joint statement was produced from the meeting.
- In February, its *3rd ministerial* meeting was held (virtually) in which the members agreed to strongly oppose any attempts by China to alter the status quo in the Indo-Pacific region by force, and vowed to work with ASEAN and Europe in this case.
- In November 2020, the world saw all four countries joining the *Malabar 2020* naval exercise in India (almost 3 years after Australia requested to join it). In the same month, a defence deal was agreed upon between Australia and Japan.
- By late January 2021, there was a National Security Advisor level talk (telephonic) between USA and Japan in which the latter did show its willingness to strengthen their bilateral alliance to achieve 'free and open' Indo-Pacific.
- By March 2021, the Quad members were working to develop a plan to distribute COVID-19 vaccines to countries in Asia as part of a broader strategy to counter China's influence.
- The *1st meeting* (virtual) of the leaders of the four countries was planned to take place in March 2021.

China has been busy cancelling out the importance of the forum with the claim that 'all the talk of a free and open Indo-Pacific is so much ocean spume (froth or foam)', as its foreign minister, Wang Yi, once put it. If such a claim of China looks off mark, as per some experts, so too is the claim of an Asian NATO in the process of making! Though the forum has got force after a new regime came to power in the USA (under Joe Biden), the world needs to wait for some more time to see the forum being heard and felt across the region!

DEGLOBALISATION AND INDIA

Global factors are yet to stabilise since the financial crisis hit the developed economies. Recovery among these economies is getting tough—even unconventional monetary policies have been tried (pursuing for negative interest rate regime). Meanwhile, several of these economies have signalled 'protectionist' rhetoric—the Brexit. The new government in the USA has already taken various protectionist measures by now and many more are supposed to come in the coming times.

Besides, in the past few years, the world has seen increased debate on the drawbacks of the globalisation process. Among experts as well as several nations, a general feeling looked evolving against globalisation. The negotiations related to the WTO look almost stalled. At the end of the tunnel, by late 2016, the world witnessed rise in the 'protectionist sentiments' among important economies.

The two events mentioned above show as if the world (or at least the economies which matter most) has started to move slowly away from the much-celebrated idea of globalisation—*de-globalisation* taking over the world—shrinking scope for multilateral trade and economic inter-dependence. Again, this lack of willingness towards globalisation among different economies is not of the same degree nor universal to every economy—better say it looks selective.

India's prospects of export growth depends on its trading partners' carrying capacity of globalisation to it. Today, for India, three external developments are of significant consequence:

1. In the *short-run*, global interest rates (as a result of the US elections and the implied change in its fiscal and monetary policy) will impact India's capital flows and exchange rates. Experts are already expecting high fiscal stimulus, more dependence on unconventional monetary policy, etc. to follow in the developed world.
2. The *medium-term* political outlook for globalisation and in particular for the world's 'political carrying capacity for globalisation' may have changed in the wake of recent developments. A strong US dollar and declining competitiveness might incline many countries to follow protectionist policies. This will result in declining global trade hitting India hard.
3. Developments in the US, especially the rise of the dollar, will have implications for China's currency and currency policy which will impact India and the world—if China is able to successfully re-balance its economy, the spillover effects will be positive; otherwise quite negative. China, with its underlying vulnerabilities, remains the country to watch for its potential to *unsettle* the global economy.

India's trade in goods and services both will be important in this case. India's services exports growth will test the world's 'globalisation carrying capacity' in services—depending on the restrictions in developed countries on two variables—*firstly,* the labour mobility and *secondly,* outsourcing.

It is possible that the world's carrying capacity will actually be *much greater* for India's services than it was for Chinese goods. After all, China's export expansion over the past two decades was imbalanced in several ways:

- The country exported far more than it imported.
- It exported manufactured goods to advanced countries, displacing production there, but imported goods (raw materials) from developing countries.
- When it did import from advanced economies, it often imported services rather than goods (though capital goods is a major exception).

As a result, China's development created relatively a few export-oriented jobs in advanced countries, insufficient to compensate for the jobs lost in manufacturing—and where it did create jobs, these were in advanced services (such as finance), which were not possible for displaced manufacturing workers to obtain. In contrast, India's expansion may well prove much more balanced:

- India has tended to run a current account deficit, rather than a surplus.

- While its service exports might also displace workers in advanced countries, their skill set will make relocation to other service activities easier; indeed, they may well simply move on to complementary tasks, such as more advanced computer programming in the IT sector itself.
- On the other hand, since skilled labour in advanced economies will be exposed to Indian competition, their ability to mobilize political opinion might also be greater.[31]

Precisely speaking, the *political backlash* against globalisation in advanced countries, and China's difficulties in rebalancing its economy, could have major implications for India. And it will be advisable for India to close track of the changing global dynamics.

COVID-19 AND MULTILATERALISM

In the wake of the COVID-19 pandemic, the Government gave a serious call for self-reliance and launched an ambitious campaign, the ***Atmanirbhar Baharat Abhiyan***. At the face of it, the campaign indicates the rise of a protectionist India. But that is not the case.

India still remains very much committed to a fair and vibrant multilateral world and is actively engaged in negotiating favourable deals in its regional trade agreements. As every country is busy protecting its socio-economic interest in the globalising world, India too wishes the same. The changed stance in its approach is seen by the experts in the backdrop of the ongoing coronavirus crisis which is expected to make the emergence of a new global economic order. India seems busy securing a suitable and favourable place in the post-COVID-19 global economic order.

WAY FORWARD

The ongoing COVID-19 pandemic has impacted[32] external sector of different countries differently—while countries witnessed contraction in exports and imports, AEs (Advance Economies) suffered larger contraction and EMDEs (Emerging Market and Developing Economies) less, especially the East-Asian economies. To promote a sustainable external sector, the future concerns and related policy actions[32] of India should be in the following direction:

- Trade partners of India have been building pressure for custom cuts in recent years. In this regard, the Government needs to keep defending the custom regime as it is necessary for protecting its trade interests.
- The practice of 'inverted duty' structure (i.e., lower custom duties on finished goods and in comparison, higher on the intermediate goods to produce them) has been hampering India's trade interests, under which custom duties are higher on the intermediate goods rather than the finished goods. At present, for several sectors, import elasticity of exports is greater than 1 (which means that with 1 per cent increase in imports of raw materials and intermediate goods exports of finished goods from India increase more than 1 per cent).
- Improving supply chain of the economy and integrating it with the 'global value chain' will enable India to enhance its export competitiveness. In past, several of the free trade agreements signed by India could not

31. Based on the discussion given in the Economic Survey 2016-17, Government of India, Ministry of Finance, N. Delhi, Vol. 1, pp. 6-9.

32. ***India's Exports,*** Gita Gopinath and Amartya Lahiri in Abhijit Banerjee, Gita Gopinath, Raghuram Rajan and Mihir S. Sharma edited **What the Economy Needs Now,** pp. 86-94, Juggernaut Books, N. Delhi, 2019; relevant recent official documents of Ministry of Commerce & Industry, GoI and the **Economic Survey 2019-20,** Vol. 1, pp. 102-124 and Vol. 2, pp. 71-109, Ministry of Finance, GoI, N. Delhi.

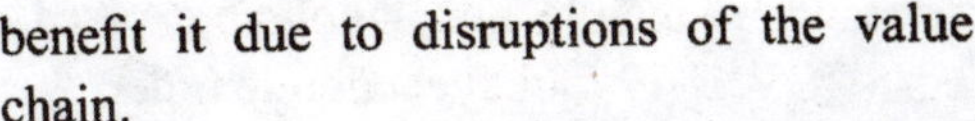

benefit it due to disruptions of the value chain.

- Decreasing the delays related to clearances at ports and airports to speed up the movement of shipments. Several steps have been taken by the Government in this regard but still much needs to be done.
- The MSMEs should be getting healthy access to loans and structure of the GST regime should be streamlined for them.
- Macroeconomic environment should be made conducive for trade by signing suitable trade agreements, avoiding arbitrary taxes, restrictions and tariff.
- Attempting effective labour reforms and raising skills of the workforce will be giving an edge to India's exports.
- The disruption of global manufacturing *value chains* due to the pandemic presents a tremendous opportunity for India to become one of the key nodes in the chain— for tapping this opportunity the country needs to work effectively on the plan which has been chalked out by the Government by now— trade facilitation, ease of exporting, regulatory reforms being its main parts.[33]

33. **Economic Survey 2020-21,** vol. 2, pp. 120-21, Ministry of Finance, GoI, N. Delhi.

CHAPTER 16

INTERNATIONAL ECONOMIC ORGAN ISATIONS & INDIA

*If, as T.S. Eliot said, humankind cannot bear too much reality, recent events suggest that the world cannot bear too much globalisation either.**

In this Chapter...

- International Monetary System
- Bretton Woods Development
- International Monetary Fund
- World Bank
- Asian Development Bank
- OECD
- World Trade Organisation (WTO)
- Nairobi Negotiations & India
- Buenos Aires Conference and India
- India and WTO
- BRICS Bank
- Asian Infrastructure Investment Bank
- Reforming IMF & WB

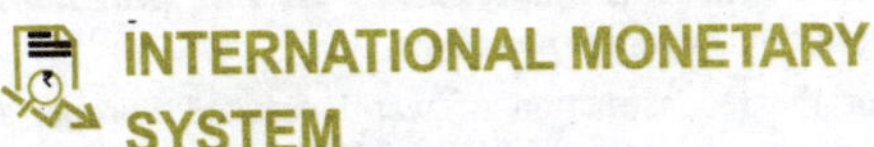

INTERNATIONAL MONETARY SYSTEM

The international monetary system (IMS) refers to the customs, rules, instruments, facilities, and organisations facilitating international (external) payments. Sometimes, the IMS is also referred to as an international monetary *order* or *regime.*[1] IMS can be classified according to the way in which exchange rates are determined (i.e., fixed currency regime, floating currency regime or managed exchange regime) and the form foreign reserves take (i.e., gold standard, a pure judiciary standard or a gold-exchange standard).

An IMS is considered good if it fulfils the following *two objectives*[2] in an impartial manner:

1. maximises the flow of foreign trade and foreign investments, and
2. leads to an *equitable* distribution of the gains from trade among the nations of the world.

1. D. Salvatore, ***International Economics*** (New Jersey: John Wiley & Sons, 2005),. pp. 737–38; Samuelson and Nordhaus, ***Economics*** (New Delhi: Tata McGraw-Hill, 2005) pp. 609–12.

2. D. Salvatore, ***International Economics***, p. 738.

* Economic Survey 2016-17, *Government of India, Ministry of Finance, N. Delhi, Vol.1,p.7.*

The evaluation of an IMS is done in terms of ***adjustment, liquidity*** and ***confidence*** which it manages to wield.

Adjustment

Adjustment refers to the process by which the balance-of-payment (BoP) crises of the nations of the world (or the member nations) are corrected. A good IMS tries to minimise the cost of BoP and time for adjustment for the nations.

Liquidity

Liquidity refers to the amount of foreign currency reserves available to settle the BoP crises of the nations. A good IMS maintains as much foreign reserves to mitigate such crises of the nations without any inflationary pressures on the nations.

Confidence

Confidence refers to the faith the nations of the world should show that the adjustment mechanism of the IMS is working adequately and that foreign reserves will retain their absolute and relative values. This confidence is based on the transparent knowledge information about the IMS.

BRETTON WOODS DEVELOPMENT

As the powerful nations of the world were hopeful of a new and more stable world order with the emergence of the UNO, they were also anxious for a more homogenous world financial order after the Second World War. The representatives of the USA, the UK and 42 other (total 44 countries) nations met at Bretton Woods, New Hampshire, USA in July 1944 to decide a new international monetary system. The International Monetary Fund (IMF) and the World Bank (with its first group-institution IBRD) were set up together—popularly called the ***Bretton Woods' twins***[3]—both having their headquarters in Washington DC, USA.

INTERNATIONAL MONETARY FUND

The International Monetary Fund (IMF) came up in 1944 whose Articles came into force on the 27 December, 1945, with the main functions as exchange rate regulation, purchasing short-term foreign currency liabilities of the member nations from around the world, allotting special drawing

3. For the new international monetary system, basically two plans were presented in the meeting—one by the US delegation led by ***Harry D. White*** (of the US Treasury) and the British delegation led by ***John Meynard Keynes.*** It was the US plan which was ultimately agreed upon.

J.M. Keynes had proposed a more impartial, practical and over-arching idea via his plan at Bretton Woods. His suggestions basically included three things:

(i) Proposal to set up an International Clearing Union (ICU), a central bank of all central banks, with its own currency (Keynes named this currency ***'bancor'***)—to mitigate the balance of payment crises of member nations.

This bank was supposed to penalise (***no such provision in the IMF***) the countries holding trade surpluses (with a global tax of one per cent per month) on the ground that such countries were keeping world demand low by under-purchasing the products produced by other countries. The corpus collected via this tax was to be used to maintain an international buffer stock of primary goods (i.e., food articles)—to be used in the periods of food shortages among the member nations. (***In place, under the IMF provisions trade deficit countries are penalised.***)

(ii) For the reconstruction of war-devastated Europe, a ***fund*** was to be set up, on the basis of this plan for Relief and Reconstruction (in place of it the US-sponsored ***Marshall Plan*** took care of the needs of Europe).

(iii) There was a proposal of creating Commodity Buffer Stock to be operated by an International Trade Organisation (ITO). This stock of primary goods was to be used to stabilise their prices in the international market.

The operation of this ITO was making purchases when the world prices were low and selling when the prices became high. The buffer stock operations, however, were to be helpful to the poor countries. Keynes was primarily interested in stabilising the input prices of the rich countries. (***Though the charter of the ITO was drawn up and other formalities completed, it was never born because of US opposition.***) ***For further reading, see*** D. Salvatore, ***International Economics,*** 742–43; B. Dasgupta, ***Globalisation : India's Adjustment Experience*** (New Delhi: Sage, 2005), p. 48.

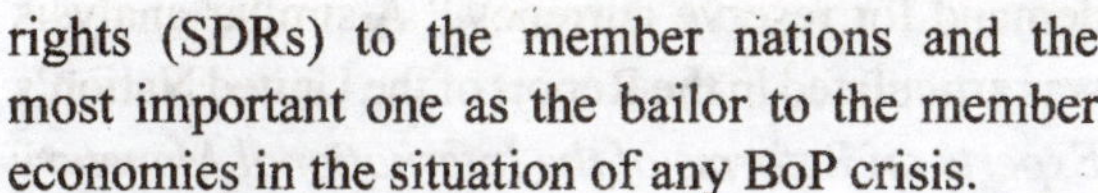

rights (SDRs) to the member nations and the most important one as the bailor to the member economies in the situation of any BoP crisis.

The ***main functions***[4] of the IMF are given below:

1. to facilitate international monetary cooperation;
2. to promote exchange rate stability and orderly exchange arrangements;
3. to assist in the establishment of a multilateral system of payments and the elimination of foreign exchange restrictions; and
4. to assist member countries by temporarily providing financial resources to correct mal-adjustment in their balance of payments (BoPs).

The Board of Governors of the IMF consists of one Governor and one Alternate Governor from each member country. For India, Finance Minister is the Ex-officio Governor while the RBI Governor is the Alternate Governor on the Board.

The day-to-day management of the IMF is carried out by the Managing Director who is Chairman *(currently, Ms Christine Lagarde)* of the Board of Executive Directors. The Board of Executive Directors consists of 24 directors appointed/elected by member countries/group of countries.—is the executive body of the IMF. India is represented at the IMF by an Executive Director (*currently Arvind Virmani*), who also represents three other countries in India's constituency, viz., Bangladesh, Sri Lanka and Bhutan.

India's Quota & Ranking

IMF reviews members' quotas once in every five years—last done in December 2010—here, India consented for its quota increase. After this, India's quota (together with its 3 constituency countries) has increased to **2.76** per cent (from 2.44 per cent) and it has become the **8th** (from 11th) largest quota holding country among the **24** constituencies. In absolute terms, India's quota has increased to SDR 13,114.4 million (from SDR 5,821.5 million), which is an increase of approximately US $ 11.5 billion or ₹56,000 crore). While 25 per cent of the quota is to be paid in ***cash*** (i.e., in 'Reserve' currency), the balance 75 per cent can be paid in ***securities.***[5]

Once a member nation has signed the ***EFF*** (Extended Fund Facility) agreement with the IMF, borrowing[6] can be done by the member nation—India signed this agreement in the fiscal 1981–82. ***India has been borrowing*** from the IMF due to critical balance of payment (BoP) situations—once between 1981–84 (SDR 3.9 billion) and next during 1991 (SDR 3.56 billion). India is now a *contributor* to the IMF as it has been participating in the Financial Transactions Plan (FTP)[7] of the IMF since September 2002—at this time India was in strong balance of payment situation and in a comfortable forex reserves position.

Current US/EU Financial Crises: Challenges Regarding International Payments

The recent financial crises of the US and the EU nations have raised the questions of the challenges of international payments once again. At this crucial juncture, the world seems tossing the idea of a reserved currency for all international

4. ***Basic Facts About the United Nations*** (New York: United Nations, 2000), pp. 55–137.

5. These securities are non-interest bearing note purchase agreements issued by the RBI which can be encashed by the IMF anytime as per its requirement. They do not entail any cash outgo unless the IMF calls upon India to encash a portion of these notes. The 'Reserve' (paid in 'cash') asset portion of the quota is counted as a part of country's 'Reserves'.

6. Such facility from it is available once the member country has signed the agreement with the IMF called the Extended Fund Facility (EFF). Popularly, this is known as the ***'Conditionalities of the IMF'*** under which India started its Economic Reform Programme in 1991–92 once it borrowed from the IMF in the wake of the BoP crisis of 1990–91.

7. FTP is the mechanism of the IMF through which it finances/repays its operations—member nations contribute money into it from their 'quota resources' on which they get 'interest'.

payments—as if the famous Keynesian idea of such a currency (Bancor) is going for a kind of revival. The **Bancor** was a supranational currency that John Maynard Keynes and E. F. Schumacher[8] conceptualised in the years 1940–42, which the United Kingdom proposed to introduce after the Second World War. The proposed currency was, to be used in international trade as a unit of account within a multilateral barter clearing system, the *International Clearing Union*, which would also have to be founded. The Bancor was to be backed by barter and its value expressed in weight of gold. However, this British proposal could not prevail against the interests of the United States, which at the Bretton Woods conference established the US Dollar as the world key currency. Milton Friedman[9], the famous US economist insisted that Keynes' theories were incorrect who believed that, 'inflation was highly destructive and that only monetary policy could control it and that monetary policy is a heavyweight instrument and cannot be used for short-term economic management.'

Since the outbreak of the financial crisis in 2008, ***Keynes's proposal*** has been revived—in a speech delivered in March 2009 entitled *Reform the International Monetary System,* Zhou Xiaochuan, the Governor of the People's Bank of China, called Keynes's Bancor approach **farsighted** and proposed the adoption of International Monetary Fund (IMF) special drawing rights (SDRs) as a global reserve currency as a response to the financial crisis of 2007–2010. He argued that a national currency was unsuitable as a global reserve currency because of the *Triffin dilemma*[10] —the difficulty faced by reserve currency issuers in trying to simultaneously achieve their domestic monetary policy goals and meet other countries' demand for reserve currency.[11] A similar analysis was articulated in the Report of the United Nation's *Experts on Reforms of the International Monetary and Financial System*[12] as well as in a recent IMF's study.[13]

 WORLD BANK

The World Bank (WB) Group today consists of *five* closely associated institutions propitiating the role of development in the member nations in different areas. A brief account is as follows.[14]

IBRD

The International Bank for Reconstruction and Development (IBRD) is the oldest of the WB institutions which started functioning (1945) in the area of reconstruction of the war-ravaged regions (World War II) and later for the development of the middle-income and credit-worthy poorer economies of the world. Human development was the main focus of the developmental lending with a very low interest rate (1.55 per cent per annum)—the areas of focus being agriculture, irrigation, urban development, healthcare, family welfare, dairy development, etc. It commenced lending for India in 1949.

After the process of reforms started in the World Bank in 2010, India was allotted additional shares in IBRD (now holds 56,739 shares accounting to US $ 6,844.7 million). With this India emerged as the 7th largest shareholder

8. ***E. F. Schumacher,*** *Multilateral Clearing Economica,* New Series, Vol. 10, No. 38 (May, 1943), pp. 150-165.
9. ***M. Friedman,*** (1968) *The American Economic Review,* Vol. 58, No. 1, pp. 1-17.
10. ***Zhou Xiaochuan,*** 'Reform the International Monetary System', BIS Review 2009, Bank of International Settlements, Basel, Switzerland, 28 November, 2011.
11. ***Zhou Xiaochuan,*** *Financial Times, 12th Dec. 2011.*
12. Recommendations by the Commission of Experts of the President of the General Assembly on reforms of the international monetary and financial system, UNO, 20th March, 2009.
13. ***Reserve Accumulation and International Monetary Stability,*** *IMF,* Washington DC, 13th April, 2010.
14. Based on ***Basic Facts About the United Nations,*** 52–55; Publication Division, ***India 2004*** (New Delhi: Government of India, 2007); Publication Division, ***India 2013*** (New Delhi: Government of India, 2014).

(up from the 11th position) in IBRD with voting power of 2.91 per cent (up from 2.77 per cent).[15]

IDA

The International Development Agency (IDA), which is also known as the *soft window* of the WB, was set up in 1960 with the basic aim of developing infrastructural support among the member nations, long-term lending for the development of economic services. Its loans, known as *credits,* are extended mainly to economies with less than $895 per capita income. The credits are for a period of 35–40 years, *interest*-free, except for a small charge to cover administrative costs. Repayment begins after a 10-year grace period. In the beginning there was a human angle to its lending, but now there remain no hard and fast differences between the purposes for the IBRD and IDA lending.

Every year developing nations make enough diplomatic attempts to carve out maximum loan disbursal for themselves. India had been the ***biggest beneficiary*** of the IDA support. The total support (IBRD + IDA) for India had been $ 91.81 billion till date.[16] Since 2015 India did not avail any financial support from the IDA as it 'graduated' from the agency in the financial year 2014.[17]

IFC

The International Finance Corporation (IFC) was set up in 1956, which is also known as the *private arm* of the WB. It lends money to private sector companies of its member nations. The interest rate charged is commercial but comparatively low. There are many attractive features of IFC's lending. It finances and provides advice for private-public ventures and projects in partnership with private investors and, through its advisory work, helps governments of the member nations to create conditions that stimulate the flow of both domestic and foreign private savings and investment.

IFC focuses on promoting economic development by encouraging the growth of productive enterprises and efficient capital markets in its member countries. It participates in an investment only when it can make a special contribution that complements the role of market investors [as a foreign financial investor (FFI)]. It also plays a catalytic role, stimulating and mobilising private investment in the developing world by demonstrating that investments there, too, can be profitable.

We have seen a great upsurge in the IFC investments in India which has undoubtedly strengthened the foreign investors' confidence in the Indian economy.

MIGA

The Multilateral Investment Guarantee Agency (MIGA), set up in 1988, encourages foreign investment in developing economies by offering insurance (guarantees) to foreign private investors against loss caused by *non-commercial (i.e., political) risks,* such as currency transfer, expropriation, war and civil disturbance. It also provides technical assistance to help countries disseminate information on investment opportunities.

ICSID

The International Centre for Settlement of Investment Disputes (ICSID), set up in 1966, is an investment dispute settlement body whose decisions are binding on the parties. It was established under the 1966 *Convention on the Settlement of Investment Disputes between States and Nationals of Other States*. Though recourse

15. Publication Division, ***India 2014*** (New Delhi: Government of India, 2015), p. 322.
16. Publication Division, ***India 2013***, p. 415.
17. International Development Agency, World Bank, Washington DC, USA, March 2019.

to the centre is voluntary, but once the parties have agreed to arbitration, they cannot withdraw their consent unilaterally. It settles the investment disputes arising between the investing foreign companies and the host countries where the investments have been done.

India is not its member (that is why the Enron issue was out of its preview). It is believed that being signatory to it encourages the foreign investment flows into an economy, but risks independent sovereign decisions, too.

ASIAN DEVELOPM ENT BANK

Set up in 1966 with 31 founding members (India being one of them), today (by *March 2017*) it has grown to encompass 67 members—of which 48 are from Asia and Pacific and 19 from outside. It has its headquarters situated at Manila, Philippines.

The *purpose* of the Bank is to foster economic growth and co-operation in the region of Asia and the Far East and to contribute to economic development of the developing member countries, collectively and individually. The six *functions* of the Bank are clubbed below:

1. Promoting investment—public and private—and harmonious regional development with special regard to less developed member countries;
2. Coordinating development policies and plans (on request); promoting intra-regional trade; providing technical assistance in financing, execution and project proposals;
3. Co-operating with the UNO and other international institutions—public and private—and undertaking other activities and provide other services advancing its purpose.

India's subscription to the Bank's capital stock is 6.331 per cent with a voting power of 5.363 per cent (as per the *ADB Annual Report, 2018*).

India started borrowing from ADB's Ordinary Capital Resources (OCR) in 1986. The Bank's lending has been mainly in the energy, transport and communications, finance, industry and social infrastructure sectors.

The Bank has extended technical assistance to India in addition to loans from its OCR window. The technical assistance provided includes support for institutional strengthening, effective project implementation and policy reforms as well as for project preparation.

India holds the position of Executive Director on the Board of Directors of the Bank—its constituency comprises India, Bangladesh, Bhutan, Lao PDR and Tajikistan. The Finance Minister is India's Governor on the Board of Governors of the Asian Development Bank and Secretary (EA) is the Alternate Governor.

OECD

The roots[18] of the Organisation for Economic Co-operation and Development (OECD), Paris, go back to the rubble of Europe after World War II. Determined to avoid the mistakes of their predecessors in the wake of World War I, European leaders realised that the best way to ensure lasting peace was to encourage co-operation and reconstruction, rather than punish the defeated.

The Organisation for European Economic Cooperation (OEEC) was established in 1947 to run the US-financed **Marshall Plan** for reconstruction of a continent ravaged by war. By making individual governments recognise the interdependence of their economies, it paved the way for a new era of cooperation that was to change the face of Europe. Encouraged by its success and the prospect of carrying its work forward on

18. Publication Division, *India 2012* (New Delhi: Government of India, 2013), p. 418.

a global stage, Canada and the US joined OEEC members in signing the new OECD Convention on 14 December, 1960. The Organisation for Economic Co-operation and Development (OECD) was officially born on September 30, 1961, when the Convention entered into force.

Other countries joined in, starting with Japan in 1964. Today, **35** OECD member countries worldwide regularly turn to one another to identify problems, discuss and analyse them, and promote policies to solve them. The track record is striking. The US has seen its national wealth almost ***triple*** in the five decades since the OECD was created, calculated in terms of gross domestic product per head of population. Other OECD countries have seen similar, and in some cases even more spectacular, progress.

There are many countries that a few decades ago were still only minor players on the world stage—China, India and Brazil have emerged as new economic giants. Most of the countries that formed part of the former Soviet bloc have either joined the OECD or adopted its standards and principles to achieve the common goals. Russia is negotiating to become a member of the OECD, and now the organisation has close relations with Brazil, China, India, Indonesia and South Africa through its 'enhanced engagement' programme. Together with them, the OECD brings around its table **40** countries that account for **80** per cent of world trade and investment, giving it a pivotal role in addressing the challenges facing the world economy.

India & OECD India has got 'enhanced engagement' (since 2007) with the body, however, 'accession' (membership) to it is distinct—though it has the potential in future leading to it. The accession process to it is complex and longer as it involves a series of examinations to assess a country's ability to meet its OECD standards in a wide range of policy areas. Meanwhile, India's relationship with the OECD has developed steadily since 1998 (when it joined its Steel Committee)—since 2007 being its 'Key Partner'. Since 2017, India has been participating as an *Associate* or *Participant* in 21 OECD bodies and adheres to 9 OECD legal instruments, making it an important contributor to several areas of importance—from corporate governance to fiscal matters to nuclear energy. Furthermore, India plays an active role in OECD's regional activities in Asia together with co-operation on various international fora.

WORLD TRADE ORGANISATION (WTO)

The World Trade Organisation (WTO) came into being as a result of the evolution of the multilateral trading system starting with the establishment of the General Agreement on Tariffs and Trade (GATT) in 1947. The protracted Uruguay Round negotiations spanning the period 1986–1994, which resulted in the establishment of the WTO, substantially extended the reach of multilateral rules and disciplines related to trade in goods, and introduced multilateral rules applicable to trade in agriculture (Agreement on Agriculture), trade in services (General Agreement on Trade in Services—GATS) as well as Trade Related Intellectual Property Rights (TRIPS). A separate understanding on WTO dispute settlement mechanism (DSU) and trade policy review mechanism (TPRM) was also agreed upon.

The WTO provides a rule based, transparent and predictable multilateral trading system. The WTO rules envisage non-discrimination in the form of National Treatment and ***Most Favoured Nation (MFN)*** treatment to India's exports in the markets of other WTO members. National Treatment ensures that India's products, once imported into the territory of other WTO members, would not be discriminated vis-à-vis the domestic products in those countries. MFN treatment principle ensures that members do not discriminate among various WTO members. If a member country believes that the due benefits are not accruing to it because of trade measures by another WTO member, which are violative of WTO rules and disciplines, it may file a dispute under the Dispute Settlement Mechanism (DSM) of the WTO. There are also contingency provisions built into WTO rules, enabling member countries to take care of exigencies like balance of payment problems and situations like a surge in imports. In the case of unfair trade practices causing injury to the domestic producers, there are provisions to impose Anti-Dumping or Countervailing duties as provided for in the Anti-Dumping Agreement and the Subsidies and Countervailing Measures Agreement.

Membership The present membership[19] of the WTO is **164**. The last member to join was Afghanistan (March 2016) after a long negotiation process of eleven years. Other than its members, at present, there are 22 observer governments including Afghanistan, Holy See (Vatican), Iran, Iraq, Libya, Uzbekistan, etc. As per the guidelines of the WTO, observers (except Holy See) must start accession negotiations within *five years* of becoming observers.

Ministerial Conferences Ministerial Conferences are the highest decision-making body of the WTO which is to meet at least every two years. These conferences bring all members together which are countries or separate customs territories. During these conferences, decisions on all matters can be taken. By now, there have been 11 such conferences of the body—the *11th Ministerial Conference* took place in Buenos Aires, Argentina (December 10-13, 2017).

The ***12th Ministerial Conference (MC12)*** will take place in the week of 29 November 2021 in Geneva, Switzerland (which was endorsed by its General Council on March 1st, 2021). MC12 was originally scheduled to take place in June 2020 in Kazakhstan's capital, *Nur-Sultan,* but was postponed due to the COVID-19 pandemic. However, the conference has been approved to be chaired by Kazakhstan itself.

Previous conferences *Nairobi*(15–19 December, 2015); *Bali* (3–6 December 2013); *Geneva* (15–17 December 2011); *Geneva* (30 November–2 December 2009); *Hong Kong* (13–18 December 2005); *Cancun* (10–14 September 2003); *Doha* (9–13 November 2001); *Seattle* (30 November – 3 December, 1999); *Geneva* (18–20 May 1998) and *Singapore* (9–13 December 1996).

NAIROBI NEGOTIATIONS & INDIA

The WTO held its 10th Ministerial Conference in Nairobi, Kenya during 15–19 December 2015. This was the first such meeting to be hosted by an African nation. The outcomes of the Conference, referred to as the ***Nairobi Package***, are given below[20]:

1. The Nairobi Declaration reflects divergence amongst the WTO membership on the relevance of reaffirming the *Doha Development Agenda (DDA)* as the basis of future negotiations. This was despite the fact that India, along with many other developing countries, from groups such as the G-33, LDCs, and the Africa Group, wanted a reaffirmation of the mandate of the Doha Round. While reflecting that there are divergences, the Ministerial Declaration also notes the "strong commitment of all Members to advance negotiations on the remaining Doha issues". It records that WTO work would maintain development at its centre. It also reaffirms that provisions for special and differential treatment shall remain integral.
2. As the future of the Doha Round appeared in doubt, India sought and succeeded in obtaining a re-affirmative Ministerial Decision on *Public*

19. As per the WTO website, April 2021.

20. Ministry of Finance, **Economic Survey 2015-16** (New Delhi: Government of India, 2016), Vol. 2, pp. 73–75.

Stockholding for Food Security Purposes honouring both the *Bali* Ministerial and General Council Decisions. The decision commits members to engage constructively in finding a *permanent solution* to this issue.

3. A large group of developing countries has long been seeking an SSM (Special Safeguard Mechanism) for *agricultural products*. In order to ensure that this issue remains on the agenda of future discussion in the WTO, India negotiated a Ministerial Decision which recognises that developing countries will have the right to have recourse to an SSM as envisaged in the mandate. Members will continue to negotiate the mechanism in dedicated sessions of the Committee on Agriculture in Special Session.

4. It was also agreed to eliminate *agricultural export subsidies* subject to the preservation of special and differential treatment for developing countries such as a longer phase-out period for transportation and marketing export subsidies for exporting agricultural products. Developed countries have committed to removing export subsidies immediately, except for a few agricultural products, and developing countries will do so by 2018.

5. Developing countries will keep the flexibility to cover *marketing and transport subsidies* for agriculture exports until the end of 2023, and the LDCs and net food-importing developing countries would have additional time to cut such export subsidies. The Ministerial Decision contains disciplines to ensure that other export policies are not used as a disguised form of subsidies. These disciplines include—
   (i) terms to limit the benefits of financing support to agriculture exporters;
   (ii) rules on state enterprises engaging in agriculture trade; and
   (iii) disciplines to ensure that food aid does not negatively affect domestic production.

6. One of the Decisions adopted extends the relevant provision to prevent *'ever-greening'* of patents in the pharmaceuticals sector. This decision would help in maintaining an affordable and accessible supply of *generic medicines*.

7. India supported outcomes on issues of interest to LDCs, including enhanced preferential rules of origin for LDCs and preferential treatment for LDC services providers. India already offers duty-free, quota-free access scheme to all LDCs, which provides a comprehensive coverage with simple, transparent and liberal rules of origin. India has also recently (late 2015) made available substantial and commercially meaningful preferences in services to LDCs.

8. The issue of *fisheries* subsidies could not be resolved due to lack of consensus. Including India, several other countries (China, Egypt, South Africa, Korea and Saudi Arabia, etc.) were opposed to disciplining rules on fisheries subsidies due to lack of clarity.

9. On the issue of *Anti-dumping*, India strongly opposed a proposal that would give greater power to the WTO's Anti-Dumping Committee to review Members' practices. Due to lack of convergence, no outcome was achieved.

10. A group of 53 WTO members, including both developed and developing countries, agreed on the timetable for implementing a deal to *eliminate tariffs* on 201 Information Technology products. This duty-free market will be available to all WTO members (even to India, which was not party to the agreement).

11. As regards the introduction of other ***new issues*** for discussion, the Declaration acknowledges the differences in views and states that any decision to launch negotiations multilaterally on such issues would need to be agreed by all members. The rich (developed) countries wanted the introduction of new issues of their interests which included—*global value chain, e-commerce, competition laws, labour, environment* and *investments.*

BUENOS AIRES CONFERENCE AND INDIA

The 11th Ministerial Conference (MC11) of World Trade Organisation (WTO), which took place in Buenos Aires, Argentina (10-13 December, 2017), ended *without* a Ministerial Declaration or any substantive outcome, though the unanimous view was that it was extremely well-conducted with complete openness and transparency and the process afforded everyone ample opportunity to express their views. Major developments (as per the *Economic Survey 2017–18*) at the conference were as given below:

- In the run-up to MC11, decisions were expected on a permanent solution on food security and other agriculture issues. Unfortunately, the strong position of one of the member (the USA) against agricultural reforms based on current WTO mandates and rules, led to a deadlock without any outcome on agriculture or even a work programme for the next two years. However, the existing mandates and decisions ensure that work will go forward and members will continue to work on issues such as the permanent solution on public stockholding for food security purposes, agricultural Special Safeguard Mechanism and agricultural domestic support.
- Some of the other decisions that were taken included a Work Programme on disciplines on Fisheries Subsidies with a view to arriving at a decision by MC12.
- It was also decided to continue with the non-negotiating mandate of the existing Work Programme on e-commerce.
- On new issues like investment facilitation, MSMEs, gender and trade, which lacked a mandate or consensus, Ministerial Decisions were not taken forward.
- India stood firm during the Conference on its stand on the fundamental principles of the WTO, including multilateralism, rule-based consensual decision-making, an independent and credible dispute resolution and appellate process, the centrality of development, which underlies the Doha Development Agenda (DDA), and special and differential treatment for all developing countries. Meanwhile, India continues to negotiate with the countries with similar views at mini-Ministerial Conferences to reach a consensus on the issues which derailed the Buenos Aires Conference of the trade body.

INDIA AND WTO

India has played an important part in the effective formulation of major trade policies. Increasing protectionism, inadequate members in the Appellate Tribunal for dispute resolution, increasing number of Regional Trade Agreements (RTAs) and Free Trade Agreements (FTAs), etc. have resulted in member countries questioning the efficacy of WTO as an institution meant to ensure free trade and promote multilateralism. Some of the initiatives[21] taken by India during 2020-21 to strengthen the WTO are given below:

TRIPS Waiver India and South Africa jointly proposed 'Waiver from Certain Provisions of the TRIPS Agreement for the Prevention, Containment

21. **Economic Survey 2020-21**, vol. 2, pp. 119- 20, Ministry of Finance, GoI, N. Delhi.

and Treatment of COVID-19' for a limited time period, with a view to ensuring that the intellectual property rights do not become a barrier in the timely and affordable access to medical products, including vaccines and therapeutics (the proposal received broad-based support from many, civil society and international organisations).

Appellate Body The AB (Appellate Body) of the WTO is a permanent body intended by the DSU (Dispute Settlement Understanding) to resolve appeals on issues of law. It is ordinarily composed of 7 members having a 4-year term, with the possibility of 1 reappointment. Since July 2017, the United States has been *stalling* AB appointments on the pretext that it has not been functioning in accordance with the DSU norms—precipitating the 'Appellate Body crisis'. With fewer than 3 members to hear any appeal (since 10th December, 2019), the AB is not able to function as mandated. In the wake of this crisis, around 23 WTO members have created an MPIA (Multiparty Interim Arbitration) mechanism that closely replicates the substantive and procedural aspects of appellate review under the AB (with the EU, China, Brazil, Australia, New Zealand being some of the key members of it).

India has *not joined* MPIA yet, which supports the *restoration and preservation* of the normal functioning of the two-stage binding WTO dispute settlement mechanism.

Agriculture In the case of agriculture, India, along with many other developing countries, has been demanding a *permanent solution* on the issue of public stockholding for food security purposes. This has become even more relevant in the wake of the ongoing pandemic, as the government had to step up disbursement of foodgrains under the public distribution programmes for ensuring food security of the masses.

India has also been raising the issue of imbalances and asymmetries in the existing AoA (Agreement on Agriculture) and their implications for developing countries.

Fisheries As per the Buenos Aires Ministerial Decision (MC11) of December, 2017, WTO Members agreed to continue to engage constructively to frame disciplines on *fisheries subsidies* by the next Ministerial Conference (MC-12) in 2020. The negotiations are ongoing and are being conducted in the form of monthly cluster meetings under NGR (Negotiating Group on Rules) in the WTO.

Electronic Transmission WTO members agreed not to impose customs duties on electronic transmissions in 1998 and since then, the moratorium has been extended periodically at the ministerial meetings. India and South Africa made a joint submission under the Work Program on E-Commerce titled, 'The E-Commerce Moratorium: Scope and its Impact' in March, 2020, which argues that reconsideration of the moratorium is important for developing countries to preserve policy space for their digital advancement.

e-Commerce In response to the failure to obtain a multilateral mandate for rule-making in e-commerce, in January 2019, a Joint Statement on e-commerce was issued on behalf of 76 members of the WTO supporting rule-making on e-commerce.

India has not joined the said plurilateral initiative, which believes that developing countries need to focus on improving domestic physical and digital infrastructure, creating supportive policy and regulatory frameworks and developing digital capabilities to bridge the digital divide and enable shared benefits of digitalisation.

Trade Safeguards India conducts anti-dumping, anti-subsidy and safeguard investigations on the basis of applications filed by the domestic industry with prima facie evidence of dumping and subsidisation of goods (which damage the domestic industry). The DGTR (Directorate General of Trade Remedies) introduced an online portal – ARTIS (Application for Remedies in Trade for Indian industry and other Stakeholders) in April 2020 – to submit online petitions in this regard.

Reforms In the ongoing discussions on WTO reforms, India's proposal seeks to re-affirm the importance of development and promote inclusive growth. The broad elements of India's proposal include—

1. Preserving the core values of the Multilateral Trading System;
2. Resolving the impasse in the Dispute Settlement System;
3. Safeguarding development concerns; and
4. Transparency and Notifications.

BRICS BANK

Together with the process of globalisation, world regional forces have also been asserting their power through different short of alignments—the *Fortaleza Declaration* of heads of state (late July 2014) from Brazil, Russia, India, China, and South Africa (the BRICS countries) is another such attempt—creation of a BRICS Bank, i.e., New Development Bank (NDB). Major highlights about the bank are given below:

1. The bank will have initial subscribed capital of $50 billion—equally shared by the five nations.
2. The capital base is to be used for funding infrastructure and 'sustainable development' projects in the BRICS countries initially.
3. Other low and middle-income countries will be able to get funding as time progresses.
4. A *Contingent Reserve Arrangement* (CRA) of $100 billion is to be also created to provide additional liquidity protection to member-nations during balance of payments problems.
5. The CRA is being funded 41 per cent by China, 18 per cent each from Brazil, India, and Russia, and 5 per cent from South Africa.
6. CRA, according to the Declaration, is 'a framework for the provision of *currency swaps* in response to actual or potential short-term balance of payments pressures.'

More than the establishment of the NDB, the Fortaleza Declaration is remarkable for adoption of ***one-nation one-vote*** prescription for the proposed bank. The Bretton Woods institutions (the World Bank and the International Monetary Fund) have structures that are not equitable.

As per the experts, *two factors* have triggered the birth of the NDB:

1. BRICS have *emerged as a big economic power*, and solidified their ties in terms of commerce with the emerging market economies and developing countries (EMDCs) and they are a force to reckon with in the global economy.
2. Their *disenchantment* with the Bretton Woods institutions has been growing over the years.

Two statements of the *Fortaleza Declaration* make the situation more clear—

1. "We are confronted with persistent political instability and conflict in various global hotspots and non-conventional emerging threats. On the other hand, international governance structures designed within a different power configuration show increasingly evident signs of losing legitimacy and effectiveness, as transitional and ad hoc arrangements become increasingly prevalent, often at the expense of multilateralism."

2. "We believe the BRICS are an important force for incremental change and reform of current institutions towards more representative and equitable governance, capable of generating more inclusive global growth and fostering a stable, peaceful and prosperous world."

The BRICS bank development comes at a time when reforms at the Bretton Woods institutions fail to fructify for one reason or the other and with the US and European nations still not reconciled to concede BRICS nations a greater voice in the governance structure of the Bretton-Woods institutions.

Whether the BRICS-sponsored NDB will be a fitting alternative to the Bretton Woods twin depends on a host of factors. Major ones of these factors, among others, are its ability—

1. to put in place a conflict resolution mechanism,
2. to devise a robust credit appraisal mechanism, and
3. to put in place an effective supervisory regime.

The BRICS-sponsored development bank is not an isolated and unique initiative. Similar initiatives had sprung up in the past to blunt the might of Bretton-Woods twin. *Development Bank of Latin America* (created by *Andean* nations) in the 1960s, the Chiang Mai Initiative in early 2000s (of 10 ASEAN nations plus China, South Korea and Japan) to establish a network of bilateral *currency swap pacts* in the wake of Asian currency crisis, and the establishment of the *Bank of South* by Latin American countries in 2009 were the result of escalating dissatisfaction with the US-dominated IMF and World Bank.

India & the NOB India is supposed to be the biggest beneficiary of the bank. This looks quite possible as certain priorities of India match well with the priorities and lending provisions of the bank such as the bank aims at prioritising environmentally sustainable projects (75 per cent of its funds dedicated to this cause alone) while India is working today on the world's biggest plan of promoting 'green energy' through multiple means. By ***March 2021***, India had availed a total fund of US$ 4.9 billion to promote projects across a variety of sectors—renewable and green energy, transportation (roads and bridges), etc.—with several projects in the pipeline of approval for funding.

ASIAN INFRASTRUCTURE INVESTMENT BANK

The Asian Infrastructure Investment Bank (AIIB) was officially launched in 2014 by China with 21 Asian nations as the founding members. By *March 2019*, the bank had a total of 93 members from across the world (inclusive of the 23 prospective members). Still, the USA, Japan and Canada have not joined it rather. The experts suggested them to support it especially when the existing mechanism (the World Bank and Asian Development Bank) is not able to cater to the infrastructural needs of the continent.

The AIIB is aimed at providing finance to infrastructure projects in the Asia region, as a multilateral institution. It is planned to operate broadly in the same manner as existing multilateral development banks (MDBs) such as the World Bank and the Asian Development Bank (ADB). While much of the debate is centred on whether the AIIB will complement or compete with existing organisations, it is intended to be more a commercial bank—with nations as shareholders, than a purely development aid institution. In the wake of the COVID-19 pandemic a proposal under consideration as per which the bank may start financing 'social infrastructures' also. The AIIB will start with an authorised **capital base** of US$ 1 billion to be enhanced to **US $ 100 billion.**

Experts have termed it as a rival for the International Monetary Fund (IMF), the World Bank (WB) and the Asian Development Bank (ADB), which are regarded as dominated by developed countries like the United States.[22] The United Nations has addressed the launch of the AIIB as 'scaling up financing for sustainable development' and for the concern of Global Economic Governance.[23]

As per the experts and analysts, there are **several factors** which are behind such an initiative coming from China. The major ones are given below:

1. The Chinese government has been frustrated with what it regards as the slow pace of reforms and governance, and wants greater input in global established institutions like the IMF, World Bank and Asian Development Bank which, it claims, are dominated by American, European and Japanese interests.
2. The ADB, a Manila-based regional development bank designed to facilitate economic development in Asia, estimated in a report that developing Asian countries have an infrastructure demand of about US$ 8 trillion between 2010–2020— $2.5 trillion for roads and railroads, $4.1 trillion for power plants and transmission, $1.1 trillion for telecommunications, and $0.4 trillion for water and sanitation investments.[24]
3. Oxford Economics reported that by 2025, the region will constitute 60 per cent of global infrastructure investment, with China's share alone is expected to increase from around 22 per cent to 36 per cent over the next decade.
4. Despite the significant economic growth enjoyed by countries such as China, India, and South Korea in recent decades, many countries among the developing Asian regions are still mired in poverty, suffering from a profound lack of access to modern-day necessities such as sanitation, a reliable power grid, and adequate transportation and communications networks.
5. It is believed that the new bank could allow Chinese capital to finance these projects and allow it a greater role to play in the economic development of the region commensurate with its growing economic and political clout.

Size of the AIIB Based on the lending capital ratios of the World Bank and European Development Bank, the AIIB could extend loans for infrastructure spending at around 100 per cent to 175 per cent of its subscribed capital. This would mean having outstanding loans of up to $US175 billion. With Public Private Partnerships and increased subscriptions, considerably larger amounts could be leveraged for projects in the future.

By March 2021, the bank had promoted 59 infrastructure projects across Asia with a total investment capital of US$ 11.3 billion.

An edge to China The Bank is supposed to give China an edge in the global economy in the following ways:

1. The AIIB will be a better way for China to deploy its massive foreign exchange reserves which are currently earning next to nothing in US Treasury bonds. China believes that the commercial financing of infrastructure differentiates the AIIB from the likes of the

22. The Guardian, 'Support for China-led development bank grows despite US opposition', UK edition, 13 March, 2015.
23. United Nations Financing for Development Office, 'Global Economic Governance', New York, 20 March, 2015.
24. ***The Economist***, *'An Asian Infrastructure Bank: Only Connect'*, 4 October, 2013; Biswa N. Bhattacharyay, ***Estimating Demand for Infrastructure in Energy, Transport, Telecommunications, Water and Sanitation in Asia and the Pacific: 2010–2020***, Asian Development Bank Institute, 9 September, 2010.

ADB which places a greater emphasis on poverty reduction.

2. The AIIB also supports China's strategic interests in its hugely ambitious 'Silk Road Economic Belt' policy.

3. By exporting technology, transferring development know-how, and facilitating industrialisation using Chinese long-term finance to the under-developed economies, China will not only find a bigger market, promote prosperity of all nations along the 'Belt and Road', but also diversify its foreign asset portfolio.

4. It will make China emerge a much bigger global power player which is supposed to be keen to challenge America's long-established strategy of institutionalising power in a rules-based order. The case of the AIIB shows that China now seeks to define this order for itself, with the battle for influence in Asia increasingly fought through rules and institutions.

5. The so-called 'rules-based order' was set up after the 2nd World War through policies such as the Bretton Woods agreement which established US dominated organisations such as the World Bank and IMF in which China plays a very small role.

India & AIIB India is one of the 21 founding members of the bank and is believed to benefit maximum from it. India holds 8.6794 per cent of its shares (with a total investment of US$ 8.3673 billion) and avails a 7.614 per cent voting rights (with a total of 86,214 shares) in it. India's shareholding is the *second highest* after China which holds 30.8913 per cent shares.

India is presently the *largest* borrower of the bank—for diverse projects it had borrowed a total of US$ 6.2 billion till ***March 2021*** with many more infra projects in the pipeline of consideration for financial support. Unlike most other multilateral development banks set up by developed countries, AIIB is the first major multilateral development bank where principal contributors are the borrowing members themselves.

REFORMING IMF & WB

Demand for suitable reforms in the Bretton Woods institutions—International Monetary Fund (IMF) and World Bank (WB)—is long overdue. Majority of the experts believe that the disillusionment from the delay in reforming them led the emerging market economies to look into alternatives and the outcome was the creation of the two new international financial institutions, the AIIB (Asian Infrastructure Investment Bank) and NDB (New Development Bank). The biggest hurdle in the path of reforms, the USA, at last came in favour of reforms (by early 2017) after the G20 Summit on it had already commenced (London, 2016). The *major reforms proposed* in the IMF and WB are given below[25]:

1. **Reforms in the IMF:** Proposal of a far-reaching reform of the IMF in order to restore its legitimacy and effectiveness so that it can help member nations fight immediate and future crises—touching the following areas:

   (i) Increasing its resource base so that it is able to help out (bail out in the case of balance of payment situations) nations in times of crisis. G20 wishes to increase its resources from the current level of US$250 billion to US$750 billion. It should be remembered that just after the 'sub-prime crisis' of 2008, the WB had estimated the resource shortfall of upto US$700 billion in 2009 alone!

25. The write-up is based on multiple sources *(upto April 2021)* such as—**The Economist, The Guardian, The Wall Street Journal**, several volumes of the **Economic Survey** of India and other media sources.

(ii) Merit-based selection of the head of the IMF, irrespective of nationality.

(iii) Eliminating the veto of the U.S. in key decisions.

(iv) Broadening the application of double-majority voting as a way to increase the role of smaller members.

(v) Revising the rule of quota and vote distribution to reflect accurately and fairly the current and future economic weight of the members.

(vi) Transforming its Board of Directors from a bureaucratic body to a high-level policy decision-making forum of ministers.

2. **Reforms in the WB:** In the case of the WB, the following reforms have been proposed:

(i) Need of Shareholders to replenish the capital base for 'soft' loans (while the IDA disburses interest-free, the IBRD disburses concessional loans to the eligible member nations and in recent years the WB has faced a resource crunch as several developed countries, especially the USA, proposed fund cuts).

(ii) Merit-based selection of the World Bank president—without regard to nationality.

(iii) Revamping of shareholdings and voting rights in the executive boards (to give a greater voice to emerging market economies and to borrowers).

(iv) Overhauling its operational modalities (so that it can react with less bureaucratic and time-consuming burdens to the legitimate needs of its borrowers).

It is believed that the successful launching and operation of the AIIB and NDB played an instrumental role in expediting the process of deliberations on reforming the IMF and WB. For reforms to take place, the US and Europe will need to move away from their long-held positions towards these institutions which looks a bit difficult as nations have their own priorities to support the moves towards reforms.

CHAPTER 17

TAX STRUCTURE IN INDIA

*Through taxes, government in reality decides how to draw the required resources from the nation's households and businesses for public purposes—the money raised so is the 'vehicle' by which real resources are transferred from private goods to public goods.**

In this Chapter...

- Tax
- Methods of Taxation
- A Good Tax System
- Methods of Expenditure
- Value Added Tax
- Goods and Services Tax
- Commodities Transaction Tax
- Securities Transaction Tax
- Capital Gains Tax
- Minimum Alternate Tax
- Corporate Tax Reform
- Dividend Distribution Tax
- Legitimacy and Taxation
- Ease of Paying Taxes
- Tax Administration Reforms
- Fifteenth Finance Commission
- Outlook for Future

TAX

Modern economics ***defines*** tax as a mode of income redistribution.[1] There might be other ways also to look at it—the usual meaning of tax people think is that a tax is imposed by the government to fulfil its important obligations on the expenditure front.[2] We may take an example to see how taxes redistribute income:

Suppose an economy has a flat rate of 30 per cent income tax. Just see the impact of this tax on the income disparity of two people A and B earning ₹50,000 and ₹80,000, respectively.

1. P.A. Samuelson and W.D. Nordhaus, ***Economics,*** (New Delhi: Tata McGraw Hill, 2005), p. 327.

2. For further reference, J.E. Stiglitz and C.E. Walsh, ***Economics,*** (New York: W.W. Norton & Company, 2006), pp. 378-79.

* **Economic Survey 2016-17,** *Government of India, Ministry of Finance, N Delhi, Vol. I, p. 7.*

Indivi-duals	*Nominal Income*	*Income Disparity before Tax*	*Income after paying Tax*	*Income Disparity after Tax*
A	₹50,000	₹30,000	₹35,000	₹21,000
B	₹80,000		₹56,000	

The table given above shows how the income disparity between two individuals A and B decreases from ₹30,000 to ₹21,000 after paying taxes—this is the *first level* when incomes of these individuals have got re-distributed.

Now the money the government has got by tax collection, i.e., ₹39,000 (₹15,000 + ₹24,000) will be spent on different sectors—infrastructure, education, health, etc.—which will provide services to one and all alike. Here income is re-distributed at the *secondary level*. Consider a person who pays income tax, but does not take services of government schools for his children's education, nor goes to the government hospitals for medical services and compare him with a person who has no option other than the government schools and the hospitals—the higher tax payer getting no government services and a lower tax payer getting all the services. Here income looks re-distributed from the consumption side.

Incidence of Tax

The point where tax looks as being imposed is known as the incidence of tax—the event of tax imposition.[3]

Impact of Tax

The point where tax makes its effect felt is known as the impact of tax—the after-effect of tax imposition.[4]

Direct Tax

The tax which has both incidence and impact at the same point is the direct tax—the person who is hit, the same person bleeds.[5] For example, income tax, interest tax, etc.

Indirect Tax

The tax which has incidence and impact at different points is the indirect tax—the person who is hit does not bleed[6] someone else's blood. For example, excise, sales tax, etc. are imposed on either the producers or the traders, but it is the general consumers who bear the burden of tax.

METHODS OF TAXATION

There are three methods of taxation prevalent in economies with their individual merits and demerits.

Progressive Taxation

Progressive taxation has increasing rates of tax for increasing value or volume on which the tax is being imposed.[7] Indian income tax is a typical example of it. The idea here is less tax on the people who earn less and higher tax on the people who earn more—classifying income earners into different slabs. This method is believed to discourage more earnings by the individual to support low growth and development unintentionally. Being poor is rewarded while richness is punished. Tax payers also start evading tax by showing lower unreal income. But from different angles, this tax is pro-poor and taxes people according

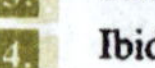

3. Samuelson and Nordhaus, ***Economics***, pp. 75-77.
4. Ibid.
5. Ibid., p. 329.
6. Ibid., p. 329.
7. Samuelson and Nordhaus, ***Economics***, 329; Stiglitz and Walsh, ***Economics***, p. 380.

to their affordability/sustainability. This is the most popular taxation method in the world and a populist one, too.

Regressive Taxation

Regressive taxation is just opposite to the progressive method having decreasing rates of tax for increasing value or volume on which the tax is being imposed.[8] There are not any permanent or specific sectors for such taxes. As a provision of promotion, some sectors might be imposed with regressive taxes. For example, to promote the growth and development of small scale industries, India at one time had regressive excise duty on their productions—with increasing slabs of volume they produced, the burden of tax used to go on decreasing.

This method, while appreciated for rewarding the higher producers or income-earners, is criticised for being more taxing on the poor and low-producers. This is not a popular mode of taxation and not as per the spirit of modern democracies.

Proportional Taxation

In proportional taxation there is neither progression nor regression from the point of view of rate of taxes. Such taxes have fixed rates for every level of income or production; of they are neutral from the poor or rich point view or from the point of view of the levels of production.[9] Usually, this is not used by the economies as an independent method of taxation. Generally, this mode is used as a complementary method with either progressive or regressive taxation. If not converted into proportional taxes, every progressive tax will go on increasing and similarly every regressive tax will decrease to zero, becoming completely futile tax methods. That is why every tax, be it progressive or regressive in nature, must be converted into proportional taxes after a certain level.

A GOOD TAX SYSTEM

What are the characteristics of a good tax system? There has always been a debate among economists and policymakers on the issue of design of the tax system. Taxation in developing economies has been even more debated as the trade-off assessment generates enough controversy. The main debatable issues in the design of a tax system are whether progressive or regressive taxation, direct tax or indirect tax collections should be higher, whether revenue deficit is better, etc. The controversies apart, there is a broad consensus on five ***principles***[10] of a good tax system among economists and policymakers. These are fairness, efficiency, administrative simplicity, flexibility and transparency.

Fairness

Though fairness (i.e., the first criterion of a good tax system) is not always easy to define, economists suggest the inclusion of two elements in the tax system to make it fair, namely, ***horizontal equity*** and ***vertical equity.*** When individuals in identical or similar situations pay identical or similar taxes, it is known as ***horizontal equity.*** When 'better off' people pay more taxes, it is known as ***vertical equity.***

Efficiency

The efficiency of a tax system is its potential to affect or interfere the efficiency of the economy. A good tax system raises revenue with the least cost on the taxpayers and least interference on the allocation of resources in the economy. The

8. Ibid.
9. Samuelson and Nordhaus, ***Economics***, p. 329.
10. Stiglitz and Walsh, ***Economics,*** p. 382. A comprehensive analysis of good tax structure is also given in ***Meade Committee Report,*** Institute for Fiscal Studies (IFS), Washington DC, 1978.

tax system affects the economic decisions of individuals and groups by either encouraging or discouraging them to save, spend, invest, etc. Taxes can improve efficiency of the economy—taxes on pollution or on smoking give revenue to the government and serve broader social purposes, too. This is known as the *double dividend* of a tax.

Administrative Simplicity

Administrative simplicity the third criterion which includes factors such as computation, filing, collection, etc. of the taxes that should be as simple as possible. Simplicity checks tax evasion too. Tax reform in India has simplification of tax as its major plank—also recommended by the Chelliah Committee.

Flexibility

A good tax system has the scope of desirable modifications in it if there is any such need.

Transparency

How much tax taxpayers are actually paying and what are they getting against it in the form of the public services should be ascertainable, i.e. the transparency factor.

METHODS OF EXPENDITURE

Similar to the methods of taxation, the modes of government expenditure are also of three types—progressive, regressive and proportional.[11]

At first instance, it seems that as a country achieves better levels of development, sectoral and the item-wise expenditure of the economy must have decreasing trends. But practical experience shows that the level of expenditure needs enhancement every day and the economy always needs more and more revenues to fulfil the rising expenditures. That is why for economies, the best form of government expenditure is the progressive expenditure.

The best way of taxation is progressive and the best way of government expenditure is also progressive and they suit each other beautifully. Most of the economies around the world are having progressive taxation with progressive expenditure.

VALUE ADDED TAX

The value added tax (VAT) is a method of tax collection as well as the name of a state level tax (*at present*) in India. A tax collected at every stage of value addition, i.e., either by production or distribution is known as value added tax.[12] The name itself suggests that this tax is collected on the value addition (i.e., production).

The production of goods or services is nothing but the stages of value additions where the production of goods is done by the industrialists or manufacturers. But these goods require value addition by different service providers/ producers (the agents, the wholesalers and the retailers) before they reach the consumers. From production to the level of sale, there are many points where value is added in all goods. VAT method of tax collection is different from the non-VAT method in the sense that it is imposed and collected at different points of value addition chain, i.e., *multi-point tax collection*. That is why there is no chance of imposing tax upon tax which takes place in the non-VAT method—*single point tax* collection. This is why VAT does not have a 'cascading effect' on the prices of goods and thus it does not increase inflation—and is therefore highly suitable for an economy like India where, due to high level of poverty, a large number of people lack the market level purchasing capacity. It is a pro-poor tax system without being anti-rich because rich people do not suffer either.

11. Based on the discussion on Government Expenditure in Samuelson and Nordhaus, *Economics.*

12. Ibid., p. 333

Need of VAT in India

Over 160 nations in the world have implemented the VAT system of taxation regarding collecting their indirect taxes. There have been valid reasons why India should move towards the VAT method of tax collection. We may see some of the major reasons:[13]

1. Due to single point tax collection, Indian indirect tax collection system was price-increasing (having *cascading effect* on the price) which was highly detrimental to the poor masses. The implementation of VAT will improve the purchasing capacity and thus living standard of the poor people.[14]
2. India is having a federal political system where side by side the central government, states have also been given power to impose taxes and collect them. At the central level, there had been uniformity of taxes for the economy. But there was no 'uniformity' at the state level taxes (i.e., state excise, sales tax, entertainment tax, etc.). This was detrimental to the development of a single market for Indian economy as a whole. India basically had many markets, but no Indian market as such. To bring in uniformity at the state-level taxes, VAT was a necessary step in India.
3. With the process of economic reforms, India moved towards the market economy. And for this, firstly India needed to have a single market. Without uniformity at the state level taxes (***uniform VAT***), this was not possible.
4. Indian federal design has resulted in economically weaker states and a stronger centre. As VAT increases the total tax collection (experience of the world suggests so), it was fit to be implemented at the state level.
5. India has been a country of high level tax evasion. By implementing VAT method of indirect tax collection, it becomes almost impossible to go for large-scale tax evasion. To prove one's level of value addition, the purchase invoice/receipt is a must which ultimately makes it cross-check the level of production and sale in the economy.[15]
6. If some of the state level taxes (which are many) are converted into state VAT, the complexity of taxation will also be minimised. And at the end, it is possible to merge some of the centre's indirect taxes with it, i.e., arrival of the ***single VAT***.

Keeping all such things in mind, India started tax reform (*Chelliah committee* and *kelkar Committee*) and a certain level of success has been achieved in this area.

1. In the year 1996, the central government started collecting its excise duty on the VAT method and the tax was given a new name—the CENVAT.
2. The next proposal was to merge the states' excise duty (imposed on intoxicants only) and their sales taxes into one tax—the state VAT or VAT. This could not take place due to states' lack of political will. Finally, only states' sales taxes could be modelled on value-added method and re-named as the VAT. With a time lag, all states went with this reform (in 2008–09) with apprehensions of shortfalls in their tax collections, making Centre to compensate them. In the beginning, a few states claimed for compensations in their revenue shortfall but by 2011–12 itself, VAT started

---

13. Derived from the points forwarded by the ***GoI*** and the ***Empowered Group of State Ministers.***
14. Raja C. Chelliah, Pawan K. Aggarwal, Mahesh C. Purohit and R. Kavita Rao, ***Introduction to Value Added Tax***, in Amaresh Bagchi (ed.). ***Readings in Public Finance*** (New Delhi: Oxford University Press, 2005), pp. 277-78.
15. Ibid.

generating higher tax collections in comparison to the erstwhile sales tax. Before the implementation of the GST (in which the VAT of states got merged into, except on petroleum and alcohol), the VAT collection was growing with a rate of 15 per cent per annum.

3. The GST (Goods and Services Tax) was finally implemented in 2017–18 (on July 1st, 2017) merging 17 of the existing central and state indirect taxes.

GOODS AND SERVICES TAX

After implementing the state VAT, the GoI wanted to go for the proposed GST (Goods and Services Tax). This is aimed at integrating the indirect taxes of Centre and states into a *single national tax*—popularly known as the *Single VAT* of India. By creating a *single market* at the pan-India basis, it will help the business and industry in a big way. The tax has the potential to increase GDP up to 2 per cent (conservative estimates by some experts). All the benefits which the state VAT brought to the market and economy are the same in the case of the GST, too. The *first proposal*[16] of the GST had suggested the following tax arrangements under it:

1. To be collected on the VAT method (will have all the same features of the VAT).
2. To be imposed at *pan-India* level with uniformity in tax—better say a *single rate* of indirect tax—replacing the multiple central and state indirect taxes.
3. *Four* taxes of Centre (cenvat; service tax; stamp duty and central sales tax) and *nine* taxes (excise duty, sales tax/vat; entry tax; lease tax; works contract tax; luxury tax; turnover tax; octroi and cess) of the states to be merged into the GST.
4. To have a single rate of 20 per cent (12 per cent to flow to Centre and 8 per cent to the states).

Implementation Process

After studying the Kelkar Committee report, the Government in 2006 decided to introduce the new tax from the financial year 2010–11. The lack of consensus between the centre and states kept the process delayed—to sort out the contentious issues, one after another, two independent *expert committees* submitted[17] their advice to the Government. Finally, the Constitution (101st Amendment) Bill, 2016 was cleared by the Parliament by early August 2016—paving the way for its implementation. By late September 2016, the GST Council (GSTC) was created by the Government. The Council has been entrusted with the power to make recommendations to the Union and the States on various issues—rates, floor rates, exemption, etc.—related to GST.

Finally, the new federal indirect tax GST was enforced[18] by the Government on July 1, 2017. The major features of the tax are as given below:

1. To apply to all goods other than 'alcoholic liquor for human consumption' and 'five petroleum products', viz. petroleum crude, motor spirit (petrol), high speed diesel, natural gas and aviation turbine fuel.
2. A total of 8 central taxes subsumed under it [Central Excise Duty; Duties of Excise (Medicinal and Toilet Preparations); Additional Duties of Excise (Goods of Special Importance); Additional

16. *Vijay Kelkar Task Force on the FRBM Act 2003*, Ministry of Finance, Economic Survey 2004-05, (New Delhi: Government of India, 2005), p. 40.

17. First it was from the National Institute of Public Finance and Policy (NIPFP), followed by the Subramanian Committee, during 2016-17.

18. ***Ministry of Finance***, Government of India, N. Delhi, July, 2017.

Duties of Excise (Textiles and Textile Products); Additional Duties of Customs (commonly known as Countervailing Duty, i.e., CVD); Special Additional Duty of Customs (SAD); Service Tax; and Central Surcharges and Cesses so far as they relate to supply of goods and services].

3. A total of 9 state taxes subsumed under it [State VAT; Central Sales Tax; Luxury Tax; Entry Tax (all forms); Entertainment and Amusement Tax (except when levied by the local bodies); Taxes on advertisements; Purchase Tax; Taxes on lotteries, betting and gambling; and State Surcharges and Cesses so far as they relate to supply of goods and services].
4. Concept of 'declared goods of special importance' dropped.
5. On inter-sate transactions of goods and services, an 'Integrated GST' will be levied.
6. The threshold limit for exemption from levy of GST would be ₹20 lakhs for normal States and ₹10 lakhs for the Special Category States.
7. The threshold for availing the Composition scheme would be ₹50 lakhs—with the Service providers kept out of it.
8. States to get compensation for 5 years for the loss of revenue due to, the implementation of GST (for this base year will be 2015–16 with growth rate of 14 per cent).
9. Minor changes in rules and regulations may be permitted with the approval of the Chairperson, if required (due to suggestions from the stakeholders or from the Law Department).
10. All exemptions/incentives on indirect taxes will rest withdrawn with obligation to pay GST. If any of them continues it will be administered by way of a reimbursement mechanism.
11. Bands of rates (in per cent) of goods under GST shall be 5, 12, 18 and 28 and in addition there would be a category of exempt goods. Further, a cess would be levied on certain goods such as luxury cars, aerated drinks, pan masala and tobacco products, over and above the rate of 28 per cent (for payment of compensation to the States).
12. Keeping in mind the federal structure of India, there will be two components of GST—Central GST (CGST) and State GST (SGST)—both Centre and States levying GST across the value chain on every supply of goods and services. States will assess 90 per cent of assessees with annual turnover below ₹1.5 crore while the remaining 10 per cent by the centre. For taxpayers with over ₹1.5 core turnover, the split is 50:50 between the centre and states.

GST Collections Tax collections were severely hit by the COVID-19 pandemic—GST collections being the lowest in April 2020 (₹36,000 crore). As economy started recovering, the monthly GST collections crossed the ₹1 lakh crore mark consecutively for the last 3 months, reaching its *highest ever* in December 2020 (₹1.15 lakh crore)— a 12 per cent growth over December 2019.[19]

An analysis was done by the Government to estimate the impact of GST rationalisation on GST revenue collection. It was found that a positive shock to the GST rationalisation variable (implying increasing the number of goods under

19. Economic Survey 2020-21, vol. 2, p. 54, Ministry of Finance, GoI, N. Delhi.

GST) leads to an increase in GST collection in first few months (one to three months) after the shock and then the impact tappers off.

Increased GST collections may be the result of concerted efforts made by the Government to improve tax compliance such as—extensive automation of business processes, application of e-way bill, targeted action on compliance verification, enforcement based on risk assessment and proposed introduction of electronic invoice system.

Inducing Voluntary Compliance To enhance voluntary compliance, Government took several *behavioural initiatives* (based on taxpayer's behaviour) in recent times, incorporating factors such as—deterrence; developing social and personal norms; reducing complexity; and enhancing fairness and trust. Some of the major initiatives[20] in this direction are as summarised below:

1. **E-Way bill:** For the transportation of goods above a certain threshold of value, electronic generation of bill (e-Way bill) is put in place. Through this, physical verification is possible which works as a deterrence against misreporting by the taxpayers.
2. **'PIN code to PIN code' distance mapping:** Mentioning origin and destination PIN Codes in e-Way bill is compulsory. This deters misuse of the bill for multiple trips and evading tax.
3. **Returns made public:** The return filing status of the taxpayer has been made a available in public domain (on the GST Portal). This enables the buyers to choose the compliant taxpayers for doing business. This helps the buyers to minimise business risk by increasing the probability of availing a timely 'input tax credit' (ITC). This measure uses *social* and *market* pressures to enhance compliance.
4. **Caution against mismatch in tax filing:** Making taxpayers informed about mismatch in their tax filing and 'induce' (i.e. encourage) them to correct it to avoid future litigation. This is done by cross-checking the tax filing forms (GSTR-2A & GSTR-3B; and GSTR-1 & GSTR-3B).
5. **Repeat reminders:** Taxpayers are sent repeat reminders through SMSs of due date of monthly filing and non-filing of return. This is aimed at inducing taxpayers to inculcate the habit of timely return filing.
6. **Free software:** In order to *ease* the compliance in the technology- driven GST regime, free software has been offered to taxpayers which takes care of services such as—preparing invoices, GST returns, Income Tax returns, Balance sheet and Profit & Loss statement. This eases compliance pressure on taxpayers, especially small businesses (which constituted more than 80 per cent of all GST taxpayers in March 2019).
7. **Questionnaire-based return filing:** To reduce complexity and simplify return filing process, a questionnaire-based return filing system has been put in place. Based on reply given by the taxpayer in it, only relevant tables are visible to taxpayers on return dashboard. This is meant to *ease* compliance for taxpayers.
8. **Compliance rating put in public domain:** GST Act provides for *public display* of compliance rating score of taxpayers based on record of compliance. This will work as a *deterrence* and induce punctual behaviour from taxpayers. Besides, public display of this information enhances transparency and improves trust of businesses in the tax administration, leading to evolution of a social norm of good compliance in the long run.

20. **Economic Survey 2019-20**, Vol. 2, pp. 48-51, Ministry of Finance, GoI, N. Delhi.

9. **Acknowledging contribution of compliant taxpayers:** A certificate is being issued to compliant taxpayers acknowledging their contribution in nation building. This appreciation serves to motivate taxpayers to continue their compliant behaviour in future as well.

GST-Induced Formalisation The need of GST[21] has commenced a vigorous process of formalisation in the economy— as increasing number of 'non-formal' firms have been registering for the new tax. This will not only enhance the level of tax compliance in the country but have effect, in medium- to long-term on income of people, tax collections (direct taxes also), social security of the employees, etc. Data made available in the process of GST collections are already giving the experts and Governments a new understanding (through data mining) about the economy.

COMMODITIES TRANSACTION TAX

The *Union Budget 2013-14* introduced (basically, *reintroduced*) the Commodities Transaction Tax (CTT), however, only for ***non-agricultural*** commodity futures at the rate of **0.01** per cent (which is equivalent to the rate of equity futures on which a *Securities Transaction Tax* is imposed in India). Along with this, transactions in commodity derivatives have been declared to be made *non-speculative*, and hence for traders in the commodity derivative segment, any losses arising from such transactions can be set off against income from any other source (similar provisions are also applicable for the securities market transactions).

Like all financial transaction taxes, CTT ***aims*** at discouraging excessive speculation, which is detrimental to the market and to bring parity between securities market and commodities market such that there is no tax/regulatory arbitrage. *Futures contracts* are financial instruments and provide for price risk management and price discovery of the underlying asset commodity/ currency/stocks/interest. It is, therefore, essential that the policy framework governing them is uniform across all the contracts irrespective of the underlying assets to minimise the chances of regulatory arbitrage. The proposal of CTT also appears to have stemmed from the general policy of the government to widen the tax base.

Commodities Transaction Tax (CTT) is a tax similar to Securities Transaction Tax (STT), proposed to be levied in India, on transactions done on the domestic commodity derivatives exchanges. Globally, commodity derivatives are also considered as financial contracts. Hence, CTT can also be considered as a type of 'financial transaction tax'.

The concept of CTT was ***first*** introduced in the *Union Budget 2008-09*. The government had then proposed to impose a commodities transaction tax (CTT) of 0.017 per cent (equivalent to the rate of equity futures at that point of time). However, it was withdrawn subsequently as the market was *nascent* then and any imposition of transaction tax might have adversely affected the growth of organised commodities derivatives markets in India. This has helped Indian commodity exchanges to grow to global standards [MCX is the world's ***No. 3*** commodity exchange; globally, MCX is ***No. 1*** in gold and silver, ***No. 2*** in natural gas and ***No. 3*** in crude oil].

SECURITIES TRANSACTION TAX

The Securities Transaction Tax (STT) is a type of 'financial transaction tax' levied in India on transactions done on the domestic stock exchanges. The rates of STT are prescribed by the central government through its budget from time to time. In tax parlance, this is categorised as a ***direct tax.*** The tax came into effect from *1 October, 2004*. In India, STT is collected for the

21. **Economic Survey 2019-20,** vol. 2, pp. 285-87, and **Economic Survey 2017-18,** vol. 2, pp. 32-42, Ministry of Finance, GoI, N. Delhi.

Government of India by the stock exchanges. With charging of STT, long-term capital gains tax was made *zero* and short-term capital gains tax was reduced to 10 per cent (subsequently, changed to 15 per cent since 2008).

The STT framework was subsequently reviewed by the central government in the year 2005, 2006, 2008, 2012 and *2013*. The STT rates were revised upwards in the year 2005 and 2006 while it was reduced for certain segments in 2012 and 2013. The STT provisions were altered in the year 2008 such that for professional traders (brokers), STT came to be treated as an *expense* which can be deducted from the income instead of treating the same as an advance tax paid. [The 2004 STT provisions provided that the STT payments of professional traders, whose 'business income' arising from purchase and sale of securities could be set off against their total tax liability.]

As on date, STT is not applicable in the case of *preference shares, government securities, bonds, debentures, currency derivatives, units of mutual fund other than equity oriented mutual fund,* and *gold exchange traded funds* and in **such cases,** tax treatment of short-term and long-term gains shall be as per normal provisions of law.

Transactions of the shares of listed companies on the floor of the stock exchange or otherwise, mandated under the regulatory framework of SEBI, such as *takeover, buyback, delisting offers,* etc. also do not come under STT framework. The *off-market* transactions of securities (which entails changes in ownership records at depositories) also do not attract STT.

CAPITAL GAINS TAX

Capital gains tax is a direct tax and applies on the sales of all 'assets' if a profit (gain) has been made by the owner of the asset—a tax on the 'gains' one gets by selling assets. The tax has been classified into two:

1. **Short Term Capital Gain (STCG):** It applies 'if the asset has been sold within 36 months of owning it'. In this case, the 'rate' of tax is similar to the normal income tax slab. But the period becomes '12 months' in cases of shares, mutual funds, units of the UTI and 'zero coupon bond'—in this case the 'rate' of tax is **15** per cent.
2. **Long Term Capital Gain (LTCG):** It applies 'if the asset has been sold after 36 months of owning it'. In this case, the 'rate' of tax is **20** per cent. In cases of shares, mutual funds, units of the UTI and 'zero coupon bond', there was 'exemption' (zero tax) though, recently, an LTCG of 10 per cent (above ₹1 lakh of capital gains) was introduced[22] on them by the Government.

MINIMUM ALTERNATE TAX

The Minimum Alternate Tax (MAT) is a direct tax imposed on the 'zero tax' companies at the rate of 18.5 per cent on their book profit. This was first imposed in 1997–98.

Basically, income tax is paid as per the provisions of the Income Tax Act (IT Act), but companies calculate their profit (through profit and loss account) as per the provisions of the Companies Act. The IT Act allows several kinds of exemptions and other incentives from total income together with deductions on the gross income. Again, the rate of 'depreciation' under the Companies Act is higher than the IT Act. As a result of these exemptions, deductions and other incentives under IT Act together with higher depreciation under the Companies Act, companies show their taxable income either 'nil' or 'negative', and this way, the 'zero tax' companies emerge.

22. ***Union Budget 2018-19*** introduced this tax (other than the Security Transaction Tax which these financial instruments already attract).

Practically, 'zero tax' companies might be having high 'book profit' and distributing huge dividends (under the Companies Act) to their shareholders, too, but by showing 'nil' or 'negative' taxable income (under the IT Act), they might not pay any income tax! To bring such companies under the income tax, *Section 115JB* was introduced in the IT Act in 1997–98 and MAT was imposed accordingly.

MAT is a way of making companies pay minimum amount of tax. It is applicable on all companies except those engaged in infrastructure and power sectors, free trade zones, charitable activities, venture and angel funds. Foreign companies with income sources in India also come under it. In 2015, the Government rationalised the MAT provisions for the FIIs (Foreign Financial Institutions)—now they do not need to pay MAT on their profits from capital gains on transactions in securities (which are liable to lower tax rate).

We may take an example – suppose a company has a 'book profit' of ₹10 lakh. And, after claiming the deductions, exemptions and depreciation, its 'gross taxable income' comes down to ₹6 lakh, its taxable income becoming ₹4 lakh. In this case, the applicable income tax would be ₹1.2 lakh (if rate of income tax is 30 per cent flat). But the company will pay a MAT of ₹1.85 lakh (at the rate of 18.5 per cent on its 'book profit' of ₹10 lakh). The company concerned needs to pay the tax which is higher—here, the tax to be paid will be ₹1.85 lakh.

At present, the tax is collected as an advance tax. The tax can be carried forward and set off (adjusted) against regular tax payable during the subsequent 10-year period (known as MAT credit). There has been a strong demand to abolish this tax in the country. In April 2017, the Government started phasing out the exemptions available to the companies on it from April 2017. In order that companies are able to use MAT credit, the carry forward period has been also increased to 15 years.

CORPORATE TAX REFORM

The joint stock companies (more popular as 'companies' and 'corporate' sector in India) pay a direct tax known as *corporate income tax* (popular as 'corporate tax') on their annual profits. The existing rates used to be 30 per cent for the domestic and 35 per cent for the foreign companies, operating in the country. Following the ongoing process of corporate tax reforms, the Government, in September 2019, affected a major change in the corporate income tax (CIT). The change[23] which was enforced from fiscal 2019–20 is being briefly summarised below:

- For the existing companies (with gross turnover over ₹400 crores), the base corporate tax was cut from 30 to 22 per cent. Thus, the effective rate (i.e. inclusive of surcharge and cess) fell down from 34.61 to 25.17 per cent. Companies can opt for the new tax rate by forgoing the deductions and exemptions availed by them. This will benefit 0.9 per cent of the companies (i.e. large ones) operating in the country (their number being 4,698).
- For the new manufacturing companies (with gross turnover below ₹400 crores), registered on or after 1st October 2019, the rate was cut from 25 to 15 per cent. In this case, the effective rate of tax fell down to 17.16 per cent. This will benefit 99.1 per cent companies (i.e. small and medium ones) of the country.

This drastic move was aimed at three major objectives—firstly, boosting the production volume of the manufacturing sector which involves a large number of MSMEs (including the newly launched start-ups); secondly, attracting higher investments in manufacturing industries; and thirdly, creating more job opportunities.

---

23. **Economic Survey 2019-20**, Vol. 2, pp. 46-48, Ministry of Finance, GoI, N. Delhi.

- The rate structure was left unchanged for the foreign companies.

Logic behind the reform In recent times, the corporate tax was cut by many countries across the world to attract investment and create jobs. India's move was an immediate response to rate cuts initiated by Asian developing countries, which compete with India in the global export markets. After the reform move, the corporate tax rate in India (for new manufacturing companies in particular) is lower than most of the ASEAN countries.

Countries	Tax Rate (%)
Timor	10
Singapore	17
Brunei	18.5
Vietnam	20
Thailand	20
Cambodia	20
Malaysia	24
Laos	24
Myanmar	25
Indonesia	25
Philippines	30

Source: Department of Revenue, Ministry of Finance, GoI, N. Delhi, April 2020.

Other than attracting investment and enhanced job creation, the move is also expected to have a multiplier effect on the economy—increased income levels and higher tax collections in the medium to long term.

DIVIDEND DISTRIBUTION TAX

The ownership of joint stock companies (i.e. the Ltd. firms) rests in the hands of their shareholders. Thus, such companies pay dividend (i.e. a part of profit) to their shareholders once they book operating profits. The dividend paid (distributed) by the companies to the shareholders used to attract a direct tax in India known as the dividend distribution tax (DDT). It means, before dividend to get paid to the shareholders, the DDT was to be paid to the tax department (that is known as payment of DDT in the 'hands of the companies'). The rate of tax *till March 2020* used to be 15 per cent.

Starting with the financial year ***2020-21,*** the Government affected a major change[24] in regard to the DDT—now companies don't need to pay this tax anymore. Now, the joint stock companies will transfer the dividend directly to the shareholders without deducting the tax. This way, the dividend earned by shareholders will be part of their personal income which will attract personal income tax (in place of dividend tax). It means, dividends will still attract the direct tax (i.e. individual income tax) in the hands of the recipients in place of the companies (which used to pay the DDT). But still, it will make a revenue loss to the Government as the tax will not apply now with a flat rate of 15 per cent, rather get paid as per the income slabs of the recipients. The change is estimated to entail a revenue loss of ₹25,000 crores annually.

Experts and stakeholders used to argue that the DDT resulted in increasing the tax burden for investors who already pay an income tax (i.e. corporate income tax) on their annual profits. This used to pinch those investors who are liable to pay tax less than the rate of DDT if the dividend income is included in their personal income—as personal income tax has various slabs. Further, non-availability of credit of DDT to most of the foreign investors in their home country resulted in reduction of rate of return (ROR) on equity capital for them. The move is aimed at making Indian equity market more attractive for investors—domestic as well as foreign. This move is supposed to provide a channel to Indian population to be part of the formal process of wealth creation in the

24. Union Budget 2020-21, Ministry of Finance, GoI, N. Delhi.

country besides routing investment in the nation building.

LEGITIMACY AND TAXATION

India commenced with a broad-based tax reforms programme in 1991 as an important part of the economic reforms process. Simplifying tax structure, cutting rate of taxes, enhancing tax compliance and broadening the tax base are the major contours of this reform programme. But even today, India has not fully translated its democratic vigour into commensurately strong fiscal capacity. The tax base of India is still not adequate. To build fiscal capacity, it is essential to create legitimacy in the state. In this regard the *Economic Survey 2015–16* presented a very timely and suitable piece of analysis. The document adds that to build fiscal capacity, the government needs to put in place a better tax regime which is only possible once the government is able to enhance its legitimacy among the citizens. The suggestions[25] forwarded by the Survey in this regard are briefly being given here.

1. The *spending priorities* of the government must include essential services which are consumed by all citizens. For that matter, action needs to be taken on public infrastructure, law and order, less pollution and congestion, etc.
2. *Reducing corruption* must be a high priority. However, this will be fiendishly (clever and imaginative) difficult. This is needed not just because of its economic costs but also because it undermines the legitimacy of the state. The more citizens believe that public resources are not wasted, the greater they will be willing to pay taxes. Improving transparency through efficient auctioning of public assets will help create legitimacy, and over time strengthen fiscal capacity.
3. *Subsidies to the well-off* need to be scaled back. At present[26], it is estimated to be around ₹1 lakh crore. Phasing down these bounties and targeting subsidies for the poor is important in strengthening legitimacy.

   In the same way, the existing regime of tax exemptions redistributes income towards the richer private sector—it dilutes the legitimacy of the state in the eyes of the poor citizens. There is a need of putting in place a reasonable taxation provision for the 'better off' section in the country regardless of where they get their income from—industry, services, real estate, or agriculture.
4. *Property taxation* needs to be developed. India lacks systematic data on property tax and whatever is there, it is very sparse. This proves the low attention the country has given to this issue. As property taxes are 'progressive', they are desirable. It makes more sense because evading this tax is difficult as they are imposed on immovable (non-mobile) assets. With the help of today's technologies, such properties can be easily identified.

Higher rates on properties (with values updated periodically) can be the foundation of local government's finances. This can provide local public goods and strengthen democratic accountability and more effective decentralisation. Higher property tax rates would also put sand in the wheels of property speculation. *Smart cities* require smart public finance and for India's urban future, a sound property taxation regime will be vital.

25. **Ministry of Finance,** Department of Revenue, Government of India, N. Delhi, April 2016.

26. Ministry of Finance, **Economic Survey 2015-16,** Vol. 1, pp. 105-117.

One low hanging fruit is to avoid raising exemption threshold and allow natural growth in income to increase the number of the taxpayers. The Survey has suggested a simple method for it—*inaction*. In 2016–17 itself, the Government began this process—exemption limit for individual income tax has been left unchanged together with a programme to link corporate tax cut and phase out of the exemption regime existing for the companies.

EASE OF PAYING TAXES

India has given high attention to improving its rank in the Doing Business report of the World Bank. It jumped up 79 positions (out of 190 countries) in the latest report improving from 142nd of 2014 to 63rd in 2019 *(Doing Business 2019)*. However, its rank still continues to trail on four parameters, one being Paying Taxes (rest of the three being Starting Business, Registering Property, and Enforcing Contracts). A comparative picture[27] of *ease of paying taxes* in India and a few other countries (especially, the peers like China, Brazil and Indonesia) are being summarised below:

- India's rank in ease of paying taxes has, however, improved from 156 in 2014 to 115 in 2019 but it has been much below expectations.
- India performs lowly in the case of a number of tax payments—while in India the number is 12 (from 59 of 2009), it is only 7 in China, 10 in Brazil and 26 in Indonesia.
- Hours taken per year in paying taxes are also comparatively higher in India— 250-254 hours in India, while only 138 in China, 1501 in Brazil (quite higher) and 191 in Indonesia.
- In New Zealand, it takes only 140 hours per year in paying taxes. On this front, however, the situation has deteriorated in the country—time spent in paying taxes got just doubled in the last decade (2009–19).
- India trails in the case of total tax payable (per cent of gross profits) in comparison to most of the peers also—while it is 49.7 for India, it is 59.2 for China, 65.1 for Brazil and 30.1 for Indonesia.
- In the case of paying taxes, although Indonesia (26) has more than double the number of payments per year than India (10-12), its citizens spend far less time in paying them than India. Brazil seems to fare particularly poor in this segment.

These parameters provide a measure of the scope for improvement. To emerge an economy of US$ 5 trillion, India needs to channelise all of its resources and focus on improving the ease of paying taxes—businesses, industries together with individuals and companies all feel good if it takes less time in paying taxes.

TAX ADMIN, STRATION REFORMS

Making tax administration more transparent, efficient and tax-payer friendly has been one of the major coordinates of India's tax reforms. A major step in this direction was taken by the Government in August 2020 with the launching of the platform 'Transparent Taxation- Honouring the Honest'. The platform[28] has the objective to impart greater efficiency, transparency and accountability, and to eliminate physical interface between taxpayers and tax officers and has *two key* features:

1. Usage of technology, data analytics and Artificial Intelligence, and
2. Recognising taxpayers as partners in nation-building.

There are *3 pillars* on which this platform is based, which are briefly discussed below:

27. Economic Survey 2019-20, Vol. 1, pp. 130-155, Ministry of Finance, GoI, N. Delhi.

28. Economic Survey 2020-21, vol. 2, pp. 62-67, Ministry of Finance, GoI, N. Delhi.

A. Faceless Assessment

The existing *e-assessment* scheme was renamed in August 2020 as the Faceless Assessment scheme. The older scheme was based on the idea that automated random allocation of cases across income tax teams with dynamic jurisdiction and elimination of face-to-face contact between the income-tax authorities and the taxpayer can lead to an efficient, non-discretionary, unbiased single window system of assessment. This was broadened in the new scheme by bringing 'all the pending assessment cases' across the country within its purview with declaring that any order passed outside the scheme shall be *invalid*.

A National Faceless Assessment Centre (NFAC), headed by Principal Chief Commissioner of Income Tax, has been set up under it, as the sole point of contact between the tax department and the taxpayer— with all notices or communications to and from the taxpayer, and internal communications related to assessment process routed through the centre. Regional Faceless Assessment Centres have also been put in place to facilitate and streamline the process.

B. Faceless Appeals

The Faceless Appeals scheme, 2020 has been set up to finalise all income tax appeals in a faceless manner under a faceless ecosystem with exception of appeals relating to serios frauds, major tax evasion, sensitive and search matters, international tax and black money.

The National Faceless Appeal Centre (NFApC) has been established as the apex body for conducting e-appeal proceedings in a centralised manner— with Regional Faceless Appeal Centres (RFAC) under it to facilitate the process. The NFApC will be the *only point* of contact between the taxpayer and the underlying Appeal Units; and Appeal Units and NeAC/Assessing Officer. Under it all internal and external communications take place electronically and the assessee or the Assessing Officer is not required to attend the proceedings personally or through an authorised representative.

C. Taxpayers' Charter

While regulating and enforcing tax laws, traditionally, tax administration used to pay limited attention on the aspect of the tax services it was providing. However, in the last few decades, due to increased demand for better services to tax payers, there has been worldwide recognition of the 'rights of the tax papers'— accordingly, formal taxpayers' charters have been published or the expected behaviour from tax officials has been inserted in the 'mission statement' of the tax department. India's taxpayer's charter comprises *commitments* by the income tax department and *obligations* of the taxpayers, which are as given below:

1. Courteous, fair and reasonable treatment to taxpayers.
2. Treatment of taxpayers as honest unless the department has a reason to believe otherwise.
3. Fair and impartial appeal procedure and review mechanism.
4. Accurate and complete information for fulfilling tax compliance obligations.
5. Timely decisions in every income tax proceeding.
6. Collection of the correct amount of due tax.
7. Respect for taxpayer's privacy and ensuring no more intrusive than necessary in inquiry, examination, or enforcement action.
8. Maintaining confidentiality by not disclosing any taxpayer's information to the department unless authorised by law.
9. Ensuring accountability for the actions of the tax authorities.
10. Provision to allow a taxpayer to choose an authorised representative of his choice.

11. Provision for a mechanism to lodge a complaint and its prompt disposal.
12. Fair and impartial system to resolve tax issues in a time-bound manner.
13. Periodical publishing of the service standards and report.
14. Reduced cost of compliance as the department shall duly take into account the cost of compliance when administering tax legislation.

The Charter obliges the taxpayer:

(i) to honestly disclose full information and fulfil compliance obligations.

(ii) to be aware of compliance obligations and seek the help of the department if needed.

(iii) to keep accurate records.

(iv) to know the information and submissions made by his authorised representative.

(v) to make submissions in a timely manner.

(vi) to pay amount due in a timely manner.

Need of Ombudsman

To ensure enforcement of taxpayers' rights are taxpayers' perspective, a dedicated institution is essential. This can be done by establishing an effective Ombudsman. Though it was established in 2011 (after getting created by the Government in 2003 itself) but in absence of law to support its functions and independence from the department, it proved *ineffective* and its decisions reamining *only advisory* in nature. It could settle complaints either through agreements between the complainant and the tax department through conciliation and mediation or by passing an award, with a token compensation for loss suffered by the complainant not exceeding ₹5,000. Thus, the institutions of Ombudsman for direct and indirect taxes were, therefore, abolished in February 2019.

The present tax grievance redressal system consisting of grievance cells are the Aaykar Sewa Kendras (headed by tax officials) and the *e-nivaran* portal (a separate dedicated window for income tax grievance redressal).

Global experience (Australia, Canada, UK, Brazil, South Africa, Belgium and France) regarding ombudsman system. To make the 'Honouring the Honest' platform more successful, India needs to put in place this institution with adequate teeth and independence from the tax department— to ensure trust between taxpayers and tax authority.

FIFTEENTH FINANCE COMMISSION

The 15th Finance Commission (Chaired by Mr. N. K. Singh) submitted two reports. While the first report, consisting of recommendations for the financial year 2020-21, was tabled in Parliament in February 2020, the final report with recommendations for the 2021-26 period was tabled in Parliament on February 1, 2021. Its key recommendations[29] are given below.

Devolution Criteria The criteria for distribution of central taxes among states for 2021-26 period a same as those for 2020-21. The Commission has used 2011 population data for determining the share of states during its entire award period. To reward efforts made by states in controlling their population, the Commission has used the Demographic Performance criterion. States with a lower fertility ratio will be scored higher on this criterion.

Grants-in-aid The Commission has recommended grants from the centre to states and local bodies worth ₹10.3 lakh crore for the 2021-26 period. These include:

1. revenue deficit grants to 17 states,
2. grants to urban and rural local bodies,

29. Fifteenth Finance Commission, Ministry of Finance, GoI, N. Delhi, February 2021.

3. disaster management grants,
4. grants for eight sectors including health, education, and agriculture, and
5. certain state-specific grants.

Funding of defence and internal security A dedicated non-lapsable fund called the Modernisation Fund for Defence and Internal Security (MFDIS) will be constituted to primarily bridge the gap between budgetary requirements and allocation for capital outlay in defence and internal security. The fund will have an estimated corpus of ₹2,38,354 crores over the five years (2021-26). Of this, ₹1,53,354 crores will be transferred from the Consolidated Fund of India. The rest of the amount will be generated from measures such as disinvestment of defence PSUs and monetisation of defence lands.

Fiscal consolidation The Commission suggested that the Centre bring down fiscal deficit to 4 per cent of GDP by 2025-26. It recommended the fiscal deficit limit (as per cent of the GSDP, i.e., Gross State Domestic Product) for states to be:

1. 4 per cent in 2021-22,
2. 3.5 per cent in 2022-23, and
3. 3 per cent during 2023-26.

Extra annual borrowing worth 0.5 per cent of GSDP will be allowed to states during 2021-25 for undertaking power sector reforms.

The Commission observed that the recommended *path for fiscal deficit* for the Centre and states will result in a reduction of total liabilities of:

1. the Centre from 62.9 per cent of GDP in 2020-21 to 56.6 per cent in 2025-26, and
2. the states on aggregate from 33.1 per cent of GDP in 2020-21 to 32.5 per cent by 2025-26.

The Commission recommended forming a *high-powered inter-governmental group* to:

1. review the fiscal responsibility legislation (FRBM Act), and
2. recommend a new fiscal responsibility framework and oversee its implementation.

OUTLOOK FOR FUTURE

Though the process of tax reforms has been slower (similar to the process of the economic reforms), especially in the case of indirect taxes, its positive outcomes have encouraged the country to go for further reforms. Together with enhancing legitimacy in state, there is a need to making taxpayers aware about the need of filing their tax returns. Certain suggestions[30] to improve the taxation system in current time are being briefly summarised below:

- Structural reforms done recently in corporate tax are commendable but slowly all of the deductions and exemptions enjoyed by the taxpayers should be withdrawn and reduction in the base rate should be attempted.
- The ease of filing GST should be enhanced on priority basis.
- The technical glitches related to the GST filing system should be corrected as soon as possible to lessen unnecessary harassment faced by the tax filers.
- Enhancing ease of paying taxes is an essential part of a good tax system. In this regard, India should take lessons from the peers like China, Brazil and Indonesia other than New Zealand.
- Enhancing tax compliance is the need of the hour, especially in the case of the personal income tax. There needs a policy framework to be initiated to induce behavioural change in the taxpayers. The clamour for cutting

30. Based on the Economic Survey 2020-21; Economic Survey 2019-20; Union Budget2020-2 1 ; EconomicSurvey 2018-19 and Union Budget 2019-20; Ministry of Finance, GoI, N. Delhi.

personal income tax rates will not be practically possible for the Government (due to possible fall in revenue) till the base of this tax is not broadened for which encouraging non-taxpaying citizens to start paying tax will be required. This move will be further strengthened by withdrawing the existing deductions and exemptions enjoyed by the taxpayers.

- The presence of trust between taxpayers and the tax department is essential for encouraging voluntary compliance from the tax filers. For this to be done, Government should put in place an effective and transparent tax administration—reducing 'human interface' should be tried with increased pace.
- The presence of 'fear' and 'distrust' for the tax department in the minds of taxpayers dilutes tax filing and they need to be corrected in medium to longer term.
- Litigations and involved delays cause enormous damage to the exchequer besides harassing the taxpayers and wasting precious time of the appellate and various courts. All possible alternatives should be utilised to resolve them in speedier manner.

The growth recovery seen till January 2021, would facilitate buoyant revenue collections in the medium term, and thereby enable a sustainable fiscal path, as per the *Economic Survey 2020-21.* Moreover, the roadmap for the long-term fiscal policy strategy for both the Centre and the States, laid down by the 15th Finance Commission, is expected to support the expenditures of the governments and help a smoother recovery of the economy in 2021-22.

CHAPTER 18

PUBLIC FINANCE IN INDIA

*The way the modern governments manage all money they get-the public money-is the subject matter of public finance. The policy stance taken in this regard is declared annually by the governments via their 'fiscal policy' popularly known as the Budget.**

In this Chapter...

- Introduction
- Budgeting
- Union Budget
- Deficit Financing
- Fiscal Policy
- Indian Fiscal Situation: A Summary
- Fiscal Consolidation in India
- Zero-Base Budgeting
- Output-Outcome Framework
- Cut Motion
- Trilemmas
- Direct Benefit Transfer
- Change in Fiscal Year
- Public Debt
- Independent Debt Management
- Central Government Debt
- Central Transfer to States
- General Government Finances
- COVID-19 Fiscal Stimulus
- Outlook for 2021-22

INTRODUCTION

Public finance is a much wider title which includes all those matters which are connected with public money, i.e., the money a government gets, spends, borrows, lends, raises or prints. Public finance, i.e., finances of the government, now named as *public economics*, does not only discuss the issue that how much of the country's resources the government should acquire for its own use but also discusses the 'efficiency' with which the money should be used. Public finance gets reference in the ancient treatise *Arthashastra*[1] of Kautilya which covers 'treasury, sources of revenue, accounts and audit' in a very detailed way. However, the subject has gathered much significance in the post Second World War period once the governments' role in

1. L. N. Rangarajan (ed.), ***The Arthashastra***, Penguin Books, (New Delhi, 1992).

* *See Amaresh Bagchi (ed.),* ***Readings in Public Finance,*** *(New Delhi: Oxford University Press, 2005). Also see, Paul A. Samuelson and William D. Nordhaus,* ***Economics,*** *(New Delhi: The McGraw-Hill Company, 2005), 412-711. Also see Joseph E. Stiglitz and Carl E. Walsh,* ***Economics,*** *(New York: W. W. Norton, 2006) pp. 695-697.*

the economy started expanding[2] due to various reasons, namely, the rise of public sector, the delivery of public goods, law and order, defence, etc. By the Second World War, the importance of the government's role in the economy was urgently felt and it was believed that all needs of the people cannot be met if the economy is left to the market (i.e., the private sector) in its entirety. For example, national defence, law enforcement and other major areas which must be cared for by the national government besides the supplies of ***affordable or free*** healthcare, education, social security measures, etc. could only be taken care of by the governments (***as they are not profit driven***). That is why there was an agreement among the experts and the policymakers to expand the government's role in the economy. This led to the ultimate rise of the public sector around the world.[3] Here we will be looking into the major concepts related to the area of public finance with special reference to India.

BUDGETING

Budget is an annual financial statement of a government's income (revenue) and expenditure – even[4] companies, organisations, etc. have such documents. The word 'budget' has its origin in the British parliamentary exercise of preparing such statement way back in the mid-18th century from the French word *'Bugeut'*, meaning a leather bag out of which the financial statement was brought out and presented in the Parliament. Today, this word is used to mean the annual statement in all economies around the world.

The constitution of India has a provision (Art. 112) for such a document called Annual Financial Statement to be presented in the Parliament before the commencement of every new fiscal year—popular as the Union Budget. Same provision is there for the states, too.

Data in the Budget

The Union Budget has ***three sets***[5] of data for every sector or sub-sector of the economy concerned:

1. Actual data of the preceding year (here preceding year means one year before the year in which the Budget is being presented). Suppose the Budget presented is for the year 2019-20, the Budget will give the final/actual data for the year 2017-18. After the data we write either **'A'**, meaning actual data/final data or write nothing (India writes nothing).
2. Provisional data of the current year (i.e., 2018-19) since the Budget for 2019-20 is presented in 2018-19 itself, it provides Provisional Estimates for this year (shown as **'PE'** in brackets with the data).
3. Budgetary estimates for the following year (here the following year means one year after the year in which the Budget is being

2. The size of government expenditure for the developed economies stood at almost 10 per cent of their GDPs at the beginning of the 20th century—which could rise to 18 per cent only at the outbreak of the Second World War—went for a steep rise by 1980 to 40 per cent. The government expenditure was barely 9 per cent of the GDP in India at the time of Independence, nearly doubled in 1970s and reach 75 per cent in the 1980s—when questions were raised about their sustainability as revenue receipts failed to grow adequately resulting in rising budgetary deficits (see Amaresh Bagchi (ed.), ***Readings in Public Finance***, Oxford University Press, (New Delhi: 2005) pp. 1–4.

3. It should be noted here that the world which had the form of the state economy (i.e., the Socialist countries at this time), majority of the economic activities were under government control. As the communist form of the state economy emerged by the late 1940s (i.e., Peoples Republic of China, 1949), it had 100 per cent state control over the economic activities.

4. *Collins Dictionary of Economics*, op. cit., & ***Oxford Dictionary of Business***, op. cit.

5. Based on the budgetary documents of the Ministry of Finance, Government of India, New Delhi.

presented or the year for which the Budget is being presented, i.e., 2019-20). This is shown with the symbol **'BE'** in brackets with the data concerned.

One comes across certain other kinds of data, too, in day-to-day government economic literature which are given below:

1. **Revised Estimate (RE):** Revised Estimate is basically a current estimation of either the budgetary estimates (BE) or the provisional estimates (PE). It shows the contemporary situation. It is an interim data.
2. **Quick Estimate (QE):** Quick Estimate is a kind of revised estimate which shows the most latest situation and is useful in the process of going for future projections for some sector or sub-sector. It is an interim data.
3. **Advance Estimate (AE):** Advance Estimate is a kind of quick estimate but done ahead (is advance) of the final stage when data should have been collected. It is an interim data.

Developmental and Non-developmental Expenditure

Total expenditure incurred by the government is classified into two segments—developmental and non-developmental. All expenditures of productive nature are developmental such as on the heads of new factories, dams, bridges, roads, railways, etc.—all *investments*.

The expenditures which are of consumptive kind and do not involve any production are non-developmental, i.e., paying salaries, pensions, interest payments, subsidies, defence expenses, etc.

This classification is not used in the Indian public finance management now (see *Plan* and *Non-Plan Expenditure,* in the next entry).[6]

Plan and Non-Plan Expenditure

Every expenditure incurred on the public exchequer is classified into two categories—the plan and the non-plan. All those expenditures which are done in India in the name of *planning* are the *plan expenditures* and the rest of all are *non-plan expenditures*. Basically, all asset creating and productive expenditures are planned and all consumptive, non-productive, non-asset building are non-plan expenditures and are developmental and non-developmental expenditures, respectively.

In the financial year 1987-88, there was a terminology change in Indian public finance literature when developmental and non-developmental expenditures were replaced by the new terms plan and non-plan expenditures, respectively. (It was suggested by the Sukhomoy Chakravarti Committee.)[7]

Meanwhile, a high-power panel headed by Dr. C. Rangarajan (Chairman, Prime Minister's Economic Advisory Council), in *September 2011* suggested for redefining ***Plan*** and ***Non-Plan*** expenditures as ***Capital*** and ***Revenue*** expenditures, as the former set of terms 'blur the classification'—this will facilitate linking expenditure to 'outcomes' and better public expenditure, the panel suggested. Major suggestions of the panel are:

1. *Plan* and *Non-Plan* distinction in the Budget is neither able to provide a satisfactory classification of 'developmental' and 'non-developmental'

---

6. Ministry of Finance, ***Union Budget 1987-88*** (New Delhi: Government of India, 1987).

7. ***Review of the Working of the Monetary System,*** headed by Sukhomoy Chaktravarthy, Reserve Bank of India, Government of India, New Delhi, 1985.

dimensions of government expenditure nor an appropriate budgetary framework. It has therefore become 'dysfunctional'.

2. Suggests for *redefining the roles* of the Planning Commission (PC) and the Finance Ministry (FM). According to the panel the PC should be responsible for the formulation of the five-year plan, and the task of firming up the annual budgets should be entrusted to the FM.
3. The PC should dispense with the exercise of approving annual plans of states and it could make a strategy or hold review meetings with the representatives of the states.
4. Public expenditures should be split into *capital* and *revenue* expenditures.
5. Public expenditure should have 'management approach' based on measurable 'outcomes', indicating that the responsibility should be assigned to the FM.

Analysis of the Situation While the need for looking beyond the budget is well accepted, there are many factors raising doubts on the 'efficacy' and 'relevance' of the five-year plans as the instrument. The division of expenditure between *Plan* and *Non-Plan* is artificial and creates problems, such as:

1. Plan expenditure tends to get priority especially when austerity and expenditure reduction has to be done periodically for fiscal consolidation. Non-Plan expenditure gets the *cut* even if it is vitally needed for economic development. An example is budget provision for the maintenance of assets such as hospitals, schools and irrigation dams already created under Plan, but whose maintenance is treated as Non-Plan.
2. Review and implementation of schemes is another area of direct responsibility for the Ministry of Finance and the Ministry of Statistics and Programme Implementation. The Finance Minister himself had, in the budget speech for 2005-06, promised to ensure that programmes and schemes were not allowed to continue indefinitely from one Plan period to another without an independent and in-depth evaluation. The Planning Commission, serving as the *focal point for Plan allocations*, dilutes the role of the Finance Ministry in this case.
3. 'Output' and 'Outcome Budgeting' was introduced by the Central Government the Budget for 2005-06. Non-Plan expenditure remains out of its purview. This means, for example, the outcome of expenditure on running schools and hospitals will not be evaluated. This, again, is another fallout of the artificial division into Plan and Non-Plan.

This classification used to adversely affect the whole budget process, formulation and implementation. Looking at this anomaly, the Government switched over from the 'plan' and 'non-plan' classification of expenditure to 'revenue' and 'capital' since the fiscal 2017-18 (as announced in the *Union Budget 2017-18).*

Revenue

Every form of money generation in the nature of income, earnings is revenue for a firm or a government which does not increase the financial liabilities of the government, i.e., the tax incomes, non-tax incomes along with foreign grants.

Non-revenue

Every form of money generation which is not income or earnings for a firm or a government (i.e., money raised via borrowings) is considered a non-revenue source if it increases the financial liabilities.

Receipts

Every receiving or accrual of money to a government by revenue and non-revenue sources is a receipt. Their sum is called *total receipts*. It includes all incomes as well as non-income accruals of a government.

UNION BUDGET

As a practice, the annual financial statement (Art. 112) of the Government of India is called the Union Budget. Though, the budgeting process in India traces its origin from the British tradition—today, most budgets in the world are technically similar in nature. The budget is broadly classified into two parts—*A. Revenue Budget* and *B. Capital Budget*— which all Revenue and Capital kinds of Receipts and Expenditures, respectively. A concise description of the items covered under both the budgets are given below:

A. Revenue Budget

The budget has two sets of descriptions, namely the *revenue receipts* and *revenue expenditures* consisting of the following items:

1. **Revenue Receipts:** These consist of all revenue kinds of receivings (tax and non-tax) of the Government, which are of two types:

   (i) ***Tax Revenue Receipts:*** All revenues received via collections of the direct and indirect taxes are shown here (such as income tax, corporate tax, dividend tax, interest tax, expenditure tax, GST, central excise/cenvat, custom duty, anti-dumping and countervailing duties, etc.)

   (ii) ***Non- Tax Revenue Receipts:*** Here, we find all of the receivings of the Government which accrue from sources other than taxes, which are:

   (a) *Profits* and *dividends* which the government gets from its public sector undertakings (PSUs).

   (b) *Interests* received by the government out of all loans forwarded by it, be it inside the country (i.e., internal lending) or outside the country (i.e., external lending). It means this income might be in both domestic and foreign currencies.

   (c) *Fiscal services* also generate incomes for the government, i.e., currency printing, stamp printing, coinage and medals minting, etc.

   (d) *General Services* also earn money for the government as the power distribution, irrigation, banking, insurance, community services, etc.

   (e) *Fees*, *Penalties* and *fines* received by the government.

   (f) *Grants* which the governments receive—it is always external in the case of the Central Government and internal in the case of state governments.

2. **Revenue Expenditures :** All expenditures incurred by the government are either of *revenue kind* or *current kind* or *compulsive kind.* The basic identity of such expenditures is that they are of consumptive kind and do not involve the creation of productive assets. They are either used in running of a productive process or running a government. A broad category of things that fall under such expenditures in India are:

   (i) *Interest* payment by the government on the internal and external loans

(ii) *Salaries, Pension* and *Provident Fund* paid by the government to government employees

(iii) *Subsidies* forwarded to all sectors by the government

(iv) *Defence* expenditures by the government

(v) *Postal Deficits* of the government

(vi) *Law and order* expenditures (i.e., police and paramilitary)

(vii) Expenditures *on social services* (include all social sector expenditures as education, healthcare, social security, poverty alleviation, etc.) and *general services* (tax collection, etc.)

(viii) *Grants* given by the government to Indian states and foreign countries

Revenue Deficit If the balance of total revenue receipts and total revenue expenditures turns out to be negative, it is known as revenue deficit, a new fiscal terminology used since the fiscal 1997-98 in India.[8]

This shows that the government's *Revenue Budget* (see the next topic) is running in losses and the government is earning less revenue and spending more revenues—incurring a deficit. Revenue expenditures are of immediate nature (this has to be done) and since they are consumptive/non-productive, they are considered as a kind of expenditure which sums up to a heinous crime in the area of fiscal policy. Governments fulfil the gap/deficit with the money which could have been spent/invested in productive areas.

A government might have its revenue expenditures less than its revenue receipts, i.e., having (*revenue surplus*) budget. Such fiscal policy is considered good where the government has been able to manage some money out of its revenue budget which could be spent for the creation of productive assets. Yes, another thing that should be kept in mind is as to how the government has managed this surplus and whether the policies which made this happen are judicious enough or not. In the Second Plan, India emerged as a revenue-surplus state, but experts did not appreciate it as it had many bad impacts on the economy—higher tax rates culminated in tax evasion, corruption, creation of black money, etc.

Revenue deficit may be shown in the quantitative form (as how much the gross/total deficit is in currency terms) or in percentage terms of the GDP for that particular year (shown as percentage of GDP). Usually, it is shown as a percentage of the GDP for domestic as well as international analyses.

Effective Revenue Deficit Effective revenue deficit (ERD) is a new term introduced in the *Union Budget 2011-12*. Conventionally, 'revenue deficit' (RD) is the difference between revenue receipts and revenue expenditures. Here, revenue expenditures include all the grants which the Union Government gives to the state governments and the UTs—some of which ***create assets*** (though these assets are not owned by the Government of India but the state governments and the UTs concerned). According to the Finance Ministry *(Union Budget 2011-12)*, such revenue expenditures contribute to the growth in the economy and, therefore, *should not be treated as unproductive* in nature like other items in the revenue expenditures. And on this logic, a new methodology was introduced to capture the 'effective revenue deficit', which is the Revenue Deficit 'excluding' those revenue expenditures of the Government of India which were done in the form of **GoCA** (grants for creation of capital assets).

The GoCA includes the Government of India grants forwarded to the states and UTs for the implementation of the centrally-sponsored

8. Raja J. Chelliah, 'The Meaning and Significance of the Fiscal Deficit', in Amaresh Bagchi (ed.), ***Readings in Public Finance***, (New Delhi: Oxford University Press, 2005), pp. 387-88. Also see Ministry of Finance, ***Union Budget 1997-98***, (New Delhi: Government of India, 1997).

programmes such as Pradhan Mantri Gram Sadak Yojana, Accelerated Irrigation Benefit Programme, Jawaharlal Nehru National Urban Renewal Mission, etc. These expenses, though they are shown by the Government of India in its Revenue Expenditures, are involved with *asset creation* and cannot be considered completely 'unproductive' like other items put in the basket of the Revenue Expenditures—the reason why a new 'terminology' was created.

It is believed that the term was innovated by the Government to *justify* the higher revenue deficits of the period— by outlining that all of it were not having the 'typical' nature (i.e., consumptive kind) of being revenue deficit— as some of it were used to create 'assets' also (shown as the GoCAs). The Government of the time has set a **zero** per cent effective revenue deficit by 2017-18, while revenue deficit will be still 1.5 per cent— which implied that by 2017-18, all of the revenue deficit would have been used for the creation of assets. Since 2014-15 onwards, the new Government does not seem giving much significance to the concept, though the concept continues to exist— for *2020-21,* it is estimated to be 1.6 per cent.

B. Capital Budget

The part of the Budget which deals with the receipts and expenditures of the capital by the government is called capital budget. This shows the means by which the capital is managed and the areas where capital is spent.

1. **Capital Receipts :** All non-revenue receipts of a government are known as capital receipts. Such receipts are for investment purposes and supposed to be spent on plan-development by a government. But the receipts might need their diversion to meet other needs to take care of the rising revenue expenditure of a government as the case had been with India. The capital receipts in India include the following capital kind of accruals to the government:

   (i) ***Loan Recovery:*** This is one source of the capital receipts. The money the government had lent out in the past in India (states, UTs, PSUs, etc.) and abroad comes back to the government when the borrowers repay them as capital receipts. The interests which come to the government on such loans are part of the revenue receipts.

   (ii) ***Borrowings by the Government:*** These include all long-term loans raised by the government inside the country (i.e., internal borrowings) and outside the country (i.e., external borrowings). Internal borrowings might include the borrowings from the RBI, Indian banks, financial institutions, etc. Similarly, external borrowings might include the loans from the World Bank, the IMF, foreign banks, foreign governments, foreign financial institutions, etc.

   (iii) ***Other Receipts by the Government:*** These include many long-term capital accruals to the government through the Provident Fund (PF), Postal Deposits, various small saving schemes (SSSs) and the government bonds sold to the public (as Indira Vikas Patra, Kisan Vikas Patra, Market Stabilisation Bond, etc.). Such receipts are nothing but a kind of loan on which the government needs to pay interests on their maturities. But they play a role in capital raising process by the government.

2. **Capital Expenditure:** All the areas which get capital from the government are part of the capital expenditure. It includes so many heads in India.

   (i) ***Loan Disbursals by the Government:*** The loans forwarded by the government might be internal (i.e., to the states, UTs, PSUs, FIs, etc.) or external (i.e., to foreign countries, foreign banks, purchase of foreign bonds, loans to IMF and WB, etc.).

(ii) *Loan Repayments by the Government:* Again, loan payments might be internal as well as external. This consists of only the *capital* part of the loan repayment as the element of interest on loans is shown as a part of the *revenue expenditure.*

(iii) *Plan Expenditure of the Government:* This consists of all the expenditures incurred by the government to finance the planned development of India as well as the central government financial supports to the states for their plan requirements.

(iv) *Capital Expenditures on Defence by the Government:* This consists of all kinds of *capital* expenses to maintain the defence forces, the equipment purchased for them as well as the modernisation expenditures. It should be kept in mind that *defence* is a non-plan expenditure which has capital as well as revenue expenditures in its maintenance. The revenue part of the expenditure in the defence is counted in the revenue expenditures by the government.

(v) *General Services:* These also need huge capital expenditure by the government—the railways, postal department, water supply, education, rural extension, etc.

(vi) *Other Liabilities of the Government:* Basically, these include all the repayment liabilities of the government on the items of the Other Receipts. The level of liabilities depends on the fact as to how much such receipts were made by the governments in the past. The amount of payment liabilities in the year also depends on the fact as to which years in the past the governments had other receipts and for what duration of maturity periods. For example, the *PF liabilities* were not an item of such liabilities for almost first three decades after Independence. But once the government employees started retiring, it went on increasing. Future India (especially 1960s and 1970s) saw the expansion of the PSUs and excessive employment generation in them (devoid of the logic of labour requirement). We see the PF liabilities expanding extensively throughout the 1990s—the governments had been under pressure to manage this segment either by cutting interest on PF or at present trying to make it a matter of market economy. The same thing happened with the element of *pension* and we have been able to devise a market mechanism for it once pension reforms took place and the arrival of a pension regulatory authority for the area.

2. **Capital Deficit:** There is no such term in public finance or in economics as such. But in practice, one usually hears the use of the term capital crunch, scarcity of capital in day-to-day economic news items. Basically, the government in the news is facing the problem of managing as much funds, money, capital as is required by it for public expenditure. Such expenditure might be of revenue kind or capital kind. Such difficulties have always been with the developing economies due to their high level requirement of capital expenditures. Had there been a term to show this situation, it would naturally have been *Capital Deficit.*

3. **Fiscal Deficit:** When balance of the government's total receipts (i.e., revenue + capital receipts) and total expenditures (i.e.,

revenue + capital expenditures) turns out to be negative, it shows the situation of fiscal deficit, a concept being used since the fiscal 1997-98 in India.[9]

The situation of fiscal deficit indicates that the government is spending beyond its means. To be more precise, we may say that the government is spending more than its income (though, in practice, all receipts of the government are not income. Basically, receipts are all forms of money accruing to the government, be it income or borrowings).

Fiscal deficit may be shown in the quantitative form (i.e., the total currency value of the deficit) or in the percentage form of the GDP for that particular year (percentage of GDP). In general, the percentage form is used for domestic or international (i.e., comparative economics) studies and analyses.

Fiscal deficit of the governments (Centre and States) has been rising continuously due to diverse socio-economic reasons. The issue has been hotly debated during the period of economic reforms (which will be discussed under a separate title later on). After the fiscal responsibility law was enacted in 2003, we find a concerted effort (fiscal consolidation) from the Government to contain it.

The *Union Budget 2021-22* has set a fiscal deficit target of **6.8** per cent for 2021-22. The budget has revised the fiscal deficit for 2020-21 to **9.5** per cent (a whopping 6 per cent increase from the budgetary target)— due to 'unforeseen and unprecedented circumstances' caused by the COVID-19 pandemic. However, the budget has committed to continue on the path of fiscal consolidation, achieving a fiscal deficit level below *4.5* per cent by *2025-2026.*

9. Raja J. Chelliah, 'The meaning and significance of public deficit', p. 381 & p. 387. Also see Ministry of Finance, ***Union Budget 1997-98.***

Primary Deficit

The fiscal deficit excluding the interest liabilities for a year is the primary deficit, a term India started using since the fiscal 1997-98.[10] It shows the fiscal deficit for the year in which the economy had not to fulfil any interest payments on the different loans and liabilities which it is obliged to—shown both in quantitative and percentage of GDP forms.

This new concept of deficit has not only helped Governments to measure their dependence on loans but led them to introspect into the pattern of expenditures and possible cuts in them. We see primary deficit increase to the peak of 3.2 per cent in 2009-10, since when it has been declining (which shows Governments' increasing dependence on borrowings)— for *2021-22,* the Government has set its target at ***0.3*** per cent (lower from 0.4 per cent for 2020-21)— due to increased government expenditures aimed at supporting the economy to recover out of the disruption caused by the COVID-19 pandemic.

Primary Surplus

Primary surplus is a situation in budgeting process when the tax receipts of a government are higher than its total expenditures excluding interest payments. This concept is also being used in India since 1997-98 as an indicator to understand the fiscal health in a better way.

The data related to it helps governments in understanding the impact of interest payments on its revenues (income) together with prioritising the expenditures. It means that had governments not having the interest payment liabilities, it would have run into budgetary surplus. Rather, it also hints at the fiscal space available for government to go for revenue or capital expenditures. A variety of other information can be obtained by going into primary surplus data of a period such as—situation of tax base, debt to GDP ratio, health of

10. Ministry of Finance, ***Union Budget 1997-98.***

tax compliance, fiscal capacity of the government, tax expenditure, sizes of revenue and capital expenditures, etc.

Monetised Deficit

The part of the fiscal deficit which is provided by the RBI to the government in a particular year is Monetised Deficit, a new term adopted since 1997-98 in India.[11] This is shown in both the forms—in quantitative and a percentage of the GDP for that particular financial year.

To finance its expenditures, the Government of India depends on short- and long-term borrowings. To borrow, Government issues short-term (Treasury Bills) and long-term (G-Secs) securities. These securities were to be subscribed (purchased) by the RBI on compulsory basis. The value of investment made by the RBI in the year used to be the monetised deficit of the Government. Once the fiscal responsibility law was enacted (in 2003), the situation has changed much.

Since 1997, the RBI stopped being the primary subscriber of the Treasury Bills (rather RBI invests in them voluntarily) as an integral part of the ways and means advances (WMAs). Since 2013, an ad-hoc '14-Days Intermediate Treasury Bills' has been put in place to meet the short-term needs of the Government, which are not subscribed by the RBI. The compulsion for RBI to subscribe the G-Secs was also dropped in 2007 (now RBI just manages the borrowing programmes of the Government). Thus, as RBI no longer subscribes the primary issuance of either Treasury Bills or the G-Secs, technically speaking, monetised deficit looks *phased out.* But in practice, for the need of regulating monetary policy, RBI keeps buying and selling all of the Government securities (short- and long- term)— under the open market operations (OMOs). It means, on de-facto basis, RBI is not under any compulsion to invest in the Government securitie, in reality it needs to deal with them (thus in reality, monetised deficits have kept occurring since 2007 also). It all depends on fiscal deficit—till budgets run in deficits, in reality, monetised deficits will be there.

For the year 2021-22, the Government *(Union Budget 2021-22)* has set a market borrowing target of ₹12 lakh crores (to support its total expenditures of ₹34.83 lakh crores)— almost two times higher than ₹5.36 lakh crores target for 2020-21 (which actually turned out to be ₹9.35 lakh crores due to increased revenue expenditure on account of the COVID-19 pandemic). The *Contingency Fund of India* is also proposed to be enhanced to ₹30,000 crores (from ₹500 crores) in the year. Today, around 95 per cent of the Government expenditures are financed through market borrowings which ultimately create challenge for the RBI in chalking out the right monetary policy for the economy.

Deficit and Surplus Budget

When a budget proposes higher expenditures than the receipts, it is known as a *deficit budget.* Opposite to this, if the budget proposes lesser expenditures than the receipts, then it is called a *surplus budget.*[12]

In practice, governments the world over usually do not present a surplus budget as it symbolises government's lower concerns towards development. But at times, as a political weapon, a government might come out with such a budget (for example, the Uttaranchal Budget for 2006-07 was a surplus budget). How can a government propose for a surplus budget in a developing state when even developed countries still need

11. Raja J. Chelliah, p. 389. Also see Ministry of Finance, ***Union Budget 1997-98.***

12. In the US economy if tax revenue falls short of government expenditures, the government has a *fiscal deficit,* and it means that the government needs to borrow in the capital market to cover the difference. Opposite to it, if the government runs a *fiscal surplus* (i.e., its tax revenues exceed its expenditure) then the government, like the household sector, will be a net saver and will represent a source of saving for the economy (see Stiglitz and Walsh, ***Economics,*** P. 549).

development and are going for deficit budgets? The Union Budget in India has never been presented as a surplus budget.

DEFICIT FINANCING

The act/process of financing/supporting a deficit budget by a government is deficit financing. In this process, the government knows well in advance that its total expenditures are going to turn out to be more than its total receipts and enacts/follows such financial policies so that it can sustain the burden of the deficits proposed by it.

First used in the area of public finance in the early 1930s in USA,[13] today the term is being used by the corporate sector, too, and such a financial management of a firm might be followed by it as part of its business strategy. Again, a sick firm might need to follow deficit financing route for many years to come as required by the firm to make it come out of the red (i.e., doing away with the losses).

Need of Deficit Financing

It was in the late 1920s that the idea and need of deficit financing was felt. It is when government needs to spend more money than it is expected to earn or generate in a particular period, to go for a desired level of growth and development. Had there been some means to go for more expenditure with less income and receipts, socio-political goals could have been realised as per the aspirations of the public policy. And once the growth had taken place, the extra money spent above the income would have been reimbursed or repaid. This was a good public/government wish which was fulfilled by the evolution of the idea of deficit financing.

It was by the early 1930s that the US first tried its hand at deficit financing soon to be followed by the whole Euro-American governments.[14] Through this route the developed world was able to come out of the menace of the Great Depression (1929).[15] The idea became popular around the world by the 1960s. India tried its hand at deficit financing in 1969 and since the 1970s, it became a routine phenomenon, till it became wild and illogical, demanding immediate redressal. The fiscal deficits in India did not only peak to unsustainable levels but its composition was also not justified and not based on sound fundamentals of economics. Finally, India headed for a slow but confident process of fiscal reforms that is also known as the process of fiscal consolidation (to be discussed later on).

Means of Deficit Financing

Once deficit financing became an established part of public finance around the world, the means of going for it were also evolved by that time. These means are basically the ways in which the government may utilise the amount of money created as the deficit to sustain its budget for developmental or political needs. These means are given below in order of their suggested and tried preferences.

1. *External Aids*[16] are the best money as a means to fulfil a government's deficit requirements even if it is coming with soft

13. J. K. Galbraith, ***A History of Economics***, (London: Penguin Books, 1987) p. 226. (*The whole Chapter XVII on J.M. Keynes (pp. 221-36) is interesting to refer on the topic.*)

14. For a detailed discussion on the topic, one may refer to Joseph. E. Stiglitz, ***Economics of the Public Sector***, (New York: W.W. Norton, 2000).

15. It should be noted here that although the governments had run deficits (i.e., budget deficit) even before the Keynesian idea of the deficit, the pre-Keynesian thinking was that in peacetime the budget should generally be *balanced* (i.e., neither deficit nor surplus), or even in surplus so that the government debt created by wartime deficits could be paid off. For further reference on the topic and its constraints, Stanley Fischer and William Easterly, ***Economics of the Government Budget Constraints***, World Bank Research Observer, Vol. 5, No. 2, July 1990, pp. 127-42; also reproduced in Amaresh Bagchi (ed.), ***Readings in Public Finance***, pp. 301-19.

16. Ibid.

interest. If they are coming without interest, nothing could be better.

When India went to borrow from the IMF in the wake of the financial crisis of 1990-91, the body advised India to keep its fiscal deficit to the tune of 4.5 per cent of its GDP and noted it to be sustainable for the economy. What was the rationale behind this data? Basically, in those times with the foreign aids (soft loans either from the *WB* or from the *Aid India forum*) India was able to manage its budget to the tune of 4.5 per cent of its GDP. In 2002, when India's fiscal deficit was around 6 per cent (5.7 per cent to be precise), the IMF validated it to be sustainable. There were two reasons—first, India was able to show a check on fiscal deficit and secondly, at the same time, the forex reserves of the country were suitably higher to neutralise the negative impacts of the higher fiscal deficit than the suggested levels (4.5 per cent).

External Grants are even better elements in this case (which comes free—neither interest nor any repayments) but it either did not come to India (since 1975, the year of the first Pokhran testings) or India did not accept it (as happened post-Tsunami, arguing grants/aids coming with a tag/condition). That is why here this segment has not been discussed as a means to manage deficit.

2. ***External Borrowings***[17] are the next best way to manage fiscal deficit with the condition that the external loans are comparatively cheaper and long-term.

   Though external loans are considered an erosion in the nation's sovereign decision making process, this has its own benefit and is considered better than the internal borrowings due to two reasons.

   (i) External borrowings bring in foreign currency/hard currency which gives extra edge to the government spending as by this, the government may fulfil its developmental requirements inside the country as well as from outside the country.

   (ii) External borrowings are preferred to the internal borrowings due to 'crowding out effect'. If the government itself goes on borrowing from the banks of the country, from where will others borrow for investment purposes?

   The Government proposed (in the *Union Budget 2019-20*) to raise part of its borrowings from the external markets. It means, the Government was in favour of issuing 'Sovereign Bond'— a proposal put forth for the *first time*. Such an initiative of the Government might be based on the fact that the sovereign external debt of India is at quite comfortable level (5 per cent of the GDP).

   Though, till **April 2020**, no such action was taken by the Government in the direction (*Union Budget 2020–21* also remained muted on the proposal), there has been a heated debate among economists on the pros and cons of such a move (for more details on it, see GLOSSARY).

3. ***Internal Borrowings***[18] come as the third preferred route of fiscal deficit management. But going for it in a huge way hampers the investment prospects of the public and the corporate sector. It has the same impact on the expenditure pattern in the economy. Ultimately, economy heads for a double negative impact—lower investment (leading to lower production, lower GDPs and lower per capita income, etc.) and lower demands

17. Ibid.

18. Ibid.

(by the general public as well as by the corporate world) in the economy—the economy moves either for *stagnation* or for a *slowdown* (one can see them happening in India repeatedly throughout the 1960s, 1970s, 1980s). The situation improved after the mid-1990s.

4. ***Printing Currency*** is the last resort for the government in managing its deficit.[19] But it has the biggest handicap that with it, the government cannot go for the expenditures which are to be made in the foreign currency. Even if the government is satisfied on this front, printing fresh currencies does have other damaging effects on the economy:
   (i) It increases inflation proportionally. (India regularly went for it since the early 1970s and usually had to bear double digit inflations.)
   (ii) It brings in regular pressure and obligation on the government for upward revision in wages and salaries of government employees—ultimately increasing the government expenditures necessitating further printing of currency and further inflation—a vicious cycle into which economies entangle themselves.

Now, it remains a matter of choice and availability of the above-given means, and which means a government adopts and in what proportion for fulfilling its deficit requirements.

Composition of Fiscal Deficit

The Keynesian idea of deficit financing, though he advocated it, had a catch in it also which was usually missed by third world economies or intentionally overlooked by them. The catch is related to the question as to why an economy wants to go for fiscal deficit. Thus, it becomes essential to go for an analysis of the composition[20] of the fiscal deficit of a government.

Out of the two broad expenditure obligations of a government—revenue expenditure and capital expenditure—the following combinations of expenditure composition are suggested:

1. A fiscal deficit with a surplus revenue budget or a zero revenue expenditure is the best composition of fiscal deficit and the most suitable time for deficit financing.
2. The deficit requirements for lower revenue expenditures and higher capital expenditures are the next best situation for deficit financing, provided revenue deficit is eliminated soon.
3. The last could be the situation when major part of deficit financing is to fulfil revenue expenditures and a minor part to go for capital expenditures. The total money of the deficit might go to fulfil revenue expenditure, which could be the worst form of it.

Basically, there should be a judicious mix of plan and non-plan expenditure as well as revenue and capital expenditures in India. Lesser non-plan expenditures or higher plan-expenditures are better reasons behind deficit financing in India (though India has a typical feature of capital expenditure which makes this combination of deficit financing not a suggested form—discussed ahead).

Third world economies (including India) though went for higher and higher fiscal deficits and deficit financing, they either did not address or failed to address the composition of deficit favourable towards capital and non-revenue expenditures.

19. L.N. Rangarajan, ***The Arthashastra***, pp. 259–62.

20. J. Cullis and P. Jones, ***Public Finance and Public Choice*** (New York: Oxford University Press, 1998).

FISCAL POLICY

The real meaning, significance and impact of fiscal policy emerged in the wake of the Great Depression and the Second World War. Fiscal policy has been **defined** as 'the policy of the government with regard to the level of government purchases, the level of transfers, and the tax structure'—probably the best and the most acclaimed definition among experts.[21] Later, the impact of fiscal policy on macro-economy was beautifully analysed.[22] As the policy has a deep impact on the overall performance of the economy, fiscal policy is also **defined** as the policy which handles public expenditure and tax to direct and stimulate the level of economic activity (numerically denoted by the Gross Domestic Product).[23] It was J. M. Keynes, the ***first*** economist who developed a theory linking fiscal policy and economic performance.[24]

Fiscal policy is also **defined** as 'changes in government expenditures and taxes that are designed to achieve macro-economic policy goals'[25] (such as growth, employment, investment, etc.). Therefore, we say that 'fiscal policy denotes the use of taxes and government expenditures'.[26]

How the taxes and the government expenditures influence the overall economy, has been explained in brief here.[27] Let us first discuss the ***taxes*** and their impact on the economy:

1. Taxes have a direct bearing on people's income affecting their levels of disposable incomes, purchase of goods and services, consumption and ultimately their standard of living.
2. Taxes directly affect the savings of individuals, families and firms which affect investment in the economy—as investment affects the output (GDP) thereby influencing the per capita income.
3. Taxes affect the prices of goods and services as factor cost (production cost) is affected, thereby affecting incentives and behaviour of economic activities, etc.

Government expenditures affect/influence the economy in two ways:

1. There are some expenditures on government purchases of goods and services, for example, construction of roads, railways, ports, foodgrains, etc. in the goods category and salary payments to government employees in the services category.
2. There are some expenditures due to government's income support to the poor, unemployed and old-age people (known as government ***transfer payments)***.

Deficit Financing in India

India was declared to be a planned economy right after Independence. As development responsibilities of the government were very high, there was a need of huge funds in rupee as well as in foreign currency forms. India faced continuous crises in managing the required fund to support its Five-Year Plans—neither foreign funds came nor internal resources could be mobilised in sufficient amount. (Due to lower tax collections, weaker

---

21. The acclaimed definition first came up in the widely used work *Macroeconomics* by Dornbusch and Fisher which is now available as R.S. Dornbusch, S. Fisher and Richard Startz, ***Microeconomics***, (New Delhi: Tata McGraw-Hill, 2002).
22. John Hicks, the British Nobel Laureate did show it, referring changes in taxes and government expenditure using the framework of the famous IS-LM model (Ibid).
23. S. R. Maheshwari, ***A Dictionary of Public Administration*** (New Delhi: Orient Longman, 2002), p. 227.
24. In his acclaimed work ***The General Theory of Employment, Interest and Money***, 1936.
25. Stiglitz and Walsh, ***Economics***, p. 729.
26. Samuelson and Nordhaus, ***Economics***, p. 412.
27. Based on the elaboration by Samuelson and Nordhaus, ***Economics***, pp. 412-13.

banks that too privately owned, and negligible saving rate, etc.)[28]

By the late 1960s, the government headed for deficit financing and from the 1970s onwards, India started going for higher and higher fiscal deficits and became more and more dependent on increased deficit financing with every fresh year. we may classify deficit financing in India into three phases.

The First Phase (1947-1970)

The first phase had no concept of deficit financing and the deficits were shown as Budgetary Deficits. Major aspects of this phase were as follows:

1. Trying to borrow from inside and outside the economy but unable to meet the target.
2. In the 1950s, a serious attempt was made to increase tax collections and check revenue expenditures to be ultimately able to emerge as a surplus revenue budget economy. But huge cost was paid in the form of tax evasion, rise in corruption, stagnating standard of life and a neglected social sector.
3. Taking recourse to heavy borrowings from the RBI and finally nationalisation of banks so that their money could be used by the government to support the plans. This not only increased the interest burden of the governments but also ruptured the whole financial system in coming years—banks did not remain commercial entities and became part of the government's political statement.
4. Establishing giant PSUs with higher revenue expenditures (salaries) which increased the revenue expenditures of the future governments when the pensions and the PFs needed to be serviced.
5. Unable to go for the required level of investment even after taking recourse to all the above given means.

The Second Phase (1970-1991)

The second phase is considered the period of deficit financing, follow up of unsound fundamentals of economics and finally culminating in severe financial crisis by the year 1990-91. Major highlights of this phase may be summed up as follows:

1. This phase saw the nationalisation policy and simultaneous revival of an increased emphasis on the expansion of the PSU (two points should be noted here specially—*first*, many of the South-East Asian economies have officially declared their acceptance of capitalism and privatisation. *Secondly*, China had declared that investment in the government-controlled companies are a loss of money at this time).
2. Upcoming PSUs increased the total expenditure of the government's revenue as well as capital.
3. Existing PSUs were taking their own due from the economy—the illogical employment creation excessively increased the burden of salaries, pensions and PF. Many of them had started fetching huge losses by this time. As the public sector does not have profit as its primary goal, there was a lack of profit and loss analysis. The PSUs had no connection between their need of labour force and the existing labour force. Ultimately, the responsibility of profit or loss did not remain the onus of the officers, thus making them centres of intentional losses and an institutionalised centre of corruption.
4. The governments have failed on both the fronts—checking population rise and mass employment generation—the burden of

28. For a detailed data-based discussion, refer to Sudipto Mundle and M. Govinda Rao, '*Issues in Fiscal Policy*' in Bimal Jalan (ed.), ***The Indian Economy: Problems and Prospects*** (New Delhi: Penguin Books, 2004), pp. 258-85.

different *subsidies* went on increasing making them unmanageable and highly illogical. Self-employment programmes could not pick up, or better said, it was politically suitable to go for piece-meal wage-employment programmes with different names.

5. Planned development remained highly centralised and devoid of any place for local aspirations—frustrations of masses started showing up in the form of extremist and radical organisations raising their heads, creating a law and order problem and excessive expenditure on them. The outcome was a burdened police force and lagging judicial set-up.
6. The plan expenditures which governments were going for were through investments in the PSUs which were not committed to profit motive; deficit financing for the PSUs was not based on sound economics. Majority of the plan expenditures in a sense turned out to be non-economic, i.e., non-plan expenditure at the end.

Due to the reasons, it was tough to say whether it was sound to go for huge fiscal deficits in India.[29]

The Third Phase (1991 onwards)

The third phase started with the initiation of the economic reforms process under the conditionalities put forth by the IMF (controlling fiscal deficit was one amongst them). As the economy moved from government dominance to market dominance, things needed a restructuring and public finance also needed a touch of rationality.

29. This was the general feeling among experts, policymakers and the IMF alike.

In the wake of economic reforms process, encouraging investment from the private sector was to be Government's priority. To enable the private sector to invest in the economy, they should be made available with enough fund. It means, the Government needed to drain the financial system less (i.e. reducing 'crowding out' of fund) so that the private sector gets the investible funds. For this to occur, Government took a variety of actions starting with the early 1990s, such as—rationalising expenditures of the governments (centre and state), raising its own tax and non-tax revenues, strengthening and expanding financial markets, etc. (which will be discussed later).

INDIAN FISCAL SITUATION: A SUMMARY

In December 1985, the Government of India presented a discussion paper in the Parliament titled 'Long-Term Fiscal Policy'. It was for the *first time* in the fiscal history of India that we see a long-term perspective coming on the fiscal issue from the government. This also included the policy of government expenditure. The paper was bold enough to recognise the deterioration in India's fiscal position and accepted it among the most important challenges of the eighties—the paper set specific targets and policies to set the things right. This paper was followed by a country-wide debate on the issue and it was in 1987 that the government came ahead with *two* bold steps in the direction:

1. a virtual freeze was announced on government expenditure, and
2. a ceiling on the budgetary deficit.

The above steps had a positive impact on the situation, but it was temporary as since mid-1988, the situation again started deteriorating. The BoP crisis at the end of 1990 was generated partly by the alarmingly high *fiscal deficit*[30] and due to a high level of external borrowings. The IMF support to fight the crisis came in but with many macro-economic conditionalities, checking the fiscal menace being a major one among them. With the process of economic reforms which started in 1991-92, the government also announced its commitment to reduce fiscal deficit to 3-4 per cent (of GDP) by the mid-1990s (from the level of about 8 per cent during 1987-90). This step was among the many measures which the government started with the objective of stabilising the economy. We may have a look at India's fiscal situation upto 1990-91 in the following way:

1. The fiscal deficits of the central government, after averaging below 4 per cent of the GDP till the 1970s, started climbing up by being 5.77 per cent in 1980-81, 8.47 per cent in 1986-87 ending up at 7.85 per cent in 1990-91 after being above 7 per cent in the second half of the 1980s.[31]
2. The revenue (i.e., current) expenditure of the government (Centre and states combined) increased from 11.8 per cent of GDP to 23 per cent between 1960 and 1990. The revenue receipts of the government also went up, on an average, from 14.6 per cent in 1971-75 to 20 per cent in 1986-1990. But the gap between revenue receipts and expenditures remained negative—financed largely by domestic borrowings (as a result, the interest payments on domestic debt increased from 0.5 to 2.5 per cent of the GDP during 1975-90).[32] The revenue deficit went on increasing after 1979-80 and reached the highest level of 3.26 per cent of the GDP in 1990-91.[33]
3. The fiscal situation of the states was not good either. State governments which are primarily responsible for health, education and other social services had an aggregate revenue expenditure of 5 per cent of GDP on these accounts while their capital expenditure accounted for 2.5 per cent on social and other sectors.[34] The states' expenditure on the social sector went down while their interest payments had increased during the 1980s.[35]

As per the experts, the debt situation in the states would have been even worse, but for the fact that the states, unlike the Centre, did not have independent powers to borrow either from the RBI or the market because of the statutory overdraft regulatory scheme.[36] Thus, their deficits have been self-limiting—whenever the states tried to cut down their deficits, the care of the social sector and capital expenditure suffered and development prospects in the states also suffered.

30. The proximate cause of the payment crisis in the mainstream perspective, was faulty macro-economic policies, specially large fiscal deficits of the government during 1984-91, deficits that spilled over in country's current account of the balance of payment. (See Mihir Rakshit, 'The Micro-economic Adjustment Programme: A Critique', ***Economic and Political Weekly** 26*(34) (August), quoted by Mihir Rakshit, ***'Some Microeconomics of India's Reform Experience'*** in Kaushik Basu (ed.), ***India's Emerging Economy: Performance and Prospects in the 1990s and Beyond*** *(New Delhi:* Oxford University Press, 2004), p. 84.

31. S.D. Tendulkar and T.A. Bavani, ***Understanding Reforms*** (New Delhi: Oxford University Press, 2007) p. 73.

32. Bimal Jalan, ***India's Economic Policy*** (New Delhi: Penguin Books, 1992) p. 48.

33. ***Handbook of Statistics on the Economy 2002-03,*** Reserve Bank of India, Table 221 (cited by Tendulkar and Bhavani, ***Understanding Reforms***, p. 74).

34. Bimal Jalan, ***India's Economic Policy***, p. 50

35. Reserve Bank of India, ***The Report of Tenth Finance Commission*** (New Delhi, Government of India, 1994) (as quoted in Bimal Jalan, *India's Economic Policy*, p. 50.

36. This scheme has changed now. After the implementation of the suggestions of the ***12th Finance Commission,*** states are now allowed to go for market borrowings to take care of their plan expenditures once they have passed and enacted their Fiscal Responsibility Acts (FRAs) in consonance with the FRBM Act, 2003.

Now the question arises that why the government has not been able to check the menace of fiscal deficits even though there has been a consensus to do so? ***There are reasons***[37] which as follows:

1. **Political factor:** The political lobbies and sectional politics as well as the subsidies are supposed to be one big factor for rising government expenditure. We see this on a higher scale if there is a probable mid-term election or closer to a general election.
2. **Institutional factor:** The administrative size combined with the processes of reporting, accounting, supervising and monitoring is getting greater importance than the production and delivery of goods and services.[38]
3. **Ethical factor:** This is a more powerful factor as it easily generates wide public support for the government expenditure. There are many heads of such expenditures such as subsidies (food, power, fertilizer, irrigation, etc.), poverty alleviation programmes, employment generation programmes, education, health and social services. The logic for such expenditure comes from the idea that the government should function as the protector of the poor and provider of jobs for them implying that such government expenditures benefit the poor.

It was in 2000 that the double menace of revenue and fiscal deficits got attention from the government at the Centre and some constitutional/statutory safeguards looked necessary. Consequently, the Fiscal Responsibility and Budget Management Bill, 2000 was proposed in the Parliament.

FRBM Act, 2003

The fiscal policy of an economy has been considered as the building block for enabling macro-environment by economists, policymakers and the IMF alike. It does not only provide stability and predictability to the policy regime, but also ensures that national resources are allocated in terms of their defined priorities through the tax transfer mechanism.

Unproductive government expenditures, tax distortions and high deficits are considered to have constrained the Indian economy from realising its full growth potential. At the beginning of the fiscal reforms in 1991, the fiscal imbalance was identified as the ***root cause*** of the twin problems of inflation and the difficult balance of payments (BoPs) position.[39] Since then, the ***medium-term fiscal policy stance*** of the government has been on the following lines:[40]

1. Reducing the deficits (revenue and fiscal)
2. Prioritising expenditure and ensuring that these resulted in intended outcomes.
3. Augmenting resources by widening tax base and improving tax-compliance while maintaining moderate rates.

The fiscal consolidation which followed in 1991 failed to give the desired results as there was no defined mandate for it. Neither was there any statutory obligation to do so.[41] This is why the Fiscal Reforms and Budget Management Act (FRBMA) was enacted on 26 August, 2003 to provide the support of a strong institutional/statutory mechanism. Designed for the purpose of

37. Based on the points raised by Bimal Jalan, p. 49.
38. This factor seems getting redress with the starting of ***outcome*** and ***performance*** budgeting 2004-05 onwards.
39. Ministry of Finance, ***Economic Survey 2006-07***, (New Delhi: Government of India, 2007), p. 18.
40. Ibid.
41. Ibid.

medium-term management of the fiscal deficit, the FRBMA came into effect on 5 July, 2004.

The FRBM Bill, 2000 was passed by the Parliament with all political parties voting in favour, and is considered a watershed in the area of fiscal reforms in the country. Main highlights of the FRBMA, 2003 are below:[42]

- GoI to take measures to reduce fiscal and revenue deficit so as to eliminate revenue deficit by 31 March, 2008 (which was revised by the UPA Government to March 31, 2009) and thereafter build up adequate revenue surplus.
- Rules to be made under the Act to specify annual targets for the reduction of fiscal deficit (FD) and revenue deficit (RD), contingent liabilities and total liabilities (RD to be cut by 0.5 per cent per annum and FD by 0.3 per cent per annum).
- FD and RD may exceed the targets only on the grounds such as national security, calamity or on exceptional grounds.
- GoI not to borrow from RBI except by Ways and Means Advances (WMAs).
- RBI not to subscribe to the primary issue of the GoI securities from 2006-07 (it means that these government bonds/papers will become market-based instrument to raise long-term funds by the government).
- Steps to be taken to ensure greater transparency in fiscal operations.
- Along with the Budget and Demands for Grants, the GoI to lay the following three statements before the Parliament in each financial year:
  - Fiscal Policy Strategy Statement (FPSS);
  - Medium-Term Fiscal Policy Statement (MTFPS); and
  - Macro-economic Framework Statement (MFS).
- The Finance Minister to make quarterly review of trends in receipts and expenditure in relation to the Budget and place the review before the Parliament.

Experience of the FRBM Together with the central compliance to the FRBM Act, we see the states also enforcing their fiscal responsibility Acts (FRAs). Though these developments[43] brought in fiscal discipline[44] among the governments; however, follow-ups to the fiscal targets gave mixed results— barring a few years, in most of the years the targets were crossed by both of the governments. Based on this experience, the *Union Budget 2016-17* proposed to set up an expert committee to *review* the fiscal targets mandated under the FRBM Act— as many times, domestic or/and global environments[45] may make Government helpless in following the prescribed fiscal discipline without compromising the goals of development and economic stability. The committee (under the chairmanship of N. K. Singh) handed over its report by late 2017–18 advising certain flexibility in the fiscal regime with the following major advices:

- Debt should be the *anchor* of the fiscal policy (i.e., fiscal targets moving up or down depending on sustainable borrowings by the governments).
- Debt to GDP target of 60 per cent for General Government (Centre + States)— 40 per cent in the case of Centre and 20 per cent for states— till 2020–21.

42. Ministry of Finance, ***Economic Survey 2003-04,*** (New Delhi: Government of India, 2004).

43. ***Economic Survey 2013-14; 2014-15*** and ***2015-16.***

44. The acceptance of the recommendations of the **13th** and **14th Finance Commissions** by the Government of India in this regard the been highly effective.

45. We find similar views being forwarded by the Ministry of Finance, ***Economic Survey 2015-16***, Vol. 1 & Vol. 2 (New Delhi: Government of India, 2016).

- A flexibility of 0.5 per cent in the fiscal deficit target (i.e., the introduction of 'escape clause').

Accordingly, the FRBM Act was amended and these new mandates were introduced in 2018–19. As fiscal deficit of 2020–21 is estimated to be *9.5* per cent (up from the target of 3.5 per cent), the Act is slated for further amendment (under the clause mentioned 'unforeseen and unprecedented circumstances' in the Act) in 2021–22 so that the Government is able to cover the extra expenditures incurred in the process of supporting economy on account of the disruption caused by the *COVID-19 pandemic*.

The fiscal consolidation mandate is further slated for change in near future as the *15th Finance Commission* has recommended to form a 'high-powered inter-governmental group' to:

1. review the fiscal responsibility legislation (FRBM Act), and
2. recommend a new fiscal responsibility framework and oversee its implementation.

FISCAL CONSOLIDATION IN INDIA

The average combined fiscal deficits, of the Centre and states after 1975, had been above 10 per cent of the GDP till 2000-01. More than half of it had been due to huge revenue deficits. The governments were cautioned by the RBI, the Planning Commission as well as by the IMF and the WB about the unsustainability of the fiscal deficits. It was at the behest of the IMF that India started the politically and socially painful process of fiscal reforms, a step towards fiscal consolidation.[46] A number of steps were taken by the government at the Centre in this direction and there had been incessant attempts to do the same in the states' public finances too. Major highlights in this direction can be summed up as given below:

1. Policy initiatives towards cutting revenue deficits:

   (i) **Cutting down revenue expenditure:**

   (a) Cutting down the burden of salaries, pensions and the PFs (down-sizing/right-sizing of the government, out of every 3 vacancies 1 to be filled up, interest cut on the PF, pension reforms-PFRDA, etc.)

   (b) Cutting down the subsidies (Administered Price Mechanism in petroleum, fertilizers, sugar, drugs to be rationalised; it was done with mixed successes);

   (c) Interest burden to be cut down (by going for lesser and lesser borrowings, pre-payment of external debts, debt swaps, promoting external lending, minimal dependence on costlier external borrowings, etc.)

   (d) Defence being one major item of the expenditure, bilateral negotiations initiated with China and Pakistan (the historical and psychological enemies against whom the Indian defence preparedness was directed to, as supposed) so that the defence force cut could be completed on the borders, etc.

   (e) Budgetary supports to the loss-making PSUs to be an exception than a rule

   (f) Expenditure reform started by the governments in different areas and departments

46. IMF imposed some macro-economic conditions on the economy while India borrowed from it for its BoP correction in 1990-91. One among the conditions was cutting down the government expenditure (i.e., salaries, pensions, interest and subsidies, etc.) by 10 per cent every year.

(g) General Services to be motivated towards profit with subsidised services to the needy only (railways, power, water, etc.)

(h) Postal deficits to be checked by involving the post offices in other areas of profit

(i) Higher education declared as non-priority sector; fees of institutions of professional courses revised upward; etc.

(ii) **Increasing revenue receipts :**

(a) Tax reforms initiated (Cenvat, VAT, Service Tax, GST proposed, etc.)

(b) The PSUs to be disinvested and even privatised (if a political consensus reached which alludes today)

(c) Surplus forex reserves to be used in external lending and purchasing foreign high quality sovereign bonds, etc.

(d) State governments allowed to go for market borrowing for their plan expenditure, etc.

2. The borrowing programme of the government:

(i) The Ways and Means Advances (WMA) scheme commenced in 1997 under which the government commits to the RBI about the amount of money it will give as part of its market-borrowing programme, to bring transparency in public expenditure and to put political responsibility on the government.

(ii) The RBI will not be the primary subscriber to government securities in the future—committed way back in 1997.

3. The fiscal responsibility on the governments:

(i) The Fiscal Responsibility and Budget Management (FRBM) Act was passed in 2003 (voted by all political parties) which puts constitutional obligation on the government to commit so many things as fiscal responsibility comes in the public finance—fixing annual targets to cut revenue and fiscal deficits the government not to borrow from the RBI except by the WMA, government to bring in greater transparency in fiscal operations, along with the Budget the government to lay statements regarding fiscal policy strategy in the House, and Quarterly Review of trends of receipts and expenditures of the government.

(ii) A mechanism (to include state governments under the umbrella of fiscal responsibility) was advised (now implemented, too) by the 12th Finance Commission which allowed the state governments to go for market borrowing (without central permission) for their need of plan development provided they pass their fiscal responsibility Acts (FRAs) and commit to the fiscal responsibility regarding cutting their revenue and fiscal deficits. By March 2016, all states and UTs had implemented their FRAs.

In order to make a balance between fiscal consolidation and developmental needs, the fiscal legislative regime was changed by the Government in 2018-19 by introducing debt-based fiscal targets with a scope to cross the fiscal deficit target by 0.5 per cent. Meanwhile, the existing regime is again slated for change as the *15th Finance Commission* has recommended to form a 'high-powered inter-governmental group' to review the fiscal responsibility legislation (FRBM Act), and recommend a new fiscal responsibility framework and oversee its implementation.

ZERO-BASE BUDGETING

The idea of zero-base budgeting (ZBB) first came to the privately owned organisation of the USA by the 1960s. This basically belonged to a long list of guidelines for managerial excellence and success, others being Management by Objectives (MBO), Matrix Management, Portfolio Management, etc., to name a few.[47] It was the US financial expert ***Peter Phyrr*** who first proposed this idea for government budgeting and Jimmy Carter, Governor of Georgia, USA was the first elected[48] executive to introduce ZBB to the public sector. When he presented the US Budget in 1979 *as the US President,* it was the first use of the ZBB for any nation state. Since then, many governments of the world have gone for such budgeting.

Zero-base budgeting is the allocation of resources to agencies based on periodic re-evaluation by those agencies of the need for all the programmes for which they are responsible, justifying the continuance or termination of each programme in the agency budget proposal—in other words, an agency reassesses what it is doing from top to bottom from a hypothetical *zero base.*[49]

There are three essential principles of ZBB. Some experts say it in a different way. There are three essential questions which must be answered objectively before going for any expenditure as per the techniques of ZBB:

1. Should we spend?
2. How much should we spend?
3. Where should we spend?

There are *three* special features of this budgeting which distinguishes it from the traditional budgeting. These features, in brief, are as under:

1. The conventional aggregate approach is not applied in it, in which each department of the government prepares their own budget for many activities in the aggregate and composite form, making it difficult to scrutinise each and every activity. In place of it, every department needs to justify its existence and continuance in the budget document by using the mathematical technique of econometrics, i.e., cost-benefit analysis. In a nutshell, every activity of each department is 'X-rayed' and once the justification is validated, they are allocated the funds.
2. *Economy* in public expenditure is the *raison d'etre* of this budgeting. This is why the ZBB has provisions of a close examination and scrutiny of each programme and public spending. Finally, the public spending is cut without affecting the current level of benefits of various public services accruing to the public.
3. *Prioritising* the competing needs is another special feature of ZBB. Before allocating funds to the different needs of the economy, an order of priority is prepared with utmost objectivity. As the resources/funds are always scarce, in the process of prioritised allocation, the item/items at the bottom might not get any funds.

Besides its benefits, there are certain ***limitations*** too before the ZBB which prohibit its assumed success, according to experts. These

47. George R. Terry and Stephen G. Franklin, ***Principles of Management*** (New Delhi: AITBS, 2002), pp. 9-10.
48. See Peter A. Phyrr, 'The zero Base Approach to Government Budgeting', *Public Administration Review, 37 (Jan./Feb., 1977)*, 7; and Thomas P. Lauth, 'Zero-Base Budgeting in Georgia State Government: Myth and Reality', *Public Administration Review,* 38 (Sept./Oct., 1978) pp. 420-30; (cited in Nicholas Henry, ***Public Administration and Public Affairs*** (New Delhi: Prentice-Hall, 2003), p. 217.
49. Nicholas Henry, ***Public Administration and Public Affairs,*** p. 218.

limitations have made it subject to criticism. The limitations are given below:

1. There are certain expenditures upon which the government/parliament does not have the power of scrutiny (as the 'charged Expenditure' in India).
2. There are certain public services which defy the cost-benefit analysis—defence, law and order, foreign relations, etc.
3. Scrutiny is a subjective matter and so this might become a prey to bias. Again, if the scrutinisers have a complete utilitarian view, many long-term objectives of budgeting and public policy might get marginalised.
4. It has scope for the emergence of the Ministry of Finance as the all-powerful institution dictating other ministries and departments.
5. Bureaucracy does not praise it as it evaluates their decisions and performances in a highly objective way.

Despite the above-given strong limitations, the ZBB has a sound logic and should be considered a long-term budgetary reform process. The basic idea of this form of budgeting is to optimise the benefits of expenditure in every area of activity and in this sense it is exceptional. To the extent the corporate world is concerned, this has been a very successful financial management tool.

In India, it is believed to be in practice since 1997-99. We cannot say that India is a success in ZBB, but many of the profit-fetching PSUs have been able to use it successfully and optimise their profits.

OUTPUT-OUTCOME FRAMEWORK

Economising expenditures and enhancing performance of expenditures have fascinated governments of the world, especially since the early 1960s, which resulted in the idea of zero-based budgeting. India also has its share of experiments in this direction. By 2019-20, the Government of India developed the idea of the Output-Outcome Framework (OOF). The OOF is an important reform[50] towards outcome-based monitoring of developmental actions of the ministries and departments. This is a creative modification of a similar effort of the past (i.e. the 'Outcome & Performance Budgeting' initiated in 2005-06). The DMEO (Development Monitoring and Evaluation Office) at Niti Aayog has been working on it since 2017, which actively supports the Government agencies in the process.

Under it, a framework of 'measurable indicators' has been put in place monitoring the objectives (i.e. 'Outcomes') of the Central Sector (CS) and Centrally Sponsored Schemes (CSSs) which account for around 40 per cent of the Government's budget expenditures. This is a paradigm shift from measuring simply 'physical and financial' progress, to a 'governance model based' on outcomes. Actively tracking progress against defined targets, the framework provides two key benefits to improve governance:

1. Enhancing the development impact, and
2. Improving accountability and transparency.

Thus, the Output-Outcome Framework 2019-20 lays the foundation of the journey towards a stronger portfolio of Government's development programmes. It enables performance-based 'budgetary allocations' and can also be used to drive budgetary and administrative convergence among existing schemes and programmes. With the cooperation of line ministries and implementing actors, a robust monitoring mechanism based on this framework can revolutionise the governance and implementation process.

---

50. As put forward by the **Union Budget 2019-20,** Ministry of Finance, GoI, N. Delhi.

CUT MOTION

In democratic political systems, there is a provision of Cut Motion in the House/Parliament (usually it is the opposition but floor might be crossed by members of the House belonging to the government due to presence of inner-party politics). In the US, the budget provisions presented by the government must be passed by the Congress. Only then they can be enacted. Unlike this, in the British parliamentary system though the budget of the government is voted by the House, usually this is considered a political document and passed unchanged. India has mixed provisions of voting on the budget after discussion in both the Houses. There are different constitutional provisions by which the Parliament starts discussion to reduce the demands, grants, etc. proposed by the government in the Budget:[51]

1. **Token Cut:** This motion intends to *'reduce the demand by ₹100'*. Such a motion is moved in order to express a specific grievance which is within the sphere of the responsibility of the Government of India—the discussion remains confined to the particular grievance specified in the motion.
2. **Economy Cut:** This motion intends to *'reduce the demand by a specified amount'* representing the economy (in expenditure) that can be affected. Such specified amount may be either lump sum reduction in the demand or omission or reduction of an item in the demand—the discussion remains confined to the matter in which the economy can be affected.
3. **Disapproval of Policy Cut:** This motion intends to *'reduce the demand to Re. 1'*. This represents *disapproval* of the policy underlying the demand—the discussion remains confined to the particular policy and is open to members to advocate an alternate policy.
4. **Guillotine** is the process in which the Speaker puts all the outstanding demands made by the Budget *directly to vote* in the House—ending further discussions (intended to cut short the discussion on the Budget). Through this, the Speaker may put the whole Budget to vote (i.e., allowing 'no discussion' on the Budget by the House). In recent years, this route was taken time and again by the Government of India, to avoid the aggressive mood of the Opposition.

Though this is a *short route* to get the Budget passed by the House (avoiding criticism by the opposition benches), it may turn out to be very dangerous—as the voting process may take the form of 'no confidence motion' and the government may be routed out of power. But, till date, *Guillotines* never resulted in routing a government out of power in India (as India follows the British Model of Parliamentary system).

TRILEMMAS

Putting the right kind of fiscal policy has always been the most challenging policy decision to be taken by the democratic governments around the world. There are some famous 'trilemmas' related to this aspect. Economics have by now many 'trilemmas' developed and articulated by economists from time to time and the process still continues. Let us see some highly popular and newsmaking ones:

1. The '**financial stability trilemma**', put forward by Dirk Schoenmaker[52] (2008), explains the incompatibility within the Euro zone of :

32. Rules of Procedure and Conduct of Business in Lok Sabha, Parliament Secretariat, New Delhi.

32. Dirk Schoenmaker, "A New Financial Stability Framework for Europe", ***The Financial Regulator***, p. 13(3), 2009.

(i) a stable financial system,

(ii) an integrated financial system, and

(iii) national financial stability policies.

2. By far the most high profile current trilemma of the Eurozone (by Edward Chancellor[53]) was believed to be the seeming irreconcilability between its **three wishes,** namely,

(i) a single currency,

(ii) minimal fiscal contribution to bail outs, and

(iii) the ECB's commitment to low inflation.

3. Martin Wolf[54] spoke about the US Republican Party's **fiscal policy trilemma:**

(i) large budget deficits are ruinous;

(ii) a continued eagerness to cut taxes; and

(iii) an utter lack of interest in spending cuts on a large enough scale.

4. Then we have the **Earth Trilemma** (EEE), which posits that for:

(i) economic development (E),

(ii) we need increased energy expenditure (E),

(iii) but this raises the environmental issue (E).

5. Above all these more recent trilemmas in economics, the prima donna of all of them is Mundell's **'impossible trinity'**. This old trilemma asserts that a country cannot maintain, simultaneously, all three policy goals of:

(a) free capital flows,

(b) a fixed exchange rate, and

(c) an independent monetary policy. The impossible trinity has seen enough waters flowing down the time since it was articulated almost five decades ago which has a strong theoretical foundation in the *Mundell-Fleming Model* developed in the 1960s.

Dani Rodrik[55] argued that if a country wants more of globalisation, it must either give up some democracy or some national sovereignty. Niall Ferguson[56] highlighted the **trilemma** of a choice between commitment to globalisation, to social order and to a small state (meaning limited state intervention).

DIRECT BENEFIT TRANSFER

In 2015, the new government in Centre introduced[57] the game-changing potential of technology-enabled Direct Benefits Transfers (DBT), namely the *JAM (Jan Dhan-Aadhaar-Mobile) Number Trinity* solution. It offers possibilities for effectively targeting public resources to those who need them most, and including all those who have been deprived in multiple ways. Under it, the beneficiaries will get the money 'directly' into their bank or post-office accounts linked to their 12-digit biometric identity number (Aadhar) provided by the Unique Identification Authority of India (UIDAI). The idea was first initiated by the GoI in 2013 (UPA-II) on pilot basis with seven schemes in 20 districts of the country.

53. Edward Chancellor, "Germany's Eurozone Trilemma", ***Financial Times***, 6 November, 2011.

54. Martin Wolf, "The Political Genius of Supply Side Economics", ***Financial Times***, 2010.

55. Dani Rodrik, "The Inescapable Trilemma of the World Economy", 27 June, 2007, *(Erodrik.typepad.com/dani_rodriks_weblog.*

56. *Niall Ferguson*, "Conservatism and the Crisis: A Transatlantic Trilemma", Centre for Policy Studies, Ruttenberg Lecture, 24 March, 2009.

57. Ministry of Finance, ***Economic Survey 2015-16***, pp. 28, 123, 213; Publication Division, ***India 2016*** (New Delhi: Government of India, 2017) pp. 718.

Part of the technological platform—the *Digital India*—it is expected to provide integration of various beneficiary' databases with Aadhaar and appropriate process re-engineering. It would result in:

- removal of fake and duplicate entities from beneficiary lists
- prevention of leakage and wastage
- substantial saving of effort, time and cost
- ensuring full traceability of flow of funds to the beneficiary
- checking the element of corruption through transparency
- accountability of flow of funds
- expenditure rationalisation

Meanwhile, the *Aadhaar (Targeted Delivery of Financial and Other Subsidies, Benefits and Services) Bill, 2016* was passed by the Parliament and enforced by late 2016. This is a *transformative* piece of legislation which will benefit the poor and the vulnerable.

The Government announced its clear stand in *2021-22* to increasingly use the Aadhar-based DBT tool to transfer subsidies to the beneficiaries. Experts believe that the platform may be used in future to launch basic income scheme also.

CHANGE IN FISCAL YEAR

To examine the 'desirability and feasibility' of having a new financial year[58], the Government did set up a high-level committee headed by the former Chief Economic Adviser Shankar Acharya in July 2016 with the following terms of reference:

1. To examine the genesis of the current financial year and the studies made in the past on the desirability of a new financial year;
2. To examine the suitability of the existing financial year from the point of view of—estimation of receipts and expenditure of the governments; impact on agricultural crops, businesses, taxation, statistics and data, budgetary process; and other relevant matters; and
3. Recommend a suitable financial year together with the changes needed in tax laws during transitional period, changes in the coverage of the recommendations of the Finance Commission and the appropriate timing of change.

The Committee submitted its report (still not available in the public domain) by end-December 2016 is under the consideration of the Government. For shifting to a new financial year, there needs to be a consensus among the governments—the reason this proposal was floated by the PM in one of the meetings of the Governing Council of the NITI Aayog. The NITI Aayog proposed for the January–December fiscal year backed by an in-depth discussion paper (released by late 2016)—followed by a survey of *Deloitte* as per which 84 per cent of Indians being in its favour.

Aimed at aligning monsoon forecast (this way the agricultural prospects) with the budget and the fact that more than 156 countries and MNCs following the calendar year as the accounting period, the committee is supposed to go in favour of the January–December fiscal (as the experts believe, taking clues from the comments of Shankar Acharya while he was interacting with the media after submitting the report). Majority of the experts believe that the fiscal year of a government should be closely aligned to its major economic

58. This is not the first time India has looked at changing its fiscal year—in 1985, the L K Jha committee had recommended moving to a January-December format. In March 2017, a Parliamentary panel (Standing Committee on Finance, chaired by M Veerappa Moily, Congress MP) also advocated to end with the decades-old tradition of April-March fiscal introduced by the Britishers—adopted in 1867 principally to align the Indian financial year with that of the British government. Prior to this change, the financial year in India used to be May-April.

activities as is done by most of the nations in the world.[59]

In the case of such a change, the budget will have to be presented in November together with a reworked Parliament session along with changes in data collection and working of state governments. For the common man, the change will not have any big impact.

It is believed that opposition from the states and the expected disruption due to the implementation of the GST were the major reasons for putting the proposal on the back burner. Otherwise, from 2018-19 or 2019-20 India would have shifted to a new fiscal year.

PUBLIC DEBT

Public debt[60] is the total loans of the government of a country. Since this government is national, at times, this is also called 'national debt'. But in a broader sense, the concept of national debt includes the non-government debt also.

Debts of the Governments While the Union Government of India is mandated to borrow inside and outside the country the amount specified by the Parliament (Article 292), States are mandated (Article 293) to borrow only inside the country. Beginning the financial year 2005-06, States were given access to external loans also (on the recommendations of the 12th Finance Commission, 2005-10) for which sovereign guarantee is given by the Centre. While the 'general category' states get external loans on a back-to-back basis (i.e. cost of interest and risk of exchange rate fluctuations borne by States), the 'special category' states get from the Centre in the combination of 90 per cent loan and 10 per cent grant.

Public Debt of India The liabilities of the Centre have three segments of it, namely—Internal Liabilities, External Liabilities, and Public Account Liabilities. To the extent **Public Debt of India** is concerned, it includes only Internal and External liabilities incurred by the Central Government. The composition of the public debt is given below:

1. **Internal segment** includes a variety of 'instruments' used by the Centre to mobilise resources inside the economy, namely:
   (i) ***Dated Securities:*** Popularly known as G-Secs (Government Securities), they are primarily issued by Centre as fixed coupon bonds of different maturities (short-, medium- and long-term). They are today the single-most important source of deficit financing (more than 90 per cent) for the Centre.
   (ii) ***Treasury Bills:*** T-Bills are zero coupon securities issued by the Centre at a discount and are redeemed at their face value at maturity. Issued for short-term (less than 365 days), today they have three tenures—91, 182 and 364 days.
   (iii) ***14-Day T-Bills:*** These 'non-transferable' T-Bills (introduced by the RBI in 2013 to finance Centre's ways and means advances as issuance of 'on-tap' treasury bills was phased out) are issued by the Centre to only States, foreign central banks and other specified bodies at an interest rate fixed at 3 per cent below the average yield of 91-days T-Bills in the preceding quarter.
   (iv) ***Securities issued to International Financial Institutions:*** Securities issued by Centre as India's contributions to the international financial institutions

[58] Different countries follow different financial years to serve their differing priorities—the USA follows October-September, Australia from July-June (as the IMF and WB) while China follows a January-December. Like India, Canada, the UK, New Zealand, Hong Kong follow April-March period as their fiscal year.

[60] Based on the documents of the Ministry of Finance and the Reserve Bank of India.

such as the IMF, World Bank, Asian Development Bank, etc.

(v) ***Securities issued against 'Small Savings':*** The deposits under small savings scheme (SSSs) are credited to the NSSF (National Small Savings Fund) from which withdrawals also keep taking place. The rest of the fund (net withdrawals) of the NSSF is invested in special G-Secs issued by the Centre.

2. **External segment** of the public debt includes the external liabilities created through external borrowings by the Centre for its own uses (excluding those taken by the States). This constitutes a variety of 'multilateral' and 'bilateral' loans from IMF, World Bank, ADB, Sovereign Funds, foreign governments, etc.

Adjusted Debt In 2010, Government articulated the concept of adjusted debt which indicates the debt amount after factoring in the impact of external debt (at current exchange rate of rupee) and netting out Market Stabilization Scheme (which was abolished in 2014) and NSSF (National Small Savings Scheme) liabilities not used for financing the deficit of the Central Government. While analysing the General Government Debt (consolidated debt for Central and State Governments), 14 days T-bills investment by States and Central loans to State Governments are also netted out to avoid double accounting.

Along with a quarterly report on public debt, an 'Annual Status Paper on Government Debt' (since 2010-11) is also published by the Government. The status paper aims to enhance transparency by providing a detailed account of debt operations during the year and an assessment of the health of the public debt based on internationally accepted debt performance indicators.

INDEPENDENT DEBT MANAGEMENT

Debt management has been in news for some time now. However, the idea for a public debt management agency (PDMA) was proposed in the *Union Budget 2015-16* itself but it was put on the back burner probably due to clear objections from the Reserve Bank of India (RBI). By *March 2019,* the issue of having an independent debt management agency outside the preview of the RBI was again voiced by the policy think tank, the NITI Aayog, saying it was *an idea whose time has come*. There looks strong logic in this:

- At present, the RBI manages the government debt, including market borrowing (RBI has been reluctant to part with this function).
- There is a case of clear conflict of interest in this arrangement—on the one hand RBI decides the key interest rates (i.e., policy rates under monetary policy mechanism), while on the other it trades in the government bonds (treasury bills, cash management bill and G-Secs) also.
- Lack of alignment between India's domestic bond market (which is controlled by RBI's policy rates) and the external bond market/ external commercial borrowings (which is linked to the global variables). India has seen a rise in its external commercial borrowings in past years primarily due to interest rates in the global market being much lower than in India. This discrepancy looks awkward in today's times when the global financial market is converging.
- The size of fund which India needs for her infrastructural development depends much on the deepening of the bond market which is not possible due to RBI having a hold on it which is linked to its monetary policy.

It is believed that once the debt management office is separated from the RBI, the Government will be able to pay much more attention on the aspect of debt having an eye on the changing needs of fund over the time. It will help the Government to cut the cost of fund also. Such a step from the Government may be expected in 2021-22 by looking at the timing of the debate (in a sense the NITI looks preparing an atmosphere amidst the news of a kind of tussle between the RBI and the Government).

CENTRAL GOVERNMENT DEBT

The debt liabilities of the Central Government include all borrowings of the government contracted against the Consolidated Fund of India (technically defined as '**Public Debt**'), as well as liabilities in the Public Account of India. These liabilities include external debt but exclude part of the NSSF (National Small Savings Fund) liabilities to the extent of States' borrowings from the NSSF and investments made out of the NSSF, which do not finance Central Government deficit. The latest position (by end March 2020) and features of the Centre's debt[61] are briefed below:

- The total liabilities stood at ₹97.05 lakh crore (88.67 per cent of which was public debt).
- As ratio of GDP, the liabilities have been consistently declining—to 45 per cent by 2019-20 (from the peak of 55 per cent in 2004-05 and moderated level of 46.5 per cent in 2014-15). However, it increased to 47 per cent on account of increased borrowings in the aftermath of the COVID-19 economic description. This is an outcome of both fiscal consolidation efforts and relatively high GDP growth—a clear contribution of the FRBM Act, 2003.
- The liabilities are characterised by low currency and interest rate risks. This is owing to low share of external debt in the debt portfolio and almost entire external borrowings being from official sources. Most of the public debt has been contracted at 'fixed' interest rates which keeps them insulated form interest rate volatility.

- The maturity profile of the liabilities has also 'elongated' gradually, leading to reduced rollover risk. G Secs maturing in less than 5 years has been on consistent decline—the weighted average maturity has increased from 9.7 years at end March 2010 to 10.7 years at end March 2020.

CENTRAL TRANSFER TO STATES

States in the country enjoyed comparatively lower financial headroom in comparison to the Centre. However, this issue was addressed by the upcoming Finance Commissions in a very progressive way, either by higher devolution from the central pool of taxes or grants-in-aids. During the period of economic reforms, states got new tools to mobilise resources but on the terms of increased responsibilities and transparency. But still, States keep facing fiscal pressure due to various reasons. In this regard, the Central transfer of funds to states plays a very crucial role. Transfer of funds to States comprises essentially of *three* components[62] (except other transfers[63] which include the Additional Central Assistance and Special Central Assistance):

1. Share of States in Central taxes devolved to the States
2. Grants awarded by the Finance Commission
3. Centrally Sponsored Schemes (CSSs).

61. **Economic Survey 2020-21,** Vol. 2, pp. 75-76, Ministry of Finance, GoI, N. Delhi.

62. **Economic Survey 2019-20,** Vol. 2, pp. 43-44, Ministry of Finance, GoI, N. Delhi.

63. For more details on the 'Other Transfers', see **Chapter 5** on *Planning in India* in the book.

The Central Government accepted the recommendations made by the ***Fifteenth Finance Commission (FC-XV)*** for the year *2020-21*, relating to the Post Devolution Revenue Deficit Grant, Grants to Local bodies and Disaster Management Grants, which were[64] as given below:

- The 'Grant-in-Aid' amounting to ₹1.99 lakh crore for transfer to States (that was around 50 per cent higher than recommended by the 14th Finance Commission (FC-XIV) for the award year 2019-20).
- Out of the corpus of ₹90,000 crore allocated as 'grant for local bodies', 32.5 per cent were for urban local bodies and the remaining for rural local bodies.
- Unlike that of the FC-XIV, the local bodies grant during the year were also allocated to *Fifth* and *Sixth* Schedule Area as well as Mandal/Tehsil and District/Zila Panchayats in the case of rural local bodies, and also allocated to 59 Cantonment Boards in the case of the urban local bodies.
- For the *first time* Finance Commission grants were also allocated for the purpose of improving *ambient air quality* in million plus cities/urban agglomerations.
- Share of states in central taxes for the year was envisaged by the Government to rebound to 6.0 per cent of GDP (from 5.7 per cent in 2019-20).

GENERAL GOVERNMENT FINANCES

Though States are also following their fiscal responsibility laws enacted by them, they also have been facing pressure on fiscal front due to a variety of reasonable and populist reasons. Deterioration in States, fiscal position ultimately drains the resources of the Centre and the overall fiscal situation of the economy gets deteriorated.

Thus, to get an overview of fiscal position of the Government as a whole, it is critical to analyse the General Government (Centre plus States) finances. The General Government liabilities as a proportion of GDP have been increasing over the last few years— the latest situation[65] in 2019-20 being as given below (compared with the year 2011-12):

- Debt-to-GDP ratio was at 73.8 per cent (increasing every year form 67.4 per cent).
- Nominal interest rate was at 6.85 per cent (decreasing every year from 8.52 per cent).
- Nominal economic growth rate was at 7.21 per cent (decreasing almost every year from 15.74 per cent).
- Interest rate–growth rate differential (IRGD) was at 'negative' 0.4 per cent (decreasing almost every year from 'negative' 7.2 per cent).

The Government pledged to reduce the general Government liabilities in 2020-21. However, in the wake of the COVID-19 pandemic, it is expected to further increase on account of the shortfall in revenue and higher expenditures as the fiscal deficit estimates for the year (i.e., 2020–21) has seen a steep upward revision to 9.5 per cent (from the budget target of 3.5 per cent). The revised estimate for Government's total borrowing for the year is ₹9.35 lakh crore (up from the Budget estimate of ₹5.36 lakh crore). This has to naturally deteriorate the liabilities of the General Government.

---

64 **Economic Survey 2020-21,** vol. 2, p. 74, Ministry of Finance, GoI, N. Delhi.

65 **Economic Survey 2020-21,** vol. 2, pp. 80-81, Ministry of Finance, GoI, N. Delhi.

COVID-19 FISCAL STIMULUS

In order to facilitate a resilient recovery of the economy from the impact of COVID-19 pandemic and the following lockdown, Government of India and RBI together announced a total stimulus[66] worth ₹29.87 lakh crore (i.e., 15 per cent of the GDP). Out of this, stimulus worth 9 per cent of GDP was provided by the Government under AtmaNirbhar Bharat Package.

India's fiscal policy approach to the pandemic has been different from many other countries of the world (which launched one-time large stimulus to support demand)— India introduced fiscal stimulus in a phased manner. India's fiscal stimulus measures reflected flexibility of adapting to an evolving situation in order to enable resilient economic recovery in the following phases:

1. Special *economic and comprehensive package* announced in the initial phase (mid-May 2020) was aimed to primarily provide a cushion to the vulnerable sections of the society and the small businesses— direct food transfers to the poor and vulnerable, livelihood programmes, guarantees and liquidity enhancing measures.
2. Measures to *stimulate consumer spending* (mid-October 2020) were announced as steady unwinding of lockdown and restrictions started.
3. Measures under *AtmaNirbhar Bharat 3.0* (mid-November 2020) was announced as economic recovery began, which was aimed at boosting investment through measures like Production Linked Incentives (PLI), enhancing capital expenditure and steps to encourage investment in infrastructure sector.

66 **Economic Survey 2020-21,** vol. 2, pp. 58-62, Ministry of Finance, GoI, N. Delhi.

OUTLOOK FOR 2021-22

From the fiscal perspective, 2020-21 has been a difficult year— the *Economic Survey 2020-21* predicted a likely fiscal slippage. The prediction of the survey became correct once the *Union Budget 2021-22* estimated the fiscal deficit for 2020-21 at 9.5 per cent (a hopping 6 per cent higher than the budgetary target). Not only this, for the year 2021-22, the Government has set a fiscal deficit target of 6.8 per cent and a borrowing plan of around ₹12 lakh crores (to support the economy recover out of the pandemic shock). Given the situation, the economy will be faced with the following fiscal challenges in the upcoming year 2021-22:

- Though GST collections crossed ₹1 lakh crore mark in October 2020, the future collections depend on the pace of economic recovery.
- Slippage in direct tax collections is possible as corporates have declared lower profits and job market has been hit hard due to the pandemic.
- Excessive government borrowings are expected to not only harden interest rates but crowd out funds also.
- By mid-March, a price rise was seen in the crude oil which may push India in higher current account deficit.
- Investments from the private sector have remained subdued together with the lower credit offtake from the banking industry— threatening a subdued growth in the coming years.
- Government requirement of fund will go up in order to implement the recommendations of the 15th Finance Commission also.
- The benefits from the increased capital expenditures planned by the Government for the year depend on timely completion of the projects undertaken.

- Various key reforms introduced during 2020-21 and 2021-22 are likely to impart growth momentum and strengthen the fiscal position of the Government.
- A roadmap for long-term fiscal policy strategy is the need of the hour for both Centre and States (the recommendation of the 15th Finance Commission in this regard needs to be followed.

In the wake of COVID-19 pandemic, the fiscal policy response of the Government has been a combination of demand and supply side policies (under the ambit of *AtmaNirbhar Bharat*) to cushion against the economic shock, and subsequently fuel the economic recovery. Going forward, in order to sustain the recovery in aggregate demand, the Government looks committed to an expansionary fiscal stance in 2021-22. The growth recovery is projected to facilitate buoyant revenue collections in the medium term, and thereby enable a sustainable fiscal path in the coming times. [67]

---

67. Based on diverse sources such as corporate results, media reporting and the Economic Survey 2020-21, vol.2, pp.51-89, Ministry of Finance, GoI, N. Delhi.

CHAPTER 19

SUSTAINABILITY AND CLIMATE CHANGE: INDIA AND THE WORLD

".., this is the only home we have and, as environmentalists are fond of saying, Mother Nature doesn't do bailouts ... so we better find a better way to grow."

In this Chapter...

- Introduction
- COVID-19 Impact on Climate Initiative
- Sustainable Development Goals (SDGs)
- India and SDGs
- Paris Agreement (COP 21)
- COP24
- COP25
- Green Finance
- Climate Finance
- Green Climate Fund
- Global Environment Facility
- INDCs
- India and Climate Change
- International Initiative of India
- India's Forests
- Agricultural Residue Burning
- Climate Risk Insurance
- Future Outlook
- Development with Wisdom

INTRODUCTION

Improving living standards for mankind has been the single minded goal of all nations and world bodies. After defining development in numerous ways for over two decades, there seems to be a consensus on 'Human Development'. While a large population on earth is still to get the 'bare minimum' for development, humanity is at the crossroads where it is faced with the first of its kind challenge—the challenge of 'climate change'. The dilemma is that whatever we can do for our development, there has to be a repercussion on nature. An even bigger dilemma is in achieving a global consensus on how to check or restrict and finally reverse the process of climate change.

A survey of the global comparative opinion shows that people in India and indeed all countries have a marked and rising concern about sustainable development and climate change in recent years. However, the challenges are also formidable, especially in the context of finding the matching resources of the required magnitude given the economic conditions. Climate science has rightly

**Thomas L. Friedman, Hot, Flat, & Crowded, (London: Penguin Books, 2009), p. 23.*

taken up an important position in the public debate. Even as the science of climate change grapples with uncertainties, the world is witnessing more extreme events. With rising extreme events and rising citizen demand, the world has little option but to listen to the voice of evolving science and respond adequately with strategies and policies rooted in the principles of multilateralism with equitable and fair burden sharing.[1]

Since 2010 onwards, the world has witnessed increasing numbers of natural disasters and extreme weather conditions—frequently getting news headlines across the world. Policy-makers have been facing enormous pressure on availability of clean air, water and energy together with the problems of poverty and hunger, especially in the developing world.

The *year 2015* witnessed two landmark international events—the historic climate change agreement under the *UNFCCC in Paris* in December 2015 and the adoption of the *SDGs* (Sustainable Development Goals) in September 2015. The Paris Agreement aims at keeping the rise in global temperatures well below 2°C, which will set the world towards a low carbon, resilient and sustainable future, while the Sustainable Development Goals, which replace the MDGs (Millennium Development Goals), set the development agenda for the next fifteen years. On the domestic front too, some important climate-related initiatives were taken, including the launching of the historic *International Solar Alliance* (an initiative taken by India) and the submission of the ambitious INDC (Intended Nationally Determined Contribution).

COVID.19 IMPACT ON CLIMATE INITIATIVE

The year 2020 was the 4th anniversary of the official adoption of SDGs. The World Health Organisation declared the outbreak of the COVID-19 on 30th January 2020 resulting in a public health emergency, which was later pronounced to be a pandemic. It has led to considerable human and economic costs setting countries back on their developmental goals and creating serious impediments to the attainment of the SDGs.

In 2020, the developed country Parties were supposed to fulfil the goal of jointly mobilising US$ 100 billion a year for climate finance, an essential component of the commitments made by the developed countries, which remained elusive due to the pandemic. The postponement of *COP 26* to 2021 also gives less time for negotiations and other evidence-based work to inform the post-2025 goal.

India is no exception to the unprecedented crisis unleashed by the pandemic. It is faced with remarkable challenges emerging from the need to provide substantive economic stimulus, address livelihood losses, introduce and implement wide -ranging economic reforms. The need to develop sustainably, however, remains at the core of the country's development strategy.[2]

SUSTAINABLE DEVELOPMENT GOALS (SDGs)

The UN General Assembly in its 17th session in September 2015 announced a set of *17 SDGs* (Sustainable Development Goals) and 169 targets which will stimulate action over the next 15 years. This set of goals replaces the Millennium Development Goals (MDGs) which were coming to an end in 2015 and will try to work in the areas which could not be completed earlier.

The SDGs were adopted after one of the largest consultation exercises in UN history. The goals were proposed in the United Nations Conference on Sustainable Development (*Rio+20*) in June 2012. The SDGs will be effective between 2016 and 2030.

1. Oliver Morton, 'Megachange: The World in 2050', in Daniel Franklin and John Andrews, ***The Economist*** in London: 2012), pp. 92–110.

2. **Economic Survey 2020-21,** vol. 2, pp. 204-55, Ministry of Finance, GoI, N. Delhi.

The *17 Goals* agreed under the SDGs are given below:

1. No Poverty
2. Zero Hunger
3. Good Health and Well-being
4. Quality Education
5. Gender Equality
6. Clean Water and Sanitation
7. Affordable and Clean Energy
8. Decent Work and Economic Growth
9. Industry, Innovation and Infrastructure
10. Reduced Inequality
11. Sustainable Cities and Communities
12. Responsible Consumption and Production
13. Climate Action
14. Life Below Water
15. Life on Land
16. Peace, Justice and Strong Institutions
17. Partnerships to achieve the Goal

The 17 goals have a total of 169 targets and thus are very comprehensive in comparison to the MDGs. Countries need to evolve proper monitoring mechanism to track and achieve these targets under the set goals—a very challenging task. The major challenges faced by the countries in this regard will be like—financing the implementation process, mustering participation from the stakeholders, and evolving an administrative structure.

INDIA AND SDGs

India has taken several proactive steps at the national and sub-national levels to mainstream the SDGs into the policies, schemes and programmes of the Government. The major initiatives in this regard are given below:

- **SDG India Index:** The index was developed by the NITI Aayog to measure[3] the progress of states and union territories in the direction of achieving the goals and monitor their actions in this regard. There are 100 indicators[4] across the goals in which the states/UTs are given performance score (between 0 and 100) and are ranked accordingly.
- **SDGs Nexus:** As there exists a 'nexus' between the SDGs targets and social indicators (such as education-electricity, health-energy, etc.), India has accordingly acquired a 'nexus approach' to the goals and started streamlining its social sector schemes and initiatives accordingly.
- **Voluntary National Review:** In *July 2020,* India presented its second VNR (Voluntary National Review) to the UNHLPF (United Nations High-Level Political Forum) on Sustainable Development which is the highest international platform for review and follow-up of the SDGs under the auspices of the UNESCO (United Nations Economic and Social Council). Besides highlighting India's achievements, the review presented the Indian model of *SDG localisation,* stakeholders' perspectives,[5] strategies of integrating businesses, and the means of implementation.
- **Localisation:** Localisation of the SDGs is crucial for the realisation of the goals under 2030 Agenda. In this regard, the *SDG*

3 The salient features of the *SDG India Index Report, 2018* (which was developed by the NITI Aayog) have been discussed in detail in the **Economic Survey 2018-19,** Vol. 2, pp. 105-108, Ministry of Finance, GoI, N. Delhi.

4 **Economic Survey 2019-20,** Vol. 2, pp. 168-172, Ministry of Finance, GoI, N. Delhi.

5 India in this regard had consultations with over 1000 CSOs (Civil Society Organisations) which was the cornerstone of the VNR Report preparation process. The consultations involved 14 groups and had the principle of ***Leaving No One Behind*** as its focus (which lies at the heart of SDGs), as per the **Economic Survey 2020-21,** vol. 2, pp. 205-07, Ministry of Finance, GoI, N. Delhi.

India Index and *Dashboard,* designed and developed by NITI Aayog, is the principal tool through which not only the local bodies are being connected but their performance is being measured and monitored.

- **COVID-response:** The pandemic threatened the very backbone of livelihood and sustainability. In this regard the governments initiated several measures starting with the arrangement of free food to agricultural and MSMEs related reforms which were directly or indirectly connected to the SDG goals.

PARIS AGREEMENT (COP 21)

The 21st Conference of Parties *(COP 21)* under the UNFCCC (United Nations Framework Convention on Climate Change) took place in Paris in December 2015. The Paris Agreement on post-2020 actions on climate change will succeed the *Kyoto Protocol*. Unlike the Kyoto Protocol, it provides a framework for all countries to take action against climate change. Placing emphasis on concepts like climate justice and sustainable lifestyles, the Paris Agreement, for the *first time,* brings together all nations for a common cause under the UNFCCC. One of the main focus of the agreement is to hold the increase in the global average temperature to well below 2°C above pre-industrial level and on driving efforts to limit it even further to 1.5°C.

The Agreement comprises 29 articles and is supported by 139 decisions of the COP. It covers all the crucial areas identified as essential for a comprehensive and balanced agreement, including mitigation, adaptation, loss and damage, finance, technology development and transfer, capacity building and transparency of action and support.

A marked departure from the past is the Agreement's *bottom-up approach,* allowing each nation to submit its own national plan for reducing greenhouse gas emissions, rather than trying to repeat a top-down approach advocated by the Kyoto Protocol, giving each country an emission reduction target. The *sailent features* of the Agreement[6] are as follows:

1. It acknowledges the development imperatives of developing countries by recognising their right to development and their efforts to harmonise it with the environment, while protecting the interests of the most vulnerable.
2. It seeks to enhance the 'implementation of the Convention' while reflecting the principles of equity and CBDR-RC (Common but Differentiated Responsibilities and Respective Capabilities), in the light of different national circumstances.
3. Countries are required to communicate their climate action plans to the UNFCCC known as Nationally Determined Contributions (NDCs) every five years. Each Party's successive NDC will represent a progression beyond the Party's then current NDC, thereby steadily increasing global effort and ambition in the long-term.
4. It is not mitigation-centric and includes other important elements such as adaptation, loss and damage, finance, technology development and transfer, capacity building and transparency of action and support.
5. Developed countries are urged to scale up their level of financial support with complete road map towards achieving the goal of jointly providing US$ 100 billion by 2020. At the same time, a new collective quantified goal based on US$ 100 billion floor will be set before 2025.

6 Ministry of Finance, **Economic Survey 2015-16,** Vol. 2, pp. 179-181.

6. It mandates that developed countries provide financial resources to developing countries. Other Parties may also contribute, but on a purely voluntary basis.
7. Developed countries are urged to take the lead in mobilisation of climate finance, while noting the significant role of public funds in the mobilisation of finance which should represent a progression beyond their previous effort.
8. It includes a robust transparency framework for both action and support.
9. Starting in 2023, a global stock-take covering all elements will take place every five years to assess the collective progress towards achieving the purpose of the Agreement and its long-term goals.
10. It establishes a compliance mechanism, overseen by a committee of experts that operates in a non-punitive way, and is facilitative in nature.

COP24

The Paris Agreement of 2015 (COP21) became quite controversial due to several reasons, one being the delay in finalising the 'rulebook' for its implementation (for it, there already have been COP22, COP23 and now COP24). The 24th meeting of Conference of Parties **(COP24)** to the United Nations Framework Convention on Climate Change (UNFCCC) was held at Katowice, Poland (December 2–15, 2018). The key focus of the meeting was to finalise the guidelines for the implementation of the ***Paris Agreement of 2015*** in post-2020 period. The major agreements[7] which the countries were able to reach at the conference were:

- Agreement on the *rulebook* which ensures that each tonne of emissions released into the atmosphere is accounted for (making emission measurable). It also includes certain other provisions related to cut in emission—how governments will measure, report and verify their emissions-cutting efforts. This deal will apply from 2020 (for now, it is guided by the Kyoto Protocol, 1997).
- To initiate the work on setting up the new collective finance goals post-2020 from the floor of US$ 100 billion.
- Conducting the Global Stocktake (GST) of the effectiveness of climate action in 2023 and how to assess progress on the development and transfer of technology.

India reiterated its commitment to the Paris Agreement in a collective manner and followed an approach guided by the principles of Equity and Common but Differentiated Responsibilities and Respective Capability (CBPR-RC).

COP25

The 25th session of the Conference of the Parties **(COP25)** to the UNFCCC was held at Madrid, Spain under the Chilean Presidency. The COP25 decision[8], titled *Chile Madrid Time for Action*, emphasises the following two special areas of concern, namely:

1. The continued challenges that developing countries face in accessing financial, technology and capacity-building support, and
2. The urgent need to enhance the provision of support to developing country Parties for

7 *United Nations Framework Convention on Climate Change (UNFCC) Secretariat*, Bonn, Germany, December 2018.

8 **Economic Survey 2019-20**, Vol. 2, pp. 179, Ministry of Finance, GoI, N. Delhi.

strengthening their national adaptation and mitigation efforts.

The major decisions agreed upon by the Parties are given below:

- Commitment made by developed country Parties to a goal of mobilising jointly US$ 100 billion per year by 2020 to address the needs of developing countries.
- In the case of combating *climate change,* support from developed Parties to developing country Parties for mitigation, adaptation and implementation.
- Urgency of scaling-up of action and support, including finance, technology and capacity-building, for developing countries for averting, minimising and addressing loss and damage—under the review of Warsaw International Mechanism (WIM) for Loss and Damage.
- Establishing the *Santiago Network* for catalysing technical assistance for the implementation of relevant approaches in developing countries.
- On *adaptation* matters, it recalls that the provision of scaled-up financial resources should aim to achieve a balance between adaptation and mitigation, taking into account country-driven strategies, and the priorities and needs of developing country Parties, considering the need for public and grant-based resources for adaptation.
- On *technology* matters, the adopted decision requests the Technology Executive Committee (TEC) and the Climate Technology Centre and Network (CTCN) to continue to implement their mandates with strengthened efforts on all themes of the technology framework.
- GCF (Global Climate Fund) has been requested to collaborate with CTCN and TEC for strengthening cooperative action on technology development and transfer at different stages of the technology cycle.

India reiterated its commitment to implement the Paris Agreement in its letter and spirit and to act collectively to address climate change including consideration of principles of equity and common but differentiated responsibilities and respective capabilities. India hosted the *India Pavilion* at COP25 with the theme "150 years of celebrating the Mahatma", designed to depict Mahatma Gandhi's life and messages around sustainable living.

COP26 Due to COVID-19 pandemic, the COP26 got postponed and now it is scheduled to take place in Glasgow, Scotland by late 2021. Major issues for discussions and consensus for the COP will be— transparency mechanism, market and non-sustainable market mechanisms (Article 6), common time frames for nationally determined contributions, long-term climate finance; governance of Warsaw International Mechanism for loss and damage, consensus on the *definition* of climate finance, common accounting methodology for assessment and evaluation of climate finance.

GREEN FINANCE

In the past few years, the term 'green finance' has gained a lot of attention across the world. The idea gets its first mention in the UN document at the UN Conference on Sustainable Development (also known as *Rio+20*), 2012. Though it lacks a universal definition, green finance mostly refers to financial investments in projects and initiatives that encourage more sustainable economy.

There is no universal *definition* of green finance, though it mostly refers to financial investments flowing towards sustainable development projects and initiatives that encourage the development of a more sustainable economy[9]. By now, several working definitions have come up—China's Green Credit Guidelines, the Climate Bonds Taxonomy of Green Bonds, the International Development Finance Club's (IDFC) approach to reporting on green investment, the World Bank/International Finance Corporation's (IFC) Sustainability Framework, and the UK Green Investment Bank Policies.

India and Green Development Green finance is yet to pick up in India. Attaining the ambitious solar energy target, development of solar cities, setting up wind power projects, developing smart cities, providing infrastructure which is considered as a green activity and the sanitation drive under the 'Clean India' or 'Swach Bharath Abhiyan' are all activities needing green finance.

India created a corpus called the NCEF (National Clean Energy Fund) in 2010–11 out of the cess on coal produced/imported ('polluter pays' principle) for the purpose of financing and promoting clean energy initiatives and funding research in the area of clean energy. Some of the projects financed by this fund include innovative schemes like:

1. a green energy corridor for boosting the transmission sector,
2. Jawaharlal Nehru National Solar Mission's (JNNSM) installation of solar photovoltaic (SPV) lights and small capacity lights, installation of SPV water pumping systems, SPV power plants, grid-connected rooftop SPV power plants, and
3. pilot project to assess wind power potential.

By **April 2021,** most of the banks had issued *green bonds* in India. Proceeds from these bonds are mostly used for funding renewable energy projects such as solar, wind and biomass projects and other infrastructure sectors, with infrastructure and energy efficiency being considered as green in their entirety. By early 2016, the SEBI (Securities and Exchange Board of India) approved the guidelines for green bonds. India needs to take care of ***certain issues***[10] involved with the mobilisation of green finance:

1. For a developing country like India, poverty alleviation and development are of vital importance and resources should not be diverted from meeting these development needs. Green finance should not be limited only to investment in renewable energy, as, for a country like India, coal-based power accounts for around 60 per cent of the installed capacity. Emphasis should be on *greening coal technology*.
2. Green bonds are perceived as new and attach higher risk and their tenure is also shorter. There is a need to reduce risks to make them investment grade.
3. There is also a need for an internationally agreed upon definition of green financing as its absence could lead to over-accounting.
4. While environmental risk assessment is important, banks should not overestimate risks while providing green finance.
5. Green finance should also consider unsustainable patterns of *consumption* as a parameter in deciding finance, particularly conspicuous consumption and unsustainable lifestyles in developed countries.

---

9 ***Green Finance Study Group***—as quoted by the Ministry of Finance, **Economic Survey 2015-16,** Vol. 2, pp. 182–83.

10 Ibid.,

CLIMATE FINAMCE

The world is alive to the compulsion of combating climate change as unmitigated climate change risks pose irreversible costs. Complexity arises in the case of financing for addressing adaptation and mitigation of GHG emissions. Provision of finance is embedded in the convention and has also been mentioned in the *Paris Agreement* for addressing the adaptation and mitigation needs of developing countries. Tracking of climate finance is equally important. Lack of a clear **definition** of climate finance has led to controversies in recent estimates of climate finance.

The Paris Agreement mandates that transparent and consistent information on support provided and mobilised through public interventions for developing country Parties be provided by developed countries. However, it is silent on the definition of climate finance. While the question of what counts as climate finance would be decided at a later stage by the Standing Committee on Finance under the UNFCCC, it is important that it should highlight certain basic elements like:[11]

1. Sources of funding, terms of funding and purpose of funding in addition to resources being committed/disbursed/new.
2. While defining climate finance, it is also important to define what cannot be counted towards climate finance.
3. Aid money meant for development purpose should not be counted as climate finance. With reference to funds provided for multiple purposes, only the share provided solely for climate change should be included under climate finance.
4. Systems should be in place to check for double counting or treatment of ODA as climate finance.

[11] Ibid., pp. 185–86.

There is an even greater gap in tracking adaptation finance and segregating it from development funds as a whole. As a result, very often, the entire amount allocated to a project is erroneously treated as adaptation finance. Any climate finance tracking exercise needs to carefully account for these problems.

GREEN CLIMATE FUND

The Green Climate Fund (GCF) is a global fund[12] created to support the efforts of developing countries to respond to the challenge of climate change—by helping them limit or reduce their greenhouse gas (GHG) emissions and adapt to climate change. It seeks to promote a paradigm shift to low-emission and climate-resilient development, taking into account the needs of nations that are particularly vulnerable to climate change impacts.

It was set up by 194 countries who are parties to the United Nations Framework Convention on Climate Change (UNFCCC) in 2010. It aims to deliver equal amounts of funding to mitigation and adaptation. It has been given an important role in serving the agreement and supporting the goal of *Paris Climate Agreement-2015* by keeping climate change well below 2 degrees Celsius.

The fund was launched in 2014 with a pledge of US$ 10.3 billion (from both public and private sectors in the form of grants, loans, equity or guarantee)—the highest contribution was pledged by the USA (US$ 3 billion), followed by Japan (US$ 1.5 billion), the UK (US$ 1.2 billion), France (US$ 1.03 billion), and Germany (US$ 1.0 billion) while small amounts came from some developing nations also and one city (Paris). In 2019, the GCF Board approved US$ 5.2 billion to support the implementation of 111 climate change adaptation and mitigation projects and programmes in 99 developing countries. GCF's first replenishment (2020-23) process so far witnessed 28 countries

[12] Green Climate Fund, Incheon, South Korea, March 2019.

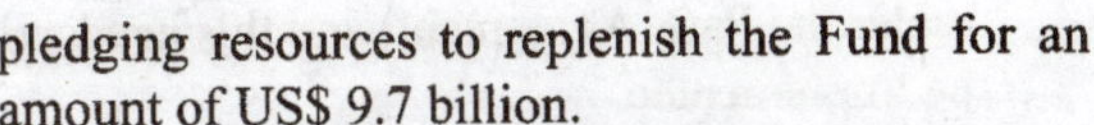

pledging resources to replenish the Fund for an amount of US$ 9.7 billion.

In recent climate talks, the issue of targeting emissions to limit temperature rise by 1.5 to 2 degree Celsius above pre-industrial level was intensely debated. However, climate finance (the real enabler in this direction) could not be resolved as desired.

GLOBAL ENVIRONMENT FACILITY

The Global Environment Facility (GEF) was established[13] on the eve of the 1992 *Rio Earth Summit* to help (mainly the developing countries) tackle earth's most pressing environmental problems. Both developed and developing countries are donors (39 in number) to the GEF. Its fund is replenished after every 4 years. At the last replenishment (GEF-7), it was pledged with a fund of US$ 4.1 billion for the period 2019 to 2023.

Today, it has become an international partnership of 183 countries, international institutions, civil society organisations and the private sector that addresses global environmental issues. By *March 2019*, the fund had provided over US$17.9 billion in grants and mobilised an additional US$ 93.2 billion in co-financing for more than 4500 projects in 170 countries.

INDCs

The INDCs (Intended Nationally Determined Contributions) are plans by governments communicated to the UNFCCC regarding the steps they will take to address climate change domestically. As per the *COP19* decision (Warsaw 2013), all Parties were requested to prepare their INDCs, without prejudice to the legal nature of the contributions towards achieving the objectives of the Convention and communicate well in advance of COP21.

India's INDC India submitted its INDC to the UNFCCC in October 2015 which is quite exhaustive and covers elements such as adaptation, mitigation, finance, technology and capacity building. The highlights[14] are given below:

1. To put forward and further propagate a healthy and sustainable way of living based on traditions and values of conservation and moderation.
2. To adopt a climate-friendly and cleaner path than the one hitherto followed by others at a corresponding level of economic development.
3. To reduce the emissions intensity of its GDP by 33 to 35 per cent of the 2005 level by 2030.
4. To achieve about 40 per cent cumulative electric power installed capacity from non-fossil fuel-based energy resources by 2030 with the help of transfer of technology and low cost international finance including from the Green Climate Fund (GCF).
5. To create an additional carbon sink of 2.5 to 3 billion tonnes of CO_2 equivalent through additional forest and tree cover by 2030.
6. To better adapt to climate change by enhancing investments in development programmes in sectors vulnerable to climate change, particularly agriculture, water resources, the Himalayan region, coastal regions, health and disaster management.
7. To mobilise domestic and new and additional funds from developed countries for implementing these mitigation and adaptation actions in view of the resources required and the resource gap.
8. To build capacities, create a domestic framework and an international architecture for quick diffusion of cutting-edge climate technology in India and for joint collaborative R&D for such future technologies.

13. **Global Environment Fund,** Washington DC, USA, March 2020.

14. *Economic Survey 2015-16*, vol. 2, p. 183-84, MoF, GoI, N. Delhi.

Implementation Challenges

India's developmental approach puts adequate emphasis on all the *three pillars* of sustainable development— economic, social and environmental. A great deal of stress is also being laid upon the inter-generational equity in regard to the emerging climate actions proposed to be taken by the present generation. However, the imperatives of the intra-generational equity (i.e., eradication of poverty and equitable social and economic development) cannot be brushed aside. This way, the implementation of the climate targets is intertwined with national and global economic scenario— with the following challenges[15] in future:

- First priority being *adaptation,* the cost is supposed to increase in coming times as India is highly vulnerable to extreme weather events which are expected to worsen with the passage of time because of the momentum due to carbon stock continuing to increase the temperature. India is relying on domestic resources which have come under strain due to increased expenditures on livelihood on account of COVID-19 pandemic.
- The mobilisation of **fund** will be the critical element in the implementation of India's NDC which commenced on January 1, 2021. Preliminary estimates provided by NDC indicate that India will need US$ 2.5 trillion (at 2014–15 prices) till 2030 for it.
- As per India's second *Biennial Update Report (BUR),* India achieved a reduction in emission intensity of GDP by **21** per cent between 2005–14. However, to fully implement the NDC, the country will need new and additional financial resources, technological support (which were committed to by the developed countries under the Paris Agreement) and this needs to be implemented.

Besides having an integrated approach to mobilise adequate fund (at the domestic and international levels) for appropriate climate action, the developed countries need to do much more than what they are currently committed to. The present scope, scale and speed of international *climate finance* is, however, insufficient as the climate finance requirements run into trillions of dollars as against a commitment of US$ 100 billion each year by 2020 by the developed countries (that, too, is yet to materialise).

INDIA AND CLIMATE CHANGE

India has been very sensitive to the issue of climate change and has been active in mitigating the crisis with the global community. The National Action Plan on Climate Change (NAPCC), launched in 2008, was India's first multi-dimensional step in this direction. The action plan has objectives of *adaptation and mitigation* through focused National Missions. The missions also focus on key adaptation requirements and creation of scientific knowledge and preparedness. India decided to ***revise the NAPCC*** in line with its INDCs (Intended Nationally Determined Contributions) under the Paris Agreement to make it more comprehensive in terms of priority areas. The progress of implementation of the *eight national missions* is briefly explained[16] below:

1. **The Perform, Achieve and Trade (PAT)** scheme under National Mission for Enhanced Energy Efficiency (NMEEE) is designed on the concept of 'reduction' in energy consumption. By April 2019, 110 Designated Customers (DC) were notified under it. The total energy consumption of these DCs comes out to be 15.244 Million Tons of Oil Equivalent (Mtoe) and it is expected to get a total energy savings of 0.5130 Mtoe. By

15. **Economic Survey 2020-21,** vol. 2, pp. 214-15, Ministry of Finance, GoI, N. Delhi.

16. **Economic Survey 2020-21,** vol. 2, pp. 208-11, Ministry of Finance, GoI, N. Delhi..

2020, about 20 Mtoe of energy savings is estimated under the scheme.

2. **National Solar Mission**aims to increase the share of solar energy in the total energy mix.

   The target has been set at 100 GW via Grid Connected Solar Power Projects, Grid Connected Rooftop projects, large and medium size land based solar power projects. The total investment in setting up 100 GW will be around ₹6 lakh crores. A cumulative 32.5 GW of solar electric generation capacity was installed (by November 2019).

3. **National Water Mission** focuses on monitoring of ground water, aquifer mapping, capacity building, water quality monitoring and other baseline studies. There are 1071 assessment units categorised as over exploited as per the assessment (last done in 2011) of Central Ground Water Authority (CGWA). Directions have been issued for mandatory Rain Water Harvesting/Roof Top Rain Water Harvesting for all target areas in the country. Rain water harvesting has been made mandatory for drawing ground water.

4. **National Mission for a Green India** envisages a holistic view of greening and focuses on multiple ecosystem services along with carbon sequestration and emission reduction. The mission emphasises the landscape approach to treat large contiguous areas of both forest and non-forest, public and private lands with a key role of the local communities in planning, implementation and monitoring. Actions taken under it are—afforestation activities (convergence with the MGNREGS also done), promoting alternate energy at household level, etc.

5. **National Mission on Sustainable Habitat** is being implemented through three programmes: Atal Mission on Rejuvenation and Urban Transformation, Swachh Bharat Mission, and Smart Cities Mission. The actions under it consists of mandatory energy conservation for commercial buildings having load of 100 KW or above, Mass Rapid Transit Systems and six sub-sectors launched (solid waste management, water and sanitation, storm water drainage, urban planning, energy efficiency and urban transport).

6. **National Mission for Sustainable Agriculture**aims at enhancing food security and protection of resources. Key targets include covering 3.5 lakh hectare of area under organic farming, 3.70 under precision irrigation, 4.0 lakh hectare under System of Rice Intensification, 3.41 lakh hectare under diversification to less water consuming crop, 3.09 lakh hectare additional area under plantation in arable land and 7 bypass protein feed making. The mission has resulted in the formation of the network project NICRA (National Innovations on Climate Resilient Agriculture).

7. **National Mission for Sustaining the Himalayan Ecosystem** aims to evolve suitable management and policy measures for sustaining and safeguarding the Himalayan Ecosystem. The key achievements include setting up of Centre of Glaciology at Wadia Institute of Himalayan Geology, thematic task forces in 6 lead institutions, State Climate Change Centres in 11 out of 12 Himalayan States, 40 Training Programmes under State Climate Change Centres organised with 5500 people trained, formation of Inter-University Consortium of 4 universities on Himalayan Cryosphere and Climate Change.

8. **National Mission on Strategic Knowledge for Climate Change** seeks to build a *knowledge system* that would inform and support national action for ecologically sustainable development. The key achievements include—setting up of 11 Centres of Excellence and 10 State Climate Change Centres, Training programme, 7

Human Capacity Building and National Knowledge Network programmes in the areas of climate change science, adaptation and mitigation, 8 Global Technology Watch Groups in the areas of Renewable Energy Technology, Advance Coal Technology, Enhanced Energy Efficiency, Green Forest, Sustainable Habitat, Water, Sustainable Agriculture and Manufacturing have been set up.

Climate Change Action Programe

The central sector scheme Climate Change Action Programme (CCAP) was launched in 2014 with the aim to build and support capacity at central and state levels, strengthening scientific and analytical capacity for climate change assessment, establishing appropriate institutional framework and implementing climate actions. Major actions[17] under the scheme are:

- Energy audit studies have revealed an end-use saving potential to the extent of 40 per cent in the country—the Energy Conservation Building Code, 2018 has started setting minimum energy performance standards.
- Schemes like UJALA for LED bulb distribution and replacing conventional streetlights by LED lights are being implemented.
- As part of the National Electric Mobility Mission Plan (NEMMP) 2020, Faster Adoption and Manufacturing of (Hybrid &) Electric Vehicles in India (FAME India) scheme was formulated in 2015 to promote manufacturing and sustainable growth of electric and hybrid vehicle technology.
- The National Bio-fuels Policy 2018 targets 20 per cent blending of ethanol in petrol and 5 per cent blending of biodiesel in diesel by 2030.

National Adaptation Fund on Climate Change (2015) supports concrete adaptation activities for the States/UTs that are particularly vulnerable to the adverse effects of climate change and are not covered under on going schemes. The Scheme has been taken as central sector scheme with NABARD (with domestic and multilateral funds) as the National Implementing Entity.

Aligning Financial System with Sustainability

A sound financial system is required for cleaner forms of production. This is more so, as estimates point towards the requirement of trillions of dollars to achieve SDGs globally. Hence, the spotlight[18] is now on aligning the financial system with sustainable development with the following steps:

- The RBI (in 2007) sensitised banks to the various international initiatives and asked them to modify their lending plans in the light of such developments.
- The SEBI (in 2012) mandated the Annual Business Responsibility Reporting (ABRR), a reporting framework based on the National Voluntary Guidelines (NVGs) for listed companies for pursuing sustainable management practices. The Indian Institute of Corporate Affairs (in 2011) developed a concept of NVG for adoption by the corporate sector.
- 'Climate Bonds' remain focused on green bonds, which are specifically linked to climate-change mitigation, adaptation and resilience. India (US$ 10 billion) has the second largest emerging green bond market after China (US$ 110 billion), with a very high potential of growth. 'Green bonds' are being issued by financial, non-financial or public entities where the proceeds are used to finance 100 per cent green projects and

17 **Economic Survey 2019-20,** Vol. 2, p. 176, Ministry of Finance, GoI, N. Delhi.

18 **Economic Survey 2020-21,** Vol. 2, pp. 217–20, Ministry of Finance, GoI, N. Delhi.

assets. "Social bonds' are yet another variant of the climate bonds, getting popular in the country. Climate bonds are supposed to gain popularity in coming years as issuers and investors both are inclined to adopt policies and strategies linked to SDGs.

Aimed to scale up the environmentally sustainable investments, India joined the *International Platform on Sustainable Finance (IPSF)* in October 2019. It aims to mobilise resources from the international financial market to help finance the transition to a green, low carbon and climate resilient economy. Its twin objectives are:

1. Exchange and disseminate information to promote best practices in environmentally sustainable finance; and
2. Compare the different initiatives and identify barriers and opportunities to help scale up environmentally sustainable finance while respecting national and regional contexts.

INTERNATIONAL INITIATIVE OF INDIA

In order to mitigate the climate change risk and integrate the power of global community, India has taken some very vital initiatives at international stage. These initiatives are discussed briefly below.

International Solar Alliance

The International Solar Alliance (ISA) is the *first* treaty based inter-governmental organisation headquartered in India. With 83 signatory countries, the alliance creates a multi-stakeholder ecosystem where sovereign nations, multilateral organisations, industries, policymakers and innovators work together to promote the common and shared goal of meeting energy demands of a secure and sustainable world. It aims to pave the way for future solar generation, storage and technologies for member countries' needs by mobilising over US$ 1000 billion by 2030. The achievement of its objectives will also strengthen the climate action in member countries, helping them fulfil the commitments expressed in their INDCs. Some **major initiatives** under the Alliance[19] are as given below:

- It has signed an MoU with the UNESCAP and enjoys a permanent Observer Status at the UN General Assembly with funding agreements with the World Bank, Asian Development Bank and European Development Bank.
- *World Solar Bank* and *One Sun One World One Grid Initiative* were initiated aimed at global solar energy revolution. While the former would cater to the need for dedicated financing window (including low-cost fund) for solar energy projects, the latter aspires to develop an interconnected 'green grid'.
- Its solar rooftop programme has been noteworthy, with a demand of more than 1 GW aggregated from member countries. ISA has diversified its programmatic focus on health sector, cold storage chains for agriculture and vaccines and other innovative applications of solar energy.
- 'Coalition for Sustainable Climate Action' was launched in 2020, comprising global public and private corporates, to institutionalise its partnership with the corporate sector.
- *First World Solar Technology Summit (WSTS)* was organised in September 2020 to showcase next-generation solar technologies and deliberate on increasing access to new technologies at an affordable cost.

---

19 **Economic Survey 2020-21,** vol. 2, pp. 222–23 and **Economic Survey 2019-20,** vol. 2, pp. 179–80, Ministry of Finance, GoI, N. Delhi.

Coalition for Disaster Resilient Infrastructure

In September 2019, India launched the Coalition for Disaster Resilient Infrastructure (CDRI) on the side lines of UN Secretary General's Climate Action Summit. This international partnership of national governments (35), UN agencies, multilateral development banks, private sector, and knowledge institutions aims to promote the *resilience* of new and existing infrastructure systems to climate and disaster risks. The coalition has the following[20] objectives:

- Enabling measurable reduction in infrastructure losses from disasters, including extreme climate events.
- Enabling universal access to basic services and prosperity as enshrined in the SDGs, working under the Sendai Framework for Disaster Risk Reduction and the Paris Climate Agreement.
- Conducting country-specific and global activities and providing member countries. technical support and capacity development, partnerships to facilitate and encourage investment in disaster resilient infrastructure systems.

In its formative stage, CDRI will focus on developing resilience in ecological and social infrastructure with a concerted emphasis on health, education, transportation, telecom, energy, and water. Within 2-3 years, the coalition aims to have a 3-fold impact of achieving considerable changes in member countries' policy frameworks, future infrastructure investments and high reduction in economic losses from climate-related events and natural disasters.

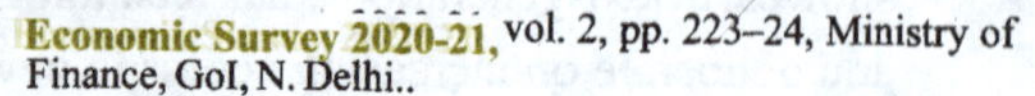

20. **Economic Survey 2020-21,** vol. 2, pp. 223–24, Ministry of Finance, GoI, N. Delhi..

INDIA'S FORESTS

Forests play a crucial role in adaptation and mitigation to climate change. They help to store more carbon (i.e. carbon sink) than any other terrestrial ecosystem (as per the *India State of Forest Report-2019*). India accounts for 2 per cent of the total global forest area in 2015 as per the Global Forest Resource Assessment-2019 of the FAO. The major features[21] of the forests in India are summarised below:

- In terms of canopy density classes the area covered by Very Dense Forest (VDF) is 99,278 sq. km (3.02 per cent), Moderately Dense Forest (MDF) is 3,08,472 sq. km (9.39 per cent) and Open Forest (OF) is 3,04,499 sq. km (9.26 per cent).
- The forest and tree cover have reached 80.73 million hectare, which is 24.56 per cent of the geographical area of the country. The total forest cover of the country, as per current assessment 2019, is 7,12,249 sq. km, which is 21.67 per cent of the total geographic area of the country. There has been an increase of 3,976 sq. km (0.56 per cent) of forest cover, 1,212 sq. km (1.29 per cent) of tree cover and 5,188 sq. km (0.65 per cent) of forest and tree cover put together, at the national level as compared to the previous assessment 2017.
- The States/UTs showing significant gain in forest cover are Karnataka (1,025 sq. km), Andhra Pradesh (990 sq. km), Kerala (823 sq. km) and Jammu & Kashmir (371 sq. km) whereas States showing loss in forest cover are Manipur, Meghalaya, Arunachal Pradesh and Mizoram.

21. **Economic Survey 2019-20,** Vol. 2, P. 181-185, Ministry of Finance, GoI, N. Delhi.

- India is one of the *17 mega diverse* countries in the world. This is evident in the *Shannon-Weiner Index* for Diversity which is used for measuring species richness and abundance. The index also compares diversity of species among various habitats.
- The latest report assessed Shannon-Weiner Index for 16 bio-diverse areas. The Index shows that Tropical Evergreen forest is *high* in Karnataka, followed by Kerala. Tropical moist deciduous forest cover is *high* in Arunachal Pradesh, Karnataka and Maharashtra. Tropical dry deciduous forest is *high* in Arunachal Pradesh and semi-evergreen forests are *high* in Karnataka. Tropical Littoral and swamp forests are *high* in UP and tropical thorn forests are seen widely in Andhra Pradesh.
- The total carbon stock in forest is estimated as 7,124.6 million tons (an increase of 42.6 million tons compared to the last assessment for 2017). India's carbon stock is ranked at 8th among the top 10 countries in the world.
- Net change in carbon stock in India shows that net change is highest in soil organic carbon, followed by Above Ground Biomass (AGB) and Dead Wood. Litter carbon registered negative growth rate as compared to 2017 assessment.

India is among a few countries in the world where, despite ongoing developmental efforts, forest and tree cover are increasing considerably. A comparison with some other emerging and advanced economies shows that India's growth in forest cover has been in positive territory.

AGRICULTURAL RESIDUE BURNTNG

India, being the second largest agro-based economy with year-round crop cultivation, generates a large amount of agricultural waste, including crop residues. Due to cropping pattern related reasons and input provisioning policies followed by the governments, farmers across many states in the country burn lakhs of tonnes of agricultural residues in agricultural fields. Open burning of crop residues has become an environmental concern in India, particularly during paddy harvesting season. The situation[22] in this regard is summarised below:

- A variety of crop residues are burnt, especially in northern states of Punjab, Haryana, UP, and Rajasthan depending on the agro-climatic region. However, about 50 per cent of all crop residue burnt in the country are residues of rice crop (TIFAC, 2018)[23].
- The use of combine *harvesters* leaves the crop residues in field, and in order to clear the fields for the next crop in the easiest way, farmers' burn the residues. About 178 million tonnes of surplus crop residues are available in the country (TIFAC, 2018). Burning of these residues leads to rise in pollutant levels and deterioration of air quality.
- Various source apportionment ***studies*** at city scales have shown that agricultural burning contributes significantly in PM2.5 (particulate matter, diameter measurements of 2.5 micrometres or less) concentrations.
- Because huge volumes of residues are burnt in a very short duration (of a few weeks), it leads to significant contributions in pollutant

22. **Economic Survey 2019-20,** Vol. 2, P. 186-189, Ministry of Finance, GoI, N. Delhi.
23. **TIFAC** (Technology Information, Forecasting and Assessment Council) was set up in 1988 as a registered society under the Department of Science and Technology as an autonomous body. It is mandated to assess the state-of-art of technology and set directions for future technological development in India in important socio-economic sectors.

levels like PM2.5 (TERI, 2018; SAFAR, 2019).

- The effect of stagnant atmospheric condition over Delhi during the harvest season of kharif crop aggravates the deterioration of the ambient air quality in the region. As per TERI (2019), emission pollutants vary according to the type of crop residue (e.g. PM2.5 emission (g/Kg) followed in this order— Sugarcane (12.0 per cent), Maize (11.2 per cent), Cotton (9.8 per cent), Rice (9.3 per cent), Wheat (8.5 per cent). There are studies which have reported that open burning of crop residues has ill-effects on soil organic carbon and soil fertility. These studies are supported by the NASA images also.

Suggestions to check residue burning Various suggestions which came from the studies to address crop residue burning and check air pollution have been given below:

1. Promoting the practice of conservation of agriculture with low lignocellulosic (fibrous) crop residues like rice, wheat, maize, etc. Agricultural *machineries* can help farmers to sow the seeds of the next crop without any problem associated with residues of the previous crops and also without affecting the crop productivity. This can improve or sustain the productivity of the crop land in the long term, as *in-situ* management. Apart from this, there are other options to utilise the crop residues *ex-situ* from the crop land.
2. Creating markets for crop residues and mandating nearby thermal power plants to undertake co-firing them with coal.
3. Promoting infrastructure for setting up biomass depots for storage of bailed crop residues in areas that have shown high fire incidents or high production of a particular crop.
4. Providing special loans for financing farm equipment and working capital for private sector.
5. Promoting use of crop residue-based biochar briquettes in local industries, brick kiln and hotel/dhaba as an alternate fuel.
6. Promoting pollution control as a parameter for deciding incentives and allocation to States and UTs.

Government Steps We see government taking two categories of steps to check residue burning:

1. Three *legislative initiatives* have been undertaken, namely— NPMCR (National Policy for Management of Crop Residue), 2014 guidelines; NGT (National Green Tribunal) prohibited (2015) agricultural residue burning in any part of the NCT of Delhi; and burning crop residue was made a crime under Section 188 of the IPC and under the Air and Pollution Control Act of 1981.
2. A subsidy-based central sector scheme, the 'Promotion of Agricultural Mechanisation for In-Situ Management of Crop Residue in the States of Punjab, Haryana, Uttar Pradesh and NCT of Delhi', launched for the period 2018-20 (which had visible impact on the incidence of crop residue burning).

the idea is much similar to the concept[1] of 'human development' articulated by the UNDP. In recent times, the world has started accepting the role of people's *attitudinal* and *behavioural* dimensions, too, in the gamut of development promotion.[2] Further, we see an increased and consensual acceptance among the nations on the issue of delivering 'happiness' and 'life satisfaction' to the citizens.[3] It means, over the last few decades the whole idea about the 'ultimate' aim of the economies has gone for a kind of metamorphosis. Making growth and development percolate to the *'marginalised and disadvantaged sections'* of society (i.e., the SCs, STs, OBCs, Minorities and Women) remains the official policy of 'inclusive growth' for India.[4]

The GoI has been conscious about the development of the social sector which includes areas, like health, education, shelter, social welfare, social security, etc. Once the economy commenced the process of economic reforms, we see an increased attention to the strengthening of social sector—enhancing the social infrastructure and situation.[5] But India is faced with a variety of interconnected and interdependent issues and challenges in the areas, such as inclusion, expansion, implementation, accountability, governance, decentralisation, etc.[6]

By 2020, India is projected to be the youngest nation in the world in terms of size—while this 'youth bulge' provides India great opportunities, it also 'poses challenges'. These young people need to be healthy, suitably educated and appropriately skilled to contribute optimally to the economy[7]. The proportion of economically active population (15–59 years) in India has increased from 57.7 per cent to 63.3 per cent during 1991 to 2013, as per Sample Registration System (SRS) data for 2013. If India has to reap the benefits of this *demographic dividend* in the years ahead, it is imperative that investments in social infrastructure are made in appropriate measure to achieve the desired educational and health outcomes.

India has to evolve a multi-pronged strategy with focus on bridging the gaps in access to social infrastructure through appropriate use of innovative technologies for enhancement of human potential for productive employment in various sectors and for improving the quality of life. Mobilising the civil society, media and other stakeholders of society in this regard will play a huge supportive role.

HUMAN DEVELOPMENT

The ***Human Development Report 2020,*** titled *The Next Frontier: Human Development and the Anthropocene,* was launched on December 15, 2020. The **major highlights**[8] from the report *(more on India)* are given below:

- India is at 131st rank (out of 189 countries)— 2 ranks lower than the previous report.
- Ranks of some other countries in 'medium human development' are— Sri Lanka (72nd), Thailand (79th), China (85th), Indonesia and Philippines (both 107th), Vietnam (117th), Bangladesh (133rd), Pakistan (154th).
- India's HDI (0.645) in the South Asia is more than the region's average (0.641),

1. Amartya Sen, ***Development as Freedom***, Oxford University Press, N. Delhi, 2000, pp. 3–11.
2. ***World Development Report 2015: Mind, Society, and Behaviour***, World Bank, Washington DC, 2015.
3. ***World Happiness Report-2012 and 2013***, Sponsored by the UNO, N. York, 2013 and 2014.
4. ***Eleventh Five- Year Plan (2007–12)***, Planning Commission, GoI, N. Delhi.
5. Increased allocations of fund as well as enhanced performance is reported by the ***Economic Surveys of 1991–92 to 2014–15***, MoF, GoI, N. Delhi.
6. Amartya Sen and Jean Dreze, ***An Uncertain Glory: India and its Contradictions***, Allen Lane, Penguin Books, London, 2013, pp. vii-xiii.
7. ***Economic Survey 2014–15***, MoF, GoI, N. Delhi, pp. 131-146.
8. **Human Development Report 2020**, UNDP, New York, USA, December 15, 2020.

CHAPTER 20

HUMAN DEVELOPMENT IN INDIA

*The basic purpose of development is to enlarge 'people's choices'. In principle, these choices can be infinite and can change over time. People often value achievements that do not show up at all, or not immediately, in income or growth figures-greater access to knowledge, better nutrition and health services, more secure livelihoods, security against crime and physical violence, satisfying leisnre hours, political and cultural freedoms and sense of participation in community activities. The objectiue of development is to create an enabling environment for people to enjoy long, healthy and creative lives.**

In this Chapter...

INTRODUCTION

Economic growth still remains the immediate focus of the world economies. But, income enhancement can only bring the desired development in the country once it is supported by a conscious public policy aimed at it. Again, the presence of 'good governance' in the policy framework can hardly be missed. After the increased acceptance of welfare economics, the standard of life of the masses has emerged as the most popular tool to measure developmental achievements of the economies—

** Mahbub ul Haq (1934-1998), Founding Editor of the Haman Development Report, UNDP, 1990.*

CLIMATE RISK INSURANCE

With looming climatic aberrations, the time[24] for introducing a climate risk insurance in the country has come— the country incurs losses to the tune of around US$ 10 billion annually due to extreme weather events— about 80 per cent Indians remain uninsured. It is an important tool for providing security against loss of livelihoods and assets as a consequence of disasters.

This is of great significance especially for the farm community which mainly faces the risks of 'weather variability' and the 'uncertainty of crop yield'— the magnitude and intensity of the same being higher in India. As an overwhelming majority of farmers (contributing significantly to the economy and livelihood) depend on farming and have extremely limited means and resources to cope with the disastrous consequences of crop failure, it is high time for such an insurance.

Driven by agriculture and the process of development, natural (i.e., primary) forests are increasingly being converted into secondary forests inviting an increased risk of new[25] infectious diseases, which also needs to be included in the climate risk insurance.

Agriculture insurance in the country is very challenging because of a large number of small and scattered landholdings, varying climatic and soil conditions, lack of basic data, and variety of agricultural practices, making it *practically impossible* to implement the scheme on a wide scale. Further, there is widespread lack of knowledge about the nature and functions of crop insurance amongst the farmers, a majority of whom are illiterate and poor.

The *Weather Index Insurance* for agriculture introduced in 2003 did not find much success as it suffered from complex processes, moral hazard, adverse selection, and low penetration of institutional credit.

Studies suggest moving towards *parametric insurance* that agrees to make payment on 'just the occurrence of a climate event' (data for which is easily accessible). Further, the use of climate information services could also be useful. The example of the Karnataka State Natural Disaster Monitoring Centre's *Varuna Mitra,* which has not only benefitted 3.5 lakh farmers through its weather advisories but also provides data to insurers at Panchayat scale to improve pay-outs to farmers, is a case in point.

FUTURE OUTLOOK

India very well understands that action towards sustainability is an undeniable concern for humanity. India's National Agenda of development (evolved by the Niti Aayog) mirrors the SDGs and its policies ensuring the balance among *three pillars* of development— economic, social and environmental. India's future concerns together with performance commitments are given[26] below:

- India reduced emissions intensity of GDP by 21 per cent during 2005-2014 and it is on track to achieve the emission reduction goals. The 175 GW targets for renewables by 2022 will play a very positive role in this direction.
- India is among a few countries in the world where, despite ongoing developmental

24. **Economic Survey 2020-21,** vol. 2, p. 221, Ministry of Finance, GoI, N. Delhi. It was the *Economic Survey 2016-17* which pitched for it in the country for the ***first*** time; the insurance industry has been deliberating on such possibilities since 2015 itself.

25. An example in this regard is the insurance bought by ***Wimbledon*** tennis tournament against a pandemic occurrence in 2003 following the **SARS** outbreak, thus receiving an insurance pay-out of US$ 142 million in 2020 which was utilised to pay the prize money and staff wages *(Insurance Journal 2020).*

26. Based on the **Ministerial documents, Economic Survey 2020-21, Vol. 2, pp.204-25** and **Economic Survey 2019-20,** Vol. 2, p. 190, Ministry of Finance, GoI, N. Delhi.

efforts, forest and tree cover is increasing considerably. The forest and tree cover have reached 80.73 million hectare which is 24.56 per cent of the geographical area of the country. In 2019, total carbon stock in forest is estimated as 7,124.6 million tons (an increase of 42.6 million tons as compared to 2017).

- Agriculture *crop residue burning* and construction and demolition (C&D) *waste* continues to be major concerns. Many countries are already using recycled C&D products in construction. The *Delhi PPP model* in C&D waste management can be a beacon for the other States and cities to replicate, enabling the Swachch Bharat Mission and supporting the SDGs.
- Scarce *financial resources* continue to be the biggest constraint despite the efforts of stakeholders from various walks of life. Developed countries should honour their financial obligations and promises under the multilateral environmental agreements. The world that benefited from carbon emissions (that made them developed) *must repay*.
- Development and *transfer of technology* at affordable costs is also crucial for developing countries.
- India needs high standards of governance, monitoring and implementation at all levels to achieve the SDG goals. An effective spirit of cooperative federalism will be also needed where together with centre, states and local bodies also come on board—invoking participation of the biggest stakeholder, the common people.

To facilitate the effective implementation of the *SDGs* and *Paris Agreement* on climate change, adequate provision of finance, technology transfer, and capacity building to developing countries are critical. India has done and will continue to do its fair share of responsibilities, but it strongly calls for the lead to come from the developed countries.

DEVELOPMENT WITH WISDOM[27]

Hardly anything makes economic sense unless its continuance for a long time can be projected without running into absurdities. Growth and development can happen to a 'limited objective', but it cannot be stretched upto an 'unlimited extent'. How can the 'finite' earth support mankind's 'infinite' physical needs? Long before this was postulated by the 'Club of Rome' in 1972, exactly the same thing Gandhiji had said in the thirties itself, 'Earth provides enough to satisfy every man's need, but not for every man's greed'. Mankind needs to introspect not only about its present needs but the way those needs are being met.

Besides, we also need to 'differentiate' between our 'needs' and 'aspirations'. Our physical needs have a direct 'link' with the resources we have at our disposal to meet them. If mankind is to survive and prosper, we need to be aware of the repercussions of our activities on Mother nature. Humanity needs to be wiser not only in selecting the tools for development but also in setting the goals of development.

27. These virtuous opinions can be seen in a number of contemporary thinkers and writers since the 1970s:

E. F. Schumacher, ***'The Economics of Permanence'***, *Resurgence*, 3(1), May/June 1970, reprinted in Robin Clarke, Editor, ***'Notes for the Future: An Alternative History of the Past Decade' (London:*** Thames and Hudson, 1975. Schumacher invoked Gandhi while advocating for the 'economics of permanence'.

Jeffery Sachs, ***Common Wealth: Economics for a Crowded Earth,*** (London: Penguin Books, 2009, pp. 29-35, pp. 55-155.

Jeffery Sachs, ***The End of Poverty***, Penguin Books, 2005, pp. 280-284.

Tim Harford, ***'The Undercover Economist'***, Abacus, GB, London, 2006, pp. 90-104.

Thomas L. Friedman, ***'The World is Flat'***, Penguin Books, GB, London, 2006, pp. 383-385, pp. 495-504

Ramachandra Guha, ***' The Ecology of Affluence'*** in ***'The Ramachandra Guha Omnibus'***, Oxford University Press, N. Delhi, 2005, pp. 69-97.

while India is also above the average value of 0.631 among the medium HDI category countries.

- *From 1990 to 2019*, the HDI value of India has increased to 0.645 (from 0.429), registering an increase of over 50 per cent. During this period, the life expectancy at birth rose by nearly 12 years; mean years of schooling rose by 3.5 years; expected years of schooling rose by 4.5 years; and gross national income (GNI) per capita increased by 274 per cent.
- *Inequality-adjusted HDI* (IHDI) value for India fell by 26.4 per cent, causing the value to reach 0.475 (Bangladesh's value to fall by 24.4 per cent, but remains above India's IHDI value standing at 0.478; Pakistan's IHDI value fell to 0.384, decreasing by 31.1 per cent). The IHDI value for India was at par with the average IHDI value of the South Asia, the medium HDI countries' IHDI value stood at 0.465. The IHDI was developed by the UNDP, on the consideration that inequality found across a country is a shortcoming in the actual value of its HDI.
- *Gender Development Index* (GDI) value at 0.820— for female 0.573 and male 0.699— showcasing a wide contrast. In this case, India was ahead of Pakistan (0.745) but below Bangladesh (0.904). The average GDI for the South Asia was 0.824, while that for medium HDI countries it was 0.835.
- *Life expectancy* at birth at 69.75 years— 71.0 years for females and 68.5 years for males.
- While the *expected years of schooling* were 11.7 years for males and 12.6 years for females, the *mean years of schooling* were 8.7 years for males and 5.4 years for females.
- GNI per capita (at PPP) was US$ 10,702 for males and US$ 2,331 for females (showing a huge gender-based income disparity).
- *Gender Inequality Index* (GII) highlights gender-based inequalities in the countries, which is derived using three measures— economic activity, reproductive health and empowerment.
  - India's GII was 0.488 which made it rank at the 123rd place out of the 162 nations.
  - Economic activity is measured by the labour market participation, which stood for males at 76.1 per cent and for females at 20.5 per cent.
  - Reproductive health is measured using maternal mortality ratio and adolescent birth rate, which were at 133 deaths per 1 lakh live births and 13.2 births per 1,000 women, respectively.
  - For empowerment, the index measures the percentage of female seats in the Parliament, which was at 13.5 per cent in India— with at least some secondary education, it was 47 per cent for males and 27.7 per cent for females.

PHDI The *Planetary Pressures-Adjusted Human Development Index* (PHDI) is an *experimental* index (introduced for the ***first*** time) that adjusts the HDI for planetary pressures in the Anthropocene. The PHDI is the level of human development adjusted by *carbon dioxide emissions* per person (production-based) and *material footprint* per capita to account for the excessive human pressure on the planet. It should be seen as an 'incentive' for transformation. In an ideal scenario where there are no pressures on the planet, the PHDI equals the HDI. However, as pressures increase, the PHDI falls below the HDI. In this sense, the PHDI *measures* the level of human development when planetary pressures are considered. The performance of some countries on the new index is given below:

- Norway (1st on HDI) falls 15 places, leaving Ireland at the top.
- USA (17th on HDI)) and Canada (16th on HDI) fall 45 and 40 places, respectively (which reflect their disproportionate impact on natural resources).
- China (85th on HDI) drops 16 places.
- **India** moves up by **8** places. It should be noted that under the *Paris Agreement,* India has pledged to reduce the emission intensity of its GDP from the 2005 level by 33–35 per cent and obtain 40 per cent of electric power from non-fossil fuel sources by 2030. Between 2014 and 19, solar capacity of India has increased from 2.6 GW to 30 GW (target of adding 20 GW achieved 4 ahead of the schedule)— the country is 5th in the world in installed solar power capacity.

Important Comments of The Report

Anthropocene People's agency and empowerment can bring about the action we need if we are to live in *balance with the planet* in a fairer world— we are at an unprecedented moment in history, in which human activity has become a dominant force shaping the planet, which leaves its impacts on the existing inequalities and threatens significant development reversals. The list of crises (including climate, biodiversity collapse, ocean acidification, etc.) is long and growing longer, so much so that many scientists believe that for the *first time,* instead of the planet shaping humans, humans are knowingly shaping the planet. This is the Anthropocene— the Age of Humans— a new geologic epoch.

COVID-19 Though humanity has achieved incredible progress, we have taken the **Earth** for granted, destabilising the very systems upon which we rely for survival. *COVID-19,* which 'almost certainly' sprang to humans from animals, offers a glimpse of our future, in which the strain on our planet mirrors the strain facing societies. While the devastating effects of COVID-19 have taken the world's attention, other layered crises, from climate change to rising inequalities, continue to take their toll. The challenges of 'planetary and societal imbalance' are intertwined— they interact in a vicious circle, each making the other worse.

Way out How should we react to this new age? Do we choose to strike out on bold new paths striving to continue human development while easing planetary pressures? Or do we choose to try—and ultimately fail— to go back to business as usual and be swept into a dangerous unknown? The report is firmly behind the first choice, and its arguments go beyond summarising *well-known lists* (indicating the long-drawn and contentious global climate deliberations) of what can be done to achieve it.

POVERTY ESTIMATES

Since India commenced the process of economic reforms, a major shift has taken place in the country's policy-orientation towards poverty alleviation and employment generation—in place of *wage employment*, the focus has shifted to *self-employment* – so that 'gainful employment' could be created and poverty could be alleviated permanently[9].

 *Economic Survey,* 1999–2000, Ministry of MoF, GoI, N. Delhi.

The Planning Commission used to estimate poverty using data from the large sample surveys on household consumer expenditure carried out by the National Sample Survey Office (NSSO) *every five years*. It *defines* poverty line on the basis of monthly pei capita consumption expenditure (MPCE). The methodology for estimation of poverty followed by the Planning Commission has been based on the recommendations made by experts in the field from time to time—the recent estimates based on the recommendations of the Expert Group headed by *Prof. Suresh D. Tendulkar* which submitted its report in December 2009.

As per this methodology, poverty estimates (NSSO, 68th Round, 2011–12) for the period 2004–05 to 2011–12 are as given below:

1. Total poverty declined from 37.2 to 21.9 per cent.
2. Rural poverty declined from 41.8 to 25.7 per cent.
3. Urban poverty declined from 25.7 to 13.7 per cent

Looking at the controversy and confusion related to per day monetary estimates of poverty line criteria, late 2015, the GoI did set up a task force under the vice-chairman of the NITI Aayog (Arvind Panagariya) to suggest a new method for poverty estimates.

MULTIDIMENSIONAL POVERTY

Poverty is often defined by 'one-dimensional' measures – usually based on income, but no single indicator can capture the multiple dimensions of poverty. In place, the idea of multidimensional poverty encompasses the various deprivations experienced by poor people in their daily lives – such as poor health, lack of education, inadequate living standards, disempowerment, poor quality of work, the threat of violence, and living in areas that are environmentally hazardous, among others. This measure of poverty can incorporate a range of indicators that capture the complexity of this phenomena in order to inform policies aimed at reducing poverty and deprivation in a country. Depending on the context of a country and the purpose of the measure, *different indicators can be chosen* to reflect the needs and priorities of a nation, as well as its constituent regions, districts, provinces, etc.

It was in 2010 for the first time that such a measure was developed by Oxford Poverty and Human Development Initiative (OPHI) and United Nations Development Programme (UNDP)— and a global multi-dimensional poverty index (GMPI) was prepared and used since then in the HDRs published (since 1990) by the latter. It is released at the HLPF (High-Level Political Forum) on Sustainable Development of the United Nations every year in July.

India The GMPI is computed by scoring each surveyed[10] household on ***10 parameters*** based on— nutrition, child mortality, years of schooling, school attendance, cooking fuel, sanitation, drinking water, electricity, housing and household assets. In the case of India, it utilises the National Family Health Survey (NFHS), which is conducted under the aegis of Ministry of Health and Family Welfare and International Institute for Population Sciences (IIPS). According to the *GMPI-2020* which covers '107 developing' countries:

- India is 62nd with an MPI score of 0.123 and 27.91 pr cent headcount ratio, based on the NFHS 4 (2015/2016) data.
- Neighbouring countries like Sri Lanka (25th), Bhutan (68th), Nepal (65th), Bangladesh (58th), China (30th), Myanmar (69th) and Pakistan (73rd).

As per the Niti Aayog, the latest NFHS 5 (2019/2020) is set to see remarkable improvement brought about by focused schemes and interventions in these parameters since NFHS 4,

10 **NITI Aayog,** Press Note on Global Multidimensional Poverty Index and India, PIB, September 7, 2020.

especially in sanitation, cooking fuel, housing, drinking water and electricity (the survey was paused due to the COVID-19 pandemic).

The Niti Aayog as the nodal agency is assigned with the responsibility of leveraging the monitoring mechanism of the GMPI to drive reforms— Government uses the index to monitor the performance of the country in 29 select Global Indices. Meanwhile, the Niti Aayog has constituted a *Multidimensional Poverty Index Coordination Committee (MPICC)* having members from relevant ministries and departments together with the experts from OPHI and UNDP (for their technical expertise). By *April 2021,* the preparation of a MPI Parameter Dashboard to rank States and UTs, and an State Reform Action Plan (SRAP) was at an advanced stage of development.

PROMOTING INCLUSIVE GROWTH

The focus of the Indian development planning has been on the formulation of programmes and policies aimed at bringing the 'marginalised and poor sections' of society into the mainstream. The government has been implementing many such programmes for social and financial inclusion. The disbursement of benefits needs a systematic channel which will provide for financial empowerment and make monitoring easier and the local bodies more accountable. The *Pradhan Mantri Jan Dhan Yojna (PMJDY)* launched in August 2014 and the *RuPay Card* (a payment solution) are important schemes in this regard. These two schemes are complementary and will enable achievement of multiple objectives such as financial inclusion, insurance penetration, and digitalisation.

We find an increased Government emphasis on the socio-economic empowerment of the ***minorities.*** In this regard several new schemes have been launched in recent times—the 'Nai roshni' scheme for leadership development of minority women; *Padho Pardesh*, a scheme of interest subsidy on educational loans for overseas studies for the students belonging to the minority communities; for skill development and of the minorities, schemes like *Seekho Aur Kamao* (Learn and Earn), *USTTAD* (Upgrading Skill and Training in Traditional Arts/Crafts for Development) and *Nai Manzil.*

Other than implementing programmes aimed at inclusive growth, enhancing economic growth and efficiency of market, governments need to assure equitable accessibility of these benefits to all citizens in this regard.

Accessible India Campaign

The number of persons with disabilities in India constituted 2.2 per cent of the population (Census 2011). It is imperative to promote, protect and ensure the full and equal enjoyment of all human rights and fundamental freedoms by all persons with disabilities, and to promote respect for their inherent dignity *(UN Convention on rights of Persons with Disabilities).* In this direction, the Department of Empowerment of Persons with Disabilities (DEPwD) launched *Accessible India Campaign* (Sugamya Bharat Abhiyan) as a nation-wide campaign for achieving "universal accessibility for Persons with Disabilities (PwDs)" with a focus on three verticals—built Environment, Public Transportation and ICT (Information and Communication Technologies).

The Government has launched an *Inclusiveness and Accessibility Index* as part of this campaign. The index helps the industries and corporates to participate in the campaign by voluntarily evaluating their readiness for making the workplace accessible for PwDs. The index enables the organisations to introspect over their inclusive policies and organisational culture in aid of PwDs, employment of such workforce and adaptations to meet the needs of PwDs. Further, the *Rights of Persons with Disabilities Act, 2016* has been enacted by the Government aimed at securing and enhancing the rights and entitlements of PwDs (it includes the provision of increasing the reservation in government vacancies from 3 per cent to 4 per cent).

DEMOGRAPHTCS

The population of India has gone for some major changes in the recent decades. These changes have not only restructured the contours of Indian demographics but have brought new openings and challenges regarding it.

1. As per provisional results of *Census 2011,* the following facts regarding the Indian population dynamics are of high importance. The 2001–11 is the *first* decade in independent India wherein the population momentum, coupled with declining fertility, has dampened the pace of net additions to population. Thus, the net addition in this decade is less than that of the pervious decade by 0.86 million. At present, a little more than *one out of every six* persons in the world is an Indian.
2. As per *Sample Registration System-2013* (SRS) data:
   (i) There has been a gradual decline in the share of population in the age group 0–14 from 41.2 to 38.1 per cent during 1971 to 1981 and from 36.3 to 28.4 per cent during 1991 to 2013.
   (ii) On the other hand, the proportion of economically active population (15–59 years), or India's 'demographic dividend', has increased from 53.4 to 56.3 per cent during 1971 to 1981 and from 57.7 to 63.3 per cent during 1991 to 2013.
   (iii) On account of better education, health facilities, and increase in life expectancy, the percentage of *elderly* (60+) has gone up from 5.3 to 5.7 per cent and 6.0 to 8.3 per cent, respectively, in the same two periods.
   (iv) The growth rate of the *labour force* will continue to be higher than that of the population until 2021.
3. According to an *Indian Labour Report* (Time Lease, 2007):
   (i) 300 million youth will enter the labour force by 2025, and 25 per cent of the world's workers in the next three years will be Indians.
   (ii) Population projections indicate that in 2020 the average age of India's population will be the lowest in the world—around 29 years compared to 37 years in China and the United States of America, 45 years in West Europe, and 48 years in Japan.
   (iii) Consequently, while the global economy is expected to witness a shortage of young population of around 56 million by 2020, India will be the only country with a youth surplus of 47 million *(Report on Education, Skill Development and Labour Force (2013–14) Volume III, Labour Bureau, 2014).*

As per the *Economic Survey 2014–15*, the main issue to address, then, is not just providing employment but increasing the employability of the labour force in India. To garner the 'demographic dividend', the Survey suggested the following ***policy initiatives*** in this regard:

1 A declining 0–14 population will impact both elementary (5–14 age group) and higher education (15–29 age group). Elementary education can be further subdivided into primary (5–9 age group) and middle/upper primary (10–14 age group). The focus should be on:

(i) Improving access to education considering the high dropout rates among senior students

(ii) Removing gender disparity especially in the higher age group and in rural areas

(iii) Improving quality of education, including pupil-teacher ratios and provision of amenities in schools, especially in view of the declining learning levels.

2. The *lag in demographic transition* between different states necessitates state-specific policies to optimally garner the benefits of the demographic dividend. Owing to substantial fertility decline in the south during the last two decades, the south is ahead in the demographic transition compared to the north, so the window is already wide open in the south compared to the north. India is better placed in this respect than most other countries. Thus, two sets of policy initiatives emerge for the states.

(i) The states which are already well into the demographic window should actively pursue policies for employment generation to the already bulging labour force.

(ii) The states just entering the window period have some time to plan and must pursue policies simultaneously in several areas like education, health (including reproductive health), gender issues, and employment generation from now on so that they can fully utilise the opportunity.

SOCIO-ECONOMIC AND CASTE CENSUS

The identification of the real beneficiaries is of paramount importance for the success of any targeted approach. In line with this approach, the *Dr. N. C. Saxena Committee* was constituted to advise on the 'methodology for a BPL census in rural areas'. Since June 2011, for the first time, a Socio-Economic and Caste Census (SECC) is being conducted through a comprehensive 'door-to-door' enumeration in both rural and urban India, and authentic information is being made available on the socio-economic condition and educational status of various castes and sections through the SECC.

The exercise was completed by *late 2016* and presently, the errors are in the process of rectification—the reason the report of the census has not been put in the public domain yet. Once the census is fully ready, its findings are expected to be used as guidelines in several areas such as—identifying the level of poverty, target population for the disbursal of subsidies, selection for eligibility for educational scholarships, old age pension, re-orienting the existing reservation policy, better implementation (by correct identification the beneficiaries) of the MGNAREGA, National Food Security scheme, etc.

EDUCATION FOR ALL

To improve life quality and inclusiveness in general and to enjoy the benefits of the demographic dividend, quality education of all has been declared by the Government. India is committed to achieve the *Goal-4* of the SDGs (which seeks 'to ensure inclusive and equitable quality education and promote lifelong learning opportunities for all' by 2030) also well within the time.

Free and compulsory education starts in India at the age of 6 and ends at the age of 14 years under the ambit of the Right of Children to Free and Compulsory Education (RTE) Act, 2009. The Act stipulates norms and standards for a recognised school imparting elementary education. The RTE norms provide for an all-weather building in elementary schools. The school building should, *inter-alia*, consist of at least one classroom for every teacher and an office-cum-store-cum-Head teacher's room, barrier free access, separate toilets for boys and girls, safe and adequate drinking water facility to all children, and playground. India's achievements in the direction, together with various policy actions of the Government, are summarised[11] below:

Infrastructure As per the *U-DISE+ (Unified District Information for Education Plus)-2018-19*, the physical infrastructure of more than 9.72 lakh government elementary schools (schools with Primary or Upper Primary classes have been referred as 'Elementary Schools') has improved significantly. Out of these, 90.2 per cent have girls' toilet, 93.7 per cent have boys' toilet, 95.9 per cent have provision of drinking water facility, 88.1 per cent have hand wash facility, 82.1 per cent have wash (drinking water, toilet and hand wash) facility, 84.2 per cent have medical check-up facility, 20.7 per cent have computer and 67.4 per cent have electricity connection, 74.2 per cent have ramps, 56.5 per cent have boundary wall, 69.3 per cent have playground, 83.8 per cent have library, 21.5 per cent have kitchen garden and 13.9 per cent have rainwater harvesting structure, 23.6 per cent have facility for testing of water and 14.8 per cent have incinerator.

Attendance The age specific attendance ratio (ASAR) indicates the proportion of children of a particular age group actually attending schools/ colleges irrespective of the level or class in which they are studying. Children in the age-group of 6–13 years have reported almost 95 per cent and above attendance across States. But the attendance rate in the early childhood education is low and diverging irrespective of the achievement in education status of the states concerned. While Punjab reported a high attendance rate of 61.6 per cent of the children in the age groups of 3–5 years (i.e., early childhood education), Karnataka reports the *lowest attendance* rate of only 18.3 per cent. In the 18–23 years age bracket, which comprises students pursuing higher education, Kerala and the hilly States have reported higher attendance compared to the rest of India.

Enrollment The NSS (National Sample Survey) Report on 'Key Indicators of Household Social Consumption on Education in India 2017–18' reflects the increased participation in education system across various indicators and highlights some challenges in terms of affordability, quality, distribution of educational infrastructure, etc. As per it, there were about 13.6 per cent persons of age 3 to 35 years who were *never enrolled.* The reasons they cite for not enrolling were 'not interested in education' and 'financial constraints.' Among those who were enrolled, *drop-out rate* was as high as 10 per cent at the primary level, 17.5 per cent at the upper primary/middle and 19.8 per cent at the secondary level.

Cost of education The poor and underprivileged section of people prefer to engage themselves in economic activities for their survival. The absence of suitable financial support system and high burden of course fee, especially in higher education, pushes them out of the education system. As per the NSS Report, the composition of various components of expenditure on education indicates that the course fees which is 50.8 per cent at all India level (including tuition, examination, developmental fees and other compulsory payments) among others contributes about half of the average expenditure of a basic course.

Higher education The NSS Report also throws interesting findings on the challenges faced in affordability in higher education sector. Students pursuing education in private aided institutions are spending significantly higher as compared to government institutions across rural-urban India. Also, due to the absence of competition in government schools/institutions, the quality of education in government schools/institutions is

11. Economic Survey 2020-21, vol. 2, pp. 329-31 and Economic Survey 2019-20, vol. 2, pp. 276-281, MoF, GoI, N. Delhi.

low. As a result, more and more students prefer to enrol themselves in *private institutions*.

School Education The recent initiatives taken by the Government for improving the quality of learning and teaching at school level (i.e. the old primary and secondary education) are summarised below:

- *Integrated Scheme for School Education (ISSE),* i.e. 'Samagra Shiksha' was launched in 2018–19 by subsuming three erstwhile Centrally Sponsored Schemes, namely Sarva Shiksha Abhiyan (SSA), Rashtriya Madhyamik Shiksha Abhiyan (RMSA) and Teacher Education (TE). Till 2017–18, the Sarva Shiksha Abhiyan (SSA) was the designated Centrally Sponsored Scheme to meet the objectives of the RTE Act in *elementary schools* (which provided assistance to State/UTs for universalisation of elementary education).

  The ISSE envisages school education as a ***continuum from pre-school to senior secondary level*** and aims to ensure inclusive and equitable quality education. Under it, States and UTs are supported (with grants) for strengthening of existing government schools, and for creation and augmentation of infrastructure facilities.
- Class-wise and subject-wise *Learning Outcomes* added in the RTE norms. This serves as a guideline for States/UTs to ensure that all children acquire appropriate learning level.
- The RTE Act, 2009 was amended in 2017 to ensure that all teachers acquire the minimum qualifications (prescribed under the Act) by 31st March, 2019 to reinforce the Government's emphasis on improvement of *quality* of elementary education.
- The Navodaya Vidyalaya Scheme provides for opening of one Jawahar Navodaya Vidyalaya (JNV) in each district of the country to bring out the best of *rural talent*. Its significance lies in the selection of talented rural children as the target group and aims to provide them quality education comparable to the best in a residential school system.
- A National Mission called 'NISHTHA' (National Initiative for School Heads' and Teachers' Holistic Advancement), under the Centrally Sponsored Scheme of *Samagra Shiksha,* was launched in 2019–20 to improve learning outcomes at the elementary level.
- The Integrated Teacher Training Programme envisages to build the capacities of around 42 lakh teachers and heads of schools, faculty members of SCERTs, DIETs, Block Resource Coordinators, and Cluster Resource Coordinators. The aim of this training is to motivate and equip teachers to encourage and foster *critical thinking* in students, handle diverse situations and act as first level *counsellors*.
- Promoting *joyful learning* through cultural activities including art, music, dance and theatre is playing a very critical role in a student's life and school activities. (National Curriculum Framework emphasised the importance of such activities and how they helped to enhance learning.)
- Pradhan Mantri Innovative Learning Programme (DHRUV) was launched to identify and encourage talented students to enrich their skills and knowledge.
- To broad an *technology aided teaching and learning*, States and UTs are being actively involved to contribute and use the Digital Infrastructure for Knowledge Sharing

(DIKSHA) platform. Steps are also being taken to improve the quality and diversify the nature of e-content on DIKSHA. Other e-content sites like *e-pathsala*, National Repository of Open Educational Resources (NROER) are also being integrated with DIKSHA to ensure easy access.

Higher Education The recent initiatives taken by the Government for improving the quality of learning and teaching in higher education including technical education are summarised below:

- 'Pandit Madan Mohan Malaviya National Mission on Teachers and Teaching (PMMMNMTT)' was launched which aims at building a strong professional cadre of teachers by setting performance standards and creating top class institutional facilities for innovative teaching and professional development of teachers in higher education. It provides capacity building to all existing teachers (central, state and private teachers can take part in it as well as in induction training).
- Higher Education Financing Agency (HEFA) was established to provide sustainable financial model for higher education institutions, Kendriya Vidyalayas, Navodaya Vidyalayas, AIIMS and other educational institutions.
- National Educational Alliance for Technology (NEAT) was announced on *PPP mode* for using technology for better learning outcomes in Higher Education. The objective is to use 'Artificial Intelligence' to make learning more personalised and customised as per the requirements of the learner.
- Education Quality Upgradation and Inclusion Programme (EQUIP), a 5-year vision plan (2019–24) put in place, *aimed* at ushering 'transformation' in India's higher education system by implementing strategic interventions.
- Some other scheme launched in 2019–20 were—*SWAYAM 2.0* to offer 'online degree programmes' with enhanced features and facilities by top ranking universities; *DEEKSHARAMBH,* a guide to student induction programme and *PARAMARSH* to mentor institutions seeking NAAC (National Assessment and Accreditation Council) accreditation.

COVID-19 AND SCHOOLING

As schools are closed since March 2020 due to COVID-19, the school education has got badly hampered in the country as per ASER (Annual Status of Education Report, October 2020). The percentage of enrolled children from government and private schools owning a smartphone increased enormously from 36.5 per cent in 2018 to 61.8 per cent in 2020 in rural India. If utilised well, the resultant reduction in the *digital divide* between rural and urban, gender, age and income groups is likely to reduce inequalities in educational outcomes. To enable this process, the Government has launched the following initiatives to make education accessible to children during this pandemic (as per the *Economic Survey 2020-21*):

PM eVIDYA Launched under the Atma Nirbhar Bharat Abhiyan (May 2020), this initiative for school and higher education tried to unify all efforts related to digital/online/on-air education to enable multi-mode and equitable access to education for students and teachers. It has got 4 components as given below:

1. **One nation, one digital education infrastructure:** All States/UTs have free access to a single digital infrastructure, i.e., *DIKSHA* under it. This artificial intelligence -based and highly scalable system can be

accessed through a web-portal and mobile application. Since lockdown till December 2020, it got over 800 crore hits.

In April 2020, *Vidya Daan* portal was launched on Diksha as a national content contribution programme to seek and allow contribution/donation of e-learning resources for school education by educational bodies, private bodies, and individual experts.

2. **One class, one TV channel through Swayam Prabha TV Channel:** ***Swayam Prabha*** DTH channel was launched in October 2020 to support and reach those who do not have access to the internet.
3. **Extensive use of Radio, Community radio and Podcasts** 12 GyanVani FM Radio Stations, over 300 Community Radio Stations, *iRadio* and *Jio Saavn* Mobile apps, etc. have been launched under it.
4. **For the differently-abled:** One dedicated DTH channel is being operated specifically for hearing impaired students in sign language, and for visually and hearing-impaired students, study material has been developed in Digitally Accessible Information System (DAISY) and in sign language.

SWAYAM This portal provides dedicated services to students of grades 9 to 12 on it— 1.5 crore students got enrolled in over 92 courses on it.

NROER The National Repository of Open Educational Resources (NROER) is an open storehouse of e-content— nearly 17,500 pieces of e-content are available for various school subjects in all grades.

PRAGYAT These guidelines on digital education were developed with a focus on online/blended/ digital education for students who are presently at home due to the closure of schools.

MANODARPAN This is an initiative for psychosocial support launched under the Atmanirbhar Bharat Abhiyan to strengthen and empower the human capital in the education sector.

NATIONAL EDUCATION POLICY-2020

The National Education Policy–2020 was announced by the Government in July 2020 which will replace the 34-year-old National Policy on Education (NPE) 1986. The **major highlights** of the policy[12] are summarised below:

- Universalisation of education from pre-school to secondary level with 100 per cent Gross Enrolment Ratio (GER) in school education by 2030.
- To bring 'out of school' (2 crores) children back into the mainstream through universalisation of access and expanding the open schooling system.
- The current 10+2 system to be replaced by a new 5+3+3+4 curricular structure corresponding to ages 3–8, 8–11, 11–14, and 14–18 years, respectively.
- Class 10 and 12 board examinations to be made easier to test core competencies rather than memorised facts.
- School governance is set to change, with a new standard framework based on online self-declaration in the public domain for both public and private schools.
- Emphasis on foundational literacy and numeracy, and no rigid separation between academic streams, extra-curricular, vocational streams in schools.

---

12. **Economic Survey 2020-21,** vol. 2, p. 333, Ministry of Finance, GoI, N. Delhi and *Ministry of Human Resource Development*, July 20, 2020, GoI, N. Delhi.

- Vocational Education to start from Class 6 with Internships.
- Teaching up to at least Grade 5 to be in mother tongue/regional language, wherever possible. No language will be imposed on any student.
- Assessment reforms with *360-degree Holistic Progress Card,* tracking students progress for achieving learning outcomes.
- A new and comprehensive National Curriculum Framework for school education, Early Childhood Care & Education, Teacher Education and Adult Education.
- By 2030, the minimum degree qualification for teaching will be a 4-year integrated B.Ed. degree.
- The *National Research Foundation* will be created as an apex body for fostering a strong research culture and building research capacity across higher education.
- A new body, the *Higher Education Commission of India* (HECI), will be set up as a single overarching umbrella body for entire higher education, excluding medical and legal education with 4 independent verticals:
  - National Higher Education Regulatory Council (NHERC) for regulation.
  - General Education Council (GEC) for standard setting
  - Higher Education Grants Council (HEGC) for funding
  - National Accreditation Council (NAC) for accreditation.

Public and private higher education institutions will be governed by the same set of norms for regulation, accreditation and academic standards.

The new education policy has come out after an unprecedented process of consultations and deliberations, which aims to usher the country into a new regime of education and skill required for future— India has hopes from it.

SKILL DEVELOPMENT

As per the ILO (2020), the future labour market situation of young persons is highly influenced by their initial experiences, including how quickly and how well they are able to access the labour market, and the skills and competencies acquired through education and training. General education improves knowledge of the people while *skill training* enhances their employability and equip them to tackle the requirements of the labour market. The Government has been giving extra emphasis on skilling the labour force as the country faces a major skill gap (outlined in detail by the *Economic Survey 2016-17*). The current *skill situation* in the country and the *recent steps* taken by the Government for its development are summarised[13] below:

- There is an improvement in the proportion of skilled people over the annual cycle of Periodic Labour Force Survey (PLFS) across rural, urban and gender classification. However, the level of skill acquirement remained low, as only 2.4 per cent of the workforce of age 15–59 years have received formal vocational/technical training and another 8.9 per cent of the workforce received training through informal sources.
- Out of the 8.9 per cent workforce who received non-formal training, the largest chunk is contributed by on-the-job

13. **Economic Survey 2020-21,** vol. 2, p. 335-37, Ministry of Finance, GoI, N. Delhi.

training (3.3 per cent), followed by self-learning (2.5 per cent) and hereditary sources (2.1 per cent) and other sources (1 per cent).

- Among those who received formal training, the most opted training course is IT-ITeS among both males and females, followed by, electrical-power and electronics, mechanical engineering, strategic manufacturing, automotive, etc.

Policy Reforms To translate India's demographic advantage by various skill development initiatives, the Government has initiated the following major reforms related to skill development in the country:

- **Unified Skill Regulator:** The unified skills regulator, the National Council for Vocational Education and Training (NCVET) has been set up (October 2020) to make the skill ecosystem more dynamic and credible. It aims to award more credible certifications, assessments and standardisation in the area.
- **PMKVY 3.0:** The Pradhan Mantri Kaushal Vikas Yojana 3.0 (PMKVY 3.0) aims to skill 8 lakh candidates in 2020–21. As a paradigm shift, this 'demand driven' scheme is being followed with bottom-up approach for identification and mapping of job roles—being implemented for classes 9 to 12.
- **Quality Enhancement:** To enhance the quality of long-term training programmes and provide a choice to learners about the institutes, the grading of ITIs has been undertaken (to improve their quality and transparency). For ensuring 'greater industrial connect', a new model of Dual System of Training (DST) and Flexi MoUs is being implemented.
- **Integration with Vocation:** Education at both school and higher levels are being integrated with vocation. The VET (Vocational Education and Training) in general education has received a big fillip with the *New Education Policy-2020* (which envisions giving 50 per cent of school and higher education candidates exposure to VET over the next 5 years).

STATUS OF EMPLOYMENT

Generating sufficient number of wage- and self-employment has been one of the prime aims in the Government in the direction of inclusive growth. As things have not been going as per the expectations in the job market, we saw increased debate on the issue of 'jobless growth' in recent past— which is believed to get worse due to lack of quality data regarding the status of employment and unemployment in the country. That is why the Government launched a new regular employment survey, namely the *PLFS (Periodic Labour Force Survey)* in 2017–18. Based on the PLFS for *2017-18* and *2018-19*, the state of labour force, employment and unemployment, separately for rural and urban sectors in usual status (ps+ss),[14] is given below:

- Size of labour force in 2018–19 was estimated at about 51.8 crore persons (48.8 crore employed and 3.0 crore unemployed)—which increased by 0.85 crore between 2017 and 19 (0.46 crore in urban and 0.39 crore in rural sector).
- Gender composition of the increased labour force— 0.64 crore males and 0.21 crore females.

---

14 The workers in the usual status (ps+ss) are obtained by considering the usual principal status (ps) and the subsidiary status (ss) together. The workers in the usual status (ps+ss) include (a) the persons who worked for a relatively long part of the 365 days preceding the date of survey and (b) the persons from among the remaining population who had worked at least for 30 days during the reference period of 365 days preceding the date of survey. *Source:* Economic Survey 2020-21, vol. 2, pp. 337-41, Ministry of Finance, GoI, N. Delhi.

- Number of unemployed declined by 0.79 crore between 2017 and 19, largely in the category of females, and in rural sector.
- Female labour force participation rate increased from 17.5 per cent in 2017–18 to 18.6 per cent in 2018–19.
- *Industry-wise* estimates on workforce:
  - 21.5 crore employed in 'Agriculture' (the largest employer with 42.5 per cent of workforce).
  - 6.4 crore employed in 'other services' (13.8 per cent) were engaged.
  - 'Manufacturing' and 'Trade, hotel and restaurants' each employed about 5.9 crore (with 12.1 per cent and 12.6 per cent shares, respectively)
  - 'Construction' employed 5.7 crore (12.1 per cent share).
- Among the total employed, about 25 crores are self-employed (52 per cent of the workforce), 12.2 crore regular wage/salaried employees and 11.5 crore casual workers.
- Self-employment is still the major source of employment with close to was self-employed. The proportion of regular wage/salaried employees saw an increase in both rural and urban areas and for both males and females. This increase was more among urban females which increased from 52.1 per cent in 2017–18 to 54.7 per cent in 2018–19. This also indicates the improvement in quality of employment.
- Proportion of casual labour declined, which was more in the case of urban females from 13.1 per cent in 2017-18 to 10.7 per cent in 2018-19, as compared to males from 15.1 per cent in 2017-18 to 14.2 per cent in 2018-19.

Formal Employment The net payroll data of Employees' Provident Fund Organisation (EPFO) as on 20th December, 2020 shows a net increase of new subscribers in EPFO of 78.58 lakhs in 2019-20 as compared to 61.1 lakhs in 2018-19.

As per the data from Department for Promotion of Industry and Internal Trade, employment reported by *start-ups* increased from 1.52 lakh in January–December, 2019 to 1.75 lakh in January–December, 2020 due to increase in the number of active recognition of start-ups from 11,694 to 14,784 in the same period.

Unemployment Unemployment rates at all India level, for all ages, as per usual status, *declined* marginally to 5.8 per cent in 2018–19 from 6.1 per cent in 2017–18. In the case of rural, urban, youth, SC, OBC, etc. (between 2017 and 19), unemployment rates have remained the same or declined. The highest decline occurred among those who have received formal vocational/technical training.

The level of unemployment is recorded the highest, 20.2 per cent, among urban youth (age 15–29 years) and the lowest for the subgroup 'not literates' at 1.1 per cent among the persons of age 15 years and above with different educational attainments. Youth unemployment in 2018–19 was on high extremes in Arunachal Pradesh, Kerala, Manipur, and Bihar and on the lower extreme in Gujarat, Karnataka, West Bengal and Sikkim.

Gender Dimension of Employment

To achieve faster economic growth and wealth creation, the presence of gender equality in labour market is considered smart economics. Gender equality has the potential to impact upon poverty, inequality and economic well-being of a country through increase in income of the household, spending on health and education of children, improvement in saving, investment and consumption growth. As per the *World Development Report* (World Bank, 2011), in an era of globalisation, no country can develop and achieve its full potential if half of its population (i.e., women) is locked in non-remunerative, less productive and non-economic activities. The *latest facts* (2018-19) related to this aspect[15] in the country are given below:

- Labour Force Participation Rate (LFPR) of females in the productive age (15-59 years) was 26.5 per cent in 2018-19, as compared to 80.3 per cent for males (rural+urban).
- While 54.7 per cent of urban women were employed in the regular wage/salaried category, about 59.6 per cent of rural females were not only self-employed but 37.9 per cent among them were helpers in household enterprises.
- The low female LFPR is attributed to high participation of women (15 years and above) in *domestic duties* (55.7 per cent in rural areas and 59.1 per cent in urban areas).

As per the *TUS* (Time Use Survey) of the NSO, conducted during 2019 (January–December), we observe that the time spent by a female on *unpaid domestic services* and *unpaid caregiving services* to household members is prominent and higher than male counterparts during a 24-hour time period had the following features:

- The unpaid domestic and caregiving services provided by women are not influenced by their level of education—even with education level of 'secondary and above', women spent 295 minutes in unpaid domestic services and 146 minutes in unpaid caregiving services.
- In terms of contribution to the economy, while women of productive age group spent 337 minutes in unpaid *non-SNA* activity, it was only 41 minutes in the case of males. Similarly, males spent 305 minutes in paid activities, while it was only 68 minutes for females.
- The time spent on unpaid domestic and care giving services (340 minutes or 5.6 hrs) is high for females in the workforce as compared to males but relatively less than females who are not in the labour force (457 minutes or 7.60 hours). Thus, women in the workforce shoulder the responsibility of domestic activities as well as paid work, which leaves them with less time to spend on employment related activities.

GIG EMPLOYMENT

With the change in technology, evolution of new economic activities, innovation in organisation structures and evolving business models, the nature of work has also been changing. Digital platforms have emerged as enablers for employment creation with the power to easily discover job seekers and job providers— in the absence of middlemen. These *new forces* have created massive opportunities for the consumer and the service provider to interact through innovative ways. The new digital technology enables two-sided markets [16]which has helped the e-commerce platforms (such as Amazon, Flipkart, Ola, Uber, Urban Clap, Zomato, Swiggy etc.)

15. Unpaid activities include taking care of children, elderly in the household, production of goods and services for own consumption, while paid activities include self-employment, regular wage/salary jobs and casual work. **SNA** production activity includes employment, Unpaid direct volunteering for other households for production of goods or for production of goods/services for market/non-market units, Unpaid community and organisation-based volunteering for production of goods or for production of goods/services for market/non-market units, etc. and **Non- SNA** Production includes Unpaid domestic services for household members, Unpaid caregiving services for household members, Unpaid direct volunteering for other households for production of services for the households and Unpaid community- and organisation-based volunteering for production of services for the households **(Source: TUS,2019)**.

16. **Two-sided market** is one in which (i) two sets of agents interact through an intermediary or platform, and (ii) the decisions of each set of agents affect the outcomes of the other set of agents, typically through an externality (*Source:* Marc. Rysman, 'The Economics of Two-Sided Market', 2009, *Journal of Economic Perspectives*, 23 (3): 125-143).

to emerge. The labour force works with them under the *flexi-staffing* model (in which India is today one of the world's largest markets). The economy which evolved in the process is known as the **gig economy** and the workforce working in this segment is called *gig workers.* During the COVID-19 induced lockdown, we saw the increasing role of this economy.

- A significant growth happened in the online retail business.
- Preference to 'work from home' resulted in cutting staff strength, engaging freelancers, outsourcing tasks (to reduce overhead costs) as well as hiring skilled services.
- With increasing demand in industries for on hire project-specific consultants, logo/ content designers, web designers, etc. for the white-collar workers, the delivery boys and taxi drivers engaged in platforms like Uber/Ola, Swiggy, Big Basket, Pizza Hut etc. are now showing potential as well.

As a result, the gig economy has been popular amongst the workers in India. The benefit of the gig economy is that it allows *flexibility* in employer-employee relationship to both service seeker and service provider.

Job Contract The nature of *job contract* for a gig worker is different from the contract between an employer and an employee/worker in the following ways:

- Labour contract is usually shorter and more specific to the task or job assigned.
- Employment type might be either temporary or contractual and certainly not regular.
- Nature of payment against the work is more of piece rate, negotiable, may be as wage or partly as profit/reward than a fixed salary.
- Control over employees' work by the employer varies in degree but in any case, is not full.
- Most of the time, workers are flexible to decide on when to work, where to work, etc.

As gig or platform workers were neither considered as *workers* nor *employees* (for more on this, see *Glossary*) under the definition of employee in the labour laws of India, they were not entitled to legal protections under labour laws. This is why they were devoid of their basic rights and social security protections also. For the *first time*, these class of workers were given the missing legal protection— they were defined as unorganised workers for providing them social security benefits (by the newly introduced *Code on Social Security, 2020*).[17]

LABOUR REFORMS

The multiplicity of labour laws and difficulty in complying with them has always been cited as an impediment to industrial development in India. This is why labour reforms has been made an active part of the ongoing economic reform process in the country. In a major initiative for *ensuring compliance* and promoting *ease of doing business*, the government has initiated a number of labour reform measures. In the past few years, several new initiatives[18] have been taken by the GoI in this directions which may be ***summed up briefly*** as given below:

1. The *Apprentice Act 1961* was amended in December 2014 to make it more responsive to industry and youth. The 'Apprentice Protsahan Yojana' was also launched to support MSMEs in the manufacturing sector in engaging apprentices. Government is also working affirmatively to bring a *single uniform law* for the MSME sector to ensure operational efficiency and improve

17. Economic Survey 2020-21, vol. 2, pp. 346-47, Ministry of Finance, GoI, N. Delhi.

18. Ministry of Labour and Employment, GoI, N. Delhi, March 2017 and Economic Survey 2016-17, MoF, GoI, N. Delhi, Vol. 1, p. 162.

productivity while ensuring job creation on a large scale.

2. A unified labour portal scheme called ***Shram Suvidha** Portal* has been launched for timely redress of grievances and for creating a conducive environment for industrial development. Its main features are:
   (i) Unique Labour Identification Number (LIN) allotted to around 0.7 million units facilitating online registration
   (ii) Filing of self-certified, simplified single online return instead of 16 separate returns by industry
   (iii) Transparent labour inspection scheme via computerised system as per risk-based criteria and uploading of inspection reports within 72 hours by labour inspectors

3. **Under Employees' State Insurance Corporation (ESIC) Project Panchdeep:** Digitisation of internal and external processes to ensure efficiency in operations, especially services to employers and insured persons.

4. **Under Employees Provident Fund (EPF):** Digitisation of complete database of 56.4 million (*by March 2019*) EPF subscribers and allotment of universal account number (UAN) to each member, which facilitates portability of member accounts. UAN is being seeded with bank account, Aadhar Card and other KYC details to promote financial inclusion. Direct access to EPF accounts will enable members to access and consolidate previous accounts.

5. **For Unorganised Workers:** The Rashtriya Swasthya Bima Yojana (RSBY) is a scheme under the Unorganised Workers' Social Security Act, 2008. It is a smart card-based cashless health insurance scheme, including maternity benefit, which provides a cover of ₹30,000 per family per annum on a family floater basis to below poverty line (BPL) families in the unorganised sector.

6. **National Council for Vocational Training-Management Information System (NCVT-MIS)** portal has been developed for streamlining the functioning of Industrial Training Institutes (ITIs), Apprenticeship Scheme, and assessment/certification of all NCVT training courses.

7. **National Career Services Portal:** The National Career Service (NCS) Portal was launched to provide a nationwide *online platform* for job seekers and employers for job matching in a dynamic, efficient and responsive manner.

8. **Payment of Bonus (Amendment) Act 2015:** The Act passed in December 2015, has redefined the eligibility for bonus payment of the Payment of Bonus Act 1965 from ₹10,000 to ₹21,000 per month. This will not only enhance the bonus payment to the employees but make more eligible to the same.

Recent Reforms Last two years (2019 and 2020) were *landmark years* in the history[19] of labour reforms as the Government amalgamated, rationalised and simplified 29 existing central labour codes (i.e., laws) into 4 labour codes, namely—

1. Code on Wages, 2019
2. Industrial Relations Code, 2020
3. Occupational Safety, Health and Working Conditions Code, 2020
4. Code on Social Security, 2020.

The move was aimed at bringing these laws in tune with the changing labour market trends and at the same time accommodating the

19 **Economic Survey 2020-21**, vol. 2, p. 341, Ministry of Finance, GoI, N. Delhi.

minimum wage requirement and welfare needs of the unorganised sector workers, including the self-employed and *migrant* workers, within the framework of the legislation. The reforms were a long-drawn process spread over nearly a period of three decades. The draft rules are presently open for comments from general public and various category of the stakeholders.

COVID-19 and Labour Market

How vulnerable urban casual workers are, was exposed by the COVID-19 pandemic. As per the PLFS (Periodic Labour Force Survey), January–March 2020, the size of such workers was **11.2** per cent of the total labour force in the country— a significant proportion of them is supposed to be 'migrants' who were impacted by the lockdown. From May to August 2020, about 63.19 lakh migrant workers travelled through *Shramik* Special trains. With limited data available on inter-state migration and employment in informal sectors, it is difficult to figure out the numbers of migrants who lost jobs and accommodation during the pandemic and returned home. To mitigate the hardships, the Government took the following initiatives[20] for the welfare of workers during the pre-lockdown and lockdown period:

- **AtmaNirbhar Bharat Rojgar Yojana (ABRY)** was announced in October 2020, as a component of AtmaNirbhar Bharat 3.0 had two segments of it:
  - Entire employees' and employers' contribution (i.e., 24 per cent— 12 per cent each) of wages towards EPF was paid by the Government (in respect of new employees and also to re-employee who lost their jobs due to COVID-19, in establishments employing *up to 1000* employees during October, 2020 to June, 2021).
  - Only employees' share of EPF contribution (i.e., 12 per cent) of wages towards EPF was paid by the Government (in respect of new employees and also to re-employee who lost their jobs due to COVID-19, in establishments employing *up to 1000* employees during October, 2020 to June, 2021).
- **Pradhan Mantri Rojgar ProtsahanYojana (PMRPY)** was launched (August 2016) with the objective to incentivise employers for creation of new employment— under it, Government was paying 8.33 per cent of the employer EPS contribution for all sectors in respect of these new employees earning upto ₹15,000 per month. Government contribution was increased to 12 per cent (in 2018) and extended to the textile sector also.
- EPFO members were allowed to withdraw non-refundable advance of 75 per cent of outstanding balance or 3 months' wages whichever is lower, in order to provide relief to the organised sector employees.
- Statutory rate of contribution in EPF was reduced to 10 per cent (from 12 per cent) for May–July, 2020.
- Under *Prime Minister's Garib Kalyan Package* (PMGKP), financial assistance was given to building and other construction workers (BOCW), which largely included migrant workers, from the funds collected under BOCW's cess.
- *Shramik Special Trains* were operated on the request of states to facilitate migrant labourers/stranded passengers from May 2020.

HEALTH FOR ALL

The draft approach paper to the 12th Plan proposed the idea of 'universal healthcare' in 2012, for the

20. **Economic Survey 2020-21,** vol. 2, pp. 347-49, Ministry of Finance, GoI, N. Delhi.

first time. The funding situation did not seem conducive enough and that is why the government did not think to launch it—falling growth rate in the wake of the western recession and many domestic factors. However, providing accessible, affordable and equitable quality health care, especially to the marginalised and vulnerable sections of the population, is one of the key objectives of the Government. There are innumerable challenges to the delivery of efficient health services in India, given the paucity of resources and the plethora of requirements in the health sector. Population health is also significantly influenced by social and environmental determinants such as age at marriage, nutrition, pollution, access to potable water and hygienic sanitation facilities. However, the *National Health Policy 2017* clearly aims to go for 'universal healthcare' and mobilise the required fund (around 2.5 per cent of the GDP as was estimated by the 12th Plan) for the cause modelled on public private partnership (PPP).

The Indian health sector has a *mix* of both public and private providers of health services. The private sector and the quality of care provided is variable, ranging from informal providers (quacks) to individually run nursing homes to large polyclinics and multiplex hospitals. The regulation for cost and quality of care is largely weak in most of the states. In the case of public sector, the health services are delivered through a network of health facilities including ASHA (a volunteer health worker) at the community level, Health Sub-Center (HSC), Primary Health Centres (PHCs), Community Health Centres (CHCs), District Hospitals, Government Medical College Hospitals and the state and central government assisted Employees' State Insurance (ESI) hospitals and dispensaries. Outreach and community level services are provided through coordination between ASHA, Anganwadi Workers (AWWs) and the Auxiliary Nurse Midwife (ANM) at the HSC.

Burden of Diseases

The report[21] *India: Health of the Nation's States-2017* provides the first comprehensive set of findings for the distribution of diseases and risk factors across all States from 1990 to 2016. The concept of Disability Adjusted Life Years (DALYs)[22] provides a framework for analysing the disease burden and risk factors. DALYs is the sum of years of potential life lost due to premature mortality and the years of productive life lost due to disability. One DALY represents the loss of the equivalent of one year of full health. Major findings of the report are given below.

- There has been significant improvement in the health status of the individual as life expectancy at birth (LEB) has increased by approximately 10 years during the period 1990 to 2015. The significance of DALYs as a critical health policy indicator is reflected by the inverse relationship between life expectancy and DALYs rates.

21. The ***India: Health of the Nation's States-2017*** report is a collective effort of Indian Council of Medical Research (ICMR), PHFI and IHME, University of Washington (as per the ***Economic Survey 2017–18***, Vol. 2, pp. 176-183).

22. DALYs express the premature death and disability attributable to a particular cause, and are made up of two components: years of life lost (YLLs) and years of life lived with disability (YLDs). YLLs measure all the time people lose when they die prematurely, before attaining their ideal life expectancy. Ideal life expectancy is based on the highest life expectancy observed in the world for that person's age group. YLDs measure years of life lived with any short- or long-term condition that prevents a person from living in full health. They are calculated by multiplying an amount of time (expressed in years) by a disability weight (a number that quantifies the severity of a disability). Adding together YLLs and YLDs yields DALYs, a measure that portrays in one metric the total health loss a person experiences during their life.

- The per person disease burden measured as DALYs rate dropped by 36 per cent from 1990 to 2016 in India, after adjusting for the changes in the population age structure during this period.
- Of the total disease burden in India measured as DALYs, 61 per cent was due to communicable, maternal, neonatal, and nutritional diseases (CMNNDs) in 1990, which dropped to 33 per cent in 2016.
- There was a corresponding increase in the contribution of non-communicable diseases (NCDs) from 30 per cent of the total disease burden in 1990 to 55 per cent in 2016, and of injuries from 9 per cent to 12 per cent.
- In 2016, *malnutrition* still remained the most important risk factor (14.6 per cent) that results in disease burden in the country though the disease burden due to it has dropped in India substantially since 1990.
- Neonatal disorders and nutritional deficiencies as well as diarrhoea, lower respiratory infections, and other common infections are manifestation of maternal and child malnutrition.
- The contribution of *air pollution* to disease burden remained high in India between 1990 (11.1 per cent) and 2016 (9.8 per cent), with the levels of exposure remaining among the highest in the world. It causes burden through a mix of noncommunicable and infectious diseases, mainly cardiovascular diseases, chronic respiratory diseases, and lower respiratory infections.
- The *behavioural and metabolic risk factors* associated with the rising burden of Non Communicable Diseases (NCDs) have become quite prominent in India. In 2016, the dietary risks, which include diets low in fruit, vegetables, and whole grains, but high in salt and fat, were India's third leading risk factor, followed closely by high blood pressure and high blood sugar (high fasting plasma glucose).
- Unsafe water, sanitation, and handwashing (WaSH), causing 5 per cent of health loss, was the *second leading* risk factor in 1990, but its ranking has dropped to seventh position in 2016.

Efficiency in the use of resources along with measures for preventive and curative health care is necessary to translate enhanced expenditure into improved health outcomes. In this context, the increase in use of antibiotics in developing countries like India where health care spending is low, is a cause for concern.

Universal Healthcare

Announcement of *National Health Policy 2017* is a watershed step in the direction of assuring health to all—aimed at 'universal access[23] to good quality health care services'. Subsequently, the Government launched 'Ayushman Bharat' with two components:

1. Health & Wellness Centres to provide comprehensive primary health care, and
2. Pradhan Mantri Jan Arogya Yojana (PMJAY) to provide health cover to 10.74 crore poor and vulnerable families upto ₹5 lakh per family per year for secondary and tertiary hospitalisation.

The focus of healthcare is on *four* important pillars, namely—(i) preventive healthcare, (ii) providing affordable healthcare, (iii) building

23. Economic Survey 2019-20, Vol. 2, pp.294-299, Ministry of Finance, GoI, N. Delhi.

medical infrastructure, and (iv) mission mode interventions. These are briefly discussed below:

1. **Preventive Health Care:** Major steps taken by the Government in this regard are:

   (i) To promote preventive healthcare, one and a half lakh Ayushman Bharat-Health & Wellness Centres (AB-HWCs) are proposed to be set up by 2022. A total of 28,005 have already been set up (as on January 14th, 2020) to deliver comprehensive Primary Health Care services with focus on universal high quality screening, prevention, control and management of common NCDs such as Hypertension, Diabetes, and the three common Cancers–Oral Cavity, Breast and Cervical Cancer, while continuing to provide services for Reproductive, Maternal, Adolescent and Child health (RMNCH+A) and for communicable diseases.

   (ii) Under *Mission Indradhanush*, 3.39 crore children and 87.18 lakh pregnant women in 680 districts across the country (including Gram Swaraj Abhiyan & extended GSA) have been vaccinated.

   (iii) Apart from the above, recognising the need for addressing the social determinants of health, the government has adopted a *multi-sectoral approach* and is increasingly synergising its efforts with other Mission Mode initiatives of the Government such as *Eat Right & Eat Safe, Fit India, Anaemia Mukt Bharat, Poshan Abhiyan* and *Swacch Bharat Abhiyan,* etc.

   (iv) Recognising the threat of 'nicotine addiction' among youth and children through gateway products such as *e-cigarettes*, the government banned all commercial operations in e-cigarettes. Large pictorial warnings and quit line number on tobacco packs and the resulting increased call volumes from 20,000 to 2.50 lakh calls per month at the quit line services, indicate that government's efforts to reduce tobacco use are starting to bear fruit.

2. **Health Care Affordability:** Affordability is a major dimension of health care, especially in the case of India where a vast population lives below the poverty line. To make health care affordable, the Government has taken a number of initiatives in years as given below:

   (i) As per the latest National Health Accounts (NHA) 2016–17, the *out of pocket expenditure (OoPE)* as a percentage of total health expenditure has declined from 64.2 per cent in 2013–14 to 58.7 per cent in 2016–17. This shows improvement in affordability.

   (ii) Free Drugs Service, Free Diagnostics Service, Free Laboratory Services, Pradhan Mantri Bharatiya Jan Aushadhi Pariyojana (PMBJP) and Pradhan Mantri National Dialysis Programme (PMNDP) are some important initiatives launched to address the high OoPE.

   (iii) Primary health care accounts for 52.1 per cent of India's current public expenditure on health as per the National Health Estimates, 2016–17. The National Health Policy, 2017 recommended to spend at least two-thirds of Government's health expenditure on primary healthcare.

   (iv) Ayushman Bharat-Pradhan Mantri Jan Arogya Yojana (PM-JAY), the world's largest health insurance scheme, is a major step towards providing affordable healthcare to the identified poor. The Scheme has been rolled out based on the deprivation and occupational criteria of the *Socio-Economic Caste Census* for rural and urban areas, respectively.

3. **Medical Infrastructure:** Lack of healthcare infrastructure has been a major hurdle in front of the country. In recent times, the Government has taken several concerted efforts to improve it:

(i) The doctor-population ratio in India is **1:1456** (population estimated to be 1.35 billion) against the WHO recommendation of 1:1000. To address the shortage of doctors, the government has embarked on an ambitious programme for upgradation of district hospitals into medical colleges. In the last 5 years, government has sanctioned 141 new medical colleges.

(ii) The norms for graduate and post graduate seats in medical colleges have also been revised. The maximum intake capacity at MBBS level has been increased from 150 to 250 and the norms for setting up of Medical colleges in terms of requirement of land, faculty, staff-bed strength, etc. have also been rationalised.

(iii) The Government operates Centrally Sponsored Scheme–establishment of New Medical Colleges attached with existing District/Referral Hospitals' with fund sharing between Centre and States. As a result, the number of MBBS and PG seats have increased by 27,235 and 15,000, respectively. These efforts would go a long way in addressing the shortage of doctors.

(iv) The Pradhan Mantri Swasthya Suraksha Yojana (PMSSY) was launched to augment the *tertiary healthcare* capacity in clinical care, medical education and research in underserved areas of the country, under which *AIIMS like* institutions are built and Government Medical Colleges are upgraded by setting up 'Super Speciality' Blocks.

(v) *National Medical Commission Act, 2019* was promulgated to enable constitution of 'National Medical Commission'. Reforms have also been brought about with the introduction of a common entrance test NEET-UG for admission to all MBBS courses including AIIMS and JIPMER.

4. **Mission Mode Interventions:** Mission mode interventions aim to deal with maternal health, child health and combat communicable and non-communicable diseases—with the Government now focused on addressing this epidemiological transition from communicable diseases (CDs) to non-communicable diseases (NCDs). Major initiatives taken by the Government in this regard are:

(i) Under Ayushman Bharat marks a paradigm shift in the way health care is delivered. It targets universal health coverage with dual focus—*firstly,* by focusing on preventive, promotive and palliative care apart from ambulatory care; and *secondly,* by providing protection against catastrophic health expenditure for secondary and tertiary hospital care.

(ii) The new paradigm recognises and addresses the emerging challenges of NCDs due to changing epidemiology and also targets to sustain the efforts for RMNCH+A (Reproductive, Maternal, New-born Child plus Adolescent Health) and communicable diseases through initiatives such as Surakshit Matritva Aashwasan (SUMAN), Social Awareness and Action to Neutralise Pneumonia Successfully (SAANS) and TB Harega Desh Jeetega.

(iii) The AB-HWCs would follow a well-defined referral and return linkages to ensure continuum of care.

(iv) *Tele-consultation* to be used at all levels to improve 'referral advice' and undertake 'virtual consultation' including case management support by doctors and specialists.

WATER AND SANITATION

The World Health Organisation has repeatedly stressed the importance of clean water, sanitation, and clean environment, as a pre requisite to achieving universal health. Showing high faith in the idea of the WHO, the Government has accorded high priority to provisioning of drinking water and sanitation together with clean air in the country. In order to prioritise the tasks, the Government launched a '10-Year Rural Sanitation Strategy' for the decade 2019-29 for rural areas. Similarly, the Universal coverage of Water Supply has also been launched. Some highlights[24] in this regard are given below.

SBM-G Under SBM-G (Swachh Bharat Mission-Grameen), rural sanitation made an incredible leap in the target achievement from 39 per cent in 2014 to 100 per cent in 2019 (more than 10 crore toilets were built). The *Phase-II* of the mission is being implemented for the period 2020-25. Its focus is Open Defecation Free (ODF) sustainability and Solid & Liquid Waste Management (SLWM) through convergence between different verticals of financing and various schemes of Central and State Governments (such as 15th Finance Commission grants to local bodies, MGNREGS, Corporate Social Responsibility funds, etc.).

As per the *UNICEF* study ('Access to Toilets and Safety, Convenience and Self-respect of Women in Rural India', February, 2020), 91 per cent of the women reported that they have been able to save upto an hour and do not have to travel up to a kilometre for defecation after the construction of toilets.

SBM-U Under the SBM-U (Swachh Bharat Mission-Urban), to further enhance sanitation, the *Union Budget 2021-22* announced to focus on complete faecal sludge management and waste water treatment, source segregation of garbage, reduction in single-use plastic, reduction in air pollution by effectively managing waste from construction-and-demolition activities and bio-remediation of all legacy dump sites. Called the ***SBM-U 2.0,*** it is to be completed over a period of 5 years from 2021 to 2026.

Jal Jeevan Mission The mission accords highest priority to improve the quality of life and enhance ease of living of people especially those living in rural areas with the following objectives:

- To enable every rural household get assured supply of potable water with functional tap water connection (FTWC), at a service level

24. Economic Survey 2020-21, vol. 2, pp. 357-58, Ministry of Finance, GoI, N. Delhi.

of 55 litres per capita per day (lpcd) regularly on long-term basis.

- To provide FTWC to every rural household in partnership with States.

It is a decentralised, demand-driven and community-managed programme with the Gram Panchayat playing a key role in planning, implementation, management, operation and maintenance of water supply systems.

- It functions on the 'no one is left out' principle under which 'Har Ghar Jal Block', 'Har Ghar Jal Panchayat' and 'Har Ghar Jal Gaon' sub-schemes are being run. In 2020-21, Goa became the first state in the country to have 100 per cent FTWC, i.e., 'Har Ghar Jal Rajya'.

At the time of roll out of the scheme (in August 2019), about 3.23 crore (17 per cent) households out of total 18.93 crore rural households had tap water supply. The remaining 15.70 crore (83 per cent) rural households were to be provided with functional tap water connections (FTWC) by 2024.

Jal Jeevan Mission-Urban The *Union Budget 2021-22* announced the launching of this new drinking water supply mission for urban areas. The scheme aims at 'universal water supply' in all Urban Local Bodies (4,378) with 2.86 crores household tap water connections, as well as liquid waste management in 500 *AMRUT* cities.

HOUSING FOR ALL

'Housing for All' is the slogan of the Government for which the cut off year is 2022. Two schemes, Pradhan Mantri Awaas Yojana-Gramin (PMAY-G) and Pradhan Mantri Awaas Yojana-Urban (PMAY-U) are being run to achieve the objective. The recent NSO survey on 'Drinking Water, Sanitation, Hygiene and Housing Condition in India 2018' has given the following performance report[25] in this direction:

- About 76.7 per cent of the households in the rural and about 96.0 per cent in the urban areas had the house of pucca structure.
- More than four times increase in the number of houses completed in a year under PMAY-G, from 11.95 lakh in 2014–15 to 47.33 lakh in 2018-19. In 2019–22, the cumulative target is 1.95 crore houses (5,27,878 houses were delivered by 17th January, 2020).
- Under PMAY-U, against assessed demand of 1.12 crore, 1.03 crore houses were sanctioned, 61 lakhs grounded for construction and 32 lakhs have been delivered as on 1st January, 2020. This scheme covers a range of social groups, comprising senior citizens, construction workers, domestic workers, artisans, differently-abled (Divyang), transgender and leprosy patients. Women empowerment by giving them ownership of the house is slated to turn out to be a major push in the direction of inclusiveness.

COVID-19 and Rental Housing In the wake of the ongoing coronavirus pandemic, a mass return migration of the labourers from the urban areas was seen in the country. It looked really ridiculous as the country was under lockdown. Other than drying up of source of income (in this case state governments ran free distribution of cooked food and rations), the labourers faced uncertainty regarding their accommodation as they were unable to pay rent for their dwellings and their landlords asked them to just vacate. This made the Government notice the problem of migrant labour and urban poor face in getting houses nearby place of work at affordable rent. To look after this issue,

25. **Economic Survey 2019-20**, Vol. 2, pp. 298-299, Ministry of Finance, GoI, N. Delhi.

the *Affordable Rental Housing Complex(ARHC)* scheme was launched in May 2020, as one of the several measures announced under the campaign *Atmanirbhar Bharat Abhiyan*. For more details on the scheme, refer *Chapter 9*.

SOCIAL SECTOR EXPENDITURE

India's expenditure on social sectors has not reflected a major increasing trend during the past few years (2008–2019), an increase in expenditure *per-se* may not always guarantee appropriate outcomes and achievements. The efficiency of expenditure incurred so far can be assessed by the performance of social sectors through various social indicators. An overall assessment of social sector expenditures in terms of achievements shows that wide gaps still exist in educational and health outcomes and there is a need for substantial improvement and the need to remove inequalities in the country.

The latest data[26] regarding General Government (i.e., Centre plus States) expenditures of India on the social services[27] for the year ***2020-21 BE*** (where BE stands for Budget Estimates) in comparison to 2019-20 RE (where RE stands for Revised Estimates) were as given below:

Total budgetary expenditure ₹64.70 lakh crores (up from ₹58.76 lakh crores of 2019-20).

- *Total expenditure* (as % of total expenditures): 26.5 (up from 26.1 of 2019-20).
- *Expenditure on Education* (as % of total expenditures): 10.4 (same as in 2019-20).
- *Expenditure on Health* (as % of total expenditures on social services): 5.4 (up from 5.3 of 2019-20).
- *Expenditure on Social Services* (as % of total expenditures): 26.5 (up from 26.1 of 2019-20).

Total expenditure (as % of GDP) 8.8 (up from 7.5 of 2019-20).

- *Expenditure on Education* (as % of GDP): 3.5 (up from 3.0 of 2019-20).
- *Expenditure on Health* (as % of GDP): 1.8 (up from 1.5 of 2019-20).

In the wake of *COVID-19* pandemic, the General Government expenditures on social services went up unprecedently— a big part of the expenditure (around 10 per cent GDP) was accorded for it. While the *National Education Policy-2020* has pledged to increase the General Government expenditure on education to 6 per cent of the GDP, the increasing coverage of the *Ayushman Bharat* is estimated to enhance the expenditure on health above 2.5 per cent of GDP by the end of 2021-22.

POLICY SUGGESTIONS

Social infrastructure has positive externalities. It has a significant role in the economic development and welfare of a country. It is empirically proven and widely recognised that education and health impact the growth of an economy. Investing in *human capital* by way of education, skill development, training and provision of health care facilities enhances the productivity of the workforce and welfare of the population. In this regard, contemporary documents ***suggest*** the

26. **Economic Survey 2020-21,** Vol. 2, pp. 326-28, Ministry of Finance, GoI, N. Delhi.

27. **Social services** include areas such as—education, sports, art and culture; medical and public health, family welfare; water supply and sanitation; housing; urban development; welfare of SCs, STs and OBCs; labour and labour welfare; social security and welfare, nutrition, relief on account of natural calamities, etc. **Education** pertains to expenditure on 'education, sports, arts and culture'. **Health** includes expenditure on 'medical and public health', 'family welfare' and 'water supply and sanitation'.

following actions[28] for the governments in the country:

1. Action is needed in the direction of improving the quality of education—an important contributor to improvement in the quality of education would be an increase in the percentage of *qualified teachers*.
2. India needs to overcome the development challenges through innovative models of *delivery of services*. It has a critical role to play in India's march towards double-digit growth.
3. Without improvement in social infrastructure, development of a country is incomplete—expenditures on education, skill and health need to be enhanced.
4. Overhauling of the subsidy regime is needed with faster pace. It will not only rationalise the subsidies but bring in a variety of *other benefits* in the service delivery system—inclusion of the needy population; exclusion of the fake accounts; prevention of corruption and leakages; traceability; authentication of delivery; transparency and accountability. The idea of technology-enabled Direct Benefits Transfers (DBT), namely the JAM (Jan Dhan-Aadhaar-Mobile) number trinity solution, introduced by the GoI in this regard is believed to be a game-changing move.
5. India needs to include the *behavioural dimensions* of the target population in its framework of policy-making to realise the desired results in the area of promoting the cause of the social infrastructure. India has already included this aspect in its sanitation campaign (especially, in checking open defecation)—the same is needed in other areas of importance, too.
6. There is a need of *integrating* the social sector initiatives of the Centre, states and the local bodies. The new 'think tank' NITI Aayog can provide a suitable platform in this regard.
7. Strengthening of the *local bodies* (the PRIs) will not only boost the social sector but it will have an effect of externality in the form of an aware, awakened and participative citizenry. Through them, India can garner the support of civil society and the NGO.
8. There is a need to orient the *private sector* (corporate world) towards this cause. Their inclusion in this area will not only bring in fund to this fund-scarce sector but enable the country to use their expertise in the promotion of the social infrastructure.
9. Aimed to bridge the gap of information divide, the use of information and communication technology (ICT) needs to be encouraged at mass scale.
10. Need of sensitising all stakeholders about the ensuing dangers of climate change and promoting sustainable behaviour for promoting and sustaining inclusive growth.
11. The ongoing *COVID-19* pandemic has shown the vulnerability of India's health sector. It is high time that expenditures on the sector were enhanced and a mission mode approach was applied to fight any such pandemic in future.
12. The disruption caused by the ongoing *COVID-19* pandemic has made the education sector to think away from the classroom or at least a dependable alternative of it.

Considering the role of investment in social infrastructure in development, the government is committed to invest in social sector in order

28. Based on various official documents such as— **India 2021** and past 6 volumes of it, **Economic Survey 2020-21**, and past 6 volumes of it, the latest **India Development Report-2017**, **Niti Aayog** among others.

to bring overall improvement in socio-economic indicators and achieving SDGs. In spite of *COVID-19* pandemic, public spending on social sector increased in 2020-21 and efforts continued through AtmaNirbhar Bharat Rojgar Yojana, higher allocation under MGNREGS, Garib Kalyan Rozgar Abhiyan and path-breaking labour reforms etc. The Government believes that India's progress towards vibrant economy is deep-seated in investing in social capital.

CHAPTER 21

BURNING SOCIO-ECONOMIC ISSUES

*Indian Planners pursued growth as an end in itself, ignoring poverty reduction and other social objectives.**

In this Chapter...

- Process Reforms in India
- India as Currency Manipulator!
- Taxpayers' Services Enhance Trust in Tax System
- India's Self-Reliance vs. Multilateralism
- Resolving the Menace of Bad Loans
- Preparing Healthcare for Future
- Reforming India's Public Debt Management
- Monetisation of Public Assets – The Significance
- The Circularity of Economy
- Fulfilling the Minimum Needs of Citizens

- **Note:** Several of the Burning Issues of high socio-economic importance have been given in the regular chapters of the book itself at their natural places aimed at promoting their connectivity with broader scheme of the subject matter and enhancing readers' ease of understanding. These issues (with the Chapters given in brackets along with them) are—***Social stock exchange; Environmental, social and governance investment (14); PLI Scheme (9); Commercialising space sector (10); Consolidation of banks, Credit rating biasness against India (12); Digital health mission (13); Forex management and the impossible trinity, Trade facilitation, India as pharmacy of the world, The Quad (15); Tax administration reforms, Taxpayers' charter, 15th Finance Commission (17); Climate risk insurance (19); Human Development Report-2020, National Education Policy-2020, Gig employment (20).***

PROCESS REFORMS IN INDIA

Introduction

Regulation has always remained among the most essential functions of the governments. Experiences and illustrations suggest that it is just not possible to have complete regulations in a world which is full of uncertainties, making it almost impossible to account for all possible outcomes. India has been a case of over-regulation, which makes regulations ineffective even after complying with the administrative process (as the *Economic Survey 2020-21* has concluded by quoting various comparative studies). For ease of living, India needs immediate reforms in the area.

Regulatory Framework of India

It is often believed that India's regulatory problems are due to the lack of regulatory standards and poor compliance to process. However, international comparisons show that India ranked better than its peers on these two parameters. Rather, the real

* *Jagdish Bhagwati and Arvind Panagariya, India's Tryst with Destiny, Collins Books, N. Delhi, 2014, p. 9.*

issue seems to be 'effectiveness' of regulations caused by undue delays, rent seeking, complex regulations, and quality of regulation (as per the 'World Rule of Law Index' of World Justice Project, World Bank's Worldwide Governance Indicators, and various studies of the World Bank).

We find unnecessary regulation in India. A study of *Quality Council of India* (conducted for the *Economic Survey 2020-21*) shows that voluntary closure of a company in the country with no dispute/litigation takes 1570 days (i.e., around 51 months) to complete— the comparative figures for Singapore, UK, and Germany are 12 months, 15 months, and 12–24 months, respectively.

Causes & Remedies

The root cause of over-regulation has been the approach to account for every possible outcome. However, economic theory and real-life evidences show that in an 'uncertain and complex' world, it is just not possible to frame laws which can account for all possible outcomes. Therefore, the decision making involves 'discretion', which is rather not considered good. Thus, laws are carefully framed to avoid discretionary powers given to official, resulting in enacting more complex laws which make discretion even more non-transparent.

Evidences show that complex laws (i.e., over-regulation) make decisions more opaque, while the simpler laws enhance transparency. In practice, policymakers in the country have given primacy to regulation *by default* over 'supervision' (aimed at avoiding discretion in decision making, at all costs). Regulation got this importance due to one more reason— unlike supervision, it can be easily measured. After all, regulations provide criteria (or checklists), making it easier for regulators to follow and reduce their accountability. In contrast, it is difficult to quantify the amount and quality of supervision. The optimal solution lies in:

1. Simple regulations combined with transparent decision-making process.
2. Discretionary powers of decision makers need to be balanced with improved transparency, stronger systems of *ex-ante* accountability (such as bank boards) and *ex-post* resolution mechanisms.

The new initiative of Government, the *e-Marketplace* portal, is a very good example in this direction which has been successful in serving three goals— increasing price-related transparency in government procurement, reducing procurement cost, and easing decision making by honest officials.

Recent Initiatives

At present, the administrative process reforms are being taken by the Government very seriously and a few structural moves have already been taken:

1. **Labour Law:** Labour falls under the Concurrent List of the Constitution and therefore, both Parliament and state legislatures can make laws regulating labour. There were over 100 state and 40 central laws regulating various aspects of labour such as— the resolution of industrial disputes, working conditions, social security, and wages— which make labour regulation very complex. To rectify this, Government merged the existing 29 central labour laws into 4 labour codes.
2. **Other Service Providers:** India's regulatory framework for OSPs (Other Service Providers) was, till recently, outdated and complex. For instance, the BPO (Business Process Outsourcing) industry usually runs on global cloud-based systems but India's regulations restricted its use and insisted on its localisation. Besides, there were cumbersome registration requirements and restrictions on 'Work from Home'.

The sector was liberalised by the Government initiating (November 2020) a few effective steps— no registration requirement for OSPs, BPO industry taken out of the ambit of OSP regulations, majority of requirements for 'Work from Home' and 'Work from Anywhere' abolished, etc.

3. **Institutional architecture:** Since Independence, a plethora of autonomous bodies had proliferated and there is a need to prune them consistently not just from a cost perspective but in order to maintain transparency, accountability, and efficient supervision.

   Taking effective steps in this regard (in 2020–21), the organisations such as the All-India Handloom Board, All India Handicrafts Board, Cotton Advisory Board and Jute Advisory Board were *closed* by the Government and the existing 4 film media units (Films Division, Directorate of Film Festivals, National Film Archives of India, and Children's Film Society) merged into one body, the NFDC (National Film Development Corporation).

In this direction, a very effective move will be to enact a law aimed at 'transparency of rules' so that asymmetry of information can be abolished (as was proposed by the *Economic Survey 2016-17*). Due to frequent changes made in rules, citizens are forced to follow a long paper trail of circulars and notifications to know the current requirements. Once a law related to transparency of rules is enacted, it will simplify citizens' understanding of regulations by bringing transparency as all departments will need to mandatorily put all citizen-facing rules on their website; any rule not explicitly mentioned on the website will not be imposed by officials; all laws, rules and regulations will have to be always presented in an updated and unified form.

Conclusion

It means that the regulatory framework of India should be made simpler, which will lead to certain discretionary powers given to officials undoubtedly. But with the help of effective supervision, transparency and fixing accountabilities regulation can improve the ease of living for citizens besides promoting the cause of 'minimum government and maximum governance' also. The process reforms started by the Government need to be implemented in all possible areas.

INDIA AS CURRENCY MANIPULATOR!

Introduction

Exchange rates of world currencies have always been sensitive issues. Its criticality got enhanced even more once globalisation commenced. The issue of currency manipulation has been often reported in media more in the case of the USA, which did put several countries on the list of currency manipulators (including India) in past four years.

Currency Manipulation

Under currency manipulation, a country influences its currency deliberately. Though the act is declared unfair by the UN economic institutions, economies do it to gain advantages of the following kinds:

1. **Trade benefit:** Devaluation in currency boosts exports as domestic goods and services become cheaper for the buyers of foreign countries.
2. **Interest benefit:** If the economy concerned is a net lender to foreign countries, it earns more interest on the overseas loans forwarded by it (in the case of being a net borrower, the economy loses more through interest payment— results in higher outflows of foreign exchange).
3. **Forex flow benefit:** Under-valuation of the domestic currency brings in enhanced flows of foreign currencies in the economy as

interest rates tighten and investors get the chance to earn more by investing in the security market.

India as Currency Manipulator!

The USA, in December 2020, included India (together with Taiwan, Thailand, China, Japan, Korea, Germany, Italy, Singapore and Malaysia) in its monitoring list of countries with potentially 'questionable foreign exchange policies' and 'currency manipulation' (a year after India was removed from the watchlist in May 2019). Once an economy meets *two* of the following *three criteria* (of the US Trade Facilitation and Trade Enforcement Act of 2015), it is put on the monitoring list by the country:

1. A 'significant' trade surplus with the US (at least $20 billion over a 12-month period). *[Over a 12-month period ending June 2020, India had a $22 billion trade surplus with the USA].*
2. A 'material' current account surplus equivalent to at least 2 per cent of the GDP (Gross Domestic Product) over a 12-month period. *[Over a 12-month period ending June 2020, India had a current account surplus but of only 0.9 per cent of its GDP.]*
3. 'Persistent', one-sided intervention (when net purchases of foreign currency totaling at least 2 per cent of the country's GDP over a 12-month period are conducted repeatedly, in at least six out of 12 months). *[Over a 12-month period ending June 2020, net purchases of foreign exchange by the RBI were of $64 billion i.e., 2.4 per cent of India's GDP.]*

Data show India meeting two criteria. But the charge of currency manipulation against India does not sustain by some simple facts— the benefits it might get out of increased exports will get more than offset by the increased payment costs of its external debts!

India's Exchange Management

India switched from fixed to floating currency system in the year 1993–94. In 'dual exchange rate' system of India while one exchange rate is announced by the RBI every day, the other is determined by the market (i.e., the demand and supply of rupee and foreign currencies in India's foreign exchange market), which is recognised by the IMF as *free float* (i.e., floating currency system).

As India gave an emphatic call for *Make in India,* followed by *Atmanirbhar Bharat Abhiyan,* the Government looks pushing in favour of boosting exports and attracting higher foreign investments. Like every other country, India also aspires to hold enough forex reserves to boost the confidence of the foreign investors and expand essential imports of technology and capital goods. But there does not seem any manipulation in its exchange regime— no such hint has come from any of the international financial institutions (i.e., IMF, World Bank or Bank for International Settlements).

Conclusion

In recent times, the US has hardened its stance against all its trade partners who generated a sizeable trade surplus with it and shown protectionist tendencies, which has resulted in a kind of declared trade and currency war against its main trading partner China. However, the US has not been able to prove any claim of currency manipulation on either China or India. This time round too, experts believe that the US administration will put India away from the currency manipulator watchlist— the changed political dispensation in US under *Joe Biden* is also expected to play a more constructive role in this regard.

TAXPAYERS' SERVICES ENHANCE TRUST IN TAX SYSTEM

Introduction

Tax is defined by modern economics as a method of income redistribution— serving the larger goal of welfare. But it took modern economies several more decades to change their traditional approach which gave 'limited attention to tax services' as regulator and enforcer of tax laws. It was by the late 1980s that the attention shifted towards the need of providing *better tax services* to taxpayers, with the Washington Consensus and deliberations for the WTO playing the roles of facilitators in this regard.

The Need for Better Tax Services

On the increased demand for better services to the taxpayers, there has been a worldwide recognition of the 'rights' of the tax payers-beginning with the UK (1986), several countries took initiatives towards this such as US (1988), New Zealand (2002), Canada (2007), etc.

Besides recognising taxpayers' rights, the arrangement of an 'independent institution' like *Ombudsman* has proved very useful in many countries. The ombudsman looks upon tax issues from the taxpayers' perspective besides ensuring that taxpayers understand their tax rights well and are treated fairly by the tax department.

As per the OECD, the countries with an independent tax Ombudsman have performed *better* on the tax administration front through better *trust* between taxpayers and tax authorities, have exhibited a higher average Tax to GDP ratio and lower time taken to file taxes. The Ombudsman in Australia, Canada, UK, Brazil, South Africa, while *tax mediators* in Belgium and France function independent of the tax administration.

Case with India

Though late, but initiative towards this was taken by India also— in *2020-21* (which was proposed in the year's Union Budget) a formal 'taxpayers, charter' was notified and 'expected behaviour' from the tax officials were inserted in the 'mission statement' of the tax department. India's taxpayers' charter consists of '14 commitments' of the income tax department and '6 obligations' of the taxpayers.

As far as a tax Ombudsman is concerned, India's experience has not been good. After instituting Ombudsman for income tax (in 2003) and indirect taxes (in 2011), they were abolished in February 2019. The Ombudsman was appointed from amongst the serving officers responsible to investigate the grievances and complaints against the functioning of the tax authority. In the absence of an Act of law empowering its functions, the institution was *ineffective*, and its decisions were *only advisory* in nature. The Ombudsman could settle complaints either through agreements between the complainant and the tax department through conciliation and mediation or by passing an award, with a token compensation (not exceeding ₹ 5,000) for the loss suffered by the complainant.

Looking into the vital role which the Ombudsman plays in enhancing tax compliance and trust of taxpayers in the tax system, it is high time that India set up such an independent institution, with adequate teeth and independence.

Conclusion

Experts feel that there is a need to revitalise grievance redress system and incorporate a more holistic view of enhancing customer experience and protecting taxpayers rights in the country. It is imperative to reform the redress mechanism to make the pledge of *Honouring the Honest* (Union Budget 2020-21) more successful.

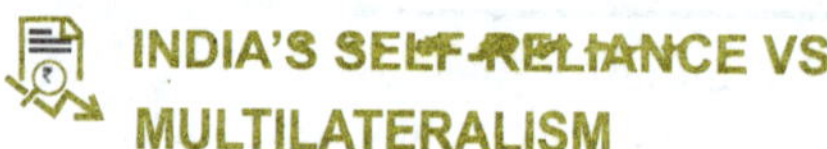

INDIA'S SELF-RELIANCE VS. MULTILATERALISM

Introduction

During the COVID-19 pandemic, serious bottlenecks were faced by countries due to their dependence on the global supply chain— some also learnt hard lessons from it. Assessing the fault lines of the global supply chain, the Government of India thought to use the crisis as an opportunity and launched a long-term policy in the direction of self-reliance under the AtmaNirbharta campaign. Such a call from India, which has been an ardent votary of globalisation and multilateralism, was interpreted by many as the rise of protectionism in India.

Self-Reliance vs. Multilateralism

Experts have seen India's recent push towards self-reliance antagonistic to its stand on multilateralism and globalisation. However, it was not for the first time that India gave such a call. Self-reliance has been among the *six major objectives* of planning in India since independence itself. But the timing of this call from India makes the world think this move in the colour of India's rising belief in 'protectionism'. This belief is emboldened by recent trade-related skirmishes of India with USA and other countries where India has been blamed to be against the normal principles of multilateralism and for being protectionists. This makes global investors and governments feel as if India is reneging on its commitments to multilateralism and globalisation. However, this has not been the case. The world needs to interpret India's stance in the new and changing global perspectives.

The Changing Global Economic Order

Post-cold war times have not been stable due to political as well as trade related reasons (in the case of trade, it has been due to the new body WTO). The state of global economic order got another element of *fluidity* by the Great Recession (of 2008) of the western developed economies which was further accelerated by the unprecedented rise of China as an economic power. It got further coloured by a global suspicion towards China in the aftermath of the *COVID-19* pandemic. Thus, the world has changed much since India gave its first call for self-reliance by the late 1940s. As another emerging global economic power, India needs to recalibrate its approach to multilateralism and carve out a favourable place for her in the emerging global economic order. The world needs to read India's recent push in favour of self-reliance in the light of the following co-ordinates:

- The self-reliance campaign is India's attempt to mend her rising trade deficits with China.
- In the wake of *COVID-19 pandemic*, some major multinational companies are exploring the possibilities to relocate their production centres away from China – India is busy attracting them with the help of her 'Make in India', 'Assemble in India' and 'self-reliance' push (as India is not against foreign investment, rather supports it with one of the most competitive policy frameworks in the region). In traditional sense, self-reliance means no foreign investment.
- Global economic order, which has been already fluid since the mid-1980s, is going through a process of new *churning* due to increasing Sino-US trade tensions and rising protectionism across the developed world – and India wishes to occupy a favourable place for herself in this emerging global economic order.
- Given the challenges of unemployment, demography and *surplus agricultural*

production, India is wilful of restructuring its trade.

- India has been quite willing to play a more vibrant role on the international fora and in recent years there has been increased activism from India towards it.
- India still remains very much committed to the cause of multilateralism–the reason it is considered among the staunchest votaries of globalisation in the WTO. India remains actively engaged in negotiating its free and preferential trade agreements.

Conclusion

Thus, India's recent emphasis on self-reliance is not antagonistic to either globalisation or multilateralism; rather, it is a way to protect her own socio-economic interests like other countries of the world. This time round, India's approach to self-reliance is smartly intertwined with domestic interests propelled by global funds (foreign investments) with the ultimate objective of situating herself favourably in the emerging global economic order.

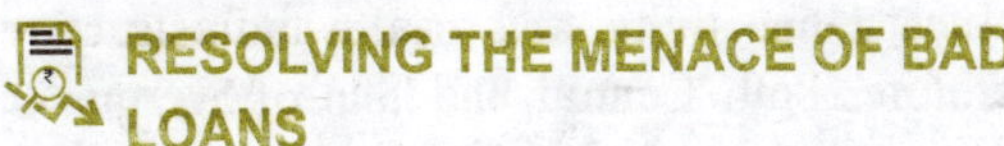

RESOLVING THE MENACE OF BAD LOANS

Introduction

The rising size of bad loans (i.e., non-performing assets) of specially the public sector banks (PSBs) has hit the investment prospects in the country in a very big way. Being the main lenders to the infrastructures sector, the speed of infra expansion has been hit hard, more so in the last 5 years. As per the latest estimates (RBI, April 2021), 9.4 per cent of loans forwarded by the PSBs were non-performing while their stressed assets were at 9.96 per cent.

To solve the crisis of the high NPAs, the Reserve Bank of India (RBI) had introduced multiple schemes over the last few years—flexible Refinancing of Infrastructure (5/25 scheme), Asset Reconstruction Companies (ARC), Strategic Debt Restructuring (SDR), Asset Quality Review (AQR) and Sustainable Structuring of Stressed Assets (S4A).

As these measures could not be effective, the Government initiated two *new steps* in this regard— enforcement of the insolvency and bankruptcy law (IBC, 2016) and proposal to set a bad bank— for the resolution of the bad loan menace.

The Concept

Theoretically, bad banks work on a simple concept, i.e., banks' loans are classified into two categories, good and bad. The bad loans of the banks are bought or taken over by the bad bank while the good loans are left with the bank itself. This way, bad loans do not contaminate the good assets of banks. As banks hit by the problem of bad loans become financially viable entities, they restart their lending process. While the concept of a bad bank is simple, the implementation can be quite complicated. A variety of organisational and financial options are there to design them. The RBI has signalled in favour of setting up such a bank, but it has also highlighted the concern of 'designing it properly'.

There are different models of creating a bad bank. India needs to go for the model which suits her needs—a bad bank which can serve two purposes, firstly, putting away the loads of the NPAs from the balance sheet of banks (so that they can *technically* be fit to lend again) and secondly, infusing fresh capital into them (to make them *really* start lending). This model has been most used by the countries across the world—during South East Asian crisis (1996-97) as well as in the USA—when the Government of the countries did set up band banks under their ownership. Such a move served both of the purposes. The advice (of the *Economic Survey 2016–17*) to set up a public sector rehabilitation agency (PARA) falls under this category.

Since 2017-18, the Government had been hinting at the idea of the bad bank but the final decision to set it up was still awaited. Recently, the *Union Budget 2021-22*,proposed setting up of a *bad bank* under the ARC (asset reconstruction company), AMC (asset management company) and AIF (alternative investment funds) model to acquire, manage and turnaround bad loans.

The ARC will acquire bad loans from banks at a negotiated price (at a discount) and pay by way of cash and security receipts. The funds for buying the bad loans will come from the sponsors (government, banks, etc.) as well as alternative investment funds. The AMC will acquire, manage and turnaround bad loans against which it will charge a fee.

Conclusion

Majority of the experts believe that the experiment of band bank may be successful in making the banks come out of the NPAs menace but at a high cost as the ARCs are supposed to ask for high discounts for the bad assets of banks as happened in the case of the insolvency and bankruptcy law where high haircuts have been seen to leverage a bank out of the defaulted loans.

PREPARING HEALTHCARE FOR FUTURE

Introduction

The ongoing COVID-19 pandemic has emphasised the importance of the healthcare sectors and its inter-linkages with other key sector of the economy, showcasing how a healthcare crisis can get transformed into an economic and social crisis. A line from Mahatma Gandhi— it is health that is real wealth and not pieces of gold and silver— looks having enough wisdom for the world in this regard.

Lessons from the Hard Times

The pandemic has put India kind of countries in a state of complete dilemma. While the wretchedness of the countries with one of the highest investments in healthcare was a cause of fear and scale of investments they need, the support system of their available health infrastructure gave them some rays of hope also. India has been no exception to this dilemma. Though India's healthcare has shown resiliency in these hard times, this should not be forgotten once the pandemic subsides.

The pandemic has helped showcase the role of technology-enabled platforms as an alternate distribution channel for remote delivery of healthcare services. These technology-enabled platforms offer a promising new avenue to address India's last-mile healthcare access and delivery challenges. These platforms, coupled with digitisation and the promise of artificial intelligence at-scale, have led to a drastic uptake in the utilisation of *telemedicine* for primary care and mental health.

As telemedicine depends crucially on internet connectivity and health infrastructure. Therefore, both Central and State governments need to invest in telemedicine on a mission mode to complement the government's digital health mission and thereby enable greater access to the masses. The National Health Mission (NHM) has played a critical role in mitigating inequity in healthcare access. Therefore, in conjunction with Ayushman Bharat, the emphasis on NHM should continue.

Outline for Future

A country like India needs to prioritise its policy focus and resource deployment very carefully not only to fight the current pandemic but also to prepare itself for the health crises of future. In this regard, the following areas need attention:

- **Financial impact:** From a financial perspective, India has one of the highest levels of OOPE (Out of Pocket Expenditures) in the world (65 per cent), which directly contributes to the high incidence of catastrophic expenditures and poverty. A negative correlation exists between the level of public expenditure on health and OOPE. Even a small increase in public expenditure on health can have high impact on OOPE—as per the estimates of the *Economic Survey 2020-21*, an increase from 1 per cent to 2.5–3 per cent of GDP (as envisaged in the National Health Policy-2017) can decrease the OOPE from 65 per cent to 30 per cent.
- **Information asymmetry:** As a bulk of healthcare in India is provided by the private sector, it is critical for policymakers to mitigate information asymmetry in healthcare, which creates market failures and thereby renders unregulated private healthcare sub-optimal. The newly launched National Digital Health Mission can be utilised with the aid of artificial intelligence and machine learning algorithms to mitigate information asymmetry with respect to the patients. A standardised system for quality reporting on healthcare for hospitals, physicians and insurance companies can start with basic input indicators to be reported mandatorily by every healthcare stakeholder.

  Over time, this can evolve to cover *output* and *outcome* indicators such as infection rates and re-admission rates. A start has been made in this direction by the Niti Aayog through the Health Index at the state level.
- **Insurance infrastructure:** With limited visibility into patients' medical records and no standardised treatment protocols, insurance companies have a risk of 'adverse selection' (see *Glossary* for it) at the time of policy issuance and a risk of 'moral hazard' (see *Glossary* for it) at the time of claims. To safeguard against this risk, insurance companies ask for higher premiums and put restrictions on insurance coverage in the insurance policy. Addressing this information asymmetry can help lower premiums, enable the offering of better products, and help increase the insurance penetration in the country.
- **Regulator:** Finally, a sectoral *regulator* to undertake regulation and supervision of the healthcare sector must be seriously considered. This is especially pertinent as regulation has grown in importance as a key lever for governments to affect the quantity, quality, safety, and distribution of services in health systems.

Conclusion

Considering the significance of healthcare system in striving to achieve the Sustainable Development Goals of Universal Healthcare Coverage, India needs to take steps not only to improve healthcare accessibility but its affordability also.

REFORMING INDIA'S PUBLIC DEBT MANAGEMENT

Introduction

Modern economies depend on loans in a big way for meeting various needs and responsibilities. In the post-war period, the Governments' dependence on loans has also increased many times on account of various reasons such as welfare measures, growth promotion, defence, etc. One such category of loan is known as the public debt (which is called Government debt) which, in the case of India, is all debts created by the Government of India—

short-term, long-term, internal, or external. Public debt leaves a deep impact on the economy. That is why experts and policy makers scrutinize the issues such as its size, interest rate, independence of the body managing it, etc.

The Case with India

The issue of public debt management has been debated by experts since the Union Budget 2015-16 first proposed to set up a public debt management agency implying that this responsibility will shift away from the Reserve Bank of India. The debate mainly revolves around the degree of independence such an agency will be given in this regard. It also touches upon the contentious issues related to the arrangement of it.

In 2019-20, the issue of having an independent debt management agency 'outside the preview' of the RBI was again voiced by the policy think tank, the Niti Aayog, which said that it was *an idea whose time has come*. Majority of the experts find strong logic in such a proposal which can be understood by going into *four major roles* which the RBI plays today:

1. At present, public debt is managed by the RBI.
2. Government's market borrowings are also managed by the RBI.
3. Announcing the monetary policy already remains among the chief functions of the RBI as country's Central bank.
4. Under open market operations, RBI trades in the Government bonds also (such as treasury bills, cash management bill and G-Secs).

Given the roles which RBI plays today, we find a clear case of 'conflict of interest'. While on one hand it decides the key policy/interest rates (such as repo rate, reverse repo rate, term repo rate, marginal standing facility rate and bank rate) as central bank, on the other hand it trades in the government bonds also (interest rates of which are influenced by the policy rates set by the RBI itself). Such contradictions have created practical problems for India's financial market in particular and economic development in general, in the following ways:

- We find a lack of alignment between India's domestic bond market (which depends on interest rates which are set by RBI) and the external bond market/external commercial borrowings (which is linked to the global variables).
- India has seen a rise in its external commercial borrowings in past few years primarily due to interest rates in the global market being much lower than in India. This discrepancy looks awkward in today's times when the global financial market is converging.

The economic potential of India remains untapped due to dearth of investible funds. That is why India started liberalising the rules of foreign investments also. More than that, the potential cannot be tapped till enough investment is not mobilised for the development of requisite infrastructure base. In this case, Governments have always agreed with experts' opinion which favoured deepening of India's bond market. But practically, it does not seem possible till the RBI has hold on it— which is directly linked to its other responsibility, the monetary policy. So, it looks kind of vicious cycle— RBI borrowing at the interest rates set by RBI!

As policy rates leave impact on every penny anybody mobilises right from individual to corporates to governments, its ramifications and overall impact on the economy and its financial relations with global economy out there may be just imagined.

Conclusion

Majority of the experts believe that once the debt management office is separated from the RBI, the Government will be able to pay much more attention to the aspect of debt— by having an eye on the changing needs of fund over the time. It will help the Government to cut the cost of fund also. Though the RBI is believed to have shown reluctance to part with its role of Government debt manager, still such a step from the Government is expected anytime given the increased emphasis we see on self-reliance (under the AtmaNirbhar campaign) and an aspiration to replace China as the global production hub— all of which depend on requisite availability of funds.

MONETISATION OF PUBLIC ASSETS - THE SIGNIFICANCE

Introduction

Public assets, in simple words, are all the assets which are owned by the governments (centre, states and the local bodies) raised out of their capital expenditures. Some of them are the central public sector enterprise (CPSEs) and public sector enterprises (PSUs) owned[1] by the central government of India. Once the process of economic reforms commenced in the early 1990s, the Government has taken several steps to orient them towards efficiency and profit— one recent step being their monetisation.

Comprehensive Management

We find a paradigm shift in the Government's approach towards public assets in 2016 when the 'mandate' of the existing Department of Disinvestment (DoD) was changed from managing disinvestment to 'comprehensive management of the Governments investment in the public assets' (CMPA) with a subsequent change in its name to the Department of Investment and Public Asset Management (DIPAM). In brief, the CMPA involves the following four steps to be taken with respect to the CPSEs:

1. Achieving optimum return and accelerating growth.
2. Leveraging assets by capital and financial restructuring.
3. Improving investors' confidence through capital market exposure.
4. Rationalising decision-making process for efficient management.

Asset Monetisation

One of the actions under the CMPA is 'monetising' these assets. Under it, the Government decided to hand over some of the existing national highways to private bidders (to earn revenues out of their operation) on *toll-operate-transfer* (TOT) basis. Under the TOT model, stretches of national highway are to be bidded out to private players. The private players (infrastructure developers, private equity, institutional investors like pension and wealth funds) operate, maintain, and collect toll on the stretches of roads during the concession period (15 to 30 years).

The model has been designed to create an opportunity for the private sector to invest in *low-risk assets* and at the same time provide for efficient operations and maintenance of highways, which has broadly two benefits:

1. Plugging the leakages and enhancing transparency in government toll collection system, and
2. Helping government to securitise the assets and get fresh cash for creating new assets.

---

1. To understand the CPSEs and PSUs in detail, refer ***GLOSSARY*** of the book.

The TOT model has been tried by other countries also such as USA, Puerto Rico, Malaysia, etc. with varying degrees of success. In the case of India, certain hurdles have been faced as the country lacks a strong line of contactors with experience in such business pursuits. Bidders show lack of interest also as private road operators have not been able to generate profitable revenues from roads since 2010.

The Significance

The policy of monetising the public assets is a very significant move by the Government which will leave a lasting impact on the ongoing process of economic reforms and accelerating the process of development in the country in great many ways:

- **Providing a level-playing field:** The existence of many non-toll roads operated by the NHAI and states has been discouraging the private operators to invest in the road infrastructure. In this way, this move is an integral part of the 'factor market' reforms which were initiated under the second[2] generation of the economic reforms in 2000 which aimed at orienting economic activities towards market mechanism (by dismantling the regime of subsidies).
- **Boosting economic viability:** Roads have not been doing well on the front of toll collections due to several reasons for the last more than one decade and a large part of loans forwarded to the sector turned into non-performing assets of the PSBs (public sector banks). The move of monetising some of the roads will help these assets become economically viable.
- **Attracting foreign investment:** Road sector has not been able to attract foreign investment even after offering very liberal policy framework— lack of a 'business model' in the sector cited as a prominent reason for this. Such a business model is being expected form the TOT model.
- **Attempting to operate public assets on business line:** Public assets never got attention from the government as wealth builders or generators of income, however, some of the assets have been generating good revenues. In recent policy shift, Government has started seeing these assets as 'engines of growth' and 'sources of revenue' generation.
- **Strengthening inclusive growth:** This process will add wealth to the masses (through listing of these assets on stock exchanges) as well as generate fresh revenues which can be used for furthering the goal of inclusive growth.

Conclusion

Monetisation of public assets looks like Government going to do business but this is not the case as neither all public assets can be run on profit line nor the Government can afford relinquishing its role of promoting welfare. This should be a rebalancing act of the Government to optimise economic and social outcomes for the country.

THE CIRCULARITY OF ECONOMY

Introduction

Recently, the policy think tank of India, the *Niti Aayog* proposed (2019-20) to adopt the idea of circular economy in the country— by emphasising the need of sustainable development and resource circularity as the need of the hour. For the Aayog, it implies reusing waste back into the production cycle to produce new products and uses instead of wasting such materials with embedded resources.

2 For more details on the *Generations of Economic Reforms* in the country, see Chapter 6.

As per the Aayog, by 2050, the world population would reach 9.7 billion of which 3 billion people would prosper to middle class consumption level. This would require 71 per cent more resources per capita, thereby raising total mineral and material demand from 50 billion tons in 2014 to 130 billion tons in 2050.

The Hypothesis

The idea of circular economy is originally based on 'steady-state economy' which is itself rooted in ecological economics. Steady-state economy suggests the use of materials and energy in such a way that they are held constant. Today, the idea of circular economy is applied by a diverse group of researchers and professionals emphasising different aspects of it. Therefore, it has got several definitions which make it difficult to measure also. However, most of its definitions focus on the 'use of resources' or 'system change'. The resource use view follows the *3-R approach*— Reduce (minimum use of raw materials); Reuse (maximum reuse of products and components); and Recycle (high quality reuse of raw materials).

A circular economy tries to follow the example of an ecosystem. In it, there is nothing like *waste* because every residual item can be used to make a new product (but after eliminating the toxic substances)— such as producers taking back their products after use and repairing them for a new useful life. This way, only recycling is not its part, rather assuring quality is also taken care of.

Vis-a-Vis the Traditional Approach

The idea of circularity is opposite to the 'linear' (or growth) economy. While the origins of the circular economy concept are to be found in the 1960s environmentalism, it evolved under the influence of ecology and cybernetics which shaped the public environmental discourse of the period. The economy draws attention to the background of the present 'linear economy' in post-war policies that encouraged reconstruction and a social and economic democratisation across the West, including an expansion of 'mass-consumption'. The view of circularity emphasises the role of the 1960s counterculture in generating a popular reaction against this expansionary growth-based agenda, and its influence in shaping subsequent environmentalism, including the 'metabolic' and ecological economic understanding of the environmental crisis.

Conclusion

To ensure that the material needs of the humanity are supplied with, this is high time the world moved towards circularity of the economy. Several corporates have taken steps towards it, but they can be called just baby steps— an integrated effort, combining the forces of government and non-government entities, is required in this regard.

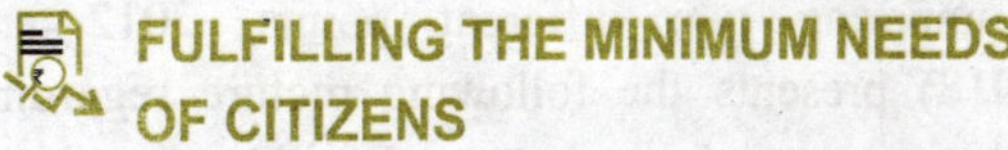

FULFILLING THE MINIMUM NEEDS OF CITIZENS

Introduction

Given the rampant poverty in the country, the Governments have always been careful about provisioning of meeting the 'minimum needs' (i.e., the essential goods and services) of citizens. Today, the very ability of someone to access these needs (such as housing, water, sanitation, electricity, and clean cooking fuel) is regarded as an important barometer of economic development in academic and policymaking circles.

Basic Needs Approach to Development

Some of the renowned economists of the world have tried to define development in terms of 'basic needs'. This approach to development puts emphasis on the 'minimum' specified quantities of *necessities* such as food, clothing, shelter, water, and sanitation that are necessary to prevent ill health and undernourishment (Paul Streeten, 1981; Louis Emmerij, 2010) and defines poverty as a failure to achieve certain minimum *basic needs* or *capacities* (Amartya Sen, 1999). Taking inspiration from this approach, the Government has got a "Bare Necessities Index" (BNI) developed to measure the achievements in this regard (the index has been used by the *Economic Survey 2020-21*).

Progress in Provision of Minimum Needs

The bare necessities index has been prepared sourcing data from two NSO Rounds on *drinking water, sanitation, hygiene,* and *housing* condition in India— 69th (2012) and 76th (2018). Similarly, the data on the indicator 'household using *LPG for cooking*' for 2011-12 has been taken from NSO Report on Energy Sources of Indian Households for Cooking and Lighting 2011-12. The index (comparing two different points, 2012 and 2018) presents the following picture regarding provisioning of the bare necessities (i.e., basic needs, minimum needs):

- Compared to 2012, access has improved across all states in the country in 2018 (the highest being in Kerala, Punjab, Haryana, and Gujarat and the lowest in Odisha, Jharkhand, West Bengal, and Tripura).
- Improvements have been widespread for all five dimensions (water, housing, sanitation, micro-environment, and other facilities).
- Inter-State disparities have declined in 2018 compared to 2012 across rural and urban areas but they still exits.
- Improvement has been seen disproportionately more for the poorest households in comparison to the richest households across rural and urban areas. The improvement in equity is particularly noteworthy because while the rich can seek private alternatives, lobby for better services, or if need be, move to areas where public goods are better provided for, the poor rarely have such choices.
- Improved access to these necessities has improved health and education.

As the needs of housing, water, sanitation, electricity, and clean cooking fuel are jointly consumed by all the members of a household, these, thus, touch the life of every member in the household. As these are durable assets, they deliver services to the household over long periods of time.

Focused efforts Improving access to these necessities has remained among the prime aims of the successive Governments in the country. The ongoing schemes designed to deliver these necessities include— the Swachh Bharat Mission (SBM), National Rural Drinking Water Programme (NRDWP), Pradhan Mantri Awaas Yojana (PMAY), Saubhagya, and Ujjwala Yojana. As these schemes have been equipped with some *new features* (such as use of technology, real-time monitoring, geo-tagging of assets, social audit, embedded digital flow of information, and direct benefit transfers wherever possible), a clear improvement has been seen in their efficiency, effectiveness, and governance.

Deepening of the idea Government should target the population in need of these minimum needs across the country and prioritise them— in rural as well as urban areas. As civic amenities in urban areas are provided by the local self-governments, there is a need of convergence in implementation of schemes at centre-state and local levels. To assess the progress in enabling people access these necessities at local levels, a dedicated index can be developed at district level using suitable indicators and methodology.

Conclusion

Putting focus on the accessibility of minimum needs will not only improve the general well-being of the masses but will also strengthen the broader goal of inclusive growth in the country. Experts believe that a focused approach and use of the networks of schemes will enable India to achieve the SDG goals of reducing poverty, improving access to drinking water, sanitation, and housing by 2030.

SELECTED MCQs (ECONOMIC AND SOCIAL DEVELOPMENT)

Readers can try testing their ability to solve objective type questions through these multiple type questions (MCQs). The sets consist, only those questions which are high on relevance for the examinations which will take place in 2020 and 2021. In order that most of the questions look familiar and chances of solving them correctly remain in good range, it is advised to try solving them once the whole book has been read and revised properly— right from Chapter 1 upto the Glossary.

*A thing may look specious in theory, and yet be ruinous in practice; a thing may look evil in theory, and yet be in practice excellent.**

In this Chapter...

SET -1

1. Select the correct statement (s) about the state of the *start-up ecosystem* in the country by using the code given below:
   1. The number of unicorns in India kept stagnating at 28 during 2020 due to the hardships caused by the COVID-19 pandemic.
   2. 7 new unicorns were added in India during 2020.

   Code:
   (*a*) Only 1 (*b*) Only 2
   (*c*) Both 1 and 2 (*d*) Neither 1 nor 2

2. Standing deposit facility scheme (SDFS) has been in news recently. Select the correct statement(s) related to it by using the code given below:
   1. A new small saving scheme (SSS) announced by the Government in the Union Budget 2018–19.
   2. This will allow 'uncollateralised deposit' of the liquidity by the RBI.

   Code:
   (*a*) Only 1 (*b*) Only 2
   (*c*) Both 1 and 2 (*d*) Neither 1 nor 2

** Edmund Burke (1729-1797)*

3. Select the correct statements about the *'hybrid annuity model'* (HAM) which the government has launched recently to promote the road projects in the country by use the code given below:
   1. It is an improvement over the existing 'engineering-procurement-construction' model of the PPP.
   2. Investment participation in this model is between the GoI and the private firm in the ratio of 40:60.
   3. Toll is to be collected by the government while the private participator gets a fixed amount of annuity for a defined period of time.
   4. Risks related to clearance, compensation, commercial and traffic are to be borne by the government.

   Code:

   (*a*) 1 and 2 (*b*) 1, 2 and 4

   (*c*) 2, 3 and 4 (*d*) 1, 2, 3 and 4

4. Select the correct statement (s) about *carry trade* by using the code given below:
   1. A financial act to earn profit by arbitrage.
   2. Borrowing and investment both are done back-to-back in it.

   Code:

   (*a*) Only 1 (*b*) Only 2

   (*c*) Both 1 and 2 (*d*) Neither 1 nor 2

5. The term 'hair cut' was much in news recently. Select the correct statement(s) about it using the code given below:
   1. It is used to show a fall in the asset's price.
   2. Used in share market when companies offer shares to their employees at a lower price than the prevailing market price of the share.

   Code:

   (*a*) Only 1 (*b*) Only 2

   (*c*) Both 1 and 2 (*d*) Neither 1 nor 2

6. Consider the fbllowing statements regarding the 'Taylor Rule'.
   1. A rule that suggests appropriate adjustments to interest rates, based on various economic factors such as inflation and employment rate.
   2. The rule indicates that if inflation or employment rates are higher than desired, interest rates should be increased in response to these conditions, and the opposite action should be taken under the opposite conditions.

   Select the incorrect statement/statements using the code given below:

   (*a*) Only 1 (*b*) Only 2

   (*c*) Both 1 and 2 (*d*) None of these

7. Which of the following existing schemes have been subsumed under the recently launched programme Samagra Shiksha? Select your answer using the code given below:
   1. Sarva Shiksha Abhiyan
   2. Rashtriya Madhyamik Shiksha Abhiyan
   3. Teacher Education

   Code:

   (*a*) 1 and 2 (*b*) 1 and 3

   (*c*) 2 and 3 (*d*) 1, 2 and 3

8. Select the correct statement(s) related to the recently launched scheme *Affordable Rental Housing Complex (ARHC)* using the code given below:
   1. It was launched under the *Atmanirbhar Bharat Abhiyan.*
   2. It aims at arranging rented houses for the migrant labour.
   3. It comes under the PM Awas Yojana.
   4. It is fully funded by the Centre and includes urban poor as its beneficiaries.

   Code:

   (*a*) 1 and 2 (*b*) 2 and 3

   (*c*) 1, 2 and 3 (*d*) 1, 2, 3 and 4

9. Consider the following statements about the idea of 'inclusive growth'.
   1. The idea of 'inclusive growth' entered into the domain of planning with the Eleventh Plan.
   2. This is not only about economics but also about 'social' inclusion.
   3. The main idea behind inclusive growth is to include SCs, STs, OBCs, minorities and women in the country's development process.
   4. The 3rd Generation of Economic Reforms runs parallel to the idea of inclusive growth.

   Select the correct statements using the code given below:

   (a) 1, 2 and 3 *(b)* 2, 3 and 4
   (c) 1, 3 and 4 *(d)* 1, 2 , 3 and 4

10. 'Bad bank' was recently in news. Select the correct statement(s) about it, using the code given below:
    1. It is a bank which buys the bad loans of the banks.
    2. Government of India is presently considering to set up such a bank.
    3. It will help India come out of the twin balance sheet problem.

    Code:

    (a) 1 and 2 *(b)* 2 and 3
    (c) 1 and 3 *(d)* 1, 2 and 3

11. LoU (Letter of Undertaking) was recently in news. Select the correct statement(s) about it by using the code given below:
    1. It is issued by a customer in the name of a bank or financial institution.
    2. It guarantees the creditworthiness of the drawee of the LoU.

    Code:

    (a) Only 1
    (b) Only 2
    (c) Both 1 and 2
    (d) Neither 1 nor 2

12. Consider the following statements about 'effective revenue deficit'.
    1. Effective revenue deficit is a Western idea of public finance management, which India used for the first time in the Union Budget 2011–12.
    2. It is a modified kind of revenue deficit which excludes that part of revenue deficit by which assets have been created.

    Select the correct statement(s) using the code given below:

    (a) Only 1 *(b)* Only 2
    (c) Both 1 and 2 *(d)* Neither 1 nor 2

13.. Consider the following statements about 'farm subsidies' in India.
    1. The input subsidies in India such as on fertilizers fall under indirect farm subsidies.
    2. Reduction in power and irrigation bills offered to farmers falls under direct farm subsidies.
    3. The agricultural provisions of the WTO, though allow direct farm subsidies, prohibit indirect subsidies.
    4. All subsidies forwarded by the governments in India fall under the indirect category.

    Select the correct statements using the code given below:

    (a) 1 and 2 *(b)* 2 and 3
    (c) 3 and 4 *(d)* 1 and 4

14. Cut in the cash reserve ratio may allow banks to cut the interest rates for loans because:

    (a) RBI controls the reserve ratios.
    (b) banks get additional fund without any additional cost.
    (c) it decreases banks' cost of operation.
    (d) it has a direct bearing on the repo rate which, in turn, affects the interest rate of loan.

15. Select the correct statement (s) related to India's *self-reliance* acquired during COVID-I9 pandemic by using the code given below:
    1. Hand sanitizers
    2. PPE Kits
    3. Ventilators
    4. COVID testing and treatment facilities

    Code:
    (*a*) 1, 2 and 3 (*b*) 2, 3 and 4
    (*c*) 1, 3 and 4 (*d*) 1, 2, 3 and 4

16. Participatory Notes (P-Notes) were in news recently. Consider the following statements about P-Notes.
    1. SEBI has classified three possible categories of P-Notes issuing FIIs in the country.
    2. Category-I are the offshore government entities/institutions investing solely on behalf of a country's central bank.
    3. Category-II are regulated entities as Mutual Funds, supervised by their regulatory bodies in their countries of origin.
    4. Category-III entities neither fall in Category-I or Category-II, which have been recently asked by the SEBI not to issue P-Notes.

    Select the correct statements using the code given below:
    (*a*) 1, 2 and 3 (*b*) 2, 3 and 4
    (*c*) 1, 3 and 4 (*d*) 1, 2 , 3 and 4

17. Select the correct statement/s related to the current monetary policy announced by the RBI by using the code given below
    1. Banks were asked to use an external benchmark to cost their loans in place of their MCLRs.
    2. As per the RBI, the idea of MCLR could not help in improving monetary policy transmission.

    Code:
    (*a*) Only 1 (*b*) Only 2
    (*c*) Both 1 and 2 (*d*) Neither 1 nor 2

18. 'Accommodative' monetary policy stance of the RBI means:
    (*a*) Interest rate may be cut down or increased.
    (*b*) Interest rate will increase in coming times.
    (*c*) It is another name for contractionary stance.
    (*d*) Interest rate will fall in coming times.

19. If interest rate is increased in an economy, it will:
    (*a*) increase the consumption expenditure in the economy.
    (*b*) increase tax collection of government.
    (*c*) decrease the savings in the economy.
    (*d*) decrease the investment expenditure in the economy.

20. Arrange the following according to their increasing order of 'liquidity', using the code given below:
    1. Saving deposits with the banks
    2. Currency and coins with the public
    3. Demand deposits with the banks
    4. Term deposits with the banks

    Code:
    (*a*) 4-1-3-2 (*b*) 2-3-4-1
    (*c*) 3-4-1-2 (*d*) 1-2-3-4

21. *Swiss Challenge* was recently in news. Select the correct statements related to it. using the code given below:
    1. It is a method of public procurement through awarding contracts.
    2. Bidders face challenge of improving upon the first bidder.
    3. The new method of awarding contacts is being first time used in India.
    4. This can be used for PPP and non-PPP projects.

Code:

(a) 1 and 3 (b) 1, 2 and 4

(c) 3 and 4 (d) 1, 2, 3 and 4

22. Select the correct statement(s) using the code: given below:
    1. Infrastructure sector has the highest share in the non-performing assets of the public sector banks in the country, at the start of the year 2021-22.
    2. From 2001 till March 2021, banks' lending to the infrastructure sector has grown annually around 43 per cent.

Code:

(a) Only 1 (b) Only 2

(c) Both 1 and 2 (d) Neither 1 nor 2

23. Consider the following statements related to the current provision of using the disinvestment proceeds.
    1. The allocations out of the NIF will be decided by the Union Budget.
    2. Only the profits accruing out of the NIF can be used, that too only on the social sector.
    3. During 2013–14, the government approved allocations from the NIF towards spending on recapitalisation of public sector banks.
    4. Fund of the NIF can be used for equity infusion in the Metro projects.

Select the correct statements using the code given below:

(a) 1, 2 and 3 (b) 2, 3 and 4

(c) 1, 3 and 4 (d) 1, 2 , 3 and 4

24. Select the correct statements using the code given below:
    1. Increasing primary deficit is considered a better trait of fiscal consolidation.
    2. Revenue deficit pushing fiscal deficit upward is considered bad.
    3. Falling monetised deficit is needed to promote the process of economic reforms in India.

Code:

(a) 1 and 2 (b) 2 and 3

(c) 1 and 3 (d) 1, 2 and 3

25. Select the correct statement (s) about a *prudential fiscal policy* stance in the case of India by using the code given below:
    1. Even high government debts can be sustained if growth is there.
    2. Government debts have a built-in dynamic to make growth happen.

Code:

(a) Only 1 (b) Only 2

(c) Both 1 and 2 (d) Neither 1 nor 2

ANSWER KEY WITH EXPLANATIONS

1. (c) Even during the COVID-19 pandemic, the Indian start-up ecosystem was progressing well. India is today home to 38 unicorns— adding a record number of 12 start-ups to the unicorn list in 2020. Unicorns are companies with valuation of US$ 1 billion or above.

2. (b) Need of the 'standing deposit facility' (SDF) was proposed by the RBI in November 2015 for the first time. The Union Budget 2018–19 announced to put this scheme in place. RBI will be able to hold 'uncollateralised' deposit under it in case the economy is flush will excess fund (as was seen during demonetisation in November 2016).

3. (c) Hybrid Annuity Model (HAM) is a PPP model to develop road projects while the 'engineering, procurement, construction' (EPC) was fully funded by the GoI. Private sector, in this model, has the responsibility to build the road and hand it over to the government. The selection takes place on the basis of bidding—the bidder which asks for lowest annuity

gets the project. The new PPP model was announced by the GoI by late ***January 2016***.

4. *(c)* Carry trade is an action in which an investor borrows money in a market where interest rate is relatively low and invests the borrowed money in a market where interest rate is higher.

5. *(a)* The term was in news in reference to the Insolvency and Bankruptcy Law of India. Under insolvency proceedings, banks could recover only a part of their loans given to the borrowers (as borrowers, assets were sold off with 'hair cuts').

6. *(d)* Both the statements are correct about the Rule. The US Federal Reserve Board seems to take this rule under consideration (as many other central banks of the world) but does not always follow its suggestions when adjusting the interest rate. This rule was developed by John Taylor, a 20th century economist.

7. *(d)* Launched in 2018–19, the scheme aims to treat school education holistically without segmentation from pre-nursery to Class 12—with the broader goal of improving school effectiveness measured in terms of equal opportunities for schooling and equitable learning outcomes.

8. *(c)* The scheme has been launched as a measure of the *Atmanirbharata Bharat Abhiyan* in May 2020 on public private partnership (PPP) mode and aims at providing housing to 'migrant labour' and 'urban poor' on affordable rent.

9. *(d)* The 3rd generation of economic reforms articulated the idea of 'decentralised' development planning—parallel to the idea of inclusive growth. The concept got reference while the government decided to go for the 2nd and 3rd generations of economic reforms (in the year 2000–01)—the benefits of reforms were found to be non-inclusive in nature.

10. *(d)* The *Economic Survey 2016–17* advised the government to set up such a body which it called 'public sector asset reconstruction agency (PARA)'. It will serve twin purposes—on the one hand it will buy the 'non-performing assets' (i.e., bad debts) of the government banks while, on the other, it will help the corporate sector of the country to come out of the 'red' (their balance sheet in unsustainable)—this way helping India to come out of the 'twin balance sheet' (TBS) problem.

11. *(b)* LoU is issued by banks/financial institutions to firms which gives guarantee of firms' creditworthiness. This makes it possible for the firms to borrow as per their needs. In case the firm defaults in servicing the loans, the LoU-issuing bank/institution is supposed to compensate the lending banks/financial institutions. It was in news by late February 2018 when a firm (led by Nirav Modi) was accused of ₹11,500 crore borrowings from several overseas branches of the Indian banks on the basis of an LoU issued by the Punjab National Bank (PNB) in the name of his firm (Gitanjali).

12. *(b)* The idea was for the first time used by the GoI in the Union Budget 2011–12, but it was not borrowed from the Western nations—this is an Indian idea.

13. *(d)* The agricultural provisions (i.e., the Agreement on Agriculture) of the WTO have put a ceiling on the amount of farm subsidies (both direct and indirect) of the member country as they distort the free market prices of farm goods.

14. *(b)* The CRR has got no connection to repo rate. Rather, in case the CRR is cut,

banks get additional fund without any additional cost—in other way, banks get an additional profit which they may give to borrowers—and interest rates of loans may fall down.

15. *(d)* During the COVID-19 pandemic, India acquired self-reliance in the areas of protective masks and several medicines.

16. *(d)* All of the statements are correct about the P-Notes.

17. *(d)* Banks are shifting to *(from April 2019)* the either of the four benchmarks (which they have to opt themselves) replacing the existing benchmark, the MCLR. These four options are—Repo rate, 90-day Treasury Bill yield, 182-day Treasury Bill yield, any other benchmark designed by the FBIL (Financial Benchmarks India Private Ltd).

18. *(d)* Such stance indicates RBI's willingness to cut down interest rate in coming times. Normally, such stance is seen when inflation rate is estimated to fall in coming times.

19. *(d)* As interest rate goes up, the investment decreases because the cost of fund increases.

20. *(d)* Demand deposits will have more liquidity than the saving deposits as the former includes the 'current accounts' of the firms (the most liquid deposit with the banks).

21. *(b)* This method is being used by the GoI for the first time, though it has been already used by the states (Andhra Pradesh, Bihar, Gujarat, MP, Punjab, etc.). By late ***January 2016,*** the Ministry of Railways used this method to award contracts for development of 400 railway stations in the country. However, the government has been discouraged by the Vijay Kelkar Expert Committee (set up on 'Revisiting and Revitalising the PPP Model of Infrastructure Development'). The committee submitted its report in January 2016 itself.

22. *(c)* Both of the statements are correct.

23. *(c)* In January 2013, the government restructured the National Investment Fund (NIF) and decided that the disinvestment proceeds with effect from the fiscal year 2013–14 will be credited to the existing *'Public Account'* under the head NIF and they would remain there until withdrawn/invested for the approved purpose by a Union Budget. It was decided that the NIF would be utilised for subscribing to the shares of the CPSE, including public sector banks (their recapitalisation, too) and insurance companies, to ensure 51 per cent government ownership in them; investment by the government in RRBs, IIFCL, NABARD, Exim Bank; equity infusion in various Metro projects; investment in Bhartiya Nabhikiya Vidyut Nigam Ltd. and Uranium Corporation of India Ltd.; investment in railways towards capital expenditure.

24. *(d)* Increasing primary deficit means falling interest burden. Economic reforms promote more investments from the private sector—it means lesser market borrowing by the governments (market borrowing by the government is known as monetised deficit).

25. *(d)* Growth makes debts sustainable but not vice-versa (as debts taken by governments may be spent on consumption such as in paying subsidies, salaries, interests, etc.).

SET-2

1. The *AT-I bond* was in news recently. Select the correct statement (s) about it using the code given below:
   1. They are Basel III compliant bonds issued by banks in India.
   2. They are unsecured and perpetual in nature.

   Code:
   (*a*) Only 1 (*b*) Only 2
   (*c*) Both 1 and 2 (*d*) Neither 1 nor 2

2. For which of the following purposes Indian currency is fully convertible? Select the correct answer using the code given below:
   1. Repatriation of remittances
   2. Interest payments of foreign loans
   3. Direct foreign investment
   4. Indirect foreign investment
   5. Trade

   Code:
   (*a*) 1,3 and 5 (*b*) 1, 2, 4 and 5
   (*c*) 3, 4 and 5 (*d*) 2, 4 and 5

3. In the situation of supply of money remaining the same when there is an increase in demand of money in the economic system, there will be:
   (*a*) An increase in the level of prices
   (*b*) A decrease in the rate of interest
   (*c*) An increase in the rate of interest
   (*d*) An increase in the deposits of banks

4. Consider the following statements regarding the Marginal Standing Facility (MSF).
   1. MSF functions as the last resort for banks to borrow short-term funds.
   2. MSF is on the line of the existing LAF and is part of it.
   3. Being a penal rate, MSF is a costlier route than repo.
   4. MSF is linked to the net demand and time liabilities of the banks.

   Which of the above statements are correct?
   (*a*) 1, 2 and 3 (*b*) 2, 3 and 4
   (*c*) 1, 3 and 4 (*d*) 1, 2, 3 and 4

5. RBI recently announced revised norms for Priority Sector Lending in India. Consider the following statements in the light of the announcement.
   1. Foreign banks' PSL target has been increased to 40 per cent at par with Indian banks irrespective of their number of branches.
   2. Food and Agro-processing and overdrafts up to ₹50,000 in no-frill accounts have been included in it.
   3. Off-grid solar and other renewable energy solutions, together with vocational education, are now under the PSL.
   4. MSE loans up to ₹2 crore have also been added under the PSL lending of the banks.

   Which of the above statements are correct?
   (*a*) 1, 2 and 3 (*b*) 2, 3 and 4
   (*c*) 1, 3 and 4 (*d*) 1, 2, 3 and 4

6. Which of the following segments of money is considered as the 'Other 'deposits with the RBI?
   1. Deposits of quasi-government bodies
   2. Other financial institutions and primary dealers
   3. Balance in the accounts of foreign central banks and governments
   4. Accounts of international agencies

   Select your answer using the code given below:
   (*a*) 1, 2 and 3 (*b*) 2, 3 and 4
   (*c*) 1, 3 and 4 (*d*) 1, 2, 3 and 4

7. As per the New Monetary Aggregates of the RBI, which of the following is not regarded as 'broad money'?

1. Bankers' deposits with the RBI
2. Demand and Time Deposits of the banks
3. Other Deposits with the RBI
4. Currency and coins with the public
5. Currency in circulation
6. Savings of Post Offices

Select your answer using the code given below:

Code:

(*a*) 1, 2 and 4 (*b*) 3, 4 and 5
(*c*) 1, 5 and 6 (*d*) 2, 3 and 4

8. Which of the following statements is correct about the situation of inverted custom duty'?
(*a*) When custom duties are higher on the raw materials and lower on the finished goods.
(*b*) When, due to some exemptions, custom duties on the similar goods are lower for the multinational firms in comparison to the domestic firms.
(*c*) When the countries with low tax regime (tax havens) give high export subsidies making the indigenous industries suffer in trade.
(*d*) None of the above.

9. Which one of the following statements correctly explains the concept *Brown Revolution*?
(*a*) Use of digital ecosystem in mining industry
(*b*) Extracting hydrogen energy from the hydrocarbon resources
(*c*) Using Artificial Intelligence in precision farming
(*d*) Dovetailing the digital revolution with farm machinery

10. Which of the following statements is correct about the term 'bank run'?
(*a*) The net balance of money a bank has in its chest at the end of the day's business.
(*b*) A panic situation when deposit holders start withdrawing cash from the banks.
(*c*) The ratio of a bank's total deposits and its total liabilities.
(*d*) The period in which a bank creates the highest credit in the market.

11. Which of the following statements is correct about the 'liquidity coverage ratio' which was in news recently?
(*a*) Corporate houses measure the availability of their working capital needs by it.
(*b*) Banks maintain enough liquidity under it for their needs upto 30 days.
(*c*) RBI uses this to measure the liquidity supply in the country's money market by it.
(*d*) This is ratio of the short-term and long-term liquidity available in an economy.

12. Consider the following statements regarding the operations of the various money market components in India.

Commercial Paper route of borrowing working capital is profitable once inflation has peaked.

Cost of operation for the banks in the Call Money Market falls in the wake of rising inflation.

Earnings from Money Market Mutual Funds may fall down as inflation rate increases.

Interest payment liabilities of the GoI on account of the Cash Management Bill increases in the case of decreased inflation.

Select the correct statements using the code below:

(*a*) 1, 2 and 3
(*b*) 2, 3 and 4
(*c*) 1, 2 and 4
(*d*) 1, 2, 3 and 4

13. Consider the following statements
    1. Government's cost of loan repayment is minimum once the inflation is maximum.
    2. Tax collections of governments increase with increased inflation.
    3. Seignorage is a double-edged technique to increase governments' income.

    Select the correct statements using the code given below:
    (*a*) 1 and 2 (*b*) 2 and 3
    (*c*) 1 and 3 (*d*) 1, 2 and 3

14. Consider the following statements related to the functions of RBI.
    1. The final decision regarding Credit and Monetary Policy is taken by the Union Ministry of Finance.
    2. Open Market Operations by the RBI comes under its autonomous powers.
    3. Ultimate power of issuing fresh currency notes in India remains with the RBI.
    4. RBI has been given full autonomy in the area of regulating the All India Financial Institutions.

    Which of the above statements are incorrect?
    (*a*) 1, 2 and 3 (*b*) 2, 3 and 4
    (*c*) 1, 3 and 4 (*d*) 1, 2, 3 and 4

15. Which of the following statement (s) is/are correct about *fire* sale? Select your answer by using the code given below:
    1. Selling goods or assets at heavy discounts.
    2. Discount sale of goods that were damaged in fire.
    3. Any discount sale where the seller is in financial stress.

    Code:
    (*a*) Only 1
    (*b*) Only 2
    (*c*) 1 and 2
    (*d*) Neither 1 nor 2

16. Consider the following statements regarding Commodity Future Trading in India.
    1. It is the best tool of maintaining stable prices for the commodities.
    2. Price discovery at Commodity Exchanges discounts the local and global factors in the process of price search.
    3. This is highly suitable for the agricultural commodities in India where highest price fluctuations happen due to various natural and man-made reasons.
    4. At times, GoI bans trading in certain agricultural commodities as in short-term it may lead to speculative price rises.

    Which of the above statements are correct?
    (*a*) 1, 2 and 3
    (*b*) 2, 3 and 4
    (*c*) 1, 3 and 4
    (*d*) 1, 2, 3 and 4

17. In the situation of interest rate being increased in an economy:
    (*a*) Consumption expenditure increases in the economy.
    (*b*) Tax collections of government decrease in the economy.
    (*c*) Investment expenditure decreases in the economy.
    (*d*) Savings decrease in the economy.

18. Consider the following statements related to a *limited liability firm*.
    1. Nominal Capital of a company is the limit up to which a company can issue shares.
    2. Registered Capital and Authorised Capital of a company are synonyms.
    3. Paid-up Capital of a company can never be more than its Issued Capital.
    4. Upper limit of Paid-up Capital of a company is its Authorised Capital.

Select the correct statements using the code given below:

(a) 1, 2 and 3 (b) 2, 3 and 4
(c) 1, 3 and 4 (d) 1, 2, 3 and 4

19. Arrange the following according to their increasing order of 'liquidity', using the code given below:
1. Saving deposits with the banks
2. Currency and coins with the public
3. Demand deposits with the banks
4. Term deposits with the banks

Code:
(a) 1-2-3-4 (b) 2-3-4-1
(c) 3-4-1-2 (d) 4-1-3-2

20. The 'accrual-based'accounting was in news recently. Select the correct statement(s) about it using the code given below:
1. Under such accounting practice, transactions are counted as they happen.
2. In this system, income is counted when cash is really received.

Code:
(a) Only 1 (b) Only 2
(c) Both 1 and 2 (d) Neither 1 nor 2

21. Net stable funding ratio (NFSR) was in news recently. Which of the following statements is not correct about it?
(a) This is a clause of the Basel III norms for banking regulation.
(b) This is an obligatory provision for Indian banks.
(c) It is a ratio which shows the resilience of banks to their long-term needs of funds.
(d) India is not committed to follow this provision.

22. A new disinvestment policy was announced by the Government recently. Select the correct statements related to it. using the code given below:
1. As per the new policy, the PSUs can be now privatised.
2. Government of India can sell the shares of the PSUs upto 100 per cent, too.
3. PSUs will be used to attract more investment in the economy.

Code:
(a) Only 1 (b) 2 and 3
(c) Only 2 (d) 1, 2 and 3

23. Consider the following statements about 'capital consumption'.
1. A situation, when due to the losses of a company in consecutive years make it obliged to pay its current expenses using its capital base.
2. A situation when the listed firms under-report their losses so that they can take higher benefits of depreciation.
The process by which a company shows higher loss in its operation to withhold payments of dividends to its various shareholders.

Which of the above statements are incorrect?
(a) 1 and 2 (b) 2 and 3
(c) 1 and 3 (d) 1, 2 and 3

24. Consider the following statements about the idea of 'micro-finance' in India.
1. Micro-finance is a small-scale financial intermediation, inclusive of savings, credit, insurance, business services and technical support provided to the needy borrower.
2. The thrust of the micro finance initiative is to channelise production and consumption credit in multiple doses based on the absorption capacity of the prospective borrower.
3. It has evolved through following different models at different times—a 'charity-based model' to a 'thrift-based model' and finally to the 'trust and creditworthiness model'.
4. It was in Australia where the link between microfinance institutions and the formal financial institutions evolved.

Select the correct statements using the code below:

(a) 1, 2 and 3 (b) 2, 3 and 4
(c) 1, 3 and 4 (d) 1, 2, 3 and 4

25. Consider the following statements related to the Angel Investors.
    1. Such investors are focused on helping the business succeed rather than reaping a huge profit from their investment.
    2. Conceptually, in profit motive, they are exact opposite of a 'venture capitalist'.
    3. They usually invest in 'person' rather than in the viability of the business.
    4. In India, they are classified as a category of 'venture capital funds'.

Select the correct statements using the code given below:

(a) 1, 2 and 3 (b) 2, 3 and 4
(c) 1, 3 and 4 (d) 1, 2, 3 and 4

ANSWER KEY WITH EXPLANATIONS

1. *(a)* It was in news in the case related to the Yes Bank scam. Though investors earn interest on them, they cannot liquidate them.

2. *(b)* Rupee is fully convertible in the following cases—interest payment, remittances, grants and indirect foreign investment (though it belongs to the capital account).

3. *(c)* As the level of money supply remains unchanged and demand for money goes up, the same amount of fund will be demanded by many resulting in an increase in the cost of loan, i.e. interest rate.

4. *(c)* RBI announced this route in 2011–12 as a 'penal' route for banks to borrow once they have exhausted all borrowing options, i.e., the repo route. MSF rate is regulated by the RBI above the current repo rate. This route can be used by banks for only overnight borrowings and is linked to their net demand and time liabilities (NDTL).

5. *(b)* Only those foreign banks which have 20 or more branches in the country have been brought at par with domestic banks regarding PSL (in a phased manner over a maximum period of 5 years starting April 1, 2013 to March 31, 2018). The foreign banks with less than 20 branches have no sub-targets within the overall priority sector lending target of 32 per cent. It is known that the RBI in August 2011 did set up a committee to re-examine the existing classification and suggest revised guidelines with regard to PSL and related issues (chaired by S. M. V. Nair). The committee submitted its report in February 2012.

6. *(d)* The stock of money in 'Other deposits' with the RBI is the liquidity which is available at its disposal for day-to-day uses and are not of any use for long-term purposes. Accounts in international agencies include agencies like IMF and other such bodies.

7. *(c)* In the new monetary aggregate, M^3 is the 'broad money' (like the old one). Bankers' deposit is part of the 'reserve money'. Post Offices' saving deposits (excluding National Saving Certificates) are part of M^4. For 'other deposits', see the explanation of Q. No. 8.

8. *(a)* This is a situation when the import (custom) duty applicable on the finished product is lower than on the raw material (or intermediate product). This discourages domestic manufacturers. In the case of India, it occurs not solely because of basic custom duty but in some cases as a result of other additional duties.

9. *(b)* It is all about combining tractor services for ploughing and sowing to using

sensors, cloud computing and artificial intelligence for precision farming. The term was first used by Howarth Buffet (a farmer and brother of the US billionaire Warren Buffett). It was in news in India in the case of the small farmers.

10. *(b)* This happens when there is a fear that the bank has insufficient funds with it—depositors lose confidence in the bank and start withdrawing their deposits in the bank concerned. This term has been used in contemporary journalism recently in the wake of the high loss fetched by the United Bank of India. Similar situations were seen in the wake of the sub-prime crisis in the US economy—by now, over 300 banks have been closed down in the economy due to losses.

11. *(b)* This is one of the provisions of the Basel III norms of prudential regulation of the banking sector.

12. *(d)* This question is based on the idea of relationship between 'inflation' and 'real interest rate' which borrowers pay on their borrowings. Components of money market are tools of borrowing 'short-term' (i.e., working capital) money from the financial market—thus inflation affects them in similar ways.

13. *(d)* The idea is the same as 'inflation premium'. Seignorage is a technique by which government intends to increase its tax revenues by issuing fresh currency notes, which brings in extra cash to the government in two ways, one via printed currency and the other through increase in tax income.

14. *(b)* RBI avails no autonomy in its functioning—though the Narasimhan Committee-I in 1991 had suggested autonomy in the areas of critical importance, similar to many Western economies. It is believed that it has been given a kind of working autonomy in the area of making and announcing the Credit and Monetary Policy (though there is no change in the official stand hitherto).

15. *(d)* The term *originally* means the discount sale of goods damaged in fire but, over the time, got diversified meanings in commercial world. In financial market it refers to securities that are trading well below their *intrinsic value.*

16. *(d)* All the statements are correct. In the case of India's agricultural commodities, such trading doesn't seem functioning well because other related institutional developments have not happened in time and farmers are not yet active players on the commodity exchanges of India (partly due to operational difficulties, smaller capital base and lack of knowledge). Once big farmers (contract/corporate farmers) emerge, it will start functioning in a better way for such commodities.

17. *(c)* Investment decreases in the economy as the cost of fund increases.

18. *(d)* All the options are correct.

19. *(d)* Demand deposits will have more liquidity than the saving deposits as the former includes the 'current accounts' of the firms (the most liquid deposit with the banks).

20. *(a)* It is one of the two methods of accounting. The governments in India follow the *cash-based accounting* system, through which income is counted when cash (or a cheque) is actually received, and expenses are counted when actually paid. An alternative method is an *accrual-based accounting* system, wherein transactions are counted as they happen, regardless of when the money is actually received

or paid. It was in news recently, as it was advised by an expert committee to switch over to this system (to the Government of India by the Jalan Committee on expenditure management).

21. *(d)* This is one of the clauses of the Basel III norms (of the Basel based Bank for International Settlement) aimed at prudential regulation of the banking sector. Banks are supposed to maintain sufficient long-term (one year) liquidity under it so that they could be sure of stable source of fund in times of financial stress if such situations arise in the economy.

22. *(d)* As per the new policy announced by the Government in 2016–17, any amount of shares can be sold in the public sector undertakings (PSUs). Disinvestment is now seen as the part of 'comprehensive management of Government's investment in the PSUs'.

23. *(d)* Capital consumption is the other term for 'depreciation'. In the process of their uses, fixed assets depreciate (go for wear and tear) at the rate decided by the government of the economy—the rates for the same assets may vary across economies.

In the new system of national income accounting, it is written as CPC (Consumption of fixed capital)–in use since 2015–16 after the advice of the IMF.

24. *(d)* Microfinance (MF) is a small-scale financial intermediation, inclusive of savings, credit, insurance, business services and technical support provided to the needy borrower. The thrust of the MF initiative is to channelise production and consumption credit in multiple doses based on the absorption capacity of the prospective borrower. The presumption here is that the borrowers possess basic financial literacy and requisite capacity to operate their self-determined economic ventures profitably. The formal existence of MF was found in 1972. A *charity based model* (interest free loans where repayment was based on peer pressure) of MF was evolved in Ireland. Later on, in *Germany*, a *thrift-based model* was developed with the establishment of saving funds. Bangladesh Grameen model is based on the principle of trust and creditworthiness of poor with both obligatory and voluntary saving schemes. The Foundation for Development Cooperation (FDC) of Australia evolved a research project, The Banking With the Poor (BWTP) network to link microfinance institutions with formal financial institutions.

25. *(d)* Such investors are usually found among an entrepreneur's family and friends, but they may be from outside also providing financial backing to entrepreneurs for starting their business. The Union Budget 2013–14 promised a provision for them. As per *SEBI (Alternative Investment Funds) Regulations, 2012 (AIF Regulations)*, Category I AIF are those AIFs with 'positive spill over effects' on the economy, for which certain incentives or concessions might be considered by SEBI or the GoI or other regulators in India, which shall include *Venture Capital Funds, SME Funds, Social Venture Funds, Infrastructure Funds* and such other *Alternative Investment Funds(AIFs)* as may be specified.

SET-3

1. Which of the following is the correct equation for India's NNP at market prices'?
   (a) Total GVA at basic prices + Production taxes (less Production subsidies)
   (b) CE + MI + CFC + Product taxes + Production taxes (less Product and Production subsidies)
   (c) Total GVA at basic prices + Product and Production taxes (less all subsidies)
   (d) CE + MI + CFC + Product taxes (less Product subsidies)

2. Select the correct statement(s) related to banking industry of the country by using the code given below:
   1. Banks can borrow upto their statutory liquidity reserves if there is no ceiling on repo borrowings.
   2. Monetary system is more sensitive to changes in overnight repo rate than the reverse repo rate, rather, both help bank cut their operational cost.

   Code:
   (a) Only 1 (b) Only 2
   (c) Both 1 and 2 (d) Neither 1 nor 2

3. Select the correct statement (s) about the nature of government's.fsc:al polict; stance by using the code given below:
   1. In the counter-cyclical fiscal policy, government spends less during contractionary times and more during expansionary times.
   2. Under a pro-cyclical fiscal policy, government spends more during expansionary times and less during contractionary times.

   Code:
   (a) Only 1 (b) Only 2
   (c) Both 1 and 2 (d) Neither 1 nor 2

4. Consider the given statements regarding subsidies.
   1. They are essential parts of public policy to the extent they are ad hoc arrangements.
   2. While everybody benefits from it, they are not paid by all.
   3. Capital part of subsidies is counted in the capital expenditure of the government.
   4. The FRBM Act has strict provisions regarding subsidies.

   Select the incorrect statements using the code given below:

   Code:
   (a) 1, 2 and 3 (b) 1, 3 and 4
   (c) 2, 3 and 4 (d) 1, 2, 3 and 4

5. Select the correct statement(s) related to the measures taken recently under the *Atmanirbhar Bharat Abhiyan,* by using the code given below:
   1. A *Fund of Funds* was created for the MSMEs.
   2. Defence sector has been allowed 74 per cent foreign direct investment under automatic route.
   3. Revised investment for the medium enterprises has been increased by five times to ₹ 50 crores.
   4. In the case of the collateral-free loans disbursed to the MSMEs, the loans will be ultimately guaranteed by the Centre.

   Code:
   (a) 1 and 2 (b) 2 and 3
   (c) 1,3 and 4 (d) 1, 2, 3 and 4

6. If the RBI decides to adopt an 'expansionist' monetary policy, which of the following it would not do?
   1. Cut CRR and optimise SLR.
   2. Increase MSF Rate.

3. Cut Bank Rate and increase Reverse Repo Rate.

Select the answer using the code given below:

(a) 1 and 2 (b) Only 1
(c) 2 and 3 (d) Only 2

7. Which of the following 'redistributive' policies the government will not adopt if it wants to bridge economic inequality?
1. Rationalising subsidies
2. Progressive tax policies
3. Regressive expenditure

Select the answer using the code given below:

(a) 1 and 2 (b) Only 2
(c) 2 and 3 (d) Only 3

8. Which of the following will be the outcome once an economy is under an inflationary pressure?
1. Domestic currency heads for depreciation.
2. Exports become less competitive with imports getting costlier.
3. Cost of borrowing decreases.
4. Bond-holders get benefitted.

Select the answer using the code given below:

(a) 1 and 2 (b) Only 2
(c) 1 and 3 (d) Only 3

9. Select the correct statement (s) about the *Union Budget 2021-22* by using the code given below:
1. Health and Wellbeing is among its nine pillars for which the allocation has been increased by a hopping 57 per cent.
2. 'National Institution for One Health' has been proposed.

Code:

(a) Only 1 (b) Only 2
(c) Both 1 and 2 (d) Neither 1 nor 2

10. Consider the following statements regarding the marginal standing facility rate of the RBI.
1. It is similar to the repo rate for the financial institutions.
2. It is on the lines of the liquidity adjustment facility and part of it.
3. Though it is a costlier route to fulfil overnight requirement of funds, it is not a penal rate.
4. Banks use this route once they exhaust all channels to raise short-term fund.

Select the incorrect statements using the code given below:

(a) 1, 2 and 3 (b) 1, 3 and 4
(c) 2, 3 and 4 (d) 1, 2, 3 and 4

11. Which one of the following statements is not true about Game Theory?
(a) It is a branch of economics that uses models to study interactions between countries, individuals and organisations.
(b) It was devised in 1944 by John Von Neumann and Oscar Morgenstern.
(c) It was often used in political or military context to explain conflicts between countries but has of late been used to map trends in the business world, ranging from how cartels sell prices to how companies can better their goods and services in new markets.
(d) Robert J. Aumann and Thomas C. Schelling were awarded Nobel Prize in Economics in 2005 for their work on this theory.

12. Select the correct statements about 'countervailing duty'.
(a) A tax imposed on import by the importing country to neutralise the benefit of export subsidies offered by the exporting country.
(b) Another name of the anti-dumping duty.

(c) It does not come under the preview of the WTO.

(d) It is opposite to custom duty.

13. Select the correct outcomes of depreciation in a country's currency using the code given below:

1. Export of the country goes up as the value of the exportable items falls in the international market.
2. At times, countries use it as a means to promote their exports.
3. Promoting exports through depreciation in one's currency is like selling national assets at throwaway prices to the world.

Code:

(a) Only 1 (b) Only 3

(c) 2 and 3 (d) 1, 2 and 3

14. Consider the following statements about derivatives in India.

1. A security derived from a debt instrument, share, secured or unsecured loan.
2. A contract which derives its value from the prices or index of underlying assets.
3. A security derived from exchange rates and interest rates.
4. It may be derived from monsoon forecasting.

Select the correct statements using the code given below

(a) 1, 2 and 3 (b) 1, 3 and 4

(c) 2, 3 and 4 (d) 1, 2, 3 and 4

15. 'Net income' term was recently in news. Which of the following statements is correct about it?

(a) It is balance of a company's total income and its total expenditure.

(b) The profit of a company after paying corporate tax.

(c) The income earned by a company over its losses and interest payments.

(d) The income of a company without deducting its losses.

16. Consider the following stater-nents regarding 'angel investors'.

1. Investors who provide financial backing to entrepreneurs for starting their business.
2. They are investors with positive spillover effects.
3. They may provide finance as loan or as share capital in the upcoming business.
4. They usually invest in person rather than the economic viability of business.
5. They are usually from the entrepreneur's family and friends, but may be from outside, too.
6. Venture capital funds serve similar purpose to the extent arrangement of investible capital is concerned.

Select the incorrect statements using the code given below:

(a) 1, 2 and 5 (b) 2, 3 and 4

(c) 3, 5 and 6 (d) None of these

17 . Consider the following items with respect to India's capital account.

1. Foreign currency deposits of the banks
2. Private remittances
3. Security market investments by the RFPIs and QFIs
4. Foreign direct investment
5. External bonds issued by the GoI
6. Merchandise trade balance
7. Interest liabilities of the external loans

Which among the above items is associated with India's capital account?

(a) 1, 3, 4 and 5 (b) 2, 4, 6 and 7

(c) 1, 5, 6 and 7 (d) 1, 3, 6 and 7

18. Select the correct statement (s) about India's *Interest Rate Growth Rate Differential* (IRGD) by using the code given below:

1. India's IRGD has remained negative not due to higher growth rate but lower interest rate.
2. Over the last 25 years, India had a negative IRGD.

Code:

(a) Only 1 (b) Only 2
(c) Both 1 and 2 (d) Neither 1 nor 2

19. As per the circular of the RBI. which of the following statements is correct about the Core Investment Companies (CICs)'/
(a) All those companies with a paid-up capital of over ₹1,000 crore, which invest primarily in the core industries.
(b) All those NBFCs which invest not less than 90 per cent of their total assets in the form of shares and securities for non-trading purposes.
(c) All the corporate houses with net-owned fund not less than ₹1,000 crore invested in the core sector for at least 10 years.
(d) All the Foreign Institutional Investors (FIIs) with a minimum of ₹1,000 crore paid-up capital base with at least 80 per cent of it invested in the core industries for long-term purposes.

20. For which of the following purposes Indian currency is fully convertible? Select. the correct answer using the code given below:
1. Repatriation of remittances
2. Interest payments of foreign loans
3. Direct foreign investment
4. Indirect foreign investment
5. Trade

Code:

(a) 1,3 and 5 (b) 1, 2, 4 and 5
(c) 3, 4 and 5 (d) 2, 4 and 5

21. Which of the following statements are incorrect when the government starts repurchasing its bonds before their maturity periods?
1. Promotion of an 'expansionist' monetary policy
2. An attempt to increase the saving rate of the economy
3. A tool to check the rising inflation
4. Promotion to credit creation by the banks

Select the answer using the code given below:

(a) 1, 2 and 3 (b) 1, 3 and 4
(c) 2, 3 and 4 (d) 1, 2, 3 and 4

22. NITI Aayog has suggested a new method, the '*price deficiency payment*' for farmers which is consistent with India's agricultural obligations to the WTO. Select the correct statements regarding it, using the code given below:
1. It suggests to pay a bonus price above the minimum support price (MSP) announced for a crop which will be not more than the market price of the crop.
2. It looks into the prices in the mandis regulated by the Agriculture Produce Market Committee (APMC) of the states.
3. Farmers to get a maximum payment of the difference between the MSP and market price of a crop.
4. The technology platform of direct benefit transfer (DBT) is to be used for the purpose.

Code:

(a) 1 and 2 (b) 1, 2 and 4
(c) 2, 3 and 4 (d) 1, 2, 3 and 4

23. Which of the following is/are correct about the concept 'invisible hand'? Select the answer using the code given below:
1. The intrinsic human motivation to work for gains.
2. It cannot work in the absence of the market forces.
3. It is also known as 'animal spirit.

Code:
(a) 1 and 2 (b) 2 and 3
(c) 1 and 3 (d) 1, 2 and 3

24. Nutri Cereals were in news recently. Select the correct statement(s) about them using the code given below:
1. These are organically grown cereals which have high fibre content.
2. Government of India announced a few cereals to be known by this name.

Code:
(a) Only 1 (b) Only 2
(c) Both 1 and 2 (d) Neither 1 nor 2

25. Select the correct statement (s) about the employee stock option plans (ESOPs) by using the code given below:
1. It involves the employees of limited stock company in the affairs of the company as stakeholders and enhances the latter's efficiency and performance.
2. It exposes the company to the risks of insider trading and share scams.

Code:
(a) Only 1 (b) Only 2
(c) 1 and 2 (d) Neither 1 nor 2

ANSWER KEY WITH EXPLANATIONS

1. *(b)* As per the new methodology, this is the correct formula to derive the Net National Product (NNP) of a nation.
2. *(b)* Liquidity Management Framework of the RBI for Repo borrowings has double ceilings which prevent banks from borrowing upto the value of their SLRs. Benefits of overnight repo are a taken by more banks than that of the reverse repo rate.
3. *(b)* In the counter-cyclical fiscal policy, governments spend more during contractionary (i.e., falling growth rate) and less during expansionary (i.e., rising growth rate) times.
4. *(b)* Basically, subsidies benefit some people while they are paid by the whole population of the economy. Subsidies have been advised by the economists provided they are used as short-term measures—if the economy uses them as a long-term measure, they make the population handicapped (those who get them). Subsidies are like putting someone on pain-killers in place of providing the real treatment for the pain! That is why it is always advised by economists that besides subsidies there should be an effective and time-bound long-term policy to impart market-linked purchasing capacity to the population getting subsidy benefit. All subsidies fall under the non-planned expenditure. The FRBM Act has no direct provisions regarding subsidies—it talks about the revenue and fiscal deficits only.
5. *(d)* Foreign direct investment in the defence sector was increased from existing 49 per cent to 74 per cent (India already allows 100 per cent) foreign direct investment in the defence sector on case-by-case basis. The definition of the MSMEs has gone for upward revision [for details, see relevant sub-topic in *Chapter 9*].
6. *(d)* Following the 'expansionist' policy means encouraging the circulation of money in the economy. Here, except the MSFR increase, all other measures are dedicated to increase liquidity in the system.
7. *(d)* Regressive expenditure will never serve the purpose. The government will need to tax the higher income bracket with higher rate of taxes and rationalise the subsidies so that they go to the needy only and in adequate amount. All these measures are already being operationalised by the GoI.

8. *(c)* Inflation is directly seen converting into proportionate depreciation in the domestic currency. In such situations, exports become cheaper for other countries (which make it more competitive in the world market), besides imports becoming costlier (as the domestic currency loses value in front of the external currency). Real cost of borrowing is calculated by deducting the current rate of inflation (which is higher) from the 'nominal rate of interest/borrowing' (that is the rate of interest banks announce on a certain category of loan). Bond-holders are basically lenders, so they suffer—interest income sees dilution.

9. *(b)* For Health and Wellbeing, the allocation of fund is 137 per cent more than the previous Budget.

10. *(a)* This route is only for banks, on the lines of the LAF, but it is not its part. It is a penal rate, that is why it remains always higher than the repo rate. While putting this route in place, the RBI has permitted banks to borrow maximum 1 per cent of their Net Demand and Time Liabilities, in coming times it was cut down, too. Similarly, it commenced with a rate of 1 per cent higher than the current repo rate, but over the time it went upto 3 per cent higher than the current repo (in the process of checking inflation, by end 2013).

11. *(a)* Game Theory is a branch of Applied Mathematics which uses models to study interactions between countries, individuals and organisations. It has been used by applied economists in different areas.

12. *(a)* Anti-dumping duty is imposed in a similar case but not due to export subsidy given by the exporting country, rather when the country is exporting (dumping) something 'below fair market price'. In both of the taxes, an investigation is provisioned by the WTO.

13. *(d)* Depreciation makes a country's exports become cheaper in the international market (i.e. the value of exportable items falls for the importers)—this makes the country export more (increase in 'volume' of the exportable). Countries use depreciation as a tool to promote their exports (in present times, China has been doing the same)—but such a policy is not healthy in long-term.

14. *(a)* The derivatives in India have not been allowed to derive their value from the weather forecasting (it is allowed in many developed economies, for example, the USA).

15. *(a)* It is derived by deducting the expenses of the company from its total revenue in a particular period (usually one year). It is also called *earnings, net earnings* or *net profit*.

16. *(d)* All the statements are correct about angel investors—a term introduced in the Union Budget 2013–14. SEBI puts them in the Category I AIF (Alternative Investment Fund) with 'positive spillover effects'. The venture capital funds also come under this. A venture fund invests in business rather than in the person (opposite of the angel investor).

17. *(a)* Private remittances, interest liabilities of foreign loans and trade balance are shown in the current account.

18. *(b)* IRGD is the difference between interest rate (on Government loans) and the growth rate of the economy, which has remained negative in India due to growth rate being higher than the interest rate (as

per the *Economic Survey 2020-21, vol. 1, pp. 43-83*).

19. *(b)* CICs are basically the NBFCs carrying on the business of acquisition of shares and securities, which satisfies some conditions, i.e., it holds not less than 90 per cent of its total assets in this form; its investments in the equity shares in group companies constitute not less than 60 per cent of its total assets; it does not trade in its investments in shares, debt or loans in group companies except through block sale for the purpose of dilution or disinvestment; and it does not carry on any other financial activity except investment in bank deposits, money market instruments, government securities, loans and investments in group companies.

20. *(b)* Rupee is fully convertible in the following cases—interest payment, remittances, grants and indirect foreign investment (though it belongs to the capital account).

21. *(c)* The money which flows from the government into the system was called the 'cheap currency' by J. M. Keynes. By doing so, governments promote economic activities, which supports business and trade.

22. *(c)* This advice was given by a 'Task Force on Agriculture' of the NITI by late 2015. It suggested that farmers can be made a payment (say 50 per cent) of the difference between the market price and APMC regulated price for a crop, to encourage them produce more. This way, India will be able to promote more food crops as well as not violate the agricultural provisions of the WTO.

23. *(d)* The origin of this concept is traced back to the work *(An Inquiry into the Nature and Causes of the Wealth of Nations, 1776)* of the Scottish philosopher-economist Adam Smith (1723–90). The same concept is considered the seed behind capitalism which later got modified into market economy.

24. *(b)* By late 2018–19, Government of India named the *millets* as such. For details, see the entry *NUTRI CEREALS* in the *Glossary*.

25. *(c)* ESOPs (under which the share of the firm is sold off to its employees) increase the risk-taking capacity of the employees. The Economics Survey 2019–20 suggested the Government of India to use it in the case of the public sector banks to improve their performance.

SET-4

1. Consider the following statement.

'Process of industrial mutation that incessantly revolutionises the economic structure from within, incessantly destroying the old one, incessantly creating a new one.'

Which of the following is correct about the statement given above?

(a) This is how Albert Einstein defined technological research and development.

(b) A passage quoted from the World Economic Forum document on the 4th industrial revolution.

(c) Description of innovation by Joseph Schumpeter.

(d) Quote from the speech of Nobel Laureate for economics Abhijit Banerjee.

2. Which of the following statements is correct about the situation of inverted custom duty'?
   (a) When custom duties are higher on the raw materials and lower on the finished goods.
   (b) When due to some exemptions custom duties on the similar goods are lower for the multinational firms in comparison to the domestic firms.
   (c) When the countries with low tax regime (tax havens) give high export subsidies to making the indigenous industries suffer in trade.
   (d) None of the above.

3. Select the correct statement(s) about India's new, method of national income accounting by using the code given below:
   1. Subsidies are not added in it.
   2. Firms' income are taken after deducting their depreciation.

   Code:
   (a) Only 1 (b) Only 2
   (c) Both 1 and 2 (d) Neither 1 nor 2

4. Consider the following statements regarding depreciation.
   1. Fixed assets losing monetary value over time.
   2. Loss of value in a domestic currency in front of a foreign currency.
   3. Fall in the monetary value of the equipment of a plant due to their use.
   4. It does not happen in the case of non-fixed assets.

   Select the correct statements using the code given below:

   Code:
   (a) 1, 2 and 3 (b) 2, 3 and 4
   (c) 1, 2 and 4 (d) 1, 2, 3 and 4

5. Deficit financing leads to inflation in general. but it can be checked if:
   (a) Government expenditure leads to increase in the aggregate supply in ratio of the aggregate demand.
   (b) Only aggregate demand is increased.
   (c) All expenditures are used for the national debt payment only.
   (d) Fresh currencies are printed to fulfil its deficit financial needs.

6. Consider the following options if all banks in an economy are nationalised and converted into a monopoly bank.
   1. Deposits will decrease in the new bank.
   2. Deposits will increase in the new bank.
   3. There will be no effect on either saving rate or lending.

   Select the correct option/options using the code given below:
   (a) Only 1 (b) 1 and 2
   (c) Only 2 (d) 1 and 3

7. Which of the following defines credit rationing in the best way?
   1. When banks offer loans only to the companies with strong financials and performance.
   2. Companies with weak financials and performance are given loans at comparatively lower interest rates under it.
   3. Such actions are prevalent when there is a liquidity crunch in the financial system.

   Select the correct statements using the code given below:

   Code:
   (a) 1 and 2 (b) 2 and 3
   (c) 1 and 3 (d) 1, 2 and 3

8. Which ofthe following factors is responsible for a surplus in the current account of an economy?

1. Its exports are compulsory imports for other economies.
2. It imports low-technology items and exports high-technology items.
3. It has a huge domestic market.
4. Its imports are non-compulsive in nature.

Select the answer using the code given below:

(a) 1, 2 and 3 *(b)* 2, 3 and 4
(c) 1, 3 and 4 *(d)* 1, 2 and 4

9. If RBI cuts down the cash reserve ratio. it will have the- following impact on the economy.
   1. Banks will have higher leverage to liquidity.
   2. Economy may see increased investment.
   3. Supply of currency in the economy may broaden.
   4. Real interest rates may decline.

   Select the answer using the code given below:

   (a) 1, 2 and 3 *(b)* 2, 3 and 4
   (c) 1, 2 and 4 *(d)* 1, 2, 3 and 4

10. Which of the following items appears in a company's balance sheet?
    1. Value of raw materials held by the company
    2. Cash held in the banks in the company's current account
    3. Sales revenue of the company
    4. Issued capital of the company

    Select the answer using the code given below:

    (a) 1, 2 and 3 *(b)* 2, 3 and 4
    (c) 1, 2 and 4 *(d)* 1, 2, 3 and 4

11. Select the correct statement (s) related to the newly launched *Planetary Pressures-Adjusted Human Development Index (PHDI)* by using the code given below:
    1. India moves up by 8 ranks form its HDI ranking on it.
    2. China moves up by 16 places from its HDI ranking on it.

    Code:

    (a) Only 1 *(b)* Only 2
    (c) Both 1 and 2 *(d)* Neither 1 nor 2

12. Which of the following statements defines the term 'insurance penetration'?
    (a) The number of insured per one hundred population in an economy
    (b) Insured people per one thousand of the population of an economy
    (c) Number of alive and insured per hundred population in an economy
    (d) None of the above

13. The exchange rate of a currency in its. forex market depends on:
    1. Its twin deficit.
    2. The currency regime economy follows for exchange determination
    3. Inflation, printing of fresh currencies, levels of forex earnings.

    Select the answer using the code given below:

    (a) 1 and 2 *(b)* 2 and 3
    (c) 1 and 3 *(d)* 1, 2 and 3

14. Consider the following statements regarding the state of full convertibil'ity of the rupee in the current account.
    1. 100 per cent foreign currency is made available by the government at official rate of exchange for all visible and invisible imports.
    2. Foreign investment in the Indian security market, though an issue of capital account, is considered as a matter of the current account for convertibility purpose.
    3. In the case of foreign grants, rupee is partially convertible in India.

4. Rupee is fully convertible if someone needs foreign currency to go for medical treatment abroad.

Select the incorrect statement/statements using the code given below:

(a) 1, 2 and 3 (b) 2, 3 and 4
(c) 1, 2 and 4 (d) 1, 3 and 4

15. The Reserve Bank of India calculates four components of money supply, viz., M_1. M_2, M_3 and M_4. Select the incorrect pair out of the following.

(a) M_1 consists of the currency and coins with the public; demand deposits of the banks and other deposits with the RBI.
(b) M_2 consists of M_1 and demand deposits of the post offices.
(c) M_3 includes the sum of M_1 and M_2.
(d) M_4 includes the sum of M_3 and demand as well as time deposits of post offices.

16. Consider the following statements in a situation when a currency goes for devaluation.

1. Fall in the value of currency vis-á-vis a foreign currency.
2. Exports become less competitive.
3. Trading partners see fall in their export.
4. Imports become costlier.

Select the correct statements using the code given below:

(a) 1, 2 and 3 (b) 2, 3 and 4
(c) 1, 2 and 4 (d) 1, 3 and 4

17. In the case of India, the lag between the rate of fixed investment and its impact on GDP is seen to be:

(a) 1–2 years (b) 2–3 years
(c) 3–4 years (d) None of these

18. A state of 'equilibrium' for a consumer means:

(a) A state of saving rate equal to the growth rate of the economy for the consumer.
(b) A state of zero saving for the consumer and full expenditure.
(c) The consumer is unable to fulfil has needs with the given income.
(d) The consumer is able to fulfil his needs with a given level of income.

19. Modern economics defines 'tax' as:

(a) A mode of income redistribution
(b) A method of effecting transfer pricing
(c) A way to mobilise resources for government expenditures
(d) A tool of meeting the social obligations of modern governments

20. Consider the following statements about 'Sensex'.

1. Sensex is the representative share index of the Indian stock market.
2. Its rise means an overall rise in the prices of shares of a group of companies registered with the Bombay Stock Exchange.
3. The shares which are kept in it are of the high net-worth companies.
4. It is a privilege to be in this 30-shares index.

Select the incorrect statement/statements using the code given below:

(a) Only 1 (b) 1 and 2
(c) Only 2 (d) None of these

21. 'Structural reform measures' was one of the two categories of measures announced by the government to be taken under the process of economic reforms in India. These measures deal with:

1. Redefining the role of the state in the economy
2. Attempting higher participation of private capital—Indian and foreign
3. Increasing aggregate supply in the economy
4. Checking the excessive demand in the economy leading to inflation

Select the answer using the code given below:

(a) 1, 2 and 3 (b) 2, 3 and 4
(c) 1, 2 and 4 (d) 1, 3 and 4

22. Which of the following statements is correct about the term 'ex-factory price'?
(a) It is 'factory price' added with all indirect taxes of the Centre and the state.
(b) It is the 'ex-showroom price' after deducting the weight of indirect taxes from it.
(c) It is 'factor cost' added with the weight of current rate of inflation.
(d) None of the above.

23. Recently, the government allowed the formation of a new type of 'firm' (business entity) in India- LLP. Select the correct statements related to it. using the code given below:
1. It is a partnership firm.
2. Liability of partners does not extend to their personal assets.
3. It can enter into contracts and hold property in its own name.
4. This will enable smaller firms higher access to credit.

Code:
(a) 1 and 2
(b) 1, 2 and 4
(c) 2, 3 and 4
(d) *1, 2, 3 and 4*

24. Which of the following policy steps a government usually takes to boost demand and support the economy in deflationary situations?
1. Lowering interest rates together with cutting direct taxes
2. Emphasising savings and enhancing salaries
3. Increasing government expenditure
4. Going for tapering of fiscal stimulus

Select the answer using the code given below:

(a) 1 and 2 (b) 3 and 4
(c) 1 and 3 (d) 1 and 4

25. Which of the following refers to the *Gold Tranche?*
(a) The physical reserve of gold maintained by the Central Banks
(b) A system of credit made available by the IMF to its members
(c) A special loan forwarded by the WTO to its members
(d) A system of credit granted by the World Bank to its members

ANSWER KEY WITH EXPLANATIONS

1. (c) The Austrian economist gave innovation a new name 'creative destruction'.

2. (a) This is a situation when the import duty (custom) applicable on the finished product is lower than on the raw material (or intermediate products). This makes domestic manufacturing non-competitive against the imported finished products.

3. (a) In the new methodology of national accounting, subsidies are not added with (it is 'less subsidies').

4. (d) This is 'wear and tear' in fixed/immovable assets due to their use. For different assets, the rates of depreciation are announced by the countries—the rates may vary across countries. Depreciation is also used by countries as a toll of economic policy—for example, to boost the sales of heavy vehicles the Government of India has doubled the rate of depreciation of the vehicles (from 20 per cent to 40 per cent).

5. (a) The basic reason for price rises in the situations of deficit financing is that governments fail to equalise the total

6. *(c)* demand of the economy by the total supply.

   Monopoly will discourage the depositors from putting money in the bank. The saving rate of the economy, together with the lending activities of the bank, will also get hampered.

7. *(c)* Credit rationing results when companies with robust financial and operating performance get loans while the less robust ones are denied credit by banks and financial institutions.

8. *(d)* Having a huge domestic market never supports current account positively; it may impact the account negatively if its consumers are demanding more of the items which are being imported by the economy. In the case of India, the situation is: its imports are compulsive and most of its exports are non-complusive for its trade partners.

9. *(d)* The CRR provides more money in the hands of banks, which may be now lent out for investment and increase the supply of currency in the economy. As the supply of money increases to the banks, they may cut interest rates (cost of money remaining the same).

10. *(c)* The revenues a company gets out of its sale of the manufactured items are not shown in the balance sheet of the company.

11. *(a)* On PHDI India is ranked 123rd while its rank is 131st on the HDI (Human Development Index), but rank of China falls down to 101st on it, which is ranked 85th on the HDI. This difference is there due to India's higher commitment and performance towards implementing the Paris Climate pact.

12. *(d)* 'Insurance penetration' is defined as the ratio of underwritten premium in a given year to the GDP of an economy.

13. *(d)* Exchange rate of a currency depends on so many variables as given in the question. If the economy follows the 'floating currency regime' for the exchange rate determination, the exchange rate is directly linked to all those factors which affect the availability of domestic and foreign currencies in the economy—the higher the supply of foreign currency, the higher the value domestic currency will have and vice versa.

14. *(c)* Foreign investments are of two types, viz., one is in the direct form and another in the indirect form (i.e., in security market), both are considered capital inflows. But in the case of convertibility, the security investment part of the foreign investment is considered a matter of current account to make it liquid in which rupee is fully convertible (otherwise, no foreign investor will come to invest in the share market). Going abroad is a matter of current account, thus rupee is fully convertible for this purpose.

15. *(c)* M_3 stands for the sum of M_1 and total deposits of the banks (i.e., demand and time deposits of banks). These components of money in India were defined by the 2nd Working Group on Money Stock set up by the RBI in 1972. The 3rd Working Group on the Money Stock submitted its report to the RBI in 1998—as per it, the new components of money in India are—M_0, M_1, M_2 and M_3. Together with the new stock of money, the Working Group has suggested liquidities formula for the stock, too, namely—L_0, L_1, L_2 and L_3.

16. *(c)* Though devaluation in currencies is discouraged and negated with excessive pressure coming from the trading partners of the country, it ultimately makes goods of the country cheaper in the world market— the economy earns profit from exports. The increase in profit of export takes place due to increase in 'volume' of the exports (but in reality, exporters forego more goods to earn the same amount of foreign currency). As foreign currency becomes costlier, the country sees decrease in its imports (provided its imports are non-compulsive in nature) due to import substitution.

17. *(c)* As per the *Economic Survey 2019–20*, Vol. 2, p. 20, Ministry of Finance, GoI, N. Delhi.

18. *(d)* Though this ideal stage is reached only in hypothesis—with the changing times, consumers not only demand new goods and services, but new times come with the alternatives of it, too.

19. *(a)* Incomes of citizens get redistributed after tax—this happens at two levels: once after paying tax and once when the governments use this money to provide essential services to the population. The poorer population uses more of the government services than the richer. Option (c) is also correct but comes later in order.

20. *(b)* Being in this index does not bring any privilege to a company. The shares put here are just for representation purposes of the industry.

21. *(a)* Government never did intend to check the demand—it basically went for a set of reforms known as the 'macro-economic stabilisation measures', which attempt to boost demand in the economy. The whole process of economic reforms in the economy is all about demand and supply management.

22. *(d)* 'Ex-factory Price' and 'Ex-showroom Price' are the same. Factory price is basically the factor cost.

23. *(d)* All of the statements are correct. Such a business entity was allowed by the GoI through the Limited Liability Partnership (LLP) Act, 2008. By *May 2016*, over 36,000 such firms were operative in the country. This firm has certain legal qualities of the 'limited liability' firms with the ease of a 'proprietorship partnership' firms.

24. *(c)* Statement 2 will have contradictory/neutralising effects on the economy as savings cut demand and salary enhancement increases demand. All these measures were taken by the government during 1996–99 in India when aggregate demand in the economy had fallen down to a very low level and inflation was, at one time, just 0.5 per cent (the second fortnight of December, 1999). Tapering in the fiscal stimulus cuts demand in the economy as it syphons out liquidity from the market.

25. *(b)* Reserve Tranche (also called Gold Tranche) is made available to the member nations by the IMF which is of 25 per cent value of the Special Drawing Rights (SDRs) assigned to them by the IMF. The part of money belonging to the tranche can be withdrawn by a nation at its will without paying any charge upto one year.

SET-5

1. Select the correct equation for the Gross Value Added at the factor cost in the new method of national accounts.
   (a) CE + MI + CFC + Production Subsidies
   (b) CE + MI + CFC + Production Taxes
   (c) CE + MI + CFC + Product Taxes
   (d) CE + MI + CFC + Product Taxes

2. What is correct about 'mandatory foreign currency' hedging?
   1. Government compulsory rule for an entity to cover the risk of its foreign currency liabilities.
   2. Currency derivatives make it easier for companies to do it.

   Select the correct statements using the code given below:

   Code:
   (a) Only 1 (b) Only 2
   (c) Both 1 and 2 (d) Neither 1 nor 2

3. Consider the following statements about the concept acid test ratio..
   1. The metric is used to measure the ability of a firm to meet its short-term liabilities.
   2. This is part of the overall liquidity position of a firm.

   Select the correct answer by using the code given below:

   Code:
   (a) Only 1 (b) Only 2
   (c) Both 1 and 2 (d) Neither 1 nor 2

4. Consider the following statements.
   1. The value of total goods demanded in an economy is always identically equal to the total value of goods supplied.
   2. Statement 1 is correct in the case of modern economies only, where use of currencies is the mode of exchange, but does not hold true if it is a barter economy.

   Select the correct statement/statements using the code given below:
   (a) Only 1 (b) Only 2
   (c) Both 1 and 2 (d) None of these

5. Select the correct statement(s) about India from the *World Happiness Report 2020*, using the code given below:
   1. In comparison to the last report, India has lost four ranks.
   2. In the case of current life evaluation, Delhi is ranked 180th among the 186 cities of the world.

   Code:
   (a) Only 1 (b) Only 2
   (c) Both 1 and 2 (d) Neither 1 nor 2

6. Which among the following policy decision/decisions a government should take to promote foreign investments in the economy?
   1. Allowing full convertibility to its currency in current and capital accounts.
   2. Reducing or withdrawing the 'withholding tax'.
   3. Prohibitory laws for its nationals for overseas investments.

   Select your answer using the code given below:
   (a) 1 and 2 (b) 2 and 3
   (c) 1 and 3 (d) 1, 2 and 3

7. An economy is following the policies given below:
   1. Creating self-employment sources with high speed.
   2. Cutting its expenditures on the heads of salaries, subsidies and pension.
   3. Promoting public-private partnerships in the infrastructure sector.

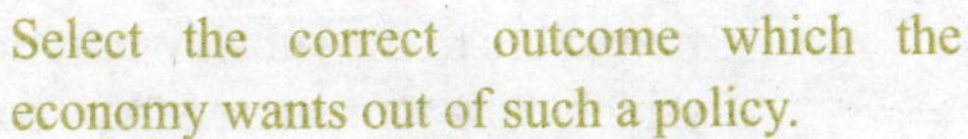

Select the correct outcome which the economy wants out of such a policy.

(a) Promoting revenue expenditure at the cost of capital expenditures.
(b) Cutting revenue expenditures to promote capital expenditure.
(c) Promoting development expenditures without risking welfare.
(d) Both (b) and (c)

8. Select the correct statement about 'zero-coupon bond' from the following.

(a) A bond with zero coupon rate which is sold at a price lower than its face value and investors get face value price at maturity.
(b) A bond with zero rate of interest but of the highest value of liquidity for which investors get other concessions like tax breaks.
(c) A special category of bond used as 'express money' to finance immediate needs of the economy which carries zero interest but gives tax credits to investors in their income tax returns.
(d) A kind of bond which is generally issued by governments in the times of financial crises to the high income group citizens, which carries no interest but investors get tax concessions for investing in it.

9. Which of the fol lowing action (s) contribute to wealth creation in an economy? Select your answer by using the code given below:

1. Listing a firm on the stock exchange
2. Conversion of a limited stock company into a private limited firm
3. Disinvestment of the central public sector enterprises (CPSEs)

Code:

(a) 1 and 2 (b) 2 and 3
(c) 1 and 3 (d) 1, 2 and 3

10. Select the correct statement(s) about corporate borrowings in the economy by using the code given below:

1. Most of corporate borrowings are secured.
2. Pledging of shares as secondary security for loans is very weak in design.

Code:

(a) Only 1 (b) Only 2
(c) Both 1 and 2 (d) Neither 1 nor 2

11. External commercial borrow ings (EEC Bs) have been made much easier by the RBI in recent times. Select your answer using the code given below:

1. Public sector oil marketing companies can borrow upto US$ 10 billion every year as their working capital under automatic route provided the loan has a maturity period of minimum 3 years.
2. Sector-wise cap on ECBs has been abolished now.

Code:

(a) Only 1 (b) Only 2
(c) Both 1 and 2 (d) Neither 1 nor 2

12. Select the correct components of the 'mission mode interventions' launched by the Government in the health care sector, using the code given below:

1. It deals with maternal, child, communicable and non-communicable diseases.
2. Its central idea is addressing the ongoing transition from communicable to non-communicable diseases in the country.

Code:

(a) Only 1 (b) Only 2
(c) Both 1 and 2 (d) Neither 1 nor 2

13. Consider the following statements about the process of issuing shares through 'private placement'.

1. This is one among three routes through which a company raises capital in the primary market by issuing shares.
2. Companies directly negotiate with the investors which may be financial institutions as well as individuals.
3. This is completely opposite to the public issue route to issue shares.

Select the correct statements using the code given below:

(a) 1 and 2 (b) 2 and 3
(c) 1 and 3 (d) 1, 2 and 3

14. Consider the following statements and select the incorrect one (s) among them using the code given be low:
    1. Banks maintaining a minimum reserve cash ratio in order to mobilise adequate liquidity to meet the customer's cash demands in their day-to-day business is known as 'fractional banking'.
    2. The Cash Reserve Ratio provision in India for the banks is a part of the 'fractional banking'.

Code:

(a) Only 1 (b) Only 2
(c) Both 1 and 2 (d) Neither 1 nor 2

15. Consider the following statements.
    1. 'Trade creation' has taken place in India via the provisions of the WTO.
    2. Growth stories of the industrialised economies were the outcome of follow-up to 'creative destruction'.
    3. 'Trade creation' may be led by 'creative destructions'.

Select the correct statements using the code given below:

(a) 1 and 2 (b) 2 and 3
(c) 1 and 3 (d) 1, 2 and 3

16. What is correct about the term 'transfer payments' which was in news recently?
    (a) The payments which take place indirectly from the high bracket direct taxpayers to the subsidy-based sectors which are consumed by someone else.
    (b) The expenditure by government for which it receives no goods or services, such as tax collection, unemployment allowance, etc.
    (c) The minimum return an asset must earn to prevent its transfer to the next best alternative use.
    (d) Tax is a mode of income redistribution through which payments get transferred from high to low income group directly and indirectly, both ways.

17. Which of the following statements is a correct description of the *Manodarpan*?
    (a) An initiative to enhance tax compliance through rewarding the honest tax payers.
    (b) A psychological support initiative in education sector.
    (c) A role model created to encourage sense of sanitation among the citizens.
    (d) An initiative of AYUSH to promote natural living.

18. Which of the following statements is correct about the external concessional loans India gets as Official Development Assistance?
    (a) Only central government can use them.
    (b) Both Centre and the States can use such loans.
    (c) Such loans can be used by Centre, States as well as the private sector.
    (d) They can be used in only social sector.

19. Select the correct statement about the 'unemployment trap'.
    (a) A situation in the economy when the rate of employment growth is less than the rate of increase in the unemployed population.

(b) A situation of frictional unemployment when there is a heavy rush of labour force from the primary to the secondary activities.

(c) A situation when existing job loss is higher than the new jobs created.

(d) A situation when unemployed population of an economy does not feel encouraged to become employed.

20. Consider the following statements.

1. The risk of a government defaulting on overseas loan is known as sovereign risk.
2. All kinds of overseas borrowings by private companies also carry the burden of sovereign risk.
3. A member nation may insure its sovereign risk with the World Bank arm known as Multi-Lateral Insurance Guarantee Agency.

Select the correct statements using the code given below:

Code:

(a) 1 and 2 (b) 2 and 3
(c) 1 and 3 (d) 1, 2 and 3

21. Select the correct statements regarding India's present composition of the external debt, using the code given below:

1. Concessional part is around 9 per cent.
2. Forex reserves provide around 82.5 per cent cover to it.
3. Long-term part of the debt is around 80 per cent.

Code:

(a) Only 1 (b) Only 3
(c) 2 and 3 (d) 1, 2 and 3

22. Consider the following statements.

1. Expenditures done on advertisement, research and development are known as 'essential costs'.
2. The costs which are borne on account of salaries, fringe benefits, pensions and provident funds are known as 'sunk cost'.

Select the incorrect statement/statements using the code given below:

(a) Only 1 (b) Only 2
(c) Both 1 and 2 (d) None of these

23. Consider the following statements

1. 'Product swap' functions just opposite to the system of barter.
2. 'Currency swap' is a mode of hedging against exchange rate fluctuations.
3. 'Subsidy swap' is a method of cross-subsidising two products.

Select the correct statementusing the code given below:

(a) 1 and 2 (b) Only 2
(c) 2 and 3 (d) Only 3

24. Consider the following statements.

1. 'Market cost' is 'factory price' added with all the indirect taxes.
2. 'Market cost' and 'ex-factory price' are different things.
3. 'Maximum retail price' and 'market cost' are the same things.

Select the correct statement/statements using the code given below:

(a) Only 1 (b) 1 and 2
(c) Only 3 (d) 1 and 3

25. Select the correct statement/s about the concept 'primary surplus' which is related to government budgeting using the code given below:

1. A situation when the tax receipts of government are higher than its total expenditures in a year.
2. Interest payment liabilities of the governments are part of it.

Code:

(a) Only 1 (b) Only 2
(c) Both 1 and 2 (d) Neither 1 nor 2

ANSWER KEY WITH EXPLANATIONS

1. *(a)* When 'production taxes' are added to it (less 'production subsidies'), we get the value of GVA at Basic Prices.

2. *(c)* This way, the risk involved with the re-payment of foreign currency loans is minimised.

3. *(c)* The Acid Test Ratio refers to a financial metric that is used to measure the ability of a firm to meet its various short-term obligations. It is calculated by dividing the sum of a firm's most liquid assets (like cash and short-term receivables) by its short-term liabilities. Other short-term assets like inventory, which are not readily convertible into cash, are usually not included in the calculation of this ratio. Financial analysts use it to measure a firm's liquidity position.

4. *(a)* This is known as the *'Walras's Law'* which is correct only in the case of a barter economy. This is so because the economies which have currency as a mode of exchange, currency supplies depend on so many factors and not on the level of the goods and services produced in the economy. The best example is shown by the instances of inflation.

5. *(c)* In the latest *World Happiness Report 2020*, India is ranked 144th (its rank was 140th in the report of 2019). Delhi's rank remains among the 6 lowest cities in the world in the case of 'future life evaluation' also.

6. *(a)* The 3rd statement is neutral to the issue of attracting foreign investment and its promotion. Once the domestic currency becomes fully convertible in the capital account, such prohibitory laws are not possible—that is why India is believed to not allowing such convertibility at the full scale—as the economy does not want foreign exchange taking flight from the economy (since it is itself trying to attract it).

7. *(b)* The Government of India also wants to do the same but its subsidy rationalising programmes have not taken place on the expected lines.

8. *(a)* G-Secs are issued by the GoI through this route, too.

9. *(c)* Here, wealth creation means more income and growth creation. By listing a firm on stock exchange and disinvesting the CPSEs, a greater number of people get chance to share the profits of these firms. But, on the other hand, the size of ownership shrinks when a public limited firm converts into a private limited firm.

10. *(c)* The practice of allowing corporates to pledge shares of the same company to borrow is weak in design due to two reasons—firstly, the pledged shares do not corelate properly to the project's value and secondly, in this case promoters bear no liability beyond their pledged shares.

11. *(c)* By late February 2019, RBI took several steps to liberalise the ECB norms. Now all entities eligible to receive foreign direct investment (FDI) can borrow upto US$ 750 million per annum under automatic route without any sectoral cap/limit.

12. *(c)* The *Mission Mode Interventions* is the fourth pillar of the Government approach to health care under the National Health Policy 2017 (the other three being—preventive healthcare, providing affordable healthcare, and building medical infrastructure).

13. *(d)* In a 'public issue' the company does not negotiate directly with the public who want to purchase the shares.

14. *(c)* In 'fractional banking' the reserve/ liquidity is maintained by the bank but not in cash form but it may be in non-cash form (assets), too. The Statutory Liquidity Ratio (SLR) of the Indian banks is the part of such banking.

15. *(d)* The increase in international trade which results from the elimination or reduction of trade barriers (such as quota, customs, surcharge, etc.) is 'trade creation'. Innovation is known as 'creative destruction' (the term was coined by the Australian economist J. Schumpeter).

16. *(b)* All loss-making activities done by the government under the head of social sector come under it—poverty alleviation, healthcare, education, social security, etc.

17. *(b)* The Manodarpan is an initiative for psychosocial support launched under the Atmanirbhar Bharat Abhiyan to strengthen and empower the human capital in the education sector.

18. *(b)* Private sector cannot avail its use. There is no sectoral compulsion though the areas are outlined before the loan is availed.

19. *(d)* This is another term for 'poverty trap'. Such a situation arises in an economy where there are provisions of unemployment allowance—disposable income (income after paying direct taxes) becomes less than the allowance they get.

20. *(a)* World Bank arm, MIGA, provides insurance services, but to the companies which go for foreign direct investment; it covers non-commercial risk.

21. *(d)* As per the *RBI, December 2019*, India's external debt was US$ 557.4 billion by end-September 2018, while its forex reserve was US$ 461.2 billion.

22. *(c)* The expenditures on the items discussed in Statement 1 are 'sink costs'. There is nothing like 'essential costs' in business economics.

23. *(b)* 'Product swap' is similar to barter while there is nothing like 'subsidy swap' in public finance management.

24. *(a)* 'Market Cost' and 'ex-factory price' are same things. 'Market cost' added with the traders margins and effect of the current inflation is 'maximum retail price' (MRP).

25. *(d)* This is a situation in government budgeting process when the tax receipts of government are higher than its total expenditures excluding interest payments. This concept is being used in India since 1997–98 as an indicator to understand the fiscal health in a better way.

SET-6

1. Select the correct statement (s) about the new index the *Planetary Pressures-Adjusted Human Development* Index launched recently by the UN DP, using the code given below :
   1. It is human development adjusted by carbon dioxide emissions per person.
   2. Norway's rank on human Development Index falls by 15 ranks on it.

   Code:
   (a) Only 1 *(b)* Only 2
   (c) Both 1 and 2 *(d)* Neither 1 nor 2

2. Select the items which India shows in its current account, using the code given below:
   1. Inflows due to exports and outflows due to imports

2. Inflows and outflows due to income repatriation
3. Inflows and outflows due to foreign portfolio investment
4. External lending and borrowings

Code:

(*a*) 1 and 2 (*b*) 2 and 3
(*c*) 3 and 4 (*d*) 2 and 4

3. Select the correct statement (s) related to India from the latest *Human Development Report* 2020 by using the code given below :
   1. India's rank has fallen by 3 ranks from the last year's report.
   2. India's value on the *Inequality-adjusted HDI* (IHDI) has fallen by around 11 per cent in the report.

   Code:

   (*a*) Only 1 (*b*) Only 2
   (*c*) Both 1 and 2 (*d*) Neither 1 nor 2

4. Amalgamation of the public sector banks are aimed at multiple gains. Select the correct gains using the code given below:
   1. Economies of scale
   2. Improved access to capital
   3. Covering larger geographical areas
   4. Banks of global size

   Code:

   (*a*) 1 and 2 (*b*) 2 and 3
   (*c*) 1, 2 and 4 (*d*) 1, 2, 3 and 4

5. Consider the following statements.
   1. 'Liquidity trap' is a situation when people prefer to hold money rather than invest it.
   2. 'Liquidity preference' is the situation when people prefer to invest money rather than hold it.
   3. 'Liquidity crunch' is a situation of short-supply of money in the money market.
   4. 'Credit crunch' is a situation of short-supply of money in the loan market.

   Select the correct statements using the code given below :

   (*a*) 1, 2 and 3 (*b*) 2, 3 and 4
   (*c*) 1, 2 and 4 (*d*) 1, 3 and 4

6. Consider the fol lowing statements about the 'Lorenz curve'.
   1. A straight line on it represents complete equality of income.
   2. With greater curvature in it, inequality of income rises proportionally—this inequality is measured by the 'Gini Coefficient'.

   Select the incorrect statement using the code given below :

   (*a*) Only 1 (*b*) Only 2
   (*c*) Both 1 and 2 (*d*) Neither 1 nor 2

7. What does the term 'Ninja' mean which became a common word in the financial world after the US sub-prime crisis?
   (*a*) A loan given on false claims of credit-worthiness by the banks.
   (*b*) Borrower with no assets, no income or no job.
   (*c*) Highly competitive form of lending, compromising the financial funda-mentals.
   (*d*) A loan given to someone who is on the brink of bankruptcy.

8. Select the correct effect of fal l in the rate of inflation.
   (*a*) Government's interest payment liabilities increase.
   (*b*) Interest income on saving bank accounts goes down.
   (*c*) Lending and bank business grows.
   (*d*) Bondholders' incomes decrease.

9. Select the correct global agency/report from which the fol lowing has been quoted.
   "To fight poverty, one needs to know where poor people live as they are not evenly

spread across a country, not even within a household."

(a) Global Climate Risk Index 2020
(b) Human Development Report 2019
(c) World Happiness Report 2020
(d) Global Multidimensional Poverty Index 2020

10. Consider the following statements about the 'penny stocks'.
   1. The shares listed on a stock exchange which show high market capitalisation with relatively low volume of shares.
   2. The shares which are issued at a par value of rupee one.
   3. Their trading price shows high volatility.

   Select the incorrect statements using the code given below :
   (a) 1 and 2 (b) 2 and 3
   (c) 1 and 3 (d) 1, 2 and 3

11. Consider the following statements about a 'preference share' in India.
   1. These shares bear a stated dividend.
   2. They get priority over equity shares.
   3. Such shares can be issued for a period of less than 1 year.

   Select the correct statements using the code given below:
   (a) 1 and 2 (b) 2 and 3
   (c) 1 and 3 (d) 1, 2 and 3

12. Which of the following defines an economy in the situation of a 'population trap'?
   (a) When the population control policies of the economy almost fail and it goes for a situation of population boom.
   (b) When the population of an economy starts increasing after achieving the stage of 'replacement level'.
   (c) When the 'natural rate of increase' in an economy starts falling drastically below the 'replacement level'.
   (d) None of the above

13. Consider the following statements.
   1. A situation when people think that they are getting richer during the times of inflation is known as 'money illusion'.
   2. It is believed that lower levels of 'money illusion' are beneficial to 'grease the wheels' of the economy.

   Select the correct statement using the code given below:

   Code:
   (a) Only 1 (b) Only 2
   (c) Both 1 and 2 (d) Neither 1 nor 2

14. Which one of the following decisions follow the idea of 'prisoner's dilemma'?
   1. Companies fixing prices of their products at the levels less than they could in the trust that other companies do not fix lower prices.
   2. The dilemma, ultimately, hampers the companies which fix the higher prices.

   Select the answer using the code given below :

   Code:
   (a) Only 1 (b) Only 2
   (c) Both 1 and 2 (d) Neither 1 nor 2

15. Recently, India shifted to a new method for measuring its national income. The new method classifies taxes into 'product' and 'production'. Select the correct statements using the code given below:
   1. Both of the taxes are imposed on the producers.
   2. While product taxes are variable, the production taxes are fixed.
   3. Land revenue, profession tax, stamps and registration fees are some of the examples of production taxes in India.
   4. Sales tax, excise duty, service tax, export and import taxes are the examples of product taxes in India.

Code:

(a) 1 and 2 (b) 1, 2 and 3

(c) 2, 3 and 4 (d) 1, 2, 3 and 4

16. Select the correct situation which defines 'poverty trap'.
 (a) When the population in an economy continues to remain poor even after increase in its 'nominal income'.
 (b) When the rise in income of the poor people is equitably neutralised by inflation.
 (c) When unemployment rate starts increasing together with the inflation.
 (d) When unemployed population getting unemployment allowance does not feel encouraged to become employed.

17. Select the correct statement/s by using the code given below:
 1. Setting up new PSUs goes against the spirit of the economic reforms.
 2. Process of disinvestment may not lead to de-nationalisation.

 Code:

 (a) Only 1 (b) Only 2

 (c) Both 1 and 2 (d) None of these

18. Select the correct statement(s) taken from the new *Labour Force Participation Survey* evolved by the Government, using the code given below :
 1. Labour force includes both those who are in workforce and those who are unemployed.
 2. Worker population ratio (WPR) is the proportion of employed persons to the total population.
 3. Labour force participation rate is the proportion of population in the labour force to the total population.

 Code:

 (a) 1 and 2 (b) 2 and 3

 (c) 1 and 2 (d) 1, 2 and 3

19. Select the correct statement (s) related to India's *social sector spending* of 2020- 21, using the code given below:
 1. General Government exp.....iture on it fell down steeply to 5.3 per cent of the GDP due to economic disruption caused by the COVID-19 pandemic.
 2. General Government expenditure on health more than doubled in the year in comparison to the previous year, on account of the COVID-19 pandemic.

 Code:

 (a) Only 1

 (b) Only 2

 (c) Both 1 and 2

 (d) Neither 1 nor 2

20. Consider the following statements (s) about the concept *Interest Coverage Ratio* of a firm.
 1. Lending institutions evaluate the risk in lending to a new company.
 2. It is used by the lending firm to evaluate the emerging risk of a borrowing firm.
 3. Higher the interest coverage ratio of a company, safer the loan is considered by the lending institutions to it.

 Select the correct answer using the code given below :

 (a) 1 and 2 only

 (b) 2 only

 (c) 1 and 3 only

 (d) 1, 2 and 3

21. 'Bad' money forces 'good' money out of circulation proposes the Gresham 's Law.
 1. It analyses the circulation of 'black' money in the Indian economy—usually getting deposited in the tax havens through hawala route.
 2. The Chinese currency Yuan headed to replace the dominance of the US dollar in the world foreign exchange market.

In light of the law, select the incorrect statement given above using the code given below:

(a) Only 1 (b) Only 2
(c) Both 1 and 2 (d) Neither 1 nor 2

22. Select the correct statement (s) related to the *Gig economy,* using the code given below:
   1. Employment type in it is normally temporary or contractual in nature.
   2. Flexi-staffing is a kind of norm in it.
   3. Labour contract is usually shorter and more specific to the job.

   Code:
   (a) 1 and 2 (b) 2 and 3
   (c) 1 and 3 (d) 1, 2 and 3

23. Consider the following statements about 'earth tri lemma'.
   1. For economic development, the world needs increased energy expenditure but this raises the environmental issues.
   2. The 'EEE' trilemma is synonymous to it.
   3. Without limiting the levels of consumption, earth as a system, cannot sustain.
   4. Three issues need attention to sustain the earth—low consumption, high saving and an attitude of conservation.

   Select the correct statements using the code given below :
   (a) 1 and 2 (b) 3 and 4
   (c) 1 and 4 (d) 1 and 3

24. Which of the following is correct about the 'impossible trinity'?
   (a) A country cannot maintain all three policy goals–stable financial market, global integration and stable exchange rate.
   (b) A country cannot maintain all three policy goals–free capital flows, a fixed exchange rate and an independent monetary policy.
   (c) A country cannot maintain all three policy goals–stable exchange rate, global integration and continuous economic growth.
   (d) A country cannot maintain all three policy goals–small fiscal deficits, social welfare and high economic growth.

25. Select the correct statement regarding the process of 'disinflation'.
   (a) Prices fall towards the upper limit of the healthy range of the headline inflation
   (b) Price levels fall below the lower limit of the healthy range of inflation.
   (c) Retail inflation index falls down to single digit.
   (d) It is similar to deflation.

ANSWER KEY WITH EXPLANATIONS

1. (c) The PHDI (Planetary Pressures-Adjusted Human Development Index) basically discounts the per capita material footprint to account for the excessive human pressure on the planet, from a country's rank on the HDI (Human Development Index).
2. (a) Foreign portfolio investments and loans are part of the capital account.
3. (a) India is ranked 131st on the Human Development Index (HDI) in the HDR 2020. India's *Inequality-adjusted HDI* (IHDI) value fell by 26.4 per cent to reach 0.475 (its value on Human Development Index is 0.645) as per the HDR-2020.
4. (d) All of the statements are correct about the ongoing process of amalgamation of the public sector bank.
5. (c) 'Liquidity trap' and 'liquidity preference' are used synonymously. Liquidity crunch is short-supply of money in the money as well as capital market.

6. *(d)* The 'Lorenz Curve' is a graphical representation of wealth distribution (US economist Max Lorenz, 1905) in which a straight diagonal line represents perfect equality of wealth distribution—the Lorenz curve lies beneath it, showing the reality of wealth distribution. The difference between the straight line and the curved line is the amount of inequality of wealth distribution, a figure described by the Gini coefficient. The curve is used to show what percentage of a nation's residents possess what percentage of that nation's wealth.

   'Gini Coefficient' (developed by the Italian Statistian and Sociologist, 1912) measures the inequality in income in an economy (also known as the Gini index or Gini ratio). This is a measure of statistical dispersion intended to represent the income distribution of a nation's residents. This measures the inequality among values of a frequency distribution (for example levels of income)—a Gini coefficient of zero expresses perfect equality, where all values are the same (for example, where everyone has the same income) while a Gini coefficient of one (i.e., 100 per cent) expresses maximal inequality among values (for example, where only one person has all the income). However, a value greater than one may occur if some persons represent negative contribution to the total (e.g., have negative income or wealth). For larger groups, values close to or above 1 are very unlikely in practice. This is commonly used as a measure of inequality of income or wealth.

7. *(b)* Banks require the borrower to show a stable income source or sufficient collateral, a 'ninja loan' ignores the verification process. A ninja loan is often found in the mortgage market. In such loans, generally, interest rate initially remains lower and is increased later. Such borrowers hope to pay their loan once their property appreciates. But in case the property doesn't appreciate, many borrowers default repayments. This is why such loans are very risky for lenders.

8. *(a)* Due to fall in inflation, 'real cost of borrowing' increases which makes Government's loan payment costly. Other statements are written just their opposite.

9. *(d)* The report said that the traditional concept of poverty is outdated which used to label countries or even households as rich and poor—as it is an oversimplification. Poverty varies inside a family also. *Global Multidimensional Poverty Index* is jointly published by the United Nations Development Programme (UNDP) and Oxford Poverty and Human Development Initiative (OPHI).

10. *(d)* They are low-priced shares of small companies with very low market capitalisation. They were in news recently as some of such shares did show high rise in their trading prices on the security bourses.

11. *(a)* Such shares may get dividend even if the company has gone in loss and they are issued for a period upto 10 yrs.

12. *(d)* This is a situation of population growth rate (i.e., natural rate of increase) greater than the achievable growth rate in the economy.

13. *(c)* The phrase was coined by the economist J.M. Keynes.

14. *(a)* This is a famous example in the 'game theory' which concludes that why co-operation is difficult to achieve even if it

is mutually beneficial, ultimately making things worse for the parties involved.

15. *(d)* All of the statements are correct. While the product taxes are imposed on the producers, they are ultimately paid by the consumers of the goods and services—these taxes are linked to the production volumes of the producers (so they are variable). Production taxes are paid by producers are not linked to the volume of their productions. That is why they are 'fixed cost' of production.

16. *(d)* Such situations occur since the after tax income (i.e., disposable income) turns out to be less than the benefit of the unemployment allowance.

17. *(b)* Setting up a new PSU is not antagonistic to the process of reform. After the 'Comprehensive Management of Public Assets' started in February 2016, the orientation towards the PSUs has also gone for a change.

18. *(d)* In 2017–18, the Government launched a new regular employment-unemployment survey namely, 'annual' *Periodic Labour Force Survey-2017–18* with certain changes in survey methodology, data collection mechanism and sampling design vis-à-vis the earlier quinquennial (once in every five years) Employment and Unemployment Surveys (EUS) of NSO (National Statistics Office).

19. *(d)* General Government (Centre+States) expenditure on social sector is estimated to be 8.8 per cent of the GDP in 2020–21 (up from 7.5 per cent of 2019–20), while on health it reached 3.5 per cent of GDP (up from 3.0 per cent of the previous year).

20. *(d)* Interest cover ratio is used by lenders to determine a borrower's (i.e., a company) capability to service its loan. It is calculated by dividing a company's *earnings before interest and taxes* (EBIT) during a given period by the company's interest payments due within the same period.

21. *(c)* The Law proposed by Sir Thomas Gresham (an advisor to Queen Elizabeth—I of England) does not deal with 'black', 'white' or any weakening world currency, nor it is correct in the case of paper currencies. The law is correct once metallic currencies are in circulation which have proportional intrinsic value—such currencies are hoarded (as in the case of price rise).

22. *(d)* It is the economy of digital platform (such as e-commerce platforms, Swiggy, Ola etc.). India has emerged among the largest markets in the world in Gig economy, the rise especially happened faster during the COVID-19 induced lockdowns and restrictions on the movement of the people.

23. *(a)* The 'EEE' trilemma is also known as the 'Earth Trilemma' which says that for economic development, mankind needs to increase energy consumption but this accelerates environmental degradation. In a sense, energy model needs re-thinking.

24. *(b)* This remains the prima donna of all 'trilemmas' articulated by the economists. This is also known as 'Mundell's Impossible Trinity' which has strong theoretical foundations in the Mundell-Fleming Model developed in the 1960s.

25. *(a)* For example, in the case of India, retail price index falling towards 6 per cent (that is the upper limit of India's healthy range of inflation) from above 6 per cent levels (such as 7 or 8).

SELECTED MODEL ANSWERS*

*Reading maketh a full man; conference a ready man; and writing an exact man.***

Q.1 Write a short note on the environmental, social and governance (ESG) criteria of investment and development regarding it in the case of India.

Ans. In the last few years, a new concept for investing in the listed companies has emerged in some western stock markets—known as the environmental, social and governance (ESG) criteria. The concept which is also known by its other name, *impact investing,* explores the following aspects of the company:

1. Environmental criteria look into its approach towards the nature (energy use, pollution, waste disposal, conservation, treatment of animals, etc.).
2. Social criteria examine its relations with employees, suppliers, customers, privacy, data protection and the communities where it operates.
3. Governance deals with its leadership, executive pay, audits, internal controls, and rights of shareholders.

The value-laden criteria of ESG are being increasingly (especially in western countries) analysed and screened by the 'socially conscious investors' before making their investment decisions. These criteria help investors find companies with values that match their own. Such investments, in a sense, make investors believe that they are able to avoid and discourage the companies whose practices signal risk factors (as seen in the cases— the 2010 oil spill of BP and 2015 emission scandal of Volkswagen—share prices of both falling by over 10 per cent as investors' backlash).

As business practices are getting more conscious of these criteria, investment firms are increasingly tracking their

* *The answers given to some of the questions may be comprehensive. Readers are suggested to cut it short as per the requirement of the question. Questions in the civil services examination are generally asked in parts, i.e., budgetary measures, monetary measures, administrative measures, etc.*

** *Francis Bacon (1561-1626), 'Of Studies'* ***Essays,*** *London, UK, 1625.*

performance— in 2020, financial services companies such as *JPMorgan Chase, Wells Fargo,* and *Goldman Sachs* published their annual reports in which extensive review was given in this regard.

In India, as per the SEBI, the focus on it has further increased— in line with global trend, investors in India also did show increased interest in ESG investment during 2020–21. As a consequence of this, the regulator in April 2021 committed to announce relevant ESG guidelines soon. As per the experts, given India's high commitment to the Paris Climate pact, this becomes even more valid for the country.

Q.2 Briefly discuss the measu res taken by the Government to check inflation in 2020-21.

Ans. By June 2020, an increase was seen in the food prices led especially by pulses, onion and potato— rising over 10 per cent across the board. In the wake of rising prices, the Government took several steps to improve the availability of these commodities and make them available to consumers at affordable prices, such as:

1. Banning the export of onion September 2020 – December 2020).
2. Imposition of stock limit on onion under the Essential Commodities Act (October 2020 – December 2020).
3. Easing of restrictions on imports, facilitating imports at integrated check-posts, issuance of licenses for imports and reduction in import duties.

Some other measures taken by the Government in this regard were:

1. Price Stabilisation Fund (PSF) Scheme has succeeded in achieving its objective of stabilising the prices of pulses.
2. Use of pulses from the central buffer for uses in PDS distribution, Mid-day Meal Schemech and in ICDS Scheme, PM Garib Kalyan Yojana and AtmaNirbhar Bharat package (aimed at giving relief to the poor people hit with *COVID-19 pandemic*) besides supplies to Army and Central Para-Military Forces.
3. The creation of buffer stock of pulses has helped in moderating the prices of pulses.
4. States and UTs are also being encouraged to set up their own PSF.
5. MoU signed with Mozambique to ensure assured supply of pulses during 2020–21 (2 lakh tons).
6. Maintaining buffer stocks of onion under PSF for making appropriate price stabilising market interventions.

These measures resulted in increased imports of onion, tur and masur dal in the country and resulted in cooling of prices by October 2020.

Q.3 Write a short note on the newly launched scheme, the *One District One Product* and discuss its main features.

Ans. The Prime Minister-Formalisation of Micro Food Processing Enterprises (PM-FME) was launched by late 2020–21 (under the Atmanirbhar Bharat Abhiyan) as a Centrally Sponsored Scheme for the period 2020–25. *One District One Product* (ODOP) approach is to be adopted under it to reap the 'benefit of scale' in terms of procurement of inputs, availing common services and marketing of products. States identify 'one food product per district' keeping in view the existing clusters and availability of raw material under it. The scheme also places focus on *waste to* *wealth* products, minor forest products and *Aspirational Districts* (112 most backward districts of the country have been identified by the Niti Aayog as Aspirational Districts). The existing micro food processing units are to get the following supports under it:

- Credit-linked capital subsidy (35 per cent of the project cost with a maximum of ₹ 10 lakh) to be given to the units led by individuals, FPOs (Farmers Producer Organisations), producer cooperatives and SHGs (Self Help Groups).
- Credit-linked grant (35 per cent of the project cost) for the development of common infrastructure including common processing facility, lab, warehouse, cold storage, packaging and incubation centre through FPOs/SHGs/ cooperatives or state-owned agencies or private enterprise for use by micro units in the cluster.
- SHGs to get seed capital (₹ 40,000) for working capital and purchase of small tools.
- 50 per cent grant for branding and marketing.

The scheme has picked popularity very fast and by *April 2021,* a total of 35 States/UT had identified hundreds of food products under it.

Q.4 'We see a complete change in paradigm in the Government 's policy towards the public sector enterprises.' Comment.

Ans. The policy of the Government towards the public sector enterprises (PSEs) went for paradigm shift in November 2020— which goes beyond the policies of past which were import substitution and self-sufficiency (the ideas on which the Mahalanobis Plan of 1956 was based). Though, after 1991, the enterprises saw their disinvestment and privatisation starting given their inherent inefficiencies, leading to low productivity. By now, several measures have been taken to reduce Government's presence in commercial activities— this 'policy to withdraw' has been a subject of discussion in several volumes of the *Economic Surveys* (which shows the deep deliberations on the issue).

Under the *Atmanirbhar Bharat Mission,* the government has proposed to *rationalise* the participation of the CPSEs in commercial activities with their presence limited only in the 'strategic sectors'— numbers cut down to only ***four***— others to be either merged or privatised or brought under the holding companies. The enterprises of 'non-strategic sectors' would be privatised. This initiative is expected to bring healthy competition in sectors and will also assist the Government to focus extensively on 'strategic sectors.' In order that the retained enterprises are able to meet the expectations of the Government, certain other reforms have also been suggested by the *Economic Survey 2020-21* such as:

1. Revamping their Boards and structure
2. Enhancing operational autonomy of their Boards coupled with strong norms of corporate governance
3. Listing on stock exchange for greater transparency

Besides disinvestment and rationalisation, certain separate steps have also been taken by the Government in the case of the PSEs in recent times— revamping of 'performance monitoring system' to make it more objective and forward-looking (based on sectoral indices and benchmarks); timely closure of sick and loss-making enterprises; and disposal of their assets being the major ones.

Q.5 Discuss India's stance towards globalisation and multilateralism in the backdrop of recently launched *Atmanirbhar Baharat Abhiyan.*

Ans. In the wake of the ongoing COVID-19 pandemic, we saw a very emphatic call coming from the Government towards self-reliance and the *Atmanirbhar Bharat Abhiyan* launched in May 2020 for the cause. It was not for the first time that India gave such a call. Self-reliance has been among the six major objectives of planning in India since independence itself. But the time when this call has been given by the Government, makes the world think this move in the colour of rising 'protectionism' in the country. This makes global investors and governments feel as if India will take a back seat in the case of promoting the cause of multilateralism and globalisation. But that is not the case, and the latest push by India for self-reliance needs to be understood in a new light.

- This campaign is India's attempt to mend her rising trade deficits with China.
- In the wake of *COVID-19 pandemic*, some big major multinational companies are exploring the possibilities to relocate their production centres away from China – India is busy attracting them with the help of her 'Make in India', 'Assemble in India' and 'self-reliance' push (as India is not against foreign investment; rather, she supports it with one of the most competitive policy frameworks in the region). In the traditional sense, self-reliance means no foreign investment.
- Global economic order is going through a process of churning due to increasing Sino-US trade tensions and rising protectionism across the developed world – and India wishes to occupy a favourable place for herself in the emerging global economic order.
- Given the challenges of unemployment, demography and surplus agricultural production, India is wilful of restructuring its trade and role at the global scale.
- India remains still committed to the cause of multilateralism and this is the reason she is considered among the staunchest votary of globalisation and WTO – India remains actively engaged in negotiating its free and preferential trade agreements.

Thus, India's emphasis on self-reliance is not antagonistic to either globalisation or multilateralism; rather, it is a way to protect her own socio-economic interest like any other country.

Q.6 'By dovetailing Assemble in India into the Make in India scheme, India can garner unprecedented economic gains.' Comment.

Ans. India faces numerous challenges such as high incidence of poverty, under-nutrition, drinking water and lack of health care, to name a few of them. To take care of these concerns, India needs high growth together with faster job creation. Given the economic potential of the domestic economy, India needs to tap the global market for this. At present, global trade is faced with some typical issues such as—increased trade tension between USA and China, increasing protectionism among several western economies (which may not be as bad as it is for China), the MNCs exploring an alternative to shift their China-based production centres (due to increasing labour cost in China, mainly), India's improving ease of doing business, etc.

The current global environment presents India an 'unprecedented' opportunity to chart a China-like, labour-intensive, export trajectory and thereby create unparalleled job opportunities. As per the *Economic Survey 2019–20,* for this India needs to integrate 'Assemble in India' for the world into 'Make in India'. By doing so, India can garner the following benefits:

- By doing so, there is a possibility for India to raise its export market share (in the world exports) to about 3.5 per cent by 2025 and 6 per cent by 2030.
- This will create 4 crore well-paid jobs by 2025 and 8 crores by 2030. Other than suggesting to make India's trade policy as an enabler, the Survey has articulated a clear-headed strategy to grab this opportunity.
- A boost to Make in India may not only enhance exports but replace imports of products in which India has sufficient scope for expansion in domestic manufacturing.

Q.7 Write a note on India's recent efforts related to trade facilitation as its commitment to the World Trade Organisation.

Ans. The Trade Facilitation Agreement (TFA), negotiated at the WTO, came into force in February 2017. The agreement is aimed at reducing trade barriers caused by inefficient and overly burdensome regulatory administrative procedures. In the process of complying to the agreement, India in August 2016 did set up a National Committee on Trade Facilitation (NCTF). Further a National Trade Facilitation Action Plan (NTFAP) for 2017-2020 containing specific activities to further ease out the bottlenecks to trade was prepared.

For the period 2020 to 2023, a new NTFAP is under preparation, to take additional reforms to bolster trade facilitation efforts and transform the cross-border clearance eco-system through efficient, transparent, risk based, coordinated, digital, seamless and technology driven procedures. India has been making proactive strides in TFA implementation under the guidance of NCTF. Many of the commitments, as per the *Economic Survey 2020-21,* which are otherwise due by 2022, have already been notified to WTO as implemented such as:

- Single Window and Risk Management for clearance of goods were put in place.
- Transparency notifications covering information on import and export procedures, enquiry points, single windows etc., were also set up in April, 2019.
- Various regulatory relaxation measures were extended for facilitating trade during COVID-19, which include—24x7 clearance; dedicated single window; condonation of delay in filing import declarations; waiver of late filing fees; undertakings instead of bond; being the major ones.

Increased emphasis of India on transparency, openness, predictability and automation in trade reflect India's high commitment towards facilitation of trade.

Q.8 Write a note on the current situation of monetary transmission in the country.

Ans. Monetary policy plays a very vital role in the allocation of funds from the financial system. For this, lending rates decided by the banks must be sensitive to the policy rates (i.e., repo, reverse repo, MSF and bank rate) announced by the central bank—known as 'monetary transmission'. But in recent years, a healthy monetary transmission has been lacking in the system. Since 2015–16 itself, the RBI has been concerned about a general lack of monetary transmission in the financial system. Till *April 2021*, steps like enforcing the MCLR and external benchmarks on banks for deciding their lending rates, have been taken by the RBI.

As per the RBI (January 2021), monetary transmission remained weak throughout 2019–20 and continued to be so till December 2020. Though the RBI reduced the repo rate by a hefty 2.5 per cent, banks reduced their lending rates on fresh and outstanding loans by only 0.94 per cent and 0.83 pe cent, respectively— among private banks the transmission was greater. The major reasons for lower monetary transmission cited by the *RBI* and *Economic Survey 2020-21* are given below:

- Banks' unwillingness to lend together with reducing lending rates due to unpredictable impact of the COVID-19 disruption.
- Banks are apprehensive of the real size of their non-performing assets on account of relaxation announced by the Government to save borrowers from the economic hardship caused by the COVID-19 pandemic.
- Banks are not in a position to measure their actual profit and loss due to the disruption caused by the pandemic.
- Economy was already in the grip of slowdown even before COVID-19 pandemic hit the economy.
- Since the confidence of investors' and consumer's both are lower, experts believe that the lending rates are presently not much responsive to the monetary policy.

It is believed it will be more apt to assess the issue of monetary transmission once the economy comes out of the grip of pandemic. Meanwhile, the RBI was following an accommodative monetary policy stance and was eager to enhance monetary transmission.

Start-ups drive economic growth (wealth creation), create employment and foster a culture of innovation which will turn the youths 'from job seekers to job givers' and thus can emerge as the tool to tap the demographic dividend.

Q.9 Write a critical note on the need of independent debt management in the country.

Ans. The issue of independent debt management for the country has been a critical topic for discussion since it was proposed first by the Government in the Union Budget 2015–16. The proposal was to set up a public debt management agency (PDMA) out of the Reserve Bank of India (RBI which currently manages the public debt). But it was put on back burner probably due to clear objections coming from the central bank, as experts feel. By *March 2019*, the issue was again pushed by the policy think tank Niti Aayog (by saying that 'it was an idea whose time has come'). There looks *strong logic* in having an independent debt management body:

- At present, the RBI manages the government debt through the Public Debt Management Cell, including market borrowing (RBI has been reluctant to part with this function).

- There is a case of clear *conflict of interest* in this arrangement—at one hand RBI decides the key interest rates (i.e., policy rates under monetary policy mechanism) while, on the other hand, it trades in the government bonds (treasury bills, cash management bill and G-Secs) also.
- Lack of alignment between India's domestic bond market (which is controlled by RBI's policy rates) and the external bond market/external commercial borrowings (which is linked to the global variables). India has seen a rise in its external commercial borrowings in past years primarily due to interest rates in the global market being much lower than in India—rather India's financial market needs to converge with the global financial market.
- The size of fund which India needs for her infrastructural development depends much on the deepening of the bond market which is not possible due to RBI having a hold on it, which is linked to its function of announcing the monetary policy.

It is believed that once the debt management office is separated from the RBI, the more dynamism will enter into debt and fund management for the economy which will help both public and private sectors. Such a piece of advice was first proposed by the Tarapore Committee, 1997 (set up on the capital account convertibility) and in recent times by B.N. Srikrishna chaired FSLRC (Financial Sector Legislative Reforms Commission report, 2013).

Q. 10. "Today, capitalism is more taken as a tool of growth promotion rather than an economic system." Elucidate .

Ans. Capitalism as an economic system is considered a failure in the wake of the Great Depression (1929) after it was slowly modified into the mixed economy. But the system has influenced several countries in by now. Two such clear spells can be cited:

1. The *first* under the influence of the Washington Consensus (post-1985)
2. The *second* after the official acceptance of Globalisation (via the WTO, post-1995).

Experts believe that the ensuing Great Recession (after the US sub-prime crisis of 2007) among the developed countries was largely caused by the extreme capitalistic inclinations (neo-liberal policies) found among them.

Thus, we can say that by now the world has witnessed the negative effects of capitalism twice. Over the time, a kind of agreement has emerged across the world that though capitalism is not an ideal (or sustainable) type of an economic system, such policies can be quite helpful in promoting the cause of growth. This is why today, we find countries across the world having capitalistic policy orientation (i.e., *pro-business* policies) under the overall design of a mixed economy having:

- one set of policies (capitalistic) aiming higher growth, and
- the other aiming at effective welfare.

Such a clear policy shift has been seen in India too where the Government has been following *pro-corporate* and pro-poor policy stance (since 2014–15). Basically, over the time, experts seem to take capitalism less as an economic system and more as a tool of promoting growth.

Q.11 Briefly discuss the rationale behind the RBI's shift to an external benchmark for banks for deciding their lending rates.

Ans. Finding lack of monetary policy transmission, on the advice of the RBI, since April 2016, banks started deciding lending rates of their loans on the marginal cost of fund-based lending rate (MCLR). By late 2018, it was realised by the central bank that this arrangement has not served the aforesaid purpose. In the aftermath, RBI advised banks (in its 5th bi-monthly monetary policy statement, December 2018) to shift from the MCLR to an 'external benchmark' since April 2019 for deciding their lending rates. Accordingly, banks can opt for any one out of four such external benchmarks prescribed by RBI:

1. Repo rate
2. 91-day Treasury Bill yield
3. 182-day Treasury Bill yield
4. Any other benchmark produced by the FBIL (Financial Benchmarks India Private Ltd).[1]

Actual interest rates of loans offered by the banks will be on a spread over these benchmarks. It means that the actual lending rates will not remain linked to the 'internal' dataset of the banks (as the case has been in the case of the MCLR), rather to an external benchmark which is determined by market. This arrangement is believed to enhance the element of monetary policy transmission, and make lending more transparent together with adding value to the banks.

Q. 12 "A hard and fast control on the government's fiscal freedom may be counterproductive to the economy." In light of this statement, discuss the changing idea about the FRBM Act in the country.

Ans. Aimed at fiscal consolidation, India passed the Fiscal Responsibility and Budget Management (FRBM) Act in 2003—soon states also passed their fiscal responsibility Acts (FRAs) on the similar line. To the extent 'exact' follow-up to the FRBMA-linked targets are concerned, the performance has been mixed. The targets were exceeded many times due to fiscal escalations (either due to natural calamities or on exceptional ground), while many times they were better than the mandated figures. The implementation of the Act has also been postponed thrice by now. But this Act brought the element of higher fiscal discipline among the governments and there is no doubt about it. In the past few years, a view has emerged as per which binding the government expenditures to a fixed number may be counterproductive to the economy at large. Due to a hard and fast discipline regarding fiscal targets, some highly desirable expenditures by the government may get blocked, for example—expenditures on infrastructure, welfare, etc.

Accordingly, on the advice of an expert committee (chaired by N. K. Singh), the following changes were affected in the existing Act by late 2017–18:

- Debt *anchored* to the fiscal policy (i.e., fiscal targets moving up or down depending on sustainable borrowings by the governments).

1. RBI recognises FBIL as an 'independent benchmark administrator'. The company (set up in December 2014) has been jointly promoted by Fixed Income Money Market & Derivative Association of India (FIMMDA), Foreign Exchange Dealers' Association of India (FEDAI) and Indian Banks' Association (IBA).

- Debt to GDP target was set at 60 per cent for General Government (Centre + States— 40 per cent in the case of Centre and 20 per cent for states)— till 2020-21.
- A flexibility of 0.5 per cent was allowed in the fiscal deficit target (i.e., the introduction of 'escape clause').

On account of the COVID-19 pandemic, the Act was to be amended (under the 'unforeseen and unprecedented circumstances' clause) further in 2021–22 to finance the General Governments' rise in expenditures. Meanwhile, the *15th Finance Commission* has recommended to form a 'high-powered inter-governmental group' to— (i) Review the fiscal responsibility legislation (FRBM Act), and (ii) Recommend a new fiscal responsibility framework and oversee its implementation— a further amendment can be expected in the Act in near future.

Q. 13 Write a short note on the new initiatives taken by the RBI in recent times aimed at streamlining the credit and monetary policy.

Ans. In the past two and a half years, several new initiatives have been taken by the RBI aimed at strengthening the current regime of credit and monetary policy. The major ones are given below:

- Now, RBI announces the policy on *bi-monthly* basis.
- The *glide path for disinflation* policy adopted under which the CPI (C) is used by the RBI as the 'Headline Inflation' for monetary management.
- A *Monetary Policy Framework* has been put in place—under it, the RBI is to *'target inflation'* at 4 per cent with a variations of 2 per cent. It means, the 'range of inflation' is to be between 2 and 6 per cent (of the CPI-C).
- Besides the existing repo route, *term repos* have been introduced for three set of tenures—7, 14 and 28 days.
- Banks, overnight access to liquidity is being progressively *reduced* and in place they are being encouraged to *increase* their dependency on the term repos. By *March 2016*, banks were allowed to borrow only up to 1 per cent of their NDTL from the Call Money Market—0.25 per cent through *repo* and the rest of 0.75 per cent through *term repo*. This aims to improve the trans-mission of policy impulses across the interest rate spectrum and provide stability to the loan market.
- RBI has allowed individuals to participate in the Government Security market (similar to the developed economies like the USA).
- The initiation of the *MCLR* (Marginal Cost of fund based Lending Rate) from the financial year *2016–17*. This is aimed at quickening the transition of the interest rate signalling from the RBI to the loan market.
- Asking banks to shift to one of the four external benchmarks (repo rate or 91-day Treasury Bill yield or 182-days Treasury Bill yield or any other benchmark produced by the FBIL) for deciding lending rates in place of the MCLR—to enhance monetary policy transmission.

Q. 14 "The idea of the NITI Aayog has given a completely new dimension to the process of development planning in the country." Comment.

Ans. The economic 'think tank' set up by the GoI in January 2015 has the potential and imagination to change the very process of development planning in the country. This can be understood by the following *major initiatives* which have been taken under it:

- For the *first* time, a central think tank has tried to integrate the strength and aspirations of the Centre, states and the local bodies towards 'shared national agenda' of development. Through this, India will usher into a new era of 'decentralised planning'.

  In place of the old design of one size fits all ('top-down' approach), now India goes for flexible and decentralised model of development (based on 'bottom-up' approach).
- It is for the *first* time that India is trying to evolve a 'development model' which could include what is integrative in nature, rooted in India's ethos and open to the new ideas of the world.
- Development planning of the Centre has got more 'legitimacy' due to the inclusion of the states and UTs in the Governing Council of the NITI Aayog—it should be noted that the decisions of the NITI Aayog are to come out after due negotiations in the Council.
- The idea of 'Team India' is a timely innovation in it—a federal political system can neither realise its developmental desires nor utilise its strength of diversities without integrating the central and state governments.
- The idea of 'competitive and co-operative federalism' has already given a new impetus among the states of India to search for a better way and method of development promotion (as the *Economic Survey 2015–16* concluded on the basis of empirical proofs).
- Some of the new ideas, such as—*conflict resolution, sounding board, vision and scenario planning* will make development planning more 'result-oriented' and suited to the changing times.
- It has high potential to strengthen the cause of socio-political development in the country as the planning has now become a 'socio-economic' process (unlike only economic in the past).

Experts believe that the workings and achievements of the NITI Aayog will depend on the federal maturity shown by the governments in the country.

Q.15 Briefly discuss the impact of agricultural crop residue burning and suggest measures to check its impact on the ambient air:

Ans. Open burning of crop residues has become an environmental concern for India, particularly during kharif season (especially, paddy).

- The problem is more in northern states of Punjab, Haryana, UP, and Rajasthan. Around 50 per cent of all crop residue burnt in the country are residues of rice crop, as per TIFAC (2018).
- The use of combine *harvesters* leaves the crop residues in field, and in order to clear the fields for the next crop in the easiest way, farmers' burn the residues, leading to deterioration in air pollution. About 178 million tonnes of surplus crop residues are available in the country (TIFAC, 2018).
- Various *studies* (TERI, 2018 and SFAR, 2019) at city scales have shown that agricultural burning contributes significantly in PM2.5 (particulate matter,

diameter measurements of 2.5 micrometres or less) concentrations.

- Delhi remains enveloped with high PM2.5 air pollution (range of 250–600) during kharif harvesting season, contributed by the stagnant atmospheric condition.

Various *suggestions* which came from the studies *(Economic Survey 2019–20)* to address the problem are as follows:

- The use of agricultural *machinery* can help farmers to sow the seeds of the next crop without any problem associated with residues of the previous crops and also without affecting the crop productivity.
- Creating markets for crop residues and mandating nearby thermal power plants to undertake co-firing them with coal.
- Promoting infrastructure for setting up biomass depots for storage of bailed crop residues in areas that have shown high fire incidents or high production of a particular crop.
- Providing special loans for financing farm equipment and working capital for private sector.
- Promoting use of crop residue-based biochar briquettes in local industries, brick kiln and hotel/dhaba as an alternate fuel.
- Promoting pollution control as a parameter for deciding incentives and allocation to States and UTs.

Government has taken various legislative and promotional steps to check the instances of crop residue burning. The instances of crop residue burning have fallen but much needs to be done yet.

Q. 16 Write a note on the current policy regarding the use of disinvestment proceeds and justify the same.

Ans. The current policy regarding the use of the disinvestment proceeds is of January 2013. The proceeds of disinvestment with effect from the fiscal year 2013–14 are credited to the existing *'Public Account'* under the head NIF and they remain there until withdrawn/invested for the approved purpose—to be decided by the Union Budgets. Currently, the proceeds are used for the following purposes:

- Subscribing to the shares being issued by the CPSE including PSBs and Public Sector Insurance Companies, on *rights basis* so as to ensure government ownership in them at 51 per cent.
- *Recapitalisation* of public sector banks and public sector insurance companies.
- Investment by Government in RRBs, IIFCL, NABARD, Exim Bank.
- Equity infusion in various Metro projects.
- Investment in Bhartiya Nabhikiya Vidyut Nigam Limited and Uranium Corporation of India Ltd.
- Investment in Indian Railways towards capital expenditure.

The Union Budget 2021–22 clearly declares the disinvestment proceeds among its major sources of revenues for financing the budgetary expenditures. With fiscal deficit estimated to rise in 2020–21 (9.5 per cent of GDP) and 2021–22 (6.8 per cent of GDP), we find an increased emphasis from the Government on strategic disinvestment leading to privatisation and asset monetisation of the PSUs. Thus, the use of proceeds now depends on the needs and nature of the Government's expenditure.

Q.17 Critically examine the recently annou nced disinvestment policy for the public sector u ndertakings.

Ans. A new disinvestment policy was announced by the Government by February 2016—pushing in favour of the 'strategic disinvestment'. It will be better to call it a modification in the existing policy of 2009. As per the government, such policy implies "the sale of substantial portion of Government share holding of the PSUs of upto 50 per cent, or higher along with transfer of management control". The main features of this policy are—

- To be undertaken through a consultation process among different Ministries, Departments and the NITI Aayog.
- NITI Aayog to identify PSUs and advice on the mode of sale, percentage of shares to be sold and method for valuation.
- Core Group of Secretaries on Disinvestment (CGD) to consider the recommendations of NITI Aayog to facilitate a decision by the Cabinet Committee on Economic Affairs (CCEA) on strategic disinvestment and to supervise/monitor the process of implementation.

The changed stance of the government regarding disinvestment policy is a borrowing from the past experiences of disinvestment. Strategic mode of disinvestment was started by the GoI in 1999–00 itself which was put on hold by the next Government in 2004. The new government announced a new policy which aimed at GoI owing at least 51 per cent stake in the divested PSUs believing in the 'ideology' that *public has right* to own national assets. The new policy has not changed this ideology but has taken a more dynamic stance.

The new policy of disinvestment should be seen in the *backdrop* of the newly begun process of the "comprehensive management of government investment in the PSUs". Under it, the government has recognised its investment in the PSUs as an important asset and aims to optimise returns from it by its efficient use and attracting investment in the economy.

Q.18 "India's income and consumption pattern shows a huge anomaly." Analyse with suitable illustrations .

Ans. India's tax to GDP ratio is very low, and the proportion of direct tax to indirect tax is not optimal from the view point of social justice. The recent data released by the Government *(Union Budget 2017–18)* indicate that India's direct tax collection is not commensurate with the income and consumption pattern of the people:

- 'Corporate tax' filing pattern is very weak—out of 5.6 crore informal enterprises, only one-third filed tax returns. Similarly, out of total registered company (13.94 lakh), around half filed tax returns—of which around 20 per cent did show zero income and only 7781 companies did show profit above ₹10 crores.
- In the case of 'individual income tax', the situation is not better—out of 4.2 crore employees of the organised sector (formal sector), around 45 per cent filed income tax returns. Only 3.4 core Indians filed income tax returns out of which around half had income below

exemption limit; only 24 lakh people had income above ₹10 lakhs and only 1.72 lakh had income above ₹50 lakhs.

- The above-given data can be contrasted with the fact that in the last five years, more than 1.25 crore cars were sold in the country, and the number of Indian citizens who flew abroad (either for business or tourism) was 2 crore in the year 2015.

From the figures cited above, it can be concluded that India is largely a tax *non-compliant* society. The predominance of *cash* in the economy makes it possible for the people to evade their taxes. When too many people evade taxes, the burden of their share falls on those who are honest and compliant. The demonetisation process has given the government new data related to people's income and it is believed that the data mining will help the Government in increasing the tax net and tax revenue in future.

Q. 19 'India's economic policies are neo-liberal.' Examine.

Ans. The process of economic reforms started by India in 1991 was a follow-up to liberal policies influenced by current world ideas of neo-liberalism via the IMF (as it agreed with Washington Consensus, 1985). This is why critics of the reform process call Indian economic policies neo-liberal (it was also remarked by the *Supreme Court of India*, in one of its judgements in 2012).

Through reform, India started redefining the economic role of state in the economy—a predominant role was assigned to the 'private sector', but the state today has a different and bigger role. We may cite some examples to show why India's policies are still not neo-liberal.

- State still manages majority stakes in the PSUs and many 'very big PSUs' have been newly set up.
- Higher degree of regulation gives more economic authority to the government.
- Even after liberalisation, India is ranked very low in being a liberal economy, what to ask of a neo-liberal economy.
- Subsidies are still on the higher side.
- Government expenditure on education, healthcare, social security has increased hugely post-1991.
- Even liberal policies of the government are under several official checks and controls.
- Had India followed neo-liberal policies, it would also have faced some financial crisis after the US 'sub-prime' crisis.

Since 2016–17, we find a new stance in the fiscal policy of the GoI.

- Now, the government believes in doing all needful welfare works with a more performance-oriented policy framework. Rationalising the subsidy regime is an important part of the policy (with the help of Aadhar-enabled technology platform, the DBT).
- On the other hand, the government is trying to tweak all possible options to enhance the 'ease of doing business' in the economy—so that the business and industry are able to realise their full potential.

This new stance in the fiscal framework has been termed by the government 'pro-poor and pro-corporate'. Basically, to do welfare, the government needs revenues—in this backdrop the changed stance looks quite suitable.

Q.20 Discuss the transformational reforms initiated by the Government in recent times.

Ans. We have seen a major change in the Government's stance towards the need of reforms—several steps of reforms have been taken which have been termed transformational. These reforms are 'transformational' in the sense that they are aimed at transforming the very outlook to policy making and are taken in a long-term perspective. We may have a look on the major ones.

- Inflation targeting and setting up the Monetary Policy Committee by amending the RBI Act, 1934.
- Restarting of the 'strategic disinvestment' of the PSUs.
- Demonetisation of the high denomination currency notes (aimed at checking corruption, black money, tax evasion, fake currency and terrorism).
- Enactment of the new Benami Law (aimed at checking black money).
- Bankruptcy Law (aimed at promoting the 'ease of doing business')
- Enactment of the Aadhar Act (aimed at rationalising and weeding out corruption in the present subsidy regime)
- Attempts in the direction influencing the 'behavioural pattern' of the citizens to promote the cause of socio-economic well being, etc.

The *Union Budget 2017–18* has clearly termed them transformational reforms. As these reforms are aimed at long-term gains, there might be some political backlash on them. But this is the way, economies grow up and get matured. Remark from the latest *Economic Survey 2016–17* looks quite correct in this case—economic reforms are not, or not just, about overcoming vested interests, they are increasingly about shared narratives and vision on problems and solutions.

Q.21 "The gradual approach to economic reforms has given its own dividends to India." Comment with suitable illustrations.

Ans. The economic reforms which commenced in the world by the mid-1980s reached several other countries in the next decade, more so after the arrival of the WTO. Over the time, experts, together with the World Bank and the International Monetary Fund, have classified such countries into two categories—one which went for the 'gradualist' approach and the other which followed the 'stop-and-go' approach.

India's reform process has been termed gradualist (also known as 'incremental'). We see the traits of occasional reversals in the reform policies of India. There has been a lack of consensus among the different coalitions as well as the Centre and the states. It reflects the compulsions of India's highly pluralist and participative democratic policy-making process.

Though such an approach helped India avoid socio-political upheavals, it either delayed or did not allow it to realise the desired objectives of reforms. The first generation of reforms could not bring the expected results out of the reforms due to the absence of some other kind of reforms which India goes for after almost one decade. This has created a mood of disillusionment among the general public towards the benefits of the reforms—failing governments to muster enough political support in favour of it. But the gradualist nature of reform has given India certain other benefits which are considered bigger than gaining only the economic fruits out of it.

- India, being a welfare state, does not seem to follow reforms for only wealth creation which is the essence of reforms.
- With a huge population of poor and marginalised people, subsidised or free delivery of essential goods and services becomes necessity on the part of the government.
- In India kind of economy, market forces cannot be believed to have remedy for every economic issue. This makes a strong case for the intervention from the government.
- India has been able to avoid several economic crises too by following such an approach—first the impact of South East Financial Crisis (1996–97) and second, the western recession (2007–08) led by the US sub-prime crisis.
- In a sense, the incremental approach to reform made India delay adopting highly 'neo-liberal' policies and turned out to be a blessing in disguise.

Excessive inclination towards gradualist reforms may hamper the growth prospects of the economy. This is why the new government at the centre looks committed to the cause of essential reforms in a speedy manner—at times, even taking high political risks, too.

Q.22 "Of late, India has realised that influencing social norms will bring in multiple socio-economic dividends to the economy." Comment with the help of suitable current illustrations.

Ans. Mankind is basically a social and psychological byproduct. It means, our actions have high influence of socio-psychological factors. This has been validated by the recent studies, too. Lately, even the international agencies have also suggested the world governments to include the behavioural dimensions of their citizens into their policy framework.

Several factors related to our behaviour are directly and indirectly related to the prospects of growth and development. For example, 'social norms' are considered a major factor of maternal health in India—young women are accorded low status in joint households. Within-household nutritional differentials are stark. A recent study *(Economic Survey 2015–16)* shows that children of younger brothers in joint family households are significantly more likely to be born underweight than children of their older brother. This is attached in part to the lower status of younger daughter-in-laws in families.

Like several other countries in the world, India too has recognised the importance of influencing 'social norms' in a wide variety of sectors.

- Persuading the rich to give up subsidies they do not need
- Motivating citizens to take care of old people
- Inculcating a tendency to do good to others and philanthropic actions
- Enhancing the level of trust among the citizens. For this, the GoI took initiative to first trust its own citizens (self-attestation of documents, etc.)
- Reducing social prejudices against girls
- Educating people about the health externalities of keeping public spaces clean
- Appealing to go against open defecation. India's attempt in this regard has been

appreciated by the World Bank, too *(WDR-2015)*.

The government has a progressive role to play in changing norms, and indeed governments all over the world have embarked on systematic ways of studying how to promote behavioural change.

Q.23 'Niti Aayog has been imagined as a vehicle of good governance in the country.' Comment.

Ans. The Government of India has visualised Niti Aayog as the vehicle of good governance. Governance has improved a lot at the Central level but at the state level, it has not improved much (as was found by the special volume on governance published by the 10th Plan also). As the lives of citizens depend more on the supplies from the state governments, the poor governance at this level hits their lives in a big way.

The Central government's push in favour of good governance has been practically crippled by the inability or unwillingness of the state governments in this regard. It means that the state of governance cannot be improved much till there is an effective co-operation among the governments of the country. Once a very willing beginning has been started under the Niti Aayog ('co-operative federalism' being one of the *three foundations* on which it is imagined to be built) in this direction, it is believed that the quality of governance should improve in the coming years. We find an intentional attempt by the Government to intertwine the aspect of good governance in the very idea of the Niti Aayog. Not only the word governance but the *established traits of governance* find clear mentions at several places.

- In the *Foundations* the Niti Aayog is supposed to be built on (a collaborative platform facilitating implementation),
- In the *Guiding Principles* (Participation, Inclusion, Governance and Antodaya); in its *structural composition* (Governing Council as a tool to promote participatory federation), and finally,
- In its *Functions* (co-operative and competitive federalism, best friend of states at the Centre, decentralised planning, harmonisation, conflict resolution, internal consultancy, capacity building, monitoring and evaluation are effective in improving governance).

This way, the very idea of Niti Aayog looks very sensitive to the need of good governance in the country—as Niti Aayog is able to play the role desired from it as the state of governance will improve in the country. This is why experts believe the Niti Aayog as the 'vehicle of good governance'.

Q.24 "Comprehensive management of public assets is basically aimed at operating public enterprises on the business line." Comment.

Ans. In 2016–17, we find the Government changing the very mandate of disinvestment process. The Department of Investment and Public Asset Management (the new name of the existing Department of Disinvestment) was given the *mandate* to manage the government investment in the public sector enterprises (PSEs) to realise the following objectives:

- accelerating economic growth,
- their efficient use, and
- achieving optimum return from them.

In the process of realising the aforesaid objectives, the department is supposed to take the following measures in regard to the PSEs:

- Financial restructuring,
- Attracting fresh investment by enhancing investors' confidence, and
- Rationalising their decision-making process.

Under it, the Government has already started monetising the public assets wherever it is possible (as the National Highways, Airports, Ports, etc are being handed over to prospective operators from the private sector to increase the revenues of the Government). Such a move will not only provide a level playing field to the private sector companies in the sector concerned but will also help the Government cutting the losses fetched by the PSEs.

Q.25 'Use of nudge in making public policy can be highly effective in India.' Explain with the help of suitable illustrations.

Ans. Behavioural economics provides insights in to nudge (which literally means to prod someone gently with one's elbow in order to attract attention) people towards desirable behaviour. By now, nudge has been successfully used in India as an instrument of public policy (in the Swachh Bharat Mission (SBM) and Beti Bachao Beti Padhao (BBBP) campaigns) and it can be further used to aim even higher goals such as:

- from BBBP to BADLAV (Beti Aapki Dhan Lakshmi Aur Vijay Lakshmi),
- from Swachh Bharat to Sundar Bharat,
- from 'Give it up' (for the LPG subsidy) to 'Think about the Subsidy', and
- from tax evasion to tax compliance.

Nudges can be used in policy making with effective outcomes by taking the following three policy actions:

1. People's behaviour is influenced by social and religious norms. Thus, beneficial norms can be used as positive influencers (friends and neighbours as role models) to modify people's behaviour.
2. As people have an inclination to go for 'default' option in their actions, changing the default can be a very effective policy.
3. Policy of reminders and repeated reinforcements help sustained change in behaviour as people find it difficult to sustain good habits.

Common people fail to connect to policy actions of the Governments. For an effective use of nudges in public policy, it is essential to relate economics to common person using something that he or she encounters every day, for example, a plate of food (as the *Economic Survey 2019–20* did show and *Economic Survey 2020-21* continues with).

Q.26 Briefly discuss the recent reasons due to which a tremendous rise has been seen in the food subsidy bill of the Government.

Ans. In the last few years, there has been steep rise in the food subsidy bill— estimated to be ₹ 1,65,000 lakh crores for 2020–21 (which is already at ₹ 98,000 crores by November 2020) in comparison to ₹ 45,000 crores in 2013–14. As per the *Economic Surveys 2019–20* and *2020–21*, the steep rise in food subsidy has been caused by the following reasons:

- The NFSA has a wider coverage than the erstwhile TPDS.
- The Antyodaya beneficiaries also get foodgrains at the NFSA prices.

- Under NFSA, the categorisation of APL and BPL was abolished.
- Coverage under the Act was also delinked from the poverty estimates as it was substantially high to ensure that all the vulnerable and needy sections of the society get its benefit.
- The build-up of the foodgrain stocks much higher than their buffer norms.
- Increase in economic cost and real MSP.
- Decline in the sale to the APL households.

While the economic cost has increased, — proportionate to increase in MSP (per kilogram wheat and rice being ₹ 37.24 and ₹ 26.84 per in 2020-21 in comparison to ₹ 26.16 and ₹ 19.08 in 2013–14, respectively), the selling prices (CIP) for NFSA beneficiaries have not been revised from ₹2 and ₹3 per kg for wheat and rice, respectively. These rates were fixed under the Act initially for a period of three years from the date of commencement of the Act (July, 2013) and thereafter were to be fixed by the Government from time to time, while not exceeding the MSP. As no revision has been done since then, it has resulted in widening of the gap between the economic cost and the CIP and increasing food subsidy bills.

While the interests of the vulnerable sections of the population need to be safeguarded, the food subsidy also needs to be rationalised as it distorts market for foodgrains, pulls inflation down and challenges the sustainability of food security in the country.

Q.27 'Greater wealth creation, together with increased formalisation of the economy, will lead to greater inclusiveness in the country.' Comment.

Ans. Increasing economic growth is considered the simplest way a country can create wealth. But wealth is created by generating fixed assets also. In a nutshell, generating higher income and creating fixed assets are complimentary to each other.

In modern economy, one time-tested method to create wealth is followed by the formal agencies of growth—namely, the public limited companies which are also known as the corporate sector. As these firms are joint stock companies owned by a large number of shareholders other than the promoters, the wealth created by them is also shared by a large number of stakeholders including the common shareholders. Besides, they contribute in the GDP of the country via their production process other than creating jobs. For that matter, even non-public limited firms can also do the same provided they become formal part of the economy—at least in the eyes of the tax department (i.e. being GST registered, filing income tax returns, etc.).

The other benefit of formal firms is that they need to provide social security benefits to their employees. Such employees, this way, start getting all public benefits which are offered by either the Centre or State governments. As the number of formal agencies increases, the number of beneficiaries also expands. This way, it is believed that higher formalisation of the economy leads to higher degree of inclusive growth in the country.

Q.28 Briefly discuss the reason due to which a disconnect has been seen recently between the stock markets and economy.

Ans. A clear disconnect has been seen between the stock markets and the economy in the country— since March 2020 till February 2021— while economic growth rates have been going down (even in negative territories), the stock indices were rising up and up.

As per the SEBI, such a disconnect was never witnessed before. Typically, stock markets have been barometers of the economy and move in the direction the economy moves or at least it is expected to move this way. Several institutions, including the Financial Stability Board and the RBI, have raised concerns on the disconnect of the financial markets with the real economy and a possible risk it may pose to systemic stability. Meanwhile, the jury is out and is busy in guessing game— the country is yet to get an official version of explanation for the phenomenon. However, experts have cited certain reasons behind it:

- World markets, especially of the developed economies, are flush with funds (due to large fiscal stimulus announced by the governments) and this fund is flowing towards the emerging markets in expectations of a steeper recovery in the post-pandemic period.
- The changing global trade dynamics are also fuelling more flow of funds towards India in the forms of direct and indirect foreign investments— in the hope that the country might emerge as an alternative to China as a global production hub.
- The emphasis given by the Government on structural reforms being done in either agriculture sector or labour markets is encouraging investments in the stocks.
- India's pharma has seen encouraging investments, especially in the vaccination sector.
- The 'gig economy' (i.e., e-commerce, digital platforms, etc.) of India has emerged among the largest in the world and has attracted high investments in recent times.

Q.29. Write a note on the challenge which the RBI faced du ring the COVID-19 pandemic related to forex management and the impossible trinity.

Ans. During most parts of 2020–21, India saw a rise in its foreign exchange (forex) reserves— India's surplus in its trade account resulting in a large balance of payment surplus. In such a situation, the RBI is faced with *two* options:

1. Absorb the surplus (by buying it from the forex market) and accumulate more forex reserves or
2. Let the ₹ appreciate.

With inflation largely attributed to supply-side disruptions and expected to stabilize, RBI chose to intervene in the forex market, accumulate reserves, which prevented one-sided appreciation of ₹ and supplemented expansionary monetary policy (i.e., reduction in the repo rate). Though RBI had to fine balance the headline inflation in a sustainable manner and yet stimulate growth.

As per the *Economic Survey 2020-21*, accumulation of forex reserves resulted in concomitant release of ₹ in the system which helped the Government's higher borrowings as inflation remained lower. But once the headline inflation went above the policy band (of 4+/-2 per cent), RBI had to confront the classic conundrum of *impossible trinity*[2] (i.e., the Mundell-Fleming trilemma) – maintain an open capital account, stable exchange rate, and still conduct independent monetary policy.

2. * See *Chapter 18* for more on the **Impossible Trinity**.

Overall, the RBI was able to manage this conundrum— an almost stable exchange for ₹, inflation remaining under check and keeping an independent monetary policy— with little bit of difficulties.

Q.30 Write a critical note on the ongoing process of banking consolidation followed by the Government.

Ans. In the backdrop of the recommendations of financial sector reforms (M. Narasimham, 1991 and 1998), we find a broader process of banking consolidation of the public sector banks (PSBs) commencing in the country by 1993–94 itself— with the following paradigm emerging over the time:

Merger: It is aimed at creating bigger and stronger banks besides reducing operational cost and broadening capital base of the banks. Mainly starting with the mergers of the Associates of SBI (all 7 such banks merged into 1 by 2017–18), the biggest such exercise was affected in August 2019 when 10 PSBs were merged into four (their number came down to 12). As per the *Union Budget 2021–22,* in 2021–22, other 2-3 banks are to be merged.

Disinvestment: Both of the routes of disinvestment are to be followed in the case of the banks— 'minority' stake sale and 'strategic' (which may result in privatisation also) aimed at infusing fresh capital and managerial professionalism. The Government has clearly announced in the *Union Budget 2021–22* to privatise all 'non-strategic' public sector enterprises (which include some of the PSBs too) while maintaining ownership control in the 'strategic' ones limited to only *four* in number (which will include few of the PSBs also besides some other financial institutions).

The Government believes that India needs global sized banks to become a US$ 5 trillion economy by 2024–25. Today, India has only one bank in top 100 global bank list (i.e., SBI at 55th position) while China and the USA have 18 banks and 12 in the list, respectively.

As per the *Chief Economic Adviser K.V. Subramanian* (August 2020), India is the 5th largest economy in the world— so, if the Indian banking sector was proportional to the size of its economy, it should have been where South Korea is, which has 6 banks in the global top hundred. He further added that even countries that are a fraction of India's size, for example, Finland, Denmark, Belgium, Austria, Norway have at least 1 bank in the global top hundred— Sweden and Singapore which are one-sixth and one-eighth the size of Indian economy, respectively, have 3 banks in the list.

Q.31 Briefly outline the importance of the social stock exchange in the case of India with suitable illustrations.

Ans. The idea of social exchange is rather new to India. They came up by the last decade in countries like UK, Canada, Singapore, Kenya, etc. Social Stock Exchange (SSE) allows the listing of *social enterprises* (non-profit and for-profit, both) on stock exchanges aimed at providing them additional channel to raise fund.

These enterprises depend mainly on philanthropic funds from governments, international donors or companies (chiefly through their corporate social responsibility) and a dearth of funding has always been felt by them in the country. Given the sustainable development goals of the UNO, India has also been realising the need of inclusive and socially responsible development. In tandem, the corporate sector has begun to adopt a variety of measures to ensure that their activities are not causing harm to society or the environment— nature of investing also shifting towards the environmental social governance (ESG) criteria.

It was in the *Union Budget 2019–20* that the Government proposed to set up a social stock exchange under the ambit of the SEBI for social enterprises so that they can raise capital as equity, debt or as units like a mutual fund. Accordingly, on the recommendations of a Working Group (under the Chairmanship of Ishaat Hussain), the SEBI announced (in June 2020) the guidelines (which was in the stage of public feedback by April 2021) for setting up of the SSE in the country. As per the SEBI, the exchange can be housed within the existing stock exchanges (such as BSE and/ or NSE), which will help it leverage the existing infrastructure and client relationships of the exchanges to onboard investors, donors, and social enterprises (for-profit and non-profit). The SSE will have two primary roles.

ECONOMIC SURVEY 2020-21

The Economic Survey 2020-21, which is dedicated to the COVID Warriors, was presented in Parliament on January 29, 2021. Following the tradition since the past few years, this Survey also contains two volumes. While the first volume deals with the theoretical issues, assessment of the existing policies and suitable advice for the future, the second one mainly aims to present a performance report of the closing year. The key highlights of both the volumes are presented here in a format which will be helpful at various levels of the civil services examinations.

In this Chapter...

VOLUME-1

Volume 1 consists of a total of ten chapters touching diverse areas of importance to the economy. A chapter-wise summary is given below.

SAVING LIVES AN D LIVELIHOODS AMIDST A ONCE-IN-A-CENTURY CRISIS

- India focused on saving lives and livelihoods by her willingness to take **short-term pain for long-term gain,** at the onset of the COVID-19 pandemic.
- Response stemmed from the **humane principle** that:
  - **Human lives lost cannot be brought back.**
  - GDP growth will recover from the temporary shock caused by the pandemic.
- An **early, intense lockdown provided a win-win strategy** to save lives, and preserve livelihoods via economic recovery in the medium to long-term.
- Strategy also motivated by the Nobel-Prize winning research by Hansen & Sargent (2001): a policy focused on *minimising losses in a worst-case scenario* when uncertainty is very high.
- India's strategy **flattened the curve,** pushed the peak to September 2020.
- After the September peak, India has been unique in experiencing **declining daily cases despite increasing mobility.**
- **V-shaped recovery,** as seen in 7.5% decline in GDP in Q2 and recovery across all key economic indicators vis-à-vis the 23.9% GDP contraction in Q1.
- COVID pandemic affected both demand and supply:
  - India was the only country to announce **structural reforms to expand supply** in the medium-long term and avoid long-term damage to productive capacities.
  - **Calibrated demand side policies** to ensure that the accelerator is slowly pushed down only when the brakes on economic activities are being removed.
  - A public investment programme centered around the **National Infrastructure Pipeline** to accelerate the demand push and further the recovery.
- **Upturn in the economy, avoiding a second wave of infections**–a sui generis case in strategic policymaking amidst a once-in-a-century pandemic.

DOES GROWTH LEAD TO DEBT SUSTAINABILITY?-YES,BUT NOT VICE-VERSA!

- **Growth leads to debt sustainability** in the Indian context but not necessarily vice-versa:
  - Debt sustainability depends on the 'Interest Rate Growth Rate Differential' (IRGD), i.e., the difference between the interest rate and the growth rate.
  - In India, **interest rate on debt is less than growth rate** - by norm, not by exception.
- **Negative IRGD in India** – not due to lower interest rates but much higher growth rates – prompts a debate on fiscal policy, especially during growth slowdowns and economic crises.

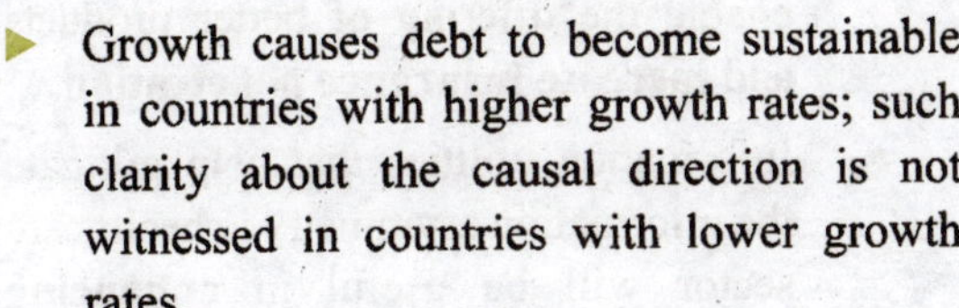

- Growth causes debt to become sustainable in countries with higher growth rates; such clarity about the causal direction is not witnessed in countries with lower growth rates.
- Fiscal multipliers are disproportionately higher during economic crises than during economic booms.
- **Active fiscal policy** can ensure that the full benefit of reforms is reaped by limiting potential damage to productive capacity.
- Fiscal policy that provides an impetus to growth will lead to **lower debt-to-GDP ratio**
- Given India's growth potential, **debt sustainability is unlikely to be a problem** even in the worst scenarios
- **Desirable to use counter-cyclical fiscal policy** to enable growth during economic downturns.
- Active, counter-cyclical fiscal policy – not a call for fiscal irresponsibility, but to break the intellectual anchoring that has created an **asymmetric bias against fiscal policy**.

DOES INDIA'S SOVEREIGN CREDIT RATING REFLECT ITS FUNDAMENTALS? NO!

- The **fifth largest economy in the world** has never been rated as the lowest rung of the investment grade (BBB-/Baa3) in sovereign credit ratings:
  - Reflecting the economic size and thereby the ability to repay debt, the fifth largest economy has been predominantly rated AAA.
  - China and India are the only exceptions to this rule – China was rated A-/A2 in 2005 and now India is rated BBB-/Baa3.
- **India's sovereign credit ratings do not reflect its fundamentals:**
  - A clear outlier amongst countries rated between A+/A1 and BBB-/Baa3 for S&P/ Moody's, on several parameters.
  - Rated significantly lower than mandated by the effect on the sovereign rating of the parameter.
- Credit ratings map the **probability of default** and therefore reflect the willingness and ability of the borrower to meet its obligations:
  - India's **willingness to pay** is unquestionably demonstrated through its **zero sovereign default history.**
  - India's **ability to pay** can be gauged by low foreign currency denominated debt and **forex reserves.**
- Sovereign credit rating changes for India have **no or weak correlation with macroeconomic indicators.**
- India's fiscal policy should reflect Gurudev Rabindranath Tagore's sentiment of ***'a mind without fear'.***
- Sovereign credit ratings methodology should be made **more transparent, less subjective** and better attuned to reflect economies' fundamentals.

INEQUALITY AND GROWTH: CONFLICT OR CONVERGENCE?

- The relationship between inequality and socio-economic outcomes vis-à-vis economic growth and socio-economic outcomes, is different in India from that in advanced economies.
- Both inequality and per-capita income (growth) have similar relationships with

socio-economic indicators in India, unlike in advanced economies.

- **Economic growth has a greater impact on poverty alleviation than inequality.**
- India must continue to focus on **economic growth to lift the poor out of poverty.**
- ***Expanding the overall pie***-redistribution in a developing economy is feasible only if the size of the economic pie grows.

HEALTHCARE TAKES CENTRE STAGE, FINALLY!

- COVID-19 pandemic emphasised the importance of healthcare sector and its inter-linkages with other sectors – showcased how a health crisis transformed into an economic and social crisis.
- India's **health infrastructure must be agile** to respond to pandemics – healthcare policy must not become beholden to 'saliency bias'.
- **National Health Mission** (NHM) played a critical role in mitigating inequity as the access of the poorest to pre-natal/post-natal care and institutional deliveries increased significantly.
- Emphasis on NHM in conjunction with **Ayushman Bharat** should continue.
- An **increase in public healthcare spending from 1% to 2.5-3% of GDP** can decrease the **out-of-pocket expenditure from 65% to 35%** of overall healthcare spending
- A **regulator for the healthcare sector** must be considered given the market failures stemming from information asymmetry.
    - Mitigation of information asymmetry will help **lower insurance premiums,** enable the offering of better products and **increase insurance penetration.**
    - Information utilities that help mitigate the information asymmetry in healthcare sector will be useful in **enhancing overall welfare.**
- **Telemedicine** needs to be harnessed to the fullest by investing in **internet connectivity** and **health infrastructure.**

PROCESS REFORMS

- India over-regulates the economy resulting in regulations being ineffective even with relatively good compliance with the process.
- The root cause of the problem of overregulation is an approach that attempts to account for every possible outcome.
- Increase in complexity of regulations, intended to reduce discretion, results in even more non-transparent discretion.
- The solution is to **simplify regulations** and **invest in greater supervision** which, by definition, implies greater discretion.
- Discretion, however, needs to be balanced with **transparency**, systems of ex-ante accountability and ex-post resolution mechanisms.
- The above intellectual framework has already informed reforms ranging from labour codes to removal of onerous regulations on the BPO sector.

REGULATORY FORBEARANCE AN EMERGENCY MEDICINE, NOT STAPLE DIET!

- During the Global Financial Crisis, regulatory **forbearance** helped the borrowers to tide over temporary hardship.

- Forbearance continued long after the economic recovery, resulting in unintended consequences for the economy.
- Banks exploited the forbearance window for window-dressing their books and misallocated credit, thereby damaging the quality of investment in the economy.
- Forbearance represents emergency medicine that should be discontinued at the first opportunity when the economy exhibits recovery, not a staple diet that gets continued for years.
- To promote judgement amidst uncertainty, **ex-post inquests must recognise the role of hindsight bias** and not equate unfavourable outcomes to bad judgement or malafide intent.
- An **Asset Quality Review** exercise must be conducted immediately after the forbearance is withdrawn.
- The **legal infrastructure** for the recovery of loans needs to be strengthened de facto.

INNOVATION: TRENDING UP BUT NEEDS THRUST, ESPECIALLY FROM THE PRIVATE SECTOR

- **India entered the top-50 innovating countries for the first time in 2020** since the inception of the Global Innovation Index in 2007, ranking **first in Central and South Asia**, and third amongst lower middle-income group economies.
- India's gross domestic expenditure on R&D (GERD) is lowest amongst top ten economies.
- **India's aspiration must be to compete on innovation with the top ten economies.**
- The **government sector contributes a disproportionately large share in total GERD** at three times the average of top ten economies.
- The business sector's contribution to GERD, total R&D personnel and researchers is amongst the lowest when compared to top ten economies.
- This situation has prevailed despite higher tax incentives for innovation and access to equity capital.
- **India's business sector needs to significantly ramp up investments in R&D**
- Indian resident's share in total patents filed in the country must rise from the current 36% which is much below the average of 62% in top ten economies.
- For achieving higher improvement in innovation output, India must focus on **improving her performance on institutions and business sophistication innovation inputs.**

JAY HO: AYUSHMAN BHARAT'S JAN AROGYA YOJANA (JAY) AND HEALTH OUTCOMES

- **Pradhan Mantri Jan Arogya Yojana (PM-JAY)** – the ambitious programme launched by Government of India in 2018 to provide healthcare access to the most vulnerable sections demonstrates **strong positive effects on healthcare outcomes in a short time.**
- PM-JAY is being used significantly for high frequency, low-cost care such as dialysis and continued during the COVID pandemic and the lockdown.
- Causal impact of PM-JAY on health outcomes by undertaking a Difference-

in-Difference analysis based on National Family Health Survey (NFHS)-4 (2015-16) and NFHS-5 (2019-20) is following:

- *Enhanced health insurance coverage:* The proportion of households that had health insurance increased in Bihar, Assam and Sikkim from 2015-16 to 2019-20 by 89% while it decreased by 12% over the same period in West Bengal.
- *Decline in Infant Mortality rate:* From 2015-16 to 2019-20, infant mortality rates declined by 20% for West Bengal and by 28% for the three neighbouring states.
- Decline in under-5 mortality rate: Bengal saw a fall of 20% while the neighbours witnessed a 27% reduction.
- Modern methods of contraception, female sterilisation and pill usage went up by 36%, 22% and 28%, respectively, in the three neighbouring states while the respective changes for West Bengal were negligible.
- While West Bengal did not witness any significant decline in unmet need for spacing between consecutive kids, the neighbouring three states recorded a 37% fall.
- Various metrics for mother and childcare improved more in the three neighbouring states than in West Bengal

- Each of these health effects manifested similarly when we compare all states that implemented PM-JAY versus the states that did not.
- Overall, the comparison reflects **significant improvements in several health outcomes in states that implemented PM-JAY versus those that did not.**

BARE NECESSITIES

Access to the 'bare necessities' has improved across all States in the country in 2018 as compared to 2012.

- It is highest in States such as Kerala, Punjab, Haryana and Gujarat while lowest in Odisha, Jharkhand, West Bengal and Tripura.
- **Improvement in each of the five dimensions,** viz., access to water, housing, sanitation, micro-environment and other facilities.
- Inter-State disparities declined across rural and urban areas as the laggard states have gained relatively more between 2012 and 2018.
- Improved disproportionately more for the poorest households when compared to the richest households across rural and urban areas.

- Improved access to the 'bare necessities' has led to **improvements in health indicators** such as infant mortality and under-5 mortality rate and also **correlates with future improvements in education indicators.**
- Thrust should be given to reduce variation in the access to bare necessities across states, between rural and urban and between income groups.
- The schemes such as **Jal Jeevan Mission, SBM-G, PMAY-G,** etc. may design appropriate strategy to reduce these gaps.
- A Bare Necessities Index (BNI) based on the large annual household survey data can be constructed using suitable indicators and methodology at district level for all/targeted districts to assess the progress on access to bare necessities.

VOLUME-2

Volume 2 contains the performance report of the economy in 2020-21, which has been summarised below:

STATE OF THE ECONOMY IN 2020-21: A MACRO VIEW

- COVID-19 pandemic ensued **global economic downturn**, the most severe one since the Global Financial Crisis.
- The lockdowns and social distancing norms brought the already slowing **global economy to a standstill.**
- Global economic output estimated to fall by 3.5% in 2020 (*IMF January 2021* estimates).
- Governments and central banks across the globe deployed various policy tools to support their economies such as lowering policy rates, quantitative easing measures, etc.
- India adopted a **four-pillar strategy** of containment, fiscal, financial, and long-term structural reforms:
    - **Calibrated fiscal and monetary support** was provided, cushioning the vulnerable during the lockdown and boosting consumption and investment while unlocking.
    - **A favourable monetary policy** ensured abundant liquidity and immediate relief to debtors while unclogging monetary policy transmission.
- As per the advance estimates by NSO, India's GDP is estimated to grow by (–) 7.7% in FY21 – a **robust sequential growth of 23.9%** in H2: FY21 over H1: FY21.
- India's **real GDP** to record a **11.0% growth in FY2021-22** and **nominal GDP** to grow by **15.4%** – the **highest since independence**:
    - Rebound to be led by low base and continued normalisation in economic activities as the rollout of COVID-19 vaccines gathers traction.
- **Government consumption** and **net exports** cushioned the growth from diving further down, whereas investment and private consumption pulled it down.
- The recovery in second half of FY2020-21 is expected to be powered by **government consumption**, estimated to grow at **17% YoY.**
- Exports expected to decline by 5.8% and imports by 11.3% in the second half of FY21
- India expected to have a **Current Account Surplus of 2% of GDP** in FY21, a **historic high after 17 years.**
- On supply side, Gross Value Added (GVA) growth pegged at -7.2% in FY21 as against 3.9% in FY20:
    - **Agriculture set to cushion the shock of the COVID-19 pandemic on the Indian economy in FY21 with a growth of 3.4%.**
    - **Industry and services estimated to contract by 9.6% and 8.8%, respectively, during FY21.**
- Agriculture remained the silver lining while **contact-based services, manufacturing, construction** were **hit hardest**, and recovering steadily.
- India remained a **preferred investment destination** in FY 2020-21 with FDI pouring in amidst global asset shifts towards equities and prospects of quicker recovery in emerging economies:
    - Net FPI **inflows** recorded an **all-time monthly high of US$ 9.8 billion** in

November 2020, as investors' risk appetite returned.

- **India was the only country among emerging markets to receive equity FII inflows in 2020.**

- Buoyant SENSEX and NIFTY resulted in India's **market-cap to GDP ratio crossing 100% for the first time since October 2010**
- **Softening of CPI inflation** recently reflects easing of supply side constraints that affected food inflation.
- Mild contraction of 0.8% in investment (as measured by Gross Fixed Capital Formation) in 2nd half of FY21, as against 29% drop in 1st half of FY21.
- Reignited **inter and intra state movement** and record-high monthly **GST collections** have marked the unlocking of industrial and commercial activity.
- The **external sector** provided an effective cushion to growth with India recording a **Current Account Surplus of 3.1% of GDP** in the first half of FY21:
  - **Strong services exports** and weak demand leading to a sharper contraction in imports (merchandise imports contracted by 39.7%) than exports (merchandise exports contracted by 21.2%).
  - **Forex reserves** increased to a level so as to cover 18 months' worth of imports in December 2020.
  - **External debt** as a ratio to GDP increased to 21.6% at end-September 2020 from 20.6% at end-March 2020.
  - Ratio of forex reserves to total and short-term debt improved because of the sizable accretion in reserves.
- **V-shaped recovery** is underway, as demonstrated by a sustained resurgence in high frequency indicators such as power demand, e-way bills, GST collection, steel consumption, etc.
- India became the **fastest country to roll-out 10 lakh vaccines** in 6 days and also emerged as a **leading supplier of the vaccine** to neighbouring countries and Brazil.
- **Economy's homecoming to normalcy** brought closer by the initiation of a mega vaccination drive:
  - **Hopes of a robust recovery** in services sector, consumption, and investment have been rekindled.
  - Reforms must go on to enable India realise its potential growth and erase the adverse impact of the pandemic.
- India's **mature policy response** to the 'once-in-a-century' crisis provides important. lessons for democracies to avoid myopic policymaking and demonstrates benefits of focusing on **long-term gains.**

FISCAL DEVELOPMENTS

- India adopted a **calibrated approach** best suited for a resilient recovery of her economy from COVID-19 pandemic impact, in contrast with a front-loaded large stimulus package adopted by many countries.
- **Expenditure policy** in 2020-21 initially aimed at supporting the vulnerable sections but was re-oriented to boost overall demand and capital spending, once the lockdown was unwound.
- **Monthly GST collections** have crossed the **₹1 lakh crore** mark consecutively for the last 3 months, reaching its **highest levels in December 2020 ever since the introduction of GST.**
- **Reforms in tax administration** have begun a process of transparency and accountability

and have incentivised tax compliance by enhancing honest tax-payers' experience.

- Central Government has also taken consistent steps to impart support to the States in the challenging times of the pandemic.

EXTERNAL SECTOR

- COVID-19 pandemic led to a sharp decline in global trade, lower commodity prices and tighter external financing conditions with implications for current account balances and currencies of different countries.
- India's **forex reserves at an all-time high of US$ 586.1 billion as on January 08, 2021,** covering about 18 months' worth of imports
- India experiencing a Current Account Surplus along with robust capital inflows leading to a **BoP surplus since Q4 of FY2019-20.**
- Balance on the capital account is buttressed by **robust FDI and FPI inflows:**
  - Net FDI inflows of US$ 27.5 billion during April-October 2020: 14.8% higher as compared to first seven months of FY2019-20.
  - Net FPI inflows of US$ 28.5 billion during April-December 2020 as against US$ 12.3 billion in corresponding period of last year.
- In H1: FY21, steep contraction in merchandise imports and lower outgo for travel services led to:
  - Sharper fall in current payments (by 30.8%) than current receipts (15.1%).
  - Current Account Surplus of US$ 34.7 billion (3.1% of GDP).
- **India to end with an Annual Current Account Surplus after a period of 17 years.**
- India's **merchandise trade deficit was lower** at US$ 57.5 billion in April–December, 2020 as compared to US$ 125.9 billion in the corresponding period last year.
- In April-December 2020, **merchandise exports** contracted by 15.7% to US$ 200.8 billion from US$ 238.3 billion in April-December, 2019:
  - Petroleum, Oil and Lubricants (POL) exports have contributed negatively to export performance during the period under review.
  - Non-POL exports turned positive and helped in improving export performance in Q3 of 2020-21.
  - Within Non-POL exports, agriculture and allied products, drugs and pharmaceutical and ores and minerals recorded expansion.
- Total **merchandise imports** declined by (-) 29.1% to US$ 258.3 billion during April-December 2020 from US$ 364.2 billion during the same period last year:
  - Sharp decline in POL imports pulled down the overall import growth.
  - Imports contracted sharply in Q1 of 2020-21; the pace of contraction eased in subsequent quarters, due to the accelerated growth in Gold and Silver imports and narrowing contraction in non-POL, non-Gold and non-Silver imports.
  - Fertilizers, vegetable oil, drugs and pharmaceuticals and computer hardware and peripherals have contributed positively to the growth of non-POL, non-Gold and non-Silver imports.
- **Trade balance with China and the US improved as imports slowed**
- **Net services receipts** amounting to US$ 41.7 billion remained stable in April-September 2020 as compared to US$ 40.5 billion in corresponding period a year ago.

- **Resilience of the services sector** was primarily driven by software services, which accounted for 49% of total services exports.
- **Net private transfer receipts**, mainly representing remittances by Indians employed overseas, totaling US$ 35.8 billion in H1: FY21 declined by 6.7% over the corresponding period of previous year.
- At end-September 2020, India's **external debt** placed at US$ 556.2 billion – a decrease of US$ 2.0 billion (0.4%) as compared to end-March 2020.
- Improvement in **debt vulnerability indicators**:
  - Ratio of forex reserves to total and short-term debt (original and residual)
  - Ratio of short-term debt (original maturity) to the total stock of external debt.
  - Debt service ratio (principal repayment plus interest payment) increased to 9.7% at end-September 2020, compared to 6.5% at end-March 2020.
- **Rupee appreciation/depreciation:**
  - In terms of 6-currency nominal effective exchange rate (NEER) (trade-based weights), Rupee depreciated by 4.1% in December 2020 over March 2020; appreciated by 2.9% in terms of real effective exchange rate (REER).
  - In terms of 36-currency NEER (trade-based weights), Rupee depreciated by 2.9% in December 2020 over March 2020; appreciated by 2.2% in terms of REER.
- **RBI's interventions in forex markets** ensured financial stability and orderly conditions, controlling the volatility and one-sided appreciation of the Rupee.
- **Initiatives undertaken to promote exports:**
  - Production Linked Incentive **(PLI) Scheme.**
  - Remission of Duties and Taxes on Exported Products (**RoDTEP**).
  - Improvement in logistics infrastructure and digital initiatives.

MONEY MANAG EMENT AND FINANCIAL INTERMEDIATION

- **Accommodative monetary policy** during 2020: repo rate cut by 115 bps since March 2020.
- **Systemic liquidity** in FY2020-21 has remained in surplus so far. RBI undertook various conventional and unconventional measures like:
  - Open Market Operations
  - Long-Term Repo Operations
  - Targeted Long-Term Repo Operations
- **Gross Non-Performing Assets** ratio of Scheduled Commercial Banks decreased from 8.21% at end-March 2020 to 7.49% at end-September, 2020.
- The monetary transmission of lower policy rates to deposit and lending rates improved during FY2020-21.
- NIFTY-50 and BSE SENSEX reached **record high closing** of 14,644.7 and 49,792.12, respectively, on January 20, 2021
- The recovery rate for the Scheduled Commercial Banks through IBC (since its inception) has been over 45%.

PRICES AND IN FLATION

- **Headline CPI inflation:**
  - Averaged 6.6% during April-December, 2020 and stood at 4.6% in December, 2020, mainly driven by rise in food inflation (from 6.7% in 2019-20 to 9.1%

during April-December 2020, owing to build up in vegetable prices).

- CPI headline and its subgroups witnessed inflation during April-October 2020, driven by substantial increase in price momentum – due to the **initial disruptions caused by COVID-19 lockdown.**
- Moderated price momentum by November 2020 for most subgroups, coupled with positive base effect, helped ease inflation.

▶ **Rural-urban difference in CPI inflation** saw a decline in 2020:

- Since November 2019, CPI-Urban inflation has closed the gap with CPI-Rural inflation.
- Food inflation has almost converged now.
- Divergence in rural-urban inflation observed in other components of CPI like fuel and light, clothing and footwear, miscellaneous, etc.

▶ During April-December 2019 as well as April-December 2020-21, the major driver of CPI-C inflation was the **food and beverages** group:

- Contribution increased to 59% during April-December, 2020, compared to 53.7% during April-December, 2019.

▶ **Thali cost increased** between June 2020 and November 2020, however a sharp fall in the month of December reflecting the fall in the prices of many essential food commodities.

▶ **State-wise trend:**

- CPI-C inflation increased in most of the states in the current year.
- Regional variation persists.
- Inflation ranged from 3.2% to 11% across States/UTs during June-December 2020 compared to (-) 0.3% to 7.6% during the same period last year.

▶ **Food inflation** driving overall CPI-C inflation due to the relatively more weight of food items in the index.

▶ Steps taken to stabilise prices of food items:

- Banning of export of onions
- Imposition of stock limit on onions
- Easing of restriction on imports of pulses

▶ **Gold prices:**

- Sharp spike as investors turned to **gold as a safe haven investment amid COVID-19** induced economic uncertainties.
- Compared to other assets, gold had considerably higher returns during FY2020-21.

▶ Consistency in import policy warrants attention:

- Increased dependence on imports of edible oils poses risk of fluctuations in import prices.
- Imports impacting production and prices of domestic edible oil market, coupled with frequent changes in import policy of pulses and edible oils, add to confusion among farmers/producers and delay imports.

SUSTAINABLE DEVELOPMENT AND CLIMATE CHANGE

▶ India has taken several proactive steps to **mainstream the SDGs** into the policies, schemes and programmes.

▶ **Voluntary National Review** (VNR) presented to the United Nations High-Level Political Forum (HLPF) on Sustainable Development.

- **Localisation of SDGs** is crucial to any strategy aimed at achieving the goals under the 2030 Agenda.
  - Several States/UTs have created institutional structures for the implementation of SDGs and also nodal mechanisms within every department and at the district levels for better coordination and convergence.
- Sustainable development remains core to the development strategy despite the unprecedented COVID-19 pandemic crisis.
- Eight National Missions under **National Action Plan on Climate Change (NAPCC)** focused on the objectives of adaptation, mitigation and preparedness on climate risks.
- **India's Nationally Determined Contributions** (NDC) states that finance is a critical enabler of climate change action.
- The financing considerations will therefore remain critical especially as the country steps up the targets substantially.
- The goal of jointly mobilising US$ 100 billion a year by 2020 for climate financing by the developed countries has remained elusive.
- The postponement of COP26 to 2021 also gives less time for negotiations and other evidence-based work to inform the post-2025 goal.
- Despite overall growth in the global bond markets, green bond issuance in the first half of 2020 slowed down from 2019, possibly as a result of the on going COVID-19 pandemic.
- **International Solar Alliance (ISA)** launched two new initiatives – **'World Solar Bank'** and **'One Sun One World One Grid Initiative'** – poised to bring about solar energy revolution globally.

AGRICULTURE AND FOOD MANAGEMENT

- India's **Agricultural (and Allied Activities) sector** has shown its resilience amid the adversities of COVID-19 induced lockdowns with a **growth of 3.4% at constant prices during 2020-21 (first advance estimate).**
- The share of Agriculture and Allied Sectors in Gross Value Added (GVA) of the country at current prices is **17.8%** for the year 2019-20 (CSO-Provisional Estimates of National Income, 29th May 2020).
- **Gross Capital Formation (GCF)** relative to GVA showing a fluctuating trend from 17.7 % in 2013-14 to 16.4 % in 2018-19, with a dip to 14.7 % in 2015-16.
- **Total food grain production** in the country in the agriculture year 2019-20 (as per Fourth Advance Estimates) is **11.44 million tons** more than during 2018-19.
- The **actual agricultural credit flow** was **₹13,92,469.81** crores against the target of ₹13,50,000 crores in 2019-20. The target for 2020-21 was ₹15,00,000 crores and a sum of ₹ 9,73,517.80 crores was disbursed till 30th November 2020:
  - **1.5 crore dairy farmers** of milk cooperatives and milk producer companies were targeted to provide Kisan Credit Cards (KCC) as part of Prime Minister's AtmaNirbhar Bharat Package after the budget announcement it in February 2020.
  - As of mid-January 2021, a total of **44,673 Kisan Credit Cards (KCCs)** have been issued to fishers and fish farmers and an additional 4.04 lakh applications from fishers and fish farmers are with the banks at various stages of issuance.

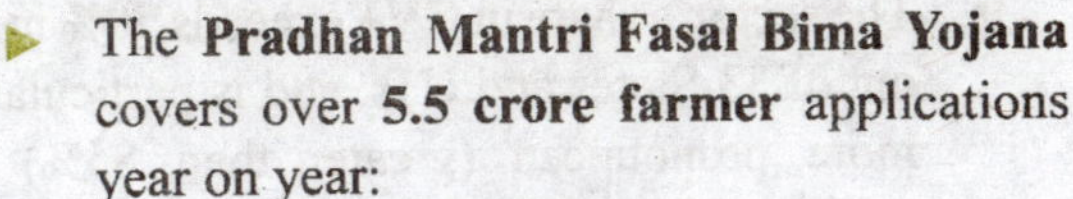

- The **Pradhan Mantri Fasal Bima Yojana** covers over **5.5 crore farmer** applications year on year:
  - Claims worth ₹ **90,000 crores** paid, as on 12th January 2021.
  - Speedy claim settlement directly into the farmer accounts through Aadhar linkage.
  - **70 lakh farmers** benefitted and claims worth ₹ 8741.30 crores were transferred during COVID-19 lock-down period.
- An amount of ₹ **18000 crores** have been deposited directly in the bank accounts of **9 crore farmer families** of the country in December 2020 in the 7th instalment of financial benefit under the **PM-KISAN** scheme.
- **Fish production** reached an all-time high of 14.16 million metric tons during 2019-20:
  - GVA by the Fisheries sector to the national economy stood at ₹2,12,915 crores constituting 1.24% of the total national GVA and 7.28% of the agricultural GVA.
- **Food Processing Industries (FPI)** sector growing at an Average Annual Growth Rate (AAGR) of around 9.99 % as compared to around 3.12 % in Agriculture and 8.25 % in Manufacturing at 2011-12 prices during the last 5 years ending 2018-19.
- **Pradhan Mantri Garib Kalyan Anna Yojana:**
  - 80.96 crore beneficiaries were provided foodgrains above NFSA mandated requirement free of cost till November, 2020.
  - Over 200 LMT of foodgrains were provided amounting to a fiscal outgo of over ₹ 75000 crores.
- **AtmaNirbhar Bharat Package:** 5 kg per person per month for four months (May to August) to approximately 8 crore migrants (excluded under NFSA or state ration card) entailing subsidy of ₹ 3109 crores approximately.

INDUSTRY AND INFRASTRUCTURE

- A strong **V-shaped recovery** of economic activity further confirmed by IIP data.
- The **IIP & eight-core index** further inched up to pre-COVID levels.
- The broad-based recovery in the IIP resulted in a growth of (-) 1.9 % in November-2020 as compared to a growth of 2.1 % in November-2019 and a nadir of (-) 57.3 % in April-2020.
- Further improvement and firming up in industrial activities are foreseen with the Government enhancing capital expenditure, the vaccination drive and the resolute push forward on long pending reform measures.
- **AtmaNirbhar Bharat Abhiyan** with a stimulus package worth **15 of India's GDP** announced.
- India's rank in the **Ease of Doing Business** (EoDB) Index for 2019 has moved upwards to the **63rd position in 2020** from 77th in 2018 as per the Doing Business Report (DBR):
  - India has improved its position in 7 out of 10 indicators.
  - Acknowledges India as one of the top 10 improvers, the third time in a row, with an improvement of 67 ranks in three years.
  - It is also the highest jump by any large country since 2011.

- **FDI equity inflows were US$49.98 billion in FY20** as compared to US$44.37 billion during FY19:
    - It is US$30.0 billion for FY21 (up to September-2020).
    - The bulk of FDI equity flow is in the non-manufacturing sector.
    - Within the manufacturing sector, industries like automobile, tele-communication, metallurgical, non-conventional energy, chemical (other than fertilizers), food processing, petroleum & natural gas got the bulk of FDI.
- Government has announced a **Production-Linked Incentive (PLI) Scheme** in the 10 key sectors under the aegis of **Atma Nirbhar Bharat** for enhancing India's manufacturing capabilities and exports:
    - To be implemented by the ministries concerned with an overall expenditure estimated at ₹ 1.46 lakh crores and with sector specific financial limits.

SERVICES SECTOR

- India's services sector contracted by nearly 16 % during H1: FY2020-21, during the COVID-19 pandemic mandated lockdown, owing to its **contact-intensive nature.**
- **Key indicators** such as Services Purchasing Managers' Index, rail freight traffic, and port traffic, are all displaying a V-shaped recovery after a sharp decline during the lockdown.
- Despite the disruptions being witnessed globally, **FDI inflows** into India's services sector grew robustly by 34% Y-o-Y during April-September 2020 to reach US$ 23.6 billion.
- The services sector accounts for over **54% of India's GVA** and nearly **four-fifths of total FDI inflow into India.**
- The sector's share in GVA exceeds 50% in 15 out of 33 States and UTs, and is particularly more pronounced (greater than 85%) in Delhi and Chandigarh.
- Services sector accounts for **48% of total exports**, outperforming goods exports in the recent years.
- The **shipping turnaround time** at ports has almost halved from 4.67 days in 2010-11 to **2.62 days** in 2019-20.
- The Indian **start-up ecosystem** has been progressing well amidst the COVID-19 pandemic, being home to **38 unicorns** – adding a record number of 12 start-ups to the unicorn list last year.
- India's **space sector** has grown exponentially in the past six decades:
    - Spent about US$ 1.8 billion on space programmes in 2019-20.
    - Space ecosystem is undergoing several policy reforms to engage private players and attract innovation and investment.

SOCIAL INFRASTRUCTURE, EMPLOYMENT AND HUMAN DEVELOPMENT

- The combined (Centre and States) **social sector expenditure** as % of GDP has increased in 2020-21 compared to last year.
- India's rank in HDI 2019 was recorded at 131, out of a total 189 countries:
    - India's **GNI per capita** (2017 PPP $) has increased from US$ 6,427 in 2018 to US$ 6,681 in 2019.
    - **Life expectancy at birth** improved from 69.4 years in 2018 to 69.7 years in 2019.
- The access to data network, electronic devices such as computer, laptop, smart phone, etc. gained importance due to **online**

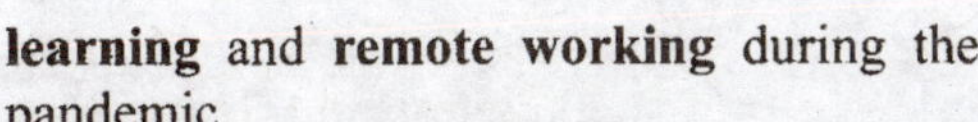

learning and **remote working** during the pandemic.

- Major proportion of workforce engaged as regular wage/salaried in the urban sector during the period of January 2019-March 2020 (quarterly survey of PLFS).
- Government's incentive to boost employment through **Atma Nirbhar Bharat Rozgar Yojana** and rationalisation and simplification of existing labour codes into 4 codes.
- Low level of female LFPR in India:
    - Females spending disproportionately more time on unpaid domestic and care giving services to household members as compared to their male counterparts (Time Use Survey, 2019).
    - Need to promote non-discriminatory practices at the workplace like pay and career progression, improve work incentives, including other medical and social security benefits for female workers.
- Under **PMGKP** announced in March 2020, **cash transfers of upto ₹ 1000** to existing old aged, widowed and disabled beneficiaries under the National Social Assistance Programme (NSAP).
- An amount of ₹ 500 each was transferred for three months digitally into bank accounts of the women beneficiaries under **PM Jan Dhan Yojana**, totaling about **₹ 20.64 crores.**
- **Free distribution of gas cylinders** to about **8 crore** families for three months.
- Limit of collateral free lending increased from ₹ 10 lakhs to ₹ 20 lakhs for **63 lakh women SHGs** which would support 6.85 crore households.
- **Wages under Mahatma Gandhi NREGA** increased by ₹ 20 from ₹ 182 to ₹ 202 w.e.f. 1st April, 2020.
- **India's fight against COVID-19:**
    - Initial measures of lockdown, social distancing, travel advisories, practicing hand wash, wearing masks reduced the spread of the disease.
    - Country also acquired **self-reliance in essential medicines**, hand sanitizers, protective equipment including masks, PPE Kits, ventilators, COVID-19 testing and treatment facilities.
    - **World's largest COVID-19 vaccination drive** commenced on 16th January 2021 using two indigenously manufactured vaccines.

Concluding remarks After going into the economic havoc wrecked by the COVID-19 pandemic, the Survey ends on an optimistic note— by advising the Government to follow an 'expansionary' fiscal approach to help economy recover out of it smoothly. It has also advised the Government to not be afraid of the impact which a higher fiscal deficit may leave on the economy by linking the cost of borrowings (which will be needed to finance the higher fiscal deficit) with the growth rate of the year— by putting forth the idea of 'interest rate growth rate differential' (IRGD). In line with the suggestions of the Survey, we find the Government announcing a major fiscal plan in the *Union Budget 2021-22* aimed at faster economic recovery by increasing its expenditures.

UNION BUDGET 2021-22

The Union Budget 2021—22 was presented by the Union Finance and Corporate Affairs Minister in Parliament an February 1, 2021. Presenting the first ever digital Union Budget, the minister stated that India's fight against COVID-19 continues into 2021 and that this moment in history, when the political, economic, and strategic relations in the post-COWD world are changing, is the dawn of a new era—one in which India is well-poised to truly be the land of promise arud hope.

In this Chapter...

- Health and Wellbeing
- Physical and Financial Capital and Infrastructure
- Inclusive Development for Aspirational India
- Reinvigorating Human Capital
- Innovation and R&D
- Minimum Government, Maximum Governance

The **key highlights** of the budget have been given below:

6 pillars of the Union Budget 2021-22:

1. Health and Wellbeing
2. Physical & Financial Capital, and Infrastructure
3. Inclusive Development for Aspirational India
4. Reinvigorating Human Capital
5. Innovation and R&D
6. Minimum Government and Maximum Governance

HEALTH AND WELLBEING

- **₹ 2,23,846 crore** outlay for *Health and Wellbeing* in BE 2021–22 as against **₹ 94,452 crore** in BE 2020-21 – an **increase of 137%.**
- Focus on strengthening three areas: **Preventive, Curative, and Wellbeing.**
- Steps being taken for improving health and wellbeing.

Vaccines

- **₹ 35,000 crore for COVID-19 vaccine** in BE 2021–22.
- The **Made-in-India Pneumococcal Vaccine** to be rolled out across the country, from present 5 states – **to avert 50,000 child deaths annually**.

Health Systems

- **₹ 64,180 crore** outlay over 6 years for **PM AtmaNirbhar Swasth Bharat Yojana –**

a new centrally sponsored scheme to be launched, in addition to NHM.

- Main interventions under PM Atma Nirbhar Swasth Bharat Yojana:
  - **National Institution for One Health.**
  - 17,788 rural and 11,024 urban Health and Wellness Centres.
  - **4 regional National Institutes for Virology.**
  - 15 Health Emergency Operation Centres and **2 mobile hospitals.**
  - **Integrated public health labs** in all districts and 3382 block public health units in **11 states.**
  - **Critical care hospital blocks** in 602 districts and **12 central institutions.**
  - Strengthening of the **National Centre for Disease Control (NCDC),** its 5 regional branches and 20 metropolitan health surveillance units.
  - Expansion of the **Integrated Health Information Portal** to all States/UTs to connect all public health labs.
  - **17 new Public Health Units** and strengthening of 33 existing Public Health Units.
  - **Regional Research Platform** for WHO South-East Asia Region.
  - 9 Bio-Safety Level III laboratories.

Nutrition

- **Mission Poshan 2.0** to be launched:
  - To strengthen nutritional content, delivery, outreach, and outcome.
  - Merging the Supplementary Nutrition Programme and the Poshan Abhiyan.
  - Intensified strategy to be adopted to improve nutritional outcomes across 112 Aspirational Districts.

Universal Coverage of Water Supply

- **₹ 2,87,000 crore** over 5 years for **Jal Jeevan Mission (Urban)** - to be launched with an aim to provide:
  - **2.86 crore household tap connections.**
  - Universal water supply in all 4,378 Urban Local Bodies.
  - Liquid waste management in 500 AMRUT cities.

Swachh Bharat, Swasth Bharat

- **₹ 1,41,678 crore** over 5 years for **Urban Swachh Bharat Mission 2.0.**
- Main interventions under Swachh Bharat Mission (Urban) 2.0:
  - Complete **faecal sludge management** and **wastewater treatment.**
  - **Source segregation** of garbage.
  - **Reduction in single-use plastic.**
  - **Reduction in air pollution** by effectively managing waste from construction-and-demolition activities.
  - **Bioremediation** of all legacy dump sites.

Clean Air

- **₹ 2,217 crore** to tackle air pollution, for **42 urban centres with a million-plus population.**

Scrapping Policy

- **Voluntary** vehicle scrapping policy to **phase out old and unfit vehicles.**
- **Fitness tests** in automated fitness centres:
  - After **20 years** in the case of **personal vehicles.**
  - After **15 years** in the case of **commercial vehicles.**

PHYSICAL AND FINANCIAL CAPITAL AND INFRASTRUCTURE

Production Linked Incentive scheme (PLI)

- **₹ 1.97 lakh crore** in next 5 years for PLI schemes in **13 Sectors.**
- To create and nurture **manufacturing global champions** for an **AtmaNirbhar Bharat.**
- To help manufacturing companies become an integral part of **global supply chains,** possess core competence and **cutting-edge technology.**
- To bring **scale and size** in key sectors.
- To provide **jobs to the youth.**

Textiles

- **Mega Investment Textile Parks (MITRA)** scheme, in addition to PLI:
  - **7 Textile Parks** to be established over 3 years.
- Textile industry to become **globally competitive,** attract **large investments** and **boost employment generation & exports.**

Infrastructure

- **National Infrastructure Pipeline (NIP)** expanded to 7,400 projects:
  - Around 217 projects worth **₹ 1.10 lakh crore** completed.
- Measures in three thrust areas to increase funding for NIP:
  - Creation of institutional structures.
  - Big thrust on monetising assets.
  - Enhancing the share of capital expenditure.

Creation of institutional structures: Infrastructure Financing

- **₹ 20,000 crore** to set up and capitalise a **Development Financial Institution (DFI)** – to act as a provider, enabler and catalyst for infrastructure financing.
- **₹ 5 lakh crore** lending portfolios to be created under the proposed DFI in 3 years.
- **Debt Financing** by Foreign Portfolio Investors to be enabled by amending InvITs' and REITs' legislation.

Big thrust on monetising assets

- **National Monetisation Pipeline** to be launched.
- Important **asset monetisation** measures:
  - 5 operational toll roads worth **₹ 5,000 crore** being transferred to the **NHAIInvIT.**
  - Transmission assets worth **₹ 7,000 crore** to be transferred to the **PGCILInvIT.**
  - **Dedicated Freight Corridor** assets to be monetised by Railways, for operations and maintenance, after commissioning.
  - Next lot of **Airports** to be monetised for operations and management concession.
  - Other **core infrastructure assets** to be rolled out under the Asset Monetisation Programme:
    - **Oil and Gas Pipelines** of GAIL, IOCL and HPCL.
    - **AAI Airports** in Tier II and III cities.
    - Other **Railway Infrastructure** Assets.
    - **Warehousing Assets** of CPSEs such as Central Warehousing Corporation and NAFED.
    - **Sports Stadiums.**

Sharp Increase in Capital Budget

- **₹ 5.54 lakh crore** capital expenditure in BE 2021–22 – sharp **increase of 34.5%** over ₹ 4.12 lakh crore allocated in BE 2020-21.
  - Over **₹ 2 lakh crore** to States and Autonomous Bodies for their Capital Expenditure.
  - Over **₹ 44,000 crore** for the Department of Economic Affairs to provide for projects/programmes/departments exhibiting good progress on Capital Expenditure.

Roads and Highways Infrastructure

- **₹ 1,18,101 lakh crore**, highest ever outlay, for Ministry of Road Transport and Highways – of which ₹ 1,08,230 crore is for capital.
- Under the **₹ 5.35 lakh crore Bharatmala Pariyojana**, more than 13,000 km length of roads worth ₹ 3.3 lakh crore awarded for construction:
  - **3,800 km** have already been constructed.
  - Another **8,500 km** to be awarded for construction by March 2022.
  - Additional **11,000 km of national highway corridors** to be completed by March 2022.
- **Economic corridors** being planned:
  - **₹ 1.03 lakh crore** outlay for 3,500 km of NHs in Tamil Nadu.
  - **₹ 65,000 crore** investment for 1,100 km of NHs in Kerala.
  - **₹ 25,000 crore** for 675 km of NHs in West Bengal.
  - Over **₹ 34,000 crore** to be allocated for 1300 km of NHs to be undertaken in next 3 years in Assam, in addition to ₹ 19,000 crore works of NHs currently in progress in the State.
- **Flagship Corridors/Expressways:**
  - **Delhi-Mumbai Expressway** – Remaining 260 km to be awarded before 31.3.2021.
  - **Bengaluru-Chennai Expressway** – 278 km to be initiated in the current FY; construction to begin in 2021–22.
  - **Kanpur-Lucknow Expressway** – 63 km expressway providing an alternate route to NH 27 to be initiated in 2021–22.
  - **Delhi-Dehradun economic corridor** – 210 km to be initiated in the current FY; construction to begin in 2021–22.
  - **Raipur-Vishakhapatnam** – 464 km passing through Chhattisgarh, Odisha and North Andhra Pradesh, to be awarded in the current year; construction to start in 2021–22.
  - **Chennai-Salem corridor** – 277 km expressway to be awarded and construction to start in 2021–22.
  - **Amritsar-Jamnagar** – Construction to commence in 2021–22.
  - **Delhi-Katra** – Construction will commence in 2021–22.
- **Advanced Traffic management system** in all new 4 and 6-lane highways:
  - Speed radars.
  - Variable message signboards.
  - GPS enabled recovery vans will be installed.

Railway Infrastructure

- **₹ 1,10,055 crore** for Railways of which ₹ 1,07,100 crore is for capital expenditure.
- **National Rail Plan for India (2030)**: to create a 'future ready' Railway system by 2030.

- **100% electrification** of Broad-Gauge routes to be completed by December, 2023.
- Broad Gauge Route Kilometers (RKM) electrification to reach 46,000 RKM, i.e., 72% by end of 2021.
- Western Dedicated Freight Corridor (DFC) and Eastern DFC to be commissioned by June 2022, to bring down the logistic costs – enabling **Make in India strategy.**
- Additional initiatives proposed:
  - The Sonnagar-Gomoh Section (263.7 km) of Eastern DFC to be taken up in PPP mode in 2021–22.
  - **Future dedicated freight corridor projects** –
    - East Coast corridor from Kharagpur to Vijayawada.
    - East-West Corridor from Bhusaval to Kharagpur to Dankuni.
    - North-South corridor from Itarsi to Vijayawada.
- Measures for **passenger convenience and safety**:
  - Aesthetically designed **Vista Dome LHB coach on tourist routes** for better travel.
  - High density network and highly utilised network routes to have an **indigenously developed automatic train protection system**, eliminating train collision due to human error.

Urban Infrastructure

- Raising the share of public transport in urban areas by **expansion of metro rail network** and augmentation of city bus service.
- **₹ 18,000 crore** for a new scheme, to augment public bus transport:
  - Innovative **PPP** models to run more than **20,000 buses.**
  - To boost automobile sector, provide fillip to economic growth, create employment opportunities for our youth.
- A total of 702 km of conventional metro is operational and another 1,016 km of metro and RRTS is under construction in 27 cities.
- **'MetroLite'** and **'MetroNeo'** technologies to provide metro rail systems at much lesser cost with similar experience in Tier-2 cities and peripheral areas of Tier-1 cities.
- Central counterpart funding to:
  - Kochi Metro Railway Phase-II of 11.5 km at a cost of ₹ 1957.05 crore.
  - Chennai Metro Railway Phase –II of 118.9 km at a cost of ₹ 63,246 crore.
  - Bengaluru Metro Railway Project Phase 2A and 2B of 58.19 km at a cost of ₹ 14,788 crore.
  - Nagpur Metro Rail Project Phase-II and Nashik Metro at a cost of ₹ 5,976 crore and ₹ 2,092 crores respectively.

Power Infrastructure

- 139 Giga Watts of installed capacity and **1.41 lakh circuit km** of transmission lines added, and additional **2.8 crore households** connected in past 6 years.
- Consumers to have alternatives to choose the Distribution Company for enhancing competitiveness.
- **₹ 3,05,984 crore** over 5 years for a revamped, reforms-based and result-linked new **power distribution sector scheme.**
- A comprehensive **National Hydrogen Energy Mission 2021–22** to be launched.

Ports, Shipping, Waterways

- **₹ 2,000 crore** worth 7 projects to be offered in **PPP-mode** in FY21–22 for **operation of major ports.**

- Indian shipping companies to get ₹ **1624 crore** worth subsidy support over 5 years in global tenders of Ministries and CPSEs.
- To **double the recycling capacity** of around 4.5 Million Light Displacement Tonne (LDT) by 2024; to generate an **additional 1.5 lakh jobs**.

Petroleum & Natural Gas

- Extension of **Ujjwala Scheme** to cover **1 crore more beneficiaries.**
- To add **100 more districts** to the City Gas Distribution network in next 3 years.
- **A new gas pipeline project in J&K.**
- An independent **Gas Transport System Operator** to be set up for facilitation and coordination of booking of common carrier capacity in all-natural gas pipelines on a non-discriminatory open access basis.

Financial Capital

- A single **Securities Markets Code** to be evolved.
- Support for development of a **world-class Fin-Tech hub at the GIFT-IFSC.**
- A new permanent institutional framework to help in the development of Bond market by purchasing investment grade debt securities both in stressed and normal times.
- Setting up a system of **Regulated Gold Exchanges**: SEBI to be notified as a regulator and Warehousing Development and Regulatory Authority to be strengthened
- To develop an **investor charter** as a right of all financial investors.
- **Capital infusion** of ₹ **1,000 crore** to Solar Energy Corporation of India and ₹ **1,500 crore** to Indian Renewable Energy Development Agency.

Increasing FDI in Insurance Sector

- To increase the permissible **FDI limit from 49% to 74%** and allow foreign ownership and control with safeguards.

Stressed Asset Resolution

- Asset Reconstruction Company Limited and Asset Management Company to be set up.

Recapitalization of PSBs

- ₹ **20,000 crore** in 2021–22 to further consolidate the financial capacity of PSBs.

Deposit Insurance

- **Amendments to the DICGC Act, 1961**, to help depositors get an easy and time-bound access to their deposits to the extent of the deposit insurance cover.
- Minimum loan size eligible for debt recovery under the Securitisation and Reconstruction of Financial Assets and Enforcement of Security Interest **(SARFAESI) Act, 2002** proposed to be reduced **from ₹ 50 lakh to ₹ 20 lakh** for NBFCs with minimum asset size of ₹ 100 crore.

Company Matters

- To **decriminalise the Limited Liability Partnership (LLP) Act, 2008.**
- **Easing Compliance requirement of Small companies** by revising their definition under the Companies Act, 2013 by increasing their thresholds for Paid up capital from "not exceeding ₹ 50 Lakh" to "not exceeding ₹ 2 Crore" and turnover from "not exceeding ₹ 2 Crore" to "not exceeding ₹ 20 Cr".
- **Promoting start-ups and innovators by incentivising the incorporation of One Person Companies (OPCs):**

- Allowing their growth without any restrictions on paid up capital and turnover.
- Allowing their conversion into any other type of company at any time.
- Reducing the residency limit for an Indian citizen to set up an OPC from 182 days to 120 days.
- Allowing Non-Resident Indians (NRIs) to incorporate OPCs in India.

▶ To ensure **faster resolution of cases** by:

- **Strengthening NCLT** framework.
- Implementation of **e-Courts** system.
- Introduction of **alternate methods of debt resolution** and special framework for MSMEs.

▶ Launch of data analytics, artificial intelligence, machine learning driven **MCA21 Version 3.0 in 2021-22**.

Disinvestment and Strategic Sale

▶ **₹ 1,75,000 crore** estimated receipts from disinvestment in BE 2020-21.

▶ **Strategic disinvestment** of BPCL, Air India, Shipping Corporation of India, Container Corporation of India, IDBI Bank, BEML, Pawan Hans, Neelachal Ispat Nigam limited, etc. to be completed in 2021–22.

▶ Other than IDBI Bank, two Public Sector Banks and one General Insurance company to be privatised.

▶ **IPO of LIC** in 2021–22.

▶ **New policy for Strategic Disinvestment** approved; CPSEs except in four strategic areas to be privatised.

▶ NITI Aayog to work out on the next list of CPSEs to be taken up for strategic disinvestment.

▶ Incentivising States for disinvestment of their Public Sector Companies, using central funds.

▶ **Special Purpose Vehicle** in the form of a company to monetise idle land.

▶ Introducing a revised mechanism for ensuring **timely closure of sick or loss making CPSEs**.

Government Financial Reforms

▶ **Treasury Single Account** (TSA) System for Autonomous Bodies to be extended for universal application.

▶ **Separate Administrative Structure** to streamline the 'Ease of Doing Business' for Cooperatives.

INCLUSIVE DEVELOPMENT FOR ASPIRATIONAL INDIA

Agriculture

▶ Ensured **MSP at minimum 1.5 times** the cost of production across all commodities.

▶ **SWAMITVA Scheme** to be extended to all States/UTs, 1.80 lakh property-owners in 1,241 villages have already been provided cards.

▶ **Agricultural credit** target enhanced to **₹16.5 lakh crore** in FY22 - animal husbandry, dairy, and fisheries to be the focus areas.

▶ **Rural Infrastructure Development Fund** to be enhanced to ₹ **40,000 crore** from ₹ 30,000 crore.

▶ To **double the Micro Irrigation Fund to ₹ 10,000 crore.**

▶ **'Operation Green Scheme'** to be extended to **22 perishable products**, to boost value addition in agriculture and allied products.

Froam 43 Side B

- Around **1.68 crore farmers** registered and **₹ 1.14 lakh crore** of trade value carried out through **e-NAMs**; **1,000 more mandis** to be integrated with e-NAM to bring transparency and competitiveness.
- APMCs to get access to the **Agriculture Infrastructure Funds** for augmenting infrastructure facilities.

Fisheries

- Investments to develop modern fishing harbours and fish landing centres – both marine and inland.
- **5 major fishing harbours** – Kochi, Chennai, Visakhapatnam, Paradip, and Petuaghat to be developed as hubs of economic activity.
- **Multipurpose Seaweed Park** in Tamil Nadu to promote seaweed cultivation.

Migrant Workers and Labourers

- **One Nation One Ration Card** scheme for beneficiaries to claim rations anywhere in the country - **migrant workers** to benefit the most.
  - Scheme implementation so far covered 86% of beneficiaries across 32 States and UTs.
  - Remaining 4 states to be integrated in next few months.
- **Portal to collect information** on unorganised labour force, migrant workers especially, to help formulate schemes for them.
- Implementation of **4 labour codes** underway
  - Social security benefits for gig and platform workers too.
  - Minimum wages and coverage under the Employees State Insurance Corporation applicable for all categories of workers.
  - Women workers allowed in all categories, including night-shifts with adequate protection.
  - Compliance burden on employers reduced with single registration and licensing, and online returns.

Financial Inclusion

- Under **Stand-Up India Scheme** for SCs, STs and women,
  - Margin money requirement reduced to 15%.
  - To also include loans for allied agricultural activities.
- **₹ 15,700 crore** budget allocation to MSME Sector, more than double of this year's BE.

REINVIGORATING HUMAN CAPITAL

School Education

- **15,000 schools** to be strengthened by implementing all NEP components. Shall act as exemplar schools in their regions for mentoring others.
- **100 new Sainik Schools** to be set up in partnership with NGOs/private schools/ states.

Higher Education

- Legislation to be introduced to set-up **Higher Education Commission of India** as an umbrella body with 4 separate vehicles for standard-setting, accreditation, regulation, and funding.
- Creation of formal umbrella structure to cover all Govt. colleges, universities, research institutions in a city for greater synergy.

- Glue grant to implement the same across 9 cities.
- **Central University** to come up in **Leh** for accessibility of higher education in Ladakh.

Scheduled Castes and Scheduled Tribes Welfare

- **750 Eklavya model residential schools** in tribal areas:
  - Unit cost of each school to be increased to **₹ 38 crore.**
  - For hilly and difficult areas, to **₹ 48 crore.**
  - Focus on creation of robust infrastructure facilities for tribal students.
- Revamped **Post Matric Scholarship Scheme** for welfare of SCs.
  - **₹ 35,219 crore** enhanced Central Assistance for 6 years till 2025-2026.
  - **4 crore** SC students to benefit.

Skilling

- Proposed amendment to **Apprenticeship Act** to enhance opportunities for youth.
- **₹ 3000 crore** for realignment of existing **National Apprenticeship Training Scheme (NATS)** towards post-education apprenticeship, training of graduates and diploma holders in Engineering.
- Initiatives for partnership with other countries in skilling to be taken forward, similar to partnership:
  - With UAE to benchmark skill qualifications, assessment, certification, and deployment of certified workforce.
  - With Japan for a collaborative Training Inter Training Programme (TITP) to transfer of skills, technique and knowledge.

INNOVATION AND R&D

- Modalities of **National Research Foundation** announced in July 2019:
  - **₹ 50,000 crore** outlay over 5 years.
  - To strengthen overall research ecosystem with focus on national-priority thrust areas.
- **₹ 1,500 crore** for the proposed scheme to promote digital modes of payment.
- **National Language Translation Mission (NTLM)** to make governance-and-policy related knowledge available in major Indian languages.
- PSLV-CS51 to be launched by **New Space India Limited (NSIL)** carrying Brazil's Amazonia Satellite and some Indian satellites.
- As part of the **Gaganyaan** mission activities:
  - **4 Indian astronauts** being trained on Generic Space Flight aspects, in Russia.
  - **First unmanned launch** is slated for **December 2021.**
- **₹ 4,000 crore** over five years for **Deep Ocean Mission** survey exploration and conservation of deep sea biodiversity.

MINIMUM GOVERNMENT, MAXIMUM GOVERNANCE

- Measures being undertaken to bring reforms in Tribunals to ensure speedy justice.
- **National Commission for Allied Healthcare Professionals** already introduced to ensure transparent and efficient regulation of the 56 allied healthcare professions.
- The **National Nursing and Midwifery Commission Bill** introduced for the same in nursing profession.

- **Conciliation Mechanism** with mandate for quick resolution of contractual disputes with CPSEs.
- **₹ 3,768 crore** allocated for first digital census in the history of India.
- **₹ 300 crore** grant to the Government of Goa for the diamond jubilee celebrations of the state's liberation from Portuguese.
- **₹ 1,000 crore** for the welfare of Tea workers especially women and their children in Assam and West Bengal through a special scheme.

Fiscal Position

- RE for Expenditure is ₹ **34.50 lakh crore** as against original BE expenditure of ₹ **30.42 lakh crore.**
    - Quality of expenditure has been maintained as Capital Expenditure estimated as per RE is ₹ **4.39 lakh crore** in 2020-2021 as against ₹ **4.12 lakh crore** in BE 2020-21.
- Estimates of ₹ **34.83 lakh crore** BE for expenditure in 2021-2022 including ₹ **5.5 lakh crore** as capital expenditure, an increase of 34.5% to give required push to economy.
- The fiscal deficit in BE 2021-2022 is estimated to be **6.8% of GDP**. The fiscal deficit in RE 2020-21 is pegged **at 9.5% of GDP** - funded through Government borrowings, multilateral borrowings, Small Saving Funds and short-term borrowings:
    - Gross borrowing from the market for the next year to be around 12 lakh crore.
    - Plan to continue the path of fiscal consolidation, achieving a fiscal deficit level **below 4.5% of GDP by 2025-2026** with a fairly steady decline over the period.
    - It will be achieved by increasing the buoyancy of tax revenue through improved compliance, and secondly, by increased receipts from monetisation of assets, including Public Sector Enterprises and land.
    - Deviation Statement under Sections 4(5) and 7(3) (b) of the FRBM Act tabled, necessitated by this year's unforeseen and unprecedented circumstances.
    - Amendment to FRBM Act proposed to achieve targeted Fiscal Deficit levels.
- The Contingency Fund of India is to be augmented from ₹ **500 crore** to ₹ **30,000 crore** through Finance Bill.

Net borrowing of the States

- Net borrowing for the states allowed at **4% of GSDP for the year 2021-2022** as per the recommendation of 15th FC.
    - Part of this earmarked for incremental capital expenditure.
    - Additional borrowing ceiling of 0.5% of GSDP will be provided subject to conditions.
- States expected to reach a **fiscal deficit of 3% of GSDP by 2023-24**, as recommended by the 15th Finance Commission.

Fifteenth Finance Commission

- The final report covering **2021-26** was submitted to the President, retaining vertical shares of states at **41%.**
- Funds to UTs of Jammu and Kashmir and Ladakh would be provided by Centre.
- On the Commission's recommendation, ₹ **1,18,452 crore** have been provided as Revenue Deficit Grant to 17 states in 2021–22, as against ₹ **74,340 crore** to 14 states in 2020-21.

Tax Proposals

Vision of a transparent, efficient tax system to promote investments and employment in the country with **minimum burden on taxpayers.**

1. Direct Taxes

- **Achievements:**
  - **Corporate tax rate** slashed to make it among the lowest in the world.
  - Burden of taxation on **small taxpayers** eased by increasing rebates.
  - Return filers almost **doubled to 6.48 crore** in 2020 from **3.31 crore** in 2014.
  - **Faceless Assessment** and **Faceless Appeal** introduced.
  - **Relief to Senior Citizens:**
    - **Exemption from filing tax returns** for senior citizens over 75 years of age and having only pension and interest income; tax to be deducted by paying bank.
- **Reducing Disputes, Simplifying Settlement:**
  - **Time limit for re-opening cases** reduced to **3 years** from 6 years.
  - **Serious tax evasion cases,** with evidence of concealment of income of ₹ 50 lakh or more in a year, to be re-opened only up to 10 years, with the approval of the Principal Chief Commissioner.
  - **Dispute Resolution Committee** to be set up for taxpayers with taxable income up to ₹ 50 lakh and disputed income up to ₹ 10 lakh.
  - **National Faceless Income Tax Appellate Tribunal Centre** to be established.
  - Over **1 lakh taxpayers** opted to settle tax disputes of over ₹ 85,000 crore through **Vivad Se Vishwas Scheme** until 30th January 2021.
- **Relaxation to NRIs:**
  - Rules to be notified for removing hardships faced by NRIs regarding their foreign retirement accounts.
  - **Incentivising Digital Economy:**
    - **Limit of turnover for tax audit** increased to **₹ 10 crore** from ₹ 5 crore for entities carrying out 95% transactions digitally.
  - **Relief for Dividend:**
    - Dividend payment to REIT/ InvIT exempt from TDS.
    - Advance tax liability on dividend income only after declaration/ payment of dividend.
    - Deduction of tax on dividend income at lower treaty rate for Foreign Portfolio Investors.
- **Attracting Foreign Investment for Infrastructure:**
  - **Infrastructure Debt Funds** made eligible to raise funds by issuing **Zero Coupon Bonds.**
  - Relaxation of some conditions relating to prohibition on private funding, restriction on commercial activities, and direct investment.
- **Supporting 'Housing for All':**
  - Additional deduction of interest, up to ₹ 1.5 lakh, for loan taken to

buy an affordable house extended for loans taken till March 2022.

- **Tax holiday** for Affordable Housing projects extended **till March 2022.**
- Tax exemption allowed for notified Affordable Rental Housing Projects.

Tax incentives to IFSC in GIFT City:

- **Tax holiday for capital gains** from incomes of aircraft leasing companies.
- Tax exemptions for aircraft lease rentals paid to foreign lessors.
- Tax incentive for relocating foreign funds in the IFSC.
- Tax exemption to investment division of foreign banks located in IFSC.

Ease of Filing Taxes: Details of capital gains from listed securities, dividend income, interest from banks, etc. to be pre-filled in returns.

Relief to Small Trusts: Exemption limit of annual receipt revised from ₹1 crore to ₹5 crore for small charitable trusts running schools and hospitals.

Labour Welfare:

- Late deposit of employee's contribution by the employer not to be allowed as deduction to the employer.
- Eligibility for tax holiday claim for start-ups extended by one more year.
- **Capital gains exemption** for investment in start-ups extended **till 31st March, 2022.**

2. Indirect Taxes

GST:

- Measures taken till date:
  - Nil return through SMS.
  - Quarterly return and monthly payment for small taxpayers.
  - **Electronic invoice system.**
  - Validated input tax statement.
  - **Pre-filled editable GST return.**
  - Staggering of returns filing.
  - Enhancement of capacity of GSTN system.
  - Use of **deep analytics and AI to identify tax evaders.**

Custom Duty Rationalisation:

- **Twin objectives**: Promoting domestic manufacturing and helping India get onto global value chain and export better.
- **80 outdated exemptions** already eliminated.
- Revised, distortion-free customs duty structure to be put in place from 1st October 2021 by **reviewing more than 400 old exemptions.**
- **New customs duty exemptions** to have validity up to 31st March following two years from its issue date.
- **Electronic and Mobile Phone Industry:**
  - Some exemptions on parts of chargers and sub-parts of mobiles withdrawn.

- **Duty on some parts of mobiles revised to 2.5% from 'nil' rate.**

Iron and Steel:

- **Customs duty reduced** uniformly to 7.5% on semis, flat, and long products of non-alloy, alloy, and stainless steels.
- **Duty on steel scrap exempted** up to 31st March, 2022.
- **Anti-Dumping Duty (ADD) and Counter-Veiling Duty (CVD) revoked** on certain steel products.
- **Duty on copper scrap reduced** from 5% to 2.5%.

Textiles:

- Basic Customs Duty (BCD) on caprolactam, nylon chips and nylon fiber & yarn reduced to 5%.

Chemicals:

- Calibrated customs duty rates on chemicals to encourage domestic value addition and to remove inversions.
- **Duty on Naphtha reduced** to 2.5%.

Gold and Silver:

- Custom duty on gold and silver to be rationalised.

Renewable Energy:

- **Phased manufacturing plan** for solar cells and solar panels to be notified.
- **Duty on solar invertors raised** from 5% to **20%**, and on **solar lanterns** from 5% to **15%** to encourage domestic production.

Capital Equipment:

- Tunnel boring machine to now attract a customs duty of 7.5%; and its parts a duty of 2.5%.
- Duty on certain auto parts increased to general rate of 15%.

MSME Products:

- Duty on steel screws and plastic builder wares increased to 15%.
- Prawn feed to attract customs duty of 15% from earlier rate of 5%.
- Exemption on import of duty-free items rationalised to incentivise exporters of garments, leather, and handicraft items.
- Exemption on imports of certain kind of leathers withdrawn.
- Customs duty on finished synthetic gemstones raised to encourage domestic processing.

Agriculture Products:

- Customs duty on cotton increased from nil to 10% and on raw silk and silk yarn from 10% to 15%.
- Withdrawal of end-use based concession on denatured ethyl alcohol.
- Agriculture Infrastructure and Development Cess (AIDC) on a small number of items.

Rationalisation of Procedures and Easing of Compliance:

- **Turant Customs** initiative, a Faceless, *Paperless, and Contactless Customs* measures.
- New procedure for administration of Rules of Origin.

Achievements and Milestones during the COVID-19 pandemic

- **Pradhan Mantri Garib Kalyan Yojana (PMGKY):**
  - Valued at ₹ **2.76 lakh crore.**
  - Free food grain to **80 crore people.**
  - Free cooking gas for **8 crore families.**
  - Direct cash to over **40 crore farmers, women, elderly, the poor and the needy.**
- **AtmaNirbhar Bharat package (ANB 1.0):**
  - Estimated at ₹ **23 lakh crore** – more than **10% of GDP.**
- PMGKY, three ANB packages (ANB 1.0, 2.0, and 3.0), and announcements made later were like **5 mini-budgets** in themselves.
- ₹ **27.1 lakh crore** worth of financial impact of all three ANB packages including RBI's measures – amounting to **more than 13% of GDP.**
- **Structural reforms:**
  - **One Nation One Ration Card.**
  - Agriculture and Labour Reforms.
  - Redefinition of MSMEs.
  - Commercialisation of the Mineral Sector.
  - Privatisation of Public Sector Undertakings.
  - Production Linked Incentive Schemes.
- **Status of India's fight against COVID-19:**
  - **2 Made-in-India vaccines** – medically safeguarding citizens of India and those of 100-plus countries against COVID-19.
  - **2 or more new vaccines expected soon.**
  - **Lowest death rate per million** and the lowest active cases.

2021 - Year of milestones for Indian history

- **75th year of India's independence**
- 60 years of Goa's accession to India
- 50 years of the 1971 India-Pakistan War
- Year of the **8th Census** of Independent India
- India's turn at the **BRICS Presidency**
- Year for **Chandrayaan-3 Mission**
- **Haridwar Maha Kumbh**

Vision for AtmaNirbhar Bharat

- **AtmaNirbharta** – not a new idea – ancient India was self-reliant and a business epicentre of the world.
- AtmaNirbhar Bharat – an expression of 130 crore Indians who have full confidence in their capabilities and skills.
- Strengthening the **Sankalp** of:
  - Nation First.
  - Doubling Farmer's Income.
  - Strong Infrastructure.
  - Healthy India.
  - Good Governance.
  - Opportunities for Youth.
  - Education for All.
  - Women Empowerment.
  - Inclusive Development.
- 13 promises made in the Union Budget 2015-16, and resonating with the vision of Atmanirbharta, to materialise during the **Amrut Mahotsav of 2022** – on the 75th year of our independence.

"Faith is the bird that feels the light and sings when the dawn is still dark." – *Rabindranath Tagore*

Concluding remarks We find a strong theoretical imprint of the latest ***Economic Survey 2020-21*** on the Budget. Without being afraid of the fiscal slippage which may occur, the Government has announced high expenditures on the capital front to boost demand and help economy recover out of the pandemic shock. Due to unforeseen expenditures, the fiscal deficit estimate for 2020-21 has been already revised to 9.5 per cent (from the budgetary target of 3.5 per cent). In the same direction, for 2021–22, the Government has set a higher fiscal deficit target of 6.8 per cent— on account of the increased expenditures proposed in the budget. The Government looks in full agreement with the theoretical base of 'interest rate growth rate differential' (IRGD), which is predicted to remain favourable to India, provided by the latest Economic Survey in this regard.

GLOSSARY

*Concepts are the constituents of thoughts---consequently, they ore crucial to such psychological processes as categorisation, inference, memory, learning, and decision-making.**

Abuse of Dominance A situation when a dominant firm/company (or a group of firms) is engaged in promoting its market position through 'anti-competitive' business practices, such as—predatory pricing, price squeezing, charging unreasonable prices, etc. Such practices hamper healthy competition in the economy and non-dominant firms face difficulties in their growth—they finally may shut down their operations. In recent times, it was in news globally—the US company *Microsoft* was facing litigation (under 'anti-trust' provision) for its Windows Operating System.

Though India used to regulate/restrict several such practices (under the MRTP Act, 1969), exact use of the term 'abuse of dominance' was not in practice. But the Competition Act, 2002 (which replaced the MRTP Act) has clear use of it—it defines such situation in clear terms.

Accounting systems There are two prevailing systems of accounting followed by the governments—cash-based or accrual-based. In the *cash-based system,* income is counted when cash (or a cheque) is actually received and expenses are counted when actually paid. On the other hand, in the *accrual-based system,* transactions are counted as they happen regardless of when the money is actually received or paid. Government of India is switching over from the cash-based system to accrual-based system (which is the popular practice across the world).

Accredited Investors Taking clues from other financial markets of the world the SEBI proposed to introduce a new category of investors' known also as 'qualified investors' or 'professional investors' in February 2021— *accredited investors*. As per it, they are those who understand various financial products, risks and returns associated with them and thus, are able to take 'informed' investment decisions.

Acid Test Ratio It is a metric used to measure the ability of a firm (company) to pay back its short-term liabilities (i.e., loans). It is calculated by dividing the firm's most liquid assets (like cash)

** See Eric Margolis and Stephen Laurence, 'Concepts', in the Edward N. Zalta The Stonford Encyclapedia of Philosophy, Metaphysics Research Lab, Centrefor the Study of Language and ldormation (CSLI), Stanford, USA, 2012.*

and short-term receivables (payments from sales) by its short-term liabilities.

This metric might be differentiated for the same firm due to differences in opinion of the financial analysts as how they classify various assets of the firm (for example, short-term assets like 'inventory' are not considered liquid assets by some since they may not be readily converted into cash).

Activity rate The labour force of a country is known as the activity rate or *participation rate*. It is in per cent and always a proportion of the total population of the country—the economically active population. This rate varies from one country to another, depending upon several factors such as school leaving age, retirement age, popularity of higher education, social customs, opportunities, etc.

Adverse selection One among the two kinds of the market failure, often associated with insurance business which means doing business with the people one would have better avoided.

Adverse selection can be a problem when there is an asymmetry in information between the seller and the buyer of an insurance policy—as insurance will not be profitable when buyers have better information about their risk of claiming than does the seller of the insurance policy. In the ideal case, insurance premiums are set in accordance with the risk of a randomly selected person in the insured bracket (such as 40-year-old male smokers) of the population.

The other kind of market failure is *moral hazards* associated with the insurance sector.

Agricultural labourer A person who works on another person's land for *wages* in money or kind or share is regarded as an agricultural labourer. He or she has no risk in the cultivation, but merely works on another person's land for wages. An agricultural labourer has no right of lease or contract on land on which he/she works.

Alpine Convertible Bond An ACB (Alpine Convertible Bond) is a Foreign Currency Convertible Bond (FCCB) issued by an Indian company exclusively to the Swiss investors.

Amortisation Payment of a loan in installments by the borrower. It is usually done in an agreed period and every installment includes a part of the total loan plus the interest.

Angel tax Angel tax is applicable (in India, by March 2019) on the unlisted companies that raise capital through sale of shares at a value above their fair market value. This excess capital is treated as 'income' and thus attracts income tax. This tax predominantly affects start-ups and the angel investments they attract.

Animal spirit 'Confidence', considered as one of the essential ingredients of economic prosperity, was called by J. M. Keynes animal spirit. For Keynes, this is a 'naive optimism' by which an entrepreneur puts aside the fact of loss as a healthy man puts aside the expectation of death.

But from where does this animal spirit come has been a mystery—can it be created artificially from outside or whether it is an innate thing some are born with, etc.

Antitrust A category of the government policy which deals with monopoly. Such laws intend to stop abuses of 'market power' by big companies and at times to prevent corporate mergers and acquisitions that would strengthen monopoly. The US has such laws and recently it was in news when Microsoft was its target.

Appreciation It shows increase in the value and is used in economics in the following two senses:

1. It is an increase in the price of an asset over time, such as price rises in land, factory building, houses, offices, etc. It is also known as *capital appreciation*.

2. It is an increase in the value of currency against any foreign currency or currencies. It

is market-based if the economy follows the floating-currency exchange-rate system.

Arbitrage Earning profits out of the price differences of the same product in different markets at the same time. For example, buying and selling any product, financial securities (as bonds) or foreign currencies in different markets/economies. As globalisation is promoting liberalised cross-border movement of goods and services around the world, arbitrage is prevalent today. To avoid arbitrage, the WTO member countries (i.e. the official countries in the process of globalisation) are under compulsion to chalk out homogenous economic policies--and a level-playing field at the international level is emerging.

Asset Anything which has a 'money value' owned by an individual or a firm is an asset. It is of *three* types:

1. **Tangible Asset:** All physical assets such as land, machinery, building, consumer durables (refrigerator, car, TV, Radio, etc.), etc. (*the assets which are in the material form*).
2. **Intangible Assets:** All non-physical/ immaterial assets such as brand names, goodwill, creditworthiness, knowledge, know-how, etc.
3. **Financial Assets:** All financially valid valuables other than tangibles and intangibles such as currencies, bank deposits, bonds, securities, shares, etc.

Assigned revenue The term is used to refer to various tax/duty/cess/surcharge/levy, etc. proceeds which are (traditionally) collected by state government (on behalf of) local bodies (the PRIs), and subsequently adjusted with/assigned to the PRIs. The collection of such revenue is governed by relevant Acts of the local bodies.

Some examples of assigned revenue in India include entertainment tax, surcharge on stamp duty, local cess/surcharge on land revenue, lease amount of mines and minerals, sale proceeds of social forestry plantations, etc. State Finance Commissions recommend *devolution* of assigned revenue to local bodies on objective criteria, which may be specified by them in specific context.

Autarky The idea of self-sufficiency and 'no' international trade by a country. None of the countries of the world has been able to produce all the goods and services required by its population at competitive prices; however, some tried to live it up at the cost of inefficiency and comparative poverty.

Back-to-back loan A term of international banking, is an arrangement under which two firms (i.e., companies) in different economies (i.e., countries) borrow each other's currency and agree to repay (such loans) at a specified future date. Each company gets full amount of the loan on the repayment date in their domestic currency without any risk of losses due to exchange rate fluctuations. It has developed as a popular tool of minimising the exchange-rate exposure risk among the multi-national companies. This is also known as the *parallel loan*.

Bad bank A bank created specially to buy the *bad debts* (called 'non-performing assets' in India) of the existing banks to clear such loans of the latter. This way, the banks with NPAs clear their 'balance sheet' and again start lending to the customers. The bad bank now tries to recover the bad debts it has bought through available legal means. Though such banks were set up in 20th century itself in the USA, it came in recent use once the US central banks' chief (Ben Bernanke) proposed the idea of using a government-run bad bank to clean up the 'sub-prime' loans of the private banks in the country (in wake of the sub-prime crisis of 2007).

It made news in India once the *Economic Survey 2016–17* suggested the Government of India to set up such a body—public sector asset rehabilitation agency (PARA)—to solve the 'twin balance sheet' (TBS) problem the country is faced with. [For more discussion, see *Chapter 21*].

Bad debt An accounting term to show the loans which are unlikely to be paid back by the borrower as the borrower has become insolvent/bankrupt. Banks might write off such bad debts against the profits of the trading as a business cost.

Balanced budget The annual financial statement (i.e., the budget) of a government which has the total expenditures equal to the taxes and other receipts.

Most governments, in practice, run unbalanced budgets, i.e., deficit budgets or surplus budgets–either the expenditures being higher or lower than the taxes and the other receipts, respectively. It is done to regulate the economic activities.

Balance of payments A balance sheet of an economy showing its total external transactions with the world–calculated on the principles of accounting.

Balloon payment When the final payment of a debt is more than the previous payments, it is balloon payment.

Basing point price system A method of pricing in which a differential (i.e., varying) price is fixed for the same product for the customers of the different locations—nearer the customer, cheaper the product. This is done usually to neutralise the transportation cost of the bulky products such as cement, iron and steel, petroleum, etc.

Beer The bond equity earnings yield ratio (BEER) is a measure to compare the earnings on government bond (normally, 10-year G-Sec are taken as reference) and equities. BEER is calculated by dividing the yield (interest) of a government bond (10-year G-Sec) by the current earnings of a stock benchmark (such as the 50-share index Nifty).

Theoretically, if the reading is at 1, it means that both equity and bond markets are fairly valued. A reading greater than 1 would mean that the equity market is overvalued, while below 1 means that equity market is undervalued. BEER is the reverse of the PE (price-to-earnings) ratio (refer it in the *Glossary* itself).

Bellwether stock A share which often reflects the state of the whole stock market. The technical analysts, associated with the stock market, usually keep a track-record of such shares and go on to forecast the future stock movements.

BFS For the purpose of supervision and surveillance of the Indian financial system, a Board for Financial Supervision (BFS) was set up by the RBI in November 1994. The board supervises commercial banks, non-banking financial companies (NBFCs), financial institutions, primary dealers, and the clearing corporation of India (CCI).

Bond An instrument of raising debt on which the bond-issuer pays a periodic interest (known as *'coupon'*). In theory, bonds could be issued by governments as well as private companies.

Bonds generally have a maturity period; however, some bonds might not have any definite maturity period (which are known as *'Perpetual Bonds'*).

Bracket creep Increasing incomes due to inflation (via increased dearness allowances, individual income goes for an increase) pushes individuals into higher tax *brackets* and leaves them worse off (as their real income has not increased and their disposable income, i.e. income after tax payments, falls). This phenomenon is known as the bracket creep.

Brown Revolution Simply put, introducing the digital revolution in the farm sector is being called Brown Revolution— the term is believed to have been first used by the US farmer *Howarth Buffet* (brother of the billionaire global investor Warren Buffet).

Already introduced in USA and Europe, under it the tractor industry is expected to soon include combining tractor services for ploughing and sowing seeds to using sensors, cloud computing and artificial intelligence for precision farming. It is a kind of combining the forces of the fourth industrial revolution with the existing farm machines and tools.

Brownfield location A derelict industrial area that has been demolished to accommodate new industries. This is opposite to the *greenfield location* where a new industry is set up in a new area.

Bubble The price rise of an asset unexplained by the fundamentals and still people interested in holding the assets. After the bursting of the bubble, assets cool down to their real prices.

Budget line A line on the dual axis graph showing the alternate combinations of goods that can be purchased by a consumer with a given income at given prices.

Bullet repayment 'Bullet repayment' means a lump-sum payment for the *entire loan amount* at the time of maturity. Such arrangements may be put in place by the banking regulator (RBI in case of India) to fasten the process of recovery of the non-performing assets (NPAs) process of the banks. The distressed assets, in this way, come back to bank, may be with a lower profit element to them.

Bullion Precious metals such as gold, silver, and platinum that are traded in the form of *bars* and *coins* for investment purposes and are used for jewellery as base metals.

Business cycle See *chapter 7, Section-B* with the same title.

Buyer's market A short period of market situation in which there is excess supply of goods/services forcing price fall to the advantage of the buyers.

Camels An acronym derived from the terms capital adequacy (C), asset quality (A), management (M), earnings (E), liquidity (L) and systems for control (S). The acronym is used as a technique for evaluating and rating the operations and performance of banks all over the world.

Capital Capital is one of the three main factors of production (*labour* and *natural resources* are the other two), classified into *physical capital* (i.e., factories, machines, office, etc.) and *human capital* (i.e., training, skill, etc.). Different ways to look upon a company, listed on a stock exchange, are given below (from capital point of view):

1. **Authorised Capital:** This is the amount of share capital fixed in the Memorandum of Association (MoA) and the article of association of a company as required by the Companies Act. This is also known as the *Nominal* or *Registered Capital.*

   This is the limit (i.e., nominal value) upto which a company can issue shares. Companies often extend their authorised capital (via an amendment in the MoA) in advance of actual issue of new shares. This allows the timing of capital issue to be fixed in light of the company's need for new capital and the state of the capital market and allows share options to be exercised accordingly.

2. **Paid-up Capital:** The part of the authorised capital of a company that has actually been paid up by the shareholders. A difference may arise because all shares authorised may not have been issued or the issued shares have been only partly paid-up by then.

3. **Subscribed Capital:** The capital that has actually been paid by the shareholders (as they might have committed more than this to contribute). It means, the subscribed capital is the actually realised paid-up capital (paid-up capital is subscribed capital plus credit/due on the shareholders).

4. **Issued Capital:** The amount of the capital which has been sought by a company to

be raised by the issue of shares (it should be kept in mind that this cannot exceed the authorised capital).

5. **Called-up Capital:** The amount of share capital the shareholders have been *called* to pay to date under the phased payment terms. It is usually equal to the 'paid-up capital' of the company except where some shareholders have failed to pay their due installments (known as *calls in arrears*).

Capital adequacy ratio A regulation on commercial banks, co-operative banks and the non-banking financial companies to maintain a certain amount of capital in relation to their assets (i.e., loans and investments) as a cushion (shock-absorber) against probable losses in their investments and loans.

A concept devised by the Bank for International Settlements (BIS), Basel, the provision was implemented in India in 1992 by the RBI (for a more detailed discussion, see the chapter on 'Banking').

Capital consumption The capital that is consumed by an economy or a firm in the production process. Also known as *depreciation*.

Capital-output ratio A measure of how much additional capital is needed to produce each extra unit of the output. Put the other way round, it is the amount of extra output produced by each unit of added capital. The ratio indicates how efficient new investment contributes to the growth of an economy.

A capital-output ratio of 3:1 is better then the 4:1 as the former needs only three units extra capital to produce one extra output in comparison to the latter which needs four units for each extra unit output.

Carry Trade Borrowing funds at cheaper interest rate from one market and investing in another where interest rate is relatively higher is called carry trade. Such returns are made by arbitraging [see *Arbitrage* in Glossary itself] on the interest rate differentials seen across the countries. Therefore, we see increased foreign investments in India (in debt securities such as corporate bonds, government securities, etc.) from the countries whenever an interest rate cut is announced by their central banks.

Cash cow A profitable business or firm (may belong to either public or private sector) which gives regular cash flow to the owner (this happens either due to regular demand of the popular goods produced by the firm or the compulsions of the consumer to buy the products). For example, the antiseptic lotion 'Dettol' is a cash cow for Reckitt and Colman in the private sector and LPG is a cash cow for the manufacturing and marketing government companies (provided there is no subsidy on LPG).

Caveat emptor A Latin phrase which means *'let the buyer beware'*. Simply put, it means that the supplier has no legal obligation to inform buyers about any defects in his goods or services; the onus is on the buyer to himself determine the level of satisfaction out of the products.

Chinese wall The segregation of the different activities of a financial institution (such as, jobbing, stockbroking, fund management, etc.) in order to protect clients' interest.

Circuit limit A limit of regular fall in share indices of Stock Exchanges around the world after which the exchange a are closed for further trading. For example, circuit limit decided for the BSE (Bombay Stock Exchange) has been fixed at 10 per cent. The time there is a continuous fall in the BSE Sensex and it reaches 10 per cent, the exchange is closed to further trading.

Such a limit/provision prevents the share market from crashing down.

Circular economy Several definitions of circular economy are used in scientific and professional literature because the concept is applied by a diverse group of researchers and professionals, emphasising different aspects of it. This makes it difficult to measure also. But most of its definitions focus on the 'use of raw materials' or 'system change'. Definitions that focus on resource use often follow the *3-R approach*—Reduce (minimum use of raw materials); Reuse (maximum reuse of products and components); and Recycle (high quality reuse of raw materials).

A circular economy tries to follow the example of an ecosystem. In it, there is nothing like waste because every residual item can be used to make a new product (but after eliminating the toxic substances)—such as producers taking back their products after use and repairing them for a new useful life. Thus, only recycling is not important in this system, rather assuring quality is also taken care of.

Classical economics A school of thought in economics based on the ideas of Smith, Ricardo, Mill, etc. The school dominated the economic thinking of the world until about 1870, when the *'marginalist revolution'* took place.

Clean coal Underground coal gasification and liquefaction, which converts coal into liquid and gaseous fuel alternatives, is a recognised 'clean coal' technology—handy in extraction of energy from coal seams which cannot be mined through conventional methods.

Collateral Any item/asset which accompanies/subordinates/supplements a primary item is known as collateral. The term is used in banking industry while providing loans. This is also known as 'secondary/subordinate security'— which borrowers/guarantors provide in the form of an asset (like land, building, etc.) while seeking a loan. The principal/primary security is usually the borrower's personal guaranty, or the cash flow of a business.

Except for highly creditworthy customers (who can get loans against their signatures), lenders always demand a collateral if the primary security is not considered to be reliable or sufficient enough to recover the loan in the case of a default—lenders have the legal right to seize the collateral.

Closed shop The requirement that all employees of a given firm be members of a specified trade union. It is a method of restricting labour supply and maintaining high wages applied by a powerful trade union.

Collection Rate It is the ratio of customs earnings and imports' value of a country. This metric is used to understand the impact of special custom duties, countervailing duties and custom exemptions offered on imports by a country. Due to such exemptions offered by India on essential imports, we see the country's customs collections not increasing as much its imports increase, which makes collection rate lower or falling (if number of such exemptions increased due to some reason). For the year 2019, India's collection rate was 6.6 per cent (up from 5.5 per cent of 2014).

Collective products A product which can only be supplied to a group. Many goods and services provided by the governments fall in this category, such as national defence, police administration, etc.

Committed expenditure The expenditures of the governments from which they cannot deny (as they have already committed them to pay) are known as committed expenditure. The liabilities such as 'interest' (of the internal as well as external loans) and 'pension' (of the retired personnel of the governments) are examples of such expenditure.

Commodities transaction tax [See Chapter 17, *Tax Structure in India*]

Commodity money Products being used as the means of payment as in the traditional barter system. Such practices take place generally when the confidence in money has fallen down (as for example in the situations of high inflation and high depreciation).

Communitisation A method of privatising public service delivery without going for the tendering process. It is done by transfering powers including financial powers to the user community who will take up the job of revenue collection along with an effective and more practical governance of the service delivery. This model is bereft of profit motive and so, more transparent.

Service delivery in communitised elementary schools, health services and power tariff collection (which increased by 100 per cent) considerably improved since it was done (in 2002).

Comparative advantage Comparative advantage refers to the ability of a company or an economy to produce something at a lower opportunity cost (i.e. by forfeiting potential benefit). By this, the company/economy gets the ability to sell its products cheaper than the prices offered by its competitors. It can be understood with the help of 'trade off' also—given two options (with their own set of advantages and disadvantages), the best option has the comparative advantage.

Articulated by James Mill, this concept was popularised by David Ricardo (his mentor was James Mill) by early 19th century. Among the key concepts of economic theory, this advocates the belief that 'all countries can mutually benefit from cooperation and voluntary trade.' Over the time, it became the foundational tenet of international trade. The concept gives the insight that trade will still occur even if one country has an 'absolute advantage' in all products. For example, China has the comparative advantage in global export market due to its 'lower wages' but China also keeps importing so many goods and services (where it has lower comparative advantage).

Consortium An *ad hoc* grouping of firms, governments, etc. brought together to undertake a particular project by pooling their resources and skills for major construction projects, loans, etc.

Conspicuous consumption Consumption for the purpose of showing off ostentatiousness but not for the utility aspect – for example, the use of diamond-studded sandals, watches, pens, etc.

Contagion A situation or an effect of economic problems in one economy spreading to another, also known as the *domino effect*.

Contrarian A person following an investment strategy (specially in share market) just opposite to the general investors in a given period. For example, when a share is generally being sold by the investors, a contrarion keeps on buying them—the logic is that due to selling pressure, the price will fall below the intrinsic value of the share and there is a prospect of future profit out of the share.

Core Investment Companies (CICs) An NBFC carrying on the business of acquisition of shares and securities which satisfied the conditions: it holds not less than 90 per cent of its total assets in this form; its investments in the equity shares in group companies constitute not less than 60 per cent of its total assets; it does not trade in its investments in shares, debt or loans in group companies except through block sale for the purpose of dilution or disinvestment; and it does not carry on any other financial activity except investment in bank deposits, money market instruments, government securities, loans to and investments in group companies.

Correction A term usually used in stock market which shows a reversal of share prices in reaction to an excessive rise or fall in the past.

Countervailing duty Countervailing duty (CVD) is imposed by the importing nation on imports if the exporting nation is found to offer export subsidies to their exports. This measure aims at balancing the price of imports with the domestic products. This duty is imposed in such a way that imported item also remains competitive.

A similar duty, with the same aim, once imposed by the importing nation in case the exporting country is found to export at *below fair market price* (it means the exporting nation is dumping the item in the importing nation) is known as 'anti-dumping' duty.

Both the duties are imposed after fulfilling the proper provisions of investigation conducted as per the specifications of the WTO.

Creative destruction The process by which an innovative entrepreneur takes risks and introduces new technologies to stimulate economic activity, replacing old technologies, is known as 'creative destruction'. As per *Schumpeter, Joseph A.* (1883–1950), creative destruction is the key to economic growth. But due to irregularity in such innovations, business cycle is followed by both collapse and crisis (J. A. Schumpeter, *Capitalism, Socialism and Democracy,* 1942).

Crony capitalism An approach of doing business when the firms look after themselves by looking after their own people (i.e., families and friends). Used in a negative sense.

Cross subsidy The process of giving subsidy to one sub-area and fulfilling it through the profits from the other sub-area. For example, in India kerosene oil is cross-subsidised against petrol and aviation fuel.

Crowdfunding This is a method of mobilising finance/fund. Crowd-funding refers to the collective effort of individuals who pool money—mostly through the Internet—to support start-ups. There are two basic forms of crowdfunding—'community' crowdfunding and 'financial return' crowdfunding. The *former* includes donation-based concepts (donators get no financial returns in it) while in the *latter* contributors of funds get financial returns (from the project set up with the fund). In the financial model of crowdfunding, contributors might be given equity/share in the upcoming project.

Crowding-out effect A concept of public finance which means an increase in the government expenditure which has an effect of reducing private the sector expenditure.

CSR The concept of corporate social responsibility (CSR) is fast gaining popularity among the corporate sector of the world. As per the experts, CSR is qualitatively different from the traditional concept of passive philanthropy by the corporate houses. Basically, CSR acknowledges the *debt* that the corporates owe to the community within which they operate. It defines the corporates' partnership with social action groups (i.e., the NGOs) in providing financial and other resources to support development plans, especially among disadvantaged communities. There is stress on long-term sustainability of business and environment and the distribution of well-being.

Decoupling theory Decoupling theory holds that Asian economies, especially emerging ones, no longer depend on the United States economy for growth, leaving them *insulated* from a severe slowdown there, even recession—looked true for some time as Asian stocks rose while socks in the US fell. However, as fears of recession mounted in the US, stocks declined heavily. Looking this happen in late 2008, the decoupling theory regarding the Asian as well as the EU economies has now lost ground. But still, the emerging economies are able to have higher growth rates and exports in comparison to the US– that is why the theory is still debated by experts.

Deindustrialisation Sustained decrease in the share of the secondary sector (i.e., industry) in the total output (GDP) of an economy.

Demat account It is a way of holding securities in an electronic or dematerialised form. Demat form of shares can be traded online. As such, the transactions are concluded much faster, which prevents theft, misuse, forging of original shares certificates or other documents, and allows an investor to buy or sell shares in any quantity. Demat accounts are offered by banks, and the dematerialised stock is held by the depository (National Securities Depository Ltd. [NSDL] or Central Securities Depository Ltd. [CSDL]).

Demerger The breaking-up of a company into more separate companies. Such companies are usually formed through mergers.

Derivatives The financial assets that 'derive' their value from other assets, such as shares, debentures, bonds, securities, etc. traded on the platforms of stock and commodity exchanges.

DIIs Domestic Investment Institutions (DIIs) are the financial institutions of Indian origin investing in India in different derivatives such as share, securities, corporate bounds, etc. They may be owned by governments or private entities in the form of mutual funds, pension funds, and insurance companies are the major examples in India.

Dirty float A term of foreign exchange management when a country manipulates its exchange rate under the floating currency system to take leverage in its external transactions.

Discount house A financial institution specialising in buying and selling of short-term (i.e., less than one year) instruments of the money market. The SBI Discount and Finance House of India (SBI DFHI) is India's largest discount house.

Disgorgement Disgorgement is a common term in developed markets, though for most market participants in India it is a new thing. Disgorgement means repayment of illegal gains by wrongdoers. Funds that were received through illegal or unethical business transactions are 'disgorged', or paid back, with interest to those affected by the action. In the case of India, SEBI is responsible for this job unlike international practice of civil courts and market regulator both looking into it

Disgorgement is a 'remedial' civil action, rather than a 'punitive' civil action. In the US, individuals or companies that violate Securities and Exchange Commission regulations are typically required to pay both civil money penalties and disgorgement. Civil money penalties are punitive, while disgorgement is about paying back profits made from those actions that violated securities regulations.

Interestingly, disgorgement payments are not only demanded of those who violate securities regulations. In the US, anyone profiting from illegal or unethical activities may be required to disgorge their profits. The money disgorged from the violating parties is used to create a 'Fair Fund'–fund for the benefit of investors who were harmed by the violation.

Dissaving The situation of higher current consumption over current disposable income by the households–the difference is met by withdrawals from the past savings (*i.e., decrease in saving*).

Domino effect An economic situation in which one economic event causes a series of similar events to happen one after the other. For example, experts believe that the falling of share indices around the world in early-2008 was a domino effect of the sub-prime crisis faced by the US economy. A similar case is cited from the mid-1996 when all major stock markets crashed around the world due to the domino effect emanating from the South East Asian currency crisis.

Dow-Jones index The US share price index which monitors and records the share price movements of all companies listed on the New York Stock Exchange (*with the exception of high-tech companies which are listed on the nasdaq stock exchange*). India has its equivalent in the BSE *Sensex*.

D-SIBs Since 2015, every year, the RBI releases a list of banks operating in the country as the Domestic Systemically Important Banks (D-SIBs). For foreign banks operating in India, there is a similar provision to declare them G-SIBs (Globally Systemically Important Banks). By April 2020, in India there were three banks in this category (SBI, ICICI Bank and HDFC Bank).

In simple words, this means that these banks are *too big to fail*. It has the implied meaning that failure of any of these banks would have a cascading effect on the whole financial system of India. Inclusion of banks in this list gives additional comfort to investors and depositors as they think that these banks will not be allowed to fail (immediately by the RBI and ultimately by the Government). This gives such banks an advantage to mobilise funds cheaper (through deposits) over their peers in the banking industry.

As per the norms, such banks need to set aside 'more capital' for their continued operation as part of the 'capital to risk-weighted assets ratio' (CRAR). Higher CRAR, which is more commonly used as the CAR (Capital Adequacy Ratio), provides banks the strength to tide over acute economic and financial stress. There are five 'buckets' created by the RBI into which the banks are put depending upon their Systemic Importance Scores (SISs). While the SBI (being in the 'third bucket') needs to set aside 0.60 per cent extra capital of its risk-weighted assets, ICICI and HDFC banks (being in the 'first bucket') need to set aside 0.20 per cent extra capital of their risk-weighted assets—form April 1, 2019.

Dumping Exporting goods at a price lower than its price in the domestic market. To neutralise the effects of dumping, the importing country may impose a *surcharge* on such imports which is known as the *anti-dumping duty*.

Dutch disease When an increase in one form of net exports drives up a country's exchange rate, it is called the Dutch Disease. Such instances make other exports non-competitive in the world market and impairs the ability of domestic products to compete with imports.

The term originated from the supposed effect of natural gas discoveries on the Netherland's economy.

EASE-Index EASE-Index (Enhanced Access & Service Excellence-Index) was published for the first time for the public sector banks (PSBs) in March 2019. Prepared by the *Boston Consulting Group*, the index measures the performance of the PSBs on 140 objective metrics across 6 themes, including customer responsiveness, credit off-take and digitalisation, among others.

The index which ranks the banks will be published every year. The Punjab National Bank was ranked 1st with a score of 78.4 (out of 100), followed by Bank of Baroda (77.8), Oriental Bank of Commerce (74.6). Dena Bank had the lowest score of 53.8.

e-Business Using computers and the Internet to link both the *internal* operations (i.e., transactions and communications between the various departments/divisions of the business firm) and its *external* operations (i.e., all its dealings with the suppliers, customers, etc.).

e-Commerce Method of buying and selling goods and services over the Internet – a kind of direct marketing, i.e. without the help of any middle arrangement of sales.

Economies of scale The long-run reduction in average/unit cost that occurs as the scale of the firm's output increases. The opposite situation is known as *diseconomies of scale*.

Economies of scope The long-run reduction in average/unit cost that occurs as the scope (diversification) of the firm's activities increases.

Edgeworth box A concept for the purpose of analysing the possible relationships between two individuals or countries. It is done using indifference curve.

The concept was developed by Francis Ysidro Edgeworth (1845–1926) who is also credited for analytical tools of *indifference curves* and *contract curves*.

Effective revenue deficit [See Chapter 18, *Public Finance in India*]

Elephants This term is used as a 'slang' in financial market for big companies with huge funds which they may use for diverse kinds of investments. Usually used for their huge investments in stock markets, they leave big impact on a country's security market. Professionally managed entities like mutual funds, pension funds, insurance companies and banks are some of its examples.

The concept can be understood by comparing it to the situation when an elephant enters the pool (i.e., buys stocks), the water level (stock price) increases, and once the elephant exits the pool (i.e., selling stocks), the water level (stock price) decreases. In this perspective, for individual investor the term mouse is used (as it leaves comparatively a very low impact on stock market).

Engel's law The law which says that people generally spend a smaller part of their budget on food as their income rises. The idea was suggested by Ernst Engel, a Russian statistician in 1857.

Environmental accounting The method of accounting which includes the ecological and environmental damages done by the economic activities in monetary terms. The *green GDP* of an economy is measured by the same method—experimented in Costa Rica, Mexico, Netherlands, Norway, and Papua New Guinea, among others. Indicative estimates suggest that conventionally measured GDP may exceed GDP adjusted for natural resources depletion and environmental degradation by a range between 1.5 per cent and 10 per cent.

Environmental audit Assessment of the environmental impact of a firm/public body through its activities. This is done with an objective to reduce or eliminate the pollution aspect.

Environmental taxes As against the Command and Control approach to managing environment, the Economic or Market Based Instruments (MBIs) approach sends economic signals to the polluters to modify their behaviour. The MBIs used for environmental taxes include pollution charges (emission/affluent & tax/pollution tax), marketable permits, deposit refund system, input taxes/product charges, differential tax rates, user administrative changes and subsidies for pollution abatement, which may be based on both price and quality. India has been already collecting taxes on *water* and *air* via the Water Act and the Air Act. Due to its experience, India is among the chief participants in devising the MBIs in the world.

Equity share A security issued by a company to those who contributed capital in its formation shows ownership in the company. The other terms for it are 'stock' or 'common stock'.

Such shares might be issued via public issue, bonus shares, convertible debentures, etc. and may be traded on the stock exchanges.

Such shareholders have a claim on the earnings and assets of the company after all the claims have been paid for. Therefore, such shareholders are also known as the *residual owners*.

Escrow account In simple terms, an 'escrow account' is held by a *third party account*. It is a separate bank account to hold money which belongs to others and where the money parked will be released only on the fulfilment of certain conditions of a contract. The term ***escrow*** is derived from the French word 'escroue' meaning a scrap of paper or roll of parchment, an indicator of the deed that was held by a third party till a transaction is completed. An escrow account is an *arrangement for safeguarding* the 'seller' against its 'buyer' from the payment risk for the goods or services sold by the former to the latter.

ESOPs Employee Stock Option Plans (ESOPs) is a provision under which a foreign company (i.e., MNC) offers shares to its employees overseas. Till February 2005 in the case of local firms, an MNC needed a permission from the RBI before allotting ESOPs, but since then, it does not need any permission provided the company has a minimum of 15 per cent holding in the Indian arm.

Exploding arms A term associated with the mortgage business which became popular after the subprime crisis hit the US financial system in mid-2007. Exploding arms are mortgages with initial low, fixed interest rates which escalate to a high floating rate after a period of two to three years.

Externalities Factors that are not included in the gross income of the economy but have an effect on human welfare. They may be *positive* or *negative*– training personnel is an example of the former while pollution falls in the latter.

FCCB Foreign Currency Convertible Bond (FCCB) is an unsecured instrument to raise long-term loan in foreign currency by an Indian company which converts into shares of the company on a predetermined rate. It is counted as the part of external debt. It is a safer route to raise foreign currency requirements of a company.

Federal Fund Rate The federal fund rate (also popular as *Fed Fund Rate* or *Fed Rate*) is the rate of interest banks charge each other on overnight loans in the USA. The rate is fixed by the US central bank Federal Reserve. This is equivalent to the *Repo rate* of India which is fixed by the RBI.

Fiduciary issue Issuance of currency by the government not matched by gold securities, also known as *fiat money*.

Financial closure Financial closure is defined as a stage when all the conditions of a financing agreement are fulfilled prior to the initial availability of funds. It is attained when all the tie-ups with banks or financial institutions for funds are made and all the conditions precedent to initial drawing of debt are satisfied.

Fire sale Selling goods or assets at heavily discounted prices is called fire sale. Originally, it referred to the discount sale of goods that were damaged by fire, but over the time it generally means any sale where the seller is in financial distress— even 'clearance sales' offered by showrooms belong to it. In financial markets, we use this term when some stock or security is available well below its intrinsic value (as happens in the case of prolonged bear markets).

Fiscal drag The restraining effect of the progressive taxation economies feel on their expansion—fall in the total demand in the economy due to people moving from lower to higher tax brackets and the government tax receipts go on increasing. To neutralise this negative impact, governments usually increase personal tax allowances.

Fiscal neutrality A stance in policy making by governments when the net effect of taxation and public spending is neutral—neither encouraging nor discouraging the demand. For example, a *balanced budget* is the same attempt of fiscal policy when the total tax revenue equals the total public expenditure.

Fiscal stance Economies across the world pick their fiscal policy stance (i.e., approach, orientation) as per their needs. One element of it is giving stimulus (with differing kinds of economic support) to the economy or sectors concerned. Broadly speaking, the nature of such stimulus/ measures can be of two categories, namely— *'above-the-line'* and *'below-the-line'*.

Above-the-line measures include those for which full cost is reflected in the fiscal deficit, government debt, and increased borrowing needs in the short-term— which include additional spending (on health services, unemployment benefits etc.); capital grants and targeted transfers (for example, wage subsidies or direct transfers); or tax measures (for example, tax cuts or other relief) provided through standard budget channels.

Below-the-line measures involve the creation of assets, like equity injections, loans, asset purchase, etc. which may have little or no upfront impact on the fiscal deficit although they can later increase debt or reduce liquidity (as per the *IMF Fiscal Monitor,* April 2020).

Fisher effect A concept developed by *Irving Fisher* (1867–1947) which shows the relationship between inflation and the interest rate, expressed by an equation popular as the *fisher equation,* i.e., the nominal interest rate on a loan is the sum of the real interest rate and the rate of inflation expected over the duration of the loan:

$$R = r + F$$

where R = nominal interest rate, r = real interest rate and F = rate of annual inflation.

The concept suggests a direct relationship between inflation and nominal interest rates—changes in inflation rates lead to matching changes in nominal interest rates.

The Fisher effect can be seen each time one goes to the bank; the interest rate an investor has on a savings account is really the nominal interest rate. For example, if the nominal interest rate on a savings account is 4 per cent and the expected rate of inflation is 3 per cent, then money in the savings account is really growing at 1 per cent. The smaller the real interest rate, the longer it will take for savings deposits to grow substantially when observed from a purchasing power perspective.

Flag of convenience Shipping rights in oceans and seas are governed by international treaties. Flag of convenience is a grant of a shipping 'flag' by a member of these treaties to a non-member nation establishing the legality of shipping to the latter (*usually used for illegal activities*).

Forced saving The enforced reduction of consumption in an economy. It may take place directly when the government increases taxes or indirectly as a consequence of higher inflation—a tool usually utilised by the developing countries to generate extra funds for investment. Also known as *involuntary saving.*

Foreign currency hedging The firms/companies which own a liability in foreign currency (such as foreign loans they might have borrowed) are asked, at times, by the Government to 'reduce the risk' (hedge) involved due to such exposures—known as 'mandatory hedging'. Government might ask different proportion of foreign currency hedging (30 per cent, 50 per cent or even 100 per cent).

There are a few ways how the companies do it. One very popular way is signing a forward contract in the currency of need in advance—and this way the risk of exposure to foreign currency risk is neutralised.

FOB This is the abbreviation of 'free-on-board'—when in the balance of payment accounting, only the basic prices of exports and imports of goods (including loading costs) are counted. It does not count the 'cost-insurance-freight' (CiF) charges incurred in transporting the goods from one country to another country.

Forward contract A transaction contract of commodity on an agreed price which binds both the seller and the buyer to pay and deliver the commodity on a future date. The price agreed upon is known as *forward* rate.

One must not confuse this with the term 'future contract' as in it, the term of the contract cannot be decided by the mutual needs of the parties involved (which is possible in a 'forward contract').

Forward trading A trading system in certain shares (as allowed by the SEBI in India) in which buyers and sellers are allowed to postpone/defer payment and delivery respectively after paying some charges. If the buyer wants deferment, it is known as *badla* (an Indian term for *contango*) and if the seller goes for deferment of delivery of shares, it is known as *undha badla* (in India, elsewhere it is known as *backwardation*).

Fractional banking A system of banking in which banks maintain a minimum reserve asset ratio in order to maintain adequate liquidity to meet the customer's cash demands in its everyday business (*the SLR in India is such a provision,*).

Free goods The goods which are in abundance (*as air and water*) and are not considered as scarce economic goods. As such, goods have *zero supply price* and they will be used in large volumes resulting in rising environmental pollution (point should be noted that today air and water may not be considered as the typical free goods, at least the 'pure air' and 'pure water').

Free trade The international trade among an agreed-upon group of countries without any barriers (such as tariffs, quotas, forex controls, etc.), promoted with the objective of securing international specialisation and an edge in their foreign trade.

Free port A port that is designated as such is the one where imports are allowed without any duty, provided they are re-exported (i.e., *entrepot*). If the same is correct in the case of an area, it is known as the *free trade zone.*

Gallup poll A method of survey in which a representative sampling of public opinion or public awareness concerning a certain subject/ issue is done and, on this basis, a conclusion is drawn.

The credit of developing this research methodology goes to *George H. Gallup* (1901–84), a US journalist and statistician who in 1935 did set up the *American Institute of Public Opinion.* Through his efforts, the method developed in the period 1935–40. In the coming times, the poll technique was immensely used by business houses for their market research and the psephologists for election forecasting, around the world.

Game theory The analysis of situations involving two or more interacting decision makers (that may be individuals, competing firms, countries, etc.) who have conflicting objectives. It is a technique which uses logical deduction to explore the consequences of various strategies that might be adopted by game players having competing interests.

Game theory is a branch of *Applied Mathematics* that studies strategic interactions between agents–where the agents try maximising their pay off. It gives *formal modelling approach* to social situations in which decision makers interact with other agents. The theory generalises maximisation approaches developed to analyse markets such as supply and demand model.

The field dates back from the 1944 classic *Theory of Games and Economic Behaviour* by John von Neumann and Oskar Morgentern (Princeton University Press, N. Jersy, 1944 & 2004; 60th Anniversary Ed.). Neumann was a mathematician and Morgenstern an economist and this book was based on the former's prior research published in 1928 on the *Theory of Parlour Games* (in German).

The theory has found significant applications in many areas outside economics as usually construed, including formulations of nuclear strategies, ethics, political science, and evolutionary theory.

Giffen goods The goods for which the demand increases as its price increases, rather than falls (opposite to the *general theory of demand*)—named after Robert Giffen (1837–1910). It applies to the large proportion of the goods belonging to the household budget (as flour, rice, pulses, salt, onion, potato, etc. in India)—an increase in their prices produces a large *negative income effect* completely overcoming the normal substitution effect with, people buying more of the goods.

Gig economy A considerably new concept which came into being once the digital platform emerged. Inferring from the literature of the ILO and World Bank, this constitutes the economy of the digital world, which includes 'diverse category of platforms today, engaged in retailing, aggregating, contracting, freelancing, lending, facilitating payments, etc. (Amazon, Ola, Swiggy, Paytm, being a few examples). The economy made increased news globally during the COVID-19 induced lockdowns and restrictions on human movement when people were forced to work from home— making India emerge among the world's largest economies.

A largely unregulated segment, countries across the world have started formalising it regarding labour rights (with India formally classifying them with the unorganised labour force in 2020) of the employees engaged in it, tax provisions, data security and privacy etc.

Gini coefficient An inequality indicator in an economy. The coefficient varies from 'zero' to 'one'. A 'zero' Gini coefficient indicates a situation of perfect equality (i.e., every household earning the same level of income) while a 'one' signifies a situation of absolute inequality (i.e., a single household earning the entire income in an economy).

Golden handshake A payment (usually generous) made by a company to its employees for quitting the job prior to their service.

Golden handcuff A royalty/bonus payment by a company to its staff (usually top ranking) to keep them with the company or to save them from poaching by other companies.

Golden hello A large sum paid by a company to attract a new staff to its fold.

Golden rule A fiscal policy stance which suggests that over the economic cycle, government should borrow only to 'invest' and not to finance the 'current expenditure'. The attempts towards 'balanced budgeting', 'zero-based budgeting' developed under the influence of this rule.

Goodhart's Law The idea of Goodhart which suggests that attempts by a central bank (as RBI in India) to regulate the level of lending by banks imposing certain controls can be circumvented by the banks searching the alternatives out of the regulatory preview.

Go-Go fund The highly speculative mutual funds operating in the USA with the objective of earning high profits out of capital appreciation–adopt risky strategies for the purpose (investing in volatile unproven and small shares, etc.), also called the *performance funds*.

Grandfather clause This is a clause normally found in a newly introduced law from which certain entity (individual, company, etc.) may be exempt from abiding— such actions of governments are called grandfathering. We may take an example— suppose a government bans owning a cat, a clause of the law may exempt (grandfather clause) those who already own a cat. Though this remains a controversial clause, we find it prevalent across the world [as per the *Farlex Financial Dictionary*, Farlex Inc., N. York, USA, 2012].

Greater Fool theory A theory evolved by the technical analysts of stocks/shares according to which some even buy overvalued stocks with the conviction that they will find a *greater fool* who will buy them at even higher prices. This is also popular as *castle-in-the-air theory*.

Greenfield investment An investment by a firm in a new manufacturing plant, workshop, office, etc.

Greenfield location An area consisting of unused or agricultural land (*i.e., 'greenfield'*) developed to set up new industrial plants.

Greenshoe option A term associated with the security/share market. This is a clause in the underwriting agreement of an initial public offer (IPO) by a company which allows to sell additional shares (usually 15 per cent) to the public if the demand for shares exceeds the expectation and the share trades above its offering price. It gets its name from the *Green Shoe* company which was the first company to be allowed such an option (in the USA, early 20th century). This is also known as *'over-allotment provision'*.

The company availing this option uses the proceeds (i.e. from the greenshoe option) to prevent any decline in the market price of shares below the issue price in the post-listing period (in such cases, the aforesaid company uses the money to purchase its own shares from the market—as demand increases, the market price of its shares picks up).

Gresham's law The economic idea that 'bad' money forces 'good' money out of circulation, named after Sir Thomas Gresham, an adviser to Queen Elizabeth I of England. This law does not apply to the economies where paper currencies are in circulation. The economies which circulate metallic coins (gold, silver, copper, etc.) of proportional intrinsic values face such situations when people start hoarding such coins.

Greenspan Put A financial market terminology named after the former chairman of the US central bank, Federal Reserve, to mean the helpful way he responded to big declines in the stock market by delivering a cut in interest rates.

Grey market The 'unofficial' market of the newly issued shares before their formal listing and trading on the stock exchange.

Growth recession An expression coined by economists to describe an economy that is growing at such a slow pace that more jobs are being lost than are being added. The lack of job creation makes it 'feel' as if the economy is in a recession, even though the economy is still advancing. Many economists believe that between 2002 and 2003, the United States' economy was in a growth recession.

In fact, at several points over the past 25 years the US economy is said to have experienced a growth recession. That is, in spite of gains in real GDP, job growth was either non-existent or was being destroyed at a faster rate than new jobs were being added.

Hair cut The term is used in two senses. *Firstly,* it is used to show the difference between market value and collateral value of an asset. For example, when we go to borrow a loan to bank against gold as collateral what banks do is that they consider the collateral value of gold lower (₹25,0000 than its market value (₹35,000). *Secondly*, it is used to measure the 'spread' (i.e., margin) at which market makers (a type of share broker) trade a stock in the security market.

The term has been in news recently in India in the case of the insolvency proceedings of the banks' bad loans (NPAs). The assets of the borrowers (who borrowed from banks to invest in those assets) have been sold off at much lower prices than their investment values—it means assets have been sold off at hefty 'hair cuts'.

Herfindahl index This is a measure of the level of seller concentration in a market which takes into account the total number of firms and their relative share in the total market output. Also known as *Herfindahl-Hirschman Index.*

Hidden price rise A quantitative or qualitative decrease in a product without changing the price.

Hidden tax Addition of an indirect tax into the price of goods or service without fully informing the consumer as, for example, the magnitude of the excise duty in tobacco and alcoholic products is so high that the taxes are added to the products directly.

Historic cost The original cost of purchasing an asset such as land, machine, etc. which is shown in the balance sheet of a firm under this title with an adjustment for the replacement cost of the asset.

Hoarding An act of unproductive retention of *money* or *goods.*

Hog cycles The cycles of over and under production of goods. This takes place due to time lag in the production process–this happens in the case of agricultural products specially.

Impossible trinity See the topic *Trilemmas* in *Chapter 18.*

India's sovereign rating Presently, India is rated by six international credit rating agencies, namely Standard and Poor's (S&P), Moody's

Investor Services, FITCH, Dominion Bond Rating Service (DBRS), the Japanese Credit Rating Agency (JCRA), and the Rating and Investment Information Inc., Tokyo (R&I).

Indifference curve A curve on the graph showing the alternative combinations of two products, each giving the same utility/satisfaction.

Induced investment The part of investment (increase or decrease) which takes place due to a change in the level of national income.

Inferior product The goods or service for which the income elasticity of demand is negative (i.e., as income rises, buyers go to purchase less of the product). For such products, a price cut results in lesser demands by the buyers.

Inflation For all types of inflation, see chapter *7* of the book.

Insider trading A stock market terminology which means transactions of shares by the persons having access to confidential information which are not yet public—such persons stand to gain financially out of this knowledge (the person might be an employee, director, etc. of the share issuing company or the merchant bank or the book runner to the issue, etc.). Such kind of trading in stocks is illegal all over the world.

Insolvency The situation when the liabilities of an individual or a firm to creditors exceed its assets—inability to pay the liabilities from the assets. Also known as *bankruptcy*.

Insurance intermediary Insurance intermediary functions between insurance firm (company) and its customers— the entities such as insurance agent, banks, surveyors, third party administrators, etc. being its examples. In 2019–20, the Government of India allowed 100 per cent FDI (foreign direct investment) in this segment, which was always facing requirement of huge capital base and technical expertise.

Inventory The stocks of finished goods, goods under the production process and raw materials held by a firm.

Invisible hand A term coined by Adam Smith (in his magnum opus *The Wealth of Nations, 1776*) to denote the way in which the market mechanism (i.e., the price system) coordinates the decisions of buyers and sellers without any outside conscious involvement. For him, this maximises individual welfare.

IPO An IPO or initial public offering refers to the issue of shares by the promoters of a company for the first time. The shares may be made available to the investors at face value of the share or with a premium as per the perceived market value of the share by the promoters. The IPO can be in the form of a fixed price portion or book building portion. Some companies offer only demat form of shares, others offer both demat and physical shares.

I-S schedule Here 'I-S' stands for 'investment saving'. This graphic schedule displays the combinations of levels of national income and interest rate where the equilibirium condition for the real economy (investment = savings) holds.

Islamic banking It is banking practiced as per the Islamic principle as prescribed in the *shariah* known as *Fiqh al-Muamalat* (Islamic rules on transaction). The Islamic law prohibits interest on both loans and deposits. Interest is also called *riba* in Islamic discourse. The argument against interest is that money is not goods and profit should be earned on goods and services only, not on control of money itself. But Islam does not deny that capital, as a factor of production, deserves to be rewarded. It, however, allows the owners of capital a share in a surplus which is *uncertain*.

It operates on the principle of sharing both profits and risks by the borrower as well as the lender. As such, the depositor cannot earn a fixed return in the form of interest as happens in conventional banking. But the banks are permitted to offer incentives such as variable prizes or bonuses in cash or kind on these deposits. The depositor, who in the conventional banking system is averse to risk, is a provider of capital here and equally shares the risks of the bank which lends his funds.

Investment finance is offered by these banks through *Musharka* where a bank participates as a joint venture partner in a project and shares the profits and losses. Investment finance is also offered through *Mudabha* where the banks contribute the finance and the client provides expertise, management, and labour, and the profits are shared in a prearranged proportion while the loss is borne by the bank.

Trade finance is also offered through a number of ways. One way is through *mare up*, where the bank buys an item for a client and the client agrees to repay the bank the amount along with an agreed profit later on. Banks also finance on lines similar to *leasing, hire purchase,* and *sell and buyback*. *Consumer lending* is without any interest, but the bank covers expenses by levying a service charge. Besides, these banks offer a host of fee-based products like money transfer, bill collections, and foreign exchange trading where the bank's own money is not involved.

Islamic banks have come into being since the early 1970s. There are nearly 30 Islamic banks all over the world within the conventional banking system. The whole banking system in Iran has moved over to the Islamic system since the early 1980s and even Pakistan is Islamising its banking system.

Many of the European and American Banks are now offering Islamic banking products not only in Muslim countries, but also in developed markets such as the United Kingdom. The concept is also catching up in countries like Malaysia and Dubai.

As per the Islamic experts, with growing indebtedness of many governments and with bulk of the borrowing going to servicing of the past debt and payment of huge interests, it could be an alternative to conventional banking as practiced in the rest of the world. Wherever it is practiced, *studies* have shown that the rate of return is often comparable and sometimes even higher than the interest rate offered by conventional banks to depositors.

India has no such full-fledged banks, though a few non-banking financial firms have been operating in Mumbai and Bangalore on Islamic principles. We find the traces of such financial operations by co-operatives even during pre-Independence era, too. In November 2017, the proposal of introducing such banking in the country was rejected by the RBI. It was in 2015–16 that an expert panel of the RBI (headed by Raghuram Rajan, the then RBI Governor) had stressed the need of thinking in the direction of introducing Islamic Banking in the country.

Isocost line A line on the two-axis graph which shows the combination of factor inputs that can be purchased for the same money.

Isocost curve A curve on the graph showing the varying combinations of factors of production (i.e., labour, capital etc.) that can be used to produce a given quantity of a product with a given technology.

J-curve effect The tendency for a country's balance of payments deficit to initially deteriorate following a devaluation of its currency before moving into surplus.

Junk bond An informal term denoting the financial securities issued by a company/bidder as a means of borrowing to finance a takeover bid. Such securities generally include high-risk, high-interest loans, that is why the term 'junk' is used. It is also known as *mezzanine debt*.

Kerb Dealings All the transactions taking place outside the stock exchanges.

Khilji Effect The rulers of the Delhi sultanate didn't understand formal macroeconomics.

But they knew one lesson very clearly—it was important to "signal the government's intent to keep expectations in check". Alauddin Khilji personally inspected markets and it worked—checking prices from rising. Such an effect on market is popular in India as the 'Khilji Effect'.

India saw these time-tested lessons followed by the GoI in 2014–15—Central Ministers publicly stated that matters are under control with sufficient quantity of 'onions' and 'potatoes'. The Government brought these two commodities under the purview of the Essential Commodities Act, too. This did show the 'strong intent' of the government to control prices.

However, the routine statements claiming that 'prices will rise' often started the inflationary spiral (it was repeatedly done by the then Union Minister of Agriculture).

Kleptocracy A government which is corrupt and thieving—the politicians and bureaucrats in charge using the powers of the state to earn personal benefits/profits. Russia, after the disintegration, is considered to be a clear-cut example when Mafia-friendly government allotted valuable shares of the government companies when they were privatised.

Kondratieff wave A business cycle of 50 years, named after the Russian economist Nikolai Kondratieff (wrote so in his book *The Long Waves in Economic Life*, 1925).

He argued that capitalism was a stable system (the business cycle of 50 years implied it) in contrast to the Marxist view that it was self-destructive and unstable—he died in one of Stalin's prisons.

Labour force As per the newly introduced (in 2017–18) PLFS (Periodic Labour Force Survey) of India, labour force refers to those who are either engaged in any economic activities or are willing to pursue an economic activity in a reference period. It includes both (i) those who are in workforce; and (ii) those who are unemployed. Of these, *workforce* refers to the population who are actively engaged in any economic activities and producing goods and services in a reference period while *unemployed* refers to all those who are seeking and available for work but had not worked in a reference year due to lack of work. Hence, Labour force participation rate (LFPR) can be *defined* as the proportion of population in the labour force to the total population. Similarly, *worker population ratio* (WPR) can be defined as the proportion of employed persons to the total population.

LAF The abbreviated form of the Liquidity Adjustment Facility, is part of a financial policy provided to the banks by the RBI in India. The facility commenced in June 2000 under which the banks operating in India are allowed to park their funds with the RBI for short-term periods (i.e., less than one year which is usually from one day to seven days, in practice), known as the *Reverse Repo*. On such deposits to the RBI, the banks get an interest rate of 6 per cent per annum at present.

Laffer curve A curve devised by the economist Arthur Laffer in 1974 which links average tax rates to total tax revenue. It suggests that higher tax rates initially increase revenue but after a point, further increases in tax rates cause revenue to fall (for instance by discouraging people from working). But it is tough to know whether an economy is on the Laffer curve, as higher taxation breeds evasion of taxes too.

Liar loans A term associated with the financial world which created news after the US financial system was hit by the subprime crisis in mid-2007.

These are the loans wherein borrowers fraudulently mis-state their incomes often egged on by the lender or broker to the bank. Such frauds have been detected along the entire US mortgage financing chain by September 2007–websites freely advertised that for a nominal fee, they could produce sufficient proof of income by generating bank statements, pay slips, income tax returns, and provide references. Lenders in turn *lied* about the real terms and conditions of the loans to borrowers and lied about the quality of loans sold to investors. The whole gamut of these deeds makes such mortgage loans the *'liar loans'*.

LIBOR The London Interbank Offered Rate (LIBOR) is the interest rate on dollar and other foreign currency deposits at which larger banks are prepared to borrow and lend these currencies in the Euro-currency market. The rate reflects market conditions for international funds and are widely used by the banks as a basis for determining the interest rates charged on the US dollar and foreign currency loans to the business customers.

Life-cycle hypothesis An idea which states that current consumption is not dependent solely on current disposable income of the consumers but is related to their anticipated lifetime income. This hypothesis has its high applied value in the real life economic management.

Life Insurance Some important terms:

- **Endowment policy:** Insurance policies where a lump sum is payable either at the end of the policy term or if the insured dies during the policy tenure, are termed endowment policies.
- **Beneficiary:** A person or organisation legally entitled to receive benefits.
- **Term life insurance:** In most cases, term life insurance refers to a product that provides death benefit protection for a specified period of time, say for 30 years. Benefits are doled out under this scheme only if the insured dies during the term.
- **Whole life insurance:** It is a policy that provides insurance coverage for the entire life of the individual for a fixed premium throughout his life insurance, coupled with an investment component. Investments could be made in stocks or bonds that lead to accumulation of cash values. The augmented cash reserves are returned once one decides to surrender the policy.

  Universal life insurance was created to provide more flexibility than whole life insurance by allowing the policy owner to shift money between the insurance and saving components of the policy.
- **Variable universal life insurance policy:** A form of whole life insurance policy, this is a policy for those who weigh high risk threshold. It offers cash values that fluctuate based on the performance of the underlying mutual funds in the investment account. It is this investment of premiums in the equity market that carries with it an element of uncertainty.
- **Premium:** This is the amount that the policy holder pays to the insurance company for the benefits provided under an insurance policy. The frequency of premium payments is opted by the individual. Typical premium modes include monthly, quarterly, semi-annual, and annual.
- **Annuity:** An agreement sold by a life insurance company that provides fixed or variable payments to the policy holder, either immediately or at a future date.
- **Group life insurance:** A life insurance policy issued to a group of people, usually through an employer.
- **Lapse:** Defaulting on premium payments leads to the termination of an insurance policy. A lapse notice is sent in writing to the policy holder when the policy has lapsed.
- **Lump sum:** It refers to the proceeds of the policy that is paid to the beneficiary all at once rather than in installments. Typically, most life insurance policies make lump sum payment settlements.

Liquidation A process of 'winding up' a joint-stock company as a legal entity.

Liquid asset The monetary asset that can be used directly as payment.

Liquidity The financial term is used in three different senses. At a very general level it means 'cash' (when banks face shortage of fund" they say there is liquidity crunch). At another place, it shows an asset's quality to convert into 'cash' (in this sense it is used in the concept of SLR in the case of banks in India). And lastly, it also means the readiness (or speed) of money to be available for use (in this sense it is used in the case of stock of money i.e., M_1, M_2, M_3 and M_4).

Liquidity Coverage Ratio Liquidity coverage ratio (LCR) is a clause of *Basel III* norms (of the Basel based Bank for International Settlement) which aims at prudential regulation of the banking sector. Under it banks are supposed to maintain enough short-term liquidity (their needs of the next 30 days) so that they can survive acute financial stress if such situations arise in the economy.

Liquidity preference A term denoting a preference among the people for holding money instead of investing it.

Liquidity trap A situation when the interest rate is so low that people prefer to hold money rather than invest it.

In such situations investors do not go to increase investment even if the interest rates on loans are decreased. J. M. Keynes suggested for increased government expenditure or reduction in taxes to fight such a situation.

L-M schedule Here 'L-M' stands for 'liquidity-money'. This is a schedule showing the combinations of levels of national income and interest rates where the equilibrium condition for the monetary economy, L = M, holds.

Local area bank Announced in the Union Budget 1996–97 to ensure a focussed savings and credit mobilisation by defining the clear boundary of operation, the Local Area Bank (LAB) operates to a narrow geographical area of three contiguous districts. The private sector is also allowed entry in the segment.

Locomotive principle The idea that in a situation of worldwide *recession* (see the chapter *Business Cycle*), increase in the total demand in one economy stimulates economic activities in the other economies via foreign trade.

Lorenz curve A graph showing the degree of inequality in income and wealth in a given population or an economy. It is a rigorous way to measure income inequality. In this method (for example), personal incomes in an economy are arranged in increasing order; the cumulative share of total income is then plotted against the cumulative share of the population. The curve's slope is thus proportional to per capita income at each point of the population distribution. In the case of complete equality of income, the Lorenz curve will be a straight line and with greater curvature the inequality rises proportionally–the *Gini Coefficient* measures this inequality.

LoU Letter of Undertaking (LoU) is basically a kind of guarantee/promise given by the LoU-issuing bank/financial institution about the credit-worthiness of a firm (corporate body). By showing the LoU the drawee of the LoU can borrow from the eligible banks/financial institution inside India or abroad. In the case of a default in repaying the loan by the drawee (of the LoU), the bank/financial institution compensates the lending body. This term came in news in February, 2018 in a financial fraud with a public sector bank (Punjab National Bank).

Lump of labour fallacy The fallacy in economics that there is a 'fixed amount of work' to be done, i.e. a lump of labour—this may be shared in different ways to create fewer or more jobs in an economy. An economist, D.F. Schloss in 1891 called it the lump of labour fallacy because in reality, the amount of work to be done is not fixed.

Macro and microeconomics In economics, two different ways of looking at the economy have been developed by economists i.e., macroeconomics and microeconomics.

Macroeconomics ('macro' in Greek language means 'large') looks at the behaviour of the economy *as a whole* such as the issues like inflation, rate of unemployment, economic growth, balance of trade, etc. It is the branch of economics which studies the economy in its *total* or *average* term.

Microeconomics (in Greek language 'micro' means 'small') looks on the behaviour of the *units,* i.e. the individual, the households, the firms, a *specific* industry, which together make up the economy.

Marginal Standing Facility(MSF) Operationalised on the lines of the existing Liquidity Adjustment Facility (LAF – Repo) in May 2011 under which all Scheduled Commercial Banks can avail overnight funds, up to one per cent of their Net Demand and Time Liabilities (NDTL). Though it operates like the 'repo' and serves similar purpose also for banks, it is a penal rate, the reason this rate is always set by the RBI a bit higher than the repo rate of the time. Banks are supposed to use this route once they have exhausted all other options to mobilise short-term fund.

Marginal utility The increase in satisfaction/utility a consumer derives from the use/consumption of one *additional* unit of a product in a particular time period–it goes on decreasing, i.e., the *diminishing marginal utility.*

Market capitalisation A term of security market which shows the market value of a company's share—calculated by multiplying the current price of its share to the total number of shares issued by the company.

Market maker An intermediary (may be an individual or a firm) in the secondary market who buys and sells securities/shares simultaneously quoting two-way rates. For example, on the Over the Counter Stock Exchange of India (OTCEI) only 'market markers' are allowed to operate. The Discount and Finance House of India (SBI DFHI) is the chief market maker in the 'money market' of India.

A market maker plays a very vital role by providing sustainability to liquidity in the secondary market.

Marshall Plan A programme of international aid named after General George Marshall (a US Secretary of State) under which North America contributed around 1 per cent of its GDP in total (between 1948–52) to western Europe to rebuild the economies ravaged in the Second World War.

Menu cost The cost a firm bears in changing the prices of its product—it includes retraining the sales staff, reprinting of the new price list, labelling of goods, and informing the customers about the price change. Higher menu costs discourage the firms going for frequent price changes.

Merchant banks Merchant banks are a kind of financial institution/company which are involved in providing a variety of financial services in an economy. Such as underwriting issuance of new shares, credit syndication, mezzanine financing (see this *entry* in Glossary), portfolio management, managing private placements, corporate advisory services, etc. In India, they are registered and regulated by the Security and Exchange Board of India (SEBI).

Mezzanine financing Mezzanine financing is defined as a financial instrument which is a *mix* of 'debt and equity' finance. It is a debt capital that gives the lender the rights to convert to an ownership or equity interest in the company. It is listed as an asset on the company's balance sheet. As it is treated as equity in a company's balance sheet, it allows the company to access other traditional sources of finance.

In the hierarchy of creditors, mezzanine finance is subordinate to *senior debt* but ranks higher than *equity*. The return on mezzanine finance is higher in relation to debt finance but lower than equity finance. It is also available quickly to the borrower with *little* or *no collateral*. The concept of mezzanine financing is just catching up in India. Mezzanine financing is used mainly for small and medium enterprises, infrastructure and real estate. *ICICI Venture's Mezzanine Fund* was the first fund in India to focus on mezzanine finance opportunities.

MIBID The Mumbai Inter Bank Bid (MIBID) is the weighted average interest rate at which certain banks in Mumbai are ready to borrow from the call money market.

MIBOR The Mumbai Inter Bank offer Rate (MIBOR) is the weighted average interest rate at which certain banks/institutions in Mumbai are ready to lend in the call money market.

Microcredit Smaller credit/loan to small and needy borrowers who are outside the reach of commercial banks, for the purpose of undertaking productive activities.

Misery Index An index of economic misery that is sum of the rates of inflation and unemployment for an economy–higher the value greater is the misery.

Modern Monetary Theory Quite popular today in the developed economies, the modern monetary theory states that national governments in place of targeting 'arbitrary' fiscal deficit should rather target 'full employment' by going for higher expenditures. The belief is based on the fact that a national government cannot go bankrupt as it has the legal power to print its currency. It means, without being concerned about its tax revenue, government should keep on spending to promote general well-being of the citizens.

Under such a monetary theory, money is made available by the central bank at cheaper cost (to boost demand in the economy) and governments increase their expenditures (by financing via increased internal borrowings). The central banks continue buying government debts (i.e. government securities) which is ultimately supplied with printing of fresh currency—this process can go on endlessly (as national governments have legal power to print as much currency as much they need! Though the sustainability of such a monetary policy is being hotly debated across the world, we find governments getting more and more attracted to it. The only challenge this policy faces is the concern of a rise in the rate of inflation.

The idea of universal basic income is based on the world's increasing faith in the capability of the modern monetary theory. Now, even the governments in developing world are getting attracted to it— recently not only the Government of India but several states launched quasi-basic income schemes for farmers (either as income or investment support).

Monetary neutrality The idea that changes in money supply have no effect on real economic variables (such as output, real interest rates, unemployment, etc.) if money supply increases by 10 per cent, for example, the price will increase by the same level.

A core belief of Classical Economics, the idea was put forth by David Hume in the 18th century. Today, this is not considered a valid idea.

Money illusion A phrase coined by J. M. Keynes to denote the misleading thinking among people that they are getting richer as a result of inflation when in reality the value of money decreases.

The phrase is used by some economists to argue that a small amount of inflation may not be a bad thing and could even be beneficial as it may help to 'grease the wheels' of the economy—a feeling of getting richer (let it be illusory itself!).

Moral hazard This is a situation in which someone takes risk knowing that the cost of risk will be borne by someone else— one of two challenges insurance companies face (the other being 'adverse selection', see the term in Glossary itself). This hazard arises when both the parties (Insurance firm and the insured) have incomplete information about each other. Banks also face similar challenges while lending.

In practice, when our houses are not insured, we take more precautions against fire, burglary, etc. but not as much if the houses are insured (due to which the cost of our negligence is borne by the insurance firm)!

Most Favoured Nation As per the WTO agreements, member countries cannot *normally* discriminate between their trading partners. If any country grants one country a special favour such as a lower customs duty rate for one of their products, the same would need to be extended to all other WTO members. This principle is known as Most Favoured Nation (MFN) treatment.

MFN governs trade in ***goods***. MFN is also a priority in the General Agreement on Trade in ***Services*** (GATS) and the Agreement on Trade-Related Aspects of ***Intellectual Property*** Rights (TRIPS). However, there are some *exceptions* under WTO regime which allow member countries to:

1. Set up a 'free trade agreement' that applies only to *goods* traded within the group (discriminating against goods from outside).
2. Give developing countries special access to their markets.
3. Raise barriers against products that are considered to be traded unfairly from specific countries.
4. To discriminate, in limited circumstances, in services.

But the agreements only permit these exceptions under strict conditions. In general, MFN means that every time a country lowers a trade barrier or opens up a market, it has to do so for the same goods or services for all its trading partners whether developed or developing.

Narrow banking Short-term lending in risk-free asset is narrow banking. A suggestion for such banking was given by the committee on Financial System (CFS) in 1991 for the weak banks of India.

Nash equilibrium A concept in game theory named after John Nash, a mathematician and Nobel prize winning economist, which occurs when each player is pursuing their best possible strategy in the full knowledge of the strategies of all the other players—once the equilibrium is reached, none of the players has any incentive to change their strategy.

Neo-classical economics The school of economics based on the writings of Alfred Marshall (1842–1924) which replaced the classical economics by the 19th century, also known as the *'marginal revolution'*.

Net income This is related to a limited liability firm/company (i.e., Ltd.). It is derived by deducting the expenses of the company from its total revenue in a particular period (usually one year). If income tax and interest are not deducted, it is called *'operating profit'* (or 'loss', as the case may be). Net income is also called *earnings, net earnings* or *net profit*.

Net Stable Funding Ratio Net stable funding ratio (NSFR) is one of the clauses of the Basel III norms (of the Basel based Bank for International Settlement) aimed at prudential regulation of the banking sector. Banks are supposed to maintain sufficient long-term (upto one year) liquidity under it so that they could be sure of the stable source of fund in times of financial stress if such situations arise in the economy.

Net worth Net worth for a company is its total assets minus total liabilities. This is an important determinant of the value of a company, considering it is composed primarily of all the money that has been invested since its inception, as well as the retained earnings for the duration of its operation. Net worth can be used to determine creditworthiness because it gives a snapshot of the company's investment history. This is also called *owner's equity, shareholders' equity,* or *net assets.*

In the case of an individual, net wroth is the value of a person's assets, including cash, minus all liabilities – the amount by which the individual's assets exceed his liabilities is considered the net worth of that person.

Ninja A mortgage business terminology became a common word after the US subprime crisis of mid-2007, which is an acronym for the borrowers with no income, no job or assets.

Nominal value The value of anything calculated at the current prices. It does not include the effect of inflation during the periods and gives a misleading idea of value.

Non-monetary liabilities of RBI Non-monetary liabilities (NNML) of the RBI are liabilities which do not have any monetary impact. These comprise items such as the Reserve Bank's paid-up capital and reserves, contribution to National Funds (NIC-LTO Fund and NHC-LTO Fund), RBI employees' PF and superannuation funds, bills payable, compulsory deposits with the RBI, RBI's profit held temporarily under other deposits, amount held in state Governments Loan Accounts under other deposits, IMF quota subscription and other payments and other liabilities of RBI *less* net other assets of the RBI.

Similarly, NNML of banks includes items such as their capital, reserves, provisions, *etc.* NNML of the banking sector includes NNML of the Reserve Bank and that of other banks.

Non-workers The *Census of India* defines non-workers as the persons who did not 'work at all' during the reference period. They constitute:

1. Students who did not participate in any economic activity paid or unpaid.
2. Household duties who were attending to daily household chores like cooking, cleaning utensils, looking after children, fetching water, etc. and are not even helping in the unpaid work in the family farm or cultivation or milching.
3. Dependent such as infants or very elderly people not included as *worker*.
4. Pensioners drawing pension post-retirement, not engaged in any economic activity.
5. Beggars, vagrants, prostitutes and persons having unidentified source of income and with unspecified sources of subsistence and not engaged in any economically productive work.
6. Others, which include all non-workers who may not come under the above categories such as rentiers, persons living on remittances, agricultural or non-agricultural royalty, convicts in jails or inmates of penal, mental or charitable institutions doing no paid or unpaid work and persons who are seeking/available for work.

[Also see entry *'Worker'*]

Normal goods The goods whose demand increases as the income of the people increases. It is just opposite of *inferior goods.*

Numeraire A monetary unit which is used as the basis for denominating international exchanges in a product and financial settlements on a common basis. For example, the US dollar being used as the numeraire of international oil trade, the Special Drawing Rights (SDRs) and the IMF transactions.

Nutri Cereals The existing 'coarse cereals' are now known as 'nutri cereals' (as per a GoI notification of April 20, 2018). The cereals put under this category are the millets—Sorghum (Jowar), Pearl Millet (Bajra), Finger Millet (Ragi/ Mandua), Minor Millets/Foxtail Millet (Kangani/ Kakun), Proso Millet (Cheena), Kodo Millet

(Kodo), Barnyard Millet (Sawa/Sanwa/Jhangora), Little Millet (Kutki) and two Pseudo Millets (Black-wheat (Kuttu) and Amaranthus (Chaulai). Now, the new nomenclature will be used for production, consumption and trade purposes. The move is aimed at removing a lingering perception that these grains are inferior to rice and wheat, even as their health benefits are larger.

As per the ICAR (Indian Council of Medical Research), compared to **rice** Foxtail millet has 81 percent more protein, Little millet has 840 percent higher fat, 350 percent higher fiber and 1,229 percent higher quantity of iron. The Council highlighted that recent research findings show millets contain 'anti-diabetic' properties and millet-based foods have low 'GI' (Glycaemic Index) and reduce the 'postprandial blood glucose' level and 'glycosylated haemoglobin'.

There has been demand in the country to declare these crops as 'Nutri Cereals' to boost their demand and allow farmers to get higher prices. Promotion of these cereals enhances sustainability in farming (as they need less water in comparison to rice and wheat) also. Besides, they have in-built mechanism to enhance farm income (crop loss will decline as they are climate resilient). The noted agriculture scientist *M.S. Swaminathan* had also suggested the name change in 2006 (National Commission on Farmers).

To popularise the consumption of these nutritious cereals, the government has already announced to include millets in the PDS (Public Distribution System) with the objective of improving nutritional security of the country. India produced around 48 million tonnes of these crops in 2018–19 (with a growth rate of around 11 per cent—much higher than other cereals).

NVS Non Voting Shares (NVS) are the equity shares not having the right to vote at the general meetings of the company. But these shares get higher dividend than the shares having voting rights. A company in India may issue such shares maximum to the 25 per cent of the total issued share capital and such shares cannot get more than 20 per cent higher dividend than the shares with voting rights.

Okun's law Based on the empirical research of *Arthur Okun* (1928–80), the law describes the relationship between unemployment and growth rate in an economy. According to it, if GDP grows at 3 per cent p.a., the unemployment rate would not change. In the case of faster growth rates, every extra above the 3 per cent will have a decrease in the unemployment rate by its half (i.e., a 4 per cent growth rate will decrease unemployment by 0.5 per cent–half of 1 which is the extra above 3 per cent). Similarly, a growth rate below 3 per cent will have the same but opposite impact on unemployment (i.e., increases it).

Though the law was perfectly correct for the period of the US economy Okun studied, it may not be valid today in either US or anywhere else. But in general, the law is still used by experts and policy makers as a rule of thumb to estimate the relationship between growth rate and job creation.

Open market operation An instrument/tool of monetary policy under which the sale/purchase of government Treasury Bills and bonds is done by the central bank (the RBI in the case of India) as a means of regulating money supply.

Operation twist This is an act related to monetary policy responsibility of the central bank. Under it, the central bank purchases long-term government securities and sells short-term government securities—aimed at making long-term borrowing cheaper. The act aims at 'twisting' the prevailing interest rates (yields) on the short- and long-term securities in the financial system.

It was the central bank of USA (Federal Reserve Board) which took the *world's first* such step in 1961 (under the US President J.F. Kennedy). Since then, such actions have been taken by other central banks across the world as per their needs. After 2008 (the US sub-prime crisis), we find almost all recession-hit western economies trying this quite widely. It is believed to be named after the famous song 'Twist' of 1961 (of Ernest Evans who was popularly known as Chubby Checker).

The term made news in India when by late December 2019, the RBI announced a similar measure—*first* such step taken ever. Under it, the RBI announced to 'purchase' 10-year Government securities (G-Secs) of ₹10,000 crores (maturing 2029) and 'sell' short-term G-Secs (maturing 2020) of the similar amount. Soon after, interest rate on the long-term G-Secs (10-year) started moderating.

In the process of activating the desired kind of monetary policy, central banks keep studying the movement of interest rates on short- and long-term G-Secs—anchoring the interest rates to the current policy rate (i.e. repo rate in the case of India). Once the divergence in interest rates is against the objective of the monetary policy, central banks may go for 'operation twist'.

Opportunity cost A measure of the economic cost of using scarce resources to produce particular goods or service in terms of the alternative thereby foregone, also known as the *economic cost.*

Over the counter The financial papers/securities which can be bought or sold through a private dealer or bank rather than on a financial exchange. The term has its use in the non-financial world too–purchasing medicines from a medical store without the doctor's prescription is an over-the-counter deal in drugs.

Parallel importing A type of arbitrage where an independent importer buys products of a particular supplier at low price in one country and resells it in direct competition with the supplier's distributors in another country where prices are higher.

It promotes free trade and competition by breaking down barriers to international trade and undermines price discrimination between markets covered by the suppliers.

Pareto Principle The maximisation of the economic welfare of the community. Named after the Italian economist Vilfredo Pareto (1843–1923), this points to a situation in which nobody can be made better off without making somebody else worse off.

By an efficient use of resources, an economy is able to do so, i.e., without making somebody else worse off, somebody might be made better off. In reality, change often produces losers as well as winners. Pareto optimality does not help judge whether this sort of change is economically good or bad.

Parkinson's Law A proposition by C. Northcote Parkinson which suggests that work expands according to the time available in which it is done.

PLFS In 2017-18, the Government of India launched a *new* regular employment-unemployment survey, namely, annual *PLFS (Periodic Labour Force Survey)* with certain changes in survey methodology, data collection mechanism and sampling design vis-à-vis the earlier quinquennial (once in every 5 years) EUSs (Employment and Unemployment Surveys) of NSO (National Statistics Office).

In the new survey, households are selected in both *rural* and *urban* areas by providing 75 per cent weightage to households where at least one member has secondary education (Class 10) or above. In the EUS, *affluence level* and earning from non-agricultural activities in rural areas and Monthly Per Capita Consumption Expenditure (MPCE) of household in selected blocks in urban areas were used for stratification of households. Due to the changes in methodology and sampling design, labour market estimates based on PLFS are not strictly comparable with the results of earlier EUSs.

P/E ratio Also called 'price multiple' or 'earnings multiple', the *price-to-earnings ratio* (P/E Ratio) measures the current share price to its per-share earnings (earning per share, i.e. EPS). It is used in the stock market by analysts to determine the relative value of a company's shares in one to one comparison. This ratio is derived by dividing the market value per share (numerator) with earnings per share (denominator). A high P/E ratio could mean that a company's stock is over-valued, or investors are expecting high earnings in future. In the case of loss making companies, there is no P/E ratio (as there is no denominator).

Penny stocks Very low-priced shares of small companies which have low market capitalisation. The term made news in mid-2006 when some of the 'penny stocks' did show a high rise in their trading prices in India at the BSE as well as the NSE.

Petroleum pricing Petroleum products pricing in India follows a dynamic method which is based on the *Indian Crude Basket* (called *Indian Basket* also). Indian Basket is weighted average of the prices of *Oman & Dubai* (for sour grade) and *Brent* (sweet grade) crude oils. Actual price depends on the ratio in which sour and sweet grades of crude were used by the oil refineries in the previous financial year (for 2017–2018, the ratio was 74.77: 25.23 for sour and sweet, respectively) used for pricing in 2018–19.

Crude oil with high amount of *sulphur* is termed 'sour' and with less sulphur is called the 'sweet' grade. The dynamic price is maintained by the Petroleum Planning and Analysis Cell (attached to the Ministry of Petroleum and Natural Gas), set up in 2002 by the Government as dismantling of the 'administered pricing mechanism' (APM) for petroleum began.

Philtips curve A graphic curve depicting an empirical observation of the relationship between the level of unemployment and the rate of change of money wages and, by inference, the rate of change of prices.

It was in 1958 that an economist from New Zealand, A. W. H. Phillips (1914–75) proposed that there was a trade-off between inflation and unemployment–the lower the unemployment rate, the higher the inflation rate–governments simply need to choose the right balance between the two evils.

Piggyback loan A term associated with mortgage business got popular in the wake of the US subprime crisis mid-2007. Piggyback loan is a second mortgage enabling a borrower to buy a house with little or no equity.

Pigou effect Named after Arthur Cecil Pigou (1877–1959), a sort of wealth effect resulting from deflation/disinflation (i.e., price fall) – a fall in price level increases the real value of people's money, making them wealthier and inducing increased spending by them; higher demand creation leads to higher employment.

Ponzi Scheme It is an investing or deposit scheme (usually offered in India by the non-banking financial companies such as Chit Funds) which offers *high returns with very low risks*. Such schemes are able to give high returns to their 'older investors' by mobilising funds from the 'newer investors'—creating a kind of pyramid of investors. The day they stop getting new investors, the existing investors stop getting returns and may lose their entire invested capital as the scheme collapses. This way, such schemes are a kind of financial scams. The Government has proposed to check such schemes from cheating innocent investors in the country.

Preference shares The shares which bear a stated dividend and carry a priority over equity shares (in matters of dividend and assets), are also known as hybrid securities (since they have the qualities of equity shares as well as bond). Such shares in India cannot have a life over 10 years.

Price-earning ratio A concept used in the share market to equate various stocks–is a ratio found/ calculated by dividing the market price of a share by the earning per share.

Primary and secondary market Primary market refers to buying of shares in an initial public offering. The shares are bought by applying through a share application form. Secondary market refers to transactions where one investor buys shares from another investor at the prevailing market price or at an agreed price. The shares are bought and sold in the secondary market on the stock exchanges. The investors may buy and sell securities on the stock exchanges through stock brokers.

Primary Dealer Primary Dealer (PD) is an intermediary participating in the *primary* auctions of the government securities (i.e., G-See or the Gilt-edge securities or the Gilt) and the Treasury Bills (TBs); through a PD, these instruments reach the secondary market.

Primary dealers are allowed participation in the call money market and notice money market. They get liquidity support from RBI via repos or refinance (against the G-Secs.).

Prisoner's dilemma A popular example in *game theory* which concludes why co-operation is difficult to achieve even if it is mutually beneficial, ultimately making things worse for the parties involved. It is shown giving an example of two prisoners arrested for the same offence held in different cells. Each prisoner has two options, i.e., confess, or say nothing. In this situation, there are *three* possible outcomes:

1. One could confess and agree to testify against the other as a state witness, receiving a light sentence while his fellow prisoner receives a heavy sentence.
2. They can both say nothing and may turn out to be lucky getting light sentences or even be let off due to lack of firm evidence.
3. They may both confess and get lighter individual sentences than one would have received had he said nothing and the other had testified against him.

The second outcome looks the best for both the prisoners. However, the risk that the other might confess and turn state witness is likely to encourage both to confess, landing both with sentences that they might have avoided had they been able to co-operate by remaining silent.

In reality, firms behave like these prisoners, not setting prices as high as they could do if they only trusted the other firms not to undercut them. Ultimately, the firms are worse off, i.e. all firms suffer.

Population trap A situation of population growth rate greater than the achievable economic growth rate. This makes it difficult to alleviate poverty. Government is suggested to implement population control measures.

Positive pay This concept (which was introduced by the RBI by early 2021) involves a process of 'reconfirming key details' of large-value cheques. The issuer of the cheque under it submits electronically, through channels like SMS, mobile app, internet banking and ATM, certain minimum details of that cheque (like date, name of the beneficiary, or payee and amount) to the drawee bank, details of which are cross-checked with the presented cheque by Cheque Truncation System (CTS). Any discrepancy is flagged by CTS to the drawee bank and presenting bank, who then take redressal measures.

Poverty trap A situation where an unemployed getting unemployment allowance is not encouraged to seek work/employment because his/her after-tax earnings as employed is less than the benefits as unemployed, also known as the *unemployment trap*.

Predatory pricing The pricing policy of a firm with the express purpose of harming rivals or exploiting the consumer. By price-cutting, firstly the rivals are ousted from the market and later the consumers are exploited as monopolistic suppliers by the firm.

PPP Purchasing power parity (PPP) is a method of calculating the correct/real value of a currency which may be different from the market exchange rate of the currency. Using this method economies may be studied comparatively in a common currency. This is a very popular method handy for the IMF and WB (introduced by them in 1990) in studying the living standards of people in different economies.

The concept of the PPP was developed by the great European conservative economist, Gustav Cassel (1866–1944), belonging to Sweden. This concept works on the assumption that markets work on the *law of one price,* i.e., identical goods and services (*in quantity* as well as *quality*) must have the same price in different markets when measured in a common currency. If this is not the case, it means that the purchasing power of the two currencies is different.

Let us look at an example. Suppose sugar is selling $1 in US and ₹20 in India a kilo, then the PPP-based exchange rate of rupee will be $1 = ₹20. This is the way how *The Economist* of London has prepared its 'Big Mac Index' (comparing the Mc Donald's Big Mac burger prices in different economies).

In theory, the value of currencies in terms of their market exchange rate should converge with their value in terms of the PPP in the long run. But that might not happen due to many factors like the fluctuations in inflation; level of money supply; follow-up to the exchange rate regimes (fixed, floating, etc.), and other.

For the calculation of the PPP, a comparable basket of goods and services is selected (a very difficult task) of the identical qualities and quantities. The other difficulty in computing PPP arises out of the flaw in the 'one price theory', i.e., due to transportation cost, local taxes, level of production, etc. The prices of goods and services cannot be the same in different markets (This is correct in theory only, not possible in practice.)

PSEs & PSUs The public sector undertakings (PSUs) or public sector enterprise (PSE) refers to a 'government company' in which minimum 51 per cent of the paid-up capital is owned by the government—exclusively or jointly by Centre and State in the case of India (Section 2(45) of the Companies Act, 2013). The term is not intended to mean a 'public company' (i.e. 'Limited' company, where shares are freely transferable and has a shareholder base of more than 200 people), though most of them are today public companies. Central public sector enterprises are classified as *maha-ratnas, nav-ratnas, mini-ratnas,* and *other enterprises,* depending on their performance track record based on guidelines approved by the Government from time to time.

PSUs refer to commercial ventures which charge 'user fees' for the services they provide—the user charges may be market-based or subsidised. Usually, they are fully owned and managed by the Government such as— Railways, Posts, Defence Undertakings, Banks, etc. PSEs, on the other hand, refer to those companies which are registered under the Companies Act, 1951. Predominantly owned by the Government, they are managed by a Board of Directors with Government-appointed Chairmen and Managing Directors together with nominees of Government on board to represent the interests of the Government such as—NTPC, ONGC, SAIL, BHEL, Indian Oil, Coal India, etc.

While the audit of the PSUs is done by the CAG (Comptroller and Auditor General of India), in the case of the PSEs, it is done first by CAs (Chartered Accountants), followed by a supplementary audit done by the CAG.

Purchase tax A tax collected by states in India on goods. This is imposed on the *purchases* done by traders/manufacturers—basically collected by the seller and given to the states concerned. This is deducted once the traders/manufacturers pay value added tax (VAT) to the states—as VAT is paid on the differential value of the traded/manufactured goods. This tax is among the 9 state taxes merged into the indirect tax, the GST.

Q Theory As investment theory for firms proposed by the Nobel prize winning (1981) economist James Tobin (1918–2002). He theorised that firms would continue to invest as long as the value of their shares exceeded the replacement cost of their assets–the ratio of the market value of a firm to the net replacement cost of the firm's assets is known as *'Tobin Q'*. If Q is greater than 1, then it should expand the firm by investment as the profit it should expect to make from its assets (reflected by share price) exceeds the cost of the assets.

If Q is less than 1, the firm would be better off by selling its assets which are worth more than shareholders currently expect the firm to earn in profit by retaining them.

Random walk When it is impossible to predict the next step. As per the Efficient Market Theory, the prices of financial assets (such as shares) follow a random walk–there is no way of knowing the next change in the price. The reason this theory provides is that in an efficient market, all the information that would allow an investor to predict the next price move is already *reflected in the current price.* Such belief has led some economists to conclude that investors cannot outperform the market consistently.

As opposed to this, some economists argue that asset prices are predictable and that markets are not efficient–they follow a *non-random walk* perspective.

Redlining The act of not lending to people in certain poor or troubled neighbourhoods shown on the map with a 'red line'. Even if their credit-worthiness has been judged based on other criteria, they are not considered as borrowers by the banks, simply because they live in that area.

Rent It has two different meanings in economics:

1. The first is layman, i.e. the income accruing from hiring land or other durable goods.
2. The second (also known as *economic rent*) is a measure of *market power,* i.e. the difference between what a factor of production is paid and how much it would need to be paid to remain in its current use.

For example, a cricket player may be paid ₹40,000 a week to play for his team when he would be willing to turn out for only ₹10,000, so his economic rent will be ₹30,000 a week.

Rent-seeking Spending time and money not on the production of real goods and services, but rather on trying to get the government to change the rules so as to make one's business more profitable.

It is like cutting a bigger slice of the cake rather than making the cake bigger, trying to make more money without producing more for customers. The term was coined by the economist Gordon Tullock.

Rent-seeking behaviour The behaviour which improves the welfare of someone at the expense of someone else. A protection racket is the most extreme example of it, in which one group (i.e., the protected one) betters itself without creating welfare-enhancing output at all.

Replacement cost The cost of replacing an asset (such as machinery, etc.). Opposite to *historic cost* (i.e., the original cost of acquiring an asset), replacement cost adjusts the effects of inflation.

Residual risk What is left after one takes out all the other shared risk exposures to an asset, also known as *alpha* (a).

When one buys an asset, one is exposed to a number of risks, many of them not unique to the asset but reflect broader possibilities (such as the future behaviour of stock market, interest rate, inflation or even government policies, etc.). Exposure to this risk can be reduced by diversification.

Retail banking A way of doing banking business where the banks emphasise the individual-based lending rather than corporate lending–also known as *high street banking.* Such banking focusses on consumer loans, personal loans, hire-purchase, etc., considered more cumbersome and risky.

Retrocession The term has got *three* different meanings in which it is used:

1. The purchase of 'reinsurance' by a 'reinsurance company' (as in the case of India, the GIC going for 'reinsurance' on the 'reinsurance' it has provided to other 'insurance companies' operating in India). This limits the risk that a reinsurance company may face, since it has purchased insurance against an 'event' that might affect a company that it had underwritten (reinsured). If a reinsurance company *continues* to purchase insurance, it might 'unknowingly' buy back its own risk, which is known as 'spiraling'.
2. The 'voluntary' act of returning ceded property by one to another which may be a result of 'request' to have property returned. But, by definition, it is not the result of a 'forced' transaction. Returning of Hong Kong to China by the UK in 1997 is the best such example of the recent times.
3. The act of 'differentiating' and 'diversifying' assets by consolidating and then dividing them amongst a number of stakeholders – by doing so the risk involved is 'retroceded' (i.e., cut down or minimised). This is, usually, done by the 'hedge funds' in their day-to-day portfolio management.

Reverse takeover The term is used to mean two different kinds of takeovers:

1. Takeover of a public company by a private one, and
2. Takeover of a bigger company by a smaller one.

Residual unemployment Unemployment of those who remained unemployed even in the times of full employment (as for example employing a severely handicapped person may far outweigh the productivity obtained from him).

Reverse mortgage A scheme for senior citizens in India announced in the Union Budget 2007–08. Under this scheme, the senior citizens go to mortgage their house owned by them in reverse to a bank and the bank pays them the agreed money either in installments or lumpsum. Guidelines for reverse mortgage announced by the National Housing Bank (NHB) in May 2007 has a provision of maximum period of 15 years for such mortgage. Once the period of mortgage is complete, either the house should be vacated or the bank will sell the house at the market price and the loan of the bank will be settled. If the value of the house is more than the loan, the difference is paid to the senior citizens or their heirs. If the heir wants to possess the house, he/she needs to pay the loan.

Reverse yield gap An excess of returns on gilt-edged (government) securities above those on equities. This occurs during periods of high inflation because equities provide capital gains to compensate inflation while the gilt-edged securities do not.

Revealed preference The notion that what one wants is revealed by what one does, not by what one says–actions speak louder than words.

Ricardian equivalence An idea which (generated too much controversies) was originally suggested by David Ricardo (1772–1823) and more recently by Barro, that government deficits do not affect the overall level of demand in an economy.

This is because tax-payers know that any deficit has to be paid later, and so they increase their savings in anticipation of a higher tax bill in future; thus government attempts to stimulate an economy by increasing public spending or cutting taxes, will be rendered impotent by private sector reaction.

The equivalence can be seen as part of a thread of economic thinking which holds that only decisions about real variables (e.g., consumption and production) matter, and that decisions about financing will, in a perfectly functioning market, never have an effect.

Risk seeking An act whereby investors prefer an investment with an uncertain outcome to one with the same expected returns and certainty that it will deliver them – the act which cannot get enough risk.

Round tripping Literally, round tripping means the ending of a journey (trip) at the place where it began from. In economics, it is related to external sector which comes under the regulatory control of the RBI in India (in the case of companies, SEBI also joins as regulator). Under it, the money (mostly black money) leaves a country of origin through various channels such as over-invoicing (showing higher prices of goods in bills), payments to shell (i.e. fake) companies located overseas, hawala route, etc. After remaining overseas for some time (known as the cooling period), the fund returns back to the country of origin (as white money)—completion of the trip. For return trips, normally, the legal instruments of foreign investment like Global Depository Receipts (GDRs) and Participatory Notes (PNs) are used.

In recent past companies like United Spirits, Unitech, Sterlite and Reliance ADAG were alleged to have indulged in stock price manipulation channelising funds through this route—using their shell companies, P-Notes and international investment banks.

Round-trip trading Round-trip trading is an unethical trading of shares. Under it, the same trader or two traders sell and buy a share same day simply to push the trading volumes of the share upward. This is done to manipulate observers into believing that the share is in high demand (rather the company might not be running in profit). This increases the profit aspect of the company which gets reported through their balance sheet. The most infamous global case of it was the Enron power company of the USA (in India, the Satyam Computers was the first such reported case). This act is illegal across the world.

Rule of thumb A rough-and-ready decision-making aid that provides an acceptably accurate approximate solution to a problem. Where refined decision-making processes are expensive (in terms of information gathering and processing them), such a method looks justified.

Rounding error The error which comes up due to rounding off the figures in decimals, for example, considering 3.6 as 4 and 3.4 as 3. Such rounding off the data is never going to be mathematically correct.

Salary The payment made to employees of an organisation, firm, etc. for the use of labour as a factor of production. It differs from *wage* in the following two ways:

1. It is not paid on hourly basis (or for the actual number of hours worked by the employee) as wages are paid, and
2. It is usually paid on monthly basis whereas wages are paid on daily or weekly basis.

Satisfying theory A theory which suggests that firms do not want only 'satisfactory' profits but maximum profits as well as other objectives such as sales increase, size increase, etc. might be having equal or greater importance than profits.

Say's law Named after the French economist Jean Baptise Say (1767–1832), the law proposes that aggregate supply creates its own aggregate demand.

The logic of the law goes like this–the very act of production generates an income (in the form of wages, salaries, profits, etc.) exactly equal to the output which, if spent, is just sufficient to purchase the whole output produced. Ultimately, it gives an important clue, i.e., in order to reach full-employment level, all that is needed is to increase the aggregate supply.

The key assumption behind the law is that the economic system is 'supply-led' and that all income is spent. But in practice, some income 'leaks' into saving, taxation, etc., and there is no auto-guarantee that all income is 'injected' back as spending. Therefore, others suggest for a 'demand-led' idea of the economic system under which demand creation is attended vigorously.

Second-bestTheory The idea was put forward by Richard Lipsey and Kelvin Lancaster (1924–99) in 1956 which suggests a way out of the situation when all the assumptions of an economic model are not met. As per the theory, the second-best situation is meeting as many of the assumptions as possible (but it might not give the optimum or the desired results).

Securities transaction tax

[See Chapter 17, *Tax Structure in India*]

Seigniorage A method of generating resource by a government through printing of fresh notes/ currency notes. Money printing at higher rate to pay the government expenditures leads to inflation that enables the government to secure extra resources though that is called 'inflation tax' also.

Sequestration The process under which a third party (*the sequestrator*) holds a part of the disputed assets till the dispute is settled.

Shadow banking When financial institutions create credit (forward loan) like a bank but are not under the banking regulatory framework of the country, they are supposed to be involved in shadow banking. Hedge funds are one such example. It also includes unregulated activities of regulated entities. Credit default swaps (CDSs) are the examples of it—regulated entities (like banks) provide loan protection in it to other lenders against default risks by the borrowers.

As such institutions do not accept traditional bank deposits, they easily escape the regulatory design of a country. Such acts are financially risky to the economy, as in it 'capital requirements' (of CRR, SLR, etc.) are bypassed by the institutions. Therefore, in cases of default, there remains no standby capital/asset to counter it. After the 'sub-prime' crisis in USA (2007–08), shadow banking came under increasing scrutiny and regulation across the world. The NBFCs (non-banking financial companies) in India are an example of such banking.

Sharpe Ratio The idea of William Forsyth Sharpe (Nobel Economist) which checks whether the rewards from an investment justify the risk. For this, Sharpe uses the past data of rewards and calculates it using standard deviation. Therefore, the ratio says nothing about the future performance of the investment.

Short selling Selling shares without possessing them. After the prices fall to a certain extent, the short-seller covers his position by cheaper shares booking the difference in price as profits. It is also known as *bear operation*. Short-sellers, however, could get caught on the wrong foot if the market reverses the downtrend.

Shutdown price That lower level of the prices for the product of a firm at which the firm decides to close (*shut*) down – as it has become impossible to recover even the short-run variable cost at the price. Many such instances we get in the Euro-American economies during the period of the Great Depression (1929).

Skimming price A pricing method of charging high profits—adopted by a firm when consumers are not price-sensitive and demand is price-inelastic.

Smurfing Smurfing (also called structuring) is a method in which small sizes of money is kept in several number of bank accounts to hide the real identity of the real owner. This has been a very commonly used method of money-laundering. During the reform period, as more prudential norms of banking regulation evolved, such acts declined in India. 'Smurfer' (or 'money mule') is a person who does this.

Social costs The costs borne by the society at large resulting from the economic activities of the firms–pollution being a prominent example.

Solvency margin The term made news in the 1970s concerning a life insurance company. The only requirement, till then, by a life insurance company was that the value of its assets should not be less than the value of its liabilities. The regulators in many countries felt that the value of assets should exceed the value of liabilities by a certain margin. This margin which came to be known as *'solvency margin'* became a useful device to force shareholders of a life insurance company either to keep in reserve a certain portion of the profit or to bring in additional capital if there is not sufficient profit to meet unforeseen contingencies. The European Union developed an empirical formula taking recourse to the past experience to determine the quantum of margin required. The IRDA has stipulated that the excess of assets (including capital) over liabilities should not be less than 150 per cent of the solvency margin arrived at by the EU formula.

Sovereign bond The securities (backed by assets or/and legal guarantee) issued (i.e. sold off) to borrow are known as bonds. Bonds are issued by both government and non-government agencies. When a national government issues it in overseas markets, it is known as Sovereign Bond. Buyers of the bond enjoy the profit element on bonds which is popularly known as 'bond yield'.

Today, the world has a highly developed bond market in which national governments issue such bonds to borrow in either foreign or their domestic currencies (in the case of India, the bonds by which rupee-denominated loans are borrowed from the overseas markets are known as 'masala bonds'). The term came in news when the Government of India proposed (in the *Union Budget 2019–20*) to finance a part of its expenditures by issuing such bond; however, these bonds are yet to be issued.

Sovereign risk The risk of a government defaulting on its debt or a loan guaranteed by it (all international loans by the private companies are basically guaranteed by the government of an economy).

Spot price The price quoted for anything in a transaction where the payment and delivery is to be done now.

Spread A frequently used term of financial market which is the difference between two items, for example, the spread (i.e., the difference) an underwriter pays for an issue of bonds from a company and the price it charges from the public. Similarly, the returns on two different bonds if they are different; the difference is known as spread.

Standard deviation It is a statistical technique to measure how far a variable moves over time away from its mean (average) value.

Standing Deposit Facility Scheme The Standing Deposit Facility Scheme (SDFS) is a new monetary tool given to the RBI (announced by the Union Budget 2018–19). Such a facility was proposed by the RBI in November 2015 itself. Such a tool was needed at the disposal of the RBI which it can use when the economy is flush with excess fund. This will allow 'uncollateralised deposit' of the liquidity in the economy if such a need arises.

The need of such a tool was felt last time when the Government demonetised the high value currency notes of ₹500 and ₹2000 denominations in November 2016. As people were depositing the demonetised currencies in their bank accounts, the banking industry was flush with excessive fund (temporarily). To handle the situation, RBI increased banks, CRR (Cash Reserve Ratio) temporarily to syphon out the excess liquidity with the banks.

Stealth tax A popular name given to an obscure tax increase for example, stamp duty, property tax, etc. They get implemented months later by the time they usually fade out from the public memory.

Sterilised intervention This is an act of the central bank of India (RBI) related to its dual responsibilities, namely regulating monetary system through the right monetary policy and stabilising the exchange rate of rupee. Under sterilised intervention, the RBI intervenes in foreign exchange in a typically different way. Under it, to stabilise the exchange rate of rupee, RBI keeps buying foreign currencies while, it keeps selling government securities (to syphon out rupee pumped in the monetary system while purchasing foreign currencies). This way, the RBI aims to stabilise exchange rate while not allowing inflation to go out of bound (target). This process may be run in the reverse also (when foreign exchange is outflowing from the country).

Due to increased integration of the economy with the global economy, India has seen increase in external transactions (inflows and outflows of foreign currencies) also. As India has been following an active policy of attracting foreign investment (direct and indirect both), the exposure of economy to global economy has increased over time—getting very difficult for the RBI to fulfil its responsibility. Due to increased volatility in the global economy (caused by the Great Recession hitting the western economies), India started facing the volatile inflows and outflows of foreign exchange. Faced with the typical situation, the RBI commenced this act (suggested by the *Urjit Patel Committee* in 2014).

Stochastic process It is a process that shows random behaviour. For example, *Brownian* motion, which is often used to describe changes in share prices by the experts in an efficient market (random walk), is such a process.

Sub-Prime crisis The word 'sub-prime' refers to borrowers who do not have sound track record of repayment of loans (*it means such borrowers are not 'prime', thus they could be called 'less than prime' i.e. 'sub-prime'). The* 'sub-prime crisis', which has been echoing time and again recently, has its origin in the United States housing market by late 2007—being considered as the major financial crisis of the new millennium.

Subsidy bidding It is competitive bidding for subsidies, where companies bid against one another to serve an area at the lowest price—the lure is the subsidy and other benefits. This system is a way of administrating subsidies without leaving any room for some competitors or technologies gaining an edge over others. But competitive bidding has anticompetitive effects, since it gives a special advantage to one company. Regulators should adopt a consumer choice system, under which any subsidy for each high cost customer it served. If the customer moved to a competing carrier, the subsidy would move, too.

Substitution effect The replacement of one product for another resulting from a change in their relative prices.

Sunk costs The costs in commercial activities that have been incurred and cannot be reversed. The cost on advertisement, research and development, etc. are examples of such costs. Sunk costs are a big deterrent to new entrants in the commercial world as after the venture has failed, these costs cannot be recovered—there is no two-way process here.

Surety It is the guarantee of a debt of one party by another. A surety can be an organisation or person that assumes the responsibility of paying the debt in case the debtor defaults or is unable to make the payments. This is also known by its other name, *guarantor*.

Swap The act of exchanging one by another. It could be of many economic items:

- **Currency swap:** The simultaneous buying and selling of foreign currencies could be *spot* or *forward/future* currency swaps. This is used by MNCs to minimise the risk of losses arising from exchange rate changes.

- **Debt swap:** Exchanging one debt by another for a fresh term of repayment schedule at the same or usually lower interest rates.
- **Interest rate swap:** Exchanging one debt of a particular interest rate for another at lower interest rate.
- **Product swap:** Exchanging one product for the other as wheat for milk (similar to barter).

Swift The Society for Worldwide Inter-bank Telecommunication (SWIFT) is a messaging network which connects banks and financial institutions across the world. International transactions of the banks and institutions are ultimately based on this network. The network was in news in India after the LoU (Letter of Undertaking) related banking fraud occurred with the Punjab National Bank in February 2018. Meanwhile, the RBI has enforced (February 2018) a new guideline under which all banks and financial institutions of India need to link their core banking system to the SWIFT to protect themselves from occurrence of any future financial fraud.

Swiss formula Tariff cut formulae are either linear or non-linear. A Swiss formula is a non-linear formula. In a linear formula, tariffs are reduced by the same percentage irrespective of how high the initial tariff is. As opposed to a linear formula, in a non-linear formula, tariff cuts are directly or inversely proportional to the initial tariff rate.

In the Swiss formula, tariff cuts are proportionally higher for tariffs which are initially higher. For instance, a country which has an initial tariff of 30 per cent on a product will have to undertake proportionally higher cuts than a country which has an initial tariff of 20 per cent on the same product.

Systemic risk The risk of damage to the health of the whole financial system. In modern financial world, the collapse of one bank could bring down the whole financial system.

Takeover The process of one firm acquiring the other, also known as *acquisition.* As opposed to the merger which is an outcome of 'mutual agreement', takeovers are 'hostile' moves.

Takeovers may be classified into three broad categories:

1. *Horizontal takeovers* involve firms which are direct competitors in the same market;
2. *Vertical takeovers* involve the firms having supplier-customer relationship; and
3. *Conglomerate takeovers* involve the firms operating in unrelated markets but intend diversification.

Takeover bid An attempt of acquiring the majority share in a firm by another firm. There are various *terms* to show the *'tactics'* applied in such bids either by the bidder or the bidded firms:

- **Black knight:** The launch of an unwelcome takeover bid (as Mittal's for the Arcelor in recent past).
- **Golden parachute:** A generous severance term written into the employment contracts of the directors (of a firm) which makes it expensive to sack them if the firm is taken over.
- **Green mail:** A situation of takeover bid when the bought-up shares by a potential bidder is actually being bought by the directors of the firm itself.
- **Leveraged bid:** A takeover bid being financed primarily by the loan.
- **Pac-man defence:** A situation when the firm being bidded for takeover, bids for the bidder firm itself–also known as *reverse takeover bid.*

- **Poison pill:** A tactic used by the firm being bidded of merging with some other firm in order to make itself less attractive (financially or structurally) to the potential bidder.
- **Porcupine:** Any agreements between the firm being bidded and its suppliers, creditors, etc., which are so complex that after the takeover, the bidder firm feels difficulties integrating it.
- **Shark repellants:** The measures specially designed to discourage takeover bidders (e.g., altering the firm's articles of association to increase the proportion of shareholder votes needed to approve the bid above the usual 50 per cent level, etc.).
- **White knight:** The intervention of a third firm in a takeover bid which either merges with or takes over the victim firm to rescue it from the unwelcome bidder.

Tax expenditure Tax expenditure, which is also known as *revenue forgone*, is the difference between the official tax rate (which is imposed) and the effective tax rate (which is actually collected). This difference mainly occurs due to tax exemptions offered by the governments, basically to promote certain sectors in the absence of which they may not grow or even come up.

As such exemptions increase complexity and distort tax system, the Government has started withdrawing them in India since the past few years.

Tax inversion This is a situation of tax structure. This takes place when a firm bases its headquarters in a low tax country while keeps its material operations in the high tax countries (generally their country of origin). This way, firms cut their tax payment liabilities. This is legal and is a method of tax avoidance. Multinational corporations (MNCs) keep doing this—several MNCs of the US-origin shifted their headquarters to the UK, during the 1970s and 1980s. The countries in the world which have very low tax regime for corporations have emerged as very attractive locations for the headquarters of big corporations. Bermuda, Virgin Islands, etc. are such countries (popularly known as the 'tax havens').

Taylor Rule A rule/concept aimed at establishing a relationship between the rate of inflation in an economy and in its aftermath the nominal interest rate announced by the Central Bank of the country. Proposed by J.B. Taylor (1948), this rule suggests that when there is an one percent increase in the inflation rate, the central Bank increases nominal interest rate by more than one per cent. Though such a relationship between inflation rate and nominal interest rate of the Central Bank is difficult to establish, the concept has an academic importance.

Technological unemployment Unemployment which results from the automation of the production activities (*i.e., machines replacing men*).

Third-party insurance Motor third-party insurance or third-party insurance is a statutory requirement under the Motor Vehicle Act in India–also known as *'act only'* cover. A person purchasing a motor vehicle has to go for this compulsory insurance which benefits the third person (i.e. neither the vehicle owner nor the insurance company)–the person who becomes a victim of an accident by the vehicle. The amount of compensation is largely decided by the earning capacity of the accident victim.

Third way An economic philosophy (better say rhetoric) which propagates it is neither capitalism nor socialism but a third (pragmatic) way.

The idea was popularised in the late 20th century by some political leaders having leftist leanings, including Bill Clinton and Tony Blair. Though it has been hard to pin down, it was earlier used to describe the economic model of Sweden.

Tight money When money has become difficult to mobilise, the term is used to show the 'dear money' when the rates of interest run comparatively on the higher side.

Till money The notes and coins the commercial banks keep to meet everyday cash requirements of their customers (this is counted as part of their CRR).

Tobin tax A proposal of imposing small tax on all foreign exchange transactions with the objective to discourage destabilising speculation and volatility in the foreign exchange markets.

Proposed by the Nobel prize-winning economist James Tobin (1918–2002), the tax has never been implemented anywhere in the world so far.

Total product The main/core product supported by many peripheral products/services, for example, a car, coming with loan facility, warranties, insurance, and after-sales service, etc.

Trade creation The increase in international trade that results from the elimination or reduction of trade barriers (such as quota, customs, etc.).

Tragedy of the commons Refers to the dangers of over-exploitation of resources due to lack of property rights over them ('commons' are the resources neither owned privately nor by the state but are open for free use by all). A rationing or imposing of levy on such resources as a check.

The concept was proposed by a 19th century amateur mathematician William Forster Lloyd.

Transfer payments The expenditure by the government for which it receives no goods or services. For example, the expenditures on tax collection, social sector, unemployment allowance, etc.

As such expenditures are not done against any products, they are not counted in the national income of the economy.

Transfer earnings The return that an asset must earn to prevent its transfer to the next best alternative use. Any earning above the transfer earnings is known as its *'economic rent'*.

Transfer price A term of international economics via which an MNC charges lesser prices for its exportables to its arm in another economy where tax rates are high, for increasing income. The East India Company did it heavily in pre-independent India.

Underwriting The process of acceptance by a financial institution of the financial risks of a transaction for a fee. For example, merchant banks underwrite new share issues, guaranteeing to buy up the shares not sold in a public offer (i.e., in the situations of under-subscription).

Unicorn A term of mythology is today used to mean a firm (company) which has valuation (as per the investors) of US$1 billion or more. Usually a *start-up*, such firms do not have an established performance record but as they look attractive due to diverse reasons (such as being a sunrise industry), accessing loans or investments is relatively easier for them. The term was *first* used by the venture capitalist Aileen Lee in 2013, as per whom, a firm with valuation over US$ 100 billion is 'super unicorn' (the companies such as Facebook, LinkedIn, etc.).

By April 2021, India was home to a total of *38 unicorns,* adding a record number of 12 start-ups to the list in 2020 (in 2019, 9 new unicorns got created), as per the *NASSCOM Tech Start-up Report 2021*. The number of unicorns in US and China were 243 and 227, respectively.

Unorganised sector According to India's NCEUS (National Commission for Enterprises in Unorganised Sector) classification, the "unorganised sector' consists of all *unincorporated* private enterprises owned by individuals or households engaged in the sale and production of goods and services operated on a proprietary or partnership basis and with less than ten total workers". However, "*informal workers* consist of those working in the unorganised enterprises or households, excluding regular workers with social security benefits, and the workers in the formal sector without any employment benefits/social security provided by the employers".

Unsecured loan The loan which is forwarded by banks only against the creditworthiness of the borrower is known as 'unsecured' loan. Such loans are also known as *signature loans* and *personal loans*. If the loan is supported by some form of collateral (of secondary security, such as land, building, etc.), then it is a 'secured' loan.

Basically, loans are provided by banks against two kinds of securities—the creditworthiness of the borrower (known as the 'primary security') and collateral (known as the 'secondary security').

Usual status This is a term used in India's labour force surveys where the Usual Status gives an idea about average working condition of an individual for the entire reference year. It is further subdivided into two categories— one being *principal status (ps)* and other the *subsidiary status (ss)*. While the principal status measures the activity in which an individual has spent relatively longer time of a reference year (major time criterion), the subsidiary status measures the activity status of an individual who has spent majority of days out of work force but have worked for a short period of time (more than 30 days).

Usury Charging an exorbitant rate of interest or even charging interest. Decried by many ancient philosophers and many religions, today most modern economies have some law regulating the upper limit of the interest rates and they consider interest as a reward to the lender for the lending risk.

VGF The Viability Gap Funding (VGF) is a fund assistance facility provided by the GoI to the private players in the infrastructure projects being developed under public private partnership (PPP). The fund is given by the GoI as one time 'grant' and it could be maximum 20 per cent of the project cost (in special cases, an additional 20 per cent might be approved by the states/ministries/ authorities).

The facility, which was operationalised in September 2006, was aimed at attracting private investment towards this socio-economically desirable sector. Several infra projects were economically 'non-viable' which used to discourage private players away from such projects—this facility encourages them to take part.

Veblen effect Named after the American economist Thorstein Bunde Veblen (1857–1929), this is a theory of consumption which suggests that consumers may have an 'upward-sloping demand curve' as opposed to a 'downward-sloping demand curve' because they practise conspicuous consumption (*a downward - sloping demand curve means that the quantity demanded varies inversely to the price i.e. demand falls with price rise*). The concept suggests that quantity demanded of a particular goods varies directly with a change in price (*i.e., as price increases, demand increases*).

Velocity of circulation A measure of the average number of times each unit of money is, used, to purchase the final goods and services produced in an economy in a year.

Venture capital Generally, a private equity capital which lends capital to the entrepreneurs who are innovative and cannot get the required fund from the conventional set-up of the lending mechanism.

In India, it was the Government of India which did set up the first such fund in 1998–the IVCF.

Vostro account *Vostro is an account that one party holds for another.* With a view to giving more operational leeway, the RBI decided to dispense with the requirement of prior approval of the RBI for opening and maintaining each rupee

vostro account in India of non-resident exchange houses in connection with the rupee drawing arrangements (RDAs) that banks enter into with them. The approved dealer banks could now take its permission the first time they entered into such an arrangement with non-resident exchange houses from the Gulf countries, Hong Kong, Singapore and Malaysia. Subsequently, they may enter into RDAs, and inform the RBI immediately.

Walras' Law As per this law, 'the total value of goods demanded in an economy is always identically equal to the total value of goods supplied'. For this to happen, the economy should be in equilibrium. It also means that if there is an excess supply of certain things in one market, there must be excess demand for it in another market. Here 'another market' does not mean the market of another economy—it is taken as apple's market, grape's market (as 'separate' markets). This could be only correct in a barter economy (it does not work in an economy with currency as its mode of exchange).

The idea was part of the 'general equilibrium theory' developed by the French mathematical economist *Marie-Esprit-Leon Walras* (1834–1910), after whom it is named.

Wasting asset The natural resource which has a finite but indeterminate life span depending upon the rate of depletion (such as coal, oil, etc.).

Weightless economy The situation of an economy when the output is increasingly produced from intellectual capital rather than physical materials–a shift in production from iron and steel, heavy machines, etc. to microprocessors, fibre optics and transistors, etc. This is the weightless economy, i.e., the *new economy* which arrived in the US (specially) by the end of the 20th century.

Welfare economics The branch of economics which is concerned with the way economic activity ought to be organised so as to maximise economic welfare. The idea applies to the welfare of individuals as well as countries.

This is normative economics, i.e., it is based on value judgements. It is also called *'economics with a heart'*. This focuses on questions about *equity* as well as *efficiency*.

It employs value judgements about what *ought* to be produced, how production *should* be organised, the way income and wealth *ought* to be distributed, both in present times and in future. As different individuals in different communities have unique set of value judgements (guided by their attitudes, religion, philosophy, and politics), it has been difficult for the economists to reach a consensual idea upon which they could advise the governments in policy making, known as the *welfare criteria*. Economists and philosophers have been suggesting their brands of the *welfare criteria* since long–Vilfredo Pareto, Nicholas Kaldor, John Hicks, Scitovsky, Amartya Sen, as the few famous ones.

Wildcat strike A strike called on by a group of employees without the support of their organised trade union.

Williamson Trade-off Model A model for evaluating the possible benefits and detriments of a proposed merger that could be used in the application of a discretionary competition policy. The model was developed by Oliver Williamson.

Winner's curse The possibility that the winning bidder in an auction will pay too much for an asset since the highest bidder places a higher value on the asset than all other bidders.

Withholding tax A tax imposed on the income on a foreign portfolio (investments). This tax is imposed to discourage foreign investments, to encourage domestic investment, and to raise money for the government.

Worker (Census definition) The *first* definition of 'worker' by *Census* was given in 1872. Over time, the terms 'work' and 'worker' as defined by ***Census of India*** have undergone several amendments to suit the changing dimensions of work. 'Work' is defined as participation in any *economically productive activity* with or without compensation, wages or profit. Such participation may be physical and/or mental in nature. Work involves not only actual work but also includes:

1. Effective supervision and direction of work;
2. Part time help or unpaid work on farm, family enterprise or in any other economic activity; and
3. Cultivation or milk production even solely for domestic consumption.

Accordingly, as per Census of India, all persons engaged in 'work' defined as participation in any economically productive activity with or without compensation, wages or profit are workers. The reference period for determining a person as worker and non-worker is one year preceding the date of enumeration.

The Census *classifies* 'Workers' into two groups, namely, *Main Workers* (those workers who had worked for the major part of the reference period, i.e, 6 months or more) and *Marginal Workers* (those workers who had not Worked for the major part of the reference period i.e. less than 6 months). The *Main* workers are classified based on Industrial category of workers into the following four category: (i) Cultivators; (ii) Agricultural Labourers; (iii) Household Industry Workers; and (iv) Other Workers.

[See entry *'Non-Worker'* also.]

Worker (NSO definition) The NSO (National Statistics Office) data classifies the *workers* based on employment status into three categories—self-employed workers; regular wage/salaried employees; and casual labourers.

1. *Self-employed* category includes those who work for themselves and do not sell their labour power to anyone else in return for wage. This category of workers includes all those workers who operated their enterprises or are engaged in a profession or trade, either on own account, individually or with partners, or as home-based workers.
2. *Regular wage/salaried* employees are those who receive predetermined wages/salary on a regular basis. Such workers are better in qualitative terms than the rest as they receive pre-determined wages/salary with or without other benefits like social/job security.
3. *Casual worker* includes those who are hired for very short time period on daily or monthly basis.

The *own account workers* include those workers who operated their enterprises on their own account or with one or a few partners and ran their enterprise without hiring any labour during the reference period while *own account employers* are those own account workers who ran their enterprise by hiring labourers. However, *unpaid family labourers/helpers* included those who were engaged in their household enterprises, working full or part time and did not receive any regular salary or wages in return for the work performed during the reference period.

Worker (NSO definition) The employment-to-population ratio is defined as the proportion of an economy's working-age population that is employed. As an indicator, the employment-to-population ratio provides information on the ablity of an economy to create jobs. Worker population ratio (WPR) is defined as the number of persons employed per thousand persons [WPR= No. of employed persons ¥ 1000/Total population]. Worker Population Ratio is an indicator used for analysing the employment situation in the country. This is also useful in knowing the proportion of population that is actively contributing to the production of goods and services in the economy.

Workfare Government programmes which make the receipt of unemployment-related benefits (as unemployment allowance) conditional upon participation in some local work scheme.

X-inefficiency A graphic representation of the 'gap' a firm shows in its actual and minimum costs of supplying its products. As per the traditional theory of supply, firms always operate on minimum attainable costs. As opposed to this, x-inefficiency suggests that firms typically operate at higher costs than their minimum attainable costs. This takes place due to many *inefficiencies* (such as organising the works, lack of co-ordination, lack of motivation, bureaucratic rigidities, etc.). Large corporates usually face this problem as they lack effective competition which could 'keep them on their toes'.

Yield gap A method of comparing the performance of bonds and shares in an economy. It is defined as the average returns on shares minus the average returns on bonds.

Zero-coupon bond A bond bearing zero coupon rate (i.e. no interest) sold at a price lower than its face value. Investors book profit when they sell it at its face value). Such bonds are popularly used by the governments to raise long-term funds. In a situation of rate cut by the RBI, zero-coupon bonds gain value—it means, they sell at higher prices. When there is an increase in the rate, the opposite happens.

Zero-sum game A situation in the *game theory* when the gains made by winners in an economic transaction are equal to the losses suffered by the losers. This is considered a special case in game theory. Most economic transactions are in some sense *positive-sum games.* But in popular discussion of economic issues, there are often examples of mistaken zero-sum mentality, such as profit comes at the expense of wages, 'higher productivity means fewer jobs', and 'imports mean fewer jobs here.'

Zero tilling A relatively new farm production process, is a one-time operation in which a small drill places the seed and the fertiliser in a small furrow, saving the farmer a lot of time and other resources. At first utilised in Haryana in 1999–2000, by now it has spread to the other wheat growing states. The technique gives higher yield (by over 5 per cent) than the conventional wheat farming.